T0384284

WORLDWIDE DESTINATIONS

Worldwide Destinations: The Geography of Travel and Tourism is a unique text that explores tourism demand, supply, organisation, and resources for every country worldwide in a logically structured and accessible format.

The ninth edition is fully updated to include the following features:

- Greater exploration of current issues such as climate change, the impact of COVID-19 on destinations and subsequent recovery strategies, regenerative tourism, changes in consumer behaviour, and sustainability.
- New and updated case studies throughout.
- Increased emphasis on South America and a new chapter focussing on the tourism geography of Antarctica.
- Enhanced online resources for lecturers and students including PPTs, web links, video links, MCQs, and discussion questions.

The first part of this book comprises thematic chapters that detail the geographic knowledge and principles required to analyse the tourism appeal of destinations. The subsequent division of this book into regional chapters enables the student to carry out a systematic analysis of a particular destination by providing insights on cultural characteristics as well as information on specific places.

This volume is an invaluable resource for studying every destination in the world, explaining tourism demand, evaluating the many types of tourist attractions, and examining the trends that may shape the future geography of tourism. This thorough guide is a must-have for any student undertaking a course in travel and tourism.

Brian Boniface is a tourism consultant and educationalist with wide experience in teaching geography on vocational courses for the tourism industry in colleges of further education.

Chris Cooper is a Professor in the School of Events, Tourism and Hospitality Management at Leeds Beckett University. He possesses extensive international research and consultancy experience and has a well-established reputation as an international leader in tourism education. He was awarded the United Nations World Tourism Organization Ulysses Prize for contributions to tourism education and policy in 2009.

Ninth Edition

WORLDWIDE DESTINATIONS

The Geography of Travel and Tourism

BRIAN BONIFACE AND CHRIS COOPER

Routledge
Taylor & Francis Group

LONDON AND NEW YORK

Cover: © Getty Images/Mitch Dann

Ninth edition published 2024
by Routledge
4 Park Square, Milton Park, Abingdon, Oxon, OX14 4RN

and by Routledge
605 Third Avenue, New York, NY 10158

Routledge is an imprint of the Taylor & Francis Group, an informa business

First edition published by Heinemann as *The Geography of Travel and Tourism* 1985
Eighth edition published by Routledge 2021

British Library Cataloguing-in-Publication Data
A catalogue record for this book is available from the British Library

ISBN: 978-1-032-52489-4 (hbk)
ISBN: 978-1-032-52491-7 (pbk)
ISBN: 978-1-003-40685-3 (ebk)

DOI: 10.4324/9781003406853

Typeset in Stone Serif, Avenir and Rockwell
by codeMantra

Contents

FIGURES

TABLES

PHOTOGRAPHS

CASE STUDIES

Preface

In the mid-1980s when we set out to write the first edition of the *Geography of Travel and Tourism*, we were pioneering a new territory, following the footsteps of a very small band of geographers who had discovered tourism as a field of research. Back then, 'those faraway places with the strange-sounding names' rarely featured in the curriculum at school or college. Nowadays, tourism as a subject has been well and truly explored by a host of authors writing textbooks, reports, and papers for specialist journals. Moreover, in the mid-1980s, the Cold War was very much a reality, and the demand for international tourism was largely concentrated in a few developed countries, mostly in Western Europe and North America. The vast majority of the world's people had neither the income nor the opportunity to travel far from their home region; nowadays, demand is much more widely spread. The growing middle class in China, for example, is set to become the world's biggest spender on international tourism. In the ninth edition, we have endeavoured to place less emphasis on Europe and given more space to emerging destinations, including Antarctica – now with a dedicated chapter for the first time – and countries in sub-Saharan Africa. Yet, tourism is now at a crossroads, due to the impact of the COVID-19 pandemic in the short- and long-term threats posed by climate change. The Ukrainian war has revived the spectre of disruption to a generation, which had grown accustomed to peace, stability, and growth.

While the scope of tourism is widening, at the same time, the focus on tourism is becoming narrower, with most authors specialising in ever-smaller areas of the subject, and with very few geographers taking a comprehensive and popular market approach to travel and tourism. As in previous editions, we aim to fill this gap in the market. Nonetheless, we have retained many of the ingredients of previous successful editions and highlighted themes such as climate change and the impact of the COVID-19 pandemic in certain countries.

The regional chapters are written to a flexible template that generally describes the setting for tourism and analyses both the demand and the supply-side of tourism, including transport, organisation, and resources. We have aimed for greater consistency in the regional chapters than in previous editions. We make no apology for this comprehensive approach, as we feel it is needed more than ever before in a subject area dominated by increasing specialisation. Therefore, *Worldwide Destinations* complements the more detailed treatment of tourism found in the host of textbooks, reports, and academic papers that deal with specific themes or destinations. Each chapter offers a number of mini case studies to highlight certain areas or topics, and discussion points to encourage greater student involvement. Each chapter includes learning objectives and concludes with a series of summary points and review questions. Up-to-date URLs are provided wherever possible to allow for a deeper examination of the destination.

Supplemented with a good atlas, *Worldwide Destinations* provides a framework for understanding most aspects of travel and tourism. Geography can make a unique contribution to the study, not only of tourism but also of those man-made and natural events around the world that make the news headlines. One example is the young British girl who was able to warn other holidaymakers on a beach in Thailand of the impending disaster on December 26, 2003, because she had learned about tsunamis at school as part of her geography course. The study of geography not only gives information on places but also provides the insight to understand other cultures.

As before, family, friends, and colleagues have supported us in writing this edition. Nicholas East and Sara Monteiro have provided helpful suggestions, while Maria Boniface has proved invaluable as a translator. Our students, including those on distance learning courses from many countries around the world, have provided feedback on current trends in tourism. Chris has relished updating this edition despite the groans from his long-suffering family – clifftop and beach walks with Coco, as always, provided great thinking time.

Brian Boniface and Chris Cooper

PART **I** The geographical
principles of travel
and tourism

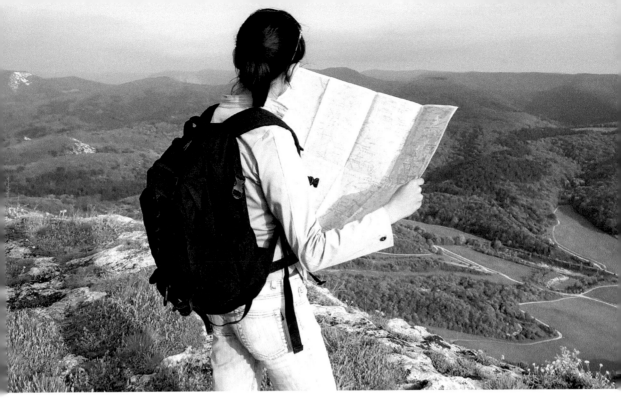

1 An introduction to the geography of travel and tourism

Learning objectives

After reading this chapter, you should be able to:

- Define and use the terms leisure, recreation, and tourism and understand their interrelationships.
- Distinguish between tourism, migration, and other types of mobility.
- Distinguish between the different forms of tourism and the relationship of different types of tourists with the environment.
- Recognise the importance of scale in explaining patterns of tourism.
- Identify the three major components of the tourism system.

DOI: 10.4324/9781003406853-2

- Explain the push and pull factors that give rise to tourist flows.
- Appreciate the methods used to measure tourist flows and be aware of their shortcomings.

Leisure, recreation, and tourism

Tourism is seldom the dream world of the holiday brochure, and it is the connection with the real world that makes the geography of travel and tourism such an exciting and vibrant area to study. Travellers to remote places and backpackers often do not regard themselves as tourists – which they are – and tourism is intimately linked with the leisure activities that play such an important role in our lives.

What exactly is meant by the terms 'leisure, recreation, and tourism', and how are they related? *Leisure* is often seen as a measure of time and usually refers to the time remaining after work, sleep, household chores, and personal obligations have been completed (Figure 1.1). In other words, leisure represents free time for individuals to spend as they please. However, this introduces the question of whether all free time is leisure. A good example of this dilemma is whether the unemployed perceive their free time as 'enforced' leisure, or whether volunteers at a sporting event view their activity as 'serious leisure'. This perceptive has led to the notion that leisure is as much an attitude of mind as it is a measure of time, and it requires an element of 'choice'. In fact, the relationships between work and leisure have changed over the last two centuries in most of the world. The Industrial Revolution brought about a sharp contrast between the home, the workplace, and the leisure environment, which became more widely separated as transport facilities improved. In pre-industrial societies, the pace of life is attuned to the rhythm of the seasons rather than being governed by the clock, and personal mobility is limited. In post-industrial countries such as Britain and the United States, one aspect of the so-called '24/7 culture' is the blurring of the boundaries between work and leisure, and the *work-life balance* is increasingly under threat as a result. Highly paid executives are expected to be in contact with the office during their vacations, while some corporate employers provide leisure opportunities based at the workplace.

The COVID-19 pandemic of 2020–2022 impacted leisure and tourism in ways that we will discuss in the next chapter. The home necessarily became the centre of leisure activities, while many were forced or chose to work from home, further blurring the distinction between work and leisure.

Recreation is normally understood as the variety of activities undertaken during leisure time (Figure 1.1). Basically, recreation refreshes a person's strength and spirit and can include activities as diverse as watching television at home to holidaying abroad. We can draw a useful distinction between leisure pursuits that involve the arts, cultural activities, entertainment, and physical activities. Additionally, we can distinguish *sports* from other types of physical recreation as they involve competition and participants must follow rules laid down by a recognised authority.

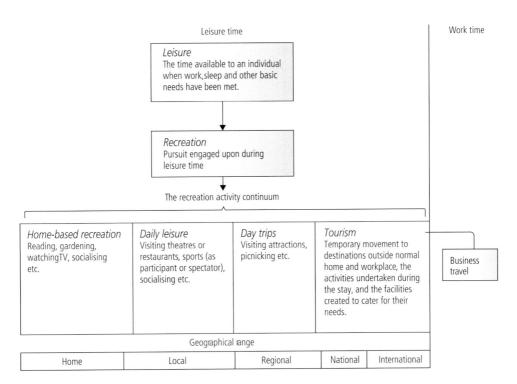

Figure 1.1
Leisure, recreation, and tourism

If we accept that leisure is a measure of time and that recreation embraces the activities undertaken during that time, then tourism is simply one type of recreational activity. However, it is more challenging to disentangle the meanings of the terms, recreation and tourism, in practice. Perhaps the most helpful way to differentiate is to envisage a spectrum. At one end, you have recreation based at home or in the local area, while at the opposite end, you have recreational travel that involves some distance and may require overnight accommodation. This distinction is based on the time required for the activity and the distance travelled, and it places tourism firmly at one extreme of the *recreational activity spectrum* (Figure 1.1). The spectrum also allows us to consider the role of same-day visitors or *excursionists*. These travellers are increasingly a consideration in the geography of tourism; they visit for less than 24 hours and do not stay overnight. In other words, they utilise all tourism facilities except accommodation, putting pressure on the host community and the environment.

Clearly, tourism is a distinctive form of recreation and demands separate consideration. Particularly, from the geographical perspective, tourism is just one form of temporary or leisure mobility, recognising that technology and changes in society have given people the capacity to travel extensively. In other words, we can think of tourism as a form of voluntary, temporary mobility in relation to where people live.

Discussion point: tourism and mobilities – a new way of thinking

Geography is rediscovering tourism as an area for research by combining social and spatial elements in a new 'mobilities' approach. This approach considers tourism as just one form of 'mobility', located within a spectrum ranging from permanent migration to daily shopping. In this framework, tourism is re-examined as a form of 'voluntary temporary mobility in relation to home'. In other words, the mobilities approach regards tourism as one dimension of our 'connections' with the world, ranging across many different localities. The key message behind the idea of tourism 'as a form of mobility' is that tourism is no longer treated as a distinct and special activity, but simply one that is a part of a range of other activities in society. However, the mobilities approach creates several issues for tourism:

- Firstly, the approach places movement at the centre stage and increases our understanding of the underlying processes driving patterns of tourism movement. The key question is to understand and explain what influences these movements, from personal resources at a micro scale to geo-politics at a macro scale.
- Secondly, mobilities blur the distinction between home, work, and tourist destinations; as well as between different types of travellers – whether they are commuters, shoppers, or migrants.
- Not everyone can be part of this world of movement. Travelling involves mustering the personal resources needed, and yet, some argue that the mobilities approach ignores these inequalities. Only 2 or 3 per cent of the world's population engage in international tourism, and some that do are 'hypermobile', engaging in many trips in any one year.
- Much of this world of movement is also involuntary. In addition to refugees fleeing political or religious discrimination, there are economic migrants seeking a better life, and a modern form of the slave trade, involving women and children trafficked to provide unpaid labour or forced into prostitution.

Is tourism still a 'special' activity or does the mobilities approach devalue it to being a part of everyday life and expectations?

The mobilities approach brings into focus the international debate as to the definition of tourism. There are two ways to investigate the problem:

1. Firstly, we can define tourism from the **demand side**, i.e., the perspective of the person who is the tourist. This approach is well developed, and the United Nations Statistical Commission now accepts the following definition of tourism: 'The activities of persons travelling to and staying in places outside their usual environment for not more than one consecutive year for leisure, business and other purposes'. This definition raises several issues:

   - What is a person's usual environment?
   - The inclusion of 'business' and 'other' purposes of visit demands that requires us to conceive of tourism more broadly than simply as a recreational pursuit.

- Certain types of travellers are excluded from the definition. Tourism is only one part of the spectrum of travel, which ranges from the daily journey to work, or for shopping, to migration, where the traveller intends to take up permanent or long-term residence in another area (see Figure 1.2).

2. We can also define the tourism sector from the **supply-side** perspective. Here the difficulty lies in disentangling tourism businesses and jobs from the rest of the economy. After years of debate, the accepted approach is the *tourism satellite account* (TSA), adopted by the United Nations in 2000. The TSA measures the demand for goods and services generated by visitors to a destination. It allows tourism to be compared with other sectors of the economy by calculating its contribution to investment, consumption, employment, gross domestic product (GDP), and taxation.

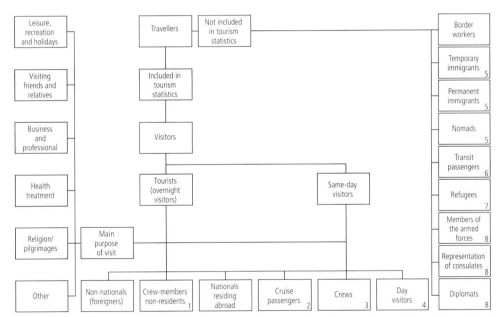

1. Foreign air or ship crews docked or in lay over and who use the accommodation establishments of the country visited.
2. Persons who arrive in a country abroad cruise ships (as defined by the International Maritime Organization, 1965) and who spend the night aboard ship even when disembarking for one or more day visits.
3. Crews who are not residents of the country visited and who stay in the country for the day.
4. Visitors who arrive and leave the same day for: leisure, recreation and holidays; visiting friends and relatives; business and professional; health treatment; religion/pilgrimages and other tourism purposes, including transit day visitors en route to or from their destination countries.
5. As defined by the United Nations in the Recommendations on Statistics of International Migration, 1980.
6. Who do not leave the transit area of the airport or the port, including transfer between airports and ports.
7. As defined by the United Nations High Commissioner for Refugees, 1967.
8. When they travel from their country of origin to the duty station and vice versa (including household servants and dependants accompanying or joining them).

Figure 1.2
Classification of travellers

Discussion point: defining tourism experiences

Traditional definitions of tourism fail to incorporate the idea of tourism as an 'experience', yet experiences now define what many tourists are seeking. In fact, the tourist is as much a creator of the experience as the tourism industry itself. This is known as 'co-creation' of the tourism experience and has been enabled in part by technology, whereby tourists construct their own product. Can you devise a new definition of tourism that takes this idea into account?

Geography and tourism

Geography is concerned with **location**; by this, we mean not just the global position of a place in terms of latitude and longitude, but also its situation relative to other places, particularly major centres of population.

When we study the geography of travel and tourism, three key concepts need to be considered:

- Spatial scale
- The geographical components of the tourism system
- Spatial interaction between the components of the tourism system

Spatial scale

Geographers study the spatial expression of tourism as a human activity, focussing on both tourist-generating and tourist-receiving areas, as well as the links between them. We can undertake this study at a variety of scales, namely:

- The global or continental scale – the distribution of major climate zones and ecosystems, air and shipping routes, and patterns of migration.
- The national scale – the identification of a country's transport networks and tourist regions and population distribution.
- The regional scale – the assessment of tourism resources in part of a country.
- The local scale – the location of particular attractions and the configuration of holiday resorts.

This issue of scale has become important in the global versus local debate. As the tourism sector embraces the tools of globalisation, such as the forging of global airline alliances, we must never forget that the tourism product is delivered at the local scale, often by local people and within a local cultural context.

We have used the idea of scale to organise the material presented in this book because at each scale we can gain a distinctive perspective and insight on tourism. In other words, as a more detailed explanation is required, attention is drawn to increasingly smaller parts of the problem. This idea of scale, or geographical magnitude, keeps in focus the area being dealt with, and can be likened to increasing or decreasing the magnification on a microscope, or the area covered by a map. Even in this digital age, an understanding of maps and their uses is essential for the tourism student. A small-scale map in an atlas will cover a large area, such as an entire country or continent, with only generalised information on locations being shown, whereas a large-scale *topographic* map will cover only a small area, but in detail.

Flows of leisure tourism in Europe provide a good example of the importance of scale. At the international scale, the dominant flow of tourists is from north to south. However, at the regional scale, a variety of other patterns emerge, such as travel between cities or out of cities to the coast or countryside. Meanwhile, at the local scale, we can consider day-trip patterns, with people travelling relatively short distances from their accommodation in the holiday area.

The geographical components of the tourism system

From a geographical point of view, tourism has three major components: first, the places of origin of tourists, which we call *generating areas*; second, the tourist destinations themselves or *receiving areas*; and third, the routes travelled between these two sets of locations, known as *transit routes* (Leiper, 1979). These components relate to differing economic, environmental, and social contexts, and in each part of the system, the tourist will interact with different parts of the travel and tourism industry. This simple model is illustrated in Figure 1.3, and the components form the basis for Chapters 2–5:

- *Tourist-generating areas* represent the homes of tourists, where journeys begin and end. The key issues to examine here are the features that stimulate *demand* for tourism, including the geographical location of an area as well as its socio-economic and demographic characteristics. These areas represent the main tourist markets in the world, and naturally enough, the main marketing functions of the tourism industry are found here (such as tour operation and travel retailing). We consider tourist-generating areas in Chapter 2.
- *Tourist-receiving areas* attract visitors to stay temporarily and will have features and attractions that may not be found in the generating areas. The tourism industry located in such an area will comprise visitor attractions, the accommodation sector, retailing and service functions, as well as entertainment and recreation facilities. In our view, destinations deserve more attention than the other two components; not only do they attract the tourist – thus energising the system – but also because the impacts of tourism on the host community and environment explain why the sustainable planning and management of tourism is so important. We examine the features of destinations in Chapters 3 and 4.
- *Transit routes* are a key element in the system as their effectiveness and other characteristics shape the volume and direction of tourist flows. These routes represent the transport sector of the tourism industry, which we consider in Chapter 5.

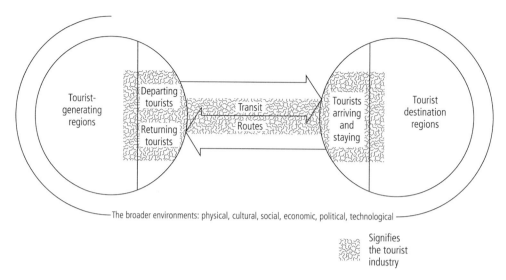

Figure 1.3
The tourism system

The characteristics of each component of the tourism system are determined by the context. For example, a tourism system in a developing country is likely to have a generating component more dominated by domestic travel than would be the case in a developed country of comparable size and population. External factors, such as the international political and economic situation, also affect the tourism system in terms of a range of issues, notably terrorism and security, and this means all components should develop crisis and risk management plans. Of course, change in one part of the system will impact on the other parts. For example, enhanced security arrangements in the transit route will affect both the demand and supply sides of the system.

Spatial interaction between the components of the tourism system: tourist flows

The consideration of tourist flows between countries and regions is fundamental to the geography of tourism and allows us to see the all-important interrelationships between the three components we have identified. An understanding of tourist flows is critical for managing the environmental and social impacts of tourism, securing the commercial viability of the tourism industry and for planning new developments.

Tourist flows are a form of spatial interaction between two areas with the destination area containing a surplus of a commodity or *resource* (surfing beaches or ski slopes, for example) and the generating area having a deficit or demand for that commodity. In fact, it is possible to detect regular patterns of tourist flows. They do not occur randomly but follow certain rules and are influenced by a variety of 'push' and 'pull' factors:

- **Push factors** are mainly concerned with the stage of economic development in the generating area and will include such factors as levels of affluence, mobility, and holiday entitlement. Moreover, an advanced stage of economic development will not only give the population the means to engage in tourism but the pressures of city life will provide the urge to 'get away from it all'. An unfavourable climate will also provide a strong impetus to travel. However, we must add a note of caution here as awareness of climate change and the carbon emissions from air transport is moderating these push factors, as the debate about whether to fly or not is gaining attention.

- **Pull factors** include accessibility, and the attractions and amenities of the destination area. The relative cost of the visit is also important, as is the effectiveness of marketing and promotion by the destination.

Explaining tourist flows

The movements of people between places are highly complex and are influenced by a wide variety of interrelated variables. Numerous attempts have been made to explain the factors that affect tourist flows and to provide rules governing the magnitude of flows between regions. An early attempt by Williams and Zelinsky (1970) selected 14 countries that had relatively stable tourist flows over several years and which accounted for the bulk of the world's tourist traffic. They identified the following factors:

- Distances between countries (the greater the distance, the smaller the volume of flow)
- International connectivity (shared business or cultural ties between countries)
- The general attractiveness of one country for another

The *gravity model* is another way of explaining tourist flows (see Figure 1.4). Push and pull factors generate flows, and the larger the mass (population) of country 'A' or country 'B', the greater the flow between them. The second factor, known as the friction of distance, refers to the cost in time and money of longer journeys, and this acts to restrain flows between the country of origin and more distant destinations. We can also use other models based on travel itineraries.

Measuring tourist flows

As tourism has become more prominent, national governments and international organisations have introduced the measurement of both international and domestic flows. There are three main reasons why statistics of tourism flows are important:

- Statistics are required to evaluate the **magnitude of tourist flows** and to monitor any change. This allows projections of future flows to be made and the identification of market trends.
- Statistics serve as a basis of hard facts that enable tourism planners and developers to operate effectively and **plan for the future of tourism**.
- Both the public (government) and private (business) sectors use the statistics as the basis for their **marketing efforts**.

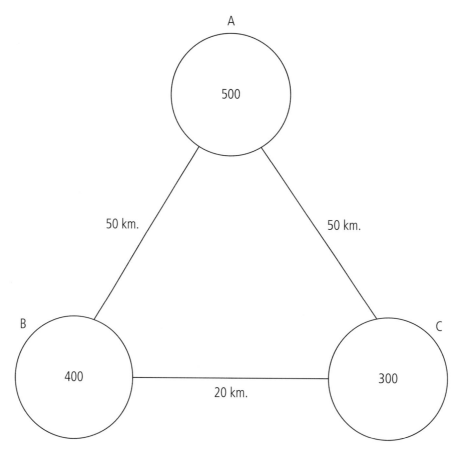

Figure 1.4
The gravity model

There are three main categories of tourism statistics:

Volume statistics provide the number of tourists visiting a destination in a given period of time, including the length of stay of visitors at their destinations. Various methods are available to measure tourist flows.

For volume statistics, tourists can be counted as they enter or leave a country, and immigration control often provides this information. However, measuring domestic travel is more problematic. In destination areas, an alternative method is to enumerate tourists at their accommodations using registration cards. This method is only effective with legal enforcement and normally omits visitors staying in private villas, Airbnb, and apartments, as well as 'VFR' tourists (those visiting and staying with friends or relatives).

Statistics of domestic volume may be obtained through national travel surveys or destination surveys. National travel surveys involve interviewing a representative sample of the population in their homes or on the Internet. People are asked questions about the nature and extent of their travel over a past period, and the results not only provide statistics on volume, along with information on expenditure. Examples of national travel surveys include the *UK Tourism Survey* (UKTS) and Germany's *Reiseanalyse*. In destination surveys, visitors to a tourist area, a specific site, or attraction are interviewed to establish the volume, economic value, and characteristics of traffic to that location.

Statistics of tourist characteristics refer to the detailed composition of the tourists themselves. While statistics of volume measure the quantity of tourist flows, this category measures the quality of the flow, including information on the gender, age, and socio-economic group of the tourists, the structure of the trip, and their attitudes to the destination. It is not uncommon for statistics of tourist characteristics and volume to be collected together.

Surveys of tourist characteristics have evolved from straightforward questioning that provides basic factual information, for example, the age profile of visitors, to surveys that now concentrate on questions that are designed to assist the marketing and management of a destination, or to solve a particular problem. Statistics of tourist characteristics are obtained in a various ways. Additional questions can be added to accommodation registration cards or border checks, but more commonly, a sample of travellers is asked a series of questions about themselves, their trip, or their opinions of the destination. An example of this approach is the *UK International Passenger Survey* (IPS), which measures the volume, economic value, and characteristics of inbound and outbound tourism for the United Kingdom.

The third category is **expenditure statistics**. Tourist flows are not simply movements of people; they also have an important economic significance for the tourism system. Quite simply, tourism represents a flow of money that is earned in one place and spent in another. Thus, a major generating country may well have a deficit on its international tourism account (meaning residents spend more on foreign travel than their country receives from tourists), while a developing country will probably have a credit, thereby helping its overall balance of payments. To make comparisons easier, expenditure is usually expressed in US dollars rather than in national currencies. Measurement of tourist expenditure can be obtained directly, by asking visitors how much they have spent on their trip, or indirectly by asking hoteliers and other suppliers of tourist services for estimates of tourist spending. Bank records of foreign currency exchange may also serve as another indirect method of obtaining statistics on international expenditure.

Despite the variety of methods available to measure tourist flows, producing accurate statistics is not easy. In the first place, the tourist has to be distinguished from other travellers, including returning residents, and while internationally agreed definitions of tourists do exist, they are not yet consistently applied worldwide. Furthermore, there has been no real attempt to co-ordinate international surveys until recently. To add to these problems, survey methods change over the years, even within a particular country, making it difficult to compare results over time. Another problem is that surveys count 'events' rather than 'people', so a tourist who visits the same country twice in a year will be counted as two arrivals. Travellers on touring holidays may be counted as separate arrivals in various destinations, inflating the overall visitor arrival figures. The relaxation of border controls for trade purposes, allowing freedom of movement between countries, further complicates the statistician's task of enumerating tourists. A good example of this is travel within the European Union under the provisions of the Schengen Treaty.

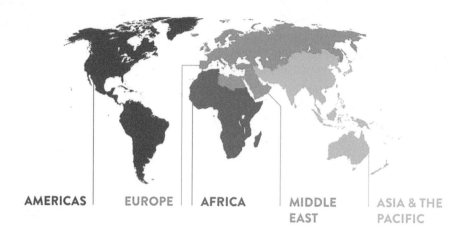

AMERICAS | EUROPE | AFRICA | MIDDLE EAST | ASIA & THE PACIFIC

Figure 1.5
UNWTO regions

The National Tourism Organization (NTO) of a country is usually our first source of information. However, it is important to mention the co-ordinating role of two international bodies:

- The United Nations World Tourism Organisation (UNWTO), based in Madrid, a specialised agency of the United Nations with 160 member countries, is the world's leading international organisation in the field of tourism. The UNWTO promotes tourism as a driver of economic growth while considering sustainability and offers support to the sector in advancing knowledge worldwide. The UNWTO divides the world into five regions, which do not always correspond to continental divisions (see Figure 1.5).
- The World Travel and Tourism Council (WTTC), based in London, is a non-governmental organisation (NGO) comprised of members of the global business community. It collaborates with governments to raise awareness of the industry, promote 'sustainable tourism', and create jobs.

Forms of tourism

The geographical components of tourism, combined with the idea of scale and tourist flows, result in a wide variety of different forms of tourism that can be categorised according to:

- Type of destination
- Characteristics of the tourism system
- Market
- Distance travelled

Type of destination

Here, we can make an important distinction between international and domestic tourism. *Domestic tourism* embraces those travelling within their own country, whereas *international tourism* comprises those who travel to a country other than their country of residence. International tourists can be viewed as non-residents travelling in a given country, constituting its *inbound tourism* sector, or as residents of a particular country travelling abroad to other countries, which is defined as *outbound tourism*. International tourists have to cross national borders and may encounter different currencies and languages. Clearly, the size of a country is important here. Larger countries are more likely to have a variety of tourist attractions and resorts, and quite simply, greater physical distances involved in travel may deter international tourism. For instance, we can compare the volume of domestic tourism in the United States (almost 90 per cent of all tourism) with the Netherlands (around 50 per cent), where travel to neighbouring countries is so much easier. Increasingly though, the distinction between domestic and international tourism is diminishing as restrictions on movement between countries are removed.

Concern for the environmental and social impact of tourism has focussed attention on ways of classifying tourists according to their relationship with the destination. For example, Smith (1978) groups tourists along a continuum ranging from explorers, with virtually no impact, to mass tourists, where the impact may be considerable (see Table 1.1). Interestingly, we can now consider a seventh type of tourist to add to Smith's classification: the 'enlightened mass tourist' who is aware of sustainability issues and travels with more concern for the destination.

Characteristics of the tourism system

Here, we can consider forms of tourism based largely on the destination visited. However, the nature of the destination will influence the other components of the tourism system, namely the market with its particular motivations to travel and the means of transport used. In other words, the tourism product determines the nature of the tourism system. Thus, we can distinguish many types of tourism, including the following:

- Rural tourism – focussed on the countryside.
- Urban tourism – focussed on towns and cities.
- Health and wellness tourism – travel that is not just for medical or dental treatment but for a holistic approach involving beauty, fitness, and mindfulness. In the past, health tourism was mainly focussed on spas and resorts that were based on water sources with therapeutic properties.
- Heritage tourism – travel to experience the tangible aspects of a country's history.
- Cultural tourism – travel to experience a different way of life.
- Sport tourism – concerned with spectators travelling to sports events as well as the participants.
- Ecotourism – based on nature.
- Dark tourism – focussed on places where tragic events have occurred.
- Faith-based tourism – focussed on places regarded as sacred and motivated by religion.

Table 1.1 Smith's typology of tourists

Type of tourist	Numbers	Adapt to local destination	Tourist impact decreases	Tourist volume increases
Explorer	Very limited	Accepts fully		
Elite	Rarely seen	Accepts fully	↑	
Off-beat	Unknown, but visible	Adapts well		
Incipient mass	Steady flows	Seeks Western amenities		
Mass	Continuous influx	Expects Western amenities		
Charter	Massive arrivals	Demands Western amenities		↓

Explorer
These include academics, climbers, and true explorers in small numbers. They totally accept local conditions, and are self-sufficient, with portable chemical toilets, dehydrated food, and walkie-talkies.

Elite
Travelling off the beaten track for pleasure, they have done it all, and are now looking for something different. While they use tourist facilities, they adapt easily to local conditions – if they can eat it, we can.

Off-beat
Not as rich as the elite tourist, they are looking for an added extra to a standard tour. They adapt well and cope with local conditions for a few days.

Incipient mass
A steady flow of tourists, often in small groups or individuals, is seeking accommodations with central heating, air conditioning, and other amenities. They will cope for a while if they are absent and consider it part of the 'experience'.

Mass tourism
Large numbers of tourists, often European or North American, with middle-class values and relatively high incomes. The flow is highly seasonal, with tourists expecting Western amenities and multi-lingual guides.

Charter tourism
This is full blown down-market, high-volume tourism. It is totally dependent upon the travel trade. The tourists have standardised tastes and demands, and the country of destination is irrelevant. This type of tourism is less common in developing and undeveloped counties.

Source: Smith (1978)

Discussion point: forms of tourism and the tourism system
Each form of tourism is expected to have distinctive components in various parts of Leiper's tourism system. Take ecotourism, for example. In the destination area, nature will be the main attraction, and the ancillary services (accommodation, transport, etc.)

will be well managed, employ local people, and be 'green' or 'environmentally friendly'. In the generating area, the ecotourist will be motivated by responsible attitudes towards the environment and will be educated to an above-average level. In the transit zone, the ecotourist will seek out locally owned companies that attempt to minimise the environmental impact of their transport operations.

Now, let us analyse sport tourism in a similar way, giving specific examples for the areas generating the demand, the transit routes, and the destinations.

The Market

Here, we are examining a section of the population expressing a demand for a particular tourism product or range of products. We can express this in terms of the *purpose of the visit*:

- *Holiday tourism* is perhaps the most commonly understood form, where the purpose of the visit is leisure or recreation. We can broadly classify holidays or vacations as either 'sun, sand, and sea' where good weather and beach-related activities are important or as 'touring, sightseeing, and culture' where new destinations and different lifestyles are sought. In addition to the beachgoers and culture-seekers, there is a trend for the more adventurous to seek physical challenges in the world's more remote places, offering opportunities for adrenalin-fuelled 'extreme sports' that carry a high element of risk. Some view this as a reaction against the comfort and predictability of everyday life in post-modern societies. We should also distinguish the traditional 'long vacation' from *short breaks* lasting less than four nights, and there is now a tendency for people to take several short holidays during the year.

- *Common-interest tourism* comprises individuals travelling with a shared purpose with those they visit at the destination. This purpose could include visiting friends and relatives, or travelling for reasons related to religion, health, or education. Common-interest tourists, especially the VFR category, may make little or no demands on serviced accommodation or other tourist facilities at the destination.

- *Business and professional tourism* includes 'MICE' tourism, which includes individuals attending trade fairs, exhibitions, associate meetings, corporate conferences, and those participating in incentive travel schemes. The inclusion of business travel complicates the simple idea of tourism being just another recreational activity. Business travel is work-related and is, therefore, not regarded as part of a person's leisure time and cannot be thought of as recreation. However, because business travellers do use the same facilities as those travelling for pleasure, and are not permanent employees or residents of the host destination, they must be included

Table 1.2 Leisure and business tourism

	Leisure tourism	Business tourism	But.....
Who pays?	The tourist	The traveller's employer or association	Self-employed business travellers are paying for their own trips
Who decides on the destination?	The tourist	The organiser of the meeting, incentive trip, conference/convention, and trade fair	Organisers will often consider delegates' wishes
When do trips take place?	During holiday periods and at weekends resulting in seasonal demand	Year-round, no seasonal fluctuations, but less demand at weekends	Peak holiday months are avoided for major events
Lead time (period of time between booking and going on the trip)	Holidays often booked months in advance, short breaks, a few days	Some business trips must be made at very short notice	Major conferences are booked many years in advance
Who travels?	Anyone with the necessary free time or money	Those whose work requires them to travel or members of associations; most business travellers are men, unaccompanied by family members	Not all business trips involve managers on white-collar duties; in the United States, women now account for over 50% of all corporate business trips
What kinds of destination, accommodation, and transport are used?	Wide choice of destinations – coast, city, mountains, and countryside; all types of serviced and self-catering accommodation; wide variety of transport modes	Little choice of destination, except for conferences; largely centred on major cities, using hotels; in transport speed and flexibility are important	Incentive destinations are much the same as for up-market holidays
How important is price in influencing demand?	Sensitive to price, resulting in elasticity of demand	Less sensitive to price – time is more crucial	Economic recession can cause a downturn in demand or a switch to cheaper transport (e.g., from business to economy class)

Adapted from Davidson (1994) *Business Travel.*

in any definition of tourists (Figure 1.1). However, the business traveller, unlike the holidaymaker, faces significant constraints in terms of where and when to travel. We summarise the differences between business and leisure tourism in Table 1.2.

A further market-based approach involves considering market segments, which encompass two aspects:

1. The nature of the tourists themselves, such as:

    *   Youth tourism – Products geared specifically to the 15–25 years age group.
    *   'Grey' or 'third age' tourism – Products geared specifically to older or retired people.
    *   Gay tourism – Though prohibited or shunned in many parts of the world that have strict moral attitudes to sexual orientation, this segment is significant due to the strength of the 'pink dollar' in spending on leisure products.

2   The type of travel arrangements purchased, such as:

    *   An *inclusive tour* involving two or more components of the trip are purchased together and one price is paid.
    *   *Independent travel* arrangements where the traveller purchases the various elements of the trip separately.
    *   *Tailor-made travel*, which is a combination of the two and increasingly common due to the use of the Internet for travel purchases.

Distance travelled

Here, the distinction is between long-haul tourism, which is generally taken to mean travel over a distance of at least 3,000 kilometres (2,000 miles), and short-haul or medium-haul tourism involving shorter journeys. This differentiation is important in terms of aircraft operations and for marketing. Due to their geographical location, Australians and North Americans are more likely to be long-haul or intercontinental tourisms compared to their counterparts in Europe.

The personal view of the travel experience

Finally, when describing tourism as a social phenomenon and a wealth-creating activity and analysing tourism's impact on the communities visited, it is easy to lose sight of the tourist as an individual and the extent to which travel and recreation satisfy the need for self-fulfilment. All holiday trips have time as well as spatial components, and each phase has specific characteristics:

*   In the *anticipation phase* before the trip, perceptions play a crucial role. These perceptions involve how we filter the information we receive to create an overall 'mental map' of the world, and they significantly influence travel decisions, with an increasing influence of technology such as social media.
*   In the *realisation phase*, tourism experiences at the destination are the goal of the trip. However, we also need to consider impressions of the outward and return journeys as part of the overall holiday experience (Figure 1.6).
*   In the *recollection phase* after the trip, the extent to which the quality of these experiences met expectations will influence future travel decisions and be communicated on social media.

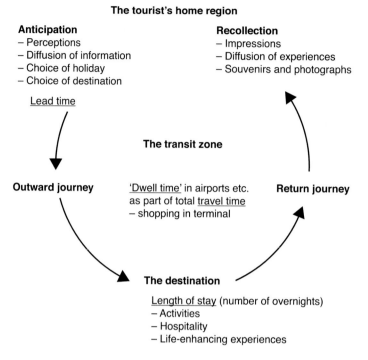

Figure 1.6
The travel experience

Summary

- Leisure has come to be accepted as a measure of free time, while recreation is seen as the activities undertaken during that time.
- Tourism is usually seen as a distinctive form of recreation involving a stay away from home, often involving long distance travel, but it also includes travel for business or other purposes.
- The geography of travel and tourism focusses on three key concepts:

  1. Tourism is a system comprising tourist-generating areas, tourist-receiving areas, and transit routes.
  2. We can consider tourism at a variety of scales, from the global to the local, depending on the level of detail required.
  3. Tourist flows are the spatial interaction that is generated between the components of the tourism system at different scales. Understanding these flows is fundamental to the geography of tourism, and this includes push and pull factors, and the methods of measuring tourism.

- We can distinguish different forms of tourism, based on the destination, the various components of the tourism system, the market, the purpose of visit, the distance travelled, and not least, the nature of the tourists themselves. These distinctions result in distinctive types of tourist experiences.

Review questions

1. How would you classify the following examples of travellers? (NB. some may not be tourists!):

    a) James Pennywise, a computer salesman from Birmingham, is visiting Bournemouth to help organise a short training course in the latest information technology.
    b) Philippa Tease, a travel agent from Miami, Florida, is attending the annual ASTA Convention in Bermuda as a delegate.
    c) Philippa and her Spanish friend Ramona are planning an 'eco-trip' later in the year to explore the Ecuadorian rainforest 'as far away from tourists as possible'.
    d) Francesca from Buenos Aires is visiting Rimini in Italy for a family reunion.
    e) Ulla Erikson from Stockholm is visiting Santorini in the Greek islands for a few hours as part of a Mediterranean cruise.
    f) Valentina from Vilnius, a student at an English language school in Poole, England, is travelling to Cherbourg in France on the 8.30 ferry and returning to Poole at 7.00 the following day.
    g) Anne-Michelle from Sydney is working as a volunteer on community projects in Thailand, as part of her Gap Year before starting university.
    h) A group of young women from a village in China pay money to a syndicate for the promise of a better life in Australia. They are flown out to a remote mining camp in Queensland, their passports are taken away, and they are made to work as 'hostesses' in a bar to repay the money they still owe the syndicate.

2. Investigate the ways in which Spanish and Japanese attitudes to work and leisure differ from those prevalent in Britain and the United States.
3. Draw up a chart comparing working hours and paid holiday entitlement (taking account of national holidays) in your own country with other countries in Asia, Europe, and North America.

Assignment

Draw up a chart based on Figure 1.6, outlining a recent holiday trip. This should indicate the time spent on various stages of the trip as well as the places you visited and the activities you took part in.

References and further reading

Cooper, C.P. (2023) Tourism essentials: Chapter 1 in *Essentials of Tourism*, Sage, London
Davidson, A. (1994) *Business Travel*, Addison, Wesley and Longman, Harlow
Jafari, J. and Xiao, H. (2016) *Encyclopaedia of Tourism*, Springer, Cham
Leiper, N. (1979) The framework of tourism, *Annals of Tourism Research* 6 (4), 390–407

Matley, I. (1976) *The Geography of International Tourism*, Association of American Geographers Resource Paper No 76-1

Pearce, P. (ed.) (2019) *Tourist Behaviour*, Edward Elgar, Cheltenham

Smith, V.L. (1978) *Hosts and Guests: The Anthropology of Tourism*, Blackwell, Oxford, www.unwto.org

Williams, A.V. and Zelinsky, W. (1970) On some patterns in international tourist flows, *Economic Geography* 46 (4), 549–567

2 The geography of demand for tourism

Learning objectives

After reading this chapter, you should be able to:

- Explain the term 'tourist demand' and distinguish between effective and suppressed demand.
- Understand the concepts of travel propensity and frequency.
- Identify the motivations and determinants of demand for tourism, including the impact of COVID-19.
- Explain the influence of stage in economic development, population factors, and political regimes on demand for tourism.

DOI: 10.4324/9781003406853-3

- Understand the influence of personal variables on the demand for tourism.
- Appreciate the main barriers to travel that lead to suppressed demand, including COVID-19.

Leisure, recreation, and tourism: a basic human right?

Leisure, recreation, and tourism are of benefit to both individuals and societies. The United Nations (UN) recognised this as early as 1948 when it adopted its Universal Declaration of Human Rights (www.un.org/en/documents/udhr/), which states that everyone 'has the right to rest and leisure including… periodic holidays with pay'. More specifically, in 1980, the World Tourism Organisation declared the ultimate aim of tourism to be 'the improvement of the quality of life and the creation of better living conditions for all peoples'. Such statements imply that everyone has the right to demand tourism, but more recently the UN and UNWTO have moderated their views with the following considerations:

1. The need to ensure that tourism is consumed in a sustainable manner. The World Tourism Organisation's 'Global Code of Ethics for Tourism' was endorsed by the UN in 1999 and designed to '…minimise the negative impacts of tourism on the environment and on cultural heritage, while maximising the benefits for residents of tourism destinations' (WTO, 2003).
2. The perception that tourism is an activity for the privileged in a socially divided world. The emergence of 'pro-poor tourism' is an attempt to redress this issue.
3. With increased awareness of global climate change, there is a growing need for tourists to change their behaviour. This involves not only in terms of the volume of travel and travelling responsibly but also in offsetting carbon emissions generated by their travel demands.

This chapter examines how participation in tourism differs between both nations and individuals and explains why, despite declarations to the contrary, tourism is an activity highly concentrated among the affluent, industrialised nations. For much of the rest of the world, and indeed many disadvantaged groups in industrialised nations, participation in tourism, and particularly international tourism, remains an unobtainable luxury.

The demand for tourism: concepts and definitions

Geographers define tourist demand as 'the total number of persons who travel, or wish to travel, to use tourist facilities and services at places away from their places of work and residence' (Mathieson and Wall, 1982). This definition implies a wide range of influences, in addition to price and income, as determinants of demand and includes not only those who actually participate in tourism but also those who aspire to do so but, for various reasons, are unable to.

We should distinguish between 'effective' and 'suppressed' demand for tourism:

- **Effective or actual demand** comprises the actual number of participants in tourism, i.e., those who are actually travelling. This is the component of demand that is most commonly and easily measured, and the bulk of tourist statistics refer to effective demand.
- **Suppressed demand** is made up of that section of the population that does not travel for some reasons. Two elements of suppressed demand can be distinguished.

  i. *Potential demand* refers to those who will travel at some future date if they experience a change in circumstances. For example, their purchasing power may increase, or they may have had a COVID-19 vaccination.
  ii. *Deferred demand* is a demand that has been postponed due to a problem in the supply environment, such as the disruption to Nepal's trekking industry caused by the earthquake in 2015.

In other words, both deferred and potential demand may be converted into effective demand at some future date.

- Finally, there will always be those who simply do not wish to travel, constituting a category of **no demand**.

Effective demand

Travel propensity

In tourism, a useful measure of effective demand is travel propensity, which signifies the percentage of the population actively engaged in tourism. Net travel propensity refers to the percentage of the population who undertake at least one tourism trip during a specific period, while gross travel propensity gives the total number of tourism trips taken as a percentage of the population. Clearly, as second and third holidays increasingly important, gross travel propensity becomes more relevant. Simply dividing gross travel propensity by net will give the travel frequency, in other words, the average number of trips taken by those participating in tourism during the period in question (see Box 2.1). The suppressed and no-demand components will ensure that net travel propensity never approaches 100 per cent and a figure of 70 per cent to 80 per cent is likely to be the maximum. Gross travel propensity, however, can exceed 100 per cent and often approaches 200 per cent in some Western European countries with numerous frequent travellers.

BOX 2.1
CALCULATION OF TRAVEL PROPENSITY AND TRAVEL FREQUENCY

Out of a population of 10 million inhabitants:

3.0 million inhabitants take one trip of one night or more	i.e. 3 × 1 = 3.0 million trips
1.5 million inhabitants take two trips of one night or more	i.e. 1.5 × 2 = 3.0 million trips
0.4 million inhabitants take three trips of one night or more	i.e. 0.4 × 3 = 1.2 million trips
0.2 million inhabitants take four trips of one night or more	i.e. 0.2 × 4 = 0.8 million trips
5.1 million inhabitants take at least one trip	8.0 million trips

Therefore:

$$\text{Net travel propensity} = \frac{\text{Number of population taking at least one trip}}{\text{Total population}} \times 100$$

$$= \frac{5.1}{10} \times 100 = 51 \, \text{per cent}$$

$$\text{Gross travel propensity} = \frac{\text{Number of total trips}}{\text{Total population}} \times 100$$

$$= \frac{8}{10} \times 100 = 80 \, \text{per cent}$$

$$\text{Total frequency} = \frac{\text{Gross travel propensity}}{\text{Net travel propensity}} = \frac{80\%}{51\%} = 1.57$$

A further refinement to the earlier calculations involves assessing the capability of a country to generate trips. This process comprises three stages. First, the number of trips originating in the country is divided by the total number of trips taken in the world. This gives an index of the ability of each country to generate travellers. Second, the population of the country is divided by the total population of the world, thus ranking each country by relative importance in relation to world population. By dividing the result of the first stage by the result of the second, the 'country potential generation index' (CPGI) is produced (Hurdman, 1979).

$$\text{CPGI} = \left(\frac{N_e / N_w}{P_e / P_w} \right)$$

where:

N_e = number of trips generated by country
N_w = number of trips generated in world
P_e = population of country
P_w = population of world

An index of 1.0 indicates an average generation capability. Countries with an index greater than 1.0 are generating more tourists than expected by their population. Conversely, countries with an index below 1.0 generate fewer trips than average.

Adapted from: Schmidhauser, H. (1975) Travel propensity and travel frequency, pp. 53–60, in Burkart, A.J. and Medlik, S. (eds) *The Management of Tourism*. Heinemann; and Hurdman, L.E. (1979) Origin regions of international tourism, *Wiener Geographische Schriften*, 53/54, 43–49.

Determinants of travel propensity

Travel propensity is determined by a variety of factors, which, for the purposes of this chapter, can be divided into two broad groups that demonstrate the importance of 'scale' in considering tourism demand. First, there are the influences that lie at the national level of generalisation, which comprise the world view of travel propensity. These include economic development, population characteristics, and political regimes. Secondly, we can examine the variations in travel propensity from a personal perspective regarding lifestyle, life cycle, and personality factors. In fact, a third group of factors relating to the supply of tourist services is also important. This group encompasses technology, the price, frequency, and speed of transport, as well as the characteristics of accommodation, facilities, and travel organisers. These factors are explored in Chapters 3 and 5.

The world view

Stage in economic development

Economic factors

A society's level of economic development significantly determines tourist demand because the economy influences various critical and interrelated factors. One approach is to consider the division of world economies used by the International Monetary Fund (IMF, 2019). The IMF classifies countries into 39 'advanced economies' and 155 'emerging markets and developing economies' (excluding Cuba and North Korea). This classification has evolved over time and is based on numerous variables, including gross domestic product, source of exports, net debt or credit, and population. Advanced economies are further divided into major advanced economies (the United States, Japan, Germany, France, Italy, the United Kingdom, and Canada); members of the Eurozone; and newly industrialised Asian economies. This classification provides a more accurate picture than the oversimplified contrast presented by the media, which highlights the distinction between the developed nations and the so-called 'Third World' of developing countries.

As a society moves towards becoming an advanced economy, several important processes occur. The nature of employment changes from work in the primary sector (agriculture, fishing, and forestry) to work in the secondary sector (manufacturing) and the tertiary sector (comprising services such as tourism). As this process unfolds, an affluent society usually emerges, with the proportion of economically active individuals increasing from around 30 per cent or less in the developing world to 50 per cent or more in the advanced economies of Western Europe or the United States. The 'emerging market' stage of development is reached, creating demand for consumer goods and leisure pursuits, such as tourism, as demonstrated by China. Development is also characterised by an increase in government investment in infrastructure and a high penetration of technology – both of which encourage tourism.

Other developments run parallel to the changing nature of employment. The population is healthier and has more time for recreation and tourism, including paid-holiday entitlement. Improving educational standards and access to technology and the media enhance awareness of tourism opportunities, while transportation and mobility rise in line with these changes. Institutions respond to this increased demand by developing a range of leisure products and services. These developments occur in conjunction with each other until, in an advanced economy at the 'high mass consumption' stage of development, all the economic indicators encourage high levels of travel propensity. Clearly, tourism is a result of industrialisation and, quite simply, the more highly developed an economy, the greater the levels of tourist demand, as shown by India's growing outbound tourism activity. For this reason, the developing countries only account for a small proportion of the demand for international tourism. The share of the developing countries in the global tourism market is increasing as more countries move towards the advanced economy stage. Effectively, this implies that more countries are joining the 'premier league' of destinations that attract over 1 million arrivals each year, thereby increasing the worldwide competition for tourists. Business travel is sensitive to economic activity, and although it could be argued that increasingly sophisticated communication systems may render business travel unnecessary, there is no evidence of this to date. Indeed, the very development of global markets and the constant need for face-to-face contact should ensure a continuing demand for business travel.

Population factors

Levels of population growth, distribution, and density affect travel propensity. Population growth can be closely linked to stages of economic development by considering the demographic transition, where population growth is seen in terms of four connected phases (Figure 2.1).

- First, the **high stationary phase** corresponds to many of the least developed countries (LDCs) in the Third World with high birth and death rates, keeping population growth at a fluctuating but low level.
- Second, the **early expanding phase** sees high birth rates but a fall in death rates due to improved health, sanitation, and social stability, leading to population expansion characterised by young, large families. Clearly, foreign travel is a luxury that most people living in these countries cannot afford, whereas, on the other hand, some governments are developing an inbound tourism industry to earn foreign exchange.
- The **late expanding phase** witnesses a fall in the birth rate rooted in the growth of an industrial society and advances in birth control technology.

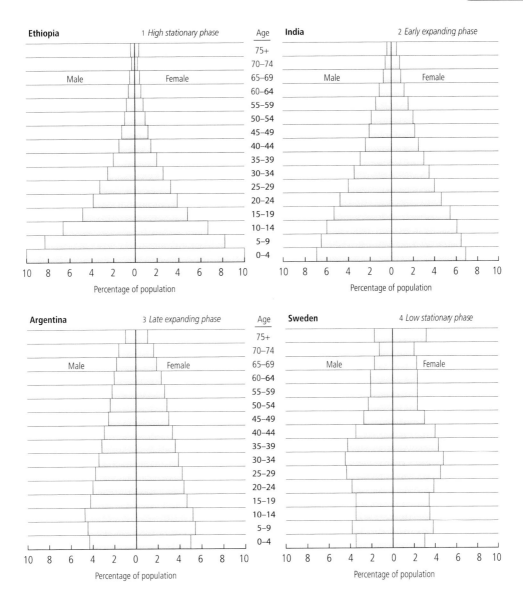

Figure 2.1
The demographic transition

Source: Demographic yearbook of the UN, 1992

Most developing countries fit into the last two phases of population growth with a transition to the late expanding phase paralleling the emerging market stage of development.

- Finally, the **low stationary phase** corresponds to the high mass consumption stage of economic development. Here, birth and death rates have stabilised to a low level. At this stage, it is the evolving demographic characteristics of the population that hold significant implications for tourism demand, because:

1. Populations are ageing.
2. These ageing populations possess a substantial discretionary income, although this may decrease in the future as governments reduce social security benefits to curb public spending.
3. The 'baby-boomer' generation (born in the years immediately after the Second World War) constitutes an important population cohort of experienced, discerning travellers exercising 'grey' power and influencing demand.
4. Household composition is evolving, with increased numbers of single and childless households and fewer families in the traditional sense.

However, some criticise the demographic transition on the basis that it does not include migration and is less applicable to very advanced economies.

Population density (the number of inhabitants per square mile or kilometre) has little influence on travel propensity compared to the distribution of population between urban and rural areas. Large urban areas normally indicate a developed economy where consumer purchasing power, along with the perceived stress of living in modern cities, give rise to a high travel propensity. Yet the trend to *urbanisation* is even more evident in developing countries, and as a result, by 2020 over 60 per cent of the world's population were living in cities. Vast numbers of people are migrating from poor rural communities to the major cities, where many live in peripheral shanty-towns without basic services. Nevertheless, even in such challenging conditions, these migrants enjoy greater access to employment, health care, and education compared to their previous circumstances. The high fertility rates often associated with subsistence farming communities are likely to decline, resulting in smaller families and eventually less poverty.

The distribution of a population within a nation not only impacts the levels of tourist demand but also influences its patterns. When the population is concentrated in one part of the country, it distorts tourism demand. This asymmetrical distribution of population is well illustrated by the United States, where two-thirds of the population live in the eastern one-third of the country. The consequent east-to-west pattern of tourist flow (and permanent migration) has placed pressure on the recreation and tourist resources of the western states. On a regional scale, the concentration of the population in cities also affects demand patterns, often leading to the development of a recreation and tourism hinterland around the city.

Political influences

Politics affect travel propensities in numerous ways:

- **Political complexion** In democratic nations, the degree of government involvement in promoting and providing facilities for tourism can vary. Typically, 'conservative' or 'neo-liberal' administrations subscribe to the principles of the free market and act to nurture an environment in which the tourism industries can flourish without the administration directly involved in tourism itself. Socialist administrations, on the other hand, tend to encourage the involvement of the government in tourism and often provide opportunities for the 'disadvantaged' to participate in tourism.

Democracies control travel propensity foreign trips by limiting the amount of foreign currency that can be taken out of a country. Commonly this occurs when a nation's own currency is weak or the economy is faltering. A weak currency will also deter people from travelling abroad. In planned economies, tourist organisations are cen-tralised and act as an arm of the administration. The government can also severely restrict its peoples' freedom of movement by controlling access to the Internet and by granting or withholding exit visas. The Chinese government, for example, controls outbound tourism by allowing its citizens to travel only to those countries that have been granted 'approved destination status'.

Discussion point: China's outbound travel
By 2018, China had become the world's leading generator of international tourism. To what extent do you think the host countries for these tourists are prepared for them? For example, should hotels be re-designed in accordance with the principles of *feng shui*, and do we understand the needs and preferences of the Chinese tourist when it comes to attractions and activities at the destination? Indeed, should we as hosts, modify our way of life to suit our Chinese guests, or any other tourists, for that matter?

- **Political groupings** Politics also influences tourism demand in terms of political and economic groupings of countries and the increased facilitation of travel between members of such groupings. The member countries of the European Union, for ex-ample, are committed to the effective abolition of border controls, and the adoption of the euro as the single currency has boosted demand for intra-European travel. However, political events such as Brexit (Britain's withdrawal from the European Union) are set to change the pattern of tourism in Europe.
- **Deregulation** The political environment for deregulation and privatisation also en-courages tourism demand through initiatives such as the deregulation of transporta-tion, which can reduce fares and thus increase demand for travel. Additionally, the increased efficiency of the sector, again, acts to boost demand through lower prices and higher quality.
- **Political instability** In a more general sense, unstable political environments ad-versely affect tourism. This impact is not limited to specific regimes where civil dis-order or war is prevalent but also includes the increased threat of terrorist attacks in this century. Tourism demand has been adversely affected across the globe, and in extreme cases, inbound travel to the world's 'trouble spots' becomes impossible.

The personal view

Two sets of personal factors influence travel propensity and, therefore, act to condition access to tourism. The first group of factors can be termed *lifestyle* and include income, employment, holiday entitlement, educational attainment, and mobility. A second group falls under the term *life cycle*, where the age and domestic circumstances of an individual combine to affect both the amount and type of tourism demanded. Naturally, these factors are interrelated and complementary. A high-status job is normally associated with an individual in middle age with a high income, above-average holiday entitlement, education, access to technology and mobility. The interweaving of these variables, coupled with their rapid growth since the end of the Second World War, has combined to make leisure, recreation, and tourism a major force in the developed world. These variables can be used to segment tourism markets, and researchers are now using sophisticated techniques to understand travel behaviour. COVID-19 has had an impact on the personal determinants of travel demand, specifically on how people perceive the risk of infection. Some people are risk-averse, whereas more educated, affluent, and younger tourists are often resistant to 'travel fear'. Others have seen their behaviour change, opting for private rather than public transport, domestic tourism rather than foreign travel, shorter stays, and self-contained accommodation rather than serviced establishments with public spaces.

Lifestyle determinants

Income

Tourism is a luxury, an expensive activity that demands a certain threshold of income before an individual can choose to take part. The key indicators are:

- **Gross income** is the total amount earned but gives little indication of the money available to spend on tourism.
- **Disposable income** is the money that actually reaches people, to use as they see fit. However, demands on disposable income include essentials such as housing, food, and clothing.
- **Discretionary income** is the most useful measure of the ability to participate in tourism. It is the income left over when tax, housing, and the basics of life have been accounted for. Clearly, two households with the same gross incomes may have very different discretionary incomes.

The relationship between income levels and the consumption of tourism is an example of *elasticity of demand*. The demand for business tourism tends to be inelastic, as it is relatively unaffected by changes in the cost of travel, while conventional leisure tourism is sensitive to price. Americans and the Japanese tend to have a higher elasticity of demand than Europeans on similar incomes, as they are more likely to forego a holiday trip with a downturn in the economy or in their financial situation. A low discretionary income markedly depresses travel propensity. As discretionary income rises, the ability to participate in tourism is associated with the purchase of leisure-oriented goods, until, with a high discretionary income, travel may reach a peak and then level off as the demands of a high-status job, and possibly frequent business trips, reduce the ability and desire to travel for pleasure.

Employment

The nature of employment not only influences travel propensity by determining income and holiday entitlement but also has an effect upon the type of holiday demanded. A more fundamental distinction is between those in employment and those who are unemployed. The impact of unemployment on the level of tourism demand is obvious, but the nature of demand is also changed, with the threat of job insecurity among the workforce encouraging later booking of trips, more domestic and VFR holidays, shorter lengths of stay, and lower spending levels.

Paid-holiday entitlement

A variety of holiday arrangements now exist worldwide, with most nations having several one-day national holidays, as well as annual paid-holiday entitlement by law or collective agreements between employers and trade unions. Individual levels of paid-holiday entitlement would seem to be an obvious determinant of travel propensity, but in fact the relationship is not straightforward. However, it is possible to make several generalisations:

- Low levels of entitlement do act as a real constraint upon the ability to travel, while a high entitlement encourages travel. This is in part due to the interrelationship between entitlement and factors such as job status, income, and mobility.
- As levels of entitlement increase, the cost of tourism may mean that more of this entitlement will be spent on leisure at home.
- Patterns of entitlement are changing. Entitlement is increasingly used as a wage-bargaining tool, and the introduction of flexitime, work sharing, long weekends, and sabbaticals will release blocks of time that may be used for short holiday breaks.

Choice of lifestyle

In pre-industrial and industrial societies, an individual's social class or socio-economic group largely determined their use of leisure. In post-industrial countries, such as Britain, the type of holiday demanded is increasingly related to an individual's choice of a particular lifestyle and the behavioural patterns associated with that lifestyle.

Other personal factors

The level of educational attainment is an important determinant of travel propensity, as education broadens horizons and stimulates the desire to travel. Furthermore, the better educated the individual, the higher their awareness and susceptibility to information, the media, advertising, sales promotions, and technology. The latter point is important as education enhances the ability to utilise technology and facilitates the demand for travel through access to the Internet, which influences travel decisions through both social media and user-generated content sites such as TripAdvisor. Personal mobility, usually expressed as car ownership, is an important influence on travel propensity, especially regarding domestic holidays. We will discuss this variable in Chapter 5.

Discussion point

Other variables, such as gender and belonging to an ethnic minority, may limit access to tourism. Women in traditional societies, and even in advanced economies, have effectively fewer leisure opportunities than men due to the way society is organised. Even in Europe, there are wide differences between countries in the amount of unpaid work (caring, household chores) carried out by women, with Sweden comparing favourably in this respect with Spain. Discuss how such gender inequality might affect the extent of women's participation in domestic and foreign tourism.

Life cycle determinants

The propensity to travel, and indeed the type of tourism experience demanded, is closely related to an individual's age. While the conventional measurement is chronological age, domestic age better discriminates between types of tourist demand and levels of travel propensity. This approach is sometimes referred to as life course analysis. Domestic age refers to the stage in the life cycle reached by an individual and different stages are characterised by distinctive holiday demands and levels of travel propensity (Table 2.1). The

Table 2.1 Domestic age and tourism demand

Adolescence/young adult

At this stage, there is a need for independence and a search for identity. Typically, holidays independent of parents begin at around 15 years, constrained by lack of finance but compensated by having few other commitments, no shortage of free time, and a curiosity for new places and experiences. This group has a high propensity to travel, mainly on budget holidays using surface transport and self-catering accommodation. They are seen as opinion leaders, and the tourism sector actively seeks their custom, hoping to gain their loyalty in later years.

Marriage

Before the arrival of children, young couples often have a high income and few other ties, giving them a high travel propensity, frequently overseas. The arrival of children coupled with the responsibility of a home means that constraints of time and finance depress travel propensity. Holidays become more organisational than geographical with domestic tourism, self-catering accommodation, and visiting friends and relatives increasingly common. As children grow up and reach the adolescence stage, constraints of time and finance are lifted and parents' travel propensity increases. In the industrialised countries, this post-Second World War 'baby boom' group is the vanguard of the new tourist – discerning, experienced and seeking quality and value for money.

Retirement

The emergence of early retirement at 50 or 55 years is creating an active and mobile group in the population that will demand both domestic and international travel. In later retirement, lack of finance, infirmity, reduced personal mobility, and often the loss of a partner act to offset the increase in free time experienced by this group. Holidays become more hotel-based and travel propensity decreases.

concept of domestic age works well for Westernised, industrialised tourist-generating countries and is therefore a useful generalisation for the leading generators of tourism worldwide. However, it has its critics for these reasons:

- The concept is less well-suited to other cultures.
- In the industrialised world, changing household composition and social norms mean that the concept has to be treated with care.

> **Discussion point: tourism and domestic age**
> To what extent does the idea of domestic age fit the holiday preferences and tourism patterns of members of your family? Furthermore, when thinking about the travel patterns of your family, is there an identifiable 'travel career' demonstrated by anyone in your family or any of your friends?

Personality factors

No two individuals are alike, and differences in attitudes, perceptions, and motivation have a significant influence on travel decisions. Attitudes depend on an individual's perception of the world. Perceptions are mental impressions of, say, a place or travel company and are determined by many factors, which include childhood, family, and work experiences. As perceptions will be influential in making the decision to travel, it is important for planners and managers in tourist destinations to foster favourable 'images' of their locations in the public's mind.

Attitudes and perceptions in themselves do not explain why people want to travel. The inner urges, which initiate travel demand, are called travel motivators. It is crucial to understand these motivators as they help explain why some destinations fall in and out of fashion. An individual's personal needs help form motivations – the 'intrinsic' influences; while 'extrinsic' influences such as peer groups and fashion are a second set of influences. Gray (1970) has outlined a classification of travel motivators:

- **Wanderlust** is simply a curiosity to experience the strange and unfamiliar. It refers to the basic trait in human nature to see, at first hand, different places, cultures, and peoples. Status and prestige motivators would be included under this heading.
- **Sunlust** can be literally translated as the desire for sunshine and a better climate, but in fact it is broader than this and refers to the search for a better set of amenities for recreation than are available at home.

As tourist consumer behaviour has changed, there has been a shift away from sunlust to wanderlust motivators, partly driven by fears of the effects of exposure to the sun, but also by the desire to fully experience the culture as well as the physical attractions of the destination.

The interaction of personality attributes, such as attitude, perceptions, and motivation, influence demand in two ways. First, they impact on a tourist's *image* of a destination – an important factor in the decision-making process of whether to visit a

Table 2.2 Cohen's classification of tourists

The organised mass tourist
Low on adventurousness, he or she is anxious to maintain his or her 'environmental bubble' on trip. Typically purchasing a ready-made package tour off-the-shelf, he or she is guided through the destination having little contact with local culture or people.

The individual mass tourist
Similar to the organised mass tourist but more flexibility and scope for personal choice are built-in. However, the tour is still organised by the tourism industry and the environmental bubble shields him or her from the real experience of the destination.

The explorer
The trip is organised independently and is looking to get off the beaten track. However, comfortable accommodation and reliable transport are sought, and while the environmental bubble is abandoned on occasion, it is there to step into if things get tough.

The drifter
All connections with the tourism industry are spurned and the trip attempts to get as far from home and familiarity as possible. With no fixed itinerary, the drifter lives with the local people, paying his or her way, and is immersed in their culture.

Familiarity

Institutionalised tourism
Dealt with routinely by the tourism industry – tour operators, travel agents, hoteliers, and transport operators.

Non-institutionalised tourism
Individual travel, shunning contact with the tourism industry except where absolutely necessary.

Novelty

Source: Adapted from Cohen (1972)

particular destination – and second, they allow different types of tourists to be identified. One classification by Cohen (1972) is particularly useful. He uses a classification based on the theory that tourism combines the curiosity to seek out new experiences with the need for the security of familiar reminders of home. Cohen proposes a continuum of possible combinations of novelty and familiarity and, by breaking up the continuum into typical combinations of these two ingredients, a fourfold classification of tourists is produced (Table 2.2). More recent research has confirmed Cohen's approach, suggesting there is a human gene associated with risk and sensation seeking.

Suppressed demand

Potential demand

Throughout this chapter, the concern has been to identify factors which influence effective tourist demand. Yet tourism is still an unobtainable luxury for most of the world's population, not just in undeveloped and developing countries but also for many in the developed world. Indeed, the concept of *potential demand* demonstrates that there are considerable inequalities of access to tourism, rooted in the personal circumstances of individuals. Lansing and Blood (1960) have identified five major reasons why people do not travel:

- Expense of travel – exacerbated by reduced disposable incomes as a result of COVID-19
- Lack of time
- Physical limitations (such as ill health)
- Family circumstances
- Lack of interest

It is not uncommon for individuals to experience a combination of two or more of these barriers. For example, a one-parent family or a person caring for a disabled relative may find that a lack of income and time will combine with family circumstances to prevent tourism. Obviously, it is just these groups who would most benefit from a holiday, and tourism planners are increasingly concerned with identifying these barriers and devising programmes to encourage non-participants to travel. Perhaps the best-known example of this is the *social tourism movement*, which is concerned with the participation in travel by people with some form of handicap or disadvantage, and the measures used to encourage this participation. In countries where state intervention is the norm, the government and its agencies are largely responsible for social tourism. In some (such as Israel), labour unions play an important role, while in others, the participation of church groups and similar voluntary organisations is more significant. Also, in response to COVID-19, social tourism in the form of travel vouchers and reduced admission charges has been introduced to reward 'front line' workers. Slovenia is one example (see https://www.gov.si/en/news/2020-06-09-slovenia-residents-receive-tourist-vouchers-44587).

Deferred demand

Of course, there are also barriers to travel based upon the supply environment, leading to deferred demand. The new millennium has seen a series of events that have markedly increased deferred demand around the world and reduced growth rates of international tourism. These events include natural disasters, such as the 2004 Asian tsunami, numerous terrorist attacks on destinations and events, wars such as those in Syria and Afghanistan, the COVID-19 pandemic, and an increased awareness of the impact of travelling on climate change.

The effect of a crisis on demand has been for tourists to either defer travel or to change the nature of their trip and:

- Book later.
- Travel to what are perceived to be safer destinations closer to home.
- Use surface transport modes such as railways, which are more 'carbon-neutral' than air transport.
- Use 'flexible' booking channels such as the Internet.

CASE STUDY 2.1
THE COVID-19 PANDEMIC AND ITS IMPACT
ON TOURISM DEMAND

Tourism is potentially at risk from natural and man-made disasters, particularly in developing countries that can ill-afford the loss of foreign exchange. Crisis and risk management plans have been developed in many destinations after the events of 9/11 drastically impacted the demand for international tourism. The four elements of such plans are:

- Reduction – the identification of a potential crisis and the strengths and weaknesses of a destination to reduce the impact of the crisis.
- Readiness – the development of a plan and continual assessment of the strategies to deal with the risks.
- Response – involves an operational response focussed on damage limitation, and a communications response focussing on reassuring the potential tourist.
- Recovery – the speed with which the destination resumes normal operations. In successive crises since 9/11, the tourism sector has proved resilient, but in the case of COVID-19, this did not mean 'business as usual' prior to the epidemic.

The COVID-19 pandemic has had an unprecedented impact on tourism worldwide, both on demand (restrictions on freedom of movement plus the fear of infection) and on supply (the closure of tourism facilities). The industry faced a crisis much longer in duration than previous disruptive events, and one that few experts could have foreseen. The pandemic caused a 74 per cent decline in the number of international tourists in 2020, and a loss of 1 trillion US dollars in export revenues from tourism (Ketter and Avraham, 2021). The impact of the pandemic has not only been transformative, but it has also accelerated trends that were already emerging, such as video-conferencing and working from home. We also need to recognise that, while tourism is a victim of the pandemic, it is also a vector as the movement of travellers helps spread pathogens around the world.

The first cases of a previously unknown lung disease were reported in Wuhan, a major city in south China, in December 2019. A wholesale market that sold live animals among other goods was identified as the source. By February 2020, the virus had been recognised as a pandemic by the World Health Organisation and had spread to cruise ships and over a hundred countries. Pandemics have the following characteristics:

- They are widely distributed or even global in scope.
- The disease is spread by transmission that can be traced from one location to another.
- Multiple cases appear within a short period of time.
- The populations affected have initially little or no immunity to the disease. (This was true historically of the indigenous peoples of the Americas and the Pacific islands, who were decimated shortly after contact with Europeans by diseases such as smallpox.)
- They are new diseases or are associated with new variants of existing organisms.

The connection between foreign travel and the spread of infection has been recognised for centuries with the imposition of **quarantine** restrictions on travellers arriving at a country's ports. These restrictions originated in Venice, in medieval times a cosmopolitan centre of international trade, and were rigidly enforced. Ships had to wait for 40 days (*quaranta giorni* in Italian) at the island of Lazzaretto Nuovo before passengers and crews were permitted to enter Venice itself to protect the city from bubonic plague.

The introduction of mass vaccination programmes proved to be the most effective response to the pandemic crisis. Prior to a variety of vaccines being officially sanctioned, the preventive measures imposed by governments had a particularly damaging effect on tourism, and the economy in general. These included:

- Lockdowns of whole communities, quarantine restrictions, and the social isolation of households.
- Travel bans, suspension of international flights, and border closures.
- Closure of schools and tourism-related businesses, causing major changes to employment and disposable income.
- Cancellation of events (for example, the Tokyo Olympics was postponed to 2021).
- Bans on social gatherings; this had a major impact on religious practice and the sport and entertainment sectors of tourism.
- Social distancing; this reduced the physical capacity of businesses in the hospitality sector and visitor attractions. Many found it difficult to adapt, and uneconomic to provide reduced services.

In the face of worldwide travel bans and lockdowns, destinations were unwilling to receive tourists but continued to market themselves on-line during the pandemic. During lockdown, videos and advertisements tried to ensure that potential visitors were not only aware of the destination, but that it remained at the top of their minds. For example, Malta's video campaign in 14 different languages used the emotions of longing and nostalgia with the slogan 'Dream Malta Now-Visit Later'. The Greek NTO's video 'Discover Greece from Home' portrayed Greeks living in their homes to create an authentic interaction with the destination. The approach post-lockdown by many NTOs was to restore confidence, emphasising health checks, hygiene, and social distancing to show that the destination was not only safe but also uncrowded (Ketter and Avraham, 2021).

It is evident that digital tourism has received a massive impetus from the COVID-19 crisis, and that the pre-booking of attractions and the use of contactless payments for every transaction are here to stay. In the meantime, we must learn to live with the virus. It is also clear that the pandemic has provided destinations with a unique opportunity to rebuild tourism to be a positive force for good for the environment, economies, and societies. The UN World Tourism Organisation has declared that innovation and sustainability must become the 'new normal'. We must not waste this opportunity, as it probably will not come round again in our lifetimes.

- Consider the cost and carbon emission impact of travel carefully.
- Take shorter trips and avoid travel to long-haul destinations.
- Opt for domestic rather than international tourism.
- Cease travelling altogether.

The pattern of tourism demand

Determinants of tourist demand, allied to the characteristics of the mosaic of tourism destinations around the world, combine to produce the global rhythms and patterns of tourism. The end of the Second World War represented the beginning of a remarkable period of growth for international tourism, with an annual average growth rate approaching 7 per cent for the second half of the twentieth century. However, this growth was severely impacted by the COVID-19 pandemic as Table 2.3 dramatically represents. Until the early years of the twenty-first century, international tourism was remarkably resilient to factors that might have been expected to depress growth – recession, oil crises, wars, and terrorism. However, the 9/11 attacks changed everything, destabilising demand and enhancing the importance of security while travelling. As we enter the third decade of the twenty-first century, the long shadow cast by the COVID-19 pandemic and concerns about climate change may well see previous decades being viewed as a period of unprecedented freedom to travel. Particularly, COVID-19 has impacted tourism flows around the world, not simply by significantly reducing volumes but also the pattern of flows, as some destinations are perceived to be safer, having managed the crisis better than others.

International tourism arrivals and departures are concentrated into relatively few countries, mainly in Europe and North America. This produces an unbalanced picture that

Table 2.3 International tourism demand: the historical trend

Year	International tourism arrivals (millions)	International tourism receipts (US$ millions)
1950	25.3	2,100
1960	69.3	6,867
1970	159.7	17,900
1980	284.8	102,372
1985	321.2	116,158
1990	454.8	255,000
1995	567.0	372,000
2000	696.8	477,000
2005	806.0	680,000
2010	940.0	868,400
2019	1465.9	
2021	446.3	

Source: UNWTO

Table 2.4 International tourism demand: the changing regional picture percentage share of international arrivals by UNWTO region

Region	1950 %	1960 %	1970 %	1980 %	1990 %	2000 %	2010 %	2019 %	2021 %
Europe	66.5	72.5	70.5	68.4	63.5	57.8	50.6	50.8	67.9
Americas	29.6	24.1	23.0	18.9	18.8	18.4	15.9	15.0	18.4
East Asia & Pacific (EAP) (including South Asia)	1.0	1.3	3.6	7.8	12.1	16.6	21.7	24.5	4.6
Africa	2.1	1.1	1.5	2.5	3.4	3.9	5.3	4.7	4.2
Middle East	0.9	1.0	1.4	2.4	2.1	3.3	6.5	5.0	4.8

Source: UNWTO

favours developed Western economies and disadvantages the developing world, which is left to compete for the long-haul market – and this accounts for a minor share of the total market. For both generators and destinations of international tourism, as more countries, such as the Russian Federation, have entered the market, the dominance of the leading players has been gradually reduced.

- **Generators** The major tourism-generating countries are those with advanced economies. However, as countries approach this stage, they become significant generators of international tourism, such as China and India.
- **Destinations** The post-war period has been marked by the rapid emergence of the East Asia and the Pacific region (EAP) as an international tourism destination, largely at the expense of the Americas and Europe (Table 2.4). This trend was checked by the COVID-19 pandemic, with EAP experiencing a severe decline in arrivals.

Summary

- Tourism is a major contribution to the quality of life in the twenty-first century, and demand for tourism is made up of those not only who participate but also who do not travel for some reason.
- Travel propensity is a useful indicator of tourism participation, as it gives the proportion of a population who actually engage in tourism. Travel frequency refers to the average number of trips taken by those participating in tourism during a specified period.
- Travel propensity is determined by a variety of factors that can be viewed at two scales. At the world scale, those countries with a high level of economic development and a stable, urbanised population are major generators of tourism demand. The political regime of a country is also relevant here. At the individual scale, a certain

level of discretionary income is required to allow participation in tourism, and this income, and indeed, the type of participation, will be influenced by such factors as the type of employment, life cycle stage, mobility, level of educational attainment, and personality.

- Even within the developed world, many are unable to participate in tourism for some reason. Demand for tourism is, therefore, concentrated in developed Western economies and predominates among those with high discretionary incomes.

Assignments

Using the UNWTO web site, plot the flows of international tourism from the major tourist-generating countries to significant destinations on a world map. Explain the patterns that you see in terms of:

1. Short-haul (intra-regional) and long-haul (intercontinental) flows;
2. The reasons for the dominance of developed Western economies in the ten leading generating countries; and
3. The competitive advantages of the 'top ten' world destinations.

References and further reading

Cohen, E. (1972) Toward a sociology of international tourism, *Social Research* 39 (1), 164–183

Gray, H.P. (1971) *International Travel-International Trade*, Heath Lexington Books, New York

International Monetary Fund (2019) *World Economic Outlook 2018*, IMF, Washington

Ketter, E. and Avraham, E. (2021) StayHome Today so we can TravelTomorrow: Tourism destinations digital marketing strategies during the Covid-19 pandemic, *Journal of Travel and Tourism Marketing* 38 (8), 818–832

Lansing, J.B. and Blood, D.M. (1960) *The Changing Travel Market*, Institute for Social Research, Washington

Pearce, P.L. (2011) *Tourist Behaviour and the Contemporary World*, Channel View, Bristol

Song, R. (2018) Emerging markets in tourism, pp. 111–28, in Cooper, C., Volo, S., Gartner, W.C. and Scott, N. (eds) *The Sage Handbook in Tourism Management: Applications of Theories and Concepts to Tourism*, Sage, London

World Tourism Organisation (2003) *Global Code of Ethics for Tourism*, WTO, Madrid

World Tourism Organisation (2011) *Tourism Towards 2030: Global Overview*, WTO, Madrid

3 The geography of resources for tourism

Learning objectives

After reading this chapter, you should be able to:

- Appreciate the nature of resources for tourism.
- Distinguish the methods used to classify and evaluate resources for tourism.
- Outline the main factors favouring the development of tourism resources.
- Appreciate the impact of the COVID-19 pandemic on the destination.
- Understand the way that destinations evolve.
- Appreciate the need for destination planning, marketing, and sustainability.
- Match specific types of recreation and tourism to the appropriate resources.

DOI: 10.4324/9781003406853-4

Introduction

Technology now allows tourists to reach most parts of the world, yet only a small fraction of the world's potential tourism resource is developed. Nonetheless, with growing demand for tourism focussed on a small resource base, tourist destinations are under pressure. In part, this is because tourism does not occur evenly or randomly in time or space, but pressure is focussed seasonally and at special and unique places. This demands the effective planning and management of tourism resources and, in particular, the matching of appropriate types of tourists to particular types of resource. Different types of tourism will have distinctive requirements for growth, and certain sites, regions, or countries will be more favourable for development than others. This chapter examines tourism resources at three scales: global, national, and local.

The characteristics and management of tourism resources

Characteristics

Tourism resources have three main characteristics:

1. By tourism resources we usually mean tangible features that are considered to be of economic value to the tourism sector. The sector, and indeed the tourist, therefore has to recognise that a place, landscape, or natural feature is of value before they can become tourism resources. For example, rugged mountains were viewed by most people in the West as barriers to be feared, rather than as scenic attractions, until the eighteenth century. Similarly, until sunbathing became fashionable in the 1920s, the combination of sun, sand, and sea was not seen as a valuable tourism resource, and we are now beginning to see people's perceptions of the beach holiday change due to fears of skin cancer.
2. Most tourism resources are not used exclusively by tourists. Apart from resort areas or theme parks where tourism is the dominant use of land, tourism shares the resource with agriculture, forestry, water management, or residents using local services. In many parts of the world, beaches continue to be more important as a resource for local fishing communities or the construction industry than for tourism. Tourism is a significant land use but rarely the dominant one, and this can lead to conflict. Tourism, as a latecomer, is 'fitted in' with other uses of land. This is known as *multiple use*, and needs skillful management and co-ordination of users to be successful.
3. Tourism resources are perishable. Not only are they vulnerable to alteration and destruction by tourist pressure, but, in common with many service industries, some resources are also perishable in another sense. Tourist services such as beds in accommodation or ride seats in theme parks are impossible to stock and have to be consumed when and where they exist. As unused resources cannot be stored, yield management systems have been developed to maximise their consumption.

Planning

Clearly, the components of the tourist destination can only be effective if careful planning and management deliver a sustainable tourism product. Inevitably, tourism is attracted to fragile and unique resources throughout the world. In the period following the Second World War, many countries sought international tourism as an ideal solution to economic problems. Tourism was seen as an 'industry without chimneys', which brought economic benefits in employment, income, and development. However, this economic imperative overlooked the environmental, social, and cultural consequences of tourism in many countries. In part, this was due to the ease of measuring the economic impacts of tourism and the difficulty of quantifying other types of impact. There is now an increasing awareness of the need to consider the environment and the host community to complement the economic needs of destinations. Consumer pressure is shunning ethically unsound destinations, and environmental impact assessments are being completed for major tourism projects. Since the late 1980s, sustainable tourism development has become the organising framework, as mainstream concepts of sustainability have been applied to tourism. The concept of sustainability demands a long-term view of tourism and ensures that consumption of resources does not exceed the ability of a host destination to provide for future tourists. In other words, it represents a trade-off between present and future needs. A key priority is to translate the principles of sustainable development into action. For example, in the tourism industry, this is being done in several ways:

- Codes of conduct and guidelines: providing the industry with practical measures for, say, recycling.
- Accreditation and certification: inspecting and certifying businesses based on sustainable practices.
- Licences: licensing businesses operating in environmentally sensitive areas.
- Best practice dissemination: educating and communicating examples of best practice in sustainable tourism throughout the industry.

Carrying capacity is a key concept of sustainable tourism; in other words, planners determine the levels of use that can be sustained by a resource and manage it to that level (see Table 3.1). Once these numbers are exceeded, the resource suffers from 'overtourism' – a fashionable word for exceeding carrying capacity.

Tourism planning must be central to these issues. Tourism planning has evolved from an inflexible, physical planning approach to a flexible approach which seeks to maximise the benefits and minimise the costs of tourism, while at the same time recognising the holistic nature of tourism, whereby we must plan for the visitor as well as the resource. The benefits of tourism planning are clear (Table 3.2). Ideally, tourism planning is characterised by:

1. A basis in sound research
2. The involvement of the local community in setting goals and priorities
3. A holistic approach, considering all aspects of the destination
4. Implementation by the public sector (government) in partnership with the private sector (business)

Table 3.1 Carrying capacity

The concept of carrying capacity has a long pedigree. It was originally developed by resource managers in agriculture and forestry to determine the cropping levels that plots of land could sustain without nutrients and other food sources being depleted. In tourism, carrying capacity refers to the ability of a destination to take tourism use without deteriorating in some way. In other words, it defines the relationship between the resource base and the market and is influenced by the characteristics of each. One of the best definitions is by Mathieson and Wall (1982, 21): 'The maximum number who can use a site without unacceptable deterioration in the physical environment and without an unacceptable decline in the quality of experience gained by visitors'. This definition raises two key points:

1 Carrying capacity can be managed, and there is no absolute number for any destination. For example, open heathland can appear crowded with very few visitors present, while a wooded area can absorb many more visitors.

2 We can look at carrying capacity in different ways, in terms of the resource itself, from the point of view of the visitor and from the point of view of the host community:

    a Physical carrying capacity refers to the number of facilities available such as aircraft seats or car parking spaces. It is easy to measure and can be calculated on a simple percentage basis.

    b Environmental or biological carrying capacity is more difficult to measure and refers to limits of use in the ecosystem. There is increasing interest in the capacity not only of the vegetation cover to take tourism use but also of the animal life, such as tourism based on whale or dolphin watching, or the African game reserves.

    c Psychological or behavioural carrying capacity refers to the point at which the visitor feels that additional visitors would spoil the experience. This is less straightforward than may appear at first sight. Completely empty spaces are just as problematic as crowded ones, and the type of tourist also influences perceptions of crowding. To take beaches as our example, the European Union stipulates a density of 0.6 square metres per person as a minimum standard; however, people from Mediterranean cultures are usually prepared to accept much greater levels of crowding than would be acceptable for, say, Scandinavians.

    d Social carrying capacity is a measure of the ability of the host community to tolerate tourism. It is a more recent addition to typologies of capacity but is becoming an important issue. Indeed, one of the most important tests of a sustainable tourist destination is the level of involvement of the local community in plans and decisions relating to tourism development. While there is a concern that local residents have a lack of knowledge about tourism, new techniques such as 'destination visioning' (where the locals determine the future of tourism) and 'limits to acceptable change' (where they determine levels of future development) are increasingly being adopted and are a form of capacity management.

    e Economic carrying capacity refers to the point at which the investment needed to sustain environmental quality becomes prohibitive.

Despite the many approaches to tourism planning, the planning progress can be reduced to six basic questions:

1.   What type of tourist will visit?
2.   What is the scale of tourism?

Table 3.2 The benefits of tourism planning

For those involved in delivering and developing tourism at the destination, tourism planning:

- Provides a set of common objectives for all at the destination to follow.
- Co-ordinates the many suppliers of tourism at the destination.
- Encourages partnerships between *stakeholders* at the destination (these might include, for example, representatives of the local community as well as tour operators and others actually involved in the tourism industry and government).
- Encourages effective organisation at the destination.
- Provides an integrating framework for future actions and decisions.

For the destination itself, tourism planning encourages a high-quality tourism environment because it:

- Optimises the benefits of tourism to a destination.
- Minimises the negative effects of tourism on the economy, environment, and host community.
- Encourages the adoption of the principles and practice of sustainable tourism.
- Provides a plan based on land use for zoning areas for development, conservation, and protection.
- Encourages design and other standards for the tourism sector to work on.
- Encourages careful matching of the development of the destination and its markets.
- Allows for the consideration of issues such as manpower and investment.
- Upgrades the destination environment.
- Encourages a monitoring system to be implemented at the destination.

3. Where will development take place?
4. What controls will be placed on development?
5. How will development be financed?
6. What will be the government's role?

The answer to these questions will depend, from place to place, on the government's approach to tourism and the importance of tourism to the economy. The planning process is summarised in Figure 3.1.

Unfortunately, despite the emergence of tourism planning as a profession, many plans for tourism either fail or are opposed. They may fail because policy changes, demand changes, unforeseen competition emerges, investment is not available, or the plan was too ambitious or inflexible in the first place.

If tourism planning fails, these consequences may follow:

- The quality and integrity of the tourism resource are put at risk.
- The role of tourism in multiple land use may be threatened as other uses dominate.
- The tourist suffers from a poor-quality experience.

Figure 3.1
Tourism planning flowchart
Source: Based on Mill and Morrison (1985)

As we have become more sophisticated in the management of tourism, the emphasis has moved from the protection and preservation of resources to the management of visitors, and, in particular, the need to deliver an enjoyable, worthwhile experience. Figure 3.2 outlines the approaches used to manage visitors.

Discussion point: valuing tourism resources
The value of a resource cannot always be expressed in terms of money. For example, how can we compare the value of a work of art with a natural attraction such as a waterfall or an area of rainforest threatened by the development of a hydroelectric power plant?

Tourism resources at the global scale

Physical features

We can view the Earth as a system made up of the following subsystems:

* The biosphere (all living things)
* The atmosphere (air)

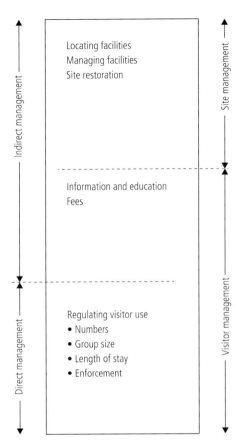

Figure 3.2
Visitor management strategies and actions

- The hydrosphere (water)
- The lithosphere (the Earth's crust)
- The cryosphere (ice)

Nearly three quarters of the Earth's surface consists of sea, including the five oceans, namely the Pacific (by far the largest), the Atlantic, the Indian, the Southern, and the Arctic (which is largely ice-covered). Land makes up the remaining 29 per cent, comprising the seven continents and associated islands, namely Asia (the largest both in terms of population and land area), followed by Africa, North America, South America, Antarctica, Europe, and Australasia. Strictly speaking, Europe is part of the greater landmass known as Eurasia. Almost 40 per cent of the Northern Hemisphere, but less than 20 per cent of the Southern Hemisphere, is made up of land. This uneven distribution of land and sea has important implications for climate, population distribution, economic development, communications, and thus tourism.

The topography of the Earth's land surface is composed of a variety of landforms, which we can broadly group into four categories: mountains (areas of elevated, rugged terrain), more gently sloping hill lands, elevated plateaus, and lowland plains. Within each category, there are features resulting from natural forces such as erosion and variations in the composition of the underlying rock. It is worth looking at some of these features in more detail.

- *Geothermal* features comprise volcanoes, crater lakes and calderas, lava formations, geysers, and hot springs. They are caused by disturbances from deep within the Earth's crust. The world's most spectacular mountains are generally associated with geologically unstable areas characterised by earthquakes and volcanic activity. This includes the 'Pacific Ring of Fire', which is situated close to the western and eastern margins of the world's largest ocean. Even in areas where volcanic eruptions have ceased for many millennia, they have left a legacy of hot springs and other water sources rich in minerals. These are thought to have therapeutic properties, and in many instances have given rise to a spa (by this, we mean a health resort rather than a facility for health and beauty treatments).
- *Karst* features are found in areas composed of hard limestone, where surface streams have 'disappeared' through sinkholes to carve out impressive gorges and caverns.
- *Glaciated* features are the result of action by frost and slow-moving masses of ice. Most are the legacy of the last Ice Age, which ended in Europe and North America some ten millennia ago. They include spectacular mountain peaks, bowl-shaped cirques at the head of former glaciers, moraines of deposited material in the valleys, lakes, and waterfalls. The scenic variety offered by mountains in middle latitudes is particularly attractive for tourism development and encourages activity and adventure holidays. Most activities involve a limited number of visitors and are the concern of 'niche' tour operators dealing directly with their customers. In contrast, skiing and snowboarding attract a mass following, and a major winter sports industry has burgeoned in most developed countries, even where suitable resources are in short supply. In summer, regions such as the Alps attract tourists interested in sightseeing for a 'lakes and mountains' holiday.

The sparse population of most mountain regions has made it easier for governments to designate areas as *national parks* for their outstanding natural beauty, unique geological features, wildlife habitats, or their 'countryside capital' – the rural fabric of traditional buildings and landscapes. This last point highlights the fact that very few national parks are areas of pristine wilderness that have remained unaltered by human activity, and many do not satisfy the strict criteria laid down by the International Union for the Conservation of Nature (IUCN). Tourism has to compete with other demands on resources, including forestry, pasture for grazing, hydroelectric power generation, and mineral extraction. Since mountain areas have a limited carrying capacity, over-development involving the construction of dams, roads, and cableways is a matter of growing concern. This has led many authorities to discourage the more popular forms of tourism in favour of activities that are more in harmony with the natural environment and will sustain the resource for future generations.

The coast

The coastal zone is where the processes of the sea and the land interact, resulting in a great diversity of landforms and scenery. At least 60 per cent of the world's population is estimated to live on or near the coast, so tourism is but one of many economic activities making demands on its resources.

The quest for the 'perfect beach' is a recurring theme in international tourism. The beach, the world's favourite playground, appeals to all the physical senses more than any other environment and is associated in people's minds with images of carefree hedonism. In contrast, the 2004 tsunami in the Indian Ocean is a reminder that the sea has always been a potential source of danger. Most coastlines are rugged and indented, so that sandy beaches are restricted to small 'pockets' between headlands. Even where the land is flat and conditions are favourable for large-scale tourism development, coastal sites are sought for industrial use, such as oil refineries and nuclear power stations. Moreover, with climate change resulting in rising sea levels, the coast is a vulnerable resource.

A beach extends from the foreshore to a landward boundary formed by a line of cliffs, protective sand dunes, or a man-made feature such as a sea wall. There are significant differences between beaches in terms of texture, from fine-grained sand to coarse shingle, while colours can vary from tan or buff to white and pink (where the sand is derived from fragments of coral), contrasting with black beaches of volcanic origin. The gradient of the beach is important, as this influences the amount of wave energy that reaches the shore. A steeply-sloping beach with waves breaking over an offshore reef is sought by surfers, but is unlikely to provide safe bathing conditions for families with young children.

Although beaches have a high carrying capacity, the same is not true of dunes, where the protective plant cover is highly vulnerable to trampling. Overcrowding and the litter produced by a throwaway society are features of popular holiday resorts in peak season. Furthermore, coastal waters are prone to pollution from a variety of sources. The World Health Organization reports that industrial waste and faecal contamination from untreated sewage are a serious risk to swimmers on many beaches, particularly in Asia. In response to the pollution threat, a growing number of countries have adopted the 'Blue Flag' scheme, which closely monitors water quality, safety (for example, the presence of lifeguards), environmental management to prevent conflict between different types of water-based recreation, and, not least, environmental education. Beaches are also severely eroded by winter storms, and this has led many local authorities, with the help of central government, to invest in costly beach replenishment schemes which import material from elsewhere (see Figure 3.3).

Coral reefs are a feature of oceanic islands and most mainland coasts in the tropics, where sea surface temperatures range between 23°C and 29°C, and the water is clear and of moderate depth. Locations near the mouth of a large river such as the Amazon, or

Figure 3.3
Before and after beach replenishment: aerial view of Miami Beach. Courtesy of the City of Miami Beach Historical Archive MB 991.6 (1982)

where there is a cold current offshore, are not favourable for their growth. Typically, the reef encloses a sheltered lagoon and slopes steeply as a 'drop-off' to the sea bed. This provides an ideal setting for water sports, particularly snorkelling and scuba diving. Coral reef ecosystems are extraordinarily diverse but highly vulnerable, not only to a rise in sea temperature of only 2°C caused by 'global warming', but also a number of other dangers, mostly man-made. These include sediment from beachfront development in places like Florida, over-fishing, pollution from sewage, oil spills, and physical damage by careless holidaymakers. Several countries have designated *marine reserves* to protect the reefs and sea life in general, but enforcement is problematic, given the scale of commercial fishing worldwide.

Coastal *wetlands*, consisting of estuaries, marshes, and swamps, have long been under-valued as a tourism resource, but are now attracting the attention of developers. Although important as natural sea defences, and as habitats for wildlife, including many species of birds – a fact recognised by the Ramsar Convention – the world's wetlands are under threat. In many tropical countries, mangrove swamps have been dredged to provide harbours and yacht marinas or to expand the lucrative shrimp-farming industry. Elsewhere, wetlands have been reclaimed for use by airports, industry, and intensive agriculture.

Discussion point: cultural behaviour and beach resources
The ways in which people use the beach for recreation and the type of amenities on offer vary considerably from country to country. This raises the following points for discussion: Should some beaches be privately owned, or should access be freely available to everybody? How can we maintain or improve the quality of our beaches? When have you been on holiday in a foreign country, how does the use of the beach differ from your experience at home, is this due to cultural differences, different weather patterns, or other reasons?

Inland water resources

In landlocked countries, lakes and rivers provide a substitute for a coastline as a recreational resource; indeed, shallow lakes tend to warm up more rapidly in summer than the sea. We can regard inland water resources for tourism as nodes, namely lakes and reservoirs; as linear corridors, rivers and canals; or simply as landscape features (such as Victoria Falls). Lakes are particularly numerous in recently glaciated areas such as the Alps, northern Europe, and North America. Where lakes are accessible to major cities, they attract second home owners and a wide range of recreational activities, which may not be compatible (for example, anglers and jet-skiers). Spatial zoning and temporal phasing – planning and resource management that restricts certain activities to a particular area and time – will be necessary to avoid conflict between users. Maintaining water quality is also a major problem, as unlike the tidal nature of the seas and oceans, lakes have no natural cleansing mechanism. Rivers are more widely available than lakes, but usually tourism and recreation have to take second place to the needs of industry, commerce, and agriculture. Even so, boating holidays and river cruises on the inland waterways of Europe and North America are growing in popularity, while rivers previously regarded as unnavigable are sought out by adventurous tourists for the challenge of white-water rafting and canoeing.

The safeguarding of those natural resources is mainly the concern of national governments, often working with UNESCO to designate specific ecosystems as Biosphere Reserves.

Cultural features

A country's resources in the arts, culture, and entertainment – the so-called 'creative industries' – are at least as important as its physical resources and sport facilities in attracting tourists. The problem is defining culture, which means different things to specific interest groups. To some, it relates to activities that demand intellectual effort, in contrast to most forms of popular entertainment. In the context of tourism, culture in its broadest sense refers to the whole way of life of particular societies. Although only a minority of tourists are primarily culture-seekers, most travellers are interested in the everyday differences between their country of origin and the lifestyle of the people in the countries they visit. These are usually expressed in gastronomy, the performing arts (including dance and music), the visual arts and handicrafts, markets, folklore, and festivals. UNESCO has designated many of these popular living traditions as 'intangible cultural heritage'. Two examples from Spain are flamenco and the Fallas festival in Valencia.

On a global scale, we can recognise a number of cultural regions, where there is a broad similarity in lifestyles, architecture, agricultural systems, and often a shared historical background and religion. These regions rarely correspond to continental boundaries. For example, 'Western' culture since the Renaissance in the fifteenth century has spread well beyond the confines of Europe, because of overseas trade, colonial expansion, emigration, and advances in technology. Tourism thrives in the absence of barriers to communication, so the existence of a common language is an advantage, although the dominance of English – partly as a consequence of globalisation – poses a threat to minority languages. Nevertheless, in most of Africa and Asia, and parts of Latin America, Western influence is superficial and strong cultural differences persist. This is evident in the Muslim countries of Africa and the Middle East, as well as the countries of south and east Asia where Buddhism has long been the dominant influence. In many countries, indigenous tribal groups continue to live outside the mainstream culture, which often regards them as primitive, backward, or uncivilised. Identified as a 'Fourth World' by some anthropologists (Graburn, 1976), these tribes are increasingly sought as a unique resource by tour operators and included in itineraries, but unfortunately tourism could present another threat to a way of life which is already endangered. Examples of such minority cultures include the hill tribes of Southeast Asia, the Andaman Islanders of India, the Aborigines of Australia, the Koi San (Bushmen) of southern Africa, and the Amerindians of the Amazon rainforest.

Tourism is a major factor encouraging cultural change in traditional societies. On the other hand, tourism has done much to revive local festivals and handicrafts. Nevertheless, in many instances these have been modified to suit the taste of foreign tourists, so that culture becomes just another commodity for sale, losing its authenticity as part of the travel experience. Younger members of host communities are keen to imitate what they perceive as the desirable lifestyle of the tourist, the so-called 'demonstration effect', often disrupting the community's social cohesion.

Tourism based on a cultural motivation has a long history. A shared religion can encourage travel between countries, so *pilgrimages*, here defined as journeys with a religious motivation, were arguably the earliest form of organised tourism. Most of the great religions have sacred sites – a shrine, a holy mountain, or a holy city. Pilgrimages tend to be highly concentrated in time as well as space, a notable example being the annual Muslim *hajj* to Mecca (which is a forbidden city to non-believers). Perhaps as a reaction to a secular, materialistic world, *faith-based tourism* – travel emphasising spiritual values – would appear to be on the increase, as shown by the revival of the pilgrim route to Santiago de Compostela, the greatest Christian shrine of medieval Europe.

Travellers to 'secular shrines', such as the former home of a celebrity, famous writer, or national leader, are often called pilgrims, but are more correctly described as cultural tourists, who are also attracted to destinations noted for their art treasures, historic sites, and architectural achievements. Cultural tourists are following in the tradition of those wealthy travellers who undertook the 'Grand Tour' of Europe in the eighteenth century. Thomas Cook, taking advantage of improved means of communication, brought the cultural attractions of Europe and the Middle East within reach of the Victorian middle class. Today's young backpackers taking a Gap Year from work or college have similar motivations, but the numbers involved are on an altogether vaster scale than was ever the case with the Grand Tour, and their journeys are truly global in scope.

Research and discussion

Compare the travel experiences of today's Gap Year tourists with those undertaking the Grand Tour in the eighteenth century. See if you can detect any similarities and describe the ways they differ, taking into account the following:

- Gender, age, and social class
- Motivations for travel
- Sources of information available
- Destinations chosen
- Modes of transport used
- Documentation required
- Types of accommodation used
- Activities undertaken
- Respect for the host community's social conventions, dress codes, and taboos
- Recollections of travel experiences

Heritage tourism has grown up with people's curiosity about places, nature, and the past (often highly romanticised). It is about much more than an interest in history and old buildings. In effect, legends loosely based on historical fact, mythology, and literary invention (such as *Game of Thrones*) play as great a part in creating heritage attractions as actual events and the findings of archaeology. Here the tourist trail spawned by *The Da Vinci Code*, including the hitherto little-known Rosslyn Chapel in Scotland, is one notable example of the influence of the mass media. In its wider sense, heritage includes those natural as well as man-made features that are considered worthy of preservation. Some features are so unique, spectacular, or well-known that they are of worldwide significance, and their loss or desecration would affect humankind as a whole. For this reason, UNESCO has designated most of these for special protection as World Heritage Sites. While this designation does bring with it management responsibilities, lack of the ability to enforce conservation measures means that some monuments are in a poor state of preservation, or their integrity is threatened by inappropriate development nearby.

Controversies about the recent past are very much part of the growing interest in *dark tourism*. As the name implies, this focusses on places associated with death, suffering, and disaster. The best-known examples commemorate the sites of the Jewish Holocaust during the Second World War, such as the concentration camp at Auschwitz in Poland. This type of tourism raises moral questions regarding visitor motivation, appropriate methods of interpretation that avoid sensationalism and commercial exploitation, and the extent to which buildings should be preserved or even reconstructed in the pursuit of authenticity (see Stone et al., 2018).

Finally, many tourists, especially those in the younger age groups, are less interested by a country's past than in its contemporary culture, as reflected in sport, fashion, and popular music. Again, the influence of the mass media is evident. The national tourism organisation of a country may have a large promotional budget, but this will have considerably less impact than the free publicity and exposure provided by a movie or television series (such as *Game of Thrones*) seen by a worldwide audience. This, in turn, creates a demand for 'film/screen tourism' in locations as diverse as Dubrovnik and Iceland.

Discussion point: whose heritage?

In heritage tourism, we also need to consider the art treasures and artefacts that form part of national collections like the British Museum and the Louvre. Many of these were acquired from indigenous cultures, for example, in Africa during the period of colonial expansion or as the spoils of victory in war. Should these museums and art galleries comply with demands that the artefacts should be returned to their countries of origin? To what extent should the need to preserve the integrity of collections for future generations take precedence over the principle of restitution to the 'rightful owners', whoever these might be?

Tourism resources at the national scale

In Part 2, we investigate resources as part of the supply side of tourism, focussing on the key attractions of specific countries. Inevitably, those countries which have become major destinations will be given more detailed treatment than others.

Tourist attractions

Attractions are the *raison d'etre* for tourism; they generate the visit, give rise to excursion circuits, and create an industry of their own. The simplest approach to identifying attractions in an area is to draw up an inventory or checklist, by defining the range of attractions, counting them, and either tabulating or mapping the result.

Swarbrooke (2002) has classified attractions into the following categories:

- Natural, including beaches, caves, scenic features, and wildlife (the flora and fauna).
- Man-made, but not originally designed to attract tourists, such as historic houses, castles, and cathedrals.

- Man-made and purpose-built to attract tourists; this includes museums, art galleries, exhibition centres, casinos, and a growing range of leisure attractions for a family 'day out' such as theme parks and aqua-parks.
- Special events. These 'event attractions' differ from the others, which are 'site' or 'point' attractions, in that they occur only periodically and, in some cases, change venues. The latter includes sporting events, notably the FIFA World Cup, the Commonwealth Games, and the Summer and Winter Olympics. These present unique

CASE STUDY 3.1
CAVES AS 'NATURAL' TOURIST ATTRACTIONS

Caves as a recreational resource are usually limited to those with specialist knowledge and equipment. On the other hand, caves have been valued in many parts of the world as dwellings and repositories since early times, partly because they are characterised by only small seasonal variations in temperature.

The subterranean networks of caverns in areas of hard limestone are one of the 'last frontiers' of tourism, as only a small fraction have as yet been explored, let alone exploited and made safe for tourists as 'show caves'. Among the features formed by solution and deposition are slender stalactites, contrasting with stalagmites rising from the cave floor. In some caves – Drach in Majorca is a fine example – there are underground lakes. Caves have often yielded valuable evidence of prehistoric cultures, including those of the Dordogne region in France and Altamira in Spain. These contain rock paintings dating back to the Ice Age, which archaeologists believe may have had religious significance. Deep caves accessible only to divers and speleologists contain life forms that are adapted to an extreme environment. Many caves are therefore sites of scientific importance and subject to strict controls.

Caves differ from most natural attractions in the following ways:

- They are a hidden feature of the landscape.
- Physical alterations to the resource, including roped-off trails and some form of artificial lighting, are necessary to provide access from the cave entrance to the interior 'chambers' containing the most impressive formations.
- Visitors are restricted to guided tours to ensure their safety and to protect this fragile resource from damage. In extreme cases, some of the 'painted caves' had to be closed after a few years of public access, to preserve the artefacts from deterioration as a result of exposure to light and the exhaled breath of visitors. Replica caves can be constructed physically at the destination or virtually, using augmented or virtual reality (VR).

A few caves have the physical capacity to stage event attractions such as concerts – St Michael's Cave in Gibraltar and the Dachstein high in the Austrian Alps are good examples. In the area around a show cave, there is often demand for facilities and other visitor attractions, some of which may be inappropriate for the setting.

opportunities to promote the host country and have a spin-off effect encouraging other attractions nearby. They also require considerable investment in buildings and infrastructure, planning and organisation to safeguard the health, safety, and security of visitors and participants. The bombing of the Boston Marathon in 2013 was an early example of how events can be targeted by terrorists. Cultural event attractions of major international significance would include Rio de Janeiro's Carnival and the Edinburgh Festival.

Tourism development based on a cluster of attractions is more likely to be successful than one based on a single world-class attraction. Increasingly, tourist attractions and the resource base, in general, are suffering from intensive use and need effective visitor management. This can only be achieved if these attractions are considered as an integral part of the resource base rather than dealt with in isolation.

A broader view of the tourism resource base

The tourism resource base allows for a multitude of different outdoor recreation activities, ranging from abseiling to zorbing. Some of these activities – notably skiing, golf and yachting – require specialised facilities as well as equipment and skills, whereas others – canoeing, for example – are not associated with development on any scale. All types of sport and outdoor recreation are based on some kind of physical resource that may be natural, man-made, or a combination of both. The 'arts, culture, and entertainment' sector of tourism focusses more on a destination's human resources.

Clawson provides one of the most useful ways of thinking about the total resource base for tourism (Clawson and Knetsch, 1966). He viewed resources as forming a continuum from intensive resort development at one extreme to wilderness at the other, and his scheme, therefore, incorporates both resource and user characteristics. Clawson's three basic categories are:

- User-oriented areas of highly intensive development close to population centres.
- Resource-based areas where the type of resource determines the use of the area.
- An intermediate category, where access is the determining factor.

In Table 3.3, we relate a selection of recreation activities to Clawson's classification.

Another way of thinking about resources, related to Clawson's ideas, is to distinguish *reproducible* resources (those which can be replaced, such as theme parks) from *non-reproducible* resources that, if lost, are irreplaceable, such as elements of the natural and cultural heritage mentioned earlier.

An equally broad view of tourism resources is the 'systems approach', which views the supply side of tourism as a complex system. Here, the components of the system are autonomous agents, such as businesses or community groups who interact but pursue their own objectives. Hence, the difficulties faced by any organisation in trying to manage the tourism sector or a destination. The nature of tourism as a complex system means it has

Table 3.3 A classification of recreational resources

User orientated	Intermediate	Resource based
Based on resource close to the user. Often artificial developments (city parks, stadiums, etc.). Highly intensive developments. Activities often highly seasonal, closing in off-peak.	Best resources available within accessible distance to users. Access very important. Natural resources more significant than user-orientated facilities, but these experience a high degree of visitor pressure.	Outstanding resources. Based on their location, not that of the market. Primary focus is resource quality. Often distant from user, the resource determines the activity.

Reproducible ⟵――――――――――――――⟶ Non-reproducible

Activity paramount ⟵――――――――――――――⟶ Resource paramount

Artificiality ⟵――――――――――――――⟶ Naturalness

⟵――― Intensity of development ⟶

Proximity ⟵――― Distance from user ――⟶ Remoteness

Examples of activities:	Examples of activities:	Examples of activities:
Golf	Yachting	Sightseeing
Tennis	Windsurfing	Mountain climbing
Spectator sports	Boating	Trekking
Visits to theme parks, zoos, resorts, etc.	Camping	Safaris
	Hiking	Expeditions
	Angling	Surfing
	Field sports	Whitewater rafting
	Downhill skiing	Canoeing
	Snowboarding	Potholing
		Scuba diving
Typical resource:	**Typical resource:**	**Typical resource:**
Theme park	Heathland	Unique historical monument
		National park

to be conceptualised and understood as a whole; it is impossible to break it down into constituent parts without losing the integrity of the system. This is why, when tourism is being taught as a discipline, educators have to break it down for ease of communication, but the use of case studies allows for the whole system to be understood.

The evaluation of resources for tourism

Measurement of the suitability of the resource base to support different forms of tourism is known as resource evaluation. The main issue here is to match the varied requirements of different users with the characteristics of the resource base. For example, pony trekkers need rights of way, footpaths, or bridleways, and attractive scenery. The aim of a resource evaluation system is to satisfy these various needs, which can be plotted on a *recreation opportunity spectrum*. This provides planners with a management tool for matching specific locations in an area to particular types of recreation use.

The tourism product and destination marketing

An area may have tourism potential, with a favourable climate, attractive scenery, hospitable people, and a range of resources awaiting discovery but it will not become a viable tourist destination unless it has:

- At least one attraction that can be promoted as a unique selling proposition (USP).
- Support facilities, including accommodation.
- Accessibility to a major tourist-generating country.
- Favourable pre-conditions for development, which means the provision of basic infrastructure, a tourism organisation, and a measure of political stability, which are largely lacking in parts of Africa, for example.

These elements combine to provide the *tourism product* of a destination. While individual enterprises within the tourism industry supply products to the consumer, notably airlines and hotels, the destination product is the sum of these many parts. Nevertheless, the marketing of places demands a very different approach to the marketing of tangible consumer products such as cars. Firstly, the nature of the product is different. Destination products comprise a set of tangible and non-tangible components based around an activity at the destination. That activity could be a skiing vacation or a spa visit, and for each, the mix of components will vary. Using Innsbruck in Austria as our example, we can see that this destination product is made up of the following components:

- The *core destination product* – the winter sports experience.
- The *facilitating destination product* – the transportation services and accommodation in Innsbruck.
- The *supporting destination product* – the high-quality shopping and restaurants in Innsbruck.
- The *augmented destination product* – the overall ambience of Innsbruck communicated through the urban design and conservation of the old town (Kotler et al., 2020).

Secondly, there is a range of stakeholders who feel they should all have a say in the marketing of 'their' destination. Thirdly, destination marketing is commonly done by a public sector agency, though they often lack marketing expertise, and political considerations may override marketing issues. Finally, the real challenge for the marketer is to achieve 'differentiation' – in other words, to demonstrate that destination A is truly different from destination B – and create a *brand* that is widely recognised, a problem for Caribbean destinations which are all viewed as basically the same.

Tourism resources at the local scale

For the tourism resource to be developed, someone or some organisation must act. These agents of development can be either in the private sector or in the public sector, which includes central government, state-funded organisations acting on its behalf, and local authorities.

The public sector is involved not only in tourism development at the local scale, but at all levels, including the international. Developing countries receive assistance for projects through agencies such as the World Bank or the United Nations Development Programme. Many governments actively encourage tourism projects in their own countries by providing finance at generous rates and tax breaks to developers. Typically, at the national and international levels, government involvement is with the planning and co-ordination of tourism development. At the local level, the role of the public sector is usually limited to providing the initial *infrastructure*; this includes all development on or below ground, such as roads, parking areas, railway lines, harbours, and airports, as well as the provision of utilities. Adequate water supplies are crucial, bearing in mind that the requirements for a luxury hotel and golf course may be excessive, and conflict with the needs of the local population. Where basic services have failed to keep pace with a spate of hotel building, a destination will suffer bad publicity regarding its standards of health, hygiene, and safety. The public sector is also responsible for ensuring adequate security from crime and terrorism. Even an isolated incident affecting tourists can receive widespread negative coverage by the media in their countries of origin.

As tourism projects are costly, private sector developers typically provide the *superstructure*. This includes the accommodation sector (of which hotels are normally the most important component), entertainment venues, sports facilities, shops, restaurants, and passenger transport terminals. Clearly, this division of responsibilities reflects the motives of the two sectors. The private sector looks for profit and a return on investment, while the public sector is anxious to provide the basic services in an environment favourable for tourism development. In some developed countries, the *voluntary sector*, consisting of non-profit making organisations, has a subsidiary role in the development process. As their main interest is conservation, these organisations are much more likely to oppose large-scale tourism projects than to initiate development. The National Trust is an outstanding British example, but differs from most such organisations in being a major landowner.

At the local scale, accessibility is all-important and may be the deciding factor in the success of a tourism project. Resorts in destination areas such as the Mediterranean owe much of their popularity to their location near an airport with direct flights to the major tourist-generating cities in northern Europe. We should point out here that accessibility is a relative term, which is determined by cost as well as distance. Exclusive 'up-market' resorts are often located in areas away from the main tourist routes.

Other factors encouraging the development of tourism resources at local level include land availability, suitable physical site attributes (soil, topography), and a favourable planning environment with zoning for tourism use. Normally, undeveloped *greenfield* sites are chosen, but there is an increasing number of tourism projects in inner city areas, often utilising a waterfront location previously occupied by dockyards and industry. Such *brownfield* sites usually require costly reclamation treatment before building work can take place.

Finally, tourism development should take place with the consent of the local community. However, in most developing countries (and some developed ones), democratic structures of government are weak at the local level, and even the ownership of land may be the subject of dispute. This became evident in southern Asian fishing communities in the aftermath of the 2004 tsunami, when it was alleged that local people were excluded from the benefits of reconstruction. Local authorities may lack the expertise and financial 'muscle' to take on business interests from outside the region whose activities may have a negative social and environmental impact.

Resorts and other tourist centres

Whereas ecotourism and many outdoor recreation activities are dispersed throughout rural space, most types of tourism are concentrated to some degree in resorts or in centres of population. It is difficult to classify tourist centres, as categories frequently overlap, and may also change over time (see Table 3.4). Resorts are places that are frequented by health and pleasure seekers, and recreational tourism is the reason they came into being. In Britain, the term 'resort' usually means a seaside town, while in the United States, it denotes a self-contained leisure complex. In our definition, resorts differ from other urban or rural communities in that they have evolved, or been deliberately planned, in response to the needs of tourists. As a result, they are distinct in layout and townscape, and are often characterised by eclectic styles of architecture, in contrast to more workaday places. This is not to say that leisure tourism does not play an increasingly important role in a great many towns and cities, particularly national capitals and *historic tourist centres* such as Oxford, Florence, and Kyoto, which are visited for their rich cultural and architectural heritage, regardless of their primary function. Even manufacturing and mining towns, long shunned by tourists (other than business travellers), are developing attractions that exploit the growing interest in a country's industrial heritage.

One way of measuring the importance of tourism to a destination is the Tourism Intensity Index, which divides the number of guest nights spent in tourist accommodation by the number of inhabitants. Although this is a fairly accurate measure for holiday resorts, it seriously underestimates the impact of tourism in major cities with a large resident population or in historic towns such as Bruges that attract large numbers of day visitors.

In developing countries, many planned holiday resorts are in effect 'tourist ghettos', separated physically and culturally from the support communities that provide the workforce for the hotels. Elsewhere, the distinction between 'hosts' and 'guests' is less marked. However, typically in resorts, we find a concentration of tourist-orientated land, and

Table 3.4 A typology of tourist centres	
Spa resorts	Reached their peak prior to 1914 as 'watering places' catering for health-seekers; now most visitors are short-stay and attracted for other reasons, including health, fitness, and 'wellness' tourism (e.g. Bath, Baden-Baden, Vichy, Hot Springs)
Mountain resorts/hill stations	Mainly established in the colonial era to provide a cool, healthy refuge for expatriates in hot climates; now cater for domestic visitors (e.g. Darjeeling)
Winter sports resorts	Located in mountainous areas with facilities geared to skiing and other snow-based activities; now adapting to the market and climate change to provide all-year sport and leisure facilities (e.g. St Moritz, Aspen)
Seaside resorts	Depend on the quality of their beaches, climate, and water sport facilities. Can be categorised as either (a) exclusive, with high class accommodation (e.g. Cannes, The Hamptons) or (b) popular, with a wide range of accommodation and many purpose-built facilities (e.g. Blackpool, Benidorm, Atlantic City, Acapulco, Surfers Paradise)
Lake resorts	Appeal based on scenery and access to major cities; attract 'second homers'; facilities for water sports (e.g. Bellaggio)
Gaming and entertainment resorts	Based on market-oriented activities rather than a particular resource, tend to be heavily regulated (e.g. Las Vegas, Sun City)
Service centres	Mainly rural communities providing support facilities for visitors to national parks (e.g. Gatlinburg)
Centres of pilgrimage	Facilities geared to groups of visitors with a religious motivation (e.g. Lourdes, Varanasi)
Cultural and historic centres	Primary function may be education, administration, or distribution – tourism has to compete for space; historic towns and cities attract a high proportion of foreign visitors to their heritage or cultural attractions (e.g. Oxford, Florence, Kyoto, Fez)
Primary cities	Usually, national capitals; primary function is administration and finance, and tourism is one of many functions; concentration of national culture in theatres, museums, and art galleries; business tourism important; tourists typically short-stay, with a high percentage of foreign visitors (e.g. Washington, New York, Madrid, Tokyo)
Industrial centres	Some short-stay leisure tourists attracted by manufacturing or mining heritage (e.g. Bradford, Rio Tinto, Ballarat, Calico)
Ports and border towns	Gateways for tourists in transit; shopping opportunities for cross-border travellers due to price differentials between countries

building uses close to the focus of visitor attraction. This area of tourist-related functions is termed the *recreational business district* (RBD), distinct from the main office and shopping area, which in larger towns is called the central business district (CBD). The RBD develops under the twin influences of the major access route into the resort and the central tourist feature. For example, in seaside resorts the RBD often develops parallel to

Photo 3.1
On the heritage trail in Poole

Source: Brian Boniface

the beach, behind a promenade or boardwalk, and contains premier hotels and shops. Beyond the beachfront, the intensity of tourist functions and land values decreases in a series of zones around the RBD (Figure 3.4). In the case of historic tourist centres, the RBD usually corresponds to the ancient core of the town, which in most European examples is focussed on a castle, university, or cathedral. In practice, it is difficult to distinguish the RBD functions from the CBD as they overlap (Figure 3.5). Conservation is of primary concern, with 'heritage trails' linking sites with the most historical significance. Methods of interpretation that use costumed guides, or re-enactments of historical events, bring the 'heritage experience' to life for the tourist. Nevertheless, 'the attraction may be medieval, but few tourists are prepared to eat, sleep and travel in medieval conditions' (Ashworth and Tunbridge, 1990). Modern support facilities, while necessary, may be an intrusive feature in the skyline and street scene of the historic city. In large cities, especially national capitals such as London, the tourism function is polycentric. Tourist facilities are widely dispersed between several *quarters* or districts catering for recreational or cultural tourism, while the business traveller gravitates to the CBD with its range of financial and commercial services.

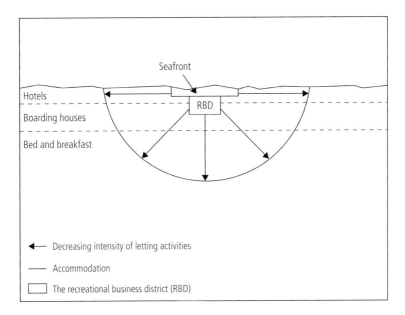

Figure 3.4
The recreational business district

Source: Wall, 'Car owners and holiday activities', in Lavery (1971)

Figure 3.5
The RBD and CBD in an historic tourist centre

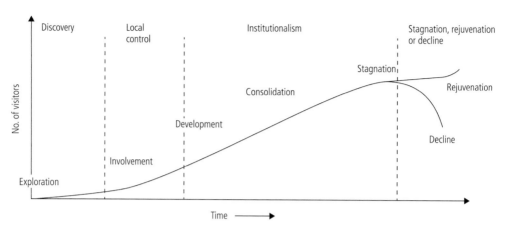

Figure 3.6
The tourist area life cycle

Source: Butler (1980)

The development of resorts over time is an important consideration for geographers concerned with tourism. Butler (1980) has suggested a *tourist area life cycle* where resorts evolve from 'discovery' through development to eventual decline. Although the life cycle approach has its critics who feel it is difficult to operationalise, the main utility of this approach is a way of thinking about resorts, an explanatory framework for their development, and as a means of integrating supply-side trends with the changing market of a resort. After all, the type of tourist who visits in the exploration phase will be very different from those visiting during consolidation or decline (Figure 3.6). We can summarise the tourist area life cycle as follows:

- Exploration: Small number of adventurous tourists; main attraction is unspoilt nature or cultural features.
- Involvement: Local initiatives provide facilities and some advertising ensues; larger numbers of visitors, a tourist season, and public sector involvement follows.
- Development: Large numbers of tourists and control passes from locals to national or international companies. The destination begins to change in appearance. Overuse may begin.
- Consolidation: The destination is now a full-fledged part of the tourism industry; the rate of growth in visitors is reducing. A recognisable recreational business district has emerged.
- Stagnation: Peak visitor numbers have been reached and the destination is now unfashionable with environmental, social, and economic problems. Major promotional efforts are needed to maintain visitor numbers.
- Decline: Visitors now visit newer resorts as the destination goes into decline. It is dependent on a smaller geographical catchment and repeat visits.
- Rejuvenation: Here, the authorities attempt to 're-launch' the destination by providing new facilities, attracting new markets, and re-investing.

The impact of COVID-19 on destination resources

The impact of COVID-19 on tourism destinations from 2020 onwards has been significant, affecting demand, the resources on offer, and destination management. While the impact will reduce over the coming years, it is still an important consideration when considering the destination and its resources. It is evident that every destination will have to rebuild its tourism from the ground up, pressing the restart button for the new normal.

The enforced closure during the pandemic of tourism-related businesses such as hotels caused a chain reaction throughout the whole economy from wholesalers to farmers. Destinations where tourism is the mainstay of the economy were particularly vulnerable, such as coastal resorts, the more remote rural areas, small islands, and winter sports resorts. In developing countries where the government was unable to provide a financial 'safety net' for struggling businesses, the consequences were dire; workers in tourism had no alternative but to return to their home villages for subsistence.

The ability of many destinations to recover is hampered by poor resilience, the lack of diversity in the economy, undiversified source markets, and a high percentage of both SMEs and tourism employment characterised by seasonal and part-time work.

The problem of overtourism

Thanks to the COVID-19 pandemic, many thought the problem of 'overtourism' had been resolved. It first attracted media attention in the summer of 2017, particularly in Barcelona, but its symptoms have affected many cities, historic towns, and island destinations for much longer, and are likely to revive after the pandemic has become a distant memory. Excessive numbers of visitors concentrated in time and space have a negative impact on the quality of life for local residents, provoking a backlash against the tourism industry with slogans such as 'tourists go home'. Activists claimed that local people and students were being priced out of the property market, as thanks largely to Airbnb, thousands of apartments have been made available by homeowners to short-stay tourists, undercutting the hotel sector without being subject to any kind of regulation. A further contributory factor of Airbnb is the fact that many units rented to tourists are in residential areas, not the RBD. The influx of tourists often exceeded the population of the destination, as for example in Venice, Dubrovnik, and Nassau in the Bahamas, where cruise ship arrivals have been blamed for the negative impact. Visitors compete for limited resources, namely physical space, viewpoints, access to beaches, and entry to heritage attractions, and art galleries, where the intrusion of the 'selfie' diminishes the experience for other visitors. Overtourism is the consequence of uncontrolled mass tourism, with information technology acting as the driver of change, exemplified by:

• The availability of cheap flights provided by the proliferation of low-cost carriers.
• The access to cheap accommodation through agencies such as Airbnb. On any given night, 2 million visitors were staying in other people's homes thanks to Airbnb,

which offers the tourist market more rooms than the world's top hotel chains combined (Poon, 2018, 13).

- The facilitation of movement within cities by cheap taxi services such as Uber.
- The ability to book holidays online through the Internet.

Overtourism can be prevented by ensuring the level of visitation does not exceed the social and psychological carrying capacity of the destination. This involves setting quotas on visitor numbers, both zoning and limiting the supply of accommodation. Several cities have imposed measures to replace uncontrolled mass tourism by *responsible tourism* that will benefit local residents, 'creating better places for people to live in and better places for people to visit' (Poon, 2018, 23).

Summary

- Certain factors favour the development of tourism resources, and this explains why the world pattern of supply is uneven.
- Developed resources are cultural appraisals, considered by society to be of economic value. They are usually shared with other users and are both fragile and perishable.
- As countries realise the negative impacts of tourism, planning to safeguard these resources has become vital. Planning aims to minimise the costs of tourism and to maintain the integrity of the resource base.
- At the world scale, both physical and cultural features are key factors influencing tourism development, with attractive coastlines, mountains, and lakes being the most popular locations for recreation and tourism.
- At the national scale, classifications of tourist attractions which include the whole resource base are useful. Evaluations of the potential of the resource base to satisfy tourist's demands allow possible future areas for recreation and tourism to be identified. These evaluations can then be applied at the local scale to resort developments with their distinctive morphology and mix of service functions.
- It is also possible to identify a cycle of resort development.

Review questions

1. Devise a method to increase the capacity of the trails in an area of heath land where excessive numbers of hikers, horse riders, and other recreational users have caused severe erosion.
2. Give examples of island destinations where the wildlife resource is vulnerable to even small numbers of visitors, and suggest ways of managing the problem.
3. There is an increasing trend to involve all stakeholders at a destination in the tourism planning process. How can this be done in a balanced way to ensure that it is not just the loudest and most influential voices that are heard?

4. Popular tourist attractions sometimes reach saturation point in terms of carrying capacity and are at risk of deteriorating. How might such attractions introduce 'demarketing' to reduce the number of visits?

References and further reading

Ashworth, G.J. and Tunbridge, J.E. (1990) *The Tourist-Historic City*, Belhaven, London
Butler, R.W. (1980) The concept of a tourist area cycle of evolution, *Canadian Geographer* 24 (1), 5–12
Butler, R.W. (2015) Tourism area life cycle, pp. 183–226, in Cooper, C. (ed.) *Contemporary Tourism Resources*, Volume 1, Goodfellow, Oxford
Clawson, M. and Knetsch, J. (1966) *The Economics of Outdoor Recreation*, John Hopkins University Press, Baltimore
Cooper, C. (2022) The destination. Chapter 22 *Essentials of Tourism*, Sage, London
Croes, R. and Semrad, K. (2022) Destination competitiveness, pp. 77–90, in Cooper, C., Volo, S., Gartner, W.C. and Scott, N. (eds) *The Sage Handbook of Tourism Management: Application of Theories and Concepts to Tourism*, Sage, London
Crouch, G. and Ritchie, J.R.B. (2012) *Competitiveness and Tourism*, Edward Elgar, Cheltenham
Fennell, D. and Cooper, C. (2020) *Sustainable Tourism: Principles, Contexts and Practices*, Channel View Publications, Bristol
Fyall, A. (2019) Tourism destination repositioning and strategies, pp. 271–284, in Fayos-Sola, E. and Cooper, C. (eds) *The Future of Tourism: Innovations and Sustainability*, Springer, Cham
Graburn, N. (1976) *Ethnic and Tourist Arts: Cultural Expressions from the Fourth World*, University of California Press, Berkeley
Hall, C.M., Scott, D. and Gossling, S. (2020) Pandemics, transformations and tourism: be careful what you wish for, *Tourism Geographies* 1–23, 577–598
Kotler, S. Makens, J., Bowen, D. and Baloglu, S. (2020) *Marketing for Hospitality and Tourism*, 8th edition, Prentice Hall, Englewood Cliifs
Lavery, P. (ed.) (1971) *Recreational Geography*, David and Charles, Newton Abbot
Mathieson, A., and Wall, G. (1982) *Tourism, Economic, Physical and Social Impacts*. Longman, Harlow
Mill, R.C., and Morrison, A.M. (1985) *The Tourism System: An Introductory Text*. Prentice Hall, Englewood Cliffs
Poon, A. (2018) *Overcoming Overtourism*, LEVE-Global, Trinidad and Tobago
Ron, A. and Timothy, D. (2019) *Contemporary Christian Travel*, Channel View Publications, Bristol
Stone, R., Hartmann, P., Seaton, A., Sharpley, R. and White, L. (eds.) (2018) *The Palgrave Handbook of Dark Tourism Studies*, Palgrave, London
Swarbrooke, J. (2002) *The Development and Management of Visitor Attractions*, 2nd edition, Elsevier Butterworth-Heinemann, Oxford

4 Climate and tourism

Learning objectives

After reading this chapter, you should be able to:

- Understand the importance of latitude and the distribution of land and sea areas in determining climatic differences.
- Be aware of the major elements of climate and explain how these affect the various types of recreational tourism.
- Understand the problems of classifying world climate zones.
- Describe the distribution of world climates and their significance for tourism.
- Discuss the possible impact of climate change on tourism patterns.

DOI: 10.4324/9781003406853-5

Introduction

It is important to make a distinction between weather and climate. We can think of climate as a system in which the atmosphere interacts with the hydrosphere, the biosphere, and the cryosphere, with the sun as the ultimate energy source. Most of this activity takes place in the atmosphere's lowest layer – less than 16 kilometres (10 miles) in thickness – known as the *troposphere*, which contains the gases essential for life on our fragile planet. Nevertheless, the *stratosphere* at altitudes between 10 and 50 kilometres contains Earth's protective ozone layer, and changes in circulation in the lower stratosphere affect the troposphere. Weather is conditions in the troposphere at a given time and place. Climate is the pattern of weather phenomena synthesised over a period of time, and we usually base our choices of when and where to go on holiday on climate information. In contrast, outdoor recreation trips are sensitive to changes in the weather, while some activities are dependent on particular weather conditions, so we need to rely on short-term forecasts. We can view climate as a:

- Resource and 'pull' factor encouraging the development of tourism.
- As a constraint limiting the appeal of a destination.
- As a consideration in whether or not to travel due to concerns about climate change.

Despite the widespread use of air conditioning and other forms of climate control (as, for example, in Dubai and Las Vegas), tourists spend some time in an outdoor environment which may be considerably warmer or colder than their country of origin. On a world scale, we can see the importance of climate as a 'push' factor in the tourist flows from the colder, cloudier tourist-generating countries to warmer, sunnier destinations; and at a local scale, the weather will attract city-dwelling families to a nearby beach on a hot summer day. Climate determines the activities at the destination and the length of the holiday season (although this is also influenced by other factors such as the timing of school holidays in the generating areas). The providers of leisure goods and services are usually faced with seasonal variations in demand. In most destinations, this problem of *seasonality* influences development and operating costs, impacting profitability and employment in the tourism industry. The relationship between climate and tourism is changing as both travellers and the tourism sector become more aware of climate change and its effects. Indeed, tourism, particularly where it involves air travel, is itself a major contributor to climate change, and is becoming criticised as a high carbon activity.

The world climate scene

Tourists tend to need information on the *average* rainfall and temperatures they can expect at a particular location, rather than the extreme weather events that make headline news. Nevertheless, in recent years, heat waves, severe storms, and floods have become increasingly frequent, and this has been attributed to climate change as the atmosphere has become less stable. For some destinations at least, we should consider the extremes of temperature we might experience as well as the average for a particular month.

Since the beginning of the twentieth century, average temperatures for the world as a whole have risen by 0.6°C, and the rate of change appears to be accelerating. Most scientists link this global warming to the emissions of carbon dioxide (CO_2), methane (CH_4), and nitrous oxides into the atmosphere resulting from the burning of fossil fuels since the Industrial Revolution. It is known that CO_2 is largely responsible for the 'greenhouse effect' that prevents excessive radiation of heat from the Earth's surface back into space. On the other hand, sceptics argue that episodes of warming and cooling have occurred throughout history, as shown, for example, by the retreat and advance of glaciers in the Alps. These were, however, almost certainly due to natural cycles, such as sunspot activity, rather than human interference with the environment. Regardless the causes of climate change, the impact of rising temperatures is potentially very significant and is already being felt in some parts of the world. The undesirable side-effects of climate change include:

- Rising sea levels, resulting in coastal erosion and the loss of beaches. Venice is a good example of a major cultural resource that faces an increased risk of flooding. Furthermore, remember that most tourism developments are on the coast. The highest costs will be borne by those communities who have contributed least to the problem. Island nations such as Kiribati and Tuvalu in the Pacific are threatened with disappearance. This has led some to argue that the wealthier developed countries should pay reparations to those developing countries most affected by climate change.
- Higher sea surface temperatures resulting in coral bleaching, making the reefs less attractive to divers.
- Increased growth of algae in coastal waters depleting water quality.
- Prolonged heat waves, especially in cities, with episodes of poor air quality.
- Invasions of insects and pathogens spreading disease.
- The increased risk of drought due to erratic rainfall. This will mean tourism having to compete with other sectors of the economy for scarce water resources.
- An increasing number of extreme weather events.
- Retreat of the snowline impacting upon winter sports resorts.

Climate change therefore presents the tourism industry with a formidable challenge, and destinations will need to adapt, both to minimise the risks and maximise the opportunities that change can bring. Moreover, climate change and the loss of natural ecosystems are closely linked. More diverse habitats typically store more carbon and are more resilient to climate change. Some of the responses to climate change are described in the regional chapters and are summarised in Box 4.1.

Climate is determined by three main factors:

1. Latitude or distance from the Equator
2. The distribution of land and sea
3. Relief

Latitude is the primary factor, as this determines the angle of the sun's rays at any given time of the year; if this is too oblique, the sun's heating power will be limited. Due to the

Earth's rotation, the Northern Hemisphere is tilted towards the sun in June, when it is overhead at noon on the Tropic of Cancer (latitude 23.5° North). At high latitudes north of the Arctic Circle (66.5° North), there is daylight for 24 hours at midsummer, while Antarctica (south of 66.5° South) experiences continual darkness. By December, the sun's overhead path has moved south of the Equator to the Tropic of Capricorn (latitude 23.5°

BOX 4.1
THE RESPONSE TO CLIMATE CHANGE

The tourism sector is responding to climate change in two ways. The first is to attempt mitigation of the effects of climate change by altering behaviour, such as reducing the carbon footprint of travellers. The second is in terms of adaptation, where destinations develop strategies to cope with the realities of climate change, as presented in the following chart:

Adaptation approach	Coastal and small island destinations	Mountain and winter destinations
Examples of technological adaptation approaches	Development of new weather-independent attractions including theme parks, casinos, and sports facilities. Development of new facilities for business, particularly conferences. Development of facilities to support niche markets such as food and wine, adventure, and marine tourism.	Ski slope developments to reduce snow needs. Snow-making equipment. Development of ski facilities at higher altitudes. Development of facilities for year-round tourism such as trails, nature-based attractions, spa facilities, and year-round accommodation. Landscaping with native vegetation and reforestation.
Examples of business model adaptation approaches	Scenario planning to review competitive positioning for 'beach-plus' tourism. Market diversification strategies away from beach tourism. Season extension strategies, including event programmes. Development and marketing of non-weather-dependent products. Visitor education. Withdrawal from tourism.	Scenario planning to review competitive positioning for year-round tourism. Market diversification to attract those not participating in winter sports. Season extension strategies, including festival and event programmes. Development of non-weather-dependent products such as hiking, health, and spa facilities. Withdrawal from tourism.

Partly adapted from Abegg, B (2006) *Climate Change and Winter Tourism*, OECD Wengen Workshop, OECD, Paris.

South). This marks the onset of summer in the Southern Hemisphere, and in contrast a period of continuous cold and darkness north of the Arctic Circle. The low latitudes between the Tropics of Cancer and Capricorn enjoy a warm climate all year round as the sun is high in the sky for most of the day, with only a very brief period of twilight before nightfall. The result of increasing distance from the Equator is a shorter summer, a greater difference in day length between the seasons, and a longer period of twilight.

The simple model of a steady decrease in temperature from the Equator to the poles is complicated by the fact that most of the world's landmass is concentrated in the Northern Hemisphere. Land surfaces heat and cool more rapidly than large areas of water. The oceans therefore act as a reservoir of warmth, so that windward coasts and islands have a *maritime* climate which is equable. Furthermore, warm ocean currents, notably the Gulf Stream and the North Atlantic Drift, distribute some of the warmth of tropical seas to higher latitudes (see Figure 4.1). As a result, Britain and Ireland experience a much milder climate than their position relatively near the Arctic Circle would suggest. Cold currents have a chilling effect, the most well-known example being the Labrador Current off the east coast of Canada (icebergs carried by this current caused the 1912 *Titanic* disaster). The Pacific Ocean, due to its much larger size than any other body of water, exerts a worldwide influence on climate, as demonstrated by the El Niño phenomenon. The heartlands of Eurasia and North America at similar latitudes to the British Isles are far removed from the influence of the sea and undergo a *continental* climate, characterised by extreme variations in temperature.

In many parts of the world where there are high mountains, *relief* has a major effect on weather patterns. Climbers are well aware that air temperatures are considerably lower on the summit of a mountain. As a rough guide, the temperature falls by 6.5°C per 1,000 metres of altitude (equivalent to 3.5°F per 1,000 feet). There is also a reduction of barometric pressure with increasing altitude; at 5,000 metres, the density of the air is less than 60 per cent of its sea level value. The thinner atmosphere at such altitudes means that, although more solar radiation reaches the ground by day, heat is lost more rapidly to the sky at night. Because there is less oxygen in the air, physical exertion becomes more difficult. Great contrasts in temperature, moisture, and sunshine are found within short distances in mountain regions, providing a variety of habitats or *life zones* for plants and animals. Mountain barriers profoundly modify the climates of adjacent lowlands since moist air from the sea is forced to rise over them, becoming drier and warmer as it descends. At a local scale, the position of a slope or valley in relation to the direct rays of the sun has important consequences for land use and resort development.

Additionally, at a local scale, the energy consumption of large cities results in a climate that is appreciably warmer than the surrounding rural areas, the so-called *heat island* effect. Most of the acute problems that occurred in Europe's cities during the heat wave of the summer of 2003 – such as 15,000 deaths in France alone – were attributed to very warm nights with minimum temperatures over 25°C, 5 to 10°C above the summer average. In Paris, the measures carried out in readiness for a similar heatwave in 2019 led to a 90 per cent fall in the death rate. Nevertheless, the demand for air conditioning in Europe is now set to approach American levels, which in itself would be a significant contributor to climate change.

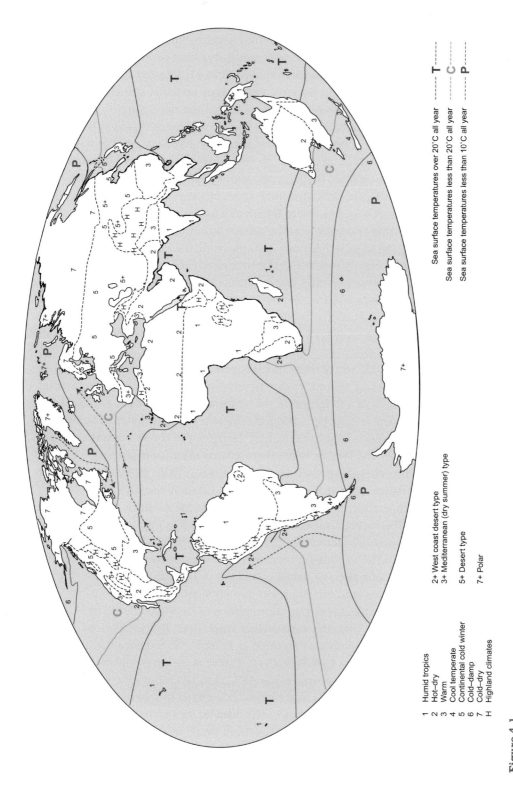

Figure 4.1
World climate zones

1   Humid tropics
2   Hot–dry
3   Warm
4   Cool temperate
5   Continental cold winter
6   Cold–damp
7   Cold–dry
H   Highland climates

2+ West coast desert type
3+ Mediterranean (dry summer) type

5+ Desert type

7+ Polar

Sea surface temperatures over 20°C all year ----- T ------
Sea surface temperatures less than 20°C all year ----- C ------
Sea surface temperatures less than 10°C all year ----- P ------

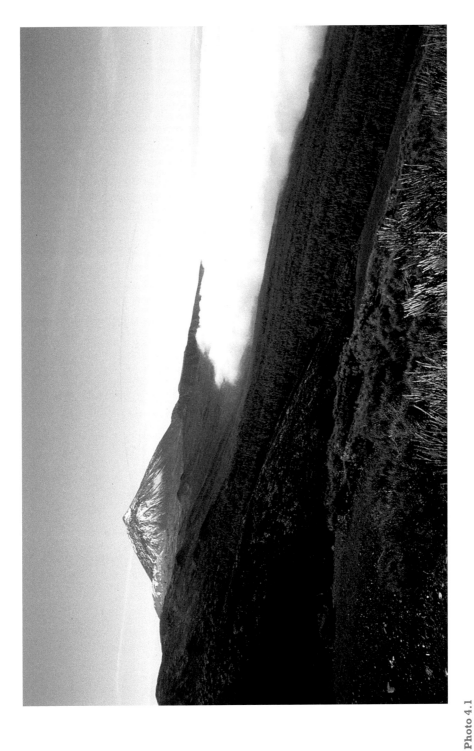

Photo 4.1
Orographic cloud formed by moist air ascending Mount Teide, Tenerife

Source: Brian Boniface

Climate elements and tourism

Temperature is the element of climate that exerts the greatest influence on tourist activity. It is important to mention that exposure to direct sunlight on a hot day can make you feel much warmer than being in the shade, even when the air temperature remains the same.

The insulation value of the clothing necessary for thermal equilibrium is expressed in *clos*, units of thermal resistance (see Figure 4.2). In this context, our primary focus is on average *maximum* (daytime) temperatures. A subtantial number of people participate in beach activities and sunbathing only when the maximum temperature exceeds 20°C (68°F). Even if the air temperature is well above this figure, the sea surface temperature in summer is often 5°C lower. Away from tropical shores, a *wetsuit* providing insulation is essential for surfers, replaced by a *drysuit* when the water is extremely cold (below 12°C). This is due to the fact that water chills the body through conduction 30 times faster than dry, still air at the same temperature.

The young beachgoer's concept of the ideal climate would probably not be shared by older people more interested in sightseeing than 'sun, sand and sea'. The comfort zone for most people, wearing standard business clothing, is a narrow band of temperature, varying slightly as we acclimatise from winter to summer, where the air is neither excessively dry nor too humid. 'It's not the heat, but the humidity' is a complaint often made

Average daytime temperatures:

Figure 4.2
Temperature and clothing for holiday travel in January

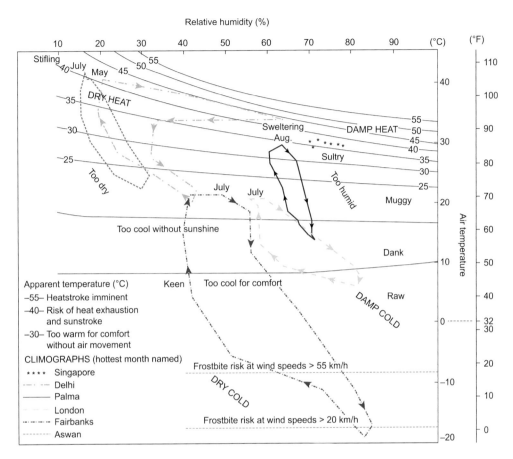

Figure 4.3
Bioclimatic chart

about summer weather. This acknowledges the importance of *relative humidity*, which is a measure of the moisture content of the air as a percentage of the total amount it could hold at a given temperature. Thus, tropical air at 35°C can hold nine times more water vapour than cold air at 0°C. A dry heat, where the relative humidity is less than 30 per cent, is widely recognised as more tolerable than the humid heat typical of many tropical countries. When moisture levels in the air are nearing saturation, it is difficult to keep cool despite profuse sweating, and failure to maintain the body's heat balance will result in heat exhaustion or, in extreme cases, heatstroke. A more common problem, resulting from wearing unsuitable clothing, is the skin condition known as 'prickly heat'. We can express the effect of humidity on heat perception as the *effective temperature*, which also takes into account air movement, or more simply, as the *apparent temperature* shown in the bioclimatic chart (Figure 4.3). The significance of this for human well-being is evident when comparing the *climographs* for Delhi and Aswan. These graphs use the average daytime temperature and relative humidity as co-ordinates for each month of the year. In August, Delhi would feel more uncomfortable than in Aswan, where the actual air temperature is 5°C higher.

Tourists do vary considerably in their ability to acclimatise, according to their age, gender, body mass index, rate of metabolism, and ethnic origin. The human body can adapt fairly readily to tropical conditions through an increase in the sweat rate and the supply of blood to the skin but much depends on how we modify our lifestyle and patterns of behaviour. The body responds to cold mainly by shutting off the blood supply to the hands and feet to maintain the core temperature at 37°C (98°F). In cold climates, adding layers of clothing is much more effective than physiological adaptation in achieving thermal equilibrium. Radiant heat from the sun and air movement also influences comfort levels.

Sunshine is particularly crucial at the beach, where ultraviolet light is reflected from the water surface and the sand, adding to the heat load that exposed skin receives from the sky. Despite the advantage of long summer days, the British Isles experience a cloudy climate compared to southern Spain, where the sun shines brightly for as much as 80 per cent of the daylight hours. Ultraviolet (UV) radiation is even more intense in tropical latitudes, although skies are often overcast, and the duration of bright sunshine is usually less than in the Mediterranean. The UV Index is a simple numerical scale that measures the ultraviolet radiation reaching the Earth's surface in terms of its potential for skin damage. It can be incorporated into local weather forecasts to warn people about the risk of sunburn. Sunscreen preparations protect the outer skin from the short-wave UVB rays, which cause sunburn, but allow the long-range UVA rays to penetrate, stimulating melanin production for a sun tan. Prolonged exposure to UVA radiation will, however, result in premature ageing of the skin. Skiers, trekkers, and mountain climbers at high altitudes are particularly at risk from sunburn, since the air is clear and sunlight is strongly reflected from snow and bare rock. Such 'incident radiation' can provide considerable warmth to the skin, allowing sunbathing and skiing to take place at the same location.

Climate change has caused a thinning of the ozone layer, allowing more of the sun's harmful rays to reach the Earth. This phenomenon is influencing the behaviour of beachgoers, making them more reluctant to spend prolonged periods sunbathing (see the case study).

CASE STUDY 4.1
THE PROS AND CONS OF SUNBATHING

In Britain and other northern countries, media often feature alarming stories about skin cancer and premature ageing as consequences of indulging in the sun's rays after a long, dark winter. Conversely, there is ample evidence that a moderate amount of exposure allows the skin to produce vitamin D, essential for health and well-being. Indeed, in the early part of the twentieth century, medical opinion positively encouraged sunbathing in the fight against tuberculosis and rickets, a bone disease resulting from a deficiency of vitamin D. This condition was common among children living in large cities who were deprived of sunlight due to overcrowding and the blight of industrialisation.

Like much else in tourism, sunbathing is subject to the vagaries of fashion. Throughout recorded history, the leisured elite in most civilisations have valued a pale complexion and avoided the sun, whereas a tan was the characteristic of those who had to perform outdoor manual work. This perception changed in the 1920s, following the First World War, partly as a reaction against Victorian attitudes. The French Riviera was reinvented as a summer destination by artists, writers, and the fashion designer Coco Chanel, who played a significant role in making *le bronzage* fashionable. The cult of sunbathing soon spread to the rest of Europe and the Americas. However, it was not until the 1950s, following the Second World War, that holidays in sunny, exotic destinations became accessible to most North Europeans and North Americans. Here too, France was a driver of social change, with the 'invention' of the bikini and the Club Méditerranée holiday village concept based on sun, sea, sports, food, and wine. This epitomised the cult of the body, free from the constraints of social class, and represented an escape to a pre-industrial 'Polynesian' lifestyle. By the 1970s a deep 'mahogany' tan had become a status symbol, and the manufacture of sun creams a major industry.

This began to change in the 1980s, particularly in Australia, where the Queensland Cancer Society raised awareness of the risks of excessive exposure through their SunSmart campaign. The industry's response has been to shift the emphasis from tanning to skin protection, marketing sunscreens with a high sun protection factor (SPF) that indicates the damage caused by both UVA and UVB radiation, and making 'fake tans' fashionable.

On a global scale, the ozone layer in the stratosphere filters out lethal UVC radiation, preventing it from reaching the Earth's surface and reducing the impact of harmful UVB rays. The discovery of an 'ozone hole' over Antarctica, increasing the risk of cataracts and skin cancer, led to international action to ban CFCs. The effects of the thinning of the ozone layer are particularly evident in Southern Hemisphere countries such as Chile, New Zealand, and Australia. Fair-skinned visitors need to be aware of the increased risk of sunburn and wear clothing with a high SPF, as a standard T-shirt offers little protection.

Discussion point

With climate change, do you think that sunbathing will once again become unfashionable, particularly among young people?

Winds are influenced in their direction and strength by the Earth's rotation, topography, and the gradient between high and low-pressure areas (indicated by the spacing of isobars on a weather map). A global perspective on air circulation reveals that in tropical latitudes, the trade winds are blowing from the north-east in the Northern Hemisphere and from the south-east in the Southern Hemisphere, whereas in middle latitudes, the prevailing winds are from the west. This simple model is greatly modified, particularly in the Northern Hemisphere, by the great seasonal contrasts in temperature and pressure between the continents and the oceans. These contrasts result in notable shifts in wind direction in West Africa and much of Asia, where the **monsoon** is the dominant feature of the climate. At the local scale, mountain and valley winds are characteristics of many highland regions, while onshore sea breezes during the day and weaker offshore land breezes at night are features of many coastal areas during periods of warm, settled weather. Coastal locations with a particularly windy climate tend to be shunned by beach tourists, but this is changing with the growth in popularity of aerial and water sports, notably windsurfing and kite surfing. Tarifa at the southern tip of Spain is a good example (see Gómez Martín, 2005). In the case of surfing, although the swells are the result of storms in mid-ocean, local offshore winds provide a smooth face for surf riders by holding off the incoming waves.

Onshore sea breezes moderate the humid summer heat of the Mediterranean and tropical islands like Singapore, resulting in cooler effective temperatures at certain times of the year. At high latitudes and in middle latitudes during the winter months, strong winds combined with low temperatures exert a pronounced chilling effect on exposed skin, leading in extreme cases to frostbite. Even in the relatively mild conditions typical of maritime locations such as the British Isles, this *wind-chill* factor is a major constraint on outdoor recreation.

While many tourists from the Arabian Peninsula find rainy weather appealing, people generally regard **precipitation** in its various forms of rain, hail, sleet, and snow as a constraint, although much depends on its intensity, duration, and seasonal distribution. In the tropics, there is usually a well-defined division of the year into 'wet' and 'dry' seasons, where the rain typically falls in short heavy downpours following strong convectional heating of the air and the build-up of cumulus clouds during the afternoon. In contrast, most of the rain that falls in the British Isles is cyclonic in origin; it may be smaller in total amount but is spread over many more rainy days.

We can view snow as an expensive hazard for transport or as a valuable recreational resource. Suitable locations for winter sports resorts are found mainly in accessible mountain regions, where there is snow cover to a depth of more than 30 cm for at least three months of the year. As the provision of facilities for skiers is costly, the resort operator needs accurate information on the local climate, including temperature (with average minima below –2°C), sunshine, wind speeds, and relative humidity. The type of snow cover is important and skiers favour *powder* (loose, low-density snow). Such is the demand for skiing that artificial 'snow domes' have proliferated even in countries where snowfall never occurs, such as Dubai. Although the introduction of winter sports has brought economic benefits to remote mountain communities, it has also led to environmental degradation, especially in the Alps. Deforestation to create ski runs has increased the risk of avalanches, while the use of snow-making equipment to guarantee snow cover inhibits the growth of delicate alpine plants. Many ski resorts, such as those in Scotland and Australia, are climatically marginal, where the reliability of snow is vulnerable to the impact of global warming.

Unlike other elements of the climate, fog invariably has a negative effect on tourist activities. As a natural phenomenon, fog is a feature of many coastal areas and enclosed valleys in mountain regions, but human interference with the environment has greatly aggravated the problem. Due to pollution, the monitoring of **air quality** is increasingly crucial as part of the concern about environmental issues and the quality of life generally. The motor vehicle is widely regarded as a major polluter, emitting nitrous oxide, hydrocarbons, and ground level ozone (not to be confused with the ozone in the upper atmosphere). More recently attention has focussed on the growth of air transport, and frequent fliers are being encouraged to reduce their 'carbon footprint' in response to the threat of climate change. An older problem in most of the world's large cities, especially in those countries undergoing rapid development, is the emission of sulphur dioxide from 'smoke-stack industries'. Smogs or episodes of severe air pollution are particularly common in regions where anticyclonic conditions, inhibiting air movement, prevail for much of the year. Examples would include the Mediterranean countries and California in summer, and the continental heartlands of North America and Eurasia in winter. An unpleasant cocktail of gases and particulates poisons the air of our cities, reducing visibility, blighting vegetation, eroding historic buildings and monuments, and threatening the health of people suffering from respiratory problems. Prior to the enforcement of strict clean air regulations, 'acid rain' degraded forests and lakes in many areas downwind of sources of industrial pollution in Europe and North America. Even the Arctic is under threat from pesticides and other pollutants carried north by winds and ocean currents; as these are slow to break down at low temperatures, the snow is contaminated, with disastrous consequences for the food chain.

CASE STUDY 4.2
SMOG IN BEIJING

Pollution is widespread throughout China's cities, due to runaway industrial growth, the recent proliferation of motor vehicles, and the prevalence of coal-fired power stations. The situation is particularly dire in Beijing, which has a continental climate characterised for much of the year by anticyclonic conditions with very little precipitation. Contamination of the air results in an acrid smog, with the Air Quality Index (AQI) exceeding 300, a level which is positively hazardous for health, necessitating the wearing of face masks. In November 2014, Beijing hosted the Asia-Pacific Economic Co-operation (APEC) Summit, attended by the world's most powerful leaders. The conference aimed to reduce the emission of 'greenhouse gases' as a response to global warming. To avoid adverse publicity, the city authorities enforced the following measures:

*   Restrictions on the use of private cars
*   Taking 70 per cent of the city's buses out of circulation
*   A ban on construction work
*   Halting production from the factories causing most of the pollution

Although these drastic measures caused much inconvenience, there were clear skies for a few days, a welcome effect which was dubbed 'APEC blue'. The citizens of Beijing are now less ready to accept pollution as the price of economic progress, as they have discovered the problem can be resolved, given the will to do so.

World climates

Classifying climates

Even in a small country like Britain, temperatures, rainfall, and exposure to wind or sunshine vary a good deal, resulting in many local climates. However, these differences are less significant on a global scale than those between, say, the south of England and the French Riviera. It is also true that areas of the world separated by vast distances have such similar features that we regard them as belonging to the same climate zone. Thus, the climate of California resembles that of Spain, and the South Island of New Zealand shows broad similarities to England, once we appreciate that the seasons are reversed in the Southern Hemisphere.

It is relatively simple to draw a series of world maps showing the various elements of climate, but much more difficult to synthesise this information to determine the best overall conditions for tourism. Numerous attempts have been made to classify climates from the standpoint of human physiology, rather than the widely-used system devised by Köppen, which is based on vegetation zones.

- Of particular relevance is the work of Lee and Lemons (1949), who devised a scheme relating temperatures to clothing requirements.
- Terjung (1966) utilised data on temperature and relative humidity to produce a 'comfort index' for each month of the year for both daytime and night-time conditions. This was further refined, where the data were available, to take account of the effects of wind-chill and solar radiation. Terjung's classification is the most comprehensive, but produces an excessive number of climate zones, even when the features of the comfort index are summarised for the year as a whole.
- An approach gaining wide acceptance is the 'tourism climatic index' (TCI) devised by Mieczkowski (1985), which employs values for temperature, relative humidity, sunshine, precipitation, and wind speeds. The TCI is now being used by destinations to build resilience against climate change (see Cavlek et al., 2018).
- The tourist's satisfaction with weather conditions is given more prominence in the climate index for tourism (CIT) devised by De Freitas et al. (2008), which is particularly geared towards beach tourism.

The bioclimatic chart (Figure 4.3) is the starting point for our classification scheme. We can think of the world's climates as a continuum, from hot, humid conditions at one extreme to cold and dry at the other. However, most parts of the world have climates which lie somewhere between these extremes, and which are characterised by distinct seasonal variations. This is evident in the *climographs* for Delhi, Palma, London, and in an extreme form, for Fairbanks, Alaska. Such climates are conventionally described in terms of their temperature and rainfall characteristics. We have grouped them into seven major zones that can be related more closely to human comfort and clothing needs. Figure 4.1 displays the world distribution of these zones, but it is essential to be aware that the boundaries drawn on the map indicate wide areas of transition rather than abrupt changes.

The humid tropics (Zone 1)

The tropical climates have perhaps the greatest potential for tourism development. In this context, the main problem is keeping buildings and their occupants cool, as temperatures tend to remain above 20°C throughout the year even at night, while humidity is generally high (see the *climograph* for Singapore in Figure 4.3). Buildings should be designed to take advantage of any breezes, so usually an open plan is adopted with rooms having access to a veranda. Sometimes buildings are elevated on stilts and orientated to capture any air movements above the vegetation. Clothing for the tourist should be lightweight, of open texture and made of absorbent materials. Most of the diseases for which the tropics are notorious are mainly due not to the climate but to the poor standards of sanitation prevailing in many Third World countries. Nevertheless, the hot, moist environment does favour the growth of harmful bacteria and parasites, while diseases such as malaria are carried by insects that cannot thrive in cold temperatures. Tourists can protect themselves from malaria by taking prophylactic drugs and by preventative measures, for example, by 'covering up' in the evenings when the mosquitoes are active. For other tropical diseases such as yellow fever, vaccination is essential.

With the exception of some areas near the Equator, the tropics have a dry season of varying length when conditions are not unfavourable for tourism. The rainy season is largely determined by the position of the **Intertropical Convergence Zone** (ITCZ), the belt where the trade winds meet. Corresponding to the period of 'high sun', the ITCZ sweeps north of the Equator during the Northern Hemisphere summer, and then south of the Equator roughly from November to February. The ITCZ is significant as the breeding ground of many tropical storms.

We can distinguish between the 'trade wind' climate of many tropical islands and coastal areas, and the tropical 'wet-dry' climate, which is characterised by much greater seasonal variations in rainfall, temperature, and humidity. It is during the long dry season that the savanna grasslands, typical of much of Africa, provide the best conditions for game viewing or 'safari tourism'. In the Caribbean, West Africa, and Southern Asia, the dry season coincides with the winter months in North America and Europe, so these destinations are well placed to attract winter-sun seekers from the main tourist-generating countries. Tropical countries south of the Equator are less favoured, as their best months for beach tourism coincide with the summer in the countries of the Northern Hemisphere.

Extensive coral reefs fringing the coastline are a feature of many tropical destinations. The exuberant vegetation and diversity of species of the tropical rainforest is nowadays perceived as a unique resource for ecotourism. Most natural habitats in fact are threatened by the growing pace of development in the tropical 'South', which is still perceived primarily as a source of raw materials for the industrialised countries of the 'North'. The destruction of the rainforests of the Amazon Basin and Indonesia are two well-known examples. The environmental consequences may well be serious, not just for the tropical zone but for the Earth as a whole, in terms of loss of biodiversity. The problem of erratic rainfall, however, hits the least developed economies hardest.

Tropical highland climates

Health resorts have been developed in mountain areas in the tropics that enjoy a cooler climate, and where malaria was not a problem until recently. Tropical highland climates occur wherever mountains or plateaus rise more than 1,500 metres above sea level, as this is the altitude at which the effects of reduced air pressure become perceptible. Many cities in Latin America, East Africa, and Asia are situated at altitudes of between 2,000 and 4,000 metres, where it is advisable for the tourist and business traveller to spend a few days adjusting to the rarefied air. At higher altitudes further acclimatisation becomes problematic, and some visitors are likely to experience the symptoms of acute mountain sickness.

At high altitudes in the tropics, the air temperature is considerably cooler than at the coast, particularly at night, although the seasonal rhythm is similar (see Figure 4.4). We can think of the arrangement of climate zones in tropical mountain regions as a series of layers, corresponding to the mean annual temperature at different altitudes. For example, in Mexico, Central America, and the Andes of South America, the following climate zones are generally recognised:

1   The *tierra caliente*, or tropical zone up to 1,000 metres
2   The *tierra templada* or subtropical zone between 1,000 and 2,000 metres, where coffee is one of the main crops
3   The *tierra fria* between 2,000 and 4,000 metres
4   The *tierra helada* above 4,000 metres

Ascending a high mountain in the tropics has been compared to a journey towards the poles, but with one important difference. Unlike the polar regions, high altitude locations are exposed to intense solar radiation throughout the day all year round. Notable examples of a 'cold region where the sun is hot' would be Tibet, and the Altiplano of Bolivia, where the traditional poncho provides protection from the sun, shade, and strong winds. Mountain summits above cloud level in the tropics have been likened to 'islands in the sky' containing some unusual vegetation adapted to a daily freeze-thaw regime. These ecosystems are particularly vulnerable to climate change due to the very restricted area of the habitat. One such example is Kilimanjaro, where the snow cap of this iconic mountain is in danger of disappearing. This may also be true of glaciers in the Peruvian Andes and the Himalayas, which has consequences for the water supply of many cities in South America and the Indian sub-continent.

The hot dry climates (Zone 2)

Areas of constant drought account for over a quarter of the Earth's land surface, and the threat of *desertification* affects many countries outside the arid zone. The 'hot deserts' in tropical and subtropical latitudes occur wherever the air is dry because of subsidence from the permanent high-pressure belts. The hot dry regions can claim the sunniest places on Earth – both Upper Egypt and Arizona receive more than 4,000 hours of bright sunshine annually. They are also subject to great extremes of temperature. Due to the intensity of solar radiation, air temperatures often reach 45°C by mid-afternoon in the summer but

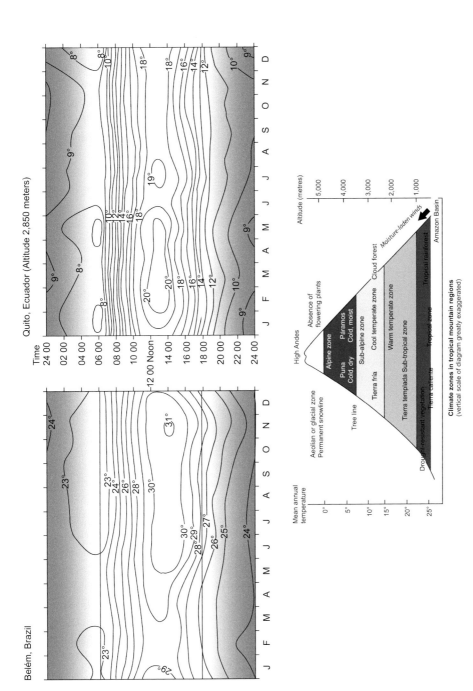

Figure 4.4

Tropical lowland and highland climates. The thermoisopleths (lines of equal temperature) on the charts indicate average variations in air temperature (°C) during the day throughout the year. As both cities are situated on the Equator, seasonal variations in temperature are very small compared to the differences between day and night. This is evident in the chart for Quito (upper right), where the close spacing of the lines indicates a rapid rise in temperature after sunrise

Source: Adapted from Trewartha (1954): 243, 271

fall rapidly after dusk as a result of radiation from the ground to the clear night sky; during the winter months, frost may occasionally be recorded before dawn. The relative humidity is generally very low during the daytime (see the *climograph* for Aswan in Figure 4.3). The main exceptions are coastal areas, particularly those adjoining an enclosed sea where humidity is high due to evaporation from the water surface. Very little of this moisture can rise to produce rainfall, so that summers in places like Aden and Bahrain are particularly oppressive. The western coasts of continents in these latitudes, flanked by cold ocean currents, normally experience much milder temperatures and a good deal of mist; the rainless Atacama and Namib Deserts are striking examples. Here, the *upwelling* of cold water from the ocean depths is associated with strong offshore winds. These provide world-class conditions for surfing, although sea temperatures may be 20°C lower than air temperatures on the beaches (see Butt, 2002).

In the heat of a desert summer, the dryness of the air, aggravated by strong dust-laden winds, results in the rapid evaporation of moisture from the skin. To prevent dehydration, a high daily intake of water is necessary, ranging from 5 litres when at rest in the shade to an impressive 24 litres for hard physical activity while exposed to the sun. The intense glare from the sky can also cause eye disorders. The clothing most suited to the climate is loose fitting, to allow evaporative cooling from the skin; the material should be of close texture and moderate thickness. It should also be light in colour to reflect radiation, and cover as much of the body as possible. A variety of shading, cooling, and insulation devices have traditionally been used by architects in hot dry regions to even out the daily variations of temperature and reduce the impact of solar radiation.

Areas of sand dune devoid of vegetation, in fact, account for only a small proportion of the desert regions that support a surprising variety of plant and animal life adapted to drought conditions. Strong winds and flash floods, after the sporadic rains, have, over the millennia, produced many spectacular landforms by erosion. In places where ground water is available, the vegetation can be luxuriant, and some of these oases can support large urban communities based on complex irrigation systems.

The more accessible areas of the deserts are increasingly sought after by tourists, who value the space, the winter sunshine, and the scenery which they can offer. At night, the stars shine with a clarity no longer experienced in Europe, where 'light pollution' from brightly lit urban areas and motorways is the norm. Some dry regions, such as Arizona, are perceived to have a healthy climate free of respiratory diseases, whereas in the irrigated areas of the Sahara and parts of the Middle East, there is a substantial risk of malaria. Tourism development has taken place in those regions where adequate supplies of water and power can be provided at reasonable cost and where good external communications are available from the main tourist-generating countries. Coastal areas generally have the best prospects as water can be obtained from the sea by desalinisation, although this could be prohibitively expensive for countries deficient in exportable resources such as petroleum.

The warm climates (Zone 3)

Situated mainly between latitudes 25° and 40°, these regions come under the influence of air masses of tropical origin in summer and the westerly winds of middle latitudes in winter. Unlike the tropics, there is a definite cool season, but winters are rarely cold enough to prevent outdoor activities such as golf and tennis from being enjoyed in comfort. One standard layer of clothing (or 1 clo of thermal resistance, equivalent in insulation value to a business suit) is sufficient for average winter temperatures that range between 10°C and 20°C. Most of the zone is actually too cool for beach tourism in winter, despite the impression given by some 'winter-sun' holiday brochures. The main exceptions are the Canary Islands, Madeira, southern Florida, and Bermuda, which can be described as 'subtropical'.

Within this zone, the Mediterranean climate, with its dry summers and abundant sunshine, acts as a strong 'pull' factor, since it offers the best all-round conditions for most types of tourism and outdoor recreation. As the name implies, this climate is best developed around the Mediterranean Sea, which allows the influence of the Atlantic Ocean to penetrate as far as south-west Asia. It is also found in California and, to a lesser extent, in equivalent latitudes of the Southern Hemisphere. During the autumn and winter months, these regions lie in the path of depressions that bring a good deal of rain. The summers are very warm, although the afternoon heat is moderated by sea breezes and fairly low humidity, while the nights are pleasantly cool. Lack of rain causes problems in ensuring adequate water and power supplies to meet the needs of agriculture, local communities, and tourism, aggravated by the growing demand for golf courses, aqua-parks, and for second or retirement homes. The dry evergreen vegetation characteristic of these climatic conditions is vulnerable to devastating fires. With climate change, more frequent episodes of extreme summer heat, combined with the effects of air and water pollution, will probably make the Mediterranean resorts much less attractive for foreign holidaymakers

CASE STUDY 4.3
MEGA-FIRES: SYMPTOM OF CLIMATE CHANGE OR MAN-MADE DISASTER?

A lethal combination of high temperatures (over 30°C), high winds (exceeding 30 kilometres per hour), and low humidity (under 30 per cent) breeds devastating wildfires that have grown in ferocity and frequency in recent years. Some claim the fires that occurred in Portugal and Greece in the summer of 2018, in California in the autumn of 2018, and the Australian bushfires of 2019 are symptomatic of global warming. In the western United States, imported grasses have replaced much of the natural scrub vegetation which easily regenerated itself after fire. In the Mediterranean region, tourism and the building of second homes for city-dwellers must share part of the blame. It is even alleged that many of the fires in the Mediterranean region have been set deliberately, to clear land designated as forest for development. In the United States and Australia, environmentalists could share some of the responsibility. Conservation practices now discourage the controlled burning of forests, allowing a vast quantity of tinder-dry vegetation to accumulate.

from northern Europe, although prospects for tourism in the 'shoulder season' months in spring and autumn might improve.

On the eastern margins of the continents in these latitudes, the warm temperate, humid summer climate zone differs from the Mediterranean in having adequate rainfall throughout the year. In some regions, notably southern China and Japan, summer is the rainy season and winters are relatively dry, thanks to the monsoon. Summers can be oppressive due to the high humidity, and there is generally more cloud cover than in the Mediterranean. If less than ideal for tourism, the prevailing warm moist conditions are very favourable for agriculture.

The cool temperate and continental cold winter climates (Zones 4 and 5)

Countries in middle latitudes are significant mainly as generating areas for sun-seeking tourism. Yet it was in the cool temperate zone that the beach holiday was invented in the nineteenth century, although sea temperatures rarely exceed 20°C during the summer months. Nowadays, many of these 'cold water' coastal resorts, such as the Isle of Man, are re-inventing themselves to meet the challenge of warmer, sunnier destinations, by diversifying their tourism product and investing in all-weather attractions. Climate change should result in a longer and more reliable holiday season, particularly benefitting domestic tourism.

The main difference between the maritime climates on the western margins of the continents and the continental climates of their heartlands and eastern margins in these latitudes is the relative mildness of winter in the west compared to its severity elsewhere. In Europe, the prevailing westerlies and their associated depressions can penetrate far to the east, in the absence of any significant north-to-south mountain barrier. It is therefore difficult to draw any meaningful boundary between the maritime climate of Western Europe, best exemplified by the British Isles, and the continental climate of Eastern Europe. Indeed, anticyclones centred over Scandinavia can occasionally block the westerlies and bring spells of very cold winter weather to parts of Britain. In North America, high mountains run parallel to the west coast, shutting out the moderating influence of the Pacific Ocean and confining mild, moist climatic conditions to a narrow coastal strip. You may find it surprising that the coastal margins of eastern North America and East Asia have a severe winter climate, but this is because the prevailing winds are offshore, bringing very cold air from the continental heartlands. The Atlantic and Pacific Oceans do have a slight warming effect, and this is sufficient to trigger heavy snowfalls in the mountains of New England and northern Japan. The situation is quite different at equivalent latitudes in the Southern Hemisphere, where there are vast expanses of ocean, interrupted only by the peninsula of Patagonia and the islands of Tasmania and New Zealand. These areas experience a maritime climate that is generally milder, more equable, and certainly less prone to air pollution than the British Isles.

In the maritime or cool temperate zone, average winter temperatures range from 0°C to 10°C, and there is little snowfall except on high ground. Two standard layers of clothing (1.6 clos) are normally sufficient for these conditions. However, the mild temperatures are often associated with overcast skies, drizzle, fog, and strong winds. Due to the continual progression of warm and cold fronts, the weather is very changeable. Rainfall is generally adequate at all seasons, and it is often excessive on west-facing coasts and mountain slopes. Summers tend to be rather cool and cloudy, with maximum temperatures rarely exceeding 25°C. Such a climate is invigorating, and is better suited to the more active forms of outdoor recreation.

Continental climates in mid-latitudes show much greater seasonal contrasts in temperature (see Figure 4.5). Winter temperatures are below 0°C (32°F) for several months, so that snow, icy roads, and frozen waterways are to be expected – and dealt with – as a matter of course. Buildings are well insulated and, in some regions, have traditionally been designed to withstand heavy snowfalls. Winter clothing consists of three standard layers (equivalent to 2 clos) separated by 6 mm of trapped insulating air. An overcoat, adequate head covering and protection for the extremities are essential at these low temperatures. However, the winter weather is generally more settled, due to the prevailing anticyclonic conditions, than in the cool temperate zone. This provides opportunities for a variety of snow-based activities such as cross-country skiing and snowmobiling. Summers are appreciably warmer than in the British Isles with maximum temperatures often exceeding 25°C; nevertheless, a good deal of rain falls during this season, and hailstorms are frequent. Autumn in forested areas is a colourful season and is characterised by crisp, stimulating weather.

The continental heartlands of North America and Asia have little or no rainfall due to the 'rain shadow' effect of mountain barriers. These mid-latitude deserts, such as the Gobi of Mongolia, differ from those of the hot dry zone in the severity of the winter climate.

Mid-latitude highland climates

In middle latitudes, both the permanent snowline and the tree line in mountain regions such as the Alps and Rockies are at much lower altitudes than is the case in the tropics, providing favourable conditions for skiing. The upper ski slopes are generally located in the alpine zone above the tree line, and while those resorts situated above 1,500 metres in the forested sub-alpine zone have a reliable snow season, many in the Alps are at much lower altitudes. During the winter months, the upper mountain slopes are often much warmer and sunnier than the valleys, due to the temperature inversions that occur under anticyclonic conditions in mountain regions.

The cold damp climates (Zone 6)

Small in terms of land area, these maritime climates are dominated by the permanent low-pressure belts over the North Atlantic, North Pacific, and Southern Oceans, which generate a great deal of stormy weather throughout the year. The islands situated here receive less sunshine than any other part of the world, while temperatures rarely fall below −5°C in winter or rise much above 10°C in summer. The climate is too cold and windy for tree growth, and there is much boggy terrain due to the constant precipitation. Rain and wet snow can easily penetrate clothing, removing its insulating qualities. Heat loss also occurs from the feet if these are not adequately protected from the waterlogged ground,

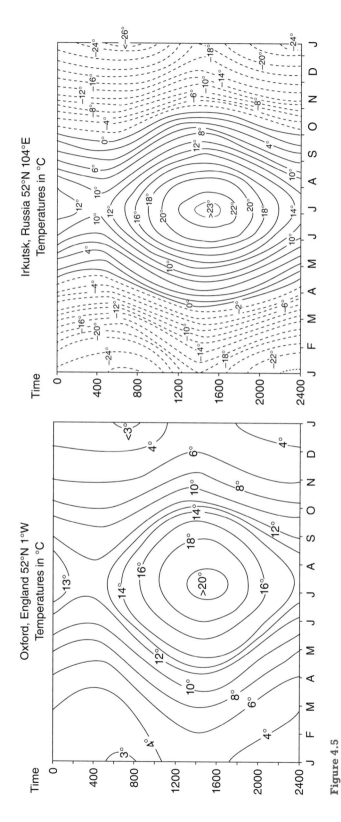

Figure 4.5

Temperature variations in two mid-latitude cities

Source: Adapted from Trewartha (1954): 314,350, Oxford typifies the cool temperate climate where there is a gradual change from winter to summer temperatures. In contrast, Irkutsk is an extreme example of the continental climate. The thermoisopleths (lines of equal temperature) are closely spaced, indicating abrupt changes in temperature causing serious skin damage or 'trench foot'. Suitable clothing for these bleak conditions consists of material with small air spaces that prevents heat loss due to the wind and at the same time allows the skin to 'breathe' freely, plus a water-repellent layer that can be easily removed. Despite the unfavourable climate, the rich bird and marine life of the Faroes, Aleutians, and the islands of the Southern Ocean offer potential for ecotourism.

The cold dry climates (Zone 7)

Until the late twentieth century the polar regions were the frontier of tourism; while the 'Near Arctic' fringes in northern Scandinavia and Alaska had been developed to an extent, the 'High Arctic' (north of 75° latitude) and Antarctica remained the preserve of scientific expeditions.

Cold climates, where the mean annual temperature is below 0°C, account for a third of the Earth's land surface, including 10 per cent (mainly in Antarctica and Greenland), which is permanently ice covered. Although temperatures in the sub-arctic regions of North America and Eurasia can reach 25°C during the brief summers, the length, darkness, and extreme severity of the winters is the dominant fact of life in high latitudes. In the polar regions, the sun's rays are oblique even in summer, but expeditioners must guard against the risk of snow blindness due to the strong incident radiation. In the Southern Hemisphere, Antarctica has an even colder climate than those northern lands adjoining the Arctic Ocean. Although the icy seas of both polar zones are surprisingly rich in marine life, their ecosystems are distinct. The Arctic islands support a variety of land mammals as well as marine species, with the polar bear at the top of the food chain. In contrast, the interior of Antarctica is virtually sterile and only its coastal fringes provide a habitat for penguins and other bird life.

Provided the weather is calm, temperatures as low as –40°C are bearable, as the air is very dry. However, this causes dehydration, as moisture is lost from the body to the atmosphere in exhaled breath, and this, together with heat emitted from vehicles and buildings, produces 'human habitation fog', as in the urban areas of Siberia. Extreme cold has a punishing effect on people and materials; for example, steel becomes brittle and shatters like glass. Under blizzard conditions, exposed flesh can freeze in less than a minute. The extremities have to be protected from frostbite; the ears by a hood and the hands and feet by two insulating layers. Cold weather clothing tends to be bulky as several layers are needed under a wind-proof parka, and with physical exertion large quantities of sweat are produced. Furs and down are, therefore, being replaced by lighter synthetic materials with similar insulating properties. The clothing should fit fairly loosely when active, but can be drawn in when at rest to trap insulating air. However, no amount of clothing will keep an inactive person comfortable for long at temperatures much below –15°C, and high energy foods are essential (over 5,000 calories a day may be needed).

Throughout the Arctic and most of the sub-arctic regions, the summers are not warm enough to thaw the ground to more than a shallow depth, so that the moisture beneath this 'active layer' remains frozen year round. This condition, known as *permafrost*, presents costly engineering problems. Buildings and utilities must be insulated from contact with the ground, otherwise the permafrost would melt and the structure subside. Because moisture cannot drain down, there is much waterlogged ground in summer, attracting swarms of biting insects. The southern part of the sub-arctic zone is dominated by vast, rather sombre forests of spruce, birch, or larch, trees that can withstand a short growing season and poor soils. As summer temperatures decrease, these are replaced by the stunted vegetation of the tundra and the polar deserts of the High Arctic.

Fur trapping has long been the only source of income for the native peoples of Alaska, northern Canada, Greenland, and Siberia. Tourism offers them alternative employment as guides and outfitters to groups of hunters, anglers, and expeditioners from the south. There is also a growing demand for ecotourism in the polar regions, particularly from the United States. Although the market for this continues to be small, there is evidence that even minimal numbers of tourists can have a damaging effect on the fragile ecosystems, even where their movements are strictly controlled, as in Antarctica. This is a problem simply because the ecosystem takes such a long time to recover from any damage.

Polar ecosystems are also under threat from climate change, particularly in the Arctic, where temperatures have risen by twice the world average. The ice sheets of Greenland and Antarctica, together with the year-round floating pack ice of the Arctic and Southern Oceans, make up most of the Earth's *cryosphere* and as such, form an important part of the global climate system as they have a high *albedo*, reflecting solar energy rather than absorbing it. The decline in the thickness and extent of the Arctic Sea ice in summer means that greater expanses of open water are exposed to the warming influence of direct sunlight, causing further melting. Glaciers in Alaska and northern Canada have retreated considerably since the 1970s, while the flow of melt water from the Greenland ice sheet has increased significantly. Furthermore, much of the permafrost of Alaska and Siberia is thawing, releasing methane and CO_2 into the atmosphere and amplifying the 'greenhouse effect'. In Antarctica, the evidence for climate change is less apparent, with the exception of the Antarctic Peninsula.

CASE STUDY 4.4
GREENLAND AS AN INDICATOR OF CLIMATE CHANGE

Over 80 per cent of Greenland is covered by a vast ice sheet larger than Alaska in area, and up to 3,000 metres in thickness, with huge glaciers reaching the sea in numerous locations. Only a narrow coastal strip is inhabited, mainly in the south-west. The ruins of abandoned Viking farms amid the tundra are evidence of warmer climatic conditions early in the last millennium.

Although the ice mass covering Antarctica is ten times larger in volume, climate change in Greenland is likely to have a much greater global impact in the foreseeable future. Whereas Antarctica is isolated from the rest of the world by a cold circumpolar ocean current, Greenland occupies a strategic location between North America and Eurasia and is influenced by air masses and ocean currents from the North Atlantic. Greenland's ice sheet influences global climate patterns, as it reflects 80 per cent of the solar radiation it receives, but it is also affected by global warming. Greenland has experienced several changes in recent decades. These are already having an impact on the mainly Inuit population and the country's fledgling tourism industry, which is based on the spectacular coastal landscape of fiords, serrated mountains, and glaciers, and the scope for wilderness adventure.

The shrinking of the ice sheet. About 7 per cent of the ice in the interior is drained by the Jakobshavn Glacier. In Disko Bay, this glacier, which has greatly increased its output since 2000, 'calves' to produce a myriad of icebergs. The spectacular location has been designated a World Heritage Site, attracting visitors who come by cruise ship or stay in accommodation at the nearby town of Ilulissat. Until recently, ice loss through glacier calving at the edges of the ice sheet was offset by increased snowfall in the interior. However, glacier calving in coastal waters now contributes less to ice loss than physical and biological processes acting on the interior ice sheet. In many places, this is no longer a pristine white wilderness; in summer, the surface is veined with channels and lakes of meltwater, with patches of 'dirty ice' covered with soot, dust, and algae blown in from warmer latitudes. All of this reduces the albedo of the ice sheet, resulting in further warming. The flow of meltwater widens crevasses in the ice, forming *moulins* that act much like sinkholes in a limestone plateau. Vast quantities of water are funnelled to the base of ice sheet, facilitating the movement of glaciers by lubricating the bedrock beneath. The ice sheet is evidently becoming more unstable.

The thinning of the sea ice. Sea ice is forming later in autumn and breaking up earlier in spring, so that there is now open water near the coastal settlements for six months of the year rather than three months as in the recent past. The habitat of wildlife such as the walrus, narwhal, and the polar bear is increasingly at risk. A key element of the traditional Inuit culture, particularly in the north and east of the country, are the teams of sled dogs used primarily for travel on the ice; these will become less relevant to a new generation of Greenlanders.

The thawing of the permafrost. The boggy 'active layer' of the tundra is increasing in thickness as the underlying permafrost responds to rising temperatures. This active layer contains a great deal of peaty material, which is drying out, causing wildfires and releasing greenhouse gases such as carbon dioxide and methane into the atmosphere.

From a global perspective, Greenland acts as an 'early warning system' for the consequences of 'global warming'. Scientists drilling deep into the ice sheet have extracted a record of world climatic conditions over many millennia. These show that, in the past, changes have sometimes been abrupt rather than gradual. In the worst-case scenario for the future, the ice sheet could melt entirely, raising sea levels around the world by 7 metres (23 feet). It is possible that freshwater from the melting Greenland ice could weaken the flow of the Gulf Stream, deflecting this 'conveyor belt' of warm ocean water well to the south of its present path across the North Atlantic. Northern Europe and the British Isles would experience deteriorating climatic conditions, despite 'global warming' elsewhere in the world.

Discussion point

In the short term, climate change will benefit Greenland's economy, reducing its dependence on Denmark. The fishing industry has expanded, while the retreat of the glaciers has opened up areas for the exploitation of minerals such as cryolite. Warmer temperatures in west Greenland could encourage more outdoor activities, although dogsled expeditions will probably become less viable. How should the tourism industry respond to the challenge?

Summary

- At the world scale, climate is one of the key factors influencing tourism development and holiday travel.
- In developed countries with cold winters and unreliable weather, climate is more likely to be a 'push' factor for recreational tourism than a 'pull' factor.
- Climatic conditions are determined by latitude, altitude, and the interrelationship of coasts and mountains.
- Climate is made up of several factors, of which temperature and humidity are most significant for human well-being, while others strongly influence particular types of recreation activity.
- Seasonal variation is an important characteristic of most climates and this is used as a basis for classification, so that useful comparisons can be made between different destinations.
- The optimal climate for tourism is the Mediterranean type, but this is particularly vulnerable to the impact of global warming.
- Tour operators are increasingly seeking out 'exotic' locations where conditions are much less favourable. The hot climates, formerly regarded as unhealthy, are now highly regarded as destinations for beach holidays, cultural tourism, and ecotourism. The cold climates of high latitudes and high mountain regions are attracting the more adventurous tourists who value the unpolluted natural environment despite its hazards.
- Like other tourism resources, climate is subject to change. It remains to be seen whether these changes will be beneficial to the tourism industry, or to tourists themselves. Some destinations will gain as a result, whereas others will lose out, depending on their location in the world. It is certain that tour operators and tourism generally will have to adapt, as the climate is beyond human control.

Assignments

1. Some recreational activities are more weather dependent than others, notably beach volleyball, surfing, and snow-based 'winter sports' such as skiing. Using data from

meteorological offices, investigate when are the best months of the year to enjoy particular activities in the following destinations:

   a. The Costa del Sol, Spain, for golf and beach tourism
   b. Cornwall, England, for surfing
   c. Kenya for safari tourism
   d. St Moritz, Switzerland, for winter sports
   e. Napier, New Zealand, for surfing and beach tourism

2. Design a leaflet giving climate advice and information to a group of American tourists, varying in age and physical fitness, who are planning to climb Mount Kilimanjaro.
3. The Paris Agreement on climate change (2016) set an agenda for the reduction of greenhouse gases emitted by transport as well as other sectors of the global economy, and prescribed several sustainable development goals (SDGs). Failure to achieve these would result in a global temperature increase greater than 1.5°C. Discuss the effectiveness of international cooperation in tackling climate change, and at a national/regional level investigate the measures the various stakeholders in tourism can take to alleviate the effects of climate change in various parts of the world.
4. Explain why air conditioning is not an adequate long-term response to the growing incidence of heat waves in urban areas.

References and further reading

Butt, T. (2002) The Cape Doctor and other bloody events, *Surfers Path* (December–January), 48–51

Cavlek, N., Cooper, C., Krajinovok, V., Smec, L. and Zaninovic, K. (2018) Destination climate adaptation, *Journal of Hospitality and Tourism Research* 43 (2), 314–322

De Freitas et al. (2008) A second generation index for tourism (CIT): Specification and verification, *International Journal of Biometeorology* 52, 399–407

Early, K. (2022) Too hot to handle, *Geographical Magazine* 94 (4), 38–42

Gómez Martín, A. (2005) Weather, climate and tourism a global perspective, *Annals of Tourism Research* 32 (3), 571–591

Hopkins, D. and Higham, J. (2018) Climate change and tourism: Mitigation and global climate agreements, pp. 422–436, in Cooper, C., Volo, S., Gartner, W.C. and Scott, N. (eds) *The Sage Handbook of Tourism Management: Theories, Concepts and Disciplinary Approaches to Tourism*, Sage, London

Lee, D. and Lemons, H. (1949) Clothing for global man, *Geographical Review* 39, 181–213

Mieczkowski, Z. (1985) The tourism climatic index: A method of evaluating world climates for tourism, *Canadian Geographer* 29 (3), 220–233

Terjung, W. H. (1966) Physiological climates of the conterminous United States: A bioclimatic classification based on man, *Annals of the Association of American Geographers* 56, 144–179

Trewartha, G. (1954) *An Introduction to Climate*, McGraw-Hill, Chicago

UNWTO (2009) *From Davos to Copenhagen and Beyond: Advancing Tourism's Response to Climate Change*, UNWTO, Madrid

5

The geography of transport for travel and tourism

Learning objectives

After reading this chapter, you should be able to:

- Appreciate the close relationship between tourism and transport.
- Understand the principles of spatial interaction between places and their importance to the geography of tourism.
- Describe the four main physical elements of any transport system.
- Identify the costs involved in running a transport system.
- Describe the distinguishing features of the main transport modes and recognise their particular contributions to tourism.

DOI: 10.4324/9781003406853-6

- Identify the Greenwich Meridian, the various time zones, and the International Date Line and illustrate their importance for the traveller.
- Outline the characteristics of each mode of transport for the different types of travellers.
- Appreciate the environmental implications of different modes of transport.

Introduction

In Chapter 1, three components of tourism were identified: the tourist-generating area, the tourist destination area, and the linkages between them. This chapter is about the linkages and introduces some of the basic principles of transport geography, illustrating their application to tourism.

Tourism and transport are inseparable. Tourism is about being elsewhere and transport bridges the gap between origin and destination. We need to consider transport for these reasons:

- In a historic sense, transport has developed together with tourism. Improvements in transport have stimulated tourism and, in turn, tourism demand has prompted such transport developments as the growth of low-cost airlines to serve the leisure market.
- Transport renders tourist destinations accessible to their markets in the tourist-generating areas. All tourism depends on access. Indeed, accessibility or the lack of it can make or break a destination; island destinations are particularly vulnerable.
- Transport for tourism involves considerable public and private investment and represents a major sector of the tourism industry in terms of employment and revenue generated. Transportation, therefore, is a major industry in its own right, with concerns extending well beyond tourism and influencing most aspects of everyday life. Tourism, then, is transformed by and has helped to transform the world communications map, and increasingly, all elements of the system are integrated to create a seamless experience.
- Transport for tourism can become an attraction in itself – for example, heritage railways.
- Yet transport also has significant environmental implications. Tourism transport accounts for around 5 per cent of the world's carbon emissions. However, it is estimated that 80 per cent of those emissions are caused by 20 per cent of all trips, and these trips are mostly long haul (Peeters et al., 2007). It is, therefore, important that tourists understand the consequences of their transport choices. Whilst the COVID-19 pandemic severely reduced travel and therefore carbon emissions, by 2023 both were back to pre-pandemic levels.

Discussion point: Hypermobility – to fly or not to fly

Towards low carbon air transport

Until the world moves to a low-carbon economy, the use of traditional sources of energy – those that are based on fossil fuels such as oil – will increase. The energy that is used by the tourism sector is predominantly based on fossil fuels, with aviation delivering the majority of greenhouse gas emissions from tourism and motor transport almost one-third. There is no doubt, therefore, that a transition to a tourism sector based on low carbon energy is needed. This involves a shift in energy production away from fossil fuels towards cleaner forms of energy. For tourism, the biggest challenge is the transport sector, particularly aviation, which needs to move to a low-emission mode and begin to use the most fuel-efficient technology possible.

To fly or not to fly

As the public awareness of climate change grows, attention has turned to carbon emissions from aircraft. It is now recognised that flying is bad for the environment, and consequently, there has been considerable media attention directed to whether we should still fly or seek alternative forms of transport. Indeed, tourism – 'to fly or not to fly' has become an important public debate. Whilst a majority of people support freedom to fly, an increasing number feel that flying, particularly frequent fliers, should be taxed or even curtailed.

However, this will involve a major social movement against flying, a new way of thinking, which in turn will influence policy and practice. There are already signs that this movement is gaining traction. In Sweden for example, 'the Greta Thunberg effect' means that Swedes refer to the 'shame' of flying – *flygskam* as well as *flygfritt* (flight free), and *vi stannar på marken* (we stay on the ground).

Resistance is already evident in the business community. A large number of frequent fliers do so on business, with fares paid by their organisation. Business travel is frequently seen as a benefit of the job, a 'perk' that is enjoyed by senior executives enjoying a glamourous life in business class. Of course, this does not help the case of those who argue that flying should be curtailed. Indeed, they argue that this 'hypermobility' can have negative medical and psychological effects on the individuals concerned, including 'jet lag' (disruption of circadian rhythms), travel fatigue, exposure to radiation, loneliness, and isolation. Realisation of these impacts of flying has prompted leading companies to develop policies to safeguard against the adverse effects of frequent flying.

If flying becomes too toxic, then long-haul destinations – many in the developing world – will suffer. Similarly, air transport delivers food and supplies to remote destinations, such as Australia, and if flying stops, the economies of many long-haul destinations will be hit. These areas are often reliant on tourism as the only viable economic option, and tourism is an important earner of foreign exchange and driver of development. Therefore, climate adaptation must take this into account by creating other options for sustainable livelihoods.

Principles of interaction

In Chapter 1, the basic principle of spatial interaction between two places was outlined in terms of a supplying area containing a surplus of a commodity and a generating area having a demand for that commodity. In geography, this is known as spatial differentiation, with transport linking the two areas. Ullman (1980) has suggested that three main factors are necessary for spatial differentiation and transport development:

1. **Complementarity:** This is a way of saying that places differ from each other, and that in one place, there is the desire to travel and in the other, the ability to satisfy that desire. This complementarity of demand and supply will produce interaction between areas, and a transport system will be required. Examples of complementarity are the flows of tourists from north-eastern states of the United States to Florida, or from north-west Europe to the Mediterranean.
2. **Intervening opportunities:** While Ullman's idea of complementarity makes interaction possible, there may be competing attractions. To take an example, for a resident of Munich wishing to take a summer holiday in a Spanish resort, mainland Spain is closer than one of the Canary Islands. Mainland Spain is, therefore, an intervening opportunity, even though perfect complementarity exists between Munich and the Canary Islands.
3. **Transferability or the friction of distance:** This refers to the cost of overcoming the distance between two places in time, effort, and money. If the cost of reaching a destination is too high, then even complementarity and lack of intervening opportunities will not persuade movement to take place.

The elements of transport

If interaction does take place, a transport system will be needed. Faulks (1990) has identified four basic physical elements in any transport system:

- The way
- The terminal
- The carrying unit
- Motive power

For each *mode* or form of transport, the characteristics of these elements vary and it is, therefore, useful to examine them in turn.

The way

The way is the medium of travel used by the various transport modes. It may be artificial, such as roads, railways, tramways, and cableways; it may be a natural way, i.e., the air, the sea, lakes, and rivers; or it can be a combination of the two, such as inland waterways. The following distinctions are important:

- If the way has to be provided artificially, a cost is incurred.
- The cost of the way is influenced by a second distinction: whether the user shares the way with others (for example, roads) or has the sole use of a specialised way (such as railways).
- Vehicles on roads and boats on inland waterways are controlled almost exclusively by their drivers or operators. In contrast, the movement of aircraft, trains, and to some extent shipping is subject to traffic control, signalling or some other navigational aid.

The way is usually the responsibility of an organisation that is independent of transport operators such as the airlines and bus companies. Examples in the United Kingdom would include the Civil Aviation Authority and National Highways.

The terminal

A terminal gives access to the way for the users, while a terminus is the furthest point to which that system extends – literally the end of the line. Terminals can also act as interchanges where travellers transfer from one mode to another (for example, from aircraft to coach/train at an airport, or in the case of the Channel Tunnel, from coach or car to the shuttle train). Terminals vary considerably in size, layout, and the amenities they provide, as these are determined by the length and complexity of the journey, and the expectations of passengers. A terminal for riverboat passengers in a developing country might be little more than a landing stage. International airports, on the other hand, are often showpieces of modern engineering design, although the traveller rarely experiences a 'sense of place' because of standardisation. A century ago, the monumental railway stations of London, Milan, and New York and the Cherbourg terminal for the great ocean-going liners were the national showpieces of their time.

The carrying unit

Each type of way demands a particular type of carrying unit: aircraft; ships and smaller vessels for waterways; cars, buses/coaches, and other vehicles for the roads; and rolling stock for the railways. Aircraft have to be designed to particularly high specifications to ensure safety and comfort, and are, therefore, costly. Aircraft, ships, and road vehicles are flexible to operate compared to trains, monorails, and trams, where breakdowns on the track cause extensive delays.

Motive power

The historical development of motive power technology reads almost like a history of tourism, with a marked acceleration of the pace of change after the 1950s (see Table 5.1). Motive power combines with the 'way' and the carrying unit to determine the speed, range, and capacity of the transport mode in question.

The motive power for most transport modes is now dependent on petroleum as the energy source. Geology determines that this natural resource is unevenly distributed, with the Middle East supplying almost two-thirds of the total world output. We are facing the possibility of an energy crisis even more severe than that of the early 1970s. Oil reserves are being depleted by competing demands not only from transport but the rest of the global economy. The United States is the world's largest consumer of petroleum, importing 50 per cent of its requirements and is concerned to secure the flow of oil from the effects of political turmoil in the Middle East by tapping alternative suppliers in the Caspian Basin and the Gulf of Guinea. Heavy oil sources such as the tar sands of northern Canada are becoming commercially viable, but this would release unacceptably high levels of carbon dioxide into the atmosphere. In the meantime, Japan and the European Union are seeking to harness alternative energy sources, notably hydrogen and battery power, but these as yet are not realistic prospects for transport on a large scale. Another alternative, the development of biofuels, is becoming a controversial issue as there is a danger that the diversion of agricultural land for this purpose will raise food prices. What this does mean, however, is that tourism is seen as a high carbon sector, and there are increasing calls to curb travel, particularly by air.

In terms of the capacity of a transport system, the most important consideration is to find the combination of carrying unit and motive power that can hold the maximum number of passengers while still allowing sufficient utilisation of the transport system. Increasing size does bring its own problems; larger aircraft, such as the Airbus A380, for example, require reconfigured airport access.

Transport costs and pricing

Transport costs and pricing are fundamental to the geography of tourism. The distinctive cost structure of each mode influences consumer choice and thus determines the volume of traffic on a route. There are two basic types of transport cost:

1. **Social and environmental costs:** These costs are not paid for by the transport operator or user but are borne by the community. Examples would be the unquantifiable cost of aircraft noise to residents living near an international airport or the carbon emissions from cars.
2. **Private costs:** Those who operate the transport system pay private costs, which are then passed on to the customer as fares. A basic distinction needs to be made here between fixed and variable costs:

    a) Fixed costs (or overheads) are incurred before any passengers are carried or indeed before a carrying unit moves along the 'way'. These costs are 'inescapable' and include items such as interest on capital invested in the system and

Table 5.1 The historical development of transport and tourism

Mode of transport	Pre-industrial era	1840–1920	1920–1940	1950	1960–1970	1980–2000	The future
Air			Propeller technology; civil aviation begins; travel is expensive and limited; airships enjoy a brief period of acceptance; basic terminal facilities	Speeds of 400 km/h	Jet aircraft (B707); speeds 800 km/h; cheap fuel; rapid expansion of charter services; development of CRS and GDs	Wide-bodied jets (B747); extended range; fuel efficiency; no increases in speed except for Concorde; extensive terminal services	Hypersonic aircraft; space tourism; global alliances of airlines; new generation jumbo jets with large capacity; increased deregulation
Sea		Steamships and packet boats	Ocean liners and cruisers; little competition from air; short sea ferry speed less than 40 km/h with very basic facilities; no increase in speed for passenger liners		Air overtakes shipping on North Atlantic routes; hovercraft and hydrofoils being developed	Fly-cruise established; larger and more comfortable ferries; fast catamarans developed	Amphibious 'ground effect' craft; sub-marine tourism; themed cruising
Road	Horse-drawn carriages; unpaved roads		Cars achieve speeds of 55 km/h but remain unreliable; coaches develop from charabancs		Cars improve in speed and performance, 100–115 km/h; cars increasingly used for domestic tourism in place of public transport; roads improve; motorways introduced	Speed limits in the United States; steep rise in car-ownership rates; urban congestion; green fuel; improved coaches; re-introduction of trams	Urban gridlock; automated road systems; personal rapid transit; demand-responsive transport; resurgence of road-based public transport
Rail		Steam locomotive	'Golden age' of rail; speed exceeds that of cars		Electrification of rail networks; continuous welded tracks	High-speed networks develop in Europe; business products offered; dedicated rail tourism products developed based on nostalgia for steam	Development of medium-haul tourism products; enhanced motive-power technology

Source: Adapted from Cooper et al. (1997, 277)

depreciation of assets. The most important feature of fixed costs is that they do not vary in proportion to the level of traffic on a route, the distance travelled, or the numbers of passengers carried. For example, the railway track and bed have to be maintained irrespective of the number of trains that use it.

b) Variable or running costs depend on the level of service provided, distance travelled, and the volume of traffic carried. In this context, costs include fuel, crew wages, and maintenance. These costs are escapable because they are only incurred when the transport system is operating and can be avoided by cancelling services.

Since each mode has a different ratio of fixed to variable costs, the distinction is a very important one. Railways, for example, have to provide and maintain a track. This means that a railway system must sustain a high proportion of fixed costs, whereas for road transport, the fixed costs are low. The outcome is that the cost per passenger-kilometre decreases rapidly for rail but more slowly for road transport. In other words, railways are uneconomic if they are only carrying a few passengers, as each one has to make an unacceptably large contribution to fixed costs.

On the other hand, road transport is much more competitive as the greater part of the costs are variable, and fleets of buses, coaches, or taxis can be deployed more readily to meet changes in demand.

It is interesting to note that the success of low-cost carriers in the air transport business is due to their distinctive business model, which allows them to significantly reduce the fixed costs of operating (paperless tickets and internet booking, for example) whilst also reducing the variable cost by cutting out many services to passengers, such as free catering and seat allocation.

In fact, the distinction between fixed and variable costs is blurred; for example, costs of staffing and equipping a terminal may increase with the volume of traffic. These costs are known as semi-fixed. While we could say that wages are a variable cost, crew have to be retained and paid irrespective of the utilisation of the transport system in the short term. In the longer term, staffing can normally be adjusted to the volume of business.

The ratio of fixed to variable costs is an important consideration for transport operators in the tourism business. Compared to many activities, transport has a high proportion of fixed costs. The product is also perishable, because if a seat is not sold on a flight, it cannot be stored and sold at a later date. This means that operators must achieve a high utilisation of their systems, if carrying units are idle for long periods, they do not contribute to fixed costs. Finally, it is important to achieve a high *load factor* (i.e. the number of seats sold compared to the number available).

The link between load factor and pricing is clearly illustrated by the *marginal cost principle*. Using an air-inclusive tour as our example, marginal cost is the additional cost incurred by carrying one extra unit of output (in this case, a passenger). The operator determines a load factor that covers the fixed costs of the journey and the variable cost of each passenger carried. If the flight is budgeted to break even at a load factor of 80 per cent, then every passenger carried over this level will incur a small marginal cost, because variable costs are low, and this represents a substantial profit for the tour operator. Unfortunately, for the tour operator, the opposite also applies; for every passenger below the 80 per cent level, a loss will be incurred.

A related problem is the fact that tourism demand tends to be highly peaked on a daily, weekly, and annual basis. This means that airline fleets may only be fully utilised at certain times of the year. Both in Europe and North America, one solution to this was the creation of the winter holiday market in the late 1960s to utilise idle aircraft and contribute to fixed costs. Another solution is to use *differential pricing*. Here, operators offer low fares for travel in the off-peak period to increase the traffic at those times. The trend in all transport modes is for fares to match distinctive market segments, each of which have their own travel requirements. This is done through 'yield management', which uses sophisticated computer programming to optimise the fares charged.

Transport modes, routes, and networks

Modes

Each transport mode has different operational characteristics, based on the different ways in which technology is applied to the four elements of any transport system (Table 5.2). Technology determines the appropriateness of the mode for a particular type of journey. It also ensures that some modes overlap in their suitability for the needs of travellers, and this may lead to competition between airlines and surface transport operators on some routes, such as London to Paris. In other cases, transport modes are complementary, for example, the road or rail links between airports and city centres. Another example would be fly-drive holidays, where the tourist has the advantages of air transport to reach the destination and the convenience of a hired car for touring the holiday area.

Transport integration

An important issue for transport planners is to provide smooth transfers between transport modes. It is more common to find a lack of integration between modes in terms of poor co-ordination between operators, timetables, and the physical siting of terminals. Integrated transport systems are an ideal solution, though in practice they are expensive to deliver.

Discussion point – Environmental considerations and choice of transport mode
Carbon emissions are a recognised source of global warming, and transport modes used by tourists, particularly cars and aircraft, are known polluters. The question for the future will be whether some forms of transport that are not as polluting, trains, for example, will be favoured by tourists over aircraft or the car. The choice is complicated by the fact that companies now offer 'carbon offsetting' services where tourists can purchase, say tree planting or low energy light bulbs for the developing world, to 'offset' the carbon they have used during their flight. At the same time, governments may also influence the decision by applying 'green' taxes to cars and aircraft, effectively increasing the cost of their use. In other words, transport choice is both a victim and a vector of climate change.

Table 5.2 Characteristics of transport modes

Mode	Way	Carrying unit	Motive power	Advantages	Disadvantages	Significance for tourism
Road	Normally a surfaced road, although 'off road recreational vehicles' are not restricted	Car, bus, or coach; low capacity for passengers	Petrol or diesel engine; some use of electric vehicles	Door-to-door flexibility; driver in total control of vehicle; suited to short journeys	Way shared by other users leading to possible congestion	Door-to-door flexibility allows tourist to plan routes; allows carriage of holiday equipment; acts as a link between terminal and destination; acts as mass transport for excursions in holiday areas
Rail	Permanent way, with rails	Passenger carriages; high passenger capacity	Diesel engines (diesel/electric or diesel/ hydraulic); also electric or steam locomotives	Sole user of the way allows flexible use of carrying units; suited to medium or long journeys, and to densely populated urban areas; non-polluting	High fixed costs	Mid-nineteenth century opened up areas previously inaccessible for tourism; special carriages can be added for scenic viewing; trans-continental routes and scenic lines carry significant volume of tourist traffic
Air	Natural	Aircraft; high passenger capacity	Turbo-fan engines; turbo-prop or piston engine	High speed and range; low fixed costs; suited to long journeys	High fuel consumption and stringent safety regulations make air an expensive mode; high terminal costs	Speed and range opened up most parts of the world for tourism; provided impetus for growth of mass international tourism
Sea	Natural	Ships; can have a high degree of comfort; high passenger capacity	Diesel engine or steam turbine	Low initial investment; suited to either long-distance or short ferry operations	Slow; high labour costs	Confined to cruising (where luxury and comfort can be provided) and ferry traffic

Routes

Transport routes do not occur in isolation from the physical and economic conditions prevailing in different parts of the world. Mountain ranges, extensive hilly terrain, deep river valleys, waterlogged ground, and climatic factors influence their direction, as do the locations of major cities and political boundaries. However, not all modes of transport are equally affected by these factors. For example, mountains do not deflect air transport routes although they will influence the location of airports. In contrast, railways are very much influenced by topographical features. These factors, combined with considerations of technology and investment, ensure that transport routes remain relatively stable channels of movement.

The fact that some modes of transport have a restricted 'way', namely roads, railways, and canals, will automatically channel movement. For navigational purposes, those modes that use natural ways, the air or the sea, are also channelled, and movement does not take place across the whole available surface of the earth. We can examine transport route systems at a variety of scales:

- At the world scale, there is a network of inter-continental air routes, and those countries with a coastline are also linked by the long-haul sea routes (line routes) nowadays used mainly by oil tankers and to transport freight.
- At the regional scale, many countries have nationwide bus, coach, and rail services.
- At the local scale, there are excursion circuits based on a particular city or resort.

Networks

Each transport network is made up of a series of links (along which flows take place) and nodes (terminals and interchanges). The accessibility of places on a network is of particular interest to geographers as once a node is linked to another, it becomes accessible. Scale is important here; at a local scale, many places may be highly accessible, but when viewed at the world scale, they become relatively inaccessible.

Geographers analyse these networks in a variety of ways:

- The most straightforward technique is a flow map, which shows the volume of traffic on each route. Examination of the map gives a rough indication of major nodes and links.
- A more accurate approach is to analyse the network using *graph theory*. However, before this can be done, the transport network must be reduced to its basic structure of nodes and links on a *topological* map. Although such a map retains contiguity of relationships, it is not true to scale like the familiar topographic map of an area. A well-known example is the map of the London Underground system, where the different lines are colour coded and straightened out, diagonals are featured, and where the distance between stations is much less important than their relationship to each other on the route network. In theory, the more links there are in a network, the

greater the connectivity of that network. In fact, even dense transport networks can be badly connected, making some cross-city or cross-country journeys difficult. For example, London south of the River Thames is poorly served by the Underground compared to the central area and the north.

The remainder of this chapter provides a detailed consideration of transport systems for each mode and their relationship to tourist demand.

Air transport

Developments in civil aviation have brought about far-reaching changes in the nature of international tourism and the structure of the travel industry since the Second World War. Few parts of the world are now more than 24 hours flying time from any other part, and it is estimated by the UN World Tourism Organisation that around 20 per cent of international tourists use air transport. The jet aircraft has opened up many formerly remote areas as holiday destinations. Here it is instructive to compare 'Concorde' with the Boeing 747. Although the supersonic airliner captured the public imagination in the last quarter of the twentieth century, it had limited range and capacity, and the high fares ensured that it accounted for only a small share of the market for air travel compared to wide-bodied jets. Concorde was in the last analysis unsustainable for environmental as well as economic reasons. Despite the current massive growth in air travel, it is true to say that only a small percentage of the world's population have experienced flying, and even in developed countries surface modes of transport carry much greater volumes of traffic than the airlines. This situation is, however, changing as low-cost carriers make air travel a real option on short-haul routes that used to be the preserve of surface transport.
   The following are the main advantages of the air transport mode:

*   The way allows the aircraft a direct line of flight unimpeded by natural barriers such as mountain ranges, oceans, deserts, or jungles.
*   Superior speeds can be reached in everyday service.
*   Air transport has a high passenger capacity and is ideally suited to journeys of over 500 kilometres, travel over difficult, road-less terrain (as in Papua-New Guinea), and journeys between groups of islands separated by stormy seas from the mainland (such as the Shetlands of Scotland).

Air transport does, however, have disadvantages:

*   It needs a large terminal area that may be some distance from the destination it serves.
*   It is expensive due to the large amounts of power expended and the high safety standards demanded.
*   Payload restrictions mean that vehicles cannot be carried, in contrast to sea-going ferries and some rail services.

- It has negative environmental impacts. The true cost of air travel for the airlines and their passengers has been masked by the fact that the airlines, unlike other business enterprises, are exempt from certain taxes, particularly on kerosene. The continued rapid growth of air traffic may not be sustainable, given the contribution of aircraft emissions to climate change. It has been estimated that a passenger on a single trans-Atlantic flight contributes as much to global pollution as a motorist driving 16,000 kilometres (10,000 miles) in a year.
- Air transport is particularly vulnerable to terrorism and to fluctuating fuel prices.

The world pattern of air routes

The shortest distance between two places lies on a great circle, which drawn on the surface of the globe, divides it into equal hemispheres. Aircraft can utilise *great circle routes* fully because they can ignore physical barriers, with the improvements in range and technical performance that have been achieved since the Second World War. For example, the great circle route between Britain and the Far East lies over Greenland and the Arctic Ocean. Aircraft can fly 'above the weather' in the extremely thin air, uniformly cold temperatures, and cloudless conditions of the stratosphere at altitudes of between 10,000 and 17,000 metres. In middle latitudes, pilots take advantage of westerly winds in the stratosphere that attain speeds as high as 450 kilometres per hour. These *jet streams* reduce the flying time from California to Europe by over an hour compared to the journey in the opposite direction.

However, air routes are influenced not only by the operational characteristics of jet streams but also by safety and security factors. The movement of aircraft, particularly over densely populated countries, is channelled along designated airways. The development of commercial routes is determined by:

- The extent of the demand for air travel
- Adequate ground facilities for the handling of passengers and cargo
- International agreements

The Chicago Convention of 1944 defined five freedoms of the air that are put into practice by bilateral agreements between pairs of countries (Figure 5.1). These freedoms are:

- The privilege of using another country's airspace.
- To land in another country for 'technical' reasons.
- The third and fourth freedoms relate to commercial point-to-point traffic between two countries by their respective airlines.
- The fifth freedom allows an airline to pick up and set down passengers in the territory of a country other than its destination.

In many parts of the world, these freedoms are greatly affected by international politics, including the Ukraine war. With the ending of the Cold War, commercial considerations

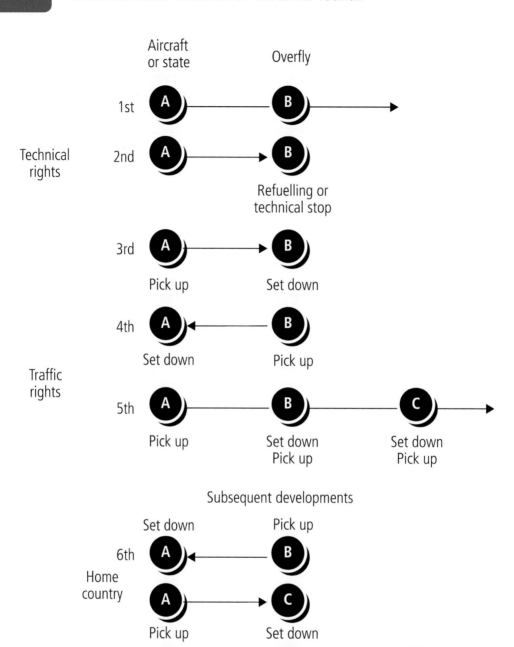

A = Home country
B and C = Other countries

Figure 5.1
The five freedoms of the air

became even more important. The sixth and seventh freedoms allow an airline to pick up in a country other than the country of origin, take passengers back to its home base or 'hub', and then take them on to another destination. For example, the German airline Lufthansa may pick up passengers in London, then fly them back to their Frankfurt hub where they change planes, and are taken on to say, Singapore. This is known as 'hub and spoke' operations and has encouraged the development of hub airports at a regional and intercontinental scale.

International agreements are becoming less important with the deregulation of the air transport system. This means that governments are no longer allowed to control routes, fares, and volumes of traffic on flights within and across their borders. The first major country to deregulate was the United States in the late 1970s followed by the European Union in the 1990s. Deregulation:

- Encourages competition among airlines.
- Has led to the building of strategic alliances between airlines such as the 'Star Alliance' and the 'One World' alliance.
- Encourages the growth of regional airlines and regional airports.
- Has favoured the development of 'budget' or low-cost carriers (LCCs) on busy routes because it not only allows competition on the routes, but also opens up the possibility of using smaller, cheaper, regional airports.

Nevertheless, many countries have yet to agree to an 'open skies' policy for reasons of military security, or to protect the national 'flag-carrier' – usually state-owned and heavily subsidized – from foreign competition.

The routes and tariffs of the world's scheduled international airlines are, to an extent, controlled by the International Air Transport Association (IATA) (https://www.iata.org) to which most belong. IATA has divided the world into three Traffic Conference Areas for this purpose:

- Area 1, with its main office in Montreal, includes North America, Greenland, the Caribbean islands, Bermuda, South America, and the Hawaiian Islands in the north Pacific.

Discussion point – The impact of low-cost carriers on transport routes and choices

Low-cost carriers (LCCs) sometimes known as budget or no-frills carriers have changed the pattern of air transport. By significantly lowering fares they have opened up air travel as an option to markets that otherwise would have used surface transport. In Australia, for example, the advent of LCCs has significantly reduced the long-haul overland bus services beloved of backpackers. In deregulated skies, the LCCs are able to fly point-to-point to regional airports, so opening up new destinations for tourism. Of course, whilst this may seem to be an advantage for tourist and destination alike, we must remember that more aircraft in the sky has environmental implications.

In class, debate the case for the expansion of low-cost carriers.

- Area 2, based in Geneva, includes Europe, Africa, and the Middle East.
- Area 3, based in Singapore, includes Asia, Australia, New Zealand, and the islands of the south-west Pacific.

Most of the world's air traffic is concentrated in three main regions: the eastern part of the United States, Western Europe, and East Asia. This is partly due to market forces originating from their vast populations and partly due to the strategic location of these areas. The situation of London is particularly advantageous as it is at the centre of the earth's 'land hemisphere' in which over 90 per cent of the world's population, and an even greater proportion of the world's industrial wealth, are concentrated.

The 'air bridge' between Europe and North America across the North Atlantic is the busiest intercontinental route, linking the greatest concentrations of wealth and industry in the world. The capacity provided by wide-bodied jets and vigorous competition between the airlines has brought fares within reach of the majority of the population of these countries, while the Atlantic has shrunk, metaphorically speaking, to a 'pond' that can be crossed in a few hours.

Time zones

International travel usually necessitates a time change if the journey is in any direction other than due south or north. These differences in time result from the earth's rotation relative to the sun; at any given moment at one locality, it is noon, while half the world away to the east or west, it is midnight. The sun appears to us to be travelling from east to west and making one complete circuit of the earth every 24 hours. Viewed from space, the earth is, in fact, making a complete turn on its axis through 360 degrees of longitude. This means that for every 15 degrees of longitude, the time is advanced or put back by one hour; places that lie to the east of the Greenwich Meridian have a later hour, those to the west an earlier hour due to this apparent motion of the sun. Nowadays, we take satellite navigation for granted to fix our position, so it is difficult to appreciate the problems that sailors faced until the invention of a reliable timepiece – the chronometer – in the eighteenth century. This made it possible to determine longitude accurately and was as important as any technological advance in making possible the development of travel and tourism across the globe.

Theoretically, every community could choose its own local time. The development of the railways made standardised timetables essential, using an international system of time zones based on the Greenwich Meridian. Since 1884, the world has been divided into 24 time zones in which standard time is arbitrarily applied to wide belts on either side of a particular meridian, which is usually a multiple of 15 degrees. Often, these correspond to political units rather than strictly following the meridians (for example, Paris is one hour ahead of London despite being on the same longitude). Several countries are too large for one standard time to be conveniently acceptable. Russia has the greatest west to east spread of any country, with no less than 11 time zones, followed by Canada with six, while the contiguous United States (excluding Alaska and Hawaii) has four, namely Eastern, Central, Mountain, and Pacific. (In contrast, China applies Beijing time to all its territory.)

Countries in the Western Hemisphere have time zones that are designated with a minus number as so many hours 'slow' behind Greenwich Mean Time (GMT), which is the standard time on the Greenwich Meridian passing through London. Countries in the Eastern Hemisphere have time zones designated with a plus number as so many hours 'fast' on GMT. Only when it is noon on the Greenwich Meridian is it the same day worldwide; at all other times, there is a 24-hour difference between each side of the 180° meridian. In 1884, the International Date Line (IDL) was established as the boundary where each day actually begins at midnight and immediately spreads westwards across the globe. By coincidence, the IDL passes conveniently through the world's largest ocean and corresponds to the 180° meridian, except where deviations are necessary to allow certain territories and groups of Pacific islands to have the same calendar day. The calendar on the western (Asian) side of the IDL is always one day ahead of the eastern (American) side.

Whereas travellers by road or rail simply adjust their watches by one hour when crossing time zone boundaries, long-haul air travel presents more of a problem. For example, the time difference between London and Singapore is eight hours, and this needs to be taken into account when calculating the *elapsed flying time* (how long the flight actually takes between London and Singapore). Jet travel across a large number of time zones also causes disruption to the natural rhythms of the human body, which respond to a 24-hour cycle of daylight and darkness. The effect of *jetlag* varies considerably between individual travellers and appears to be more disruptive on long west-east flights than on westbound journeys.

CASE STUDY 5.1
CROSSING THE INTERNATIONAL DATE LINE

When it is 21.00 (9 PM) GMT on Sunday, June 6

WEST	International Date Line	EAST
Auckland GMT +12 hours		Los Angeles GMT – 8 hours
Monday, June 7, 0900		Sunday, June 6, 1300
Earth's rotation		

The time difference between New Zealand and California is 20 hours. This should explain why you take a day from the calendar (you 'gain' a day) when travelling from west to east across the IDL, and add a day to the calendar (you 'lose' a day) when travelling from east to west.

Problem-solving

1. On Monday, June 7, a cruise liner crosses the IDL from east to west en route from Tahiti to Tonga. The calendar should be changed to which new day?
2. At 1200 noon local time on Monday, June 7, a patrol aircraft takes off from the Chatham Islands (Time Zone GMT + 12.45) and flies east. Five minutes after crossing the IDL, the pilot reports a vessel engaged in illegal whaling in the Pacific Ocean. Give the approximate time, the day, and the date of the incident.

The location of international airports

A major international airport acts as the primary *gateway* to a country for most foreign visitors, so that first impressions are important. Such an airport needs several passenger terminals, a cargo terminal, hotels with conference facilities, and convenient interchange with long-stay car parks, bus, and rail transport. It provides thousands of jobs in the retail, catering and transport sectors, and has all the problems associated with a large urban area, including a large environmental footprint and significant carbon emissions. Also, security has been given a high profile since 9/11. At the same time, passenger terminals increasingly resemble shopping malls, providing a stream of revenue to the airport authorities, and with a captive market of travellers faced with a lengthy 'dwell time' due to delayed or cancelled flights. This means that airports are attractive commercial propositions and many are now privatised (for example, Brisbane in Australia).

The largest jet aircraft in operation need runways at least 3,000 metres in length. In tropical countries, and especially at high altitudes, runways have to be even longer, as the lower density of the air means that jets have to make longer runs to obtain the lift to get airborne. A major airport, therefore, requires a great deal of land. The physical nature of the site is important; it should be as flat as possible with clear, unobstructed approaches. Such land is not abundant in the small islands that are popular with holidaymakers, or for that matter near many of the world's cities. In Rio de Janeiro, Osaka and Hong Kong airports have been built on land reclaimed from the sea. Runways are aligned so that aircraft can take off against the prevailing wind and airports are located up-wind of large concentrations of industry, which cause smog and poor visibility. The local weather record is, therefore, important.

At the same time, the airport must be in a location that is readily accessible to the large centres of population it is primarily meant to serve. However, most are 20–30 kilometres distant (for example, Kuala Lumpur, Milan), while Narita is 50 kilometres from the centre of Tokyo. Investment is needed to construct or improve rapid surface transport links with the city centre to minimise total travel time. This is particularly important for business travellers on short-haul flights. Generally, there is a motorway link or in densely populated areas, a dedicated high-speed railway, separated from the main network.

The growth of air traffic has meant that many airports are now reaching or have exceeded their passenger and aircraft capacity for safe and efficient operation. This is beginning to pose a real constraint on the development of air transport. Despite their importance for tourism and the national economy, proposals for new airports or for airport expansion are fiercely opposed in developed countries. This opposition is mainly due to the problem of noise pollution and scarcity of land, particularly in Western Europe. Consequently, on short and medium-haul routes, there is a definite role for short take-off and landing (STOL) aircraft, and possibly vertical take-off and landing (VTOL) aircraft. Indeed, VTOL is now being introduced as air taxis in cities, as seen in initiatives like 'uber elevate' (Prideaux, 2018; Cohen and Hopkins, 2019).

Helicopters require minimal ground facilities but are noisy and expensive to operate, and have only a limited range and capacity. The helicopter is, however, widely used for premium business travel, and in North America for sightseeing flights, or to reach

CASE STUDY 5.2
THE IMPACT OF A NATURAL DISASTER ON AIR TRANSPORT

The eruption of the Icelandic volcano Eyjafjallajökull in April 2010 is a reminder of the vulnerability of mankind to the raw forces of nature, and the dependence of a global economy on air transport. A plume of fine silica ash was ejected high into the atmosphere, and then carried into the path of the jet stream at an altitude of 8000 metres over western and northern Europe. This was an unprecedented event, and the International Civil Aviation Authority (ICAO) (www.icao.int) had recommended a 'zero tolerance' approach to volcanic ash, as even minute quantities of the silica can cause serious damage to jet engines. Following the advice of the UK Meteorological Office, most of European airspace was closed for several days, causing massive disruption to airline operations. According to IATA, this cost the industry 1,700 million dollars, with Lufthansa as one of the airlines most affected. The loss of working hours by well over a million travellers who were delayed in airports around the world had a significant economic impact. However, this should be compared to the hardships faced by farmers in developing countries such as Kenya, who were unable to export their produce to British supermarkets. The effect on the tourism sector of various European countries, such as Spain, was soon felt. The shutdown's impact was made more severe as a consequence of globalisation, the dependence of countries, particularly Britain, on air transport, and the weak European economy. Other aspects of the shutdown include:

- The piecemeal response by governments in resuming services demonstrated the need for a Europe-wide air traffic control system to replace the existing 27 national systems.
- A re-assessment of the risk to aviation by determining safe levels of volcanic ash. The shutdown had been criticised by the airlines as an over-reaction by governments and as a symptom of a risk-averse culture. In the United States, for example, the authorities do not close airspace after volcanic eruptions in Alaska, but allow the airlines to make decisions based on ash forecasts.
- Ferries, car hire companies, and rail transport were the main beneficiaries of the crisis as stranded passengers sought alternative ways of getting home.
- Plans for airport expansion, for example at Heathrow, had to be re-assessed. During the shutdown, scientists were able to determine from the decrease in nitrogen oxide emissions that London's airports, rather than its road traffic, are the main factor causing air pollution levels that already exceed EU limits.

A volcanic eruption on a much larger scale – as has occurred several times in Iceland since the eighteenth century – is a distinct possibility, with catastrophic consequences if the ash cloud persists for several months, through its impact on global weather patterns, agriculture, and the wider economy.

mountain areas for hiking and skiing that would otherwise be inaccessible. On environmental grounds, there is scope for new versions of seaplanes and airships. Airships are slow but are ideally suited for luxury cruising, and unlike their ill-fated predecessors in the 1930s, they would use helium for motive power.

Land transport

Unlike air transport, which is truly worldwide in its scope, travel by road or rail is constrained to some extent by national boundaries. Although few borders are 'no go areas' like the Iron Curtain of the Cold War era, most do not provide unrestricted access. Following '9/11' surface, transport was perceived as safe from terrorism, but this changed with the bombings of the rail networks in Madrid and London and the use of vehicles as terrorist weapons in London and Barcelona, when the authorities realised that to implement security measures for surface transport is, if anything, more difficult than it is for air transport. Road and rail transport is subject to a greater degree of control by national governments than the airlines and is, therefore, described in more detail in the regional chapters in Part 2.

Road transport

The main advantage of road transport is the possibility in ideal conditions of door-to-door flexibility, and travel by other transport modes almost invariably begins and ends with a road journey. This, combined with the fact that road vehicles can only carry a small number of passengers and have a relatively low speed, makes them particularly suitable for short- to medium-distance journeys. Additionally, the development of recreational vehicles (RVs) allows a form of motorised accommodation. The main disadvantage of road transport is that many users share the way and this can lead to congestion at periods of peak demand. As tourism is subject to annual and weekly peaks, this can be a major handicap. Since the Second World War, the automobile or private car has become the dominant transport mode for most types of tourism, while coach travel accounts for a much smaller share of the holiday market (note that 'coach' means economy class air travel in the United States). Coach operations differ from scheduled bus services in that they are very much part of the tourism industry and provide higher standards of comfort and service. Coach travel not only provides a transfer service at airports and other terminals, but is also used for excursions from resorts, and for touring holidays as a product in its own right. Modern fleets of buses and coaches are now highly efficient environmentally; the Greyhound Bus Company in the United States, for example, takes pride in its environmental credentials (see www.greyhound.com).

    The main impetus towards an international system of highways has come about through the demands of an increasingly motorised population and the development of long-distance coach/bus services and road haulage. The popularity of the car is because it can provide comfort, privacy, flexibility in timing, the choice of routes and destinations, and door-to-door service. The car is perceived as an inexpensive form of travel, especially for family holidays, because running costs and vehicle depreciation are not included as part of the cost of individual trips. It is certainly more convenient compared to public transport for carrying surfboards and other recreational equipment to the destination. On the other hand, we tend to overlook the cost to society of the millions of serious injuries a year in road accidents worldwide. The demands of the private car have resulted in a tourism landscape of motels and other drive-in facilities dedicated to personal mobility.

There are over a billion cars worldwide, with the largest growth taking place in China, India, and other developing countries. Nevertheless, car ownership in most developing countries is a luxury and public transport systems are often rudimentary. Passenger service vehicles may be improvised from former American school buses, jeeps, or even trucks. Climatic conditions also affect road transport systems and the type of vehicles that may be used. In large areas of the tropics, there are fairly extensive networks of roads made from the laterite subsoil; these are viable during the dry season but impassable after the rains. In sub-arctic regions, highways have a gravel surface which is less damaged by frost and thaw than tarmac. Many developing countries have by-passed 'the age of the locomotive', investing heavily in road building to achieve national unity and economic progress. Brazil is one such example, with an extensive network of long-distance bus and coach services on offer. International road projects include the Pan-American Highway system in Latin America and trans-continental routes in Africa and Asia that can be used, when the political situation allows, by overland expeditions and the more adventurous traveller.

In Western Europe and North America, a network of motorways or freeways – limited access highways – connects most major cities and industrial areas, though holiday resorts are sometimes less well-served. Motorways have shortened journey times and appreciably reduced accident rates. Roads designed especially for sightseeing have been built in scenically attractive coastal and mountain areas. However, too much road building, and the development that invariably goes with it, can destroy the very beauty the tourist has come to see.

The private car has brought about greater individual freedom but at a cost to both society and the environment. Some allege that the West is already characterised by 'hypermobility', implying that many trips for shopping or recreation are unnecessary and could be reduced by a change in lifestyle. The demand for car *ownership* may have reached a peak across Europe, the United States, and Australia, and car *use* can be reduced at destinations in several ways:

* 'Park and ride' schemes;
* Improving access to bus, tram, and train services; or through
* Disruptive innovations, namely a gradual re-thinking of the whole concept of individual ownership, for example ride sharing (see waze.com and zipcar.com for examples of car sharing).

In some cities, measures to limit car use include road pricing or congestion charges, while the development of autonomous (self-driving) vehicles will reduce congestion and pollution, and indeed, they are predicted to lead the next transport revolution.

In developing countries, antiquated diesel buses, 'collective taxis', and taxi-motorcycle combinations (such as tuk-tuks and trishaws) add to the traffic problems. Although in some countries, for example, Egypt, this type of transport is being banned. The environmental cost of road transport is increasingly understood, and governments in some countries are taxing cars according to their carbon emissions, whilst manufacturers are now designing 'zero' emission and hybrid cars.

Car use can also be controlled in national parks and other attractions in rural areas by imaginative traffic management schemes. However, the most sustainable forms of transport are cycling and horse riding; these are growing in popularity as activity holidays, although artificial motive power is still needed to reach the destination area and provide logistical support to tour groups. In Europe, a network of 'green routes', some reclaiming former railways, is being developed for the use of hikers, cyclists, and horse riders.

Rail transport

In contrast to the road, the railway track is not shared and extra carriages can be added or removed to cope with demand. This is particularly important in holiday areas where special trains may be run. Additionally, special facilities can be provided on rolling stock such as dining cars or viewing cars on scenic routes. The railway's main disadvantage is that the track, signalling, and other equipment must be maintained and paid for by the single user of the way. Providing railway track is particularly expensive as the motive power can only negotiate gentle gradients. This means that engineering work for cuttings, viaducts, and tunnels is a major cost consideration, especially on long routes and in mountain regions. Railways are, therefore, characterised by high fixed costs and a need to utilise the track and rolling stock very efficiently to meet these high costs. The railway's speed and capacity to move large numbers of passengers make it suitable for journeys of 200–500 kilometres between major cities.

In the nineteenth century, the introduction of railways revolutionised transport and enabled large numbers of people to travel long distances relatively cheaply. The great trans-continental railways were built before 1914, when there was no serious competition from other modes of overland transport. The first was the Union Pacific between Chicago and San Francisco, completed in 1869, which opened up the American West to settlement and tourism. The introduction of the Pullman car at the same time allowed long distance journeys to be made in comfort. The Canadian Pacific was built for political as well as economic reasons, as, to a large extent, was the Australian Trans-continental linking Perth to Sydney. The world's longest line – the Trans-Siberian linking Moscow to Vladivostok – took 15 years to complete (1891–1905) and still remains the vital lifeline of Siberia.

After the Second World War, the railways came under increasing competition from the airlines for long-distance traffic and from the private car for short journeys. New railway construction virtually ceased in most countries, but improvements were made to track, and steam was replaced as motive power by diesel fuel or electricity. The decline in passenger rail transport has been most significant in the Americas. In France, China, and Japan, on the other hand, there has been considerable government investment in applying new technology to the development of high-speed trains and upgrading the trunk lines between major cities. In Western Europe, the Channel Tunnel between England and France has encouraged the development of rail-based tourism products such as the 'Eurostar' service between London and Paris, Amsterdam, and Brussels. There is also a niche market based on nostalgia for the 'golden age' of travel in the 1920s, with products such as the revived 'Orient Express'. The growth of environmentalism and concern at a future energy crisis may yet prompt a modal switch from congested airspace and roads; indeed, the Eurostar has been marketed as the 'green alternative' to air travel. It is perhaps ironic that high speed trains – namely the TGV in France – have themselves been opposed by environmentalists.

Civic authorities, even in countries as dominated by the automobile as the United States, are investing in **rapid transit** – automated light railways with a high-passenger capacity, rather than building more car parks and multi-lane highways. Due to their operational inflexibility, monorails are rarely used for urban transport, but can be an important part of the leisure environment, for example, the Disneyworld theme park in Florida (see Photo 5.1).

In mountain regions, specially designed railways have long been used, as in Switzerland, to overcome the problem of steep gradients, and these are tourist attractions in themselves. However, aerial cableways are more versatile and cost-effective, as well as being faster in transporting large numbers of skiers and other tourists.

Water-borne transport

Voyages by sea are slow compared to air travel – an aircraft can make 20 crossings of the Atlantic in the time a ship makes one return journey. By the late 1960s, most of the long-haul market on the North Atlantic routes had been lost to the airlines. Furthermore, many travellers are badly affected by the six types of motion that characterise a ship in heavy seas (namely surge and roll, heave and yaw, pitch and sway). However, the advantages of this mode are that:

- Ships expend relatively little power.
- Ships can be built to much larger specifications than any vehicle or aircraft to carry as many as 10,000 passengers and crew at a time over long distances. Increasing size does bring safety and pollution problems, and few of the world's ports are equipped to accommodate very large ships.
- They can also provide a high degree of comfort. This has led to the development of the cruise market, which is travel for travel's sake in 'floating resorts'.
- Ships can be designed as roll-on roll-off ferries accommodating large numbers of motor vehicles – in effect 'floating bridges'. This has led to marketing directed at motorists using the short sea routes, such as those crossing the English Channel.

Technological advances are beginning to overcome some of the natural disadvantages of sea transport. For example, a conventional vessel has to displace a volume of water equivalent to its own weight. This can be partly overcome by vessels using the hydrofoil principle, where the hull is lifted clear of the water by submerged foils acting like aircraft

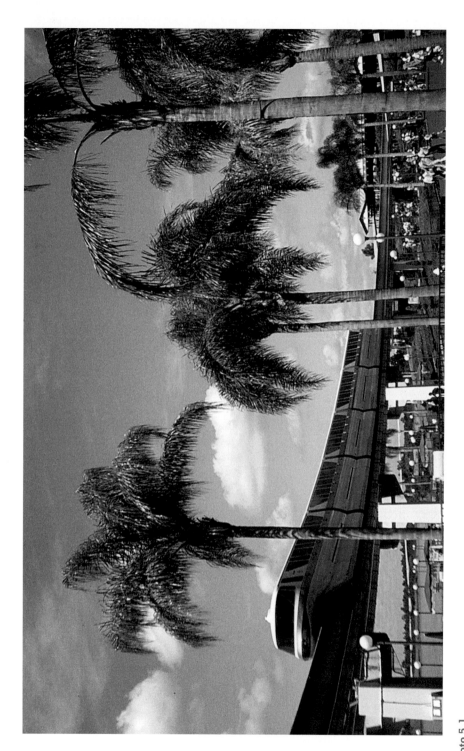

Photo 5.1
Monorail at Disneyworld, Florida

Source: Brian Boniface

wings, or hovercraft, where the entire vessel uses a cushion of air to keep it clear of the water. So far, neither hydrofoils nor hovercraft are used on long ocean voyages due to their vulnerability in rough seas and strong winds, as well as their limited capacity and range of operation. They are successful on short sea crossings where their speed (up to three times that of a conventional ship), manoeuvrability, and fast turn-round in port give them the advantage. Wave-piercing catamarans have proved to be more versatile than hydrofoils or hovercraft on some routes. As a result, hovercraft is being phased out of car ferry services, but their amphibious characteristics are well-suited for specialist roles, such as transport in areas of marshy terrain. Hydrofoils cannot carry vehicles, but they have proven advantages operating on lakes such as those of northern Italy, and on the wide waterways of Russia. There is obvious potential for ocean-going high-speed craft, combining the advantages of air and sea modes, currently under development.

The world pattern of sea routes

We must make a distinction between the long-haul or line routes plied by shipping and the short sea routes, especially those of Europe and the Mediterranean, where ferries provide vital links in the international movement of travellers by road and rail. Cruising is a separate category as it is essentially a type of holiday and not a point-to-point voyage.

Long-haul routes

Despite having the advantage of the freedom of the high seas outside a country's territorial waters, ships rarely keep to great circle routes. Instead, they ply sea-lanes determined by the availability of good harbours en route and which avoid sea areas characterised by storms and ice hazards. Economic considerations are foremost; the most important routes are those linking Europe with its main trading partners. Many ports on the long-haul routes, including Liverpool and Valparaiso, have declined due to changing patterns of trade. Tourists and legal emigrants now account for only a small fraction of the business due to competition from the airlines and the high labour costs involved in operating a passenger liner. (Some cargo liners or freighters do take up to 12 passengers, and voyages on these ships attract a significant niche market in the United States.) The Straits of Malacca, and the Panama and Suez Canals are vital links between the oceans on the line routes, with the shipping canals providing an alternative to much longer (and often stormy) voyages around Cape Horn or the Cape of Good Hope. Climate change could soon make the centuries-old dream of a commercial sea route through the Arctic Ocean a viable proposition; this would shorten the sailing time from Europe to the Far East by a week or more. By 2019, small cruise ships were already navigating the 'Northwest Passage' linking the Atlantic and Pacific oceans via the Canadian Arctic.

Generally speaking, international regulations on shipping have been less effective than those for civil aviation. Many ship owners operate under 'flags of convenience' to avoid strict adherence to safety standards, pollution controls, and labour laws in their countries of origin.

Discussion point

Piracy on the high seas is no longer a subject just for writers of historical adventure stories. How big a threat is piracy to tourism on the world's shipping routes, and how should it be dealt with?

Short sea routes

Passenger traffic on the short sea routes is increasing rapidly throughout Western Europe largely as the result of the popularity of motoring holidays and the growth of trade between the countries of the European Union. The introduction of roll-on roll-off facilities has enabled ports on these routes to handle a much greater volume of cars, coaches, and trucks, and most ferries now operate throughout the year with greatly improved standards of comfort and service. The opening of the Channel Tunnel in 1994 caused shipping companies to transfer investment to the western English Channel. Ferries are often the only transport option available to groups of small or remote islands where airports may be few and far between. In the case of the Aegean Islands of Greece, a popular holiday destination, large capacity ferries provide a link to the mainland ports, while smaller vessels offer an inter-island service, especially during the peak summer season. Services making greater use of fast catamarans connect the many islands along the Adriatic coast of Croatia. In developing island nations such as the Philippines, ferries are popular due to their low fares compared to domestic air services, although safety standards are below those considered acceptable in Western countries. Ferries are not widely used by business travellers for whom time is money; one notable exception is the jetfoil service linking Hong Kong to Macau.

Discussion point

Western countries are too dependent on air transport. In the near future, people may re-discover the benefits of 'slow travel' by train, ship, seaplane, or airship, where the journey becomes a positive and enjoyable part of the travel experience, much the same way as 'slow food' is now an important part of the dining experience. In class, debate this proposition.

Cruising

The chartering of ships for inclusive tours began in the 1860s. Prior to the Second World War, such cruises typically lasted for several months and catered exclusively for upper income groups with abundant leisure and wealth. The sea voyage, often undertaken for health reasons, was more important than the places visited. Faced with increasing competition from the airlines in the 1950s, ship owners diversified from operating passenger liners into cruising, although this was not an easy transition as the ships were often unsuitable. Few ports of call could accommodate 30,000 tonne vessels.

The introduction of *fly-cruising* in the 1960s was important as it allowed the cruise ship to be based at a port in the destination region, so that clients no longer had to make a long, possibly stormy voyage from a port in their home country. The cruise market has proved resistant to recession with a loyal, repeat clientele. There has been massive investment in large purpose-built cruise ships, designed with a great deal of open deck space for warm water voyages. As well as a high standard of service and accommodation, a variety of sports, activities, and entertainment is available. In 2019, there were over 300 purpose-built vessels carrying 29.7 million passengers on the world's seas and waterways, compared to 19.1 million passengers in 2010. This impressive growth was halted by the COVID-19 pandemic, and the cruise sector was effectively closed down for 18 months.

Many of the ocean-going ships are huge, supplying up to 6000 berths (bed spaces). At the same time, prices have fallen, and there are more passengers in the younger age groups, so that cruising is less of a 'grey market' than in the past. Themed and special interest cruises are increasingly promoted as the ship provides an ideal viewing platform. For example, there is an increasing number of cruises to Antarctica and the Arctic Ocean, and whale and dolphin-watching are popular activities in many parts of the world, but these are controversial in view of their possible ecological impact.

The Caribbean is the most popular cruising destination, due to its location close to the North American market, the warm climate, and the wide variety of scenery offered by the islands. The two other main cruising destinations are the Mediterranean and the Far East/Pacific. The North European market dominates cruising in the Mediterranean, where many ports of great cultural, historic, and natural interest can be visited on shore excursions. The western Pacific and South China Sea are mainly popular with the Australians and the Japanese.

Areas for summer cruises include the Baltic and Norwegian coast in northern Europe, and the even more spectacular coastline of British Columbia and Alaska in North America.

In the future, larger ships will be built to benefit from economies of scale; there will be greater differentiation in the cruise product, and new itineraries will be developed to avoid crowded routes such as the Caribbean. Cruising will also take its environmental and social responsibilities more seriously; in the past, it had a poor environmental reputation (see Wozniak, 2018). Examples here include P&O who have launched 'Fathom', where passengers work alongside NGOs and locals on environmental and social projects (see Fathom.org), and Hurtigruten was the first cruise line to introduce hybrid battery power on its ships.

Ports

There are relatively few seaports with deepwater harbours, and most are located on river estuaries where improvements are necessary to accommodate modern shipping. For example, the English Channel port of Poole boasts one of the world's largest natural harbours and has shown impressive growth as a container port and ferry terminal. However, shipping is restricted to a narrow channel less than 10 metres in depth that requires constant dredging. Ports need considerable investment in terminal facilities and improved transport links with major cities in the hinterland. The popularity of leisure sailing may involve conflicts of use, justifying the development of purpose-built marinas, where yachts can be safely moored and serviced in a location separate from the commercial activities of the port.

Inland waterways

In pre-industrial times, rivers were used wherever possible by merchants and other travellers in preference to the hazards of the road. Improvements to these natural waterways, and the development of canals in the eighteenth century, provided cities located in the interior with a commercial route to the sea, but locks and other engineering devices were needed to ensure constant water levels. Most inland waterways are now used as a recreational resource (for example, the narrow canals of Britain). At the regional scale, the world's great rivers serve as a lifeline for many communities. Cruises on the Rhine, Danube, and the Nile have been part of the international tourism scene since the nineteenth century, and in recent years, the Volga, Yangtze, Mekong, and Amazon have been promoted as river cruise destinations. Boats powered by clean energy are being introduced on some inland waterways, such as the canals of Amsterdam.

Summary

- Transport satisfies a need for spatial integration between two places, which can be explained by the principles of complementarity, intervening opportunity, and transferability.
- A transport system consists in general terms of four basic physical elements – a way, a terminal, a carrying unit, and motive power.
- There are yet few alternative sources to petroleum as an energy source, and carbon emissions have become a major concern for some transport modes, particularly air.
- Increased mobility is an advantage to the individual and the economy, but transport development takes place at a cost to the community. The fixed and variable costs of the transport system are borne by the operators and the users, while the cost structure determines the suitability of a particular transport mode for different types of journeys.
- Transport routes are determined by economic considerations, the nature of the way, or navigational convenience.
- The development of rapid means of communication, especially in civil aviation, has done much to revolutionise the scale and structure of the travel industry.
- It has also meant that almost all countries have adopted a system of time measurement based on the Greenwich Meridian.
- Airports are closely integrated with surface forms of transport, but the expansion of major international airports leads to demands on scarce land, energy, and human resources that are increasingly difficult to resolve.

- Airlines and shipping are part of worldwide networks based on market forces and need to be examined on an international scale. This is less true of road and rail transport operators, which are subject to more scrutiny by national governments and, therefore, best dealt with on a country-by-country basis.
- The private car is the dominant mode in domestic tourism, while coaches and some forms of rail transport have significant roles in reducing the environmental impact of car use.
- In shipping, we need to distinguish between the long-haul routes that have long ceased to carry much passenger traffic, and the short sea routes used mainly by holiday motorists.
- Some forms of transport such as the hydrofoil have highly specialised roles, while cruising is a type of holiday rather than a means of transport in the true sense.

Review questions

1. Explain why airport expansion in developed countries with a democratic form of government is a controversial issue.
2. Discuss why individual ownership of cars is likely to increase, even in developed countries, whereas shared ownership would offer financial advantages to the motorist as well as benefitting the environment.
3. Identify the elements of transport as applied to a specific short sea ferry route with overland connections to major cities in countries 'A' and 'B'.

References

Cohen, S.A., and Hopkins, D. (2019) Autonomous vehicles and the future of urban tourism, *Annals of Tourism Research* 74 (1), 33–42

Cooper, C., Fletcher, J., Gilbert, D., and Wanhill, S. (1997) *Tourism: Principles and Practice*, Pearson, Harlow

Faulks, R.W. (1990) *The Principles of Transport*, 4th edition, McGraw Hill, New York

Lohmann, G. and Duval, D.T. (2015) Tourism and transport, pp 129–182, in Cooper, C. (ed) *Contemporary Tourism Reviews*, Volume 1, Goodfellow, Oxford

Peeters, P., Szimbo, B. and Duijinisveld, D. (2007) Major environmental impacts of European tourism transport, *Journal of Transport Geography* 15 (1), 83–93

Prideaux, B. (2018) Tourism and surface transport, pp. 297–313, in Cooper, C., Volo, S., Gartner, W.C. and Scott, N. (eds) *The Sage Handbook of Tourism Management Theories, Concepts and Disciplinary Approaches to Tourism*, Sage, London

Ullman, E. (1980) *Geography as Spatial Interaction*, University of Washington Press, Washington

Wozniak, D. (2018) The economic, social and environmental impacts of cruise tourism, *Tourism Management* 66, 387–404

The regional geography of travel and tourism

Europe

6

An introduction to the tourism geography of Europe

Learning objectives

After reading this chapter, you should be able to:

- Identify the major physical features of Europe and the impact of climatic differences on the flow of tourists.
- Identify the cultural features of Europe and explain regional differences.
- Understand how tourism demand in Europe is influenced by social and demographic trends, including the effects of the COVID-19 pandemic.
- Identify the main features of the transport system in Europe.

DOI: 10.4324/9781003406853-9

- Describe the main features of the tourism sector in Europe.
- Understand the role of the European Union.

Introduction

Within relatively narrow physical confines, Europe is a continent of immense economic, social, and cultural diversity. In part, this diversity explains why Europe has long been a crucible of conflict, culminating in two world wars in the twentieth century. On the other hand, the devastation of the Second World War brought about a movement towards economic and political integration, which is still in progress. As the twenty-first century unfolds, Europe faces new challenges from the following:

- A resurgent Russia to the east, which unleashed a full-scale invasion of Ukraine on February 24, 2022. This has turned out to be the most dangerous conflict for Europe since the Second World War due to the scale of the devastation and the influx of refugees. Long term, it is creating major problems regarding the security of energy supplies.
- Islamic fundamentalism and its intolerance of Western values.
- Immigration from Africa to the south, caused by rural poverty (due partly to climate change), the aspirations of a youthful population for a better life, and internal political changes.
- Recovery from the impact of COVID-19 (see case study 6.2).

Europe is experiencing strong economic competition from both North America and the newly industrialising BRIC countries (Brazil, Russia, India, and China), and this is reflected in its failure to maintain market share in international tourism:

- In 1960, Europe accounted for 72 per cent of international tourism arrivals.
- By 2019, this share had fallen to just over 50 per cent, but as Europe recovered from the pandemic more quickly than competing regions, it subsequently rose to 67 per cent.

Europe, as defined by the UN World Tourism Organisation, includes the Russian Federation and the Central Asian republics. Still, in this chapter, we are concerned with the geographical continent of Europe, which continues to dominate world tourism, despite representing less than 10 per cent of the world's population and an even smaller share of the total land area. It includes five out of the world's top ten destination countries and accounts for half the world's receipts from international tourism. The strong economies in the region still account for most of the world's top tourist-generating countries, dominating the outbound flow of international travel and also generating massive demand for domestic trips.

Europe is pre-eminent in the world's tourism system for the following reasons:

- Most of Europe's economies are advanced. The population, though ageing, is in general affluent, mobile, and has a high propensity to travel.

- Europe consists of a rich mosaic of languages, cultural resources, and tourist attractions of world calibre.
- The adoption of the single European currency, the Euro, in many European countries has facilitated tourism.
- Europe comprises many relatively small countries in close proximity, encouraging a high volume of short international trips.
- The climatic differences within the region are significant, leading since the 1950s to a considerable flow of sun-seeking tourists from northern Europe to the south.
- Europe's tourism infrastructure is mature and of a high standard.
- The tourism sector throughout most of the region is highly developed, and standards of service – though not the best in the world – are good.
- Most European governments have well-funded, competent tourist authorities with marketing and development powers.

With a few striking exceptions, Europe's political and economic structures are stable, providing a safe environment for investment in tourism. The dismantling of the Iron Curtain in 1989 and the opening up of Eastern Europe, along with the advent of the Single European Market and the adoption of the Euro, have removed barriers to tourism movement within the region. With the admission of 11 former Eastern bloc countries since 2004, the European Union includes most of the continent. We should mention here the role of the European Travel Commission (www.etc-corporate.org), which is an independent non-profit organisation promoting Europe as a tourist destination to markets outside the region such as China. The NTOs of the 34 member countries of the ETC (which include Ukraine and the micro-states of San Marino and Monaco) co-operate in sharing information and expertise to ensure Europe remains competitive as a destination.

Physical features

Physically, but not culturally, Europe is a western extension of Asia, a peninsula surrounded on three sides by sea. Its eastern boundary is rather indeterminate, and is in fact straddled by two important nations – Russia and Turkey. Within Europe, we can distinguish two major physical/climatic divisions – north and south – separated by a series of mountain ranges such as the Alps.

The dominant feature of northern Europe is a lowland plain, crossed by many rivers, and extending from southern England to the Urals in Russia, with the remnants of worn-down mountain systems along its periphery. It is on this plain that the major industries and cities are located, and, therefore, it acts as the source of many tourists to the rest of Europe. Southern Europe, on the other hand, is hilly or mountainous, containing only small pockets of fertile lowland, and with few inland waterways of any length.

Europe's mountain ranges act as a major influence on weather systems; in the past, they were barriers to communications, and nowadays they are seen as a recreational and tourism resource for both winter sports and 'lakes and mountains' summer holidays. The most important are:

- **The Alps** – a series of high mountain ranges extending in an arc from south-eastern France to Austria and Slovenia. Their great height is due to geologically recent earth movements, while the valleys were widened and deepened by glaciers during the last Ice Age. A number of large lakes were formed as a result of moraines – accumulations of glacial debris – blocking the valleys.
- The **Pyrenees** – the mountain ranges extending from the Bay of Biscay east to the Mediterranean, and forming the boundary between France and Spain.
- The **Balkan Peninsula** consists of a complex system of mountain ranges in south-eastern Europe bordered by the Adriatic, Aegean, and Black Seas. Earthquakes are frequent in this region. There is a striking contrast between the coastlands that enjoy a Mediterranean climate, and the interior that experiences harsh winters.
- The **Carpathians** – a series of mountain ranges forming a crescent around the plains of the Pannonian Basin in the heart of Europe.
- The **Caucasus** lie far to the south-east, between the Black Sea and the Caspian (which is not really a sea, but a vast, partially saline lake). These mountains rise to even greater altitudes than the Alps.
- The Kjolen Mountains form the spine of the **Scandinavian Peninsula**. They differ from the other ranges in being geologically stable, the remnants of a much older mountain system than the Alps, and over the ages they have been worn down to a series of high plateaus rather than forming rugged mountain peaks.

Europe's seas also deserve consideration in view of the importance of coastal tourism. In most countries with a coastline, more than two-thirds of the accommodation stock is found at the seaside. Tourism is, however, only one of many uses of the coast, with the result that pollution and degradation of the marine ecosystems are serious problems.

- This is especially true of the **Mediterranean**, which is virtually an inland sea. Not only are there several large industrial cities on the coast, but the Mediterranean also attracts over 160 million holidaymakers each summer, far more than any other body of water of similar size. In other words, the Mediterranean accounts for only 0.7 per cent of the world's sea area, but its shoreline attracts almost 20 per cent of the world's international tourism arrivals. Over 500 rivers flow into this enclosed sea, carrying all manner of pollutants. The natural cleansing action of the sea is reduced by the weakness of the tides, and the water is changed only once in every 90 years, through the Mediterranean's only outlet – the Straits of Gibraltar – to the Atlantic Ocean. The scope for international co-operation to mount clean-up operations and prevent further pollution is limited, as less than half of the shoreline belongs to EU countries. The Mediterranean's reputation for calm weather is a misconception, as it is frequently disturbed by strong regional winds, such as the Sirocco (blowing from the Sahara) and the Mistral.
- The importance of the **Baltic Sea** as a major focus for summer tourism is likely to increase as a result of climate change. Like the Mediterranean, it is almost enclosed, but the water is brackish rather than saline, and it is rather shallow, so its northern reaches are often ice-covered in winter. It is also the repository of many rivers and much industrial waste, particularly from the countries of the former Eastern bloc, where environmental controls are less stringent than those of Germany and Scandinavia.

Climatically, Europe is very varied. On the western fringes of the European plain, Atlantic influences keep the climate mild but unpredictable, while the further east one travels, the more extreme are the temperatures in both summer and winter. In the mountains, long periods of high pressure bring clear skies and excellent visibility, while the Mediterranean climate is considered to be just about perfect for most tourism activities, with hot sunny summers and mild winters. Nonetheless, Europe has not escaped the effects of climate change with many winter sports resorts suffering from unreliable snow cover and countries in the south of the region experiencing prolonged heat waves in summer. Southern Europe is the most climatically favoured area, characterised by a *pleasure periphery* of resorts in every country fringing the Mediterranean with an extension along the Black Sea. Add to this the cultural and heritage attractions of many of these countries – for example, Greece and Italy – and the classic mix of a tourist destination is created. It is, therefore, doubly tragic that the pollution and low-cost development on much of the Mediterranean coast has detracted from these natural and cultural resources.

Cultural features

Europe has resisted the trend towards homogenisation, with national and even regional cultures, languages, and traditions continuing to flourish. These cultural differences are rooted in history and partly determined by language and religion. The most striking differences in life styles, cultural traits, and perhaps national temperaments are:

- Those between northern Europe and the 'Latin' south-west, so called because its languages – notably French, Italian, Portuguese, and Spanish – are derived from Latin, the language of the Roman Empire, which once dominated southern Europe, and later the language of the Roman Catholic Church. Whereas the Protestant Reformation of the sixteenth century came to dominate most of northern Europe, it failed to take root south of the Alps.
- Between Western and Eastern Europe, the differences go much further back in time than the Cold War division of Europe between Russia and the Western powers between 1945 and 1989. Whereas Roman Catholicism dominated Western Europe in the Middle Ages, the eastern part of the continent was much more influenced by the Orthodox version of Christianity based at Constantinople. In the east, subsequent political and economic development was also disrupted by invaders from Asia. The differences between east and west were shown in the civil wars between Catholic Croats, Orthodox Serbs, and Muslims that ravaged the Balkan Peninsula in the 1990s, following the break-up of Yugoslavia. In Western Europe, the tensions between Catholics and Protestants that culminated in the Thirty Years War (1618–1648) largely have disappeared, with the notable exception of Northern Ireland.
- Many of the mountain regions of Europe contain communities that are culturally different from those of the surrounding lowlands. Their former isolation helped preserve traditional lifestyles, but these are now increasingly under threat, partly because of tourism and, second home development by affluent city-dwellers.

A complex history of interaction between the different cultures spanning more than two millennia has left a rich architectural heritage throughout Europe, which is now an important tourism resource (see Box 6.1).

BOX 6.1
STAGES IN EUROPE'S CULTURAL DEVELOPMENT

Timescale	Major developments	Cultural features	Examples
20000 BP	Culmination of the Palaeolithic hunting culture	Cave paintings	Altamira, Lascaux
10000 BP	End of the last *Ice Age*		
5000 BP	Introduction of agriculture and later, metal working in the *Bronze Age*	Megalithic monuments Minoan civilisation in Crete and Aegean Islands	Stonehenge, Skara Brae, Newgrange, talayots of Minorca Knossos
3000 BP	*Iron Age Rise of Classical Greece*, extending throughout the western as well as the eastern Mediterranean	Celtic hill forts Overland trade route in amber linking Baltic to the Mediterranean Temples, theatres	Maiden Castle, Dorset Acropolis, Athens Taormina, Sicily
30 BC	*Rise of the Roman Empire*, extending literacy and order beyond the Mediterranean to the Rhine and Danube in the north	Road system, bridges, aqueducts, public baths, military fortifications, arenas	Pont du Gard, Nîmes, Alcantará, Ephesus, Hadrian's Wall, Coliseum, the Pantheon, Rome, Hadrian's villa at Tivoli
500 AD	*The Dark Ages* – a period of cultural regression in Western Europe, following the invasion of barbarian tribes from the north and east and the break-up of the Roman Empire. In the eastern Mediterranean, civilisation continued, based on *Constantinople*	Romanesque architecture, characterised by churches and monasteries of a simple but robust design	Sutton Hoo treasure Viking longships The churches on the pilgrim route to Santiago
The more elaborate Byzantine style of architecture, which eventually spread to Russia and other parts of Eastern Europe	Santa Sophia		

Timescale	Major developments	Cultural features	Examples
1100 AD	*High Middle Ages* – triumph of Catholicism in the West, the Crusades	Gothic style of architecture, originating in northern France, emphasising the vertical (notably soaring spires and an abundance of stained glass) Castles and walled towns, the first universities	Chartres Cathedral
1500 AD	*The Renaissance* – the rediscovery of classical learning – starting in Italy, followed by the global expansion of European power during the Age of Discovery	Classical architecture inspired by the design of ancient Greek and Roman temples, followed by the Baroque style that emphasised colour and exuberant ornamentation	St Peter's, Rome, Vicenza, Versailles
1800 AD	*The Industrial Revolution*	Technological changes resulting in the use of mass-produced building materials. Engineering achievements, particularly applied to transport, impressive civic buildings	
2000 AD	*Post-industrial*	Social as well as technological changes have led to a great emphasis on individuality of design in architecture and experimentation in new materials, often expressed in airports and other public buildings	Guggenheim Museum, Bilbao, Millau Viaduct

The **Council of Europe**, based in Strasbourg, is the organisation that has been most active in the search for a common European heritage, with a membership that extends beyond the European Union to embrace the entire continent, including Russia. It has developed a number of cultural itineraries or themed routes that are representative of European culture as a whole. The medieval pilgrim routes to the tomb of St James at Santiago de Compostela in Spain are seen as crucial to the making of a European identity, and they were the first cultural itinerary to be designated in 1987. The pilgrimage route from Canterbury to Rome, the Via Francigena, was designated in 1994.

Within contemporary Europe, there are striking regional differences in economic development. Geographers have identified a core region extending from Birmingham to Milan where there is a pronounced concentration of industrial wealth, aided by excellent communications. The contrast between this central axis and the peripheral regions may become less evident in the future, and a secondary axis of development is already in evidence along the 'sunbelt' – the north shore of the Mediterranean from Barcelona to Genoa.

CASE STUDY 6.1
THE EUROPEAN CAPITAL OF CULTURE INITIATIVE

Since 1985, many cities have competed for the title of European City of Culture, later renamed European Capital of Culture (ECoC). To be considered for this annual award, and the subsidy that goes with it, the European Commission stipulates that cities must prepare a cultural programme with the following criteria:

• It must reflect the European character of the event.
• It must involve the participation of the community.
• The programme must also have a lasting and sustainable impact on the city's long-term cultural, social, and economic development.

The ECoC iniatitive was intended to highlight both the diversity of European culture and the features that the countries of Europe share. The emphasis is on cross-cultural exchange as a means of bringing the peoples of Europe together. However, in practice, the host cities have tended to use the ECoC designation to gain competitive advantage over other urban destinations.

The ECoC designation acts as a catalyst for the cultural and economic regeneration of the host city. For example, as a result of Liverpool winning the title over many rivals in 2008, the value of tourism to the city's economy increased by 25 per cent, generating a total spend of £617 million during that year and creating 11 per cent more jobs.

Liverpool was already well-known worldwide for its achievements in sport and popular music. The opportunities for promotion and development through ECoC designation are potentially even greater for cities that are important regional centres in their own countries, but which rarely feature on the international tourism circuit, such as Graz, Austria (designated in 2003), Pécs, Hungary (2011), and Kosice, Slovakia (2013). On the other hand, cities such as Prague and Santiago de Compostela receive large numbers of visitors and need to 'demarket', rather than raise their international profile still further through ECoC designation.

Tourism demand

With a population approaching 700 million, Europe represents a major tourism market for both the region and elsewhere in the world. There are a number of demographic trends impacting upon tourism:

- Decreasing propensity to marry
- Increasing diversity of lifestyles and living arrangements
- A trend to marrying later in life
- A decline in fertility
- An increase in the number of divorces
- An increase in immigration from less developed countries outside Europe, where fertility rates are much higher

This means that the traditional family holiday will no longer be the norm in many countries, the elderly will become an important consideration in tourism, and also that the European market is not growing as fast as other regions of the world. To some extent, the rise of the eastern European market has offset the slower growth characteristic of Western Europe.

These social and demographic factors have resulted in a complex pattern of tourism demand in Europe, although the methods of collecting tourism statistics differ between countries, making comparisons difficult. Western Europe takes the lion's share of international tourism with around one-third of arrivals, followed by southern Europe, with a share of over a quarter. However, there are clear signs that the traditional flow of tourists from the northern industrial areas to the south is diminishing for the following reasons:

- Consumers are tiring of the inclusive-tour format.
- The Mediterranean is becoming increasingly polluted.
- Traditional 'sun, sea and sand' holidays are less popular, as people become more aware of the risk of skin cancer.
- Competing destinations for other forms of tourism have become increasingly available.
- New destinations are opening up in the east of Europe.
- Long-haul destinations are growing in popularity.
- The adoption of the Euro has made what had been reasonably-priced destinations, such as Spain, more expensive.

The bulk of tourism in Europe is generated from within the region, while the United States is by far the largest market from outside it. Most countries are important destinations in their own right, but Spain, Italy, and France are clearly in the lead, not just for the region but also for the world as a whole. Estimates suggest that two-thirds of European international tourism is for leisure purposes, around 20 per cent is business travel, and

15 per cent is VFR. The car is the dominant mode of transport because of the many short, cross-border trips, followed by air travel.

International tourism is an important feature of the European economy with a re-distribution of wealth from north to south, which varies in significance from country to country. For example, in Spain and Portugal, tourism is a significant source of export earnings in the form of foreign exchange, yet for the major generators of tourism (such as the Netherlands and Germany), tourism represents only a small percentage of the expenditure on imports, despite the volume of outbound travel. Tourism is, therefore, a vital ingredient in Mediterranean economies and any fall in arrivals is a major problem for these countries, demanding imaginative solutions. It is also these countries in southern Europe, particularly Portugal, Spain, and Greece, that still have comparatively low levels of holiday taking by populations who are less urbanised and more family-centred than other parts of Europe. Seasonality is a major issue in European tourism, fuelled not only by climate but also by traditions. Although beach tourism (increasingly augmented by sports and activities) still dominates the European product, other sectors of tourism are on the increase. These and other trends include:

- Europeans will continue to take more, but shorter tourism trips.
- Short-break city and cultural tourism is growing rapidly.
- Traditional north-south holidays are still a significant feature of European tourism, but east-west and west-east travel is growing rapidly.
- Significant market segments for the growth of tourism will be those aged over 55 years, and those aged under 25 years.
- Intra-regional flows of tourism dominate Europe's international tourism, but their share is decreasing.
- The market is moving increasingly towards holidays that involve active pursuits, and/or exposure to local society and culture.
- The popularity of the car for leisure-based trips is decreasing, with an increase in the use of air travel encouraged by the growth of the low-cost carriers.
- Demand for business tourism in Europe will continue to be strong despite the growth of communication technologies.
- Capacity ceilings are being reached in some Western European countries, whereas countries in eastern and southern Europe have considerable potential for growth.

CASE STUDY 6.2
THE IMPACT OF COVID-19 ON TOURISM IN EUROPE

The decade 2010–2019 prior to the pandemic was a period of steady growth, and tourism accounted for 11 per cent of employment in the European Union. As a result of the pandemic, international tourism arrivals and receipts from tourism fell by around two-thirds between 2019 and 2020. Tourism proved resilient in 2021, fuelled by pent-up demand, but lagged well behind pre-pandemic volumes, with intra-regional travel showing stronger growth than long-haul tourism. Governments and NGOs played an important role in supporting businesses, protecting jobs, implementing health, and safety measures and ensuring that national borders were opened with some degree of coordination. Nevertheless, the roll-out of a variety of vaccines was the key factor aiding recovery. To standardise the response, the European Commission based in Brussels introduced the EU Digital COVID Certificate, which helped to facilitate the free movement of tourists' resident within the European Union. (This offers proof that the holder has been vaccinated or has received a negative test result.) The Commission also led on COVID-19 recovery plans, supporting the efforts of individual nation states to build back tourism following the pandemic.

The supply side of tourism

Transport

The transport sector in Europe has been heavily influenced by deregulation. For air transport, deregulation has encouraged the development of regional airports and airlines and is taking pressure from the very busy routes between major cities and from the north to southern holiday destinations. There are three key trends evident in the air transport sector in Europe:

- The rapid growth of low-cost carriers is one result of deregulation and increased competition on routes, and they are taking passengers away from the traditional charter airlines. Thanks to their flexibility in operation and affordability, low-cost carriers have benefitted from the post-COVID-19 recovery, whereas the national scheduled airlines have found it difficult to retain their customers.
- Congestion in the skies over Europe is likely to become acute, necessitating a more unified system of air traffic control.

Discussion point
Some travel commentators have asserted that low-cost carriers, and the wide choice of city breaks that are available as a result, have done more to increase a cultural awareness of Europe in countries such as Britain than any number of directives from the European Union. Discuss whether there is any truth in this assertion.

Although deregulation also applies to surface modes of transport, its impact is less obvious, but other events are significant. The cross-Channel ferry industry, for example, has moved its activities to the western Channel to counter the effect of the Channel Tunnel. The European rail network is investing in high-speed routes, which will eventually link the major European countries and could conceivably extend into Eastern Europe. Indeed,

143

the continued investment in rail transport will see a gradual switch from road and air to rail travel. Although this is being done partly for environmental reasons, it is not clear whether these lines will be cost-effective, and they may even create their own pollution problems. For road transport, the disappearance of border controls across the region with the expansion of the European Union is an important factor in encouraging international travel. There is already a network of Continental highways bearing the 'E' designation (for example, E 1 running from Le Havre to Sicily and E 2 from Paris to Warsaw via Nuremberg). Mountain ranges act as a constraint on overland transport, although the Alps separating northern and southern Europe are no longer a formidable barrier, with a number of tunnels, bridges, and passes allowing year-round travel. However, any further road developments in the Alps will exacerbate the environmental problems, which are already acute.

Accommodation

The accommodation and catering sectors are mainly characterised by small businesses throughout Europe. In the United Kingdom, over one-half of accommodation establishments are independently owned, and in the Netherlands, two-thirds have less than 16 rooms. There is, however, a trend towards dominance by large hotel chains such as the French Group Accor. These can take advantage of the opportunities offered by globalisation and an expanding European Union to extend their operations all over Europe, including the former Eastern bloc countries. A further trend is the rapid penetration of a disruptive new player – Airbnb – in Europe's major cities and resorts.

The organisation of tourism in Europe

The organisation of tourism in Europe is complex. Each country has its own distinctive administration and traditions that influence both the public and private sectors in tourism. Every country in Europe has a national tourism organisation, supported by both regional and local organisations. Generally, the functions of these organisations are to develop and promote tourism, although in some cases their powers are more wide-ranging and include the registration and grading of accommodation as well as education and training. There is an identifiable trend towards devolution of tourism powers from the national level to regions, and a move to involve the private sector in the activities of the tourist boards. The individual organisations are described in the relevant chapters, but since the early 1980s, the European Union has also become involved in the organisation and administration of tourism.

The European Union is one of the few organisations that has attempted to devise a policy for tourism that is truly international in its scope. The Treaty of Rome in 1957 founded the European Economic Community, which became the present European Union, and in the ensuing decades, the number of member countries grew from the original six signatories to 28 with the admission of Croatia in 2013. 'Brexit' (the withdrawal of the United Kingdom from the European Union in 2020) is likely to have an impact on tourism, while the COVID-19 pandemic, along with a major immigration problem has called into question the wisdom of lax border controls. Nevertheless, the Lisbon Treaty recognises the need for the European Union to co-ordinate the actions of member states in maintaining Europe as 'the world's Number 1 destination'. In practice, tourism policy *per se* has been a minor part of the EU's business, and is generally regarded, under the *subsidiarity* principle, as a matter for individual countries and not for the European Union as a whole. On the other hand, EU policies on regional development and transport have a major impact on the tourism sector.

The setting up of the Single European Market entailed legislation to remove the various barriers that impede the free movement of goods and services between member countries. The following EU institutions have an important role:

- The European Commission, based in Brussels, which is effectively the 'civil service of Europe', initiating and implementing EU legislation.
- The European Parliament, based in Brussels and Strasbourg, amends European legislation and has generally been supportive of tourism initiatives at EU level.
- The Council of Ministers represents the national interest of member countries.
- The European Court of Justice, based in Luxembourg, adjudicates disputes over tourism policy.
- The European Investment Bank (EIB), based in Luxembourg, provides long-term loans and supports regional development, including tourism projects.

The free movement of travellers within the European Union involves the abolition of border controls under the Schengen Treaty. The harmonisation of taxes and duties provides a 'level playing field' for competition. The introduction of a single European currency removes the need for currency exchange, but several countries remain outside the 'Eurozone', which was adversely affected by the 2009 financial crisis. The EU's social legislation has encouraged labour mobility in the tourism sector across member states. Nevertheless, some have argued that certain health and safety regulations, with restrictions on working hours, in an industry that is characterised by 'anti-social' hours, could make European countries less competitive with North America and the EAP region in the international tourism market.

Summary

- Europe is pre-eminent in world tourism, representing half of international world arrivals, and has a large outbound and domestic tourism industry. This is because most of the region's economies are either in the high mass-consumption stage or the drive to maturity, so the population, though ageing, is in general affluent, mobile, and has a high propensity to travel.
- Europe also comprises many relatively small countries in close proximity, encouraging a high volume of short international trips.
- The region's climatic differences are significant and have led to a flow of tourists from the industrialised countries of northern Europe to the south.

- In terms of the organisation of tourism in Europe, most governments have well-funded, competent tourist authorities with marketing and development powers and, as the region attempts to compete with other world destination regions, the role of the European Union will become increasingly important to tourism.
- Europe's tourism infrastructure is mature and of a high standard, with a fully developed transport network.
- The tourism industry is also highly developed, with the largest regional concentration of accommodation in the world.
- Europe's rich mosaic of culture and physical features produces many tourist attractions of world calibre.
- Despite the trend towards increasing international co-operation, it should be stressed that a number of European countries, for example, Switzerland, are not members of the European Union.

Assignment

Draft a map of Europe outlining national boundaries, marking stages in the growth of the European Union with the year of accession for each member state. Countries should be indicated on the map by the national vehicle registration code, for example, CH (Switzerland), D (Germany), and HR (Croatia). Show which countries belong to the Eurozone, and indicate those countries that are members of the European Free Trade Area (EFTA).

References and further reading

European Travel Commission and Atout France (2022) *Restarting Tourism for the Better Performance of European Tourism Before, During and Beyond COVID-19*, European Travel Commission, Brussels and Atout France, Paris

7 An introduction to the tourism geography of Britain

Learning objectives

After reading this chapter, you should be able to:

*   Describe the physical regions of Britain and understand their importance for tourism.
*   Grasp the social and economic changes in Britain since the Second World War and their implications for the demand for domestic and international tourism.

DOI: 10.4324/9781003406853-10

- Identify the historical trends in inbound tourism from the 1960s to the present day.
- Understand the visitor characteristics of inbound tourism to Britain.
- Identify the historical trends in domestic and outbound tourism in Britain since the 1970s.
- Understand the visitor characteristics of domestic tourism in Britain.
- Describe the major features of the tourism industry in Britain including transport, accommodation, and organisation.

Introduction

Geographically, Great Britain and Ireland constitute the two largest islands in the group known as the British Isles, situated off the north-west coast of Europe. Within this group, there are two sovereign states – The United Kingdom of Great Britain and Northern Ireland and the Republic of Ireland. *Britain* comprises the three nations of England, Scotland, and Wales, excluding Northern Ireland, which is covered along with the Republic in Chapter 9. Additionally, the islands of Guernsey, Jersey, and the Isle of Man are semi-independent states associated with the United Kingdom.

Although only a narrow stretch of water separates Britain from the continent of Europe, this has been sufficient to give the British the following characteristics:

- A strong maritime outlook with interests in all parts of the world, while the heritage of the Royal Navy in the defence of the realm, protection of the seas, and exploration, is an important part of Britain's identity and tourist appeal.
- A cultural identity quite different from other west Europeans, perhaps reflected in the 2016 decision to leave the European Union. The North Sea and English Channel are often stormy, and, in the past, have acted as a barrier against unwelcome invaders from the mainland of Europe.

The British with their long tradition of travel and exploration invented holidays in the modern sense, since Britain was the first country to experience the consequences of the Industrial Revolution. The importance of tourism is clearly illustrated by these statistics for 2021. The impact of COVID-19 drastically reduced the volume and value of tourism to and from the United Kingdom.

- Overseas arrivals to the United Kingdom were 6.1 million in 2021.
- The British took almost 19 million trips abroad.
- The British took around 119 million domestic trips.
- Tourism was estimated to support over 3.8 million jobs directly and indirectly and contribute 9 per cent of gross domestic product (GDP).

The physical setting for tourism

Britain has a large population relative to its area, although over 85 per cent of this is concentrated in England. Only 11 per cent of the country is actually classified as urban, thanks to planning controls. Britain offers great scenic variety, but we can recognise three landscape zones as the physical setting for tourism:

- **The highland zone** includes Central and North Wales, the Southern Uplands, and the Highlands and Islands of Scotland. Here, rocks are older, often impermeable, and high rainfall gives leached, infertile soils. The population is thinly scattered, and land use is dominated by livestock rearing.
- **The upland zone** includes Exmoor, Dartmoor, the Brecon Beacons, the Black Mountains, and the Pennines; and in Scotland, Caithness, Sutherland, and the Orkneys. Here the rocks are younger, landforms more rounded, and distinctive regional differences are apparent (contrast the Yorkshire Dales with Dartmoor). Britain's national parks are mainly in the highland and upland zones where they have been designated for their natural beauty and characteristic landscapes.
- **The lowlands** nowhere exceed 300 metres in altitude and encompass much of southern and eastern England. The lowlands are characterised by a warmer and drier climate, with intensive agriculture and sprawling conurbations dominating land use.

The coasts are of major importance, particularly for domestic tourism. The western coasts are deeply indented and rugged, featuring sandy coves and many offshore islands. In contrast, the east and south exhibit smooth, low-lying coasts with typical characteristics such as long beaches, spits, chalk cliffs, or dunes. Most of the more attractive stretches of coastline have been given protection as 'Heritage Coasts', and plans are in place to designate areas of the sea and seabed as marine conservation areas.

Climate and weather

The latitudinal extent of the British Isles (from 50° to 60° North) results in a diversity of climatic influences and conditions. Being located off the coast of mainland Europe means that the climate is tempered by maritime influences, especially in the south-west of England, where moist, mild conditions predominate. The British Isles are a battleground of different air masses, and conditions are dependent upon either the nature of the dominant air mass at the time or the wet and stormy weather which results from the 'fronts' where the air masses meet. Low-pressure systems constantly arrive from the Atlantic, and the western highlands and uplands bear the brunt of these systems, providing shelter to the lowland zone.

In winter, temperatures are lowest in the north-east of the British Isles and mildest in the south-west. However, in summer, the gradient changes to west-east, with cooler air temperatures in the west. Although bathers should note that sea temperatures are often lower along the North Sea coast, as the prevailing westerly winds are offshore. During the summer, sunshine figures become a source of keen competition between resorts. The south coast boasts the highest average duration of bright sunshine, with the number of sunshine hours decreasing inland, to the north, and with altitude.

If sunshine is the goal of many holidaymakers, precipitation is to be avoided (apart from snow in winter sports resorts). The highest precipitation is found in the higher ground of the west (the Lake District, Wales, and the Scottish Highlands), which receives around 2,500 millimetres per year, about four times as much as parts of eastern England. Precipitation falling as snow is more common in the highland and upland zones, and the colder east. In the Cairngorms in Scotland, snow can persist for more than 100 days of the year, leading to a major of concentration of winter sports in the Aviemore area. Climate statistics can be deceptive, and the variety of influences upon weather in the British Isles means that there are considerable differences from the average experience.

Changes in British society since the Second World War

Demand for tourism and recreation in Britain has grown at a phenomenal rate since 1945, not only in terms of volume but also in variety. The cause of this growth is rooted in the social and economic development of Britain since the Second World War; specifically, two major influences can be identified: social/economic and technological.

Social and economic influences

Social and economic changes in Britain have combined to boost demand for both domestic and international tourism. Since 1945, rising per capita incomes have brought higher purchasing power. The 1960s were a particularly prosperous period of high employment in which the first real stirrings of mass demand for holidays abroad were experienced. The following decades suffered the setbacks of energy crises, recession, and unemployment, but even so, real household disposable incomes per head have increased steadily, fuelling demand for tourism.

The dramatic increase in *car ownership* over the period has played its part in revolutionising holidaying habits. By 2021, there were 32.2 million cars, and facilities for motorists have grown accordingly. For example, the length of motorway in Britain exceeds 3,700 kilometres bringing many holiday destinations within reach of the conurbations. As a consequence of these developments, the number of passenger-kilometres driven increased considerably. However, rising concerns about the environmental impact of traffic have slowed government road building schemes, and attempts are being made to curb the use of the car, especially in the cities, as in London with the introduction of a 'congestion charge' in 2003. Environmental taxes on motorists are also designed to reduce the use of the car and this will impact upon its leisure or non-essential use, whilst the drive to reduce carbon emissions has led to the introduction of electric cars and associated infrastructure across the United Kingdom. In 2022, it was estimated that there were over 735,000 battery electric cars and an additional 480,000 hybrid vehicles in the United Kingdom.

Increased affluence and personal mobility have been paralleled by an increase in both educational levels and access to education. Consequently, there has been heightened awareness of opportunities for tourism. Around 2.3 million students are enrolled in full-time higher education.

The *time available* for holidays has also grown with increased holiday entitlement, three-day weekends, and various flexible working arrangements providing blocks of time for trips away from home. Through the 1960s, for example, industry and services (such as retailing and banking) transitioned to a five-day working week. This shift is significant for the shorter-holiday market, but for the traditional long holiday, it is the annual entitlement is crucial, and this has greatly increased since the Second World War. Since the 1990s, legislation at the European level has augmented workers' entitlement to holiday and leisure time, but this could change as a result of Brexit.

Perhaps surprisingly, the increase in demand for tourism and recreation has been driven both by changes in society resulting from the aforementioned factors and by increases in the population itself. Indeed, between 1951 and 2021, the population of Britain grew by over 35 per cent, including large-scale immigration, and is projected to exceed 70 million by 2030. More important to tourism is the changing composition of the population. For example, the post-Second World War baby boom produced a generation that demanded tourism and recreation from the late 1970s onwards. Similarly, people are healthier and living longer than previous generations, and almost one-third of the population will be over the present retirement age (60/65) by 2030. Given the problem of pensions, most older people may not be able to afford an active, leisured, and affluent lifestyle, and the options available to government and society generally, faced with the situation of a declining birth rate and fewer economically active citizens, are limited. The COVID-19 pandemic in 2020 caused a major disruption to these trends, severely restricting travel both within and beyond the United Kingdom.

Technology

These changes in society have gone hand in hand with technological innovations (aside from transportation, which we examined in Chapter 5). For example:

- Breakthroughs in product design have brought a range of leisure goods within reach of the majority of the population (such as fibreglass boats, mountaineering equipment, and specialist outdoor clothing).
- Technology, too, through the media and the Internet, has brought awareness of holiday and recreational opportunities to all, specifically through newspaper and magazine travel sections, television and radio programmes featuring holiday opportunities, the guidebooks produced by tourist boards and motoring organisations, and many web sites featuring tourism destinations.
- Digitisation. The Internet and social media have empowered both the tourism industry and the consumer to allow the assembly of tailor-made travel itineraries, the formation of on-line travel communities and user-generated review sites, and rapid response to consumer demand.

- Finally, not only has technology released the work-force from mundane tasks as microprocessors and robot engineering are introduced, but labour-saving devices have also helped to reduce the time spent on household chores and released that time for leisure and tourism.

Discussion point

Since 1990, the growth of the Internet has transformed both the demand for and supply of tourism in the United Kingdom. In addition, it has provided destinations and companies with a cheap and effective promotional and information tool. It is interesting that technology experts feel that the technology is running ahead of the tourism sector's ability to design and create content for websites. Looking at websites for destinations that you are familiar with, do you agree with this statement?

Demand for tourism in Britain

Overseas visitors

Britain is a major recipient of international tourists in the global scene, whilst nationally tourism is an important earner of foreign currency. Overseas visitors come to Britain for heritage, culture, the countryside, and ethnic reasons. The ebb and flow of tourist movements in and out of Britain is due to the relative strength of sterling against other currencies, the health of the economy, special event attractions, the impact of international and national crises, and the marketing activities of both public and private tourist organisations.

The historical trend

- **The 1960s:** The early 1960s saw between 3 and 4 million overseas visitors coming to Britain, but with the devaluation of sterling in 1967, Britain became a very attractive destination.
- **The 1970s:** The number of overseas visitors had increased to almost 7 million visits by 1970. By the mid-1970s, the weakness of the pound against other currencies made Britain the 'bargain basement' of the Western world and arrivals leapt to 11 million. This boom in inbound travel easily outpaced the depressed demand for overseas travel by British residents, and Britain enjoyed a surplus on its balance of payments travel account. In other words, spending by overseas visitors to Britain was greater than spending by British residents overseas. This was compounded by the Queen's Silver Jubilee in 1977, which increased arrivals to 12 million. By 1978, sterling was a stronger currency, and Britain was experiencing high inflation.
- **The 1980s:** These latter two factors had the effect of increasing the real price of tourism services and goods in Britain, and increased taxation on goods in the early 1980s led to a 'price shock' for overseas visitors. Britain was no longer a cheap destination, and both visitor numbers and spending (in real terms) declined accordingly. This decline resulted in a deficit on the balance of payments travel account, the first in many

years. The world economic recession also depressed visits in the early 1980s, but an upturn began in 1982, driven by a weaker pound and allied to economic recovery in the main generating areas of Western Europe and North America. Only in 1986 was this growth rate checked by the Pan-Am bombing over Lockerbie, the Chernobyl disaster, and the weakening of the US dollar.

- **The 1990s:** The period saw significant events that have profoundly influenced the trend of tourism to the United Kingdom. The opening of the Channel Tunnel changed the mode of transport of visitors to the United Kingdom and took market share from both air and sea arrivals, whilst deregulation of air travel within Europe and the emergence of budget airlines encouraged the growth of arrivals to regional gateways.
- **The new millennium:** At the beginning of the new millennium, world events – notably 9/11 and the bombing of the London transport system – depressed international travel, whilst the outbreak of foot and mouth disease in the British countryside also had a negative impact. As a result, overseas visits to the United Kingdom fell back to 23 million. Recovery began in 2002, with over 24 million arrivals and by 2018 approached 38 million, boosted by a weaker pound as a result of the Brexit decision. With the outbreak of COVID-19 in 2020 and the consequent travel restrictions, numbers fell drastically and are recovering slowly through 2022 and 2023. Even though arrivals were boosted by a weak pound, there were only 6.1 million arrivals in 2021. We can recognise the following trends for incoming tourism:

  - The origin of overseas visits to Britain is changing. Not only are the sources of travel becoming more diverse, but also visits from all major source areas have increased steadily. Visits from Western Europe form the majority of the market at around two-thirds of the total but are declining. Visits from North America have remained relatively stable at between 15 and 20 per cent of the total, whilst new markets such as Eastern Europe and the Russian Federation have made a major contribution to arrivals over the decade. In the rest of the world, the major markets are Australia, New Zealand, the Middle East, and Japan.
  - Length of stay is decreasing.
  - Independent travel is increasing.
  - Visitor spend is increasing.

Visitor characteristics

Aggregate figures conceal variations in the different segments of incoming tourism:

- Holiday visits grew rapidly up until 1977 (constituting almost half of total arrivals), but have since declined slowly, with considerable annual fluctuations, reaching 38 per cent by 2022.
- Visiting friends and relatives is a reliable and growing segment that has reached a plateau at 36 per cent of total arrivals. This is a particularly important sector of the Scottish market.
- Business travel has also grown steadily over the decade, but the COVID-19 crisis had a severe impact upon visitation, with numbers falling to 17 per cent by 2022.

Within the United Kingdom, both the geographical and seasonal distribution of overseas visitors is very concentrated. Geographically, the majority of visitors go to England, with Scotland and Wales receiving much smaller shares. Even within England, the pattern is concentrated on London, which as the capital, international gateway, and world business centre, receives almost half of all overseas visits, especially first-time arrivals. However, tourist authorities are anxious to spread the benefits of this spending to other areas by encouraging motoring and touring holidays (especially from Western Europe). Equally, encouraging traffic through the English Channel and North Sea ferry terminals, the Channel Tunnel, and use of regional airports by low-cost carriers may reduce the dominance of London. Indeed, there is evidence that these measures are meeting with some success, with Glasgow and Edinburgh increasing their share of overseas visits. Seasonality is less of a problem than before, but the third quarter of the year still accounts for the highest percentage of overseas visitors to Britain.

Around 85 per cent of visitors to Britain arrive by air and 8 per cent by sea, with 7 per cent arriving through the Channel Tunnel. The share of seaborne visits is declining due to:

- Competition from the Channel Tunnel, which continues to increase its share of traffic.
- Growth of budget airlines and regional air services.
- Deregulation of Ireland/UK air services.

British residents' demand for tourism

Britain's tradition of tourism has led to a high level of travel propensity in the population. Around 60 per cent of the British take a holiday in any one year, but, taken over a period of three years, this figure rises to 75 per cent as some enter and others leave the market in a particular year. Even so, there is a hard core of those who do not travel, especially the poor and the elderly.

Until the COVID-19 pandemic, the main growth in tourism was overseas travel at the expense of the domestic long-holiday market. For the British tourism, market as a whole, the underlying factors fuelling growth – leisure spending, holiday entitlement, and mobility – continue to rise. However, whilst outbound tourism continued to grow in the post-COVID-19 period, domestic tourism did well.

Domestic tourism in Britain

Domestic tourism contrasts sharply with international tourism out of Britain in the following ways:

- The length of stay is shorter.
- The level of spending is lower.
- Measuring it becomes more challenging – in 1989, the four UK national tourist boards launched the United Kingdom Tourism Survey (UKTS). This was replaced by the Great Britain Tourism Survey (GBTS) in 2012.

The historical trend

Holidays in Britain are inextricably linked with disposable income and general economic health.

The 1970s: The decade began with strong demand for domestic holidays in Britain. However, over the decade, demand fluctuated, and, in the face of changing economic factors, the share of domestic tourism experienced an absolute decline as that of overseas tourism by British residents increased.

The 1980s: Recessions adversely affected demand for domestic tourism, and several factors came into play. First, domestic tourism is dominated by those in the lower socio-economic groups who are more sensitive to price and changes in income or economic circumstances. Second, the industrial heartlands of the North, the Midlands, Scotland, and South Wales, which traditionally generated high levels of demand for holidays at home, were particularly badly hit by the recessions. Consequently, demand for holidays in Welsh and northern resorts fell. Finally, not only did inflation push up the cost of a holiday at home but also, at the same time, recession bred uncertainty about employment, and holiday decisions were delayed. The mid-1980s saw a significant upturn in domestic tourism due to the increased cost of travel overseas, a weak pound, and vigorous promotion of holidays in Britain. Hopes for the continuation of this increase were dashed in the late 1980s/early 1990s, as recession and the Gulf War severely reduced domestic volumes and spending across the whole of the United Kingdom.

The 1990s and the new millennium: Whilst world events in the new Millennium might have been expected to keep the British to holidaying at home, the outbreak of foot and mouth disease rendered large parts of the British countryside out of bounds, and the bombing of the London transport system was a deterrent to visit the capital in the early years of the century. With economic recovery following the 2008 financial crisis, the volume of domestic trips grew to 122 million in 2014. However, the COVID-19 crisis in 2020 and 2021 meant that Britons holidayed at home and boosted the domestic market. In the new Millennium, there have been important structural changes in the domestic tourism market that will continue in the post-COVID-19 years:

- A continued decline in length of stay.
- Growth in the market for short holidays.
- Growth of business and conference tourism.
- A shift away from traditional coastal destinations towards towns and countryside.
- A response by the coastal resorts to upgrade and reposition their facilities.
- The impact of the 2016 Brexit decision and the COVID-19 pandemic, boosting the appeal of the 'staycation'.
- An increased volume of trips to friends and relatives.

Visitor characteristics

Aggregate totals do disguise differences between the various sectors in Britain, but an important distinction in the domestic market is between a long holiday (four nights or more) and a short holiday (one to three nights). For some time, the general trend has been a gradual decline in domestic long holidays and an increase in short, often additional, holidays. Clearly, many short holidays are taken as 'additional' holidays to complement the 'main' holiday (which may be taken in Britain or overseas). The generation of domestic holiday trips is broadly proportional to the distribution of population across the British Isles. However, some areas have a relatively high holiday-taking propensity (London and the Southeast of England), whilst others are comparatively low (Scotland, the North-west of England).

England is the dominant domestic holiday destination for the United Kingdom, with over 80 per cent of mainland trips. Scotland accounts for 10 per cent of trips and Wales 8 per cent, with Northern Ireland approaching 2 per cent of the market. Within England, the West Country is by far the most popular destination. Britain's holiday islands – Guernsey, Jersey, the Isle of Man, and the Isles of Scilly – together account for over 2 million trips a year from the mainland.

Of course, holiday choices are challenging to explain and are subject to the vagaries of changing tastes and fashion. However, the basic principle of spatial interaction operates in the domestic market, with a supplying area containing a surplus of a commodity and the tourist-generating area possessing a demand for that commodity. For example, the South of England and the West Country are perceived to be sunny and warm, with additional advantages of an attractive coast, established resorts with a range of amenities, and opportunities for touring. But set against these attractions is the problem of overcoming distance to reach the holiday destination from home.

Domestic tourism demonstrates a clear pattern in time as well as space. The trend towards short, additional holidays has gone some way towards reducing the acute seasonal peaking of domestic holidays, rooted in the timing of school and industrial holidays. Around two-fifths of long holidays begin in July or August, but for short holidays, this figure falls to one-fifth.

The business and conference sector of the domestic market has grown steadily, representing 14 per cent of total trips but a greater percentage of total expenditure. Resorts, towns, and cities fiercely compete for this lucrative sector across Britain for these reasons:

- It is not concentrated in the summer peak.
- Business and conference tourists tend to use serviced accommodation.
- This type of visitor spends much more per capita than the average holidaymaker.

Demand for overseas travel

The United Kingdom consistently features among the world's top tourist-generating countries. Indeed, the greatest market growth in tourism has been in trips overseas, which approached 70 million in 2018. However, the impact of the COVID-19 pandemic was devastating and cut the number to just 19 million. Since the 1950s, the holiday sector, in particular, has exhibited strong growth and is expected to recover in the post-COVID years. This growth has been fuelled by:

- Competitive pricing of inclusive tours, especially to short-haul (mainly Mediterranean) destinations.

- The growth of budget airlines.
- A strong consumer preference for overseas destinations.
- An increasingly experienced outbound market, which can manipulate the Internet to book and create their own trips.

In the future, growth in the market will be by an increase in travel frequency, rather than through newcomers to overseas travel attracted by the low fares offered by budget airlines.

Discussion point

A succession of warm summers, escalating fuel costs and concerns over the impact of travel on the world's climate, allied to fears over terrorism and a weak pound caused by the Brexit decision, could mean a renaissance for the UK's tourism destinations. In class, debate whether they are prepared for this and whether they can deliver.

The historical trend

Growth in the holiday sector stems from economic factors. However, the activities of the travel trade since the 1950s have brought a holiday overseas within reach of a large percentage of the population. What has happened is that the increased organisation of the travel industry coupled with the growth of travel intermediaries, such as travel agents and tour operators, has taken much of the responsibility for organising a holiday away from the tourist. Add to this sophisticated marketing, pricing, reservation systems, and the Internet, and it is clear that the travel industry has done much to convert suppressed demand for a foreign holiday into effective demand. Taking the critical 20 years when growth was at its height, in 1970 only one-third of the population had ever taken a holiday overseas; by 1990, this figure was well over two-thirds. Clearly, this has implications for both products and destinations as the market matures.

The 1970s: Between 1965 and 1972, the real price of inclusive tours fell by 25 per cent, due to increased use of jet aircraft, fierce price competition, and the increased availability of winter holidays. This encouraged demand, only to see it dashed by the oil crisis of 1973/1974 and the bankruptcy of a major tour operator. The mid-1970s saw fluctuations in the numbers of holidays taken overseas as higher oil prices, weak sterling, economic recession, and higher holiday prices took their toll. In the late 1970s, a strong pound, cheaper holidays/air fares, and vigorous marketing increased demand to a growth rate of 20 per cent per annum. At the same time, high inflation pushed up the price of a domestic holiday, and with the British beginning to view the annual holiday as a priority, overseas holidays grew in popularity.

The 1980s: The decade of the 1980s saw virtually uninterrupted growth in overseas holiday trips. Four key underlying causes can be identified:

- Thanks partly to North Sea oil, Britain was a wealthier country with relatively strong currency vis-à-vis popular holiday destinations.

- Real discretionary income rose for those sections of the population with a preference for overseas travel (the young, the upwardly mobile, and the higher socio-economic groups).
- A sophisticated tour operation and distribution system, allied to high spending on promotion, made overseas travel accessible also to lower socio-economic groups.
- Competitive pricing of inclusive tours.

The 1990s and the new millennium: The market continued to grow into the twenty-first century, despite the setbacks of '9/11' and other world events, leaving a considerable deficit on the UK's travel account. The financial crisis of 2008 impacted negatively on departures and imposition of air passenger duty (APD) increased the overall cost of travelling. By 2014, economic recovery was evident and APD was reduced for popular holiday destinations and, as a result, departures began to grow. Growth was then checked by the uncertainty surrounding the Brexit decision and the consequent weakening of the pound, and the drastic impact of the COVID-19 pandemic. The outbound market is influenced by several factors:

- Acquisition and merger in the tour operator/travel agency sector leading to an increased concentration of capacity in the hands of a few companies.
- The deregulation of European airlines, blurring the distinction between charter and scheduled services and allowing the growth of budget airlines.
- Opening of the Channel Tunnel leading to a response by the ferry companies in terms of new ships and routes in the western English Channel.
- Introduction of green taxes such as those on air passenger departures as mentioned earlier.
- Introduction of the Euro as European currency.
- Increasing the use of the Internet to evaluate and book travel.
- Competitive pricing of long-haul destinations such as Florida and the Far East.

Visitor characteristics

The level of spending on overseas trips confirms the high priority given to overseas travel by the British. Examining the reason for the visit, leisure tourism is growing, representing 64 per cent of trips, whilst business tourism accounts for only 6 per cent of trips.

In total, almost 85 per cent of trips are by air, compared to 10 per cent of trips by sea, whilst 7 per cent use the Channel Tunnel. The modal split changed in the 1990s due to the influence of the Channel Tunnel (which provided the first fixed link to the Continent) and European airline deregulation. Holiday arrangement – inclusive tour or independent – has also changed with a growth in independent travel, as the relative share of inclusive tours shrinks, and the boundary between the two forms of travel blurs as travellers use the Internet to create their own travel. The fact that a large majority of the British population has experienced a holiday overseas has led to an increased number who feel confident to travel independently, particularly for short haul trips. For these travellers, France is the most important destination. However, this new breed of experienced travellers now travels further and to a greater range of countries.

In the new millennium, the most popular destinations continue to be Spain, France, Ireland, North America, Italy, and Greece. Clearly, Western Europe dominates, with the United States the only non-European country with considerable drawing power. In line with this and recent trends worldwide, long-haul destinations are a sector showing considerable growth. Business trips have remained buoyant over the decade, and trade with EU member states generates a significant volume of surface travel for business purposes.

Three key influences will determine the volume and nature of the UK market for travel overseas in the future:

1. Prospects for the UK economy, particularly as it responds to the Brexit decision.
2. Changes in consumer habits and attitudes, particularly regarding green issues.
3. The growing maturity of leisure markets in terms of the products offered and the response of consumers.

The supply of tourism in Britain

The components of tourism

This section examines the various components of tourism in Britain from a geographical viewpoint. Those involved in the industry now have an organisation – the Tourism Alliance – that can represent their views to the government.

Resources

Britain's tourism resource base is remarkably diverse, including numerous national parks and other areas subject to varying degrees of protection under planning law. In England and Wales, national parks are required both to preserve their landscapes and to enhance their enjoyment by the public. It is not always easy to balance these objectives, as unlike those of North America and Africa, Britain's national parks contain sizeable communities, most of the land is in private ownership, and the landscape has been primarily modified by farming and mining activities over the centuries. This was recognised in 1995 by an Act of Parliament committing the parks to the economic and social wellbeing of their communities. Multiple use is also characteristic of the areas managed by the British Forestry Commission, whose primary aim is to reduce the country's dependence on timber imports. The Commission is charged with opening up the forests for recreation and tourism, and it has developed self-catering cabins in holiday areas for this purpose. A specialist agency – Forestry England – has been established to achieve this. 'Community forests' have also been designated on the edge of conurbations on land previously used for agriculture and industry. Widening public access to the countryside and Britain's waterways is a controversial issue, with Scotland favouring legislation, whereas England places more emphasis on voluntary agreements with landowners.

Britain also boasts many scenic lakes and reservoirs, but demand for their recreational use outstrips supply. This has led to intensive management of lakes such as Windermere and Lake Bala, as well as the Norfolk Broads. Other linear features include rivers and canals, both of which are extensively used for recreation, as are the Heritage Coasts and national hiking trails, such as the Pennine Way. Government provision for tourism and recreation is complemented by conservation trusts and charities, notably the National Trust, which has purchased extensive areas of attractive coast and countryside, as well as a large number of historic buildings.

Britain's built heritage includes:

- Many ancient monuments, of which Stonehenge is the best known.
- Medieval castles, abbeys, and cathedrals.
- The great country houses of the landowning class. Many of these 'stately homes' are now major attractions with a much wider appeal than simply history-based tourism.
- The examples of Georgian and Regency architecture from the eighteenth and early nineteenth centuries in Britain's spas, seaside resorts, market towns, and cities.
- The legacy of the Industrial Revolution. The art and architecture of Victoria's reign are now widely appreciated after a period of neglect, along with its engineering achievements.

Separate government agencies are involved in the protection of the countryside and the conservation of historic buildings and ancient monuments, namely Natural England, Historic England and the English Heritage Trust, and their equivalents in Wales and Scotland.

Assignment

Britain's battlefield sites are an important but neglected part of the national heritage, offering a window into a violent past that includes the Norman Conquest, the Scottish wars of Independence, the Wars of the Roses, and the English Civil War. However, there are often problems of access, inadequate interpretation, and a lack of even basic facilities for visitors. This is not due to a lack of interest in history, as shown by the popularity of staged tournaments and the re-enactment of Civil War battles by volunteer enthusiasts.

1. Plot the location of what you consider to be the most significant battlefields in British history, starting with Stamford Bridge (1066) and ending with Culloden (1746). Give reasons for your choice.
2. Discuss how battlefield sites could be improved as tourist attractions, using specific examples in England, Scotland, and the Welsh border country.

Regional landscapes and character feature in the novels of British writers and the marketing of a particular area often capitalise on these literary associations; for example, South Tyneside has been promoted for many years as 'Catherine Cookson Country' and

Carmarthenshire in Wales as 'Dylan Thomas Country'. 'Film tourism' is now a major factor in attracting visitors to numerous country houses and other historic places. Examples here include tourists following the locations of the Harry Potter films, such as Alnwick Castle.

In concentrating on heritage, which many criticise as nostalgia for an imagined past in 'theme park Britain', we could easily overlook the major economic contribution made by contemporary Britain's creative industries and achievements in art, music, the media, and sport. These are increasingly appreciated worldwide, thanks in part to the status of English as a world language. Students from all over the world are attracted to English as a foreign language (EFL) schools, which have proliferated in response to demand; many of these are accredited to the British Council.

Attractions

It is in areas such as national parks and the hinterlands of major cities and resorts that the most successful point tourist attractions lie. Since the 1990s, tourist attractions in the United Kingdom have received a major funding boost from the Heritage Lottery and Millennium funds, which have directed money to develop new attractions and improve many existing ones. Indeed, these initiatives have begun to transform the leisure landscapes of Britain. The United Kingdom has many tourist attractions, and their very diversity of size, type, and ownership makes classification difficult. However, Patmore (1983) identified three basic types:

- Many attractions simply result from the opening of an existing resource – an ancient monument, stately home, or nature reserve.
- Some attractions have begun to add developments (such as the motor museum and monorail at Beaulieu Palace) to augment the attraction and broaden their appeal. The varying shades of provision in the English and Welsh *country parks* mean that they should also be included in this second category.
- The third type of attraction is one artificially created for the visitor, including theme parks such as Alton Towers, the London Zoo, or pseudo-heritage attractions such as the London Dungeon. The government and the tourist boards are anxious to improve the professionalism of tourist attractions and to diversify the range on offer, which now include coal-mining museums, capitalising on Britain's rich industrial heritage.

Accommodation

Although the major cities account for much of the stock of serviced accommodation, around two-fifths of beds in hotels and guest houses are located at the seaside, especially on the south and south-western coasts of England and in North Wales. However, much of this accommodation is in outmoded Victorian and Edwardian buildings – establishments that do not meet the aspirations of contemporary holidaymakers. Both the public and private sectors are trying to remedy this problem and ensure that accommodation supply matches demand. The real change in holiday tastes has been towards self-catering accommodation. Between 1951 and 2018, the proportion of main holidays in England based on self-catering rose from 12 to over 40 per cent, boosted by the entry of Airbnb into the market. Self-catering developments initially appeared in holiday camps, later in caravan parks, and more recently in purpose-built leisure complexes with provision for a range of sports and other activities. The first of these all-weather complexes was opened by the Dutch company Centre Parcs in Sherwood Forest. This has since expanded its operations, attracting competitors who have adopted and replicated the format. At the same time, the holiday camps, pioneered by Butlin before the Second World War, have had to upgrade their facilities, and reposition themselves in the marketplace as tastes have changed. In major towns and cities, demand from business and overseas travellers keeps bed occupancy rates high. Here provision tends to be in the larger, expensive hotels (often with more than 100 bedrooms).

Accommodation is also dispersed along routeways and in rural areas. Initially, board and lodging for travellers was found on stage-coach routes and later, during the nineteenth century, at railway termini and major seaports. More recently, airports and air terminals have attracted the development of large, quality hotels (as seen at Heathrow and in west London), and motorway service areas now also offer budget accommodations – the equivalent of the old coaching inns. This heralded the growth of large budget chain hotels – such as travelodge and Premier Inn – across the United Kingdom. In rural areas, accommodation is concentrated in south-west England, Scotland, and Wales. There is a growing demand for farm holidays, self-catering cottages, and 'time-share' developments. It is also the rural areas that bear the brunt of second-home ownership, with social consequences for declining village communities.

Transport

Travellers entering Britain can do so through a variety of gateways, but in fact, both air and surface transport networks focus on the south-east of England.

- **Air:** Over 80 per cent of international passengers travelling by air are channelled through the London airports, and the major airlines are reluctant to move out from these gateways. Manchester has been identified as the UK's second major airport, and Glasgow's international status has stimulated major growth. Airports on Guernsey, Jersey, and the Isle of Man complete the network, and although holiday traffic to these islands is not inconsiderable, it has a highly seasonal pattern. Overall, Britain's major airports handled almost 297 million passenger movements in 2022.
- **Sea:** For sea traffic, there is again a concentration of passengers in southern England due to the dominance of cross-Channel ferry routes. Elsewhere, there is a diversification of routes such as those from Hull and Harwich on the east coast. A second concentration of routes is from the west coasts of mainland Britain to the Republic of Ireland and Northern Ireland. On the sea routes, the upgrading of ships and the introduction of high-speed 'catamarans' is a response to both the threat of the Channel Tunnel and the rise in the expectations of travellers.

- **The Channel Tunnel:** The 'Chunnel' opened in 1994 and has not only stimulated new traffic, but also taken traffic from both air and especially sea services to Europe. Its impact is expected to continue as high-speed rail links are developed on the English side of the Tunnel. Interestingly, the response of ferry operators to develop routes in the western English Channel has been less successful than expected. Other responses have been mergers on the short sea routes, closure of some routes (Newhaven to Dieppe for example), and price competition.
- **Land Transport:** In the domestic holiday market, and for overseas travellers touring Britain, road transport dominates. Since the Second World War, the use of the car has become more important than either rail or coach services, as road improvements have been completed and the real cost of motoring has fallen. The 1980 Transport Act revolutionised bus/coach operations in the United Kingdom by deregulating services. Coach travel poses a very real alternative to the railways on journeys of up to 400 kilometres, and the new generation of luxury coaches have increased passenger numbers for this type of public transport. Privatisation of British Rail in the mid-1990s resulted in train services being operated by a multiplicity of companies, whilst the permanent way and terminals remained the responsibility of a separate organisation. There has been much private sector investment, particularly on some inter-city routes and those serving coastal and inland holiday areas. There are also over 40 small private railways outside the network, which are tourist attractions in themselves, trading on nostalgia for the 'age of steam'.

Organisation

Public agencies with responsibility for tourism in Britain play a vital role in shaping the tourist 'product', through their promotional activities and advice to business enterprises. Increasingly, government is 'devolving' these functions from national level to regional and local organisations (see OECD (annual)).

National level

In Britain, the 1969 Development of Tourism Act formed three statutory national tourist boards, (English, Scottish, and Wales Tourist Boards) and the British Tourist Authority (BTA), which was given sole responsibility for overseas promotion and any matters of common interest between the national tourist boards. The Scottish and Wales Tourist Boards (STB and WTB) reported to the Scottish Office and the Welsh Office, respectively. The Northern Ireland Tourist Board predates these bodies, having been created in 1948.

Since the 1990s, the administration of tourism throughout mainland Britain has been reorganised a number of times as a result of changes in the perception of the role of the public sector, and with the devolution of power to Scotland and Wales in 1999, their tourist boards could undertake overseas promotion. In England, the focus has been changed to be more strategic and less operational. The British Tourist Authority is the national tourist board, a non-departmental public body, funded by the Department of Digital,

Culture, Media and Sport (DCMS). Its responsibilities are to encourage tourists to Britain and improve tourist amenities. VisitBritain markets Britain overseas, whilst VisitEngland undertakes domestic marketing and provides advice to the tourism sector. As tourism is a devolved power, Scotland, Wales, and Northern Ireland all have independent tourist boards. The Mayor of London also has a promotional agency – London & Partners, acknowledging the special role of the capital (www.londonandpartners.com). Guernsey, Jersey, and the Isle of Man each continue to have small, relatively independent boards reporting directly to their island governments.

Regional and local level

The increasing emphasis on devolution is shown by the structure of regional tourist boards (RTBs). There are regional tourism agencies in England such as Visit South East England, and four regional teams in Wales. In Scotland, a major restructuring at the regional level has given rise to six regions and three island areas. At the local level throughout Britain, county and district councils have considerable powers that they can use for tourism promotion and development. In the next chapter, we describe in more detail the tourism resources and attractions for each of Britain's component countries, regions, and offshore islands.

Summary

- Britain is a major generator of both domestic and international tourism. Demand for tourism has grown rapidly since the Second World War for social and economic reasons.
- Around 60 per cent of the British population now take a holiday in any one year, but, even so, there is a hard core of those who do not travel.
- The long-established pattern of domestic holidays spent at the seaside is changing with the trend towards shorter holidays.
- The demand by residents of Britain for holidays abroad has increased steadily since the Second World War, and the United Kingdom is consistently one of the world's top tourist generators. A combination of economic circumstances and the response of the travel industry has converted suppressed demand into effective demand for holidays abroad.
- Britain is a major recipient of overseas tourists on the global scene, and this demand is influenced by the relative strength of currencies, the health of the economy, special events, external world events such as '9/11', and the marketing activities of tourist organisations.
- Britain offers a rich variety of landscapes and weather conditions, but the climate is everywhere tempered by maritime influences.
- The main components of tourist supply in Britain are a diversity of attractions from national parks to purpose-built theme parks; a wide accommodation base focussed on the coasts and the major cities; and a comprehensive internal transport network, as

well as international gateways of global significance, including the major innovation of the Channel Tunnel.

• Tourism in Britain is administered by a newly reorganised structure of organisations involving the private as well as the public sectors.

Assignments

1. Explain how changes in British society since the 1950s have influenced leisure, outdoor recreation, and the choice of holiday destination.
2. Describe the various ways the public, private, and voluntary sectors protect Britain's coast and countryside.

References

Organization for Economic Co-operation and Development (annual) *Tourism Policy and International Tourism in OECD Member Countries*, OECD, Paris

Patmore, J.A. (1983) *Recreational Resources*, Blackwell, Oxford

8 The regional geography of tourism in Britain

Learning objectives

After reading this chapter, you should be able to:

- Explain the tourist appeal of England in terms of heritage and other factors.
- Identify the tourist regions of England and describe their key attractions.
- Demonstrate knowledge of the regions, resorts, business centres, and tourist attractions of Scotland.
- Demonstrate knowledge of the regions, resorts, business centres, and tourist attractions of Wales.
- Explain the tourist appeal of Britain's offshore islands.

DOI: 10.4324/9781003406853-11

England

England's great variety of scenery is partly due to differences in geology – for example, the contrast between chalk downlands, sandstone or limestone ridges, and clay vales. These have not only influenced the shape of the countryside but also the traditional building materials used in rural communities. However much of the English countryside we see today was the creation of the Enclosure Acts of the eighteenth century. This important resource is increasingly under threat from development pressures and changes in farming practices, such as the removal of hedgerows.

Tourism resources

For convenience, we have divided England for tourism purposes into a number of geographical regions. These are broadly based on the areas covered by the nine economic regions, but sometimes regional boundaries are arbitrary and the historic counties have greater significance for both visitors and local communities.

The South

Aside from London, which has its own promotional partnership, two regional tourist boards, Tourism South East and VisitSouth-west, cover southern England. The South is the UK's main gateway region for all modes of transport and is also a major concentration of population, wealth, and commercial activity. Consequently, this part of England suffers more than other regions from the problems of economic growth, including congestion on air and surface transport routes. These problems are particularly evident in London and the adjacent Home Counties for the following reasons:

1. London is the focus of national communications, including the main railway termini, the Channel Tunnel terminal at St Pancras, a major coach interchange, and the busiest motorways. It is circled by airports (Heathrow, Gatwick, Stansted, London City Airport, and Luton), which are fundamental to the international network of air services.
2. London is one of the world's great cosmopolitan cities, with a population of almost 9 million, attracting overseas and domestic tourists as well as day visitors. The capital offers the ceremonial and architectural heritage of Britain's imperial past, world-class tourist attractions, shopping, and nightlife. As well as the great showpieces of Church and State – notably St Paul's Cathedral, Westminster Abbey, the royal palaces, and the Houses of Parliament – most of the nation's leading museums and art galleries are located here. Since 2000, a range of new attractions have been developed, some as a result of Millennium funding, including:

   • The London Aquarium
   • Churchill's Cabinet War Rooms, commemorating his leadership in the Second World War
   • Rock Circus

- The London Eye – like the Eiffel Tower in Paris a century earlier, this was not originally meant to be a permanent attraction but very soon became a feature of the city's skyline
- The Millennium Bridge, enhancing the appeal of the River Thames
- The Olympic Park in the east of the city
- The Tower Bridge exhibition
- The Gunpowder Plot – an immersive experience at the Tower of London
- The Immersive Gamebox
- The Young V&A at Bethnal Green
- Shrek's Adventure London
- Shakespeare's Globe Theatre
- London Zoo's Millennium Conservation Centre (Photo 8.1)

Tourism does add to the capital's traffic problems, especially in the central area, where most of the attractions and quality hotels are situated. This area includes:

- The City of London, which was the original trading nucleus on the north bank of the Thames and is now a major centre of international finance. Since it has only a small resident population, it is almost traffic-free at weekends. The annual Lord Mayor's Show is a reminder of the traditions of 'The City' and its separate identity. The City is now home to many iconic buildings changing the London skyline, while 'The Shard', situated on the south bank of the Thames near London Bridge offers a spectacular viewpoint for visitors.
- The City of Westminster, which was once the seat of royal power and is now the nation's administrative centre; it includes most of the 'West End', where luxury trades and entertainment originally developed to serve the court and the aristocracy.
- The Royal Borough of Kensington and Chelsea, with its quality shopping and world-class museums.
- The River Thames itself, an increasingly important transport artery with pleasure cruises, ferries, 'rib experiences' (speedboat rides), and 'city cats' (riverbus services).

Tourist pressure is a particular problem for London's historic buildings but set against this is the fact that tourism contributes to London's economy through spending and jobs. It also helps to support the West End theatres, department stores, and other amenities that Londoners enjoy.

Following the abolition of the Greater London Council in 1986, it was challenging to co-ordinate the tourism policies of the 33 London boroughs. With the formation of the Greater London Authority (GLA) in 1999, there is once again a single body, with an elected London Assembly and mayor, to implement strategies for tourism and transport covering the metropolitan area. Here, Visit London plays an important role co-ordinating the capital's tourism. Even so, the GLA has a limited budget for tourism compared to say, New York City. Efforts have been made to 'spread the load' of tourist pressure to lesser-known attractions outside central London, such as Islington, Greenwich, and the former dock area to the east. London Docklands is one of the world's largest examples

Photo 8.1
Natural History Museum, London

of inner-city regeneration, including facilities for water sports and attractions based on London's historic role as a great port. To the west of London, there is a cluster of well-established attractions, including Hampton Court, Kew Gardens (now a World Heritage Site), the Thames at Richmond, and the London Wetlands Centre.

London is the setting for many special events in the sporting and arts calendar, which draw hundreds of thousands of visitors (notably the Notting Hill Carnival, Wimbledon, Twickenham, soccer finals, and cricket test matches). London was the first city to stage an international exhibition (in 1851), and continues to attract business and conference tourism on a vast scale. While there are a number of purpose-built facilities – ExCeL, the Barbican Conference Centre, the Queen Elizabeth II Conference Centre, Olympia, and Earl's Court – much of the activity takes place in the capital's larger hotels that have world-class facilities for meetings. Even with more than 400,000 bed spaces presently available, there is a shortage of accommodation in London. There are new developments to address this problem, notably in the expanding budget hotel sector and in converted buildings such as the former County Hall.

The countryside of the Home Counties has been protected by a 'green belt' from the sprawl of Greater London. This includes two Areas of Outstanding Natural Beauty (AsONB), the Chilterns to the north west of London and the North Downs in Surrey, where country parks, picnic sites, and trails focus visitor pressure. The range of tourist attractions includes:

- St Albans Cathedral
- 'Stately homes' such as Blenheim Palace (Churchill's birthplace), Knebworth, Luton Hoo, Polesden Lacey, and Woburn Abbey – one of the first to appeal to the mass market by providing additional attractions to the house and gardens
- The 'Intelligence Factory' at Bletchley Park, recalling its vital role in the Second World War
- Whipsnade Wild Animal Park
- The Making of Harry Potter at Warner Brothers Studio, Leavesdon
- The Grand Union Canal, one of England's most popular waterways

The Thames flows through several towns, which feature prominently on the *milk run* – the standard excursion circuit for foreign tourists. In Oxford, the university's colleges, libraries, and museums are the main attraction; here the conflict between tourist pressure and the historic townscape is recognised but yet unresolved. Windsor further downstream is a classic example of the tension between tourism and local interests. Windsor's key attractions – associated with royalty over the centuries – are the Castle and St George's Chapel. This small town is inundated with coaches in the summer months and has introduced a strict management regime. Henley is famous for its regatta, in an area noted for boating activities celebrated in the town's Museum of River and Rowing. Other attractions in the Thames Valley include the historic site of Runnymede (where Magna Carta was sealed in 1215), Ascot racecourse and developments such as the Lookout Discovery Centre and the Roald Dahl Gallery. Numerous theme parks, such as Legoland, Thorpe Park, and Chessington World of Adventures, have been located in the Windsor/north Surrey area to take advantage of the motorway ring around London and the access this provides to a major concentration of demand. The city of Guildford is also well situated as a focus for business tourism and tourism education.

To the south east of London, **Kent** is both the 'Garden of England' – with its orchards, hop farms, and country houses – and the historic gateway for visitors from the Continent. As a result, this county has been the focus of considerable development pressure in association with the Channel Tunnel and its rail link to London. It is also the focus of the demand for 'out of town' shopping, with the Bluewater leisure and shopping centre. The Channel ports, notably Folkestone, have declined in the face of severe competition from the Channel Tunnel and stricter passport controls following Brexit are causing delays. To mitigate the loss of jobs, Dover is highlighting its dual role as a gateway and fortress from Roman times to the Second World War. Many of the coastal towns of Kent are attractive centres of tourism (Broadstairs, Ramsgate, Whitstable, Herne Bay) or historic and important resorts such as a revitalised Margate with the 'Turner Contemporary' art gallery and Dreamland. Nevertheless, the industrialisation of the south side of the Thames estuary conflicts with tourism, while the improvement in communications is a mixed blessing, as the area now faces competition from northern France as a destination for Londoners. The Historic Dockyard at Chatham is an example of how England's naval heritage has been adapted to become a popular tourist attraction. Rochester has capitalised on its associations with Charles Dickens, although the 'Dickens World' theme park based on his novels is located at Chatham.

Kent boasts many historic buildings, of which the most famous are Hever Castle and Leeds Castle – a major heritage attraction and conference venue. The following market towns are important tourist centres:

- Ashford – now given added importance as a Channel Tunnel rail terminal.
- Tonbridge with its Norman castle.
- Royal Tunbridge Wells with its chalybeate spa.
- Canterbury, which is the spiritual capital of England and the worldwide Anglican community. The cathedral and the themed 'Canterbury Tales' exhibition, recalling its importance as a centre of pilgrimage in pre-Reformation times, are a major attraction for domestic and overseas visitors.

Westwards along the coast in Sussex, historic towns such as Rye compete for attention with the large well-established resorts of Eastbourne, Brighton, Hove, Littlehampton, Worthing, and Bognor Regis. Brighton, in particular, has been successful in attracting a younger clientele, while other resorts have declined. It has good transport links to London and is arguably more sophisticated than other English seaside resorts, with a readiness to accept alternative lifestyles. Brighton has the usual holiday attractions (except for a good beach) but it can also offer a unique architectural fantasy (the Royal Pavilion), a purpose-built marina and conference centre, a new outdoor heated lido, the Brighton i360 viewing platform (https://brighton360co.uk). It is also the stage for cultural events such as the Brighton Film Festival. In a bid to attract new markets, Hastings has developed themed attractions – the 1066 Story, Smugglers' Adventure, the Shipwreck Museum, and the Blue Reef Aquarium. Although much of the Sussex coastline has been overdeveloped, significant natural features such as the Seven Sisters are protected by the National Trust and through designation as Heritage Coast. A short distance inland, the South Downs National Park owes its character as open, rolling grassland to centuries of farming practice. Opponents of the national park have long argued that the area's new status would increase visitor impacts and antagonise local farmers. Historic towns in the area include Chichester with its cathedral and Festival theatre, and Arundel, which features a castle and a cathedral in a spectacular setting.

The counties of Dorset and Hampshire form a major part of the vaguely defined region known as **Wessex**, which is loosely based on the Anglo-Saxon kingdom of that name and the novels of Thomas Hardy. The two counties offer a variety of resources for tourism, including:

- A number of harbours with facilities for sailing, such as Christchurch, Lymington, Poole, and Cowes, with its famous yachting Regatta. The Solent separating the Isle of Wight from the mainland is one of Europe's finest coastal waterways.
- Large areas of unspoiled countryside, particularly Cranborne Chase and the much-visited New Forest. The New Forest is an environmentally sensitive area with a unique landscape under severe pressure from tourism and recreation. Today, the landscape, flora and fauna are conserved under a variety of pieces of legislation, underlined in 2005 with the granting of national park status. Visitor pressure in the Forest arises from the adjacent Bournemouth and Southampton conurbations, and the fact it is easily accessible through the national motorway network. Managing the growing numbers of visitors is vitally important, given their possible impact on local communities and the sensitive wildlife habitats that visitors find so appealing.
- The Dorset coast is a classic fieldwork area for geographers and geologists, attracting many educational visits to the fossil beds near Lyme Regis, Chesil Beach, and Lulworth Cove. It has gained international recognition as a World Heritage Site and re-branding as the 'Jurassic Coast'. Careful management is needed to reduce the impact of visitors on the Dorset Coastal Path and at popular sites such as Studland and Lulworth Cove.
- Portsmouth is a major gateway to France and the Channel Islands. Here England's naval heritage is the focus of a maritime leisure complex regenerating the harbour area, where visitors can inspect historic ships from different eras, namely Henry VIII's *Mary Rose*, Nelson's *Victory*, and *HMS Warrior*, overlooked by the spectacular viewing platforms of Spinnaker Tower. The adjoining seaside resort of Southsea has invested in attractions such as the Blue Reef Aquarium, the Pyramids leisure pool, and the D-Day Museum, which highlights Portsmouth's role in the Second World War.
- Southampton also has an important maritime heritage relating to the era of the great ocean liners, but this tends to be eclipsed by the city's role as a regional administrative and shopping centre.
- The Bournemouth conurbation (embracing Poole and Christchurch) is the region's major holiday destination with one of the largest concentrations of tourist accommodation outside London. It is also a major provider of English language schools, so that the spend of foreign students contributes significantly to the local economy. Bournemouth has successfully adapted to change, updating its former genteel image,

to attract the youth market with a vibrant club scene. At the same time, the resort has retained its appeal to the family market and senior citizens. Although Bournemouth's beachfront remains less commercialised than other major resorts, the council has invested in a major international conference centre among other attractions and has been foremost in launching sports events and festivals. To some extent, Poole has been overshadowed by Bournemouth, partly because its beach is far from the town centre. However, the redevelopment of the historic quay has raised its tourism profile significantly.

- Weymouth is both a historic seaport and one of England's oldest seaside resorts. Regeneration initiatives include speciality shopping at Brewer's Quay, while the sailing events of the 2012 Olympics took place in Portland Harbour.
- Swanage is a small family resort in an attractive setting backed by the Purbeck Hills.
- Winchester is the most important of the region's historic towns. At one time, a royal capital, with a famous castle and cathedral, it has moved with the times as shown by Winchester Science Centre and Planetarium. Other tourist centres include Dorchester, with its Thomas Hardy associations, Wimborne, Sherborne, and Bridport.
- The Isle of Wight is an important holiday destination in its own right, offering a choice of family resorts such as Ryde, Shanklin, and Ventnor, and is responding to the challenge of its competitors with attractions based on local finds of dinosaur fossils. The island is linked to Lymington, Portsmouth, and Southampton by car and passenger ferry services.

The West Country

The area covered by VisitSouth-west includes the counties of Cornwall, Devon, Somerset, west Dorset, Gloucestershire, and Wiltshire. The South West Peninsula corresponds geographically to the major part of the region, offering two attractive coastlines, fine scenery, including two national parks, and a mild, relatively sunny climate (which has given rise to such advertising slogans as 'The Cornish Riviera' and more recently 'The English Riviera'). The M5 motorway and increased car ownership have made the region much more accessible and ensured its continued popularity with the domestic market. Tourism is important for employment and income generation in a largely rural region with few alternative industries, although seasonality is a problem. The countryside is a major tourism resource throughout the region, encouraging farm stays and activity holidays. Many of the picturesque villages with their craft workshops are linked by themed routes for cycling, hiking, or riding. Perhaps the best known of these is the 'Tarka Country' trail in north-west Devon, which is held up as a classic example of sustainable tourism. As the West Country largely escaped the Industrial Revolution, many of the market towns have preserved a rich architectural heritage, and some now act as regional tourism centres – for example, Truro, Barnstable, Taunton, Marlborough, and Salisbury. However, the coast of the South West Peninsula is the best-known feature, through the experiences of successive generations of British holidaymakers since Victorian times. Most of this varied and often beautiful coastline is protected by National Trust ownership or Heritage Coast policies, which effectively prevent the encroachment of industry or insensitive tourism development. The coast provides many recreational opportunities, notably surfing off the more exposed beaches, sailing in the sheltered estuaries, and long-distance paths for hiking.

Cornwall epitomises the beach tourism product of south-west England, but it is different in character from other parts of the region, with its granite cliffs and Celtic heritage, where the Cornish language is recalled by the distinctive place names. As a peninsula, Cornwall has the advantage of both an Atlantic and Channel coastline, but a peripheral location is also a disadvantage in terms of accessibility and possibilities for touring. A new airport at Newquay has nevertheless enhanced Cornwall's appeal to up-market tourists. The county faces unemployment with the decline of its traditional mining and fishing industries, while the growth of second home ownership in places like St Ives has aroused controversy and policy responses. Several attractions are based on this maritime and industrial heritage, while the small fishing ports of the south coast, such as Fowey, Looe, Mevagissey, and Polperro have preserved much of their character. Cornwall's tourism resources also include:

- The surfing beaches along the Atlantic coast, focussing on the resorts of Bude, Newquay, and Polzeath.
- The large family resorts of Falmouth and Penzance.
- The impressive coastal features of Land's End and St Michael's Mount.
- The mild climate that has made possible an ambitious garden restoration project – the Lost Gardens of Heligan with their subtropical vegetation.
- The Eden Project, backed by Millennium funding, is another example of reclamation. In this case, a former china clay pit has been transformed into a series of climate-controlled 'biodomes' representing the world's major ecosystems.
- Bodmin Moor and Tintagel are associated with the legends of King Arthur.
- The county's dramatic landscapes and seascapes have been an inspiration to writers and artists. St Ives, in particular, is a well-established 'artists' colony', with a branch of the Tate Gallery and the Barbara Hepworth Museum attracting many visitors.

With the exception of Dartmoor, Devon and Somerset are characterised by a gently undulating, more wooded landscape, where dairy farming is the predominant land use. Areas of outstanding natural beauty account for a large part of the two counties, while the two national parks differ greatly in character. Dartmoor is a bleak, treeless moorland punctuated by granite masses known as 'tors'. Exmoor is visually appealing and has been romanticised for tourism promotion as 'Lorna Doone Country'.

The maritime heritage includes reminders of the Elizabethan age of overseas expansion, during which the small ports of north Devon – Appledore and Bideford – played an important role, as well as Bristol, Dartmouth, and Plymouth. There is a wide choice for beach holidays; in south Devon, the large resorts around Torbay – Brixham, Paignton, and Torquay – are distinct in character and cater for different market segments, yet they are promoted together as The English Riviera. They have been the focus of a tourism development plan and share the Riviera International Conference Centre, with the purpose of diversifying their product to attract new clients. East Devon includes part of the 'Jurassic Coast' and a number of smaller resorts such as Exmouth that cater for the traditional

CASE STUDY 8.1
BATH: THE ROLE OF FASHION IN TOURISM

Bath has played a major role in the history of tourism in England. The Romans first recognised the value of a thermal resource, which is unique in Britain, and the Roman Baths now rank as a world-class heritage attraction. Bath reached its zenith as a spa resort in the eighteenth century, when 'taking the waters' was the fashion among the aristocracy, followed by the rising middle class. The fine Georgian architecture dates from this period, earning UNESCO designation as a World Heritage City. The city authorities improved the road to London, making it physically more accessible, while 'Beau' Nash, as master of ceremonies controlled social access. However, by the early 1800s, Bath was no longer the undisputed centre of fashion. Jane Austen was a one-time resident of Bath and a keen observer of the foibles of society. Her novels have been brought to a wider audience through television and movie adaptations, and the city's townscapes have attracted film tourism as a result.

Spa tourism is expected to revive with a new state-of-the-art facility, but event attractions such as the Royal Bath and West Show, shopping, and sightseeing are the main reasons visitors come to Bath. One of the most popular museums is devoted to fashion as its theme. Residents are ambivalent towards tourism; for example, the open-topped buses popular with visitors have met with opposition. In class, discuss why some residents see tourism as a threat rather than an opportunity.

family market. The north Devon coast offers more spectacular scenery and good surfing beaches, with Ilfracombe as the major resort. Clovelly is an example of a picturesque village that has become a popular 'honeypot' for swarms of day-trippers, and where a new visitor centre should ensure that residents are less exposed to the tourist gaze. Further along the Bristol Channel in Somerset, Minehead has the Butlin's themed accommodation, while Weston-super-Mare is investing in new initiatives such as the controversial Tropicana arts and culture development.

Apart from Bath, we should mention some other places noted for their heritage:

- Bristol is a major commercial centre with a functioning port at Avonmouth. Its tourism industry is based on business travel; transport heritage (particularly that associated with the great Victorian engineer, Brunel); the city's role in the expansion of the British Empire; Aerospace Bristol celebrating the city's aviation heritage, and contemporary museums (for example, the 'At-Bristol' hands-on science centre).
- Wells is a small historic town noted for its cathedral and other medieval buildings.
- The Mendips nearby offer impressive limestone scenery, featuring Cheddar Gorge and show caves such as Wookey Hole with their stalagmite and stalactite formations.
- Glastonbury has been regarded as a sacred site since ancient times, when the imposing hill known as Glastonbury Tor was an island amid the former marshes of the Somerset Levels (which are still highly vulnerable to flooding today). In medieval times, the abbey attracted pilgrims as the burial place of King Arthur. The town has

now become a destination for 'New Age' devotees, and the Glastonbury music festival also attracts a wide following.

- Exeter is the county town of Devon, featuring an imposing cathedral, and Roman remains among its attractions.
- Plymouth promotes its naval heritage, focussing on the Hoe, the historic Dockyard, and the *Mayflower* connection. The large natural harbour of Plymouth Sound is ideal for sailing, while the National Marine Aquarium is a long-established tourist attraction.

The chalk downland of Salisbury Plain is a dominant feature of Wiltshire. Although Salisbury has one of the finest cathedrals in Europe, surrounded by a spacious Close, the city is mainly visited for its proximity to Stonehenge. Contrasting attractions in Wiltshire include Longleat, a stately home with a popular safari park attached; the National Trust village of Lacock Abbey (which is associated with one of the pioneers of photography); and the restored Kennet and Avon Canal.

CASE STUDY 8.2
STONEHENGE: AN EXAMPLE OF CONTESTED HERITAGE

The stone circle known as Stonehenge, standing alone on the open landscape of Salisbury Plain, is the best-known feature in an extensive World Heritage Site containing many prehistoric remains. The monument dates from around 2000 BC, and the alignment of the stones in relation to the rising sun at the summer solstice suggests it had ritual significance. In the course of the twentieth century, the mystique of Stonehenge was dispelled by intrusive road traffic, due to the monument's situation in an angle between two busy highways, and the impact of mass tourism. There are tensions between English Heritage, which is responsible for the day-to-day management of Stonehenge itself, and the National Trust, which owns 600 hectares of farmland around the site, while the Ministry of Defence uses large areas of Salisbury Plain for military training. There are tensions between the local community and the visitors. These include quasi-religious groups such as the 'Druids', who claim that Stonehenge was a temple for the religion of ancient Britain (notwithstanding the fact that the Celts worshipped in forests and sacred oak groves), and New Age travellers. Problems with the latter led to the site being fenced off in the 1980s. The former visitor centre was described in Parliament as a 'national disgrace', and visitors did not have the value-for-money experience they might have anticipated from viewing a world-class attraction.

For Stonehenge to retain its mystique, effective traffic control and visitor management are essential, and in 2013, the following measures were put in place:

- The closure of the A344 highway.
- The introduction of 'road trains', with a capacity of 400 passengers/hour to carry visitors from a car park situated 2 kilometres from the site.

- The opening of a new state-of-the-art visitor centre using improved methods of interpretation.

Nevertheless, some would argue that these measures do not go far enough to cope with record numbers of visitors. The A303 highway needs to be diverted, but this would involve tunnelling, at a cost successive governments have regarded as excessive. Ideally, a large area of Salisbury Plain and its most significant monuments need to be protected as a 'sacred landscape', through land purchase and management agreements between the various stakeholders. This would enable visitors to view Stonehenge in something like its original setting.

East Anglia

Facing the North Sea and within easy reach of London, East Anglia is well-placed to attract Continental visitors through Stansted Airport and the ports of Harwich and Felixstowe. In medieval times, the region was the most prosperous part of England, thanks to the wool trade with the Low Countries, and this explains the rich architectural heritage of small towns such as Lavenham. East Anglia largely escaped the developments of the Industrial Revolution and has preserved much of its rural character. Predominantly low-lying, the landscape is nonetheless varied, including the former marshlands of the Fens to the north west, the sandy heaths and forests of Breckland in west Suffolk, and the fertile countryside along the River Stour in east Suffolk, an area made famous by Constable's paintings. We can consider the following as important tourist centres:

- Cambridge, where the university's historic colleges and museums, such as the Fitzwilliam, are located in a beautiful riverside setting.
- Ely, famous for its cathedral dominating the Fens.
- King's Lynn, once a major port, now featuring the 'North Sea Haven' regeneration scheme.
- Norwich is the regional capital with many historic buildings.
- Colchester with a heritage dating back to Roman times.

The north Norfolk coast, with its low cliffs of boulder clay, and the sandy coast of east Suffolk are quite different in character. Both have been designated as Heritage Coasts, and the latter boasts an internationally renowned bird reserve. North Norfolk has several small resorts, Cromer, Hunstanton, Sheringham, and Holt, which are linked by a coastal steam railway. The Essex coast is characterised by marshes and river estuaries, on which are situated the yachting centres of Burnham on Crouch and Maldon. Essex resorts illustrate different approaches to tourism; for example, Clacton has developed to attract the mass market, while neighbouring Frinton has banned any commercialisation of its seafront. Southend, boasting the world's longest pier, is primarily a day-trip destination for Londoners.

Great Yarmouth is one of eastern England's largest and oldest resorts and is also the gateway to the **Norfolk Broads**. These shallow lakes of medieval origin are Britain's best-known area for water-based recreation and holidays. There are over 200 kilometres of navigable waterways, and over 2000 powered craft are available for hire. However, the commercial success of tourism has been achieved in competition with agriculture, which makes heavy demands on water supplies in an area with a relatively low rainfall, and at a cost to the environment, for example:

- Detergents, human sewage, discarded fuel, and a lowered water table have upset the ecological balance.
- Banks are eroded and wildlife disturbed by the wash from the boats.
- The sprawl of boatyards and other development despoils the landscape.

In an effort to balance the conflicting demands of tourism, agriculture, and wildlife, this unique wetland area was designated a national park in 2011, carefully managed by the Broads Authority.

The Midlands

The Midlands are usually associated more with manufacturing than with tourism, presenting the tourist boards covering the west and east of the region with an image problem. However, imaginative theming of short breaks, investment in attractions and accommodation, and effective marketing is attracting tourists and day visitors to the countryside, historic towns, and industrial heritage of the region. The Midlands boasts one of Britain's most popular theme parks, Alton Towers, which takes advantage of the national motorway network. For both domestic and overseas tourists, the Cotswolds are famous for their mellow limestone buildings in tourist centres such as Broadway and Chipping Campden. In comparison, Cannock Chase scarcely ranks as a tourist destination but is an important recreational resource for the region, as it is located near the West Midlands conurbation. Other countryside areas in the West Midlands include the Malverns and the Shropshire Hills, while the Wye Valley near the Welsh border attracts canoeing and other activity holidays.

Of the many historic towns, the best known is Stratford-on-Avon, which is popular with overseas visitors for its literary associations, underlined by the redeveloped Royal Shakespeare Theatre. Other important tourist centres in the West Midlands are:

- The cathedral cities of Gloucester, Hereford, and Worcester, which host the Three Choirs Festival celebrating the music of Elgar.
- The elegant spa town of Cheltenham.
- Warwick and its castle, now a major themed attraction.
- Shrewsbury and Ludlow, in medieval times, were fortress towns guarding the Welsh Marches (the border country with Wales) and preserve a rich architectural heritage. Ludlow is also noted for its quality restaurants.

The industrial heritage of the West Midlands is undergoing radical change, with the restoration of canals for recreation and a new breed of museum such as:

- The Ironbridge complex, which interprets the beginnings of the Industrial Revolution.
- The Potteries Museum at Stoke-on-Trent showcases the ceramics industry of north Staffordshire.
- The Black Country Museum at Dudley portrays life and work in this former area of heavy industry.

Modern engineering industries are still thriving in the West Midlands conurbation, which includes Birmingham, Coventry, and Wolverhampton. The National Exhibition Centre and National Arena at the heart of the motorway system enhance Birmingham's importance as a centre for business tourism and event attractions. This is complemented by the redeveloped Bull Ring shopping complex in the city centre, the Jewellery Quarter focussing on Birmingham's speciality trades, and new attractions such as 'Think Tank' (an interactive discovery museum), Cadbury World, and the National Sealife Centre. For many people, Coventry and its cathedral symbolise urban recovery after the Second World War, but the city's museums also celebrate its contributions to transport technology, while Millennium Place is an outdoor arts complex.

The East Midlands region includes the Lincolnshire coast, with the resorts of Skegness, Mablethorpe, and Cleethorpes providing traditional seaside recreation for the industrial cities of Derby, Leicester, and Nottingham. Lincoln is a major tourist centre with a magnificent cathedral dominating the city's skyline. Nottingham has exploited its association with the legendary Robin Hood, while Leicester has appropriated one of England's most controversial monarchs – Richard III – as a tourist icon (he was killed in battle at Bosworth Field nearby, and his remains interred more than five centuries later in the city's cathedral). Countryside areas for recreation include Charnwood Forest, the Vale of Belvoir, and Sherwood Forest, while the artificial lake known as Rutland Water is an important resource for water sports.

The North

The northern part of England, which includes three regional tourist boards, is one of contrasts, from industrial heartlands, through the spectacular scenery of national parks, to its bustling resorts. The region also forms an important gateway to Britain for Scandinavian, German, and Dutch tourists who enter through the ports of Newcastle and Hull. The scenery of the area is evidenced by the fact that it contains five national parks, which are the focus of tourism and day trips, and several areas of outstanding natural beauty, such as the Solway Firth, noted for its golf courses, and the Eden Valley and North Pennines, which are popular with anglers.

In many rural upland areas, government funds are supporting the development of farm-based tourism. Tourism and recreation bring income and jobs, supports rural services, and stems depopulation, but herein also lie seeds of conflict, as some argue that tourism interferes with farming operations and destroys the very communities that tourists visit. This may occur through the purchase of second homes and the reorientation of rural services towards weekend and summer visitors. The opportunities for outdoor recreation and the threats from tourist pressure are greatest in the national parks:

1. The **Lake District** is intensively managed for tourism and recreation with 'honeypot' areas designed to take pressure, for example, Ambleside and Bowness, along with traffic management and car-parking schemes. Access to the park from the north is through the market town of Penrith, and from the south through the historic town of Kendal. Keswick is the major service centre for the park, and there is an interpretation facility at Brockholes. There are attractions based on the literary associations with Wordsworth, Ruskin, and Beatrix Potter, but the Lake District is mainly popular for active tourism and recreation – walking, water sports, outdoor pursuits, and mountaineering. In the past, these activities have interfered with the upland farming regime of the area, but management schemes run by the park's authorities have solved many of these problems. The landscape is on a human scale with attractive towns and villages, *fells* (low moorland hills), and lakes, each with its own character. Windermere, for example, is intensively used and managed, while remoter lakes and tarns are little visited.

2. The **Yorkshire Dales** National Park is characterised by a gentler landscape than the Lake District. It is criss-crossed by limestone walls and dotted with field barns (some converted to shelters for walkers). Touring centres in the park include Richmond, Skipton, and Settle, and popular villages such as Malham with its cove and tarn which are spectacular relics of the Ice Age. In and around the park are literary sites linked to the Brontes and also locations associated with a popular series on British television. Like its southern neighbour, the Peak District National Park, the Dales are popular for outdoor pursuits and field studies. The Settle/Carlisle Railway is a major scenic route linking two national parks.

3. The **Peak District** is the most visited of Britain's national parks due to its proximity to the industrial cities of both the North and the Midlands, with some valleys, notably Dovedale, experiencing visitor pressure. The White Peak is the southern and central area of limestone dales and crags with important centres such as Matlock and Castleton. The Dark Peak in the north is a more rugged and spectacular area with a number of lakes and reservoirs. Some caverns and mines are open to visitors, and the industrial heritage is featured in attractions such as the Crich National Tramway Museum. At Matlock Bath, the Heights of Abraham is a country park with theme park attractions. The main touring centres are Bakewell, Ashbourne, Matlock, and Holmfirth – home to another popular television series. The spa town of Buxton has revived its opera house and conference facilities. Hardwick Hall in Chesterfield is one of Britain's foremost Elizabethan country houses, while Chatsworth is one of its most visited stately homes.

4. The **North York Moors** National Park is characterised by heather-covered, rolling countryside with picturesque villages. It also offers a spectacular coastline, summits such as Roseberry Topping, and natural features such as the Hole of Horcum, popular

with hang gliders. The North Yorkshire Moors steam railway runs through the park from Pickering to Grosmont.

5. The **Northumberland** National Park lies on the Scottish border and contains Kielder Forest and Kielder Water, both recent additions to the landscape. Hadrian's Wall to the south is of unique historic interest as a Roman military achievement, with associated archaeological attractions, but in places under intense tourist pressure. Hadrian's Wall runs from Hexham westwards to Carlisle, which is an important regional centre and historic gateway to Scotland.

> **Discussion point**
> The designation of national parks in the United Kingdom began in the 1950s and then stalled for many years until the New Forest was granted this status in 2005, beginning a new wave of designations. Nevertheless, national park designation is not universally welcomed by local residents. Devise a list of the key stakeholders in a selection of national parks and identify their main concerns. Where might the main areas of conflict be?

The coasts of northern England include both major resorts and areas of scenic interest that have been conserved as Heritage Coast or as wildlife sanctuaries, such as Spurn Head and the Farne Islands. Many of the North's resorts – Blackpool is a major example – have faced the problem of declining traditional markets in nearby industrial cities by investing in new facilities, upgrading accommodation, and marketing aggressively to attract new market segments:

- Scarborough is one of Britain's oldest resorts, an elegant town between two bays, offering a Sealife Centre, the Alpamare water park, and open-air theatre among its modern attractions. The redeveloped Spa Conference Centre adds a business dimension to its market (Photo 8.2).
- There is a range of smaller resorts, such as Bridlington, Hornsea, Whitby, and Filey on the North Sea coast and Morecambe on the less bracing Irish Sea coast.
- Day-trip resorts close to conurbations include New Brighton and Southport serving Merseyside, and Whitley Bay for Newcastle. Southport has been re-branded as 'England's Classic Resort', and with seven championship courses in the vicinity, as the capital of 'England's Golf Coast'.
- The North of England is mainly known for its great industrial cities and their role in sport and popular culture, but the region can also boast many historic buildings and sites of national importance, which increasingly attract overseas tourists as well as day visitors. These include:

1. Numerous castles, particularly in areas close to the Scottish border, Alnwick and Bamburgh, are fine examples;

Photo 8.2
Scarborough

Source: Chris Cooper

2. Reminders of pre-Reformation England in ruined abbeys such as Fountains and Riev-
    aulx in Yorkshire, and the pilgrimage centre of Holy Island off the Northumberland
    coast.
3. Great country houses such as Castle Howard, which has been used as a location for
    costume dramas.
4. More modest buildings from different parts of the region have been brought to-
    gether on one site at the Beamish North of England Open Air Museum in County
    Durham.
5. The spa towns of Ilkley and Harrogate – now a major conference venue.
6. The historic centres of Beverley, Chester, Durham, Lancaster, and York. Chester has
    significant Roman remains, but tourism focusses on 'The Rows', which are medieval
    shopping arcades. Durham boasts an impressive castle and Romanesque cathedral,
    reflecting the power of its prince-bishops in the Middle Ages. However, **York** is out-
    standing for these reasons:

    •   It has retained its medieval walls, city gates, and street pattern.
    •   York Minster is one of Europe's largest Gothic churches.
    •   The Jorvik Viking Centre has transformed an archaeological site into a visitor
        attraction featuring 'authentic' sights, sounds, and smells.

183

York has also exploited its part in the Industrial Revolution through the National Railway Museum, although the industrial heritage is more obvious in larger, less historic cities. Bradford, for example, has shown an imaginative approach to tourism based on its woollen textile industry, but also utilising its proximity to 'Bronte Country' and the contribution of the large Asian community to contemporary culture, particularly food. Indeed, the resurgence of tourism, sport and leisure-related projects on 'brownfield' sites reclaimed from industrial use characterises most northern cities. Regional centres such as Hull, Leeds, Newcastle, Liverpool, and Manchester have major tourist developments leading their drive for reinvestment. For example, in Merseyside, the Liverpool Garden Festival and Albert Dock schemes were designed to attract investment in other sectors of the economy. As a result, the city now features the 'Tate Liverpool' art gallery and museums celebrating its maritime and musical heritage (including the Beatles), as well as an impressive collection of civic buildings from the Victorian era. Manchester raised its international profile by hosting the Commonwealth Games in 2002, and its city centre was redeveloped following an IRA terrorist attack. At Castlefield, there is now an urban heritage park and a new exhibition venue – the GMex Centre. Further along the Ship Canal the BBC has relocated much of its production to Salford Quays, where the 'The Lowry' is also situated, celebrating one of the region's most famous artists. A new arts venue – 'Factory International' – opened in 2023. Manchester has set out to attract specific markets – for example, sport tourism with the National Football Museum, music lovers, youth tourism with a vibrant club scene, and gay tourism. Developments elsewhere in the North West include Wigan Pier – a themed heritage attraction based on life in Victorian England, and at Preston, the Riversway Preston Docklands and Marina.

On the other side of the Pennines, Newcastle has expanded its leisure and shopping attractions, while 'The Baltic' in Gateshead is at the cutting edge of the contemporary arts scene. In Yorkshire and Humberside, the following tourism developments are significant:

- Wakefield's National Coal Mining Museum in a former colliery, celebrating one of England's major industries prior to the 1980s.
- The Royal Armouries Museum and the Thackray Medical Museum in Leeds.
- Sheffield is developing special event tourism and boasts the Meadowhall leisure and shopping complex – one of Europe's largest.
- Rotherham's 'Magna' is a visitor attraction based on the achievements of British industry.
- Hull's designation as European City of Culture in 2017 transformed its cultural product, focussed on the refurbished Ferens Art Gallery. The city is probably better known as a port and hosts 'The Deep', an exhibition interpreting the life of the oceans and the nineteenth century whaling industry. Similarly, Grimsby's trawlermen are celebrated in the Grimsby Fishing Heritage Centre. These attractions have helped to alleviate the loss of jobs and income caused by the decline of the North Sea fishing industry.

CASE STUDY 8.3
BLACKPOOL: THE REJUVENATION STAGE IN
THE TOURIST AREA LIFE CYCLE?

Blackpool is famous primarily for the iconic tower that has dominated the seafront since 1895. It has long claimed to be Britain's most popular resort, and the statistics are impressive:

- In 2022, the resort attracted 18 million staying visitors and excursionists.
- The visitor economy is worth £1.5 billion.
- The hospitality sector provided 67,000 bed spaces, of which 54,000 were in serviced accommodation.
- Tourism is interwoven in Blackpool's economy, supporting over 25,000 jobs.
- It boasts the Pleasure Beach, Britain's most popular amusement park and visitor attraction.

Although the beach attracted a few visitors for sea bathing (for health reasons) in the eighteenth century, it was not until the late nineteenth century, with the coming of the railways, that Blackpool grew rapidly. The Grand Theatre, the Winter Gardens, and Blackpool Tower were outstanding examples of Victorian architecture and interior design, providing entertainment for a largely middle-class clientele. Blackpool became a destination for mass tourism with the introduction of 'Wakes Weeks', when factories in northern England and the Midlands were closed temporarily so machinery could be serviced, allowing workers and their families to spend a few days at the seaside. The timing of these closures varied from town to town, assuring hotels and guest houses of a steady stream of holidaymakers throughout the summer. The 'Illuminations' were an innovative and successful attempt to extend the holiday season and nowadays continue to attract around 3 million visitors each year. Blackpool was constantly developing new attractions and promoting the top names in 'show business'. The 'Golden Mile' – the Recreational Business District extending along the seafront between the North and South Piers – was the focus of activity. Blackpool was the recognised venue for trade union and political party conferences. However, by the 1990s, it had reached the stagnation stage in the tourist area life cycle and was facing possible decline. This can be attributed to several factors:

- Growing competition from package holidays to overseas beach destinations.
- Improved road links, primarily the M55 motorway, facilitated day trips rather than the traditional two-week holiday.
- The industrial towns, particularly those dependent on textiles, were no longer an assured market, with changing work practices leading to a fall in demand.
- Competition from newer, purpose-built venues for the lucrative conference market.

In the new millennium, Blackpool recognised that the market was changing and becoming more demanding. Blackpool's weaknesses include:

- A scarcity of good quality restaurants and bars.
- A night-time economy that is over-dependent on hen and stag parties.
- A predominance of lower spend visitors.
- An over-supply of low-grade holiday accommodation.
- Social problems, with Blackpool having some of Britain's most deprived neighbourhoods.

Faced with falling visitor numbers and the impact of the COVID-19 pandemic, the local authority put in place a number of initiatives to 'rejuvenate' the resort, including a bid to re-invent Blackpool as a 'British Las Vegas'. In 2022, an ambitious new destination plan for a 'Blackpool Tourism Business Improvement District (BID)' was approved (www.blackpooltourismbid.co.uk). The BID is designed to develop a thriving destination that appeals to different market segments, from traditional holidaymakers to upscale conference delegates. It aims to change negative perceptions of Blackpool and create a high quality, year-round family destination, by investing in covered walkways, more open space and retail, hospitality, and entertainment venues. The BID builds on previous civic achievements. For example, Blackpool Tower and the Winter Gardens are multi-functional assets to the resort. They were acquired by Blackpool Council in 2010 and have since undergone extensive refurbishment. The popularity of a TV show featuring dance competitions has ensured that the ornate Tower Ballroom has become the focus of nationwide interest. Blackpool's accessibility by rail has greatly improved with the electrification of the line to Preston, and it is now within three hours travel time from London by high-speed train. In terms of internal transport, previous plans have improved connectivity within the resort through investment in public transport, including electric buses and the modernisation of the tramway network, while retaining the iconic 'heritage trams', allowing seamless travel from Blackpool North station to the promenade. Blackpool is meeting the challenge of a decline in its traditional markets and is embracing change, through the commitment to tourism shown by the local authority. It has been prepared to make the necessary investments in new transport infrastructure, conference facilities, and a new 'Museum of Entertainment', while recognising the resort's heritage as a centre of entertainment and memorable family holidays.

Discussion point

Only 1 per cent of Blackpool's visitors originate from foreign countries, whereas Bournemouth and Brighton attract greater numbers of foreign visitors, including a high proportion of young people. Discuss ways in which Blackpool could appeal to particular markets, for example, Australia and the Netherlands.

Scotland

Scotland, Wales, and the Isle of Man are situated in the rugged north and west of Britain and form part of the 'Celtic fringe' of western Europe. Neither the Romans in the second century AD, nor Edward I of England in the thirteenth century, succeeded in conquering Scotland, and it remained an independent country until the Act of Union in 1707. However, a form of the English language became dominant except in the more remote western and northern parts of the country, where the Gaelic language and culture still survive. The Scots developed a separate legal system, and with the Reformation in the sixteenth century, they had their own Church, which placed a high value on education. Styles of architecture were influenced by France rather than England. There is a strong sense of national identity, expressed in sport, music and dance, food, and literature, and with devolution in 1999, Scotland has regained most of its former independence, although in 2014, the independence referendum returned a vote to remain as part of the United Kingdom.

Outside the conurbations of Glasgow and Edinburgh, Scotland is a much less crowded country than England, with plenty of space for outdoor recreation. Two-thirds of the country is mountainous, and the Highlands are one of the largest areas of unspoiled mountain and lake scenery in Europe. Many potential visitors are deterred by the reputation of the climate such that, outside of the Central Lowlands, leisure tourism is very seasonal. In fact, the west coast of Scotland boasts fine beaches and enjoys more spring sunshine than most parts of Britain. Apart from the scenery, Scotland can also offer a wealth of folklore and a romantic history – re-interpreted by Hollywood films in the 1990s.

Tourism in Scotland is the responsibility of the Scottish Tourist Board (VisitScotland), which also administers EventScotland. There are a range of regional and local agencies, while the Scottish Tourism Forum represents the industry to government, and the Scottish Tourism Alliance leads on industry issues. Tourism is important economically, directly supporting almost 200,000 jobs and accounting for almost 5 per cent of GDP. The Scottish tourism product is delivered primarily by small businesses and this places a question over the quality of the product at times and has also held back investment in the sector. For example, there are few all-weather developments. Scottish tourism is based on scenery, cultural heritage, and the large ethnic market formed by the descendants of emigrants, especially in Canada. Special interest and activity holidays are also important, particularly those based on fishing, whisky, and golf. Scotland's tourists visit mainly for leisure purposes, as the country was a late entrant into the conference and exhibition market. The overseas market has remained healthy for Scotland, with North America and Continental Europe providing most of the demand. Most visitors arrive by air, as there is only one port (Rosyth) providing a ferry service to mainland Europe. Scotland also attracts domestic tourism, of which around one-half originate from within the country. Increasingly, Scotland faces a dilemma: the traditional image of lochs, tartan, and heather is inappropriate for the newer forms of tourism, based on short city-break products as developed in Glasgow and Edinburgh.

Tourism resources

We can identify three main tourism regions in Scotland, based mainly on differences of geology:

- The Southern Uplands, mainly high moorlands with only a few pockets of lowland.
- The Central Lowlands, which is actually a rift valley formed between two faults or lines of weakness in the earth's crust. Although this region occupies only 10 per cent of the total area, it contains 80 per cent of Scotland's population of 5.2 million.
- The Highlands and Islands of the north and north-west, where ancient rocks form rugged mountains and a magnificent coastline, and the nearest, there is to true wilderness in the British Isles.

The Southern Uplands

The Southern Uplands lie between the Cheviots on the English border and the southern boundary fault of the Central Lowlands, which approximates to a line drawn between Girvan in Ayrshire to Dunbar. Granite is the rock most commonly found in Galloway in the west, forming a rugged landscape. To the east of Dumfries, the hills are more rounded and broken up by areas of lowland, the most extensive being the Merse of the Tweed valley. The Southern Uplands as a whole are thinly populated, the towns are quite small, and the main lines of communication with England keep to the valleys.

This area forms the gateway to Scotland, and tourist developments at Gretna have exploited this, although the centuries of border battles and cattle raiding are still much less well-known outside Scotland than the clan warfare of the Highlands. The main tourist attractions in the border country to the east include:

- The abbeys at Jedburgh, Kelso, and Melrose, immortalised by the great Romantic novelist Sir Walter Scott.
- The spa town of Peebles.
- The textile weaving towns of Hawick and Selkirk.

On the route west to Galloway, Dumfries has a 'Burns Trail' celebrating its associations with Scotland's national poet. Galloway has a milder climate and gardens are an attraction. The area has facilities for sailing and other activity holidays, and there are important archaeological sites and the Galloway Forest Park. Stranraer is a major ferry port for Northern Ireland.

North of Galloway, the Ayrshire coast has notable seaside resorts such as Girvan, and Ayr has one of Scotland's few all-weather facilities at Haven's Craig Tara Holiday Park. There are also golf courses, as at Troon.

The Central Lowlands

Despite the name, the Central Lowlands include a good deal of high ground, since the formation of this rift valley was accompanied by extensive volcanic activity. The isolated 'necks' of long-extinct volcanoes can still be seen, the crag on which Edinburgh Castle stands being a good example. The Ochils and Sidlaws to the north of the estuary known as the Firth of Forth, and the Pentland Hills to the south, rise to 500 metres – high by English standards. Parts of the eastern Lowlands are quite fertile, notably the Carse of Gowrie in Fife and the Lothians around Edinburgh. The coastline is deeply indented by three great estuaries – the Firths of Forth, Clyde, and Tay, on which are situated Scotland's major ports, Leith (for Edinburgh), Glasgow with its outport at Greenock, and Dundee.

The Central Lowlands contain by far the greater proportion of Scotland's industry and population. The main centres, namely, Glasgow, Edinburgh, Dundee, and Stirling, are linked by a good communications system, which involved bridging the Forth and Tay. Here too are the main international and domestic air gateways to Scotland. Both Edinburgh and Glasgow have shuttle services to London, while Glasgow Airport has developed international services since the deregulation of air services in Scotland and the demise of Prestwick. Budget airlines also operate to Dublin, Luton, and regional airports in the British Isles.

The region is dominated by the two rival cities of Glasgow and Edinburgh. Both are significant cities for tourism but have very different products and approaches. Each has its own tourist board and tourism strategy.

Edinburgh, as the capital of Scotland, is home to the Scottish Parliament and is a major cultural centre, attracting a large number of overseas visitors especially to the International Festival and Military Tattoo. The old city is built on a narrow ridge on either side of the 'Royal Mile' connecting the Castle to the palace of Holyrood House and is crammed full of picturesque buildings. It is separated from the 'New Town' to the north by the Norloch Valley, now occupied by public gardens and the Waverley railway station. The New Town, built according to eighteenth-century ideas of planning and architecture, contains Princes Street, a major shopping area, but other speciality shopping streets now compete with Princes Street's multiple stores. In particular, the area to the north of Princes Street, the Grassmarket area in the old town, and Stockbridge abound with restaurants and speciality retailing. Edinburgh has a wealth of historic buildings and national attractions such as the Royal Scottish Museum and the newly developed 'Dynamic Earth' story of the planet. The Edinburgh International Conference Centre has been a major boost to business tourism. There are also many attractions on the outskirts, including:

- Edinburgh Zoo
- The Forth road and rail bridges
- Dirleton, Tantallon and Crichton Castles
- Linlithgow Palace, associated with Mary Queen of Scots
- The restored Royal Yacht Britannia
- Ocean Terminal shopping centre at Leith
- Jupiter Artland, including a unique sculpture gallery
- The National Mining Museum of Scotland

Discussion point

The traditional image of Scotland is of tartan, heather, lochs and mountains, bagpipes, and shortbread. Yet for the cosmopolitan cities of Edinburgh and Glasgow, some argue that this image is counterproductive. These two cities have tourism markets based upon short breaks, conference, and business tourism – markets that are not attracted by Scotland's 'traditional' image. How can this 'clash' of communication be resolved?

Across the Forth Estuary lies Dunfermline, a former capital of Scotland. The Fife coast has a string of picturesque fishing villages – Elie and Crail – and the historic university town of St Andrews with its golf course. Dundee is the regional centre, boasting the Victoria and Albert Museum of Design, the royal research ship *Discovery*, and the Dundee Science Centre among its attractions. Perth is another former Scottish capital and acts as the gateway to the Highlands.

Glasgow is a much larger city than Edinburgh and has acquired a much grittier image. It developed mainly during the nineteenth century as Scotland's major port and industrial centre. Glasgow's renaissance as a city was well-publicised in 1990 with its selection as European City of Culture. With the vision of the local authority and the tourist board, a fine Victorian city now has a wealth of attractions, accommodation, restaurants, and tourist facilities including the new Riverside Museum.

ASSIGNMENT

Investigate why Glasgow was chosen as European City of Culture, and why this was important for Glaswegians. In your research, evaluate what the city has to offer, including cultural attractions such as the Burrell Collection, the Glasgow Science Centre, sports facilities, exhibition venues, heritage attractions, entertainment, and shopping opportunities. How does Glasgow compare in these respects with, say, Liverpool?

Stirling, with its strategically located castle, played a major role in the Scottish Wars of Independence during the thirteenth and fourteenth centuries and was given worldwide recognition by the film *'Braveheart'*.

The Highlands and Islands

Geologically speaking, the Highlands include the whole of Scotland to the north of a line drawn from Helensburgh on the Firth of Clyde to Stonehaven on the North Sea coast, which represents the northern boundary fault of the Central Lowlands. The region is made up of very old, highly folded rocks and was severely affected by glaciation during the Ice Age, which formed its landscape of rugged mountains (the highest in the British Isles), lochs, and broad, steep-sided glens. Most of the forests of Scots pine, which formerly covered much of the Highlands, have disappeared, with the significant exception of the Cairngorms area, leaving a treeless, heather-covered landscape.

The Highlands are divided into two by Glen More, the great rift valley extending right across Scotland from Fort William to Inverness, which is followed by the Caledonian Canal. The North-west Highlands to the west of Glen More are more rugged than the Grampians to the east. The Atlantic coast from Kintyre to Sutherland is deeply indented by sea lochs and is fringed by innumerable islands, with very little in the way of a coastal plain. Along the North Sea coast, the coastline is more regular and less spectacular; there are fairly extensive lowlands in the north-east 'shoulder' of Scotland between Aberdeen and the Moray Firth, where the climate is drier and better suited to farming.

By comparison with other mountain regions of Europe such as the Alps, most parts of the Scottish Highlands are sparsely populated, for historical reasons. Despite a difficult climate and poor soils, the glens, the coastal lowlands, and islands once supported substantial communities whose way of life was quite different from that of the Lowlands. The Highlanders spoke Gaelic and had a strong feeling of loyalty to the clan or tribal group. In the nineteenth century, many such communities were evicted in the Clearances to make way for large private sheep farms and reserves for field sports. Traditionally, many Highlanders have gained a living from 'crofting', a self-sufficient type of agriculture on smallholdings supplemented by fishing. In some localities, weaving and whisky distilling have been important activities.

Tourism has become an important source of income and provider of jobs. In 1965, the Highlands and Islands Development Board was established by the British government to encourage public and private investment in the seven 'crofting counties' (Argyll, Inverness, Ross and Cromarty, Sutherland, Caithness, Orkney, and Shetland). In the past, this area was very short of quality accommodation, so the Board financed new hotels and self-catering accommodation. In 1991, it became the Highlands and Islands Enterprise (HIE), which is also concerned with investigating ways of extending the short tourist season and ensuring that tourism does not damage the beauty of the scenery.

The main tourism centre for the Highlands is Inverness, where the majority of accommodation and services are found. South of this university town, Loch Ness has a tourist industry based on the world-famous 'monster' with visitor centres at Drumnadrochit.

Transport is a problem in the Western Highlands on account of the deeply indented coastline; so wide detours have frequently to be made to get from one place to another. With the exception of Skye, which now has a bridge to the mainland, the Hebrides are not easily accessible, although some of the small scattered communities are linked by 'air taxi' services and ferry connections. The ports of Ullapool, Kyle of Lochalsh, Mallaig, and Oban are the main bases for visiting the Hebrides. Islands have a great attraction for holidaymakers, despite, in this instance, the unpredictable weather and lack of facilities:

- Skye is popular because of its historical associations with the clans and the 1745 Jacobite rising to restore the Stuart dynasty, as well as the magnificent mountain scenery of the Cuillins.
- Iona is a place of pilgrimage.
- Staffa is noted for its basalt sea caves.
- Crossing the Minch, the Outer Hebrides or Western Isles have a bleaker environment. Harris is noted for its tweed, cloth hand woven into distinctive patterns, while Lewis

has a major prehistoric site at Callanish. The remote islands of St Kilda, uninhabited since 1930, are a World Heritage Site.

- The Orkneys and the Shetlands, separated from mainland Scotland by some of the stormiest seas in Europe, were once ruled by Norway. In the Shetlands, the Scandinavian influence remains strong even today (one manifestation being the 'Up Helly Aa' festival in Lerwick). The Orkneys are fairly low-lying and fertile and contain unique prehistoric sites at Skara Brae and Maes Howe. The magnificent harbour of Scapa Flow was once an important naval base. The Shetlands lie 140 kilometres further north and are bleaker and much more rugged. Oil has brought wealth to a community where fishing has traditionally been the mainstay of the economy, and the distinctively small, hardy island sheep and ponies are reared. These northern islands are linked by regular air services from Edinburgh and Glasgow, as well as ferries from Scrabster (near Thurso) and Aberdeen. They are increasingly attracting cruise ships.

The scenic attractions of the Grampians are more readily accessible to the cities of the Lowlands than the Western Highlands. This part of Scotland was made fashionable as a holiday destination by Queen Victoria, and the Dee Valley west of Aberdeen is particularly associated with the British royal family. Hollywood films based on Scottish heroes have also stimulated renewed interest in the area. During the nineteenth century, numerous hotels were built, notably on the shores of Loch Lomond, in the Trossachs (an area of particularly fine woodland and lake scenery designated as a national park in 2002), where Loch Lomond seaplanes are a recent innovation, and at Gleneagles near Perth, which is a noted centre for golf. The Spey Valley (famous for its whisky and salmon fishing) was another area that particularly benefitted from Victorian tourism. It has good road and rail communications to Glasgow and London. After the 1960s, this area became important for winter sports since the Cairngorms can provide a suitable climate and terrain.

Elsewhere in the Scottish Highlands, winter sports facilities have been developed at Glenshee near Braemar and at Aonach Mor near Fort William, where a new attraction, the Nevisrange Gondola provides access for walkers to the mountain peaks such as Ben Nevis.

Wales

Wales was able to maintain a separate national identity, thanks to centuries of successful resistance to the Anglo-Saxon invaders who took over the rest of southern Britain. However, the last of the principalities into which the country was divided was conquered by King Edward I in the thirteenth century. Despite this and the 1536 Act of Union with England imposed by Henry VIII, who was himself of Welsh descent, Welsh cultural traditions continued to flourish. Welsh national identity is evidenced by:

- The vigour of Welsh as a living language, especially in the mountainous north and west of the country.
- The Celtic heritage, expressed in a strong literary and musical tradition, and the national gatherings known as *eisteddfods*.

CASE STUDY 8.4
TOURISM VERSUS CONSERVATION IN THE
CAIRNGORMS

The Cairngorms are unique in Britain as an example of an arctic-alpine ecosystem, one of the reasons for the designation of these mountains as a national park in 2008. However, there is scope for conflict here with the growing winter sports industry, which demands sophisticated infrastructure and facilities. The ski fields lie in the Coire Cas, a corrie or cirque that acts as a 'snowbowl', located high above the treeline on the northern slopes of Cairngorm Mountain. The season is from December to April, but climate change means that snow-cover cannot be guaranteed. The Aviemore Centre in the valley below is a purpose-built resort offering a full range of services. Conferences are held in spring and autumn, while in summer, the Centre is used as a base for activity holidays, including pony-trekking, mountain biking, gliding, and nature study – for which the Cairngorms nature reserve is probably unrivalled in Britain. Unlike other Scottish resorts, Aviemore has a year-round season and adequate wet-weather facilities, so that it can take full advantage of tourism. However, proposals to expand ski facilities have received considerable opposition from environmentalists, concerned about the fragile nature of the mountain ecosystems.

- The strength of Nonconformist Christianity, with simple chapels featuring in the landscape rather than imposing cathedrals.
- The world-famous choirs.
- The importance of rugby football as a focus for national pride.

In the course of the twentieth century, the Welsh language and culture have been encouraged by the British government, although Wales has not yet achieved the same degree of devolution as Scotland. Overall tourism policy and product development is the responsibility of the Wales Tourist Board (VisitWales), a public body reporting to the Welsh Assembly.

Tourism resources

We can divide Wales into three tourist regions based on geography and culture.

North Wales

North Wales, consisting of the counties of Gwynedd and Clwyd, is scenically the most interesting part of the country. Gwynedd is the most important tourist region in Wales. It is often regarded as the cultural 'heartland' of Wales, where the people continue to speak Welsh as their first language. The traditional culture has persisted partly because the region is isolated to some extent by the rugged mountains of Snowdonia, which rise abruptly from the coast. North Wales contains Britain's largest national park and impressive castles dating from Edward I's conquest of Gwynedd in the thirteenth century. A number of these castles – Conwy, Harlech, Beaumaris, and Caernarfon – are World Heritage Sites.

The mountains of Snowdonia form the core of the Snowdonia National Park. They have a craggy appearance quite different from the rounded outline of the Cambrian Mountains to the south and the Hiraethog or Denbighshire moors to the east. Radiating from Snowdon itself are several deep trough-like valleys carved out by the glaciers of the Ice Age; examples include the Llanberis Pass and Nant Ffrancon, which contains a number of small lakes. In such a valley is Lake Bala, offering facilities for water sports and fishing. The beautiful scenery has encouraged touring and activity tourism in such centres as Beddgelert, Llangollen, and Betws-y-Coed. For the less active, the Snowdon Mountain Railway takes visitors to the summit of the highest mountain of Wales from Llanberis, but visitor pressure has caused serious erosion.

Tourism dominates the economy of North Wales and takes advantage of both the rural and industrial heritage. Most of the high land in North Wales is of little agricultural value. In the upper valleys, there are isolated sheep farms, with their characteristic stone buildings and small irregular fields separated by roughstone walls. As in northern England, hill farms cater for tourists as a way of supplementing their incomes. The other major industry is based on mineral resources; large areas near Bethesda, Llanberis, and Ffestiniog are the sites of slate quarries, some of which have become important tourist attractions – as at Llechwedd. In Llanberis, the Welsh Slate Centre interprets this once important industry for the tourist, while in the Conwy Valley, a former quarry has been flooded to create a major surfing centre. Other industrial features that are now tourist attractions are the narrow-gauge railways, promoted as 'the Great Little Trains of Wales'. Today, Wales is a source of both power and water for England, and these resources are also used for tourism, as the power stations welcome visitors. In contrast to these examples of Victorian and modern industry, the Centre for Alternative Technology at Machynlleth is an important attraction with true 'green' credentials.

Discussion point

There is no doubt that national parks such as Snowdonia are under increased visitor pressure. One management approach to this problem is to 'spread the load' to ensure that visitor pressure is not focussed at particular points; the other is to use the 'honeypot' approach where visitors are focussed and funnelled into particular areas, which are then intensively managed to cope with the increased visitor load. In class, debate the pros and cons of each approach.

The coastline of North Wales is particularly attractive and easily reached from the conurbations of Merseyside and Manchester. There are a number of popular seaside resorts along the coast east of the estuary of the Conwy:

- Llandudno is perhaps best known as a conference venue but boasts a fine beach situated between two headlands – the Great and Little Orme.
- Colwyn Bay is the site of the Welsh Mountain Zoo.
- Rhyl pioneered all-weather tourism facilities with its Sea Life Centre, as part of a substantial redevelopment programme and the new Zipworld. Much of the narrow coastal strip around Rhyl accommodates large caravan sites.

These resorts, and particularly Llandudno, have benefitted from the upgrading of the A55, traditionally the route from the conurbations of North-west England, although this does mean that day visitors now easily outnumber staying holidaymakers.

Anglesey and the Lleyn peninsula are less commercialised, with smaller resorts, such as Pwllheli, devoted to sailing or other 'activity' holidays. Bardsey Island, off the coast, is a nature reserve. In parts of North Wales, the purchase of country cottages as 'second homes' by visitors from outside the region is controversial (partly because it is felt to weaken the Welsh language and culture). Although some villages (for example, Abersoch on the Lleyn peninsula) are dominated by second homes, others argue that the rural area benefits economically by bringing business to local suppliers. Holyhead, with its marina and important ferry service to Ireland, is the only significant commercial centre.

Mid Wales

Mid Wales is also mountainous and thinly populated, except for the narrow coastal plain around Cardigan Bay, and the upper valleys of the Wye and the Severn. Around Cardigan Bay, Welsh culture is strong, while much of Powys has been English speaking for centuries. North-south communications are difficult, especially by rail, and there are no large towns. There are a number of small seaside resorts on Cardigan Bay, such as Aberdovey and the university town of Aberystwyth, which are popular with visitors from the English Midlands. Inland, there are some small market towns, such as Newtown, Llanidiloes, and Welshpool, and several former spas, such as Builth Wells. These have become centres for touring the Cambrian Mountains but are important historic towns in their own right; Montgomery, for example, has many Georgian buildings. Other attractions in Mid-Wales include Powis Castle, Lake Vyrnwy, and the Glywedog Gorge.

South Wales

South Wales contains the majority of the Welsh population of 3 million and most of the industries. The region is separated from the rest of Wales by the Black Mountains and the Brecon Beacons but is easily accessible from southern England via the two Severn-road bridges. In the centre of the region lies the South Wales coalfield, which is crossed from north to south by a number of deep narrow valleys, including those of the Taff, Rhondda, and Rhymney. Mining communities straggle almost continuously along the valley bottoms, and the landscape was formerly disfigured by spoil heaps, tips, and abandoned workings. Both British and European Union initiatives have transformed this landscape of dereliction with:

- Landscaped country parks.
- The development of a museum of coal mining at Big Pit: National Coal Museum at Blaenavon.
- The Rhondda Heritage Park.

A similar transformation has occurred in the two main urban centres of Wales. In Swansea, dockland areas have been redeveloped as a maritime quarter with water sports, retailing, restaurants, and hotels. West of Swansea, the Gower Peninsula is an area of outstanding natural beauty with good beaches. **Cardiff** owes its growth as a major city to the Industrial Revolution and was not officially designated as the capital of Wales until 1955. Now, the seat of the Welsh Assembly, Cardiff is the location of major developments such as:

- The Millennium Stadium.
- The Wales Millennium Centre for the performing arts.
- The large-scale redevelopment of Cardiff Harbour and the former dock area with museums (such as Techniquest), restaurants and hotels, and international exposure as the location for Dr Who, a science fiction TV series.

The capital has good international links through Cardiff Wales Airport. The city centre is dominated by Cardiff Castle, which despite appearances is largely a Victorian creation rather than a medieval fortress, and the National Museum and Art Gallery of Wales. On the outskirts of the city is another national institution – the Welsh Folk Museum at St Fagans and Castell Coch, a Victorian fantasy castle. Penarth is a small seaside resort, while Barry Island boasts a major pleasure park.

Historically, the region has a great deal to offer. There are important Roman remains at Caerwent and Caerleon, and in the eleventh century, the Normans, following their conquest of England, built many castles to control the coastal plain and the valleys leading into the mountains of Mid-Wales. Near the Welsh border, Tintern Abbey, Monmouth – with its fortified bridge – and Chepstow Castle are notable examples of heritage attractions.

The Brecon Beacons National Park rises to over 900 metres at Pen-y-Fan; to the west is the old hunting ground of Fforest Fawr, in the north-east the broad valley of the River Usk, and to the south spectacular waterfalls and caves. Hay-on-Wye is the touring base for the park, the centre for the second-hand book trade, an iconic literature festival, and inspiration for the 'book city' concept. On the Usk, Abergavenny is also a touring and trekking centre. East of Brecon, Llangorse Lake is developed for water sports and is an important centre for naturalists.

In Dyfed in the south-west, the National Botanic Garden for Wales is an attraction of international significance. The Pembrokeshire Coast National Park is Britain's only linear national park, extending from Pen Camais in the north to Amroth in the south.

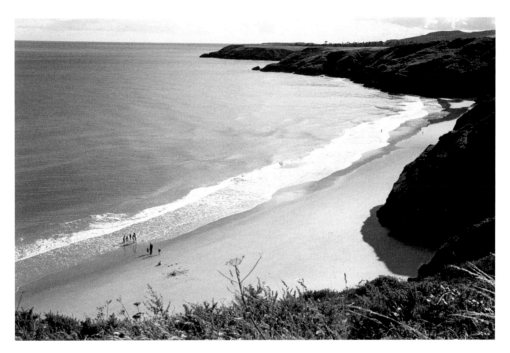

Photo 8.3
Rhossili beach, South Wales

Source: Brian Boniface

It includes some offshore islands, such as Caldey, famous for its monastery, and the bird sanctuaries of Skokholm and Skomer. The most important cultural attraction is the small city of St David's, whose cathedral was a major place of pilgrimage in medieval times. A coastal path around the park links a number of attractions such as the resorts of Tenby and Saundersfoot, Manorbier Castle, the lily ponds at Bosherston, and Pendine Sands, where attempts on the world land speed record have taken place (Photo 8.3).

ASSIGNMENT

Eating out is an important part of the tourism experience and although standards in restaurants and hotels have improved considerably in recent years throughout Britain, there are skills shortages and other problems in these sectors. Discuss how Wales can draw on locally sourced food specialities and its cultural traditions to give visitors, such as a group of foreign students based in Bournemouth, or a Japanese tour group, an authentic 'Taste of Wales'.

The Offshore Islands

Britain's offshore island destinations include the Channel Islands, which are geographically much closer to the Cherbourg Peninsula in France than to southern England, the Isles of Scilly lying some 60 kilometres to the south west of Cornwall in the Atlantic Ocean, and the Isle of Man, situated in the Irish Sea, midway between England, Scotland, and Ireland.

The Channel Islands

The Channel Islands capitalise on their favourable climate (they enjoy more sunshine than other parts of the British Isles), their Norman-French traditions, and their culinary attractions. Jersey and Guernsey are officially dependencies of the British Crown, with their own parliaments, postal services, and fiscal systems offering low rates of tax, which attracts business visitors, an influx of retired people, and duty-free shoppers. The islands have attractive coastal scenery and fine beaches (although the strong tides are hazardous to bathers). The Channel Islands were the only part of the British Isles to be occupied by Germany during the Second World War, and the Occupation from 1940 to 1945 features in several heritage attractions. Tourist facilities are well developed, with a range of accommodation (except for camping). Jersey and Guernsey are linked by air, fast ferry, and shipping services to ports in northern France and southern England. Tourism has helped to boost an economy once largely dependent on dairy farming and horticulture, but hotels depend mostly on imported labour, and visitors' cars add to the pressure of traffic on the road networks of the islands.

- **Jersey's** tourist centre is the capital, St Helier, which features Elizabeth Castle in the bay and the Fort Regent Leisure Centre above the town. The waterfront includes a marina development, illustrating the importance of the yachting market. The island's history is interpreted at numerous sites, particularly Jersey's Living Legend themed attraction. Other key attractions are Jersey Zoo, beaches such as St Brelade's and the sweep of St Ouen's Bay, and a number of secluded coves. Jersey has lost market share to Mediterranean destinations; however, the island's tourist board has developed an imaginative strategy to claw back tourists, facilitated by the introduction of budget-priced air services.
- **Guernsey's** tourism industry is on a smaller scale than that of Jersey but offers similar attractions. These include several craft centres and museums based on the island's literary associations, while the introduction of gambling casinos may attract higher spending visitors. The focus of tourism is the capital, St Peter Port.
- The smaller Channel Islands can be visited on day excursions from Guernsey or Jersey. Sark boasts spectacular coastal scenery, and along with Alderney, Herm, and Jethou, can offer a limited amount of accommodation.

The Isles of Scilly consist of 200 small islands, of which five are inhabited. They belong to the Duchy of Cornwall, and tourism, along with other matters affecting the islanders, is the responsibility of the Council of the Scillies based at Hugh Town on the island of St Mary's. The main attractions are the mild climate, (as shown by the subtropical gardens of Tresco), the unspoiled maritime scenery and bird life, and the many shipwreck sites awaiting investigation by scuba divers. St Mary's provides boat services to the other islands, and is linked to Penzance on the mainland by air and shipping services.

The Isle of Man

The Isle of Man – 50 kilometres long and 20 kilometres wide – is often described as 'northern England' in miniature, but it is administratively and culturally distinct, with a Celtic and Viking heritage. It has its own language, postal service, parliament (Tynewald), and an independent fiscal system, allowing it to develop as an offshore finance centre. In Victorian times, holidaymakers reached the Isle of Man by steamship, sailing out of Liverpool, Heysham, Belfast, and Dublin. In recent years, fast catamarans have also been introduced, and the island's airport, Ronaldsway, is linked to many regional airports in the United Kingdom, Ireland, and the Channel Islands. The island provides a variety of attractions:

- **Douglas and other coastal resorts.** Douglas, with its sweeping Victorian promenade of guest houses and terraced hotels, is the capital and major seaport of the Isle of Man, featuring the Manx Museum and 'The Story of Mann' exhibition. It represents the main concentration of bed spaces and offers a range of restaurants and entertainment facilities that are used by residents and visitors alike. Other coastal towns, each with a range of small visitor attractions, craft workshops, and accommodation, include Port Erin, Peel, Ramsey, and Castletown.
- The **cultural heritage** includes many historic buildings, for example, the castle and cathedral in Peel and Castle Rushen at Castletown, which was the former capital. The best-known feature is the world's largest working waterwheel at Laxey. There are a number of museums and craft centres, while the Cregneash Folk Village interprets the crofting way of life of islanders in the past.
- The **natural heritage** provides the setting for special interest holidays, and both walking and cycling trails are available.
- The **transport heritage** includes horse-drawn trams and narrow-gauge railways, but the most famous attraction is the annual Tourist Trophy (TT) motorcycle races, which started in 1904 as a way of extending the holiday season. This event takes place on a road circuit around the northern half of the island and fills hotels to capacity during 'TT Week' in June. The new Isle of Man Motor Museum is located at Jerby.

The Isle of Man has a varied accommodation base ranging from luxury country house hotels to value-for-money guesthouses. The Manx government has a long-standing scheme to assist the tourism sector both to adjust to the demands of the contemporary holidaymaker and to support small businesses. The tourism authorities also operate a compulsory registration and grading scheme for accommodation. The thriving business tourism market has encouraged a range of excellent restaurants.

The Department of Economic Development has led the island's process of adapting its tourism product to the tastes of twenty-first-century holidaymakers, spearheaded by the 'Visitor Economy Strategy 2022–2032'. The island's traditional markets sought an English seaside product, and while this still forms part of the island's appeal, other elements of the destination mix are now seen as more important in attracting visitors. The Isle of Man is, therefore, an excellent example of a destination that has successfully repositioned itself to become more competitive.

Summary

- England, Scotland, Wales, and the larger offshore islands are well endowed with most types of tourist attractions, and an increasingly professional approach to their management is evident.
- We can identify a number of common themes that include (1) the growth of heritage attractions, often based on declining industries, (2) the increasing use of rural resources for tourism and recreation, and (3) the growth of what we may broadly call cultural as well as recreational tourism to cities that, until recently, were associated solely with commerce and industry.
- The resorts that traditionally provided a British seaside holiday are re-investing in improved facilities to attract new markets.
- With devolution, Scotland, Wales, and the Isle of Man have much greater scope for product development, marketing, and promotion than hitherto.

Assignments

1. Compile a series of maps to show places associated with the 'greats' in British literature, music, and painting.
2. Explain why Britain's industrial heritage is an important part of its tourism appeal.
3. A group of Australians wish to visit places associated with the legendary King Arthur. Arrange a tour route to meet their requirements.
4. Discuss the strengths and weaknesses of London as a venue for a major international sport event.
5. Explain the rise of the British seaside resort and its decline since the 1950s, and suggest how particular resorts could be revitalised.

9 The tourism geography of Ireland

Learning objectives

After reading this chapter, you should be able to:

- Describe the major physical regions and climate of Ireland and understand their importance for tourism.
- Understand the nature of the Irish economy and society, and their significance for tourism demand, particularly in relation to the Irish diaspora.
- Outline the major features of demand for domestic and international tourism in the Republic of Ireland and Northern Ireland.

DOI: 10.4324/9781003406853-12

- Describe the major features of the tourism industry in the Republic and Northern Ireland.
- Demonstrate knowledge of the tourist regions, resorts, business centres, and tourist attractions of the Republic and Northern Ireland.

Introduction

As an island situated on the western periphery of Europe, Ireland is geographically isolated from the rest of the European Union and the world's main tourist-generating countries, with the exception of Britain. Since 1921, it has also been a divided island. The 26 predominantly Catholic counties that made up Eire (later the Republic of Ireland) chose the path of independence after centuries of English rule, and neutrality in the Second World War, whereas six out of the nine counties of Ulster opted to remain part of the United Kingdom as the Province of Northern Ireland. This partition never achieved widespread support among the Catholic community of Northern Ireland, who were subjected to economic and political discrimination by the Protestant majority. The differences between the two communities even extended to sport, with Catholics supporting Gaelic football and hurling, while Protestants favoured soccer. The outbreak of violence in Northern Ireland in 1969 proved detrimental to both its tourism industry and that of the Republic, with considerable disruption to cross-border communications. The division of Ireland remains an unresolved problem, but the Good Friday Agreement in 1998 effectively ended 'The Troubles' and co-ordinated the development of tourism, with an 'all-island' agency – 'Tourism Ireland' (www.tourismireland.com) – jointly funded by the Irish Government and the Northern Ireland Executive.

After centuries of relative poverty, between the 1980s and the 2008 global financial crisis, the Republic of Ireland experienced substantial economic growth, due to EU membership, attractive investment opportunities for foreign companies, and a highly educated workforce, to become the so-called 'Celtic Tiger'. Many feared that the traditional lifestyle and countryside were threatened by runaway development, materialism, and large-scale immigration during the boom years at the beginning of the twenty-first century. Northern Ireland experienced less growth, despite considerable investment by the British government.

Nevertheless, Ireland remains more rural than other West European countries, with few major cities. There is generally less pressure on resources, although some parts of the coastline have been adversely affected by unplanned development. The low population density, uncrowded roads, unspoiled countryside, and slower pace of life make Ireland a destination that is particularly well suited to rural tourism. It also provides favourable locations for movies and TV series. The people have a reputation for hospitality and conviviality, and the legendary *craic* is itself an attraction. It is, therefore, no accident that Irish 'themed' pubs are now found all over the world, while Irish music and dance have gained an international following.

The central feature of Ireland is a low-lying plain, dotted with drumlins (rounded hills of glacial origin), lakes, and expanses of peat bog. These lowlands are almost encircled by mountains, which are not particularly rugged, and breached by the valley of the Shannon in the west and the coast around Dublin in the east, traditionally the gateways for visitors. Ireland's reputation as the 'Emerald Isle' is due to the mild damp climate, which favours the growth of lush dairy pasture throughout the year, and in the south-west, sub-tropical vegetation. However, the unpredictable weather, particularly cool cloudy summers, is one of Ireland's weaknesses as a holiday destination.

Ireland is poor in natural resources compared to Britain, and from the seventeenth century onwards, many of its young people emigrated to seek greater economic opportunities, including enlistment in the British and foreign armies. The Protestant 'Scots-Irish' from Ulster played a major role advancing the frontier of settlement in North America. Following the Great Famine of 1845–1848, much larger numbers, mainly from the Catholic south and west, were forced to emigrate overseas. The descendants of those emigrants in the United States, Canada, Australia, and Britain are now many times more numerous than the population of Ireland itself. Ethnic tourism and genealogy (tracing family roots) is, therefore, a lucrative business in both the Republic and Northern Ireland. The epic theme of emigration also plays a major role in the heritage attractions of both countries.

Ireland's heritage is an important part of its tourism industry, though Catholics and Protestants in Northern Ireland interpret this differently. We can identify the following themes:

- **The Ireland of myth and legend:** Ireland is particularly rich in archaeological sites from the Neolithic period, the Bronze Age, and Iron Age, which probably had ritual or religious significance. These include many stone circles, the passage graves at Newgrange north of Dublin, the hill fort of Navan near Armagh, and the Hill of Tara in Meath, capital of the high kings of Ireland in pre-Christian times.
- **Religion in Ireland as the 'Land of Saints and Scholars':** Many of Ireland's religious monuments – Celtic crosses, monasteries, and 'round towers', together with works of Celtic art such as the Book of Kells – date from the centuries following the collapse of the Roman Empire, when Ireland was a centre of Christian missionary endeavour to the rest of Europe. The monastic cells clinging to the remote, rugged Skellig Islands, and The Rock of Cashel in County Tipperary are remarkable examples of this religious heritage.
- **Nation building**: The Gaelic language and Celtic heritage in music and dance are seen as central to Ireland's national identity. Nevertheless, the Vikings contributed by founding Dublin, Limerick, and Cork. Moreover, the great majority of the population are English speaking, due to the long period of rule by England, starting with Henry II in 1170, but not consolidated until the sixteenth and seventeenth centuries, with the imposition of English law, the Anglican Church, and an influx of settlers from other parts of the British Isles. The Anglo-Irish landowning class left a legacy of castles and great country houses that are now important tourist attractions, but which were

viewed at the time by the dispossessed Catholic peasantry as symbols of oppression. The struggle for land and freedom, particularly the 1798 rebellion, is a major theme in heritage interpretation.

- **The literary and artistic heritage**: Ireland has produced many of the great writers and dramatists of the English-speaking world, and tourist trails and guides are available.

Transport

The mode of travel to Ireland has changed since the 1970s, as low-cost carriers and aggressive marketing have seen air transport increase at the expense of the ferry services. The only direct sea routes to Ireland from the Continent are:

- Cork/Roscoff
- Rosslare/Cherbourg
- Rosslare/Roscoff

In contrast, there is a much wider choice of sea routes from Britain.

On many of these sea routes, operators are investing in state-of-the-art vessels, including high-speed catamarans and are also cutting fares in a bid to regain market share from the airlines. Deregulated airlines have also reduced fares, sparking a price war, and opened up access to Ireland's regional airports. Ryanair, for example, pioneered the low-cost carrier as a business model and the development of regional airports – supported by EU funding – namely Waterford, Kerry (Farranfore), Galway, Sligo, Donegal (Carrickfinn), and Ireland West. The four main airports are Belfast, Dublin, Shannon, and Cork. Dublin serves as the international gateway, not just to the Republic but to the whole of Ireland and acts as the hub for Aer Lingus, the national carrier. Belfast City Airport is the gateway specifically for Northern Ireland and is well served by routes to the rest of the United Kingdom (including a shuttle service to Heathrow) and the Continent. The expansion of air services has encouraged the growth of business and conference traffic. Ireland's location on the western periphery of Europe does give it the advantage of uncongested skies and, with the development of route networks between European regional airports, the authorities intend that Ireland will become less isolated from its tourist markets. Road transport is much more important for tourism than the limited rail network, and Dublin is now the focus of a national motorway network. Some measure of integrated travel is possible through Córas Iompair Eireann (CIE)-(www.cie.ie), which operates rail and bus services throughout the Republic, closely linked to transport providers in Northern Ireland.

Discussion point

Account for the success of Ryanair (www.ryanair.com) as a low-cost carrier. Investigate the impact of Ryanair on tourist routes and tourism development in Ireland and continental Europe.

The Republic of Ireland

The demand for tourism

Domestic and outbound tourism

Travel propensity and travel frequency are fairly high. Domestic tourism remains the mainstay of tourism in the Republic, with 11.6 million trips in 2019. Two-thirds of the population take at least one holiday trip, with the South-west being the most popular region. Only 36 per cent of overnight stays are in hotels, and the great majority of trips are by private car.

The growth of the Irish economy allied to airline competition has encouraged outbound tourism, with 9.3 million trips in 2019, although this fell sharply with the onset of the COVID-19 pandemic. The most popular destinations are the United Kingdom (around half of all trips) and mainland Europe, but with budget and charter flights to long-haul destinations, a greater range of destinations became available. There is also a substantial volume of cross-border traffic by road and rail between the Republic and Northern Ireland. Factors differentiating the nature of tourism demand in Ireland from that in Britain include:

- A much higher proportion of young people in the population (35 per cent are under 25 years of age), resulting in an expanding market for family holidays.
- Although the role of the Roman Catholic Church has diminished since the 1980s, pilgrimages to shrines such as Lourdes and Fatima continue to have great popular appeal. The most important of these in Ireland itself are the holy mountain of Croagh Patrick and Knock in County Mayo where an apparition of the Virgin Mary occurred in 1879. This pilgrimage centre has its own airport – Ireland West (formerly Horan International).

Inbound tourism

In contrast to the United Kingdom, Ireland achieved only very slow growth in overseas arrivals over the decade of the 1970s, and high inflation and unfavourable exchange rates led to slight reductions in arrivals in the early 1980s. However, the deregulation of Ireland/UK air services and the development of regional airports, along with substantial investment in the Irish tourism product, improved marketing – and not least, the prospects for peace in Northern Ireland, boosted inbound tourism to 11.6 million arrivals in 2019. The COVID-19 pandemic had a severe impact, particularly on the aviation sector. Recovery from the crisis was delayed due to staff shortages and the availability of accommodation and car rental services.

Revenue from tourism substantially exceeds the expenditure by Irish tourists overseas. However, we should note that Ireland's tourism industry is characterised by:

- Heavy dependence on the British market, which accounts for over 40 per cent of arrivals but only 25 per cent of tourism revenue.
- The increasing domination of the airlines, leading to a response by the ferry companies to improve quality and introduce faster services.

- Acute seasonality.
- The high percentage of 'ethnic' visits, especially from Britain and the United States. Dependence on the US market leaves Ireland vulnerable to external crises such as '9/11'.

The Republic of Ireland's tourism industry employs 5.6 per cent of the economically active population and is characterised by small businesses. The tourism sector has received considerable assistance from the government and the European Union, providing Ireland with a competitive edge in the twenty-first century.

Organisation

In the Republic, the policy-making body for tourism is the Department of Tourism, Culture, Arts, Gaeltacht, Sport, and Media. There are two significant agencies for tourism:

- Tourism Ireland is responsible for promoting the whole of Ireland as a destination overseas, with new markets emerging in Japan, Eastern Europe, South Africa, and the Middle East.
- Fáilte Ireland is the national tourism development authority for the Republic. Unlike the situation in most of the United Kingdom, hotels and guesthouses are classified under a statutory registration scheme, while the NTO provides marketing training, advice, and support for tourism enterprises.

In the wake of the peace process, local authorities on both sides of the Irish border are co-operating in tourism development aided by considerable investment from Interreg (The European Structural Fund's assistance for border regions) and other EU schemes.

The injection of money into the tourism sector has led to greater professionalism, widened the product range, and improved quality generally. It has also had the effect of changing the distribution of tourism across Ireland. While inbound tourism is more evenly spread than in most other European countries, the west and the south-west have lost market share to Dublin.

Tourism resources

The Republic's tourism resource base includes a long coastline with many unspoiled surfing beaches facing the Atlantic Ocean and the Irish Sea, six national parks, numerous forest parks, and an extensive system of inland waterways. Among the most important linear attractions are the Grand Canal linking Dublin to the River Shannon, and the Wicklow Way, a long-distance footpath. The 'Wild Atlantic Way', launched by Tourism Ireland in 2016, is a major project to encourage touring holidays in western Ireland. This scenic coastal route, 2,500 kilometres in length, runs from Malin Head to Kinsale and is divided into six sections, each with its own distinctive characteristics. The objectives are to improve infrastructure and signage, co-ordinate the activities of the many stakeholders along the route, and divert attention to less visited areas. Other tourism initiatives include 'Ireland's Ancient East', focussing on the heritage of eastern Ireland, and 'Ireland's Hidden Heartlands', promoting the midland counties of the Republic.

The following tourism products are available:

- Rural tourism supports the local economy, helps stem depopulation from more re-mote parts of the country, and keeps alive traditions and handicrafts such as embroi-dery and knitwear.
- Activity holidays include fishing in the many unpolluted lakes and rivers, golf (with ample space for development), sailing, canoeing, and horse riding (see the case study).
- Cultural activities based on the theatre, folk museums, and international festivals.
- Ethnic activities based around the many centres of genealogy.
- English language schools in competition with the United Kingdom.
- Culinary activities sourcing local produce and characterised by high standards of service.

We will now look at the key attractions of the Republic of Ireland within regions that are based on the historic provinces of Leinster, Connacht, and Munster rather than the six regional tourist authorities (RTAs):

1. Dublin and the east
2. Western Ireland
3. The South-west

Dublin and the East (Leinster)

Dublin is not only the capital of the Republic of Ireland and home to a third of its popu-lation but has also become one of the world's great tourist cities, with a major airport and ferry access through the port of Dun Laoghaire. The Dublin region has seen the largest growth of tourism in Ireland, so that by 2018, the city received almost 6 million overseas visitors and 1.5 million domestic tourists.

The main tourism resources of Dublin are linked by a series of themed trails and include:

- The city´s role in Irish history, recalled by Dublin Castle (the seat of government un-der British rule), Kilmainham Gaol, and the General Post Office (associated with the 1916 Easter Rising). This history is brought to life in the multi-media exhibition at City Hall and several museums.
- Literary heritage showcased in the Dublin Writers' Museum, featuring the lives and works of Joyce, Sheridan, Wilde, and other celebrities, and the Abbey Theatre where many of their plays were first performed.

- The architectural heritage of fine eighteenth century buildings and squares.
- The Genealogical Office, an important resource for the ethnic tourist market retracing their Irish roots.
- The Guinness Storehouse, a themed experience based on Dublin's most famous product.

The river Liffey divides the city into the *northside* and the *southside* and was the focus for city-wide initiatives to celebrate the millennium. The southside of Dublin contains Trinity College, Ireland's oldest and most famous university, and Temple Bar, an exciting 'left bank' district that has emerged since the early 1990s. This is now one of the city's most popular tourist areas, offering a wide range of leisure facilities and entertainments. The northside includes O'Connell Street, Phoenix Park, and a cluster of cultural attractions.

The capital is a good base for tourism circuits that include some of the most attractive scenery of eastern Ireland – the granitic Wicklow Mountains with their steep-sided glens – now designated as a national park. The narrow coastal plain is fertile, with a relatively dry and sunny climate. The Vale of Avoca is famous for the beauty of its landscape, and the village of Avoca attracts many visitors as the setting for a well-known TV series. The main tourist centres include the holiday resorts of Bray and Tramore; Waterford, which is world famous for its glassware; and Wexford, which hosts an international opera festival. New Ross is one of many small towns that have capitalised on ethnic links with the United States – in this case, the Kennedy family. Kilkenny has a fine medieval heritage, also supported by international festivals.

Western Ireland (Connacht and Donegal)

The Irish government has encouraged tourist facilities to locate in the west, which is a much poorer region economically, with a high dependence on traditional peasant farming. Special incentives are available in the Gaeltacht – those areas where the people still speak the Gaelic language as their mother-tongue. This is because the west is regarded as the true repository of Irish national culture, epitomised by the *ceilidh*, rather than the Anglicised south and east. Local communities have encouraged tourism with farmhouse holidays and by providing self-catering accommodation in the form of traditional style cottages.

Discussion point

Tourism is often blamed for threatening the survival of ancient languages such as Gaelic. 'Since the tourist is unlikely to have the Gaelic, the Gael must use English more and more' (Cosgrove and Jackson, 1972, 63). It can also be a force for their revival, as language is an attraction in itself. In class, debate the two sides of this argument.

Galway is the recognised capital of the west, and its airport has developed rapidly in line with Ireland's other regional airports. It is the southern gateway to the Connemara area and, with its adjoining resort Salthill, is an important centre for touring holidays and conferences. The main touring circuits are:

- The Great Western Lakes – Corrib, Mask, and Caarra – to the north.
- To the west is a superb indented coastline and the Twelve Bens, mountains that are included in the Connemara National Park.

The Aran Islands, well known in Irish literature and folklore, can be reached by sea or air.

Donegal in the north-west is geographically part of the historic province of Ulster but is largely Gaelic-speaking. Here, a rugged coastline is interspersed with fine beaches and a number of attractive fishing harbours such as Killybegs, while the lake and mountain scenery of Glenveagh National Park is popular with visitors.

The South-west (Munster)

The South-west includes the most spectacular scenery in Ireland. County Clare boasts the spectacular cliffs of Moher (see Photo 9.1) and the Burren area of limestone scenery, which is of great interest to botanists as well as geologists. A modern visitor centre interprets this heritage, helping to reduce the impacts of tourism on this sensitive natural area, which is now a national park. However, some claim that the Wild Atlantic Way project, in encouraging more visitors to the region, has increased pressure on a few 'honeypot' attractions.

Some of Ireland's most important tourist centres are located in the South-west:

- **Killarney** was recognised as a holiday resort of international significance in the nineteenth century. Nowadays, it is an ideal touring centre, including the famous scenic road known as the 'Ring of Kerry'. Killarney has the largest concentration of bed spaces outside the capital, and its airport at Farranfore is positioned to attract the short break market from the United Kingdom. Nearby are the lakes and mountains of the Killarney National Park, Muckross House, and some of the best golf courses in Europe.
- Tralee is famous for the 'Rose of Tralee' festival, largely created by Bord Fáilte (the former national tourist board) to attract young women participants claiming Irish descent from all over the world.
- **Cork** is the second city of the Republic and the centre of a development zone that includes:
  - Kinsale – a long-established important sailing and fishing centre, finding a niche market in short breaks based on fine dining.
  - Blarney – world famous for its castle, featuring the stone which supposedly confers the gift of eloquence.
  - Cobh was historically important before the jet era as the principal staging point for passenger liners and millions of emigrants to the United States, most of whom would have travelled in steerage class. The quayside has been restored with attractions recalling its role in Ireland's social and transport history, including the voyage of the *Titanic*.

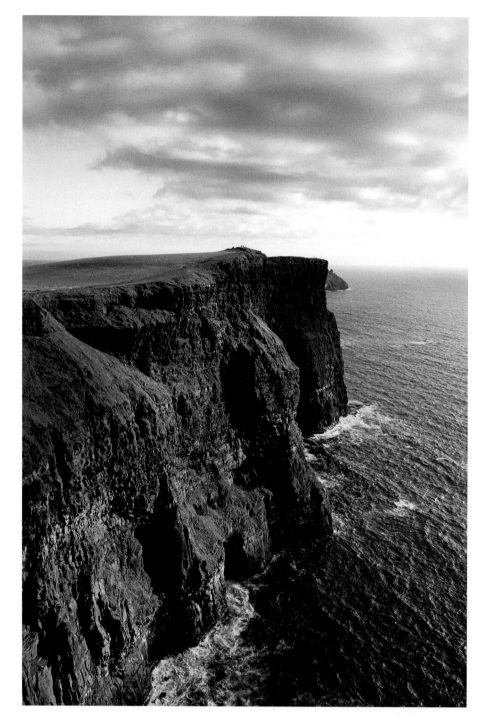

Photo 9.1

The Cliffs of Moher facing the Atlantic: western Ireland offers some of the most spectacular coastal scenery in Europe

Source: ©istockphoto.com/kelvinjay

- **Limerick and the Shannon** area offers high quality accommodation and provides good access to other areas. Shannon Airport, until the 1960s, was a compulsory stop on trans-Atlantic flights and pioneered the 'duty-free' concept of airport shopping shortly after the Second World War. The River Shannon is now more important as a tourism resource for sailing and fishing than as a commercial waterway, with Athlone and other smaller centres providing facilities. North-west of Limerick is Bunratty Castle, which pioneered the medieval banquet theme so popular with North Americans. Bunratty has now expanded its heritage attractions into a folk park and shopping complex (www.bunrattycastle.ie).

CASE STUDY 9.1
THE HORSE AS A FOCUS FOR TOURISM

In a post-industrial society, it is challenging to appreciate the central role the horse played in European and American history until well into the twentieth century. Different breeds were selected for their suitability in warfare, hunting, agriculture, transport, and racing. There is still a widespread interest in horse-related leisure activities, known as equestrianism (from *equus*, the Latin word for horse). Horse riding is an important part of countryside-based recreation, but has received less attention from policy-makers than hiking or cycling. Riding makes few demands on resources and provides income for significant numbers of farmers and small businesses, such as tack shops supplying specialist equipment. The environmental impact includes trail erosion and trampling of vegetation in areas with the greatest recreational demand. Epping Forest with its heavy clay soils close to the Greater London conurbation illustrates these challenges. Equestrian tourism is a relatively neglected field of study, bringing together a wide spectrum of horse-related activities for tourists or day visitors. These involve:

- Active participants in recreation, where the visitor does the riding or driving. This includes trail riding, hacking, trekking, show jumping, and touring by horse-drawn caravan (an Irish speciality).
- Spectators at events where the visitor watches others display their skills. This includes horse races, horse fairs, horse shows, gymkhanas, eventing competitions, rodeos, and polo matches.
- Visitors to attractions that breed and train horses or where the history of the horse is showcased along with other elements of the rural heritage.

With its mild climate and largely rural setting, Ireland is well suited to this type of tourism. The Irish have traditionally excelled in horsemanship, rider training, and horse breeding, and in few other countries is there such widespread interest in riding and racing (the Republic with a population of only 4 million boasted 25 racecourses in 2016, compared to Britain's 59). This interest is part of the national psyche and may date back to pre-Christian times when the horse was regarded as sacred by the Celtic tribes. Connemara ponies and Irish hunters are two native breeds that are renowned internationally. Events such as the Dublin Horse Show and race meetings attract many visitors from Britain and contribute significantly to the national economy. Equestrian activities accounted for 142,000 overseas participants in 2017, rivalling golf and angling in visitor spend. Ireland offers over 250 riding centres approved by the Association of Irish Riding Establishments (AIRE). Some of these are large purpose-built facilities, whereas many are attached to working farms and others form part of resort hotels. Ireland's rolling countryside of lowland heath, grassland, and wooded areas provides an attractive resource base, with less road traffic than in most parts of western Europe. Along the Atlantic coast, there are wide stretches of almost empty beaches for trail riding.

The Irish government has taken a close interest in this sector of the economy, establishing the Irish Horse Board in 2006 to co-ordinate sporting, breeding, and leisure activities. Nevertheless, equestrian tourism has played only a minor role in the promotion of Ireland's image as a destination. Like other rural activities, riding suffered from the foot-and-mouth crisis of 2001, which closed access to much of the countryside, and was slow to recover from the effects of '9/11'. This may be due to the following reasons:

- Ireland has become more urbanised, with demands from city dwellers for more recreational opportunities conflicting with the interests of farmers, who fear damage to property and litigation.
- With the exception of areas managed by Coillte (the forestry service) and the National Parks and Wildlife Service, most of the countryside is privately-owned farmland, holdings are often fragmented, and there are few legally recognised rights of way.
- The providers of the riding or race-going experience have lacked an overall vision for this sector of tourism.

In response, Fáilte Ireland has set out a strategy for equestrian tourism that identifies target markets and co-ordinates the activities of the stakeholders in the industry, with the aim of positioning Ireland as 'The Land of the Horse', where riding and race-going become part of a broader cultural experience.

Research and discussion

1. Identify the barriers that may prevent greater participation in riding as a recreational activity, and suggest ways in which demand might increase in the future.
2. A tour operator based in southern England has identified riding holidays as a niche product. This means investigating the advantages and disadvantages of Ireland as a destination for their clients. Other destinations being considered are Spain, Hungary, Argentina, and in the United States, Kentucky and Arizona, which many see

as offering serious competition. You should take account of accessibility, climate, resources, facilities, alternative activities for members of a group or family who are not horse-lovers, and 'après-ride' (the equivalent of après-ski in winter sports).

Northern Ireland

When the United Kingdom left the European Union in 2021, the Northern Ireland Protocol was designed to avoid a 'hard border' between the Province and the Republic, which remains a member of the European Union. The movement of goods from Great Britain to Northern Ireland is subject to controls, affecting the hospitality and leisure industries of the Province to some extent. Far more serious in its potential impact on cross-border movement is the Electronic Transfer Authorisation (ETA), proposed by the British government in Westminster. Most international visitors to Northern Ireland arrive via Dublin Airport, and an ETA would be required even if they spent only a few hours in the Province as part of an all-Ireland touring holiday. To avoid such an outcome, travel agents and tour operators could omit Northern Ireland from their itineraries.

The Province is often referred to as Ulster, which is misleading as this includes three of the Republic's border counties – Cavan, Monaghan, and Donegal. It is much smaller than the Republic, with a third of its population of 1.8 million living in Belfast. Northern Ireland has frequent air and shipping services to Scotland and England, and a good road and railway network. Tourism Northern Ireland (Tourism NI) is responsible for the development of tourism products and experiences, and for marketing the Province as a destination for domestic tourists and visitors from the Republic. Tourism NI is a public organisation reporting to the Northern Ireland Assembly. The Northern Ireland Tourism Alliance (NITA) represents the private sector of the industry and played an important role in mitigating the impact of the COVID-19 crisis. There are several regional tourist associations.

Tourism resources

Northern Ireland boasts the largest inland body of water in the British Isles – Lough Neagh – at the centre of a network of rivers and lakes that provide a valuable recreational resource, including a canoe trail extending from Lough Erne in the west to Strangford Lough in the east. The scenery of limestone uplands, lakeland, and basalt cliffs is an important part of the country's tourism appeal. Film tourism is also significant, as Northern Ireland provides many locations that feature in the popular *Game of Thrones* series. There are numerous forest parks and country parks providing facilities for recreation. Visitors are mainly attracted to the coast, where the National Trust plays an important role in conservation. In this context, Northern Ireland is at a disadvantage compared to the Republic, as there are as yet no national parks to attract overseas visitors. Many feel that the present designation of the Antrim Glens and the Mountains of Mourne as AONBs is too low a profile for destination marketing overseas, which since 1998 has been carried out by Tourism Ireland, and also gives these key attractions insufficient protection against development. However, proposals to designate these areas as national parks have met with opposition from local communities. Starting with 'Visit Belfast', we will now examine the six counties in more detail.

Belfast

Belfast is the seat of the Northern Ireland Assembly and Executive. The city owes its growth in the nineteenth century to the Industrial Revolution, when it became an important port and shipbuilding centre, thanks to its location on a deep, sheltered estuary. Linen manufacture here and at nearby Lisburn was also of major importance, so the industrial heritage (including the launching of the *Titanic*) is a significant part of Belfast's appeal. From 1969 to 1994, sectarian strife and the threat of terrorism caused a steep decline in tourist arrivals, especially from Britain. The Good Friday power-sharing agreement facilitated a massive investment in hotels, conference facilities, and visitor attractions. Nevertheless, Belfast remains a deeply divided city, with 'peace walls' separating Catholic and Protestant communities. Even at the height of 'The Troubles', the sectarian murals attracted sensation-seeking groups of foreign tourists, and taxi tours now are available to view the features and precincts of 'The Troubles'. More conventional attractions include Titanic Belfast on the waterfront (https://titanicbelfast.com), the redeveloped area around the cathedral, which now rivals Dublin's Temple Bar district for shopping and nightlife; the Odyssey Project – a large-scale education, science, entertainment, and sport development; and ECOS – an environmental education centre. Belfast also hosts a variety of international events such as the Cutty Sark Tall Ships Race. Attractions on the outskirts of the city include Hillsborough Castle, Carrickfergus Castle, and the Ulster Folk, and Transport Museum at Cultra.

Antrim

North of Belfast lies the Antrim Plateau where the basalt rock gives rise to impressive scenery, including:

- The Giant's Causeway, Ireland's most famous natural attraction, and because of its unique character, a World Heritage Site, but one which is under considerable tourist pressure.
- The nine glens of Antrim – deep wooded valleys sloping down to the sea, carved out of the basalt by fast-flowing streams. Glenariff is the best known of these, and at the foot of the glen one of the many *feiscanna* (festivals) of the region is held.
- The spectacular coastline between Larne and Portrush. Portrush, Ballycastle, and Coleraine are the main resorts on the Antrim coast, popular with day trippers. They have reinvested to improve facilities for family holidays and golf tourism.
- The Old Bushmills distillery is a popular visitor attraction.

Derry and Tyrone

Londonderry (Derry) is the main tourist centre in the west of the Province, set on a hill on the banks of the Foyle Estuary. This is also a divided city for sectarian reasons and a potential flashpoint, with the Protestant community occupying the walled town that withstood a historic siege in 1689. In Bellaghy, the Seamus Heaney HomePlace celebrates this popular poet. South-east of Londonderry are the touring circuits of the Sperrin Mountains, where attractions include the Sperrin Heritage Centre, Springhill House, and the historic town of Moneymore. To the south is the Ulster-American Folk Park of Omagh, one of the increasing numbers of folk museums in the Province, which explores Scots-Irish links with the United States.

Fermanagh Lakeland

Here the river Erne links several large lakes to provide an important resource for water-based recreation, nature lovers, and fishing holidays, which have long been popular with Dutch and German tourists. Castle Archdale on Lough Erne is the main centre for sailing and hire cruising, while Marble Arch is the best known of a number of caves in this limestone area. Castle Coole and Florence Court are significant attractions run by the National Trust. Enniskillen is a historic garrison town, noted for its associations with the British Army.

Armagh and County Down

This area includes the historic city of Armagh, which is the spiritual capital of Ireland with two cathedrals serving the Catholic and Anglican communities. South Armagh is a former problem area on the border, where EU funding has benefitted rural tourism initiatives by farmers' co-operatives. To the south-east rises the granite mass of the Mournes, rounded mountains sweeping down to the sea, and because of this area's closeness to the Belfast conurbation, subject to considerable pressure from a variety of outdoor recreation activities. Tourist attractions in County Down include:

- Newcastle, a seaside resort noted for sailing and golf.
- Lively Warrenpoint and the quieter Rostrevor, both situated on Carlingford Lough.
- Bangor, situated within the Belfast metropolitan area, near the scenic Ards Peninsula, which contains historic Castle Ward, Mount Stewart, and Kearney Village. The Ards Peninsula is separated from the rest of County Down by the inlet of Strangford Lough, now a marine reserve and bird sanctuary.
- The Strangford Stone, an example of communal endeavour to commemorate the Millennium and the peace process.
- The cathedral town of Downpatrick has a visitor centre interpreting the legacy of St Patrick as the bringer of Christianity to Ireland in the fifth century.

Summary

- Despite the political and religious divisions, Ireland is well-endowed with many types of tourist attractions.
- It can be divided geographically into a number of tourist regions, each with a particular blend of natural and cultural resources.
- We can, however, identify a number of common themes. These include (1) the use of European funds to develop tourism; (2) the growth of themed heritage attractions, particularly those stressing the Celtic contribution; (3) the increasing use of rural tourism to encourage the economy in remoter areas, often based on farm stays; and (4) the growth of urban tourism in terms of both short holidays, based on cultural attractions, and business trips.
- The unified development of tourism across Ireland is a significant innovation that should benefit both countries.

Assignments

1. Describe the resources and facilities available in Ireland for various types of outdoor recreation.
2. Evaluate the importance of Irish culture and traditions to its tourism industry.
3. Explain why historical ties to the United States and Britain largely determine tourism flows to Ireland.
4. Explain the appeal of Ireland as a location for film-makers.

References and further reading

Cosgrove, I. and Jackson, R. (1972) *The Geography of Recreation and Leisure*, Hutchinson, London
Fáilte Ireland (2007) *A New Strategy for Irish Equestrian Tourism*, Failte Ireland, Dublin
Organization for Economic Co-operation and Development (annual) *Tourism Policy and International Tourism in OECD Member Countries*, OECD, Paris
https://www.unwto.org/tourism-data/unwto-tourism-dashboard

10 The tourism geography of Scandinavia

Learning objectives

After reading this chapter, you should be able to:

- Describe the major physical features and climates of the Scandinavian countries and understand their importance for tourism.
- Understand the nature of Scandinavian economies and society, along with their significance for tourism demand.
- Outline the major features of demand for domestic and international tourism in Scandinavia.

DOI: 10.4324/9781003406853-13

- Describe the major features of the tourism industry in Scandinavia and appreciate the differences between the various countries.
- Demonstrate knowledge of the tourist regions, resorts, business centres, and tourist attractions in the Scandinavian countries.

Introduction

Geographically speaking, Scandinavia is a peninsula in the north of Europe that, for most of its history, has been somewhat isolated from the rest of the continent. In addition to Norway and Sweden, Scandinavia, as a cultural and political entity, includes Denmark, Finland, Iceland, and the Faroe Islands. All these countries are members of the Nordic Council (Norden), which is responsible for a high level of co-operation in policies affecting transport, tourism, education, and the environment (www.norden.org). Scandinavian Airlines – SAS, jointly owned by the governments of Denmark, Norway, and Sweden, is one such example of international co-operation and was the first to develop transpolar routes to North America and the Far East.

Until well into the twentieth century, the Scandinavian countries were relatively poor and the source of large-scale emigration to North America. The disadvantages of infertile soils, a rigorous climate, and a peripheral location have been overcome by hard work, discipline, skill, ingenuity, and a strong sense of civic responsibility. As a result, the Scandinavian countries have achieved a high level of economic prosperity based on advanced technology, combined with health and social welfare services that are among the best in the world. The region also boasts some of the most striking examples of modern architecture. High environmental standards are maintained, both in the cities, which are free of litter and graffiti, and in the countryside. Compared to the crowding which afflicts most of Europe, Scvandinavia can offer vast areas of sparsely populated coast and countryside, with almost unrestricted access to a range of recreational resources, which in Norway and Sweden are guaranteed by law. Although car ownership levels are high, public transport systems are usually integrated and provide a viable alternative for touring in the more populated areas.

The Scandinavian landscape still bears the imprint of the glaciers from the last Ice Age. The glaciers eroded the valleys of western Norway into deep troughs, later invaded by the sea to form the fjords, and scraped bare the ancient plateau surfaces of Finland and Sweden. Here, the ice sheets left masses of boulder clay, now covered by coniferous forest dotted with lakes and outcrops of rock. The climate varies from cool temperate in Jutland to sub-arctic in northern Scandinavia. Most of the region experiences a continental climate with severely cold winters and warm summers. The main negative factor affecting the development of tourism is the shortness of the summer season and the darkness of winter, owing to the northerly latitude.

The Scandinavian countries have shared similar cultural features since the Viking era (approximately 750 to 1100 AD). The Viking heritage has perhaps been over-emphasised with a view to international tourism, compared to less widely-known aspects of the region's history. In the medieval and early modern periods, Denmark, and later Sweden, dominated the whole of Scandinavia – with the result that they now have a more impressive heritage of historic buildings than the other three countries. Additionally, the Lutheran Church has provided a measure of cultural unity since the Reformation in the sixteenth century. Nevertheless, each country has developed a strong national identity, and the differences extend to international politics and attitudes towards immigration. Sweden, for example, traditionally pursued a policy of neutrality until the Russian invasion of Ukraine in 2022 exposed its vulnerability. Both Denmark and Sweden are members of the European Union along with Finland, whereas Norway and Iceland have decided that their best interests lie in a looser trade association.

Perceptions of Scandinavia fostered by the media include its supposed ethnic homogeneity, whereas the cities are now home to many ethnic minorities as a result of substantial immigration. In the 1960s and 1970s, Sweden and Denmark were renowned for their permissive attitudes towards sexual liberation and the absence of censorship, but the differences with the rest of Europe in this respect are much less evident today. More recently, the vogue for 'Scandi Noir' television dramas and the novels of Stieg Larsson have popularised a number of Scandinavian locations and the 'Sarah Lund' style of knitwear (originally Faroese).

The Scandinavian countries have a total population of almost 26 million, mainly concentrated in the towns and cities of the southern part of the region. The climate, as well as social and economic conditions, combine to make Scandinavia one of the major generating areas in the world for holiday tourism, especially to winter sun destinations. The people enjoy a high standard of living, but at the same time, place great emphasis on leisure, active participation in outdoor recreation, and the quality of life; levels of education are also high, and typical annual leave entitlement is five weeks or more. Add to this a well-developed and efficient travel trade throughout the region, and it is no surprise that levels of both domestic and foreign holiday-taking are much higher than the average for Europe. Holidays abroad represent around one-third of all holidays taken by residents of Norway, Sweden, and Denmark, and consequently, these countries have a substantial deficit on their international travel account. A large percentage of these holidays are to other countries in the region, facilitated by the abolition of passport controls for inter-Scandinavian travel. This does mean, however, that statistics for international travel between Scandinavian countries are not collected, making it difficult to measure regional tourism flows. In domestic tourism, there is a growing trend for short second holidays, especially those based on winter sports and other types of outdoor recreation.

On the other hand, the relatively high cost of living, high levels of taxation, and strong currencies combine to make Scandinavia an expensive destination for foreign visitors. The majority of tourists are from other parts of Europe, especially Germany. There is a widespread perception that Scandinavia is not only more expensive but also less accessible than other destinations, involving long journeys by road and car ferry or expensive air travel. The completion of a number of bridges and tunnels connecting the Danish islands to the mainland is greatly improving transport by road and rail between Scandinavia and the rest of Europe. With deregulation under the European Union, airfares are falling, while Copenhagen is rapidly becoming a major hub for long-haul as well as inter-regional air services. Inbound tourism to Scandinavia should also increase as interest in 'green tourism' gathers momentum. The tourism products offered by the Scandinavian countries pay more than lip service to environmental issues. They include:

- camping and self-catering holidays in the countryside; and
- a range of activity and 'wilderness adventure' holidays.

The climate and topography of the Scandinavian countries, with the exception of Denmark, have encouraged the development of winter sports, particularly 'Nordic' or cross-country skiing, which has much less impact on the environment than alpine skiing. As a cold-water destination, beach tourism is largely limited to the domestic market, but the more southerly and sheltered parts of Scandinavia may soon be 'discovered' by summer sun-seekers from outside the region as a result of climate change.

The COVID-19 pandemic impacted Scandinavia less than other regions of Europe, but there were striking differences among the various countries. In Sweden, the government favoured a 'light touch', allowing restaurants, bars, gyms, shops, and schools to remain open, whereas Denmark and Norway opted for strict quarantine measures. As a result, Sweden experienced a much higher death rate than its neighbours, without any significant economic benefit. Indeed, Denmark and Norway imposed entry restrictions on Swedish tourists.

Denmark

The smallest and most densely populated of the Scandinavian countries, Denmark lacks wilderness areas and spectacular scenery (the highest point is only 170 metres above sea level). Denmark's appeal lies in its neat, gently rolling countryside and picturesque towns and villages, while the national tourist icon is the 'Little Mermaid' on the Copenhagen waterfront, immortalised by Hans Christian Andersen. Consisting of many islands and the Jutland Peninsula, which has only a short land border with Germany, no part of the country is far from the sea. It is, therefore, not surprising to find that sailing is a popular pastime, and that the Danes have the highest rate of yacht ownership in Europe. They also have one of the highest rates of ownership of second homes (known locally as 'summer houses'). Much of the demand is generated from the capital, Copenhagen, where most families live in apartments. Cycling is also very popular – the topography is ideal even if the weather is unpredictable – and this greenest of transport modes is encouraged by a nationwide system of bikeways. Danes have the reputation for being more informal and 'continental' than other Scandinavians, with a quality of life expressed by the Danish word *hygge* (roughly translated as 'cosy'). This is experienced in the traditional inns, as drinking laws are more relaxed than elsewhere in Scandinavia. Copenhagen is particularly renowned for its exuberant nightlife and tolerance of different lifestyles.

The demand for tourism

Domestic and outbound tourism

Danes enjoy up to five weeks annual holiday entitlement, and two-thirds of the population take a holiday away from home every year. People prefer to stay with friends and relatives, in owned and rented 'summer houses', or use camping sites in preference to serviced accommodation. Along with other Scandinavian countries, Denmark encourages the principle of 'tourism for all' or social tourism for those people who, for various reasons, find it difficult to take a holiday. For example, retired people on limited incomes can even take state-subsidised holidays in the Canary Islands during the winter months, which at least reduces the cost of heating bills. Spain is the most popular holiday destination, but domestic tourism is more significant overall.

Inbound tourism

Denmark has a relatively large tourism sector and receives as many foreign visitors, around 12.8 million a year, as Norway and Sweden combined. However, Denmark is heavily dependent on Germany, followed by Norway and Sweden, for its income from tourism, which is based partly on the natural attractions of coast and countryside. These are less in demand in the face of competition from elsewhere, whereas Copenhagen is growing in popularity and accounts for two-thirds of the income from foreign visitors.

The supply side of tourism

Transport

Apart from Kastrup, serving Copenhagen, there is an increasing number of low-cost carriers offering flights to regional airports such as Aarhus, Esbjerg and Billund. Surface transport links are also excellent, with good road, rail, and ferry links to the United Kingdom and the rest of Europe. Transport within Denmark is mainly by private car, using a well-developed internal and international road system with ferry connections between the islands. Stena and DFDS Seaways operate international ferry services to the rest of Scandinavia, Germany, and the United Kingdom. However, the ferries will decline in importance due to the completion of a number of bridge and tunnel projects. These must rank as some of the world's most spectacular engineering feats; they include the Great Belt Bridge linking the islands of Funen and Zealand, and the Oresund Bridge and Tunnel connecting Zealand to Sweden. The Oresund link, positioned close to Copenhagen, is already enhancing the city's role as the gateway to Scandinavia. The Fehmarn Belt fixed link (due for completion in 2029) will drastically reduce travel times from Hamburg and Berlin to Copenhagen and Stockholm.

Accommodation

The majority of Denmark's accommodation capacity is self-catering, including summer homes and campsites, and this is where most of the growth has occurred. Hotels, inns, and youth hostels are widely available, with the highest occupancy levels in Copenhagen and, during the summer peak, on the island of Bornholm. Most yacht marinas provide accommodation, and these are popular with both foreign and domestic tourists.

Organisation

Tourism policy is the responsibility of the Ministry of Industry, Business, and Financial Affairs. The Danish National Forum leads and coordinates policy, working with the private sector. International tourism is managed by VisitDenmark. Regionally, tourism is managed by a decentralised network of 15–25 local destination management organisations.

Tourism resources

We can divide Denmark for convenience into the Jutland Peninsula and the islands of the Danish archipelago to the east, but the scenic 'Marguerite Route' allows the visitor to see virtually all the key attractions of this compact country on one short touring holiday. The dominant natural feature of Jutland is a moraine formed in the last Ice Age, which is partly covered with pine forest and large tracts of heath. These are interspersed with peat bogs that have yielded fascinating evidence about ways of life in the Bronze and Iron Ages. Interest in Denmark's archaeological heritage is widespread, forming the basis of several folk museums where buildings and traditional crafts are preserved in an authentic setting, or in reconstructed villages where students re-enact the lifestyles of the remote past. The preserved 'old town' of Aarhus is another heritage attraction, which can be enjoyed alongside a vibrant modern city. Denmark is well equipped with activity parks for children known as 'Sommerlands', but the most popular attraction is undoubtedly Legoland at Billund (www.legoland.dk). Jutland's west coast has fine sandy beaches backed by dunes, but bathing is often unsafe due to the changing winds and tides. The fishing port of Esbjerg is a major centre with ferry connections to Harwich in England and the islands of Fanø and Romø. It is also close to the medieval town of Ribe with its Viking Centre. Artists have long been attracted to the fishing community of Skagen at the northern tip of Jutland.

The islands of the Danish Archipelago offer different landscapes and attractions:

- Bornholm, situated in the Baltic Sea 200 kilometres east of Copenhagen, is particularly appealing with its rocky granite scenery but is somewhat remote from the rest of the country.
- Funen, known as the 'Garden of Denmark', is especially well equipped for tourism. The city of Odense attracts many American tourists as the birthplace of Hans Christian Andersen.
- Zealand is the largest of the islands and probably the most interesting for the foreign visitor. At Roskilde, there is much evidence of Denmark's Viking past, and 'longship cruises' are even available. There are a number of important historic buildings, the best known being Frederiksborg Castle, and Kronborg Castle at Helsingor, famous as the setting for Shakespeare's *Hamlet*. Above all, Zealand contains Copenhagen, which is a long-established short break destination. With its copper-sheathed roofs and spires, harbour, and pedestrianised shopping streets, the Danish capital has wide appeal. Specific attractions include the Tivoli Gardens, Europe's oldest amusement park (www.tivoli.dk), with its theatres and summer festivals, the Danish Royal Ballet, the Louisiana Museum of Modern Art, the Amalienborg Palace, and the Carlsberg Brewery. Unlike most European capitals, Copenhagen has fine beaches and resort attractions within easy reach by public transport from the city centre.

Discussion point

In the early twentieth century, Denmark pioneered farmers' co-operatives, which have proven successful in boosting the country's food exports. Nowadays, as in other parts of western Europe, farmers are under increasing pressure to diversify into rural tourism. Discuss the benefits and costs of farm stays in Denmark from the viewpoint of both the host farmer and their guests, in this case, a middle-income professional English couple with young children.

Norway

Of all the Scandinavian countries, Norway is probably the best known. Since the nineteenth century, tourists have visited the fjords in the western part of the country, attracted by the breathtaking combination of mountain and coastal scenery. The land is rugged, with only 3 per cent being cultivated; thus, Norwegians throughout their history have turned to the sea for their livelihoods. Norway boasts the longest coastline in Europe, deeply cut by the fjords, with chains of small offshore islands known as the *skerryguard* providing a sheltered coastal waterway for shipping. Norway has a substantial merchant navy and is a dominant player in the cruise market, while sailing is a popular pastime for Norwegians. The heritage of seafaring and exploration, from the Viking longships to Amundsen and Thor Heyerdahl (of *Kon Tiki* fame), along with the controversial whaling industry, is greatly valued. The former isolation of many areas, separated by mountain and fjord, explains why Norway has retained much of its traditional culture, including the wearing of colourful regional costumes on special occasions. Norway's vast resources of hydro-electric power are vital to the economy, but concern about the impact of the power industry on the environment has led to demands for more areas to be set aside as national parks. The nation's recent prosperity is, however, largely based on its huge reserves of oil and natural gas. The foreign exchange earnings from this mineral wealth are invested in infrastructure that will benefit Norwegian society as a whole, rather than in showpiece projects.

There are substantial variations in climate in such an elongated country. Temperatures on the coast are much milder than might be expected for such high latitudes, due to the influence of the Gulf Stream, so that the fjords and shipping lanes remain ice-free in winter, even as far north as Kirkenes on the Russian border. To experience true Arctic conditions, you need to go even further north, to Svalbard. It is worth emphasising that you can only see the midnight sun in summer, weather permitting, north of the Arctic Circle; at the North Cape, there is continuous daylight from mid-May to the end of July. Exposed coastal areas like Bergen receive an excessive amount of rain, while the sheltered heads of the fjords are much drier, sunnier, and warmer in summer – but cold in winter. In the mountainous interior, heavy snowfalls are frequent, making it possible to ski year-round in areas like the Hardangervidda plateau east of Bergen. The Norwegians claim to have invented skiing – although as a means of travel rather than as a sport – and they probably have the world's highest participation rate in skiing, with ski trails even in cities such as Oslo.

The demand for tourism

The prosperity of the Norwegian economy explains why travel propensities are high. However, holiday patterns are changing as the traditional long summer holiday gives way to shorter, more frequent trips.

Domestic and outbound tourism

Domestic tourism dominates the industry, accounting for two-thirds of commercial over-night stays. The ownership of holiday chalets, known as *hytte*, is widespread. Many of these are situated in the *saeter*, the high summer pastures above the treeline, and are a reminder of the pastoral lifestyle of the past. Hiking is a popular activity in summer, and skiing in winter. Norwegians take around 8 million foreign trips a year, resulting in a deficit on the country's travel account. Only a small percentage of trips are to other Scandinavian countries, as Norwegians prefer overseas travel to the United Kingdom, southern Europe, North Africa, and the Canary Islands.

Inbound tourism

Norway experienced a growth of inbound travel as the host country for the 1996 Winter Olympics, followed by a gradual decline. More recently, foreign arrivals have averaged 5 million a year as the kroner has weakened. However, the COVID pandemic severely reduced inbound volumes in 2020 to 1.4 million. Norway's foreign visitors come largely from Denmark, Germany, and Sweden, but those from outside Scandinavia, such as the Dutch, British, and Americans, tend to stay longer and spend more. There is a pronounced peaking of demand during the short summer season.

The supply side of tourism

Transport

In such a mountainous and elongated country, air transport is important. International air passengers are served by Oslo's two airports, boosted in recent years by low-cost carriers such as Ryanair and Norwegian (www.norwegian.com). Domestic air services, like those operated by Widerøe, link almost 50 destinations (www.wideroe.no). However, the majority of foreign visits and domestic trips are by private car, taking advantage of the improved road network, with numerous tunnels supplementing the ferry links across major fjords, as these tend to be crowded during the summer peak. The rail network run by Norwegian State Railways is more limited, terminating in Bodø and leaving northern Norway without a rail service. The Bergen to Oslo railway offers tourists one of Europe's most scenic journeys and played a major role in opening up Norway for tourism. Traditionally, shipping services have provided the country with a lifeline, notably the Hurtigruten fleet, which serves a large number of coastal communities from Bergen to Kirkenes, taking on or unloading passengers and cargo throughout the year (www.hurtigruten.com). The round trip takes 12 days and is an interesting alternative to the summer holiday cruises available to the western fjords and 'the Land of the Midnight Sun'. Large numbers of visitors also use the ferry services, which link Norway to the United Kingdom and Denmark through the ports of Bergen, Stavanger, Oslo and Kristiansand.

Accommodation

In the peak season, the majority of accommodation is in camping, although other types of self-catering have grown in popularity, leading to a shortage in the supply of holiday cabins. Other accommodation options are available on farms and in *rorbus* – fishermen's winter cabins built on stilts over the water's edge, which are a feature of coastal communities in northern Norway. Relatively few tourists, other than business travellers, use hotels, although these are generally open year-round. Even so, there is an acute shortage of accommodation capacity in popular tourist areas during the peak summer and Easter periods.

Organisation

The Norwegian government recognises the importance of the industry in aiding rural communities, transport operators, and the accommodation sector. Therefore, it has attempted to reduce the acute seasonal and geographical concentration of visits, as well as to ensure the sustainability of Norway's tourism. In an effort to boost the volume of tourism in Norway and develop professionalism in the sector, the Norwegian Tourist Board (VisitNorway) (www.visitnorway.com) was created as an independent, commercial agency, jointly supported by the Norwegian government and the tourism industry. The Ministry of Trade, Industry, and Fisheries has given the state-owned company Innovation Norway the responsibility to develop 'high yield, low impact' tourism, including closer regulation of the cruise sector to minimise pollution. Through the Ministry of Local Government and Modernisation, regional and local authorities have a key role in promoting tourism development.

Tourism resources

We can divide Norway, for convenience, into western, southern, and northern regions:

The **Western Fjords** are the most popular area for foreign visitors since they include the five most spectacular fjords (Hardanger, Sogne, Nord, Geiranger, and Romsdal), the highest mountains of Scandinavia, and Jostdalsbreen, the largest glacier in mainland Europe. Less well-known is a cultural resource unique to Norway – the *stave* churches, built entirely of wood and with Viking features in their design. The region is easily accessible by air, with airports at Trondheim, Alesund, Bergen, and Stavanger. The historic port of Bergen, situated between the two longest fjords – the Hardanger and the Sogne – is the gateway for exploring this region by ship, road, or rail. The Geiranger Fjord is generally recognised as the most attractive, with its towering rock faces and myriad waterfalls. Among the many villages lining the shores of the fjords, Laerdal, Olden, and Ulvik are the most popular resorts, while Balestrand has retained much of the ambience that attracted British tourists in Victorian times. A short distance inland lies the Jotunheim National

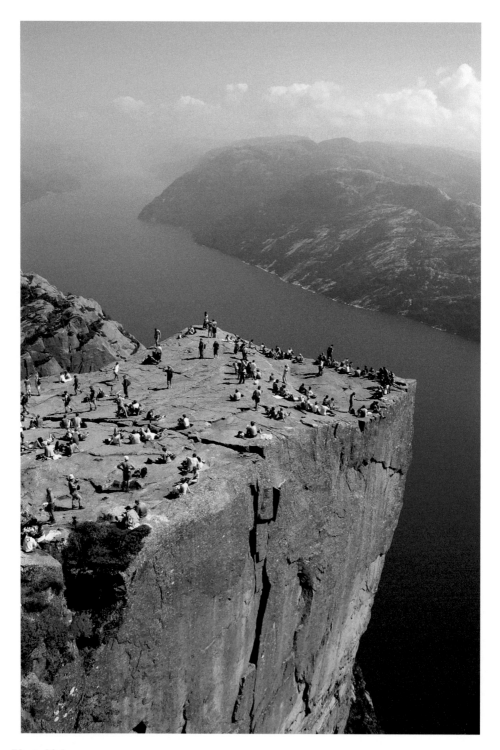

Photo 10.1
Pulpit Rock, often regarded as Norway's most iconic landmark

Source: ©istockphoto.com/Harald Tjøstheim

Park, consisting of an extensive plateau above the tree line. It is Norway's most visited wilderness area and a favourite with hikers and climbers. Alesund, with its art nouveau architecture, and Stavanger are growing in popularity as tourist centres for the UK market. The fortunes of Stavanger were transformed in the late 1960s by the discovery of vast oil and gas reserves in the North Sea. Close to Stavanger is the Lysefjord and the spectacular Pulpit Rock, often regarded as Norway's most iconic landmark. Trondheim in the north of the region is a historic cathedral city and former capital of Norway.

Southern Norway offers a gentler coastline with sheltered coves and beaches, which are popular with domestic holidaymakers. Although a modern city compared to Bergen, Oslo is an established destination for cultural tourists. The main attractions are the museums celebrating Viking and maritime heritage, and the Vigeland sculpture park. Oslo serves as the gateway to Norway's main skiing areas, and a number of resorts have developed along the railways linking the capital to Bergen and Trondheim. Lillehammer, the venue for the 1996 Winter Olympics, is the most important.

Northern Norway

The part of Norway lying within the Arctic Circle has a distinct character, not least because the interior is occupied by people of an age-old, distinct culture – the *Sami* (formerly known as Lapps). Lapland also includes part of northern Sweden, Finland, and Russia, but the Sami of Finnmark have retained their semi-nomadic way of life, based on reindeer herding, to a greater extent than elsewhere. Tourism provides a welcome source of income, but as with all such indigenous peoples, it represents a potential disruption to a culture that is in delicate balance with the harsh environment.

The coastal communities of the north still largely depend on the fishing industry, but tourist numbers are growing. This is particularly true of the Lofoten Islands, with their spectacular scenery and the opportunity to sight whales and sea eagles. The North Cape is the goal of as many as 3,000 visitors a day in July and August, and therefore ranks as a mass tourism destination by Arctic standards.

CASE STUDY 10.1
TROMSØ: TOURISM DEVELOPMENT IN EUROPE'S FAR NORTH

Tromsø, with its far northerly island location and a winter climate characterised by two months of darkness, would appear to be an unlikely tourist destination. Yet clever marketing, good communications, and a positive attitude to their environment by the local community have turned these natural disadvantages into attractions. This is no remote Arctic outpost but a bustling modern city with 76,000 inhabitants.

Thanks to the influence of the Gulf Stream, Tromsø has a much milder climate than its location 300 kilometres inside the Arctic Circle would suggest (see Figure 10.1),

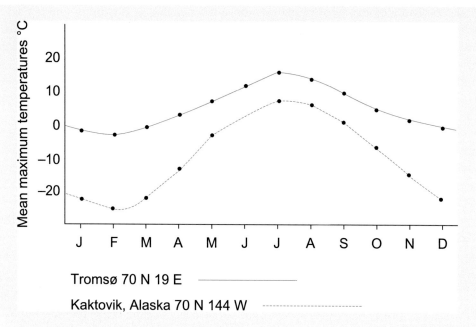

Figure 10.1
Tromsø compared to another Arctic location

making it possible to grow fruit and vegetables and raise dairy cattle. Winter temperatures are much higher than places at the same latitude in North America, Greenland, and Siberia, while summers are warm enough for outdoor recreation, including sunbathing on the beaches of Troms County (see Photo 10.2). On the other hand, at this latitude, the sun is below the horizon from November 21 to January 21, with only a few hours of twilight to relieve the darkness of the 'polar night'. Yet Tromsø, a university city with as many as 10,000 students, reduces the impact of seasonal affective disorder (SAD) with constant partying and a vibrant music and arts scene, culminating in the international film festival held in January each year. The city's most iconic building – the Tromsdalenkirke, known as the 'Cathedral of the Arctic Ocean', celebrates the theme of light in its design.

The outdoor activities on offer during the winter include the following:

- 'Chasing the Northern Lights'. Tromsø, because of its latitude, accessibility, and modern amenities, is probably the best place in the world for tourists to view the aurora borealis (Northern Lights) in the night sky between October and May. However, these spectacular displays are unpredictable, and a number of specialist operators, using various modes of transport, enable tourists to follow sightings.
- Cross-country and downhill skiing, following floodlit trails.
- Dog-sledding with teams of Alaskan huskies.
- Horse-drawn sleigh rides.
- Snowshoe trekking.

Photo 10.2
Telegraph Bay, a beach warmed by the North Atlantic Drift 300 kilometres (200 miles)
north of the Arctic Circle

Source: Courtesy of VisitTromsø © Bard Løken

- Snowmobile rallies.
- Ice fishing on the lakes and rivers of the interior.

As the regional capital of northern Norway, Tromsø has an international airport and
is also one of the country's largest cruise ports. Tourism plays a significant role in the
local economy. The city's hotels have a capacity of 3,300 bed spaces, while cabins
and campsites in Troms County are available for small numbers of visitors. Tromsø's
historic role as the 'Gateway to the Arctic' is featured in the Polar Museum, commemorating the Norwegian explorers Nansen and Amundsen, who used the city as the base
for their expeditions. The city continues to be a centre for scientific research, while
the Polaria exhibition allows the visitor to experience the Arctic environment in safety
and comfort (https://polaria.no).

Assignment

A city has features that distinguish it from lesser towns. Compare and contrast Tromsø
with Norilsk (Siberia), both of which claim to be 'the world's most northerly city',
with reference to their population characteristics, service functions, and facilities.

Svalbard

Norway's Arctic archipelago lies 1,000 kilometres north of the Norwegian mainland. Spitzbergen, the largest island, is noted for its dramatic landscape of fjords, ice-sculpted mountains, and glaciers, as well as the variety of wildlife that has adapted to an inhospitable environment. Svalbard is situated in the High Arctic north of 75° latitude, where winter is characterised by several months of continuous darkness and extreme cold. In summer, temperatures rarely rise above 10°C despite continuous daylight from April to August, and the weather is highly unpredictable. West Spitzbergen is much more accessible than the rest of the archipelago, which is hemmed in by pack ice year-round. Cruise passenger numbers in Svalbard (estimated at 57,000 in 2022) have recovered well from the pandemic. Visitors are attracted by the scenery, the heritage of the former whaling industry at Magdalen Fjord, and Ny Alesund, which was the base for a number of expeditions to the North Pole.

Although the islands are under Norwegian sovereignty, they are regarded by treaty as an international zone for commercial activities, explaining the presence of two Russian communities based on a coal mining industry that is no longer competitive. Apart from appealing to ecotourists, the extreme environment provides a challenge for adventure-seekers. Such tourists are usually aware of the risks, including the possibility of an attack by polar bears. Nevertheless, the Norwegian government has imposed a comprehensive system of regulations on tour operators as well as independent expeditioners to ensure the protection of fragile Arctic ecosystems.

Sweden

Although it is the largest of the Scandinavian countries in area, population, and GNP, Sweden lacks the clearly defined image presented by Norway and Finland. The country is known mainly for its mineral resources, the quality of its manufactured products, particularly motor vehicles and furniture, and its contribution to popular music and the film industry, rather than for any specific tourist attractions. Most of the population live within the Stockholm-Gothenburg-Malmö triangle, which serves as the economic and cultural focus of the nation.

The demand for tourism

Domestic tourism

The Industrial Revolution came late to Sweden, and most city dwellers have rural roots and a strong love of nature. By 1900, the growing middle class regularly spent summers in the countryside or in fishing communities along the west coast. They stayed in modest boarding houses, or in 'summer houses' where families catered for themselves. The large, fashionable hotels typical of continental Europe did not become a dominant part of the resort scene. It was not until the late 1930s, with the rise to power of the Social Democrats and the introduction of a statutory two-week vacation, that working-class families were able to stay at the seaside, usually in campsites (Löfgren, 2002). The development of a prosperous economy after the Second World War made it possible for the Swedes to have one of the highest travel propensities in the world (75 per cent). The majority of the working population has at least five weeks holiday entitlement, and they are more likely to take a second holiday than the citizens of other European countries. Self-catering is still the favoured type of accommodation, and over a quarter of Swedish households own a cottage or 'summer house' in the country. Sweden has one of the highest rates of second home and pleasure boat ownership in Europe. The majority of holiday trips are taken by car. Domestic business travel is focussed on the cities of Stockholm, Gothenburg, and Malmö.

Outbound tourism

Sweden is among the world's leading generators of international tourism. Destinations popular with Swedish holidaymakers include other Scandinavian countries, Germany, Spain, the United Kingdom, Italy, France, and Greece. Long-haul travel is also increasing to destinations such as Malaysia.

Inbound tourism

There were around 7 million foreign visitors to Sweden in 2019, but a much larger number of day trips from other Scandinavian countries. For overnight visitors, the main generating countries are Germany, the United Kingdom, the Netherlands, and the United States, where there is a large ethnic market. However, the COVID-19 pandemic impacted inbound tourism in 2020, reducing overnight stays by 70 per cent.

The supply side of tourism

Transport

International air transport is served by Stockholm Arlanda, Gothenburg, and Malmö Airports, and domestic flights are operated by Scandinavian Airlines to some 20 destinations. Air travel has declined in popularity among Swedes for environmental reasons, thanks to the growth of the *flygskam* (flight shaming) movement, which favours long distance rail travel. However, most foreign holiday tourists arrive by car, using the ferries on the short sea routes from Denmark and Germany. Car travel is expensive in Sweden, and government policy favours public transport by imposing controls on car use. Swedish railways have, therefore, received considerable public investment to provide high-speed routes between the major cities. There is also a nationwide system of cycle routes.

Accommodation

Sweden's serviced accommodation stock has grown since 1997, though it is still dominated by small businesses. Demand for hotel accommodation by domestic tourists is small, with the exception of business travellers. In the past, acute shortages of suitable hotels in cities like Stockholm have led to the development of company apartments. Self-catering accommodation in the form of summer cottages and log cabins is in demand for holiday tourism; timeshare and multi-ownership schemes are being developed, as are high-quality campsites.

Organisation

The Swedish Agency for Economic and Regional Growth, known as Tillvaxtverket, is responsible for developing tourism at the national level. VisitSweden, fully owned by the government, markets Sweden as a tourist destination internationally (https://visitsweden.com). Both organisations report to the Ministry of Enterprise and Innovation. The national agencies are supported by an independent network of 22 regional organisations.

Tourism resources

Sweden shares the Kjolen Mountains with Norway, but the scenery tends to be less spectacular on the eastern slopes. With 50 per cent of its area under forest, and boasting innumerable lakes, rivers, and rapids, Sweden has the largest area of unspoiled wilderness in Europe. Sweden's tourism resources also include a varied coastline on two seas and a network of inland waterways. Sweden was the first country in Europe to develop a system of national parks to protect its wilderness areas from exploitation by the powerful mining, timber, and wood pulp industries. Public access to the countryside is guaranteed by the traditional law known as *Allemansrätt* (every man's right), which allows visitors to camp overnight, hike, ride, cycle, and picnic on private land. Although winters are severely cold with abundant snow, summers are warm and sunny, especially along the Baltic coast. Midsummer Eve is the occasion for festivities throughout the country.

Sweden's cultural resources include prehistoric rock carvings at Tanum on the west coast, the heritage of the copper mining industry, the historic university towns of Lund and Uppsala, and reminders of the seventeenth-century period when Swedish military power controlled the Baltic under leaders such as King Gustavus Adolphus and Queen Christina.

The main tourist areas are found in the south, along the Baltic and North Sea coasts, and in the central lake district west of Stockholm. These three areas are linked by the Göta Canal a scenic waterway that spans 190 kilometres, connecting Gothenburg to Stockholm and the three largest lakes – Vänern, Vättern, and Mälaren. The canal was constructed in the nineteenth century to provide a short cut for shipping. Although it has lost most of its significance as a commercial waterway, some of the original vessels have been adapted for summer cruises.

The North Sea Coast

Gothenburg is Sweden's major North Sea port but offers many cultural attractions and the Liseberg theme park, one of the largest in Scandinavia. The 'golden coast' of Bohuslän nearby is popular with Swedish families, especially the resort of Tanum Strand, which is an excellent base for exploring the many offshore islands. Scania in the extreme south of Sweden has lowland landscapes similar to those of Denmark, and its capital, Malmö, now linked to Copenhagen by the famous Oresund Bridge, is a major business centre.

The Baltic coast

Here, the island of Gotland with its white sandy beaches and strange rock formations is a major destination. The well-preserved medieval city of Visby is a World Heritage Site as well as being a summer holiday resort offering a vibrant nightlife.

The Central Lake District

Lying close to the Norwegian border, the provinces of Värmland and Dalarna offer scenic lake and forest landscapes, ideal for activity holidays, including fishing, canoeing, and whitewater rafting in summer. Mora on Lake Siljan has hosted international downhill ski events but is mainly noted for the Vasalöppet, a cross-country ski race that attracts thousands of participants each March. Dalarna is regarded as the cultural heartland of Sweden, offering picturesque folk customs, heritage museums, and innumerable handicraft outlets that attract large numbers of domestic tourists. The most interesting place for the foreign visitor is undoubtedly Stockholm. The capital is attractively situated on a number of islands at the entrance to Lake Mälaren, while thousands more islands scattered along the Baltic coast provide ideal sites for summer homes. The well-planned modern city contrasts with heritage attractions such as Gamla Stan (the preserved old town), the Vasa Ship Museum (https://vasamuseet.se), and Skansen, Scandinavia's oldest folk museum (https://www.skansen.se), which has given its name to similar attractions in other countries. Stockholm also has the ABBA Museum (https://abbathemuseum.com) and the Swedish Design Museum (https://swedishdesignmuseum.com).

CASE STUDY 10.2
STOCKHOLM: A ROLE MODEL OF SUSTAINABILITY

Stockholm Visitors Board actively promotes the capital as a 'green city' by hosting a number of festivals and other events with an environmental theme. Significantly, the city was chosen as the 'European Green Capital' for 2010 by the European Commission. This annual award is presented to the city which has:

- A proven track record of environmental achievement;
- Ambitious goals for further improvements; and
- The ability to promote best practice in sustainable development to other cities.

Stockholm is a green city in the literal sense, as almost half its area is given over to parks that are well maintained and highly valued by Stockholmers. The largest of these is Ekoparken, established in 1994 as a conservation area to protect biodiversity. There are many beaches where the water quality is maintained to the highest standards.

Stockholm has been a pioneer in encouraging *sustainable transport*. Every effort is made by the civic authorities to encourage cycling through a very extensive network of cycleways and a programme that allows pass-holders to use a large number of 'borrow and return a bike' sites. Largely as a result, the number of cyclists grew by 70 per cent between 2005 and 2010. Public transport is efficient and is used daily by 80 per cent of the city's residents, so that car use, which is discouraged by a congestion charge, is much lower than in other European capitals.

Stockholm is also notable for the progress it has made in developing a *sustainable hospitality* sector. The city's hotels follow strict environmental guidelines, using district heating based on renewable energy sources and maintaining advanced standards of waste separation, energy-efficient insulation, and measures to conserve water. Scandica, a leading hotel chain in Scandinavia based in Stockholm, has succeeded in reducing CO_2 emissions by 80 per cent, energy consumption by 31 per cent, and water consumption by 22 per cent. Sustainability has become part of company culture, and Stockholm residents are 'very keen on all things eco' (Jezovit, 2010). Hotels and restaurants are committed to using locally-sourced produce, and many have been certified by the Nordic Swan eco-label, which calls for particularly high standards.

The North

Norrland, the sparsely populated northern half of Sweden, includes part of Lapland. Tourism in Swedish Lapland began in the late nineteenth century and is growing in importance because of the demand for ecotourism and adventure holidays. It is one of the largest areas of unspoiled wilderness in Europe, including six national parks. It is Europe's most northerly developed ski area, offering skiers and snowboarders the novelty of practising their sport until late June under the midnight sun. The area is guaranteed heavy snowfalls, with less risk of avalanches than in the Alps. On the other hand, the season does not start until mid-February, due to the short period of winter daylight. Riksgransen, located on the railway linking the mining city of Kiruna to the Norwegian port of Narvik, is the main winter sports resort. It offers extensive trails for ski touring and telemarking, but with a vertical descent of only 400 metres, Riksgransen's slopes have less appeal for downhill skiers. Other winter activities include ice fishing, snow-scooter 'safaris', and sledding with a team of huskies. Tourists also visit to experience the Sami culture, centred on Jukkasjärvi and Jokkmokk, where the old ways continue to flourish, and silver and leather handicrafts are sold.

CASE STUDY 10.3
THE ICE HOTEL CONCEPT

One of Swedish Lapland's major attractions is the Ice Hotel at Jukkasjärvi, promoted as the 'world's largest igloo' (www.icehotel.com). The rooms and furniture, which are unique works of art, are made from 30,000 tons of ice and compacted snow taken each November from the frozen River Torne, and the structure is used until early spring. The temperature inside the hotel is kept at a constant $-7°C$, whereas outside it may fall to −35°C. Bed furnishings are made from reindeer hides and skins, which provide insulation against the cold. Silence is another feature that distinguishes this from conventional hotels. Since 2016, this temporary structure has been complemented by Icehotel 365, a permanent building that remains open year-round.

Discuss the claim that the Ice Hotel is an excellent example of sustainable tourism, given that the concept has been widely copied, not only in Scandinavia, where Alta and Kirkenes in northern Norway offer similar attractions but in countries outside the region. Investigate why the concept appeals to certain types of tourists, including honeymoon couples from Japan.

Finland (Suomi)

Culturally, Finland differs from the other Nordic countries due to its non-Germanic language and the cultural links with Russia to the east, which ruled here for over a century. Hanko, on the Gulf of Finland, was a favourite resort of the Russian aristocracy before the 1917 Revolution. After achieving independence, Finland had to fight two wars with the USSR, resulting in the loss of eastern Karelia. Finland was under the rule of Sweden for much longer, making Swedish the second official language. Finland offers the visitor vast expanses of lakeland blending almost imperceptibly with forest, a unique landscape that inspired the music of Sibelius. The marketing campaigns of the Finnish Tourist Board emphasise unspoiled nature and the absence of air and water pollution, although the majority of the population live in the cities of the south west. Of the total area, no less than 10 per cent is inland water – lakes, marshes, rivers, and rapids – while forests of conifers and birch make up another two-thirds. Eskers, long sinuous ridges of material laid down by glaciers in the last Ice Age, separate the lakes and are a distinctive feature in a landscape which is for the most part lowland. Winters are long and severe, but the Finns are adept at dealing with them; fleets of icebreakers keep open the shipping lanes and a whole range of winter sports, including ice hockey and snowmobile rallies are popular during the cold season.

Although high-tech industries play a leading role in the economy, Finland's prosperity is based on its seemingly inexhaustible forest resources which provide timber, wood pulp, and furs. The exploitation of these in the past has caused concern among environmentalists, but as in Sweden, the timber is now harvested on a sustained yield basis. The forests and lakes are much valued as a recreational resource by city dwellers. Many families in Helsinki own a lakeside cabin as a weekend retreat, usually with a sauna attached. In Finland, the sauna is as much a social institution as a means of relaxation.

The demand for tourism

Domestic and outbound tourism

Domestic tourism accounts for over 50 per cent of overnight stays, and half the population take a holiday of four nights or more away from home. The demand for foreign holidays has increased with growing prosperity. Neighbouring Estonia is a popular destination for Finnish tourists and day visitors, using the ferries that cross the Gulf of Finland between Helsinki and Tallinn.

Inbound tourism

The proximity of Finland to the weak economies of the countries of the former Soviet Union, allied to devaluations of the Finnish mark, meant that the tourism sector suffered from overcapacity in the 1990s. In turn, this led to reductions in prices, and a formerly expensive destination became much more affordable. Foreign tourists accounted for 15 million overnight stays in registered accommodation in 2021. Germany, Britain, and Sweden are the leading markets, while there is a growing demand from the countries of East Asia. Until recently, Russian visitors were numerous, but as a result of worsening relations with the European Union, these are now subject to visa restrictions.

The supply side of tourism

Transport

Geographically, Helsinki is not only a northerly capital but is further east in longitude than Athens, so that distance is an important factor in planning a trip from the United Kingdom. Swedish and Norwegian visitors arrive mainly by sea through the ports of Helsinki, Turku, and Maarianhamina, in preference to the long road journey around the Gulf of Bothnia. Visitors from other West European countries can take the more direct ferry route from Travemünde in north Germany. Air transport has grown steadily in importance, with Helsinki acting as the gateway and Finnair as the national airline. Domestic transport arrangements are excellent, with broad all-weather highways, an improved rail system and a network of domestic air services to over 20 destinations.

Accommodation

Motels and hotels are concentrated in the major cities (Helsinki, Turku, and Tampere) where business travel means they can maintain a high annual bed occupancy rate (up to 75 per cent in Helsinki). Finland can also provide low-density holiday villages, concentrated in the central lakeland area, holiday cottages, farm accommodation, and campsites. Seasonality is high, with the majority of foreign tourists arriving between May and October, peaking in July. In consequence, roughly one-quarter of the accommodation stock is only open for part of the year. A conscious effort has been made to extend the season by developing conference and winter sports tourism. Partly because of Finland's post-Second World War neutrality in world politics, Helsinki has become a major international conference centre, offering facilities such as Finlandia Hall (www.finlandiatalo.fi) and first class hotels.

Organisation

Finland has pursued an aggressive tourism policy, spearheaded by the Ministry of Economic Affairs and Employment. The Finnish Tourist Board (VisitFinland) (www.visitfinland.com), now part of Business Finland, works to develop Finland's travel image and helps Finnish travel companies to internationalise, develop, sell, and market high-quality travel products. Tourism is seen as a means for regional development in the rural areas, and for diversification of Helsinki's economy as well. Business and conference tourism is handled by the Finland Convention Bureau (www.visitfinland.com/fcb).

Tourism resources

Finland's appeal to foreign visitors lies in its uncrowded natural resources, and it has capitalised fully on the growth of ecotourism. We can broadly divide the country for tourism purposes into northern, south-eastern, and coastal regions.

Finnish Lapland

Northern Finland, especially, offers scope for wilderness adventure holidays, both for independent travellers and package tourists. Lake Inari lies well to the north of the Arctic Circle, where the boreal forest finally gives way to tundra. Summer activities include rafting, canoeing, gold panning, and mountain-biking, while in winter, 'reindeer safaris' involving a stay in a Sami encampment, and dog-sled expeditions are on offer. Charter flights are available in December from Britain to Rovaniemi, the main tourist centre, which has been promoted with considerable success as 'the home of Santa Claus' and now has a theme park – 'Santa Park' (https://santaparkarcticworld.com). As a result, Finland has a larger share of winter visitors from the United Kingdom than any other Nordic country. There are a number of ski resorts, notably Yllas and Salla, where skiing 'under the midnight sun' is possible with a season extending into June.

Saimaa Lake District

The best opportunities for outdoor recreation are to be found in the Saimaa Lake District in the south east of the country. The lakes offer no less than 50,000 kilometres of shoreline and are forested down to the waters' edge; not surprisingly, this is a popular area in summer. The main tourist centres are Lapeenranta for summer cruises, and the spa town of Savonlinna which has an international opera festival. The Karelia forest region bordering Russia is culturally distinct, as shown by the many Orthodox churches.

The coasts

Both the southern and western coasts of Finland are characterised by clusters of offshore islands, which provide opportunities for sailing. Seafaring traditions are particularly important in the Aland Islands, which are Swedish speaking and have the status of an autonomous region. For this reason, they are popular with Swedish as well as Finnish holidaymakers, not least for the duty-free shopping available on the ferries. Other destinations include:

- the resort of Hanko
- the Moominland theme park at Nantaali
- Helsinki, which is noted more for its fine modern architecture and cultural attractions than for historic buildings, but along with other cities in Finland is promoting festival tourism
- Turku, a historic university town which was the former capital of Finland.

Iceland

Promoted as 'a land of ice and fire', exposed to the raw forces of nature, Iceland is unique. This large island is a geological 'hot spot' located on one of the major fault lines in the Earth's crust and contains over 200 volcanoes; major eruptions and earthquakes occur on average every five years. Although one-fifth of the country is covered by glaciers, Iceland is by no means as cold as its western neighbour Greenland, thanks to the warming influence of a branch of the Gulf Stream. Nevertheless, its location close to the Arctic Ocean does mean that Iceland has historically been vulnerable to climate change, and the weather is highly unpredictable. The tourist season is short and summer temperatures rarely exceed 20°C, but the air is unpolluted and remarkably clear. Iceland's abundant geothermal resources supply a third of its energy requirements and are harnessed to heat swimming pools, buildings, and greenhouses. One well-known tourist attraction is the so-called 'Blue Lagoon' outside Reykjavik, which is actually an effluent reservoir from a power plant (www.bluelagoon.com). Agriculture is largely restricted to sheep farming, and the landscape is for the most part treeless. Nearly, all the population lives on or near the coast, while the interior is made up of desert-like lava plateaux, rugged mountains, and the vast Vatnajokull ice sheet. Some of the local food specialities, and the traditional farmhouses covered with turf for insulation, are reminders of the harsh conditions that Icelanders had to endure until well into the twentieth century.

Since the Second World War, living standards have greatly improved, the demand for outbound tourism has grown, and Iceland has a substantial deficit on its tourism account.

With few resources other than the dominant fishing industry, Iceland is anxious to encourage inbound tourism. This became imperative following the financial crisis of 2009, with the government and private sector launching a vigorous promotional campaign under the slogan 'Inspired by Iceland'. As a result, the number of foreign visitors increased to over 0.7 million in 2021. The devaluation of the Icelandic krona also made the country a much more affordable destination. Only 10 per cent of visitors come from other Nordic countries, while North America, Germany, and the United Kingdom are more significant as generators of demand.

The bulk of the air transport services from Western Europe and Scandinavia are provided by Icelandair, Scandinavian Airlines, and the low-cost carrier Jet2 (www.jet2.com). The international airport at Keflavik has long been used as a stopover on transatlantic flights, and two centre holidays combining Iceland and New York are becoming a popular option. Access to Iceland by sea is much less convenient and comprises ferry services from

Bergen, the Shetlands, and Esbjerg. There is an extensive domestic air network, which is necessary as Iceland has no railways, and most of the roads are suitable only for four-wheel drive vehicles.

Iceland's tourism appeal lies in its unspoiled natural scenery and the scope this provides for ecotourism, as well as for 'soft' and 'hard' adventure. The demand for extreme sports in the rugged interior is likely to grow as life in post-industrial societies such as Britain becomes safer and more predictable. Pony trekking is a successful product utilising the native breed of horse, which is small and uniquely adapted to the broken volcanic terrain. Skiing facilities on a modest scale are available near Reykjavik and Akureyri. Bird-watching and whale-watching are popular, but Iceland's green credentials have been called into question by the decision in 2003 to resume commercial whaling, and the investment in aluminium smelters.

The most popular tourist attractions are located in the 'Golden Circle' east of Reykjavik, including the Gullfoss waterfall, the Great Geyser, and the Thingvellir National Park, a spectacular natural amphitheatre where Iceland's parliament was held in Viking times. Another cluster of natural attractions in the north of the country includes Lake Myvatn and Dettifoss, Europe's largest waterfall. Man-made attractions are few and found mainly in Reykjavik, but Iceland has made a remarkable contribution to European culture in the form of the Viking sagas, and nowadays in architecture, fashion, and popular music. Unlike most capitals, Reykjavik is a small city and close-knit community characterised by low-rise, brightly painted wooden buildings. It contains 60 per cent of the country's population and most of its stock of hotel accommodation. Thanks to its strategic location, the city has hosted a number of international conferences, including the 2005 G8 Summit.

Given that the resident population of Iceland is only 330,000, tourism has made a significant economic and social impact, with much of the housing stock being rented out as tourist apartments. There is also concern about the impact of off-road vehicles on a fragile environment. Some Icelanders question the benefits of further growth, particularly of cruise arrivals. In response, the Icelandic Tourist Board plan to improve visitor management and spread demand away from Reykjavik and the 'Golden Circle'. In 2019, a new touring route – the Arctic Coast Way – improved access to northern Iceland.

The Faroes

The Faroes consist of 18 inhabited islands in the stormy North Atlantic, halfway between the Shetlands and Iceland. They are a self-governing nation within the Kingdom of Denmark but have opted to stay outside the European Union. As yet, tourism is less important than the fishing industry, which may explain why the Faroese have rejected calls from the world's environmentalists that they should give up their whaling traditions. The excessively wet and windy climate is a major constraint on tourism, but the islands can offer some of Europe's most spectacular cliff scenery and vast colonies of seabirds. The capital, Thórshavn, is accessible by scheduled flights from Copenhagen and by summer ferry services from Esbjerg, Bergen, and Iceland. The islands receive around

111,000 arrivals a year (compared to a resident population of only 50,000). This has led to concerns about damage to the fragile environment. A unique scheme is in operation to close specific attractions to tourists for a few days each year ('closed for maintenance'), using young volunteers from many countries to help carry out conservation work such as maintaining trails and viewpoints.

Summary

- Scandinavia has a degree of political and cultural unity and was historically distinct from the rest of Europe, but the differences between the component countries of the region, for example in landscapes, are as important as the similarities.
- Scandinavia's climate is a push factor, making the region a major generator of holiday tourism.
- The physical legacy of the last Ice Age is still evident in the landscapes, particularly the fjords, glaciers, and mountains of Norway and Iceland.
- The Industrial Revolution came late to the countries of Scandinavia, so most city dwellers have rural roots and a love of nature and the outdoor life.
- The social and economic development that took place in the twentieth century has enabled Scandinavians to have one of the world's highest propensities for travel.
- Outbound tourism is more significant than inbound tourism, such that Scandinavian countries have large deficits on their travel accounts.
- Travel within the region has been facilitated by the abolition of passport controls.
- Although the region has good air transport links with other parts of the world, the majority of international tourists arrive by car, using the ferry services that are available. Inter-city transport services by rail, road, and sea are good and set to improve.
- Accommodation capacity in the short summer season is dominated by the self-catering sector, as serviced accommodation is in short supply.
- The most important of Scandinavia's tourism resources are the uncrowded, unpolluted countryside and coastlines, the spectacular scenery of the mountains, the lakes, and fjords.

Review questions

1. Identify the significant differences and similarities between the countries of Scandinavia in terms of their landscapes, cultural features, and recreation opportunities.
2. Discuss whether the reputation of the Scandinavian countries for 'green' (environmentally-friendly) tourism is always justified. Provide evidence from different countries and cities in the region.
3. Investigate the importance of improved transport links, such as the Fehmarn Belt project, in attracting more foreign tourists to Scandinavia.

Assignment

The distance by air from Kristiansand in the south of Norway to the North Cape is 1,700 kilometres (over 1,000 miles), but considerably longer if you travel by surface transport! A group of students from Leeds University in England are planning to travel from southern Norway to the North Cape by minibus during their summer vacation, returning via Sweden and Denmark.

Draw a linear map of the proposed route for the outward journey from Leeds to the North Cape, indicating ferry links, stopovers at places of interest, and the distances between each. Give a realistic estimate of the time this trip would take.

References and further reading

Jezovit, A. (2010) Sustainable Stockholm, *Leisure Management* 30 (2), 46–49

Löfgren, O. (2002) *On Holiday: A History of Vacationing*, University of California Press, Berkeley

Organization for Economic Co-operation and Development (annual) *Tourism Policy and International Tourism in OECD Member Countries*, OECD, Paris

https://www.unwto.org/tourism-data/unwto-tourism-dashboard

11 The tourism geography of the Benelux Countries

Learning objectives

After reading this chapter, you should be able to:

- Describe the physical regions of the Benelux countries and understand their importance for tourism.
- Understand the relationship between the countries of Benelux and be aware of the linguistic differences in Belgium.
- Appreciate the nature of the demand for both domestic and international tourism in the Netherlands, Belgium, and Luxembourg.

DOI: 10.4324/9781003406853-14

- Be aware of the characteristics of inbound tourism to the Benelux countries.
- Demonstrate knowledge of the tourist regions, resorts, business centres, and tourist attractions of the Netherlands, Belgium, and Luxembourg.

Introduction

Three small countries in Western Europe – Belgium, The Netherlands, and Luxembourg – have far greater economic, cultural, and political significance than we might expect from their size. Historically known as the Low Countries, the Netherlands and most of Belgium are made up of lowland plains adjoining the North Sea, while flat-topped uplands are characteristic of southern Belgium and Luxembourg. Areas of heathland separate the coastal lowlands from the uplands of the Ardennes, which rise to just over 600 metres above sea level. The region has a cool maritime climate similar to that of England. Near the coast, the cloudy weather is discouraging for tourism, with moderate rainfall throughout the year, whereas inland, the maritime influence begins to fade; winters are colder, with enough snow in the Ardennes for skiing, while summers are warmer.

Culturally, the Benelux countries are interesting for their heritage of historic buildings and art treasures, serving as a reminder that the region has played a major role in European history. However, their economic prosperity has frequently led to conflict with powerful neighbours, with the result that after the Second World War, Belgium, the Netherlands, and Luxembourg led the way to European unity with the formation of a customs union. This means that restrictions on movement between the three countries are minimal. With a combined population of 29.5 million, the Benelux states are the most densely populated countries in Europe. Not only does this lead to intense competition for land use, but it also places pressure on the environment to the extent that any proposed tourism developments are very closely scrutinised. The economies of the three countries have grown steadily since the Second World War, giving rise to increasing demands for both domestic and foreign tourism. Expenditure on outbound tourism exceeds the receipts from inbound tourism. Annual holiday entitlement averages five or more weeks, and a typical working week is less than 40 hours.

The Netherlands

The Netherlands is better known as 'Holland', although the name strictly applies to just two of the 11 provinces that united to resist Spanish rule in the sixteenth century. Holland has a strong identity; its landscapes and cultural features are known worldwide. The Dutch contribution to art, with its emphasis on scenes from everyday life, seascapes, and landscapes, has been outstanding. This reflected the tastes of middle-class patrons rather than those of monarchs, aristocrats, and cardinals. Dutch achievements in seamanship, agriculture, and engineering have also been remarkable. Much of the country, especially in the west, is made up of flat *polderlands* reclaimed from the sea. The story of this reclamation and the constant battle against the sea is proudly told in exhibitions and museums, as well as in the many engineering works (such as the Delta Plan), which are tourist attractions in themselves. The countryside is criss-crossed by dykes and canals, although relatively few windmills now survive along with the '*meers*' (lakes), resulting from early drainage schemes. However, much of the east and south of the Netherlands is scenically different, with extensive areas of heath and woodland.

The Netherlands can also offer cultural diversity. For centuries, the Dutch had ruled a major overseas empire, with colonies in the Caribbean, South America, South Africa, and Asia. The influence of their most important former colony – Indonesia – is evident, for example, in the buffet-style *rijstaffel*. More recently, the Netherlands has attracted a greater number of immigrants, in relation to its size, than any other European country. Perhaps because of their maritime outlook and the pressures of living in a small, crowded country, the Dutch have a reputation for both tidiness and tolerance, and it is probably this that has attracted young tourists from all over the world. In contrast, some of the formerly isolated fishing communities around what was once the Zuider Zee (now the ljsselmeer) have retained a strong religious outlook, along with the wearing of the traditional costumes that attract tourists. Contrary to its image, the Netherlands is a major industrial nation, boasting centres of advanced technology such as Eindhoven. High living standards, urban pressures, excellent transport systems, and an unpredictable climate have combined to encourage the development of theme parks, zoos, and innovative ideas in leisure. The best-known examples are the De Efteling Family Leisure Park near Breda (www.efteling.com), and the Center Parcs accommodation concept, which uses advanced technology to create an all-weather leisure environment in an attractive woodland setting (www.centreparcs.com). Tourism is increasingly important to the economy, providing jobs for 6.4 per cent of the workforce.

The demand for tourism

The level of economic development has fuelled the demand for leisure and tourism. Generally, although domestic tourism remains healthy, the Dutch take more foreign holidays, so that the Netherlands has a substantial deficit on its tourism account.

Domestic tourism

Domestic holidays (particularly short trips) and day excursions are an important sector of the Dutch tourism industry, and recreation is becoming a major part of the Dutch lifestyle. Most domestic holidays are concentrated in July and August, leading to congestion in popular destinations. A nationwide programme to stagger holidays was introduced in 1983 to help ease seasonal congestion, while a trend to take more winter holidays may also help combat the problem. Most people taking domestic holidays use the private car and tend to stay in self-catering accommodation (such as 'summerhouses', caravans, campsites, or holiday villages) rather than in hotels. Despite the prevalent use of the private car, the Dutch rarely take touring holidays, preferring instead single-centre stays in their small and crowded country. Business and conference tourism is an important sector of the domestic market. Good-quality conference facilities are dispersed throughout the country in both purpose-built centres and in hotels, motels, and holiday villages. International conferences are seen as a growth area, especially given the Netherlands' central position in Europe.

Outbound tourism

The Dutch have one of the highest holiday propensities in Europe, and the Netherlands is a major generator of international tourists on a world scale. Before the pandemic, outbound trips reached 23 million (2019), but fell to 10.6 million in 2021. The small size of the country encourages day excursions and cross-border trips, often for shopping, while a generous social welfare system enables all levels of society to travel abroad. There is an increasing trend for the Dutch to take winter sun and skiing holidays.

Inbound tourism

The Netherlands received around 20 million tourist arrivals in 2019; as a result of the COVID-19 pandemic, this decreased to 10 million in 2020. The majority of tourists are from other countries in Western Europe, particularly Germany. The international short-break market is important in the Netherlands, with most foreigners only staying for two to three nights on average. However, in contrast to the domestic market, they tend to use serviced accommodation. In consequence, hotels and foreign visitors are concentrated into a few centres; Amsterdam alone accounts for around 50 per cent of the commercial overnight stays in the country.

The supply side of tourism

Transport

Schiphol, Amsterdam's international airport, is not only the major gateway to the country but also a serious competitor to London Heathrow as an inter-continental hub. Likewise, KLM, the national carrier, is one of the world's leading airlines and dominates the industry in the Netherlands (www.klm.com). It serves both domestic passengers and those travelling to neighbouring countries, with an aggressive pricing policy encouraging European short breaks. Transavia is the main tourist charter airline (www.transavia.com). Other international gateways are Maastricht Airport and the ferry terminals at Vlissingen, Europort, and the Hook of Holland, mainly handling passengers from the British Isles. Surface transport arrangements are excellent throughout the Netherlands and also into neighbouring countries, with a comprehensive intercity rail network, including a direct Eurostar service from London to Amsterdam. There is a fully integrated public transport network of buses, trams, and trains. Cycling is encouraged with a nationwide system of dedicated routes.

Accommodation

Accommodation in the Netherlands is dominated by self-catering, with campsites, holiday villages, and a network of 'trekkers' huts' for cyclists and walkers. This sector of the accommodation market is well developed to meet the demand for inexpensive family holidays, but with increased affluence, preferences are switching to hotels and motels. Also, given the extensive water resources of the Netherlands, marinas are important in providing accommodation.

Organisation

The Netherlands Board of Tourism and Conventions (www.nbtc.com) is responsible for the development and marketing of the Netherlands as a destination; it uses 'Holland' as a brand for international recognition. The NBTC is backed by the provincial and local authorities, as well as by the Netherlands Congress Bureau. The government is improving tourist infrastructure by investing in 'bungalow parks', hotels, marinas, and tourist attractions, while attempting to disperse tourism across the country to benefit Dutch residents. Promotional themes focus on the country's waterland setting, its cultural heritage, cities, the seaside, and event attractions such as the 'Floriade' flower show.

Tourism resources

Each of the provinces of the Netherlands has a special appeal for foreign visitors, (except maybe for Flevoland, which consists almost entirely of polders reclaimed from the Zuider Zee in the 1930s). Most foreign tourists are attracted to the western half of the country, particularly to the cities of the **Randstad**. This is a ring of urban development that contains almost half the population of the Netherlands but on just 15 per cent of its land area. Development in the Randstad is, therefore, carefully planned to preserve its 'green heart', an area of attractive countryside inside the ring that includes the world-famous bulbfields between the historic towns of Haarlem and Leyden. The Randstad includes Amsterdam and the following major tourist centres:

- The Hague (Den Haag), the diplomatic capital of the Netherlands. Attractions nearby include Madurodam – 'Holland in miniature' (www.madurodam.nl); the picturesque town of Delft which is famous for its ceramics and associations with Vermeer; and the resort of Scheveningen.
- Utrecht – a university town celebrated for its music festivals and a major centre for trade fairs.
- Rotterdam – Europe's largest port at the mouth of the Rhine. Whereas other Dutch cities tend to promote their heritage attractions, Rotterdam was rebuilt after the Second World War, and tourism focusses on its modern architecture, shopping, and sport.

CASE STUDY 11.1
AMSTERDAM: IMAGES OF A HISTORIC CITY

Amsterdam is the commercial capital of the Netherlands and one of the world's top five tourist centres. Most of the historic area dates from Amsterdam's 'Golden Age' in the seventeenth century, when the city was the hub of a vast trading empire, and there was little expansion or rebuilding in the long period of subsequent decline. The merchant's houses, with their intricate brickwork, stepped gables, and narrow frontage along tree-lined canals, now form one of the world's most picturesque urban landscapes (see Photo 11.1).

Amsterdam boasts an excellent transport infrastructure that includes the famous trams, a network of cycleways, and a metro system that provides improved access to Schiphol Airport. The *Grachtengirdle* – the concentric ring of canals – is now mainly used for sightseeing excursions.

Compared to London or Paris, Amsterdam has few individual buildings that are internationally renowned as iconic tourist attractions. The floating flower market on the Singelgracht and the Anne Frank House – a reminder of the city's important Jewish community – are among those 'must-see' attractions for foreign visitors. Art lovers are attracted to the Rijksmuseum with its paintings by Dutch masters such as Rembrandt and Vermeer (www.rijksmuseum.nl) and the Van Gogh Museum (www.vangoghmuseum.nl). However, the main appeal of Amsterdam lies in its street life, shops, cafes, and entertainment facilities. These include the theatres around the Leidseplein, the smoke-filled *brown bars* of the Jordaen district, and the De Wallen area near the Eastern Docks, which has a long-established sex industry.

Amsterdam faces a number of problems in competing with other European cities as a tourist destination, namely:

- Tourism development is often given a low priority by the city government, whose policies are aimed at maintaining a large resident population in subsidised housing in the historic centre.
- Long-established perceptions of the city relate to a particular period – the seventeenth century – which makes change and diversification difficult.
- Since the 1960s, a very different image – of Amsterdam as a city of drugs and sex – has become deeply ingrained in the popular culture, especially among young tourists. This has led in some areas to an ambience of sleaze, litter, and drug-related crime that provides an unwelcome contrast to the traditional Dutch obsession with cleanliness and public order.
- Amsterdam, with 11 million visitors a year compared to a resident population of 1 million, has a high Tourism Intensity Index and has long experienced 'overtourism'. Part of this is due to the success of Airbnb and its competitors in converting the concept of local residents sharing their homes with visitors into a large scale commercial operation. In response, the city authorities have imposed limits on

holiday letting to a maximum stay of 60 days and a maximum of four visitors staying at a time, while also attempting to disperse tourists to lesser-known areas of the city.

Discussion point

The authorities are also proposing to make the city more liveable for residents by curbing the more undesirable aspects of tourism such as rowdy 'bachelor parties', along with sex tourism, drug taking, and alcohol abuse.

In class, debate ways in which the city authorities and the national tourism organisation could change perceptions of Amsterdam among young people and create greater awareness of its cultural attractions. Could the city be promoted more effectively as a 'family-friendly' destination?

Photo 11.1
Amsterdam

Source: ©istockphoto.com/Waltraud Ingerl

The North Sea coast with its sandy beaches backed by dunes is served by a string of resorts, which attract large numbers of German holidaymakers (mainly from the Ruhr conurbation), as well as the Dutch themselves. The busiest resorts are:

- Zandvoort – noted for its F1 motor racing circuit.
- Noordwijk – renowned for its flower gardens.
- Scheveningen – Holland's best-known seaside resort.

After a long period of decline, Scheveningen was transformed by an ambitious scheme of re-investment in exciting new leisure facilities, including a casino, and it has become a major conference venue, as a well as a classic example of the rejuvenation stage of the tourism area life cycle. Between the resorts, there are conservation areas where further development is strictly prohibited. This is because the dunes, which play a vital part in Holland's coastal defences, are very vulnerable to visitor pressure. To the south lies the province of **Zeeland**, originally a group of islands at the mouth of the Rhine, now connected by the Delta Plan to create an environment suitable for a wide range of water sports. In contrast, the medieval towns of Middelburg and Veere have much to attract the heritage tourist.

In the north east, the province of **Friesland** offers a more tranquil environment of small rural communities where the Frisian language is still spoken. The main attraction here is the Frisian Lake District around the resort of Sneek that offers facilities for boating and sailing. Separated from the mainland by the extensive mudflats of the Wadden Sea, the Frisian Islands such as Texel provide fine beaches, self-catering accommodation, and a number of important nature reserves.

Gelderland in the east of the country is under-populated by Dutch standards, and large expanses of heath and woodland have been designated as the Hoge Veluwe National Park (www.hogeveluwe.nl). The city of Arnhem was the scene of a major battle in the Second World War, and now offers a number of museums and attractions focussing on the region.

The province of **Limburg** in the extreme south is the only part of the Netherlands that can be described as hilly. Partly for this reason, the resort of Valkenburg, with its casinos and golf courses, is very popular among domestic tourists. The attractive city of Maastricht has taken advantage of its location near the borders of three countries to become an important venue for international conferences and cultural events.

Belgium (Belgique-Belgie)

It can be difficult to define the tourism product of Belgium compared to neighbouring France, Germany, and Holland. This is largely because the country is divided in language and culture between the Dutch-speaking Flemings in the north and the French-speaking Walloons in the south. In the past, the Walloons were dominant in politics, society, and the economy, but this has changed with the decline of industry in the Sambre-Meuse Valley. There is also a German-speaking minority in the border districts of Eupen and Malmedy in the east. Tensions between Flemish and French speakers have resulted in a federal compromise, with the division of Belgium into three separate regions – Flanders, Wallonia, and Brussels, which is bilingual. A British motorist driving towards Wallonia from Brugge (Bruges) in Flanders might have difficulty recognising the Flemish signage for Bergen (Mons), Luik (Liège), and Rijsel (Lille) just over the border in France.

Scenically too, the flat farmlands of Flanders and the heaths of the Kempen are quite different in character from the hills and forests of the Ardennes. Moreover, Belgium as an independent nation did not exist until 1830. In the Middle Ages, cities such as Bruges, Ghent, Antwerp, and Liège were to a large extent independent and grew wealthy on the profits of the cloth trade. However, the lack of political unity led to the region being dominated by the great powers of the time, namely Burgundy, France, Spain, and the Austrian Empire. Unlike the Dutch, the Belgians were generally ready to accept foreign rule and remained strongly Roman Catholic in religion after the Reformation in the sixteenth century. This is shown by the abundance of religious art and impressive Baroque architecture in cities such as Brussels.

Although it can offer beaches, attractive waterways, and fine scenery, Belgium's appeal is mainly cultural, in the widest sense. Like the French, the Flemish and Walloons take food and drink seriously, and it is worth noting that the country produces little wine but over 400 different kinds of beer! As this is a predominantly Catholic nation, the tourist can also enjoy many interesting festivals, although by no means all are religious in character. As in the Netherlands, theme parks are popular, attracting large numbers of tourists from neighbouring countries such as France.

The demand for tourism

Belgian travel propensities are very high, with 80 per cent of the population taking a holiday in any one year, and the rise in the number of holidays abroad has outstripped growth in the domestic market.

Domestic tourism

For domestic holidays, the car is the most popular form of transport, and self-catering accommodation (holiday villages, caravans, and camping) is increasingly used, as serviced accommodation declines in popularity. Social tourism is important in the Belgian domestic market. The Ardennes and the coast are the most popular holiday destinations.

Outbound tourism

Belgium is an important generator of international tourists, with the majority of main holidays taken abroad. Most trips are to neighbouring countries, but Italy and Spain are also important destinations. As in the Netherlands, the high number of trips abroad leaves a deficit on the travel account.

Inbound tourism

Experiencing the highest number of deaths per capita in the European Union, Belgium was severely impacted by the COVID-19 pandemic; this was particularly evident in Bruges, which depends heavily on tourism. Prior to the crisis, the performance of Belgium as an international tourist destination had been improving, with over 9 million arrivals in 2019; this fell by two-thirds in 2020, as a result of the pandemic. The majority of foreign visitors are from other European countries, particularly the Netherlands. However, visits from neighbouring countries tend to be short compared to those from the United Kingdom, Asia, or the United States. Business trips are concentrated in Brussels (particularly as it hosts the European Commission) and Antwerp. International conferences are attracted to the seaside resorts of Ostend and Knokke, as well as to new facilities in Liège and Bruges.

The supply side of tourism

Transport

Both external and internal transport links are highly developed. Brussels Airlines is the national flag carrier (www.brusselsairlines.com), and Brussels is the gateway to Belgium for the great majority of air travellers, although the airports at Antwerp, Liège, and Ostend do have some international services. More significant from the viewpoint of price-conscious British tourists are the ferry services to Ostend and Zeebrugge, including a fast catamaran connection. The Channel Tunnel provides competition for the ferry operators and the airlines, so that the Eurostar fast train service from London to Brussels has gained a large share of the lucrative business travel market. The Belgian railway network is less convenient for touring the country, as it is focussed on Brussels. Belgium has almost 1,750 kilometres of motorway, which is an extensive network for such a small country. The environmental impact of this has been considerable, but it does mean that no part of the country is more than three hours drive from the coast, and Belgium's traditional role as 'the crossroads of Europe' has been enhanced.

Accommodation

In the serviced accommodation sector, low occupancy rates mean that few new hotels are being built, and despite government assistance schemes, little investment is occurring in the existing hotel stock. The majority of new developments are taking place in Brussels. Most hotel guests are business travellers, while demand for self-catering accommodation comes from holidaymakers. Campsites, holiday villages, chalets, and apartments are available.

Organisation

The rivalry between political parties representing Flanders and Wallonia in what are often minority governments has meant that tourism policy lacks clear objectives. There are separate promotional commissions for the Flemish and French-speaking regions, effectively creating two NTOs responsible for tourism policy and marketing Belgium abroad:

- VisitFlanders (www.visitflanders.com)
- Wallonie Belgique Tourisme (www.visitwallonia.com)

Tourism resources

Belgium's strength has been the diversity of its cultural resources, and it has been less active than neighbouring countries in protecting the rural environment. The first national park was designated in 2006, not, as you might expect, in the scenic Ardennes, but in the Kempen, an area of heath with derelict quarries and coal mines in the densely populated north east. Belgium's main tourism resources can be categorised as:

- The coastal resorts of Flanders
- The art cities of Flanders
- The Ardennes, which form part of Wallonia

The **North Sea coast**, like that of Holland, is sandy, flat, and backed by dunes. However, flooding has been less of a problem in the past than the silting up of ports such as Bruges, which now lies a considerable distance inland. The coast is only 60 kilometres in length, and it has suffered from over-development and lack of planning, as shown by the ribbon development of high rise apartments and holiday villas. However, the beaches are well maintained, colourful windbreaks provide protection from the constant breezes, while the resorts provide many amenities. A tramway linking all the resorts offers a safe alternative to the car in an area where traffic can reach saturation point in peak season. In addition to domestic tourists, the coast is popular with Germans, while Ostend has long been an established favourite with the British. The resorts differ a good deal in size and character:

- De Panne, with its wide expanse of beach, can offer sand yachting as an activity for the young affluent visitor.
- Zeebrugge caters more for families.
- Ostend and Blankenberge are the busiest resorts, providing a sophisticated holiday product, including casinos.
- Knokke-Heist near the Dutch border is definitely up-market.

The main destinations for foreign tourists are the **art cities**, mostly situated in the Flanders region within easy reach of the coast. These are ideal for short breaks, or as part of an extended tour taking in Northern France and the Rhineland. The heritage of Gothic and Renaissance art and architecture is a reminder, not only of the power of the Church but also the wealth and prestige of the merchant guilds from the fourteenth to the sixteenth centuries. The art cities include:

- Bruges (Brugge in Flemish) is the best-known of the art cities of Flanders (see the case study).
- Ghent, to a greater extent than Bruges, has moved with the times and remained a major centre of commerce, with a university guaranteeing a vibrant nightlife.
- Antwerp on the River Scheldt is not only a historic city but is also a major port, rivalling Brussels in its nightlife and range of museums and exhibition centres. The important diamond industry owes a great deal to the city's close links with Belgium's former colony in the Congo.
- Brussels has the advantage of being the capital, not only of the Flanders region and of the nation, but also, in a sense, of the European Union. Flemish, French – and

increasingly English – are in use throughout the city. The European Commission has spawned a high-spending bureaucracy and encouraged many multi-national corporations to set up their head offices near the centre of power. Brussels boasts one of the finest groups of Baroque buildings in Europe around the Grand Place, and in contrast, the modernistic Atomium (www.atomium.be).

- Leuven (better known as Louvain) is famous for its university.
- Mechelen is an important cathedral city.
- Liège is the most important city in French-speaking Wallonia and is famous for its glass and gun-making industries. It is close to the Ardennes holiday region. Much of the Sambre-Meuse Valley to the west was blighted by heavy industry in the nineteenth century but is now undergoing economic regeneration.
- Namur, in an attractive setting at the confluence of the rivers Meuse and Sambre, is the official capital of Wallonia.
- Durbuy, nestled in the Ardennes, is promoted as 'the world's smallest city'.

CASE STUDY 11.2
BRUGES: THE IMPACT OF TOURISM ON A
HISTORIC CITY

Bruges is one of the best-preserved medieval cities of northern Europe, a UNESCO World Heritage Site that has become a popular short-break destination as well as a long-established attraction on European touring circuits. Unlike modern conurbations, the townscape is on a human scale, a picturesque composition of red-brick gabled buildings, church spires, cobblestone streets, and tranquil canals (see Photo 11.2). Beyond the ring road enclosing the old city lie the modern residential and industrial districts where the majority of the population lives. The historic centre is a relatively small area (430 hectares) containing only 20,000 residents but attracting over 8 million visitors annually. During the height of the tourist season, there are three times as many visitors as residents on a given day. The 2.5 million tourists staying overnight are far outnumbered by day visitors who have a much lower spend per capita but who nevertheless put pressure on the environment.

There are two public spaces at the heart of the old city that symbolise its historic role both as a trading centre and administrative capital:

- The Markt (market place), dominated by the Belfry, the iconic landmark of Bruges.
- The Burg, which is enclosed by the Stadthuis (town hall) and other outstanding examples of Gothic architecture.

Bruges reached the peak of its prosperity in the fifteenth century when it was the leading commercial centre in northern Europe. Most of the important buildings and art treasures date from this period. Later, the city lost wealth and population as the result of the silting of the Zwin estuary and the shift of international trade to Antwerp. By

Photo 11.2
Bruges

Source: Brian Boniface

the early nineteenth century, Bruges appeared to be in terminal decline, with its lace industry providing only a meagre livelihood. The citizens were too poverty-stricken to replace the old buildings, but this proved to be a blessing in disguise. The first tourists, many of them British, were influenced by the Romantic Movement in art and literature and inspired by the heritage (much idealised) of the Middle Ages. They encouraged the civic authorities to impose strict conservation measures, which remain in force today. At the close of the century, Bruges made an economic recovery, establishing a new port at Zeebrugge. However, tourism continued to grow, to become the basis for the city's prosperity.

The tourist attractions of the old city include medieval churches, almshouses, museums appealing to every taste, and art galleries featuring paintings by Van Eyck, Memling, and other Flemish artists. The Historium (see Figure 11.1) is an imaginative multi-media experience that interprets life in the city's 'golden age' for the modern tourist, featuring the studio of Van Eyck, the bustle of the port, and the bathhouses that provided rest and recreation to visiting foreign merchants (www.historium.be). Event attractions are also inspired by the medieval period. The most famous example is the 'Procession of the Holy Blood' – one of Belgium's most colourful religious festivals – that has taken place annually since the time of the Crusades. Apart from

Figure 11.1
The Historium, Bruges

Source: Courtesy of Stijn Boone, General Manager Historium Brugge

the heritage attractions, boat trips on the canals, carriage rides, the city's shops, restaurants, and markets are popular with visitors. Industries largely geared towards tourism include lace-making, chocolate-making (an art form in Belgium), and brewing. In contrast to the historic townscape, the Concertgebouw (Concert Hall) is a modern landmark and an asset to the contemporary culture of the city (www.concertgebouw.be), while the College of Europe is a reminder of the role of Bruges in the development of the European Union.

Bruges attracts visitors from all over the world, but the majority of hotel guests come from neighbouring countries, including Britain. The biggest growth is in the number of day visitors, including cruise passengers arriving from Zeebrugge. Around 15 per cent of staying tourists are business travellers or conference delegates.

Since the 1990s, the policies of the city authorities have aimed to minimise the negative impacts of tourism, which are concentrated in the southern half of the historic city. Traffic measures include a one-way street system, from which cyclists are exempt, and the diversion of cars and coaches to parking areas just outside the city centre. The residents of Bruges support tourism and realise that it is economically necessary, but many also feel that any further growth in visitor numbers would be detrimental to their quality of life.

The **Ardennes** uplands, with their forests, limestone gorges, winding river valleys, and picturesque chateaux, constitute Belgium's scenic resource. In the past, much of the region was remote and sparsely populated. Field sports were historically important, but nowadays, a wide range of activities are catered for such as riding, cycling, rock-climbing, caving, and canoeing. The Ardennes attract large numbers of Dutch tourists as well as domestic visitors, but this popularity has put increasing pressure on its resources. In the areas most accessible to the conurbations of Belgium, the Netherlands, and Germany, the unplanned proliferation of second homes has caused social and environmental problems.

Many of the villages and market towns in the region have become resorts, with Dinant being the most noteworthy, situated in an attractive setting on the River Meuse. Specific tourist attractions include the caves at Han-sur-Lesse (www.grotte-de-han.be), the castle at Bouillon, and Orval Abbey, which is noted for its beer (www.orval.be). Spa, where the mineral-rich springs set the fashion for 'taking the waters' to the rest of Europe, has given its name to similar attractions elsewhere. Like other health resorts, it offers a range of cultural and sporting activities, while the venue for the Belgian Formula 1 Grand Prix motor racing event is located nearby at Francorchamps (www.spa-francorchamps.be).

CASE STUDY 11.3
BATTLEFIELD TOURISM IN BELGIUM

The commemoration of the centenary of the First World War in 2014 brought the world's attention on the battlefields of Flanders, while celebrations for the bicentenary of Waterloo the following year proved controversial. For centuries, Belgium had been called the 'cockpit of Europe' on account of the numerous wars that took place on its soil. Without going too far back in history, we should mention the following:

- The French Revolution and the subsequent Napoleonic wars (1792–1815). This conflict ended with Wellington's victory at the battlefield of Waterloo, just south of Brussels. Ironically, Napoleon is given greater prominence in the heritage attractions commemorating the battle than the victorious British and Prussian armies.
- The First World War (1914–1918), which caused even greater devastation and loss of life. Sites include the cemeteries and war memorials around Mons and Ypres, where the Menin Gate and Flanders Fields exhibition are featured on many tourist itineraries.
- The Ardennes campaign (1944–1945), in the closing stages of the Second World War, is commemorated in the 'Battle of the Bulge' museum at Bastogne, which is of particular interest to American tourists (www.bastognewarmuseum.be).

Luxembourg

With a population of around 600,000, the Grand Duchy of Luxembourg is the smallest member of the European Union. Since 1839, it has been closely linked with Belgium, and the Belgian franc is legal tender. Due to its size (slightly less than Dorset or Rhode Island), inbound tourism is of far greater importance to Luxembourg than it is to Belgium, standing at around 1 million arrivals annually. The impact of tourism is less than you might expect for two reasons; the length of stay is short, and many visitors are business travellers to Luxembourg City. Others are transit passengers taking advantage of low-cost international flights from Luxembourg Airport, while most holidaymakers tend to be campers from the neighbouring conurbations in France, Belgium, the Netherlands, and Germany. Tourism has a major impact on the economy and represents Luxembourg's third foreign currency earner after financial services (banking and insurance) and steel exports.

Most of Luxembourg's accommodation capacity is located on campsites. Although more nights are spent in campsites than in hotels, it is the latter which are most important in terms of tourist spending. However, this is affected by the nature of the business travel market, which can afford the high tariffs.

Tourism is the responsibility of the National Tourist Office, which is part of the Ministry of Economy. It co-ordinates the activities of four local tourist offices, provides support to hospitality establishments and non-profit organisations, and develops certification schemes applicable to the tourism industry. The promotion of conference tourism is given a high priority; helped by the fact that the country has three official languages, and its people are proficient linguists and supporters of European co-operation.

Luxembourg's tourist appeal lies in its capital city and attractive countryside:

- **Luxembourg City** is an important financial centre, as well as hosting the Secretariat of the European Parliament and other EU organisations. The city has a picturesque setting among hills and valleys linked by viaducts. Although most of the massive fortifications were torn down and replaced by boulevards long ago, enough still remains to explain why Luxembourg was once called 'the Gibraltar of the North'.
- The country's other attractions are primarily located in the Oesling region in the north, which forms part of the Ardennes. They include Vianden, a noted beauty spot with an impressive castle; Clervaux, famous for its abbey; and Echternach, a pilgrimage centre, which is of unique interest for its Whitsun dancing processions (www.visitechternach.lu). The Germano-Luxembourg Nature Park is an outstanding example of international co-operation in conservation (https://www.coe.int). The Bon Pays/Gutland region in the south of the country is less impressive scenically, but it does contain the spa town of Mondorf-les-Bains, which has been rejuvenated to meet contemporary leisure demands.

Summary

- Physically, the Benelux countries comprise contrasting regions – the lowlands of the coast and the uplands of the Ardennes.
- The Benelux countries established a customs union in 1947 and stand as an outstanding example of close European integration and co-operation.
- Demand for tourism and recreation is high, but this does place pressures on the environments of these small, densely populated countries.
- In each country, demand for overseas travel is high, resulting in a deficit on their travel accounts.
- The majority of foreign tourists originate from other countries of Western Europe.
- Transport facilities are comprehensive, and the region's position in Europe attracts many transit passengers.
- Accommodation provision is dominated by self-catering capacity, particularly campsites, and holiday villages.
- There are three main areas of tourist attraction. First, the facilities and cultural resources of the historic towns and cities attract business and holiday tourists alike; second, the resorts of the North Sea coast are major holiday and day-trip centres; and third, the uplands and countryside constitute important holiday destinations for campers.

Assignment

This region of Europe contains many small historic towns and cities. Devise a sustainable tourism plan for the centre of one of these towns to ensure that the visitor experience is enhanced, and that local residents can continue to go about their daily lives.

Further reading

Organization for Economic Co-operation and Development (annual) *Tourism Policy and International Tourism in OECD Member Countries*, OECD, Paris
https://www.unwto.org/tourism-data/unwto-tourism-dashboard

The tourism geography of Germany, Austria, and Switzerland

Learning resources

After reading this chapter, you should be able to:

- Describe the major physical regions and climate of Germany, Austria, and Switzerland and understand their importance for tourism.
- Understand the nature of economies and society in the three countries and their significance for tourism demand.
- Outline the major features of demand for domestic and international travel in Germany, Austria, and Switzerland.

DOI: 10.4324/9781003406853-15

- Describe the major features of the tourism industries in all three countries, including transport, accommodation, and organisation.
- Demonstrate knowledge of the tourist regions, resorts, business centres, and tourist attractions in all three countries.

Introduction

Germany, Austria, and Switzerland occupy a key position in the centre of Europe. Germany and Austria have played pivotal roles in European history and share a similar heritage through their association in the Holy Roman Empire, which for centuries was ruled by an Austrian dynasty, the Habsburgs. Switzerland remained on the sidelines, a small country with a strategic location astride the major passes over the Alps. German is the dominant language throughout the region, but in Switzerland French, Italian and Romansch are also official languages. As a result of large-scale immigration from Southern and Eastern Europe, there is a trend towards greater cultural diversity. In the cities of Austria and Germany, the Turkish communities are often seen as a problem rather than as an opportunity, and these two countries have opposed the admission of Turkey to the European Union.

Apart from Germany's North Sea and Baltic coasts, the area under consideration in this chapter is landlocked. Three major physical regions can be identified:

1. The North German Plain and the coast are of relatively limited importance for international tourism.
2. The Central Uplands, which include areas such as the Rhineland and the Harz Mountains in Germany, the Mittelland plateau in Switzerland, and the Danube Valley in Austria, are more significant.
3. The mountainous Alpine region is of major importance for international tourism. It includes most of Austria, half of Switzerland, and the southernmost part of Bavaria in Germany.

With the exception of the North Sea coast, the region has a continental climate. Winters get colder not only as we travel further east but also as a result of altitude. In the mountains, the climate is bracing with clean air and brilliant sunshine, but the weather varies with aspect and altitude, and fogs are frequent in some valleys during the winter. The cold winters bring the snow which made possible the development of winter sports, although at low altitudes, the reliability of snow is threatened by global warming. In contrast, the resorts on the shores of the more southerly lakes bask in almost Mediterranean temperatures. The *Föhn* wind frequently blows down some of the south-facing valleys of the Alps, bringing unseasonal warmth and excessive dryness during the winter months.

Despite their very different historical backgrounds, all three countries are federal republics, with considerable devolution of powers (including tourism responsibilities) to the *länder* (states) in Germany, provinces in Austria, and cantons in Switzerland. The three countries combined have a population of around 100 million, which is concentrated in major urban areas such as the Rühr conurbation, Berlin, Vienna, and Zurich.

The economies of the three countries are highly developed and industrialised with a high standard of living and a strong interest in 'green' issues. This is reflected in the widespread demand for environmentally sound tourism. Both Germany and Austria are members of the European Union, while Switzerland – in line with its historic tradition of neutrality – has no political affiliation (although it has signed the Schengen Treaty). A central geographic location and good communications mean that levels of outbound tourism are high in all three countries. However, high prices do limit the number of inbound tourists. In Germany and Switzerland, the annual holiday entitlement is four weeks or more, and in Austria entitlement is five or more weeks. In Austria, there is a 35–40-hour working week, in Germany, 35–37 hours is the norm, but in Switzerland, working hours are relatively high and attempts are being made to reduce them.

Event attractions play an important role in tourism in all three countries, notably music festivals and sport. For example, Austria and Switzerland jointly hosted the Euro 2008 football championship, and in 2023, Germany hosted the Invictus Games.

Germany

Unlike Austria or Switzerland, Germany lacks a well-defined tourism image and is often regarded as a destination for business rather than holiday travel. This is not surprising as Germany is Europe's leading industrial nation and its largest economy. However, the tourism sector generates 4.5 per cent of Germany's GDP. The country is well-endowed with a variety of beautiful scenery and cultural attractions, particularly those based on music and the applied arts and sciences.

The Cold War political division of Germany between East and West has tended to obscure the long-standing physical and cultural differences between the Protestant northern part of the country and the predominantly Catholic south and west. Strong regional identities are also a reminder that for most of its history, Germany was a patchwork of kingdoms, duchies, prince-bishoprics, and free cities owing nominal allegiance to the Holy Roman Emperor. Many of the rulers of these states were generous patrons to artists and musicians. As a result, Berlin, which became the capital of the new united Germany in 1871, has strong rivals in several other major cities, which act as world-class cultural and business centres.

The development of tourism in Germany has also been complicated by the fact that from 1945 to 1990 the country was divided, along with the city of Berlin. The two Germanies that resulted from this division had widely differing political and economic structures:

- West Germany, officially known as the Federal Republic of Germany (BRD), prospered under a democratic style of government and a free market economy.
- East Germany, officially called the German Democratic Republic (DDR), was compelled by its Soviet masters to adopt Communism and a centralised command

economy. Tourist enterprises such as hotels were nationalised, and the whole industry was subject to state control. East Germans were discouraged from visiting other
countries, with the exception of those in the Eastern bloc, such as Romania and Hungary. Visits from West Germans were virtually prohibited, while tourism from other
Western countries was subject to many restrictions.

The structure changed rapidly after 1989, with the removal of the Berlin Wall and the
reunification of Germany a year later. A united Germany could offer a range of new tourism products and domestic markets for tourism. For example, there has been a flood of
West German tourists into East Germany, attracted by the low cost of accommodation.
Yet East Germans have a lower propensity than West Germans to travel abroad, due to
the continuing legacy of half a century of repression and a lack of financial resources.
The economy of the former DDR was badly depressed because it was based on industries
that could not compete with foreign products without the protection of state subsidies, a
pattern repeated in other countries of the former Eastern bloc. The cost of reunification
also contributed to the downturn in the German economy as a whole after the late 1990s.
The former West Germany comprises 80 per cent of the population and dominates both
tourism supply and demand in the new Germany. Three decades after reunification, in
2021 the five länder corresponding to the former DDR accounted for only 8 per cent of
overnight stays by foreign visitors to Germany.

Unlike many countries that have experienced dictatorial regimes, Germany has not
sought to cover up or deny the crimes perpetrated by the National Socialists between
1933 and 1945, and the abuses of human rights later committed by the *Stasi* (secret police) in the Communist DDR. A number of cities, notably Berlin, Munich, and Nuremberg, have museums and exhibitions confronting these issues and the phenomenon of
'dark tourism' with sensitivity.

The demand for tourism

Domestic tourism

The Germans have been among the world's greatest spenders on travel and tourism for
many years, and they attach great significance to their annual holiday, even in times
of recession. Generous holiday entitlement means that travel frequencies are high, and
holiday propensities reach almost 75 per cent, though this does vary according to age,
socio-economic status, and place of residence. The domestic market accounts for 60 per
cent of overnight stays and so dominates the industry, and one in three Germans take a
holiday within their own country. Domestic holidays are concentrated seasonally in the
summer months and geographically in the south of Germany and on the coast. Business
travel is important in the domestic market.

Germans are very health-conscious, and over 200 spa resorts, many based on abundant mineral springs, have developed to meet this demand, some of which were internationally famous in the nineteenth century as resorts for the European elite. These now
cater for a wide cross-section of the population and have been supported by generous

state-sponsored health insurance schemes. Most spas are located in the uplands of the Mittelgebirge in the central part of the country. Germans have long been renowned for 'wanderlust', here with its original meaning of 'love of walking', and the country is well provided with a network of waymarked hiking and cycling trails. Germany also initiated the youth hostel movement in the early 1900s. By way of contrast, since the 1980s, there has been considerable investment in theme parks, such as Phantasialand near Cologne (www.phantasialand.de), and visitor attractions focussing on science and technology, for example, the Bremen Space Centre and those associated with the Volkswagen assembly plant.at Wolfsburg.

Outbound tourism

Germany follows China and the United States as one the world's leading generators of international tourism. The majority of trips are to Germany's neighbours (particularly Austria) and to Mediterranean countries (particularly Italy and Spain). Many trips are package tours sold by the highly organised travel industry that has grown up to meet the demand for holidays abroad. Spain is by far the most important package holiday destination, but whereas Germans take roughly the same number of holidays in Spain as the British, they are much more likely to take a second holiday in their own country. Long-haul travel is also important to a wide range of destinations, the most popular being the United States.

The COVID-19 pandemic had a major impact, resulting in the loss of 440,000 jobs in the travel and tourism industry. However, according to the WTTC, the situation could have been far worse if it had not been for the federal government's scheme, offering short-term work allowances to businesses and employees.

Inbound tourism

The high volume of travel abroad keeps Germany's travel account in considerable deficit, even though in 2021, there were around 31 million overnight stays by foreign visitors. The main countries of origin are Germany's neighbours, and there is a significant volume of daily cross-border traffic. The United States accounts for 7 per cent of overnight stays, followed by China, Japan, and Australia in the long-haul market. Generally, average lengths of stay are short, at around two days. Business travel, including visits to trade fairs and exhibitions, is important in the inbound market but is now exceeded by the volume of holiday traffic from abroad. Sightseeing and touring are the main reasons given for visiting Germany as a holiday destination. There is a pronounced peaking of demand in July and August, although the Christmas markets for which Germany is famous attract significant numbers of foreign visitors in the Advent season.

Germany is Europe's leading conference destination and is second only to the United States in the number of meetings held. Thanks to the connections with industry and government encouragement in the past, Germany is noted for its world-class venues for motor racing. A number of international sports events have been instrumental in raising the country's international image and tourism profile, notably the Olympic Games hosted by Berlin in 1936 and Munich in 1972, and the FIFA World Cup in 2006.

CASE STUDY 12.1
TRADE FAIRS IN GERMANY

Germany accounts for a third of the European demand for trade fairs and exhibitions. As for supply, the country outstrips Italy, France, and the United Kingdom in the number of large exhibition centres. Every major town has its *messe* (exhibition ground), financially supported by local and state governments, rather than operated as a profit-making business by the private sector. Exhibitors (who are primarily there to make a sale) and visitors (who are mainly attending for work-related reasons) create a high level of demand for accommodation, catering and travel services, and thus benefit the local economy. Major venues for international trade fairs include Berlin and the following cities:

- Hanover, hosting *Deutsches Messe*, reputedly the world's largest trade fair organiser
- Cologne (Köln), noted for the biennial exhibition on photography – Photokina (www.photokina.com)
- Düsseldorf, noted for its fashion shows
- Essen, for cars
- Frankfurt, for books
- Nuremberg, the largest international fair for toys and games
- Leipzig, where two annual fairs were held as far back as medieval times. After the Second World War, these served as the showpiece for the industrial achievements of the DDR and the Eastern bloc countries generally.

Germany now faces increasing competition in this sector of business tourism and a possible over-supply of exhibition capacity. Financial constraints are forcing local and state governments to contract out some services to the private sector, and there is a trend towards greater diversification, to make more efficient use of exhibition floor space throughout the year.

The International Tourismus-Börse (ITB) hosted by Berlin is the world's largest travel trade show (https://www.itb-berlin.com). It is normally a three-day event and attracts over 20,000 participants, showcasing most of the world's destinations. Due to the COVID-19 pandemic, the show was cancelled in 2020, and for the next two years, it took place as a virtual event on-line. How does the ITB compare with similar events in Britain and other counties?

The supply side of tourism

Accommodation

Domestic business travellers and most foreign visitors are accommodated in hostels in towns and cities. Hotels, guest houses, and inns account for two-thirds of the available bed spaces. Demand for self-catering accommodation exceeds supply, as does that for most types of accommodation in the peak season. There is a concentration of hotels and guesthouses serving the holiday market in Bavaria and Baden-Württemburg, and a shortage of accommodation throughout most of the former DDR, although many hotel chains are now developing properties in this part of Germany. Holiday parks – groups of chalets around a pool and other leisure facilities – are popular with German families.

Transport

Some of the most significant innovations in transport have been made in Germany. These include the internal combustion engine, made commercially viable by Benz and Daimler in 1886, the Zeppelin airship, the oldest monorail system still in use (in Wuppertal), the *autobahn,* and the electrically powered VTOL aircraft currently planned for commercial operation.

The car is the most important form of tourist transport. The road network is excellent, including autobahns (motorways without an imposed speed limit), and also specially designed scenic routes for visitors. A major problem is seasonal congestion both on the access routes and in the popular holiday areas. Rail travel is the second-most popular form of travel, with promotional fares and inclusive package holidays available. The InterCity express (ICE) is a high-speed train that connects all major cities in Germany with speeds up to 300 kilometres/hour. The larger cities have a fully integrated public transport system of trams, buses, 'U' Bahn (underground), and 'S Bahn' (fast suburban trains). Air travel is served by ten international airports, all well-connected by rail with the urban areas they serve. The national carrier, Lufthansa (www.lufthansa.com), is based at the main gateway and hub at Frankfurt. Tourists arriving by sea can use ferries from Harwich to Hamburg, from Trelleborg in Sweden to Sassnitz, and from Roby Havn in Denmark to Puttgarten. Cruises are popular on the Rhine and the other major rivers, the canals that link these natural waterways, and on the Bodensee (Lake Constance).

Organisation

Tourism in Germany has historically lacked representation at senior levels in the federal government. The Federal Ministry for Economic Affairs and Energy holds the leading responsibility for tourism and co-ordinates across government. However, tourism responsibilities are largely in the hands of the 16 state governments, which have considerable independence to promote and develop tourism, leading to considerable fragmentation. There is, for example, no national tourism policy, as tourism is low on the list of government economic priorities. The little federal aid available for the industry is mainly used to boost accommodation in less-developed areas and stimulate farm tourism. The states provide funds for both upgrading accommodation and season-extension developments (such as indoor swimming pools) in resorts. The German National Tourist Board (DZT) is the major marketing agency for Germany, responsible for both domestic and international promotion. It is mainly financed by the federal government and promotes the brand 'Destination Germany'.

Tourism resources

Each of the länder has a strong historical identity and range of attractions, although it must be noted that the lowland landscapes of Schleswig-Holstein and the industrialised Saarland suffer in comparison with the mountains of Bavaria. This is reflected in the

267

numbers of overnight stays by foreign tourists; the first two states account for 2.9 and 0.6 per cent, respectively, of the total, compared to Bavaria, which clearly leads with 22.0 per cent of all overnight stays.

Forests cover almost a third of Germany, and as a managed resource, they are an important part of its national image and tourism appeal. The country is a leader in green issues, and there are 14 national parks protecting a great diversity of landscapes. The many small historic towns with their half-timbered buildings in a variety of styles are also an important cultural resource. Germany's cities have world-class facilities for music and the performing arts. These are becoming more prominent for international tourism, as the generous state subsidies to cultural institutions were scaled down owing to the stagnation of the economy in the 1990s.

Northern Germany

This region includes the states of Schleswig-Holstein, Lower Saxony, Hamburg, and Bremen, along with Mecklenburg-West Pomerania in the former DDR. This part of Germany accounts for just 14 per cent of overnight stays by foreign tourists, and the main tourist attractions are found in the historic cities or on the coast. Inland, there are large areas of forest, heath, and lakes – such as those of Holstein and Mecklenburg. The rivers of the region are connected by the valleys of glacial origin known as *urstromtaler*, trending from east to west, that have been utilised by a number of canals. These features offer some variety in the otherwise low-key landscapes of the North European Plain and provide opportunities for activities such as canoeing.

The North Sea is colder and rougher than the Baltic, and the coast is low-lying, with large areas of mudflats exposed at low tide. However, the North Frisian Islands have fine beaches, the most popular being those of Sylt, which is linked to the mainland by a causeway. The resort of Westerland attracts fashionable holidaymakers as well as German families, and it was here that naturism – known in Germany as *freikorpskultur* (FKK) – first appeared on the holiday scene in the 1920s. The tideless Baltic coast is scenically more attractive, with sandpits enclosing extensive lagoons. With the exception of Kiel, a major yachting centre, and Travemünde, most of the Baltic resorts, were situated in the former DDR. These flourished serving a captive domestic market, but their outdated facilities and substandard service practices left them ill-equipped to face the competition following German reunification and the introduction of a free market economy. They are now being 'rediscovered' by West German holidaymakers, who are attracted by the lack of commercialisation, ironically caused by decades of neglect under Communism.

The island of Rügen, with its chalk cliffs, deeply indented coastline, beaches, and beautiful countryside attracted Romantic artists such as Casper Friedrich and the German elite in the nineteenth century. Here, the National Socialist regime developed the resort of Prora as a regimented form of 'tourism for the people' in the 1930s as part of the 'Strength through Joy' movement. After 1945, the East German government, with a different ideology but adopting a similar policy, used these facilities for the rest and recreation of selected workers and the Communist Party elite. Resorts on the mainland near the port of Rostock include Heiligedamm and Warnemünde. Heligedamm was the first resort in Germany to adopt the English fashion of sea bathing; its fashionable reputation has been revived in recent years, and in 2007 it was chosen as the location for the G8 Summit meeting. A characteristic of the beach at many German resorts is the proliferation of *strandkörbe*, a type of mini-cabin that can be easily moved to take advantage of the sun while providing protection from the wind.

Many of the cultural attractions of northern Germany date back to the Middle Ages, when the powerful Hanseatic League of merchants from Hamburg and other cities dominated trade throughout northern Europe. This heritage is exploited for tourism in the picturesque port of Lübeck, with its well-preserved city walls and gates, church spires and red-brick merchants' houses. Similar examples, but less commercialised, can be found in Rostock, Wismar, and Stralsund.

The major cities of the region – Hamburg, Bremen, and Hanover – are primarily business centres with tourism playing a secondary role. Bremerhaven, on the Weser estuary, played an important role in the large-scale emigration of Germans for political and economic reasons to North America in the nineteenth century. This was also true of Hamburg, which deserves special mention for the following reasons:

- It is one of Europe's major ports, with worldwide trading connections and a special economic role in relation to Eastern Europe.
- It is a major cultural centre, with publishing as one of its major industries.
- The picturesque setting of the old city, between the harbour and the Alster Lakes, appeals to visitors.
- The vitality of its nightlife, centred on the Saint Pauli district and the notorious Reeperbahn.

Central Germany

To the south of the North German Plain rise the forested uplands of the Mittelgebirge. For the most part, they are not high or rugged enough to be regarded as mountains, but they are ideal hiking country. The towns of the state of Hesse and the Weser Valley are rich in legendary associations, notable examples being Hamelin and the castle at Sababurg immortalised by the brothers Jakob and Wilhelm Grimm. The German Tourist Office has promoted a tourist route from Bremen south to Marburg based on these resources as the 'Fairy-Tale Road'.

To the east, the Harz Mountains are renowned for their beautiful scenery and picturesque medieval towns such as Goslar and Quedlinburg. During the Cold War division of Germany, this region was bisected by the Iron Curtain, which severely disrupted all communications to the detriment of its tourism industry. The minefields and other barriers have long gone, replaced by nature reserves and hiking trails.

The Rhineland

This part of Germany has long been popular with foreign visitors. North Rhine-Westphalia and Rhine-Palatinate account for 20 per cent of international tourist overnights. Here, people tend to be more pleasure-loving, and *Fasching* (Carnival) is an important festive event in many of the towns and cities. The Rhine has been a major commercial artery since Roman times, and the cities on its banks featured prominently on the Grand Tour. From about 1,800 the most picturesque stretch of the river, between Bingen and Koblenz, became a focus of the Romantic Movement in art, literature, and music, and a tourist attraction in itself. In the Rhine Gorge, the river, followed closely by the autobahn and railway, meanders between terraced vineyards on south-facing slopes, and steep crags crowned by the picturesque castles that feature prominently in German legend. The northern Rhineland is less attractive as it includes the heavily industrialised Rühr Valley conurbation. This area is undergoing regeneration, with the transformation of polluting factories and mines into heritage museums, theme parks, and leisure centres, and much has been done to 'green' the landscape. There is also scenic countryside within easy reach, notably in the Sauerland, which is promoted internationally by a tourist association. The many tourist centres in the Rhine Valley include the following:

- Rŭdesheim hosts the most popular of the wine festivals in the region.
- Düsseldorf is the commercial hub of the region and is a 'must' for the serious shopper as well as business travellers.
- Cologne is one of the several cities in the Rhineland that have Roman origins. It boasts Germany's most famous cathedral.
- Bonn was a small university town, famous as the birthplace of Beethoven, when it was chosen as the capital of the new Federal Republic in 1949. Having lost its political functions after reunification, it has retained its cultural attractions.
- Aachen (known to the French as Aix la Chapelle) lies close to the border with Belgium and the Netherlands and is an example of international city promotion, in partnership with Liège and Maastricht. The city is historically important for its associations with Charlemagne, the first Holy Roman Emperor, who is widely regarded as a champion of Christendom and a promoter of European unity. The chapel containing his tomb became a focus of pilgrimage.
- Trier in the wine-producing Moselle Valley is rich in historical monuments dating back to the fourth century when it was an imperial capital, strategically located near the Rhine frontier of the Roman Empire.
- Other important historic cities in the Rhine Valley are Mainz, Wörms and Speyer, similarly located near vineyards.
- In contrast, Frankfurt on the River Main emphasises its modern role as one of the world's great financial centres rather than any particular heritage attractions. Its airport is one of the world's busiest, and it lies at the 'crossroads' of the autobahn network.

Southern Germany

South Germany comprises the states of Baden-Württemberg and Bavaria (Bayern), which account for 38 per cent of overnight stays by foreign visitors. This region vies with Italy in its wealth of Baroque churches, monasteries, and palaces. Baden-Baden is Germany's most famous spa resort, while the old university town of Heidelberg is a 'must' on the international tourist circuit. In contrast, Stuttgart is the centre of the German motor vehicle industry and the Mercedes-Benz Museum is a popular visitor attraction.

The **Black Forest**, a scenic area of pine-covered uplands, waterfalls, and picturesque villages rising to the east of the Rhine, offers ideal opportunities for skiing in winter and hiking in summer, with the world's oldest long-distance waymarked trail – the *Westweg*. The region is also famous for its folklore and clock-making industry, carried on in small towns such as Triberg.

Bavaria is the most popular state with domestic and foreign tourists, since it can offer a great variety of scenery and is noted for its folklore. A shortlist of specific attractions in Bavaria would include the following:

- Munich, the capital of Bavaria, is second only to Berlin as the city most visited by foreign tourists. It has a wealth of Renaissance architecture and is a favourite with art and music lovers. The annual *Oktoberfest* attracts around 6 million people from all over the world to consume staggering amounts of beer and food (https://www.oktoberfest.de).
- Nuremberg, the birthplace of the painter Albrecht Dürer, is another major cultural centre, containing the German National Museum (www.gnm.de).
- The '**Romantic Road**', Germany's best-known tourist route linking a number of well-preserved medieval towns, including Würzburg, Bamberg, and Rothenburg.
- Regensburg on the Danube – onetime capital of the Holy Roman Empire.
- Bayreuth, celebrated for the annual Wagner music festival (www.bayreuther-festspiele.de).

The Bavarian Alps

Although not as high or as extensive as the mountains in Austria and Switzerland, the Bavarian Alps offer spectacular lake and mountain scenery. Neuschwanstein is the best known of the romantic castles built by Wagner's patron, King Ludwig II of Bavaria (https://www.neuschwanstein.de). The resort of Garmisch-Partenkirchen is Germany's major winter sports centre.

CASE STUDY 12.2
THE OBERAMMERGAU PASSION PLAY

The small town of Oberammergau in the foothills of the Bavarian Alps is famous for its community involvement in a religious drama held every ten years. Passion plays depict the events leading to the Crucifixion and are a genre that originated in the 'miracle plays' of pre-Reformation Europe, and which have been adapted for modern film audiences. The Oberammergau Play originated in 1634 at the height of the Thirty Years War, a time when Germany was devastated by foreign armies and bubonic plague. It is not the oldest Passion Play, but it is certainly the largest, with performances running from May to October and involving over 2,000 participants. These are all established members of the community who provide not only the cast of players, choristers, and musicians but also the costumiers and stage designers. The event attracts around half a million visitors from all over the world, with performances taking place in a purpose-built auditorium holding 4,700 spectators. Over the decades, there has been a tendency towards greater professionalism, but also commercialisation, with the sale of kitsch souvenirs.

Between events, Oberammergau continues to be a major tourist destination, thanks to its appealing frescoed buildings, traditional handicrafts such as woodcarving, and a variety of attractions in the surrounding area.

Discussion point

1. Compare the Oberammergau Play with the religious events that take place during Holy Week in other Catholic countries such as Spain, for example, the *Passió* in the Catalan village of Olesa de Montserrat.
2. Explain why the Oberammergau Play has attracted controversy.

Eastern Germany

Prior to 1990, this region, consisting of the states of Brandenburg, Berlin, Saxony, Saxony-Anhalt, and Thuringia, formed the bulk of the DDR. It is crossed by the River Elbe, and cruises are now available from Hamburg to the scenic area known as the 'Saxon Switzerland' near the border with the Czech Republic. Unfortunately, much of Saxony south of the Elbe has suffered severe pollution from obsolescent heavy industrial plant using low-grade coal. Investment on a vast scale was necessary to bring environmental standards up to the level of those in the former West Germany. In contrast, the state of Thuringia is a forested upland region and has more tourist appeal Eastern Germany offers the visitor a number of towns and cities that have played an important role in German history. These include the following:

*   Weimar is associated with the German Enlightenment, including Göethe, Germany's greatest poet, and the composer Franz Liszt.
*   Eisenach and Wittenburg, where Martin Luther initiated the Protestant Reformation.
*   Leipzig, the leading commercial centre of Saxony, associated with the composer J.S. Bach.
*   Dresden, the capital of Saxony and a beautiful Baroque city with important art collections that was destroyed by Allied bombing in 1945 and now substantially restored. (Dresden porcelain is actually made 30 kilometres away in the town of Meissen.)

Berlin exerts a special fascination largely because of its place in twentieth century history. It accounts for 13 per cent of overnight stays by foreign visitors, making it second only to Bavaria as a destination. The city first became important in the eighteenth century under Frederick the Great as the capital of Prussia, the most militaristic of the German states. In the era of the Weimar Republic (1919–1933), Berlin was notorious for its avant-garde cabarets, which ended when Hitler came to power. During the Cold War era, the Berlin Wall and 'Checkpoint Charlie' epitomised the confrontation between NATO and the Soviet Union. West Berlin was a cosmopolitan 'island' of democracy and free enterprise surrounded by Communist East Germany, (although it was heavily subsidised by the federal government in Bonn), whereas East Berlin was the capital of the DDR. West Berlin's shopping and nightlife contrasted with the greyness and restrictions of life in East Germany. Shortly after the fall of the Berlin Wall, the administrative functions of a re-united Germany gradually moved from Bonn to Berlin, a process symbolised by the opening of the new *Reichstag* (Parliament Building) in 1998, and Berlin became the focus of one of the world's greatest urban regeneration projects. This was controversial, since it raised questions as to which aspects of the city's heritage should be restored or preserved. For example,

- Of Hitler's Chancellery and Bunker no trace survives, to avoid the possibility of them becoming neo-Nazi shrines. In contrast, a museum to the Jewish Holocaust was opened in the locality.
- In 2002, the Reichstag voted to demolish the 'Palace of the People' (the DDR parliament), which had been built on the site of the Stadtschloss, the former palace of Kaiser Wilhelm II and the kings of Prussia. The palace has now been reconstructed in a new guise as the Humboldt Forum, a centre for the arts.

Berlin offers the cultural tourist a number of world-class museums and music venues. While Prussia as an entity disappeared after the Second World War, the legacy of Frederick the Great includes the Brandenburg Gate, the elegant avenue known as the *Unter den Linden* and the royal palaces at Charlottenburg and Potsdam. What remains of the famous Wall is now a focus for street artists and Berlin attracts young visitors worldwide as a centre for fashion, nightlife, and the performing arts. Berlin is also a green city, with a great deal of recreational space in the form of parkland, woods, lakes, and canals.

Austria

Austria is a small country with an outsize capital, due to the historical fact that Vienna ruled the vast Hapsburg Empire until its break-up in 1918. The lavishly decorated Baroque churches, monasteries, and palaces are part of that heritage. Austrian composers – notably the Strauss family, Mozart, Haydn, Schubert, and Mahler – made an immense contribution to the world of music and are now celebrated through music festivals. But for most people, the abiding image of Austria is its scenic countryside of lakes and mountains,

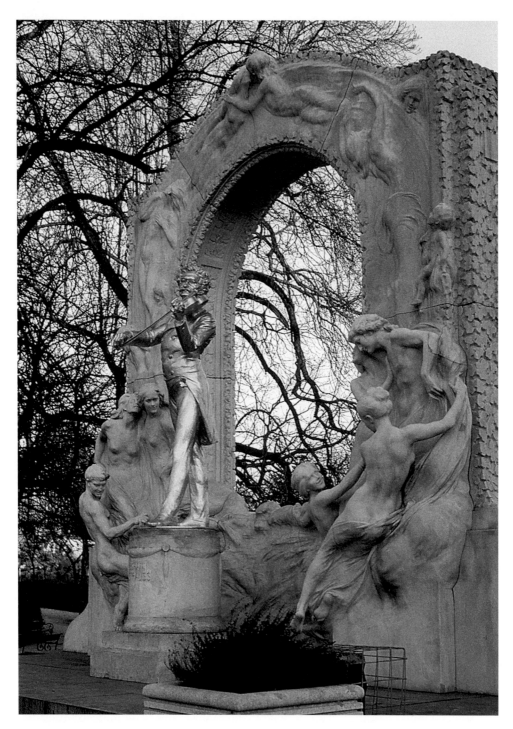

Photo 12.1
Strauss Monument in Vienna, symbolising Austria's contribution to music and dance

Source: Brian Boniface

while its reputation as one of the world's major winter sports destinations has tended to overshadow the many cultural attractions the country can offer.

Tourism plays a major role in Austria's economy, accounting for 7.5 per cent of GDP. Austria has the benefit of both a summer and a winter season; the winter sports market has grown steadily since the late 1950s and is now more significant in terms of tourist spending, than summer tourism, although it remains smaller in volume. Skiing helped to restore national pride, following the disaster of two World Wars, and ski-racing is a major spectator sport. For many years, Austria was in the top position as a skiing destination, having overtaken Switzerland in the 1950s, but more recently France has relegated it to second place. Much of the resort development took place in the years following the Second World War as part of the reconstruction of Austria's economy.

The demand for tourism

Domestic and outbound tourism

Over two-thirds of the Austrian population take a holiday, but in contrast to Germany, domestic tourists account for only 32 per cent of overnight stays. There is a growing move towards taking more than one holiday, particularly in the form of short breaks to event attractions in Austrian cities, and this is spreading the holiday pattern away from July and August. Farm stays have been successfully promoted to encourage tourism throughout the rural areas, but there is still a concentration of holidays in the Tyrol, creating considerable congestion with visitors outnumbering the inhabitants in many villages. Austria is a major generator of international tourists on a world scale, though the majority of trips are to neighbouring countries, emphasising Austria's favourable location in Europe. The majority of holidays abroad are to Mediterranean countries, particularly Italy, Greece, Spain, and Croatia.

Inbound tourism

Austria attracted 32 million international visitors and 152.7 million overnights in 2019. This fell to 15 million visitors and 97.9 million overnights in 2020 due to the impact of the pandemic.

The majority of foreign visitors are holidaymakers, and there is no doubt that proximity to Germany is important to Austria as that market accounts for just under half of all arrivals. The next three sources of tourists – Italy, Switzerland, and the United Kingdom – account for a much smaller proportion of overnight stays. New markets in Eastern Europe, coupled with marketing initiatives, also mean that Austria is receiving an increasing number of visits from this region. In addition to their proximity, Germans are attracted to Austria with its more relaxed lifestyle and absence of language barriers. This reliance on one market does leave Austria vulnerable in times of recession, and the concentration of visits determined by holiday periods in Germany causes congestion at the borders. In popular holiday areas, many resorts become totally geared to the German market.

The supply side of tourism

Transport

- With the German market so dominant, the majority of tourists arrive by car on the extensive road network (including 1,700 kilometres of tolled motorways and expressways) and experience traffic congestion at the beginning and end of the main holiday periods. The tortuous nature of some of the roads emphasises the difficulty of transportation in this elongated and mountainous country, yet the network reaches into the most remote parts, and includes Europe's highest road to the summit of the Gross Glockner. There are over 6,100 kilometres of railway including 20 private railway companies, and these are well-integrated with rural bus services reaching the most remote communities. With six airports of international standard in Austria, this is the main mode of travel for outbound tourism, although some argue that a restrictive policy on inbound flights to Vienna in the past has held back the development of the tourism industry and compounded Austria's dependence on the German market. On the other hand, Austrian Airlines is renewing its fleet and expanding its international network, with Vienna as the hub.

Accommodation

The majority of Austria's bed spaces are in serviced accommodation and except in the cities, these are mainly small, family-run hotels and guesthouses. The authorities are improving the quality of accommodation as a means of boosting both domestic and foreign tourism. Although business travel is relatively unimportant in Austria, the small conference market is being developed, particularly in Vienna, Linz, Salzburg, Innsbruck, Graz, and Villach, as well as in the larger *schlosshotels* – castles and palaces formerly owned by the aristocracy – which have been converted into hotels.

Organisation

Each of the nine Austrian provinces, including Vienna, has responsibility for tourism administered by the provincial government and a tourist board. At national level, tourism is the responsibility of the Federal Ministry of Agriculture, Regions and Tourism (www.bml.gv.at). Promotion of Austria is the responsibility of the Austrian National Tourism Office (ANTO), a joint public/private agency with funding from the government and the Chamber of Commerce. The organisation has undergone a restructuring to ensure an overtly marketing focus in the face of stagnant demand from the international market under the brand 'Holidays in Austria'. The tourism authorities in Austria are upgrading tourist infrastructure generally, particularly in the area of sports and facilities for activity holidays, and extending the network of ski lifts and funiculars. Nevertheless, some resorts (such as Mayrhofen) have halted further development in line with Austria's green image, and this may have persuaded potential skiers to choose France instead.

Tourism resources

Austria contains a third of the area covered by the Alps, and the country is famed for its lake and mountain scenery, winter sports facilities, and picturesque towns and villages. Trending east-west across the country and separated by the deep valley of the River Inn, the mountains are Austria's main attraction. Here, tourism is often the only economic land use, and its development is seen as a means of stemming the migration of young people from rural communities.

Although the landforms are due to differences in geology and the effects of glaciation, much of the landscape that tourists find so appealing, comprising alpine meadows above the tree line, wooded slopes, and fertile valleys, is the result of backbreaking toil by mountain farmers over the centuries. The High Alps provide a refuge for the marmot, the chamois, and the edelweiss – symbolic of the fragility of alpine ecosystems. For a number of reasons, these landscape and wildlife resources are increasingly at risk.

CASE STUDY 12.3
THE SOCIAL AND ENVIRONMENTAL IMPACTS
OF SKI RESORT DEVELOPMENT

Many Alpine communities have gradually changed in the course of a century from small farming villages to sophisticated ski resorts, attracting a wealthy international clientele. As agriculture yielded only a meagre livelihood, members of farming families supplemented their income with craft industries during the winter months or by temporary migration to find work in the cities. The advent of tourism provided the farmer with the opportunity to let rooms in the farmhouse to paying guests, and for family members to work part-time as mountain guides, and later as ski instructors. The farmhouse became the family-run guesthouse or hotel. Instead of out-migration from rural communities, there are now large numbers of incomers, mostly young people attracted by jobs in the tourism sector.

The ski resort of St Anton in the Tirol is an example of this transformation. It has a resident population of only 2,500 but accommodates a million tourist bed nights a year, of which 80 per cent take place in the winter season (late December to the beginning of April). The summer season (July and August) is much quieter, with a different type of clientele. The running of the family-owned guesthouse tends to be the women's responsibility, involving very long hours during the winter season. Men, on the other hand, are much more likely to have jobs that are not centred on the home, are more varied, and with working hours that allow more social contacts. This is particularly true of ski instructors who have prestige in the community and a glamorous image among foreign tourists.

Although tourism has helped to save the rural economy of mountain communities, the growth of winter sports requires considerable investment in infrastructure and facilities, and this often has a negative impact on the environment in the following ways:

- The preparation of ski runs. This involves the removal of vegetation to allow a good accumulation of snow, which causes damage to fragile alpine ecosystems, and leaves unsightly scars on the mountainsides to dismay the summer visitor. The deforestation of the lower slopes to create clear runs increases the risk of avalanches.

- The development of lift systems. The use of helicopters to ferry in materials makes it possible to develop previously inaccessible locations as high-altitude ski stations. Even glaciers can be used for summer skiing, causing damage to the watersheds of some of Europe's major rivers.

- The making of artificial snow. Faced with a shorter and less reliable season due to climate change, ski resort operators increasingly rely on technology to guarantee a supply of snow. Thousands of snow cannons use up vast quantities of water and contaminate the ground with chemicals. The artificial snow melts slowly, reducing the already brief recuperation period for alpine vegetation.

- The growing popularity of off-piste skiing. The risk of avalanches increases as skiers and snowboarders push deeper into the mountains, away from the crowds and the relative safety of the prepared ski runs. Vibrations can trigger the displacement of the snowpack from overhanging cornices, and the impact of masses of snow in motion can cause immense damage and loss of life. Although communities have coped with the danger they call the 'white death' for centuries, they have been protected primarily by the forests on the lower mountain slopes. Concrete barriers and rows of steel fences are intrusive and a poor substitute for healthy forests, but often they are the only available option.

Discussion point

The decentralisation of planning in Austria and Switzerland means that decisions regarding development are made, not by the federal government or by big business corporations, but by local communities. Ownership of the facilities in a typical Alpine resort may be divided between a number of farmers, so it is difficult to exercise uniform control over development, or agree on 'green' policies that would encourage summer tourism. Debate the pros and cons of development in a small ski resort that needs to diversify to attract a higher spend from summer visitors. Assign the roles of the various stakeholders involved in decision making (including the Church and the teaching profession) to your student colleagues.

Each of the Austrian provinces can offer distinctive attractions:

- **Tyrol** is by far the most popular destination for foreign visitors, containing the most spectacular Alpine scenery and the greatest number of ski resorts. Tyrolean folklore and costumes are the best known of Austria's traditional cultures. Most of the resorts have been developed from farming villages situated in the tributary valleys of the River Inn – the Ötztal and Zillertal for example – at altitudes of between 1,000 and 1,800 metres. Traditional building styles, based on the chalet that is well adapted to heavy winter snowfalls, provide a pleasant ambience for holidays. Summer activities in the Tyrol include hiking and gliding, while most villages are equipped with a swimming pool and facilities for tennis and other sports. The region also offers a number of scenic trails and wine routes. Tourist centres include the following:

- Innsbruck is not only the capital of the Tyrol but an important cultural centre, a reminder of its former role as a summer residence for the Hapsburg emperors; this explains the many Renaissance buildings. Along with the ski resorts on the slopes nearby, the city has twice hosted the Winter Olympics.
- St. Anton, Kitzbühl, Söll, Seefeld, and Mayrhofen are ski resorts of international significance.

- **Vorarlberg**, to the west of the Arlberg mountains, was historically isolated from the rest of Austria and has some affinity with neighbouring Switzerland. Lech and Zürs offer up-market skiing, while Bregenz on the Bodensee is a popular lake resort and a venue for music festivals.
- The provinces of **Salzburg** and the **Salzkammergut** area (so called because of the historically important salt mining industry) offer gentler lake and mountain scenery. St. Wolfgang is the most popular of the resorts in summer, but its entertainment scene is subdued compared to Söll or Kitzbühl in winter. Other attractions include the Krimml waterfalls in the Höhe Tauern National Park (https://www.wasserfaell-krimml.at), the Dachstein ice caves (https://dachstein-salzkammergut.com), the picturesque old town of Hallstatt, and the spas of Bad Ischl and Bad Gastein.
- **Styria**, the forested 'green province', is mainly visited by domestic tourists, although its capital, Graz, is Austria's second largest city and a major cultural centre, which played a key role in the defence of the Habsburg Empire against the Ottoman Turks.
- **Carinthia** is increasingly popular with foreign visitors as a summer holiday destination, where the warm sunny climate and lakes such as the Wörther See, offering many facilities for water sports, are the main attractions.
- The provinces of **Upper and Lower Austria** are noted for their vineyards, and the gently undulating landscapes provide a contrast to the Alps. A river cruise on the Danube (from Passau in Bavaria via Vienna to Budapest in Hungary) is popular with tourists, enabling them to visit the cities of Linz and Krems, along with historic castles (such as Durnstein) and monasteries (such as Melk).
- **Burgenland** is similar in its steppe landscapes to neighbouring Hungary (to which it belonged prior to 1918), while the shallow Neusiedlersee is an important nature reserve. Eisenstadt, the provincial capital, is a small town, famous among lovers of classical music for its associations with Joseph Haydn (he worked for much of his life as court conductor at the Esterhazy Palace; today this remains as an important cultural centre).

Whereas Graz, Linz, Klagenfurt, and Innsbruck are important regional centres, only two of Austria's cities – Vienna and Salzburg – attract huge numbers of visitors from all over the world, thanks to their heritage of music, art, and architecture:

- **Vienna** is full of reminders of its imperial past. These include the monumental buildings lining the Ringstrasse, encircling the old city, and the art treasures housed in the former palaces of the Hofburg, Belvedere, and Schönbrunn. Music and dance are as much a part of the city's social and entertainment scene as they were in the time of the 'Waltz King' (Johann Strauss) in the nineteenth century. The Vienna State Opera House (https://www.wiener-staatsoper.at) and St. Stephen's Cathedral (https://www.stephanskirche.at) are also part of this musical heritage. In the early 1900s, Vienna was at the forefront of new developments in art, architecture, and psychology. Although Vienna trades on nostalgia and the café lifestyle for its tourist appeal, the city is an efficiently run modern conference venue, with an international role as a United Nations centre, while geographical location makes it the recognised gateway to Eastern Europe.
- **Salzburg** has a flourishing tourism industry based on:
  - The summer music festival, which was further boosted in 1991 by the Mozart bicentenary celebrations. During festival time, accommodation in this relatively small city is at a premium.
  - The *Sound of Music* connection means that classical music lovers are outnumbered by those tourists who are attracted to the city and the scenic countryside of lakes and mountains nearby, through their associations with this popular movie.
  - The city's heritage of Baroque architecture – probably unrivalled outside Spain or Italy – which was brought into being by the powerful Prince-Bishops who once ruled Salzburg.

Liechtenstein is a small independent principality nestled in the upper Rhine Valley between Austria and Switzerland. It has strong historical ties to Austria but uses the same currency as Switzerland. The country is known mainly for its financial services, but Liechtenstein does offer the tourist medieval castles and hiking trails, as well as being a winter sports destination.

Switzerland (The Swiss Confederation – Helvetia – CH)

Switzerland is poor in natural resources and contains a diversity of languages and cultures. Yet its people have achieved a degree of political stability and economic prosperity that is envied by the rest of the world. Swiss industrial products, based on a high input of skill in relation to the value of the component raw materials, have an international reputation for quality. Similarly, the country's spectacular scenic attractions, all within a relatively small area, have been intelligently exploited by a hospitality industry that is renowned for its professionalism and training institutions. Historically, the country evolved as a confederation of cantons fighting to preserve their independence from foreign domination, yet at the same time exporting mercenaries to join foreign armies. In many respects, the 26 cantons still play a more important role in Swiss politics than the federal government in Berne. At the local level, the communes also determine tourism planning and development to a large extent, in line with the Swiss tradition of direct citizen participation in politics and national defence.

Tourism in Switzerland has a long history, and the industry was already well-established in the late nineteenth century. Its development came about as a result of a number of factors:

- From early times, Switzerland was a transit zone for invading armies, merchants, and pilgrims and later had to be crossed by wealthy travellers undertaking the Grand Tour. The Swiss were in demand as guides, as there were no serviceable roads, and the Alpine passes were often hazardous. Accommodation was also needed for travellers, the most famous example being the hospice on the St. Bernard Pass.
- As a result of the Romantic Movement in art and literature at the close of the eighteenth century, the mountains were no longer perceived as a barrier to be feared, but as a resource to be valued. For example, Byron and Shelley stayed for a considerable time by Lake Geneva, and summer resorts gradually developed for well-off tourists around other lakes in Switzerland.
- From the middle of the nineteenth century, the demand for tourism in Switzerland grew as the result of the Industrial Revolution in Western Europe, the improvement in road and rail communications and the growth of a middle class, particularly in countries like Britain, where Thomas Cook did much to popularise the country. The more adventurous tourists sought the challenges of mountain climbing, following Whymper's ascent of the Matterhorn in 1865. More remote areas of the Alps were progressively opened up to tourism with the construction of funicular and cog railways, and hotels were built at what was then the edge of the Alpine glaciers, such as the Aletsch.
- Although Switzerland had been known for its spas since Roman times, substantial development of health tourism occurred in the late nineteenth and early twentieth centuries as a result of the spread of tuberculosis in the industrial cities of Europe. The pure mountain air in spas such as St. Moritz Bad and Arosa was believed to provide a remedy for the disease.
- Skiing and other winter sports such as tobogganing and curling were introduced to St. Moritz and the resorts of the Bernese Oberland by wealthy British tourists at the close of the nineteenth century. At first, the existing mountain railways – now operating year-round – were used to transport the skiers to the slopes, but as demand grew from the 1930s onwards, they were largely superseded by faster, more efficient aerial cableways.
- International trade had long been important to Swiss cities such as Geneva. The strict neutrality of Switzerland and its multi-lingual character encouraged the growth of all kinds of business and conference tourism. Starting with the Red Cross, Geneva became the venue for many international organisations, while Zurich and Basle are

financial centres of worldwide significance. Berne and Lausanne – the headquarters respectively of the Universal Postal Union and the Olympic Committee – also provide important conference functions.

Since the 1990s, Switzerland's tourism industry has faced major challenges. These include:

- Rising costs and the nation's reputation as an expensive destination, due to the strength of the Swiss franc.
- Difficulties in recruiting labour, due to the perception of low pay in tourism compared to the industrial sector.
- An old-fashioned image of Switzerland and a need to adapt to rapidly changing market trends, such as digitalisation.
- Climate change, shown by glacier retreat, water shortages, and a less reliable snow cover for winter sports.

The demand for tourism

Domestic and outbound tourism

The Swiss have one of the highest holiday propensities in the world, with around 75 per cent taking a holiday of at least four nights. Approximately, half of all journeys with overnight stays are taken abroad. Holiday-taking is at its highest among upper-income groups, the middle-aged, and those living in the larger towns or cities. Demand for domestic tourism has grown, with the high frequency of holiday-taking meaning that most domestic holidays are second or third holidays. Around 40 per cent of all bed nights occur in the winter season (November to April), a figure boosted by the Swiss participating in winter sports. Eastern Switzerland and the Lake Geneva region are the most popular areas for domestic tourists. Swiss holidays abroad are concentrated into the summer months of July to September, and the most popular destinations are Italy and France.

Inbound tourism

Around 12 million trips a year were made by foreign visitors to Switzerland prior to the COVID-19 pandemic, accounting for 55 per cent of overnight stays in hotels. Germany accounted for the majority of visitors, followed by Britain, the United States, and France. The impact of the pandemic was somewhat less than in neighbouring countries, as winter sports locations remained open, but business and conference travel were badly affected. The fall in the number of visitors from China had severe repercussions, as they are attracted by shopping for high quality goods rather than sightseeing.

The supply side of tourism

Transport

The private car dominates domestic travel and air transport foreign travel. As in Austria, the transport networks are tortuous, and the topography often demands major engineering feats – the 18-kilometre tunnel under the St Gotthard being an outstanding example, while the roads over the Alpine passes are spectacular. Even so, roads in the High Alps are often blocked by snow from November to June. While the road network brings many remoter parts of the country within reach of day visitors, this has created congestion in holiday areas and environmental pollution from commercial vehicles on the major routes across the Alps. To meet the demand for electric vehicles, Switzerland has a dense network of charging stations, and this should help to maintain the air quality for which the country is renowned. The Swiss Federal Railways and the private railway companies operate over 5,300 kilometres of track (1,600 kilometres are narrow-gauge), and there are many mountain railways, funiculars, and rack-and-pinion systems, which are often tourist attractions in themselves. Although the cost is high, tunnels and snow-ploughs allow the railways to operate throughout the year.

There are international airports at Zurich, Geneva, Berne, and Basle. Swiss International Air Lines (SWISS) is the national carrier, with its hub at Zurich (www.swiss.com). Other features of the Swiss transport system, which is highly integrated, include the postal coaches, which penetrate the remotest villages, bicycle hire at many rail stations, and lake ferries.

Accommodation

The development of accommodation since the 1970s has led to an excess of supply over demand. About a third of the serviced accommodation capacity is only available in the winter season, particularly in the high-altitude ski resorts (such as St Moritz and Arosa). Most hotels are small with the few larger hotels found mainly in Zurich, Berne, and Geneva. Hotels and holiday chalets (mainly catering for groups of skiers) are highly dependent on foreign labour. 'Supplementary accommodation', including holiday chalets, apartments, holiday villages, and camping/caravan sites, provide a lower-cost alternative to hotels for foreign visitors, but they are also popular with domestic holidaymakers.

Organisation

Switzerland's maturity as a destination is shown by the long tradition of tourist associations and information services at regional and local levels. There are also many specialist organisations such as the Swiss Travel Fund (Reka) Cooperative that gives less privileged workers the chance to go on holiday and the Swiss Tourism Federation (STF) representing the industry. At national level, Switzerland Tourism is responsible to the State Secretariat of Economic Affairs for formulating and implementing national tourism policy, which was refreshed in 2021. It is committed to promoting Switzerland as a travel, holiday and congress destination, and the development and co-ordination of joint campaigns with market partners. As part of a national strategy for tourism, it works closely with Innotour, the federal agency responsible for promoting innovation, the Swiss Association for Hotel Credit, and the New Regional Policy, a partnership between the cantons and the federal government, which ensures an efficient distribution of investment in mountain, rural, and border regions.

Tourism resources

Swiss concern for the environment is shown by federal legislation, safeguarding the forests covering 30 per cent of the country. In addition to the Swiss National Park where conservation is the priority and where endangered alpine species such as the chamois are protected, there are 19 nature parks where rural landscapes and traditions are maintained to the benefit of local communities. The most popular tourist destination is the Alpine zone, attracting over half of all visitor arrivals. Here, lie the majestic snow-capped peaks, glaciated valleys, and winter sports developments that are Switzerland's trademark. However, tourist development has entailed social and environmental pressures and the integration of tourism into the agricultural and forest economies has needed sensitive handling.

Each of the Swiss cantons has its own range of attractions, but several major tourist areas stand out, namely:

- The **Bernese Oberland:** The most spectacular Alpine scenery is found here, south of the lake resort of Interlaken. An excellent network of funicular railways and cableways provides access to the snow fields and glaciers, the most famous ascending the slopes of the Jungfrau and Eiger. Summer visitors should be aware that the temperature at Jungfraujoch station is around 0°C due to the altitude (3,500 metres). At Lauterbrunnen, there is a classic example of a glaciated valley with spectacular waterfalls. Long popular with British tourists, the area preserves Swiss rural traditions and, at the same time, has some of the most sophisticated ski resorts in Europe, notably Gstaad, Wengen, and Grindelwald.
- **Valais** (Wallis): This canton includes the upper Rhône valley as far as the Simplon Pass and a number of small historic towns. The best-known resort is Zermatt, with its views of the Matterhorn, but the most popular ski area is Crans-Montana where considerable development has taken place. Crans-Montana has a number of acclaimed golf courses and is home to the Swiss Golf Open (https://www.omegaeuropeanmasters.com).
- **Lake Lucerne and the Forest Cantons:** The fjord-like Lake Lucerne is arguably the most beautiful body of inland water in Europe. Three cantons around the lake – Uri, Schwyz, and Unterwalden – are historically important as the cradle of Swiss independence, popularly associated with the legend of William Tell. Lucerne is a picturesque city, famous for its medieval Chapel Bridge and the Swiss Museum of Transport.
- **Graubünden (Grisons):** In some respects, it is the most traditional part of Switzerland, due to its former remoteness. The villages of the Upper Engadine Valley at altitudes of 1,500 metres are among the highest in Europe. The air here is remarkably clear and dry, the Romansch language is still spoken, and a pastoral type of rural economy persists, protected by government subsidy. In contrast are the number of spas and ski resorts, catering mainly for wealthy tourists, the most famous being St Moritz, Davos, and Klosters. Davos also has international significance as the conference venue for the World Economic Forum.
- **Suisse Romande:** The French-speaking **Suisse Romande** on the north shore of Lake Geneva (Lac Leman) attracts a wealthy international clientele to its finishing schools and the festival resort of Montreux. Historically, Geneva played a leading role in

the Protestant Reformation, with its emphasis on the work ethic, but nowadays, the city attracts visitors for shopping and nightlife. The Palais des Nations showcases Geneva's pre-eminence as a centre for the United Nations (https://www.unog.ch).

- The Italian-speaking **Ticino** (Tessin) enjoys the warmest climate in Switzerland due to its sheltered location and the moderating effect of Lakes Lugano and Maggiore. The landscape has Mediterranean features such as palm trees and lemon orchards, while the towns and villages are more colourful than in other regions. Travellers from northern Europe on their way to Italy appreciate the contrast most in early spring, when they emerge from the cold and gloomy weather prevailing north of the St Gotthard into the warm sunshine of the Ticino Valley. Bellinzona preserves much of its heritage as a medieval fortress town, while Locarno, Lugano, and Ascona are important holiday resorts and major conference venues.

Most of the Swiss population live outside the Alps in the plateau region known as the **Schweizer Mittelland**, to the north and west, where the major industries are located in the Basle–Winterthur–Zurich triangle. Apart from the Rhine Falls, the attractions are city-based rather than scenic. They include:

- Basle, Switzerland's port on the Rhine, which has a historic university and is a major cultural centre.
- Zurich on the lake of the same name contains the Swiss National Museum (https://www.landesmuseum.ch), and the FIFA Museum, showcasing the world's most popular sport.
- Berne is probably the most interesting city from a tourist viewpoint. The picturesque old town, with its medieval shopping arcades and Clock Tower, is a World Heritage Site.

The western boundary of Switzerland lies along the forested **Jura Mountains**. Less spectacular than the Alps, this region accounts for only a small percentage of tourist overnights. The small towns of the region, such as Les Chaux de Fonds, are noted for traditional Swiss crafts such as watch making.

Summary

- Apart from the relatively short German coastline, this part of Europe is landlocked. Physically, three regions can be identified; the northern lowlands; the central uplands; and the Alps.
- Forests, lakes, and spas are important tourism resources throughout the region.
- Highly developed economies and standards of living have resulted in a considerable demand for tourism and recreation.
- Of particular note is the importance of Germany as one of the world's leading generators of international tourists.

- Germany and Austria have made great contributions to music and art, attracting cultural tourists worldwide.
- Transportation in the three countries is well developed but has to overcome the harsh physical conditions and topography of the Alps.
- The federal organisation of the three countries has led to considerable devolution of tourism powers to the states in Germany, provinces in Austria, and cantons in Switzerland.
- The main tourist regions are: the coasts of northern Germany with its islands and resorts; the central uplands of Germany, including the Rhineland and the Black Forest; and the Alpine area of all three countries with its opportunities for both winter and summer tourism. The towns and cities are also important for sightseeing and as business travel centres.
- Sports facilities, museums, and cultural events are an important part of the tourism appeal of the three countries.
- Sustainability is a major consideration in the tourism policies and plans of all three countries.

Review questions

1. The response of tourism to climate change involves destinations adapting to changing circumstances (refer to Chapter4, Box 4.1). Devise a plan for the winter sports resorts in the Alps to adapt to unreliable snowfall and the retreat of the snowline.
2. Discuss the strengths (and possible weaknesses) of Switzerland as a destination for conferences, including meetings of professional associations, which generally have a limited budget compared to corporate meetings.

Further reading

Federal Ministry for Sustainability and Tourism (2019) PlanT-Master Plan for Tourism, Vienna
Organization for Economic Co-operation and Development (annual) Tourism Policy and International Tourism in OECD Member Countries, OECD, Paris
https://www.unwto.org/tourism-data/unwto-tourism-dashboard

13 The tourism geography of France

Learning objectives

After reading this chapter, you should be able to:

- Describe France's physical regions and climates and understand their importance for tourism.
- Appreciate the changing social and economic conditions of post-war France and comprehend the implications for tourism.
- Understand the major components of the French holiday market and the scale of inbound tourism to France.
- Outline the organisation of tourism in France.

DOI: 10.4324/9781003406853-16

- Be aware of the regional development role of tourism in France and be familiar with major tourism development schemes.
- Demonstrate a knowledge of the tourist regions, resorts, business centres, and tourist attractions of France.

Introduction

For many years, France has remained the world's top tourist destination in terms of visitor arrivals, and one of the leading countries in terms of tourism receipts. This means that tourism is important in the economy, representing 7.5 per cent of GDP in 2019. France was one of the first countries to recognise the importance of the industry, setting up a national tourism office as early as 1910. It is no coincidence that much of the vocabulary we use in the hotel and catering industry originates from French.

Among the factors contributing to France's success in tourism are:

- It is the largest country in Western Europe, boasting a natural resource base of 5,500 kilometres of coastline, some of Europe's finest rivers, and mountain areas such as the Massif Central, the Alps, Jura, and Pyrenees. The French refer to their country as 'the hexagon', with natural boundaries on five sides formed by the Rhine, mountain ranges, and the sea.
- France is also unique among European countries in its latitude and altitude range, which gives rise to various climates and landscape features. Mediterranean conditions are found in Provence, Occitanie, and Corsica. A long, dry summer with abundant sunshine, combined with mild winters, allows for a prolonged tourism season in world-famous resorts such as Nice and St. Tropez. The Atlantic and Channel coasts have less sunshine and a climate favouring the more active types of recreation. Eastern France has a continental climate with cold winters, while in the mountains, snow cover is uneven and variable in ski resorts situated at low or middle altitudes.
- French culture has been widely emulated, starting in the Middle Ages with the Gothic style of architecture and the ideal of chivalry. In the seventeenth century, Louis XIV's court and palace at Versailles were the role models for the upper classes throughout Europe. Despite subsequent wars and revolutions, France remained pre-eminent in the world of *haute couture* and fashion. French artists and architects were responsible for many innovations in the late nineteenth and early twentieth centuries, such as *impressionism, cubism, art nouveau*, and *art deco*.
- French is one of the most widely spoken world languages. Even in the post-colonial era, France extends beyond Europe to embrace far-flung 'Overseas Départements and Territories' (DOM-TOM) in the Americas, Indian, and Pacific Oceans, which we will describe in Chapters 19 and 22–25. Cultural and business ties between Metropolitan France and her former colonies in Africa and elsewhere remain strong, determining the pattern of long-haul tourist flows to a large extent.
- France is one of the world's leading economic powers and has been at the forefront of technological advances. However, it was not until the 1930s that the nation reached

the same level of urbanisation as England in 1851, and most industrial development has occurred since the Second World War. As a result, many city dwellers retain close links with the countryside. France has the largest agricultural sector in Western Europe, offering the tourist a landscape that owes much of its charm to the prevalence of small-scale mixed farming using fairly traditional production methods. This is particularly true of the more remote rural areas – *La France Profonde*.

France can offer a wide variety of tourism products based on these resources. We might mention the following:

- Special interest holidays, including wine-tasting tours of Burgundy and culinary short breaks for gourmets – *foodies* – in Normandy.
- The Club Méditerranée holiday village concept in beach and sport tourism.
- The importance of health and wellness tourism. Almost a hundred spa resorts are officially recognised, most developed in the nineteenth century based on mineral springs, while others on the coast offer *thalassotherapy* – seawater treatments. Although some spas have upgraded their facilities to meet changing demands for health and wellness, the sector has generally declined since the Second World War, in contrast to the situation in Germany and Italy.
- The importance of faith-based tourism in a country where, although secularism has long been official policy, two-thirds of the population are, at least nominally, Catholic. Some shrines, such as Mont St. Michel in Normandy, Le Puy in the Auvergne, Rocamadour in Aquitaine, and Vézelay in Burgundy, were well established in medieval times, acting as 'gathering points' on the major pilgrim routes to Santiago de Compostela in Spain. On the other hand, Lourdes and Lisieux did not become pilgrimage centres until the nineteenth century.
- Winter sports are offered in the mountain resorts of the Alps and the Pyrenees, and for the domestic market in the Massif Central, the Jura, and the Vosges. France has been an innovator in ski instruction (the short ski method) and in developing purpose-built ski resorts above the tree line to guarantee a longer snow season. It has overtaken Austria and Switzerland as Europe's leading winter sports destination, and in 1992, Albertville in the French Alps hosted the Winter Olympics.
- Sailing is another major activity, which has spawned massive investments by the public and private sectors in coastal marina developments. A third of these *ports de plaisance* are located in Brittany and another 28 per cent in the Provence-Côte d'Azur region.

Other activity and adventure-based types of tourism include:

- Boating on the superb network of rivers and canals
- Canoeing on fast-flowing rivers, such as the Ardèche
- Horse riding
- Cycling – here two influences are perhaps at work – the trend towards 'green tourism' and the role of the Tour de France in raising the international profile of the sport

- Surfing along the Atlantic coast
- Diving along parts of the Mediterranean coast such as Corsica
- Mountain climbing in the Alps and the Pyrenees
- Caving in the Dordogne region
- Hiking on the very extensive network of *grandes randonées* (long-distance way-marked trails), which penetrate the scenic areas of France
- Golf which is a fast-growing market, with developments in the coastal resorts of northern France

In some of these products, France has few rivals. However, effective marketing has not always matched the country's flair for style and innovation.

The demand for tourism

The French tend to take their holidays in France due to the country's range of tourism resources and also the tradition of spending the summer in the south. Consequently, the propensity of the French to travel abroad – at 10 per cent – is lower than for most other Western Europeans. As recently as 1958, only 25 per cent of the French took a holiday away from home. Since the 1990s, the travel propensity of the population has remained stable at 75 per cent, but this does mean that there is still a substantial minority who, for various reasons, do not take a holiday. There are also significant regional differences in the demand for tourism.

Domestic tourism

The changing economic and social geography of France has had implications for participation in tourism. Demographic changes since the Second World War include a population growth from 40 million to almost 68 million, the correction of the previous imbalance between males and females caused by the toll of two world wars, and an increase in the number of young people. The birth rate is much higher than in other Western European countries such as Germany. This is due largely to favourable tax rates and other family-friendly policies of successive French governments, and to an influx of over 5 million immigrants from North Africa. France has also been transformed from a largely rural society into an industrial economy, with people leaving the countryside for urban manufacturing and service centres. Accompanying these changes has been a growth in the numbers employed in the service sector, increased car ownership, social tourism initiatives, and substantial rises in both disposable and discretionary incomes. This has led to increased leisure spending as recreation, and tourism has become a significant part of the French lifestyle.

   In this respect, the increased leisure time available to the French is an important enabling factor. Successive reductions in working hours have resulted in a statutory working week of less than 40 hours. Also, the minimum school leaving age has been raised to 16 years, and there is continuing pressure for early retirement. Since its introduction in 1936, annual paid holiday entitlement has grown to five weeks, and many workers have six or more weeks. The fact that at least two weeks must be taken between May and October has led to congestion in this peak holiday period. The downside of the social legislation affecting labour is that employers may be reluctant to recruit staff, resulting in a high unemployment rate compared to the United States or the United Kingdom.

France has a very high proportion of domestic holiday-taking, with trips demonstrating a number of characteristics:

- They are lengthy, often three or four weeks, although the traditional month away in August *en famille* is decreasing.
- They are concentrated into the peak summer months (the majority of holidays are taken in July and August), although efforts are being made to spread the load with promotional campaigns, staggering of school holidays, and the growth of winter holidays.
- In a country with such varied holiday opportunities, a wide distribution of holiday destinations is evident, though a general movement from north to south, as well as to the periphery, can be discerned, with a concentration in a number of rural areas and at the coast–which comprises 40 per cent of all overnight stays.
- Half of all domestic trips are to destinations within, or close to, the tourist's home region.
- The car accounts for an overwhelming 80 per cent of domestic holiday journeys.
- Self-catering, second homes, and visiting friends and relatives account for the majority of holidays – simply because their cost commends them to families in peak season.
- The majority of holidays are arranged independently but works councils and other non-profit making organisations play an important role. These range from professional organisations, who own fully-equipped holiday accommodation and rent to members at competitive rates, to those involved in social tourism.
- Short breaks have grown in popularity at the expense of the long vacation, with many people taking three or four short breaks yearly. As a result, hotels and resorts have extended the tourist season, and tourist authorities and hoteliers have promoted a wide variety of products to meet the changing demand.

Social tourism represents a very strong movement in France and is significant for French domestic patterns of demand. There was a spectacular growth in social tourism initiatives in the 1960s. In the late 1990s, the government established a new fund to allow the unemployed and poorer citizens to take a holiday, using spare capacity in the coastal resorts. Examples of social tourism initiatives include:

- Children's hostels - *colonies des vacances.*
- Family holiday villages- *villages vacances familiales* (VVF).
- Government schemes such as *cheque vacances* boost holiday opportunities for people on modest incomes. This is administered by the National Agency for Holiday Vouchers (ANVC).

CASE STUDY 13.1
TOURISM FOR ALL?

In 1999, the French government, under a socialist prime minister, set up a state-funded agency to act as an intermediary between charities helping poor families unable to afford a holiday and facilities in coastal holiday resorts with surplus capacity. In its first year, the scheme provided holiday accommodation for up to a thousand *exclus* – people who feel excluded from society, such as single-parent families, the unemployed, low-paid workers, and immigrants. Many of these people live in grim suburban ghettos, which were the scene of rioting in the summer of 2007. Supporters of the scheme see it as a way of healing social divisions and propose that the right for all to go on holiday should be enshrined in French law. Opponents claim that the taxpayer is being asked to subsidise a project open to abuse. Government officials maintain that the overall cost of the scheme is minimal, as only low-cost accommodation such as campsites and holiday villages would be used.

In class, debate the proposition that access to culture, sports, and holidays is a fundamental human right, like access to housing, education, and medical care. What are the practical difficulties in carrying out social tourism projects in France, where individualism is a strong part of the national character?

Second homes – *residences secondaires* – continue to play an important role in domestic travel, accounting for 15 per cent of both summer and winter overnight stays. The high incidence of second home ownership (estimated at 3.4 million) and their wide distribution throughout the country are reminders that most city dwellers have rural origins. Improvements in transport have resulted in the growth of a second home belt within a radius of 100–150 kilometres of the major cities.

Outbound tourism

Before the pandemic, around 30 million trips were taken abroad each year, two-thirds of which were spent in other European countries, particularly Spain, Portugal, or Italy. This represents a growth in foreign tourism since 1945 rooted in France's changing social and economic circumstances. However, the COVID-19 pandemic severely disrupted outbound tourism, falling to 14 million trips in 2021. Spending abroad by French nationals is low compared to receipts from inbound tourists, and France runs a surplus on its travel account. Inclusive tour holidays account for a smaller percentage of French travellers abroad than in Britain or Germany; most foreign travel is by car. However, long-haul tourism has shown consistent growth, with the United States and French-speaking destinations becoming the most popular. The French travel trade is mainly concerned with outbound tourism, and in contrast to the United Kingdom, it comprises many small and medium-sized enterprises. For example, the top ten operators in France generate one-third of the total turnover in this sector. The most well-known tour operators are Nouvelles Frontières (part of the TUI group) for package holidays, and Club Méditerranée (www.clubmed.fr), which pioneered the all-inclusive concept in tourism, and has over a hundred holiday villages worldwide.

Inbound tourism

France ranks as one of the world's most popular tourist destinations, with around 90 million arrivals in 2019. The tourism sector, particularly in Paris, was severely impacted by the COVID-19 pandemic, such that arrivals fell by around 50 per cent in 2020.

The growth in inbound tourism has been helped by developments such as the Channel Tunnel and Disneyland Paris, as well as a number of sports events, such as the Rugby World Cup, that attracted worldwide TV coverage. Belgium, Germany, and the United Kingdom are the leading generating countries, followed by the Netherlands and Italy, although new generators, such as in Eastern Europe, are growing in significance. The Americans account for a smaller proportion of arrivals but generate a much higher spend per capita. Most British tourists travel independently by car and tend to fall into two distinct types:

- Day visitors to the Channel ports such as Calais, where shopping in the hypermarkets for wine and beer is the main objective.
- Those on a touring holiday or visiting their second homes in France. This type of visitor is attracted by the cultural differences between the two countries as expressed by the domestic architecture, the *charcuterie*, the bistros, the countryside, and the French lifestyle.

The geographical position of France does mean that it attracts a very large number of day excursionists and those passing through en route to Spain or Italy. Also, a high percentage of international tourists arrive in June, July, or August, exacerbating the already acute concentration of French domestic holidays. The growing popularity of winter holidays and the German trend to take second holidays in France in the off-peak may help to alleviate the problem.

France has always been popular for conventions and sales meetings, and a government-run conference bureau – the France Meeting and Convention Board co-ordinates the promotion and development of conference activities (https://int.meeting.france.fr). Business travel is an important sector of French tourism, typically concentrated in major urban centres and using higher category hotels:

- Paris has long been the world's leading destination for international congresses, offering a range of venues, with the added incentive of a short-break holiday before or after the business trip.
- Nice boasts one of Europe's largest conference and exhibition venues – the Acropolis Convention Centre (www.nice-acropolis.com).
- Other important conference cities are Lyon, Marseilles, Cannes, and Strasbourg.

The supply side of tourism

Tourism is a fragmented industry in France, comprising many small, often family-run, enterprises. It is therefore difficult to gauge levels of employment in the industry. Official figures estimate over a million jobs in hotels, catering, transport, and leisure, but this excludes the public sector and falls short of the real total. A further million jobs are generated as an indirect result or 'spin-off' from tourism.

Transport

The private car is the transport mode used by the majority of both domestic and foreign tourists. This reflects the demand for self-catering and informal holidays, as well as the asset of a road system that ranks among the best in Europe, including almost 12,000 kilometres of motorway. France has few long-distance bus services, so the rail system handles a high proportion of inter-city travel, competing effectively with the private car and domestic air services. The state-owned railway authority (SNCF) has invested in the electrification of mainline services and high-speed trains – the famous TGVs. These run partly on dedicated track at speeds of 200–300 kilometres per hour, linking Paris to Lyon, Lille, Nantes, Bordeaux, and Nice. The rail network continues to be focussed on Paris, so it is usually necessary to transfer between termini to make inter-regional connections. However, an overnight through-train runs between Calais and the French Riviera all year round, and between Calais and Languedoc in summer.

International connections by air are comprehensive, with three airports serving Paris, while Air France (www.airfrance.com) is one of the world's leading airlines. Although opposed by the French, the air transport sector has undergone deregulation as part of the European Commission's liberalisation of air transport, allowing new airlines to enter the market. The impact of low-cost carriers has been considerable in providing business for regional airports and encouraging the foreign ownership of second homes in rural areas. The French consumer now has a wide choice of destinations for a city break, such as Marrakech or Prague, and to compete, tourism providers in France have to be more imaginative and cost-effective.

Cross-Channel ferries are the preferred transport mode for tourists from Britain and Ireland. The former wide choice of routes has diminished as the car-carrying *Le Shuttle* train service through the Channel Tunnel becomes an established alternative (www.eurotunnel.com). Similarly, the airlines' share of the lucrative business travel market is being reduced through competition from the *Eurostar* train service between London and Lille and between London and Paris. Trans-Mediterranean ferry connections to Corsica, Sardinia, and North Africa are provided by Maritima Ferries from the ports of Marseilles, Toulon, Nice, and Genoa. The 9,000 kilometres of inland waterway are now mainly used for recreation and have become a tourist attraction in their own right, the most well-known being the Canal du Midi between Toulouse and Sète, built in the reign of Louis XIV to link the Atlantic and the Mediterranean. Converted barges, known as *peniches,* provide an exciting way of viewing the French countryside.

Accommodation

The bed stock in France is concentrated in Paris and the coastal resorts and is comprehensive in terms of both self-catering and serviced accommodation. Although serviced accommodation dominates, there is an increasing trend among holidaymakers towards self-catering. In total, self-catering accounts for over 3 million bed spaces, mainly concentrated in the southern and western parts of France and includes:

- Camping and caravanning, which are popular among both foreign and domestic tourists, and the number of sites – especially at the top end of the market – has increased. Most campsites are located on or near the coast, where demand can exceed supply at the height of the summer season– particularly on the Côte d'Azur.
- Gîtes are popular among British holidaymakers as they combine the advantages of self-catering with living in a small rural community. Typically, these holiday homes are converted farm buildings which are surplus to their original purpose. In the past, *gîtes* were subsidised by the state as part of a campaign to stem rural depopulation; nowadays, they are self-financing but still subject to controls by the local authorities and the non-profit-making 'National Federation of Gîtes de France' (www.gites-france.info). Some of the ferry operators and the British motoring organisations have been active in marketing this type of tourism.
- In addition, many British, Dutch, and German holidaymakers own second homes, particularly in Provence, the Dordogne, and the Ardèche regions.

Regarding serviced accommodation, only a small percentage of domestic nights are spent in hotels, so these increasingly rely on business travellers and foreign tourists. Despite this, hotel building, especially in the two-star and budget categories, has continued – both to attract the foreign market and also under social tourism schemes. Hotel capacity is concentrated in Paris, the Rhône-Alps region, and the Provence-Alpes-Côte d'Azur region. The hotel sector is very fragmented – less dominated by international chains than in most European countries, although the French-owned Accor is one of the world's leading hotel groups (https://group.accor.com). The hotel stock includes a large number of small, budget-priced hotels (*logis de France*), inns (*auberges*), and converted chateaus (*relais-châteaux*). In addition, there are a large number of *chambres d'hôte* (private houses offering bed and breakfast), most of which are unregistered. These are used mainly by French and Belgian tourists.

Organisation

At the national level, the responsibility for tourism changed to the Ministry of the Economy, Finance, and Recovery in 2022 and is shared with a variety of other ministries. Following the COVID-19 crisis, the government inaugurated 'Destination France', an ambitious plan for the recovery and transformation of the tourism sector to make France the 'number one' destination for sustainable tourism by 2030.

Atout France is the public sector agency responsible for developing the tourism sector and marketing France abroad, with 30 offices worldwide. Its responsibilities include improving the quality of tourism products, such as wine tourism.

Since 1982, policy-making has been decentralised from Paris to the 13 regions. The Regional Tourism Councils (CRTs) have more scope than other public sector organisations to carry out development. Most of these regions correspond to some extent with the historic provinces of pre-Revolution France. At the sub-regional level, the 95 *départements* into which France has been divided for administrative purposes since the Revolution have never achieved the same popular acceptance as the counties of the United Kingdom, and although each département has its tourism committee (CDT), they vary considerably in resources and effectiveness. Local sentiment identifies more with the *pays*, an area with a strong geographical identity expressed in its landscapes and food products. Le Pays d'Auge in Normandy is one of many such areas that has its tourist association. Tourism illustrates the importance of the 'mixed economy' in France, with the public and private sectors cooperating at the regional level on the regional councils and at the local level in the *syndicates d'initiatives* – which in most French towns provide information for travellers (there are over 5,000 offices nationwide). Where resorts have development potential but lack private initiative, a government-run *office du tourisme* can be set up to carry out promotion and development.

Since the time of Louis XIV, there has been a tradition of state intervention in the economy of France, with a tendency to favour large-scale projects. The best-known examples are the re-planning of Paris by Napoleon III in the 1850s and the public works carried out by President Mitterand in the 1980s. In the 1960s, the state took direct responsibility for large-scale tourism projects in Languedoc-Roussillon and Aquitaine. Partly as a result of public pressure, since the 1980s, tourism policy has moved away from large-scale initiatives towards smaller, local projects where environmental considerations are taken into account. These initiatives are spearheaded by the regional councils with financial support from the central government.

CASE STUDY 13.2
TOURISM PLANNING IN LANGUEDOC-ROUSSILLON

In 1963, the government set up an inter-ministerial commission to co-ordinate the work of various public agencies and local chambers of commerce in developing new resorts with a capacity of over 250,000 bed spaces on the Mediterranean coast west of the Rhône delta. This coastline is flat, but has the natural advantages of extensive sandy beaches backed by a series of *étangs* (lagoons). The objectives were:

- To take pressure off the congested Côte d'Azur.
- To divert holidaymakers who might otherwise go to Spain – in other words, to act as an intervening opportunity.
- To provide greater job opportunities in a region over-dependent on agriculture, particularly producing cheap wine for the domestic market.

The state financed the necessary land acquisition and preparation for development, including mosquito eradication from the coastal marshes. Other major works included a new motorway to improve access and an extensive re-afforestation programme. Mixed economy companies – bringing together the private and public sectors – provided the infrastructure for each resort. Private developers then built the accommodation and other facilities under the direction of an architect charged with giving each resort 'unity' and 'style'. La Grande Motte is the most distinctive of these new resorts, with its pyramid-style buildings. Others have the outward appearance of a traditional Mediterranean village. All provide safe and convenient access to the beach and recreational facilities, such as yacht moorings on the lagoon.

Although this is one of the world's most ambitious tourism projects, the resorts tend to be moribund outside the summer months. Many of the jobs are seasonal, and there is a danger that the region could become as over-dependent on tourism as it had previously been on agriculture.

Discussion point

Referring to what we said about tourism planning in Chapter 3, apply the flow chart (Figure 3.1) to the Languedoc-Roussillon project and evaluate the benefits of planning for the government, the local communities, and the tourists themselves.

Tourism plays an important role in regional development, enabling the economic regeneration of stagnating rural areas such as those of the Massif Central. Government grants, loans, and subsidies not only encourage the upgrading of accommodation in spas and seaside resorts throughout France but also provide much of the funding for conservation. The government showed little concern for countryside conservation until 1960 when the first national park was designated. This was due to the country's low population density, compared to England, so the need for protection was seen as less pressing, and not least, the French passion among all classes for field sports – hunting, shooting, and fishing. The majority of France's most scenic areas now have protected status as national parks or regional nature parks (PNRs).

The 11 national parks are managed by Parcs Nationaux de France (www.parcsnationaux.fr) under the overall control of the Ministry of Nature Protection. Management is designed to conserve the natural flora and fauna, and a system of zoning controls the impact of visitors:

- Tourism is encouraged in the outer zone with information points, accommodation, and recreational facilities – for example, there are a number of ski resorts in the Vanoise National Park, which is situated in the Alps.
- A second zone supports traditional rural activities, subject to regulations on field sports and activities that might be detrimental to the natural environment.
- The inner zone severely restricts entry to give maximum protection to individual species and ecosystems.

The regional nature parks generally consist of landscapes that have been greatly modified by human intervention and where multiple-use management of resources is necessary. Unlike the national parks, the 46 PNRs are widely distributed throughout France and are more accessible from the major cities. Examples include St. Amand Reismes near Lille, the Camargue, and the Parc d'Armorique in Brittany. The Corsican regional nature park has the triple aims of nature conservation, providing for tourism and preserving rural life and traditions, in an attempt to stem the movement of population from the mountainous interior to the coastal resorts.

Conservation of the built heritage has a longer history in France, although there is no real equivalent to the English National Trust. The French tend to take a more robust approach to the conservation of historic buildings, with an emphasis on full-scale restoration. Notable examples include:

- The chateaus of the Loire, which were ransacked during the French Revolution.
- The medieval city of Carcassonne – which is a nineteenth-century reconstruction.
- The port of St Malo was destroyed in the Second World War and subsequently rebuilt complete with the medieval fortifications.

Some 130 historic towns and districts of exceptional cultural or architectural significance are subject to strict planning controls as *villes d'art*. As such, they are often used as locations by the French film industry.

Tourism resources

The distribution of tourism in France shows important differences between the regions in the south and west, which attract a large international and domestic market, and the climatically less-favoured regions in the north and east. However, the part of the country most visited by foreign tourists is the Île de France, largely because it includes Paris. If we look at the pattern of domestic tourism, this region is much less significant as a destination, accounting for only 5 per cent of overnight stays. Only two regions – Alsace and the Île de France – receive more foreign than domestic tourists.

Northern France

As far as the majority of sun-seeking tourists from northern Europe are concerned, most of northern France is a zone of passage on the routes south to the Riviera, Italy, and Spain. The 'cold water' resorts along the Channel coast, once fashionable with British as well as domestic tourists, have suffered a decline since the Second World War. The heritage attractions and gentle landscapes of northern France are also overshadowed by the more dramatic scenery of the south and west. The exception is of course **Paris**, which vies with London as the world's favourite tourist city, a status which will be enhanced as the host of the 2024 Olympic Games. A short list of the attractions offered by the 'city of light' would include:

- World-famous 'icons' – such as the Eiffel Tower (www.toureiffel.paris/fr), the cathedral of Notre Dame, which was severely damaged by fire in 2019 (www.notreda-medeparis.fr), the Basilica of Sacré Coeur, and the Arc de Triomphe (https://www.paris-arc-de-triomphe.fr/).
- The city's intellectual reputation as a centre of art and music, epitomised by the Left Bank, the Louvre (www.louvre.fr), the Musée d'Orsay (www.musee-orsay.fr), and the Palais Garnier (opera).
- The romantic associations evoked by the River Seine and its bridges.
- The city's reputation as a centre of high fashion and stylish entertainment.

Compared to most world capitals, the townscapes of central Paris within the *peripherique* (ring road) consist of low-rise buildings and broad tree-lined boulevards forming a harmonious whole. Some of the historic *quartiers* (districts) have preserved their specific character – although areas like Montmartre have become commercialised due to tourism. Nevertheless, a considerable amount of urban renewal has occurred since the 1970s, including such exciting examples of modern architecture as the Louvre extension, the Pompidou Centre, the Bastille Opera, and La Defense. For many years, Paris has been the most popular city-break destination, and this is likely to continue, given its improved accessibility as a result of the Channel Tunnel to the United Kingdom.

The French capital offers the opportunity of excursions to the former royal palaces at Versailles (.chateauversailles.fr) and Fontainebleau https://www.chateaudefontainebleau.fr), or to the historic towns of Orleans, Chartres, and Beauvais. The tourism industry of Paris was boosted in 1992 by the opening of the largest theme park in Europe – Disneyland Paris (operated by Eurodisney) to the east of the city (www.disneylandparis.com/). This is an interesting example of cooperation between the public sector and a foreign-owned private corporation, with the French government providing the dedicated rail link from Roissy-Charles de Gaulle Airport. After initial teething troubles, due in part to the wide cultural gap between French and North American tastes and expectations (shown for example, in attitudes to alcohol and customer service), Disneyland Paris has established itself as the leading theme park in France, with over half of its estimated 15 million annual visitors from abroad. Much more than a theme park, it is a resort in its own right, adding 6,500 rooms to the accommodation stock in the Paris region. In 2002, a second major attraction – Walt Disney Studios Park- was added. Faced with this competition, the Asterix Park to the south of Paris has retained its market share, basing its appeal on traditional French themes (www.parcasterix.fr).

Paris is also a major destination for business travellers, and this is reflected in the availability of modern conference facilities and top-quality hotels (half of the 'de-luxe' class of French hotels are located in the capital).

The North

Consisting of the Nord-Pas-de-Calais and Picardy regions, *Le Nord* has a rather negative image among the French for poor weather and a landscape blighted by nineteenth-century heavy industry. In fact, the scenery and the architecture of the historic towns have much in common with neighbouring Flanders. In the past, the region has been a zone of international conflict, as shown by the battlefields of the Somme, as well as commerce. Calais is the major gateway to France for British tourists travelling by car, coach or train. Dunkirk also handles a significant volume of ferry traffic, but Boulogne has lost its ferry link, and, like Dover across the Channel, has had to diversify, investing heavily in the 'Nausicaa' marine-life attraction. Lille, one of a number of large manufacturing centres, has compensated for the loss of its traditional industries to become a major transport hub and business centre, thanks largely to the Channel Tunnel. Lille's cultural attractions, along with those of other historic towns such as Arras and Douai, are now more widely appreciated for short-break holidays. The 'Opal Coast' south of Boulogne, particularly the attractive resort of Le Touquet, was fashionable before the Second World War. It continues to be popular with Parisians, and golf is providing the impetus for rejuvenation.

Normandy

Normandy's history has been closely linked with that of England, as shown by the Bayeux tapestry commemorating the Norman conquest in 1066, and the battlefields of the Hundred Years War. In 1944, the Normandy beaches at Arromanches were the launch pad for the Allied campaign to liberate Europe in the Second World War. Visitors are drawn to its attractive countryside, and a number of historic towns such as Caen and Rouen, but in summer the seaside resorts provide the main appeal. The Côte Fleurie between Caen and the Seine estuary remains popular with domestic holidaymakers. A creation of the late nineteenth-century *Belle Epoque*, Deauville continues to be visited by fashion-conscious Parisians, although it has invested heavily in a marina and other modern facilities. Other resorts such as Trouville are more family-oriented and suffer from competition from self-catering complexes, a surplus of hotel accommodation, and changing holiday tastes. The port of Cherbourg, usually a brief staging point for British and Irish tourists on their way south, has invested in the *Cité de la Mer* project, whereby the former ocean terminal for passenger liners has been transformed into a marine-life exhibition (www.citedelamer.com). Normandy also boasts one of France's most unique and most visited heritage attractions – the medieval abbey of Mont St. Michel, which is daily separated from the mainland by some of the world's strongest tides. It is now the subject of a controversial project to clear the site of car parks and other modern accretions that detract from its mystique.

Brittany

With its Celtic heritage, including the Breton language, and maritime outlook, the peninsula of Brittany, with its rugged, deeply indented coastline has long been peripheral to the mainstream of French economic and social life. Yet these characteristics have considerable tourism potential, for this region with its distinctive folk costumes and religious traditions has long attracted French artists to picturesque fishing ports such as Pont-Aven, and more recently has appealed to a growing British market. The main holiday area focusses on the part of the north coast - the Côte Emeraude – which includes the resort of

Dinard and the historic seaport of St. Malo. Efforts are being made to disperse tourism away from these established centres to the more rugged coastal areas of western Brittany and the neglected interior, which, unlike Normandy, is a poor area agriculturally.

Western France

Offering among its resources the heritage attractions of Anjou, La Vendée and Aquitaine, western France has a mild but sunny Atlantic climate, some of the best beaches in Europe and is regarded by the French themselves as the land of gastronomy and the good life. On the Côte d'Argent, there are old-established resorts such as Biarritz and Arcachon, which have adapted to modern trends such as surfing and camping. North of the Gironde estuary there are a number of offshore islands, such as Île du Ré, where the number of summer visitors greatly outnumbers the local inhabitants. The scenic and cultural attractions of western France include:

- The Loire Valley, one of the best-known touring areas, where the main attractions are the chateaus and palaces associated with French royalty in Renaissance times, notably Chambord and Chenonceau (www.chenonceau.com), where history is brought to life by *Son et lumière* performances during the summer months.
- The caves of the Dordogne, which contain outstanding examples of Ice Age art. The most famous of these – Lascaux – was not discovered until 1940 and is a UNESCO World Heritage site (www.lascaux.fr). A replica cave now diverts attention from the original paintings, which otherwise would have deteriorated from the impact of visitors.
- The wine-producing area around Bordeaux, a city which is also noted for its eighteenth-century Grand Theatre.
- The Aquitaine coast boasts some of the highest sand dunes in Europe and extensive lagoons backed by pine forests. In 1967, a management plan was inaugurated to maximise these resources. Nevertheless, this has not achieved the success of Languedoc-Roussillon, due to insufficient public funding and opposition from environmentalists.
- Theme parks, namely Futuroscope near Poitiers, celebrating the film industry (https://futuroscope.com), and Le Puy du Fou, based on the heritage of La Vendée, which attracted 2.3 million visitors in 2019 (www.puydefou.com).
- Toulouse is the centre of the French aerospace industry, showcased by the European Space Park.

The Massif Central

This extensive area of mountain and plateau in south-central France offers scope for a wide variety of recreational activities, including hang-gliding, mountain biking and white-water rafting. The landscapes include deep limestone gorges, extensive forests and the strange remnants of extinct volcanoes known as *puys*. Geothermal activity is evident today in the large number of mineral springs; as a result, the Massif Central contains more than a third of French spas. The volcanic landscapes of the Auvergne provided the inspiration for the Vulcania 'science park' near the industrial city of Clermont Ferrand (www.vulcania.com). This project has attracted private-sector funding from Michelin and Volvic, both major commercial enterprises based in the region. Agrotourism has been encouraged to stem depopulation from one of France's poorest farming regions, by integrating holiday villages and second homes with rural communities. There has also been some development of winter sports tourism for the domestic market.

Vichy is probably the best known of French spas, although it now attracts fewer wealthy foreign clients than in the era prior to the Second World War. The hotels, bathing establishments, casino and opera house are grouped around the *Parc des Sources*, which is the major focus of the resort. Like other European spas, Vichy has adapted to changing demands by:

- Diversification of the product into conferences, exhibitions, and festivals.
- Modernisation of spa treatments to appeal to today's busy executives rather than the traditional three-week *cure*.
- The provision of sports facilities to attract young tourists.

Eastern France

The swathe of France extending from the Ardennes to the Jura Mountains has been for centuries a zone of passage for trade and invading armies. It includes most of the area covered by the French Alps and the Rhône-Saône corridor. The following areas are well suited for touring by car:

- The rolling countryside of **Champagne** which includes Rheims, historically important as the religious capital of France.
- **Lorraine**, although more industrialised, boasts one of the best examples of eighteenth-century town planning in the city of Nancy.
- German-speaking **Alsace** has more to offer the visitor, with its picturesque half-timbered villages and an important wine route based on Colmar, while its regional capital – Strasbourg – has acquired a major international role as a seat of the European Parliament and other EU agencies.
- **Burgundy**, lying astride the routeways connecting the Rhine to the Rhône, and thus linking northern Europe to the Mediterranean, played a major role in European history in the Middle Ages. Its rich cultural heritage includes the Romanesque abbeys of Cîteaux (www.citeaux-abbaye.com) and Cluny (https://www.cluny-abbaye.fr), and the historic cities of Dijon and Beaune, although Burgundy is best known for the wines of the Côte d'Or and Beaujolais districts.
- **Lyon** deserves special mention as the second city of France, which became of major importance through its silk weaving industry and strategic location at the junction of the rivers Rhône and Saône. It is now a major tourist and business centre, thanks to its position as an interchange on the TGV rail and motorway networks. The city

is internationally recognised as a short-break destination, noted for its fine architectural heritage and its culinary attractions.
- The **Franche Comté** is a forest and mountain region, deeply dissected by river valleys. It is much less developed for tourism than the Alps and attracts relatively few foreign visitors.

The French Alps

The traditional economy of this mountain region was based on pastoralism, with the livestock being moved to the high pastures above the tree line in summer and back to the villages in autumn. The economy is now dependent on tourism, including winter sports and in summer, lakes and mountains holidays. Most of the development has occurred in the north, where the mountains are higher, yet more accessible. Mountain climbing has been a major activity at Chamonix since the early nineteenth century, due to its proximity to Mont Blanc and the spectacular glacier known as the Mer de Glace. It has now become a major ski resort. Villages at lower altitudes – in the so-called Pre-Alps – are less used for skiing due to the unreliable snow cover but are much in demand for second home development, while Aix les Bains and Evian rank among France's most important spas.

Full-scale development for winter sports tourism began in the 1960s, involving public sector investment under the *Plan Neige*. Purpose-built resorts were planned at high altitudes above the tree line, where glacial cirques provided maximum snow cover. These were to be veritable 'ski-factories' of a uniform design appealing to sports-minded tourists, with apartment blocks sited to give direct access to the lift system. Resorts such as Tignes have been criticised for their lack of human scale, severely functional design and their impact on the fragile alpine environment. Overall, the majority of the development has been in the northern Alps, where the 15 major resorts account for over three-quarters of the industry's turnover. Since the 1990s there has been something of a reaction favouring smaller resorts of a more traditional design.

The French Alps have become Europe's most popular winter sports destination, attracting domestic and foreign skiers alike, for the following reasons:

- Proximity to the areas generating the demand. Thanks to the Channel Tunnel, British skiers have a wide choice of routes and modes of transport to the resorts. In addition to airports at Nice (serving the southern resort of Isola 2000), Lyon, Grenoble, Chambéry, and Geneva, there are Eurostar ski-trains, and 'ski-drive' arrangements are available for motorists using the excellent road network.
- Good infrastructure, including the most extensive lift system in Europe.
- Suitability for a wide range of markets, from family holidaymakers to young singles and snowboarders.
- An extensive range of accommodations, from first-class hotels to family-run *auberges*, serviced chalets, and self-catering studio apartments.

The South of France

For the tourist travelling overland, the Rhône Valley south of Lyon provides the introduction to the region known by the French as *Le Midi*. The South of France is distinguished by its Mediterranean climate, but more tangibly by the colourful landscapes, and the quality of its light, which have attracted many world-famous artists. Regional lifestyles also differ from those of northern France, while the popularity of bullfights in Nîmes, Perpignan and Arles and the use of the Catalan language in Roussillon, reflect the influence of Spain. The south includes two major tourist regions – the Languedoc-Roussillon coast, which we mentioned earlier as an example of large-scale planning, and the French Riviera.

In **Languedoc-Roussillon**, the coastal resorts have tended to draw tourists away from the interior, which includes such scenically attractive areas as the Cevennes and the Corbières. The sites associated with the Cathars are now on the tourist trail, thanks to the growing interest in medieval history and the occult. The historic cities of the interior include Montpellier with its university, Carcassonne, and Nîmes, which boasts a well-preserved Roman arena and the Pont du Gard aqueduct.

Foreign tourists account for almost half of all visitors to the Provence-Alpes-Côte d'Azur region. In **Provence**, the rural areas have successfully attracted tourists and second home owners. The cities of the region are also important tourist centres, with a wealth of heritage attractions dating back to Roman times, and a calendar of cultural events such as music festivals. The best known are Aix en Provence, which is a major artistic centre, Arles, and Avignon – where the Palace of the Popes is a reminder of the city's importance in the fourteenth century as a political and religious centre (www.palais-des-papes.com). However, tourism is of secondary importance in Marseilles, due to the dominance of industry and commerce and its reputation for crime. Provence can also offer a number of contrasting natural attractions such as the wetlands of the Camargue and the gorges of Verdon. But it is the coast, mainly the world-famous French Riviera, that draws most tourists to this region.

The **French Riviera** is the Mediterranean coast of eastern Provence, extending almost 200 kilometres from Toulon to the Italian border, and sheltered by mountains from the blustery Mistral. The Côte d'Azur is the name usually given to the section between Cannes and Menton, where the Maritime Alps almost reach the sea. Three scenic highways – the *corniches* – hug the contours of the cliffs. Well endowed with natural attractions, the Riviera is easily accessible by road, rail and air transport and has a full range of amenities. The French Riviera has experienced several stages of development in response to changing fashions in tourism:

- **Exclusive winter health tourism**. From the mid-nineteenth century to the outbreak of the First World War in 1914, the Riviera was essentially a winter destination. Wealthy British visitors began the vogue for spending the winter on the Mediterranean coast for health reasons, which is commemorated by the *Promenade des Anglais* along the seafront at Nice. Queen Victoria made several visits, confirming the Riviera's exclusive status. Grand hotels, such as the Carlton in Cannes and the Negresco in Nice (www.hotel-negresco-nice.com) catered for a wealthy clientele from all over Europe, including the Russian aristocracy. The world-famous casino in Monte Carlo opened in 1863, an initiative that almost overnight made the fortunes of the tiny principality of Monaco and its ruling family (www.montecarlosbm.com).

- **Exclusive summer beach tourism**. Until the 1920s, the elite shunned the Mediterranean summer. This changed when a number of celebrities made sunbathing fashionable. Juan-les-Pins was the Riviera's first summer resort, attracting a new moneyed clientele, including many Americans and the big names in literature, art, and entertainment, who were quite different in their outlook from the European aristocracy, whose wealth had declined as a result of wars and revolutions. The Riviera became more accessible with the construction of a new coastal highway and the inauguration of *Le Train Bleu* (the Calais-Mediterranean Express), which provided luxury travel to the resorts. The mediocre beaches of the Côte d'Azur were also improved, sometimes by importing sand from elsewhere. Market segmentation was evident as early as the 1920s, when an advertising slogan for Cannes claimed that 'Menton's dowdy, Monte's brass, Nice is rowdy, Cannes is class'. This was true to the extent that Menton had a reputation for attracting elderly invalids, whereas Monte Carlo appealed to the *nouveaux riches*. Nice on the other hand was a bustling seaport and commercial centre as well as being a major resort.
- **Popular tourism**. From the 1950s, the Riviera considerably broadened its appeal, catering for a much larger domestic market. This had been foreshadowed by the French government's decision in 1936 to introduce holidays with pay and encourage cheap rail travel to the resorts, but the Second World War was a setback to the process of democratisation. Campgrounds and a sprawl of holiday villas developed along the western Riviera, while many luxury hotels on the Côte d'Azur were converted into apartments. On the other hand, new resorts – particularly the former fishing village of Saint-Tropez – strove to retain exclusivity along with some of the established centres. Innovations in beach fashion such as the bikini ensured that the Riviera remained a focus of attention worldwide.

Today, the resorts vary considerably in character, from the exclusive hideaways of the very rich – Cap Ferrat is a good example – to unpretentious places catering for the French family market such as Saint Maxime and Saint Raphael.

- Cannes and Antibes have retained their stylish image to a greater extent than the other major resorts of the Côte d'Azur. The crescent-shaped Croisette beach at Cannes is backed by a promenade lined with palms and grand hotels, and the designer boutiques of the new town contrast with the old quarter overlooking the harbour. The Cannes Film Festival and the Nice Carnival (https://en.nicecarnaval.com) are two event attractions that are revenue earners for the Riviera.
- Nice has a range of accommodations to suit most budgets, while its airport handles not only a large volume of holiday traffic – much of it on low-cost carriers – but also a substantial amount of business travel attracted by the information technology industries that have developed in this part of France. Nice is moreover a cultural centre of some significance, with a history going back to the time of Ancient Greece and an association with some of the greatest artists of the twentieth century.
- Saint-Tropez is the leading resort of the western Riviera, offering fine beaches and a milieu that attracts a multitude of fashionistas wishing to 'see and be seen'.

Photo 13.1
Promenade des Anglais, the fashionable seafront at Nice
Source: Brian Boniface

- The **principality of Monaco** is much less dependent on gambling revenue than in the past, having diversified into international sports events and exhibitions as well as the business sector – many of its 37,000 residents are wealthy 'tax exiles'. With an area of less than 200 hectares space is at a premium, resulting in a 'mini-Manhattan' of high-rise buildings and land reclamation projects. Nevertheless, the old town of Monaco perched above the famous yacht harbour retains some of its traditional

Discussion point

1.   The Riviera's image as a tourist destination has been associated with changes in fashion since the time of its 'discovery' by English 'milords' to the present day. Discuss the influence of the following celebrities on the development of particular resorts:

-   Coco Chanel;
-   Scott Fitzgerald;
-   Painters such as Matisse;
-   Brigitte Bardot;
-   Grace Kelly.

2.   Identify the environmental and social problems affecting the Riviera that, if unchecked, could make the destination unfashionable.

character, in contrast to Monte Carlo. Visitor attractions include the Oceanographical Museum, associated with the undersea explorer Jacques Cousteau (www.oceano.org), and the Jardin Exotique, a unique collection of cacti made possible by the favourable microclimate (https://www.jardinexotique.mc).

The rural hinterland of the Riviera contrasts the sophisticated resorts, but this is changing as pressures on the coast increase. Nevertheless, the cultivation of flowers for the perfume industry at Grasse, and of fruit and vegetables for the Paris markets, are still an important part of the local economy. The numerous hilltop villages – the *villes perchés* – are a reminder of the time when the coast was menaced by Saracen pirates from North Africa rather than tourists. Some of these villages, notably Èze and Saint Paul de Vence have become artists' colonies and specialise in various craft industries aimed primarily at the tourist market.

Corsica

Known to the French as 'the island of beauty', Corsica offers some of the most spectacular scenery in the western Mediterranean. From the deeply indented western coast rise high mountains covered with forests of pine and chestnut and sweet-smelling *maquis* scrub. Tourism has underlined the differences between the coastal towns, which have always been more outward-looking, and the sparsely populated interior, where traditional lifestyles prevailed until well into the twentieth century. Tourism in Corsica is characterised by pronounced seasonality, as the majority of visitors are Parisians and Italians arriving in the months of July and August. The main resorts – Calvi, Île Rousse, and Porto Vecchio – lie on the west coast and offer facilities for water sports such as sailing and diving, while the island's capital – Ajaccio – has capitalised on its fame as the birthplace of Napoleon. Development plans for the island seek to redress the imbalance between the coast and the interior, although continuing to recognise the key role of tourism which provides about 25 per cent of jobs. Attention is focussed on the flatter East Coast, where development is taking place in a more orderly way than in the past. Improved transport links to the mainland and the growth of inclusive tours will ensure a greater role for tourism in Corsica. However, tourism must be seen to benefit the local population, who are keen to preserve their language and cultural identity.

The French Pyrenees

Winter sports play a less important role in the Pyrenees than in the Alps, and the region attracts fewer foreign skiers. Although the mountain peaks are not as high, remoteness from Paris and transport problems retarded the development of tourism. Nevertheless, a number of spas also function as ski centres during the winter months. In summer, visitors are attracted by the unspoiled scenery – notably the Cirque de Gavarnie, a spectacular natural amphitheatre resulting from glacial erosion – and the opportunities for eco-tourism and adventure sports. The major tourist centre of the region – **Lourdes** – is in fact, one of the world's leading destinations for faith-based tourism and, therefore, deserves special consideration:

- This small town – with less than 15,000 inhabitants – accounted for 2.2 million overnight stays in 2018, of which 63 per cent were foreign visitors. With some 270 hotels and a number of campsites on the outskirts, Lourdes can accommodate more than 100,000 visitors at peak times.
- Its fame as a tourist centre is based not on a tangible physical resource, but on the apparitions of the Virgin Mary to St. Bernadette. The Grotto of Massabielle, where these occurred in 1858, very soon became the focus of pilgrimage. Miraculous cures are attributed to the spring water in the grotto and although a Medical Bureau scrutinises these claims, Lourdes is not a spa in the conventional sense (unlike nearby Cauterets).
- Lourdes was the first pilgrimage centre to be created by modern means of transport and communication, which explains its rapid growth, and it has become a role model for similar developments in other countries.
- One-third of the visitors to Lourdes can be described as true pilgrims motivated by religious faith. More than 500 organised group pilgrimages take place every year, brought in by charter flights, coaches, and special trains equipped by SNCF to carry the large numbers of sick and disabled. This involves considerable organisation, in which volunteer carers play a major role.
- The distinction between the religious and secular aspects of pilgrimage is not always clear, but in Lourdes, there is some geographical separation between the two. Religious activity is centred on the 'Domain of the Sanctuary' covering an area of 20 hectares. This includes the esplanade – a vast open space for processions – and a number of large churches grouped around the entrance to the grotto. The devotion of the pilgrims provides a stark contrast to the commercialism of the town centre, with its array of shops displaying what many would regard as tasteless souvenirs.

Due to the COVID-19 pandemic and the need for social distancing, the Sanctuary was closed for two years, from 2020 to 2022. However, the Sanctuary organised the 'Lourdes United Pilgrimage' on July 26 2020, an online event that was viewed by 80 million on social media. This was a success in revitalising the rituals of the pilgrimage, but 'virtual events are an addition, not a substitute for the real thing' (Seraphin: 2021).

Summary

- Changing economic and social conditions in France since the Second World War have encouraged participation in tourism.
- The majority of French tourism is domestic, characterised by long-stay holidays concentrated in the peak summer months, although short breaks are increasing in popularity. Domestic holidays are widely distributed throughout France and tend to be organised independently.
- Social tourism plays a more important role in France than in most other countries.
- The majority of French holidays abroad are to Spain and Italy, although long-haul destinations are becoming more popular, spearheaded to some extent by Club Mediterranée.

- Incoming tourism is more significant, and France is one of the world's most popular destinations.
- The tourism industry in France is fragmented, comprising many small businesses. A wide choice of accommodation is available, with self-catering traditionally the preferred option for domestic holidaymakers, leaving the hotel sector largely dependent on the business and inbound tourism markets.
- Tourism benefits from comprehensive air, rail, and road networks.
- Tourism tends to be centralised at the government level, with the state also initiating major development projects, although both regional and local organisations are now playing a more important role.
- France can offer a great diversity of tourism resources and products, based on its countryside, coastal resorts, and cultural heritage, ranging from winter sports and adventure tourism in the Alps to sightseeing in Paris and the Loire Valley. Each region can offer different attractions, although tourism tends to play a more significant role in the coastal and mountain areas.

Assignments

1. The London-Paris route is one of the busiest in the world, with a wide choice of transport operators. Compare the advantages and disadvantages of each of the transport modes for different categories of tourists, taking into account the following factors:

    - price;
    - travel time between home or workplace and the destination;
    - convenience;
    - environmental impact.

    You could use as your examples a group of students on a European tour and a business traveller working for the government.

2. Compare the advantages of Brittany as a holiday destination with Provence, for a Swedish family with young children.
3. Explain why France has such an appeal for art lovers from all over the world.
4. Match particular types of outdoor recreation with specific areas of France, taking into account climate, topography, and facilities.

References and further reading

Organization for Economic Co-operation and Development (annual) *Tourism Policy and International Tourism in OECD Member Countries*, OECD, Paris

Potier, F.- and Terrier, C. (2007) *Atlas des mobilités touristiques en France metropolitaine* Editions Autrement, Paris

Seraphin, H. (2021) COVID-19: Impacts and perspectives for religious tourism events: The case of Lourdes Pilgrimages, *Journal of Convention and Event Tourism* 23 (1), 15–40

https://www.unwto.org/tourism-data/unwto-tourism-dashboard

14 The tourism geography of Spain and Portugal

Learning objectives

After reading this chapter, you should be able to:

- Describe the major physical regions and climates of Spain and Portugal, including the islands, and understand their importance for tourism.

- Trace the development of Spanish tourism and understand the reasons for Spain's success as a destination.

- Appreciate the characteristics of inbound tourism demand to Spain and Portugal and the impact of COVID-19.

DOI: 10.4324/9781003406853-17

- Be aware of the differences between the two countries in the nature of tourism development.
- Outline the main features of tourism organisation in Spain and Portugal.
- Demonstrate knowledge of the tourism regions, resorts, business centres and tourist attractions of Spain and Portugal.
- Understand the appeal of Andorra and Gibraltar.

Introduction

Since the 'Age of Discovery' in the sixteenth century, Spain and Portugal have made an important contribution to the world's cultural heritage. Over 600 million people in the world speak Spanish as their first or second language, mainly in Latin America. Portuguese claims 260 million speakers, mostly in Brazil, but five African nations also use it as their official language. The countries of the Iberian Peninsula, together with the Balearic and Canary Islands, are among the world's most popular holiday destinations.

Spain was one of the first countries in the world to enter the mass inclusive-tour market, taking advantage of its sunny climate and long Mediterranean coastline. However, increasingly Spain faces competition from other destinations that can offer similar attractions to north Europeans, but at lower prices. Nevertheless, Spain has been highly successful as a destination and has managed to fend off its rivals. On the other hand, Portugal entered the international tourism scene later than Spain. It not only made a determined effort to avoid some of its neighbour's worst excesses of tourism development but also attempted both to control tourism's impact on the country and to attract the more affluent tourist from the outset.

Spain

The setting for tourism

In area, Spain is the second largest country of western Europe after France, and occupies the greater part of the Iberian Peninsula. British visitors arriving by sea on the north coast, at Santander or Bilbao, should bear this in mind when planning a tour itinerary, as it is almost 1,000 kilometres by road to Málaga in the south. The dominant feature of the Iberian Peninsula is a high plateau – the Meseta – separated by rugged mountain ranges or *sierras* from the narrow coastal strips where most of the tourism development has taken place. Because of this, only the Balearic Islands and the south and east of Spain have a typically Mediterranean climate. The northern coast from Vigo to San Sebastián is not called 'Green Spain' without reason; summers are cooler and rainier, and it enjoys less sunshine than the Mediterranean coast. The Meseta experiences a more extreme climate, with rather cold winters and hot summers. These physical contrasts account for the country's great cultural diversity, with regional languages such as Basque, Catalan, and Galician flourishing alongside Castilian Spanish. The division of Spain into 17 autonomous regions acknowledges this diversity.

The rugged nature of much of the Iberian Peninsula has also helped to isolate Spain from the rest of Europe. Even today, the Pyrenees are crossed by very few roads and railways. In the south, only a narrow stretch of water separates Spain from North Africa and its Islamic culture. In fact, almost the whole of Spain, except for Asturias, was at one time under Arab domination. The *Reconquista* or struggle to oust the 'Moors' lasted from 718 to 1492. This forged the religious fervour and devotion to the Roman Catholic Church that still characterises much of Spain and explains the ambivalent attitudes of Spaniards today towards their Muslim heritage and the issue of large-scale immigration from North Africa. Despite the impressive economic development and social changes (in the role of women for example) that have taken place since the 1960s, Spain differs from other West European countries in the following ways:

- The greater persistence of craft industries, notably ceramics, guitar making and Toledo metalwork.
- The *fiestas, ferias* (fairs) and *romerías* (pilgrimages) which play such an important role in the life of many communities. These provide an opportunity to display Spain's rich heritage of regional dances and colourful costumes.
- The iconic role of the *corrida* (bullfight) in the national culture, where it is regarded as an art form and not as a sport.
- Aspects of the lifestyle, for example, the traditional afternoon siesta, whereas dining out and social activity involving families and all age groups takes place very late into the night.

Spain has achieved outstanding success as one of the world's top three destinations and can offer over 200,000 hotels. There is no doubt that tourism has contributed greatly to the transformation of the Spanish economy from that of a developing country in the 1950s to one of Europe's major industrial nations. In 2019, the tourism sector employed 11 per cent of the workforce, contributed almost one-third of the country's export earnings and accounted for 8 per cent of GDP. However, this success has been achieved at a cost to society and the environment, for example:

- Spain's rich cultural diversity in music and dance has been set aside in favour of a commercialised version of *flamenco* for tourist consumption in the resorts.
- The demands of the tourism industry have affected family life in some areas.
- Uncontrolled resort developments mar much of the Mediterranean coastline and cause pollution.
- Tourism has sharpened regional contrasts, particularly between the developed coastal areas and the interior.

Spain's success in tourism is due to a variety of factors, namely:

- There was a growth in demand for holidays in the sun from countries in northern Europe once they had recovered from the effects of the Second World War.
- Spain was well-placed to benefit from the development of civil aviation and changes in the structure of the travel industry, especially the introduction of low-cost air-inclusive tours and more recently low-cost carriers.
- Spain's relatively late entry into the European tourism market allowed it to evaluate the competition and offer lower prices than those of established destinations such as Italy and the French Riviera.
- The Spanish government strongly encouraged tourism by abolishing visa require-ments, providing advantageous credit terms to developers, regulating the industry to protect the consumer, and maintaining a favourable rate of exchange by devalua-tions of the peseta.

Some would argue that the tourism industry was able to benefit from the long period of political stability under the authoritarian rule of General Franco (Caudillo from 1939 to 1975), as industrial unrest was outlawed. After the Second World War, Spain was ostra-cised by the international community, but the politics of the Cold War soon led the US government to reappraise the Franco regime. Additionally, in exchange for American bases in Spain, much-needed investment was made available to improve the infrastruc-ture of the coastal areas that were the country's biggest tourism resource. The regime positively encouraged tourism as an engine of economic growth to lift Spain and her people out of poverty, while the slogan 'Spain is different' emphasised national charac-teristics in its appeal to foreign tourists. The government encouraged the development of large resorts where it was easier to monitor the influence of foreign tourists on local people, whose views on tourism development were also ignored in the interest of na-tional unity and economic expediency. However, although the Franco regime tried to isolate Spain from the social changes taking place in western Europe, tourism played a major role in bringing about the liberalisation of Spanish society through the demon-stration effect. Taking the province of Gerona (which includes the Costa Brava) as an example, whereas in the 1950s, 'foreign women in trousers were strongly looked down upon', a few years later 'the señoritas were wearing them as if a uniform' (Cosgrove and Jackson, 1972, 44).

The demand for tourism

Domestic tourism

Before the 1960s, only a relatively small minority of the Spanish population could afford to take holidays away from home. The middle and upper classes escaped the summer heat of the cities by visiting spas in the mountains, the beaches of the east coast, or the northern coastal resorts such as Santander and San Sebastián. The economic progress which took place after 1960 increased personal incomes and boosted car ownership, so that tourism propensity is now over 60 per cent. Despite the social changes brought about by industrialisation, family ties remain stronger than in most other European countries. Although many Spaniards work long hours by 'moonlighting' with a second job, leisure is highly valued, and the public holidays celebrating national and religious festivals are often linked by a practice known as *puente* (literally 'bridge') to increase the number of 'long weekends' in the year. The geographical pattern of holiday taking by Spaniards also contrasts with that of foreign visitors, although some Mediterranean resorts are popular with both. The Atlantic coastal resorts, on the other hand, cater predominantly for domestic demand. Many city dwellers visit the rural areas of the interior to re-connect with their family roots, which were severed due to the large-scale emigration that took place from the 1940s onwards. Domestic tourism in Spain also has the following characteristics:

- Over 80 per cent of trips are for leisure purposes.
- Only one-third of trips involve hotel accommodation, as most domestic tourists stay with friends or relatives, or in second homes (the demand for camping as a low-budget alternative is minimal).
- The most popular month is August, when one in four Spaniards is on holiday.

Outbound tourism

Well over 90 per cent of holidays taken by Spaniards are in their own country, and it was not until the 1990s that they began to view a foreign holiday as an annual event. The most visited destinations are neighbouring France and Portugal, although touring holidays in northern Europe and Morocco are becoming more popular. The countries of Latin America are important destinations for business and leisure travel. The cruise market has grown rapidly in recent years as it is unaffected by recession in the economy. History, culture, and education are the features sought by the Spanish abroad, with guidebooks stressing the culinary attractions of a destination.

Inbound tourism

Although Spain is now the world's second most popular tourism destination, it was a relative latecomer to the international tourism scene. It did not usually feature on the Grand Tour, since the generally poor state of the roads and the inns tended to deter all but the more adventurous travellers. A major improvement in the situation took place after 1928, when the government-sponsored *Patronato Nacional de Turismo* began to set up a chain of state-run *albergues* (inns) and *paradores* offering a high standard of accommodation. The small numbers of foreign visitors to Spain before the Civil War (1936–1939) were attracted by the country's picturesque traditions and not by sun, sand, and sea, unlike most of today's tourists. For example, the American writer Hemingway was largely responsible for publicising bullfighting and Pamplona's Fiesta de San Fermín, which today attract a wide international following.

Tourism growth, on a large scale, began in the early 1950s with the influx of French and British holidaymakers to the Costa Brava, spreading to the Balearic Islands and the other Costas as soon as the introduction of jet aircraft made these areas more accessible in the 1960s. By the early 1970s, Spain had become the leading holiday destination for most of the tourist-generating countries in northern Europe. However, this has left Spanish tourism vulnerable to the effects of recession in these countries, resulting in demand stagnating during the 1980s and early 1990s. This prompted the search for new markets – such as the United States and Japan – and volumes recovered in the late 1990s to exceed 40 million staying visitors and 20 million excursionists (the latter including cruise passengers and day visitors from France and Portugal). Spain has recently benefitted from unrest in Turkey and North Africa to win back tourists, and in 2019, 83.7 million arrivals were recorded. However, the increase in numbers since the 1990s has been offset to some extent by a shorter length of stay and a lower spend per capita.

The COVID-19 pandemic had a major impact on Spain's tourism sector, with international arrivals falling by 77 per cent in 2020. The Balearic Islands, Catalonia, and the Canary Islands experienced an even greater downturn, with substantial job losses. As small businesses were among those most affected by the crisis, the government provided the funding for the necessary technology, through the 2021–2025 Digitalisation Plan.

Although the tourism authorities have for many years promoted products other than beach tourism, this has proved difficult, as the image of the Spanish Costas, epitomised by the *chiringuito* (beach bar) is firmly engrained in the popular culture of northern Europe. Over 75 per cent of foreign tourists seek 'sun, sand and sea' and the majority of these are repeat visitors. The most important tourist-generating countries continue to be the United Kingdom, France, and Germany, which together account for 50 per cent of arrivals, followed by Italy, the Benelux countries, and Scandinavia. Although the Spanish-speaking countries of Latin America have contributed large numbers of immigrants to Spain, they account for only 2.5 per cent of all tourist arrivals.

Despite the efforts of both national and regional governments, tourism in Spain is highly concentrated both seasonally and geographically. Almost 50 per cent of foreign visitors arrive between June and September, coinciding with domestic holiday demand, and creating congestion in the resorts. The Canary Islands do not have this problem because of their sub-tropical climate, but other areas – notably the Costa Daurada and Costa Brava – are overwhelmingly dependent on summer visitors. Seasonality creates a problem for businesses as many find it uneconomic to remain open out of season, whereas those that do reduce their staff add to seasonal unemployment in the community. The public sector too is affected as services – such as water and power supplies – must have the extra capacity to cope with the peak demand but are under-utilised at other times of the year. One solution to the problem is for the government, through the State Secretariat of Social Services and Equality, to encourage 'third age' tourism in which Spanish senior citizens stay in resort hotels at reduced rates outside the peak season (www.imserso.es).

Four regions with a Mediterranean coastline (the Balearic Islands, Catalonia, Andalucia, and Valencia), together with the Canary Islands, account for over 90 per cent of all overnight stays by foreign tourists in hotels. In contrast, five regions in the interior of Spain (Aragon, Castilla-La Mancha, Extremadura, Navarra, and La Rioja) each receive less than 1 per cent. This implies that the benefits of tourism are not spread widely throughout the country, and that tourism has contributed to the migration of labour to the coastal resorts from the interior of Spain, where many mountain villages are virtually deserted. Rural tourism has grown in popularity in recent years and may help stem further depopulation.

However, this, in turn, leads to another problem – loss of cultural identity – if rural communities simply become second homes for north European expatriates seeking 'the good life'.

The very nature of tourism demand to Spain has reduced the economic benefits. Spanish tourism is dominated by the demands of the major north European tour operators who provide high volumes of visitors, yet demand low-priced accommodation. This encourages low-cost, high-rise hotel and apartment development in the coastal resorts and reduces the contribution of each tourist to the economy. However, the number of tourists arriving on package tours is slowly decreasing, while those taking advantage of 'dynamic packaging' where they assemble the tours themselves and take advantage of the growth of low-cost carriers and disruptive accommodation platforms such as Airbnb is increasing proportionately.

Although the authorities are aware that the mass market for beach tourism will continue to be important, attempts are being made to develop new holiday styles in order to reduce seasonality, spread tourism more evenly throughout Spain, and encourage higher-spending visitors. The market is becoming more sophisticated, and independent travellers from countries such as Britain now outnumber those on inclusive tours.

In line with this approach, conferences, sport tourism, golf, and 'five-star' luxury tourism are being promoted and much of the downmarket accommodation removed. Many Mediterranean resorts are now well-equipped with marinas for the high-spending nautical tourist, and some have invested in aqua-parks to attract the family market. Winter sports facilities have been developed in the Pyrenees, the Sierra de Guadarrama near Madrid, and the Sierra Nevada, although as yet these cater mainly for domestic demand. The Franco regime invested heavily in football stadiums, with Real Madrid gaining worldwide recognition (www.realmadrid.com). More recently, motor racing and other international sports events have featured in promotional campaigns.

The supply side of tourism

Transport

Over 80 per cent of foreign tourists arrive by air. The inclusive-tour market ensures a constant supply of tourists arriving mainly on charter airlines, owned in most cases by the major north European tour operators. However, their share of the holiday market is being eroded by the low-cost carriers such as Vueling (www.vueling.com) that can offer greater flexibility in travel arrangements for the increasing numbers of visitors staying in second homes or in rented apartments and villas. Many independent travellers touring Spain use the national carrier Iberia and its subsidiaries. Although Madrid and Barcelona are important international gateways, most north European holidaymakers fly to one of the regional airports serving a particular holiday area.

Touring Spain by car has been facilitated by the massive improvement of the road network that has taken place since the 1980s, including some 17,000 kilometres of motorways. The most important of these is the Autopista de Levante (east coast motorway) and the routes linking Madrid with the regional centres of Seville, Valencia, and Zaragoza. The Transmeditterranea shipping line provides ferry services from the Peninsula to the Balearic Islands, North Africa, and the Canary Islands (www.transmediterranea.es).

The rail system under Spanish State Railways (RENFE) (www.renfe.com) is tightly focussed on Madrid, and the change of gauge at the border with France also affects some international train services. Nevertheless, Spain now has the most extensive high-speed rail network in Europe, and its service has improved to the extent that AVE (high-speed trains) are successfully competing with the airlines for the lucrative business market on routes linking Madrid to Barcelona and other major cities. However, there is evidence that some routes were prestige projects, built to satisfy the aspirations of regional governments, with a capacity exceeding the demand for such services. Rail products geared specifically to the leisure market include the *Al Andalus Express*, which allows the visitor to view the country-side and cities of southern Spain in the style of the 'golden age' of rail travel in the 1920s.

Accommodation

Spain offers a variety of accommodation from luxury resort hotels to simple *hostales* (pensions). The official hotel classification scheme is based on the facilities provided rather than the quality of service. Sol-Meliá is the largest Spanish-owned hotel chain (www.melia.com) in a sector dominated by independent establishments and small groups, which have little bargaining power with foreign tour operators over pricing. In addition to the private sector, there are the state-owned *paradores*, situated away from the main tourist centres and providing accommodation in traditional Spanish style (often in converted castles, palaces, or monasteries). As such, they are favoured by independent travellers touring the 'real Spain' (as distinct from the Costas) by car. Hotels account for almost half of stays by foreign tourists, although their share has declined since the 1990s, and there are problems of over-supply in some areas such as the Costa del Sol. Self-catering accommodation, in the form of apartments and holiday villas, is mainly found in the resort areas of eastern and southern Spain, where Airbnb has made a significant impact, particularly in Barcelona. An almost continuous series of *urbanizaciones* (second home developments), often dominated by a particular nationality, now stretches from Denia to Estepona. Financial scandals involving several local authorities have resulted in illegal building projects and a serious problem of over-supply, bringing Spain's construction industry to the brink of disaster. Campsites are concentrated in those locations that are most accessible from France, such as the Costa Brava and the Valencia region.

Organisation

Spain's organisation of tourism has attracted attention from countries around the world and many have adopted the Spanish model. A Ministry of Information and Tourism with cabinet status was created in 1951 to provide effective co-ordination and promotion, and the national tourism plans since 1953 have set the institutional and public service frame-work for Spain's growth and continued presence in the world tourism market. At the national level, the Ministry of Industry, Trade and Tourism, through the State Secretariat for Tourism, is currently responsible for tourism policy, international promotion, and the role of tourism in national economic planning. There are three national tourism agencies:

1. Turespaña which carries out activities though the Spanish tourist offices abroad
2. Segittur which promotes innovation and research in tourism
3. Paradores de Turismo SA which runs the state-owned hotel network

Until 1978, tourism was firmly controlled by central government from Madrid, leaving the provincial authorities little scope for initiative. The Spanish Constitution of that year gave the 17 new autonomous regions (*communidades autonómas*) wide powers as part of the post-Franco democratisation of the country. Tourism is, therefore, administered by the regional governments who have the power to approve developments and determine policy. These are co-ordinated centrally via various committees and arrangements. At the local level, the *municipios* (town councils) also take on the responsibility for some aspects of tourism and can impose taxes to finance projects in their area. This may well mean that tourism receives more favourable treatment in some areas than others. In the largest resorts, there are associations of business people – *centros de iniciativas* – who promote their destination and local facilities; as in other areas of Spanish politics, much depends on the personality and connections of those in power.

Tourism resources

Northern Spain

Dominated by the Cantabrian Mountains and overlooking the Bay of Biscay to the north, the coastlands of northern Spain, known as *La Cornisa Cantábrica*, are characterised by a green countryside of meadows, woodlands, and orchards. Appropriately enough, the attractions of coast, countryside and mountains have been promoted by the regions of Galicia, Asturias, Cantabria, and the País Vasco (Basque Country) under the banner of *España Verde* (Green Spain). For an increasing number of foreign visitors, usually travelling independently by car, the appeal lies in this 'real Spain' of unspoiled scenery, rich folk traditions, and distinctive regional cuisines, in contrast to the bland international food and artificial attractions of the Mediterranean beach resorts. However, parts of Asturias and the Basque Country offer a less attractive hinterland, where declining 'smokestack industries' provide the impetus to expand tourism as a means of regenerating the area.

Galicia in the west has much in common with other areas on the 'Celtic fringe' of Europe. Although the Galicians speak a language similar to Portuguese, the folk traditions and misty landscapes are reminiscent of Ireland. This is one of the poorest areas of the Peninsula as the pocket-sized farms cannot provide a decent livelihood, so that in the past large numbers of Galicians have emigrated, particularly to South America. There is an important fishing industry based on ports such as Vigo and La Coruña, where the *rias* (submerged river valleys) provide excellent harbours. Although there are many fine beaches facing the Atlantic Ocean, few seaside resorts of significance have developed, while the region's fishing and tourism industries suffered a major setback with the *Prestige* oil spill disaster in 2003. In the interior, the historic city of Santiago de Compostela has been regenerated as a result of European initiatives to promote the pilgrim route to the shrine of Saint James, and some rural communities on or near the route have also benefitted.

The scenery becomes more rugged in **Asturias** and **Cantabria**, culminating in the spectacular Picos de Europa National Park. The area is ideal for activity holidays such as hiking and canoeing, and a number of spas and picturesque seaside resorts have developed along the fine beaches fronting the Bay of Biscay, including Laredo and Castro Urdiales. The largest resorts are Gijón and Santander, venues for numerous international festivals. The region's heritage attractions include the medieval town of Santillana de Mar and the Altamira Caves – 'the Sistine Chapel of Stone Age art' – now protected by an award-winning replica and museum (www.culturaydeporte.gob.es/mnaltamira/home).

The **País Vasco**, known in the Basque language as **Euskadi**, includes the Biscay coast from Bilbao to the French border and the western end of the Pyrenees. This region is marked off from the rest of Spain by its people, who speak a language unrelated to any other in Europe, and by their passion for gastronomy and unusual pastimes. The best-known sport, second only to football, is *jai alai* or *pelota*, an exciting ball game which has gained an international following in the Americas. Many Basques are not content with autonomy and have given support to the ETA separatist movement, which, despite a number of peace initiatives by Spanish governments, is still a potential threat. Nevertheless, the Basque Country has seen a substantial growth in visitor numbers in recent years. There are two tourist centres of international standing, namely:

*   San Sebastián (Donostia), with its wide sweep of beach between two protecting headlands, festivals, and fashionable shops, is the premier resort of northern Spain. Before the introduction of air conditioning, it served as the summer capital, with ministries and embassies moving from Madrid.
*   Bilbao, in contrast, is primarily a port and a major industrial centre, which until recently had little to recommend it for tourists. This has now changed, thanks to the ultra-modern Guggenheim Museum (www.guggenheim-bilbao.eus), showcasing international art, which has transformed the waterfront area and acted as a catalyst for urban regeneration.

Eastern and Southern Spain

The majority of foreign tourists to Spain head straight for the coastal resorts where summer sunshine is guaranteed. For this reason, the numerous cultural attractions offered by Catalonia, Valencia, Murcia, and Andalucia tend to be overshadowed by the pull of the beaches. The cities of Barcelona, Seville, and Granada are the most notable exceptions.

In the north-east, **Catalonia (Catalunya)** has a strong cultural identity, expressed in the Catalan language, festivals, and sport, and politically in a growing independence movement. Its people have often been at odds with the central government in Madrid, a recent example being the regional parliament's decision to ban bullfighting in Catalonia. Historically, the Catalans have been more outward-looking and progressive than other Spaniards, and they have made their capital, **Barcelona**, one of Europe's great seaports and centres of industry and commerce. This city has long attracted avant-garde artists and architects and is pre-eminent in fashion design and fine dining. The 1992 Summer Olympics focussed world attention on the host city and gave the impetus for many civic improvements, notably the regeneration of the run-down waterfront area and the addition of a beach using imported sand at Barceloneta.

CASE STUDY 14.1
TOURISM IN BARCELONA: BLESSING OR BLIGHT?

In contrast to the Costa Brava, Barcelona was not a major tourist destination until the 1990s. Following the success of the Olympics, the authorities launched a promotional campaign to attract more foreign visitors. This was successful, thanks partly to low-cost airlines, and Barcelona is now among the top five tourist cities of Europe, renowned for its vibrant nightlife. It is also the largest cruise port in the western Mediterranean with no less than eight passenger terminals. Cruise ship arrivals grew from 115,000 passengers in 1990 to 2.2 million in 2022. As a result, day visitors now greatly outnumber tourists staying overnight in the city's hotels. Tourism is an important part of the local economy, supporting 90,000 jobs in a city where youth unemployment is a major problem, and accounting for around 15 per cent of Barcelona's GDP. In 2019, Barcelona received 12 million visitors and 33 million overnight stays.

However, unlike London, Paris, and Rome, Barcelona is a relatively small city with 1.6 million inhabitants and lacks the capacity to deal with mass tourism. It was already densely populated with some 15,800 inhabitants per square kilometre. Tourists are mainly attracted to the historic Ciutat Vella or old town, where many buildings have been converted to holiday apartments. The problem is too many visitors concentrated in time and space around a few 'must-see' attractions. These include:

- The Barrio Gótico, a district of narrow streets and old buildings around the cathedral.
- The Sagrada Familia basilica, the unfinished masterpiece of the Catalan architect Antonio Gaudí (www.sagradafamilia.org).
- The Parc Güell, the public gardens inspired by Gaudí (https://parcguell. barcelona).
- The Ramblas, the historic artery of the city extending from the Columbus Monument on the waterfront to Plaza Catalunya and famous for its street life and floral displays. This is a jostling mass of humanity at peak times.
- The Boquería market, where stallholders are distracted by tourists seeking a photo-opportunity.

Tourists in hired mini-cars with an auto-guide and groups of cyclists add to the confusion.

The demand for accommodation, particularly for short-duration stays, has prompted residents to rent out rooms to tourists through the Internet, using agencies such as Airbnb. Unlike the hotel sector, this type of accommodation was not subject to regulation by the authorities. In 2017, there were 125,000 bed spaces in registered accommodation plus 50,000 'illegal' bed spaces. As a result, rents have escalated beyond the reach of many of Barcelona's residents, who have moved out to towns on the outskirts, such as Badalona. Some claim that businesses catering for tourists have replaced shops and restaurants serving local needs.

In 2022, Barcelona was seemingly about to return to pre-pandemic visitor numbers. Nevertheless, the city authorities now have policies to manage tourism. These include:

- A moratorium on new hotels
- Controls over the short-term rental of apartments
- Tracking down illegal accommodation
- The decision not to expand Barcelona's airport
- An agreement with tour guides to limit the size of groups

It remains to be seen whether this strategy will be supported by the business community, who fear over-regulation will deter visitors, or satisfy the activists who are suspected of having a nationalist, anti-capitalist agenda in their opposition to tourism.

Barcelona is a good base for touring other places of interest in the hinterland of Catalonia, notably Montserrat – a monastery and place of pilgrimage in a spectacular setting. Catalonia includes two major holiday areas – the Costa Brava to the north-east of Barcelona and the Costa Daurada to the south-west.

The **Costa Brava**, the rugged coastline between Blanes and Port Bou on the French border, was the first area to be developed for mass tourism in the 1950s. The scenic beauty of this coast – the pine covered hills, red cliffs, and sheltered coves – had earlier attracted artists and fashionable holidaymakers to picturesque Tossa and the resort of S'Agaró, purpose-built for tourism in the 1920s. Some resorts – notably Lloret de Mar – have been given over to the package holiday market, and their natural assets buried under concrete. Nevertheless, some stretches of coastline – as at Begur and Cadaqués – remain unspoiled, while the Medas Islands near the resort of Estartit have been designated as a marine reserve. Increasing numbers of independent holidaymakers are seeking out the cultural attractions of this part of Catalonia. These include the Salvador Dalí Museum at Figueres, the picturesque medieval city of Girona, and the archaeological site at Ampurias.

Discussion point

The Costa Brava no longer appeals to a mass market experiencing 'destination fatigue', and in 2004, it was dropped from the programmes of a leading British tour operator. Discuss why an area that had epitomised a Spanish holiday became unfashionable, and suggest ways in which the destination could be rejuvenated, by developing new products and targeting 'niche' markets.

The **Costa Daurada** is characterised by long beaches of golden sand and extends beyond Barcelona as far as the Ebro Delta. Its appeal is diminished by the proximity of industry in some areas. Sitges is the most attractive resort and one that is popular with Spaniards, but like others on this coast such as Cambrils, it is moribund out of season.

Salou is the most popular resort with foreign holidaymakers and has experienced a revival in its fortunes following the opening of the Port Aventura theme park in 1993 (www. portaventuraworld.com).

Likewise, tourism plays an important but not exclusive role in the economies of the **Valencia** and **Murcia** regions. Despite its dry climate, the narrow eastern coastal plain is one of the most productive agricultural regions of Spain, thanks to sophisticated irrigation techniques. The landscape includes citrus orchards, the villages with their blue-domed churches, the date palm plantation at Elche, and the rice fields around the Albufera lagoon. These features contrast markedly with the barren mountains to the west and Europe's only desert to the south, which is a favourite location for producers of low-budget 'western' movies. The city of Valencia is primarily a seaport and industrial centre, and its tourism appeal lies not so much in historic buildings but in the culinary attraction of *paella*, ceramic products, and the spectacular *Las Fallas* festival, which culminates in the burning of elaborate paper-mache effigies. The city's go-ahead outlook is shown by the impressive 'City of Arts and Sciences' – a science park commemorating the Millennium – and a model civic tourism administration. The Costa del Azahar to the north consists of a string of resorts, including the music festival venue of Benicassim and the historic town of Peñiscola.

The **Costa Blanca** between Denia and Alicante is one of Spain's most popular holiday areas, due in large measure to Benidorm. Elsewhere on the Costa Blanca, development tends to be low-rise, but arguably extensive villa developments have a greater social and environmental impact than 'skyscraper' hotels, as they generate large volumes of car traffic and directly compete with local agriculture for land, power, and water resources. Even the coastline of the dry south-east corner of Spain has been developed for golf tourism and water sports as the 'Costa Cálida', focussing on the resort of La Manga and the Mar Menor lagoon.

CASE STUDY 14.2
BENIDORM: A RESORT FOR ALL SEASONS

In 1950, Benidorm was a small town with less than 3,000 inhabitants, its economy based on tuna fishing and agriculture. The few summer visitors were wealthy families from Madrid, which was then an eight-hour drive away. Today, it stands as Spain's largest holiday resort, with approximately 70,000 permanent residents (2020) and is visited by around 4 million tourists annually. Benidorm boasts 40,000 bed spaces in hotels, with a much larger number in holiday apartments. By 2013, 11.9 million overnight stays in hotels were recorded; of these, 60 per cent were Spanish and 40 per cent foreign tourists, mainly from the United Kingdom, Germany, Belgium, and the Netherlands.

Benidorm's success is only partly due to its natural resources of sun, sand, and sea. There are two fine beaches, both facing south and sheltered by mountain ranges to the north. The climate is favourable for outdoor recreation year-round, with moderate temperatures ranging from 15.5°C to 29°C. Nevertheless, for a tourism resource to be developed, someone or some organisation has to act. Benidorm's transformation from a small fishing community to cosmopolitan mega-resort was largely due to a visionary mayor, Pedro Zaragoza, who held office from 1950 to 1967. By the mid-1950s, a trickle of foreign tourists started arriving on Spanish beaches. Regardless of its popularity in France, the bikini was regarded in Spain as indecent and a danger to public morals. Zaragoza not only allowed the bikini, but also protected foreign women from harassment by the locals. He was condemned for his liberal attitude by the Archbishop of Valencia, representing the conservative forces of church and state. He then took the bold step of appealing directly to General Franco and was able to convince the Caudillo that if Spain was to become a popular destination for sun-seeking north Europeans, some of the strict rules about dress and behaviour would have to be relaxed. Zaragoza's master plan for Benidorm envisaged a city of broad avenues and high-rise buildings, separated by open spaces, a 'leisure factory' for middle income tourists. During the 1960s, British tour operators provided the necessary finance for hotel development in return for a guaranteed number of rooms. A series of imaginative publicity campaigns put Benidorm firmly 'on the map', but it was the opening of the international airport at Alicante in 1967 that made it readily accessible as a destination for mass tourism.

Unlike other destinations in Spain, Benidorm achieves an average year-round occupancy rate of 90 per cent in its hotels, thanks to a loyal domestic and international clientele, with 'third age' tourists providing much of the demand during the winter months. Prices are competitive, and an uninhibited entertainment industry caters for most tastes, age groups, and nationalities. The Playa de Poniente west of the old town tends to be more popular with the Spanish, whereas the Playa de Levante (east beach) caters for the foreign mass market. The narrow streets of the old town are thronged with those seeking tapas bars and Spanish restaurants. Benidorm has readily adapted to changes in demand, with a number of visitor attractions, including the Terra Mítica theme park (www.terramiticapark.com), two golf courses, music festivals, and sports events. The Hotel Bali, one of the largest in Europe, is the flagship of a drive to attract conference business and more upmarket tourists (www.granhotelbali.com).

Andalucia

Popular with both domestic and foreign visitors, Andalucia, for many people, epitomises Spain, with its warm, sunny climate, easy-going lifestyle, and picturesque villages. Moorish rule persisted for much longer in this part of Spain, and their heritage is particularly evident in the traditional architecture. Yet this region has had more than its fair share of social and economic problems, as much of the land is dominated by large estates given over to olive production, unemployment is high, and the gypsies, who have inspired flamenco as an art form, remain a marginalised element in society. Rural tourism is growing in importance, while horse riding and trekking are popular holiday activities in the mountain areas. The many picturesque small towns and villages known as the *pueblos blancos* are accessible from the bustling resorts of the Costa del Sol, and yet a world apart. Nevertheless, tourism is mainly focussed on the major cities of the region and the coast:

Photo 14.1
Benidorm

Source: Brian Boniface

- Seville is the regional capital and was historically Spain's gateway to the Americas in the colonial period. It achieved international acclaim as the host city for the 1992 World Expo, which ingeniously used water features to cope with the notoriously hot summer temperatures. Tourists arrive in great numbers each spring for the awe-inspiring spectacle of the Holy Week processions, followed a few weeks later by the colour and excitement of the April *Feria*.
- Córdoba under Muslim rule was Europe's largest city in the tenth century and contains one of the most outstanding relics of that era – the Mezquita, inside which is the Catholic cathedral. The new Arab-style public baths epitomise the revival of interest by Spaniards in their Moorish heritage. Córdoba is also noted for its colourful patios.
- Granada is renowned for an exquisite example of Moorish architecture, the Alhambra Palace (www.alhambra-patronato.es). The adjoining gardens of the Generalife, with the snow-capped mountains of the Sierra Nevada in the background, provide an incomparable setting for festivals of music and dance. The Albaicín district nearby is also a World Heritage Site and has become an artists'quarter containing many Moroccan-style tea houses.
- Jerez is the centre for the production of one of Spain's most celebrated exports, the fortified wine known throughout the English-speaking world as sherry. The city is also renowned throughout Spain as a showcase for equestrian skills in a region devoted to horse riding and the bullfight.

Photo 14.2
The bridge crossing the gorge at Ronda, one of Andalucia's most picturesque towns

Source: ©istockphoto.com/José Luis Gutiérrez

The **Costa del Sol** extends for 300 kilometres from Gibraltar to Adra and is the holiday area that has shown the most spectacular growth since the 1960s, with resorts such as Torremolinos having experienced the various stages in the tourist area life cycle from 'discovery' to 'decline'. The location of the Costa del Sol in the extreme south of Spain is advantageous for the following reasons:

- The Sierra Nevada and other mountain ranges protect this south-facing coast, guaranteeing warmer temperatures and more sunshine in winter than elsewhere in western Europe and making it possible to cultivate sugar cane and other sub-tropical crops.
- The Costa del Sol can offer the tourist an exceptionally wide range of outdoor activities, including golf, tennis, horse riding, and sailing, while skiing can be enjoyed in the Sierra Nevada, where the snow cover lasts from December to May.
- The coastal resorts provide easy access to the many cultural attractions of southern Spain.

This part of Andalucia has long been a winter destination for wealthy tourists, starting with Málaga in the nineteenth century, while the picturesque mountain town of Ronda served as a summer retreat for British officers stationed in Gibraltar. The development of the Costa del Sol for mass tourism did not get underway until after the opening of Málaga airport in 1962. The completion of the E340 coastal road improved access to the resorts, but it soon acquired a reputation as the 'highway of death', as high-rise ribbon development extended from Málaga to Estepona. Tourism has largely replaced fishing and farming as a source of employment for local people, and greatly improved living standards. However, in some of the villages – Mijas is a notable example – expatriates from the countries of northern Europe now make up almost half the population.

The section of the Costa del Sol to the east of Málaga contains fewer resorts, and the development largely consists of holiday villas designed to blend in with the local landscape. Most of the hotel accommodation is found in the large resorts to the west of Málaga, which include:

- **Torremolinos**, which has become a byword for the ills of mass tourism and speculative development. However, this former fishing village was an upmarket, fashionable resort with a handful of luxury hotels in the early 1960s. This was followed in the 1970s by a massive expansion of accommodation in the form of high-rise hotels and apartments, using cheap mass-produced materials, to cater for an ever-growing demand from the tour operators of northern Europe. We could say that Torremolinos, along with its neighbours Benalmadena and Fuengirola, plays a vital 'honeypot' role in concentrating vast numbers of holidaymakers in a small area, providing them with familiar food and entertainment, and thereby saving the villages of Andalucia from some of the negative impacts of mass tourism.
- **Marbella** became fashionable in the 1950s and has been more successful than the other resorts on the Costa del Sol in retaining an image of sophistication, based on a large number of five-star hotels, a wealthy expatriate community, the yacht marinas of Puerto Banús – Spain's best-known example of luxury tourism, golf and cultural activities. However, even Marbella experienced a period of stagnation, if not decline, in the 1980s, caused by its association with sleaze and drug-related crime. Under energetic leadership, the resort has invested in improved facilities on its beach front, more efficient policing to ensure visitor security, and the diversification of its product to attract conferences and foreign business enterprise based on high-tech industries to the 'California of Europe'.
- **Málaga** differs from the other tourist centres of the Costa del Sol in being primarily a working seaport and commercial city. It has been shunned by the hordes of package holidaymakers heading straight from the airport to the beach resorts but has the potential to attract tourists seeking a genuine Spanish ambience. Málaga has done much to renovate its waterfront and city centre, as well as restoring such important examples of Moorish heritage as the Alcazaba citadel. The city also hopes to promote its cultural appeal as the birthplace of Picasso.

Andalucia still contains extensive stretches of unspoiled coastline along both the Mediterranean and the Atlantic. These could be at risk from developers, despite controversial legislation to determine property rights and prevent any further inappropriate building on beachfront land. Plans to develop the Cabo de Gata area between Almería and Carboneras have been halted by the growing environmental movement in Spain, and it is now designated as a nature park.

The **Costa de la Luz**, Andalucia's Atlantic coastal region, has some of the best beaches in Spain. This is a popular holiday area for the Spanish but has attracted little attention so far from foreign tour operators. Some of the existing seaports are tourist centres, while the old-established resort of Isla Cristina provides a contrast to the largely unplanned development at Matalascañas. Cadiz was the leading commercial city of Spain in the eighteenth century and is now celebrated for its Carnival, while Tarifa, exposed to the easterly *Levante* winds, is ideal for windsurfing and kite-surfing. The port of Algeciras is linked by ferry services to Tangier and Ceuta, which serve as gateways to Morocco.

CASE STUDY 14.3
A SPANISH WILDERNESS AT RISK

Further development of the coast between the Guadalquivir estuary and Huelva would threaten the sustainability of one of Europe's last wilderness areas – the Marismas, part of which is designated as the Coto Doñana National Park. This area contains a diversity of habitats, including coastal dunes, seasonally flooded marshlands, pine woods, and cork oak scrub. About half a million birds overwinter here, and it provides a refuge for endangered species such as the Iberian lynx. For centuries much of this area was a royal hunting preserve, and its ecosystems were not seriously threatened by the small-scale exploitation of its resources by local communities. This changed with the development of mining and intensive agriculture on its northern borders, while a proposed mega-resort, Costa Doñana, was successfully opposed by environmentalists in the early 1990s. The ecosystems of the national park depend on the maintenance of the water table, and during the drought of 2022, the Marismas dried up completely. Southern Spain and Portugal are on the frontlines of climate change, and this may be an early warning. However, it is more likely the disaster was due to the depletion of the water table by the digging of wells for the following purposes:

- The irrigation of rice fields, and more importantly, strawberry production for the lucrative north European market (the economic benefit to farmers far exceeds the fines imposed by the water authority on illegal wells).
- To supply the needs of the nearby beach resort of Matalascañas.

Research and discussion

1. Visitors to the Coto Doñana National Park require a permit and a professional guide. What type of visitors would be attracted to the park, given the facilities that are available?
2. Explain why the National Park's strict management policies have been unpopular with local communities and other interest groups in the area adjoining the park. Debate the issues, and assign roles to members of the class.

Spain in North Africa

The cities of Ceuta and Melilla on the North African coast have been under Spanish rule since the sixteenth century. Both enjoy free port status, and cross-border trade with Morocco is far more significant to their economy than tourism. The Spanish government has taken measures to integrate the Muslim communities who make up half the population, and to curb illegal immigration from Africa. Nevertheless, these two Spanish enclaves have been a potential flashpoint for terrorism since '11-M' (the Madrid bombings of March 11, 2004).

The Spanish Heartlands

The Meseta dominates central and northern Spain and presents an austere landscape, where the many historic towns, castles, and monasteries provide the main attractions for the cultural tourist. The northern Meseta gave rise to the warlike kingdom of Castile, which strove for centuries to dominate the Iberian Peninsula, and whose language became modern Spanish. A number of tourist routes have been promoted to link the principal places of interest, namely:

- El Camino de Santiago (The Way of Saint James) has been followed since the early Middle Ages by pilgrims from all parts of western Europe and experienced a major revival in the 1990s. The Spanish section of the route links the historic cities of Pamplona, Burgos, and León, showcasing some of Spain's finest examples of Romanesque and Gothic architecture to the shrine of St James in Santiago de Compostela. Numerous hostels provide basic accommodation, but only those pilgrims who have travelled at least 100 kilometres of the Camino on foot or 200 kilometres by bicycle are entitled to receive the certificate known as the *Compostela* on reaching the cathedral at Santiago.
- The 'Silver Route' links northern and southern Spain, passing through Mérida, with its Roman theatre, and Salamanca, home to Spain's most famous university. It crosses the region of Extremadura, land of the *conquistadors* – the adventurers who colonised the Americas in the sixteenth century.
- The 'Don Quixote Route' crosses the region of La Mancha, famous for its windmills and associations with the best-known figure in Spanish literature.

Tourism in central Spain focusses on Madrid, and Barajas Airport, now expanded as a showpiece of modern architecture, is the gateway to Europe for many visitors from the Americas. Madrid became the capital of Spain in 1560 and is a latecomer compared to other Spanish cities. Although the Madrid region accounts for only 6 per cent of overnight stays by foreign visitors to Spain, the capital is firmly established as a short-break destination. The following features give Madrid its special appeal:

- The altitude of 700 metres makes it western Europe's highest capital, with the benefits of clear skies for most of the year and invigorating mountain breezes from the Sierra de Guadarrama.
- The Prado is one of the world's finest art collections, including masterpieces by Goya and Velazquez (www.museodelprado.es).

329

- The range of restaurants offering the best of Spain's regional cuisines, speciality shopping, and first-class sports facilities.
- The vibrant nightlife, with much of the action taking place in the historic core of the city between the Plaza Mayor and the Puerta del Sol.
- The city makes an ideal base for a touring holiday.

Cultural attractions recognised by UNESCO as World Heritage Sites within easy reach of Madrid include:

- The university town of Alcalá de Henares.
- Toledo, the religious capital of Spain, which has preserved its medieval character.
- Ávila, famous as the birthplace of the great visionary St Teresa. The town still retains its medieval walls, making it a favourite location for film-makers.
- El Escorial, the monastery-palace built by Philip II as the nerve-centre of the Spanish empire (https://el.escorial.com). This austere building contrasts with the gardens of Aranjuez, the former summer palace of the Bourbon kings of Spain, which inspired Rodrigo's guitar *Concierto*.
- Segovia boasts a well-preserved Roman aqueduct and the romantic castle known as the Alcazar.
- Cuenca is noted for the picturesque 'hanging houses' overlooking the River Júcar and its reputation as an artists' resort.

The region of **Aragón** includes most of the basin of the River Ebro and a large part of the Pyrenees. This former kingdom played a major role in Spanish history, where for centuries Moors and Christians co-existed to create the *Mudejar* style of architecture typical of towns such as Teruel. The vibrant *jota aragonesa* is one of the best known of the traditional dances of Spain. Zaragoza is a historic cathedral city on the River Ebro, whose importance as a business centre was recognised internationally as the venue for the 2008 World Expo.

The Spanish Pyrenees

The mountains along the French border include the Aigüestortes and Ordesa National Parks, spas and winter sports developments, notably in the Aran Valley. Wildlife and traditional lifestyles, for long protected by isolation, are threatened by improvements in the transport infrastructure such as the Somport Tunnel, hydro-electric power projects and the growth of summer recreation.

The Spanish Islands

The two groups of Spanish islands – the Balearics in the western Mediterranean and the Canaries in the Atlantic – are different in many respects from Peninsular Spain and are therefore usually regarded as separate holiday destinations. These islands constitute only 2 per cent of the national territory and 7 per cent of the population of Spain. Yet together, they account for 30 per cent of overnights by foreign tourists in Spain.

The Balearic Islands

The Balearic Islands, consisting of Mallorca (Majorca), Menorca, Ibiza, and Formentera, account for a quarter of all tourism to Spain, and tourism is estimated to account for 45 per cent of the regional domestic product. In a few decades, the Balearic Islands have been transformed from one of the poorest regions of Spain, with a high rate of emigration, to one of the wealthiest. However, two countries dominate the market – Germany and Britain – with domestic tourists accounting for only 10 per cent of arrivals. The negative effects of tourism on the islands include:

- A coastline damaged by badly-planned development.
- Pollution resulting from emissions of carbon dioxide from tourist coaches and hired cars, inadequate waste disposal systems, and litter.
- Problems of water supply. The islands are limestone in their geology, and agriculture largely depends on ground water resources. Excessive demands have caused a lowering of the water table and penetration of the aquifer by sea water. Tourists during the peak summer season consume the equivalent of 440 litres of water daily, reaching 800 litres for those staying in luxury hotels.
- The outnumbering of the population by tourists. In mass market resorts such as Magalluf and Arenal in Mallorca, fast food outlets, tawdry souvenir shops, pubs, and *bierkellers* provide a 'home from home' for British and German holidaymakers. This, coupled with the growth of second home ownership by affluent foreigners, has led to the feeling among many islanders that they have lost their cultural identity.

Each of the Balearic Islands has distinctive landscapes, folklore, and dialects.

Mallorca is by far the largest island, with a coastline 550 kilometres in length and mountains rising to over 1,000 metres in the northwest. Between these and a lower range in the east lies a fertile plain meeting the sea in a number of fine bays. Unlike the other islands, it seemingly has the physical capacity to absorb the 13 million tourists who arrive in the Balearics each year. Mass tourism – the 'Majorca' of popular repute – is largely confined to a few mega-resorts around the Bay of Palma, within easy reach of Palma airport, which in summer is one of Europe's busiest. The 'other Mallorca' promoted by the more upmarket tour operators continues to attract wealthy celebrities and the discerning tourist.

In fact, tourism in Mallorca is not a new phenomenon, and Fomento, the island's tourist board was established in Palma in 1905; it is now the Oficina de Turismo de Mallorca (https://spain.info//en/info/palma-mallorca-tourist-office). In the years prior to the Spanish Civil War, the island attracted artists such as Joan Miró, and foreign celebrities were accommodated in the luxury hotel at Formentor. The British poet Robert Graves did much to publicise the island's attractions from his home in the mountain village of Deià when it took the best part of three days' travel to reach the island from Britain. In the period immediately following the Second World War, there were few foreign visitors to fill the hotels, so Mallorca was promoted by the government as 'the isle of love' for Spanish honeymooners, an image also guaranteed to appeal to north Europeans. By 1960, 80 per cent of tourists were foreigners. Foreign tour operators financed the building of

Photo 14.3
Formentor, Majorca

hotels in exchange for a guaranteed number of rooms on preferential terms. To induce holidaymakers on package tours to spend money in the island, hoteliers made sure they were provided with appropriate entertainment.

The worst excesses of sun, sea, and sand tourism are confined to Magalluf-Palma Nova. The rugged west coast was saved from development, because it was not easily accessible, although communications have now improved, with a direct highway link through the mountains from Palma to Soller. The east coast, indented with numerous small coves, is given over mainly to self-catering villa developments. Away from the beaches, some aspects of the island's heritage have been promoted to appeal to the average tourist. These include:

• The Caves of Drach, an outstanding example of a geological feature imaginatively developed as a showpiece attraction (www.cuevasdeldrach.com).
• The former monastery at Valldemossa, now a museum devoted to Chopin, where the composer was inspired to write his *Preludes*.
• The island's industries, notably the manufacture of artificial pearls.

Palma, the regional capital, is one of the leading seaports of the Mediterranean, with ferry services to the mainland and the other islands. It boasts an imposing cathedral and castle among its heritage attractions, and except for one small district, has been relatively unaffected by mass tourism.

In 2002, the regional government imposed an 'eco-tax' on the tourism sector, to be used specifically for environmental projects. Although this attempt to 'make the polluter pay' failed, a policy of sustainable tourism has continued; a third of the island's area has been designated for conservation, while steps have been taken to improve the environment of the most overcrowded resorts. However, it is debateable whether the further development of golf courses is truly 'green' tourism, while the buying up of rural properties, mainly by Germans, has implications for the social balance of the Mallorcan countryside.

Ibiza is relatively small in terms of area and population, and it is here that the impact of tourism has perhaps been greatest, to the extent that it accounts for 80 per cent of jobs. The island was much poorer economically in the pre-tourism era than Mallorca or Menorca and was less able to cope with the influx. Ibiza has passed through the following stages of tourism development:

- The initial period of 'discovery' by hippy-style travellers in the early 1960s, who were attracted by the island lifestyle that was perceived to be more tolerant than the rest of Spain at that time. Some of these visitors later became permanent residents, to the extent that 30 per cent of the population are expatriates, and Ibiza remains something of an artists' community.
- The introduction of direct charter flights to Ibiza airport shortly after led to the growth of the inclusive-tour market, mainly from Britain, catering for family beach holidays. The resorts of Santa Eulalia and San Carlos continue to serve this market.
- Since the 1980s, there has been a growing emphasis on the international youth market and the all-night clubbing culture, which now accounts for 12 per cent of all tourists. The binge drinking and 'hooliganism' of some north European tourists has attracted unfavourable publicity in the media, which, in turn, has deterred holidaymakers from the older age groups from visiting Ibiza.

The major impacts of mass tourism are mainly confined to San Antonio, which is a noisy, high-rise 'tourist ghetto' catering for the lower end of the market. The island's capital Eivissa (Ibiza Town) has managed to retain some of its character as a historic Mediterranean seaport and offers nightlife that is more reputable and expensive. There is concern that the traditional way of life based on agriculture has all but disappeared, while the island is reaching saturation point as far as tourism is concerned due to problems of water supply. A major highway project has met with opposition from the island's fledgling environmentalist movement.

Formentera is the smallest of the Balearics. It is comparatively barren, sparsely populated, and scenically low key. It does, however, have some good beaches, and because it is featured by few tour operators, and can only be reached by ferry from Ibiza, attracts holidaymakers seeking relative seclusion.

Menorca is scenically and culturally much more diverse, and its economy is less dependent on tourism. The island authorities have managed to secure greater control over tourism development than was the case in Ibiza, with well-planned holiday villages at Binibeca and Fornells catering for upmarket tourists. The island's main tourism resource are its fine harbours, which provide an ideal environment for yachting. The largest of these – Mahón – was an important base for the British navy in the eighteenth century, when it replaced the old city of Ciudadela as the island's capital.

The Canary Islands

While the Balearics are essentially summer sun destinations, the Canaries have the advantage of a sub-tropical climate, which favours beach tourism throughout the year. Winters are pleasantly warm, while the cool ocean current moderates summer temperatures. The islands are of volcanic origin and contain some magnificent scenery, but on the other hand, there are relatively few fine beaches. Situated some 1,000 kilometres to the south-west of Cadiz, they are much closer geographically to Morocco and the Western Sahara than to mainland Spain. The location of the islands, on important shipping routes, resulted in the 'discovery' of Tenerife and Gran Canaria as winter destinations by wealthy British travellers and returning colonial officials in the nineteenth century. Large numbers of cruise ships still call at the ports of Santa Cruz and Las Palmas, which offer duty-free shopping as their main attractions. Since the 1960s, the great majority of visitors have arrived on charter flights and are drawn from a wider range of countries and socio-economic groups. Although winter remains the high season, tourist arrivals are well distributed throughout the year. Spanish holidaymakers from the Peninsula account for about 20 per cent of hotel overnights in the islands.

- **Tenerife** is the largest of the islands and offers the greatest variety of scenery and climate, due to the effect of the spectacular peak of Teide on the prevailing trade winds. The strange volcanic landscapes of Las Cañadas National Park (www.volcanoteide.com) in the centre of the island offer a marked contrast to the desert-like south, the forested mountain slopes, and the fertile valley of Orotava, with its banana plantations to the north. In this part of the island, Puerto de la Cruz is a well-established resort catering primarily for the older age groups (see case study). Playa de las Américas in the south of Tenerife is now the most popular destination. Santa Cruz is the island's capital and has enhanced its cultural attractions with a Carnival to rival that of Rio de Janeiro and a magnificent new auditorium. Nevertheless, both Tenerife and Gran Canaria have tended to develop artificial attractions with an international mass market appeal, rather than promote the islands' folklore, traditional crafts, and architecture, or the archaeological heritage of the Guanches, the mysterious indigenous people who inhabited the islands at the time of their conquest by the Spanish in the fifteenth century.
- **Gran Canaria** has arguably more to offer mass tourism than Tenerife. Las Palmas has a fine beach and a number of heritage attractions, but since the 1970s, the city has been overtaken as a holiday destination by new developments on the south coast of the island. Here, the beaches and visitor attractions of Playa del Inglés, San Agustín, and Maspalomas attract large numbers of Germans and lesser contingents of British, Scandinavian, and Spanish holidaymakers. Away from the resorts, the interior of Gran Canaria has been described as 'a continent in miniature' offering spectacular contrasts in scenery.
- **Lanzarote** is still volcanically active, and the craters of Monte del Fuego in the Timanfaya National Park are a major attraction. This is one instance where tourism can be said to have improved a rather barren landscape of lava spreads dotted with white villages. This is largely due to the inspiration of the architect César Manrique,

who ensured that most development was planned with imagination and care for the local environment. Upmarket tourists are catered for at Costa de Teguise, and sports enthusiasts at La Santa, while Puerto del Carmen is the most popular resort.

- **Fuerteventura** is the driest of the Canary Islands, due to its closeness to the Western Sahara, and is the most sparsely populated. Persistent trade winds provide ideal conditions for windsurfing, while the vast beaches attract jeep safaris and are popular mainly with German tourists.
- **La Palma** attracts tourists looking for a more traditional culture, unspoiled nature, and unpolluted skies. The main attraction is the beautiful mountain scenery, culminating in one of the world's largest volcanic craters – the Caldera de Taburiente. However, the eruption of La Cumbre Vieja in 2021 has shown that the island is geologically unstable, and some scientists predict that earthquakes and tsunamis will at some time occur, with catastrophic consequences.
- The other islands are less developed for tourism, due to their relative isolation, as they do not have direct air connections. **La Gomera** has preserved folk traditions, and some of the native forest vegetation of the Canary Islands in the Garajonay National Park. **Hierro** is still volcanically active and attracts scuba divers to its clear coastal waters.

CASE STUDY 14.4
PUERTO DE LA CRUZ, THE NEED TO ADAPT
TO CHANGES IN DEMAND

Puerto de la Cruz is situated on the north coast of Tenerife in the shadow of Mount Teide. Unlike the purpose-built resorts in the south-west of the island, the town has a long pedigree as a commercial centre. It was the seaport serving the important town of La Orotava, 5 kilometres inland, and prospered in the eighteenth century, exporting the produce of the Orotava Valley, including wine, sugar, and cochineal. Trade and emigration to South America, particularly Venezuela, has influenced the culture of the Canary Islands. The balconied buildings in the old town around the harbour are reminders of this heritage, as are the Botanical Gardens, where exotic plants from the New World were acclimatised before dissemination to the Peninsula.

Towards the end of the nineteenth century, tourists began to visit Tenerife, and in 1893, the first luxury hotel in Puerto de la Cruz – the Taoro – was built by a British entrepreneur with the profits from the banana trade. These tourists were following in the footsteps of the scientist-explorer Alexander von Humboldt, and like him, they were attracted by the climate and landscapes of the Orotava Valley. In the course of the next 60 years, a number of celebrities were accommodated in the Taoro Hotel, including Winston Churchill and Agatha Christie. In this 'discovery phase' of the tourist area life cycle, tourism was restricted to an elite, the infrastructure for development scarcely existed, and efforts by the authorities to promote Tenerife were frustrated by political crises in Spain and abroad.

The situation changed in the 1950s, following the expansion of tourism in the Peninsula. In 1955, the Ministry of Information and Tourism in Madrid designated Puerto de la Cruz as a 'place of touristic interest', providing the impetus for planning and development. By the early 1960s, the first charter flights had arrived at Los Rodeos Airport near La Laguna, and tourist arrivals were reaching 30,000 annually. A phase of rapid and sustained hotel building took place during the next decade, mainly in the Martiánez area to the east of the old town. To compensate for the lack of good beaches, the authorities commissioned the architect César Manrique to design the magnificent lido and artificial lake known as Costa Martiánez, making imaginative use of natural materials. An artificial beach by the same architect – the landscaped Playa Jardín – was later laid out to the west of the old town.

By the mid-1980s, Puerto de la Cruz was no longer the premier resort of Tenerife, as it was facing increasing competition from new developments in the south-west of the island. This location enjoys guaranteed sunshine year-round, unlike the north coast, which is often cloudy and windy. The hotels and time-share apartments in Playa de las Américas and Los Cristianos were also much closer than Puerto de la Cruz to the new international airport – Reina Sofia or Tenerife Sur (TFS) – which was inaugurated in 1978. The previous year Los Rodeos had suffered one of the worst disasters in aviation history. Tenerife Sur soon became the international gateway to the island, relegating Los Rodeos, now renamed Tenerife Norte (TFN) to a secondary role, handling domestic services to the Peninsula and the other islands.

Around 2 million British tourists visited Tenerife in 2019, but the great majority stayed in the south-west, as Puerto de la Cruz had less to offer families and young tourists. In the mid-1980s, the resort entered the stagnation phase of the tourist area life cycle, and was soon showing symptoms of decline (Ledesma González, 2012). These included:

- A decrease in the number of bed spaces in hotels and other accommodation.
- A shorter length of stay, and a lower spend per capita by tourists, compared to the *municipios* of Adeje and Arona (which include the resorts of Playa de las Américas and Los Cristianos) in the south-west of the island.
- The obsolescence of most of the hotel stock, which was built before 1976.

Puerto de la Cruz cannot compete with the south-west of Tenerife as a beach destination and needs to diversify its product. This involves promoting the cultural heritage of this historic town and working with other local authorities to enhance the appeal of its hinterland – the Orotava Valley for hiking and other recreational activities. Event attractions include the annual Mueca festival held in the old town, which focusses on street art and music, with participants from Brazil and other countries as well as the Canary Islands (www.fetivalmueca.com). The process of urban regeneration includes improvements to the seafront promenade.

Andorra

Situated in the Pyrenees, on the border between Spain and France, Andorra (www.visitan-dorra.com) is a Catalan-speaking principality where the impact of tourism is particularly evident. It was a group of small rural communities engaged in tobacco production in the 1960s, but then improved communications transformed the country into one of Europe's tax havens. In 2021, Andorra recorded 7.5 million overnight stays, but the majority of the arrivals are day visitors from Spain and France attracted by the duty-free shopping in the capital, Andorra la Vella, where the picturesque 'House of the Valleys', the traditional seat of government, is overshadowed by modern buildings. Tourism policy is the concern of the Ministry of Tourism and Telecommunications. Andorra is changing its image as a low-cost skiing destination by promoting spa tourism based on the geothermal springs at Les Escaldes and emphasising the appeal of the country's lakes, mountains, and rural traditions.

Gibraltar

Although Gibraltar is one of Britain's few remaining overseas territories, it is largely self-governing and is physically attached to Spain, while the people are a mixture of Mediterranean cultures and equally fluent in English and Spanish. Britain's interest in Gibraltar was primarily due to its strategic location guarding the entrance to the Mediterranean. The Straits of Gibraltar continue to be one of the world's busiest seaways. Nevertheless, Gibraltar's military role is less significant nowadays, and the Royal Navy dockyard closed, forcing the colony to develop other roles as an offshore financial centre and tourist destination. The Gibraltar Tourist Board (http://www.visitgibraltar.gi) reports to the Ministry of Business, Tourism, and the Port.

Gibraltar is a small territory, only 6 square kilometres in area, dominated by the great limestone mass of the Rock, which towers 400 metres above the densely packed town and busy harbour on its western flank. Since 1985, when the frontier with Spain was re-opened, Gibraltar has attracted millions of Spanish excursionists, as well as cruise passengers and much smaller numbers of staying tourists, mostly from Britain. The Spanish are motivated by curiosity and the lure of shopping bargains, while the British, many of whom are first-time visitors overseas, are reassured by the familiar language, food, currency, British-style 'bobbies' and pubs, combined with Mediterranean sunshine.

Apart from these, Gibraltar's main attractions include:

* The world-renowned Rock, which is honeycombed with caves and 'galleries' constructed for military purposes. It also provides a habitat for Europe's only ape colony.
* The duty-free shopping in Main Street.
* The historical associations with the British army and navy.
* The relics of the Moorish and Spanish occupations.
* The facilities for water sports, including a yacht marina. On the other hand, there are only a few small beaches in the shadow of the Rock.

- Its proximity to Morocco, using the hydrofoil and ferry service to Tangier.
- Its proximity to the holiday resorts of the Costa del Sol. Prior to the 1960s, Gibraltar was the gateway to this part of Spain, and since 1985, growing numbers of British visitors have again been using it as a base for touring Andalucia.

However, the expansion of tourism in Gibraltar faces a number of problems, namely:

- The shortage of land, necessitating development on sites reclaimed from the harbour.
- The threat posed by the erosion of the Rock, caused by massive tunnelling in the past.
- The accommodation stock consists of a small number of hotels, guesthouses, and self-catering complexes that need to be upgraded and extended.
- The restricted site of the airport that lies on 'neutral territory' with its runway on land reclaimed from the Bay of Gibraltar. To the south, the airport is hemmed in by the sheer face of the Rock, while the Spanish frontier lies immediately to the north; which brings us to the most deep-seated problem.
- The long-standing political difficulties with Spain. Although Gibraltar has been British since 1703, Spain has never relinquished its claim to sovereignty. During the last major dispute, which lasted from 1969 to 1985, telecommunications were cut, the land border was closed, and the ferry service to Algeciras was severed by the Spanish government. Cut off from its natural hinterland, Gibraltar was forced to develop its own tourist attractions and recruit labour from Morocco. Another bone of contention is Gibraltar's alleged role as a tax haven in smuggling contraband from North Africa to Spain. The response of the Spanish authorities has been to subject motorists crossing the border at La Linea to lengthy delays. Spain's willingness to consider 'joint sovereignty' with Britain is rejected by the great majority of Gibraltarians, although since the UK's departure from the European Union, the status of Gibraltar is again under discussion. Nevertheless, the 2007 agreement between London and Madrid allows freedom of air travel to and from Gibraltar.

Portugal

The setting for tourism

Portugal is a much smaller country than Spain, both in population and land area. Due to its long Atlantic coastline, Portugal's climate tends to be milder and more humid, and the landscape generally greener, than is the case in most of Spain. Portugal has been a united nation for much longer than Spain, and the Moorish heritage is less evident. In culture and temperament, the Portuguese differ from the Spanish in a number of ways; for example, *fado* music is full of the melancholy or *saudade*, which is part of the national character, and the Portuguese bullfight is a milder affair than the Spanish *corrida*. Portugal's contacts with Brazil and its former colonies in Asia and Africa are reflected in its cuisine and the ornate decoration of its churches and country houses. In recent years, Portugal has co-operated with Spain in a number of projects, such as the proposed AVE high-speed rail link between Madrid and Lisbon, and motorway connections between the two countries. Historically, relations between the two countries have not been so close, and sometimes marked by hostility, as shown by the number of castles and fortified towns in eastern Portugal near the Spanish border.

Agriculture, fishing, and textiles still play an important role in the Portuguese economy, but tourism has made a major contribution, directly generating 400,000 jobs and providing 15 per cent of GDP.

The demand for tourism

Domestic and outbound tourism

Portugal is one of the few countries in Europe where out-migration has been higher than immigration in recent decades, and it has a low-wage economy. Holiday propensities at around 50 per cent are lower than those of Spain, and fewer trips are taken abroad. With over 2 million Portuguese living abroad, visiting friends and relatives (VFR) is an important component of the travel industry.

Inbound tourism

During the 1960s, upmarket tourism was encouraged by the austere, authoritarian Salazar regime, but the country remained economically and socially backward, particularly in the rural areas. The 1974 'Carnation Revolution' introduced democracy but also industrial unrest, resulting in a downturn for inbound tourism. The situation was aggravated by the influx of over a million refugees from the former Portuguese colonies of Angola and Mozambique, which had to be accommodated by the hotel sector. In line with the growth of inclusive tours and low-cost carriers to Portugal, major changes in the organisation and approach to tourism took place in the 1990s. In 2019, 27 million tourist arrivals were recorded, but due to the COVID-19 pandemic, this fell to 6.5 million the following year. Portugal's recovery has been due to a high vaccination rate, with domestic tourism taking up some of the spare hotel capacity.

Spain is by far Portugal's largest market, accounting for most of the visitors arriving by road, but these are usually short stay, including cross-border shopping excursions. Tourists from Brazil and the United States stay longer and spend more. Portugal's other main markets – Britain, Germany, the Netherlands, and France – tend to use air-inclusive tours, and there is a marked summer peak in demand.

The supply side of tourism

Transport

Portugal's location in the south-west corner of Europe necessitates a long journey if road or rail are used as travel modes. This has prompted a major road upgrading programme, including the construction of 2,000 kilometres of motorways. The rail network is fairly extensive (2,600 kilometres), and the state-owned company Comboios de Portugal (CP) operates high-speed trains between Lisbon, Porto, and other major centres. Many cruise itineraries feature Lisbon, Leixões (for Porto), and Funchal (Madeira) as ports of call. Nevertheless, air transport is the dominant mode for tourists arriving from northern Europe, and those staying in self-catering accommodation in the Algarve generally use fly-drive arrangements. The national airline is TAP Air Portugal (www.flytap.com), while low-cost carriers operate flights into Lisbon, Faro (for the Algarve), Porto, and the island of Madeira.

Accommodation

Portugal's accommodation stock is well developed, with a concentration of the larger hotels in the Algarve, Estoril, and Madeira; these cater for inclusive-tour clients, whereas those in Lisbon mainly accommodate business travellers. The government owns a chain of hotels – *pousadas* – similar in concept to the Spanish paradores. Likewise, the *estelagems* operated by the private sector often use converted country houses or *quintas*. Villas used as second homes or retirement properties have created a long-stay market, particularly in the Algarve and Madeira. Camping and caravanning are popular with German, French, and Spanish visitors to the eastern Algarve, while the many sites around Lisbon provide a cheaper alternative to the capital's hotels. The British and Dutch prefer to stay in holiday apartments, again mainly in the Algarve.

Organisation

The Secretary of State for Tourism is part of the Ministry of Economy and Maritime Affairs with overall responsibility for tourism. The national tourism agency is Turismo de Portugal. Its mission is to:

- Develop and enhance tourism infrastructure.
- Encourage and promote training.
- Support investment in the tourism sector.
- Co-ordinate the internal and external promotion of Portugal as a tourism destination.
- Regulate and inspect gambling activities.
- Plan and organise tourism.
- Organise and link to the provinces and regions.
- Organise and link to industry associations, stakeholders, and customers.

This will be achieved through the 2021 COVID-19 recovery strategy – 'Reactivating Tourism' and the 'Portugal Sustainability Tourism Plan 2020–2027'.

At the regional level, there are two directorates for tourism (Madeira and the Azores) and five regional promotion authorities (ARPTs) which are not-for-profit private agencies acting as destination management organisations.

Portugal is anxious to control the environmental and social impacts of tourism. Around 6 per cent of the country is protected in a number of nature parks. These are under the control of the Institute of Nature Conservation and Forests, which reports to the Ministry of Agriculture and Food, indicating a possible conflict of interest between conservation and rural development. Impacts are also reduced by Portugal's emphasis on the upper and middle sectors of the tourism market, in contrast to Spain's domination by mass market tourism, and this is reflected in the generally higher quality of the Portuguese tourism product compared to Spain. Portugal is also attempting to spread the load of tourism more evenly, both seasonally and geographically (well over a half of foreign arrivals are between June and September). The Algarve is already nearing saturation in terms of tourism development and stands in contrast with the more remote interior provinces, such as Tras-os-Montes, which see few foreign visitors. Counter-attractions are being developed in the Porto-Espinho area in the north and at Setúbal, south of Lisbon. Portugal has diversified its tourism product by promoting:

- Football: In 2004, Portugal hosted the European championship, which boosted arrivals, not just to Lisbon, but to lesser-known venues throughout the country.
- Golf: This helps to even out seasonal variations in demand and has raised Portugal's international profile. There are over 100 courses, generally of a high standard, with a concentration in the Algarve.
- Nautical tourism: There has been substantial investment in yacht marinas, particularly along the coast near Lisbon and the Algarve.
- Surfing: Portugal's long Atlantic coastline is almost ideal, and as a result Guincho, Peniche, Nazaré, and Ericeira attract surfers from all over the world seeking the 'big wave'.
- Music festivals: Lisbon hosts the Rock in Rio Lisboa event, alternating with Rio de Janeiro, exemplifying Portugal's close cultural links with Brazil.
- Health and wellness tourism: There are a number of spa resorts based on thermal springs where the therapeutic treatments have gained international recognition. Caldas da Rainha and Chaves are among the best-known.
- Rural tourism: It is being developed particularly in the north, rehabilitating historic villages, encouraging traditional crafts, and broadening the appeal of Portuguese wines and gastronomy.

Portugal is also encouraging a new breed of tourist – 'digital nomads', usually young professionals who travel freely while working remotely using information technology.

Tourism resources

Southern Portugal

The **Algarve** is Portugal's most popular holiday region, accounting for 30 per cent of overnight stays by foreign tourists. This success is due largely to an exceptionally sunny climate, fine sandy beaches, rocky coves, and picturesque fishing villages. Tourism did not develop until the mid-1960s when Faro Airport was opened and the April 25 Bridge across the Tagus from Lisbon greatly reduced travel times by road to what had been a remote region. In the late 1990s, a second bridge – the Vasco da Gama – opened, giving a further boost to coastal tourism south of Lisbon. Many of the resort developments (for example, near Lagos, Albufeira, and Portimão) are in the form of self-contained holiday villages. Sports facilities have been important in attracting investment from northern Europe. However, not all the development has been of a high standard – the haphazard growth of Quarteira compares unfavourably with nearby Vilamoura, planned around its yacht

Photo 14.4
Albufeira beach

Source: Brian Boniface

marina. Tourism development is concentrated in the western Algarve, whereas the low-lying coast east of Faro is less commercialised. The cultural heritage of the Algarve includes the medieval walled town of Silves, and Sagres near Cape St Vincent, where Prince Henry the Navigator initiated the great age of Portuguese exploration in the fifteenth century.

In contrast to the Algarve, the **Alentejo** region and the interior of southern Portugal has been relatively neglected for tourism. This region is characterised by wide plains, large country estates, and extensive forests of cork oak trees, a resource threatened by changes in the international wine trade. The only tourist centre of significance is Évora with its important Roman heritage, but it was envisaged that a major power project on the River Guadiana, creating a vast artificial lake, would be the catalyst for large-scale development near the Spanish border. To date, this has not materialised, but a number of rural enterprises have adapted to meet the needs of 'stargazers', tourists attracted by the absence of light pollution in this area, which has been designated by UNESCO as a 'dark sky reserve'. The coast of Alentejo, promoted as the Costa de Ouro, is attracting development on a small scale, with large stretches protected as nature reserves.

Central Portugal and Lisbon

Tourism around Lisbon has been established for much longer, and there is a wealth of attractions available for the cultural tourist as well as the sun-seeker. Lisbon, situated on the wide Tagus estuary, is one of Europe's major seaports, while Portela Airport is a hub for international flights to Europe, South America, and Africa. The capital is rich in reminders of Portugal's maritime history, notably the Tower of Belém, the Monument to the Discoveries, and the Jéronimos Monastery, which contains the tomb of the great explorer Vasco da Gama (https://wwww.mosteirojeronimos.gov.pt). Tourism received a boost with the 1998 World Expo focussing on the oceans. Planning for this international exhibition involved the regeneration of the waterfront area. Lisbon has become a popular short-break destination, with its mix of old-fashioned trams, quality shopping, and exuberant nightlife. Tourism resources close to Lisbon include:

- The strip of coast to the west of Lisbon, known as the Costa de Lisboa, has good beaches, hotels, and facilities for sport and entertainment, especially at Cascais and Estoril, which is famed for its casino. (This attracted many Spaniards during the Franco era, when gambling was prohibited in Spain.)
- South of the Tagus, the coastline around Setúbal underwent considerable development during the 1980s with much self-catering accommodation.
- North of Lisbon, and extending from Peniche almost to Porto, the **Costa de Prata** is mainly popular with Portuguese holidaymakers. Its long sandy beaches are, for the most part, exposed to the Atlantic surf. The most important resorts are Nazaré, where tourism has replaced the traditional fishing industry, and Figueira da Foz.

Away from the coast, this part of Portugal boasts many places of interest, readily accessible from Lisbon. They include:

- Sintra, in a scenically beautiful location overlooking the capital, was once favoured as a health resort by Portuguese royalty and wealthy foreigners.
- Óbidos, a picturesque medieval town.
- Coimbra is an attractive university town noted for its contribution to *fado* music.
- Fátima is an interesting example of faith-based tourism, owing its fame to the apparitions of the Virgin Mary to three shepherd children in 1917. A poor farming village was subsequently transformed into a pilgrimage centre of worldwide significance for Catholics, and which has a particular resonance for the Portuguese. Two modern basilicas, each capable of holding thousands of worshippers, face a plaza larger than that of St Peters in Rome. Many pilgrims have made the journey on foot, following recognised trails from their rural communities. In May and October each year, on the anniversary of the apparitions, vast numbers of pilgrims are attracted to the sanctuary for candle-lit processions.

The North

Tourism development is being encouraged in northern Portugal, assisted by regional development schemes, and upgraded road transport. Resources include:

- Aveiro, with its large sheltered lagoons, ideal for water sports.
- Porto, at the mouth of the river Douro, is Portugal's second city, its major commercial centre, and the gateway to the northern region. The São Bento train station is decorated

with exquisite *azulejos* (tilework panels), an art form for which Portugal is renowned. Porto's main claim to fame in the United Kingdom is its association with the port wine industry, although the actual vineyards are located 150 kilometres upstream, and the picturesque sailing barges seen on the waterfront are no longer used to transport the wine. Nevertheless, river cruises along the Douro are popular with British tourists.

- Stretching from Porto north to the Spanish border lies the **Costa Verde**, which is attracting increasing numbers of foreign visitors, travelling independently by car rather than using inclusive tours. Espinho, Povoa de Varzim, and Viana do Castelo are the chief resorts in this area.
- The Peneda Gerês National Park on the Spanish border offers wild granite mountain scenery.
- The small historic towns of the Minho region are interesting places to visit, notably Braga, the religious centre of Portugal with its spectacular Bom Jesus shrine (https://bomjesus.pt), and Guimarães, a historic town which is celebrated as the cradle of Portuguese independence.

The Portuguese Islands

There are two groups of islands of volcanic origin in the Atlantic Ocean that we can treat as separate destinations, Madeira and the Azores. Unlike the Canary Islands, they were uninhabited at the time of their discovery in the fifteenth century, but there are similarities in the native vegetation. Since 1975, the islands have enjoyed a degree of autonomy from Lisbon. In view of the limited resource base of the islands, and with fewer opportunities than in the past for the islanders to emigrate to the Americas or South Africa, tourism should play an important role in the economy. However, tourism has been much more successful in Madeira than in the Azores, and this is largely due to differences in accessibility.

Madeira

Madeira is situated 800 kilometres south-west of Lisbon and slightly nearer to Casablanca. Of greater significance is the position of the harbour of Funchal on the main shipping routes from Europe to South America and South Africa. It was largely for this reason that Madeira became a fashionable winter destination for well-to-do British travellers in Victorian times. The island was able to broaden its appeal after 1964 when the international airport was opened east of Funchal, and the number of visitors increased five-fold between 1970 and 1990. Funchal is also an important port of call on cruise itineraries. Mass tourism in the way it has occurred in the Canary Islands is ruled out by:

- The impossibility of extending the airport, which is not capable of handling wide-bodied jets.
- The shortage of land for development generally, on this mountainous but densely populated island.
- The absence of beaches, except on the small and otherwise barren island of Porto Santo, approximately 50 kilometres away from Funchal.

The regional government of Madeira has, therefore, aimed at promoting quality tourism. Foreign visitors are attracted by the beautiful scenery of mountains, coastal cliffs, and sub-tropical vegetation, and the almost ideal climate; winter is still the peak season for the British, Germans, and Scandinavians. Hiking trails follow the intricate network of *levadas* (irrigation channels), which carry water from the mountains to the pocket-sized farms. The road network is being improved to make the interior more accessible, sports facilities are being developed to attract a younger market, and traditional craft industries such as embroidery are encouraged.

The Azores

The Azores are a group of nine islands situated 1,500 kilometres west of Lisbon and 3,500 kilometres east of New York. Their mid-Atlantic location was important in the early years of trans-Atlantic flight when airports on Faial and Santa Maria acted as staging points, but with the introduction of longer-range aircraft, the islands were by-passed. Until 2015, the Portuguese government restricted scheduled air services to the islands to TAP, and Azores Airlines (formerly SATA International) based in Ponta Delgada, the regional capital on São Miguel. In 2018, Delta Air Lines initiated summer services from New York, giving Americans the opportunity to use the island of São Miguel as a stopover on the way to mainland Europe. Although Delta was subsequently replaced by United Airlines, the number of visitors is set to increase substantially. A variety of stakeholders are determined that tourism should be managed sustainably to benefit local communities and protect the natural assets of the islands (three of which are Biosphere Reserves). This includes:

- A cap of 20,000 beds on hotel capacity.
- Limits on the number of visitors to particular sites.
- Possible controls on whale and dolphin watching, which has become a popular activity (the traditional whaling industry ceased in 1982).

The islands are dispersed over 800 kilometres of ocean, making it difficult to organise multi-centre holidays, but this will change with the offer of low-cost inter-island flights. Unlike Madeira, the Azores are not regarded as a winter sun destination because, although the climate allows the cultivation of sub-tropical produce such as tea and pineapples, there is less sunshine than in most Mediterranean resorts. There are few beaches and the islands' main appeal is the spectacular volcanic scenery, the best-known examples being the crater lakes, hot springs, and geysers on São Miguel. Yachting, sea angling, hiking, and horse riding in the countryside are popular activities.

Summary

- The Iberian Peninsula and the holiday islands of Spain and Portugal are among the world's major tourist destination areas. This is partly due to Spain's early entry into mass tourism in the 1960s based upon its holiday resources of an extensive

Mediterranean coastline and accessibility to northern Europe. Portugal was a later entrant into the tourism market and is attempting to avoid mass tourism, focussing instead on more affluent markets.

- Tourist accommodation is concentrated at the coast, on the islands, and in the major cities. The principal resort areas are served by a well-developed transport infrastructure.
- In Spain, uncontrolled resort development has caused environmental damage, deepened regional contrasts, and affected Spanish lifestyles to such an extent that many other countries – including Portugal – have been anxious to avoid these negative effects of tourism.
- The attractions of both countries are mainly based on the coastline, and there are major resort concentrations on the islands, the Spanish Mediterranean Costas, and the Algarve.
- Sport tourism, particularly golf, is a major growth sector in both countries.
- Cultural tourism is reviving with the growing interest in the art treasures and historic buildings of the cities of Spain and Portugal.
- Pilgrimages are an important part of domestic tourism in both Spain and Portugal.
- Rural tourism is becoming an important sector of the market. The landscapes of the Iberian Peninsula and the islands have great natural appeal, but the level of environmental protection is variable.

Review questions

1. Describe the social and cultural impacts of mass tourism on Spanish communities.
2. Identify the advantages of Spain or Portugal as venues for international sports events.
3. Apply the tourist area life cycle to a particular Spanish resort.
4. Compare and contrast Fátima and Santiago de Compostela as centres of faith-based tourism.

References and further reading

Barke, M., Towner, J. and Newton, M.T. (1997) *Tourism in Spain Critical Issues*, CAB International, Wallingford

Cosgrove, I. and Jackson, R. (1972) *The Geography of Recreation and Leisure*, Hutchinson, London

Ledesma González, O. (2012) *El modelo túristico en el Puerto de la Cruz: presente y futuro*, Nivaria Ediciones, La Laguna

Moreira, C.O. (2018) Portugal as a tourist destination, *Journal of Mediterranean Geography* (online), 1–43, http://journals.openedition.org/mediterranee/10402

Organization for Economic Co-operation and Development (annual) *Tourism Policy and International Tourism in OECD Member Countries*, OECD, Paris

https://www.unwto.org/tourism-data/unwto-tourism-dashboard

The tourism geography of Italy and Malta

After reading this chapter, you should be able to:

- Describe the major physical regions of Italy and appreciate the differences between the north and the south.

- Understand the nature of the Italian economy and society and their significance for tourism demand.

- Outline the major features of demand for domestic and international tourism in Italy and the impact of COVID-19.

- Outline the major features of tourism infrastructure in Italy and Malta.
- Demonstrate a knowledge of the tourist regions, resorts, business centres, and tourist attractions of Italy and Malta.

Introduction

Italy is one of the largest countries of western Europe with a population of around 60 million, while the island-nation of Malta, lying 90 kilometres to the south of Sicily is tiny by comparison. Geographically, the two countries occupy a strategic position in the centre of the Mediterranean Basin, while historically the Roman Catholic Church has played a major role both politically and culturally.

Italy

As a tourist destination, Italy for many people means sunshine, good food, music, and romance. Others are attracted by the style and quality of Italian fashion and engineering products.

Tourism in Italy has a long pedigree. Domestic tourism was certainly flourishing in ancient times, when the wealthier citizens of Rome visited their summer villas in resorts such as Baia on the Gulf of Naples. After the fall of the Roman Empire, the pre-conditions for tourism – security and economic prosperity – were to cease for many centuries. Nevertheless, Rome continued to be the destination for Christian pilgrims from all over Europe. The Middle Ages were marked by the rise of the Italian city states, whose merchants grew rich as international bankers and as intermediaries in the trade in luxury goods from the Middle East. Venice, Pisa, and Genoa also made vast profits from shipping pilgrims and Crusaders to the Holy Land. Following the Renaissance, what we would now call cultural tourists were attracted to Florence and Venice, then at their zenith as the cutting edge of European civilisation. Shakespeare was strongly influenced by Italian literature, and a host of writers and artists from northern Europe, including Milton, Goethe, and Shelley, visited Italy for inspiration. In the eighteenth century, it was the custom for wealthy young aristocrats to go on the Grand Tour, accompanied by a tutor and an entourage of servants, which involved a stay of at least a few months in Italy. Here, they completed their education (in more ways than one!), buying classical sculptures (not all genuine), and paintings as souvenirs of their travels, while on their return, they renovated their country houses in the style of Palladio and other Italian architects. In a sense, the expansion of the railways in the nineteenth century allowed entrepreneurs such as Thomas Cook to popularise the idea of a European tour, bringing Italy within the reach of the expanding middle class of Victorian Britain.

Even today, most tourists to Italy have a cultural motivation, and the country's art and architectural heritage is the main reason it ranks among the world's top five destinations. Tourism products of a cultural nature include:

- Short city breaks and longer touring holidays, appealing mainly to art lovers.
- Music festivals, usually associated with a composer's home town, such as Pesaro (Rossini) and Lucca (Puccini). Italy originated opera as an art form, and there it enjoys widespread popular support.
- Courses in Italian art and literature for foreign students in university towns such as Perugia.
- Gastronomy: Italy has been a pioneer in the 'slow food' movement, focussing on locally produced and sourced ingredients, cooked to order with traditional techniques. This stands in contrast with the international fast-food eateries found in most tourist cities.
- Faith-based tourism, where Rome, Assisi, Loreto, and Padua have been joined in the twentieth century by San Giovanni Rotundo (the town in Puglia associated with the controversial Padre Pio) as the most visited destinations for Catholic pilgrims. The Italian section of the Via Francigena, the pilgrim route to Rome, passes through some of the country's most attractive landscapes, and includes Aosta, Pavia, Lucca, and Siena. Although not as well-known as the Camino to Santiago, it is often seen as a scenic and quieter alternative to the Way of St James (Ron and Timothy, 2019). Since 2005, the Italian government and local authorities have promoted the route as a tourism product. Genuine pilgrims who have completed part of the journey on foot, on horseback, or cycling qualify for a testimonial on arrival in Rome.

With some notable exceptions, such as the Gran Paradiso National Park in the western Alps, Italy's environmental record has been relatively poor compared to the countries of northern and central Europe, and ecotourism is less developed. Conservation of the nation's cultural heritage is also a major problem, given the large number of World Heritage Sites and art treasures with the limited public funding that is available.

The setting for tourism

Physical features

Italy is separated from northern Europe by the high mountain barrier of the Alps and boasts a coastline that stretches 7,000 kilometres, facing the Adriatic and the western Mediterranean. The Apennines form the rugged spine of the Italian Peninsula, presenting a formidable obstacle to east-west communications. Between these mountains and the Alps lies the North Italian Plain, which contains most of the country's productive farmland and some of Europe's largest and most prosperous industrial cities. Much of Italy is geologically unstable, as shown by the powerful earthquake that devastated Amatrice, Lazio in 2016, the frequent landslides in the Apennines, and the volcanic activity in the Naples area and Sicily. Nevertheless, Italy's abundant geothermal resources have given rise to a flourishing spa tourism industry, with resorts such as Abano, Montecatini Terme, and Ischia enjoying an excellent international reputation.

Social and cultural features

The Italian lifestyle has always been an attraction for visitors from the more reserved countries of northern Europe, as demonstrated by the elegance on display in the evening *passegiata* or parade in every town. Although Italy now has one of the lowest birth-rates in Europe due to the economic and social changes since the Second World War, family ties remain very strong. The Roman Catholic Church continues to play an important role, and religious festivals are popular. Italian culture is characterised by great regional variety, expressed in food specialities, handicrafts, and dialects. This is due largely to the fact that the Risorgimento, the reunification of Italy, was only partially achieved in 1861. Italians continue to have stronger loyalties to their city or region than to the state as a whole, and one of the biggest obstacles to national unity is the long-standing negative attitudes of northern Italians towards the South, known as the Mezzogiorno, which they regard as socially backward and a burden on the economy.

Demand for tourism

Domestic tourism

Despite Italy's appeal to the foreign visitor, it is the large domestic market that dominates and sustains the tourism industry. Italians have a legal entitlement to at least four weeks of annual leave, and well over half the population take at least one holiday away from home. The domestic market is largely seasonal, with nearly 75 per cent of trips taking place in July and August, while average lengths of stay are falling as the three- or four-week vacation becomes less popular. Seasonality is a problem, as although participation in winter sports and activity holidays is growing, summer beach holidays remain the most popular type of domestic tourism. Whereas some of the resorts of the Adriatic coast and Liguria are also very much part of the international tourism scene, many small sea-side resorts of Tuscany, Lazio, Puglia, and Calabria see few foreign holidaymakers.

Outbound tourism

An increasing number of Italians are travelling abroad, mainly to France and Spain but increasingly to long-haul destinations, and Italy ranks among the world's leading tourist-generating countries. However, it is only relatively recently that the country has become sufficiently affluent to generate a massive demand for foreign travel, and there is a wealth of attractions nearer home. In consequence, Italy has a substantial surplus on its travel account.

Inbound tourism

Tourism accounts for around 9 per cent of Italy's GDP and around 1.7 million jobs. Italy received 65 million foreign tourists in 2019, but the COVID-19 pandemic had a devastating impact on tourism, such that arrivals fell to 27 million in 2021. Starting in northern cities like Milan, the pandemic spread rapidly, bringing the country's health services to the verge of breakdown. In response, the government imposed a nationwide lockdown in early March 2020, which had a major impact on the economy. The community spirit and spontaneity of Italians, denied normal social contacts, was shown in the balcony singing, organised on social media. The tourism sector was well on the way to recovery when the Russian invasion of Ukraine occurred, imperilling energy supplies and damaging travel confidence in long-haul markets such as the United States, due to the perceived closeness of Italy to the danger zone. The loss of the Russian market, which had been growing in importance prior to the pandemic, was damaging to the Adriatic resorts such as Rimini.

There is a considerable volume of business travel to Italy, which is one of Europe's leading countries for trade fairs and exhibitions. The most important venues, with the exception of Bari and Naples, are in the north and include Milan, Turin, Genoa, and Bologna. International sports events are also important, particularly motor racing, with world-famous circuits at Monza (www.monzanet.it) and Imola (www.autodromoimola. it). For most foreign visitors, however, holidays are the main reason for visiting Italy. In contrast to the pattern of domestic tourism, foreign visitors tend to be concentrated in a few regions that are well-known for their art cities or resort attractions, namely Veneto, Lazio, and Tuscany. Before the pandemic, Germany was by far the most important market in terms of arrivals and overnight stays, on account of the good road access between the two countries. British tourists have been less inclined to be independent travellers, with over half arriving by air; here, low-cost carriers are taking market share from charter airlines. For the British, Venice, Rome, Lombardy, Tuscany, and the Sorrento Peninsula are the most popular destinations. Visitors from the United States, typically, spend only a short time in Italy, which is just one of the countries visited on a European tour, where the main attractions are the major art cities. Not surprisingly, most of Italy's luxury hotels are concentrated in Rome, Florence, and Venice.

The supply side of tourism

Transport

Domestic and international tourist travel is mainly by surface modes of transport. Italy has an excellent road network, including almost 7,000 kilometres of *autostradi,* toll motorways managed by private companies. This is effectively linked to the wider European system, despite the bottlenecks, caused mainly by excessive numbers of trucks, which occur on the approaches to the Brenner Pass and other routes through the Alps. This problem should be eased, together with the associated pollution, by the completion of a number of rail tunnel projects. The Autostrada di Sole from Milan to Reggio di Calabria is used by hordes of sun-seeking tourists from Germany and other countries of northern Europe, since it is possible to travel by car at high average speeds from Flensburg on the German-Danish border to the southern tip of the Italian Peninsula. However, accident rates in Italy are high by British or North American standards.

The rail network is also extensive and generally offers travellers an efficient service with some of the lowest fares in Europe, although overcrowding is a problem in summer. Italian State Railways (FS) own most of the network, apart from a few narrow-gauge lines. A number of high-speed trains operate between the major cities, including the *Direttissima* linking Florence and Rome; most of the funding for these high-speed rail projects comes from the private sector rather than the government.

Italy's long coastline and location in mid-Mediterranean has encouraged a history of seafaring; for example, Genoa, the birthplace of Columbus, is one of the leading ports of Europe. Although few tourists arrive by sea, cruise ships operating in the Mediterranean usually call at Italian ports such as Venice and Naples. A number of ports, namely Livorno,

Civitavecchia (serving Rome), Ancona, and Brindisi are essential nodes in a network of coastal shipping services and international ferries linking various parts of the Mediterranean. High-speed hydrofoils operate on the short sea crossings between the mainland and the smaller islands such as Capri. They are also used for sightseeing excursions on the lakes of northern Italy.

Italy is well-served by air transport. The most important airports are Fiumicino (Rome) and Linate (Milan), which rank among Europe's busiest. Alitalia, the national airline (www.alitalia.com) is active in tourism promotion, working closely with the national tourism organisation. Alitalia provides a network of domestic services, while a number of charter and low-cost airlines link the islands and resort areas to the tourist-generating areas in northern Europe. Low-cost carriers also connect Italian cities to regional airports across Europe.

CASE STUDY 15.1
PILGRIMAGES IN THE MODERN WORLD

The Vatican has a specialist agency for pilgrimages, the Opera Romana Pellegrinaggi (ORP), which also acts as the tourist office for Vatican City. It is very aware of the need to facilitate the movement of pilgrims, now the demand for faith-based tourism is becoming ever greater, and yet fewer people have the time or inclination to travel in the traditional way. In 2006, the ORP organised transport for more than 50,000 pilgrims, working with scheduled airlines. However, the airports used by these airlines are at some distance from the sacred sites that pilgrims wish to visit. The Vatican's solution to the problem was to organise its own charter flights using Mistral Air, a company owned by the Italian Post Office. As a result, the cost of the journey for pilgrims was reduced by 10 per cent in the first year of operation. Until it ceased passenger services in 2018, Mistral Air linked a number of Italian airports with the pilgrimage centres of Lourdes, Fátima, Czestochowa in Poland, Guadalupe in Mexico, Sinai, and the Holy Land. Some criticised the Vatican for its involvement in a commercial venture competing with low-cost airlines such as Ryanair for the pilgrim market.

Accommodation

Italy has 5.1 million bed spaces distributed among hotels, campsites, pensions, and *locande* (inns), favoured by domestic tourists. Hotels are most numerous in the north east of the country and are generally small family concerns, while large hotel chains are less dominant in the resort scene than elsewhere in Europe. The government agency Agriturist has done much to promote rural tourism, and a variety of accommodation is available, particularly in Veneto and Tuscany, ranging from converted farm buildings to luxury villas (www.agriturist.it). There is a trend towards greater use of self-catering accommodation, and campsites are numerous, especially along the Adriatic coast. A number of holiday villages are also available, run on similar lines to Club Mediterranée by the Italian tour operator Valtur (www.valtur.com).

Organisation

There is a clear demarcation between public sector tourism support at the national and the regional level.

NATIONAL LEVEL

Italian governments since the Second World War have usually been weak coalitions lasting on average less than a year, making it difficult to implement clear policy objectives on tourism promotion and development. In contrast to a flourishing business sector, much of the public sector is characterised by inefficiency and widespread political corruption, resulting in one of the largest unregulated 'black economies' in Europe. At the national level, a new Ministry of Tourism was created in 2021 to oversee national strategy, planning, development, marketing, and innovation. The Ministry oversees the Italian State Tourist Office (ENIT), a public sector organisation founded in 1919. ENIT's main purpose is promotion and research, aiming to diversify Italy's tourism products away from beach holidays and the 'big three' historic cities – Rome, Florence, and Venice – to other forms of tourism. With reduced public sector commitment to tourism, ENIT is involved in co-operative marketing with the private sector and the airlines. The Italian Alpine Club (CAI) is a national, non-profit organisation concerned with the conservation of the mountain environment and the maintenance of trails and refuges for climbers and hikers.

REGIONAL LEVEL

Each of Italy's 20 regional governments have devolved powers for regulating tourism businesses, developing strategic marketing activities, and managing European Structural Funds. Some regions – notably Sicily, Sardinia, Valle d'Aosta, and South Tyrol – have been more active than others in planning, development, and promotion.

Nonetheless, it is at the regional level that most activity is occurring, with funding based on the number of inhabitants of the region, rather than the number of tourists visiting.

Provinces and municipalities can also issue regulations for the tourism sector. Local associations known as **Pro Loco** work with schools and businesses, drawing on the civic pride of people living in towns and small cities. They organise festivals, revitalise traditional craft industries, and enhance the appeal of their communities. Regions and autonomous provinces are part of a 'United Conference', a public agency that ensures strategic collaboration.

Tourism resources

Northern Italy

The Italian Alps

The Italian Alps have a generally sunnier climate than the mountains of Austria and Switzerland, but this does mean that the skiing season tends to be shorter. We can divide the Alps for convenience into central, western, and eastern sections.

The central Alps are dissected by long transverse valleys that terminate in a number of lakes of glacial origin. Because of their long-established importance as a holiday destination, we need to consider the Italian Lakes as a separate entity. The central Alps include various ski resorts, such as Bormio, Livigno, and Madessimo, which are popular among price-sensitive foreign skiers and are accessible from airports in Milan and Bergamo.

The western Alps encompass the highest mountain peaks in the system. The most important resorts are easily accessible from Turin, including Sauze d'Oulx and Sestrière, which was developed by the Fiat corporation. The regional government of Valle d'Aosta has played a significant role in promoting tourism to counter rural depopulation. Cervinia, situated on the slopes of Monte Cervino (better known as the Matterhorn), is a major resort in this area, along with Courmayeur near Mont Blanc. Both resorts form part of cross-border ski circuits, with Cervinia linked with Zermatt and Courmayeur with Mégève, in the French Alps. This French-speaking region is rich in heritage attractions due to its location on the approach to the Great St Bernard Pass, historically one of the most important routes across the Alps. It also includes one of Italy's finest wilderness areas, the Gran Paradiso National Park (www.pngp.it/).

The eastern Alps offer different scenic attractions and cultural features. Although the Dolomites are by no means the highest part of the Alps, these mountains present a spectacular array of landforms resulting from erosion of the limestone rock. They present a challenge to mountain climbers and the more adventurous breed of hikers using the *via ferrata* system of trails. The area boasts one of Europe's longest ski circuits – the Val Gardena – and one of its most stylish resorts – Cortina d'Ampezzo. Merano, located in the South Tyrol, is one of Italy's most important spa towns. Until it became part of Italy in 1918, the South Tyrol had been ruled by the Austrian Habsburgs for more than six centuries. The prevalence of the German language, styles of village architecture, cuisine, and the traditional handicrafts are reminders of this heritage.

The Italian Lakes owe their elongated shape and their great depth, to glaciation of the mountain valleys during the most recent Ice Age (Lake Como, for example, is over 400 metres deep, which means the lake bed is 300 metres below sea level). The southern ends of the lakes open out into relatively flat countryside, while their northern sections are hemmed in by mountains. The vast quantities of water stored in the lakes, and a location sheltered from northerly winds, results in a milder, sunnier climate than the Lombardy Plain to the south. The most important lakes for tourism are from east to west, Garda, Como, Lugano, and Maggiore, each having specific attractions:

- Lake Garda is the largest, with a western shoreline – the 'Garda Riviera' offering high class accommodation. The best beaches are, however, on the south shore where the picturesque spa town of Sirmione is situated.
- Lake Como is only 60 kilometres from Milan and is, therefore, popular with day visitors, while its southern fringes have been affected by industrial development. In contrast, Bellagio, at a scenic location between two arms of the lake, is the most stylish of the resorts. Most tours of the lake feature a visit to the villas built by wealthy landowners in the eighteenth century, which are admired by garden-lovers worldwide.

- Most of Lake Lugano falls within Switzerland. The resorts on the Italian side are little more than villages, with the exceptions of Porlezza and the gambling centre of Campione.
- Lake Maggiore's northern tip is also Swiss territory. Much of the development is on the western shore, with Stresa being the most popular resort. Growth was rapid after the opening of the Simplon Tunnel in 1906, greatly improving access to the area.

The Italian Lakes appeal to a wide variety of visitors, including water sports enthusiasts, families travelling independently, and older holidaymakers on 'lakes and mountains' inclusive tours. The larger resorts such as Riva del Garda and Stresa offer conference facilities of international standard and feature music festivals among their attractions.

The North Italian Plain

In contrast to the Alps, the lowlands extending from Turin to the Adriatic coast are rather featureless, except in the south west of Veneto, where hills of volcanic origin noted for their vineyards rise above the plains. This part of Italy has a continental rather than a Mediterranean climate, with cold, often foggy winters and hot rainy summers. Its main river, the Po, has changed course many times over the centuries and is held in check by an extensive system of artificial embankments. Rice fields are a feature of the landscape in some areas, and this is Italy's main food producing region. Apart from the culinary attractions, the appeal to tourists lies in the many historic towns, where, despite industrialisation, the art treasures and buildings of medieval and Renaissance times have been preserved.

Venice (see case study) is a city which is truly unique, car-free, where all transport is on foot or by water, due to its island setting in the middle of an extensive shallow lagoon. It is not individual attractions that define this city's appeal but the townscape and canal network that have changed remarkably little over the centuries. The Republic of Venice was once a great power in the eastern Mediterranean, using the profits from the trade in silks and spices from Asia to embellish merchant's palaces, churches, and other public buildings.

Tourism mainly focusses on the San Marco district containing St Mark's Square, the basilica of St Marks (www.basilicasanmarco.it) and the Doge's Palace (https://palazzoducale.visitmuve.it). Event attractions such as the Venice Carnival (https://venice-carnival-italy.com) and the *Regatta Storica* (www.regattastoricavenezia.it) on the Grand Canal are an important part of the city's traditional image, while its contemporary role is exemplified by the film festival, part of the Venice biennale art exhibition, which is held in Lido di Venezia, the city's beach resort on the Adriatic. Venice tends to overshadow the other art cities of the Veneto region, notably Vicenza (showcasing Palladio's architecture) and Padua (famous for its university).

Milan is Italy's second largest city, world-famous for its fashion and engineering industries. In 2015, it hosted the World Expo. The Milanese have the reputation of putting business before pleasure and *la dolce vita*. Nevertheless, shopping is a major activity for many tourists, and this bustling city offers them a fascinating attraction – the vast domed arcade known as the Galleria Vittorio Emmanuelle. Milan also has much to attract culture-seekers, namely the multi-spired Gothic cathedral, La Scala – the world's greatest opera company (www.teatroallascala.org); and Leonardo da Vinci's masterpiece, *The Last Supper*.

Turin, as the capital of the kingdom of Piedmont-Savoy, played a leading role in the struggle to re-unite Italy, which is commemorated in the Museum of the Risorgimento (www.museorisorgimentotorino.it). The city is better known as the centre of the Fiat corporation. Turin Cathedral is a focus of pilgrimage, as it contains among its treasures the shroud venerated as a relic of the Crucifixion.

Verona boasts one of the world's best-preserved Roman arenas, capable of seating 20,000 spectators. This forms an atmospheric setting in summer for one of Europe's most popular music festivals. However, tourists are more likely to visit this beautiful city because of its associations with the legendary lovers Romeo and Juliet.

Bologna, along with the other cities of the Emilia-Romagna region, has been overshadowed as a cultural centre by Venice and Florence, despite having one of Europe's oldest universities. It is better known as a focus for Italy's railway network and for its food industries, but the city has much to offer the tourist, including medieval shopping arcades and 'leaning towers' to rival those of Pisa.

Ravenna is famous for its Byzantine art treasures. This city was the capital of the Western Roman Empire at the time of its destruction by barbarian invasions, an era vividly depicted in Manfredi's epic novel *The Last Legion*.

Trieste is set to grow as a short break destination. During the Cold War, this city's peripheral location on the border with the Eastern Bloc was a disadvantage, but this has changed with the accession of Slovenia to the European Union. Trieste was historically important as the main seaport of the Austro-Hungarian Empire.

The extensive sandy beaches of the northern Adriatic coast offer safe bathing and a wide range of facilities, appealing to families as well as young tourists. Scenically, most of the coastline is flat, and the type of development is not particularly attractive, consisting of high-rise apartments and hotels, separated by extensive camping areas. Rimini, with more hotel beds than any other Italian tourist centre, is the gateway and chief resort of the **Adriatic Riviera**, and along with Cattolica and Milano Marittima caters for mass tourism from the industrial cities of Lombardy, particularly Milan. Most beaches on the Adriatic Riviera are privately owned, and catering concessions are in the hands of family businesses. In peak season, the sand is fully occupied by serried ranks of beach umbrellas and sun loungers.

CASE STUDY 15.2
THE DEATH OF VENICE?

The city of Venice is a World Heritage Site, and an irreplaceable resource that is at risk for the following reasons:

- Flood damage: In November 2019, exceptionally high tides inundated St. Marks Square, and the cost to the city was estimated at around 1 billion euros. Venice has always been subject to flooding, but the problem is getting worse, due to the rise in sea level attributed to global warming. The combination of high tides and storm surges in the Adriatic has led to St Mark's Square being flooded much more frequently than was the case in the 1950s. The 1966 flood disaster destroyed priceless art treasures and made 5,000 people homeless, alerting the world to the possibility that the city would have to be abandoned. In response, the *Venice in Peril Fund* was set up to co-ordinate international efforts in the work of restoration and salvage. Venetians have coped by abandoning the lower floors of centuries-old buildings, but damp and subsidence continue to be major problems. In 2003, work began on Project MOSE, mobile flood barriers sealing the three entrances to the Lagoon to prevent another major flood disaster, such as occurred in November 2019. MOSE is costly and controversial, but it has prevented further widespread flooding, and the barriers are barely visible when not in use.

- Pollution of the Lagoon, which is a delicate ecosystem prone to damage from dredging and chemical effluents.
- The impact of mass tourism and the cruise industry. Venice now faces a more insidious threat than flooding – its worldwide popularity as a tourist destination. In summer, the number of visitors – estimated at 60,000 a day – exceeds the resident population. Recent taxation on overnight visitors is being extended to day visitors in an attempt to reduce visitation. Venice's importance as the major cruise port for the eastern Mediterranean has contributed to the massive influx, with the number of cruise arrivals increasing fourfold between 2010 and 2019. Ships pass within 150 metres of St Mark's Square before mooring at the Marittima terminal at the south west corner of Venice. The visual intrusion, along with safety issues prompted UNESCO to urge the Italian government to propose a re-routing of cruise ships away from the city centre. This would involve access via the southern entrance to the Lagoon and the dredging of a new channel to the west of the city; but many fear that this would cause further ecological disturbance and a loss of revenue from the lucrative cruise industry. In 2021, faced with the resumption of cruising after the COVID-19 pandemic and fearing the loss of Venice's World Heritage status, the government imposed a ban on large cruise ships carrying more than 200 passengers.

Tourism on this scale has contributed to the decline in Venice's population, which is now a third of what it was in the 1950s (or indeed the sixteenth century). The social composition of the population is also becoming less balanced. Middle income families continue to move to Mestre on the mainland, as job opportunities other than in tourism are few in the historic city, where rents are also high, fuelled by speculation. This leaves Venice increasingly to the wealthy, who can afford the upkeep of expensive palazzo-apartments, and the elderly on fixed incomes, who are unable to leave and who face physical and social isolation.

While dwellings are being converted into bed and breakfast establishments, tourism-related businesses, such as those selling papier-maché Carnival masks made in Taiwan, are replacing shops meeting everyday needs. The traditional crafts of Venice are declining due to the high rents and falling demand from a type of visitor who is much less discerning than in the past. Nevertheless, gondoliers still make a good living as an essential part of the romantic image of Venice.

Discussion point

Assign roles representing the stakeholders involved in Venice's tourism industry, and

1. Analyse the strengths and weaknesses of Venice as a tourist destination, the threats the city faces, and the opportunities there may be for more sustainable development and 'slow tourism' in the future. For example, tourists could visit in the less busy months, stay longer, slow down to appreciate the timelessness of Venice, engage with local craft industries and explore lesser-known districts away from crowded San Marco.
2. Discuss the pros and cons of the local authority imposing a tourist tax on day visitors entering the historic city.

Websites

veniceinperil.org
weareherevenice.org
fondoambiente.it
veneziaunica.it
clia.org.it (cruise industry trade association)

The Italian Riviera

The coast of **Liguria**, also known as the 'Italian Riviera', is very different in character from the Adriatic coast. Mountains to the north offer protection from cold weather, and it was the mild climate that initially attracted foreign as well as domestic tourists in the nineteenth century. It is divided into two sections:

*   The Riviera di Poniente, the western section between the French border and Genoa, which has the better beaches;
*   The Riviera di Levante, lying to the south east of Genoa, which is for the most part rocky.

Of the many resorts along this coast, San Remo is probably the best known and remains highly fashionable, with a yacht marina among its amenities. Portofino, once a small picturesque fishing village, has become an exclusive yachting centre on the most attractive stretch of the Riviera di Levante, which also contains Cinque Terre, five formerly isolated communities famed for their terraced vineyards. Resorts such as Alassio have seen better days and are suffering from over-development and overcrowding, now that much of the coast is accessible by motorway as well as by rail from the industrial cities of Piedmont and Lombardy. Genoa itself has raised its international profile through acting as host city for the G8 summit conference in 2001.

Central Italy

Tucked away in the Appenines, **San Marino** is the world's oldest and smallest republic, representing a survival of the city states that made up Italy in medieval times. The republic has a rich history of welcoming refugees, including Garibaldi during his struggle to liberate Italy, and the thousands fleeing the turmoil of the Second World War. The picturesque city of San Marino, built on the slopes of Mt Titano, boasts a number of heritage attractions. Since the 1960s, its economy has primarily been based on tourism. However, the great majority of San Marino's 2 million visitors a year are Italian day-trippers from the Adriatic beach resorts (whereas the resident population is only 34,000). About 1,300 bed spaces are on offer, but the occupancy rate is only 50 per cent. Consequently, the State Office for Tourism is keen to attract longer-stay tourists. The 'Hospitality without Barriers' promotion (www.sanmarinoforall.com) aims to make the country accessible to visitors with a disability, a challenge given San Marino's topography (Photo 15.1).

South of the Apennines, the landscape changes and is scenically much more attractive than the plains of Lombardy and Emilia-Romagna. It is characterised by small farms, vineyards, olive groves, and rolling hills crowned by a small town or village, which on first impressions appears to have changed little since medieval times. This picturesque countryside largely explains the appeal of Tuscany, Umbria, and Le Marche for rural tourism. In fact, the area of Tuscany near Siena has attracted so many British second home owners that it has been nicknamed 'Chiantishire' after the well-known local wines. The rather flat coastline gets less attention from foreign tourists despite the fine beaches, with

Photo 15.1
San Marino

Source: Brian Boniface

the exceptions of the lively resort of Viareggio, and the island of Elba, famous for its associations with Napoleon. However, it is the many historic towns and cities, rather than the coast or the countryside, which have made Tuscany one of Europe's most popular destinations. The tourist centres that have received wide international recognition for their cultural attractions include:

- **Florence**, a city on the River Arno, is the capital of Tuscany and, since the fourteenth century, has been a leading cultural centre in literature (Dante and Bocaccio) and the visual arts. Thanks to the wealth and power of its ruling dynasty – the Medicis – during the Renaissance, Florence was able to attract the best artists of the day, including Leonardo da Vinci, Michelangelo, and Botticelli. As a result, the city can boast three of Europe's finest art collections. The skyline is still dominated by the dome of the cathedral, a major achievement of fifteenth century technology. Other attractions include the covered bridge known as the Ponte Vecchio and the Palazzo Pitti. The city is also famous for its luxury trades, including leather and jewellery. Unfortunately, Florence has suffered from pollution and overcrowding due to its popularity as a tourist destination.

- **Pisa** is included on the international tourist circuit very largely because of the world-famous 'Leaning Tower' – actually one of a group of medieval buildings around the cathedral square (www.opapisa.it). Pisa's international airport is the gateway to Tuscany.

- **Siena** is a fascinating medieval city, with narrow streets opening onto the Piazza del Campo, where the *Palio* horse race is held twice every year in July and August. Facing this square are the cathedral, beautifully decorated in black and white marble, and the spectacular city hall.

- **San Gimignano** is a small hilltop town famous for its towers built by rival families in the Middle Ages, and a reminder of the strife that once characterised Tuscany. It is a favourite location for film-makers and music festivals.

Umbria and **Le Marche** are less visited by foreign tourists than Tuscany, despite their heritage attractions. Assisi's fame as a place of pilgrimage is due to its association with two great spiritual leaders – St Francis (nowadays, widely regarded as the patron of ecology) and St Clare. Urbino was a major cultural centre during the Renaissance and is famous as the birthplace of the artist Raphael. The Adriatic coast of Le Marche is scenically attractive, with a number of important resorts such as Pesaro and Gabicce Mare.

Rome is a bustling modern capital, with acute traffic problems and a heritage that presents many problems for developers. It is known as the 'Eternal City' as it has been a centre of civilisation, despite many vicissitudes, for the best part of 3,000 years. The Pope is not only the spiritual head of more than 1 billion Catholics worldwide but is also the temporal ruler of **Vatican City**, 44 hectares in area – all that remains of the formerly extensive Papal territories in Italy. The main gathering place for pilgrims is St Peter's Square, which provides a magnificent setting for the world's largest church, St Peter's Cathedral. The Sistine Chapel, part of the Vatican Palace, is famous for its paintings by Michelangelo (www.museivaticani.va/). Rome was given a makeover in the seventeenth century by Bernini, the architect and sculptor, and many of the city's monuments, fountains, public squares, and historic buildings date from this period. The Palazzo Borghese boasts a world-famous art collection. Nevertheless, traces of the ancient city can still be seen as reminders of the grandeur of the Roman Empire. They include:

- The Colosseum, where the populace spent much of their leisure time watching 'the Games', subsidised entertainment that included gladiators and other displays of violence. With over 6 million visitors a year, it ranks as Italy's most popular attraction.
- The Forum, which was the 'nerve centre' of ancient Rome (https://parcocolosseo.it/area/foro-romano/).
- The Baths of Caracalla, which are a reminder of the importance of public bathing as a recreation activity in ancient Rome.
- The Pantheon, which is the best-preserved Roman temple, largely because it was converted into a Christian place of worship.
- The Via Appia, the route taken by the Roman legions to the port of Brindisi. Although this ancient highway is protected within a regional park by the authorities and UNESCO, it is under threat from property speculators and illegal development.
- Ostia Antica, the remains of the port of ancient Rome, now 3 kilometres inland (www.ostiaantica.beniculturali.it).

In contrast, there is a modern attraction for family visits – Cinecittá World, a theme park inspired by the Italian film industry; in the 1960s, the studios attracted international celebrities to Rome as 'Hollywood on the Tiber'.

Other attractions in the Lazio region include:

- Lakes of volcanic origin
- The summer palace of the Emperor Hadrian at Tivoli
- The Abbey at Monte Cassino, founded by St Benedict as a role model of order and learning amid the turmoil of the sixth century, destroyed because of its strategic importance in the Second World War, and subsequently rebuilt (www.abbaziamontecassino.org).

Southern Italy

The Mezzogiorno or 'land of the noonday sun' tends to be more traditional than northern Italy in its outlook and lifestyle, with a much larger proportion of its population dependent on agriculture. Due to widespread poverty and a lack of resources, the region has experienced two great waves of emigration:

- To the New World, mainly the United States and Argentina, in the early 1900s.
- Mainly to northern Italy during the economic boom of the 1950s and 1960s.

The Italian government, after 1950, made great efforts to redress the economic disparities between north and south through the Cassa de Mezzogiorno, which initiated development projects and improved transport infrastructure. Funding was made available for hotel building and upgrading along with other tourism facilities. In 1984, the role of the Cassa was largely taken over by the eight regional governments. Southern Italy is now largely dependent on financial assistance from EU regional funding and private investors. Yet, despite the efforts of the agencies concerned, the South has not attracted international tourism on a large scale, with the exception of well-established areas such as the Neapolitan Riviera. Also, the stranglehold of secret societies, namely the Camorra in Naples, the 'Ndrangheta in Calabria and the Mafia in Sicily, on local business and politicians, has tended to discourage long-term investment in tourism as well as other industries.

Campania is a popular destination, as it includes the Neapolitan Riviera, the name given to the resorts and islands of the Bay of Naples. The region is subject to earthquakes and volcanic activity, and near Pozzuoli, numerous hot springs, steam jets and emissions of sulphurous gases characterise the landscape of the area known as the Phlegrean Fields. In 79 AD, the towns of Herculaneum and Pompeii were destroyed by an eruption of Vesuvius. The excavated streets and buildings of Pompeii, which had been smothered under a thick layer of ash for many centuries, now provide a fascinating glimpse of many aspects of life in Roman times. The ruined city is a must-see attraction on the tourist circuit, while other classical sites, such as Paestum and Cumae are relatively neglected.

Most of the holiday resorts are located on the Sorrento Peninsula on the south side of the Bay of Naples. Beaches are in short supply and the main attractions, especially for the older foreign visitor, are:

- The superb scenery of the coastal road from Sorrento to Amalfi.
- The picturesque resorts of Positano and Ravello, and the historic city of Amalfi.
- The easy-going lifestyle and the sentimental popular music of the Neapolitans, which for many tourists epitomises Italy.

Excursions from Sorrento offer the opportunity to visit the renowned island of Capri, celebrated for its Blue Grotto. Additionally, tours extend to Ischia, which is acclaimed for the therapeutic qualities of its radioactive springs. Both Capri and Ischia attract fashion-conscious Italians as well as large numbers of foreign visitors.

Although Sorrento is the largest holiday resort of Campania, Naples is the gateway to the region. Unfortunately, as Italy's third largest city and busiest seaport, Naples has a reputation that tends to deter, rather than attract tourists. Before the reunification of Italy, it was the proud capital of an independent kingdom and featured prominently on the Grand Tour. Since that time, the city has had more than its fair share of problems, including chronic unemployment and political corruption. Naples deserves to be better known for its cultural attractions, which include:

- The Teatro San Carlo, the nation's oldest opera house (www.teatrosancarlo.it).
- Numerous Baroque churches.
- The National Archaeological Museum, having a collection of artefacts recovered from Herculaneum and Pompeii (www.museoarcheologiconapoli.it).

CASE STUDY 15.3
POMPEII

Pompeii stands as one of the world's most remarkable archaeological sites, drawing over 3 million tourists before the pandemic (compared to around 1 million in 2021). It is also among the largest, with more than 40 hectares of the Roman town uncovered since its discovery in the eighteenth-century leaving 22 hectares yet to be excavated. The majority of foreign visitors arrive by tour bus from Rome and Salerno, allowing only two-hour window for sightseeing. However, some allege that bureaucratic inertia on the part of the authorities is responsible for a situation where the tourism experience is diminished by poor site management, poor signage, and damage due to visitor pressure and inadequate supervision. Although Pompeii receives large foreign donations, there is never enough money for maintenance, restoration, and further excavations. In fact, far fewer excavated buildings can be visited now than was the case in the 1950s. As a solution, the tourism councillor for the regional government proposes imposing a limit on the number of visitors. This approach aims to improve the tourism experience while increasing revenue from the site by leasing the ruins as a location for film-makers or as a setting for corporate business events. Debate the pros and cons of this proposal, and suggest alternative ways of protecting this fragile and unique attraction.

Puglia, the region that forms 'the heel of Italy', has long been popular with Italian holidaymakers but remained 'undiscovered' by foreign visitors until recently. Puglia is noted for its vineyards and the *trulli*, beehive-shaped village dwellings that are now much in demand as second homes. The heritage attractions include Castel del Monte, a medieval fortress designated as a World Heritage Site (www.casteldelmonteandria.it), the picturesque Baroque city of Lecce, and the many festivals of the region.

Other parts of the South can offer spectacular mountain scenery, culminating in the Abruzzi and Sila National Parks, the unspoiled beaches of Calabria, and the cave dwellings of Matera, excavated from the soft volcanic tufa. In the 1950s, Matera was the 'shame of Italy' for its squalor and deprivation, but the town has since been revitalised due to the status of the caves as a World Heritage Site.

The Italian Islands

Italy's islands, because they are widely scattered, are less important in the international tourism scene than the islands of Greece, Croatia, and Spain. With the exceptions of Capri, Ischia, and Elba, most of the smaller islands witness few foreign tourists. The two largest islands – Sicily and Sardinia – are each almost the size of Belgium and are holiday destinations in their own right. Nevertheless, together they account for only 6 per cent of overnight stays by foreign visitors in Italy.

Sicily

Only the narrow Straits of Messina separate Sicily from the Italian mainland, but it is very much a region apart from the rest of the nation. This is due to the island's closeness to North Africa and its extraordinary history under the domination of a succession of foreign invaders, notably the Arabs and the Spanish. Although Sicily's former overlords left a rich architectural heritage, the natural environment has suffered from centuries of exploitation and widespread deforestation. Many of the tightly packed hill towns rise out of a parched landscape and are over-dependent on agriculture. They have a neglected, somewhat forbidding appearance; Corleone (of *Godfather* fame) is a typical example. Tourism has made more headway on the coast, where numerous fishing villages have become beach resorts.

Sicily has much to offer the tourist. The weather is generally warm and dry, although the heat of summer is oppressive when the Sirocco wind blows from North Africa. The rich cultural mix is evident in the Sicilian dialect, food specialities, handicrafts and folklore, and the religious intensity of Holy Week. The two major cities – Palermo in the west and Catania in the east – are ports of call on Mediterranean cruises. Ferries serve the island from Genoa, Livorno, and Naples, as an alternative to the Reggio-Messina crossing and the long journey by road down the Italian Peninsula. Sicily will become even more accessible once the controversial project for a fixed link between Messina and the mainland goes ahead.

Sicily's natural attractions include Mount Etna, one of the world's largest active volcanoes, where the crater can be approached by road or by cableway. The region also includes many smaller islands. Outlying Lampedusa has become a staging point for illegal immigration from North Africa. The Lipari Islands off the north coast are volcanic and offer the spectacular scenery of Stromboli as well as opportunities for scuba diving. Sicily's heritage attractions include:

- Archaeological sites, including an array of temples and theatres built by the ancient Greeks that rival anything to be found in Greece itself. The most outstanding example is the Valley of Temples at Agrigento (www.parcovalledeitempli.it). Other important sites from the period (c. 300 BC) can be seen at Syracuse, Segesta, and Selinunte.
- The cathedral at Monreale, which is a blend of Norman-French and Arabic styles.
- Taormina is Sicily's most sophisticated and fashionable resort. With Etna as a backdrop, this is a spectacular setting for operas and other cultural events that are staged in the beautiful Greco-Roman theatre overlooking the Mediterranean.
- Cefalú caters more for families and is favoured by foreign tour operators, as it has an asset that Taormina lacks – a fine beach. It is also a picturesque fishing port with an impressive cathedral.

Sardinia

Tourism serves as an important part of Sardinia's economy. Because of its relative isolation, tour operators feature the island as a separate destination, particularly for beach tourism. Until the 1960s, Sardinia was a remote backwater, outside the mainstream of

Italian culture, while the sparsely populated interior had a reputation for lawlessness. Agritourism is now an important source of income for many rural communities. However, most of the tourism development is based on the island's white sandy beaches. One of the first areas to be developed was the Costa Smeralda, north of Olbia, which includes some of the most expensive hotels and holiday homes to be found anywhere in the Mediterranean, blending perfectly with the natural scenery. Most of Sardinia is not exclusive, and Alghero, in particular, caters for package holidays. Sardinia is well-connected by charter and low-cost flights to the cities of northern Europe and by ferry services to the Italian mainland, Corsica, and mainland France.

Malta

Despite its geographical closeness to Italy, in language and culture Malta has closer links to Britain and North Africa. Although the Maltese islands are poor in natural resources, they are strategically important due to their location in mid-Mediterranean between the Straits of Gibraltar and the Suez Canal. Malta's fine natural harbours also made it a valuable prize for foreign invaders over the centuries. The most important of these, prior to the British takeover, were the international Crusading order known as the Knights of St John who made Malta their base in the sixteenth century. As a result, the islands were in the front line of the military struggle between Christian Europe and the Ottoman Empire. In the nineteenth century and for most of the twentieth, Britain used the Grand Harbour at Valletta as a base for the Royal Navy. The smaller island of Gozo was neglected and remains something of a backwater compared to the main island of Malta, although it is greener and scenically more attractive. The first impression of Malta is an apparently barren landscape of small terraced fields, separated by drystone walls and dotted with villages built from the honey-coloured rock. Due to the limestone geology of the islands and the rather dry climate, water supply is problematic, and tourism has to compete with other demands for this resource.

Demand for tourism

Before independence from Britain in 1964, Malta was not a major destination. The departure of the British armed forces meant that the government had to transform the country's economic base, by concentrating on the service sector, including tourism. Tourism to Malta rapidly expanded during the 1970s, reaching 700,000 by 1980. Most visitors were from Britain, as Malta (along with Cyprus and Gibraltar) was part of the sterling area and, therefore, exempt from the currency controls imposed by the British government. Visitor numbers have grown since the 1980s to reach 2.8 million arrivals in 2019. The COVID-19 pandemic had a major impact on the economy, disrupting Malta's air connections. This, resulted in a decline of 76 per cent in tourist arrivals and an 80 per cent decline in outbound tourism expenditure in 2020.

Malta's membership of the European Union should boost tourism in the long term. The tourism authorities are concerned at Malta's dependence on a few markets, with the United Kingdom accounting for a quarter of all arrivals followed by Germany, Italy, and

France, with Poland in fifth place. The national carrier, Air Malta, also operates services to Libya and Egypt, demonstrating the importance of the Arab market in business travel. Valletta has been successfully promoted as an international conference venue and financial centre. However, the majority of arrivals to Malta are holidaymakers attracted by sun, sand, and sea. About a quarter of Malta's visitors are cruise passengers, with much smaller numbers, mainly Italians, arriving on ferries from Sicily and Naples. Most visitors arriving by air are on inclusive tours, but an increasing number are using low-cost carriers to visit their second or retirement homes on the islands.

The supply side of tourism

Accommodation
Malta has a large stock of hotel and self-catering accommodation, amounting to over 48,000 bed spaces. The lower end of the package holiday market is concentrated in Sliema, while there are a number of new resort developments by international companies responding to the government's strategy to upgrade facilities. In contrast, Gozo's tourism industry is much less developed as it is highly dependent on day visitors from the main island.

Organisation
The importance of tourism to Malta is reflected in the fact that the industry has its own Tourism Ministry, which is also responsible for aviation policy. The Ministry oversees various tourism agencies and companies, including the Malta Tourism Authority, Air Malta, and the Mediterranean Conference Centre (www.mcc.com.mt). The Malta Tourism Authority (MTA) was created in 1999 with the mission of marketing and planning Maltese tourism and upgrading the product (https://www.mta.com.mt). The MTA is anxious to maintain Malta as a competitively priced destination but is faced by various problems. These include:

- Water supplies, with the islands depending largely on desalinisation.
- Development pressures on the main island, which already has one of the world's highest population densities.
- Poor standards of accommodation in some areas.

These problems have led to restrictions on further development in St Paul's Bay, Sliema and the south east of the island. There is also the realisation that, if Malta has reached saturation point in terms of tourism development, then the only way the industry can expand is to use the spare capacity in the off-peak months and to attract a higher spending type of tourist. For this reason, the MTA is determined to re-brand Malta as a selective destination, with a product offer that concentrates on the islands' heritage and culture, event attractions, niche markets, and luxury accommodation. Gozo is positioned to attract upmarket tourists and scuba divers with its tranquillity. Gozo can also take advantage of EU regional funding to improve its transport infrastructure, particularly the ferry services to the main island. This should redress the social and economic imbalance between Malta and Gozo and improve employment prospects for its young people. Malta's tourism strategy will be supported by a new 'Malta Tourism Observatory', designed to monitor the progress of the strategy.

Tourism resources

Malta's main appeal for holidaymakers is the warm sunny climate, with sheltered, unpolluted bays, and harbours, providing ideal conditions for sailing, windsurfing, and diving. Sandy beaches are largely restricted to the north west of the main island, whereas most of the resort development has taken place along the east coast. Although the Maltese people are service-oriented and used to dealing with foreigners, they have retained their traditional culture that has some Middle Eastern influences as well as being characterised by a strong devotion to Catholicism. Each village has its *festa* (religious festival) and elaborately decorated church. For its size, Malta has a remarkable variety of cultural attractions that include:

* The heritage of the Knights of St John in Valetta and 'The Three Cities', as expressed in fortifications, Renaissance palaces, the Manoel Theatre (www.teatrumanoel.com.mt), and many churches. Some of the palaces and *auberges* that housed the knights have found a new role as conference centres or luxury hotels. St John's Co-Cathedral is outstanding for its works of art.
* The archaeological sites, many of which date back to 2000 BC or earlier. The most significant of these is the Hypogeum, apparently a temple linked to a fertility cult.
* The medieval walled town of Mdina, the former capital known as the 'Silent City', in contrast to the bustle of Valletta.
* The traditional *dghaisas*, which ferry tourists across the Grand Harbour.
* Handicrafts such as pottery and lace-making.

Discussion point

As a tourist destination, Malta faces problems common to many small islands that relate to its carrying capacity, and planners have to balance development needs against conservation issues. Discuss whether the MTA's strategy of re-branding can address issues such as water supply, traffic problems, population pressures, and heritage conservation to benefit all the stakeholders in the tourism sector.

Summary

* Italy has a long pedigree as a tourist destination, whereas in Malta tourism is a relative newcomer.
* In Italy, tourism is mainly cultural in nature, whereas Malta is known primarily as a beach destination despite a wealth of cultural resources.
* Italy is a major generator of international tourism, but domestic tourism is of even greater significance.

- Road and rail are the transport mode used by most tourists both to and within Italy, whereas Malta is dependent on air transport for international tourism.
- Due to its size and historical background, Italy is divided into a number of culturally distinct regions, and the contrast between the north and the south of the country is particularly significant. Even in Malta, there are contrasts between the main island and Gozo, which qualifies for EU regional funding.
- In Italy, the mountainous character of much of the country is an obstacle to surface transport, but one that has been largely overcome through superb engineering. In Malta, the small size of the islands and their limited natural resources impose a capacity ceiling for tourism development.

Assignments

1. Assess the importance of religion, including religious festivals, art, and music, in attracting tourists to Italy and Malta.
2. Identify the physical, social, and cultural features that distinguish the south of Italy from the north as tourist destinations.
3. Compare the advantages and disadvantages of different modes of transport for an elderly American couple planning a tour of Italy.
4. Arrange an itinerary for a group of fans of an Italian detective series, which is filmed on location in Sicily.

References and further reading

Organization for Economic Co-operation and Development (annual) *Tourism Policy and International Tourism in OECD Member Countries*, OECD, Paris

Ron, A. and Timothy, D. (2019) *Contemporary Christian Travel*, Channel View, Bristol

https://www.unwto.org/tourism-data/unwto-tourism-dashboard

16 The tourism geography of South-Eastern Europe

Learning objectives

After reading this chapter, you should be able to:

- Describe the major physical features and climates of the region and understand their importance for tourism.
- Appreciate the cultural background to the region.
- Understand the nature of domestic demand and inbound tourism to Greece, Turkey, and other countries in the region.
- Demonstrate knowledge of the tourist regions, resorts, business centres, and tourist attractions of the region.

DOI: 10.4324/9781003406853-19

Introduction

Apart from their location in the eastern half of the Mediterranean, we think there is justification for including Greece, the countries of the Balkan Peninsula, Turkey (now officially renamed Türkiye), and Cyprus in the same chapter. Most of these countries have developed tourism industries based on beach holidays, serving the North European market. Cultural tourism is also important, and part of their attraction for visitors is a heritage that is a blend of Western and Middle Eastern influences. During the period of Turkish expansion in the sixteenth century, almost the whole region became part of the Ottoman Empire, and some of the Greek islands and Cyprus formed the front line in the struggle waged by the Republic of Venice and the Knights of St. John in the defence of Christian Europe. The heritage of the Ottoman Empire can be seen in the architecture, cuisine, and handicrafts of south-eastern Europe, and most of these countries have large Muslim communities.

Greece (Hellas)

The setting for tourism

The location of Greece on the periphery of the European Union and its relatively weak economy, have tended to obscure the unique contribution that this small country has made to European culture:

* Greece is regarded as the birthplace of European civilisation. The Minoan culture of Crete flourished at the same time as ancient Egypt (c. 2000 BC) and was in some respects more advanced. It was followed by the more warlike Mycenean culture on the mainland, which formed the basis of legends such as the Iliad, the Odyssey, and Jason's quest for the Golden Fleece, aided by the enchantress Medea. Greece as 'the land of gods and heroes' has inspired a good deal of European art and literature.
* Later (after 500 BC), Classical Greece under the leadership of Athens developed many of the ideas and institutions that became central to the Western heritage, such as democracy and the Olympic Games. Architectural achievements, such as the Parthenon, continue to provide inspiration, and the dramas of Sophocles are still performed for modern audiences in the original open-air theatres as at Epidauros. Hellenic culture was spread far beyond Greece, particularly by Alexander the Great, and strongly influenced the Romans.
* After the fall of the Roman Empire in the West, the torch of civilisation was carried on by the Greek-speaking Byzantine Empire, based in Constantinople (now Istanbul). Orthodox Christianity spread to much of eastern Europe and to Russia, strongly influencing religious art (for example, ikons) and architecture.

Greece forms part of the Balkan Peninsula, an area which is geologically unstable. Greece shares with some other countries in the region a cultural outlook different from that of Western Europe, for example:

- Easter is given greater prominence as a religious festival than is the case in most of western Europe and is celebrated on a different date in the calendar.
- The adoption of the Cyrillic rather than the Roman alphabet.
- A legacy of centuries of domination by the Ottoman Empire.

Greece is also situated at the threshold of the Middle East, and Greek communities have long been a feature of the Levant – the eastern shore of the Mediterranean – from Alexandria to Asia Minor. Middle Eastern influences are evident in many aspects of modern Greek culture, including gastronomy and music. However, relations with Turkey have often been strained, with emotional responses based on historical grievances getting in the way of international co-operation that would benefit tourism in both countries, as well as in Cyprus. The possible entry of Turkey into the European Union (which is opposed by some of its member states) should reduce these tensions. The geographical proximity of Greece to some of the world's 'trouble spots' in the Balkans and the Middle East has also had a negative impact on the country's tourism industry, while the Western media have alleged lack of security at Athens Airport on several occasions. Greece suffered the worst economic crisis in the European Union. Greece has also had to deal, along with neighbouring North Macedonia and Bulgaria, with a stream of refugees from the war-torn Middle East. This is having a negative impact on tourism, particularly in some of the Aegean islands.

The country's geography also explains why Greece has a maritime outlook extending well beyond the Mediterranean. The 16,000-kilometre-long coastline is deeply indented and has many islands, while the interior is, for the most part, mountainous; in Greece, the sea and the mountains are never far away. The landscape has been devastated by soil erosion (largely due to deforestation), and good agricultural land is scarce. Not surprisingly, Greeks have been seafarers throughout their history, while Greece today has one of the world's largest shipping fleets and is active in cruise tourism. Due to the lack of economic opportunity, there has been a great deal of emigration, particularly from the Aegean islands, to countries such as Australia or the United States. There are over 5 million people of Greek origin living abroad, compared to the population of Greece itself (10.6 million). As far as tourism is concerned, the multiplicity of islands and harbours provides an ideal environment for sailing holidays and cruising, while the clear water of the Aegean favours diving.

Tourism is vital to the Greek economy, since it accounts for over 20 per cent of GDP and is a significant source of foreign exchange, compensating for nearly half the country's international trade deficit. Around 25 per cent of the workforce are employed in the tourism industry during the peak summer months, according to official figures. However, the contribution of tourism to job creation is even higher if we consider the 'black economy' of unregistered businesses, which is a fact of life in Greece (Buhalis, 2001, 443).

Tourism is also responsible for facilitating economic and social development in areas where other opportunities for wealth creation are lacking. Tourism has stemmed the tide of emigration from the Aegean islands, and there is now a reverse flow, including entrepreneurs from the mainland (which is not always to the advantage of the island economy).

The demand for tourism

Domestic and outbound tourism

Although nearly half the population engage in tourism, only 10 per cent of trips are to foreign countries, while the number of domestic holiday trips also fell by a third between 2008 and 2012, due to the economic crisis that had a severe impact on Greece. In some of the Greek islands, notably Rhodes, domestic tourists are far fewer than foreign holidaymakers, and their length of stay tends to be much shorter. Domestic tourists account for around a third of paid overnights for Greece as a whole, with the majority tending to stay with friends and relatives rather than hotels. Most domestic trips are made by car and include summer excursions to the coastal resorts and islands, winter skiing in the mountains, and pilgrimages to Orthodox shrines, such as Tinos in the Aegean.

Inbound tourism

Cultural tourism has a long history in Greece, and although the country was not included in the Grand Tour, it was visited by the more adventurous travellers, notably Lord Byron, who did much to promote the cause of Greek independence in the early nineteenth century. However, organised tourism did not take place on any scale until the 1950s. Along with other Mediterranean destinations, Greece developed rapidly during the 1970s, largely based on price and the attractions of the Greek islands. The hosting of the 2004 Olympics in Athens provided the impetus for major improvements in infrastructure, although the economic benefits were less evident. However, arrivals increased to over 17 million in 2006. After a subsequent decline, numbers recovered to reach 34 million arrivals in 2019, falling to 7.4 million as a result of the COVID-19 pandemic in 2020. Most tourists to Greece are visiting for recreational rather than cultural reasons – in search of sun, sand, sea, the nightlife, and possibly romance. The Greek tradition of hospitality known as *philoxenia* (literally love of strangers) has probably been an asset in developing a vast service sector dominated by small family-run enterprises. Britain and Germany supply about a quarter of the total number of visitors, most of whom arrive on inclusive tours; France and Italy are also important markets. The American market is likely to grow with the increasing availability of direct flights from the United States.

The success of the Athens Olympics boosted national pride and self-confidence. Greece is determined to downplay its image as a beach destination for north Europeans, and develop ecotourism, which is in its infancy. This will require greater investment in infrastructure.

The supply side of tourism

Transport

Over two-thirds of visitors to Greece arrive by air, encouraged by the growth of budget airline services across Europe. The most important gateways are Athens, serving southern and central Greece, and Thessaloniki for the north. Aegean Airlines dominates the domestic market. Some Greek islands can be reached by direct charter flights from the cities of northern Europe, the most significant being Corfu (Kerkira), Kefalonia, Santorini, Zante (Zakinthos), Crete (Iraklion and Chania), Mykonos, Rhodes, and Kos. Greece receives large numbers of day visitors from cruise ships plying the eastern Mediterranean. Overland travel by road or rail is also an option, but it is time-consuming as it involves:

- Ferry crossings from Ancona or Brindisi to Patras if the visitor is arriving via Italy.
- The risk of lengthy delays at border crossings if the visitor is travelling through the republics of the former Yugoslavia. Before the break-up of that country and the subsequent wars in Croatia, Bosnia, and Serbia (1991–1999), this was the preferred route, but it remains potentially unsafe, given the possibility of another crisis in the Balkans.

The rail network within Greece, operated by Hellenic Railways (OSL), has suffered from chronic under-funding, and many of the lines are single-track, reducing capacity and speed. However, fast inter-city services link Athens to Thessaloniki and Patras. Much of the road system is also poor by European Union standards, especially on the islands where the accident rate among tourists hiring mopeds, for example, is unacceptably high. On the other hand, Greece has one of the world's most extensive networks of coastal shipping services. The system is not ideal from a tourist's viewpoint, as most ferries operate from the hub of Piraeus, the port of Athens, inter-island connections can be infrequent, and shipping companies are reluctant to provide an integrated service. 'Island-hopping' is part of the attraction of Greece for many tourists, but it requires patience and an element of planning. Ferries are subject to delays and even cancellations, especially in the Aegean, when the *meltemi* wind blows during the summer months. In good weather, the more remote islands can be reached by *caiques* (converted fishing boats).

Accommodation

The accommodation and catering sectors are well represented in Greece and consist mainly of small and medium-sized enterprises. The official stock of hotels and self-catering villas, apartments, and studios is considerable (over 800,000 bed spaces in hotels alone), but it is probably exceeded by unregistered accommodation known collectively as *parahoteleria*. Most of the establishments offering rooms to let to visitors arriving in the Greek islands fall into this category, although Airbnb and a host of imitators have made disruptive inroads in this sector. A large number of campsites are also available.

Organisation

The importance of tourism is recognised by the government. The Ministry of Tourism supervises the work of the Greek National Tourism Organisation (GNTO) for promotion, planning, the implementation of policies at both national and regional levels, and co-ordination of the public and private sectors in tourism development. Government involvement is currently less than in the 1970s when it took a direct role in encouraging tourism, building facilities on a considerable scale, and offering a wide range of incentives to private developers. Tourism is included in the Five-Year Plans for economic and social development, supplemented by European Union funding.

The GNTO faces various problems brought about by both the nature of tourism to Greece and the vulnerability of many of the country's resources. They include:

- Seasonality: The emphasis on 'summer sun' tourism is a major problem, as almost 70 per cent of tourism receipts are concentrated in the months July to September. This forces those employed in the tourism sector to work excessively long hours, to the detriment of the traditional family values characteristic of the Greek way of life.
- Geographical concentration: Tourism development is mainly restricted to Athens, the coastal resorts and some of the islands. This makes it difficult to spread the benefits of tourism more evenly throughout the country and to provide adequate accommodation and other facilities to cope with demand.
- The negative social impact of mass tourism: During the off-season, the Greek islands are almost crime-free, but health and police services are stretched to the limit in some popular resorts during the peak summer months – to cope with the effects of alcohol and drug abuse by some North European holidaymakers. This type of behaviour is offensive to the host community but is tolerated because tourism brings in much needed income.
- Over-dependence on foreign tour operators: Attempts by hoteliers to introduce higher standards and prices mean that the mass market no longer perceives Greece as an inexpensive destination, while high-spending tourists are deterred from visiting the popular resorts, and the country faces competition from cheaper destinations in the region.
- Substantial leakages in tourism earnings: This results from the need to import many of the goods to supply tourists visiting the islands.
- Environmental degradation: The development of tourism has often been characterised by unplanned, haphazard building that has blighted the landscape. The rapid development of tourism, and its concentration in the dry summer season has placed severe pressure on water supply systems. Marine pollution has been caused by inadequate sewage treatment and waste disposal. Noise pollution is a feature of the popular resorts and has contributed, for example, to the decline of an endangered species of turtle on the island of Zakinthos. It is estimated that two-thirds of the forest fires that afflict Greece each summer are deliberately carried out to clear land for development.
- The lack of a co-ordinated strategy for planning and tourism development.

These issues do mean that, while Greece is endowed with superb tourism resources, the country's tourism industry does not always fulfil its potential.

Tourism resources

We should divide Greece for tourism purposes into:

- The Greek mainland, which consists of a number of regions, namely the Peloponnese in the south, Sterea Hellas (central Greece, including Athens), Epirus in the west, and Thessaly, Macedonia, and western Thrace in the northern part of the country.
- The Greek islands, which include Crete and a number of separate groups or archipelagos. The most popular of these are the Ionian Islands lying to the west of the mainland, the Cyclades in the central Aegean, and the Dodecanese to the south-east.

Mainland Greece

The mainland of Greece is divided into two by the Corinth Canal, itself a major engineering achievement. To the south is the Peloponnese, where mass tourism has as yet made little impact, largely due to the absence of good beaches. Tolon and Naplion are significant holiday resorts, easily accessible from Athens. The government has encouraged the revitalisation of traditional communities such as the Mani in the extreme south, famous for its fortified villages. This formerly remote area has been opened up for hiking and special interest holidays, which include Mystra, an important city in the Byzantine era. The Peloponnese contains some of Greece's most important archaeological sites. Some of these are included in classical tours based on Athens, namely:

- Olympia – site of the original Olympic Games, which date back to 776 BC.
- Mycenae – associated with the legends of the Trojan War.
- The well-preserved theatre at Epidauros, dating from the fourth century BC, which is still used for cultural events.

Tourism in Athens has declined significantly since the 1970s, when it was still the centre *par excellence* for sightseers. This has come about partly as a result of the growth in popularity of the Greek islands, at the expense of cultural tourism. Ugly urban sprawl and severe air pollution resulting from motor vehicles and factory emissions have also diminished the sightseeing experience. The civic authorities have regularly banned private vehicles from the city centre, usually on a rota basis, and air quality has improved, largely due to improvements in public transport. The 2004 Olympics was the catalyst for urban regeneration, with infrastructure improvements such as a new airport and metro system. Two- and three-star hotels were upgraded, while manufacturing industries were given incentives to move out of the city.

The capital's main attractions include:

- The Acropolis, the fortified hill which was the core of ancient Athens, containing a number of important temples such as the Parthenon, serving as reminders of the glory of Ancient Greece. This is interpreted by a fine museum (https://www.theacropolismuseum.gr/en). Various historic sites such as the Agora (the market place of Athens in Classical and Roman times) are now linked by an archaeological park.

- To the east of the city lie several beach resorts – the so called 'Apollo Coast', which are mainly visited by domestic tourists and day trippers.
- To the south of Piraeus are the Argo-Saronic Islands, the most popular being Aegina, while Spetses is perhaps the most attractive, providing a welcome relief from the extreme summer heat and congestion of Athens.
- To the north-west is the classical site of Delphi in its beautiful mountain setting. This was an important place of pilgrimage in ancient times due to the oracle in the temple of Apollo, which was consulted before making important decisions.

In Macedonia, the well-wooded Halkidiki Peninsula with its fine beaches has been developed for recreational tourism, with yacht marinas, golf courses, and holiday villages. The area is close to Thessaloniki, which is second in importance only to Athens as a business centre. This city tends to be overlooked by tour operators, although it is a significant cultural destination with a legacy of Classical and Byzantine architecture. On the other hand, the more recent Ottoman heritage of mosques and bath-houses is neglected, largely because Thessaloniki (formerly Salonica) was under Turkish rule until 1912.

The monasteries on Mount Athos are a special case due to their isolation, and their spiritual significance for the Orthodox Church, not only in Greece, but also in Russia. Pilgrim numbers are restricted, there are no hotels, shops, bars, and other distractions, and female tourists are prohibited from entry!

Throughout northern and western Greece, the emphasis is increasingly on agritourism and sustainable development to:

- Stem rural depopulation.
- Revive traditional village industries.
- Conserve the region's natural and cultural heritage.

Attempts to develop winter sports tourism in the Pindus Mountains as a means of reducing seasonality have not been particularly successful, and northern Greece is mainly visited for its national parks – the Vikos gorge is outstanding – and its cultural attractions, such as the monasteries of Meteora in their spectacular setting.

The Greek Islands

Of the hundreds of Greek islands, relatively few are served by regular ferry or hydrofoil services, and an even smaller number have been developed for international tourism. Each of these islands offers a unique product based on its scenery and cultural heritage, rather than the quality of its beaches.

Crete is, by far, the largest of the islands, with a coastline almost 1000 kilometres in length, and a mountainous interior where the traditional lifestyle has persisted to a greater extent than elsewhere in Greece. This contrasts with the well-developed international tourism scene along the north coast. Mallia has borne the brunt of mass tourism, while Aghios Nikalaos, with its attractive harbour, has remained more up-market. Crete can offer those tourists looking for more than beaches and nightlife:

- The heritage of Venetian rule in towns such as Chania.
- The Samaria Gorge, one of the most impressive examples of its kind in Europe. Unfortunately, its very popularity with hikers has caused ecological damage to this national park and disruption to its wildlife.
- The impressive remains of the Minoan civilisation at Knossos, the source of the Minotaur myth; this too is popular with tourists on day excursions from the nearby resorts. Phaestos, on the less visited south coast, is an uncrowded alternative.

The **Cyclades** are generally rather barren in appearance, and the small island communities are characterised by their white cube-shaped buildings, interspersed with tiny blue and white chapels. On these and other Aegean islands, two types of tourist centre can be identified, each complementing the other in terms of the facilities they provide – the port and the *chora*, the traditional focal point of island life – often situated some distance inland. The most popular islands in the group are:

- Mykonos perhaps most closely resembles the tourist stereotype of a Greek island, but it is, in fact, a sophisticated resort, with expensive bars and boutiques, and a large gay clientele.
- Paros as a hub of the Aegean ferry network is ideal for the independent traveller.
- Ios likewise attracts swarms of young backpackers during July and August, on account of its fine beaches and non-stop nightlife.
- Naxos contains more scenic variety and is the most fertile of the islands. Until the completion of a new airport with European Union funding in 1990, tourism took a backseat to agriculture and still remains relatively low-impact in nature.
- Delos at the centre of the Cyclades is uninhabited, but as the 'sacred island' was of major importance in ancient times, with a flourishing slave trade.

CASE STUDY 16.1
SANTORINI: TOURISM IN THE AGE OF THE
INSTAGRAM, BLESSING OR BLIGHT?

Santorini (Thira) is the southernmost island of the Cyclades and is one of the most visited destinations in Greece; in 2019, it recorded more than 2 million arrivals. The island is heavily dependent on tourism, which accounts for around 90 per cent of its GDP and 70 per cent of employment. In the decade following the 2008 financial crisis, it was one of the few places in Greece enjoying economic growth. On offer is some of the most spectacular scenery in the Mediterranean, the result of a catastrophic volcanic eruption that occurred circa 1500 BC. The harbour, edged by impressive cliffs is the centre of a huge caldera. The remains of a Minoan city, buried by volcanic ash have been excavated at Akrotiri. The photogenic quality of the island, particularly of certain locations such as Oia, has attracted influencers from far and wide and thousands of their followers on social media. Not only does Santorini feature on many cruise itineraries, but its airport is serviced by a number of airlines to cities in northern Europe. The steep ascent from the harbour to the villages of Oia and Fira has traditionally been made by donkey or mule, which have to cope not only with multiple journeys but with tourists who may be overweight. Fortunately, for animal welfare, cheaper alternative modes of transport are readily available.

Santorini is a small island (69 square kilometres) with a permanent population of only 15,000, and although tourism provides many opportunities for small businesses, this has come at a cost, for example:

- Overdevelopment, with urban sprawl replacing a number of small village communities. Some blame central government in Athens for failing to implement planning regulations.
- Local residents are affected by an increase in rents, due to the impact of Airbnb.
- The constant building activity and the influx of tourists creates problems of waste management.
- Energy and water consumption are reaching critical levels.

In 2017, Santorini controversially imposed a cap on cruise passenger arrivals, which contribute less to the economy of the island than staying visitors but have an adverse impact on its environmental and social capacity. The COVID-19 pandemic dealt a severe blow to the island's economy but also enabled the completion of various projects to improve the infrastructure and the sustainability of its tourism industry.

The Instagram has been more effective than the holiday brochure or DVD in reaching a mass market for places like Santorini, and the smartphone has rendered the picture postcard obsolete. Discuss whether this has been beneficial from the viewpoint of those involved in the hospitality industry and other members of the host community.

Skiathos is the most popular island in the group known as the **Sporades** in the north-west Aegean, thanks to a combination of pine-covered landscapes and fine beaches; Skyros, in contrast, has developed a niche market in 'holistic community' holidays as a solution to the stress of modern life.

The islands of the north-east Aegean include Lesbos, Samos, and Chios. Here agriculture and shipping continue to be the mainstays of the local economy, rather than tourism, which is dominated by the domestic market.

The Dodecanese are a group of 12 islands situated far from the Greek mainland and close to the coast of south-west Turkey. Their cultural heritage is different from other Greek islands as they were ruled successively by the Knights of St. John, the Ottoman Empire from the sixteenth century until 1912, and then by Italy until the Second World War. For the most part, they are relatively undeveloped for tourism, with the exceptions of Kos and Rhodes where mass tourism has made a major impact. By the late 1990s, Rhodes had a capacity of 50,000 registered bed spaces or 10 per cent of the stock for Greece as a whole. This large island offers natural attractions such as the 'Valley of the Butterflies' at Petaloudes and many heritage sites. Additionally, it hosts numerous cultural events, festivals, and *son et lumière* shows that bring history to life. The old town of Rhodes retains its medieval walls, castle, and hospital built by the Knights of St John. The main touring circuit is along the east coast to the picturesque town of Lindos, which has been carefully preserved. Almost all the accommodation consists of rented rooms with local families. In contrast, Faliraki is characterised by unplanned hotel and self-catering development and has acquired notoriety as a resort catering primarily for the British youth market. Rhodes needs to diversify its markets to reduce its dependence on package tours and overcome the problem of seasonality.

The **Ionian Islands** include three popular destinations – Corfu (Kerkira), Kefalonia, and Zante (Zakinthos). They are mountainous but fertile, with a softer climate than the Aegean islands and a greener landscape. Their cultural heritage reflects a long period of rule by the Republic of Venice and British occupation (from 1815 until 1864).

- **Corfu** has for long been a favourite with British holidaymakers, and many resorts have developed, particularly along the east coast, although the west coast has the best beaches. Mass tourism has had an adverse effect on Corfu, particularly in Ipsos and Benitses that have become mass-market resorts, while Kavos is very much an enclave for the youth market, attracted by its throbbing nightlife. In contrast, the town of Corfu has several cultural attractions.
- Kefalonia and Zante have less to offer in this respect, as they were badly affected by an earthquake in 1956 and underwent subsequent rebuilding. Zante is the more popular of the two, and much of the development for the package holiday market has been insensitive, especially in the resort of Laganas. The island serves as a notable example of the ongaoing struggle between environmentalists, who advocate for the designation of a portion of the coast as a marine national park, and local hotel developers and boat operators eager to increase their profits.

Discussion point

Compare the role of the Olympic Games in classical Greece with the modern Olympics, taking into account the following:

- The importance of the Olympic ideal
- The international scope of the event
- The inclusivity of the Games (for example, the participation of women)

The Balkan countries

Between 1945 and 1989, most of the countries of the Balkan Peninsula, with the important exceptions of Greece and Turkey, formed part of the Communist Eastern Bloc, sharply differentiated in their political and economic make-up from the countries to the west of the 'Iron Curtain'. However, this impression of unity was largely imposed by the Soviet Union, following its victory in the Second World War, and concealed the deep-seated differences between the many and varied ethnic groups, which make up the population of the region. Most countries had substantial ethnic minorities at variance with the majority culture, and all had experienced long periods of foreign rule. Most of the region formed part of the Ottoman Empire. However, Croatia, Dalmatia, Slovenia, and Transylvania were ruled until 1918 by the Habsburg Empire based in Vienna and Budapest, and as such, tended to be more advanced in their social and economic development than their neighbours to the east of the Dinaric Alps and south of the Carpathians. The period between the First and Second World Wars was marked by the political instability caused by these tensions in the new independent nations, particularly Yugoslavia. During the era of Soviet domination, the Black Sea beaches of Bulgaria and Romania were, in some respects, the East European equivalent of the Spanish costas, attracting sun-seeking tourists from the more developed socialist countries, namely Poland, East Germany, and Czechoslovakia. Since the collapse of Communism, the Balkan countries have made progress in varying degrees towards democracy, a free-market economy and closer association with Western Europe. In 2004, Slovenia was among the 'accession states' to join the European Union, followed two years later by Bulgaria and Romania. Croatia joined in 2013, while Montenegro and Kosovo have already adopted the euro as their currencies. Membership of the European Union has encouraged investment in tourism and boosted demand in countries where travel propensities are relatively low.

Albania (Shqiperia)

The change from Communism to a free-market economy has perhaps been most traumatic in Albania, which is also the poorest and least developed of the former Eastern bloc states. Although only a narrow stretch of water separates it from Corfu, the country was virtually unknown, let alone frequented by tourists until the 1990s. Albania is different in language and culture from its Greek and Slav neighbours. The majority of Albanians are Muslims and comprise two ethnic groups, Ghegs in the north and Tosks in the south, characterised by a great diversity of regional costumes. In 1991, following the fall of Communism, the government envisaged ambitious plans for tourism development, under a new Ministry of Construction and Tourism. There is little doubt that the country has considerable potential, including an extensive and yet unspoiled Mediterranean coastline where ramshackle developments have been cleared away, spectacular lake and mountain scenery, and potential for ecotourism based on the great biodiversity of the country with its bears, lynx, and golden eagles. However, Western-style tourism has been held back for the following reasons:

- Historical Communist legacy: The historical legacy of the hard-line Communist regime established by Enver Hoxha between 1945 and 1989, which imposed a policy of economic self-sufficiency, closed all mosques and churches, and isolated the Albanian people from contacts with foreigners. Numerous concrete bunkers (some of which have been put to commercial use) survive as reminders of that time.
- Inadequate infrastructure: The internal road and rail network is poorly developed, particularly in mountainous areas. External transport links by road, air, and ferry have since improved substantially.

- Lack of investment: It could be said that 40 years of collectivisation and a closed economy were followed by a period of rampant individualism, financial speculation, and unregulated capitalism. In the northern part of Albania, there was a resurgence of the traditional blood feuds between clans that characterised much of the country's history prior to 1945.

The demand for tourism

Tourism is an important driver of the economy, accounting for 8.5 per cent of GDP in 2019 and directly or indirectly for 20 per cent of employment.

Domestic and outbound tourism

Tourism propensities are relatively low, with 40 per cent of the urban population not taking a holiday trip (the figure for the rural population is probably even higher). The majority of domestic tourists choose coastal destinations such as Durres, while only 12 per cent take holidays abroad, mainly in Greece, Turkey, and Italy.

Inbound tourism

International tourism has grown rapidly, from 2.4 million arrivals in 2010 to 6.4 million in 2019. Most of the development for Western-style tourism has taken place on the 'Albanian Riviera' – the south coast between Vlore and Sarande – which has fine beaches. The tourism sector was severely impacted, not only through the COVID-19 pandemic but also by a devastating earthquake in November 2019. Since then, recovery has been slowed by the Ukraine war – both Russia and Ukraine were lucrative markets. Most tourists are of Albanian origin or from neighbouring countries – Kosovo alone accounts for 45 per cent of arrivals. However, these tend to stay with relatives or in low-budget accommodation. Albania has attracted tourists from Spain, Egypt (due to historical links), and Scandinavia. The main problem is seasonality, and Albania needs to diversify from beach tourism.

The supply side of tourism

Transport

Tourists from neighbouring countries visit Albania by road transport or, in the case of Italy, use the ferry service from Bari to the port of Durres. Air connectivity is improving with the growth of services by low-cost carriers to Mother Teresa Airport near Tirana, which is also the hub for Air Albania.

Accommodation

Hotel capacity has grown considerably, from 25,000 to 82,000 bed spaces between 2010 and 2020. Most hotels are relatively small, using expertise from Albanian expatriates and Italian financial backing. However, occupancy rates are low, and the hotel sector suffers from seasonality, labour shortages, and what is seen as unfair competition from the pro-liferation of rented apartments by Airbnb and its imitators.

Organisation

The Ministry of Tourism and the Environment is responsible for policy and the licensing of tourism enterprises. It is assisted by the Albanian Tourist Association representing the private sector.

Tourism resources

The changes that have taken place since the fall of Communism are mainly evident in the coastal towns and Tirana, which has tripled in population since 1990. Under the Hoxha regime, the city was effectively a car-free zone, but along with a vibrant café culture, it now has severe traffic problems, exacerbated by deficient planning and infrastructure. The 'Pyramid', a monumental structure built to glorify the Hoxha regime arouses controversy – should it be preserved as a heritage attraction or put to other uses? The main tourist attractions lie outside the capital, including:

- The archaeological sites at Apolonia and Butrint – the 'lost city' of the ancient Illyrian civilisation, and one of the best-preserved classical sites in the Mediterranean. Because of its accessibility from the beach resort of Ksamil and from Corfu, Butrint may have to cope with visitor numbers well beyond its present capacity.

  - The mountains of the interior contain several medieval fortress-towns, which played a major role in the Albanian struggle for freedom against the Ottoman Empire; of these Berat, Gijrokastro and Kruje are the most important.
  - The lakes on the borders with North Macedonia and Montenegro.

CASE STUDY 16.2
AGRITOURISM IN ALBANIA

The European Fund for Reconstruction and Development (ERBD) is closely involved with the funding of facilities suitable for Western tourists. Although the ERBD would like developers to concentrate on a relatively few up-market projects, the Albanian government desperately needs the foreign exchange earnings from tourism to modernise the country's infrastructure, and some fear this will put pressure on Albania's unique ecological and cultural resources. Nevertheless, the Ministry of Tourism and the Environment has identified agritourism as a sustainable economic opportunity for Albania, and it is included in the government's '100+ villages' rural development programme. Wine, honey, and locally sourced food have the potential to attract visitors, but for agritourism to be successful, as in Italy and Greece, it needs to overcome a number of problems:

- The communities that would most benefit are in northern Albania, a fair distance from Tirana.
- The basic infrastructure is poor.
- There are few attractions other than mountain scenery nearby.
- The farms are small, and there is an absence of farmers' co-operatives to share marketing expertise.

Suggest possible solutions to these problems.

The Republics of the former Yugoslavia

The pre-1991 Yugoslavia has been described as an experiment to unite many peoples of widely differing languages (including two alphabets), religions, and historical backgrounds. It was a federation of six republics – Serbia, Croatia, Slovenia, Bosnia-Herzegovina, Macedonia, and Montenegro – and two autonomous regions – Kosovo and Vojvodina. This complex arrangement was made to work largely through the authority of Marshal Tito, who ruled the country from 1945 to 1980. Furthermore, as a non-aligned country in the Cold War, following Tito's break with Stalin, Yugoslavia set out earlier to attract foreign investment and was far more successful than Bulgaria or Romania in attracting package holidaymakers from Western Europe. In 1960, Yugotours was set up to market the country and, in 1965, restrictions on the movement of foreign visitors were removed. In the same year, the Adriatic Highway was completed with Western aid, permitting the development of resort facilities along the coast from Istria to Montenegro. Another major road project – the Brotherhood and Unity Highway – linked Belgrade to Zagreb, Ljubljana, and Skopje. By 1988, Yugoslavia was attracting 9 million foreign visitors annually, but these were highly concentrated geographically on the Adriatic coast, while the former West Germany accounted for a third of the total. Although domestic tourists were mainly accommodated in low-cost holiday, villages away from the main Adriatic resorts, Yugoslavs were not discouraged from contact with Western tourists at home and had greater freedom than other East Europeans to travel to Western countries.

However, Tito's brand of socialism based on the system of 'worker's control' caused problems in hotel administration and marketing and did little to encourage private enterprise. The ending of the Cold War also brought about the revival of nationalism and ethnic rivalries, initiated by Serbia. This caused the break-up of the Federation, swiftly followed by a series of wars that lasted throughout most of the 1990s. Yugoslavia as an entity survived until 2006 when Montenegro regained its independence from Serbia. Nevertheless, the former Yugoslavia left a legacy of monumental buildings and tours with the Yugo (the Yugoslav economy car) are available, particularly in Belgrade (this probably has a similar appeal for tourists as the Trabant tours in Berlin).

Croatia

Croatia has both Mediterranean and central European characteristics in its make-up. A great diversity of landscapes and cultural attractions are on offer, but it is the sheer number of islands – many of them thriving communities – that makes the country unique. Croatia has a well-established tourism industry; for example, Opatija, with good road and rail links to central Europe, was a fashionable resort for the Austrian and Hungarian elites before the First World War, when it was known by its Italian name, Abbazia. The coastline is deeply indented, extending to 5,800 kilometres if we include the islands in the Adriatic. The coastal regions of Istria and Dalmatia are protected by the parallel ranges of the Dinaric Alps from the cold winters experienced in the interior. However, where there are gaps in the mountains, the blustery *Bora* wind can be disruptive in spring and autumn. The region of Slavonia in the north-east forms part of the lowlands of the Pannonian Basin, drained by the Danube and its tributaries. The west on the other hand is mountainous, and the karst limestone landforms here and in neighbouring Slovenia are so widespread and spectacular that the local names are often used to describe similar features in other parts of the world. Surface streams are absent, as water readily dissolves the limestone rock to form sinkholes (known as *dolines*) and *poljes* (enclosed basins).

Croatia accounted for over 80 per cent of tourist nights in registered accommodation in the former Yugoslavia during the late 1980s, but received a much smaller proportion of the revenue from tourism, which was shared out among the other republics in the federation. Nevertheless, tourism did much to benefit the economy of the Dalmatian islands and stemmed out-migration, which was a problem in the early part of the twentieth century. With the apparent resolution of the ethnic strife in Bosnia-Herzegovina and Kosovo, the country has regained its position as a major holiday destination but this time as an independent nation. Tourism plays a major role in the economy, accounting for 11.8 per cent of GDP and 6.8 per cent of employment.

The demand for tourism

Domestic and outbound tourism

The domestic market is relatively small, accounting for around 20 per cent of overnight stays. Only a small minority travel abroad, mainly to neighbouring countries, resulting in a large credit balance on Croatia's tourism account. The majority of domestic tourists stay with friends and relatives, or use second homes as accommodation rather than hotels.

Inbound tourism

In 2019, Croatia attracted 62.8 million overnight stays, of which only 30 per cent were in hotels. Germany is in the lead with 16 per cent of overnight stays, followed by Slovenia, Austria, Italy, and the Czech Republic. Croatia has been slower to regain its pre-1990 popularity with British tourists, who account for only a small percentage of arrivals, mainly on inclusive tour holidays.

The supply side of tourism

Transport

Croatia has a good transport infrastructure, with international airports at Zagreb and Dubrovnik, as well as smaller airports serving the tourism regions. Croatian Airways is the national carrier, with Zagreb as the hub. The private car and long-distance bus services play a much more important role than the limited rail network. Ferries operate from the ports of Rijeka and Split to Italy and Greece, and a network of fast catamaran services links the Dalmatian islands to the mainland.

Accommodation

There is an over-supply of hotel accommodation, as there is a growing trend for foreign tourists to rent apartments or buy second homes. Campgrounds are mainly used by tourists from central Europe, while marinas also provide a significant supply of accommodation. Proposals to privatise the holiday villages and hotels built for workers during the Tito era have been opposed by the governments of Serbia and Bosnia-Herzegovina.

Organisation

The Ministry of Tourism and Sport has overall responsibility for tourism, but there is a large degree of collaboration between government departments on issues affecting the industry, and private agencies are involved in policy making. The Croatian National Tourist Board is responsible for promotion. Tourism is highly seasonal in character, with 58 per cent of overnights in July and August, and 95 per cent of the accommodation is located on the coast.

Tourism resources

The Istrian Peninsula features good beaches, easy access to Italy, and the major resorts of Poreč and Rovinj. Dalmatia offers more spectacular scenery, but its disadvantage for family holidays is the lack of sandy beaches. The numerous sheltered deepwater harbours have encouraged cruising and sailing, while the clear unpolluted sea is ideal for diving and bathing. Some of the Dalmatian islands – such as Brioni and the Kornati group – are protected as national parks, while others – notably Hvar (famous for its lavender), Korcula, and Rab – have been developed as holiday destinations. The Makarska Riviera is a string of resorts along the narrow coastal strip between the Dinaric Alps and the sea. In contrast to the rest of Dalmatia, the Naretva delta is a lush wetland landscape, part of which is intensively cultivated and the rest designated as a nature reserve under the Ramsar Convention.
    The coast can also offer a rich cultural heritage, including:

* Important Roman remains, such as the arena at Pula, and the impressive remains of the palace of the Emperor Diocletian, which now form part of the old quarter of Split.
* The architecture of the coastal towns such as Zadar and Trogir, showing the influence of Venice, which was the major power in the region in medieval times.

- Dubrovnik, an almost perfect example of a medieval seaport, complete with city walls and pedestrianised streets and squares. It was already an international resort before the Second World War. Much of the development in the 1960s and 1970s was in the form of large hotel complexes on the Babin Kuk peninsula, 4 kilometres from the old town, which have now been modernised and partly replaced by apartments. The historic buildings in the old town were damaged by the Serbian bombardment of 1991/1992 but have been meticulously restored, while the international summer festival continues to be a major attraction. However, the popularity of Dubrovnik as a location for the TV series *'Game of Thrones'* has persuaded the city authorities to impose controls on visitation from cruise ships.

Away from the coast, tourism in Croatia mainly gravitates to the capital, Zagreb. This city is not only an attractive historic destination but also serves as an important business

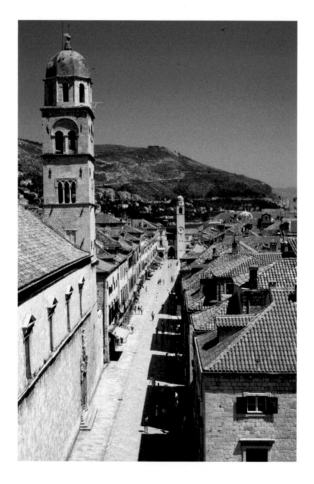

Photo 16.1
Dubrovnik

Source: Brian Boniface

centre, hosting conferences, international trade fairs, and sports events. The Plitvice National Park is renowned for its travertine terraces, lakes, and waterfalls, making it Croatia's top natural attraction.

Slovenia

With an area of 20,000 square kilometres and a population of 2 million, Slovenia is a small country with a broad tourism appeal, as it is situated at the intersection of three contrasting environments – the Mediterranean coast, the eastern Alps, and the lowlands of the Pannonian Basin. It also includes an area of karst landscapes straddling the border with Italy. Slovenia was economically advanced compared to most of the former Yugoslavia, and since independence it has energetically promoted business travel from Western Europe to replace the loss of Yugoslav markets for its products.

The demand for tourism

Domestic and outbound tourism
Despite being close to Italy and Austria, Slovenians prefer to take a holiday in their own country or in Croatia.

Inbound tourism
Foreign tourists accounted for around half of the 11.3 million overnight stays in 2019, the most important markets being Austria, Germany, and Italy.

The supply side of tourism

Transport
There are international airports serving Ljubljana and Maribor. The future of the national airline, Adria Airways, is uncertain, but the country is served by a number of low-cost carriers. Slovenia is well-served by road and rail transport linking the country to Italy and central Europe.

Organisation
The Ministry of Economic Development and Technology is the primary government department responsible for tourism policy and planning. The Slovenian Tourist Board promotes the country, and there are 12 regional development agencies. The ministry has implemented an ambitious tourism marketing and development strategy, focussing on sustainability and balanced growth, with the aim of making Slovenia a role model for 'green' tourism. Tourism businesses and destinations participate in a certification programme under the 'Slovenia Green' brand.

Tourism resources

The influence of neighbouring Austria is particularly evident in the capital Ljubljana and the mountain villages of the Julian Alps, which resemble those of the Tyrol. A large part of the mountain range is designated as the Triglav National Park, named after its highest peak. Winter sports have long been established at Kranjska Gora, Bovec, and Rogla, while the lake resorts of Bled and Bohinj provide a range of summer activities. Bled has given Slovenia its most widely recognised tourism image, but other regions have a particular appeal:

- Slovenia's section of the Adriatic coast is short but includes the popular resort of Portoroz and the seaports of Piran and Koper with their Venetian-style architecture.
- The karst region boasts numerous spectacular caves, including Postojna, which can be accessed by an underground train.
- This region also contains the stud farm at Lipica famous in equestrian tourism for the Lipizzanner breed (featured in the Spanish Riding School in Vienna).

Montenegro (Crna Gora)

Montenegro is one of the fastest-growing destinations in the region, and international tourism serves as a key driver for economic growth, accounting for 9.5 per cent of GDP and 9 per cent of employment. While the coast of Montenegro has seen many foreign occupiers in the course of history, most of the country was never effectively controlled by the Ottoman Empire. The interior, characterised by stony mountains, deep gorges, and 'eagles nest' villages, differs significantly from the lush greenery of the coast and is much less developed for tourism. The former capital, Cetinje, is a reminder that Montenegro was an independent kingdom before the First World War.

The demand for tourism

Domestic and outbound tourism

The volume of domestic tourism is small, accounting for only 5 per cent of overnight stays.

Inbound tourism

Montenegro received 2.5 million international arrivals in 2019, staying on average four days. The primary sources of tourists are Serbia and Russia, but increasing numbers are coming from Germany, France, Britain, and Scandinavia.

The supply side of tourism

Transport

Air Montenegro serves as the national airline with its hub in Podgorica, but a growing number of low-cost carriers link the country to the main markets in northern Europe. As is common in the region, road transport is more widely used than rail, and modern highways now connect the capital Podgorica to Cetinje and the 'Budva Riviera', the main resort area. However, Montenegro boasts one of the most spectacular railways in Europe. The Belgrade – Bar line was completed for strategic reasons under the Tito regime to provide the capital with direct access to a deepwater port on the Adriatic. It has the potential to attract a larger niche market for Montenegro and Serbia than is currently the case. A ferry service links Bar to Bari in Italy.

Organisation

Tourism is the responsibility of the Ministry of Sustainable Development and Tourism. The government is aware of the need to diversify and reduce the problem of seasonality: 95 per cent of overnight stays by foreign visitors are in coastal resorts, mainly concentrated in the summer months. It is, therefore, promoting nature-based tourism in the interior.

Tourism resources

Montenegro's biggest asset is its section of the Adriatic Coast, which includes some good beaches and the magnificent Gulf of Kotor (see Photo 16.2). This is a tectonic feature, and not a fjord as stated in most travel guides.

International-style resorts were developed in the 1960s at Budva and Sveti Stefan – which is unique in being a one-time fishing village converted to a luxury hotel complex.

Photo 16.2
Gulf of Kotor

Around the Gulf of Kotor, there are a number of historic seaports, including Kotor itself, Perast, and Herceg Novi. The former Yugoslav naval base at Tivat has been transformed into an up-market resort, Porto Montenegro, with marina facilities for wealthy tourists. However, the best beaches are along the south coast extending from Budva to the border with Albania.

The interior of Montenegro includes a number of national parks, such as those around the mountains of Lovcen and Durmitor, which have a special place in the national heritage. There are facilities for ecotourism and adventure tourism, including white-water rafting in the spectacular Tara Canyon.

Serbia

Serbia was the first country in the region to successfully free itself from Ottoman rule, but its subsequent history was marked by violence, with two rival families contesting the throne. As a result of the First World War, Serbia became the dominant force in the newly created Yugoslavia. Its attempt to re-assert control after the break-up of the Yugoslav federation led to economic sanctions and political isolation, culminating in the bombing of Belgrade by NATO in 1999. Since 2008, the country has returned to international acceptance, and in 2014, the government lifted visa restrictions on foreign visitors.

The demand for tourism

Domestic and outbound tourism

Domestic tourism is significant, accounting for 4.3 million overnight stays in 2019. The most popular destinations are spas and mountain resorts, where skiing is carried on during the winter months, notably at Zlatibor and Kopaonik. The government is promoting agritourism in a bid to improve living standards in the rural areas. Outbound tourism is drawn to coastal destinations such as the Greek islands, Turkey, and Montenegro, but city breaks are also popular.

Inbound tourism

In 2019, Serbia accounted for 2.4 million overnight stays, mainly from other countries of the former Yugoslavia, but Russia is an important market, due to strong cultural ties. Most visitors stay for only two days on average. Belgrade, as an important conference and trade fair destination, accounts for 50 per cent of overnight stays.

The supply side of tourism

Tourism suffers from deficient infrastructure and an accommodation sector of small family-run businesses that is under-resourced by Western standards. There is a shortage of skilled personnel due to a 'brain drain' of young people seeking better opportunities elsewhere.

Transport

Air Serbia, with its hub in Belgade, is the successor of Yugoslav Airlines but on a much-reduced scale.

Organisation

The Ministry of Trade, Telecommunications and Tourism co-operates closely with other government departments in matters affecting tourism, for example, the Ministry of Agriculture in the development of rural tourism and the Ministry of Culture and Information in the provision of cultural routes.

Tourism resources

Belgrade is the primary focus of tourism, particularly the historic fortress situated at the confluence of the Danube and its tributary, the Save. As the former capital of Yugoslavia, it is a major business centre and boasts several cultural attractions, along with a vibrant nightlife. To the east of Belgrade, the Danube has carved a series of impressive gorges, separating the Carpathians of Romania from the Balkan Mountains to the south; part of this area has been designated as the Derdap National Park. At the Kazan gorge, a formerly unnavigable section of the river has been tamed to provide hydro electric power. The Vojvodina region north of the Danube is characterised by fertile lowland landscapes similar to those of Hungary and quite different to the rest of the country, which is hilly or mountainous. The university town of Novi Sad has promoted festival tourism to attract foreign visitors, particularly the youth market. Western Serbia offers facilities for adventure tourism, including white-water rafting on the River Drina. Serbia's attractions include a number of medieval Orthodox monasteries – Studenica and Sopocani are World Heritage Sites.

Kosovo

This part of the former Yugoslavia, smaller than Yorkshire in area, is predominantly Albanian in language and culture. Its independence from Serbia in 2008 was recognised by the United States and most EU countries, but not by China and Russia. Relations with Serbia remain problematic, as the 'Field of Blackbirds', where the Serbs suffered a catastrophic defeat by the Turks in 1389, is situated in the breakaway republic, and there is a large ethnic Serb minority. Kosovo has the appeal of an 'undiscovered' destination with attractions that include the cities of Pristina and Prizren, a number of Orthodox monasteries, and a ski resort.

North Macedonia

Renaming the country may reduce the suspicion with which Greece has regarded the former Yugoslav Republic of Macedonia (FYROM). Greek sensitivities were not allayed when, in 2014, the Macedonian government erected a monument to Alexander the Great (regarded in both countries as a national hero) in the capital, Skopje. Within North Macedonia there are tensions between the Orthodox majority and the 25 per cent of the population who are ethnic Albanians and Muslim in religion. Nevertheless, the re-opening of the Greek border has allowed North Macedonia to develop its fledgling tourism industry, amounting to 750,000 international arrivals in 2019. Developing awareness of the country abroad is the responsibility of the Agency for the Promotional Support of Tourism, which reports to the Ministry of Economy. As for domestic demand, Macedonians are more likely to take holidays in Albania than in their own country. Attractions are based not so much on the capital, Skopje, which was rebuilt after a major earthquake in 1963, but on Ohrid, a historic town which is scenically located on one of the deepest lakes in Europe.

Bosnia-Herzegovina

Bosnia-Herzegovina's war-ravaged economy and refugee crises allowed even less scope for tourism than the other republics. The 1995 Dayton Agreement secured an uneasy peace after three years of civil war based on power-sharing between the three principal ethnic groups. The Federation of Bosnia and Herzegovina (FBiH) represents the Croats and Bosniak Muslims with its capital in Sarajevo, while the Republika Srpska (RS) represents the Serbs, with its de facto capital at Banja Luka. At the national level, the Ministry of Foreign Trade oversees tourism policy and co-ordinates activities, but tourism development takes place at regional or local level. As a result, the FBiH has its own Federal Ministry of Environment and Tourism, likewise the Republica Srpska has its own Ministry of Trade and Tourism.

In the former Yugoslavia, Bosnia's diversity of cultures and religions was a large part of its appeal for foreign visitors, most of whom were based in Dubrovnik and other holiday resorts on the Adriatic coast. Tourists were particularly attracted to the old Turkish quarter of Sarajevo. The Yugoslav federal government also invested heavily in Sarajevo as the venue for the 1984 Winter Olympics, as part of its policy to spread the benefits of tourism from the coast to the mountainous interior.

Since 2008, Sarajevo has experienced a tourism revival, with visitors from many countries viewing the site of the assassination of the Austrian Archduke Franz Ferdinand in 1914, which precipitated the First World War and the relics of the epic siege from 1991 to 1993. The city also hosts a major film festival as a mark of its resurgence. Other significant tourist centres include:

- Mostar – which is famous for the picturesque Turkish bridge over the River Naretva. This was a casualty of the civil war and was meticulously restored in 2005.
- Jajce – attracts tourists to its spectacular waterfall.
- Medjugorje, which accounts for 50 per cent of tourist overnights in Bosnia-Herzegovina. This formerly obscure village in Herzegovina owes its fame as a shrine of worldwide significance for Catholics to the apparition of the Virgin Mary to six local children in 1981. The Yugoslav authorities initially discouraged pilgrimages,

fearing a revival of Croat nationalism in opposition to the secular regime in Belgrade. However, they began to appreciate the economic advantages, and Yugoslav Airlines (JAT) were soon carrying groups of Italian pilgrims to Dubrovnik airport. Following a long investigation to establish the authenticity of the apparitions and subsequent miracles, the Vatican finally authorised official pilgrimages. Well over a million pilgrims now visit Medjugorje each year.

Bosnia-Herzegovina's rural landscapes, rivers, and mountains are attracting growing numbers of ecotourists and adventure-seekers from Western Europe. Activities include canoeing, white-water rafting, skiing, and climbing.

Nevertheless, Bosnia-Herzegovinas's tragic recent history has attracted attention from the followers of 'dark tourism'. Many villages were the scenes of atrocities and 'ethnic cleansing', but the town of Srebenica, where a massacre of Bosniak Muslims took place is of particular significance.

Bulgaria

Bulgaria is located in the heart of the Balkan Peninsula and is best known in Western Europe for budget-priced beach and skiing holidays. It does, however, offer a great variety of scenery and is rich in the remains of many civilisations. The country is traversed from east to west by several thickly forested mountain ranges, rising to over 2,000 metres, which attract heavy snowfalls in winter. Between the mountains lie fertile valleys enjoying a warm sunny climate, which have given Bulgaria its reputation as 'the market garden of Eastern Europe', producing fine tobacco and the famous perfume known as 'attar of roses'. The country receives a good deal of 'transit tourism' due to its location on the E5 route from Belgrade to Istanbul. Proximity to Turkey in the past was a disadvantage, resulting in Bulgaria being submerged in the Ottoman Empire for several centuries. It regained its independence, with Russian help, in 1878, a fact commemorated by the elaborate Alexander Nevsky Cathedral in Sofia, and the close ties between the two countries. Despite the presence of Turkish and Pomak (native Muslim) minorities, the Islamic contribution to the cultural heritage has been neglected. Restoration projects have focussed instead on the 'museum towns' such as Veliki Turnovo, which played a major role in the medieval period and in the National Revival leading to independence. Nevertheless, Turkish influences are re-emerging in the popular music of Bulgaria despite decades of official discouragement, and this is also evident in other Balkan countries.

The demand for tourism

Domestic and outbound tourism

The country was one of Europe's poorest and most underdeveloped before the Second World War, with over 80 per cent of the population employed in agriculture. The development of an industrial economy since the 1950s greatly improved living standards, while the introduction of the two-day weekend encouraged the ownership of second homes, which are situated mainly around the capital Sofia and on the Black Sea coast. As in other East European countries, spas play an important role in domestic tourism, the most popular being Sandanski, Kustendil, Hissarya, and Velingrad. There is now a substantial demand for foreign holidays, primarily in neighbouring countries but also in Spain.

Inbound tourism

Bulgaria recognised the importance of tourism as a source of hard currency in the 1960s and concluded agreements with several Western tour operators. Balkantourist was the state agency responsible for international tourism, owning most of the large stock of hotel accommodation, particularly on the Black Sea coast. As a result, most Western visitors are on low-budget inclusive packages, and the rate of return per individual tourist is small. Since the collapse of the Communist regime, Bulgaria has moved towards a free-market economy, encouraging joint ventures with Western hotel and banking enterprises and encouraging investment in transport and tourism infrastructure. In 2019, Bulgaria received 12.6 million tourist arrivals, mostly from neighbouring Greece and Romania. Russia and Ukraine are important markets, but recent events have focussed attention on Western Europe, where Germany is the leading source of tourists.

The supply side of tourism

Transport

Bulgaria Air is the national airline with international airports at Sofia, Varna, and Bourgas. Domestic travel is dominated by long-distance bus services, while rail transport is much less important.

Organisation

The Ministry of Tourism works with the National Tourism Council consisting of representatives from other ministries, as well as national and regional tourist associations. These are responsible for developing brands and specialised products based on local tourism resources.

Tourism resources

We can identify three key resources that Bulgaria can offer the visitor:

1.   The beaches of the Black Sea coast.
2.   Skiing in the mountains.
3.   Culture and ecology for special interest tourism.

The Black Sea coast of Bulgaria receives the majority of tourists in the country and is the location of almost two-thirds of the bed spaces. It is scenically varied, with fine beaches that are ideal for family holidays. Resort development has centred around Varna in the north – where Zlatni Pyasatsi (Golden Sands), Albena, and Drouzhba are the main resorts, and Bourgas in the south – where Slunchev Bryag (Sunny Beach) is the most popular centre. Most of these resorts offer international entertainments and are rather characterless; however, the holiday village of Dyuni has been developed in a more traditional style. Since the 1990s, some of the accommodation has been upgraded to meet international quality standards by Spanish and other western hotel chains.

Bulgaria is also a winter sports destination with major resorts at Borovets and Bansko in the Pirin Mountains, Aleko on Mount Vitosha, which caters for large numbers of weekend skiers from nearby Sofia, and Pamporovo in the Rhodope Massif. However, facilities, although improving, are not as sophisticated as those of the Alps, and the Balkan Mountains cannot offer the high-altitude skiing favoured by Western tour operators.

There is more scope for future development in promoting special interest holidays. These include 'eco-paths', spas, wine tours, musical folklore (the country is noted for its fine choirs), archaeology (the Thracian civilisation was one of the earliest in Europe), and caving. Bulgaria is also noted for its monasteries, often situated in remote mountain settings where the Orthodox Church preserved the national identity during the centuries of Ottoman rule. The most famous of these are those of Rila to the south of Sofia and Boyana on the outskirts of the capital. For such cultural tourism to be successful, more attention needs to be paid to improving accessibility and visitor management facilities to a standard appropriate for Western tourists.

Romania

Romania is the second largest country in the Balkan region, with a population of 19.9 million. The Romanian people regard themselves as different – Latins surrounded by Slavs. Although in language and temperament they have some similarities to Italians, their religion is Orthodox, and the climate is definitely continental, with severely cold winters, rather than Mediterranean. The forested Carpathian Mountains divide the country in a great horseshoe-shaped arc, separating picturesque Transylvania from the broad plains of Wallachia to the south and the rolling plateau of Moldavia to the east. Whereas Wallachia and Moldavia were separate principalities on the fringes of the Ottoman Empire until 1858, Transylvania was part of Hungary until 1918. As a result, Transylvania has substantial Magyar and German-speaking minorities who differ in religion as well as language from the Romanian majority. There are also 2 million Roma or gypsies who form a marginalised group in society (as elsewhere in the Balkans and Eastern Europe) but who play an important role in Romanian folklore.

During the 1960s, the Romanian government embarked on a major investment programme for the Black Sea coast, creating a number of new holiday resorts. In 1971, a Ministry of Tourism and Sport was established, and the state tourism organisation ONT and its subsidiary Carpati set out to increase numbers of visitors from the West as well as from other socialist countries. During the 1970s, they were successful in attracting Western tour operators. However, after 1979, the economic situation in Romania deteriorated and the Ceauçescu regime became increasingly repressive with its 'social engineering' policies. As a result, tourism receipts fell by 40 per cent between 1981 and 1986. The violent overthrow of Ceauçescu in December 1989 was followed by a slow progress toward economic reform.

The demand for tourism

Domestic and outbound tourism
Domestic tourists account for 90 per cent of overnight stays in hotel accommodation, and there is a demand by Romanians for foreign holidays, particularly to Bulgaria and Turkey, resulting in a substantial deficit in the tourism account.

Inbound tourism
Inbound tourism accounted for 5.3 million overnight stays in 2019. Tourists come mainly from Germany, Italy, France, and Israel, with the United States as the only important market outside the European Union. The average length of stay is short, at around two days.

The supply side of tourism

Tourism development faces capacity problems, particularly as regards road transport and visitor management at some of the country's heritage attractions.

Transport
Romania's road network is chronically underfunded and the country has a poor accident record. Some blame the 'brain drain' of engineers to more prosperous countries in Western Europe for the problem. The rail network does not offer a practical alternative as even inter-city services are slow.

Organisation
The government recognises the importance of tourism, which accounts for 3 per cent of GDP and 6.3 per cent of employment. The Ministry of Entrepreneurship and Tourism is responsible for the sector, with a focus on the national tourism strategy, promotion and development, infrastructure, and licensing accommodation. The master plan for tourism investment is focussed on ecotourism and health tourism. At the regional and local levels, tourism is handled by tourist associations. Sport and recreation play a major role in tourism development.

Tourism resources

The **Black Sea coast** forms part of the Dobrogea region and is scenically the least interesting part of Romania. Although it offers broad, gently shelving beaches, it has failed to compete with Bulgaria as a mass tourism destination for foreign holidaymakers. Mamaia is the largest resort, situated on a sand spit between the sea and an extensive lagoon. Like the tourist complexes of Aurora, Jupiter, Neptune, Venus, and Saturn, it offers a variety of accommodation and sports facilities which need upgrading. The older resort of Eforie with its mud-bathing establishments is well-known for health tourism. Further north, the Danube Delta is a wetland environment over 4,000 square kilometres in extent, teeming with wildlife and now protected as a nature reserve and a UNESCO biosphere reserve.

The spas and resorts of the **Carpathian Mountains** have not received as much investment as those of the Black Sea. Neither as high nor as rugged as the Alps, the Carpathians form a number of separate massifs, of which the most impressive are the Bucegi and Retezat Mountains, noted for their lakes and glaciated landforms. Exploitation of the forest resources has gone hand-in-hand with tourism, and there are a large number of dispersed mountain chalets to supplement hotels and campsite accommodation in the resorts. Before the Second World War, Sinaia attracted the Romanian aristocracy, but nowadays, the main resort is Poiana Brasov, purpose-built for winter sports but also a centre for hiking and adventure holidays. However, facilities need to be improved if they are to attract more visitors from western Europe. Between the mountain ranges lies the fertile Transylvanian Plateau, and to the north the region of Maramures, famous for its wooden churches, where the traditional culture and farming methods remain largely unchanged. In Transylvania, the historic towns of Sibiu and Sighisoara have a strong German influence in their architecture. The 'Gothic' ambience of the castle of Bran, in its picturesque mountain setting, is inevitably associated with the Dracula legend, which owes more to Bram Stoker's novel than the Romanian prince known as 'Vlad the Impaler'.

The tourist attractions of **Moldavia** include the capital, Iasi (Jassy), and the unique painted monasteries of the Bucovina region; amazingly the exterior frescoes have survived since the fifteenth century.

Bucharest, Romania's capital, lies in the plains bordering the Danube. The city boasts spacious boulevards, took much of its culture from France and was known before the Second World War as 'the Paris of the East'. Much was destroyed during the Ceauçescu era to make way for the dictator's grandiose projects such as the 'House of the Republic', which is now a tourist attraction. The Herastrau Village Museum is one of the best of its kind, showcasing the traditions of Romania. Bucharest also has an appeal for music lovers, where the creative industries are reviving after decades of repression.

Turkey (Türkiye)

The setting for tourism

Although 97 per cent of its territory is geographically part of Asia, Turkey belongs to Europe rather than to the Middle East. The country is in many ways distinct from its Arab neighbours to the south, and throughout history has acted as a cultural 'bridge' between East and West. It controls the Dardanelles and the Bosphorus, the strategic waterways linking the Mediterranean to the Black Sea. Turkey's European credentials are underlined by its participation in a number of sport and cultural events, its membership of NATO, and the selection of Istanbul as European Capital of Culture for 2010.

Turkey under the Ottoman Sultans dominated not only much of Europe between the fifteenth and nineteenth centuries but also the Middle East and most of North Africa. However, this was a multi-cultural empire quite different in character from the national state of today. The heritage of the Ottoman Empire is a major part of the fascination the country holds for Western visitors. Turkish traditional culture, including one of the world's finest cuisines, craft industries such as carpet weaving, and the vibrancy of its performing arts, help to give the country a clearly defined tourist image. Yet for many centuries prior to the arrival of the Turks from Central Asia, the region then known as Asia Minor was occupied by many earlier civilisations, including the Hittites, Ancient Greece, and the Roman and Byzantine empires. Turkey is extraordinarily rich in antiquities as a result, but not all of these are given adequate protection.

Turkey is a large country by European standards, with the natural advantage of having an extensive, and for the most part, picturesque coastline along four seas. The heartland of Turkey is less attractive, largely consisting of the semi-arid steppes of the Anatolian Plateau. This is separated from the fertile coastlands by a ring of mountain ranges. The climate is generally favourable for tourism, except in the mountainous north-east, which suffers from winters of almost Siberian intensity. The Black Sea coast receives a good deal of rain throughout the year, in contrast to the rest of the country and is noted for its forests and tea plantations.

Compared to most of its neighbours, Turkey is politically stable, although Erdogan's presidency has been characterised by internal unrest and the country's involvement in the conflict in Syria. Turkey has a strong economy, due in no small measure to the reforms carried out by Kamal Atatürk after the abolition of the Ottoman sultanate in 1923. He imposed Western institutions, the Roman alphabet, and Western dress, and removed organised religion from politics. As a result, the influence of Islam is much less evident than in neighbouring Iran and the Arab countries of the Middle East. Nevertheless, there are contrasts in lifestyles between the cities with a large Westernised middle class and the rural communities of the Anatolian Plateau where traditional attitudes still prevail. Since 2003, the moderate Islamist Justice and Development Party (AKP) has been in power, and many see its success as a challenge to the secular state. As in other developing countries, the population is growing faster than job creation and the provision of public services. This explains the continuing high rate of emigration and the growth of shanty towns (known as *gekekondu*) around Istanbul and Ankara. Another ongoing problem is the unrest among the Kurdish minority in the south-east of the country, with the separatist PKK movement instigating several terrorist incidents.

The demand for tourism

Tourism is of major importance to Turkey, accounting for 5.4 per cent of GDP and over 8 per cent of the workforce.

Domestic and outbound tourism

With a population of almost 81 million, of which 40 per cent are under 25 years of age, there is a large domestic market for tourism, but travel propensities are low by west European standards. There is a rapidly growing industrial sector, and Turkey has largely escaped the recession affecting most of southern Europe. Nevertheless, great regional disparities in wealth distribution persist, with average incomes in Istanbul being 4 to 5 times higher than in the poorest provinces in the south-east. Domestic tourism is significant, with 75 million trips taken in 2021. Domestic tourists are not only attracted to resorts such as Fethiye and Marmaris on the Aegean coast but also those on the Black Sea, which see few foreign visitors other than backpackers. Several ski resorts in the northern mountains primarily serve internal demand from Ankara and Istanbul. Domestic tourists and returning Turkish expatriates tend to stay with relatives rather than use hotel accommodation, while a rapid growth in car ownership has encouraged the frequency of holiday trips. Decades of suppressed demand have resulted in the growth of foreign travel, encouraged by the rise in disposable incomes, the expansion of Turkish Airlines, and the relaxation of currency restrictions. Nevertheless, outbound tourism is much lower in volume than incoming tourism, so that Turkey has a positive balance on its tourism account.

Inbound tourism

Despite having much to offer the tourist, Turkey did not participate in the boom in Mediterranean beach tourism that characterised the 1970s because:

• It was expensive to reach.
• The country was poorly promoted.
• Turkey did not seek to enter the inclusive tour market.

This situation changed when tourism was included in the government's Five-Year Plans, charter flights were permitted, and the country was 'discovered' by the major European tour operators. As a result, the numbers of visitors trebled during the 1980s, but growth subsequently slowed as a result of both the 1991 Gulf War and the adverse publicity about the poor standard of some accommodation in the Aegean holiday resorts of Bodrum and Kusadasi. Turkey attracted 51.2 million international visitors in 2019. As a result of the COVID-19 pandemic, this fell to 15.9 million in 2020, but the measures that were put in place by the government should ensure that the country stays firmly among the 'top 10' destinations.

Russia is the largest generator of tourism, followed by Germany and the Central Asian republics, which have cultural and business ties with Turkey. The United Kingdom was a latecomer on the scene, but despite predictions to the contrary, Turkey's popularity with the British market as a value-for-money destination shows no sign of waning. Business and conference tourism is being encouraged by new convention centres in both Istanbul and Ankara. Holiday tourism is both highly seasonal and concentrated in a small part of the country, namely the south-west coastal strip. This is largely due to short-sighted planning in the 1980s when the Ministry of Tourism envisaged coastal development on a massive scale to create jobs and maximise foreign exchange earnings.

The supply side of tourism

Transport

In the early stages of tourism development, most visitors arrived by surface transport, but since the 1990s, the majority of foreign tourists have arrived by air. Istanbul's Atatürk Airport is the busiest gateway, serving the country's leading cultural and business centre, while Ankara, despite being the capital since 1923, ranks far behind in terms of international traffic. Several regional airports have been developed to serve the west European holiday market in south-west Turkey, namely Izmir, Bodrum-Milas, Dalaman, and Antalya. The national carrier Turkish Airlines provides a network of international and domestic services. Travel by road and rail from the main generating countries to Turkey is at a disadvantage, not only because of the distances involved, but also through the delays at border crossings caused by political turmoil in neighbouring countries. Turkish State Railways operates over a limited network, but most internal travel is by road, using inter-city bus services, and over shorter distances by the *dolmus*, a type of collective taxi. Other than cruise passengers and day excursionists from Rhodes, relatively few visitors arrive by sea, although Turkish Maritime Services operate ferries from Izmir to Italy and Greece, and from Mersin to Turkish North Cyprus.

Accommodation

Turkey can offer a total of around 250,000 bed spaces in registered accommodation. Hotels are mainly used by foreign visitors.

Organisation

Tourism is the responsibility of the Ministry of Culture and Tourism with cabinet status. Tourism development is included in the government's Five-Year Plans to promote national unity and economic growth. The Promotion Directorate has a network of offices abroad. At the regional level, there are culture and tourism offices in each province.

Tourism resources

Turkey is usually divided into seven regions; however, most of the attractions visited by foreign tourists are located in the west and south of this vast country.

Eastern Thrace and Marmara

Although this region is only a small part of Turkey, it contains some of the country's most productive farmland, many of its industries and a third of the population. Although Edirne and Bursa are both historic cities and important business centres, tourism gravitates to Istanbul, which is one of the world's great tourist cities.

Istanbul is the major cultural destination for most visitors to Turkey, as the former capital of the Byzantine and Ottoman Empires. This city of 15 million people has become a popular short-break destination for the following reasons:

- It is a major meeting point of East and West, with two bridges across the Bosphorus literally linking Asia to Europe.
- It contains the finest achievement of Byzantine architecture – Aya Sofya (Holy Wisdom), built in the sixth century by Emperor Justinian as the largest church in Christendom, converted into a mosque by Sultan Mohammed II in 1453, and secularised as a museum by Atatürk. In 2020, it was re-converted to a mosque by Erdogan's government, a decision that was widely criticised, particularly by UNESCO, the Pope, and a number of Western countries.
- The Blue Mosque, with its six minarets, is one of the most outstanding examples of Islamic architecture.
- The Grand Bazaar is a 'must-see' for bargain-hunters, with over 4,000 shops under one roof.
- The Topkapi Palace evokes the splendour, intrigue, and mystery of the Ottoman Empire, particularly the *harem* or women's quarters.
- The Cagaloglü Hamman provides the experience of a Turkish bath, another traditional institution of the Muslim world, with separate sections for men and women.

The recreation hinterland of Istanbul includes numerous islands in the Sea of Marmara, attracting large numbers of day visitors from the city during the hot summer months.

The modern town of Gelibolu (Gallipoli), situated on the Dardanelles, was the scene of a major military campaign in the First World War, attracting large numbers of Australians and New Zealanders for patriotic reasons. The ancient city of Troy once stood nearby, the site now marked by a 'wooden horse' replica. Probably it was Troy's strategic location, and not 'the face that launched a thousand ships', that provoked its destruction by the Greeks in the Trojan War.

The Aegean coastlands

West European tourists are primrily attracted to the beaches of the southern Aegean coast and the Gulf of Antalya. Club Méditerranée pioneered beach tourism in the 1970s with their holiday villages at Foça, Kusadasi, and Kemer. Since that time, several resorts have experienced most stages in the tourist area life cycle, namely:

- Discovery by wealthy Turkish families, yachtsmen, and a few backpackers.
- Development by small specialist tour operators.
- Consolidation by large companies serving the mass market.

In some resorts, the environmental and cultural impact of tourism has been considerable, notably at Marmaris and Gumbet on the Bodrum Peninsula. Bodrum itself, although a lively resort, has preserved much of its Turkish ambience, due largely to its setting on a beautiful bay dominated by a Crusader castle. Elsewhere, as at Olü Deniz, famed for its beautiful beach and lagoon, development has been carefully controlled. In a rare instance, that of the Dalyan delta, development was halted altogether following protests by environmentalists.

Excursions are made from the coastal resorts to the travertine springs at Pammukale, renowned as a health resort in ancient times. There are also cultural attractions that include:

- Efes (Ephesus): In ancient times, this was one of the greatest cities of the Roman Empire, where the temple of Artemis (Diana of the Ephesians) was a place of pilgrimage. The well-preserved theatre and the Library of Celsus are 'must-see' heritage attractions. Ephesus also has religious significance for modern pilgrims due to its associations with St Paul, and as the place where, according to tradition, the Virgin Mary lived prior to the Assumption.
- Bergama (Pergamum): It is less famous and as a result much less visited.

The Mediterranean region

The 'Turkish Riviera' around the Gulf of Antalya is backed by the pine-covered Lycian and Taurus Mountain ranges. The resorts of Antalya, Alanya, and Side contain many large up-market hotels, but other resorts, such as Kalkan, lack suitable beaches and are small and less sophisticated. The purpose-built resort of Belek caters mainly for golf tourism. The Lycian mountains provide opportunities for trekking, jeep 'safaris', and white-water rafting.

The part of southern Turkey centred on the bustling city of Adana is one of the few substantial stretches of Mediterranean coastline still awaiting development, possibly because agriculture and industry have been given priority for investment. The coastal towns attract some domestic tourism, but for foreign visitors, the cultural heritage has greater appeal, such as the ancient cities of Tarsus and Antioch, associated with St Paul and the early history of Christianity.

CASE STUDY 16.3
SAILING TURKISH-STYLE: A SUSTAINABLE ALTERNATIVE

The coast of south-west Turkey has the following features that make it ideal for a sailing holiday:

- A shoreline extending for over 1,000 kilometres, with many suitable harbours and a scenic hinterland.
- Sheltered coves that are inaccessible by road, providing privacy for swimming, sunbathing, and beach barbecues.
- A warm, sunny climate with reliable afternoon breezes from May through October.

Bareboat yacht charter is available, but most holidaymakers prefer to relax, cruising on a *gület*, a motor yacht distinguished from other vessels by traditional features in its craftsmanship and design. A number of companies offer cruises lasting from 4 to 14 nights, with full board and a Turkish skipper and crew. There is sometimes the option of staying in a hotel at the start or the end of a cruise.

Discuss the 'green' credentials of a gület cruise.

Central Anatolia

The Anatolian Plateau has much to offer the cultural tourist, although the sites are widely dispersed. Apart from Ankara, the modern capital and major business centre containing Atatürk's mausoleum, they include:

- The strange lunar landscapes of Cappadocia where the soft volcanic rock known as tufa was excavated to provide a refuge for early Christian communities, complete with underground churches and cave dwellings. Balloon flights offer an interesting way of viewing the scenery.
- The city of Konya, famed for its 'whirling dervishes' – a feature of the mystical Sufi version of Islam.
- The ancient monuments at Nemrut Dagh, a World Heritage Site. Even in this remote area, visitor management and conservation are major issues.

The Black Sea coastlands

This scenic region is backed by the Pontic Mountains, which receive heavy rainfall. The relatively cool, cloudy climate is an attraction for tourists from Saudi Arabia and the Gulf states wishing to escape their notoriously hot summers. The tourist centres, linked by a new coastal highway, include the historic cities of Sinop and Trabzon (Trebizond), which was famous in medieval times for its wealth and sophistication.

Cyprus

Cyprus is the third largest of the Mediterranean islands, offering a great variety of coastal and mountain scenery and the heritage of many civilisations. The cultural ties between Greece and Cyprus go back thousands of years, far longer than the periods of Turkish and British rule. This may explain why it is a divided island, occupied by two different ethnic groups – the Greeks and the Turks – separated by language, religion, history, and since 1974 by a military/political frontier – the Green Line – which also divides the capital, Nicosia. The Greek-speaking Republic of Cyprus occupies two-thirds of the island, contains 75 per cent of its population, and accounts for perhaps 95 per cent of its tourism industry.

The Turkish Republic of North Cyprus (TRNC), on the other hand, is not recognised by the international community. The location of Cyprus, only 200 kilometres from Beirut, has meant that tourism is affected not only by the long-running dispute between Greece and Turkey over the island itself but also by the uncertain political situation in the Middle East. In the 1990/1991 Gulf War, for example, tourism suffered badly.

The demand for tourism

Domestic tourism

There is a considerable internal demand for the island's recreational resources, generated not just by the Cypriots themselves but also by the United Nations peacekeeping force in Nicosia, and the British armed forces stationed at the Sovereign Base of Akrotiri.

Inbound tourism

Before Cyprus gained independence from Britain in 1960, few tourists visited the island. In the late 1960s, it was 'discovered' by British tour operators, since Cyprus (along with Gibraltar and Malta) was part of the 'sterling area' and not subject to the strict currency exchange controls imposed by the British government at that time. After the invasion and occupation of the northern part of the island by the Turkish army in 1974, there was a drastic decline in tourist numbers, as most of the hotel stock was destroyed in the conflict. However, a major investment in tourism facilities in southern Cyprus followed, including the opening of a new airport at Larnaca to replace Nicosia, and the rapid development of Ayia Napa as a resort for the mass market. By 2019, international tourist arrivals had grown to 4 million a year. The United Kingdom is the largest source of tourists, closely followed by Sweden and Germany. The tourism industry has proved resilient despite COVID-19 and the loss of the lucrative Russia and Ukraine markets. The British inclusive tour market is well established, using charter flights to the airports at Larnaca and Paphos. There are also substantial numbers of independent British visitors travelling to their holiday villas and retirement homes on the island. As is the case in Greece, the Cyprus government discourages seat-only charters.

The supply side of tourism

The Republic of Cyprus has a more varied resource base for tourism than the TRNC, supported by a good infrastructure and a stock of accommodation providing over 80,000 bed spaces, although there are relatively few first-class hotels to attract the top end of the market.

Organisation

Tourism in the Republic of Cyprus is represented at ministerial level as it is so important to the economy (accounting for 22 per cent of GDP and 25 per cent of export earnings). This over-dependence upon tourism also causes concern regarding the industry's use of scarce resources and its social and environmental impacts. The Cyprus Tourism Organisation (CTO) has promotion, development, and licensing responsibilities. In this respect, the CTO is very concerned about the risks of overdevelopment of the coastline – already evident in resorts such as Limassol and Ayia Napa – and is aiming for high quality, high-spending tourism by upgrading the tourism product. It has successfully promoted the island as an all-year round destination, and as a result, the Scandinavian countries and Germany have become important generators of tourism to Cyprus. The CTO has actively sought new markets, notably Israel and the Arab states of the Middle East.

Tourism resources

We can summarise the primary tourism products of the Republic of Cyprus as follows:

- Beach tourism, based on major resort developments at Paphos, Limassol, Larnaca, and Ayia Napa. The trend is to go up-market with the provision of golf courses and yacht marinas, although Ayia Napa is likely to appeal mainly to the mass market, particularly young tourists interested in the vibrant club scene.
- Conferences and incentive travel are catered for by the larger resort hotels and a conference centre in Nicosia.
- Agritourism in the rural villages, which are being carefully restored to attract visitors to the 'traditional Cyprus'.
- Ecotourism, specifically birdwatching in the Akamas National Park, the one remaining undeveloped stretch of coastline in the south-west of Cyprus.
- Skiing during the winter months in the pine-covered Troodos Mountains. During the summer, mountain resorts such as Platres continue to be visited by Cypriots, escaping the intense summer heat of the plains around Nicosia. There are a number of small country hotels.
- Business tourism in Limassol and Larnaca (which is being positioned as a hub for air services to the Middle East). Tourism in Nicosia is discouraged by the political situation, but the city has, nevertheless, become an important communications and financial centre for a large part of the Middle East.
- Cultural tourism based on the heritage of Cyprus includes Ancient Greek theatres at Kourion (now used for music festivals) and Amathus; Byzantine monasteries; Crusader castles; and Islamic monuments from the Ottoman Empire.
- Cruises to the Greek islands, Israel, and Egypt from the port of Limassol.

Tourism in the TRNC

Before the 1974 Turkish takeover, Famagusta (now Magusa) and Kyrenia (Girne) were the major resorts of the island. They are much less popular nowadays, as few tour operators are prepared to provoke the Greek or Greek Cypriot authorities by including the TRNC in their programmes. Nevertheless, the best beaches are in the Turkish-occupied zone. There is also scope for cultural tourism, including:

- Othello's Tower in Famagusta with its Shakespearian associations, dating from the time of the Venetian occupation of Cyprus.
- The monasteries and castles in the mountains near Kyrenia, dating from the time of the Crusades, when the island was held by the Knights Templar.

Turkish visitors from the mainland account for two-thirds of arrivals, but substantial numbers of British and German tourists are attracted to Northern Cyprus, arriving on Turkish Airline flights at Erkan Airport via Istanbul or Izmir. Many of the British visitors have purchased second homes in the TRNC; Greek Cypriots maintain their title to the land is dubious, given the circumstances of the Turkish takeover.

The Republic of Cyprus was admitted to the European Union in 2004, but the future growth of tourism will depend primarily on the reunification of the island under a federal system of government with the agreement of Turkey. In the meantime, a limited amount of cross-border traffic is taking place.

Summary

- With the exception of Greece, which has a long tradition of cultural tourism, most countries in the region are comparative latecomers to the industry.
- The heritage of the Ottoman Empire is evident in the culinary and architectural resources of most countries in the region.
- Political instability and ethnic strife have been a feature of most countries in the region, partly as a legacy of Ottoman rule.
- Most of these countries have benefitted from their accessibility to the tourist-generating countries of central and northern Europe and the demand for 'sun, sand and sea' holidays.
- Travel propensities throughout the region are low, and outbound and domestic tourism are much less significant than incoming tourism.
- Most domestic tourists stay with friends and relatives rather than use serviced accommodation.
- The primary resources are the attractive coastal and mountain environments, while the Mediterranean climate of the islands is ideal for recreational tourism. The islands of Greece, Croatia, and Cyprus also have a rich cultural heritage, blending south European and Middle Eastern influences; however, cultural tourism tends to take second place to beach holidays.
- Cultural attractions include well-preserved archaeological sites, Orthodox monasteries, Crusader castles, and music festivals.
- One of the main problems facing tourism is a pronounced summer peak in demand, especially in Greece. Attempts to develop winter tourism have met with little success, with the notable exception of Cyprus.

- The domination of the industry by foreign tour operators makes it difficult for local entrepreneurs to respond with new quality products as the markets are price-sensitive.
- After a long period of neglect, there is a growing awareness by the authorities in each country of the need to protect the coastal and mountain environments, as well as the archaeological heritage, from the impacts of mass tourism.

Review questions

1. Compare the Greek Islands, Croatia, Montenegro, and Turkey as destinations for sailing holidays.
2. Explain why the heritage of Ancient Greece is important for the tourism industry of modern Greece.
3. Describe the cultural features, including food specialities, traditional crafts, etc. that are shared by most of the countries in the region. Suggest features that could be identified as a 'unique selling point' for each of the lesser-known countries of the region.
4. Identify the factors that are holding back the development of tourism in a number of Balkan countries.

References and further reading

Buhalis, D. (2001) Tourism in Greece: Strategic analysis and challenges, *Current Issues in Tourism* 4 (5), 440–480

Organization for Economic Co-operation and Development (annual) *Tourism Policy and International Tourism in OECD Member Countries*, OECD, Paris

https://www.unwto.org/tourism-data/unwto-tourism-dashboard

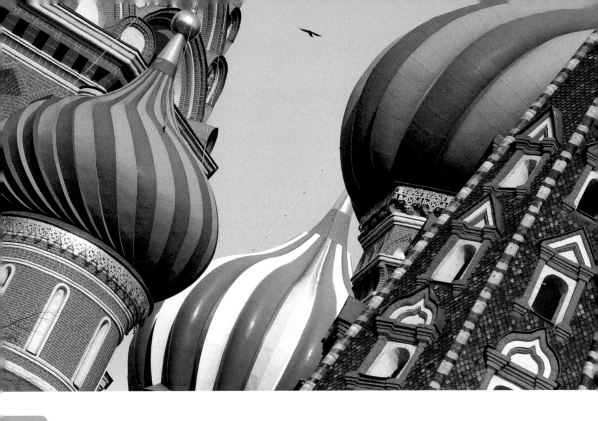

17 The tourism geography of Eastern Europe, Russia, and the CIS

Learning objectives

After reading this chapter, you should be able to:

- Describe the major physical features and climates of Eastern Europe, Russia, and the countries of the CIS.
- Understand the historical context of tourism in these countries under Communism.

DOI: 10.4324/9781003406853-20

- Understand the major features of tourism demand in the countries of Eastern Europe.
- Understand the major features of tourism demand in Russia.
- Appreciate the role of inbound tourism on the economies of the region.
- Understand the significance of the 'Silk Road'.
- Demonstrate knowledge of the tourism regions, resorts, business centres, and tourist attractions of Eastern Europe, Russia, and the CIS.

Introduction

Eastern Europe is the name given to the great tract of land, over a million square kilometres in area, extending from the Baltic to the Black Sea. It has acquired a special identity primarily for political reasons since 1945, but its historical background puts it in the mainstream of European culture. This is particularly true of Poland, the Czech Republic, Slovakia, and Hungary, which consider themselves to be part of Central Europe, because of their geographical location and a cultural heritage that these countries share with Austria and Germany. Russia, on the other hand, includes vast Asian territories extending to the Pacific Ocean, and most of the former USSR lies outside Europe. Except in a few favoured coastal areas, the climate is definitely continental, with much colder winters than are experienced in the same latitudes in Western Europe.

Between 1945 and 1989, the countries of Eastern Europe could be said to form a political and economic region sharply differentiated from those on the western side of the 'Iron Curtain'. Together with Bulgaria and Romania, these countries were closely associated with the Soviet Union (USSR) as the Eastern Bloc. However, the imposition of unity under Communism concealed the deep-seated differences between the many ethnic groups that make up the population of the region. A case can be made for dividing 'Eastern Europe' and the former Soviet Union into three groups of countries:

- The first group of countries – the Czech Republic, Slovakia, Hungary, Poland, and the Baltic States – are the most advanced economically and have a strong cultural orientation towards the West, and as we saw in the previous chapter, the same is true of Slovenia and Croatia in the former Yugoslavia.
- The second group includes Russia, Belarus, and Ukraine, which share similar east Slavic languages, history, and culture. These countries were the founder members of the Commonwealth of Independent States (CIS), following the break-up of the USSR in 1991. The 2022 invasion of Ukraine by Russia has significantly disrupted tourism in the group.
- The third group includes the countries of the former USSR south of the Caucasus and in Central Asia, which culturally have more in common with Turkey and the Middle East than with Russia.

The historical setting for tourism demand

The adoption of Communism as the political and economic model, first by Russia after 1917 and then by the countries of Eastern Europe after 1945, has had a profound effect on tourism in the region. Communism, which entails the state ownership of the means of production and distribution, influenced both the nature of the demand for tourism and recreation and the type of facilities that were on offer. Governments in the so-called 'socialist' or 'peoples' republics' had virtual monopoly control over all aspects of tourism from strategic planning to owning and managing accommodation. Public institutions were closely involved in 'social tourism' or 'trade union tourism' by subsidising workers' holidays and providing tourist facilities. The type of holidays on offer differed fundamentally from commercial mass tourism as it developed in the West.

Some East European countries had well-developed tourist industries before 1939, but, with the notable exception of Czechoslovakia, the majority of the population were too poor to afford holidays. Following the Communist take-over, the luxury hotels in spas, seaside resorts, and cities were nationalised and put to other uses. Concern for leisure and tourism revived in the 1960s when the economic restructuring was well under way, and considerations of housing, education, and health care were less pressing. The rights of all citizens to recreational opportunities had been recognised in the constitutions drawn up by the new republics. Pressure for longer holidays and two-day weekends coincided with the growing movement from the rural areas to the industrial cities. Demand also grew for the introduction of leisure goods, including cars, although choice was greatly restricted and ownership levels remained at only a fraction of those in the West. Domestic holidays were customarily spent at the seaside or in spas, where rather spartan accommodation was provided, often in the form of holiday villages or workers' sanatoria, provided by the government-controlled trade unions. However, the *nomenklatura* – the Communist Party elite and other favoured groups – had access to more luxurious facilities, including, in some cases, private beaches and hunting reserves. In the cities, the government provided generous subsidies to the performing arts and cultural attractions that, to some extent, compensated for the restrictions and consumer shortages, making everyday life drab for most citizens. The rich folklore of the various ethnic groups was also encouraged as a tourist attraction.

Demand for outbound international tourism grew slowly due to currency and visa restrictions. Inevitably, most outbound travel was to other socialist countries, and its volume was regulated by bilateral agreements between the governments of the region. Inbound tourism from the West was initially viewed with suspicion, but in most countries was actively sought from the 1960s, as it earned hard currency to purchase much-needed imports from outside the COMECON trading bloc. Indeed, Western visitors had privileges denied to most of the population, as they could buy goods from so-called 'dollar shops', which accepted only hard currencies. Giving preference to group travel, which could be carefully supervised, was one way of ensuring favourable publicity for 'socialist achievements'. However, low standards of service, outdated infrastructure, and bureaucratic controls inhibited the growth of international tourism, while the simple lack of bed spaces held back domestic tourism.

The dramatic political changes which have taken place in Eastern Europe and the former Soviet Union since 1989 have had a profound effect on the pattern of tourism development, including the invasion of Ukraine by Russia in 2022. The state tourism organisations, which were, in effect, tour operators and travel agencies like the USSR's Intourist, lost their monopoly position. A range of new organisations have since emerged, including private companies, co-operatives, and state-run concerns, all placing a greater emphasis on marketing. The prospect of local community involvement in decision-making, instead of the 'top-down' approach to planning by central government, has required a radical shift in attitudes. Changes have been most rapid in those countries such as the Czech Republic, Poland, and Hungary, which had a flourishing tourism industry before 1939, and where there is a strong entrepreneurial tradition. A flurry of tourism plans and significant investment in tourist infrastructure and accommodation has been evident as the countries of the region bring their tourism sector up to international standards. Accommodation is in short supply in some categories, so joint ventures in partnership with Western companies have often been necessary to obtain the necessary capital and expertise and act as a catalyst for other businesses to adapt their practices to a competitive market environment.

On the other hand, the switch to a market economy has had a damaging effect on social tourism. In some countries, domestic tourists were priced out of international hotels, where previously they had been charged very preferential rates. The introduction of democracy has given the peoples of Eastern Europe and the former Soviet Union much greater freedom to travel to the West, and this flow will increase as the economic outlook of the countries in the region continues to improve. The admission to the European Union of most countries in the former Eastern Bloc has accelerated this trend. Increasing levels of Internet use, which in some countries match those in the West, is another factor favouring the growth of tourism demand.

The surge in car ownership in Eastern Europe, and the growth in demand for touring holidays in the region has necessitated massive investment in road improvement schemes to meet West European standards, while public transport has been relatively neglected. Continuing economic difficulties make it difficult for governments to deal effectively with the region's already numerous environmental problems. In the long term, the demand for travel to these countries by the 'new tourists' will decline if these issues are not addressed.

In detailing the resources and the type of development that has taken place in each of the countries of the region, we start with the Czech Republic, Slovakia, Hungary, and Poland. In 1991, these four countries formed the Visegrad Group (V4) (http://www.visegradgroup.eu/) for closer co-operation, and this continues to be an influential regional association within the European Union, often disagreeing with the policies of Brussels, for example, on immigration. In 2011, the V4, along with Romania and Ukraine, agreed on a policy of sustainable tourism development to protect the environment of the Carpathians, which provides a refuge for Europe's largest populations of brown bears, wolves, lynx, and eagles.

The Czech Republic (Czechia)

In January 1993, the Federal Republic of Czechoslovakia was dissolved with the Czech Republic (https://www.czechtourism.com) and Slovakia, henceforth, following separate paths. The Czechs of Bohemia and Moravia differ from the Slovaks not only in language but also in cultural traditions. When Czechoslovakia was established in 1918, the Czech lands had been part of the Austrian Empire for four centuries, whereas Slovakia had been ruled by Hungary for much longer. The Czech Republic is not only much larger than Slovakia, with twice the population, but is also disproportionately wealthier. Since the 'Velvet Revolution' of 1989, it has attracted considerable foreign investment due to its drive to a free-market economy.

Tourism demand

Domestic and outbound tourism

Many of the tourists originating from the Czech Republic, and from other former Eastern Bloc countries, are travelling abroad for the first time and express preference for budget-priced beach holidays and touring holidays. Demand for niche products is much smaller than in Western Europe, and this is also true of long-haul travel. The Czech Republic is second only to Poland as the largest generator of outbound travel in the region, with some 10 million overnight trips a year, but this fell to just over 5 million in 2022 due to the COVID-19 pandemic. Domestic tourism is important, as an advanced industrial economy has given most Czechs a degree of affluence. Sport and an interest in physical fitness, and the outdoor life had been fostered by the Sokol movement long before Czechoslovakia achieved independence in 1918. This has resulted in a growing demand for a wide range of outdoor activities and for second homes in the countryside.

Inbound tourism

The Czech Republic has long been famous for its therapeutic springs and spas. Karlovy Vary (formerly Carlsbad) (https://www.karlovyvary.cz/en) and Marianske Lazne (Marienbad) (https://www.marianskelazne.cz/en/) in Bohemia were the favourite meeting places for the statesmen and the wealthy of Europe in the early 1900s. Under Communism, the luxury hotels were taken over by labour unions and fell into neglect, but since 1990, there has been a strong revival as a result of the growing demand for health and wellness tourism. With developments spearheaded by the Czech Tourist Authority (CTA) and Cedok (https://www.cedok.cz/), the former state tourism organisation and now the largest hotel and travel company, a wide range of products are available to today's foreign visitor, including city breaks, spa treatments, sporting holidays, stays in lake and mountain resorts, and touring holidays.

After the 1989 revolution, tourist numbers more than doubled, exceeding 20 million arrivals in the early years of the twenty-first century, and Prague (https://www.prague.eu/en) has become one of the world's most visited cities. However, the great majority of these are day excursionists, mainly from neighbouring Germany and Austria. The number of international arrivals was over 37 million in 2019 but fell to just 10 million in 2021 due to COVID-19.

The country's new-found popularity highlighted the shortage of accommodation, especially the three- and four-star hotels favoured by Western tour groups, and the need to upgrade standards is one of the most pressing needs of the tourism sector. Until recently, most of the demand has come from other East European countries where expectations are lower, and this has resulted in a proliferation of low-cost camping sites. The situation is improving as a result of joint ventures by Cedok with Western corporations for the larger hotels and privatisation of the smaller hotels and pensions, with new hotels opening in Prague and a programme of renovation of older properties.

Tourism resources

The Czech Republic offers scenic variety and a physical environment that is generally favourable for tourism. The large number of rivers and small lakes make up to some extent for the lack of a coastline. Forests cover around one-third of the country and are particularly extensive in the mountain ranges along the national borders. These forests are managed as a recreational resource, with nature reserves, waymarked trails and areas set aside for hunting – an important earner of foreign currency. Skiing is popular during the winter months in the resorts of Harrachov (https://www.harrachov.com/) in the Giant Mountains and Spicak (https://lyzovani.spicak.cz/en/) in the Sumava Mountains. Southern Bohemia and Moravia also boast spectacular limestone caves among their natural attractions.

A rich natural and cultural heritage is given a considerable degree of environmental protection, with the designation of national parks and the establishment of a 400 kilometre-long 'green corridor' linking Prague to Vienna, designed for hiking, riding, and cycling holidays, or leisurely touring by car. This tourist route includes some of the historic towns of southern Bohemia – notably Cesky Krumlov, with its unique Baroque theatre – and a number of castles. Cedok has converted some of these to luxury hotels, while others are being restored to their former aristocratic owners after a long period of neglect under Communism. Interpretation of the heritage is achieved through open-air museums. Despite these initiatives, the Czech Republic has its share of conservation problems. These include:

- Serious pollution from smokestack industries using lignite, in north Bohemia and north Moravia – Silesia.
- As a result of a lack of government funding, historic buildings have fallen into disrepair, while art treasures illegally acquired from the country's churches have found their way to the international art market.

CASE STUDY 17.1
PRAGUE

The towns and cities of the Czech Republic contain many heritage attractions, notably Kutná Hora (https://destinace.kutnahora.cz/d?lang=2), but only Prague has achieved world-wide recognition as a top-ranking tourist centre. This city's cultural appeal is due to:

- A strong musical heritage, including associations with Mozart and the Czech composers Smetana and Dvorak.

- A unique architectural heritage with outstanding examples of buildings in the Gothic, Baroque, and Art Nouveau styles. In contrast to other European cities, Prague escaped destruction in the Second World War and subsequent redevelopment of its historic centre.
- A vibrant contemporary arts scene that has attracted a large expatriate community, from other countries, particularly the United States.

As Prague has more than one historic centre, tourist attractions tend to be clustered in three distinct areas, namely:

- Hradcany – the original fortress-capital on a hill overlooking the River Vltava. This contains Prague Castle (https://www.hrad.cz/en/prague-castle-for-visitors) – seat of Bohemian kings, Holy Roman emperors, and Czech presidents, St. Vitus Cathedral (https://www.katedralasvatehovita.cz/en), and the picturesque street known as Golden Lane.
- The Old Town on the east bank of the river, which is linked to Hradcany by the highly decorative Charles Bridge. Two of the finest masterpieces of Gothic architecture in the Old Town are Tyn Church (http://www.tyn.cz/cz/) and the clock tower in Old Town Square.
- The New Town – which was actually planned as early as the fourteenth century but rebuilt in the nineteenth century. It focusses on Wenceslas Square, the setting for some of the key events in Czech history, nowadays lined with hotels, apartment buildings, restaurants, and shops. Many of these are decorated in the Art Nouveau style associated with the great Czech artist Alfons Mucha.

Tourism has brought economic benefits to Prague, including international funding of much-needed restoration work. However, the enormous influx of visitors, especially tour groups and young backpackers from all over the world, is threatening to turn the city into another Florence. This has had the following effects:

- The commercialisation of the historic city. As a result of the upsurge in land prices, neighbourhood shops have been replaced by those catering for tourists. Historic buildings have been altered in inappropriate ways and defaced with advertisements. Local residents can no longer afford the high rents for their apartments, or the prices in bars and restaurants, and have been forced to move to the suburbs.
- Wear and tear on the most popular attractions, such as Charles Bridge, which is constantly thronged with buskers, street traders, and crowds of tourists.
- A predatory attitude by many of the city's taxi operators towards Western tourists.

Other cities are mainly important as centres for business travel, namely:

- Plzen (Pilsen) (https://www.pilsen.eu/tourist/) and Ceske Budejovice (Budweis) (https://www.budejce.cz/en/) are famous for their brewing industries.
- Brno, the capital of Moravia, is noted for its engineering industries, and as an important venue for trade fairs.

Slovakia

Slovakia (https://slovakia.travel/en) made slower progress with free-market reforms than the Czech Republic, and consequently tourism was not as developed. Before the Second World War, it had a predominantly agrarian economy, and more recently the country became over-dependent on the heavy industries introduced under Communism. Slovakia is a country with great tourism potential, and while it has benefitted from the share-out of federal assets following its 'divorce settlement' with the Czech Republic, significant investment in tourist infrastructure is needed. The situation has improved since 2004, now that both countries are EU members.

The demand for tourism

Domestic and outbound tourism

Domestic tourism is important, accounting for 74 per cent of overnights in 2021. Restrictions on public spending have led to a decrease in the number of subsidised visits to spas for health reasons in both the Czech Republic and Slovakia. The emphasis tends to be on recreation rather than therapeutic treatments in Slovakian spas, thereby attracting a younger market. Nevertheless, Slovaks increasingly prefer to travel abroad, with Turkey and Croatia as their main destinations.

Inbound tourism

Slovakia received 2 million tourist arrivals in 2018, staying on average 2.5 nights, but volume fell to half a million in 2021 due to COVID-19. The Czech Republic generates the largest number of visitors, but these tend to be in the older age groups, and a generation has grown up since the separation of the two countries that now faces a language barrier, and so prefers to travel further afield.

The supply side of tourism

Organisation

The Ministry of Tourism and Construction has responsibility for tourism, while the eight municipal regions have devolved tourism powers. The Tourism Support Act also gives tourism responsibilities to local and regional destination management organisations.

Tourism resources

The main appeal of Slovakia for foreign visitors lies in its beautiful mountain scenery rather than the attractions of the capital, Bratislava (https://www.visitbratislava.com/). Unlike the Czech Republic, this is a wine rather than beer drinking nation, with some cultural similarities to neighbouring Hungary; for example, gypsy folk music is an important part of the entertainment on offer to foreign tourists in both countries. Slovaks take great pride in their rural peasant traditions, and a considerable variety of village architecture has been preserved. Other heritage attractions include medieval mining towns, the castles of the former Hungarian nobility, and in eastern Slovakia, Orthodox churches are a reminder of the region's proximity to Romania and the Ukraine.

Tourism is primarily focussed on the following areas:

- The High Tatras on the border with Poland, which contain the highest peaks of the Carpathians. Apart from the superb lake and mountain scenery, the area can provide some of the best skiing to be found in Eastern Europe. Poprad (https://www.visitpoprad.sk/en/), the gateway to this region, is a major health and wellness centre, boasting an impressive aqua park among its facilities.
- The karst limestone region of eastern Slovakia, which boasts the spectacular UNESCO-listed Dobsina ice cave (https://whc.unesco.org/en/list/725) as well as the waterfalls and rock formations of the Slovak Paradise National Park.
- The spas of western Slovakia, the most important being Piestany, which attracts large numbers of wealthy Arab and German tourists.
- Bratislava and southern Slovakia, which forms part of the Danube Plain. Bratislava is known primarily as a modern industrial city, and its cultural attractions have been overshadowed by those of Prague.

Hungary

Hungary (https://wowhungary.com/en) is famous for its spicy cuisine, and the Magyar language also marks the country as different from its neighbours. The country is only a third of its size prior to 1918, when it was Austria's partner in the Habsburg empire. Although most of Hungary, including Budapest, was under Ottoman rule for almost two centuries, their legacy here is much less apparent than in the Balkan countries to the south. The major physical feature is a great plain in the middle of the Pannonian Basin, crossed by the rivers Danube and Tisza. In the north, there are the foothills of the Carpathians and in the south-west around Pécs, uplands rising to over 800 metres. Winters are cold and cloudy, but summers approach Mediterranean conditions in heat and sunshine.

Tourism demand

Tourism has become an important part of the economy, accounting for 8.5 per cent of GDP in 2019 but falling to 5.4 per cent in 2020 due to COVID-19. Tourism accounts for 9 per cent of employment. This is due partly to the successful marketing of Hungary's two main attractions, namely the capital Budapest (https://www.budapestinfo.hu/) and Lake Balaton, which together account for the majority of foreign visitors. The tourism strategy is now to focus on quality and high yield tourism rather than mass tourism, which requires improvements in the infrastructure.

Domestic and outbound tourism

As visa and currency restrictions have been relaxed, and the economic position has improved, increasing numbers of Hungarians are travelling abroad, with Germany, Slovakia, and Austria as popular destinations and a small, but growing long-haul market. Although annual holiday entitlement averages 20 days, effective demand for domestic tourism is reduced by the widespread practice of 'moonlighting' at several jobs to make ends meet so that holiday propensities languish at around 33 per cent. The majority of domestic tourists stay with friends or relatives or in cottages in the countryside.

Inbound tourism

Even under Communism, Western tourists were encouraged by the removal of restrictions, and a limited amount of foreign investment in hotels was permitted. During the 1980s, the number of visitors from the West almost trebled, whereas those from other socialist countries actually declined. This was largely due to the low value of the Hungarian *forint* relative to Western currencies, whereas it was overvalued compared to the non-convertible currencies of the Soviet bloc. Hungary's success in attracting international tourists has continued, with around 15 million making overnight stays in 2018.

The supply side of tourism

The majority of visitors arrive by car and 40 per cent are excursionists, particularly the Austrians, who cross the border on shopping forays to towns such as Sopron and Szombathely. The gateway for air travellers is Budapest's Ferenc Liszt International Airport (https://www.bud.hu/), the hub for Wizz Air (https://wizzair.com/en-gb), one of Europe's most successful low-cost airlines. Large numbers of excursionists use the hydrofoil service on the Danube from Vienna. A high proportion of the accommodation stock is in campsites or private homes. There has been significant investment in hotels, both within and outside of Budapest, with the major chains represented.

Organisation

Before 1989, the state-owned Ibusz company (https://www.ibusz.hu/en) handled both inbound and outbound tourism, but it has since been reorganised as part of the new government's policy of economic liberalisation and faces competition from a multiplicity of independent travel agencies. Overall responsibility for tourism falls under the Cabinet Office of the Prime Minister (https://www.kormany.hu/en/cabinet-office-of-the-prime-minister). The Hungarian Tourism Agency is responsible for the development and management of tourism, formulating tourism strategy, setting budgets, and promoting the country's brand.

Tourism resources

Hungary's tourism resources include:

- Numerous spas based on the thermal springs that underlie the Pannonian Basin. Hungary has gained an international reputation for high standards of dentistry, medical treatment, and therapy, and the facilities for health and wellness tourism attract a growing conference market.
- Excellent facilities for activity holidays, such as horseriding, cycling, and watersports.
- Cultural attractions appealing more to the older tourist. These include the traditional peasant dances and crafts, notably embroidery, of the villages of the Great Hungarian Plain where rural tourism is growing.

Budapest is one of Europe's most attractive capitals. Formed from what were two separate cities, Buda, picturesquely situated on the hills above the Danube, and Pest, the commercial centre on the river's left bank, it contains many reminders of its pre-1918 role as the joint capital of the Austro-Hungarian Empire. These include:

- The magnificent neo-Gothic Parliament Building in Pest and the Fisherman's Bastion (http://www.fishermansbastion.com/) in Buda are the city's two major landmarks.
- The Hungarian State Opera (http://www.opera.hu/) is a reminder that Budapest vies with Vienna as a centre of art and music.
- The shopping boulevards, cafe society, and vibrant nightlife.
- Spa establishments such as the Hotel Gellert and the Szechenyi Baths (http://szechenyispabaths.com/), with year-round open-air bathing.
- Business opportunities in the new climate of economic liberalism. Since 1990, Budapest has attracted an international business community, and the city is growing in importance as a conference venue.

Budapest is close to the other main tourist areas of Hungary, namely:

- The Danube Bend, where the great river changes its course between mountain ranges, is a popular excursion zone. It contains some of Hungary's most historic towns including Szentendre (https://iranyszentendre.hu/en/), with its *skansen* or museum of Hungarian rural life (http://skanzen.hu/en/).
- Lake Balaton is one of Europe's largest at 77 kilometres in length, but averaging only 3 metres in depth. Its shores are fringed by beaches, modern hotels, and campsites, while several areas have been designated as nature reserves. Demand for accommodation in summer frequently exceeds supply, and the threat of pollution from intensive agriculture has to be constantly monitored. Heviz (https://www.heviz.hu/en) is the most well-known of a number of spas in the vicinity of Lake Balaton, due to its unique thermal lake.

- The Great Hungarian Plain, where the *pusztas* or vast, treeless pasturelands east of the Danube provide Hungary with many of its characteristic landscapes and traditions, such as the *csikos* (cattle herders), whose displays of horsemanship are a tourist attraction. Many of the *csardas* (country inns) feature the traditional folk music and dances that inspired Liszt and other Hungarian composers. Ecotourism is being promoted in areas such as the Hortobagy National Park (https://www.hnp.hu/en) near Debrecen, where aspects of the traditional culture and the steppe ecosystem have been carefully preserved.

> **Discussion point**
> Health and wellness is one of the fastest growing sectors of leisure and tourism, and Hungary, in particular, has pioneered low-cost medical treatments and therapies. Investigate the reasons for the growth in demand for spa tourism from the West, and carry out a SWOT analysis of a selection of spa resorts in the former Eastern Bloc countries. How well can they compete with health tourism destinations in other parts of the world?

Poland

Poland (https://www.poland.travel/en) is one of the largest countries of Europe, with a population of almost 40 million. Its exposed situation on the North European Plain between Germany and Russia has resulted in a history of invasion, fluctuating boundaries, and a long period of foreign rule when the country was partitioned between the Russian Empire, Austria, and Prussia. Over 90 per cent of the population adhere to the Roman Catholic Church, which has long been identified with Polish nationhood and resistance. Largely as a result, less than 20 per cent of Poland's' farms were collectivised by the Communist regime after 1945. At the same time, massive industrialisation brought about the Solidarity free trade union movement, which played a significant role in inspiring opposition to Communism during the 1980s. In some respects, Poland was better placed than most East European countries to make the transition to a market economy after 1989.

The demand for tourism

Domestic and outbound tourism

Domestic tourists accounted for over 46 million overnight stays in 2021. Poland generates almost 13 million outbound trips annually. The growth in demand for foreign holidays is due to rising incomes and increasing airline capacity, while long-haul travel has been encouraged by the availability of direct flights to Dubai. The most popular destinations are Germany, Italy, the United Kingdom, and the Czech Republic. The influence of the Catholic Church remains strong, and pilgrimages to Catholic shrines are an important motive for travel.

Inbound tourism

Until the early 1990s, tourism played only a minor role in the Polish economy. The majority of visitors originated from the former socialist countries and tended to be short-stay. This market has declined in importance, and the Ukraine war has resulted in a fall in visitor numbers (excluding refugees) from that country and Belarus. Tourism now accounts for over 4.5 per cent of GDP, and visitors are drawn from a wide range of countries. To a greater extent than other East European countries, Poland can attract a large ethnic market in North America, the United Kingdom, and other countries of Western Europe. Most of the tourism from these countries has been for visting friends or relatives (VFR) or business purposes, but increasing numbers are visiting Poland on inclusive tours or on tailor-made holiday arrangements, primarily for cultural reasons.

The supply side of tourism

A much greater choice of accommodation is now available to Polish holidaymakers than was the case in the past. Tourism's higher profile has led to a change in government policy, with the Polish Tourist Organization, which is responsible to the Ministry of Sport and Tourism now promoting the country. It aims to stimulate further investment and growth in the sector, in line with the government's National Development Strategy, and is involved in tourism training initiatives with West European countries. The Polish Tourism Organisation is attempting to promote tourism away from Krakow, which has become a popular destination for foreign tourists, whereas some parts of the country are little known and rarely visited.

Tourism resources

Poland has been active in conservation, with 23 national parks protecting a variety of landscapes. The main tourist areas of Poland are situated near its southern and northern borders, and a fair distance from Warsaw, the capital and gateway for air travellers.

> The Baltic Coast has been renowned since ancient times as a source of amber, hence the designation of the section along the Gulf of Gdansk as the 'Amber Coast'. The coast is by far the most popular destination, accounting for a third of all holiday overnights. On offer are 500 kilometres of sandy beaches and coastal lagoons, backed by pine forests, but the climate is often cloudy and windy. Extending east from Miedzyzdroje at the mouth of the Oder a string of resorts attract Swedish as well as domestic holidaymakers. Wolin Island is noted for its Viking heritage and further east Sopot (https://visit.sopot.pl/en/) is a popular and long-established resort adjoining the historic seaport of Gdansk. Some of Poland's most important tourism resources lie a short distance inland. The medieval fortress of Malbork (http://www.zamek.malbork.pl/en), built by the Teutonic Knights, is a reminder of the German heritage in what was East Prussia prior to 1945. In the northeast of the country, the Mazurian Lake District is an area of forests, lakes and low hills of glacial drift, which is popular for sailing, canoeing and camping.

The border country of **Southern Poland** offers more interesting scenery and facilities for winter sports. To the west lie the Sudeten Mountains, adjoining Bohemia, where a number of spas have long been established. Further east, the Carpathian Mountains, culminating in the Tatry and Beskid ranges adjoining Slovakia, rise to over 2,000 metres, and account for a fifth of all holiday overnights in Poland. Zakopane (https://discoverzakopane.com/) in the Tatry Mountains is a well-developed resort with a year-round season. In addition to skiing, organised walking tours and whitewater rafting through the gorge of the Dunajec River are available. Tourism has greatly benefitted the economy of this formerly remote and poverty-stricken mountain region.

The flatlands of **Central and Western Poland** are scenically less attractive, but the countryside does provide opportunities for fishing and riding holidays, often based on the manor houses of the former Polish aristocracy. On the eastern border with Belarus, the Bialowieza National Park (https://whc.unesco.org/en/list/33/) provides a refuge for rare animals such as the European bison.

Poland's cultural attractions are mainly to be found in the cities, although most of these suffered wholesale destruction in the Second World War. The historic cores have generally been meticulously restored and provide a welcome contrast to the bleak industrial suburbs. The most important cities from the viewpoint of international tourism are Warsaw and Krakow, whereas others such as Poznan, Lódz, and Wroclaw are primarily business centres: Lódz (https://lodz.travel/en/) has been reinvented as a cultural centre, based on a long-established film industry, where directors such as Wajda have gained international recognition and is now the location of a major new theme park.

Warsaw (https://warsawtour.pl/en/), the Polish capital, is popular as a short-break destination for art and music lovers. One of Warsaw's most impressive – if not best loved – landmarks is the Palace of Culture and Science built during the Stalinist era. The Old Town (the historic centre) is the main destination for foreign visitors (see the case study).

Krakow (http://www.krakow.pl/english/) is important for tourism as Poland's former royal capital and religious centre, which has been designated as a World Heritage Site and European City of Culture. The city, which largely escaped wartime destruction, has retained its medieval atmosphere and has attracted world-wide interest due to its association with Pope John Paul II. The major attractions include the impressive Market Square, the Cloth Hall, and Wawel Castle. In contrast, the new town of Nowa Huta was built around a steelworks as a showpiece of Communist planning. Krakow is conveniently near the ski resorts and scenic attractions of the Carpathian Mountains. In addition, a tour based on the city might include:

- The salt mines of Wielisza (https://www.wieliczka-saltmine.com/), which are famous for the art works made from this resource.
- The shrine of the Black Madonna at Czestochowa (http://jasnagora.pl/en/), which is Poland's most important pilgrimage centre.
- The former concentration camp at Oswiecim (better known by its German name of Auschwitz) (https://visit.auschwitz.org/?lang=en) – one of many established in Poland during the Nazi occupation. The buildings have been preserved along with exhibits relating to the victims, making a visit there a poignant experience. Auschwitz is regarded by the international Jewish community as the main site of the Holocaust and by the Poles as a place of national martyrdom.

CASE STUDY 17.2
THE REBUILDING OF WARSAW

The historic centre of Warsaw was almost completely destroyed during the Second World War, largely as a result of the 1944 uprising of the Polish Resistance against the Nazi occupation. Over 150,000 civilians lost their lives and 85 per cent of the Old Town was reduced to rubble. In the aftermath of the war, proposals to completely rebuild the capital on modernistic lines, as in Coventry and Rotterdam, were rejected in favour of faithfully recreating the townscape of the old city. This was because the Nazi occupation had been a deliberate attempt to eradicate a nation's culture, and the reconstruction of Warsaw was seen as an affirmation of national pride and patriotism. The bulk of the reconstruction was carried out between the late 1940s and mid 1960s. Individual buildings were meticulously restored in the Baroque style of Poland's Golden Age, on the evidence provided by eighteenth century paintings, pre-war photographs, and architects' plans. So impressive has the reconstruction been, it was granted World Heritage status by UNESCO in 1980 (https://whc.unesco.org/en/list/30/) (Photo 17.1).

The Old Town has become a major tourist attraction, with many of the restored buildings providing a vibrant ambience of shops, studios, restaurants, and jazz cafes. The major showpieces include:

- The Royal Castle (the former palace of Polish kings) (https://www.zamek-krolewski.pl/en) reconstructed at immense cost in 1980. This is linked by the 'Royal Route' to the modern centre of Warsaw and the Wilanów Palace, the former suburban residence of the royal family.
- The Old Town Market Place, regarded as the true heart of the Old Town.
- The Maria Sklodowska Museum (http://en.muzeum-msc.pl/), devoted to the Polish scientist and Nobel Prize winner better known as Marie Curie.
- The Chopin Point (http://chopin.events/en/), devoted to the great Romantic composer.
- The Warsaw Uprising Museum (https://www.1944.pl/en).
- The Historical Museum of Warsaw (https://muzeumwarszawy.pl/en/).

Discussion point
Imagine you are experiencing the aftermath of a devastating war or a natural disaster. Debate in class the case for faithfully restoring a historic townscape, compared to the advantages of a complete rebuild, with museums and other attractions using the latest ideas in technology and design. How important should the cost factor be in the decision-making process?

Photo 17.1
Warsaw Old Town
Source: Robyn Cooper

The Baltic States

Like most of Poland, the three small countries of Estonia, Latvia, and Lithuania on the eastern shore of the Baltic Sea formed part of the Russian Empire from the eighteenth century to 1918. Between the two world wars, they enjoyed a brief period of independence before being annexed by the Soviet Union in 1940. The Baltic States have much closer cultural ties with the Scandinavian countries and Germany than with Russia (although there are large ethnic Russian minorities), and since regaining their independence in 1991, they have sought economic association with those countries and see tourism as an important source of foreign currency. In 1993, all three states agreed to co-operate in the sphere of tourism policy and promotion.

The demand for tourism

Domestic and outbound tourism

The Baltic States have a high rate of economic growth and a high expenditure on foreign travel, with Estonia in the lead. Their populations are well-educated and proficient in the English language. External transport links are good, thanks to the emergence of low-cost carriers and alliances with Lufthansa (https://www.lufthansa.com/gb/en/), SAS (https://www.flysas.com/en/), and Lot Polish Airlines (https://www.lot.com/gb/en/).

Inbound tourism

Tourism is increasingly important in all three countries, but particularly in Estonia where it accounts for 5.4 per cent of GDP.

The supply side of tourism

The scenery is low-key, with the highest point reaching only 300 metres above sea level, but is made attractive by the combination of pastureland, forest, and a myriad lakes – a landscape which offers opportunities for a range of outdoor activities. Much of this is given a large measure of protection as national or regional parks. During the period of Soviet rule, the coastal resorts were popular with Russian tourists, and Intourist developed some of its best hotels in the region. The beaches have been adversely affected by the pollution of the Baltic Sea due to industrial waste from Germany, Poland, and Russia, but this problem is now being addressed.

Since the 1990s, the accommodation sector, comprising hotels, guesthouses, and holiday villages, has been upgraded with the improvement in the economy. Low-cost carriers link the capitals Vilnius, Riga, and Tallinn with cities in Western Europe, so that these cities are successfully competing for the short-break west European market. All three countries are noted for their music festivals and folklore, in which national identity was nurtured during the long period of foreign domination.

Estonia

Estonia (https://www.visitestonia.com/en/) has close affinities with Finland and has benefitted from improved ferry services. Nevertheless, it would prefer to reduce its dependence on the Finnish day visitor market – mainly attracted by cheap alcohol – by promoting itself as a cultural destination for British and other West European tourists. It has been successful to the extent that arrivals have increased from 400,000 in 1995 to over 6 million in 2018 but fell back to 1 million in 2020 due to COVID-19.

The German heritage of Estonia and Latvia is apparent in the castles built by the Teutonic Knights in medieval times, the ports which belonged to the powerful Hanseatic League, and the country houses, now mostly converted into hotels and spas, which belonged to the Baltic German landowning class. There are also many reminders of Swedish and Danish rule. International tourism mainly focusses on Tallinn (https://www.visittallinn.ee/eng/), which is one of the best-preserved medieval cities of northern Europe. It is also a major yachting centre and was chosen as the venue for the sailing events in the 1980 Olympics. The university town of Tartu, the port of Pärnu, and the fortress town of Narva, which is close to St Petersburg, are significant tourist centres.

Estonia's coastal resources include a number of offshore islands. The largest of these, Saaremaa (https://visitsaaremaa.ee/en/), has only recently been developed for tourism; under Soviet rule, it was off-limits as a military zone. The Lahemaa National Park to the east of Tallinn is noted for its lakes and waterfalls.

Latvia

Latvia's (https://www.latvia.travel/en) capital, Riga is the industrial hub of the Baltic States, while the national carrier Air Baltic (https://www.airbaltic.com/en-LV/index) operates an extensive network of international services. The city's elegant Art Nouveau architecture is a reminder of the period before 1914 when Riga was the leading port of the Russian Empire. Jurmala (https://www.visitjurmala.lv/en/) on the Gulf of Riga was then fashionable as the 'Baltic Riviera' and is now investing to improve its beachfront facilities. Kurzeme, the western part of Latvia, was known historically as the Grand Duchy of Courland and offers a number of heritage attractions in and around the cities of Liepaja (https://liepaja.travel/en/) and Ventspils (https://www.visitventspils.com/en/start/).

Promotion is the responsibility of the Ministry of Economics and the 'Investment and Development Agency of Latvia', which focusses on the country's cultural attractions. These include:

- The Latvian Song and Dance Festival (https://latviansongfest.com/), held every five years and involving many thousands of participants.
- International festivals in opera and ballet held in Riga.
- The open-air opera festival held in Sigulda.
- The Midsummer Festival, which has its roots in the country's pre-Christian past.
- The Musee Art Nouveau.
- Modern art is showcased by the Mark Rothko Art Centre in Daugavpils (https://www.rothkocenter.com/en).

Lithuania

Lithuania (https://lithuania.travel/en/) was united with Poland for much of its history and is likewise staunchly Roman Catholic. The impressive 'Hill of Crosses' (https://www.kryzi-ukalnas.lt) on the outskirts of Siauliai is the country's most visited religious site, serving as a reminder of the country's resistance to Soviet rule. The capital Vilnius (Vilna) (http://www.vilnius-tourism.lt/en/) is a major cultural centre with many fine Renaissance buildings, including the Palace of the Grand Dukes. Trakai (http://trakai-visit.lt/en/) has an impressive lakeside fortress, dating from the fourteenth century, when Lithuania was a major power.

Although Lithuania has a much shorter coastline than its neighbours, this does include the remarkable Curonian Spit, a sand feature 100 kilometres in length, which separates an extensive lagoon from the Baltic Sea. Klaipeda (http://www.klaipedainfo.lt/en/), which is the country's only seaport, and Palanga (https://www.palangatic.lt/en/) are popular beach resorts on the mainland.

Discussion point: 'Dark tourism'

A number of visitor attractions in Eastern Europe draw upon the experiences of living under totalitarian rule and the near-annihilation of the region's formerly large Jewish population during the Second World War. These attractions include the 'House of Terror' (https://www.terrorhaza.hu/en) and Holocaust Museum (http://www.hdke.hu/en/) in Budapest, the Museum of the Occupation and Freedom Fights (http://genocid.lt/muziejus/en/) (housed in the former KGB headquarters) in Vilnius, and the Vabamu Museum (https://www.vabamu.ee/) in Tallinn. Likewise, a number of sites, of which Auschwitz is the best known, commemorate the experience of Nazi occupation in Poland, along with Terezin (http://www.terezin.cz/en/index.asp) in the Czech Republic. In the former Soviet Union, there has been a greater reluctance to acknowledge the atrocities committed under Stalin. Few of the sites of the former *gulags*, the notorious labour camps, where millions of political prisoners died as a result of the appalling conditions, can be visited. In part, this is due to the inaccessibility of many locations, particularly those in north-east Siberia.

Discuss how these 'dark tourism attractions' can handle the issues of death and suffering with sensitivity, without sensationalism and a 'theme park' approach to interpretation. Should visits to such places be part of the school curriculum?

The Commonwealth of Independent States (CIS)

Russia was very clearly the dominant country in the former Soviet Union. Its role is much less evident in the loose grouping of republics known as the Commonwealth of Independent States (CIS) that replaced the USSR in 1991, but which the Baltic States refused to join. In 2009, Georgia withdrew from the CIS, followed by the Ukraine in 2014. Russia has set up the Eurasian Economic Union (http://www.eaeunion.org/) in response to the challenge from the West, while Russia's vast resources of oil and natural gas provide a means of exercising control over the countries in what Russians call their 'near abroad', such as Georgia, Ukraine, and Belarus. This section of the chapter is written during the War in Ukraine, which has effectively wiped out tourism in Ukraine but is written in the hope that Ukraine's tourism will recover once peace is restored.

Russia (The Russian Federation)

Physical features

Although much smaller than the former USSR, the Russian Federation (https://europe.russia.travel/) is still almost twice the size of the United States and spans 11 time zones. In other words, a difference of half a day separates Kaliningrad on the Baltic coast, from Petropavlovsk on the Bering Sea, 12,000 kilometres (9,000 miles) to the east. As you might expect, there is a great range of climatic conditions in a landmass that also extends across nearly 40° of latitude, and we can broadly distinguish the following life zones, starting in the north:

- Treeless boggy tundra bordering the Arctic Ocean from the Kola Peninsula in the west to the Bering Straits in the east.

- The wide zone of the *taiga* – the world's largest forest – covering 8 million square kilometres of northern Russia, including the greater part of Siberia. Due to the harsh sub-arctic climate and poor soils, this is almost entirely dominated by a few tree species such as birch, firs, and larch.
- A belt of mixed forest, typifying the more varied landscapes of central European Russia.
- A zone of treeless grassland or steppe in the south, although most of this now lies in an independent Ukraine and Kazakhstan. This zone has very fertile 'black earth' soils and was the 'bread-basket' of the USSR, but it is often prone to devastating droughts.
- The high mountains along part of the southern border, namely the Caucasus and Altai ranges.
- Landscapes and climates comparable to those of the Mediterranean are found only in sheltered pockets along Russia's short Black Sea coastline.

The continental climate that characterises almost the whole of Russia is a major constraint on tourism development. Winters are severe – for example, snow lies on average for 150 days in Moscow and 160 days in St. Petersburg. Irkutsk (https://myirkutsk.info/en) typifies conditions in southern Siberia (see Figure 4.5). The *rasputitsa* (spring thaw) causes widespread disruption to communications for a period of about two weeks. Some 7 million square kilometres of Russia are affected by permafrost, which in parts of northern Siberia reaches a depth of 1,000 metres or more. Even here, the effects of climate change are evident; the permafrost is thawing, eroding river banks (and exposing mammoth remains), triggering landslides, creating lakes, and releasing greenhouse gases into the atmosphere.

Cultural features

The world's greatest land empire had modest beginnings as a collection of principalities in central European Russia, and it was a long time before the rulers of Moscow were able to establish their supremacy. With no secure natural borders, Russia was vulnerable to invasion, culminating in two centuries of domination by Tatars from the steppes of Central Asia. This traumatic experience had a lasting impact on the Russian psyche, as a yearning for strong, centralised government under the autocratic rule of the Tsars. Ivan the Terrible, Peter the Great, and Catherine the Great made Russia a great power, bringing many non-Slav peoples under their dominion. This raises the question whether Russia is more Asian than European in its cultural orientation. In the 1990s, the country seemed to be moving towards Western models of democracy, but this coincided with a period of economic hardship and social upheaval, accompanied by rampant crime and corruption, for most ordinary Russians. In the new millennium, Russia has reasserted its role as a great power, defying the international community with the annexation of Crimea.

As a result of this history of expansion and conquest, the Russian Federation is a mosaic of over 300 ethnic groups, although Russian Slavs account for perhaps 80 per cent of the population of around 144 million. There are 21 autonomous republics and 11 autonomous regions that represent the principal non-Russian minorities. As a result of *glasnost* (the policy of open government), religion and nationalist feeling, previously suppressed under Soviet Communism and official atheism, revived in the late 1980s. The Russian Orthodox Church has regained some of the prestige it enjoyed under the Tsars before the 1917 Revolution and about two-thirds of Russians profess to be Orthodox Christians. There is also a large Muslim minority, particularly in Tatarstan, and the area to the north-east of the Caucasus, including Dagestan, Ingusettia, and Chechnya (http://www.chechentourism.ru/). Here, the Chechens have a history of resistance to Russian rule and pose an ongoing terrorist threat.

The demand for tourism

Due to climate and other physical factors, the distribution of population is asymmetrical, affecting patterns and levels of tourism demand. Whereas 75 per cent of Russia's landmass is in Asia, this vast expanse accounts for only 22 per cent of the population. Demand is concentrated in a few major cities, whereas the rural areas are declining in population, and places dependent on a single industry, such as steel-producing Magnitogorsk in the Urals, face mass lay-offs and a fall in incomes. The social composition of Russia's population is unique in that females greatly outnumber males. The life expectancy of Russian males is the lowest in the developed world, partly due to alcohol-related diseases, aggravated by the COVID-19 pandemic.

Domestic tourism

Domestic tourism under the Soviet system was mainly the responsibility of the state-controlled trade unions. Health care and rest from labour was provided in a network of sanatoria and purpose-built holiday centres, which provided groups of workers with a subsidised, if somewhat regimented, two-week vacation. Only a small proportion of this accommodation was allocated to families, while children were catered for by the Young Pioneer camps. The transition to a market economy after 1990 dealt this system of subsidised domestic tourism a severe blow. *Perestroika* (the restructuring of the economy) was accompanied by rampant inflation and the devaluation of the rouble. The consequent rise in the prices of food and other essentials drastically reduced the amount of discretionary income available to the average citizen. The Ukraine and Georgia, which contained most of the Black Sea resorts, were now independent countries. The funding for subsidised holidays from public sector organisations was curtailed. As a result, tourism propensities are low compared to the European average. On the other hand, *glasnost* encouraged rising expectations, fuelling a demand for independent holidays on the Western model.

　The amount of leisure time available to Russians has, at least in theory, increased since 1990, and about half the workforce are entitled to 24 days of holiday with pay. With the demise of Communism, the public holiday that celebrated the October Revolution was replaced by The Day of National Unity, which has its roots deep in Russian history. Until 2004, Russians enjoyed nine consecutive days off in May, beginning with International Labour Day and ending on Victory in Europe Day on May 9. Now, they have equivalent free time in January, including the Russian Orthodox Christmas. Many in the business sector are convinced that this is costly to the economy, but any changes in the situation would be highly unpopular. Nevertheless, the demands of the market economy have forced many Russians to work harder than before.

Activity holidays have grown in popularity, especially canoeing, camping, and cross-country skiing. Russians on a touring holiday prefer to use *tubaza* (tourist bungalows), which provide cheap but basic accommodation. The trend for independent holidays will increase as car ownership levels rise – at present these are low by Western standards. Most Russian city dwellers have to be content with a stay nearer home, in a *dacha* (country cottage) in one of the villages on the outskirts, which they may own themselves, part-own through a garden co-operative, or rent.

Outbound tourism

Under Soviet Communism few Russians, with the exception of favoured groups, had the opportunity to travel abroad. Although the Russian Constitution of 1993 granted the freedom to travel abroad, continuing economic problems during the 1990s ensured that foreign travel was largely restricted to the *nouveau riches* 'New Russians' who had benefitted most from the transition to a market economy. The economic recovery that took place in the new millennium, largely as a result of the rise in oil and natural gas prices, the relaxation of visa restrictions, and the granting of traffic rights to foreign airlines, enabled much greater numbers to travel, to a wider range of destinations than hitherto. In 1995, only 2.6 million Russians took a holiday outside the former USSR; by 2008, this had risen to 11.3 million, and Russia joined the top ten tourist-generating countries, with one of the highest spends per capita. However, more recently numbers have declined due to the impact of a weak rouble, COVID-19, and the economic sanctions imposed by Western governments as a response to Russia's annexation of Crimea and invasion of Ukraine. By 2021, volume had recovered to 19.2 million outbound trips.

Inbound tourism

Inbound tourism contributed only a small proportion of the Soviet Union's foreign exchange earnings, and attitudes towards foreign visitors have been ambivalent since the times of the Tsars. Bureaucracy, an obsession with state security, and travel restrictions characterised Russia even before the 1917 Revolution and seem likely to persist long after the demise of Communism. Large areas were officially closed to foreign visitors, tourists had to follow approved itineraries, and stay only in officially designated accommodation. The Soviet authorities saw tourism as a means of promoting the achievements of the world's first socialist state, and in 1929, Intourist (https://www.intourist.com) was founded as an all-purpose agency to serve foreign visitors. Although most tourists were travelling for cultural rather than ideological reasons, official itineraries included visits to factories and collective farms. In 1957, international youth travel to the USSR became the responsibility of the Sputnik organisation, part of the Komsomol (League of Young Communists), with a network of camps and low-budget hotels. From 1966 onwards, investment in tourism infrastructure and training became part of the government's Five-Year Plans. Additional impetus was given by the choice of Moscow as the host city for the 1980 Olympic Games.

In 2018, international arrivals in Russia stood at 24.5 million, more than treble the number to the whole of the former USSR in 1990, but fell back to 6.3 million arrivals in 2020 due to COVID-19. Tourists from Western Europe greatly outnumber those from the former Eastern Bloc, with Germany, Israel, Italy, and France among the leading markets. In addition to sightseeing tours, hunting expeditions, river cruises, conference tourism, adventure holidays, and homestays with Russian families are available.

The supply side of tourism

The growth of Western-style tourism faces a number of problems, namely:

- The language barrier.
- Visa restrictions – large areas are still closed to visitors, ostensibly for military reasons.
- The lack of nightlife – although casinos are springing up in many cities throughout Russia, they are not always reputable.
- A continuing shortage of accommodation, particularly in the major centres, where hotels are pre-booked by the travel companies.
- Tour itineraries still need to be pre-booked and paid for in hard currency, leaving the independent traveller at a disadvantage.
- Foreign investment in the tourism industry, as in the economy generally, is deterred by the absence of a reliable banking system, bureaucratic inertia and corruption, and uncertainty over the laws relating to private property.
- The lack of small and medium-sized business enterprises.
- The prevalent low standards of service in hotels and restaurants.
- Russia's negative international reputation after the invasion of Ukraine.

On the other hand, the younger generation in the workforce is well-educated and eager to adopt Western-style methods.

Transport

The sheer size of Russia, the difficult climate and terrain of most of the country, and the undeveloped nature of surface transport imply that aviation has long played a major role. Many communities in Siberia are only really accessible by air, since they lie more than 1,600 kilometres from the nearest railhead, the earth roads are impassable during the spring thaw and the autumn rains, while the rivers are ice-free only in the brief summer.

In the former USSR, the state-owned Aeroflot had a monopoly of domestic air services, making it the world's biggest airline. With the break-up of the Soviet Union, it was likewise divided between the various republics, and separate national airlines emerged. PJSC Aeroflot-Russian Airlines (https://www.aeroflot.com/), reorganised as a joint-stock company in 1992, still provides a world-wide network like its Soviet predecessor. How-ever, its former domestic network, which provided service to 3,600 destinations in the USSR, was divided among many regional carriers. S7 (https://www.s7.ru/en/), part of the One World alliance (https://www.oneworld.com/), has emerged as Russia's leading do-mestic carrier and provides services to a large number of destinations, mainly in the CIS and Eastern Europe. Air fares remain relatively low, even for foreign tourists paying in US dollars. On the other hand, flights can be irregular due to recurrent fuel shortages, staff morale is affected by low pay, and aviation experts have alleged that safety standards are below those considered acceptable in the West, a situation that should change with the revival of Russia's aerospace industry. The FIFA World Cup in 2018 provided the stimulus for the host country to make substantial improvements to infrastructure, including a number of new airports.

We mentioned in Chapter 5 that Russia has the world's longest railway – the Trans-Siberian – that provides the major west-to-east transport link. Although the journey from Moscow to Nakhodka – a distance of almost 10,000 kilometres – takes over a week, and the trains make few concessions to tourism, the Trans-Siberian has become one of Russia's most sought-after travel experiences. Most rail services are cheap by Western standards but also slow, and security on the trains is a problem. Although it is now possible to drive from St Petersburg to Vladivostok on all-weather highways, road transport is defi-cient in many areas, except between major cities in European Russia, and the standard of maintenance tends to be below Western standards. On the other hand, Russia has a very extensive network of inland waterways. These link the great rivers Dnieper, Don, and Volga, which have played a major role in Russian history, to the Baltic, White, and Black Seas. In the summer months, fleets of hydrofoils ply the waterways with large numbers of domestic passengers, and Russian expertise in the field of hydrofoil design may yet see a new role for this type of vessel elsewhere. River cruises on more conventional ships are becoming increasingly popular with Western tourists, especially those linking St. Peters-burg to Moscow via Lakes Ladoga and Onega, which provide a leisurely way of absorbing the timeless quality of Russia's countryside.

Organisation

With the demise of the Soviet Union, Intourist lost its state monopoly and was pri-vatised, along with Sputnik (https://www.mowsput.com/). The Russian Economic Development Ministry now oversees tourism throughout the Russian Federation. Nev-ertheless, Intourist as a commercial organisation has advantages over its competitors, with offices in a number of Western and Asian countries, as well as an established network of agencies in all the countries of the former Soviet Union. It still owns and manages hotels and restaurants, arranges surface transportation for clients, organises excursions and tickets for cultural events, and supplies guides and interpreters. In the public sector, tourism is closely linked to physical culture and sports and is regulated by the 1996 Tourism Law. There is a strong organisation at city level that recognises the fact that most Western tourists to Russia spend at least part of their stay in the cities of St. Petersburg and Moscow. Indeed, the lack of tourism infrastructure elsewhere is a major constraint on visitation.

Tourism resources

Russia's tourism resources are primarily cultural, with a major concentration in the cities of Moscow and St Petersburg.

St. Petersburg (http://www.visit-petersburg.ru/en/) is probably the most beautiful city in Russia and occupies a special place in the country's history for these reasons:

- It was founded as the capital of the Russian Empire in 1703 by the modernising Tsar Peter the Great as Russia's 'window on the west'. No expense was spared to import the best European architects of the time to design a city on classical lines, with broad streets, canals, and impressive public buildings.
- The Bolshevik attack on the Winter Palace in October 1917 brought Lenin and the Communist Party to power in Russia (for this reason the city was renamed Leningrad during the Soviet era).
- The city endured an epic siege from 1941 to 1943, epitomising the almost unimaginable sacrifices made by the Russian people in the Second World War (known in Russia as the Great Patriotic War).

Due to its northerly latitude, St. Petersburg is best visited during the season of the 'white nights' (from May to July). Among its many cultural attractions, the following are of special significance:

- The Hermitage (https://www.hermitagemuseum.org) is one of the world's largest art collections, occupying the former Winter Palace of the Tsars.
- The Maryinsky Theatre (https://www.mariinsky.ru/en/), home of the renowned Kirov Ballet.
- The Church on the Spilled Blood (http://cathedral.ru/en), built in traditional Russian style, commemorates Tsar Alexander II, who liberated the serfs but was assassinated by revolutionary extremists.
- The former palaces of the Tsars on the outskirts of the city, which were restored by the Soviet government at enormous cost after the Second World War as part of the national heritage.

St. Petersburg is also convenient for excursions to the well-preserved medieval city of Novgorod (https://visitnovgorod.com/) and the island monasteries on Lakes Ladoga and Onega.

Moscow (https://discover.moscow/en) is a much older city compared to St Petersburg and is now a sprawling metropolis of 12 million people. The historic nucleus is the Kremlin (https://www.kreml.ru/en-us/) – the walled inner city of the Tsars and later the seat of power of the rulers of the USSR and the Russian Federation. It is adjoined by Red Square and Russia's most well-known building – St. Basil's Cathedral (https://en.shm.ru/museum/hvb/), with its distinctive onion domes. Under Stalin, the city acquired its Metro system – with ornately decorated stations – and 'wedding–cake' skyscrapers, one of which accommodates the University of Moscow. After the fall of Communism, a dynamic mayor embellished the capital with some impressive new projects, including the reconstructed

Cathedral of Christ the Saviour (http://new.xxc.ru/) – symbolic of the revival of the Russian Orthodox Church after 70 years of official atheism. Other attractions include:

- The Bolshoi Theatre (https://www.bolshoi.ru/en/), renowned for its touring ballet company.
- The Moscow State Circus (https://moscowstatecircus.com/), with some 16,000 performers.
- The Pushkin (https://pushkinmuseum.art/?lang=en) and Tretyakov (https://www.tretyakovgallery.ru/en/) art collections.
- The Exhibition of Economic Achievements (https://old.vdnh.ru/en/), showcasing technology.
- The Izmaylovo market, where the tourist can buy antique samovars, icons, and Soviet memorabilia.

Moscow also has one of the world's largest conference centres – the Palace of Congresses in the Kremlin. Moscow is a good base for excursions to the following places of interest in central Russia:

- The **Golden Ring** of historic towns to the north-east of the capital, including Rostov the Great, Vladimir, Sergiev Posad, and Suzdal. These have preserved much of the Old Russia of wooden 'onion-domed' churches, fortified *kremlins*, colourful Byzantine-style monasteries, traditional craft industries, and *troika* rides during the winter months.
- The country houses of Tchaikovsky at Klin, and of Tolstoy at Yasnaya Polyana (https://ypmuseum.ru/en.html) attract lovers of Russian music and literature.
- Star City, the centre of Russia's space programme.

The River Volga provides a major tourist route linking a number of important centres, including:

- Kazan (https://visitkazan.ru/en) – which is not only the capital of the largely Muslim Tatar republic but also one of the holy cities of the Russian Orthodox Church.
- Ulyanovsk (http://welcometoulyanovsk.com/) – famous as the birthplace of Lenin but attracting fewer tourists now than in the Soviet era.
- Volgograd (http://www.welcomevolgogradcity.com/) (formerly Stalingrad), scene of one of the epic battles of the Second World War, commemorated by the iconic statue of 'Mother Russia'.

The Ural Mountains to the east are important primarily for their mineral resources and industrial cities rather than their scenic attractions. Yekaterinburg (http://its.ekburg.ru/en/) is visited as the place, where, in 1918, Tsar Nicholas II and his family were murdered by the Bolsheviks. The building where this occurred was demolished in 1971 to prevent it from becoming a place of pilgrimage, but in 2003, an Orthodox Basilica – The Church on the Blood – was built on the site. The Monastery of the Holy Royal Martyrs nearby also attracts large numbers of pilgrims.

In north-western Russia, the port of Archangel is the base for visiting the island monasteries of Solovetsky in the White Sea, which acquired a sinister reputation soon after the Bolshevik Revolution as a prison for dissidents. Murmansk, despite its location well to the north of the Arctic Circle, is one of Russia's few ice-free ports and a 'boom town', thanks to the natural gas fields of the Barents Sea. Environmentalists are concerned at the threat to marine life and the international fishing industry.

In the extreme west, the Russian enclave of Kaliningrad, faced with the decline of its military importance, hopes to become a trading gateway to the European Union, once the problem of transit through Lithuania has been resolved. It is also exploiting its German heritage for tourism (until 1945 the city, then known as Königsberg, was the capital of East Prussia).

The Black Sea coast and Caucasus

Russia's Black Sea coast has long been a major holiday destination due to its agreeable climate. In the Soviet era, this formed part of a much more extensive 'Russian Riviera' that included the Crimea and part of Georgia. In the 1980s, Sochi (https://visit-sochi.org/) alone attracted 6 million tourists from all over the USSR to its beaches. Russia's principal Black Sea resort is now repositioning itself as a destination for Western holidaymakers. It is also close to the ski slopes of the northern Caucasus, favoured by the Russian elite, and for this reason the government made a massive investment in infrastructure and facilities for the 2014 Winter Olympics, and more recently the complex has hosted Formula 1 Grand Prix. Apart from a number of spas dating from the late nineteenth century and mountain climbing centres, the number of tourists to the northern Caucasus was restricted until recently, and the natural mountain habitats were largely undisturbed. Although part of the area is designated as a national park, state-controlled corporations have been given the go-ahead for large-scale development. From the viewpoint of international tourism, the northern Caucasus will be at a disadvantage until the problems in nearby Chechnya have been resolved.

Crimea

The warm climate and beautiful coastal scenery of the Crimean Peninsula – in contrast to the uniformity of the Ukrainian steppes – attracted the Russian nobility before the 1917 Revolution. Under Soviet Communism, resorts such as Yalta and Livadia were made available to all Soviet citizens, and following the collapse of the Soviet Union, to foreign tourists with hard currency to spend.

Russia's annexation of the Crimea Peninsula has once more made it a destination for domestic tourists, with government support, including subsidised holidays. In 2019, a 19-kilometre-long road and rail bridge was built, linking the Crimea to the Russian mainland, thus avoiding travel through Ukraine.

Siberia

Siberia comprises the vast expanse of the Russian Federation lying to the east of the Urals. Since the seventeenth century, Russians have regarded the territory with its wealth of furs

and minerals as a land of opportunity, but this has been overshadowed by a fearsome reputation as a place of exile and forced labour for dissidents. The large-scale eastward migration
of peasants from European Russia did not take until the late nineteenth century (at much
the same time as the United States was experiencing its great wave of westward expansion).

The western half of Siberia is predominantly lowland, with large expanses of peat bog
covered with forest. It also contains some of the world's largest reserves of natural gas.
Eastern Siberia is physically more varied and includes a number of mountain ranges.

Since the early 1990s, Siberia has to some extent been open to Western business enterprise and tourism, although for reasons of climate and accessibility most of the development has taken place in the south, based on the cities linked by the Trans-Siberian
Railway and its extension, the Baikal-Amur line. There are now opportunities for special
interest tourism undreamed of in the old Soviet Union, including:

- Whitewater rafting and ecotourism in the Altai Mountains, an area of unspoiled wilderness bordering Kazakhstan and Mongolia.
- Summer cruises on the great rivers, the Ob, Yenisei, and Lena, that flow northwards
  for 4,000 kilometres to the Arctic Ocean.
- Ecotourism and adventure holidays based at the spa resort of Listvyanka on the
  shores of Lake Baikal, one of the world's greatest natural attractions.

The cities of Siberia are of less interest to tourists, except for those that have preserved
the traditional wooden buildings of the pre-Soviet era, such as Tobolsk and Irkutsk. No-
vosibirsk, with its modern industries and universities, is the business capital of Siberia,
while the scientific community of Academgorok nearby is a centre for space research. In
Soviet times, the mining communities of northern Siberia were heavily subsidised by the
government in Moscow but now face an uncertain future.

Norilsk, a city of 184,000 inhabitants situated 300 kilometres north of the Arctic Circle, is a possible exception, due to its vast reserves of nickel. As one of the most polluted
places on Earth, it is the antithesis of what most people would regard as a tourist destination but acts as the gateway to one of the most scenic areas of Russia – the Putorama
Plateau. This is a region dissected by deep canyons and boasting spectacular waterfalls,
while much of the Taymyr Peninsula to the north is a protected nature reserve.

The non-Russian indigenous peoples of Siberia are better adapted to the extreme environment. Under Soviet Communism, their reindeer herds were collectivised and their
religious practices, such as shamanism suppressed. Some, like the Sakha (Yakuts) and the
Buryats, are enjoying a cultural renaissance, partly due to tourism. Tourism may provide a
market for traditional textiles and handicrafts made from materials such as reindeer horn
and mammoth ivory.

With the Cold War a distant memory, Russia's sector of the Arctic Ocean is slowly
opening up to the Western market for ecotourism. Most of the island of Novaya Zemlya,
along with the Franz Josef Land archipelago, has been designated as a national park,
although a massive clean-up operation was needed to remove military hardware. As yet,
only a small number of locations can be visited, and access to these is highly dependent
on the extent of pack ice and fog. Luxury cruises for wildlife viewing to Franz Josef Land
are on offer, using a nuclear-powered icebreaker with an onboard helicopter. For some of

these tourists, reaching the North Pole is the ultimate goal, although you might question their environmental credentials. At the present time, Russia's strategic Northern Sea Route from Murmansk to the Bering Sea is navigable only with a fleet of icebreakers during the brief summer season. Global warming would bring the centuries-old dream of a commercially viable 'Northeast Passage' to reality, shortening the sailing time from Europe to the Far East by a week but also posing a serious threat to Arctic ecosystems.

The Russian Far East

The Pacific coastal region is set to grow in importance as a result of closer trade links with China and Japan. Vladivostok (http://vladivostok.travel/en/), the base of Russia's Pacific fleet, has attracted foreign investment and is re-inventing itself as a business and entertainment centre, with numerous casinos. There is a potential market of 200 million gamblers living in China, South Korea, and Japan within two hours flying time of the city. Russia's Far East is influenced by the monsoon, and the forests include species that are typical of warmer climates further south. These resources, which include the rare Amur tiger, are under threat from illegal hunting and the logging industry.

Kamchatka (https://visitkamchatka.ru/en/), along with the volcanic Kurile Islands, form part of the 'Pacific Ring of Fire' we mentioned in Chapter 3. This region, despite its raw, foggy climate, and remote location, has considerable potential for ecotourism, with the ending of Cold War travel prohibitions, as it is geographically close to Alaska on the other side of the Bering Sea. Helicopter tours provide access to Kamchatka's resources, which include glaciers, no fewer than 33 active volcanoes, a large number of geysers and hot springs, salmon fisheries, and abundant wildlife. The Kurile Islands attract Russian surfers, in the absence of alternative destinations.

CASE STUDY 17.3
LAKE BAIKAL, 'THE PEARL OF SIBERIA'

Ecotourism in Russia is not yet as developed as in the West, and the fledgling environmental movement faces many obstacles from industry and government. The controversy over development around Lake Baikal is a good example.

Lake Baikal (https://1baikal.ru/en/) is a major tectonic feature, over 1600 metres in depth, which is estimated to contain a fifth of the world's fresh water. The lake supports a variety of unique species, including seals, making it a natural laboratory for scientific research. Such an extensive body of water has a moderating effect on the local climate, giving it maritime features, but even so by late February, the lake is covered by ice 70–110 cm thick, which melts in early May.

As early as 1916, Russia's first nature reserve was established here, but it was not until 1987 that the entire lake shore was protected from logging and other development by designation as a national park. This was partly in response to many years of campaigning by local communities, who had opposed the building of a cellulose plant at the mouth of the Selenga River. Even though the water is remarkably pure by European standards, Baikal's ecology continues to be threatened by effluent from pulp mills, fertilisers, and air pollution originating in the nearby cities of Irkutsk and Ulan Ude.

Discussion point

Political and economic circumstances make the environmentalist's task more difficult in Russia than in the West. What further measures could be taken to protect Lake Baikal

Ukraine

As we mentioned earlier, this section was written during the War in Ukraine, which has effectively closed tourism and destroyed many tourism resources. Ukraine (https://www.ukraine.com/) is by far the largest of the group of countries that the European Union regards as its 'neighbours to the east' for closer co-operation, the others being Belarus, Moldova, and the countries south of the Caucasus – Georgia, Armenia, and Azerbaijan. Incomes are much lower than in the European Union, and this has fuelled a massive flow of emigrants seeking a better life in the West. The unacceptable face of this new mobility is the trafficking in young women to supply the sex tourism industry in Western Europe. Tourism development also lags behind countries in the European Union.

In the 2003 'Orange Revolution', confirmed by the 2014 'Maidan Revolution' in Kiev (Kyiv), Ukraine loosened its economic ties with Russia and made progress towards democracy and a market economy. Nevertheless, this remains a country divided between the Russian-speaking east and the Ukrainian-speaking centre and west. These differences came to a head in 2016, with dissidents in the Donbas industrial region setting up republics in defiance of Kiev, and with Russia's backing.

The western part of Ukraine was ruled by the Austro-Hungarian Empire until 1918, and subsequently, became part of Poland. Eastern and central Ukraine had been part of the Russian Empire for centuries, and the Cossacks of the Don played a major role in its expansion. As part of the USSR, Ukraine bore the brunt of Stalin's forced collectivisation of agriculture in the 1930s, and the resulting famine is commemorated by the Holodomor monument (https://holodomormuseum.org.ua/en/) in Kiev.

Tourism resources

Before the 2022 invasion, Ukraine was better known for its agricultural and industrial resources than for its tourist attractions. Yet the country's landscapes are much more diverse than the image of fields of sunflowers and wheat stretching to the horizon. Winters are less severe than in Russia, with snow lying an average of 80 days in Kiev. The State Service for Tourism and Resorts is responsible for promotion, but development is hindered by deficient infrastructure and sub-standard accommodation. Kiev is the hub of Ukraine International Airlines (www.flyuia.com), and there are a number of domestic airlines competing with the rail network and long-distance bus services. Kiev Dynamos (http://www.fcdynamo.kiev.ua/en/) is a football team that has gained international fame, and in 2012, Ukraine co-hosted (with Poland) the Euro football championship.

The Ukraine's attractions include:

- Kiev (https://visitkyiv.travel/), the capital, attractively sited on the River Dnieper, was historically the nucleus of the first Russian state before its destruction by the Tatar invasions in the thirteenth century. The surviving medieval heritage includes the Caves Monastery (https://lavra.ua/en/) and the Cathedral of Saint Vladimir (http://katedral.org.ua/).
- Lviv (https://lviv.travel/en) is the principal city of western Ukraine and boasts many Baroque buildings and a European cafe culture as reminders of its Austrian and Polish heritage.
- The forested Carpathians offer a number of ski resorts, catering mainly for domestic demand. Trans-Carpathia, lying to the south of the mountains, changed hands many times in the course of the twentieth century. Then known as Carpathian Ruthenia, it was part of Czechoslovakia from 1918 to 1938, before enjoying a very brief period of independence.
- Odessa (http://www.odessatourism.org/en/) was founded by Catherine the Great and her favourite Potemkin as the Russian Empire's major port on the Black Sea. It is renowned for its beaches, vibrant nightlife, theatres, and elegant architecture.

Belarus

Belarus (https://www.belarus.by/en/) has been slow to change from a centrally planned economy and exemplifies the problems faced by the former Soviet republics in promoting a tourist image and identifying a unique selling proposition (USP). At first sight, the resource base is not particularly promising; the country has been overshadowed by Poland and Russia and repeatedly invaded throughout its history though this has left a legacy of important castles such as Mir and Nyasvizh. On the other hand, Belarus can offer the largest remaining area of the unmodified mixed forest that once covered most of Europe, interspersed with extensive marshes and peat bogs. There is potential here for ecotourism, as well as hunting and fishing trips, as currency earners. The forest also produces the raw materials for the traditional craft industries that have largely disappeared elsewhere. As for the cities, Brest and Minsk lie on the main route from the West to Moscow, and although transit tourism is important, there is as yet little to persuade visitors to stay for longer periods.

As the host nation for the 2014 World Ice Hockey Championship, Belarus relaxed its visa requirements for foreign visitors and made much-needed improvements to transport infrastructure. Nevertheless, low-cost carriers are not encouraged, and the national airline Belavia (https://en.belavia.by/) dominates the sector.

CASE STUDY 17.4
CHERNOBYL: FROM MAN-MADE DISASTER TO 'DARK TOURISM' ATTRACTION

On April 26, 1986, a series of explosions occurred at the Chernobyl nuclear reactor in the Ukrainian SSR, then part of the Soviet Union. This incident, and the subsequent attempt by the authorities to cover-up the extent of the disaster, was one of the factors leading to the break-up of the USSR. Exposure to the radio-active fallout led to 40 immediate deaths and the prolonged suffering of many thousands. Entire towns were evacuated, and an area within a 40-kilometre radius of the reactor, including much of Belarus as well as Ukraine, was declared uninhabitable. Fast-forward to 2011, when the Ukrainian government began sponsoring official guided tours to Chernobyl when radiation levels had returned to normal, and these have since proven to be a lucrative source of foreign exchange. Tourists based in Kiev are taken to the Exclusion Zone around Chernobyl, visiting the nuclear power plant and the nearby abandoned town of Prypiat, which is like a 'time capsule' with its buildings and the Ferris Wheel in the park remaining intact. Eating, drinking, and smoking in the open air are banned to avoid the long-term risk of radiation. Some tours include visits to a missile base from the Cold War era and the opportunity to try out military hardware.

Much of the Exclusion Zone has become in effect a nature reserve. The forests have recovered and local wildlife appears to be thriving, taking advantage of the absence of people. Species include elk, wild boar, brown bear, and the rare Przewalski horse.

Moldova

Between 1918 and 1945, Romania ruled over Moldova, then known as Bessarabia, and the two countries share a similar language and culture. However, there is a large Russian minority with separatist ambitions who have created a de facto state within Moldova – Transdniestria – a potential flashpoint, since it is recognised by Russia but not the rest of the international community. Moldova has the advantage of a relatively warm, sunny climate that favours large-scale wine production, so not surprisingly, wine tours feature prominently among the country's tourist attractions. The government also plans to develop cultural tourism based on the capital, Chisinau, rural tourism, and 'health and beauty' tourism – which is problematic, given the country's poor infrastructure. Other attractions include Chisinau Zoo and Bendery Fortress.

The countries south of the Caucasus

The three countries to the south of the natural barrier formed by the Caucasus Mountains have more in common with the Mediterranean region or the Middle East than with Russia. Their European credentials are shown by participation in a number of sport and cultural events. However, while Orthodox Christianity is central to the national identity of Armenia and Georgia, Azerbaijan is predominantly Muslim and has fostered close trade links with the Central Asian republics east of the Caspian Sea. All three countries have great tourism potential – a favourable climate, spectacular scenery, a rich cultural heritage going back to ancient times, and populations with a tradition of hospitality and business enterprise. Yet the prospects for tourism and economic development have been blighted since the late 1980s by inter-communal violence, for example, the dispute between Armenia and Azerbaijan over the enclave of Nagorno-Karabagh (now the republic of Artsakh), and the separatist movements in Georgia. The failure to resolve these disputes by peaceful means is an obstacle not only to regional co-operation in tourism promotion but also to the exploitation of the oil resources of the Caspian Basin and the development of trade links with the West. Armenia has, for example, opposed the BTK (Baku-Tiflis-Kars) railway project linking Azerbaijan to Turkey.

Georgia

Georgia (https://georgia.travel/) has a well-established reputation throughout Russia for its wines and for the 'good life', in contrast to the mediocre catering that is characteristic of most of the former USSR, while its national dance troupe has achieved international fame. Since the 2003 'Rose Revolution', Georgia has been ruled by a government with strong pro-Western sympathies. However, the country's economic development has been hampered by the difficulties with Russia over the separatist movements in Abkhazia and South Ossetia, which culminated in a brief war between the two countries in 2008. Abkhazia, in Soviet times, attracted millions of Russians to the Black Sea resorts of Sukhumi, Gagra, and Pitsunda. In 1991, the tourism industry here was devastated by the civil war between the central government in Tblisi and Abkhazian separatists. The breakaway state that emerged is recognised by few countries other than Russia, and tourism has not recovered.

The Georgia National Tourism Administration (GNTA) (https://gnta.ge/) under the Ministry of Economy and Sustainable Development is responsible for promoting Georgia abroad. Tourism accounts for 6.5 per cent of GDP and 10 per cent of jobs, mitigating the loss of Russian markets to the economy. The great majority of visitors are from neighbouring countries, with Turkey in the lead. The GNTA is seeking new markets in the European Union, promoting wine tourism, ecotourism, and adventure tourism. The positioning of Georgia as a conference destination is problematic, as the capital, Tblisi, has limited hotel capacity. Most of the hotel bed spaces are in the autonomous region of Ajaria in the south-west of the country.

Tourism resources

*   Tblisi and Kutaisi, the second city, contain most of the country's cultural attractions.
*   Gudauri (https://www.gudauri.info/) in the Caucasus Mountains is a centre for winter sports and trekking.
*   Ajaria's beaches and lush subtropical landscapes, featuring tea plantations and lemon orchards, attract foreign and domestic tourists. Batumi (http://gobatumi.com/en/home), the regional capital, is a port of call for cruise ships.

- The caves of David Garej and the Uplistsikhe Cave Town-Fortress.
- Gori is significant as the birthplace of Stalin, the Georgian who rose from humble beginnings to dominate the USSR between 1928 and 1953.

Armenia

Tourism in Armenia (http://armenia.travel/en) has been overshadowed by the effects of the 1988 earthquake, the country's landlocked situation with two hostile neighbours, and historical memories of the 1915 genocide of a million Armenians, commemorated by a museum and monument in the capital, Yerevan (http://www.genocide-museum.am/eng). The snow-capped peak of Ararat is a holy mountain and national symbol for Armenians, dominating the horizon in Yerevan, yet it is virtually inaccessible as it lies across the border in Turkey. The economy is dependent on remittances from the millions of ethnic Armenians living in the United States, Canada, France, and Russia. Armenia's physical isolation as a high plateau separated by mountain barriers from its neighbours is reinforced by border tensions and the lack of rail, road, and even air links with Azerbaijan and Turkey.

Nevertheless, a number of low-cost airlines now connect Yerevan with countries in Western Europe. The National Competitiveness Foundation (NCFA), a partnership between the government and international business leaders of Armenian descent, aims to develop key areas of economic activity, with tourism as a high priority. Armenia received 1.9 million arrivals in 2019, but the majority of these are ethnic tourists, staying with friends or relatives, and in self-catering accommodation rather than hotels. The European Union accounts for 38 per cent of tourist arrivals, while 13 per cent come from the United States and Russia's share of the market is growing.

Armenia can claim to be the world's oldest Christian nation, and hoped to boost tourism by staging celebrations for the 1700th anniversary in 2003. In fact, the country's main attractions are the ancient churches and monasteries in a spectacular lake and mountain setting. Lake Sevan, at an altitude of 2,000 metres, is a popular summer destination for both domestic tourists and visitors from neighbouring Iran, who are free for a while from the restrictions imposed by Islamic rule. The mountains provide ideal conditions for paragliding, and apart from adventure tourism, there is potential for the development of agritourism and ecotourism.

Azerbaijan

Azerbaijan (https://azerbaijan.travel/) has immense oil resources, and for this reason, it has attracted a much greater amount of foreign investment than Armenia and Georgia combined. The Ministry of Culture and Tourism has ensured that a good deal of this money has gone into hotel building in the capital, Baku, for a new wave of business tourists. Some of the oil wealth is being used to conserve the rich cultural heritage that has affinities with Iran and Turkey, creating a system of ten national parks. Although Baku has been an oil boom town before, in the early years of the twentieth century, much remains from earlier periods, and the well-preserved historic quarter has a strong Middle

Eastern ambience with its minarets and bazaars. Azerbaijan has considerable biodiversity, from mountain and desert landscapes in the west to the subtropical coastlands along the Caspian Sea in the east, while ecotourism has an important role to play in stemming the depopulation of small rural communities.

Azerbaijan hosted the first European Games (http://www.european-games.org/) in 2015 and aims to attract other international sports events. To achieve this, improvements in transport infrastructure will be needed.

The Central Asian republics

Central Asia to the east of the Caspian Sea is a vast expanse of steppe and desert, punctuated by fertile river valleys, and separated from China to the east by some of the world's highest mountain ranges. Throughout recorded history, the steppes of Central Asia have been the breeding ground of nomadic warrior tribes who periodically threatened the security of the civilisations to the west, east, and south. In contrast, oasis cities such as Samarkand were important in ancient times as trading centres. Russian rule came late to the region and was imposed on civilisations that had evolved over many centuries. The Russians, particularly during the Soviet era, introduced modern industries, education, and a number of new cities, notably Tashkent and Almaty (https://visitalmaty.kz/). Nevertheless, the Muslim religion and heritage remain dominant, despite seven decades of official atheism. The Soviet authorities were also responsible for most of the environmental problems in the region. The best-known example is the shrinkage of the Aral Sea, which was brought about by vast irrigation projects for cotton cultivation. This has resulted in a deterioration of the local climate, with salt and sand-laden winds blowing in from the dried-up lake bed. With the sudden demise of the USSR in 1991, the republics were unprepared for independence. Instead of an orderly transition to democracy, there was the imposition of one-man rule by former Communist party bosses. Border disputes caused disruption to road and rail communications. The effect of 9/11 and the ongoing conflict in neighbouring Afghanistan was to align the Central Asian republics with the United States, to counter the threat of Islamic fundamentalism to their secular, authoritarian regimes.

Approaches to tourism vary, but generally tour operators in the new private sector are more efficient than the state-run organisations. A variety of accommodation is now available, including international hotel chains, small hotels and apartments in the major cities, and homestays provided by some rural communities. These include yurts, the traditional dwellings of the nomads.

Uzbekistan

Most of Uzbekistan's 35 million inhabitants are concentrated along the Syr Darya river in the west of the country and the Fergana Valley in the south-east. Prior to the Russian conquest in the late nineteenth century, cities such as Khiva and Bukhara were ruled by despotic khans and forbidden to Westerners.

Uzbekistan has the richest cultural heritage in the region and has a well-developed tourism industry, albeit one that still discourages independent travel. The country can offer ethnic diversity, colourful markets heaped with melons and other produce, and bustling bazaars, a reminder that this is a meeting place of Russian, Turkish, Middle Eastern, and Chinese cultures. In 2022, over 5 million international tourist arrivals were recorded. The capital Tashkent is a modern city and important conference venue with a Metro system and an airport that is the major hub of Central Asia. The Fergana Valley in which it is situated is a fertile agricultural region, but prone to earthquakes. However, tourism is mainly concentrated in the historic oasis cities of Khiva, Samarkand, and Bukhara:

- Samarkand is the best known of the cities on the 'Silk Road', the overland trade route that linked the Mediterranean to China. It boasts one of the world's most striking Islamic monuments – the Registan, resplendently decorated in blue tiles and gold leaf.
- Khiva with its medrassas (Islamic colleges) and former palaces is a perfectly preserved 'museum-city'.
- Bukhara in contrast is a hive of activity.

Kazakhstan

This vast landlocked country is larger than Western Europe in extent and four times the size of Texas, with a population of only 19 million. Although steppe and desert landscapes make up most of Kazakhstan (https://kazakhstan.travel/), lakes, wetlands, and spectacular mountain ranges along the border with China provide significant biodiversity and the potential for ecotourism. It is also culturally diverse; while Kazakhs make up half the population, there are considerable numbers of Russians along with ethnic Germans and other minorities from all over the former Soviet Union who were deported here en masse during the Stalin era. The republic's vast empty spaces also made it an ideal testing ground for military hardware. One legacy of this is the Baikonur space centre.

Due largely to its vast petroleum and natural gas resources, Kazakhstan more than doubled its GDP between 2000 and 2008. It is a leading member of the Eurasian Economic Community (EEC) and has ambitions to be a global player on the world tourism stage. The government has created a national brand – 'Kazakhstan – the Heart of Eurasia' based on its geographical location. A number of international conferences and sport events, notably the 7th Asian Winter Games in 2011, hosted by the cities of Almaty and Nur-Sultan (formerly Astana), have put the country firmly on the tourist map. Kazakhstan received 6.7 million tourist arrivals in 2019, mainly from neighbouring countries, but also from China, Turkey, and Ukraine, but this fell to 2 million in 2020 due to COVID-19. A growing middle class generates a significant volume of domestic and outbound tourism.

Tourism promotion is the responsibility of the Kazakhstan Tourist Association (http://www.kaztour-association.com), which is a co-operative non-profit organisation under the Ministry of Culture and Sport. Tourism activities include whitewater rafting on the River Ili, skiing and ice skating in the resort of Medeo, and trekking in the Altai and Tien Shan Mountains.

Astana (Nur-Sultan), located in the middle of the northern steppe, replaced Almaty as the capital in 1997 and boasts a range of impressive buildings. For example, the Khan Shatyr entertainment complex (http://www.khanshatyr.com/en) respects national traditions in its design, which is a response to the extreme continental climate, with temperatures ranging from -30°C in winter to 35° in summer. The complex includes a tropical beach, an attractive feature in a country which is more than 3,000 kilometres from the nearest ocean.

Kyrgystan

Most of Kyrgystan (http://www.discoverkyrgyzstan.org/) is situated at high altitudes. The country is dominated by the glaciated Tian Shan mountains and offers considerable scope for adventure tourism and equestrian activities. The main attraction is Issyk Kül, the world's second largest alpine lake. This has long been a destination for health tourism and now also offers kayaking and other water sports.

Tajikistan

Tajikistan (https://traveltajikistan.tj/) is a small country with few natural resources dominated by the Pamirs, one of the world's most rugged mountain ranges. Throughout the 1990s, it was the most politically unstable of the Central Asian republics, and this has held back the development of its tourism industry. The country was the least affected by a century of Russian rule, and traditional lifestyles still prevail.

Turkmenistan

Turkmenistan consists essentially of a ring of populated areas surrounding the empty Kara Kum desert. The country is noted for the traditional carpet weaving industry based in the modern capital, Ashqabad and the historic city of Merv. With vast reserves of natural gas at its disposal, the government sees little need to encourage leisure tourism, with the exception of a large luxury resort development on the coast of the Caspian Sea.

CASE STUDY 17.5
THE SILK ROAD

Until the sixth century AD, China was the world's only source of silk, and its manufacture was a closely guarded secret. Silk was in great demand by the ancient Mediterranean civilisations as a luxury product, to the extent that the cost of importing it may well have contributed to the decline of the Roman Empire. The 'Silk Road' linking Xian in China to the Mediterranean was, in fact, a series of overland trade routes, and in rugged mountain regions such as the Pamirs, the track could only be negotiated by camel caravans proceeding in single file. Because of the great distances and the physical dangers of desert and mountain travel, very few travellers ever undertook the complete journey. For the most part silk and other commodities such as satin, musk, and precious stones, some originating in the Indian sub-continent, were traded at a number of staging points along the route through intermediaries. Oasis towns such as Samarkand and Bukhara grew rich and culturally cosmopolitan as a result of the interchange, not only in goods but also in religious ideas and technological innovations (for example, paper manufacture, gunpowder).

In 1993, the World Tourism Organisation began a long-term project to promote the Silk Road as a tourist route. This was given additional impetus with the 2002 Bukhara Declaration that such development should be sustainable. The project has done much to relax irksome border restrictions for foreign travellers and improve professionalism among those working in the tourism sector in the participating countries. Tourists can now follow in the footsteps of Marco Polo, the thirteenth century Venetian merchant-adventurer, but travel in relative comfort and stay in international standard hotels. However, much needs to be done to improve the road networks in Central Asia and transportation links between Europe and Asia generally. This problem is being addressed by international co-operation through the United Nations Economic and Social Commission for Asia and the Pacific (UNESCAP) (https://www.unescap.org/), with funding from the Asia Development Bank (https://www.adb.org/). Much of the impetus for development is provided by China through the 'Belt and Road' programme.

Summary

- A long period of state control over tourism, lasting 40 years in Eastern Europe and 70 years in the former Soviet Union, has left a legacy that strongly differentiates these countries from those of Western Europe.
- Since 1989, this has been followed by a strong liberalising trend, characterised by economic restructuring, foreign investment, privatisation, and the encouragement of local initiative. Western involvement in the development of tourism has greatly increased.
- The Ukraine War has significantly disrupted tourism in the region.
- Entry, exit, and currency restrictions were severe under the Communist regimes but have eased with their demise.
- The former regimes encouraged social tourism linked to health and education, but as incomes rise with the successful transition to a market economy, Western-style domestic tourism will increase in significance.
- Outbound tourism in Eastern Europe and Russia is showing more rapid growth as the economy improves. Entry to the European Union by a number of countries in the region has encouraged investment in tourism and boosted demand.

- The removal of Communism has improved the image of the region in Western eyes. This needs to be reinforced by each country, emphasising its individual attractions. The differences between countries were previously concealed by the grey uniformity of Communism and are now much more evident.
- There is increasing scope for innovation in tourism products and niche marketing. Some countries, notably the Czech Republic, have made much more progress than others.
- External air links to Eastern Europe have improved, but there is a danger that the encouragement of mass tourism in the form of short city breaks might well result in the region's cities becoming a cheap playground for West Europeans.
- Environmental problems are already widespread, and ecotourism is in its infancy in most of these countries.
- Internal transport systems need to be improved, to cope with rising car ownership levels and the expectations of Western tourists.
- Future growth in tourism could also be severely constrained by the negative factors of political instability, ethnic strife, and rising crime levels, as economic growth fails to meet people's expectations.
- Poor standards of service, and mediocre products may also deter tourists, once the novelty of visiting a previously 'forbidden' destination has faded.

Review questions

1. Identify the most significant changes that have taken place since 1990 in (a) the structure of tourism and (b) tourist flows in Eastern Europe and the CIS.
2. Describe some of the environmental problems impacting on tourism in Eastern Europe and Russia, and explain why these are difficult to resolve.
3. Explain the importance of infrastructure for the development of business tourism and Western-style leisure tourism in Eastern Europe and the CIS.
4. Explain the significance of cultural attractions for inbound tourism in Russia and specific countries in Eastern Europe.
5. Analyse the factors influencing the demand for domestic and outbound tourism in Russia and specific countries in Eastern Europe.

Further reading

Organization for Economic Co-operation and Development (annual) *Tourism Policy and International Tourism in OECD Member Countries*, OECD, Paris

https://www.unwto.org/tourism-data/unwto-tourism-dashboard

Africa and the Middle East

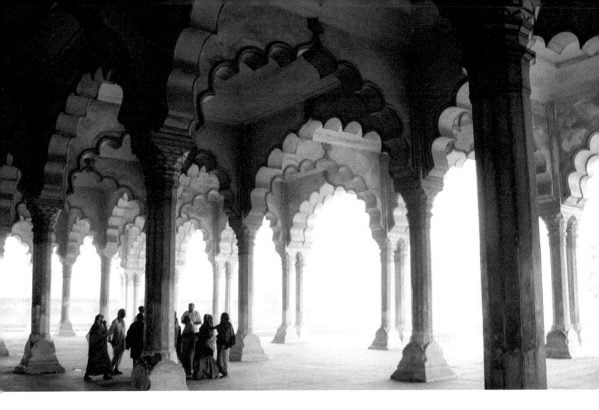

18 The tourism geography of the Middle East

Learning objectives

After reading this chapter, you should be able to:

- Describe the major physical features and climate of the countries of the Middle East region and understand their importance for tourism.
- Appreciate that inbound tourism to the region encompasses beach holidays, cultural tourism, and business travel.
- Identify the major features of tourist infrastructure in the region, particularly organisation, transport, and accommodation.

DOI: 10.4324/9781003406853-22

- Understand the impact of the political instability and recent conflicts in the region on tourism.
- Demonstrate knowledge of the tourist regions, resorts, business centres, and tourist attractions of the region.

Introduction

Our definition of the Middle East differs from that of the UN World Tourism Organisation (UNWTO) by including Iran and excluding Libya. Moreover, the UNWTO regards Israel as part of Europe, but not Palestine, which makes little sense geographically. We include the countries of south-west Asia and the Levant – the eastern seaboard of the Mediterranean (with the exceptions of Turkey and Cyprus). Vast petroleum resources and the Arab-Israeli conflict have brought the Middle East under the international spotlight since the Second World War, including the Gulf War of 1990–1991, the Iraq War in 2003, the turmoil following the 'Arab Spring' since 2011, and the civil wars in Syria and Yemen. However, these are but recent episodes in a history of trade, migration, and conquest that goes back at least to the third millennium BC. The Middle East is strategically located at the crossroads of trade routes linking the Mediterranean to the Indian Ocean and the Far East – and at the interface of three continents – Europe, Asia, and Africa. The component countries are similar in much of their physical geography. Similarities in religion, language, architecture, food specialities, and other aspects of lifestyle, plus a shared historical experience link almost all of the countries in the region, together with those of North Africa.

Cultural features

As far as the cultural similarities are concerned, you should be aware that:

- All but two of the countries in the region (Israel and Iran) are Arabic speaking. Classical Arabic is the language of the Koran, but many dialects are used in everyday speech. However, the Egyptian version of Arabic is widely understood throughout the Middle East and North Africa due to the influence of the media based largely in Cairo.
- All of these countries (except for Iran), at one time formed part of the Ottoman Empire based in Constantinople (now Istanbul). During much of the twentieth century, Britain exercised various forms of control over most of the countries in the region, while France was active in Syria and Lebanon. Events in the new millennium have confirmed the United States as the dominant power in the Middle East.
- The Middle East is predominantly Muslim in religion, except for Israel and Lebanon. It is estimated that Muslims will make up 25 per cent of the world's population by

2050. The demand for tourism in Muslim countries has several features that distinguish it from the West.

• Matters are complicated by the fact that the Muslim world is divided on sectarian lines, with the Sunni branch of Islam dominant in most Arab countries, while the adherents of Shia are more numerous in Iraq and Iran.

• There are substantial ethnic as well as religious minorities in most countries of the region (Iraq and Syria are classic examples), while the Kurds, 'a nation without a state', are divided between Turkey, Iraq, Iran, and Syria. Christians and other minorities are threatened by the rise of Islamic fundamentalism.

Western perceptions of Islam have been strongly influenced, on the one hand, by historical memories of the Crusades and the threat posed to Europe by the Ottoman Empire, and on the other, by highly romanticised images of the region created by European writers and artists in the nineteenth century. More recently, unfavourable publicity in the Western media has been a reaction to the growth of Islamic fundamentalism. Although it is true to say that, in this secular age, religion plays a greater role in everyday life in Muslim countries than in most other parts of the world, the influence of Islam does in fact vary greatly in strength from country to country. Only a few governments, for example, impose *sharia law* based on the Koran, rather than Western legal systems. Attitudes towards the status of women and towards foreign tourists also range from the strict (for example, Saudi Arabia) to the relatively liberal (Jordan, Lebanon, and the United Arab Emirates). Nevertheless, female participation in the workforce is generally much lower than in western Europe, and there is also a below average proportion of female travellers. We should take into account the following aspects of Islam as they influence the tourist experience and business practice:

• The mosque with its distinctive minaret forms a dominant feature in the skyline, but as figurative art is discouraged by the Koran, the decorative features of traditional architecture tend to be limited to abstract patterns or inscriptions in Arabic.

• The obligation of Muslims to pray five times a day with special emphasis on Friday (the Muslim Sabbath).

• The requirement to fast between sunrise and sunset during the month of Ramadan, the fifth month of the Muslim year. As this is based on a lunar calendar, the timing of Ramadan varies from year to year. In dealing with Muslim clients, the hospitality sector has to take into account *halal* dietary requirements, the timing of meal times during Ramadan, and the provision of facilities for religious observance.

• At least once in a lifetime, Muslims should make the pilgrimage or *haj* to the holy city of Mecca, the birthplace of Mohammed. The haj takes place during the 12th month of the Muslim year, resulting in a mass movement of people that is concentrated both in time and space. There are also secondary pilgrimages known as *umrah* that can be undertaken throughout the year. The pilgrim routes extending to all parts of the Muslim world became important for trade, and were therefore, well-supplied with inns (known as *khans*, *fonduks*, or *caravanserais*). Some of these traditional types of accommodation still survive (although the camel caravan has long since been replaced by motorised transport). The demand for pilgrimages has proved resilient to the economic and political crises that have afflicted the Middle East.

Another important cultural feature of the region is the contrast between the cities and the countryside, where settled and nomadic lifestyles appear to have changed little since biblical times. Even in the cities, the older districts have a seemingly chaotic street pattern, while the colourful *souks* and bazaars retain many traditional features. These are essentially covered markets, with whole sections devoted exclusively to a particular trade or type of merchandise. Traditional domestic architecture is characterised by rooms opening off an enclosed courtyard, allowing privacy for the extended family and protection from the sun. The major cities have well laid-out, modern districts similar to those of Europe – Tel Aviv is a good example here – very different in character from the adjoining Arab town of Jaffa with its maze of twisting, narrow streets.

Physical features

There is no clear physical break (the Suez Canal and Red Sea hardly count) and, as we have seen, no distinct cultural boundary between North Africa and Asia. Most of the Middle East region forms part of the arid climate zone, and irrigation is essential. Agriculturally, productive land is restricted to a few areas that, in turn, have attracted the great majority of the population, concentrated in these areas at densities exceeding those of Western Europe. They comprise:

- The coastal plains adjoining the Mediterranean and Caspian Seas, which enjoy relatively good rainfall.
- A narrow strip along the river Nile in Egypt.
- The alluvial plains of the rivers Tigris and Euphrates, which link up with the Mediterranean coastal plain in Syria to form the 'Fertile Crescent'.

To the east of the coastal strip, mountain ranges and high plateaux prevent rain-bearing winds from penetrating further into the interior. Often the dividing line between the desert 'wilderness' and the cultivated area is very distinct. Not surprisingly, water supply and distribution is a major problem in the Middle East, and this precious resource is the subject of local and even international disputes.

Most of the region is characterised by extremes of heat in summer, and even the Mediterranean coast can be oppressive. In winter, the weather is usually mild or pleasantly warm, with the important exception of some mountain areas that experience heavy snowfalls. Conditions are particularly severe in Kurdistan, where temperatures are comparable to those of Russia. Cold overcast weather is not uncommon – even as far south as Amman and Jerusalem which are situated at quite high altitudes – in contrast to the sub-tropical warmth and sunshine of the Red Sea coast.

Tourism demand and supply

Considering its location and resources, the Middle East region accounts for a relatively small share of world tourism – around 5.0 per cent of arrivals. The countries of the Middle East are close enough to the inclusive tour markets of northwest Europe to have developed a tourism industry based on sun, sea, and sand. This is a logical extension of the coastal resort developments of Mediterranean Europe, facilitated by improvements in air transport. However, the response to this opportunity has been uneven, with some countries, such as Dubai, investing heavily in tourism in an attempt to diversify the economy. Most countries with the potential to enter the market have only done so since the 1980s. Long before the expansion of mass tourism, Israel and Egypt had based their tourism industries on the attractions of the Holy Land and the relics of ancient civilisations. More recently, the oil-based prosperity of Saudi Arabia and the Gulf states has attracted a large business travel market. There is also a considerable volume of travel between countries in the region, involving business tourism, returning migrant workers visiting relatives, pilgrimages, and health tourism.

Contrary to popular belief in the West, only some of the countries in the Middle East have become affluent on oil resources, so that foreign exchange earnings from tourism are needed to even out regional imbalances. Even in the oil-rich countries, tourism is now being viewed as an opportunity to diversify the economy as the world becomes less dependent on oil. The population, as in most developing countries, contains a high percentage of young people, and tourism is seen as a means of providing much-needed employment. In fact, since the 1980s, economic development has not kept pace with population growth, leading to a decline in living standards. With only modest progress in education, telecommunications, and access to information technology, most countries in the region are ill-equipped to meet the challenge of globalisation. Nevertheless, foreign investors, as well as national governments, have provided much of the infrastructure needed for international tourism, including good roads, a large number of airports of international standard, and hotel development in the major cities and coastal resorts. You would expect external transport links to be efficient as the region is a crossroads between Europe, Africa, and Asia, and its airports are important as staging points for business on the long-haul routes between Western Europe and the East Asia-Pacific region. Although most tourists visiting the Middle East arrive by air, movements within the region are predominantly by road. The main exception is the Arabian Peninsula, due to the vast distances and difficult terrain. Throughout the Middle East, rail networks are poorly developed, and there are few international services. Given the abundance of cheap oil, an ever-growing demand for car ownership, even in the poorer countries, and a lack of environmental awareness, this situation is not likely to change.

Tourism resources

The Middle East has many strengths as a destination region, with opportunities for further development, but these are constrained by a number of serious problems. We can summarise the tourist resources of the region as:

- A wealth of cultural attractions, given that this region gave rise to the world's earliest civilisations and three major world religions – Judaism, Christianity, and Islam. Successive invaders, including the Greeks and Romans in ancient times, followed by Crusaders from western Europe defending the pilgrim routes to the Holy Land, have all left their mark. Some of the best known of these sites can be visited on a Mediterranean cruise. However, overland cultural tours, taking in several countries, have not developed to the same extent as in Europe, due to the political situation in the region.
- A generally favourable climate for beach tourism, although in some countries this is restricted by cultural and religious attitudes. A growing number of tourists now visit the region purely for the sake of recreation and relaxation. Resorts have developed to meet their needs, but with the exceptions of Israel and Dubai, facilities are generally not to the same standard as those of the western Mediterranean.
- Mountain ranges provide relief from the summer heat in the cities, and here several health resorts meet the domestic demand, such as Kasab in Syria and Taa'iz in Saudi Arabia.
- The mountains in the north of the region also provide opportunities for winter sports. At present, ski resorts have developed to meet the needs of the small domestic market and are generally not well-equipped by international standards.
- There is also scope for adventure holidays in the more accessible mountain and desert areas.
- Although some countries pay lip service to ecotourism, in practice, it has made little progress, except in Israel and Jordan.

The main threats to tourism are twofold:

- First, the political situation has been a major factor in preventing the region from realising its tourism potential. Since the Oslo initiatives in 1994, tourism has ebbed and flowed in the region depending upon the prospects for peace. The region is still torn by internal unrest, often provoked by religious fundamentalism, and since 2001, by the war on terrorism. Terrorism by groups such as Hezbollah and Hamas in Lebanon, Israel, and the Palestinian territories has resulted in much negative publicity. Most governments in the region have a poor or indifferent record on human rights. The popular uprisings in Egypt, Syria, and Bahrain, the so-called 'Arab Spring' of 2011, demanding political and economic reforms, added a new ingredient to the turmoil. This was followed by the growth of ISIS (Daesh), which aimed to re-create an Islamic state or caliphate in Iraq, Syria, and beyond. In the process, it created tourism no-go areas, not only persecuting minorities such as the Yezedi, but neglecting, and even destroying outright, world-class monuments for ideological reasons in areas under their control. In consequence, tourism has suffered, despite the region's accessibility and its wealth of natural and man-made attractions. The Gulf War of 1990/1991, for example, not only disrupted tourism throughout the Middle East but also disturbed world tourism flows, although the actual hostilities were highly localised. The civil wars in Syria and Yemen have been highly disruptive to tourism.
- Second, the unique appeal of the region lies in its antiquities and cultural sites. These need careful management and have a limited capacity to receive visitors.

This implies that there is a limit to the numbers of tourists that the region can absorb if these attractions are to remain available for future generations. The heritage is also under threat from the widespread trafficking in artefacts from archaeological sites, and from industrialisation, where dam-building by Turkey on the upper Euphrates threatens sites downstream in Syria.

Egypt

In many ways, Egypt typifies the contrasts found in the Middle East. It is a meeting place of East and West; it is mysterious and yet highly accessible. Cairo is the hub of the air routes between Europe, Asia, and Africa, while the Suez Canal, inaugurated in 1869 and enlarged in 2015, is an essential link on one of the world's most important shipping routes. With around 98 million inhabitants, Egypt is the most populous of the Arab countries and a cultural centre for the Arabic-speaking world. Its people are the inheritors of an ancient civilisation that flourished many centuries before the rise of Islam, and in many respects, the way of life of the *fellahin* (peasant farmers) along the Nile has changed little since the time of the Pharaohs. The Nile is also a reminder that Egypt has strong connections with sub-Saharan Africa to the south.

About 93 per cent of Egypt's territory is desert, but we should make a distinction between the dune-covered expanses of the Western Desert extending into Libya, and the rugged scenery of the Eastern Desert and Sinai Peninsula. In between lies the narrow green ribbon of cultivated land along the Nile, widening in the north as the Nile Delta. Just as in ancient times, Egypt is 'the gift of the Nile', highly dependent on the river's vagaries. Although it is the most highly industrialised of the Arab countries, Egypt is not self-sufficient in petroleum, and its economy cannot provide enough jobs for the rapidly growing population. In this context, the contribution made by tourism is crucial as it filters down to the lowest levels of society and employs around 9 per cent of the workforce. The government recognises this and has had a long involvement in tourism.

Tourism demand

Domestic and outbound tourism

Domestic tourism is significant, and this includes social tourism as well as travel by a relatively affluent middle class to resorts on the Mediterranean coast. Around 9 million domestic trips were made in 2015, along with 2 million trips to foreign countries; Saudi Arabia is the main destination. Due to the impact of COVID-19, outbound trips fell to less than a million in 2020.

Inbound tourism

Travellers from the West have visited the Pyramids at least since Roman times, although modern tourism did not begin until the late nineteenth century. To a large extent, this was due to the British travel company, Thomas Cook, who inaugurated steamship services on the Nile, luxury river cruises, and the development of Luxor as a winter resort. Since the 1960s, tourists from other Arab countries, visiting primarily for recreational rather than cultural reasons, have formed a growing share of the Egyptian market. Arab visitors tend to stay during the summer months, when the Mediterranean coast around Alexandria is cool by comparison with the stifling heat of the Arabian Peninsula. Most Western sightseers arrive during the winter season, which is pleasantly warm and much drier than other Mediterranean destinations.

Egypt is the dominant destination for international tourists in the Middle East. In the 1950s, there were fewer visitors, but they stayed for an average of one month, and even in the 1980s, the main reason for visiting was to view the cultural sites. However, recreational tourism has become increasingly important and international arrivals rose steadily in the 1990s, despite the setbacks of terrorist attacks and the Gulf War, and exceeded 14 million by 2010, comprising both Western and Arab markets. The unrest in Egypt following the Arab Spring, subsequent terrorist incidents, and uncertainty over airport security caused a decline in tourist arrivals to 8 million in 2013. However, confidence is returning, and arrivals rose to over 13 million in 2019, only to fall to 3.7 million in 2020 as a result of COVID-19.

Tourism supply

Egypt has over 200,000 hotel rooms. Most of this capacity is in the capital, followed by Alexandria and Luxor, but there is also significant growth in Sinai. The government encourages investment in the accommodation stock by both Egyptian and foreign companies, and tourism is given priority at the highest levels of government.

Tourism organisation

The first formal tourist authority was established in 1935, and the present agency in charge of tourism is the Ministry of Tourism and Antiquities. The Ministry has cabinet status in the government and is responsible for co-ordinating public sector tourism activities. This involves:

- Upgrading hospitality infrastructure.
- Digitising the tourism sector.
- Improving legislation.
- Rebranding and finding new markets.
- Diversifying to include new products such as medical tourism, MICE, and religious tourism.

This is part of the plan to widen Egypt's resource base and tempt tourists away from the Nile Valley, where the tourism industry is competing with other economic sectors for scarce water, power, and land resources. This is problematic as Ancient Egypt, notably the Pyramids and the Valley of the Kings, is the subject of worldwide interest, probably to a greater extent than any other bygone civilisation.

Tourism resources

To develop its full potential, tourism has to overcome a number of problems, not the least of which is Egypt's infrastructure, particularly overloaded water and power supplies and an inadequate road system. Environmental considerations are also important, especially along the Red Sea coast where there is concern for the ecology of the coral reefs. However, perhaps the main problem is the uncertain political climate of the region, causing severe fluctuations in tourist arrivals, especially from the United States. Although the government is pro-Western, and Egypt was the first Arab state to normalise relations with Israel, the country suffers from acute social and economic tensions. This has contributed to the rise of Islamic fundamentalism among the poorer classes in society, fuelling hostility to the Coptic Christian minority. All of which is causing concern for the future stability of the country and the future of its tourism industry.

Most Western tourists stay firmly on the cultural circuit, the highlights of which are:

- The Pyramids of Giza (https://whc.unesco.org/en/list/86/) just outside Cairo. These are the only survivors of the 'seven wonders' of the ancient world.
- The newly refurbished Cairo Grand Egyptian Museum (GEM).
- The temples and other antiquities near Luxor, which is the main centre for touring Upper Egypt. These include the world-famous Valley of the Kings (http://www.sca-egypt.org/eng/sca_organization.html).
- The temple at Abu Simbel near Aswan, which UNESCO campaigns saved from inundation by the Aswan High Dam project (https://whc.unesco.org/en/activities/173/).

Although the very dry climate of the Nile Valley has ensured the survival of artefacts for over 4,000 years, safeguarding the monuments from pollution for future generations is a matter of concern. Tourist pressure on the Pyramids has led the government to implement drastic conservation measures, including attempts to curb the activities of unauthorised guides and entrepreneurs. A popular way of visiting the sites in Upper Egypt is by a river cruise on the Nile, as an alternative to road transport or domestic air services from Cairo. In fact, Nile cruises have long been Egypt's best known tourism product.

The emphasis on the relics of the Pharaohs has obscured the fact that Egypt has a more recent heritage and many other attractions. This is particularly true of Cairo, although the congestion in this city of over 22 million people can be a traumatic experience. In addition to early Islamic buildings such as the Citadel of Saladin (https://whc.unesco.org/en/tentativelists/1828), there are Coptic churches, a reminder that this early form of Christianity was flourishing in Egypt centuries before Islam. However, for most tourists, the main attraction is shopping in the bazaars for an assortment of souvenirs.

Other tourist resources include:

- The Fayyûm oasis (https://whc.unesco.org/en/tentativelits/1830/), 100 kilometres to the west of the Nile Valley, is culturally interesting and a good deal less hectic than Cairo. A number of hotels have been built in this area.
- Sailing in a traditional *felucca* on the Nile offers a more authentic experience of rural Egypt than a luxury cruise in a 'floating hotel'.

- Trekking in the Sinai Desert, including a visit to St.Catherine's Monastery (https://www.sinaimonastery.com), with its biblical associations.

The greatest potential for attracting a wider market lies in the development of Egypt's coastal resorts where a year-round season is possible, and there are good facilities for water sports.

- **The Mediterranean coast** west of Alexandria has long attracted well-off domestic tourists, with beach resorts such as Mersah Matruh. This area also appeals to military history buffs as the theatre for the Western Desert campaign, culminating in the battle of El Alamein (1942) in the Second World War. Alexandria is a cosmopolitan seaport with Greek and French cultural influences, but much of its former elegance faded after the 1952 revolution, which overthrew the monarchy and brought Nasser to power. Almost nothing remains of the ancient city of Roman times, famed for its library and the long-lost palace of Cleopatra.
- The **Red Sea coast**, promoted by the Ministry of Tourism as the 'Red Sea Riviera', has clear water and coral reefs that are a major attraction for divers. Tourism on a small scale took place during the Israeli occupation of the Sinai Peninsula between 1967 and 1982, but the impetus for growth came when the Egyptian government provided generous loans for hotel development. The resorts of Hurghada, Nuweiba, and Sharm al Sheikh are now established holiday destinations for Western tourists and include luxury hotels with conference facilities among their amenities.

Israel

Within an area not much larger than that of Wales or New Jersey, two nations – Israel and the Palestine NAR (National Autonomous Region) – have so far failed to find a formula for peaceful co-existence.

With a population of over 9 million, Israel has a significance out of all proportion to its size. The country is poor in natural resources but has the asset of a workforce that is enterprising and highly skilled in the latest technology. Few other countries can offer such a great variety of scenery and climate within a short distance, including the snows of Mount Hermon in the north, the sub-tropical fertility of Galilee, and the heat and aridity of the Dead Sea, which lies more than 400 metres below sea level. People's perceptions of Israel are largely coloured by their political or religious background, for example:

- To Jews, a nation dispersed in exile since Roman times, Israel is their homeland. Jewish religious observance plays an important role in this otherwise secular state.
- To Christians the world over, Israel is largely synonymous with the Holy Land, containing most of the places associated with the Bible. Christian Arabs historically formed a significant minority of the population, which is decreasing, in both Israel and the Palestinian territories.
- To Muslims, a number of these sites are also of great religious significance. Many regard Israel as an intruder and are sympathetic to the cause of the Palestinian Arabs.

Moreover, Muslim Arabs form a substantial minority in Israel itself as well as being the majority in the Palestine NAR.

Since the founding of Israel in 1948, the Jewish state has been under siege from its Arab neighbours. Internal security is also threatened by the Palestinians in the occupied territories of the Gaza Strip, East Jerusalem, and the West Bank (known as Samaria and Judea to Israelis, and also as Cisjordania in a number of countries), which Israel acquired after the ´Six-Day War´ in 1967. The Oslo agreement in 1994 laid the foundations of a Palestinian state by giving autonomy to Gaza and most of the West Bank. However, the Palestinian *Intifada* (uprising) in 2001 was a major setback to the peace process and tourism development, and the situation deteriorated further when the hard-line Hamas party gained power in Gaza. The Palestinian authorities were unable to restrain terrorist activity, and in response to the threat from Palestinian *shaheeds* (suicide bombers), Israel implemented a security barrier around the West Bank. Security is a major consideration for travel in Israel itself, and El Al (https://www.elal.com), the national carrier routinely carried armed air marshals on its flights long before 9/11 made it a global issue.

The demand for tourism

Domestic and outbound tourism

With a GDP per capita that is higher than many European countries and a good transport infrastructure, the propensity for tourism is high. Domestic tourists accounted for over 18 million overnight stays in 2021, with hotels as the main type of accommodation used. Most Israelis have a southern European lifestyle, and trips to the beaches of the Mediterranean resorts and Eilat are a major feature of domestic tourism. Israelis took over 9 million trips abroad in 2019, leaving a deficit on the international tourism account. As a result of bilateral agreements, they can now visit most countries in the region, particularly the United Arab Emirates, Egypt, Jordan, and Turkey. Security problems at home have favoured the growth of outbound travel at the expense of domestic trips. Given its small population, Israel is well-represented in the tourist arrivals for many long-haul destinations.

Inbound tourism

Despite its security problems, Israel attracted 4.5 million international tourists in 2019 from a wide range of countries, but this fell to less than a million in 2020 due to the COVID-19 pandemic. The United States, which has a special relationship with Israel, is a major generator of demand. Russia, Ukraine, and Poland represent a large ethnic market. Other European countries, including Britain, have become important sources of tourists since the liberalisation of charter flights in 1976. The Israeli Ministry of Tourism endeavours to develop new markets, such as Japan, in close co-operation with the national carrier – indeed the majority of arrivals are by air. There is also a health spa authority to co-ordinate this important sector of tourism, particularly foreign visitors seeking treatment for psoriasis.

461

Tourism resources

Israel can offer a great variety of tourist products including:

- Summer holiday resorts along the Mediterranean coast at Herzliya and Netanya north of Tel Aviv, and at Ashkelon to the south.
- Eilat, Israel's outlet to the Red Sea, separated by 200 kilometres of desert from Jerusalem, has become a popular winter sun destination, with facilities for underwater photography, diving, and water skiing.
- Spa tourism has been developed around picturesque Lake Kinneret (better known as the Sea of Galilee) and in a more spectacular setting on the shores of the Dead Sea, utilising the unique resource provided by the mineral-rich lake and its microclimate.
- Working holidays on a kibbutz, the uniquely Israeli experiment in communal living. The kibbutz lifestyle is nowadays much less popular among Israelis than it was in the early years of the Jewish state, due to the decline of the agricultural sector and the move from socialism to a market economy. Indeed, many *kibbutzim* have departed from their socialist ideals by providing guest house accommodation to paying tourists.
- The attraction of seeing a nation in the making, composed of Jewish immigrants from all over the world, who have revived Hebrew as an everyday language. Israel's achievements in making the Negev Desert productive are particularly interesting.
- Adventure holidays, including trekking in the Negev Desert.
- Cultural tourism based on the large number of archaeological sites, many of which are mentioned in the Bible. Herod the Great's hilltop fortress at Masada (https://whc.unesco.org/en/list/1040/) is a shrine to the Jewish struggle for freedom against Rome and subsequent oppressors. In medieval times, the historic port of Acre (Akko) played a major role in the Crusades.
- Christian pilgrimages to Galilee and Jerusalem, with a peak in demand during the Easter holidays. Around a quarter of visitors to Israel are travelling primarily for religious reasons.

Business travel gravitates to the three major cities of Tel Aviv, Haifa, and Jerusalem:

- Tel Aviv is the business and financial centre of the country. The city is very much a creation of the twentieth century, with a good deal of nightlife and a Southern European beach culture.
- Haifa is Israel's largest seaport, catering for tourists arriving by ferry from Greece, Cyprus, and Turkey as well as cruise passengers. It is also a place of pilgrimage for followers of the Bahai religion.
- Jerusalem, the capital of ancient Judea and since 1967, of the modern state of Israel, is an important venue for conferences. It is a world-class tourist destination as the meeting place for three major religions and also a potential flashpoint for disputes involving Christian, Jewish, and Muslim fundamentalists. Some allege that the Israeli authorities have insensitively handled hotel expansion in the old Arab quarter of East Jerusalem. Major points of interest for the visitor include:

- Yad Vashem (https://www.yadvashem.org/) – Israel's major memorial to the Jewish Holocaust of the Second World War.
- The sites associated with Christ´s Passion, including the Mount of Olives (https://mouuntofolives.co.il), the pilgrim route known as the Via Dolorosa (https://www.seetheholyland.net/via-dolorosa/), and the Church of the Holy Sepulchre (https://churchoftheholysepulchre.net/).
- The Temple Mount (https://www.templemount.org/), an area sacred to Christians, Jews, and Muslims alike. The Al Aqsa Mosque (https://www.visitmasjida-laqsa.com) is the holiest site in Islam after Mecca and Medina. The Western Wall is all that remains of the Jewish Temple after its destruction by the Romans in 70 AD and is a place of lamentation for Orthodox Jews.

The Palestine NAR

The growth of Jewish settlements in the occupied territories, together with the security barrier around the West Bank, have in effect fragmented the territory of the Palestine NAR. The military checkpoints have made everyday travel irksome for Palestinians and severely disrupted the economy of a number of communities. This is particularly the case

Photo 18.1
The Dome of the Rock in the Old City of Jerusalem, with new buildings under construction

Source: ©istockphoto.com/Irena Kofman

with Gaza, a potential beach resort under the Oslo agreement, where tourism has since been curtailed by Israel's ongoing blockade by land, sea, and air. Tourism centres in the West Bank include:

- Bethlehem, which is a major centre for Christian pilgrims attracted to the Church of the Nativity.
- Jericho, situated in the Jordan Valley, claims based on archaeological evidence to be the world's oldest city.
- Hebron contains the Tomb of the Patriarchs, a place of religious significance to both Jews and Muslims.

Nablus and Ramullah, on the other hand, are the commercial and administrative centres for the NAR. Despite the difficulties, the Palestine NAR attracted 6 million visitors in 2018, but the majority of these spend only a few hours in the territories. The cause of the Palestinians has nevertheless attracted tourists motivated by their political sympathies rather than sightseeing, who interact with local communities. Other tourists, particularly evangelical Christians from the United States, show strong support for Zionism and the state of Israel (Ron and Timothy, 2019).

Jordan

Without significant oil resources and consisting largely of semi-arid plateaux and desert, Jordan is a small and relatively poor Arab country. The population includes two very different communities, the Palestinian refugees, mainly concentrated in the capital Amman, and the Bedouin tribes of the desert. Despite these tensions, the country has remained politically stable, largely due to the statesmanship of King Hussein who ruled from 1953 to 1999.

Tourism plays an important role in the economy, accounting for 6 per cent of GDP and second only to remittances from the large numbers of Jordanians working abroad. Over 5 million international arrivals were recorded in 2019. Over-reliance on the attractions of East Jerusalem, Bethlehem, and Jericho meant that most of Jordan's appeal, as well as its hotel stock were lost when Israel occupied those territories (the West Bank) in 1967. The government then had to redevelop tourism east of the river Jordan, on a less promising resource base. The major attractions include:

- Petra (http://visitpetra.jo/) – the ancient city of the Nabatean civilisation – in a unique setting, concealed in a deep valley. This accounts for a substantial part of Jordan's tourism revenue, and has encouraged hotel development in the area.
- The desert scenery of Wadi Rum, where ecotourism is being developed, and which is associated with the exploits of Lawrence of Arabia during the First World War.
- The eastern shores of the Dead Sea where spa tourism is being developed.
- The Crusader castle at Kerak.
- The well-preserved Roman city of Jerash with its annual festival.

- Places of particular significance for pilgrims include the site on the east bank of the river Jordan where Christ was baptised, the ruined fortress of Mukawir (associated with John the Baptist and the Jewish princess Salome), and Mount Nebo, associated with Moses.
- The beaches and water sports of Aqaba on the Red Sea coast, which has been developed as a rival to Eilat.

Tourism has been restricted by the lack of infrastructure and good hotels, although the Middle East peace initiatives have encouraged hotel investment, particularly in Amman, Aqaba, and by the Dead Sea. Most hotels are located in Amman, although a network of formerly government-run "rest houses' (now privatised) provides accommodation in the areas likely to be visited by tourists. The normalisation of relations with Israel after 1994 enabled Jordan to benefit from the millennium tourist boom, with the easing of restrictions on travel between the two countries. The Ministry of Tourism and Antiquities of Jordan (www.mota.gov.jo) has encouraged sustainable tourism. This includes community tourism projects such as the award-winning Taybeh-Zaman tourist village close to Petra, where visitors can see local craft skills in action and stay in traditional rural houses.

Although Jordan has remained relatively stable, tourism has been affected by the turmoil in the Middle East generally. The decline in the numbers of European visitors has been offset to an extent by an increase in arrivals from Arab countries. Open skies agreements with a number of European countries have affected the profitability of the national carrier, Royal Jordanian Airlines (https://rj.com/).

Syria

Although Syria is roughly the size of England and Wales, only 20 per cent of the land is cultivable. This section of the Fertile Crescent contrasts with the stony Syrian Desert in the south east. Before the civil war Syria had many tourist attractions and resources. There were beach resorts on the Mediterranean coast north of Lattakia as well as mountain resorts taking advantage of the cooler climate of the Anti-Lebanon mountains, but these were visited almost exclusively by domestic tourists. Of greater appeal to Western sightseers was Syria's cultural heritage, represented by:

- Damascus, once the capital of a powerful Arab caliphate ruled by the Ommayad dynasty and famous for its biblical association with St. Paul. Its cultural attractions include the Ommayad Mosque and the Al Azem Palace – now a museum of art and traditional crafts.
- The city of Aleppo, famous for its citadel. This has been one of the localities most severely affected by the conflict.
- The ruins of the ancient trading city of Palmyra in the Syrian Desert.
- The Krak des Chevaliers, the most spectacular of the castles built by the Crusaders.

Thanks to these resources, Syria received 8.5 million tourist arrivals in 2010, and tourism accounted for 5 per cent of the country's GDP. However, the civil war that has raged since

2011 severely impacted tourism demand, and there were only 0.7 million arrivals in 2021. The Assad regime was moving from a command to a market economy, and relations with the European Union and the United States had improved, but not with Israel, due to the continuing border dispute over the Golan Heights. Western Syria received the bulk of the investment in tourism, whereas the eastern part of the country, despite containing many archaeological sites, remained much poorer economically. Western Syria contained significant religious minorities such as the Alawites, whereas the Sunni majority were largely excluded from power.

The civil war generated an outflow of some 3 million refugees. Important heritage sites have been destroyed, and the majority of tourist-generating countries have imposed travel bans. The conflict, by damaging the economy, has reduced the demand for outbound tourism. Syrian Air (http://syriaair.com/) remains the sole airline serving the country, and this depends on expatriates travelling between Syria and their countries of residence and pilgrims visiting the holy sites in Saudi Arabia. Hotels have closed, with the exception of those accommodating families displaced by the conflict.

Lebanon

Although Lebanon is a small, mountainous country, its people have been involved in overseas trade since at least the first millennium BC, when the Phoenicians from Tyre and Sidon dominated the Mediterranean sea routes, and Lebanese communities and cuisine are now found all over the world. Lebanon is a classic example of a multi-cultural society peopled to a large extent by successive waves of refugees from other parts of the Middle East. Until 1975, when civil war broke out between the two main communities, the ruling Maronite Christians and the various Muslim groups, including Palestinian refugees, Beirut was not only the financial capital of a large part of the Arab world but also its main entertainment centre. Arab tourists came to Lebanon not only for relief from the intense summer heat of their own countries but also to escape the prohibitions on gambling and nightclubs imposed by a strict interpretation of Islam. Since the end of the conflict in 1991, the economy has made a slow recovery, and Beirut is no longer a divided city. European tour operators have added Lebanon to their stock of destinations, and Middle East Airlines (MEA) (www.mea.com.lb), the national airline, has staged a comeback based on a new airport to the south of the capital (Beirut-Rafiz Hariri International Airport), with the result that 2 million international arrivals were recorded in 2018. Aside from a revitalised Beirut, the country's tourist attractions include:

- Mount Lebanon, where a number of ski centres have developed only a short drive from the beach resorts of the coast. Both are mainly frequented by domestic tourists and visitors from other Arab countries such as Jordan and Saudi Arabia. Unfortunately, the cedar forests which covered the mountains in biblical times have largely disappeared.
- The fertile Bekaa Valley to the east includes the ancient temples of Baalbek which provide a romantic setting for cultural events.

Accommodation in Lebanon tends to be expensive, and tourism has been given little encouragement by the government, which is based on a complicated power-sharing agreement between the religious communities. Nevertheless, there are a number of rural tourism initiatives by the private sector, including the development of a hiking trail linking the coast to the mountains.

The Arabian Peninsula

Extending between the Red Sea and the Gulf, the Arabian Peninsula offers some of the most extreme contrasts to be found in the Middle East. It mostly consists of desert landscapes, culminating in the notorious Rub-al-Khali (Empty Quarter), which remained unexplored until the 1930s. There are mountain ranges along its western and south-eastern edges that attract some rainfall, and support a greater variety of vegetation. Saudi Arabia dominates the interior and contains most of the region's population, while the Gulf states – Kuwait, Qatar, Bahrain, the United Arab Emirates, and Oman – are maritime in their location and outlook. To the south, Yemen remains more traditional in its outlook and is largely undeveloped for tourism, partly as a result of political instability and civil wars.

The rapid development of the vast oil reserves of the countries around the Gulf has led to a huge growth in demand for all kinds of goods and services from a population which in the first half of the twentieth century were largely nomads, fishing communities, and peasant farmers. It has also attracted many temporary immigrants, comprising skilled professionals from Western countries, Palestinians, Egyptians, and a large number of labourers and domestic servants from Third World countries such as Pakistan and the Philippines, as well as from the poorer Arab countries such as Jordan and Yemen. In some of the Gulf states, expatriate workers form the majority of the population. The whole region has become an important generator of international travel, led by Saudi Arabia, and per capita expenditure on foreign travel is among the highest in the world. In the 1990s, the major outbound flows were to the United Kingdom and France, but since 9/11, demand for travel to the United States and Europe has fallen, and Egypt, Lebanon, and Cyprus are more significant destinations. Outbound travel is concentrated between June and September when the summer heat is intense.

In the early 1990s spending abroad by residents of the region was estimated to be almost twice that of inbound foreign visitors, who came mainly for business reasons. This is changing with the development of the winter sun holiday market in the United Arab Emirates and Oman. Tourists have benefitted from fluctuations in the business travel market after the oil boom in the 1980s, as the region´s airlines – notably Etihad (https://www.etihad.com), Qatar Airways (https://qatarairways.com), Gulf Air (https://www.gulfair.com), and Emirates (https://www.emirates.com) – are anxious to fill aircraft seats, while the luxury hotels of the Gulf states also need to increase their occupancy rates. The airport infrastructure is impressive, with terminal buildings that combine traditional design with ultramodern facilities. Bahrain and Dubai are major staging points on the intercontinental routes between Europe and the Far East, and have largely replaced Beirut as banking centres for the Middle East. Surprisingly, the impact of 9/11 was less damaging for the region´s airlines than for world aviation as a whole and carriers such as Emirates, Etihad Airways, and Gulf Air have prospered in the new millennium.

The Gulf states are well aware that oil resources will soon be exhausted and are using their wealth to diversify their economies, including investment in tourism-related projects. These countries are experiencing a tourism boom that is unprecedented in other parts of the world. Each capital now boasts a seafront *corniche* highway, marinas, luxury hotels, shopping malls, and other state-of-the-art amenities. The natural assets for tourism include a number of fine beaches along the Gulf coast, although oil spills in this shallow, enclosed sea are a potential problem – and the mountains and deserts of the interior.

Discussion point
The Gulf states are building new cities, highways, airports, resort hotels, and visitor attractions on an unprecedented scale. With local populations that lack the skills or the inclination to work in the construction industry, most of the labour required has to be imported from countries such as Pakistan or Bangladesh. Reports in the media claim this workforce is exploited, living in overcrowded, sub-standard accommodation, while health and safety issues are largely ignored to meet completion targets. Deaths and injuries occur on a scale that would not be tolerated in the West. How should tourists and the travel industry react to these issues?

Kuwait

As in the other Gulf states, a high proportion of Kuwait's population is under 25 years of age, with the propensity to use social media and the latest technology, and this is determining patterns of regional and outbound travel. Kuwait is primarily a business destination, with plans to develop leisure tourism on its offshore islands.

Bahrain

Tourism to this small island kingdom was affected by the unfavourable publicity given to the unrest here following the Arab Spring. It is a destination primarily for business travel, and like Kuwait, leisure tourism is highly dependent on visitors from Saudi Arabia. Bahrain hosts several festivals and the Formula One motor racing event.

Qatar

The Qatar Tourism Authority has used its wealth, based on vast reserves of natural gas, to encourage sustainable tourism to attract niche markets and has big ambitions to become a destination for sport tourism. Doha's international airport, built on land reclaimed from the Gulf, is designed specifically to handle the new generation of Airbus 'super-jumbos'. The emirate has hosted international conferences, a number of sports events, including the 2006 Asian Games, and its cultural attractions include a museum of Islamic arts. However, it was the 2022 FIFA World Cup that put the country firmly under the international spotlight. It was the first to be held in the Arab world and was the first to be held outside the summer months.

The United Arab Emirates

The United Arab Emirates (UAE) is now a major player in international tourism, although its constituent states of Ajman, Fujairah, Ras Al Khaimah, and Umm-al-Quwain have remained relatively inconspicuous compared to Dubai, Abu Dhabi, and Sharjah. The cities are for the most part thoroughly modern in appearance, and much of the traditional architecture, including the picturesque wind towers (a device for cooling buildings through evaporation), has been swept away. Since 2006, the UAE has invested in port terminals in Dubai, Abu Dhabi, and Sharjah to attract the lucrative cruise market.

Dubai aims to be a 'family-friendly' holiday destination. Among the Gulf states, it has done the most to attract Western tour operators and is an example of economic diversification – less than 10 per cent of its revenue now comes from oil. 'Dubai Incorporated' is a partnership between the ruling family of the emirate and the private sector through the Dubai World holding company. Dubai offers free port status, an open skies policy to foreign airlines, an environment that encourages business travellers, and not least, a tolerance of other cultures. The city has retained its historic port, but has invested massively in showpiece facilities and man-made attractions for the recreational tourist, led by the Dubai Commerce and Tourism Promotion Board. These include:

- A number of world-class golf courses in the desert (each course uses around 3 million litres of desalinated water a day).
- Yacht marinas.
- Ultramodern shopping malls and traditional markets, such as the gold souk, appealing to bargain-hunters stopping over on intercontinental flights.
- Nightlife that has made Dubai 'the playground of the Middle East', although gambling is not permitted, and the penalties for drug and alcohol abuse can be severe.
- A new generation of museums and art galleries.
- Sport tourism, including the Dubai World Cup – which showcases the Arab love of horse-racing – and the ATP tennis tournament (https://dubaidutyfreetennischampionships.com/).
- More ambitious projects include the creation of a number of artificial resort islands – notably the Palm Jumeirah – a major theme park, an indoor winter sports centre, and the iconic Burj Al Arab Jumeirah hotel (https://www.jumeirah.com). In contrast to these futuristic developments, four-wheel drive expeditions into the desert, including 'wadi-bashing', appeal to Western expatriates and adventure-seekers.

Abu Dhabi is aiming to be a centre of cultural excellence, rather than simply emulating Dubai. Operas and other musical events are held in the government-owned Emirates Palace Hotel, itself a showpiece attraction. The emirate is creating a Cultural District on Saadiyat Island that will include a maritime museum, a centre of the performing arts, a new Guggenheim (https://www.guggenheim.org/about-us) to rival that of Bilbao, and a new Louvre (with the agreement of the French government) (https://www.louvreabud-habi.ae/). Another offshore island, Yas, is the venue for Formula One Grand Prix motor racing. The Abu Dhabi Department of Culture and Tourism (https://tcaabudhabi.ae/) hopes to appeal not only to high-spending tourists but also the family market, with a new family entertainment centre development on Sir Bani Yas Island. Additionally, it is also promoting eco-friendly attractions based on the natural world. The emirate also has a number of theme parks including Ferrari World, Sea World, and the indoor Warner Brothers World.

Oman

The sultanate of Oman can offer the Western tourist greater diversity of landscapes and a more genuine experience of traditional Arab culture than is the case with the Gulf states and their largely artificial attractions. The Ministry of Tourism (https://omantourism.gov.om/) is determined to retain these traditions while at the same time investing in the hotel sector and developing cruise tourism with a terminal as part of Port Sultan Qaboos near the capital, Muscat. Snow Oman in Muscat is a new indoor ski attraction.

Oman has a long history of seafaring and traders from the port of Muscat sailed widely across the Indian Ocean many centuries before Europeans ventured into the Atlantic. In this, they were aided by the regular seasonal shift in wind direction known as the monsoon. Winds blow directly from the north east during one part of the year, and from the south west during the rest of the year, so early voyagers to India, East Africa, and Southeast Asia could be sure of returning to their home port.

The Batinah coast to the north east is being developed as an upmarket winter sun destination for Europeans, while the Musendam Peninsula appeals to adventure-seekers. In contrast, the Dhofar region in the south attracts Arabian families, who are not as a rule sun-seekers, as a summer destination. The Indian monsoon has an important influence on the climate of this part of the Arabian Peninsula. As a consequence, demand is concentrated in the rainy season from June to September, when temperatures are a 'cool' 30°C compared to a stifling 50°C in the interior. At the same time, the monsoon brings dramatic changes to the normally parched landscape.

Saudi Arabia

The Kingdom of Saudi Arabia (KSA) has the largest GDP in the Middle East, largely because it has one-quarter of the world's oil reserves. It has used some of this wealth to create six new cities in different regions of the country to diversify the economy. This is a deeply traditional country, with a government ready to modernise, but on its terms, and where the pace of change is slow in order to respect the puritanical views of the powerful Wahabi sect of Islam.

The demand for tourism

Domestic and outbound tourism

Average incomes and car ownership levels are high, and Saudis take 28 million trips a year within their own country. Many Saudis escape Riyadh and other cities at weekends to camp out in the desert or the mountains. Nevertheless, traditional destinations, such as Jeddah and Abha, face growing competition from the spectacular resort developments in the Gulf states and elsewhere. Domestic tourism is strongly influenced by the need for religious observance and family ties. The sexes are strictly separated, and tourist attractions must offer male-only and female-only days. While young men can indulge in displays of 'Mad Max' exhibitionist motoring, until 2019 women were not allowed to drive, or travel anywhere unless accompanied by a *mehram* (male guardian). Recent reforms under the government's Vision 2030 policy allow for de-segregation in restaurants and at concerts and sports events, while the power of the *mutawwain* (religious police) as enforcers of public morality has been reduced.

Not surprisingly, the trend, for Saudi families who can afford to do so, is to take holidays in destinations such as the UAE, Egypt, and Malaysia where more liberal attitudes to religion prevail. Saudis now take almost 22 million trips abroad each year, of which two-thirds are for leisure purposes and the rest equally divided between business and VFR travel. The average length of stay is relatively high at just over two weeks. Saudis tend to travel in large family groups, and shopping, rather than sightseeing, is the preferred activity. In this respect, Britain is less popular as a destination than was the case before 9/11.

Inbound tourism

As far as the West is concerned, Saudi Arabia is primarily a destination for business travellers, focussing on Riyadh and Jeddah. This is slowly changing, as the government re-evaluates the role that tourism can play in providing jobs for a rapidly growing population. Until 2019, visas had been largely restricted to resident workers and their dependents, business travellers, and Muslim pilgrims to Mecca and Medina. Tourist visas have now been extended to a large number of countries, including the United States, European Union, and United Kingdom.

A third of the 20 million tourist arrivals in 2019 – including some 100,000 British Muslims – are visiting Saudi Arabia for religious reasons, to perform the *haj* to the holy cities of Mecca and Medina, or the lesser pilgrimage known as *umrah*. The haj is concentrated in a five-day period in Mecca during the last month of the Muslim calendar and involves a major effort in logistics and organisation on the part of the Saudi authorities. The Ministry of Hajj and Umrah co-ordinates the accommodation, catering, and transport arrangements for the pilgrimage (www.haj.gov.sa). Nevertheless, security and crowd control are major problems, such that fatal accidents often occur during the climax of the rituals around the Kaaba in the Great Mosque (Masjid Al Haram), Islam's holiest shrine. For many Muslims, the cost of travelling to Mecca is prohibitive, but the number of pilgrims has nevertheless quadrupled since the 1960s despite attempts to control the numbers. The Saudi government has spent a substantial part of its oil revenues on highway construction, and the expansion of terminal facilities at Jeddah Airport, as the majority of pilgrims nowadays arrive on chartered flights rather than use the slow and perhaps dangerous land and sea routes. The *umrah* pilgrimages have the advantage of being spread over 11 months of the year, and a relaxation of visa restrictions now allows Muslim pilgrims to travel throughout the country for up to 30 days, giving much more scope for leisure tourism.

The supply side of tourism

Transport

Saudi Arabia has an extensive network of air services and no less than 28 regional airports. There is also a good road network, but with the high level of vehicle ownership traffic congestion is a serious problem. The government has, therefore, invested in rapid transit schemes in the cities of Riyadh and Jeddah and is improving and extending the state-owned railways, which were a neglected part of the transport infrastructure, mainly to cope with the volume of pilgrim traffic.

CASE STUDY 18.1
'TAMING THE DESERT': THE HARAMAIN PROJECT

The Haramain high-speed railway linking the holy cities of Mecca and Medina is one of the most challenging engineering projects to be undertaken so far this century. The line opened in 2018, crossing 450 kilometres of desert terrain, which is for the most part uninhabited. At Jeddah, the line connects with the existing system of air and rail services. The railway operates at speeds of 300 kilometres/ hour in some of the world's most extreme climatic conditions; locomotives had to be modified to cope with summer temperatures exceeding 50°C and the impact of frequent sandstorms. Moreover, the dunes are continually shifting, and special construction methods had to be used to avoid sand covering the track. Engineers also had to anticipate the effect of the rare torrential rainstorm.

Apart from the day-to-day physical problems of maintenance, there is the challenge of handling passenger flows, which may reach 250,000 a day during the haj. In accordance with Saudi law, there is strict gender segregation on the trains. Muslims are arriving from parts of the world where neither Arabic or English is spoken, and many are travelling abroad for the first time. They are often burdened with their personal possessions for the journey of a lifetime.

Organisation

As Saudi Arabia attempts to modernise its society and diversify the economy away from dependence on oil, the government's Vision 2030 provides a strategy for tourism. This includes 'entertainment cities', heritage sites, and coastal tourism. Demand is encouraged through a new electronic visa scheme. The Ministry of Tourism (http://mt.gov.sa) has responsibility for tourism at the national level, supported by the Saudi Tourism Authority (STA). At the regional level, there is a network of tourism organisations for each province.

Tourism resources

Potential niche markets for Western tourists include diving in the Red Sea, trekking in the deserts and mountains, and visits to a number of archaeological sites. The natural and cultural attractions include:

*   The relics of the ancient Nabatean civilisation, such as the city of Madain Salah.
*   Extensive coral reefs in the Red Sea.
*   State-of-the-art shopping malls, conference venues, and medical facilities.

Vision 2030 includes a number of new attractions:

*   Six Flags theme park Oidiya
*   Neom – a new city and innovation hub

Nevertheless, there are many constraints on the development of Western-style tourism. Moreover, some allege that the government, influenced by fundamentalist hardliners, has neglected Saudi Arabia's cultural heritage in the past, including sites associated with the early history of Islam.

Yemen

Yemen is much poorer than the other countries of the Arabian Peninsula, and tribal traditions persist to a much greater extent. The central government in Sana'a has been ineffective in maintaining law and order in the more remote areas; in fact, the negative publicity following the kidnappings of some Western tourists by dissident tribesmen seriously damaged the country´s fledgling tourism industry in the late 1990s. The Arab Spring resulted in further instability. Nevertheless, Yemen recorded 1 million tourist arrivals in 2013. The situation worsened in 2015 with the revolt of the Shia Houthis against the Sunni government, which is backed by Saudi Arabia. This became all-out civil war and a large-scale humanitarian disaster, and consequently, tourism has not recovered. Yet this mysterious country has much to offer the more adventurous tourist, namely:

*   A unique architectural heritage of mud-brick tower houses and palaces, particularly in Old Sana'a, Zabid and Shibam, which have been designated World Heritage Sites.

> ### CASE STUDY 18.2
> ### SOCOTRA
>
> The remote island of Socotra in the Indian Ocean belongs to Yemen but is geo-
> graphically closer to Africa. During the Cold War, it served as a military base for the
> Soviet-backed regime of South Yemen. Socotra is a World Heritage Site as many of the
> plant species, such as the 'dragon blood trees', are unique to the island. Like other
> isolated tropical islands, Socotra is highly vulnerable to the environmental impact of
> tourism, which needs to be carefully controlled. At present, access is limited, as the
> scheduled services from Aden and Sana'a provided by Yemenia, the national airline,
> are infrequent, and there is a lack of basic infrastructure and hotel accommodation.
> Nevertheless, some allege that the UAE (which has a training base on the island) has
> allowed tourist groups to fly directly to Socotra.
>
> ### Research and discussion
>
> Investigate the strengths and weaknesses of Socotra as a potential tourism destina-
> tion, by examining a number of niche markets, such as diving and ecotourism. What
> are the threats to the island's natural and cultural heritage, and what are the opportu-
> nities for tourism development?

- The remains of the ancient Sabaean civilisation, probably the biblical Sheba (although this is disputed by Ethiopians).

The capital, situated at an altitude of 2,200 metres in the northern highlands has an attractive climate and setting. This is less true of Aden in the sweltering coastal plains of the
south, which is the country's business centre.

Iraq

Two of the most important countries in the Middle East – Iran and Iraq – have strongly
influenced the development of tourism elsewhere in the region, while tourists have been
deterred from visiting by unfavourable publicity in the Western media. The war between
the two countries during the 1980s interrupted the flow of Iranian pilgrims to the Shia
shrines of Karbala and Najaf. The 2003 war and the subsequent strife between Sunni and
Shia meant that Iraq became virtually a 'no-go area' for tourism, but since 2009, a few
tour operators have negotiated access to certain areas.

The **Kurdistan Autonomous Region** in the north east of the country, which was declared a 'safe haven' for Kurds after the 1991 Gulf War, differs in many respects from the
rest of Iraq. It has two international airports, and as an area of relative stability, has attracted investment in the hotel sector. Most visitors are from other parts of Iraq, but there

are significant numbers of tourists arriving from Iran, attracted by the mountain scenery and recreational opportunities.

The major part of Iraq is made up of the fertile plains between the rivers Tigris and Euphrates, historically known as Mesopotamia. This region gave rise to one of the world's earliest civilisations, that of Sumeria, based on complex irrigation systems, in the fourth millennium BC.

Until the 1970s, Iraq was one of the most prosperous countries in the Middle East. Tourism development was encouraged by a secular government, and projects such as the Habbaniya Tourist Village near Baghdad catered for wealthy foreign visitors as well as Iraqis. Prior to the Gulf War, a number of archaeological sites were restored, such as Nineveh, capital of ancient Assyria, and more controversially, Babylon, as a showpiece for the Saddam regime. The long period of sanctions that followed the Gulf War halted any further growth, although Baghdad's hotels continued to attract business travellers from Russia and other countries circumventing the economic blockade.

Baghdad is predominantly a modern capital and little remains of the city of the Abbasid Caliphs that inspired the *Arabian Nights* in the ninth century. The major attraction for Western tourists is the National Museum, which contains the art treasures of Ur and other ancient cities of Mesopotamia. The threat to this heritage was highlighted by the Iraq War and was further aggravated by the ISIS insurgency, but in fact the pillaging of archaeological sites has been a long-standing problem.

Iran

Known as Persia until 1935, Iran is different in language, ethnicity, and culture from its Arab neighbours, with a history of powerful dynasties pre-dating the introduction of Islam by many centuries. Iran is the second largest country in the Middle East after Saudi Arabia, consisting mainly of an arid central plateau surrounded by high mountain ranges. The prevalence of desert landscapes explains the Iranian reverence for irrigated gardens. Traditionally, these were supplied by an intricate system of *qanats* – underground channels conveying water from the mountains to the plains. Before the 1979 revolution, which overthrew the pro-Western Shah and installed a fundamentalist Islamic regime under Ayatollah Khomeini, Iran attracted and generated a significant volume of international tourism.

The demand for tourism

Domestic and outbound tourism

Tehran is the modern capital of Iran and its major gateway. Since 1979, it has experienced massive growth, partly through rural out-migration. This congested, polluted city of 9 million inhabitants is the main generator of domestic tourism and a force for social change, with a predominantly young population using social media to circumvent irksome restrictions, and express a long-suppressed demand for Western-style leisure activities. As a result of sanctions imposed on Iran by the international community and the depreciation of the rial relative to other currencies, outbound tourism has tended to decrease. Iranians take over 70 million domestic trips annually, the majority staying with friends and relatives in preference to hotels.

Inbound tourism

Despite the many restrictions, international tourist arrivals reached 9 million in 2019, compared to half a million in 1995. These are mainly from neighbouring countries, attracted by a favourable exchange rate and the appeal of Iran to followers of the Shia branch of Islam, with the holy city of Masshad as its focus. (Although the Gulf states and Saudi Arabia are regarded as Sunni, they contain significant Shia minorities.) Only small numbers of visitors come from Western Europe, usually in tour groups, and even fewer arrive from the United States.

The supply side of tourism

Transport

Transport is mainly by road, with the advantage of low fuel prices. The state-owned carrier IranAir (https://iranair.com) offers a network of domestic services, but its international operations have suffered from the impact of sanctions.

Accommodation

After the 1979 revolution, Western hotel chains were expelled, and as a result, most of the accommodation is in Iranian ownership, much of it pre-dating 1979.

Organisation

Tourism is under the authority of the Ministry of Cultural Heritage, Tourism and Handicrafts with wide-ranging responsibilities for both the promotion and the development of tourism across the country.

Tourism resources

Iran has great potential as a tourist destination, as it can boast a large number of heritage sites recognised by UNESCO, opportunities for ecotourism, traditional crafts, and a distinctive cuisine. Specific attractions include:

- Some of the world's finest examples of Islamic architecture, particularly in Isfahan 'the city of mosques', and Shiraz, 'the city of roses', which is also celebrated for its associations with Omar Khayyam, famed worldwide as the author of the *Rubaiyat*.
- The remains of the pre-Islamic Persian civilisations. The most impressive of these is Persepolis, capital of the empire of Darius and Xerxes. This was the setting for the spectacular celebrations of 2,500 years of Persian monarchy staged by the last Shah in 1971.

- The ski centres of the Alborz Mountains north of Tehran; these were developed prior to the 1979 revolution and cater for a growing domestic demand.
- The summer resorts along the Caspian Sea, particularly Ramsar. These have a favourable climate, attractive scenery and are within easy reach of the capital.
- The island of Kish in the Gulf, which has been developed as a more upmarket winter destination, but as elsewhere in Iran, with strict segregation of male and female bathers.

The position of tourism in Iran mirrors the situation in the Middle East generally. Further growth will depend upon the extent to which modernisers can prevail over hard-line fundamentalists in their efforts to revive the economy, effect social reforms, and improve relations with the United States.

Summary

- The countries of the Middle East are close enough to the tourist-generating markets of northern Europe to have developed a sizeable tourism industry. Yet, only Israel, and more recently Dubai, have developed beach tourism on a scale comparable to other Mediterranean destinations.
- Cultural tourism is more significant in the region, but only Israel and Egypt have attracted cultural tourists in large numbers.
- Saudi Arabia and the Gulf states receive a considerable volume of business tourists, and this part of the Middle East is also a major generator of outbound international tourism.
- Domestic tourism is significant in most countries of the region, but is mainly VFR, rather than hotel- based.
- The region's tourism products are varied, including summer and winter sun beach holidays, spas and ski resorts in the mountains, adventure holidays in the desert, religious pilgrimages, and cultural tours.
- The Middle East can offer many natural and man-made attractions, some of which are unique. The region's history as the setting for many civilisations over thousands of years is important, while religion continues to play an important role in everyday life.
- Historically, the Middle East lies at a crossroads in world communications, where Europe, Africa, and Asia meet. Transport to and within most of the region is good, and highways and airports have been provided to meet the increased demand for international travel.
- There are many problems affecting the further growth of tourism. The prevailing warm dry climate, allied to demographic and economic pressures has put a severe strain on the region's scarce water supplies.
- Governments need to pay more attention to the conservation of the cultural as well as the natural resources on which tourism depends.
- The greatest threat is the political instability of most countries in the region, fuelled by religious fundamentalism, social and ethnic tensions, sectarianism, the unresolved conflict between Palestinians and Israelis, the legacy of the Gulf War, and the ongoing war against terrorism.

Review questions

1. Identify the constraints on Western-style beach tourism in most countries of the Middle East. How should tourists respond?
2. Discuss the importance of religion in the Middle East and the extent to which sectarianism affects the stability of countries in the region.
3. Explain the success of the UAE and Israel as tourist destinations. How much of this is due to:

    *   Each country's natural resources
    *   Cultural attractions
    *   Improved accessibility
    *   Other factors (which you should specify).

References and further reading

McManus, J. (2022) Taking the heat: Can Qatar survive climate change?, *Geographical* 94 (7), 50–56

Organization for Economic Co-operation and Development (annual) *Tourism Policy and International Tourism in OECD Member Countries*, OECD, Paris

Ron, A.S. and Timothy, D.J. (2019) *Contemporary Christian Travel*, Channel View Publications, Bristol

https://www.unwto.org/tourism-data/unwto-tourism-dashboard

19 The tourism geography of Africa

Learning objectives

After reading this chapter, you should be able to:

- Describe the major physical regions and climates of Africa and understand their importance for tourism.

- Understand the relevant social and economic background to tourism development in North Africa and sub-Saharan Africa.

- Recognise that, aside from developments in a few countries, the tourism development of sub-Saharan Africa is largely unfulfilled.

- Describe the main features of inbound tourism to the major destination countries in Africa.

DOI: 10.4324/9781003406853-23

- Appreciate the significance of the cultural resources of North Africa and sub-Saharan Africa.
- Recognise the importance of the wildlife resources for tourism in some of the countries of sub-Saharan Africa.

Introduction

Perceptions of Africa are often misleading, due to the influence, sometimes negative, of the media and the use of the Mercator Projection in world maps. This projection gives the impression that the continent is the same size as Greenland, whereas, in fact, it is 14 times larger, ranking second only to Asia in land area and population.

We mentioned in Chapter 18 that the countries of North Africa share many characteristics with those of the Middle East region. On the other hand, there are major cultural and physical differences between North Africa and the rest of the continent, in the region known as **sub-Saharan Africa.** The North African countries – Morocco, Algeria, Tunisia, and Libya – border the Mediterranean and are made up of fold mountains that are geologically similar to those of southern Europe. The climate and much of the scenery, with the exception of the desert zone, resemble that of Greece, Spain, or southern Italy, while the people are predominantly Arabs or Berbers. In contrast, most of sub-Saharan Africa consists of plateaux and block mountains, with only a narrow coastal plain separated from the interior by high escarpments. In terms of their ethnicity and culture, the emerging nations of sub-Saharan Africa are different from the Arab states of the north. The history and culture of North Africa, with the exception of Morocco, have only tenuous connections with the rest of the continent, and the Sahara Desert has acted as a formidable physical barrier to overland travel.

From the standpoint of international tourism, we need to treat the countries of North Africa separately from the rest of the continent, in view of their proximity to Europe.

North Africa

In contrast to most of sub-Saharan Africa, the North African countries, with the significant exception of Libya, have developed a sizeable tourism industry, based on beach holidays and inclusive tours for the north European market. This is an extension of the resort developments around the Mediterranean coast of Europe, although the cultural setting is quite different. This region accounts for over a third of foreign tourist arrivals to the African continent, with more than half arriving from countries across the Mediterranean, namely France, Spain, and Italy. Morocco was the first country to enter the market in the 1950s, and Tunisia soon followed.

We can divide North Africa into three main zones based on its physical geography:

- The fertile coastal plains, which have a Mediterranean climate.

- The Atlas Mountains, which reach their greatest extent in Morocco. In relation to their limited natural resources, these highlands are quite densely populated. There are frequent snowfalls during the winter months.
- The deserts of the south where productive land is restricted to the oases. The Sahara provides the region with its best-known tourist image, but, in reality, vast expanses of sand dunes are not the only landscape feature. Moreover, nomadic tribes now make up only a small minority of the population, while the camel caravan has long been superseded by motorised transport.

Morocco, Algeria, Tunisia, and Libya have formed an important part of the Muslim world, since their conquest by Arabs from the Middle East in the eighth century AD. Arabic is the official language of all four countries, and Arabs form the majority of the population, especially in the cities. However, the earlier inhabitants – the Berbers – still carry on their traditional way of life in the Atlas Mountains and the fringes of the Sahara. To some extent, they have been marginalised economically and politically, and the Berber languages, known collectively as Amazigh, receive little official encouragement. For centuries, the 'Barbary Coast' of North Africa was notorious as the source of raids by Moorish corsairs that terrorised defenceless Mediterranean villages and sometimes reached as far as the British Isles, carrying off victims for the slave markets of Marrakech and the harems of Algiers, Tunis, and Tripoli.

During the first half of the twentieth century, France ruled Algeria, Tunisia, and the greater part of Morocco. As a result, French is the second language, and some French cultural characteristics have been adopted by the educated classes of the cities. The French were also responsible for constructing a good highway system and well-planned European-style cities. To a lesser extent, the Spanish in their zone of Morocco, and the Italians in Libya, left a similar legacy. However, the influence of the Middle East remains predominant, as evidenced by the mosques and the souks, along with the crowded *medinas* and *kasbahs* (the old Arab *districts*) of the cities. Traditional handicrafts – notably leather, metalwork, and pottery – are important in the local economy and have been stimulated by the growth of tourism – often with government encouragement.

The countries of the region, known collectively as the Maghreb, have moved towards economic co-operation. However, the Arab Maghreb Union (AMG), which includes Mauritania to the South and Libya to the east, has so far been ineffective due to the long-running dispute between Morocco and Algeria over the Western Sahara. The main problem facing the Maghreb countries is the 'demographic time bomb', causing acute pressure on land and water resources; half the population of about 100 million is under 21 years of age. Poverty, illiteracy, and unemployment are widespread, both in the cities – which are surrounded by *bidonvilles* (shanty towns) – and in the countryside. The national economies cannot produce enough jobs to meet expectations, even for those with a Western-style education. This situation has contributed to the rise of Islamic fundamentalism in Algeria and the largely secular 'Jasmine Revolution' in Tunisia that initiated the 'Arab Spring' democratic movement. Popular unrest has so far been checked in Morocco. Not surprisingly, Western tourists with their relative wealth are also seen as an obvious target for exploitation by unlicensed guides, vendors, and touts of every description.

Morocco

The timeless, almost biblical scenes that can be found in Morocco (https://www.visitmo-rocco.com/en), both in the Arab *medinas* and the Berber communities of the Atlas, have a particular appeal. This has made the country a favourite location for film-makers. For the adventurous tourist travelling overland from Western Europe, it is the gateway to Africa. The influence of sub-Saharan Africa is evident, a legacy of the former slave trade routes, which crossed the desert. The markets assault the senses with a medley of sights and pungent aromas, and the widespread poverty can add to the 'culture shock' for Western visitors. Yet the cities also contain some of the most exquisite examples of Islamic architecture. This most 'oriental' of North African countries extends further west geographically than any part of the European continent and can be reached by a three-hour flight from the cities of Western Europe. Morocco is also unique among North African countries in having been an independent kingdom for many centuries, whose power at one time extended over most of Spain and the Western Sahara. It experienced only one period of foreign domination (from 1912 to 1956) when it was divided into French and Spanish protectorates. Under the rule of a monarch who has both near-autocratic powers and is revered as a religious leader, it has remained politically stable, with the government steering a course between traditional Islam and modernisation, in improving the status of women, for example.

The demand for tourism

Tourism is an important sector of the economy and earner of foreign exchange, accounting for 7.1 per cent of GDP and providing direct and indirect employment for 2 million people.

Domestic and outbound tourism

Domestic tourism is set to grow, with middle class families frequenting the beach resorts near Casablanca such as Mohammedia, and visiting mountain resorts such as Ifrane in the Middle Atlas and Oukaimaden in the High Atlas Mountains. These have both a summer season for health tourism and a winter skiing season. Those who can afford foreign travel prefer to visit Europe rather than other Arab countries.

Inbound tourism

Morocco received 12.9 million international tourist arrivals in 2019, but this fell to 2.8 million arrivals in 2020 as a result of COVID-19. Around a third of foreign visitors are Europeans, mainly from France and Spain, which dominate the market, followed by Britain and Germany. This is not surprising given the development of air-inclusive tours to Morocco, the convenient ferry links from Spain and Gibraltar, and the opening up of low-cost air routes. Algeria used to supply large numbers of tourists, but this market has largely disappeared due to the dispute over the Western Sahara. Moroccan expatriates working in Western Europe and returning for their annual holiday form a large proportion of the remaining arrivals, along with tourists from other Arab states.

The supply side of tourism

Transport

Car ownership levels and, indeed, incomes generally are much lower than in neighbouring Spain, while public transport is relatively inadequate. Nevertheless, Morocco has a good network of tarmac highways penetrating mountains and desert, while *grand-taxis* (as distinct from *petit-taxis* for short distances) play a crucial role in supplementing unreliable inter-city bus services. The national carrier, Royal Air Maroc (https://www.royalairmaroc.com/uk-en/), operates an efficient domestic air network. On the other hand, rail transport is poorly developed, and overland travel from Algeria has been disrupted by the closure of the 1,500-kilometre-long border between the two countries since 1990.

Accommodation

Two-thirds of Morocco's accommodation is in hotels, and the rest in self-catering. The French tour operator Club Méditerranée pioneered all-inclusive holiday villages on the Mediterranean coast and at Ouarzazate in the Sahara. As part of its conservation strategy, the government has encouraged the use of heritage buildings as hotels, while stays in *riads* – courtyard houses once belonging to wealthy merchants in the medinas of cities such as Fez (http://visitefes.com/en/) and Marrakech (https://visitmarrakech.com/) – are increasingly popular with Western tourists.

Organisation

The Ministry of Tourism, Handicrafts and Social and Solidarity Economy has the overall responsibility for the financing and development of tourism projects as well as promotion. The Moroccan Tourism Development Agency (SMIT) (https://smit.gov.ma/en/) is in charge of implementing policy and attracting foreign direct investment. Following a reduction in arrivals in the first-half of the 1990s, the government revised its approach to tourism. In 2001, a strategic plan for tourism – Vision 2010 – was launched on the initiative of King Mohammed VI, as part of a programme of social and economic reforms, to attract foreign investment. It aimed to create 60,000 new jobs in tourism, to increase tourist arrivals from 2.5 million in 2001 to a target of 10 million a year by 2010, and to increase the number of bed spaces by 150,000 between 2001 and 2010. The Plan Azur, a blueprint for coastal tourism, envisaged the creation of six new resorts, emphasising quality development and 'beach plus' tourism. To a large extent, the strategy, followed up by 'Vision 2020', has been successful in spreading economic growth. However, critics cite bureaucratic obstacles and inadequate infrastructure in rural areas for tourism development on the scale required. There is also a need to develop local tourism training programmes to achieve the social objectives of the plan.

Tourism resources

The heartland of Morocco is a fertile plateau separated by rugged mountain ranges from the Sahara Desert to the south and east, and the Mediterranean coast to the north. The High Atlas, rising to 4,000 metres near Marrakech, is the most spectacular of these mountain ramparts. Morocco is fortunate in having an extensive coastline on both the Atlantic and the Mediterranean. The climate of the Atlantic coast is particularly favourable for tourism, due to the influence of the cool Canaries Current, ensuring that the summers are usually free of the excessive heat and dust-laden winds found elsewhere in North Africa. Winters are much warmer, drier, and sunnier in southern Morocco than in the north, which explains why Agadir is promoted as a winter-sun destination, whereas Tangier (https://visittanger.com/en/accueil) and the resorts along the Mediterranean coast cater for summer holidays. A regional survey of Morocco shows the diversity of its natural and cultural resources, offering the tourist a variety of opportunities for recreation and sightseeing.

The Moroccan heartland

Cultural tourism to Morocco focusses on the 'Imperial Cities' circuit that combines Fez, Meknes, Rabat, and Marrakech – all of which at different times have served as the capital of Morocco.

- Marrakech has been fashionable as a winter-sun destination since the 1930s but is now mainly visited for its *souks* and the colourful market square known as the Djemaa el Fna, which is ideal for people-watching. Here, crowds gather around entertainers such as storytellers, snake charmers, acrobats, and musicians. Berber folklore features in the event attractions known as *fantasias* or *tabourida*, which feature impressive displays of horsemanship by local tribesmen. The most attractive features of Marrakech are the gardens that provide a refuge from the extreme summer heat; those of the Mamounia Hotel (https://www.mamounia.com/en/) are world famous.
- Fez has an extensive medina recognised by UNESCO as a World Heritage Site (https://whc.unesco.org/en/list/170/). The main attractions are the Attarine Medrassa (one of a number of Muslim colleges), the Karaouine Mosque, and the spice market. Those interested in Moroccan leather can visit the dyeworks and tanneries with its pungent aromas where medieval industrial methods are still carried on. Fez is also an important festival venue.
- Meknès (https://whc.unesco.org/en/list/793) is much less visited, although it includes the impressive city gate known as the Bab al Mansour, the Dar Jamal Museum, and the tomb of Sultan Moulay Ismael, probably the most despotic ruler of Morocco.

Business tourism gravitates to the modern city of Casablanca (Dar al Beida), which is Morocco's financial and commercial centre, complementing the capital Rabat (https://www.visitrabat.com/en/). Both cities have conference facilities of international standard.

Essaouira is a picturesque historic seaport, formerly known as Mogador, which has been designated by UNESCO as a World Heritage Site (https://whc.unesco.org/en/list/753/). It has long attracted artists and those seeking an alternative lifestyle and is noted for its annual music festival.

The North

This part of Morocco is dominated by the rugged terrain of the Rif Mountains, and following independence, it was neglected by the government for decades. The major tourist centres include:

- Tangier, which is a popular beach resort as well as being a major seaport, has undergone revitalisation following Vision 2010. From 1912 to 1956, the city had special status as an International Zone open to free trade and tolerant of alternative lifestyles, hence its enduring reputation as a centre for gay tourism.
- Tetouan (http://www.gotetouan.com/) was the capital of Spanish Morocco during the protectorate, and the cultural influence of Spain is still evident here and in the picturesque towns of Asilah, Chechauen, and Larache, where a new resort – Port Lixus (https://www.lixusbeachresort.com) – caters for golf and yachting. Beach tourism has developed along the Mediterranean coast near Tetouan and further east at Al Hoceima, which was badly damaged by an earthquake in 2004. These coastal resorts suffer from the problems of seasonality and under-investment, but this may change with the development, as part of the Plan Azur, of the resort of Saadia, which has received considerable attention from foreign investors.

The High Atlas

This is mainly a destination for trekking, where the attractions include spectacular mountain scenery and Berber villages that have remained apparently unchanged over the centuries. A number of tourism projects ensure that the benefits reach local people, by providing jobs, purchasing supplies, and funding community services, such as education in areas where most Berber women are illiterate.

Southern Morocco

South of the Atlas Mountains, the landscape becomes progressively more arid, until the true desert is reached. Major attractions include the oasis towns of Zagora and Ouarzazate, the gorges of the Todra and the Dadès, and the distinctive fortress-villages, built of red sun-dried clay by the local Berbers. Although it has been 'discovered' by surfers, the coast is still largely undeveloped, with the significant exception of Agadir, which is Morocco's most popular international beach resort. The old town was destroyed by an earthquake in 1960, and a modern resort of high-rise hotels and apartment blocks soon took its place to meet the demand for accommodation. Later expansion has been more sensitively designed, in the form of low-rise developments in the traditional Moorish style. To the north of Agadir, the new resort of Taghazout specialises in sport tourism, particularly golf. In the 'deep south' of Morocco near Tan-Tan, a 40-kilometre stretch of beach – Plage Blanche – was designated for ecotourism under Plan Azur, although some suspect this could be a prime location for more intensive development.

Since 1975, Morocco has occupied the **Western Sahara**, the former Spanish colony once known as Rio de Oro. However, this is disputed by the Polisario independence movement, whose claims for an independent Sahwari Arab Democratic Republic (SADR) are supported by some African countries. These include Algeria, which provides refugee camps for the many thousands of *Saharauis* opposed to Moroccan rule. The cause of this formerly nomadic people has been publicised by Javier Bardem in his documentary film *Sons of the Clouds*. Although the conflict is yet unresolved, the situation has normalised to the extent that a limited amount of tourist activity is taking place in the coastal desert zone at Dakhla, offering ideal conditions for kitesurfing and windsurfing.

Tunisia

With a long history of contact with other parts of the Mediterranean, Tunisia (https://www.discovertunisia.com/en/) is one of the most tolerant of the Arab states. This has been a factor in the development of the country as a holiday playground for Europeans seeking sun, sea, and sand. Tunisia not only has the advantages of superb beaches, and especially in the south, a favourable winter climate, but tourism development has been encouraged and carefully managed. Until the 2011 'Jasmine Revolution', Tunisia had a reputation for stability, where the government consistently applied liberal social and economic policies. Tourism is an important sector of the economy, and government involvement has been extensive. In 2019, tourism accounted for 6.5 per cent of GDP and provided employment directly or indirectly for almost 15 per cent of the workforce.

Tourism demand

Tourism caters mainly for the mass market, and this is shown by the fact that about half of the annual arrivals are mostly package holidaymakers from France, Germany, and Britain, concentrated during the summer months. Nevertheless, Tunisia has been successfully promoted as a winter-sun destination, and this has boosted arrivals between October and March. The country's dependence on the inclusive-tour European market leaves it vulnerable to recession in the generating countries and to the political situation in the Middle East. In 2015, a number of terrorist incidents directly targeting foreign tourists occurred in the capital Tunis and the beach resort of Sousse. The United Kingdom imposed a travel ban, followed by many other countries. Tunisia was no longer perceived as a safe destination, visitor numbers from Western Europe fell drastically, and tourism receipts plummeted. In response, the Tunisian government tightened security at hotels and in other sectors, and tourism subsequently recovered, with 9.4 million arrivals in 2019. The COVID-19 pandemic had a drastic impact on the tourism sector.

The supply side of tourism

Transport

As you would expect in a country dependent on the mass market, the majority of visitors arrive by air. Tunis airport (https://www.tunis-airport.com/) mainly handles scheduled services, but most holidaymakers on inclusive tours arrive at Enfidah-Hammamet (http://www.enfidhahammametairport.com/), which was specially built to handle charter flights. La Goulette and Bizerta are the ports of arrival for cruise passengers. Tunisia's professional approach to tourism includes upgrading the welcome facilities for travellers at the major gateways.

Accommodation

Hotel accommodation on the coast is mostly in low-rise developments, physically separate from the local communities, designed in the traditional style, and blending with the local environment. Other forms of accommodation include youth hostels and campsites. The French tour operator Club Méditerranée chose Tunisia as the location for several of its all-inclusive holiday villages.

Organisation

The Ministry of Tourism and Handicrafts (http://www.tourisme.gov.tn/en/) formulates the policy context for tourism, but its day-to-day implementation is carried out by the National Office of Tunisian Tourism (ONTT). Since the 1980s, Tunisia has diversified the tourism product away from the sea, sun, and sand image, by promoting:

- An upmarket marina and sports complex at Port El Kantaoui (http://www.portelkantaoui.com.tn/) adjoining the city of Sousse.
- A number of golf courses of world-class standard.
- The Tabarka area in the north-west – the 'Coral Coast' – as a scuba-diving destination.
- Soft adventure' tourism in the desert south, where a number of luxury hotels are available in oasis towns such as Tozeur.
- The rich cultural heritage of the country.
- A greater emphasis on luxury tourism for the Arabian market.

Tourism resources

Most tourists prefer to spend their time on the beaches and holiday complexes of the coast, the most important being Hammanet, Monastir, and Sousse. In the south, the island of Djerba with its myriad palm trees is an important winter-sun destination, while the Kerkenneh islands offer a less sophisticated holiday product.

Tunisia is a relatively compact country, giving the holidaymaker based on the coast a wide choice of excursions, including:

- The capital, Tunis where the spacious boulevards of the modern city provide a contrast with the medieval Arab medina. The Bardo Museum (http://www.bardomuseum.tn/)

has a world-renowned collection of finds from the site of Carthage, the great trading centre of ancient times, which under Hannibal challenged Rome for domination of the Mediterranean. After completely destroying Carthage in the last of the Punic Wars, Rome eventually built a new city on the site.

- The remains of the Roman cities of Dougga (https://whc.unesco.org/en/list/794) and El Djem (https://whc.unesco.org/en/list/38/) – where the amphitheatre is almost as large as the Colosseum in Rome. This part of North Africa was not only the granary of ancient Rome but also the supplier of many of the wild beasts that were slaughtered for public entertainment in the arena throughout the empire.

  - The holy city of Kairouan (https://whc.unesco.org/en/list/499/), famous for its Great Mosque and traditional crafts, such as saddle-making and carpet-weaving.
  - The troglodite community of Matmata and the oases of southern Tunisia. Although very few Tunisians are Saharan nomads, tour operators have exploited Western visitors' perceptions of the country by staging 'Bedouin feasts' that are really pseudo-events. Excursions by jeep or camel, from oasis towns such as Douz, provide a more genuine desert experience.

Algeria

In some respects, Algeria is the most Westernised of the North African countries. It experienced a much longer period of French rule and was, in fact, treated as part of metropolitan France. After the war of independence that ended in 1962, the FLN government established a secular, socialist-leaning state, using Algeria's considerable oil revenues to industrialise the country, expand education, and redistribute wealth. Tourism was not given a high priority, and the number of arrivals was much smaller than in neighbouring Morocco and Tunisia. The situation worsened after 1991, resulting from the vicious struggle between Islamic fundamentalists and the Algerian army.

Tourism demand

Algeria received over 2 million inbound arrivals in 2019; most of these are VFR tourists, as large numbers of Algerians work abroad, particularly in France, and return home for their annual summer holidays. French tourists visiting Algeria, and even more so Algerians visiting France, have been subjected to visa restrictions, due to the controversy over Algerian immigration.

The supply side of tourism

Transport

The majority of international tourists arrive by air, with the exception of Tunisians who use road or rail transport. Algeria has five international airports and scheduled flights are operated by the major European airlines as well as Air Algérie (https://airalgerie.dz/) – which also serves the extensive domestic network. Air transport is important in a country more than four times the size of France and allows access to remote desert and mountain areas. The country has good ferry links to Marseilles in France (operated by SNCM and Algerie Ferries (https://algerieferries.dz/)). There is a very extensive road network and excellent bus services, allowing visitors in less troubled times to travel throughout the country and into Tunisia. Rail transport is less efficient, and surface transport links with Morocco have been disrupted by the dispute over the Western Sahara.

Accommodation

Even in good times, Algeria's tourism industry has suffered from an acute shortage of accommodation. This has been made worse by the need of many foreign companies to accommodate their employees in hotels, owing to the shortage of housing. At the same time, service standards are poor. The difficulty is at its worst in Algiers, where accommodating delegates attending conferences is a continual problem. Most hotel beds are located in the purpose-built tourist centres on the coast and in some of the Saharan oases.

Organisation

Like other sectors of the economy, tourism is closely controlled by the state. Policy is decided by the Ministry of Tourism and Handicraft (http://www.mtatf.gov.dz/?lang=en), which has established a tourism development agency and is embarking on a policy of sustainable development to upgrade Algeria's product.

Tourism resources

Algeria offers a diversity of natural and cultural resources to the tourist. For example, the city of Timgad is one of the best-preserved Roman sites in North Africa.

In the extreme north, the Mediterranean coast is largely undeveloped for mass tourism, consisting of 1,200 kilometres of small bays backed by cliffs and scenically not very different from the Côte d'Azur. During the 1970s, a number of beach resorts (Tipasa, Zeralda, and Sidi Ferruch) were developed on the coast to cater for European tour operators. These were planned as self-contained towns in Arabic style, complete with well-designed souks, entertainment, and sports facilities. However, the coastal lowlands – the Tell – contain 84 per cent of Algeria's population and the bulk of its industry, so marine pollution is a serious problem.

Algiers itself – a metropolis of over 3 million people – is famous for its Kasbah, the fortified old town built under Ottoman rule. Despite having been declared a World Heritage Site, conservation has been neglected and its buildings are grossly overcrowded.

A series of mountain ramparts separate the coast from the Sahara. However, much of this mountain region, particularly the Aures Massif and Kabylie, is off-limits to tourists. The semi-arid area between the two main Atlas ranges, the Plateau of the Shotts, contains a large number of salt lakes. The true desert – and the date palms for which Algeria is famous – are reached at Laghouat, about 400 kilometres south from Algiers. From here, the Trans-Saharan Highway, the most important of the desert routes, runs a further 2,400 kilometres to Kano in northern Nigeria. Apart from the expanses of sand dunes known as *erg*, the Algerian Sahara is scenically quite varied, including the volcanic rock formations of the Hoggar rising to 3,000 metres and eroded badlands, criss-crossed by a network of wadis. Each oasis town has a distinct character, the most interesting being those of the M'zab region, while Tamanrasset is the main centre of the 'people of the veil', the Tuareg nomads. Prehistoric rock paintings at Ain Sefra and in the Tassili Mountains (https://whc.unesco.org/en/list/179/) show that the Sahara once enjoyed a much wetter climate. Although UNESCO has declared these a World Heritage Site, entire frescos have faded as a result of exposure to tourists or even been removed as part of the illicit trade in artefacts.

Libya

As a major oil producer, the government of Libya saw little need to encourage tourism until recently, while the UN trade embargo, imposed in retaliation for Kaddafi's socialist regime's support of terrorist movements throughout the Middle East, effectively restricted demand to a trickle of business travellers. After the Iraq War, the political climate changed and scheduled air services linked Tripoli and Benghazi to a growing number of cities in Europe. However, the political instability following the overthrow of Kadaffi has exposed the long-standing cultural differences between Tripolitania in the west of the country and Cyrenaica in the east, and the governments of most countries have advised against travelling to Libya.

Although 95 per cent of Libya is desert, vast reserves of ground water are believed to exist. There is a shortage of hotel accommodation and other facilities for Western holidaymakers, but the country has the following resources for tourism:

- The longest stretch of pristine Mediterranean coastline.
- Important Roman sites at Leptis Magna (https://whc.unesco.org/en/list/183), Sabratha (near Tripoli) (https://whc.unesco.org/en/list/184/) and Cyrene (near Benghazi). These were systematically excavated in the 1930s by Mussolini's Fascist regime to remind the world that Italy was an imperial power.
- The oases of Ghadames and Ghat on the former caravan routes across the Sahara.

Sub-Saharan Africa

The setting for tourism

The sheer size of Africa is at once an asset and a hindrance to developing a tourism industry. Before the advent of air travel, much of the interior of Africa was virtually inaccessible. There are very few natural harbours along the coast, and even penetration up the largest rivers – the Congo and Zambezi for example – was blocked by waterfalls and rapids. Most of the continent is sparsely populated, offering wide-open spaces, an almost unique wealth of wildlife, spectacular scenery, and a fascinating diversity of tribal cultures (around 2,000 languages are spoken in Africa). Yet apart from South Africa, with its well-developed infrastructure, the continent's tourism potential is largely untapped. This is due to the following factors:

- **Accessibility:** Although air transport has shown substantial growth, air traffic control and airport infrastructure are deficient by Western standards, and many experts consider this is holding back the development of tourism. Few airlines in Africa are run as profitable businesses, and many do not meet the safety standards demanded by the European Union and the United States. Air fares are high, despite low labour costs, and there is a lack of skilled personnel. Connectivity between African countries needs to be improved, and it is often easier to travel from one national capital to another via London, Paris, or Rome, than to fly direct. As members of the African Union (AU) (https://au.int/), most countries are signatories to the Yamoussoukro Decision that aimed to deregulate air services and open up the market to international competition. However, the agreement has yet to be implemented, as governments continue to protect the national flag carrier or even give preference to airlines from outside the continent. Road and rail infrastructure is generally inadequate in most African countries, with some areas becoming inaccessible during the rainy season. Tour operators have to face the obstacles of poor roads and high vehicle maintenance costs. In the absence of adequate public transport, improvised alternatives, such as the 'bush taxis' of the Gambia and the *matatus* of Kenya can be used by the more adventurous independent travellers.
- **A low level of economic development:** Most African countries fall in the 'least developed' category, with only a few having reached the intermediate level of development. Low incomes and high rates of illiteracy mean low participation in tourism. Although some countries do see tourism as an important source of foreign currency and a stimulus to the economy, many governments give tourism a low priority for investment compared to other economic sectors.
- **Poor organisation** There is a generally poor level of organisation, particularly at the regional level. Governments also place bureaucratic obstacles in the way of tourists, making travel between countries difficult. Education and training for the tourism sector is of a poor standard, nepotism and corruption is rife, and marketing budgets are inadequate.
- **Political instability** Some of the world's 'trouble spots' are located in Africa, fuelled by tribal unrest, ethnic rivalries, or border disputes, as the political boundaries drawn up by the former colonial rulers (Britain, France, Germany, Belgium, Portugal, Italy, and Spain) rarely correspond to natural features or tribal territories. Few African countries are, therefore, nation-states in the European sense. This instability has led to concern in the Western media over the physical security of tourists and has also discouraged Western investment in the tourism industry.
- **Perceived health and safety risks** The outbreak of ebola in 2014, although it was largely confined to three West African countries, affected travel to the region as a whole. The high incidence of AIDS, as well as insect-borne diseases such as malaria

and yellow fever, is due in large measure to the inadequate infrastructure of public health services in most of Africa.

• **Sceptical investment environment** Investors are often reluctant to invest in tourism in countries where the political climate is changeable, where a return on their investment is not guaranteed, and price inflation is not under control. This is changing, with the arrival of China on the world stage. In its demand for Africa's wealth of raw materials, China has to a large extent replaced the United States and the ex-colonial powers as a major source of investment, but this may have costs as well as benefits for the recipient countries. China is now itself facing competition from Brazil, India, and Turkey as providers of the infrastructure that Africa needs for its development.

All these constraints and structural weaknesses have frustrated Africa's ability to capitalise on the growing long-haul market, and it is evident that tourism remains still a fledgling industry. This is borne out by the statistics, for the whole of sub-Saharan Africa, there were around 40 million international tourist arrivals in 2019, while North Africa attracted almost 30 million. Indeed, for a continent that contains 15 per cent of the world's population, it receives a small share of the tourist market, amounting to only 5 per cent. Fewer than half of the 50 countries in sub-Saharan Africa have developed significant tourism industries. However, there are a number of positive factors that are boosting Africa's tourism in the new millennium:

• Interest in African peoples and cultures.
• The increasing pace and variety of tourism development.
• Africa will be attractive to segments of the population in the generating countries who have both the time and the income to travel.
• The growing importance of ethnic ties between Africa and Europe due to migration.
• The growth of an African middle class with the propensity to travel.
• The growth of sport tourism, bringing together participants from many countries in the region, as shown by the Africa Cup of Nations football event (https://www.cafonline.com/total-africa-cup-of-nations/) and the African Games (https://www.jar2019.ma).
• The pursuit of free-market economic policies in many African countries.
• Improved air access.

Population growth and climate change are two factors affecting the tourism potential of sub-Saharan Africa. The population is growing faster in Africa than in any other part of the world and is expected to reach 2 billion by 2050. Moreover, half the population of Africa are under 21 years of age, and this represents both a challenge for health and education services and an opportunity for change.

Most of Africa south of the Sahara, with the exception of South Africa, has a tropical climate. As we mentioned in Chapter 4, the rainy season is determined by the position of the Intertropical Convergence Zone (ITCZ). Any delay in the arrival of the rains can spell disaster for African farmers, particularly those in the semi-arid Sahel belt that extends from Senegal to the Horn of Africa. Climate change is already affecting much of Africa, with droughts becoming longer and more severe, and this is a push factor driving emigration.

We can divide sub-Saharan Africa into three main regions:

- East Africa, which receives around 40 per cent of international tourist arrivals
- Southern Africa
- West and Central Africa

Safaris are the primary tourism product attracting American and European visitors to Africa. However, in focussing too narrowly on long-haul tourism, we should be aware that much larger numbers of Africans are crossing national boundaries within sub-Saharan Africa, to visit friends and relatives, for business, for religious reasons, to seek medical treatment, to shop, to attend conferences, and participate in sports events.

East Africa

Tour operators regard the countries of Kenya, Tanzania, and Uganda as the core of East Africa. Their tourism resources are similar, and before independence, they had a measure of unity under British rule. The East African Community (EAC) (https://www.eac.int/), which Rwanda and Burundi joined in 2007, and South Sudan and the Democratic Republic of Congo (DRC) more recently, aims for closer economic co-operation between the member states. East Africa as a geographical region includes the countries of the 'Horn of Africa' – Ethiopia, Eritrea, Somalia, and Djibouti – where tourism is much less developed. The Swahili language is widely understood throughout East Africa, while the heritage of Islam and Arab traders is evident throughout the coastal belt.

The setting for tourism

Contrasts of scenery, climate, and culture are particularly evident in East Africa. Most of the region consists of an undulating plateau over 1,000 metres in altitude, but it also contains the most spectacular scenery to be found anywhere on the continent. Part of the Rift Valley – a deep gash in the earth's surface extending from the Dead Sea to Lake Malawi – cuts through the region as two branches. The western branch contains Lakes Albert, Edward, and Tanganyika, while the eastern branch is bounded by a high escarpment in western Kenya. The earth movements that formed the rift also raised the high mountains of volcanic origin on either side, notably Mounts Elgon, Kenya, and Kilimanjaro. The valley floor is littered with a number of craters (the most famous being Ngorongoro, which is a spectacular wildlife sanctuary), and there are numerous lakes. Some of these, for example, Naivasha, contain fresh water and are rich in fish, whereas others – Nakuru, Magadi, and Natron – have deposits of salt and soda that have attracted the attention of mineral developers, as well as of conservationists who wish to protect the millions of flamingos which breed there.

Most of East Africa has a tropical wet-dry climate but, because of its position astride the Equator, the region has two dry seasons and two rainy seasons. The coast is also influenced by the seasonal shift in wind direction known as the monsoon over the Indian Ocean. Altitude too has an important effect. Conditions in Nairobi at 1,800 metres are ideal for Europeans with daytime temperatures between 20°C and 25°C all year round. The main tourist seasons for East Africa's big-game areas are December to early March and July to early October, as these correspond to the dry seasons when the animals are concentrated around the water-holes and the grass is short, aiding visibility. Travel is also easier at this time, whereas the roads are often impassable at the height of the rainy season.

East Africa contains a large variety of habitats for wildlife, ranging from the semi-deserts of northern Kenya and Somalia which support herds of antelope and gazelle, to the dense rain forests of the Ruwenzori Mountains on the Uganda-Rwanda border, sheltering the chimpanzee and gorilla. The dominant type of vegetation is thorny scrub in the drier areas, alternating with open plains or savanna where the tall grasses, dotted with umbrella-shaped acacia trees support large herds of grazing animals and the great predators such as the lion.

Safari tourism in East Africa

Wildlife is the basis of East Africa's tourism industry. The organisation of big-game hunting safaris began at the end of the nineteenth century, although the first national parks were not designated until the 1940s. Since independence, Kenya, Tanzania, and Uganda have devoted large areas to wildlife conservation, either by designation as national parks, which conform to the high standards of protection laid down by the International Union for Conservation of Nature (IUCN) (https://www.iucn.org/), or as game reserves. This has entailed a social cost as local communities have lost their traditional rights to these lands. For example, the semi-nomadic Masai on the Kenya-Tanzania border, who have a symbiotic relationship with the wildlife, were prohibited from grazing their cattle in the Masai-Mara Wildlife Reserve (http://www.maasaimaraconservancies.co.ke/). Wildlife resources are under threat, for the following reasons:

- Poaching for bush meat, skins (mainly from leopards), ivory, and rhinoceroes horn – (the latter is greatly valued in both Yemen and the Far East, but for different reasons). It is difficult to enforce laws against poaching, which is increasingly carried out by organised criminal gangs rather than individuals.
- The encroachment of the human population (growing at the rate of 3 per cent annually) on wildlife habitats; this is a more serious long-term problem, although it is poaching that receives wide publicity in the Western media. Most of the best land has already been given over to the production of cash crops for export rather than to food staples, while African farmers see wildlife as a threat, not as a resource.

The term 'safari' has come to include the following types of products;

- Budget-priced mini-bus tours of the most accessible national parks such as Amboseli (http://www.kws.go.ke/amboseli-national-park) and Masai-Mara, based on Nairobi or one of the coastal resorts. Drivers often approach the game too closely so that tourists can get a better view. Tourists also spend most of their time looking for the 'big five', lion, leopard, elephant, rhino, and buffalo, causing bottlenecks in the process.

- In the higher price bracket, tour operators include stays in one of the government-run game lodges in the national parks. These are designed to blend in with the local environment, the most famous being 'Treetops' in the Aberdare Mountains (http://tree-tops.co.ke/) and Seronera in the Serengeti National Park. They offer a five-star service and, to an extent, tourists are cut-off from the realities of life in the African bush.
- Camping safaris, for example, in the Tsavo National Park (http://www.kws.go.ke/content/tsavo-east-national-park), are a much more authentic and sustainable alternative.
- Balloon safaris provide an ideal way to view game, but it is said that the noise from the burners frightens away the animals, while the back-up vehicles damage the terrain in the wet season.
- Other options include camel safaris in the remoter parts of northern Kenya; fishing expeditions to Lake Turkana; trekking and mountain climbing on Mount Kenya or Kilimanjaro; and escorted expeditions to privately-owned game reserves and game ranches.

The negative impacts of safari tourism can be minimised by:

- Visitor management, ensuring that tourist numbers do not exceed the carrying capacity of the area; in other words, low volume, high spending, low impact 'ecotourism' rather than mass tourism.
- Involvement of the local community, so that they derive tangible benefits from tourism. For example, in Kenya, the Masai have set up 'cultural *bomas*', villages, where they can sell their traditional crafts directly to tourists. In Rwanda, the government shares some of the revenue from visitors to the mountain gorilla sanctuaries with local communities, and this is used to fund co-operative projects. For example, instead of gathering wild honey from the forest and, thereby, upsetting the ecosystem, villagers are encouraged to take up beekeeping.

CASE STUDY 19.1
CONTROLLED HUNTING AND CONSERVATION
IN AFRICA

Many Western tourists perceive rural Africa to be a vast safari park, and are unaware that up to 70 per cent of the continent's wild animals live outside the national parks that tourists visit. African farming communities have, in fact, co-habited with the wildlife for many centuries. Animals cannot be confined within national park boundaries and, particularly in times of drought, wander onto farm land. This can pose an existential threat to rural communities; elephants trample crops and disrupt water supplies, while lions find livestock an easy prey and occasionally attack vulnerable members of the community. (In the West, we have long forgotten that our medieval ancestors faced a similar problem with wolves.) Not surprisingly, the threat to village livelihoods has led to pressure on governments to control wildlife populations by legalised hunting or in some cases their translocation to other areas.

The demand for big-game hunting has for long come mainly from wealthy individuals or syndicates in Western countries with the purpose of obtaining trophies. The sale of hunting licences is a source of revenue for the authorities, which is used to fund game wardens and anti-poaching patrols while preserving habitats for wildlife. A number of entrepreneurs have set up hunting concessions and game ranches to supply the demand. There is also a lucrative trade in live animals to supply zoos in the United Arab Emirates and the Far East.

Hunting is inevitably opposed by animal-lovers and conservationist pressure groups, but like other commodities, the trade in wildlife products is subject to supply and demand. The Convention on International Trade in Endangered Species of Wild Fauna and Flora (CITES) aims for sustainability on this issue. CITES (https://www. cites.org/) in consultation with the IUCN prepares lists differentiating between species regarding the scale of the threat:

- Species for which commercial cross-border trade is highly restricted or subject to quota systems. CITES requires both an export permit and an import permit from the authorities of the destination country.
- Species which require only an export permit, where it can be shown that the export of wildlife products plays no part in the endangerment of the species as a whole.

The international trade in ivory remains one of the biggest threats to Africa's wildlife resources. In 1989, CITES imposed an outright ban, which succeeded in halting the decline in elephant numbers, particularly in Kenya. Subsequently, four Southern African countries – South Africa, Botswana, Namibia, and Zimbabwe – were allowed to stockpile ivory for export, provided it came from 'rogue' elephants or those that had died from natural causes. Most of the demand for ivory originates in China, which has largely replaced Europe and the United States as the main trading partner for many African countries. It is estimated that 23,000 elephants are killed illegally each year to satisfy the demand for ivory, with countries such as the DRC and Sudan acting as transit points for the trade. Much of the ivory is processed in Africa by syndicates of Chinese origin, making it more difficult to intercept and identify the smuggled product. Furthermore, five Southern African countries have called for a suspension of the ban, so they can export their stockpiles and use the proceeds of the sale to fund conservation efforts. Elephant populations in these countries are stable or even increasing, so that there is a case for restricting the size of the herds.

However, opposition to big-game hunting has grown considerably in recent years in Europe and the United States. The Netherlands has banned the import of trophies from around 200 species, and the United Kingdom, Belgium, and Italy plan to introduce similar legislation. This will have unintended consequences, as much of the revenue from the sale of hunting licences goes to benefit African rural communities, and it is necessary to win their support in the fight against illegal poaching.

Discuss the proposition that controlled hunting is essential for a healthy ecosystem and provides an economic incentive for local communities to protect wildlife resources.

Kenya

Kenya (https://magicalkenya.com/) is the most developed of the East African countries and, until the eruption of inter-tribal violence following the elections in 2007, appeared to be far more stable than its neighbours. Prior to gaining independence, it had a large number of white European settlers and an Asian middle class, generating a sizeable demand for domestic tourism. Following independence in 1963, political stability and government support encouraged foreign investment in Kenya's tourism industry. The Kenyan Ministry of Tourism reflects the importance placed on tourism as the major source of foreign exchange, and it enjoys private sector support from the Kenya Tourist Board (http://ktb.go.ke/), which has responsibility for promotion. Although it has pursued a policy of 'Kenyanisation' replacing foreign nationals by Africans, the government in other respects, has had a 'laissez-faire' attitude towards the private sector and foreign tour operators. This is changing in response to the impact of mass tourism in the more accessible national parks and on the coast. The tourism authorities are also faced with a decline in arrivals as fears about crime in Nairobi, international terrorism, and political unrest have grown. Such is the problem that neighbouring countries are set to challenge Kenya's crown as the leading tourism destination in the region. This is a serious issue as tourism represents around 9 per cent of Kenya's economy. Since the early 1990s, ecotourism has been encouraged by the government's Kenya Wildlife Service (KWS) (http://www.kws.go.ke/), while the government's development plan has the following aims:

- To diversify the tourism product.
- To attract high income, low volume tourism. Here, privately-owned game ranches play an important role, as they integrate tourism, wildlife, and cattle farming. Tourists can participate in activities on the ranch, while local communities benefit, with the enterprise providing jobs and funding for schools.

Tourism resources

Kenya became one of Africa's most popular destinations (attracting over 2 million visitors in 2019), because it has a wealth of tourism resources, including some of the best-known game reserves, such as the Masai-Mara, Amboseli, and Tsavo, and an attractive coastline along the Indian Ocean. The capital Nairobi is a modern city, with facilities for shopping and entertainment, and good communications by air, road, and rail to most of the region, making it the recognised gateway to East Africa. Most foreign tourists spend one or two nights in Nairobi, and the Kenyatta Conference Centre (http://kicc.co.ke/) is a major venue for business travellers.

The old city of Mombasa, with its modern port facilities at Kilindini, and extended international airport (https://www.kaa.go.ke/airports/our-airports/moi-international-airport/), is the gateway to the Kenya coast. In the old port, Arab *dhows* can still be seen and the markets sell tourist curios such as Masai beadwork, wood and soapstone carvings, and animal trophies. The modern resort developments near Mombasa and at Malindi (https://malindians.com/) attract large numbers of winter-sun package holidaymakers, mainly from Germany, Britain, Switzerland, or Italy, while beaches and hotels tend to be dominated by a particular nationality. Tourism suffered a major setback in 2002, with the bombing of a hotel which was owned and mainly frequented by Israelis. Until then, beach tourism had been expanding in Kenya, while visits to game reserves (except by Americans) were declining. The long white sandy beaches, and lagoons protected by an offshore coral reef, provide safe conditions for diving and other water sports. Although the underwater wildlife is protected by marine national parks at Malindi and Watamu (https://www.wondersofwatamu.com/), excessive numbers of glass bottom boats, and illegal shell collecting for the lucrative souvenir trade, have caused extensive damage to the reef. Western visitors have also caused offence to a traditional Muslim society by their dress and behaviour, and social mores are changing to the extent that sex tourism is a problem. The island of Lamu (http://lamu.go.ke/trade-tourism/) has minimised these environmental and social impacts by carefully controlling tourism. The income is used for conservation projects, so that the Swahili-Arabic heritage of this attractive resort has been retained.

Tanzania

Tanzania (https://www.tanzaniatourism.go.tz/en) has a less developed tourism industry than Kenya. In part, this is due to history, until 1989, government policy encouraged African-style socialism with the state taking a major shareholding in tourism enterprises. Western-style tourism did not fit easily into this scheme, and foreign companies were reluctant to invest. Since 1990, the government has adopted a more pragmatic approach, liberalising the tourism sector, and is ambitious to become a leader in this field. This has been aided by the decline in tourism in neighbouring Kenya. The Tanzania Tourist Board, created in 1992, has revitalised the sector so that it directly supports 400,000 jobs and generates a quarter of the country's foreign exchange. By 2019, there were over 1.5 million international arrivals.

Tourism resources

Tanzania's most well-known attractions lie close to the Kenyan border, and this has made the task of promotion more difficult. They include:

- Africa's highest mountain – Mount Kilimanjaro (see photo 19.1).
- The world-famous Serengeti National Park, with its spectacular seasonal migrations of animals in search of water and grazing.
- The Ngorongoro Reserve (https://www.ngorongorocrater.org/), an extinct volcanic caldera, with excellent game viewing from the crater rim.

Ironically, it is easier to reach these attractions from Nairobi than from Tanzania's former capital, Dar-es-Salaam, on the coast. This induced the government to build an airport near Arusha (Kilimanjaro International (https://www.kilimanjaroairport.co.tz/)) and invest heavily in hotel complexes in that city. The enormous game reserves of southern Tanzania are under-utilised as they lie off the tourism circuit and are usually reached by fly-in safaris.

Photo 19.1
Kilimanjaro, Africa's highest mountain
Source: ©istockphoto.com/Graeme Shannon

Lake Tanganyika, which Tanzania shares with Burundi and the DRC, is another major attraction, yet barely developed. It is 1,500 metres in depth and is estimated to contain 18 per cent of the world's fresh water. In contrast to Lake Victoria, there are few large towns or industries to cause pollution. A small number of lakeside sites offer opportunities for diving or a beach holiday combined with a safari, usually focussing on chimpanzees in the forested mountains nearby.

Tanzania's primary focus of tourist attention is the coast, particularly the islands of Zanzibar (http://www.zanzibartourism.go.tz/), Pemba and Mafia (http://www.mafiaisland.com/), where game fishing and diving are the main attractions. Zanzibar, particularly 'Stone Town' (the old trading city) also offers major cultural attractions from the times of the Arab sultans, but development projects for Western-style beach tourism have aroused controversy because of their social and environmental impact.

Uganda

Uganda (https://www.visituganda.com/) had a flourishing tourism industry before the Amin regime brought disorder and maladministration to the country in the 1970s. Relative stability since the 1990s has led to the growth of ecotourism, based on the country's rainforest resources, which have the highest biodiversity in East Africa. Another major attraction is Murchison (Kabegera) Falls near the headwaters of the River Nile. However, the main areas of tourist interest – the Queen Elizabeth National Park and the Bwindi Impenetrable Forest National Park in the Ruwenzori Mountains – lie close to the Congolese border and are threatened by the turmoil prevalent in Central Africa. Tourism Uganda (https://utb.go.ug/) is trying to diversify the tourism product by encouraging adventure tourism and promoting the attractions of the capital, Kampala (https://visitkampala.net/). Entebbe (https://visitentebbe.net/) is the gateway to Uganda, and ferry services across Lake Victoria link the city to Kenya and Tanzania. In 2018, there were almost 1.5 million international tourist arrivals.

Rwanda

Before 1962, Rwanda (https://www.visitrwanda.com/) and Burundi were united under Belgian rule as Ruanda-Urundi. Both countries are small, densely populated, and mountainous, with few natural resources. Both countries have been affected by the ethnic tensions between the Hutu and the Tutsi (who were the dominant group under colonial rule), which culminated in the 1994 genocide in Rwanda. More recently, however, Rwanda has achieved political stability with the Tutsi regaining control and has attracted considerable foreign investment.

Rwanda has an intensively farmed landscape, including tea plantations, and its well-ordered capital, Kigali provides a contrast to the chaos evident in most African cities. The genocide is commemorated by the Memorial Centre in Kigali (https://www.kgm.rw). Tourists are mainly attracted to the Volcanoes National Park, famous for the mountain gorilla sanctuary associated with Dian Fossey, and the Nyungwe National Park with its monkeys and abundant bird life. The Rwanda Development Board (https://rdb.rw/) is also promoting health and wellness tourism in the resorts around Lake Kivu.

Burundi

In Burundi, tourism remains a fledgling industry, due mainly to political instability. Relations with Rwanda are strained; here the government is in Hutu hands. Gitega is now the capital, but Bujumbura remains the economic hub. This city is situated on Lake Tanganyika, which has potential as a tourism resource, but further development of tourism depends largely on stability within the Greater Lakes region, which includes the neighbouring DRC.

The other countries of East Africa

Tourism in Sudan and the Horn of Africa has been held back by decades of political strife, with Eritrea and Somalia generating large numbers of economic migrants and refugees.

Sudan

In 2011 after many years of conflict, Sudan was divided along religious and cultural lines between the Arab-speaking, Islamic north, and the newly independent South Sudan, which is mainly black African and Christian or animist in religion. The northern Sudan has close cultural links with Egypt and the Middle East. The capital, Khartoum, is situated at the confluence of the White Nile and the Blue Nile, which has its source in the highlands of Ethiopia. However, neither river is used to any extent as a tourist route. There are opportunities for diving along the Red Sea coast, near the old trading port of Suakin. Other attractions include the Dinder National Park, a major wildlife reserve near the Ethiopian border, and the volcanic highlands of Jebel Marra in the Western Sudan, which provide a refuge from the extreme heat of summer. However, tourism is in abeyance due to the conflict in the Darfur region.

Tourism in **South Sudan** is less developed, due to lack of infrastructure and the strife between the Dinka and the Nuer, the two main ethnic groups. The vast areas of wetlands known as the Sudd provide a contrast to the desert landscapes of the North.

Ethiopia

Ethiopia (http://www.ethiopia.travel) has great potential as a destination for a variety of tourists – culture-seekers, those interested in wildlife and adventure-seekers. The heartland of the country is a high plateau, isolated by mountains and deserts, where a unique civilisation, characterised by the Amharic language and its own version of Coptic Christianity, has survived over many centuries. Except for a brief period of Italian occupation (from 1936 to 1941), Ethiopia has never experienced foreign rule. However, it was not until the end of the nineteenth century that the diverse ethnic groups that make up the modern nation were effectively brought under the rule of Amharic monarchs from their new capital of Addis Ababa.

Most of the population of around 109 million is concentrated in the *voina dega* ('wine highland') climate zone at altitudes of between 1,800 and 2,500 metres, where temperatures remain fairly cool year round. The Rift Valley in the south-west has a tropical climate, while in the north-east on the borders with Eritrea and Djibouti, lies the Danakil Depression, one of the world's most hostile environments, reputed to be the hottest place on earth.

Air travel is vital in a country with such difficult topography. The state-owned carrier, Ethiopian Airlines (https://www.ethiopianairlines.com/), is one of the success stories of Africa, investing in the most technologically advanced aircraft, and developing regional hubs in Lomé, Togo and Lilongwe, Malawi. With this 'hub and spoke' system, the airline can connect passengers from different parts of Africa into its global network as a Star Alliance member, via Addis Ababa. In 2014, Ethiopian gained fifth freedom traffic rights to operate services to Los Angeles via Dublin.

Although Addis Ababa was developed as a conference venue for Africa by Haile Selassie in the 1960s, tourism languished for decades after his fall from power. More recently, international hotel chains have invested in cities throughout the country, but the accommodation sector suffers from a shortage of trained staff.

Tourism is co-ordinated at government level by the Ministry of Culture and Tourism (http://www.moct.gov.et/). The main tourist circuit links Addis Ababa to the former capitals of Axoum and Gondar, Lake Tana (the source of the Blue Nile), and the rock-hewn churches of Lalibela (https://whc.unesco.org/en/list/18/), which is an important place of pilgrimage. The Ethiopian Wildlife Conservation Authority manages a number of national parks offering different habitats for wildlife.

Eritrea

Eritrea's (http://www.eritrea.be/) national identity derives from half a century of Italian rule and the long struggle for independence from Ethiopia which ended in 1993, although border disputes between the two countries continue. The country offers two contrasting environments, the arid but sweltering Red Sea coast, and the cool, fertile highlands around the capital, Asmara (http://www.asmera.nl/), retaining some of its Italian heritage. The government recognises the importance of tourism and has restored as an attraction the spectacular railway linking the capital to the port of Massawa. Off the Red Sea coast, there are diving sites in the Dahlak Archipelago.

Somalia

Unlike most African countries, Somalia is not divided by language or ethnicity. However, the preconditions for tourism are lacking, and Somalis have historically resented outsiders.

Most of Somalia was an Italian colony, except for the north-west that was under British control. These former divisions and bitter clan rivalries re-surfaced in the 1990s, along with the rise of Islamic fundamentalism, leading to the breakdown of government authority outside Mogadishu (https://www.visitmogadishu.com/). Two separatist states – Somaliland and Puntland – were set up in the north, but they have not received international recognition. Somalia's long coastline has tourism potential, but its beaches are unlikely to be developed while piracy continues in this part of the Indian Ocean. In Mogadishu, the infrastructure for economic revival is being restored, mainly with Turkish assistance.

Djibouti

With few other resources, the small ex-French colony of Djibouti (https://guide.visitdjibouti.dj/) has exploited its deepwater harbour at the entrance to the Red Sea with the view to becoming a major trading centre between Africa and the Middle East. Djibouti can offer great cultural diversity.

Southern Africa

The countries of Southern Africa recognise the importance of wildlife conservation as a major part of their tourism appeal. To counter the threats of drought, poaching and development pressures to wildlife, several cross-border parks have been proposed, which would allow the animals to migrate freely within their natural ecosystems. These international 'peace parks' (http://www.sanparks.org/) now include the Kgadaladi Transfrontier Park in the Kalahari, involving South Africa and Botswana, and the Great Limpopo Transfrontier Park, with an area of 35,000 square kilometres, involving South Africa, Mozambique, and Zimbabwe.

Most countries in the region have strong economic and cultural ties with Britain and have succeeded in attracting visitors from the main generating markets. International air services to Southern Africa improved considerably during the 1990s. There is scope for more regional co-operation under the Southern Africa Development Community (SADC) (https://www.sadc.int/) in reducing border formalities to encourage travel between the various countries and in overseas promotion, by expanding membership of the Southern Africa Regional Tourism Council (SARTOC). However, the future growth of tourism will depend primarily on the continuance of political and economic stability in South Africa, which is by far the leading country in the region.

South Africa

The setting for tourism

South Africa (https://www.southafrica.net/en/) differs from the rest of the continent in having a large number of people of European origin – over 5 million or 13 per cent of the population - while Asians and those of mixed race account for another 11 per cent. Under white rule, South Africa – particularly the Cape area with its Mediterranean climate – was often perceived as an outpost of Europe. Since the coming to power of the ANC government in 1994, attitudes have changed; the country is no longer isolated by world opinion as it was in the era of *apartheid* (the policy of racial segregation), and it is now taking a larger share in the development of the African continent. We can regard South Africa as a developed country rather than part of the Third World for the following reasons:

- It has an advanced economy based on vast mineral resources, with only 14 per cent of the workforce employed in agriculture (compared to 80 per cent in Kenya, for example). South Africa also accounts for over half the electricity generated in the continent. The 'powerhouse of Africa' has attracted some 5 million immigrants from countries as distant as the Congo, but mainly from neighbouring Zimbabwe and Mozambique.
- Literacy levels are generally quite high.
- It has a well-developed infrastructure, with good air, road, and rail systems.
- There are fewer health risks than in other parts of Africa, and malaria is confined to the Lowveld region on the eastern border.

South Africa has a warm temperate climate that is almost ideal for outdoor recreation, particularly beach tourism and water sports, as sunshine hours exceed those of most Mediterranean resorts. With the exception of the Western Cape, most of the rainfall occurs in the summer months (October to April). There are important differences in climate and landscapes between the coastal areas and the high interior plateaux – the Karoo and the Highveld, where night-time temperatures frequently fall below 0°c during the winter months. The Drakensberg Mountains to the east form a high escarpment rising to 3,000 metres, offering some of South Africa's most spectacular scenery, including the Blyde River Canyon. The Atlantic coast north of Table Bay is less suitable for sea bathing than the Indian Ocean, as it is cooled by the cold Benguela Current, but conditions are generally favourable for surfing.

The demand for tourism

Tourism is a major industry in South Africa, accounting for 3.7 per cent of GDP and supporting 1.5 million jobs. Demand is influenced by the vast disparities in wealth, to the extent that most of the black majority continue to live in conditions of Third World poverty, without basic services in the tribal homelands or in the 'townships' – the urban agglomerations adjoining Cape Town and Johannesburg. Although there has been social mobility since the ending of apartheid, with the rise of a black middle class, wealth, and the ownership of land remains concentrated in the hands of the white minority. Most black South Africans are too poor to generate an effective demand for tourism.

Domestic and outbound tourism

Domestic demand accounts for a quarter of all tourism in South Africa, about 18 million trips in 2019. White South Africans travel widely throughout their country, and the great majority of trips are made by car, using the excellent road network. Self-catering accommodation is often used in preference to hotels. Sports events, and to a lesser extent cultural festivals, are an important motivation for travel. Although the climate is suitable for tourism for most of the year, the timing of school holidays in the Christmas and Easter periods results in a seasonal peaking of demand, which places pressures on accommodation, particularly in Durban (https://visitdurban.travel/) and other resorts of the Natal coast. This is the main holiday area for South Africans, especially those from the interior provinces of Gauteng (which includes Johannesburg), and the largely Afrikaans-speaking Free State. The Drakensberg Mountains are visited by large numbers of people from the coast during the hot, humid summers, and the towns of Pietermaritzburg (https://www.pmbtourism.co.za/), Estcourt and Ladysmith have a long-established tourism industry to meet their needs. Although the mountains are sufficiently high for snow during the winter months, there is only a modest winter sports industry, based in Tiffindell (https://www.tiffindell.co.za/) near the border with Lesotho, catering for domestic demand.

As regards outbound tourism, while the depreciation of the rand since the 1990s has made South Africa a competitively priced destination for international tourism, it has also made foreign travel much more expensive for South Africans. Considering their geographical isolation, they are well represented in the tourist arrivals for a large number of long-haul destinations, including Britain and the United States, as well as neighbouring African countries. There were 6.1 million departures in 2019, falling to 1.6 million in 2021 as a result of COVID-19.

Inbound tourism

In the apartheid era, much of the inbound tourism from Britain and other European countries had been for VFR or business purposes. Since the 1990s, there has been a substantial growth of interest in South Africa as a holiday destination by tour operators. Sport tourism has also played a significant role, including the Rugby World Cup (https://www.rugbyworldcup.com) in 1995, and the FIFA World Cup in 2010. In 2019, almost 15 million arrivals were recorded. The COVID-19 pandemic and its Omicron variant had a devastating impact, such that arrivals declined to 2.6 million in 2021. Around half of foreign visitors come from other African countries. The biggest overseas markets are the United Kingdom, Germany, and the United States. The Netherlands accounts for only a small percentage of overseas visitors, despite the strong historical links with the first white settlers – the Afrikaaners, whose language derives from Dutch. South Africa attracts visitors with a wide range of special interests, including botanical tours and wine-tasting in the Western Cape, industrial and transport heritage, such as steam locomotives and the gold and diamond mines, and for history buffs, the battlefields of the Zulu and Anglo-Boer wars in KwaZulu-Natal (https://www.battlefieldsroute.co.za). The ending of apartheid has also strongly influenced patterns of tourism demand. Contemporary South African culture, heritage sites commemorating the struggle for black African freedom, and township tours are now part of the tourism product. Another niche market is health tourism, particularly cosmetic surgery, in which South Africa has the following advantages:

* A good health infrastructure, with excellent medical services and clinics.
* From the viewpoint of British visitors, an English-speaking population, and a journey necessitating only a minor time-change.
* A relatively weak currency, so that five-star hotels are affordable.
* A range of post-treatment sightseeing opportunities.

The supply side of tourism

Transport

The great majority of overseas visitors arrive by air and with deregulation of South African airspace arrivals have increased. Johannesburg, at the hub of a network of intercontinental and regional services, is the major gateway to South Africa, followed by Cape Town. South African Airways (https://www.flysaa.com/) operate most of the scheduled domestic services, with several flights a day linking the main cities. Another convenient way of seeing the country is by South African Railways (https://www.southafricanrailways.co.za/). The luxury 'Blue Train' (http://www.bluetrain.co.za/) is one of the country's most famous tourist products, linking Pretoria and Cape Town and passing through some magnificent scenery on its descent from the Karoo Plateau to the coast. Nevertheless, the car is far more significant than rail transport for domestic travel. A large number of tours by coach or mini-bus are also available.

Accommodation

A wide range of accommodation is available, from luxury hotels to ecolodges and *rondavels* (African-style huts, with modern facilities) in the game reserves.

Organisation

South Africa's tourism industry is effectively organised and marketed, within the legal framework of the 1993 Tourism Act and subsequent amendments. The continuing legacy of apartheid is reflected in the politics of tourism in South Africa with different political parties and ethnic groups (there are ten official Bantu languages for example), each having their own agendas for the sector. Policy-making is largely the responsibility of the Department of Tourism, which has a mission to promote sustainable development, and South African Tourism which is charged with maintaining standards of accommodation and services, with promotion, and the development of new products.

Tourism resources

Although the early white settlers wiped out much of the game they encountered, the remaining wildlife habitats have long been given a high degree of protection by the South African government. There are 11 national parks and many game reserves, most of which are small in area compared to other countries in Southern Africa. The exception – and the most popular – is the Kruger National Park located in the Lowveld along the Mozambique border, which is served by an extensive all-weather road network and well-supplied with self-catering accommodation. Prior reservation is necessary for foreign visitors, due to the heavy domestic demand. Other notable reserves – Hluhluwe and Umfolozi – are situated in KwaZulu-Natal. There are also a large number of private game reserves – such as the Sabi-Sabi (https://www. sabisabi.com/) adjoining the Kruger National Park – which permit hunting and the viewing of wildlife on foot as well as in open vehicles. They provide luxury chalet accommodation and most have their own airstrips, while Americans generate much of the demand.

Areas increasingly sought out by tourists from Europe include:

The **Cape Peninsula**, where cold and warm ocean currents meet, and the hinterland of Cape Town, often considered to be the most beautiful part of South Africa. Contrasts of climate have created an extraordinary range of habitats for wildlife, and the coasts are ideal for whale-watching. Cape Town (https://www.capetown.travel/), situated on one of Africa's few good natural harbours, is the country's oldest European settlement, the second largest city, and its legislative capital. This cosmopolitan city is home to many ethnic groups and cultures and has a tolerant attitude to alternative lifestyles. The historic waterfront has been redeveloped as an international focus for retailing, restaurants, and entertainment. Cape Town is dominated by the world-famous landmark of Table

Mountain, and there are many fine beaches, such as Camps Bay (http://www.campsbay-info.com/). Attractions in the hinterland include the vineyards of the Hex River Valley and farmhouses in the distinctive 'Cape Dutch' style of architecture. Offshore lies Robben Island (http://www.robben-island.org.za/), the former prison of Nelson Mandela and now a museum commemorating the struggle against apartheid.

The **Garden Route** – the stretch of coast between Port Elizabeth and East London – offers rugged, attractive scenery, in which forest covered mountains alternate with fertile valleys and small sandy bays. Plettenberg Bay (https://www.plett-tourism.co.za/) is the best known of the many beach resorts. Jeffrey's Bay is noted for surfing.

Natal and Transkei (https://www.wildcoastholidays.com/) also offer resources for beach tourism. Durban is a cosmopolitan seaport as well as being a major resort, while a string of small seaside towns to the south are known as the 'Hibiscus Coast'. In contrast, the 'Wild Coast' of the Transkei is less developed. To the north of the Tugela River, the principal attractions are the game reserves, and Zulu communities have retained the traditions of a warrior nation.

On the central plateau, the main tourist centres are the cities of Johannesburg, Pretoria, and Bloemfontein:

*   Johannesburg is South Africa's largest and most prosperous city, largely due to the gold mines of the Witwatersrand. Not surprisingly, one of its major attractions is the Gold Reef City theme park (https://www.tsogosun.com/gold-reef-city-casino), which interprets this mining heritage. Johannesburg has become a regional centre for financial services, comparable with the great cities of Europe and North America. The township of Soweto nearby is actually a city of 3 million people. It is closely identified with the apartheid struggle and attracts the more adventurous and socially-aware tourists for this reason. Some tour operators encourage visitors to interact with the local community in restaurants and *shebeens* (bars).
*   Pretoria, the administrative capital of South Africa, and Bloemfontein (https://freestatetourism.org/), its judicial capital, are centres of Afrikaner culture, and as such, form a contrast to the cosmopolitan brashness and bustle of Johannesburg.
*   Sun City (https://www.suninternational.com/sun-city/) was developed in the apartheid era as a gambling centre to rival Las Vegas, in what was then the quasi-independent state of Bophutatswana, as casinos and multi-racial entertainment were illegal in the Republic itself. In the new South Africa, it continues to be a major resort, offering cabarets that attract international stars, world-class golf courses and other sports facilities, and the 'Lost City' theme park developed by a South African entrepreneur.

One of the great challenges facing the government is to balance the economic aspirations of black Africans with the need to retain white expertise and attract foreign investment, and here tourism is playing an important role. The future growth of tourism in South Africa will depend on the maintenance of political and economic stability, and the extent to which the new multi-racial 'Rainbow Nation' can offer opportunity to all ethnic groups, including the thorny issue of land reform. Since the 1990s, levels of crime have increased to become among the world's highest, particularly in Johannesburg, and the resulting insecurity is one of the biggest problems facing the country and its tourism industry.

Discussion point

To what extent can tourism satisfy black South African aspirations for a better life? For example, game reserves with luxury accommodation are located close to some of the most impoverished villages in KwaZulu. This has led to demands that local communities should benefit more from tourism, along with the townships near the big cities, which are visited by an increasing number of foreign tourists, but very few white South Africans.

The other countries of Southern Africa

Most of these countries are landlocked, so that their external surface transport links (and to an extent their economic fortunes) are vulnerable to the political situation in South Africa and Mozambique. The small kingdoms of Lesotho and Eswatini are particularly dependent on South Africa. Most of their visitors are South Africans, who tend to be short-stay and interested primarily in gambling in the hotel casinos of Maseru and Mbabane. However, these countries have more to offer, namely:

Lesotho (known as 'the Roof of Africa' or 'The Kingdom in the Sky') (https://www.visitlesotho.travel/) is situated high in the Drakensberg Mountains. Apart from the impressive scenery, there are facilities for pony-trekking and even skiing (although the season is restricted to July and August). Four-wheel drive vehicles are necessary for travel because of the rugged terrain.

Eswatini (https://www.thekingdomofeswatini.com/), formerly known as Swaziland, is rebranding itself by encouraging traditional craft industries. It is not as mountainous as Lesotho and includes a section of the game-rich Lowveld along its boundary with Mozambique. The country's tribal traditions are among the best preserved in Africa and include the Reed Dance ceremony, although this has attracted controversy from those who wish to modernise the country and end the monarch's autocratic rule.

Namibia and Botswana likewise have strong economic ties with South Africa, but with the advantage of direct air services from Europe to the capitals of Windhoek and Gaborone, they have been much more successful in attracting overseas visitors. They are mostly made up of desert landscapes, but the Kalahari is not as arid as the Sahara and supports a surprising variety of game. Because of the vast distances and sparse population, fly-in safaris are a major element in their tourism industries.

Botswana

Botswana (http://www.botswanatourism.co.bw/) is one of the more stable countries in Africa, without significant ethnic divisions and with an economy based on diamond exports. The government has sought to avoid the negative impacts of tourism by emphasising conservation and limiting the supply of accommodation. National parks and game reserves make up 17 per cent of the national territory.

This vast inland delta is formed by the Okovango River where it drains into the Kalahari Desert on the site of an ancient lake. It is one of Africa's largest and most ecologically productive wetland areas, a web of slow-flowing waterways, islands, and lagoons, many of which change shape and even disappear in response to an annual flood cycle. At the peak of the flood season, the delta can extend over an area of 16,000 square kilometres, shrinking to less than 9,000 square kilometres in the dry season. The delta supports a wide variety of wildlife that congregates on the edge of the newly flooded areas between May and October, which is the best time for game viewing. Part of the delta is designated as the Moremi Game Reserve (https://www.moremi.com/), with the Chobe National Park (https://chobenationalpark.co.za/) in the north-east. The speciality of the Okovango – its USP – is safari tours by water transport, using traditional dugout canoes and motor launches, which are restricted to the main waterways.

The policy of the Botswana government is to restrict tourism in the Okovango delta to ensure the conservation of its fragile ecosystems. This is achieved by:

- Limiting accessibility. The Okovango is difficult to reach, as Maun, the village which is the recognised gateway to the delta, is served exclusively by Air Botswana (https://www.airbotswana.co.bw/), the state carrier, and fares are kept high.
- Restricting access by price. Visitors must pay a park entrance fee of around US $ 30 a day.
- Keeping the cost of accommodation high. The operators of the 40 or so camps and ecolodges have to pay substantial concession fees, resource royalties and community charges to the government.

Nevertheless, tourism has not really benefitted the tribal communities living in or near the delta, as most supplies are not purchased locally but flown in from outside. The government has also been criticised for forcing the nomadic San (widely known as the Bushmen) to relocate and adopt a settled way of life.

Namibia

Namibia (http://www.namibiatourism.com.na/) differs from its neighbour to the east in having a long Atlantic coastline and a large white minority of mainly German or Afrikaaner origin. The country was a German colony before 1918, and subsequently, ruled by South Africa before achieving independence in 1990. In contrast to most African countries, Namibia has a good road system, encouraging self-drive touring and providing access to some of Africa's most interesting attractions, including:

- The Etosha Pan (https://www.etoshanationalpark.org/), which attracts great concentrations of wildlife during the dry season.
- The Fish River Canyon, a spectacular geological feature.
- The Waterberg Plateau (https://www.waterberg-wilderness.com/), famous for its rock paintings – created by the San hunter-gatherers who were the original inhabitants of Southern Africa.
- The 'Skeleton Coast' – where the Namib Desert meets the Atlantic Ocean. Fogs from the cold Benguela Current offshore sustain some unique plants and animals although the climate is virtually rainless. This coastal area also boasts some of the world's highest sand dunes, providing a resource for some innovative sports.

In contrast to Namibia, the countries of Zimbabwe, Zambia, and Malawi, usually receive an adequate rainfall. Since they mainly consist of highlands and plateaux rising over 1,000 metres above sea level, they have a climate which is cooler than is usual for the tropics. Under British rule, the three countries were briefly united as the 'Central African Federation of Rhodesia and Nyasaland', but after 1962, they followed different paths.

Zimbabwe

Between 1964 and 1980, Zimbabwe (then known as Rhodesia) (https://www.zimbabwe-tourism.net/) had a tourism industry, serving a sizeable domestic market, essentially the dominant white community, and South Africans. There were few overseas visitors due to the economic sanctions imposed by Britain and the country's political isolation. With the coming to power of the ZANU government in 1980 Zimbabwe's independence was formally recognised by the international community. As a result, overseas visitor numbers grew rapidly, aided by political stability and the good infrastructure laid down under British rule. The Zimbabwe Tourist Authority was formed in 1996, with responsibility for promotion and development reporting to the Ministry of the Environment, Climate Change, Tourism, and Hospitality Industry. However, the Land Distribution Act in 2000 was followed by the collapse of the economy, and unfavourable publicity in the Western media regarding the seizure of white-owned farms and the abuse of human rights. With the fragile political situation, Zimbabwe's tourism industry is in crisis, and this has put the country's wildlife resources increasingly at risk.

Hotel accommodation is concentrated in the cities of Harare and Bulawayo – which have hosted international conferences, trade fairs, and the African Games – and near the country's principal attraction – Victoria Falls (https://whc.unesco.org/en/list/509/) – on the border with Zambia. Zimbabwe can offer a variety of other tourism resources, including a system of national parks, which make up 12 per cent of its territory. These are administered by the Zimbabwe Parks and Wildlife Management Authority (https://zimparks.org/), which operates a three-tier entrance fee policy. As elsewhere in Africa, the designation of the Hwange and Gonerezhou National Parks in the 1950s and 1960s involved the eviction of thousands of people from their tribal lands, but since the 1980s government policy has changed, with local communities regaining hunting rights and becoming directly involved in ecotourism. One of the main problems facing the tourism sector is the over-commercialisation of Victoria Falls compared to the under-exploitation of some of the game reserves and the scenic attractions of the Eastern Highlands. Below the waterfall the River Zambezi attracts large numbers of canoeists and white-water rafting adventure-seekers. In comparison Lake Kariba, a vast inland sea created by the Kariba Dam in 1959, offers few facilities.

The country's cultural heritage is also viewed differently by the white and African communities. For example, the Matabo Hills (https://whc.unesco.org/en/list/306/) south of Bulawayo – an area of dramatic granite scenery – has been promoted to Western tourists as the burial place of Cecil Rhodes, the founder of the British colony, whose place in history is controversial. The Chinhoyi Caves, which played an important role in the independence struggle, are yet barely exploited as a heritage attraction. On the other hand, the mysterious ruins of Great Zimbabwe (https://whc.unesco.org/en/list/364/) are now seen as a reminder of African achievement centuries before the colonial era.

Zambia

Zambia's (https://www.zambiatourism.com/) economy is precariously dependent on the export of copper and other minerals, and tourism is increasingly seen as a more reliable way of earning foreign exchange. The government has put a high priority on conservation: almost a third of its area is devoted to national parks and game reserves, although facilities are generally not as well developed as in Zimbabwe. In the most popular national parks – Kafue and the South Luangwa – accommodation is in thatched lodges blending in with the local habitats. The main tourist centres are Livingstone (http://www.livingstonetourism.com/), situated close to Victoria Falls, which has benefitted from the deterioration of the economic situation in Zimbabwe, and the capital Lusaka which has good conference facilities.

Malawi

Malawi's (http://www.visitmalawi.mw/) main attraction is the lake of the same name, the third largest in Africa, with some of the world's best fishing, and attractive beaches along its 600-kilometre shoreline. There are good facilities for water-skiing, sailing, and windsurfing at the resorts of Salima and Monkey Bay. Compared to some other countries in Southern Africa, it is not rich in big game. However, its undulating green plateaux and mountains are ideal for riding and trekking holidays. Since the mid-1990s, a new government has liberalised the tourism sector, created a Ministry of Tourism, Wildlife and Culture, and there has been healthy growth in international arrivals.

Mozambique

Mozambique (https://www.visitmozambique.net/) retains some of the heritage of centuries of rule by Portugal. Independence in 1975 was soon followed by many years of civil war. Since the early 1990s, the government has adopted a more pragmatic approach to economic development. The country had a small tourism industry before 1975, catering mainly for white South Africans and Rhodesians. This was concentrated in the capital Maputo (then called Lourenço Marques), and to a lesser extent in Beira. The beaches along over 2,000 kilometres of coastline facing the Indian Ocean are the country's principal tourist asset. Since the ending of the civil war, there has been some development of inclusive tours, especially to the Bazaruto Islands that offer resort facilities, scuba diving, and sport fishing (https://www.bazarutopark.org/). Ecotourism is being encouraged by the government in the northern part of the country, and the Gorongosa National Park (https://www.gorongosa.org/), devastated during the civil war, is in the process of being re-stocked. Cultural attractions include Mozambique Island (https://whc.unesco.org/en/list/599/), founded by the Portuguese as a trading post in the early sixteenth century, where the balance between conservation, local community involvement, and tourism development is as yet unresolved.

The islands of the Western Indian Ocean

To the east of the African continent lie several island groups, which are very different from the mainland in geology, flora, and fauna, and where the cultures have been strongly influenced by France and Asia. All island ecosystems are vulnerable to the impact of climate change, tourism and other types of development, and the wildlife resources of the Indian Ocean islands are particularly at risk. Pressures are most severe in Madagascar, habitat of the lemur and other unique animals. In Mauritius, only 1 per cent of the original forest still survives and up to 50 per cent of the fringing coral is dead or dying. In the Seychelles, much of the coral reef around the island of Mahe was destroyed to make way for the international airport (https://seychellesairports.sc/).

Madagascar, the Comoros and Réunion, were formerly French colonies, whereas Mauritius and the Seychelles, although originally colonised by the French, later experienced a long period of British rule.

Madagascar

Officially known as the Malagasy Republic, Madagascar (https://madagascar-tourisme.com/en/) stands in a class of its own as the world's fourth largest island, with an area greater than France and a coastline 5,000 kilometres in length. The country combines the red soil of Africa and the rice fields of South-east Asia, but also has landscapes that are unique, with the 'traveller's tree' as an emblematic feature. A central spine of mountains dominates the country, separating the dry savannas of the west from the lush vegetation of the east coast. Population growth and inefficient agricultural methods have caused extensive deforestation, threatening destruction of the wildlife that is Madagascar's most important tourism resource. The island is also culturally interesting with its mix of Indonesian, African, and Arab ethnic groups. Other distinctive features are the elaborate tombs and funeral ceremonies based on ancestor worship.

The capital Antananarivo, located high on the central plateau, offers picturesque markets and the palaces of the Merina monarchs who ruled the country before it came under French control. However, this diversity of resources has not been paralleled by a thriving tourism industry. The island is expensive to reach, and once there, surface transport is poor. The principal beach resorts, situated on the offshore islands of Nosy Bé (https://nosybe-tourisme.com/en/) and Nosy Boraha (Ile Ste Marie), can only be reached by domestic air services. Since gaining independence, the government has given tourism a low priority, but this is changing now that relations with France and South Africa, Madagascar's largest potential markets, have improved.

The Comoros

The Comoros comprise four volcanic islands lying between Madagascar and Mozambique. The people are Muslims and Arabic influences are dominant in the culture. While the other islands have opted for independence, Mayotte (http://en.ilemayotte.com/) has retained its links with France and is the most prosperous of the group. Anjouan is the most picturesque island, but Grand Comore contains the international airport and most of the few hotels. Diving and sport fishing provide the main appeal for foreign tourists, mainly wealthy Americans and Europeans, although South Africa has provided much of the investment in hotels.

Réunion

Réunion (https://en.reunion.fr/) is another volcanic island, situated to the east of Madagascar. It has perhaps the most impressive scenery of any tropical island, with high mountains rising to 3,000 metres within a short distance of the coast, and boasting spectacular calderas, an active volcano, the Piton de la Fournaise, and sheer lava cliffs enclosing deep canyons. There are hiking trails between the craters and good surfing off the west coast. The island's close relationship to France (it is an overseas département) has benefitted the infrastructure and allows French tourists to take advantage of cheaper flights from Paris to the capital, St. Denis. International tourism is handicapped by the proximity of Mauritius, which has much better beaches. Réunion has potential as a stopover on flights between Europe and Australia on the island's carrier, Air Austral (https://www.air-austral.com/).

Mauritius

Mauritius (https://www.tourism-mauritius.mu/) has the advantage of direct flights from Britain and South Africa, whereas the smaller dependent island of Rodrigues (http://www.tourism-rodrigues.mu/) is remote and much less developed. Mauritius is encircled, except to the south, by a coral reef that is responsible for the island's greatest assets – 150 kilometres of attractive coastline with calm seas ideal for water sports and white sand beaches. Mauritius is a good example of how tourism, properly handled, can benefit a small developing country. In the 1960s, the island was faced with a decline for sugar, its principal export, and a seemingly inexorable pressure on resources from a rapidly growing population. Tourism (along with light industry) was seen as a solution to the grave economic situation, but the government was determined from the outset that Mauritius should be an upmarket destination. This has been achieved by:

- A ban on charter flights, while the national carrier, Air Mauritius (https://www.air-mauritius.com) is noted for its professionalism.
- The resort hotels are built to high standards of design and landscaping, taking maximum advantage of the beach and lagoon setting.
- Hotels that use local resources and local management, so that profits have stayed within Mauritius.
- A professional Ministry of Tourism (http://tourism.govmu.org), aided by the Mauritius Tourism Promotion Authority (MTPA) created in 1996.
- Standards of service and cuisine that bear comparison with the best in Europe, North America, and Asia.

By 2018, Mauritius attracted almost 1.4 million international visitors, of whom approximately half came from Europe. Mauritius has the advantage of a highly skilled workforce (120,000 are directly or indirectly employed in tourism), where the different ethnic communities – Hindus, Muslims, Chinese, Creoles (of African origin), and Europeans – live in apparent harmony. Beach resorts such as Grand Baie are the main attraction, but with the achievement of economic success, the government is giving conservation a higher priority, in a bid to attract ecotourists.

Compared to other Indian Ocean islands, the scenery of the interior is unspectacular, although there are numerous waterfalls where the central plateau of Mauritius meets the coastal plains. Away from the beaches, the main tourist centres are the multi-cultural capital Port Louis, with its markets and festivals around the calendar, Curepipe with its casino and textile shops, and the Royal Botanical Gardens at Pamplemousses (http://ssrbg.govmu.org). The possible disadvantages of Mauritius as a winter-sun destination for north Europeans are:

- Distance.
- There is high humidity and occasional cyclones from December to April.
- There is little nightlife compared to more accessible destinations such as the Caribbean islands.

The Seychelles

The Seychelles (https://www.seychelles.travel/en/) are strategically located on the major shipping routes for oil tankers from the Gulf, midway between East Africa, India, and Madagascar. The country has a small population and land area compared to Mauritius, but lays claim to over 1 million square kilometres of Indian Ocean. The islands are ecologically interesting because they contain many species of birds and plants, unique to the Seychelles. The islands fall into two main groups:

- The main islands of Mahe, Praslin, La Digue, and Silhouette are of granite formation, the possible remnants of a 'lost continent'. The combination of picturesque coves, rock formations, palm-fringed beaches, and rugged mountains provides these islands a rare beauty.
- The outer islands are low-lying coral atolls. Fresh water is scarce and the islands are mostly uninhabited. The largest, Aldabra (https://whc.unesco.org/en/list/185/), is also the most remote and is world famous for its giant tortoises.

The construction of the international airport at Mahe brought an isolated destination within reach of the main tourist-generating markets of Western Europe and South Africa, with the result that tourist arrivals increased from less than a thousand in 1970 to 350,000 in 2018. Tourism now accounts for 70 per cent of foreign exchange earnings, two-thirds of jobs and is the focus of a new integrated plan for sustainable development – Vision 21. As a result, while foreign investment in tourism is encouraged, the government has given conservation a high priority, so that only a few localities – mainly on Mahe – have been developed with low-rise hotels. However, tourism has not made the islands less vulnerable to recession in Europe than their previous dependence on agricultural exports such as cinnamon. Standards of service and facilities in the Seychelles have in the past been compared unfavourably with those of Mauritius, as tourism was grafted on to a less developed economy and social system. As in other small developing countries, tourism has caused or aggravated a number of problems, namely:

- The industry is dominated by foreign tour operators and foreign-owned hotels, so that the bulk of tourist spend does not benefit the country.
- The tourism sector has attracted workers away from agriculture, to the extent that the islands are now dependent on food imports from Europe and South Africa to meet local as well as tourist demands.
- The need to train Seychellois workers in the skills and attitudes necessary to serve affluent foreign visitors, has undermined the government's policy of socialism and nation-building based on the Creole language and lifestyle. Those involved with tourism tend to be upwardly mobile, imitating Western lifestyles – the so-called 'demonstration effect'.

West Africa

West Africa comprises two distinct zones:

- The southern forested coastal belt extending from the Gambia to Gabon.
- The northern Sahel belt extending from Mauritania to Chad along the southern edge of the Sahara Desert. The Sahel is characterised by extreme summer heat and recurrent droughts, the dry season getting progressively longer as we travel further from the Equator, so that savanna grassland, dotted with baobab trees and termite mounds, gradually merges into semi-desert.

The setting for tourism

Tourism and business travel in West Africa gravitate to the coast where commercial export-based agriculture is well developed. The climate here is characterised by sultry heat, except during the dry season – usually from December to March – when the 'Harmattan' wind blows from the Sahara, drastically lowering the humidity but also bringing dust clouds that can disrupt air transport. In Victorian times, the unhealthy reputation of the region earned it the name 'White Man's Grave'. However, conditions are by no means uniform; the coasts of Ghana and Togo, for example, are less humid than Liberia or Equatorial Guinea.

There is an important cultural divide between the northern part of the region, which is Muslim in religion and the predominantly Christian and animistic south. The rise of Islamic fundamentalism is a threat to stability, particularly in northern Nigeria with the Boko Haram movement, while in Mali and the Central African Republic similar unrest required the military intervention of France. Security fears following terrorist incidents in Mauritania caused the Paris-Dakar motor rally (https://www.dakar.com/en) to relocate to South America in 2007.

Most of the countries of West Africa are just within reach of Western Europe for winter-sun beach holidays, but for them to compete effectively for this market, good air transport links, political stability, and foreign investment are vital.

The supply side of tourism

There has been some degree of co-operation among West African countries to promote tourism to the region. This has included attempts to develop air transport. In 1961, Air Afrique was set up as a joint venture with financial backing from 11 newly independent French-speaking West African countries and Air France (https://www.airfrance.com). This Pan-African venture ceased operations in 2002, due to internal divisions and mismanagement. In 1976, the Economic Community of West African States (ECOWAS) (https://www.ecowas.int/) was formed to bring together French, Portuguese, and English-speaking countries in the region. The Francophone states constitute the majority and, with few exceptions, chose to retain close links with France after independence.

Several West African countries have state-run hotel corporations. However, their main purpose is to attract business travellers and hotel rooms are often unavailable in the major cities such as Accra due to block-booking for regional conferences. ECOWAS has aimed to regulate standards for hotels and other types of accommodation that are applicable to all 15 member states and has introduced a visa system that removes barriers to free movement, particularly for community citizens.

Lagos, Abidjan, and Dakar are the focus of air routes into West Africa. The winter-sun destinations of the Gambia, Sierra Leone, and Côte d'Ivoire are encouraging charter flights to counter the high fares of scheduled airlines. Road and rail transport is geared to the commercial objectives laid down in colonial times, so that routes lead from the interior to the seaports. This inhibits travel between the countries of West Africa, but does, to some extent, allow excursions from the coastal resorts to the hinterland.

Tourism resources

As there are some 25 countries in the region, an in-depth coverage of their tourism potential is beyond the scope of this book. The more adventurous tourist is attracted by the following 'pull factors':

- **Cultural resources**: The traditional societies of West and Central Africa fascinate the Western traveller because they are different in so many ways. This is particularly true of a country like Benin, where voodoo is recognised as an official religion. Musicians and dance rhythms from Senegal, Mali, Ghana, and Togo have gained an international following in Europe and the Americas. Similarly, the woodcarvings, ceremonial masks, and textiles of the region have inspired many Western artists.
- **Wildlife resources and wilderness adventure**: West Africa offers a considerable diversity of wildlife habitats. Gambia attracts birdwatchers to its Abuko reserve, and Mauritania has an important marine reserve for dolphin-watching, while a rainforest project in Ghana's Kakum National Park has won acclaim from environmentalists. Game parks exist in several countries, but safari tourism has not developed on any scale because the attractions are not as well publicised as those of East and Southern Africa, the 'big five' game animals are much less numerous, and the parks are less accessible.
- **The resources for beach tourism**. Much of the coastline is exposed to heavy surf from the Atlantic Ocean, so although there are many fine beaches, they are often not suitable for bathing. The International Surfing Association (https://www.isasurf. org/) recognises the region's potential for the sport, and Ghana hosted the Africa Surf Series in 2016.

For most countries in the region, there is a significant ethnic market in the populations of West African origin in Europe and the Americas. We will now look at some of these countries in more detail, starting with Cabo Verde, which is competing with the Canary Islands as a winter-sun beach destination for north Europeans.

Cabo Verde (Cape Verde Islands)

Cabo Verde (https://www.capeverde.com/) is regarded as part of West Africa but is actually a group of nine islands located in the Atlantic Ocean, 600 kilometres west of Dakar. With few natural resources and afflicted by recurrent droughts, the former Portuguese colony has historically been dependent on remittances from the large numbers of islanders who have emigrated. Realising that tourism based on sun, sand, and sea was its best economic option, the government of Cabo Verde provided generous incentives for European investors and purchased land on the islands of Sal and Boa Vista for resort development. The airport on Sal (https://www.asa.cv) was classed as Category 1 by the US government and had originally been built to serve South African Airways in the apartheid era, when the airline was prohibited for political reasons from over-flying the African continent. There are now international airports on the islands of Santiago, Boa Vista, and São Vicente. Cabo Verde operates an open skies policy, and direct charter flights are available to a number of cities in Europe, as well as scheduled services to Portugal, Brazil, and the United States. As a result, tourist arrivals grew from 67,000 in 1999 to over 750,000 in 2019, and many Europeans now have second homes on the islands. Nevertheless, there is considerable leakage from the economy as food and other goods and services have to be imported to meet the demands of the tourism sector.

Although popular with windsurfers, Sal is rather barren, and the other islands offer more attractive scenery. Mindelo (http://www.mindelocaboverde.com/) on São Vicente is the most cosmopolitan centre, with a cultural scene, expressed in music, that is reminiscent of Brazil rather than West Africa.

Gambia

This former British colony is only six hours flying time from London, and unlike the Caribbean, it has the advantage of being in the same time zone. The Gambia's (http://www.visitthegambia.gm/) dry and sunny winter climate allows it to compete with the Canary Islands as a beach destination for the British and Scandinavians – with an extra ingredient – the chance to experience African markets and village life.

No larger than Yorkshire or Connecticut in area, the country consists of little more than a narrow strip of territory along the River Gambia, and a short stretch of Atlantic coastline where the resort facilities are concentrated. Tourism is encouraged by the government to reduce the country's dependence on groundnut exports. With the help of the World Bank, Yundum Airport (https://www.banjulairport.com/) has been extended, the infrastructure improved, and a hotel training school established. Yet relatively few tourists venture far beyond the beaches on excursions up the River Gambia, one of the finest waterways in West Africa. Almost all the hotels are foreign-owned, and many of the economic benefits of tourism are not retained, while there is concern in this traditional Muslim society about some of its social manifestations such as sex tourism and beach hustling by *bumsters*. The military coup in 1994 severely affected tourism to Gambia with an estimated 40 per cent reduction in the number of foreign tourists. However, in 2019, there were around 160,000 arrivals.

Senegal

Senegal (http://www.visitezlesenegal.com) is the oldest of France's former colonies and is a mixture of French sophistication and African traditions, best exemplified in the capital Dakar. In Senegal, we can observe two contrasting approaches to tourism:

- French expatriates staff the Club Mediterranée village at Cap Skirring, and there is little contact with the local population.
- In the *campements rurales integrales* near Ziguinchor, the tourist shares the life of an African village, the accommodation being provided by a co-operative of the villagers with government support.

Senegal received nearly 1.4 million arrivals in 2019 after a downturn in tourism resulting from events in neighbouring countries, namely the conflict in Mali and the ebola out-break in Guinea.

Guinea

For many years, the former French colony of Guinea did little to encourage tourism, and it tends to be visited by only the more adventurous travellers. The beaches of the Los Islands provide a contrast to the bustling capital, Konakry, while the Futa Djallon high-lands in the interior offer waterfalls among their attractions.

Guinea-Bissau

A former Portuguese colony, Guinea-Bissau's unique geography, dissected by a number of rivers and fringed by a large number of offshore islands, makes internal transport difficult. The Bissagos Islands have gained international recognition as a World Biosphere Reserve. Unfortunately, the country's low level of economic development, porous borders, and location, midway between the producers in South America and the consumers in Europe, has encouraged large-scale drug smuggling.

Sierra Leone

The former British colony of Sierra Leone continues to have a strong emotional attach-ment to Britain. The unrest here and in neighbouring Liberia was partly due to the his-toric tensions between the Westernised Creole elites of the coast (who are mainly the descendants of freed slaves from the New World) and the tribal societies of the interior. The images of violence, the ebola epidemic in 2014, and the scandal of diamond smug-gling have overshadowed the tourism potential of both countries.

The National Tourist Board of Sierra Leone (https://ntb.gov.sl/) aims to develop responsible tourism based on nature and interaction with local communities. Among the country's attractions are a chimpanzee sanctuary and the wildlife of the Gola Rainforest National Park (https://golarainforest.org/). The capital Freetown is situated on one of Africa's finest harbours, and there are fine white sand beaches nearby.

Liberia

Both Liberia (https://visitliberia.net/) and Sierra Leone had tourism industries on a small scale before the outbreak of civil war in the 1990s. Liberia had cultural and economic ties with the United States, and its capital Monrovia was one of West Africa's leading conference venues. The Americo-Liberians controlled the country and had developed plantations on the coast in the style of Georgia and the Carolinas. More than a decade of civil war largely destroyed this legacy and the infrastructure on which a modern economy depends. Tourism is slowly recovering under the Ministry of Information, Culture and Tourism. Resources include fine surfing beaches near Robertsport and a large area of rainforest – the Sapo National Park in the south-east of the country.

Côte d'Ivoire (Ivory Coast)

Until the outbreak of tribal unrest in 2004, the Ivory Coast had been more successful than most West African countries in developing its tourism industry and its economy in general, due in part to a long period of stability following independence and very substantial foreign (primarily French) investment. State-owned hotels and travel companies are involved in the provision of tourist facilities, mainly along the coast east of Abidjan, where the beaches are protected by a series of lagoons from the heavy surf of the Atlantic. However, the resorts of the 'African Riviera' are expensive and beyond the reach of all but a privileged minority of the Ivorians themselves. In the interior, there are a number of game parks and the new administrative capital of Yamassoukro which boasts a cathedral second in size only to St Peter's in Rome. Abidjan remains the commercial centre of the country with good conference facilities.

Ghana

Ghana (https://www.ghana.travel/) is one of the most advanced countries in West Africa, with a strong agricultural sector, while the River Volta has been harnessed for hydroelectric power, creating a huge artificial lake. The Afro-American diaspora represents an important niche market, and in 2019, the Ghanaian government celebrated the Year of Return (https://www.yearofreturn.com/), marking the 400th anniversary of the arrival of the first African slaves in Jamestown, Virginia. This was designed not only to boost tourist numbers but to persuade people of Ghanaian descent to consider returning to settle in the country. As a result of the campaign, the Ghana Tourism Authority estimated that more than a million foreign tourists visited that year. Nevertheless, much greater numbers of tourists, mainly from Britain and Germany, are attracted to Ghana's rainforests, colourful markets, and the cultural attractions of Kumasi, the former capital of the once-powerful Ashanti kingdom in the interior. Tourism is important to the economy, accounting for 5.5 per cent of the total economy. The sector is promoted by the Ghana Tourism Authority, with strong government support from the Ministry of Tourism, Arts and Culture (http://motac.gov.gh/).

CASE STUDY 19.3
'DIASPORA TOURISM' – TOURISM AS A SEARCH FOR IDENTITY

The 'African diaspora', made up of the descendants of West Africans forcibly transported to the Americas as slaves, is potentially a huge market for tourism in Brazil, the Caribbean islands and the United States. The publication of Alex Haley's novel *Roots*, set in his ancestor's homeland in Gambia, stimulated interest in West Africa generally in the 1980s. The visit of President Obama to Ghana in 2009 probably had a greater impact on the growth of demand for 'ethnic tourism' among black Americans. Inclusive tours, styled 'roots packages' are now available for those wishing to connect with their origins, and a visit to the heritage sites of the slave trade is regarded as a kind of pilgrimage to be undertaken during one's lifetime.

The trans-Atlantic slave trade was at its peak in the eighteenth century, when as many as 70,000 men, women, and children a year were transported on the infamous 'middle passage' to the plantations of the New World, to satisfy the European demand for sugar, rum, tobacco, and cotton. This was part of the 'triangle of trade', in which ports such as Bristol, Liverpool, and Nantes were engaged. Guns, alcohol, and manufactured goods were traded with African chiefs for slaves obtained in inter-tribal wars. A chain of forts along the West African coast, extending from St Louis at the mouth of the River Senegal to Benguela in Angola, acted as holding points for the slave trade. On arrival in the Americas, slaves were stripped of their tribal identities and took the name and religion of their white masters. For this reason, their descendants, unlike European emigrants to the New World, are unable to identify their homelands with any precision. Britain took the lead in bringing an end to the slave trade, with Freetown in Sierra Leone providing the base for the Royal Navy's West African anti-slavery patrol. Nevertheless, the trade continued until late in the nineteenth century when slavery was abolished in Brazil and Cuba.

The tangible heritage of the slave trade is found in a number of West African countries, the Congo region and Angola. In Senegal, the island of Gorée (https://whc.unesco.org/en/list/26/) near Dakar is one of the major attractions of that country, where the picturesque buildings belie its grim history as one of the main centres of the French slave trade. In Benin, there are reminders that some of the more warlike African kingdoms such as Dahomey took an active part in procuring slaves, particularly those destined for the sugar plantations of north-east Brazil. However, Ghana is the country that is best placed to develop this type of ethnic tourism, and black Americans are an important market, accounting for around 10,000 visitors a year. The Ghana Tourism Authority has, therefore, focussed attention on the 'castles' – fortified trading posts – that were built on the Gold Coast to hold slaves. Elmina (https://visitghana.com/attractions/elmina-castle/) was founded by the Portuguese in 1482, but most date from the seventeenth century, when Denmark, Sweden, and Holland were among those who jostled with Britain for control over the lucrative trade. The 'Door of No Return' in the walls of Cape Coast Castle (https://visitghana.com/attractions/cape-coast-castle/) is a poignant reminder of the slaves' last sight of Africa. Most of these 'castles' are managed by the Ghana Museums and Monuments Board (https://www.ghanamuseums.org/) as heritage attractions, and guided tours are available.

The majority of the visitors to these heritage attractions are Ghanaians, who have different perceptions to those held by Africans of the diaspora. Black Americans tend to regard their visit, with mixed feelings of pride, sorrow, and anger, as a return to the motherland. Ghanaians, however, tend to regard them not as guests and fellow-Africans but as *obrumi*, foreigners like white tourists, marked out by their affluence, lifestyle, and behaviour from the host community, and the tourists often complain of hassle and exploitation. Whereas Afro-Americans regard the castles as places of death and suffering, to Ghanaians they are simply part of their national heritage, to be regarded as showpieces, to be restored and provided with modern lighting and tourist facilities. To many black Americans, this is 'whitewashing' history; for example, they successfully objected to a proposed restaurant above the dungeon for male slaves in Cape Coast Castle. (Bruner, 1996). There are also differences of opinion regarding the way the heritage of the slave trade should be interpreted. Elmina Castle, for example, has changed hands and been used for different purposes in the course of its long history. When the Dutch took over from the Portuguese in 1637, they converted the Catholic chapel in the castle into a slave auction market. This raises the question as to which aspects of the heritage should be preserved or reconstructed. Stakeholders with a view on this include the international aid agencies who provide most of the funding, but organisations representing the African diaspora also have a great deal of influence. This is less true of people in the local communities, who may be denied access to these heritage attractions for the convenience of foreign tourists.

Togo

Sandwiched between Ghana and Nigeria, tourism is a fledgling industry in Togo (https://www.togo-tourisme.com/) and Benin (http://www.benin-tourisme.com/). Lomé, the capital of Togo has some significance as a conference venue, and is set to grow as the

West African hub for Ethiopian Airways. The country offers fine beaches, colourful markets, and a heritage based on the voodoo religion.

Benin

In the nineteenth century, Abomey was the capital of the kingdom of Dahomey, renowned for its women warriors, while Ouidah was a centre for the slave trade. It is nowadays visited for the Snake Temple, with its strong voodoo associations.

Nigeria

The demand for tourism

Domestic and outbound tourism

Nigeria is the most populous nation in Africa, with over 224 million inhabitants, and as the world's fifth largest oil producer, it should be one of the wealthiest. Indeed, the country's GDP now exceeds that of South Africa, but this disguises great inequalities in the distribution of wealth. Income from the vast oil reserves in the Niger Delta has fuelled an enormous demand for Western consumer goods and costly development projects. It has also generated a demand for foreign travel, to the extent that Nigeria has a substantial deficit on its international tourism account. The country's growing middle class now travel widely, not just to destinations within West Africa, such as Togo, Ghana, and the 'Smiling Coast' (Gambia) but also to South Africa.

Inbound tourism

Nigeria is essentially a destination for business travellers and tourism contributes less than 1 per cent to its GDP. Around 1.5 million tourist arrivals were recorded in 2019.

The supply side of tourism

Mismanagement of the country's resources and infrastructure has led to a situation in which shortages of basic commodities and power failures are a fact of everyday life. Nevertheless, Nigeria is in the forefront of Africa's emerging economies and its people are resilient and enterprising. Lagos, a vibrant and chaotic city of 15 million people remains the country's commercial centre. As the home of Nigeria's film industry, the largest in sub-Saharan Africa, it has been dubbed 'Nollywood'. Nigerian entrepreneurs are active throughout West Africa. The federal capital was moved to Abuja, which is situated nearer the geographical centre of the country. This was done as a political compromise to satisfy the four main ethnic groups – the Fulani and Hausa, who are Muslims in the less developed north, and the mainly Christian, better-educated and more business-minded Yoruba and Ibo in the south-west and south.

Organisation

Overall responsibility for tourism policy at federal level lies with the Federal Ministry of Culture, Tourism and National Orientation (https://fmic.gov.ng/), assisted by the National Tourism Development Corporation (NTDC). The state governments play an important role in tourism development but differ greatly in their effectiveness.

Tourism resources

Calabar in Cross River State has been promoted widely due to its Carnival (http://carnivalcalabar.com.ng/). For the independent traveller, the main interest of the country lies in the traditional lifestyle of Kano and other cities of northern Nigeria, while the Yoruba city of Benin is noted for the skills of its people in metalworking. The Jos Plateau offers a cooler climate than the rest of Nigeria, while Yankari is the most visited of the country's national parks.

Cameroon

Nigeria's eastern neighbour Cameroon offers even more scenic variety and has been described as 'Africa in miniature'. In the Korup National Park, a part of the equatorial rain forest has been protected, in contrast to the unrestricted commercial logging prevalent in the Ivory Coast. Volcanic Mount Cameroon nearby is the highest mountain in West Africa. The drier northern part of the country includes extensive savannas, where a number of game reserves have been designated, the most important being the Waza National Park. Yaoundé, the administrative capital, and Douala, the country's commercial centre, attract a substantial volume of business travel, while the beaches of Kribi on the Gulf of Guinea are increasingly popular with tourists. More than most African countries, it is made up of a bewildering variety of tribal groups but has the advantage that both French and English are the official languages.

French-speaking **Gabon** with its great mineral wealth has seen little need to attract tourists, other than business travellers to the capital, Libreville. This thinly populated country has great potential for ecotourism, thanks to the biodiversity of its rainforests, and in 2002, this was recognised with the designation of 13 national parks. Similar conservation initiatives, funded mainly by the United States, are proposed for neighbouring countries in West and Central Africa.

West Africa includes a number of islands in the Gulf of Guinea. Air services link Madrid and Lisbon to Malabo and São Tomé in their former colonies, but tourism on any scale has only taken place since 2010:

- **Equatorial Guinea** (https://visitguineaecuatorial.com/) has its capital, Malabo on the island of Bioko (formerly Fernando Po), although most of its territory is on the mainland. The country's oil revenues have been used to provide much-needed infrastructure. This small country with less than a million people has big ambitions. The resort of Sipopo was built specifically for the African Union summit and is now being promoted for golf tourism. In 2015, Equatorial Guinea hosted the African Cup of Nations soccer event. There is potential for ecotourism, particularly turtle-watching on the beaches around Ureka.
- **São Tomé** and the smaller island of **Principe** have as their main assets such as fine beaches, backed by a lush setting of rainforest and cacao plantations. Principe is designated by UNESCO as a World Biosphere Reserve and the islands attract ecotourists. Some of the *roças* (plantation houses) have been converted into hotels.

The Sahel countries

In the Sahel countries, tourism is handicapped for the following reasons:

- Their landlocked situation (with the exception of Mauritania).
- The low level of economic development and poor infrastructure.
- There are few hotels outside the national capitals.
- Political instability and ethnic strife.

In most of these countries, there is a north-south divide between the Saharan nomads of the north (Moors, Tuaregs, and Arabs) and the black African farming communities of the south. This is particularly evident in Chad, whereas in Mauritania the Moors are clearly the dominant group, and the country has close ties to Morocco.

Yet this region has seen the rise of great African civilisations in the past, based on the camel caravans, which linked the region to the cities of North Africa. **Mali** can boast the legendary trading centre of Timbuktu, which now hosts a desert music festival, and the great mosque at Djenné, which is a superb example of Sudanese mud-brick architecture.

Similarly, in the **Niger Republic**, the ancient Tuareg city of Agadès attracts many tourists due to its location on the main trans-Saharan route. Compared to the Nile, the great River Niger is under-utilised as a commercial waterway and tourist route, as it is only navigable for part of the year.

Mauritania has a variety of spectacular desert landscapes, and the historic towns of Chinguetti (where the heritage is threatened by the encroaching dunes), Atar and Wadan for the adventurous tourist.

There has been some development of safari tourism in **Burkina Faso** (http://www.burkina.com/), focussing on the 'W' National Park where the country borders on Benin and Niger. The capital Ouagadougou has achieved international recognition for its film festival (https://fespaco.bf/en/).

Angola

This oil-rich country is primarily a destination for business travellers. Decades of civil war, which ended in 2002, gave Angola a bitter legacy of minefields and devastated infrastructure. The shortage of skilled labour and a long-suppressed demand for consumer goods has made Angola a land of opportunity for Chinese, Brazilian, and South African entrepreneurs. At least 100,000 Portuguese have emigrated to their former colony, attracted by far higher salaries than those available in Portugal. Luanda, which had a population of 300,000 at independence in 1975, is now a metropolis of over 4 million people, and the high cost of accommodation has made the capital one of the world's most expensive cities.

Angola has great tourism potential. The climate of the Atlantic coast is cooled by the Benguela Current, while much of the interior is a plateau averaging 1,200 metres in altitude. Improved communications and the lifting of visa restrictions should lead to greater international recognition of natural attractions such as the Kalandula National Park, which contains one of Africa's largest waterfalls.

The Congo Basin

This region is essentially landlocked with a stretch of coastline north of the mouth of the River Congo. It comprises three countries – Congo-Brazzaville, the Central African Republic (https://www.rca-gouv.net/), and the DRC. The Congo is Africa's most extensive river system and its largest area of tropical rainforest. Most of this region is virtually inaccessible, especially during the rainy season, which prevails for most of the year near the Equator. Hotels of international standard are few, and those in the major cities – Kinshasa, Kisangani, Bangui, and Brazzaville – cater for business travellers attracted by the region's vast mineral resources.

Tourism in **Congo-Brazzaville** has been revitalised by the opening of a railway (with Chinese aid) from the capital to Pointe Noire on the coast, and a new international airport at Brazzaville. Despite its wealth of wildlife resources, tourism in the **Central African Republic** remains problematic due to poor infrastructure.

The prospects for tourism in the **DRC** have been jeopardised by decades of mismanagement and civil war. In the colonial era, this vast country, then known as the Belgian Congo, had been a pioneer in wildlife conservation, and as a legacy 12 per cent of its territory is, in theory at least, designated as protected areas. The most important tourism resources lie close to the borders with Uganda and Rwanda, including the Virunga National Park (https://www.visitvirunga.org/) and two of Africa's largest lakes. The Ituri Forest is of particular interest as the homeland of the Pygmy people.

Transport on the River Congo and its tributaries is confined to small-scale local commerce, and many improvements will need to be made, to both vessels and port facilities, before this network of inland waterways is viable for international tourism. In the absence of a viable road or railway system, a large number of airlines provide domestic services, but few, if any, meet international safety standards.

The islands of the South Atlantic

To the west of the African continent lie several groups of volcanic islands, which are British-overseas territories in the Atlantic Ocean. They are isolated from the mainstream of international trade, and tourism is handicapped by the difficulty and expense of reaching them:

- **St. Helena**, (http://sthelenatourism.com/) the long-awaited airport, became operational in 2016, replacing an infrequent Royal Mail shipping service. The island is now connected by the South African airline SA Airlink (https://www.flyairlink.com/) to Johannesburg and Cape Town. Known mainly for its associations with Napoleon (who was exiled there after his defeat at Waterloo), the island has potential for tourists interested in dolphin-watching, game fishing, and the colonial heritage of the East India Company. With a population of only 4,500, there are a small number of hotels and guesthouses, along with family-run restaurants, serving a fusion of Asian and African cuisines.
- **Ascension** has a military airport, acting as a staging point between Britain and the Falkland Islands, but this barren island has little to attract visitors.
- **Tristan da Cunha** is storm swept, rugged and harbourless and must rank as one of the world's most remote communities.

Summary

- Africa is the second largest of the continents and is rich in both natural and cultural tourism resources.
- Although there is a large North African tourism industry serving the mass inclusive-tour markets of Europe, sub-Saharan Africa's tourism potential is largely unfulfilled.
- This can be attributed to a rudimentary transport network, the generally poor organisational framework, and the low level of industrial development of most African countries.
- Yet in such a vast continent, generalisations are inappropriate; South Africa, for example, has an advanced economy, a high standard of tourism organisation and infrastructure, and it also generates international tourists.
- Some African countries have identified tourism as an area for expansion to attract foreign currency and enhance their economic position. This has been most evident in Southern Africa and some of the islands of the Indian Ocean, but most of the countries of West and Central Africa have been less successful.
- The tourism resources of North Africa are based on both winter and summer beach resorts with the added ingredient of a taste of Arab and Berber culture and excursions to the Sahara.
- East Africa's tourist resources primarily comprise the national parks and game reserves, but developments at the coast allow combined beach and safari tourism.

- South Africa's attractions include beaches and wildlife, as well as spectacular scenery and a warm temperate climate.
- In West Africa, beach tourism is important, but here, as in the rest of the continent, holidaymakers can sample the colourful everyday life of African communities.
- A growing middle class in some African countries is generating a demand for intrar-egional tourism, which is to an extent suppressed by inadequate transport services.

Review questions

1. Analyse the strengths and weaknesses of South Africa as a destination for business and leisure tourism.
2. Compare the strengths and weaknesses of Mozambique and Gambia as destinations for beach tourism.
3. Identify the constraints that prevent specified African countries from realising their full potential as tourist destinations.
4. Explain why some of the countries of East Africa and Southern Africa are the world's most important destinations for safari tourism. Discuss how this type of tourism could be made more sustainable and bring greater benefits to local communities.
5. Explain the appeal of Morocco and Tunisia as holiday destinations, and why Libya has failed to attract this type of tourism.

References and further reading

Bruner, E. (1996) Tourism in Ghana: the representation of slavery and the return of the Black diaspora, *American Anthropologist* 98 (2), 290–304

Goergen, R. (2022) The elephant in the conference room, *Geographical* 94 (4), 46–54

Organization for Economic Co-operation and Development (annual) *Tourism Policy and International Tourism in OECD Member Countries*, OECD, Paris

https://www.unwto.org/tourism-data/unwto-tourism-dashboard

Asia and the Pacific

The tourism geography of South Asia

After reading this chapter, you should be able to:

- Describe the major physical features and climates of the Indian sub-continent, including the Monsoon, and understand their importance to tourism.

- Recognise that the economies of the countries in the region show many contrasts, ranging from advanced economies to some of the poorest in the world.

- Be aware of the volume and characteristics of the demand for tourism in the region.

DOI: 10.4324/9781003406853-25

- Describe the main features of the tourism industry in India, including transport, accommodation, and organisation.
- Recognise that the tourism appeal of South Asia lies in the exotic cultures based largely on religion, as well as the familiar resources of beach tourism.

Introduction

Asia is the world's largest continent, constituting 60 per cent of the world's population. In recent decades, most Asian economies have been growing rapidly, largely due to globalisation. Nevertheless, despite significant improvements, almost 320 million people are living in absolute poverty, with an income of less than US$ 2.15 a day. This indicates that, despite its economic success, Asia still accounts for two-thirds of the world's poor.

First, we need to divide Asia into regions of more manageable size, consisting of countries that are broadly similar in cultural terms. Three regions, which are geographically part of Asia – the Central Asian republics and Siberia, and the Middle East – were described in Chapters 17 and 18. This leaves South Asia, better known as the Indian sub-continent, which the UN World Tourism Organisation (UNWTO) regards as a separate world region, and South-east Asia and the Far East, which UNWTO includes as part of the East Asia-Pacific region.

The governments of most Asian countries realise the importance of tourism, and many have joined organisations such as the Pacific Asia Travel Association (PATA) (https://www.pata.org/) to promote travel to the region more effectively. From the viewpoint of the Western tourist, these countries offer interesting contrasts in landscapes and cultures, living costs are generally low, and hotel service is more personalised than in the West. On the other hand, the provision of infrastructure outside the main tourist areas is often poor. Until recently, the Asian countries themselves generated few tourists, and those that did travel abroad tended to do so within the region. As the economies of Asian countries develop, so does demand for tourism, particularly in the business sector.

Physical features of South Asia

The seasonal changes in the landscape brought about by the monsoon, and the importance of the bamboo plant in the material culture, are the defining features not only of the Indian sub-continent but also of South-east Asia and the Far East. In summer warm, humid air from the Indian Ocean and the south-west Pacific Ocean moves into southern and eastern Asia, bringing heavy rainfall – the 'summer monsoon'. In winter, the continental heartland of Asia is dominated by a strong centre of high pressure from which there is a flow of air to the south and south-east. This 'winter monsoon' brings several months of clear, dry weather.

The Indian sub-continent consists of three major physical divisions:

- **The northern mountain rampart**, which separates the sub-continent from the bulk of the Asian landmass. This includes the Himalayas to the east, and the Pamirs, Hindu Kush, and Karakoram mountain ranges to the west. These rise to over 6,000 metres and boast the world's highest summits. They also have the following important characteristics:

  - They act as a barrier to the movement of the very cold air masses, building up over Central Asia in winter, so that the lowlands to the south enjoy a warm climate throughout the year.
  - They also act as a barrier to north-south communications. Few roads cross the high mountain passes, and unlike the Alps, no railways penetrate the ranges. Even the pattern of air routes is affected to some extent.
  - Because of their altitude, the mountains themselves have a much cooler climate than the lowlands, and support a number of contrasting *life zones* based on differences in rainfall as well as temperature. The western Himalayas, for example, are much drier than those to the east – where Cherrapunji in the Assam foothills has the unenviable distinction of being one of the world's wettest places.
  - In relation to their resources, the mountain valleys are often densely populated. The growth of tourism poses a threat to local communities already under pressure, as well as providing economic opportunity.
  - In the past, the mountains contained a number of independent kingdoms, which were protected from outside influences by their remoteness and rugged terrain. At the present time, only Bhutan, and to a lesser extent, Nepal, have managed to preserve their cultural as well as political integrity. Sikkim and Ladakh have been absorbed by India, while Tibet has been forcibly integrated into China. On the other hand, some of the ethnic groups remain essentially nomadic, ignoring the modern frontiers.

- **The Northern Plains**, through which flow the great rivers Indus, Ganges, and Brahmaputra. These lowlands contain most of the historic cities and business centres of South Asia. The western part of the region has an arid climate, as shown by the Thar Desert on the India-Pakistan border. Elsewhere, winter tends to be the dry season, with a large daily range of temperature. Stifling heat (with temperatures frequently exceeding 40°C) can be expected from April to June before the onset of the summer monsoon. This provides over 90 per cent of India's water supply, so not surprisingly, it has a vital influence on the landscape and the lifestyle. The arrival of the rains is one of the world's most dramatic weather events and is also remarkably predictable, starting in Kerala at the end of May, and sweeping north to reach Mumbai (Bombay) by June 5 and Delhi by June 29. The monsoon provides some initial relief from the excessive heat but is soon followed by months of sweltering weather, as the high humidity negates any cooling effect the slightly lower temperatures might have. Each summer, torrential monsoon rains disrupt communications and leave a trail of devastation in much of the sub-continent.

- **Peninsular India and the islands** This part of South Asia is dominated by the great plateau of volcanic rocks known as the Deccan and the coastal mountain ranges known as the Western and Eastern Ghats. The region has a more moderate tropical climate than the Northern Plains, making it a suitable winter sun destination for tourists from Europe. Coastal locations such as Goa and Kerala, as well as the island states of Sri Lanka and the Maldives in the Indian Ocean have developed tourism industries based primarily on their beach resources.

Cultural features of South Asia

Despite the attractions of beaches and spectacular mountain scenery, the tourist appeal of South Asia is primarily cultural. The street life, bustling markets, colourful festivals, and distinctive foods are fascinating for Western tourists, who also experience a degree of 'culture shock' on arrival. Religion has a major impact on everyday life, and the best of the cultural heritage is to be found in temples and shrines rather than secular buildings. The perceived 'other-worldliness' of countries like India and Nepal attracts many Western tourists alienated by materialism, some of whom seek spiritual guidance in religious communities or *ashrams*. Auroville (https://www.auroville.org/) near the former French colony of Pondicherry is a much-visited example of a planned community based on religion and 'New Age' beliefs.

At this point, we feel some explanation of the major religions is necessary:

- Hinduism, with around 966 million believers, is the majority religion in India, and its rituals have profoundly influenced Indian civilisation for at least 3,000 years – far longer than Christianity in the West or Islam in the Middle East. The Hindu belief in *karma* and reincarnation often results in a fatalistic attitude to life that most Westerners find difficult to accept. Hindu temples are dedicated to a particular god or goddess (Brahma, Vishnu, and Shiva are the most important), and are sumptuously decorated with polychrome sculptures.
- Buddhism also originated in northern India, but is now much more widespread in Sri Lanka, the Himalayan kingdoms, South-east Asia, and the Far East. Common to all Buddhists is a belief in the importance of meditation as the path to *Nirvana* (enlightenment). Buddhist temples usually contain stylised images of the religion's founder – Gautama Siddhartha who is venerated as the Buddha (enlightened one). However, styles of architecture vary widely – temples in Sri Lanka and Burma are quite different from those in Bhutan, for example.
- Islam is the predominant religion in Afghanistan, Pakistan, Bangladesh, and the Maldives. The Mogul Emperors imposed Islam on northern India in the sixteenth century, and were responsible for some of the world's finest Islamic architecture, including the Taj Mahal (https://www.tajmahal.gov.in/).
- Sikhism originally arose as a resistance to the Islamic domination of northern India. Sikhs differ from Hindus in being monotheistic, placing much less emphasis on ritual, and rejecting the rigid social distinctions or castes that have characterised

traditional Indian culture. Although they account for only 2 per cent of the popu-lation of India and are based mainly in the Punjab, they play an important role in commerce and the professions.

Religious tensions also threaten the political stability of most countries in the region and, thus, reduce their appeal to tourists. Differences between Muslims and Hindus in British India led to its partition into two separate countries on independence in 1947. However, this left unresolved the status of Kashmir, causing a long-running dispute between the Republic of India and Pakistan and disrupting communications between the two coun-tries. In the late 1990s, the rise of Hindu fundamentalism in the Republic of India posed a threat to the government's policy of secularism and religious toleration, culminating in the inter-communal massacres that occurred in Gujarat in 2002. Muslim fundamentalism influences social attitudes to women and minority groups in Afghanistan and Pakistan, where religion and politics are less clearly separated than they are in India. Nevertheless, discrimination against the *dalits* or low caste Hindus, although strictly illegal, persists in some parts of India and is a barrier to their participation in many social activities, includ-ing tourism.

Western cultural influence was largely due to the British, although the Portuguese ar-rived in the region much earlier. In fact, almost the whole of the Indian sub-continent was under British rule or protection during the nineteenth and early twentieth centuries, with the exception of a few small Portuguese and French enclaves, namely Goa, Diu, Daman, Chandernagore, and Pondicherry. The legacy of the British *Raj* remains after in-dependence in the widespread use of the English language and administrative framework, sporting and military traditions, an extensive railway network, and a supply of mountain resorts known as hill-stations. These had provided British officials and their families, in the days before air-conditioning, with a refuge from the summer heat of the plains. These places still retain much of their colonial architecture, although they are now resorts for middle-class domestic tourists. They include:

- Murree in Pakistan
- Simla in the Himalayas (the summer capital of British India)
- Ootacamund in the Nilgiri Highlands of southern India
- Nuwara Eliya in Sri Lanka

Approaches to tourism

South Asia constitutes over 2 per cent of international world tourism arrivals. Over half of all tourist arrivals, and two-thirds of receipts are accounted for by the largest of the nine component countries of South Asia – the Republic of India. Elsewhere, in much of the region tourism is of little significance, notably for Afghanistan due to political unrest rendering the country unsafe for travellers, and for Bangladesh, where more pressing economic concerns overshadow tourism development. The majority of countries have encouraged inbound tourism, and most have a positive balance on their tourism account, with the notable exception of Pakistan, where outbound travel is much greater in terms of expenditure.

We can see a variety of approaches to tourism within the region including:

- Stringent restriction on visitor numbers in the case of Bhutan, in contrast to neighbouring Nepal.
- A policy of tourist segregation from the local communities in the Lakshadweep and the Maldive islands.
- Promotion of Western-style beach holidays in Goa.

India

India demands our attention for numerous reasons:

- In extent and cultural variety, it is the equivalent of Europe, but with a much older civilisation. There are at least 15 major languages, although Hindi is the most widely spoken. The country is a mosaic of different religions, ethnic groups, and castes.
- With a population of over 1.4 billion, India will surpass China as the world's most populous country by 2030. It has almost 18 per cent of the world's population on just 3 per cent of the world's land area, so that demographic pressures on the resource base are severe.
- Over half of India's population is under 25 years of age, 25 per cent of adults are illiterate, and well over 20 per cent struggle to live below the official poverty line (1.9 US dollars a day). Although India is a predominantly rural country, it also contains three major world cities – Delhi (32.9 million inhabitants), Mumbai (21.3 million inhabitants), and Kolkata (14.8 million inhabitants).
- Despite these pressures and many other socio-economic problems, India has retained a democratic form of government since independence, although the Congress Party (https://www.inc.in) has been dominant in politics for most of that time. The cultural diversity of the country is recognised in the federal system of government, in which each of the 29 states and 6 autonomous territories has a large degree of control over its internal affairs, including tourism development.
- For many years following independence, India was to a large extent a centrally planned economy. After 1991, the government embarked on a policy of liberalisation, removing many restrictions on business enterprise, and the country was opened up to foreign investment. India is set to become one of the world's leading industrial nations, with technological expertise as part of its vast human resources. Bangalore and Hyderabad, for example, are among the world's leading centres of information technology, and there are plans for 'smart cities' using advanced methods of communication in the Mumbai-Delhi corridor. In contrast, great improvements need to be made in basic infrastructure, which is inadequate by Western standards, while bureaucratic controls and inertia continue to inhibit progress.

Demand for tourism

Domestic and outbound tourism

A substantial middle class has the means to participate in domestic tourism, which is consequently many times larger in volume than inbound tourism. Domestic travel in India has been facilitated by the expansion of low-cost airlines and the rise in Internet use, such that the number of visitors is now beginning to exceed the capacity of the most popular destinations. Traditionally, a good deal of domestic travel has been undertaken for religious reasons, as all the major faiths encourage pilgrimages to shrines or holy places. The best known of these is the Hindu centre of Varanasi (Benares) on the River Ganges, where the *ghats* – the steps leading down to the water's edge are the focus for ritual bathing, readings from the sacred texts by gurus, and cremations. There are many other shrines, some in remote locations in the Himalayas and Kashmir. Often these pilgrimages entail an arduous journey, partly on foot, and embrace all classes of society, including large numbers of wandering *sadhus* (holy men). Bodhgaya is the main pilgrimage centre for Buddhists, while the Golden Temple at Amritsar is the holy place of the Sikhs. Visits to family entertainment centres, amusement parks, and places featured in 'Bollywood' movies, as well as stays in beach and mountain resorts, are expected to increase as incomes rise among a middle class with a Western-style education and aspirations.

Outbound tourism is much smaller in volume, but nevertheless accounted for 26.3 million departures in 2019, falling to 8.6 million in 2021 due to the COVID-19 pandemic. Business travel accounts for 25 per cent of these journeys. Leisure travel to countries outside South Asia has grown with the relaxation of strict foreign exchange controls imposed by the Indian government. For many years, Britain has been the most popular European destination, reflecting the cultural and family ties between the two countries. Future travel patterns may well be influenced by the fact that the United States is now India's main trading partner, and there are four times more Indian students in American universities than in British universities.

Inbound tourism

Despite having vast tourism potential, India receives only a small share of world tourism, amounting to 10.6 million arrivals in 2019. Even so, tourism has shown impressive growth since 1970, when 290,000 visitors were recorded. Tourism is now India's third largest earner of foreign exchange and provides employment directly and indirectly for over 40 million people. The impact is even greater if we consider the informal sector of the economy and the very large numbers engaged in the handicraft industries. A number of factors are holding back the expansion of tourism in India:

- Inadequate infrastructure, especially water and power supplies.
- Negative publicity in the Western media. For example, outbreaks of disease and inter-communal strife, in reality confined to specific areas, are seen as affecting the whole country.

- Promotion of this enormous and complex country as one destination, whereas India consists of many quite different destinations and tourism products. There is a need to market specific destinations and target specific types of tourists.
- The seasonal concentration of visits in the final quarter of the year, creating occupancy problems for India's hotels.
- A shortage of medium-priced accommodation, particularly in Delhi.
- Other negative factors include air pollution in the cities during the dry season, noise, poor hygiene, and harassment by beggars, and street vendors.

The main generating markets for India include Britain, Germany, France, the United States, the Middle East, and Japan. Many arrivals from the Middle East and Britain are, in fact, returning expatriates, who tend to stay with friends or relatives and make little use of tourist facilities. The most popular time to visit India is from October to December when the weather is at its best, but there is a steady flow of business travellers throughout the year. The average length of stay of tourists to India – at 28 days – is among the world's highest – backpackers, for example, from Europe, Australia, and North America, who are including India as part of an Asian tour, spend at least three weeks in the country. These young budget travellers have played an important role in opening up new destinations to conventional tourism. However, the typical backpackers of the new millennium are different from their predecessors of the 1970s in at least two respects:

- They are usually following an established route pattern, staying at hostels and cheap hotels patronised by other Western budget travellers.
- They are less concerned with a search for 'spiritual values'. Nowadays, an extended visit to India is seen more as an interesting way of filling the 'gap year' between college and a career.

Discussion point

In class, discuss the proposition that the average Western backpacker is ill-informed about the realities of life in India, is overly concerned with travelling as cheaply as possible, and often behaves in ways that cause offence to local communities. Would a code of conduct be the best solution to the problem?

The supply side of tourism

Transport

The vast majority of foreign visitors to India (other than those from neighbouring Bangladesh and Pakistan) arrive by air. Delhi and Mumbai (Bombay) are the most important gateways and have invested heavily in improving facilities for air travellers. Kolkata (Calcutta) and Chennai (Madras) serve the eastern and southern parts of the country. The Indian government has responded to the growth in air travel by adopting a liberal *open skies* policy, which allows foreign low-cost airlines to fly direct from Europe to resort areas such as Goa. The national carrier Air India (http://www.airindia.in/) has merged with Indian Airlines and operates services to over 70 destinations within the country as well as to neighbouring states. Only a small minority of Western tourists travel overland to India, due to the political situation in Afghanistan which has closed the historic route through the Khyber Pass, while the long-standing dispute between India and Pakistan over Kashmir places another obstacle in the way of travellers.

Internal transport is less fraught with difficulties. With deregulation in the late 1990s, a number of low-cost carriers such as Air Deccan (https://airdeccan.co.in/), Jet Airways, and Air Sahara entered the market, along with Kingfisher, which catered for a more up-market traveller with Western tastes and aspirations. However, only Air Deccan has survived in this highly complex and competitive market. In addition, the airlines are now competing with the state-owned Indian Railways (http://www.indianrailways.gov.in/) for a share of the domestic market, offering cheap fares and comfortable travel as well as greatly reduced journey times.

India inherited from the British Raj the most extensive railway network in Asia, amounting to over 128,000 kilometres of track, and this is used by some 24 million passengers a day. Indian Railways is vital to the national economy, providing direct employment to 1.2 million people. Trains are often grossly overcrowded, delays are frequent, and the network generally needs upgrading and investment. Nevertheless, from the viewpoint of the foreign tourist, the train provides a cheaper and more interesting way of touring than by air, with express services linking all the main cities. Foreign tourists need to purchase *Indrail* passes or make prior reservations to ensure travelling in comfort and without hassle. In some areas, steam locomotives are still used, as for example, on the narrow-gauge Darjeeling-Himalaya railway (http://www.dhrs.org/), which is a major tourist attraction in its own right. Luxury rail products such as the 'Palace on Wheels' (https://thepalaceonwheels.com/) and the 'Royal Orient' (https://www.royalorienttrain.com/) are promoted by the India Tourism Office as a way of touring the classical sites in the northwest of the country.

In contrast, India's road network of over 6 million kilometres is inadequate to cope with the great increase in traffic, resulting from rapid economic growth, as there are few four-lane highways. Livestock on the road add to the chaos, and accident levels are very high by Western standards. Nevertheless, the level of car ownership is low compared to that of China. Expectations that the Nano, a low-cost 'people's car' would reduce the number of over-burdened motor cycle combinations and satisfy a huge suppressed demand, have not materialised. Acute traffic congestion and high parking fees discourage car use in the major cities. Even affluent middle-class 'millennials' living in metropolitan areas prefer to use taxis or share rides for the daily commute, while the car is mainly used for long-distance holiday journeys.

For the foreign visitor, long-distance road travel, even by express bus, can be a noisy and exhausting experience. This situation should improve with the development of a national 'superhighway' network almost 6,000 kilometres in length, based on the 'Golden Quadrilateral' linking India's four major cities. It is hoped this will boost the country's economy and reduce the huge disparities of wealth that exist between cities such as Bangalore and the impoverished rural areas of states such as Bihar, Orissa, and Madhya Pradesh.

Accommodation

India's accommodation stock is extensive, ranging from luxury hotels to basic hostels used by young tourists on a tight budget, who are more concerned about price than fire safety standards. Modern Western-style hotels catering for both business and leisure tourists are found in all large cities and the popular tourist centres. Indian-owned chains, namely Taj (https://www.tajhotels.com/), Oberoi (https://www.oberoihotels.com/), and the state-owned India Tourism Development Corporation (ITDC) (https://itdc.co.in/), dominate this sector. More unusual types of accommodation include:

- The luxury houseboats moored on Lake Dal at Srinagar, a heritage of British and Mogul rule in Kashmir.
- The former palaces of the Indian princes or maharajas who were semi-independent rulers under the British Raj. These have now been converted into 'heritage hotels', the most famous being the Lake Palace Hotel at Udaipur in Rajahstan, in a highly romantic setting.
- *Dak* bungalows, used primarily by government officials as rest houses, are sometimes available for overnight stays by tourists in remote areas.
- Hostels provided by religious organisations.
- Tourist bungalows providing self-catering facilities and private guesthouses are available in resort areas. Campgrounds have also been developed along the main overland routes and forest lodges are available in wildlife reserves such as the Kanha National Park (https://www.kanha-national-park.com/).

Tourism organisation

In the 1960s, tourism development began to form part of the government's Five-Year Plans (whose primary objective is to raise living standards), and more recently tourism has been the subject of specific 'action plans'. The Ministry of Tourism (http://tourism.gov.in/) is responsible for formulating policy at the cabinet level and co-ordinating the tourism activities of the state and territory governments. It is supported by a network of tourist offices abroad for promotion and marketing.

The Ministry is supported by a number of other autonomous agencies including:

- The ITDC, which was set up by the government in 1965 to develop infrastructure in those areas where the private sector was reluctant to invest. Apart from hotels, the ITDC also owned resorts, restaurants, and transport operations, some of which have since been privatised.
- The Indian Institute of Travel and Tourism Management.
- The National Institute of Water Sports.
- The National Council for Hotel Management and Catering Technology.
- The National Institute of Hotel Management.

As well as supporting many projects through the ITDC, the government also provides financial incentives to domestic and foreign companies in the private sector. At the regional and local levels, the various state and city authorities have a regulatory role, and some have set up development corporations to carry out tourism projects. In recent years, however, the public sector has not been particularly active in encouraging tourism. It is perhaps not surprising that in a country with so many pressing social and economic problems, the development of tourist facilities, which the majority of the Indian population cannot afford, is seen as a low priority.

Tourism resources

On offer is a unique blend of ancient civilisations, religious monuments, spectacular scenery, beaches, mountain resorts, and wildlife reserves, that has been promoted in the West as 'Incredible India'. We can summarise the main tourism products as:

* **Cultural tourism** – Usually focussing on a particular region, and taking the form of a tour circuit linking a number of sites to a gateway city.
* **Beach tourism** – At present this is mainly found in the states of Goa, Kerala, and Tamil Nadu, and little of India's 7,500-kilometre-long coastline has been developed for tourism.
* **Adventure tourism** – Including trekking, mountain climbing, and river-running, which is mainly focussed on the more accessible parts of the Himalaya region.
* **Ecotourism** – India is second only to Africa in the variety of its wildlife resources. This is perhaps surprising given the demographic pressures and the threats of increasing pollution and deforestation (only 13 per cent of the country has any type of forest cover). The first national park – Jim Corbett to the north of Delhi – was established under British rule in 1911 due to the efforts of a hunter turned conservationist. There are now 106 National Parks and 56 wildlife sanctuaries, although most are much smaller than their equivalents in Africa. The federal government has effected a number of conservation measures; the most widely publicised is 'Project Tiger' that seeks to protect India's best-known national icon. Kanha National Park in Madhya Pradesh, the setting for Rudyard Kipling's *Jungle Book*, is the best known of these game reserves. Much of the responsibility for wildlife management has devolved to the individual states. Limited funding is a problem, and issues of economic development often conflict with conservation.
* **Health and wellness tourism** – Characterised by yoga techniques based on *ayurveda*, a holistic medical system that has been practised in India for at least two millennia.
* **Sport tourism** – The hosting of the 2010 Commonwealth Games in Delhi, and India's sponsorship of cricket and the Indian cricket 'premier league' (https://www.iplt20.com/) are examples of the country's significance as a venue for sports events.

Due to its extent, India is usually treated as four regions, based on the gateways of Delhi, Mumbai, Chennai, and Kolkata.

Northern India

This region has played a major role in the history of India, and contains the best-known cultural attractions. The 'Classic Triangle', a tour circuit linking the cities of Delhi, Agra and Jaipur, is the most popular route for foreign visitors.

- **Delhi** actually consists of two cities – the old and the new. Old Delhi was the capital of the Mogul Empire, and is a maze of narrow streets, chaotic traffic (partially alleviated by a new metro system), and bustling bazaars. Among its Islamic monuments are the Jama Masjid Mosque and the Red Fort, once a royal palace. The British planned New Delhi as the capital of India in the closing decades of the Raj. The most important of its broad ceremonial avenues is the Rajpath linking India Gate to the President's Palace (https://rashtrapatisachivilaya.gov.in/).
- **Agra** is mainly visited for the Taj Mahal, the white marble mausoleum commemorating Shah Jehan's love for his favourite wife Mumtaz. This beautiful building is under threat from:

  - Tourist pressure, leaving in its wake litter in the gardens and even graffiti on the monument itself.
  - Pollution. Although tourism provides a livelihood for many thousands employed in the craft and service sectors, Agra is also a major industrial city. Sulphur dioxide emissions have caused a massive deterioration in the stonework.

Within easy reach of Agra are other relics of historic India:

- Fatehpur Sikri, the remains of a short-lived capital of the Mogul Empire.
- Orchha, which has undergone less restoration and is not as commercialised.
- The temples at Khajuraho (https://whc.unesco.org/en/list/240), with their erotic sculptures are also a well-established stop on the tour circuit.

Jaipur is the gateway to **Rajahstan**, a state which to many epitomises India, with its colourful costumes, ethnic crafts, and the palaces of the former maharajas. It also exemplifies the problems brought about by tourism in an arid region where there are few other sources of income. Some allege that conventional organised tourism does not benefit local communities as profits mainly go to the owners of 'heritage hotels', who furthermore prefer to employ immigrant Nepalis, who are prepared to accept even lower wages than the locals. On the other hand, backpackers have also been criticised for showing little respect for Hindu traditions, while the Pushkar camel market has become a commercialised tourist event. Of the tourist centres, Jaipur itself is famous for its markets and the 'Palace of the Winds', but suffers from chronic pollution and lack of investment. Other attractions in the region include:

- Jodhpur, which gave polo to the British, is noted for its *son et lumière* performances recreating the warrior traditions of the Rajput princes.
- Udaipur, the best preserved of the Rajput cities, with a beautiful setting on Lake Pichola.
- Jaisalmer was once a major trading centre for camel caravans crossing the Thar Desert but is now a picturesque stop on the tourist itinerary. Income from tourism enabled the authorities to provide a piped water supply, but this together with vastly increased water consumption, has caused widespread subsidence, as the town's open drains cannot cope. As a result, many of the *havelis* (merchant houses) are in urgent need of repair.

The **Valley of Kashmir** offers among its attractions, beautiful mountain scenery and a cool climate, in contrast to the heat and dust of the plains of northern India. This made it the favourite resort area for the Mogul rulers, who designed the famous Shalimar Gardens in Srinagar. It has become popular with domestic tourists, despite the heavy security presence of the Indian military authorities. This was imposed as a response to a number of terrorist incidents in the late 1980s and early 1990s. However, checkpoints and curfews have made everyday life irksome for Kashmiris, many of whom depend on tourism for a livelihood. Although Gulmarg was developed in the 1970s as the premier golf and skiing resort of India, since the troubles there has been little outside investment in the region. Moreover, foreign tourists have been deterred by the chronic dispute with Pakistan. On the other hand, Ladakh, although part of the state of Kashmir, is not a disputed area and has become a trekking destination. This region offers spectacular, if rather barren, high mountain landscapes and a Tibetan culture which is still largely intact.

Eastern India

The Eastern India region is centred on Kolkata, the capital of West Bengal, which as Calcutta was the former capital of British India. In the West, the city is better known for its overcrowding and Mother Teresa's work among the destitute than for its cultural attractions, which outshine those of Delhi. Although rickshaws still feature in the traffic, Kolkata has a long-established metro system, and the city's technological achievements are showcased in 'Science City' (https://sciencecitykolkata.org/in). Within easy reach are the beach resorts of the Bay of Bengal, including Puri, which is also a major religious centre for Hindus. It is one of a number of temple-cities in the state of Orissa, the others being Konarak and Bhubaneswar. Kolkata is also the gateway to the eastern Himalayas, particularly the mountain resorts of Darjeeling and Shillong, which are noted for their tea plantations. Large areas of this sensitive frontier region are tribal territories under military control, and access is restricted for security reasons.

Southern India

The Dravidian peoples of southern India are culturally distinct, and overseas trade has played an important role in the history of the region. The port of Cochin, for example, was noted for its trade in pepper and other spices in ancient times, and in the picturesque fishing villages, Hinduism has co-existed peacefully with Christianity and other religions.

With its favourable climate, lush scenery, and fine beaches, the state of Kerala is set to rival Goa as a holiday destination. A unique asset is provided by the 'backwaters', a system of canals adapted from transporting agricultural produce to recreational use. With the introduction of charter flights in 1995, Kovalam has become a major beach resort, particularly for British holidaymakers. However, this has failed to benefit the local community to the same extent as the small-scale informal tourism of earlier years and stands in apparent contradiction to the socialist leanings of the state government. Most of the Coromandel Coast is less attractive for tourism development due to the heavy surf and was the area of India most affected by the 2004 tsunami. Nevertheless, Chennai has fine beaches as well as being a major cultural centre, offering the classical *kathakali* dance-dramas, adapted for a Western tourist audience. It is a good base for exploring the temples of Madurai and Kanchipuram (http://www.maduraimeenakshi.org/), which are spectacular examples of Hindu architecture.

Western India

Beach tourism has developed to a greater extent in western India along the Malabar Coast. The region is dominated by Mumbai, India's major port and business centre, while Goa is the leading holiday destination.

- **Mumbai** is a new city by Indian standards, with many reminders of the British Raj when, as Bombay, it served as the 'gateway to India'. The Chhatrapati Shivaji rail terminus is reputedly the world's busiest. Mumbai is perceived as a city of opportunity by rural immigrants, who pour in at the rate of a thousand a day. With little room for expansion on a narrow peninsula, the city's congestion is acute, and the contrasts between skyscrapers and grand hotels on the one hand, and the *bustees* (slums) on the other, are extreme. This may explain the dominant role of 'Bollywood' – Mumbai's booming film industry – in popular culture. Apart from shopping, the city's attractions include Chowpatty Beach, with its snake charmers and other performers, the 'hanging gardens' of exclusive Malabar Hill, the Gandhi Memorial (http://www.gandhi-manibhavan.org/), and the art collections of the Chhatrapati Shivaji Maharaj Vastu Sangrahalaya museum (http://www.csmvs.in/). The ancient history of India is brought to life at the Elephanta Caves (https://whc.unesco.org/en/list/244/), while Mumbai is a good base for visiting the Buddhist and Hindu temples of Ajanta (https://whc.unesco.org/en/list/242/) and Ellora (https://whc.unesco.org/en/list/243/).

Discussion point: poverty as a tourist spectacle

It is now possible for Western tourists to visit the slums of Mumbai on a guided tour. Here, people live in grossly overcrowded conditions, at densities of over 2000 per hectare, without basic services. The sensory experience is unpleasant, with the stench of open sewers clogged with garbage, incessant noise, the acrid smoke from pottery kilns, not to mention the health and safety hazard posed by tangles of improvised electricity cables. On the positive side, these slums provide an opportunity for thousands of small enterprises, many of them engaged in recycling useful articles out of the waste materials discarded by more affluent city-dwellers.

Debate whether these tours can be regarded as pro-poor tourism, helping to alleviate poverty. Are the organisers motivated by profit, or do they donate some of the proceeds from tourists to charitable work, such as providing street children with a basic education?

Are the tourists voyeurs motivated simply by curiosity, or are they on a guilt trip? Does visiting poverty-stricken areas and meeting some of their inhabitants provide valuable insights into the 'real India' that most tourists never experience, or does it merely exploit the slum-dwellers?

Goa's small area offers scenic variety, over 100 kilometres of fine beaches, and a re-laxed lifestyle (see photo 20.1). Culturally it is unique – a blend of Indian and 'Latin' influences. Both Catholic Carnival and Hindu festivals are celebrated here, while al-cohol is freely available, unlike the situation elsewhere in India. Portugal ruled Goa for four and a half centuries until ousted by the Indian Army in 1961, and the Portu-guese influence is evident in the architecture, music, and the cuisine. The immense Baroque church of Bom Jesu in Old Goa (http://bomjesus.org/) – the former capital – contains the tomb of St. Francis Xavier, the greatest of Jesuit missionaries to the East.

Western tourists are not attracted to Goa primarily for cultural or religious reasons; since the arrival of the 'hippies' in the 1960s, the focus has been on beach tourism. Nevertheless, we can distinguish between different categories of visitor, and a range of accommodation and services has developed to meet their needs. These include:

- Low-budget backpackers, mainly from Europe and Australia, who are stopping off in Goa as part of an extended Asian tour. They stay in cheap guesthouses in the Anjuna area, 'discovered' by the hippies of a previous generation.
- Indian domestic tourists taking seaside holidays, cultural tours, and business trips, who stay at hotels in Panaji, the state capital, or other towns.
- Package holidaymakers from the United Kingdom, Germany, and other West Eu-ropean countries arriving during the winter season on low-cost flights to Goa's Dabolim Airport. They stay in three-star hotels contracted to particular tour op-erators. Due to the rapid growth of charters since 1987, fishing villages such as Calangute have become commercialised resorts.
- Middle-class West European holidaymakers who take advantage of the cheap air fares but prefer to use locally-owned small hotels and guesthouses.

    Tourism has arguably brought economic benefits to Goa, but the state gov-ernment's policy of encouraging up-market tourism has been opposed by local non-governmental organisations (NGOs) concerned with the social and environ-mental issues associated with tourism development. These include:

- The diversion of scarce resources, such as water and power from agriculture to the hotel sector. Some claim that one five-star hotel consumes as much water as five villages.
- Violations by the hotel sector of state laws that prevent building within 200 me-tres of the shoreline.
- Unlike the locally-owned small hotels and guesthouses, the luxury hotels are linked with international chains or owned by Indians from outside Goa. The state government's attempts to control the beach shacks selling food, etc. is seen as favouring the hotels at the expense of local people's livelihood.
- The expansion of tourism has resulted in the decline of traditional occupations such as fishing and cashew nut cultivation.

- Goa is a religious, conservative society, and local people are often deeply offended by the attitude of many Western holidaymakers, expressed in drug-taking, uninhibited sexuality, and immodest dress and behaviour.
- Carnival has been exploited to promote tourist activities, rather than being primarily a religious festival for the benefit of the local community.

Discussion point

Goa has reached the stage in the tourist area life cycle where it is facing growing competition as tour operators discover more unspoiled beach locations. How should the state government and tourism sector respond?

The Islands of India

India's island territories, as yet, remain largely untouched by Western-style tourism, although they attract a growing number of domestic visitors. They include:

- The Lakshadweep (Laccadives) archipelago in the Indian Ocean, composed of small coral atolls similar to the Maldives further south. Bangaram is the only island open to Western tourists for diving holidays.

Photo 20.1
One of Goa's tropical beaches

Source: ©istockphoto.com/Tobias Helbig

- The Andaman and Nicobar Islands in the Bay of Bengal are rugged and largely forest-covered. There is potential for ecotourism and diving, but development is restricted by lack of infrastructure and the sensitive nature of relationships between mainstream India and the indigenous tribes, an example of a 'Fourth World' culture which is increasingly under threat.

Sri Lanka

Formerly known as Ceylon, Sri Lanka is a large island rich in tourism resources. Its capital, Colombo, is well-placed in relation to the air and shipping routes crossing the Indian Ocean. In the past, the island's closeness to India and fabled wealth attracted Arab traders who were followed by the Portuguese, Dutch, and British. This resulted in a mix of cultures, and one of the country's highest mountains – Sri Padu (Adam's Peak) – is sacred to all four major religions. Until the 1970s, Sri Lanka had been one of the more stable countries in South Asia, and the prospects for tourism seemed bright. The Ceylon Tourist Board (now the Sri Lanka Tourist Board) was established in 1966 when 19,000 visitors were received. By 1982, this had grown to over 400,000, most of whom were on air-inclusive holidays, organised by West European tour operators (the entrepreneur Freddie Laker was largely responsible for introducing Sri Lanka as a long-haul beach destination to the British market). However, there had long been tensions between the Sinhalese and the Tamil minority, who were originally brought in by the British from southern India to work in the tea plantations. During the 1980s, these irrupted into civil war, which rendered much of the north and east of the country off-limits to tourists. As a result, Sri Lanka lost favour with Western tour operators, and visitor numbers fell dramatically. Since the defeat of the Tamil separatists, international tourism has now largely recovered, with 2.3 million arrivals in 2019, falling to 0.2 million in 2021 as a result of COVID-19. Western Europe still accounts for a third of the demand, with the United Kingdom and Germany in the lead, but Asian countries are growing in importance.

The Ministry of Tourism and Lands has overall responsibility for the sector. It has four public sector agencies:

- Sri Lanka Tourism Development Authority
- Sri Lanka Institute of Tourism and Hotel Management
- Sri Lanka Tourism Promotion Bureau
- Sri Lanka Convention Bureau

Although Sri Lanka has suffered from the lack of a clear tourism policy, a master plan commissioned in the 1990s provided the initial framework for growth. The Ministry is now focussed on human resource development and recognises that tourism can drive the country's economic growth if supported by the development of infrastructure. The government, while encouraging foreign investment, has responded by steering development to the coastal areas close to Colombo in the west, and the port of Trincomalee in the east, in this way protecting the country's cultural and wildlife resources from the impact of tourism. The plan also stimulated a change in emphasis of tourism development to 'beach plus' products, in contrast to the sun, sand, and sea formula of earlier years.

Tourism resources

Sri Lanka's tourist attractions include:

- Extensive sandy beaches along the south and west coast, although sea conditions can be rough during the period of the south-west monsoon from May to July. Here, the Sri Lanka Tourism Development Authority has developed resort hotels of an international standard, particularly at Bentota. The beaches on the east coast are less developed, although they are more sheltered and enjoy a drier climate.
- The 'cultural triangle' of the interior, based on the historic cities of Kandy, Anuradhapura, and Polonnaruwa, each of which served at one time as capital of a powerful kingdom. The Rock Fortress at Sigiriya (https://www.sigiriya.info/), rising above the northern plain is particularly impressive, as are the remains of ancient temples, palaces, and complex irrigation systems. Traditional crafts and dances continue to flourish in Kandy, which contains the 'Temple of the Tooth' (http://www.sridaladamaligawa.lk/), a renowned Buddhist shrine.
- The wildlife resources, including the elephant orphanage at Pinnawela (http://nationalzoo.gov.lk/elephantorphanage/), and a number of national parks, such as Yala (https://www.yalasrilanka.lk/), and Gal Oya (https://www.galoyalodge.com/), which offer bungalow accommodation.
- Colombo is a major business and conference centre, as well as providing shopping opportunities for jewellery, batik, and wood-carving.

> **Discussion point**
> Although Thailand received the most media coverage, three countries of the Indian sub-continent were badly affected by the tsunami of December 26, 2004. Sri Lanka alone suffered the loss of 38,000 lives and damage to its tourism sector amounting to 250 million dollars. The state government of Tamil Nadu in southern India and the government of Sri Lanka responded by designating a coastal regulation zone, where any new development or rebuilding was prohibited within 200 metres of the sea. This was ostensibly to prevent any future disasters, but it has adversely affected the fishing communities that have been re-located. In effect, prime coastal sites have been requisitioned by the authorities to favour future luxury hotel projects rather than small tourism enterprises. In class, debate the issues involved in the reconstruction after the tsunami, from the viewpoint of the various stakeholders, including NGOs, representatives of local communities, government officials, hoteliers, guesthouse owners, and tour operators.

The Maldives

The Maldives is an independent republic, very small in land area but occupying a large expanse of the Indian Ocean south-west of the Indian sub-continent. Geographically, the Maldives is a unique collection of 26 coral atolls, containing almost 1,200 coral islands, of which only a small number are permanently inhabited. The government has done much to encourage Western tourism but on its own terms. For example, the islanders are Muslims, and no alcohol is allowed except on those islands designated for tourists as self-contained resorts. Tourists are only allowed to visit the inhabited islands on escorted tours and are expected to respect the traditions of Islam in terms of modest dress when visiting the capital, Male. This is a small town with little to attract the visitor, although it contains two-thirds of the Maldivian population and is the gateway to the islands through Velana International Airport (https://macl.aero/). The Maldives now attract around 1.5 million tourists a year, half of whom originate in Western Europe, with the United Kingdom, Germany, and Italy in the lead.

The prime tourism resource of the islands is the pristine marine environment, where the quality of the coral reefs and marine life is unrivalled anywhere in the world. The majority of visitors arrive in the Maldives to experience this marine environment and also for water sports. Each of the resort islands has a diving base, and the resort *house reef* is commonly within wading or swimming distance from the accommodation. In addition to the resorts, accommodation is available on live-aboard 'safari vessels'.

The Ministry of Tourism oversees development and regulates the resorts. In 2010, the Maldives Marketing and Public Relations Corporation (MMPRC) was created as the government body responsible for the promotion of the islands as a tourist destination. The Maldives aims to become the world's premium ecotourism destination and to diversify its markets. The authorities are acutely aware of the threat of rising sea levels resulting from climate change, as no point on the islands rises above 3 metres. The atoll of Baa, for example, has been particularly active in environmental and social programmes. These include the conservation of the mangroves, which are very effective in absorbing carbon emissions and protecting the islands from frequent cyclones; the use of renewable sources of energy in the resorts; recycling; and a ban on shark fishing.

Discussion point

With over half a million people, residents, and tourists, occupying a very limited land area, waste disposal in the Maldives is a major problem, given the vulnerability of the marine environment to pollution. Investigate how the authorities could deal with this problem.

Pakistan

Despite having a varied resource base and a fairly extensive coastline, Pakistan has been less successful than India in attracting Western tourists and the sector accounts for 2.7 per cent of GDP. In part, this is due to the strength of Islamic tradition, security concerns, poor infrastructure, and the restrictions on cross-border travel. Most of the country consists of mountain and desert landscapes, and some of the world's most difficult terrain separates Pakistan from its neighbours to the west and north.

The demand for tourism

Domestic and outbound tourism

Domestic tourism is significant and set to grow, with an estimated 50 million trips a year, including day and weekend visits. Outbound tourism is affected by visa restrictions in many countries and accounts for around a million departures annually.

Inbound tourism

Natural disasters such as floods and earthquakes, as well as internal conflicts, have had a detrimental effect on tourism, and special permits are needed to travel in some areas. In 2018, 1.9 million arrivals were recorded, with the most important generating countries being the United Kingdom, India, and the United States.

The supply side of tourism

The Pakistan Tourism Development Corporation oversees tourism following the abolition of the Ministry of Tourism. It offers a wide selection of hotels, motels, and rest houses (known as *musafir khanas*) and tours operated by its subsidiary Pakistan Tours Ltd. The national airline Pakistan International Airlines (PIA) (https://www.piac.com.pk/) provides a network of international and domestic services. Transport by road and rail is less efficient and compares unfavourably with the situation in India.

Although Urdu is the official language, Pakistan constitutes a number of ethnic groups, and the country has been less politically stable than India. In the north-west of the country, government control is only loosely exercised over the Pathans and other tribes. In the time of the Raj, this was the North-West Frontier of British India, immortalised by Rudyard Kipling; nowadays, it is an area rife with guns and refugees as a result of the continuing crisis in neighbouring Afghanistan. For this reason, the Khyber Pass has ceased to function as an overland tourist route, although the regional capital – Peshawar – is visited by the more adventurous travellers. The majority of Pakistan's population live in the irrigated valley of the River Indus, which also contains the major tourist centres:

- Lahore is the religious and cultural centre of the country, conserving much of the architectural heritage and pleasure gardens of the Mogul emperors of India.
- Multan is another historic walled city which is the focus of Muslim pilgrimages. It is situated close to the remains of the much older Indus civilisation, which flourished at Mohenjo–Daro and Harappa in the third millennium BC.
- Karachi is Pakistan's largest city and major international gateway by air and sea.
- Islamabad, which was deliberately planned as the capital of the new Muslim state, and the old city of Rawalpindi nearby, are mainly centres for business travel.
- In the north of Pakistan, Gilgit provides facilities for skiing, trekking, and mountain climbing, while adventure-seekers can follow the Karakoram Highway. This spectacular feat of engineering threads its way between some of the world's highest mountains and glaciers into China.

Bangladesh

From 1947 to 1971, Bangladesh, formerly east Bengal, was a detached part of Pakistan, but strong cultural differences led to a war of independence. The new nation had to face severe economic and environmental problems, namely:

- It is densely populated even by Asian standards, relying on an economy dominated by agriculture and with few industries other than textiles.
- Most of the country is low-lying and is effectively a 'waterland' after the monsoon rains. Unusually, devastating floods occur when tropical cyclones from the Indian Ocean coincide with heavy monsoon rains in the eastern Himalayas.
- The country's many rivers are an obstacle to an effective road and rail network, while ferry links are below Western standards.

The capital, Dhaka, is an important business centre and is the hub of Biman Bangladesh Airways (www.biman-airlines.com), the national airline. The Bangladesh Parjatan Corporation (BPC) (http://www.parjatan.gov.bd/) is responsible for promoting and developing the tourism industry under the overall control of the Ministry of Civil Aviation and Tourism. Nevertheless, tourist arrivals fall short of the target of 1 million a year, with only 0.3 million arrivals recorded in 2018.

The main areas of interest for tourists are:

- Dhaka, a city of mosques and bazaars, where decorated rickshaws are a 'green' feature of the transport system.
- The vast wetland environment of the Sundarbans, formed by the deltas of the Ganges and Brahmaputra, which provides a refuge for wildlife, including the elusive Bengal tiger.
- Cox's Bazaar, which boasts one of the most extensive beaches in Asia, where surfing has recently been introduced.
- The hill country of Sylhet in the north-east has among its attractions forests, tea plantations, and tribal minorities.

Discussion point
Bangladesh has a population of almost 170 million, most of whom are living below the poverty line, and it is one of the countries most vulnerable to the impact of climate change. Discuss how these problems can be alleviated, and whether tourism can have any role to play.

Afghanistan

Afghanistan is located where the Indian sub-continent borders on Central Asia and the Middle East, and historically, it has been both the meeting place of civilisations and a refuge for different ethnic groups. In the 1970s, Afghanistan was a transit area, and Kabul was a welcome staging point for Western tourists on the overland route to India. Since then, the country's economy and infrastructure have been devastated as a result of the Soviet invasion in 1979 and civil war arising out of long-standing tribal feuds. The fundamentalist Taliban regime from 1996 to 2001 actively discouraged tourism and even destroyed much of the country's pre-Islamic heritage, such as the Buddhist monuments at Bamian. The conditions for essential travel, let alone tourism, namely security and adequately maintained highways linking the major cities, have yet to be realised, as much of the country remains outside the control of the government in Kabul.

Although most of Afghanistan consists of arid, rugged mountains, these are punctuated by fertile valleys and historic cities such as Kandahar and Herat – celebrated in *The Kite Runner*. In the remote Wakhan corridor bordering Tadjikistan in the north-east, which was largely untouched by the conflict, a small-scale trekking industry has developed, with rest houses run by local communities.

Nepal

Although the Gurkhas had long played an important role in the British Army, their homeland, the Hindu Kingdom of Nepal was closed to the outside world until the 1950s. After its discovery by 'hippies' and overland travellers in the 1960s, there was a rapid growth of tourism. However, events such as 9/11, the massacre of Nepal's royal family, and an on-going Maoist rebellion in the west of the country have had a severe impact, such that arrivals fell from 460,000 in 2000 to only 200,000 in 2002. Numbers have since recovered to over a million arrivals in 2019.

Within an area only half that of Great Britain, Nepal can offer a great variety of climates and scenery. There are three main physical divisions running east to west, namely:

- The Himalayas, which contain eight of the world's highest mountain peaks, including Everest and Annapurna, attracting trekkers, mountain climbers, and adventure-seekers from many different countries. The popularity of Everest is creating environmental issues as the mountain is now reaching over-capacity in terms of numbers of climbers.
- The foothills, including the valleys of Kathmandu and Pokhara, contain the majority of the population. Cultural attractions abound in the form of Buddhist temples, as at Bhadgaon and Patan.
- The sub-tropical lowlands, known as the Terai, which still contain areas of jungle, including the Chitwan National Park and its famous 'Tiger Tops' game lodge (https://tigertops.com/). Buddhists from all over the world are attracted to Lumbini, the birthplace of Buddha.

The Ministry of Tourism and Civil Aviation, along with the Department of National Parks and Wildlife Conservation (https://www.dnpwc.gov.np/), is responsible for tourism organisation, and the Nepal Tourism Board is a public/private sector partnership body. In practice, Nepal relies very much on foreign aid for tourism development and on Indian tour operators to bring in the visitors. In the 1990s, air transport policy underwent a degree of liberalisation, allowing in other carriers to supplement Nepal Airlines (https://www.nepalairlines.com.np).

Poor access, pollution, inadequate infrastructure, and frequent shortages of power and water supplies are major constraints on the growth of the tourism sector. In addition, criticism from environmentalists about the pollution found on the mountains, and the lack of robust environmental policies (for example, on timber cutting to maintain tourist lodges) may also constrain tourism growth.

Adventure tourism is the mainstay of tourism in Nepal, with activities including mountain climbing, river-running, and mountain biking. Trekking, where tourists on foot are escorted and supplied by local porters and guides, is the most popular activity in the Himalayan zone of Nepal, accounting for over a quarter of all visitors. Nepal offers a great variety of trekking opportunities, including some of the world's most spectacular scenery; the trails are well-maintained, and trekkers are rarely far from a village. Although remote areas such as Mustang are being opened up to meet the demand, trekking also shows a high degree of concentration in particular areas of central and eastern Nepal, including:

- The Annapurna region west of Pokhara.
- The Everest route, from Lukha to the base camp at the foot of Mount Everest, (known as Chomolungma in the Sherpa language).

Bhutan

This Buddhist kingdom is much smaller than Nepal in area and population as well as being more remote. Culturally, it is similar to Tibet as it was prior to the Chinese takeover, with prayer flags much in evidence and numerous fortified monasteries known as *dzongs* dominating the countryside. The government has promoted a 'Gross National Happiness Index' rather than GNP as a measure of the country's well-being – a concept now being looked at by a number of Western countries. It is determined to preserve traditional lifestyles from the impact of tourism, which is therefore strictly controlled, and certain activities such as mountain climbing are prohibited, to protect the country's forest and wildlife resources. Until 2001, access was restricted to a few accredited tour operators offering special interest holidays to small groups of visitors, in contrast to trekking on the Nepalese model. The government now allows some development of up-market resort hotels, where access is controlled by price. With the king introducing democracy in 2008, pressures to improve the GNP through economic development, rather than preserving 'gross national happiness' are likely to increase.

Summary

- South Asia contains some of the world's most densely populated countries, at various stages of economic development but nevertheless poor by Western standards.
- Most countries in the region are developing an inbound tourism industry to earn much-needed foreign exchange and provide jobs for rapidly growing populations.

- The generally low level of incomes means that domestic tourism is less significant while volumes of outbound tourism are small; however, both are set to increase due to the growth of a middle class, especially in India.
- Despite a wealth of resources, South Asia accounts for only a small percentage of world tourism.
- The attractions of the region are based on the exotic cultures and landscapes, and a lifestyle in which religion plays a major role. Of particular note are the classic tour circuits in India, the beaches and gentle way of life of the Indian Ocean islands, and the spectacular scenery of the Himalayas.

Review questions

1. Investigate the strengths and weaknesses of India as a destination for business and leisure tourism.
2. Identify the natural disasters and political crises that have made an impact on tourism in South Asia, and describe how different countries in the region have dealt with these problems.
3. Discuss whether deficiencies in transport and infrastructure generally are holding back the development of tourism in the Indian sub-continent.
4. Explain the appeal of religion, cultural heritage, and lifestyle in attracting Western tourists to a number of South Asian destinations.
5. Discuss the role of the film industry, music and dance, television documentaries, and literature in publicising particular South Asian countries. Compare the images portrayed with those presented by the official national tourism organisations.

Further reading

https://www.unwto.org/tourism-data/unwto-tourism-dashboard

21

The tourism geography of East Asia

Learning objectives

After reading this chapter, you should be able to:

- Describe the major physical features and climates (noting the importance of the Monsoon) of the region and understand their importance for tourism.
- Understand tourism demand in the region, the impact of the COVID-19 pandemic and the social and economic contrasts between countries.
- Be aware of the volume and characteristics of inbound tourism to the countries of East Asia.

DOI: 10.4324/9781003406853-26

- Outline the major features of tourism in the region and identify key trends in transport and organisation.
- Demonstrate a knowledge of the cultural and natural resources, tourist attractions and business centres of the countries of East Asia.

Introduction

East Asia consists of two distinct regions – Southeast Asia – lying almost entirely within the tropics – and the countries to the north, which Europeans refer to as the 'Far East' – although this would seem geographically inappropriate to an Australian or a Californian. Most East Asian countries have experienced rapid growth since the 1970s and have adopted Western technology without sacrificing their cultural identity, which is based on older civilisations and religions than the West. Economic growth has fuelled the demand for business travel and also encouraged a significant volume of outbound leisure tourism. Now, China is the dominant force in outbound tourism to the rest of the world. Demand for tourism in the region has been affected by a number of events, which we can categorise as:

1. Man-made events, which include the financial crisis of 1997/1998; terrorism across the region, including the Bali bombings in 2002; and both the SARS (severe acute respiratory syndrome) and the 2019–2021 COVID-19 pandemic which originated in China and devastated tourism across the region.
2. A series of natural disasters, including earthquakes in China, Japan and Indonesia, the 2004 tsunami, and severe weather events including typhoons and cyclones.

Domestic tourism has become increasingly significant as living standards have risen, expressed in car ownership and the purchase of leisure equipment. The more traditional travel patterns to religious shrines and mountain resorts are changing as the growing middle class emulates Western fashions. As a result, beach resorts and theme parks combining American and Asian motifs are growing in popularity. Nevertheless, the family unit remains much stronger than in Western societies, and individual freedom is less highly regarded due to the influence of Confucian and Buddhist teachings. Regarding incoming tourism to the region, cultural attitudes may mean that those employed in the service sector try to comply with unrealistic demands by Western tourists rather than 'lose face', leaving considerable scope for misunderstanding.

East Asia offers various landscapes and attractions, although business and cultural tourism are more important than beach tourism in most countries. In 2019, international tourist arrivals approached 325 million for East Asia. This is reflected in the impressive growth of air traffic in the region with the emergence of budget carriers and new airlines, combined with growth in the supply of hotel accommodations offering excellent service standards. Demographic trends – the region already contains well over a third of the world's population – the global economy and the rise of China as an economic superpower are responsible for a rate of passenger growth, which is among the world's highest. Aircraft movements suffered temporary setbacks after 9/11 and the COVID-19 pandemic on the routes linking Europe and North America to the main East Asia hubs – Singapore, Tokyo, Osaka, Hong Kong, Seoul, Taipei, and Bangkok. Many Asian airports are reaching the limits of their capacity, and there is a flurry of airport expansion schemes and new airport plans. Only a few – notably Hong Kong's Chep Lap Kok, Singapore's Changi, Bangkok's Suvarnabhumi and Kuala Lumpur's Sepang – are equipped to handle the new breed of double-decker aircraft, seating up to 500 passengers. The airspace over the South China Sea is already one of the most congested in the world. In most countries – except for Japan, China, and Vietnam – road transport plays a more important role in domestic tourism than the railway systems. However, the Eastern Orient Express (www.belmond. com/trains/asia/eastern-and-oriental-express/), linking Bangkok, Kuala Lumpur, and Singapore, has shown there is a market among Western tourists for luxury train services.

South-East Asia

The part of Asia extending from the Andaman Sea to the Philippines was culturally influenced many centuries ago by India to the west and China to the north. Ethnic Chinese communities play a significant role in the economic life of most countries in the region and, indeed, throughout the Pacific. In the nineteenth century, the economic and political influence of Western Europe and the United States became increasingly important. During the first half of the twentieth century, the whole of Southeast Asia – except Thailand – was under the colonial rule of the following countries:

- Britain ruled Burma (now officially renamed Myanmar), Malaya, Sarawak, and North Borneo (now united as Malaysia), Singapore, Brunei, and Hong Kong.
- France ruled Indo-China; this consisted of Cochin-China, Annam and Tonkin (now united as Vietnam), Laos and Cambodia.
- The Netherlands ruled the Dutch East Indies and Western New Guinea (now united as Indonesia).
- Portugal ruled East Timor and Macau.
- The United States administered the Philippines, which it had acquired from Spain after the war of 1898.

The Western powers were soon challenged by Japan, which, although defeated militarily in the Second World War, subsequently became the major economic influence in the region. After the Second World War, most Southeast Asian countries suffered a good deal of political upheaval that was part of the wider struggle between the West and the Communist powers. This adversely affected the growth of tourism, which was also restricted or given a low priority by those countries with a socialist regime.

Ten countries in the region have joined together to form ASEAN (Association of Southeast Asian Nations), which promotes economic integration across the region. This is an important objective, given that ASEAN has a combined population of 667 million, representing around 10 per cent of global GDP. Although member countries compete for visitors, they each see the advantages of joint promotion at the main tourist-generating markets. On the other hand, ASEAN has been less effective at coping with environmental issues, notably the severe pollution in the region.

There are wide disparities in wealth between Southeast Asian countries, with some reaching the emerging market stage of development. The per capita incomes of Singapore and Brunei approach those of Western Europe, while Myanmar, Laos, and Cambodia rank among the world's least developed nations. There are also great contrasts in economic and social development within many countries, particularly between the major cities on the one hand and the impoverished rural communities on the other. Southeast Asian countries also contain tribal societies, often regarded as primitive by the mainstream culture. These include:

* The hill tribes on the Thailand-Myanmar border.
* The Montagnards (mountain tribes) of Vietnam.
* The forest-dwellers of Malaysia.
* The indigenous peoples of Western Papua (formerly known as Irian Jaya) in Indonesia.

Traditional cultures such as these fascinate Western tourists, but they are highly vulnerable to the negative impacts of tourism, as well as the exploitation of their environment by commercial logging and plantation agriculture.

Southeast Asia experiences warm to hot weather throughout the year, with frequent but brief torrential downpours. The northern parts of the region have a clearly defined cool, dry season, while the timing and duration of the rainy season in the coastal areas of West Malaysia, southern Thailand and Indonesia depend on their exposure to the monsoon winds; this has important consequences for beach tourism. During the colonial era, mountain resorts, similar to the hill stations of British India, were established to provide relief from the heat and humidity for the expatriate community. These are now important for domestic tourism, although poor road access often hampered their development. Examples include:

* Maimyo in Myanmar (Burma)
* Cameron Highlands in West Malaysia
* Dalat and Sapa in Vietnam
* Bogor in Indonesia
* Baguio in the Philippines

More important in vying for the international tourist market are the beach resort developments on the palm-fringed coasts of the region. These are based on established seaports (as at Penang) or have been planned on a comprehensive scale (as in the Langkawi Islands), using two examples from West Malaysia. Often, such development has aroused criticism not on visual grounds (usually low-rise and well-designed) but on account of their impact on local communities. This is particularly the case where golf courses have been included in the resort as they excessively demand land and water supplies. Nonetheless, they play an important role in generating much-needed foreign exchange, the primary sources of demand being Japan, Australia, Western Europe, and the United States. Tourism within the region is being encouraged by new low-cost airlines such as AirAsia (www.airasia.com), CebuPacific (www.cebupacificair.com/), and Scoot (https://www.flyscoot.com).

Singapore

Despite being a group of small islands lacking natural resources, Singapore is one of the most prosperous and stable countries in Asia. It owes its importance to its strategic location on the shipping routes linking the Indian and Pacific oceans, which have made the city one of the world's largest seaports and the gateway to Southeast Asia. The people are culturally diverse, with a Chinese majority, but united by the English language and a firm belief in the value of education, advanced technology and enterprise. Since independence, the government of the small island republic has encouraged foreign investment in a free market economy. Still, it has also imposed a degree of social discipline that many Westerners would find draconian. As a result, Singapore is less plagued by squalor, car-dominated traffic, and crime than most other urban societies worldwide and can offer Western tourists a sanitised glimpse of 'Instant Asia'. The country's high-profile national carrier – Singapore Airlines (www.singaporeair.om) – is the largest in the region in terms of passenger kilometres, and it works closely with the Singapore Tourism Board (https://www.visitsingapore.com.en/). Singapore's Stock Exchange (www2.sgx.com/) and World Trade Centre (www.wtca.org/world-trade-center-singapore) rank among the world's most important financial institutions – not surprisingly, it has become a major conference venue and business tourism destination.

The demand for tourism

Domestic and outbound tourism

Singapore is compact, densely populated and low-lying, and the lack of scenic variety and urban pressures generate a large demand for leisure tourism. Sentosa Island (the name means peace and tranquillity in contrast to the bustle of downtown) was developed in the 1970s as a recreational area for Singaporeans and visitors. Almost 20 million visitors a year are attracted to its beaches and Asian-style theme parks, although demand was impacted by the COVID-19 pandemic, with arrivals falling to 9 million in 2021. Most outbound tourism is to neighbouring Malaysia – easily reached by the causeway to Johor or to the beach resorts of Bintam and Batan in Indonesia's Riau archipelago, which are only a short distance away by hydrofoil. There is a significant volume of long-haul travel, especially to the United States.

Inbound tourism

Singapore attracts a large volume of inbound tourists – over 19 million arrivals in 2019 – but with a short stay. The majority are from other East Asian countries, with China in second place after Indonesia. Many Chinese tourists are attracted to the casinos of Singapore, as gambling is not permitted in China. Duty-free shopping accounts for a large part of the tourist spend, particularly by Western visitors, who see the city primarily as a stopo-ver rather than as a sole destination. To attract longer-stay visitors, the government has developed a tourism strategy by promoting niche markets such as education and health tourism, as well as considerable investment in four large integrated resorts. Singapore Tourism is also emphasising the city's cultural diversity and safeguarding what remains of the old-style colonial heritage, once threatened with obliteration due to the drive to modernisation. For example, several former 'shophouses' have been converted into styl-ish boutique hotels. The refurbished Raffles Hotel (www.raffles.com/singapore/), with its historical associations, markets and outdoor food stalls, contrasts markedly with the ultra-modern shopping malls and high-rise office buildings. Singapore's attractions are primarily man-made and include:

- A number of zoos and wildlife parks, including Bird Paradise and the re-wilding of the former Rail Corridor.
- The waterfront area of Clarke Quay, with its leisure, theatre, and shopping developments.
- The Suntec conference and exhibition centre (www.suntecsingaore.com/).
- The 'Gardens by the Bay' project (www.gardensbythebay.com.sg), which embodies the vision of 'Singapore – the City in a Garden'.
- The annual F1 Grand Prix (www.singapore-f1-grandprix.com/).
- The Esplanade Centre for the Performing Arts (www.esplanade.com/) epitomises Singapore's drive to become a cultural destination.

Malaysia

Like Singapore, Malaysia is a multicultural nation, but here, the Muslim Malays are the dominant ethnic group politically. The country is a federation of 13 states, but one party has dominated politics since independence, and the nine hereditary sultans have little effective power. Malaysia also consists of two culturally distinct areas, separated by the South China Sea, namely:

- Peninsular or West Malaysia, known under British rule as Malaya, which is the south-ernmost peninsula of mainland Asia.
- East Malaysia, consisting of the states of Sabah and Sarawak, which form part of the island of Borneo.

Unlike Singapore, Malaysia is rich in natural resources such as rubber, tin, petroleum, and tropical hardwoods. These provided the basis for rapid industrialisation after 1980, epitomised by the manufacture of Proton vehicles in Selangor and a number of large-scale development projects. The 'Petronas Towers' (www.petronastwintowers.com.my/) domi-nating the skyline of Kuala Lumpur and the ultra-modern shopping malls in the capital were the products of this economic prosperity.

The demand for tourism

Domestic and outbound tourism

In 1999, the government introduced a five-day working week, and this, together with rising incomes, has generated an impressive demand for domestic tourism, amounting to over 300 million trips in 2018. The majority stay with friends or relatives, and 90 per cent use cars for transport. Religious festivals, shopping, and business are the main reasons for travelling. The main destinations are the Kuala Lumpur metropolitan area and the state of Kedah, which includes the Langkawi Islands. Although the government vigorously pro-motes domestic tourism, Malaysians increasingly prefer to travel abroad. In 2019, there were over 14.5 million departures, mainly to other Southeast Asian countries, China and South Korea, but Australia is growing in importance as a destination for leisure tourism.

Inbound tourism

The choice of Kuala Lumpur as the venue for the 1998 Commonwealth Games and the opening of a new international airport at Sepang underline the importance of tourism as an earner of foreign exchange. The government has encouraged the sector through the Ministry of Culture, Arts and Tourism (MOCAT). The great majority of the 26 million in-ternational arrivals in 2019 came from other Asian countries, with Singapore accounting for more than half.

The supply side of tourism

The infrastructure for tourism is efficient, including a good highway network in Peninsular Malaysia and air services operated by Malaysia Airlines (www.malaysiaairlines.com/) and a low-cost airline 'AirAsia' which also flies internationally. Malaysia Airlines was rebranded in 2015 after two major air disasters. There has been considerable investment in resort ho-tels and golf courses, particularly by the Japanese. However, in response to tourism growth, accommodation supply has been overestimated, and occupancy rates are low. Conference facilities include the Putra World Trade Centre (https://worldtradecentrekl.com.my/) and the Malaysian International Exhibition Centre (https://mitec.com.my/) in Kuala Lumpur. In 2007, the Malaysian government inaugurated a new administrative capital at Putra-jaya, 20 kilometres to the south, providing more meeting facilities in a spacious setting. A planned high-speed rail link between Kuala Lumpur and Singapore was cancelled in 2021.

Tourism resources

Malaysia's resource base for tourism includes:

- The beaches of West Malaysia.
- A variety of cultural attractions.
- The wildlife resources of the mountains and rainforests of Peninsular Malaysia and Borneo.

Most of the tourism development has taken place in **West Malaysia**. Seasonality is not a major problem, thanks to the pattern of the monsoons, which bring heavy rain to the west coast of Peninsular Malaysia between June and September and to the east coast from November to February. Much of the west coast is low-lying, with extensive mangrove swamps along the estuaries. The best beaches are found on the offshore islands that include:

- Penang has retained its commercial importance and is a major destination for West European holidaymakers on inclusive air tours. Most of the resort development has occurred around Batu Feringhi on the island's north coast.
- The Langkawi Islands, which provide an ideal environment for scuba diving but offer much less in the way of nightlife, shopping, and cultural attractions than Penang.
- Pangkor and its small neighbour, Pangkor Laut, have developed a niche spa tourism market.

Although boasting finer beaches and attractive scenery, the east coast is less developed, and the traditional Malay lifestyle is much more evident in the villages. Tioman Island and Cherating are the main resort areas.

West Malaysia's attractions also include:

- The Taman Negara National Park (https://tamannegra.asia/) covers much of the forest-covered highlands of the interior. With a huge biodiversity of species, it attracts growing numbers of ecotourists.
- The Batu Caves, a major religious shrine for Hindus.
- The old Portuguese trading centre of Melaka (Malacca), with its colonial heritage providing a contrast to the modern architecture of Kuala Lumpur.
- The mountain resort of Genting Highlands, with its 'City of Entertainment', casino, golf course and funicular railway.
- Agro-tourism on some of the rubber plantations.

East Malaysia is much less developed, with a very limited road network, but the government is improving air links to Peninsular Malaysia as a driver for growth. The region caters mainly for adventure tourism, based on Kuching (Sarawak) and Kota Kinabalu (Sabah). From Kuching, tourists travel upriver to visit the villages of the Dyak tribes and perhaps stay in one of the traditional longhouses. Kuching is also home to the Semenggoh Nature Reserve, which shelters orangutans and many bird species. The state of Sabah boasts some of the world's largest limestone caves and Kinabalu, the highest mountain in Southeast Asia, which attracts climbing and trekking expeditions.

Brunei

The sultanate of Brunei Darussalam derives most of its considerable wealth from petroleum, and although there is potential for ecotourism, tourism development is not a priority. Royal Brunei Airlines (https://www.flyroyalbrunei.com/) and the capital, Bandar Sara Begawan, cater mainly for business travellers.

Indonesia

In contrast to Singapore and Brunei, Indonesia is one of the world's largest nations, extending 4,000 kilometres from west to east, spanning three time zones, and with a population approaching 274 million, of which 90 per cent are Muslims. There are also substantial Buddhist, Hindu, Christian and animist communities. This cultural diversity is both a strength from the viewpoint of tourism and a challenge to the process of nation building. The country is also physically very diverse, consisting of a multitude of islands, of which 6,000 are inhabited, some 400 volcanoes, and landscapes that include the rice paddies of Java, the rainforests of Kalimantan (Borneo) and the snow-capped mountains of western New Guinea. The possibilities for ecotourism are indicated by the 'Wallace Line', east of Bali, which separates islands with Asian flora and fauna from species typical of Australasia.

Tourism demand

Although Indonesia has shown significant economic growth in the new millennium, it has faced a number of socio-economic problems that affect not just the growth of international tourism but also the domestic demand for tourism:

- The Asian financial crisis of 1997–1998 affected Indonesia more severely than others in the region.
- The fall of the authoritarian Suharto regime destabilised the country, bringing to the surface ethnic and religious tensions, with attacks on the ethnic Chinese, who dominate the commercial sector, and on the Christian community in Maluku (the Moluccas).
- The political and economic dominance of Java, which contains almost two-thirds of the population and most of the country's industrial development, accounts for 55 per cent of Indonesia's GDP. The Suharto regime attempted to relieve the acute pressures of over-population and rural poverty in Java through a policy of 'transmigration', settling farmers in the more sparsely populated islands among people of very different cultural backgrounds, such as the Dyaks of Kalimantan and the Papuans of western New Guinea.
- A number of terrorist incidents by Jihadists in Java, including the bombing of hotels and embassies in Jakarta and 'Black October' – the Bali bombings.
- The COVID-19 pandemic in 2020–2022.

In addition to these problems, Indonesia has been affected by earthquakes and the 2004 tsunami, which impacted tourist arrivals. Nevertheless, tourism accounted for 6 per cent of GDP and 10.3 per cent of employment in 2019.

Domestic and outbound tourism

There is a substantial demand for domestic tourism, particularly from the growing middle class in the cities of Java. This has been encouraged by rising incomes, the growth in the number of domestic flights, and, not least, promotional campaigns. Bali, Lombok, and the historic city of Yogyakarta in Java are the main destinations. There were 11.7 million departures for foreign destinations in 2019.

Inbound tourism

A decade of stability and economic growth has encouraged international tourism to Indonesia, resulting in 16 million arrivals in 2019. Most of these are from other Southeast Asian countries, but China, Japan, and Australia are also important markets.

The supply side of tourism

Tourism development is the responsibility of the Ministry of Tourism and Creative Economy (www.kemenpar.go.id/). Despite a government policy of spreading tourism throughout the islands, most of the growth in hotel capacity has taken place in Bintam-Batan and Bali (for leisure tourism) and Java (mainly for business tourism, particularly in the major cities of Jakarta, Surabaya, and Yogyakarta). International hotel chains dominate the accommodation sector, particularly in the mid-range and luxury categories. Although the government has moved towards a more liberal civil aviation policy, the national carrier Garuda (www.garuda-indonesia.com/) and its subsidiaries dominate air transport.

Tourism resources

Relatively few of Indonesia's many islands have as yet developed significant tourism industries. Travelling from west to east includes Sumatra, Java, Bali, Lombok, Sulawesi, and some of the Lesser Sunda Islands.

Sumatra has an important oil industry, and tourism is less developed than we might expect from an island with such diverse resources. Tourism in the northern part of the island has been held back by the separatist uprising in Acheh province and the damage to infrastructure caused by the 2004 tsunami. Large areas of rainforest still remain, providing a refuge for the orang-utan and other threatened wildlife species. Lake Toba is a major natural attraction, set amid one of the world's largest craters and ringed by volcanic mountains. Sumatra also has many cultural attractions, including the Menankabau people's distinctive folklore.

Java remains Indonesia's economic and political heartland and receives most business and leisure tourist arrivals. It is dominated by a chain of high volcanic mountains, some of which – notably Mount Bromo in the east of the island – are still active. Over many centuries, land has been cultivated by an elaborate terracing system, and the island's fertility has supported a number of advanced civilisations. The most spectacular examples of this heritage are the temple at Borobodur (https://whc.unesco.org/en/list/592/), which is the world's largest Buddhist edifice, and the lesser-known Hindu temple at Prambanan (https://whc.unesco.org/en/list/642/) nearby. The palaces of former sultans at Solo and Yogyakarta also attract growing numbers of cultural tourists. The legacy of colonial rule is still evident in the historic port area of Jakarta, formerly known as Batavia when it was the hub of the Dutch trading empire in Asia. Jakarta suffers from acute traffic congestion and is vulnerable to flooding, which explains the decision of the government to relocate the capital to a new city – Nusantara – on the east coast of Kalimantan. Although sustainability is intrinsic to Nusantara's development, there are bound to be significant impacts on the biodiversity and indigenous cultures of Kalimantan.

Bali is the best known of the islands of Indonesia and the jewel in its tourism crown. Bali's appeal is based on the photogenic qualities of its landscapes and people, with resources that include:

- A tropical climate favouring beach tourism, with a dry season lasting from May to October. This coincides with the winter months in Australia to the south, which provides much of the tourism demand.
- A spectacular landscape featuring emerald-green rice terraces carved out of the hills, mountains clothed in lush vegetation, and crater lakes.
- Recreational resources include surfing beaches, offshore reefs for diving, mineral springs for spa tourism, and a range of activities that have been introduced due to demand from affluent foreign tourists and the international youth market.

Photo 21.1
Bali
Source: ©istockphoto.com/Terraxplorer

The great majority of foreign visitors to Bali, and a high proportion of domestic tourists, arrive by air. Indeed, the opening of the airport at Denpasar in 1968 catalysed the expansion of tourism on a large scale. Internal transport is by road, using a variety of vehicles such as *bemos* (mini-buses), trucks, cars, coaches, and taxis.

Bali offers a range of accommodations, from luxury five-star hotels to simple beach bungalows. Small hotels and guesthouses, known as *losmen* or 'homestays', provide inexpensive, informal accommodation, allowing visitors to sample the islanders' way of life. As they are usually run by local families, a much higher proportion of the visitor spend is retained within the local community than in the larger hotels owned by companies based in Java or outside Indonesia. The former fishing village and artists' colony of Sanur was the first resort to be developed with a mix of large hotels and bungalows, and now attracts tourists from Europe, Japan, and Australia. Kuta Beach first attracted Australian surfers in the 1970s and now offers a third of Bali's bed spaces, mostly in small hotels and guest houses. Luxury hotels are mainly concentrated in the planned resort of Nusa Dua, a good example of 'enclave tourism'.

CASE STUDY 21.1
THE IMPACT OF TOURISM ON THE CULTURE OF BALI

Can cultural tourism create what is, in effect, a tourist culture? The perception of Bali is one of a gentle, artistic people living in harmony with their environment, and the graceful *legong* dancer is its best-known tourist icon. Throughout their history, the Balinese have adopted cultural traits from other peoples – the Hindu dance dramas from India, for example – and made them part of their distinctive lifestyle. Art and religious rituals are part of everyday life in this 'island of the gods', with processions of women carrying fruit, rice cakes, and other colourful offerings to the temples that are a feature of every village. Balinese festivals integrate the visual arts, *gamelan* music, drama, and dance. The Balinese apparently do not mind the presence of outsiders at their religious ceremonies, and even the elaborate cremations have become a must-see tourist attraction.

Balinese painting and sculpture first became a commercial activity in the 1930s when the island was 'discovered' as an exotic destination for elite Western tourists. European expatriate painters encouraged local artists to experiment with new techniques and develop a greater range of styles. As a result, Ubud, with its long-established artist colony, is widely regarded as the island's cultural centre. A number of villages specialise in a particular handicraft, such as silverware, woodcarving, and stone carving.

Although the Balinese had little say in determining the overall development of their island, they have benefitted economically from tourism, which provides almost 60,000 jobs, a source of income for local farmers who can let rooms to backpackers, and a ready market for handicrafts, as well as a textile industry specialising in beachwear. The Balinese have been able to market their culture, which has been re-markably resilient to the negative impacts of mass tourism compared to other tropical island destinations.

However, the rapid growth of tourism has put a heavy strain on limited land and water resources, with negative impacts that include:

- Damage to coral reefs and coastal erosion.
- Problems of water supply, with priority given to luxury hotels and golf course projects rather than local communities.
- The 'packaging' of traditional culture, where the dance performances have been adapted for the short attention span of the average Western tourist.
- Prostitution and drug-taking.

The social impacts are most evident in Kuta Beach, where a host of traders compete to offer scantily-dressed tourists goods and services, including 'beach massage'. In some respects, Kuta is to Australians what some Mediterranean resorts are to young British holidaymakers – a tourist experience based on 'sun and fun', nightclubs, bars, and discos, rather than any respect for the local culture. Young Balinese have adopted the surfing lifestyle, and the surfboard has become another opportunity for artistic self-expression. In Nusi Dua, on the other hand, the cultural impact of tourism is mini-mised by physical separation. Here, the only Balinese allowed entry are hotel employ-ees or invited dance troupes.

Lombok has been the main beneficiary of government policy to spread tourism away from Bali. The two islands are roughly the same size and are superficially similar – indeed, Lombok is often regarded as a less developed version of Bali, but it has a drier climate and a Muslim culture. Development is focussed on the resort of Senggigi, while the offshore Gili Islands are popular with scuba divers. The authorities have set out to attract up-market tourists with luxury hotels and the associated infrastructure, including a new interna-tional airport and improvements to ferry services, port facilities and the road network.

The **Lesser Sunda Islands** to the east of Lombok remain largely undeveloped, but Flores is among those divers, surfers and sport fishing enthusiasts increasingly seek out. This island is close to Komodo, famous for its 'dragons' (which are, in fact, giant lizards). The climate is characterised by a long dry season influenced by monsoon winds from Aus-tralia, which lies not far to the south. Ecotourism has growth potential, as shown by the success of Nihiwatu on the island of Sumba (https://nihi.com/). This is a good example of responsible tourism, providing local communities with a guaranteed supply of clean water, health facilities, and education opportunities. Charter flights from Bali access the resort, and the location is sufficiently remote to give up-market guests a 'get away from it all' experience.

Sulawesi offers world-class diving, particularly in the north near Manado, where the Benaken National Park is an outstanding example of marine conservation in a region no-torious for overfishing and damage to coral reefs. Under the government's decentralising policies, the park authorities set their own entrance fees, with the proceeds benefitting the local communities. In the mountainous interior, the Toraja villages, with their unique architecture and ceremonies based on ancestor worship, provide the main attraction for tourists.

Timor Leste (East Timor)

East Timor gained independence from Indonesia after a long and bitter struggle in 2002, followed -as is often the case – by political in-fighting, which has not improved its tourism prospects. This small, mountainous country includes an enclave in Indonesian territory to the west and the island of Atauro to the north. The government sees tourism in the capital, Dili, as playing an important role in rebuilding the economy and reducing its dependence on offshore oil reserves, with technical assistance from Australia, China, Singapore, Brazil, and Portugal. Potential resources include:

- The annual Darwin-Dili yacht rally (https://www.sailtimorleste.org/), providing a sporting link and strengthening the special relationship between East Timor and Australia.
- The heritage of Portuguese colonial rule, including the revival of Carnival as an event attraction.
- Diving sites, particularly off Atauro.

Development of these resources is hampered by poor infrastructure. At the same time, the high cost of air travel from Darwin, Singapore, and Bali to Dili is a deterrent to the backpackers who often pioneer new destinations.

The Philippines

The Philippines is an island nation with a population of around 114 million, comprising many ethnic groups, with the English and Tagalog languages providing a unifying force. Volcanic mountains dominate the landscape, and the islands are prone to earthquakes and typhoons. In 2020, the eruption of the Taal volcano caused considerable disruption. The birth rate is among the highest in Asia, with economic development barely keeping pace, so there is a considerable volume of emigration. Culturally, it is quite different from the other countries of Southeast Asia. There are a few impressive monuments from pre-colonial times, and the islands have been greatly influenced by their experience of three centuries of Spanish rule, followed by half a century of administration by the United States. Although few Filipinos now use Spanish as their second language, the cultural legacy of devout Roman Catholicism is evident in the churches and religious festivals culminating in Holy Week. In contrast, the Americans introduced the English language and sports such as baseball; the result is a culture in which Western influences and attitudes are stronger than elsewhere in Asia. Metro Manila, with over 13 million inhabitants, is by far the largest centre of population and industry.

The demand for tourism

Domestic and outbound tourism

Some 40 per cent of Filipinos participate in domestic tourism, with a peak in demand over the Easter and Christmas-New Year holidays. Rising incomes and the competitive airfares provided by low-cost carriers have encouraged foreign travel, with Metro Manila generating the bulk of the demand. Hong Kong, with its large Filipino community, Singapore, Malaysia, South Korea, and Thailand accounted for the majority of the 4.5 million departures in 2018.

Inbound tourism

Tourism received a major boost under the Marcos regime in the 1970s, which hosted international events such as the Miss Universe beauty pageant, leaving Manila with a glut of luxury hotels. The main tourist markets are Japan, the United States, Taiwan, South Korea, and the millions of Overseas Filipinos working in many countries worldwide. However, natural disasters and terrorist incidents, including the kidnapping of tourists in Mindanao (where there is a large Muslim minority and separatist movement), have had a negative impact on arrivals and perceptions of the country, and compared to the rest of the region international arrivals are modest, at around 8 million a year. Damage to coral reefs is a cause for concern. Also problematic is the prevalence of sex tourism, particularly in Manila and Olongapo.

The supply side of tourism

Transport

In many areas, the transport infrastructure, including roads and domestic air services, falls short of Western efficiency standards, although ferry links between the islands have greatly improved. Philippine Airlines (www.philippineairlines.com/) provides an extensive network of services, supplemented by a number of low-cost carriers.

Organisation

The policy of the Philippine Department of Tourism (www.experiencephilippines.org) since the 1980s has been on planning clusters of resort hotels on a number of islands, which are linked to an international airport by boat and domestic air services. The Department's mission is to develop tourism for the economic benefit of the country, and the Tourism Promotion Board was established to encourage sectors such as the meetings, incentives and exhibitions (MICE) market and reduce the dependence on beach tourism.

Tourism resources

Business and cultural tourism is focussed on South Luzon, particularly in and around Manila. The capital's attractions include:

- The Malacanang Palace (https://malacanang.gov.ph/), former residence of the Marcos family.
- The Nayong Clark Park– an exhibition village showcasing the country's regional cultures.
- The historic district of Intramuros with its Spanish colonial heritage.
- The highly decorated *jeepneys* play a vital role in the city's transport system.

A number of beach resorts, Lake Taal and the volcano of that name, and the Pagsanjan waterfalls are located within easy reach of Manila. However, one of the country's major attractions and a World Heritage Site – the rice terraces at Banaue – can only be reached by a long road journey and are much less accessible. Beach tourism is focussed on the following destinations:

- The Visayas, a group of islands in the central Philippines served by the international airport at Cebu, which has direct flights to Hong Kong, Seoul, Taipei, Singapore and Tokyo. The island of Boracay is the best known, having evolved from 'discovery' by backpackers in the 1970s to become an up-market destination. However, concerns about 'overtourism' on the island led to its temporary closure in 2018. Many 'green' initiatives are now in place, and visitor numbers are restricted.
- Palawan, until recently one of the more remote islands, offers world-class diving facilities and a number of small up-market resorts that have escaped the pollution problems experienced by Boracay.

Much of Mindanao is still forest-covered and has an 'ecotourism village'. Beach tourism is being developed around the cities of Davao and Zamboanga.

The countries of the Mekong Basin

The Mekong, rising in the Himalayas and reaching the South China Sea near Saigon, is one of the great rivers of Asia and is a feature that can be used for joint promotion by the countries through which it flows, including southwest China. During the Cold War era, most of this region, except Thailand, was an area where tourism was not encouraged. These countries are now cooperating through the Mekong Delta Plan to improve international tourism by improving air links, opening more border crossings and relaxing visa regulations.

Thailand

Thailand (formerly known as Siam) is the only country in Southeast Asia not to have experienced Western colonial rule, whose monarch still exercises real power and is revered by the Thai people. On the other hand, Thailand has been the country most affected by Western-style tourism.

Tourism demand

Domestic and outbound tourism

Thailand is one of the 'tiger economies' of Asia, and economic development has seen the growth of a substantial middle class, who have the means not only to engage in domestic tourism but also to travel abroad for leisure purposes as well as for business and study. On the other hand, almost half the population are employed in agriculture and generally has insufficient income to engage in leisure tourism. Thailand has a mature tourism industry with a large domestic component, although domestic tourists spend less and stay at their destination for much shorter periods than foreign visitors. Most outbound trips are to other ASEAN countries, although Europe accounts for a significant number of departures.

Inbound tourism

The growth of international tourism has been phenomenal, from less than 500,000 arrivals in 1970 to over 40 million in 2019, with a corresponding increase in hotel capacity. Tourism has become the country's biggest foreign exchange earner and a major employer. Still, it has also exacerbated Thailand's socio-economic problems, notably the disparities in wealth between Bangkok and the rural areas of the north and east. These problems, in turn, have contributed to the growth of a flourishing sex tourism industry in Bangkok and the resort of Pattaya, with damaging consequences to the country's image as a destination. Although there is considerable cross-border traffic between Thailand and Malaysia, the majority of international tourists arrive by air on inclusive tours, and around 10 per cent are business travellers. Leisure tourists come from a wide range of generating countries, including Western Europe, North America, Japan, and Australia.

The supply side of tourism

Transport

Bangkok's new Suvarnabhumi airport is the main gateway, while the north and south of the country are visited from Chiangmai and Phuket, respectively. Thai International and its domestic arm, Thai Airways (https://www.thaiairways.com/), operate an extensive network of air routes, while express bus and overnight rail services also link Bangkok to the major regional centres of the country.

Organisation

The Tourism Authority of Thailand (TAT) (www.tourismthailand.org) is the national body for tourism and one of the oldest in the region, established in 1960. It has undergone re-organisation, and like other NTOs, it has responsibility for promotion, development, and training. TAT has strategies to develop human resources, 'electronic tourism', events and festivals, sustainable experiences, and niche markets such as medical tourism.

Tourism resources

Thailand is a multi-destination country, with different areas offering sightseeing tours (there has been substantial growth in visits to historical sites), beach tourism, and adventure holidays:

- Bangkok is the primary destination. Despite acute traffic congestion – partly relieved by a 'Skytrain' monorail system – this sprawling city has many attractions, and its Western-style hotels enjoy high occupancy rates throughout the year. Highways have replaced many of the city's canals, but the Chao Praya River remains a major artery with its long-tail boats and floating markets. As you might expect from a country devoted to Buddhist rituals and traditions, Bangkok is noted for its *wats* – temple-monasteries of a highly distinctive appearance, along with a multitude of lesser shrines. Shopping for Thai silk and other handicrafts is important to the city's appeal to Western tourists. Specific tourist attractions in Bangkok and the surrounding area include:

  - The spectacular Grand Palace (https://www.royalgrandpalace.th/), which contains the Temple of the Emerald Buddha, the most important place of pilgrimage for Thais.
  - The Rose Garden Country Resort, 33 kilometres west of the capital, features cultural shows for visitors, including traditional dances, ceremonies, and the distinctive Thai style of boxing.
  - The nearby beach resort of Pattaya, which began as a 'rest and recreation' centre for American servicemen during the Vietnam War in the 1960s. It is noisy and over-commercialised, despite attempts by the government to clean up the environment, kerb the jet skiers, and tone down the exuberant nightlife offered by the bars, discotheques, and massage parlours.
  - Hua Hin, in contrast, is a long-established, up-market resort catering mainly for domestic tourists.

Chiangmai has been developed as a counter-attraction to Bangkok in the northern part of the country, with the advantage of a cooler, less humid climate. Although the city is a major centre of Thai culture, most backpackers and Western tourists regard it as a convenient base for trekking tours among the hill tribes of the mountainous region bordering Myanmar and Laos, which forms part of the notorious 'Golden Triangle' of opium production. Concerted efforts by the government to crack down on the trade in narcotics carry the risk of fuelling border tensions and alienating ethnic minorities. It is also alleged that tourism does not benefit these communities but merely exploits them as a curiosity.

Peninsular Thailand and the offshore islands in the Andaman Sea, together with those in the Gulf of Thailand to the east, cater in varying degrees for beach tourism in response to the quest, first by backpackers and later by tour operators, for 'unspoiled' holiday destinations. This region was affected by the 2004 tsunami, but the tourism sector recovered rapidly from this setback with government support, which was not always the case with the local communities.

- Phuket was the first island to be developed, to the extent that mass tourism has now displaced its traditional mining and fishing industries. Phang Nga Bay is famous for its spectacular karst limestone rock formations.
- Koh Samui is less developed and more up-market.

Eastern Thailand is an economically poor region but offers wildlife for ecotourists and the remains of the ancient Khmer civilisation for cultural tourists. The TAT hopes that visitors will be attracted to a number of parks focussing on this heritage.

> **Discussion point**
> The Phi-Phi Islands in the Andaman Sea are said to be a classic example of a 'tropical island paradise'. As a designated marine reserve, they have been given a measure of protection by the government of Thailand, but many environmentalists fear that development is inevitable. Ironically, the movie *The Beach* has been blamed because of the worldwide interest in the islands which followed the filming. In class, debate whether this is justified or other factors are just as important.

Indo-China

Until the 1990s, the countries of Indo-China remained on the margins of international tourism as a consequence of half a century of conflict that culminated in the Vietnam War. The socialist governments of the region gave tourism a low priority, restricting the numbers of foreign visitors (by closing the border between Thailand and Laos, for example) and discouraging Western investment. These countries are now in the 'development' stage of the tourist area life cycle, with Vietnam clearly in the lead.

Vietnam

The Vietnam War was arguably the longest and the most devastating of the conflicts that took place in the second half of the twentieth century, and it was not until 1994 that the United States lifted the embargo it had imposed after the Communist victory. Nevertheless, from 1986 onwards, the Vietnamese government opened the country to foreign investment and allowed a significant amount of private enterprise to develop. As a result, Vietnam is one of the fastest-growing economies in Asia. In the cities, motor vehicles have largely replaced bicycles, *cyclos* (pedicabs), and rickshaws, but the graceful white *ao dai* costume traditionally worn by Vietnamese women remains part of the street scene.

The demand for tourism
Domestic and outbound tourism
Tourism is a fast-growing sector of the economy. Free market reforms have created a new entrepreneurial middle class with the discretionary income to visit the tourist sites in their own country, resulting in a considerable volume of domestic tourism. Visitor attractions include several theme parks with an emphasis on family entertainment. However, tour guides and others working in the tourism sector, accustomed to dealing with affluent Western visitors with cultural motivations, find it difficult to adjust to the demands of domestic tourists with very different expectations. Moreover, domestic tourism faces

competition from the number of high-spending Vietnamese travelling abroad – there were 8.6 million departures in 2019, mainly to China and other Southeast Asian countries.

Inbound tourism

The Western media have ensured that interest in the Vietnam War continued long after it ended in 1975. The locations of that bitter conflict, including the Ho Chi Minh Trail, China Beach near Da Nang, and the Cu-Chi tunnels near Saigon that sheltered the Vietcong guerrillas from American firepower, are now the basis of a lucrative niche tourism market. Vietnam is visited by some 750,000 Americans each year, including the families of war veterans and the children of refugees. However, most of the 18 million arrivals in 2019 were from other Asian countries, with China, Japan, and Taiwan as the most important markets.

The supply side of tourism

Transport

Vietnam Airlines is the national carrier (www.vietnamairlines.com), providing a network of international and domestic services, along with the innovative low-cost airline Vietjet Air. Surface transport in this elongated country tends to be slow, with the journey by train from Hanoi to Saigon (2500 kilometres) taking around 35 hours.

Organisation

The Vietnam National Administration of Tourism (VNAT) (www.vietnamtourism.gov.vn) is responsible for tourism policy, reporting to the Ministry of Culture, Sport and Tourism. VNAT works with state management bodies in four key areas:

*   Co-operation with aviation businesses, shopping centres, entertainment areas, accommodation establishments and tour operators to stimulate the development of tourism.
*   Focussing on developing new products and implementing joint promotion programmes to attract international visitors.
*   Working with the airlines to open new routes to key markets.
*   Improving the destination's reputation and service quality and ensuring environmental protection.

Accommodation capacity has increased substantially, with the major hotel chains taking advantage of tourism growth in Vietnam. Nevertheless, tourism development is hampered by an inadequate road system, unreliable power supplies, environmental damage, the limited participation of local communities, and a bureaucracy resistant to change.

Tourism resources

Vietnam can offer an impressive range of tourism resources. These include a 3,400-kilometre-long coastline, forested mountains, waterfalls, the Mekong and Red River deltas, and a rich cultural heritage. The western highlands and the mountains of northern

Tonkin have potential for ecotourism, and national parks have been designated in these areas. Trekking has already become an important source of income for many mountain tribal communities. Coastal resources include Ha Long Bay, a superb example of tropical karst topography, but designation as a World Heritage Site does not guarantee protection from excessive development. This unique natural attraction, made up of a great number of picturesque islands, attracts 6 million visitors a year and is exposed to pollution from tourist boats as well as industrial effluent. Cultural tourism is mainly focussed on the following cities:

- Hanoi was the power base of the Communist North during the Vietnam War, and with re-unification, it became the national capital, offering a number of showpiece attractions celebrating the country's heritage.
- Da Nang is located in the centre of the country and has received government invest-ment to develop it as a major tourism hub, with a new airport designed to handle 28 million passengers annually and facilities that include a marina and aqua parks.
- Hue was the scene of bitter conflict during the Vietnam War. Despite these, many Buddhist pagodas remain as reminders of the city's historic importance as the capital of the former kingdom of Annam.
- Saigon (now officially renamed Ho Chi Minh City) was the capital of South Vietnam and, following re-unification, remains the nation's main commercial centre with a population of over 9 million. Here, business enterprise is flourishing to a much greater extent than in Hanoi, and the vibrant entertainment scene has revived due to international tourism. The French colonial influence is still evident in the archi-tecture and restaurants. A number of beach resorts have developed near Saigon, and these are attracting Western investment.

Cambodia

The kingdom of Cambodia is known primarily for the majestic tiered temples of Angkor, flanked by moats and reflecting pools, built as Hindu and Buddhist places of worship by the Khmer civilisation between the ninth and thirteenth centuries. The largest temple, Angkor Wat (https://whc.unesco.org/en/list/668/), has become a tourist icon. The temple cities and the complex irrigation systems that supported them were subsequently aban-doned and taken over by the jungle until French archaeologists revealed them during the colonial period. By the late 1960s, Angkor was attracting 45,000 visitors a year, and the nearby town of Siem Reap had a flourishing hotel and restaurant trade. Tourism devel-opment was halted by Cambodia's unwilling involvement in the Vietnam War and the isolation imposed by the fanatical Khmer Rouge regime but revived in the 1990s after decades of conflict and neglect.

In the 1990s, when Angkor was designated as a World Heritage Site, the Cambodian authorities transferred responsibility for the conservation of the monuments to specific countries, such as India and Japan, which could provide the necessary expertise. This enabled the government to concentrate on developing infrastructure, including an inter-national airport at Siem Reap.

In the 1990s, Cambodia's fledgling tourism industry was dominated by cultural tourists from Western Europe and the United States, whose attention was focussed on Angkor. A range of handicrafts developed to meet this demand, taking their inspiration from the art and sculpture of the Khmer civilisation. However, by the twenty-first century, the majority of tourists were coming from other Asian countries, particularly Japan, South Korea, Taiwan and China. East Asian expatriates provide much of the investment in hotels, casinos, golf courses and other facilities, particularly in Siem Reap, and the tourism products on offer now increasingly meet the demand from the middle-range inclusive tour Asian market. Most of these tourists are less concerned with 'authenticity' than their Western counterparts, and a range of mass-produced items, usually imported, are available to meet the demand. In 2019, Cambodia received 6.6 million tourist arrivals, and a well-organised travel industry has developed to serve their needs and the growing domestic market.

Tourism resources

Angkor has greatly influenced modern Cambodian culture. The graceful *apsara* dancers of Hindu mythology are not only sculpted on the walls of ancient temples but are showcased in the performances of the Royal Ballet of Cambodia, where the dancers wear elaborate costumes inspired by the Khmer civilisation. More recent history is interpreted in the Museum of Genocide in Pnom Penh (http://tuolsleng.gov.kh/en/). This is an example of 'dark tourism', commemorating the 'killing fields' where the Khmer Rouge regime murdered an estimated 2 million people in the course of its 'de-industrialisation' policy in the late 1970s.

Cambodia also offers many natural attractions, such as the following:

- A coastline along the Gulf of Thailand, including the port of Sihanoukville and offshore islands, some of which are designated for development as luxury resorts.
- The wetland ecosystem of Tonle Sap, a lake which varies greatly in size according to the seasons. In 2019, a severe drought affecting much of the Mekong Basin had a major impact on the ecosystem, and this has been attributed to climate change.
- The country's northeast, which is being developed for ecotourism, provides jobs for impoverished rural communities.

For the benefits of tourism to be spread more widely, the road network needs to be greatly improved, training provided for those working in the sector, and small-scale community-based tourism ventures should be encouraged.

Laos (Lao People's Democratic Republic)

In contrast to much of Thailand, the Laotian lifestyle is still pre-industrial in its pace, and this is an integral part of the country's appeal to Western tourists. With a much lower population density than Thailand or Vietnam, there is less pressure on natural resources. Laos can offer great biodiversity; almost 20 per cent of its territory is protected, and ecotourism is encouraged by the Lao National Tourism Administration, which reports to the

Ministry of Information, Culture and Tourism. On the other hand, these resources are at risk from logging, wasteful 'slash and burn' farming methods, and the illegal trade in wild animals and birds. Environmentalists are also concerned about dam-building for power generation on the River Mekong, which is not only the main artery of Laos but also crucial to the economies of neighbouring countries.

The transport infrastructure is a major constraint on tourism development in Laos but has improved with a new 965-kilometre railway linking the capital, Vientiane, to the city of Kunming in the southern Chinese province of Yunnan. Nevertheless, Laos received almost 5 million arrivals in 2019, the majority coming from Thailand. The Friendship Bridge over the Mekong near Vientiane's capital is the most frequently used border crossing. Domestic tourism is facilitated by the extended family networks that provide for mutual hospitality. Western culture-seekers focus mainly on Luang Prabang, the former royal capital and religious centre, a World Heritage Site due to its wealth of Buddhist temples.

Discussion point

Sex tourism is a fact of life in many Southeast Asian cities, which mainly exploits migrants from impoverished rural areas. The unacceptable face of the 'sex industry' is a modern version of the slave trade in which people traffickers supply child prostitutes to visiting paedophiles from Western Europe, Japan and the United States. Cambodia is viewed as an alternative to Thailand, where the government has imposed stricter controls in response to campaigning by ECPAT (https://www.ecpat.org/). Visits by well-meaning tourists and volunteer workers to orphanages in Southeast Asia have contributed to the problem, as the majority of children in these institutions are not orphans but are victims of trafficking or have been placed there by their impoverished families. In effect, they are viewed as commodities in the tourism supply chain. Suggest ways in which the travel industry, and indeed tourists themselves, could help to eradicate this problem.

CASE STUDY 21.2
MEDICAL TOURISM IN SOUTH-EAST ASIA

It can be challenging to distinguish between 'health tourism' or 'spa tourism' - travel for reasons of health and well-being, and 'medical tourism', usually defined as travel to a hospital or clinic for a specific course of treatment paid for by the patient. Medical tourism has become an important niche market for many Asian countries. The TAT, among others, prefers to promote its facilities as 'wellness tourism', emphasising relaxation therapies and cosmetic surgery rather than the treatment of disease.

The demand for medical tourism has grown in Western Europe, particularly Britain, due to dissatisfaction with the long waiting lists for operations in the national health services of those countries. In the case of the United States, where many Americans lack medical insurance, it is fuelled by concern at the high cost of treatments. Even allowing for the airfare, American patients travelling overseas for treatment are making considerable savings, with the cost of an operation in Thailand being less than half the outlay in the United States. Since 9/11 and the subsequent security measures, much of the demand in the Arab countries of the Middle East for the medical services traditionally provided by the United States and Britain has been diverted to Asian countries.

Thailand is the pioneer of medical tourism in the region, featured in the 'Amazing Thailand' campaign of the 1990s, building on a centuries-old tradition of spa and massage therapies. It continues to be the leading destination in this field. Foreign visitors and expatriates now account for over 40 per cent of the patients in Bangkok's two leading private hospitals. Japan is the largest demand generator, followed by the United States, Britain, Taiwan, ASEAN countries, and the Middle East. Other important destinations in Southeast Asia for 'medical tourists' include Malaysia and Singapore – which attracted almost 1.5 million arrivals in 2018, despite costs significantly higher than in Thailand – while the Philippines hopes to increase its market share.

Information technology is a key factor in Thailand's success as a destination for medical tourism, with hospitals providing foreign patients with ready access to the treatments available and often arranging for flight tickets, the stay in the hospital, and post-operation convalescence in a holiday resort to be sold as an inclusive package. To assure foreign patients of a quality experience, the hospital has become more like a luxury hotel. This entails a makeover in design and service standards, with a central lobby, hostess service, and sometimes a food court, similar to those found in American shopping malls, becoming standard features. However, this might mean that local healthcare needs are not being met. People from poorer Asian countries are spending up to a year's wages on their medical treatment and also have to bring in their own food, while Western visitors are staying in the equivalent of luxury hotels and combining a holiday with 'bargain-basement' surgery.

Discussion point
Discuss whether medical tourism is a contradiction since it is associated with sickness, suffering and loss of personal freedom and would appear to be incompatible with tourism as a leisure activity.

Myanmar (Burma)

Before achieving independence, Burma was ruled as part of British India, and the government renamed the country, its cities and major physical features is part of a nation-building campaign, with the Burmese as the dominant national culture over more than a hundred other ethnic groups. In 2005, this was reinforced with the designation of a new capital to replace Rangoon at Naypyidaw, located deep in the country's interior. For decades after independence, the country was isolated from the West by the government's policy of socialist self-sufficiency; visas were difficult to obtain, and tourists were not permitted to stay for more than a few days. Security continues to be a major problem, with dissident ethnic groups, such as the Shans and the Karens, in the mountainous border areas. Myanmar is also physically isolated by high mountains to the north and east and an inhospitable coastline of mangrove swamps and dense forests to the west.

From the early 1990s, the military regime encouraged foreign investment in the fledgling tourism industry, primarily from Japan. Tourism development was carried out by the government using unpaid 'volunteers' (in effect, forced labour) to build the necessary infrastructure, namely much-needed roads and railway improvements, and a new airport at Bassein. In some areas, villagers were relocated to make way for tourist facilities.

The government's apparent disregard for human rights and how tourism development was carried out has aroused much controversy. Opponents of the military regime, headed by the human rights campaigner Aung San Kyi, claimed that tourism revenue simply enriched those in government circles who had invested in the new hotels, and she urged a boycott of the country. This was supported by pressure groups in the West, notably Tourism Concern. On the other hand, Lonely Planet and some tour operators believed that tourism could be a powerful force for liberalisation and social change that would ultimately benefit the Burmese people. However, tourism's contribution to the country's foreign exchange earnings is small compared to the exports of teak, precious stones and natural gas to China and India. Since 2012, Myanmar has made progress towards democracy, with Aung San Kyi, in effect, sharing power with military leaders. Nevertheless, suppression of the Rohingya, a Muslim minority living in the Arakan region, attracted unfavourable publicity from human rights groups in the West. Visitor numbers have grown significantly to reach 4.3 million arrivals in 2019.

Tourism resources

Although its transport infrastructure is poorly developed, Myanmar has much to offer both the ecotourist and the cultural tourist, including, for example:

* A number of wildlife parks and sanctuaries.
* The Irrawaddy River runs through the country's heartland, providing a major transport artery from Yangon (formerly Rangoon) to Mandalay, as in Kipling's time. River transport is now being revitalised after decades of neglect, including luxury cruises by Eastern and Orient Express.
* Yangon, the nation's largest city, boasts one of the world's most impressive Buddhist temples – the Shwe Dagon Pagoda (http://www.thesheedagonpagoda.com/), which is covered in gold and precious stones.
* Bagan is renowned for the 3,000 or so Buddhist monuments set in a vast archaeological zone, a reminder of Burma's 'golden age' during the thirteenth century.
* Mandalay was the royal capital before British rule and remains the country's religious centre. The palace has been restored as a tourist attraction.
* Inle Lake – a major scenic and cultural attraction with its unique fishing communities.
* Some of the country's tribal minorities, notably the Padaung (famed for their long-necked women), have become the focus of tourism, but some claim that this is a form of exploitation that fails to benefit these communities.

The Mergui Islands are the only part of Myanmar's long coastline with much potential for beach tourism and diving holidays.

The Far East/North-East Asia

The lands around the East China Sea and the Sea of Japan include some of the world's largest modern cities, as well as some of its oldest civilisations. Much of the region is mountainous, and populations tend to be concentrated at densities exceeding those of western Europe. In contrast to the tropical conditions prevalent in Southeast Asia, the climate is characterised by four well-defined seasons, not unlike those of Europe and North America. Spring and autumn are the best times for visiting, as winters can be bitterly cold and summers oppressively hot and humid. Japan and South Korea have long been important destinations for business travellers and cultural tourists, but since the 1990s, China has emerged as a formidable competitor for the world travel market.

Japan

The setting for tourism

Japan is the leading industrial nation in Asia after China, with an economy based on overseas trade. Despite experiencing a long period of economic stagnation since the 1990s, it boasts a GDP third only to the United States and China and four times greater than that of the United Kingdom. In response to the economic situation of the 1990s, there has been a certain amount of industrial restructuring and deregulation, and the country has become more open to foreign investment. Nevertheless, Japan is a major generator of tourists in the East Asia-Pacific region, with a very large deficit in its international tourism account.

Japan consists of four main islands located off the eastern fringe of the continent – Honshu, Hokkaido, Kyushu and Shikoku – and groups of much smaller islands, such as the Ryukyus and Iwo Jima, lying to the south. The total area of the Japanese islands is only slightly greater than the British Isles but with twice the population. The pressure on land resources is even more acute when we consider that over 80 per cent of the country is mountainous. Geological instability has produced the beautiful mountain landscapes of Japan – Mount Fuji is the best-known example – and the numerous hot springs, but it is also responsible for natural disasters such as the earthquakes which devastated Kobe in 1995 and the Tohoku region of northern Honshu in 2011. Japan has to import nearly all the petroleum it needs, mainly from the Middle East, which explains the strategic importance of the Straits of Malacca to the Japanese. The development of nuclear power as an alternative source of energy received a major setback in 2011 with the Fukushima incident.

The climate is influenced by the warm Kurosiwo Current in the Pacific Ocean and the cold Oyashio Current in the Sea of Japan, and there are considerable differences between the southeast of the country and the northern island of Hokkaido. For example, the arrival of cherry blossom, celebrated in Japan by the *Sakura* festival as a symbol of life and re-birth, usually takes place in mid-March in Kyushu but does not reach Hokkaido until mid-May.

As a nation, Japan has the following characteristics:

- It is remarkably homogenous, with one language, few social divisions, and ethnic minorities accounting for only 1.5 per cent of the population.
- It has enjoyed political stability since 1945.
- Respect for tradition co-exists with admiration for the new.
- There is a readiness to adopt the latest technological innovations.
- Society is bound by discipline and respect for authority, which keeps crime levels low by Western standards.

During its long history, Japan has absorbed some cultural influences, notably from China, but has otherwise been self-contained, with an ambivalent attitude towards the West. Following a century of encounters with European traders and Catholic missionaries, in 1640 the Tokugawa shogun ruling from Edo (now Tokyo) isolated the country and its people from almost all contact with the West, except the Dutch, whose trading activities were confined to the small island of Deshima in Nagasaki harbour. This self-imposed isolation continued until 1853 when Japan was compelled by the US Navy to open its ports to international trade. This was followed by the coup in 1868 which abolished the shogunate, restoring Emperor Meiji to effective power and greatly limiting the role of the samurai, the feudal warrior class. The new regime quickly saw the advantages of adopting Western technology, but Western-style freedoms and democracy were not introduced until after the defeat of Imperial Japan in 1945.

The demand for tourism

Due to a low birthrate and high life expectancy, the Japanese population is ageing, with a higher proportion of people aged over 65 years than in the United States and Western Europe, and the 'grey market' is well catered for. Rather than encouraging immigration as a response to future manpower shortages, there has been considerable investment in robotics for personal services, including the hospitality sector, and manufacturing. There are social trends towards a more relaxed and individualistic lifestyle, a greater emphasis on leisure and sport, particularly among young people, and a greater readiness to adopt Western fashions. Even so, the concept of an annual holiday has only slowly been accepted in Japan, which is still essentially a work-oriented society. Working hours are longer than in Europe or the United States and paid annual leave amounts to 15 days; however, Japanese workers often take only 9 days out of their full holiday entitlement out of loyalty to colleagues or to cover for illness. Holidays and leisure activities are generally sponsored by large industrial corporations for their employees; however, this paternalism is not resented by most Japanese, who are prepared to accept a degree of regimentation that Westerners would find irksome. After-work drinking parties are seen by 'salarymen' (white collar workers) as an opportunity to bond with their employers when the strict formality that usually prevails is relaxed.

Domestic tourism

Domestic tourism is more significant in volume and spending than international tourism for the Japanese travel market. Holidays account for the majority of trips, with business and VFR accounting for the remainder. Pilgrimages to Shinto and Buddhist shrines continue to be popular with family groups, while *onsen* (hot spring resorts) appeal more to the stressed executive at weekends. The Western influence is evident in the rapid growth of skiing, golf, baseball, and water sports and visits to theme parks such as Tokyo Disneyland (https://www.tokyodisneyresort.jp/en). The scarcity of land for recreation particularly affects the demand for skiing and golf:

- Some 15 million Japanese practise skiing. The mountains of Northern Honshu and Hokkaido receive abundant snowfalls during the winter months, and this has encouraged the development of a large number of ski resorts. However, apart from Nagano in the Japanese Alps and Sapporo in Hokkaido which have both hosted the Winter Olympics, few resorts approach Western standards, and overcrowding on the slopes is a major problem.
- Golf courses are few and far between, and green fees are prohibitively expensive. Most would-be players are confined to multi-storey driving ranges, and real golf can only be played on overseas trips. This goes far to explaining why the Japanese are active in purchasing tourism developments overseas and in providing Third World governments with aid for projects where golf is a major component.

Outbound tourism

During the long period of Japan's self-imposed isolation from the West under the rule of the Tokugawa shoguns, foreign travel was strictly forbidden. After 1868, a limited amount of tourism was sponsored by the government for the purpose of business or study. Tourism for leisure received no such encouragement, and it was not until 1964 that restrictions on foreign travel were lifted. In the late 1980s, the government made a positive effort to encourage overseas travel through the 'Ten Million Programme', as a way of restructuring Japan's trade balance with the rest of the world and promoting mutual understanding. Even so, partly due to recent economic problems and world events, participation in outbound travel is small by European standards, accounting for only 13 per cent of the population. The number of trips has actually decreased since 2001, and with limited holiday time available the length of stay is short, averaging eight days. Yet in 2019 20 million overseas trips were taken. In many countries, the Japanese are the largest source of tourists, and they tend to be the biggest spenders. Over half visit destinations in Asia – mainly Taiwan, South Korea, and Hong Kong; around a third go to the United States – particularly to honeymoon in Hawaii and Guam – and the remainder travel to Europe or Australasia. Group travel is important, and so is *omiyake*, the customary purchase of gifts for friends, relatives and employers. Young unmarried women, the so-called 'office ladies', constitute a major market, particularly for travel to the countries of Western Europe.

CASE STUDY 21.3
FOREIGN THEMES IN JAPANESE DOMESTIC TOURISM

It could be argued that much of the domestic tourism in Japan is a substitute for foreign travel. A large number of visitor attractions provide the Japanese with a simulated holiday experience in a foreign country without the trouble and expense of the real thing. In their everyday lives, the Japanese are fascinated by Western technology and popular culture, and they are also interested in other Asian cultures, particularly those of China and Korea (Graburn, 2008). This interest in 'foreignness' is often expressed by visiting the 'Chinatowns' that exist in Kobe and other cities and by contacts with expatriate communities. Out of a total of 2.2 million foreigners, there are some 0.2 million *gaijin* ('outside people', usually denoting Westerners) living in Japan, not just in the big cities but also in small towns, as a result of the exchange teacher's programme. Nevertheless, the Japanese continue to be curious about many aspects of Westerners' lifestyles and even their physical appearance. Japanese youth are attracted to *gaijin* communities and the US military bases, particularly in Okinawa, where they can practice their English language skills without embarrassment. This island provides numerous examples of museums, theme parks, restaurants, nightclubs and festivals celebrating American popular culture.

There are many purpose-built visitor attractions based on international themes. Tokyo Disneyland, which attracts around 18 million visitors a year, is the most popular of a number of theme parks that appeal mainly to the family market and showcase Western culture. Whereas Tokyo Disneyland offers a fantasy version of the United States, Universal Studios near Osaka (https://www.usj.co.jp/e/) aims to give the Japanese visitor a 'genuine American experience'. The *gaikoku mora* ('foreign country villages') focusses even more on international themes. The oldest of these, 'Little World' near Nagoya (https://www.littleworld.jp/english/index.html) opened in 1983 and is a collection of such attractions, each offering the regional cuisines, products, music and the performing arts of a particular country. The aim throughout is for authenticity; nearly all the villages employ foreigners as interpreters or performers and feature buildings that are replicas of foreign originals, where great attention is paid to detail. For example, Huit den Bosch near Nagasaki (http://english.huistenbosch.co.jp/) celebrates Japan's special relationship with Holland with replicas of famous Dutch landmarks such as the Royal Palace in Amsterdam. Other foreign country villages include 'British Hills' near Tokyo with its English pubs (https://wwwbritish-hills.co.jp/english/); 'Lucky Kingdom' with its Bavarian architecture and fairy tale characters; 'Parque España' with a Spanish theme (https://www.parque-net.comforeign/english/) and 'Villaggio Italia'. Nearly all the European villages have churches or chapels rented by couples for a Western-style wedding, which are viewed by the Japanese as a modern fashion statement, allowing for many photo opportunities rather than as a

Christian ceremony. At least this avoids the expense of travelling to Hawaii with the same objective.

Visiting attractions that celebrate foreignness allows the Japanese to play at being foreign as well as the opportunity to learn about other cultures. Each country is seen in terms of its unique products, images and attractions – the *meibetsu* ('famous things') that must be visited on a foreign tour. Knowledge of these has been previously obtained from the media, *manga* (adult comic books) and the travel experiences of others. Most of these visitor attractions feature famous writers or fictional characters among other tourist icons, and these have become well-known brand names in Japan. Shopping for merchandise in a foreign country village is a preparation for a future trip overseas, teaching Japanese tourists not only what they should see but also what they should bring back as gifts for friends, relatives, and work colleagues.

Inbound tourism

International arrivals stood at over 32 million in 2019, and the difference with outbound tourism is even greater in terms of spend. These relatively high volumes are despite Japan's distance from the traditional generating markets of Western Europe and the United States and the country's reputation for being expensive. Numbers have been boosted by major sporting events such as the FIFA World Cup in 2002, the Rugby World Cup in 2019 and the 2020 Summer Olympics which was postponed to 2021 due to the COVID-19 pandemic.

Business travellers account for about a quarter of incoming tourists, with the cities of Tokyo, Osaka and Nagoya as the major destinations. South Korea is the largest source of tourists due to cultural and business ties with Japan. South-east Asian countries account for half of all visitors, with a further 10 per cent coming from the United States.

The supply side of tourism

Transport

For domestic travel, road and rail are most commonly used. The northern island of Hokkaido is linked to Honshu by the world's longest rail tunnel, and bridges similarly integrate Kyushu and Shikoku with the leading transport network, supplementing the ferry services. There is an extensive network of railways (over 30,000 kilometres), including the famous *Shinkansen* (bullet train) (https://global.jr-central.cojp/en/), linking Tokyo to Fukuoka, Niigata, and Morioka in northern Japan. For foreign visitors, train travel is preferable to driving due to the problems of road congestion (there is a high level of car ownership) and inadequate signage. Most foreign visitors arrive by air, the majority through Tokyo's Narita Airport. However, other airports are growing in importance, notably Osaka's Kansai Airport (built on an artificial island), which has the advantage of being much closer to downtown than Narita, which is 60 kilometres from central Tokyo. Tokyo's other airport, Haneda handles domestic flights to a large number of destinations. The busiest air routes are from Southeast Asia, Hawaii, and the United States. The aviation sector is dominated by two airlines – Japan Airlines (https://www.jal.co.jp/en/inter/) and ANA (https://www.ana.co.jp/) – but with deregulation since 1996, they face a growing challenge from newcomers.

Accommodation

The hotel industry is driven by domestic demand, but occupancy rates for other than budget and medium-priced hotels have declined due to the economic problems and the resulting cutbacks in corporate entertainment by Japanese business executives. Tourists can stay in Western-style hotels or *ryokan* – Japanese inns where the food service, bathing facilities, and furnishings of *tatami* matting follow native traditions, and these are increasingly sought out by Western visitors. Tokyo and Osaka are the main locations for major hotel projects, some financed by international chains. These tend to be very expensive, but an alternative is available for the budget traveller in the so-called 'capsule hotels' – stacks of cubicles, each consisting of little more than a bed space. Subsidised family 'travel villages' and lodges are also available for the domestic market.

Organisation

Responsibility for the sector lies with the Ministry of Land, Infrastructure, Transport and Tourism, which supervises the external Japan Tourism Agency. The Agency oversees the promotion of Japan and carries out the Visit Japan campaigns and other marketing activities through the Japan National Tourist Organization (JNTO) (www.jnto.go.jp). The Japan Congress Convention Bureau (JCB) (https://jccb.or.jp) is leading in developing facilities for the important conference market. At the local and regional levels, local authorities work with destination management organisations in co-operation with stakeholders to design and execute strategies for particular areas.

Tourism resources

Japan's traditions are a major part of its appeal to Western tourists. These include:

*   The cuisine, where the presentation of food is treated as an art form.
*   The tea ceremony.
*   The delicacy and artistry evident in handicrafts, such as engraving on wood or silk.
*   Kabuki theatre.
*   Sumo wrestling.
*   The distinctive architecture and miniaturised landscape gardening characteristic of Shinto and Buddhist temples and shrines.

Japan has a unique human resource in the skills of the *geiko* hostesses and entertainers (better known as geishas in the West). Still, there is evidence that this is a declining tradition, with fewer girls willing to undertake the long training as *maikos* (apprentice geishas). The corporate business market for this type of entertainment was reduced considerably by the economic crisis of the 1990s and many *okiya* (geisha houses) closed as a result.

Innovation, as opposed to tradition, is evident in contemporary Japanese art forms such as animé (the animated cartoon film), the fashion scene among young people in Tokyo and other cities, and in pachinko parlours, karaoke bars, 'host bars' (exclusively for women), 'maid cafes', and other forms of entertainment. Sony (https://www.sony.net/) is one example of a Japanese corporation that has been at the forefront of developing visitor attractions employing the latest technology.

Although the drive for industrialisation has caused severe pollution problems, the Shinto religion inspires reverence for the natural world, and much has been done to preserve the country's coasts, mountains and forests, including the designation of 34 national parks in the most scenic areas. Unlike their counterparts in North America, these are not for the most part wilderness areas but contain hundreds of rural communities, such is the pressure on land and water resources.

Western visitors are mainly drawn to southern **Honshu** and its cities, which include:

* Tokyo, which is above all a business centre, but also a city of over 9 million people containing many temples and museums. The Ginza district includes the Stock Exchange, while leisure activities are concentrated in the Shinjuku district. Tokyo is also home to attractions linked to information technology, including Global Park – dedicated to animé Studios – Ghibli and a newly established digital art museum.
* Kyoto, as the former imperial capital is Japan's main cultural centre, which preserves the country's traditions, including hundreds of Shinto shrines and temples, the Gion district with its geisha houses and gardens inspired by Zen Buddhism. However, this city of one and a half million people is no museum-piece, but one that is increasingly under threat from the pressures of modernisation, despite strict planning regulations against high buildings and neon advertisements.
* Nikko, Nara and Ise are also religious centres, preserving much of the feudal past of Japan.
* The Inland Sea between western Honshu and Shikoku is probably the most scenic region of Japan, studded with picturesque islands and numerous Buddhist temples.

Kyushu has a long history of contact with other cultures, which is an important part of its appeal, particularly to the Japanese. The island offers a wide variety of attractions, including:

* Space World near Fukuoka (https://www.jnto.go.jp/eng/spot/thempark/space-world.html).
* Nagasaki, the first port to be opened to trade with the West, and the setting for Puccini's opera 'Madam Butterfly'. This city (along with Hiroshima) has been in the forefront of efforts to promote international understanding, stemming from its experience of nuclear warfare in 1945.
* Beppu, the most important of a number of spa resorts based on the island's abundant geothermal resources.

In contrast to the rest of Japan, **Hokkaido** is not densely populated and has different landscapes, with forests, cereal farming and pasture replacing rice fields. The climate is similar to that of eastern Canada, with abundant snowfalls during the long, bitterly cold winters. Moreover, the Japanese did not settle on the island until late in the nineteenth century. The indigenous Ainu people have largely been assimilated, and what remains of their culture is preserved in a few tourist villages. Tourism to Hokkaido is set to grow with the extension of high-speed rail services to Hakodate. Hokkaido's scenic attractions include:

• Lake Toya, a volcanic caldera surrounded by geothermal springs. This is a favourite summer destination for Japanese holidaymakers, as well as being a vital conference venue.
• The Daisetsuzan National Park (http://www.daisetsuzan.or.jp/english/), which in-cludes the volcanic peak of Asahi and forests that provide a refuge for brown bears and other wildlife.

Sapporo is the main commercial centre of Hokkaido and is noted for beer and the annual Snow Festival (https://www.snowfes.com/english/). Niseko is one of Japan's largest ski and snowboarding resorts, with a season lasting from November to April.

The **Ryukyu Islands** enjoy a sub-tropical climate. The people have a culture and out-look that is sufficiently different from the rest of the country for the islands to be regarded almost as a foreign destination by the Japanese. Okinawa is the group's main island and is visited by large numbers of Taiwanese tourists. It is best known in the West as the scene of some of the bloodiest fighting in the Second World War, and the economy is mainly dependent on the US bases that were set up after 1945. In 1975, Okinawa attracted world-wide attention as the venue for the International Ocean Exposition, and the islands offer many facilities for diving.

China (The People's Republic of China)

The setting for tourism

With almost 1.4 billion inhabitants, China accounts for over a fifth of the world's pop-ulation. After 1979, the government responded to a looming demographic crisis by im-plementing the one child per family policy. Although this was relaxed in 2015, the birth rate continues to fall, and the result is an uneven gender ratio of 1.2 males per female with the social problems this presents and the prospect of an ageing population. There are great disparities in wealth between the coastal 'eastern crescent' extending from Beijing to Guangzhou (Canton), which has benefitted most from the market economy, and the largely rural interior provinces which remain under-developed. Although the Han Chi-nese are the dominant group, 55 ethnic minorities live mainly in the west and southwest of the country.

Throughout the long history of the 'Middle Kingdom' under various dynasties, Chi-na's rulers had a worldview that regarded all other nations as barbarians, an attitude not unlike that of the Roman Empire. This made China resistant to change during European expansion in the nineteenth century. The Chinese Empire under the Qing (Manchu) dynasty was forced into humiliating trade and territorial concessions by the Western powers – Britain, France, and Germany – as a result of the so-called 'Opium Wars', which resulted in the loss of Hong Kong and the 'Treaty ports' of Qingdao and Wei-hai-weh. In 1911, the last emperor was replaced by a secular republic, but this did not bring stability, and for most of the twentieth century China experienced immense social and economic upheaval, culminating in the Communist revolution led by Mao Zedong who established a totalitarian state. Following the chaos of the Cultural Revolution and Mao's demise, the government, from 1978 onwards, gradually moved towards a free market economy. However, the Communist Party, backed by the People's Liberation Army (PLA) remains firmly in control. Since the 1990s the rate of economic growth has been among the highest in the world, attracting foreign investment on an unprecedented scale. By the twenty-first century, China had become the second largest economy in the world and now dominates outbound tourism in both the East Asia region and globally. China is now the world's second oil importer along with many other raw materials, to fuel its industries, with huge implications for the global economy.

The landmass of China is equivalent in size to the United States. It contains a great range of climates from the extreme winter cold of northern Manchuria to the tropical warmth of the island of Hainan in the south. It boasts some of the world's highest mountains and plateaux, one of the most inhospitable deserts – the Takla Makan – and the world's fourth longest river – the Yangtse. Throughout history, China has been prone to natural disasters on an epic scale in the form of earthquakes, floods and famines, and its rulers have been faced with the need to control the erratic flow of the rivers Yangtse and the Hwang Ho. One major constraint on development is water supply, as China, with over 20 per cent of the world's population, has only 7 per cent of the world's freshwater resources. Moreover, many of the country's rivers are polluted. The problem is particularly acute in the north, necessitating projects to divert water from the rivers of south China by a system of canals.

China has one of the world's oldest civilisations, characterised by an alphabet, a code of ethics based on the teachings of Confucius and Lao Tse, and art and medical traditions that were already well established at the time of the Han dynasty in the second century BC, which gave its name to the dominant culture of the country.

The demand for tourism

Domestic tourism

Travel for pleasure is a recent phenomenon in China, and internal migration, let alone domestic tourism, was discouraged by many restrictions under Mao's totalitarian regime. Deng Xiaoping's economic reforms in the 1980s encouraged mobility as part of the process of modernisation, and returning rural migrants from the cities were regarded as a 'civilising influence' on the countryside. Since the mid-1990s domestic tourism has increased rapidly, encouraged by the rise in living standards and, not least, by an increase in leisure time, including the introduction of the five-day working week in 1995. In 1999, the government introduced three weeks of public holidays, known collectively as the 'golden weeks', which created huge demand and congestion on the transport networks. These celebrate Chinese New Year (January/February), Labour Day (the first week in May) and National Day (the first week in October). A growing urban middle class has the means and the desire to participate in leisure tourism as part of a trend away from a 'savings culture' to one of conspicuous consumption. However, in 2020, the spread of COVID-19 seriously affected the demand for domestic travel, with much of the country closed to travellers in a draconian lockdown.

Family visits to Buddhist and Daoist shrines, such as the sacred mountain of Tai-Shan in Shandong province are popular, providing a link with Chinese tradition. Western-style beach tourism has been slow to develop, as the Chinese prefer landscapes modified by human action rather than the sea, which is often viewed as a source of danger rather than a recreational opportunity. The contrast with Western attitudes extends to sunbathing, as importance is still placed on modesty and a fair complexion. However, beach resorts within reach of the major cities attract growing numbers of middle-class families. The citizens of Beijing visit Beidahe, Wei-hai, and Qingdao. European expatriates initially developed these resorts in the 1920s. After the Communist revolution, the hotels were taken over for the use of the Party elite and favoured groups of industrial workers. Holidaymakers from Shanghai visit Xiamen in the south-east of the country.

The demand for outdoor recreation is growing, but many projects have failed because developers overestimated the spending power of China's middle class. There is now an effective demand for golf and skiing where none existed before 1990. The most developed ski resort is near Beijing at Nanshan, where snow-making machines compensate for the lack of snowfall in North China's cold but very dry winter climate.

Cultural visits are a much more significant part of domestic tourism. The authorities see these as a force for education in citizenship. Groups of workers from the same companies or work units are encouraged to visit 'patriotic education sites' and other places associated with the nation's history, particularly Mao's revolution. The emphasis on education and indoctrination combined with entertainment extends to the theme parks that have been developed on the periphery of major cities, such as 'Splendid China' and 'Windows of the World' (http://en.szwwco.com/), which replicates famous buildings from many different countries. Heritage plays an important role in tourism based on China's 'old towns' and the 'ethnic villages' inhabited by tribal minorities, but how it is conserved and interpreted differs from the approach in Europe and North America. These are standardised attractions selected by the tourist authorities at the highest level rather than as a result of local initiatives. In 'old towns', the historic core is marked off from the rest of the urban area by a ticketing gate and a reconstructed town wall, and various improvements are carried out, such as re-paving and street widening. Other typical features include a shopping street selling souvenirs and an accommodation area allocated to tour groups. Cultural performances are another element of the tourist experience, as re-enactments of ceremonies in a real or imagined past. In the ethnic villages of south-west China, the minority groups are encouraged to put on dance performances and wear their traditional costume when tourists visit. Chinese tourists realise they are being offered staged performances, but unlike Western cultural tourists who value 'authenticity', they expect and indeed appreciate such experiences as an escape from the realities of everyday life.

Since the millennium there has been a huge increase in the use of the Internet, which has encouraged the growth of independent travel, particularly among young people. Like their Western counterparts, Chinese backpackers value the freedom of travel and seek adventure and cultural experiences in relatively remote areas. They are city-based and well-educated. Participants are brought together for a specified trip by the voluntary efforts of like-minded individuals using independent websites. Nevertheless, these travellers are highly organised, with an ethos that emphasises the welfare of the group rather than encouraging the hedonistic attitudes characteristic of youth tourism in the West.

Outbound tourism

The demand for foreign travel in China has been shaped by government policy, which generally discouraged such trips until quite recently. In 1983, package tours for 'family reasons' were permitted to Hong Kong and Macau. In 1990, Thailand, Singapore, and Malaysia became the first countries to receive Approved Destination Status (ADS) by bi-lateral agreement with the Chinese government. This programme has been extended to include the European Union, Australia, and the United States in the new millennium. The relaxation of visa restrictions, the emergence of the low-cost carrier AirAsia, and the strength of the Chinese currency against the US dollar have encouraged the growth of foreign travel, although COVID-19 in 2020/2021 depressed demand. At present, only 9 per cent of the population have passports and the means to travel abroad, but growth is such that China now leads the world as a generator of international tourism in terms of both expenditure and the number of departures. Most of the demand comes from the three major urban belts of Beijing/Tianjin, Shanghai and the Yangtse Delta, and Guangzhou/Shenzhen in south China. Between 2010 and 2014 the number of trips taken abroad more than doubled, from 50 million to 109 million, and grew again by almost 40 per cent to approach 154 million in 2019. The Chinese now form the largest market in most countries of Southeast Asia. Tourism to Europe is growing despite the constraints of cost, language and cultural barriers, and the unfamiliarity of Chinese travel agents with long-haul destinations. The great majority of Chinese tourists travel in organised groups due to visa regulations and for cultural reasons, the exception being Hong Kong where independent travel has been permitted since 2003.

These factors have influenced the growth in foreign travel:

- Rising discretionary incomes among the urban middle class.
- Increasing numbers of businesses are giving their employees holidays with pay.
- The destinations popular with domestic tourists are reaching saturation point regarding the number of visitors and their capacity to provide adequate services.

As was the case in the 1950s with the 'ugly American' stereotype in Western Europe, Chinese tourists are not always viewed favourably by the host communities in the countries they visit. In Vietnam, which has a history of strained relations with its northern neighbour, they are perceived to have an attitude of superiority. On the other hand, Singapore and Hong Kong are regarded as lacking in sophistication. In Europe, where they may visit eight destinations in as many days, spending lavishly on designer brands, they expect tourism providers to adapt to meet their requirements – a situation we asked you to discuss in Chapter 2. The Chinese government views tourists as their country's representatives. It has issued tour operators and travel agencies with directives warning against anti-social behaviour (such as spitting in public spaces and queue-jumping) that would reflect badly on the PRC's image abroad. There is also the risk that Chinese tourists might be exposed to subversive foreign ideas.

Inbound tourism

Inbound tourism has been encouraged by the government since 1978 as part of the campaign to make the Chinese more receptive to Western ideas and technology and also to generate the foreign exchange needed to modernise the economy. Growth has generally been rapid, although the adverse publicity following the suppression of the pro-democracy movement in Beijing's Tiananmen Square brought about a downturn in Western visitors in the early 1990s, the SARS outbreak of 2003 and the COVID-19 pandemic significantly impacted both inbound and outbound tourism. Nevertheless, the 1997 PATA Conference was held in Beijing, highlighting the fact that China had become one of the world's leading tourist destinations, and in 2008, Beijing hosted the Olympic Games. In 2019, 65.7 million international tourist arrivals (involving a stay of at least one night) were recorded, but the strict lockdown due to COVID-19 reduced arrivals to 6 million in 2021. In addition, there were 114 million arrivals from Hong Kong and Macau, but the majority of these were day visitors, here again the COVID-19 pandemic severely impacted on this demand. The most important markets are Taiwan (which the PRC regards as a province of China), Japan, Russia, the countries of Southeast Asia, and the United States. At the same time, Britain, France and Germany together account for 5 per cent of arrivals. This success in tourism has not been achieved without growing pains. Pricing, poor service standards, and a shortage of trained personnel remain problems, as does adjusting a centrally-planned economy to one trying to accommodate free enterprise and market forces. Positive changes have taken place in the following areas:

- Improvements in the transport infrastructure.
- A greater choice of destinations, with more than 500 cities or areas open to visitors compared to 30 in 1982.
- A greater choice of attractions within established destinations such as Beijing and Shanghai.
- More competition between tour operators and travel agencies. In the past, group travel had been monopolised by the state-controlled China International Travel Service (CITS) (http://www.cits.net/) which has had to improve its performance for Western tourists.
- An increase in hotel capacity and a much-needed improvement in standards.

Business travel accounts for a third of inbound tourism and gravitates to the major cities of Beijing, Shanghai and Guangzhou. China plans to have 150 world-class conference centres catering mainly to the demand for trade exhibitions and corporate meetings. On the other hand, due to the lack of government support, the market for associate meetings, which might be concerned with controversial issues, has been slow to develop in China.

591

The supply side of tourism

Transport

Most travel in China is by rail or air, as the road network over most of this vast country is deficient by Western standards, although improvements were made in preparation for the Beijing Olympics. There has been a rapid growth in car ownership, from insignificant numbers in the 1980s to an estimated 300 million, and traffic jams are now commonplace in cities where bicycles and pedicabs used to be the only forms of transport.

Until recently rail travel was arduous and time-consuming, but the government has made a massive investment in magnetic levitation technology so that China now boasts the world's most comprehensive high-speed rail network. Fast trains already link Wuhan in central China to Guangzhou and Beijing to Shanghai. The rail journey between the capital and the nation's economic hub, a distance of over 1300 kilometres, now takes less than five hours, giving the domestic airlines serious competition. There are also ambitious plans to extend the network to the countries of south-east Asia. Nevertheless, there are concerns about safety issues, given the pressure on officials to meet central government targets. The Lhasa-Qinghai Railway linking Beijing to Tibet ranks as another significant engineering achievement. Pressurised carriages are necessary for passengers as the track at one point reaches a breathtaking altitude of 5200 metres (16,600 feet). The project also took account of the need to protect the fragile grassland ecology of the Tibetan Plateau.

China has an extensive system of domestic air services and over 200 airports, the largest of which can handle 100 million passengers annually. Air China (https://www.airchina.co.uk) and a number of regional airlines compete for the growing market for air travel. At the same time, the Civil Aviation Administration of China (CAAC) (http://www.caac.gov.cn/en/SY/), which in the 1980s exercised a state monopoly of air transport, now focusses solely on its regulatory role. The CAAC has given foreign airlines more rights to use the gateway airports at Beijing, Shanghai, and Guangzhou.

Accommodation

Most Western-style accommodation is concentrated in the major cities, notably Beijing, Guangzhou, Shanghai, and the Shenzhen Special Enterprise Zone adjoining Hong Kong. Thanks to the 2008 Olympics, there is probably an over-supply of five-star hotels in Beijing for the international tourist market. The shortage of more budget-priced hotels and motels for Chinese business and leisure tourists is being addressed by the private sector, notably by chains such as Home Inns (https://www.bthhotels.com/en/). These tend to offer a much higher standard of facilities than the 'economy-type' hotels run by local authorities or state-owned companies.

Organisation

Since 1984, the China National Tourism Administration (CNTA) has been responsible for tourism.

It is directly affiliated to the State Council and its work is firmly integrated with the Five Year Plans for the national economy. In 2018, the CNTA was dissolved and its responsibilities merged with the Ministry of Culture and Tourism (MCT) which administers China's cultural and artistic affairs.

The governments of the 26 provinces and five autonomous regions are now allowed considerable initiative, resulting in a flurry of master plans and investment schemes for tourism across China. Nevertheless, most tour operators and travel agencies are closely associated with government departments, which restricts the independence of the private sector. The industry is represented by the China Tourism Association and the National Travel Trade Association which is becoming more organised and professional.

Tourism resources

China is mainly famous for its age-old craft industries, traditional styles of architecture, and distinctive landscapes. Since the 1980s Western fashions and advertising styles have largely replaced the drab uniformity normally associated with Communist regimes. On the other hand, in the headlong rush to industrialise, air and water pollution have become major health problems in the cities, and great damage has been inflicted on the forest and wildlife resources of the mountain areas. Nevertheless, a reverence for nature is part of Chinese tradition, and the government has made great efforts to protect the habitat of the giant panda, China's most iconic animal, in the forests of the south-west. The country's cultural heritage is also at risk due to the underfunding of conservation, inappropriate restoration methods, and the urge to replace the old with the modern.

In such a vast country there are considerable regional differences in climate, landscapes, dialects, and lifestyles, including cuisine. For convenience, we have grouped China's provinces and autonomous regions according to their geographical location.

The North-East

Known historically as Manchuria, this was the homeland of the last imperial dynasty, but nowadays the Manchus are an ethnic minority in their own country. During the twentieth century, the region experienced Russian and Japanese occupation and large-scale industrial development. The main centres are Shenyang (formerly Mukden) and Harbin, noted for its annual Snow Festival. The border town of Heihe on the River Amur illustrates the changing nature of relations with Russia; past tensions between the two countries have been replaced by a thriving trade in consumer goods supplied by Chinese entrepreneurs to Russian visitors from nearby Blagoveshchensk.

North China

North China, centring on the Hwang Ho River basin, was the historic cradle of Chinese civilisation and the power base of the Chin and Han dynasties that were the first to unite the country. The region has a continental climate with severe winters and hot, humid summers. Treeless landscapes of wind-blown loess characterise the region, but it has much to attract cultural tourists, including:

- The burial place of the First Emperor at Xian, which yielded the famous terra-cotta warriors.
- The Great Wall of China – over 3,000 kilometres long – was built as a defence against the Mongol nomads to the north. The section most visited by tourists and subject to considerable pressure is at Badaling, reached by a 50-kilometre rail link from Beijing. Parts of the Wall are now illuminated to create a 'Night Tour Experience'.
- The summer resort of the Qing dynasty at Chengde, with its gardens, palaces and pagodas.

Beijing (formerly Peking) was the creation of the Ming dynasty in the fourteenth century and contains many reminders of its imperial past, including the Forbidden City (https://en.dpm.org.cn/) – the former palace compound of the emperors including the Temple of Heaven, and the Ming Tombs. In contrast, the Great Hall of the People (http://www.npc.gov.cn/zgrdw/englishpc/GreatHall/node_3072.htm), occupying one side of the vast public space known as Tiananmen Square, symbolises post-revolution China. The 2008 Olympic Games provided the impetus for improvements to Beijing's transport infrastructure. Apart from the sports facilities, the capital now boasts an array of new museums, art galleries, and theatres, and theme parks such as Universal Beijing Resort and Happy Valley. However, in the rush to modernise, most of the picturesque *hutongs* (densely packed courtyard dwellings) have been demolished to make way for faceless apartment buildings and shopping malls.

East Central China and Szechwan

This part of China centres on the River Yangtse:

- Shanghai is China's largest city and owes its rise as one of the world's great seaports to trade with the West. In the 1920s when foreign concessions dominated the city, Shanghai was renowned for its wealth and uninhibited nightlife. The impressive skyline of the new Pudong Special Enterprise Zone underlines the city's revival as an international business centre, while the historic waterfront area known as the Bund has been restored. It is home to Shanghai Disneyland Park.
- To the west of Shanghai lie a group of historic cities that have played a major role in Chinese history as capitals or cultural centres. These include Nanjing, Hangzhou (home to the Songcheng theme park), Wuxi (famous for its silk industry), and Suzhou, noted for its traditional Chinese gardens.

The Yangtse provides a popular tourist route to the fertile but mountainous province of Szechwan, deep in the interior of China. The modern cruise ships and the landing stages thronged with porters typify the contrasts between the old China and the new. The highlight of the cruise is the impressive Three Gorges between Wuhan and Chongqing. This is the location for the world's largest flood control project, involving the displacement of 1.5 million people. Taming the Yangtze will prevent repeating the 1998 floods that claimed 4,000 lives and provide 10 per cent of China's power requirements, but critics fear that the project will cause long-term environmental damage. Chongqing, the capital of Szechwan, is home to the controversial 'Flying Kiss' attraction.

Western China

Lanzhou is often regarded as the gateway to the arid and mountainous west. This includes the autonomous regions of Inner Mongolia, Ningxia, Xinjiang, and Tibet, and the province of Qinghai, which is mainly Tibetan in its traditional culture. The West is mostly inhabited by ethnic groups culturally distinct from the Han Chinese. For example, the Uighurs speak a Turkic language, are predominantly Muslim, and have a way of life based on pastoralism. The central government in Beijing has made great efforts to improve the communications infrastructure as part of a policy of integration; nevertheless, it has had to suppress Uighur dissidents. Tourist interest in the region focusses on the Silk Road (which we described in Chapter 17) and the historic towns along its route, such as Kashgar and Khotan. Domestic tourism from the cities of eastern China is encouraged by the government to boost the region's economy and provide funds to combat desertification.

   The Mogao Caves near Dunhuang are the major attraction on the Silk Road, and it was hereabouts that Chinese traders made contact with those from Persia and central Asia. Dating from the Tang dynasty, this former Buddhist sanctuary is decorated with a vast collection of wall paintings and sculptures, which was 'discovered' by a European explorer in 1907. Although the art treasures have been rescued from centuries of neglect and the encroaching desert sands, this World Heritage Site now faces a more insidious threat from mass tourism.

South China

South China is Cantonese, rather than Mandarin-speaking, with a climate and topography offering considerable potential for ecotourism, adventure holidays and beach tourism. The major tourist centres include:

- Guilin is famous for the spectacular karst mountain scenery along the River Li, inspiring a Chinese art tradition. The hidden world beneath this landscape contains a vast network of unexplored caverns and subterranean rivers extending north into Szechwan.
- Kunming is the centre for trekking tours into the rugged, densely forested, and formerly inaccessible 'hill country' of the provinces of Yunnan, Guangzhi, and Guizhou, where many tribal minorities preserve much of their original culture. The transformation of 'ethnic villages' into tourist destinations has encouraged the revival of cultural practices as a matter of local pride as well as a source of income.
- Guangzhou is the major business centre of the region, hosting two annual trade fairs in the Palace of Exhibitions which provide a showcase for the Chinese economy. It is home to theme parks including Ocean Kingdom and the Chinelong Safari Park.

In contrast, the city's markets display exotic foods and health remedies that recall an older China and which are supplied by a largely illegal trade in animal products, such as pangolin scales.

- The tropical island of **Hainan** until well into the twentieth century was neglected by the Chinese government, which regarded it as a place of exile inhabited by uncivilised tribes. Since the 1990s it has been promoted as the holiday destination of choice for China's growing middle class, particularly the resort of Sanyo. Hainan now has its regional airline, has hosted the Miss World beauty pageant, and is being promoted as a winter sun destination for the West European market.

Discussion point

The Beijing Olympics gave China the best opportunity to showcase its achievements, regain its place in the sun after centuries of being sidelined by the West, and demonstrate its green credentials. Discuss whether criticism of China's environmental record is justified, given the efforts the government is making to reduce dependence on coal and oil by harnessing renewable sources of energy. Also discuss whether there is a case for the Chinese government's attitude to ethnic minorities and human rights activists, particularly in Tibet, bearing in mind China's turbulent history and the legacy of the breakup of the USSR.

Hong Kong and Macau

Hong Kong and Macau deserve to be treated as separate destinations in their own right because of their special status within China and their former status as European colonies – Hong Kong was British from 1841 to 1997, while Macau was ruled by Portugal from the mid-sixteenth century to 1999. They include parts of the mainland of south China and a number of offshore islands. Hong Kong and Macau have a large measure of autonomy as special administrative regions (SARs) under the Chinese government's 'one country, two systems' policy, which, in effect means a 'hands-off' approach to their free enterprise economies. However, growing unease in Hong Kong about the erosion of this policy led to demonstrations in 2019 and 2020, which have affected inbound tourism.

Hong Kong

Densely built around its magnificent harbour, with The Peak in the background, Hong Kong has one of the world's most famous skylines. As a SAR, Hong Kong retains some of the features of British rule, including:

- Free port status and a free-wheeling private enterprise economy.
- Border controls with the rest of China, although visa controls have been relaxed to allow individual as well as group travel.
- The Hong Kong dollar as its official currency.

- The use of English and Cantonese as official languages shows the region's separate cultural identity from the rest of China, where Mandarin is the language of administration.
- Its own tourism authority for marketing and promotion and the development of products and experiences – The Hong Kong Tourism Board (HKTB) (http://www.discoverhongkong.com).

Most of Hong Kong's commercial growth has taken place since 1950 due to a massive influx of refugees from the PRC, liberal tax laws, and its geographical location as the focus of air and shipping routes. The SAR consists of a dozen islands at the mouth of the Pearl River, the peninsula of Kowloon, and the New Territories on the mainland. These are linked by an efficient transport system, including the famous Star Ferry (http://www.starferry.com.hk/en/), road tunnels, and the Mass Transit Railway (MTR) (http://www.mtr.com.hk), Hong Kong's underground railway network, which carries more passengers, more efficiently, than its London counterpart. The high levels of air pollution at street level and the humidity that prevails for most of the year explain the widespread use of travellators and elevated walkways in this high-rise city.

Hong Kong is one of Asia's major destinations and a base and port of call for ocean cruises. The availability of charter flights and a well-developed business travel market have encouraged inbound tourism. This provides most revenue for Cathay Pacific (https://www.cathaypacific.com), one of the leading airlines in the East Asia-Pacific region. The new international airport at Chep Lap Kok has enhanced the importance of Hong Kong, as a very restricted site had handicapped its predecessor – Kai Tak.

In 2019, Hong Kong attracted over 94 million visitors, of which over 75 per cent are from mainland China. The United States and Europe between them accounted for only 8 per cent of the market. Tourism is the second largest foreign exchange earner, but Hong Kong faces increasing competition from Macau and the Shenzhen Enterprise Zone. Rising educational and living standards, combined with urban pressures, also make Hong Kong an important generator of tourism to the rest of the East Asia-Pacific region and the United States. The challenge for the HKTB is to entice foreign tourists to stay longer and spend more and to persuade residents to take more weekend breaks and day trips within the SAR. These include visits to rural communities in the New Territories and the promotion of nature-based excursions. The government is committed to sustainable tourism, with some 40 per cent of the SAR designated as country parks, providing a much-needed recreation resource. However, most of the beaches, such as Repulse Bay are overcrowded on summer weekends and both airline and hotel capacities are reaching ceilings of development. Air and marine pollution continue to be serious problems, and Hong Kong is some way from meriting its name, which means 'Fragrant Harbour'.

For the foreign visitors, Hong Kong is a unique blend of Western business culture and Eastern traditions, such as *feng shui* in hotel and office developments and *tai chi* as a popular form of recreation. There is a great variety of attractions, which include:

- Shopping for consumer goods and Chinese items such as jade.
- The *sampans* and floating restaurants of Aberdeen.

- Museums and galleries include the Hong Kong Museum of Art, M+, a museum of contemporary art, and the Hong Kong Palace Museum.
- Themed attractions such as Ocean Park (https://www.oceanpark.com.hk/en), Hong Kong Disneyland Resort (www.hongkongdisneyland.com), Monopoly Dreams and the Space Museum.
- The outlying islands with their temples and peaceful countryside, provide relief from the hectic pace of urban Hong Kong.

Macau

The Special Administrative Region of Macau lies 120 kilometres to the west of Hong Kong, consisting of the city of Macau and the tiny islands of Taipa and Coloane. The Cotai Strip now links these with major new casinos and resort hotels opening to rival Las Vegas. Some 85 per cent of Macau's visitors are from mainland China (where there is a huge suppressed demand for gambling) and Hong Kong. Western tourists are more likely to be attracted to old Macau, which has preserved much of its Portuguese colonial heritage and a blend of Chinese and Mediterranean culture. Event attractions include the Grand Prix motor race (modelled on that of Monaco). Although Macau now has its international airport, the majority of visitors are short-stay, arriving by fast ferry or the 55-kilometre-long Hong Kong-Zhuhai-Macau Bridge and Tunnel System (HZMB) (www.hzmb.gov.hk) from Hong Kong.

CASE STUDY 21.4
TIBET: THE CULTURAL IMPACT OF CHINESE TOURISM

In 2007, anti-Chinese riots in Lhasa brought Tibet and its spiritual leader in exile, the Dalai Lama under the international spotlight. As a destination, Tibet is unique for these reasons:

- It is the highest and most extensive plateau on Earth, mostly above 5,000 metres altitude, at the upper limits of human habitation. Lhasa, situated in a deep valley at a relatively modest altitude of 3,700 metres is one of the world's highest cities.
- The region is hemmed in by even higher mountains, which made it virtually inaccessible in the past. This physical seclusion produced a civilisation based on a distinctive form of Buddhism. Until the Chinese government asserted control in 1951, Tibet was a closed society ruled by a theocracy of monks, with its people living in medieval conditions. The importance of religion in everyday life, as shown by prayer flags and red-robed monks, is an integral part of the country's appeal to Western visitors who often perceive it to be the mystical 'Shangri-La' of legend.

Given the widespread concern about the impact of Western tourism on local cultures, it is worth pointing out that only a small minority of the millions of visitors to the

Tibetan Autonomous Region (TAR) are foreign tourists, and they have to travel in supervised groups. However, the Chinese government are now promoting and developing tourism in Tibetan areas after decades of restricting access by both Han Chinese and foreign visitors alike. Chinese tourists are attracted in increasing numbers despite the negative way that the Han Chinese have long regarded Tibetans as a people.

Improved air transport, including three new airports and the railway linking Lhasa to Beijing, is part of the Chinese government's strategy to bind Tibet more closely to the national economy. However, there are few urban centres and the country has only a rudimentary road network. As a result, tourism is focussed on Lhasa, which has as its showpiece attraction the Potala Palace (https://whc.unesco.org/en/list/707), the former residence of the Dalai Lama. In its application to UNESCO for the Potala to be given World Heritage status, the Chinese government declared the monument to be an achievement of 'the peoples of China', downplaying its significance as a symbol of Tibetan cultural identity. In contravention of international guidelines for conserving historic areas, the authorities have redeveloped an adjoining district, replacing many small Tibetan-owned shops with a museum and public square. A number of monasteries have indeed been restored by the Chinese government, out of many that were closed and pillaged by Chinese Red Guards during Mao's Cultural Revolution. These include the Jokhang Temple, one of the holiest places of Tibetan Buddhism, where devout pilgrims intermingle with Chinese package tourists seeking a photo opportunity, who are seemingly unaware of the significance of the religious ceremonies. A growing number of young, independent Chinese tourists now use the small hotels and cafes that initially catered for Western backpackers. Many of these, like their Western peers, perceive the traditional culture of Tibet to be exotic and having spiritual qualities rather than regarding it as 'primitive' or 'superstitious'.

The economic development of Tibet has been accompanied by a massive influx of Han Chinese immigrants who increasingly dominate business opportunities, including the tourism sector, and thus accelerate the process of cultural change.

Taiwan

Taiwan has a population of around 24 million, occupying a largely mountainous island. Nevertheless, with an economy based mainly on its human resources and high technology, Taiwan claims to be regarded as the 'Silicon Valley of Asia'.

In 1949, following the Communist victory on the mainland, the supporters of the Nationalist government of Chiang Kai Shek retreated to the island known in the West as Formosa. Here, they established the regime which regards itself as the legitimate Republic of China in opposition to the PRC in Beijing, which in turn regards Taiwan as a province of China. The islands of Quemoy (Kinmen) and Matsu, close to the Chinese mainland became potential flashpoints during the Cold War. Since the 1990s there have been moves towards eventual re-unification, including the restoration of air and sea links and the relaxation of visa controls. In 2008, direct flights between Taipei and Beijing were inaugurated, resulting in an influx of tourists from the PRC.

The demand for tourism

Domestic and outbound tourism

In 1987, the previous restrictions on foreign travel were lifted as part of the government's transition towards democracy. Taiwan is one of the most successful Asian economies, with a well-educated population with the means and motivation to visit a wide range of overseas destinations. The country's diplomatic isolation has had little effect on the volume of outbound travel, which accounted for over 17 million trips in 2019. The Taiwanese also make around 180 million domestic trips annually.

Inbound tourism

In 2019, 12 million tourist arrivals were recorded, the majority coming from South Korea, Japan, the PRC and relatively few, other than business travellers, from Western countries.

The supply side of tourism

Transport

Taiwan has a comprehensive transport system. Taipei is the hub for China Airlines and EVA Air, while the main cities are connected by a high-speed rail network. Although car ownership is high, bus services reach most attractions, including rural communities in the central highlands.

Organisation

The Tourism Bureau of the Ministry of Transportation (https://eng.taiwan.net.tw/) promotes Taiwan abroad. The main tourist markets are the PRC, Japan (for golfing holidays) and Southeast Asian countries.

Tourism resources

The capital, Taipei, is a major business destination but has less appeal to leisure tourists apart from shopping opportunities for a wide range of electronic goods and a number of museums displaying Chinese art treasures from the former imperial capital. Taiwan has a lifestyle where Buddhism and ancient Chinese tradition co-exist with modernity and which is arguably less materialistic than the PRC. Visitors are attracted by the island's sub-tropical climate and its mountain and coastal scenery, much of which is protected in several national parks. The resources for tourism include:

*   The Taroko Gorge (https://www.taroko.gov.tw/en), on the East-West Highway crossing the island.
*   Sun Moon Lake (https://www.sunmoonlake.gov.tw/en), a favourite resort for Taiwanese holidaymakers.
*   The beaches of the east coast and offshore islands.

- The numerous hot springs that are a feature of the island's geology and which were developed as resorts by the Japanese during their occupation of Taiwan (1895–1945).
- The island's indigenous tribes now account for only 5 per cent of the population, but their tribal traditions are increasingly valued as a cultural resource.

South Korea (Republic of Korea)

The setting for tourism

Korea occupies a mountainous peninsula between China and the Sea of Japan. After centuries as an independent kingdom under the Chosun dynasty, which tried to isolate the country from foreign influences, in 1910 it became a colony of Japan. This situation lasted until Japan's defeat in 1945. Since the Second World War, the country has been divided between the Communist North and South Korea, which has become a major industrial power under a free market economy. Since the end of the Korean War (1950–1953), an uneasy stand-off persisted between North and South long after the ending of the Cold War elsewhere. In fact, Seoul, the capital of South Korea, lies only 60 kilometres from the demilitarised zone (DMZ) – in reality a heavily fortified border - that separates the two regimes. Since 2000, the two Koreas have begun a process of rapprochement. However, re-unification would seem to be a long way off, despite the Singapore summit meeting in 2018 between the US President and the leader of North Korea.

After emerging from the devastation of the Korean War, South Korea experienced an 'economic miracle' even more spectacular than Japan. Here, the business conglomerates known as *chaebol*, of which Samsung is the best known, have played a leading role. However, these have been criticised for lacking the flexibility to meet new challenges. The 1997 financial crisis badly affected the banking sector, but the government responded swiftly by reforming the economy to concentrate on advanced technology, harnessing the skills and strong work ethic of a highly educated population. At the same time, it allowed more democratic freedoms, which had been severely restricted by decades of military rule. This has resulted in a release of creative energy in the arts to the extent that South Korea, historically a recipient of culture from China, Japan, and the United States, is now a trend-setter in the fields of fashion, popular music (K-pop), and the media for other countries in East Asia, as well as exporting high quality manufactured goods to the rest of the world.

The demand for tourism

Domestic and outbound tourism

With well over 50 million inhabitants in an area slightly larger than Scotland, South Korea is one of the world's most densely populated and urbanised countries. In 2004, the five-day working week was introduced, and the travel propensity of the population now exceeds 70 per cent. As you might expect from the world's most 'wired-up' society, cyber-competitions attract as much national attention as baseball and other sports events in the country's stadiums. A high proportion of domestic trips are family visits to coastal resorts, Buddhist shrines, heritage attractions, and theme parks such as Everlands Festival World. The government has taken an active part in tourism development, creating a number of 'leisure cities' to relieve the pressure on the 'corridor' linking Seoul to Busan, the country's second city and busiest port.

Health and wellness tourism is an important feature of domestic demand, and Seoul is a major centre for cosmetic surgery in Asia. It is estimated that 20 per cent of the female population have undergone operations to achieve the 'ideal look' determined by a society which is still largely conformist.

The demand for outbound tourism was suppressed for decades after the Korean War in the interest of building up the national economy. In the late 1980s, restrictions on foreign travel, which had previously been limited to those on government or company business, were removed. South Korea soon became one of the significant tourism generators in the East Asia-Pacific region, with over 7 million departures annually. Fashion and associations with a popular movie often determine the choice of destination; for example 'Love in Prague' sparked an interest in the Czech Republic.

Inbound tourism

In 2019, over 15 million international arrivals were recorded. Most foreign visitors are from other East Asian countries, including China, Japan, Taiwan, and Hong Kong, who are mainly attracted by the entertainment scene and cultural attractions of Seoul. At the same time 'film tourism' also plays an important role. The popularity of *hallya* ('Korea Wave') culture in these countries, expressed in movies and soap operas, has even led the authorities to preserve specific film locations as visitor attractions. The United States is an important market, as it includes an estimated 2.5 million Korean expatriates and the large numbers of American veterans who have been stationed in South Korea. It would appear that Seoul ranks behind Tokyo and Beijing as a destination for European tourists, although it is not as expensive as Japan and provides less of a culture shock than China.

The supply side of tourism

Transport

South Korea has an efficient transport infrastructure, which includes Incheon and seven other international airports. There are two national airlines – KAL (https://www.korea-nair.com) and Asiana (https://flyasiana.com). High-speed trains (KTX) connect the major cities and successfully compete with domestic air services on the lucrative Seoul-Busan corridor route. Although car ownership is high, there is a nationwide network of bus services, along with rapid transit systems in the major cities.

Accommodation

The accommodation stock is also impressive, with most hotels providing the latest facilities in information technology. In contrast, tourists can experience staying in a Buddhist temple or a traditional Korean guesthouse.

Organisation

Since 2018, responsibility for tourism has come under the Ministry of Culture, Sports and Tourism. The Ministry has two main directorates – the Tourism Policy Bureau and the Tourism Industry Policy Bureau. Both work closely with the Korea Tourism Organization (KTO) (https://english.visitkorea.or.kr). The main impetus of the KTO was initially business tourism. Still, the 1988 Seoul Olympics, the Asian Games, and the 2002 FIFA World Cup provided the country with the opportunity to showcase its achievements and leisure tourism followed.

Tourism resources

Many tourists are attracted to *taekwondo*, a type of martial arts that is Korea's national sport. Seoul is a modern capital of almost 10 million people, which has preserved some of its heritage, such as the palaces that belonged to old Korea's last ruling dynasty. Other cultural attractions include the Leeum Museum of Art (https://www.leeum.org), sponsored by the Samsung corporation, and the Hyundai Gallery (http://galleryhyundai.com/en/). Seoul also has technology-based attractions, including a robot science museum.

Western tourists looking for ancient temples, craft villages and traditional landscapes may find that the Gyeongju National Park, which includes the former royal capital, has more to offer. Other destinations include:

- The port city of Busan, which is also a major holiday resort.
- Legoland Korea.
- The white sand beaches and volcanic landscapes of Cheju Island in the extreme south.
- The interior mountains, culminating in the Mount Sorak National Park (http://englis. knps.or.kr/). There are many hot spring resorts and ski centres that cater mainly for domestic demand, with a season lasting from November to April. The most important is Pyeonchang, which hosted the 2018 Winter Olympics.

North Korea (DPRK)

The distance between Seoul and Pyongyang, the capital of the People's Republic of North Korea, is only 250 kilometres. Still, the two cities are a world apart in terms of traffic, animation and the amenities of the twenty-first century. North Korea has discouraged international tourism, and only a few closely supervised tour groups from the West are allowed entry. Business travellers from China, North Korea's leading trading partner, provide the bulk of the demand for the country's hotels and limited facilities. Like all totalitarian states, tour sites extol the 'achievements' of the regime. The social controls operating under a hardline command economy minimise contact between North Koreans and tourists and also severely restrict domestic tourism. At the same time, the government effectively prevents outbound travel by withholding access to the Internet and exit visas. The growth of an unofficial parallel economy, pressure from China, and dialogue with the United States over its nuclear programme may yet reduce its self-imposed isolation.

Mongolia

Mongolia has more in common with Central Asia and Siberia than the Far East. The former 'Outer Mongolia' emerged from obscurity and moved from Communism to a free market economy during the 1990s following the collapse of the Soviet Union. The country's national hero is Genghis Khan, who in the thirteenth century conquered a vast swathe of Asia from the South China Sea to the Russian steppes. In more recent times this vast, sparsely populated and landlocked country has been overshadowed by its neighbours Russia and China. However, its people still retain much of the nomadic way of life and warrior traditions, such as displays of horsemanship, archery and wrestling. The climate is extreme, with temperatures ranging from –40°C in winter to +40°C in summer. Although the Gobi Desert and steppe landscapes are the dominant features, the Altai Mountains border the country to the north, and there are extensive forests around Lake Hovsgol, where the reindeer, rather than the horse or the camel, has defined the traditional lifestyle.

The Ministry of Environment and Tourism (https://zasag.mn) oversees the promotion and aims to attract more ecotourists from the West (https://zasag.mn/en/m/megd). Private tour companies compete with the state agency, with the result that international arrivals exceed half a million a year, with China as the main source of tourists. The hotel stock is concentrated in the capital, Ulan Bator, but alternative accommodation is available in *gers*, the portable structures of felted material traditionally used by the Mongol nomads.

Summary

- East Asia contains some of the world's most populous countries and countries at varying stages of development.
- The region is remote from the major tourist-generating countries of Europe and North America, but improved air transport is overcoming the friction of distance.
- Many countries are developing an inbound tourism industry as a source of foreign exchange and to provide jobs.
- Domestic tourism in many countries of the region is now as significant as international tourism and arguably has a great cultural impact on local host communities.
- Outbound tourism is also growing, mainly from Japan's established market and China's new market. Business travel is important throughout the region.
- Away from the more established tourist destinations, the infrastructure for tourism is of a comparatively low standard, though many countries are remedying the situation, mainly by improvements in airport facilities.
- Cultural tourism is of primary importance in the countries of the Far East, which have much to offer in the way of historic cities, temples, and landscapes.
- Cultural tourism is less significant in Southeast Asian countries where the climate favours winter sun beach tourism and where adventure travel and ecotourism increasingly play a significant role.

- Asian tourists view cultural attractions differently from Westerners, and there is less concern about 'authenticity' and staged performances.
- Although most countries in the region have national parks, more needs to be done to protect natural resources and wildlife from the pollution and excessive development that has occurred in China and some of Southeast Asian countries.
- Shopping is a major motivation for travel to and within the region, particularly for Singapore and Hong Kong.
- China, once the 'sleeping giant' of the region, has become a major economic player on the world stage and a significant force in global tourism.

Review questions

1. Evaluate the strengths and weaknesses of Japan as a destination for business and leisure tourism.
2. Discuss whether tourism can be regarded as a force for economic and social change in China and Southeast Asian countries.
3. Identify a USP and a potential niche market for tourism in the following destinations:

   - East Timor
   - Tibet
   - Mongolia

4. Explain the importance of transport in the development of tourism in the island nations of East Asia
5. Describe some of the natural disasters that have occurred recently in Japan and the countries of Southeast Asia, the response by the authorities, and the impact on tourism.

References

Graburn, N. (2008) Openings and limits: Domestic tourism in Japan, pp. 199–211, in Winter, T., Teo, P. and Chang, T.C. (eds.) *Asia on Tour: Exploring the Rise of Asian Tourism*, Routledge, London

Organization for Economic Co-operation and Development (annual) *Tourism Policy and International Tourism in OECD Member Countries*, OECD, Paris

https://www.unwto.org/tourism-data/unwto-tourism-dashboard

22 The tourism geography of Australasia

Learning objectives

After reading this chapter, you should be able to:

- Describe the major physical features and climates of Australia, New Zealand, and the islands of the South Pacific.
- Understand the economic and social background of Australia and New Zealand and how these influence tourism and travel patterns.
- Appreciate the impact of tourism on the region, particularly the islands of the South Pacific.
- Demonstrate a knowledge of the tourist regions, resorts, and business centres of Australia, New Zealand, and the islands.

DOI: 10.4324/9781003406853-27

Introduction

Australia, New Zealand, and the islands of the South Pacific form a separate geographical entity called Australasia. An alternative name – Oceania – is also appropriate as most of the constituent islands are insignificant in area compared with the vastness of the Pacific Ocean, which covers a quarter of the earth's surface and spans a distance of more than 12,000 kilometres from east to west at its widest extent. The only large land masses are:

- Australia – often called the 'island continent'.
- The eastern half of the island of New Guinea (the west is part of Indonesia).
- The two main islands of New Zealand.

The total population is small compared to neighbouring Southeast Asia – about 44 million – and there is generally less pressure on resources. Australia and New Zealand are economically, culturally and politically part of the developed Western world. Still, both countries play an important developmental role in the other countries in the South Pacific region. In the northern Pacific, the islands of Hawaii are geographically part of Polynesia, but they became the 50th state of the United States in 1959 and are therefore included in Chapter 23. Likewise in the southern Pacific, Easter Island is administratively part of Chile and is included in Chapter 25. The rest of Australasia is economically part of the developing world, consisting mainly of island mini-states with small populations and limited land resources. Most have become politically independent only since the 1960s, while some smaller islands are still governed by countries outside the region, namely France and the United States. Yet, despite their 'paradise' image, there has been civil unrest in the islands, particularly Fiji and the Solomons. With the ending of the Cold War, the islands are no longer supported by the defence industries of the Western powers and must become economically more self-sufficient. For this reason, tourism and the exploitation of the islands' potentially vast marine resources increasingly play a vital role.

The Pacific Asia Travel Association (PATA) (www.pata.org) represents all the countries in the region. There are prospects for considerable growth in tourism, as the region can offer generally favourable climates, unspoiled coastal and mountain scenery, and in the main, political stability. The market potential is certainly present with the Pacific Rim of Asia and North America as an area of impressive economic growth. Since the 1970s, Australia and New Zealand have loosened their ties to Britain and forged closer trade links with the United States and the other countries of the East Asia-Pacific region, notably Japan. This pattern of trade has resulted in a growing volume of air traffic across the Pacific, facilitated by long-range wide-bodied jets. Air transport now plays a vital role in the economy of all the countries in the region, and the peoples of Australasia are very aviation-minded. However, these Pacific destinations are still a long way from the major tourist-generating countries – particularly those of Europe – and are therefore vulnerable to downturns in travel caused by terrorism and international crises, climate change concern about long haul flights, as well as competition from more accessible parts of the world that can offer similar attractions.

The native peoples of Australasia suffered severely as a result of Western colonisation in the nineteenth century, losing most of their tribal lands and much of their culture in the process. This was particularly true of the Australian Aborigines, who became a small, marginalised minority. Since the 1970s, there has been a growing recognition of the value of indigenous arts, crafts and folklore as cultural resources, and native peoples not only take greater pride in their heritage but increasingly take an active role in the tourism industry.

Australia

Until the 1980s, Australia was unimportant as a holiday destination, with most visitors being business or VFR travellers. In the 1980s and 1990s, growth rates for inbound tourism accelerated to deliver arrivals exceeding 9 million a year by 2019. This has been partly due to the promotional efforts of both the government agency responsible for international marketing – Tourism Australia – and the Australian state governments. Their work has been aided by showcasing Australia for the 2000 Olympics and the Commonwealth Games in 2018 and competitive airfares. However, Australia's very strict lockdown policy in response to COVID-19 meant that arrivals fell to a quarter of a million in 2021. Tourism is now one of Australia's leading sources of foreign exchange, directly supporting around 500,000 jobs.

Australia is the only nation occupying a whole continent, with an area of 7.6 million square kilometres – comparable in size to the United States, but with only 7 per cent of its population. Since 1901, when the six former colonies united as the Commonwealth of Australia, the country has functioned under a federal system of government in which the states and the two territories – Northern Territory and Australian Capital Territory – enjoy much freedom to manage their own affairs, including the development and regulation of domestic tourism.

The setting for tourism

Physical features

Australia has great tourism potential, thanks to its warm sunny climates, unique wildlife, and natural features, as well as a coastline – over 36,000 kilometres in length – which includes some of the world's finest beaches and the largest coral reef. However, many of Australia's natural attractions are separated by vast distances, making tourism development in much of the continent problematic. Most of the Australian landmass has been worn down by aeons of erosion and, as a result, is relatively low-lying compared to other continents, with only a few mountain ranges and inselbergs – isolated rocky outcrops rising abruptly from the surrounding plains. More varied landscapes are to be found in the mountain system – known as the Great Dividing Range – which runs for 3,600 kilometres along the eastern margin of the continent, reaching its highest point – 2,200 metres – at Mount Kosciuszko. These mountain ranges separate the fertile coastal belt – where most of the cities and tourist facilities are located – from the interior. Australia can also claim to be the world's driest continent. Most of the outback – the vast, thinly populated bush country extending west of the River Darling - is desert or semi-desert, where the lakes shown on the map are usually expanses of salt and the rivers merely a succession of pools or *billabongs*.

Australia's most fascinating natural resources are the plants - mainly drought-resistant gums and wattles (eucalypts and acacias), resulting in very distinctive landscapes, and the marsupial animals, which are only native to the island continent. The koala, for example, is one of Australia's best known 'icons', but its habitat is increasingly under threat. Much of the natural heritage was devastated by the plants and animals introduced by nineteenth-century British settlers. In response, Australia has more than 2,000 protected natural areas, including national parks, testament to the unique flora and fauna of the continent. The World Heritage Sites designated by UNESCO in Australia are listed in Box 22.1.

BOX 22.1
WORLD HERITAGE SITES DESIGNATED BY UNESCO IN AUSTRALIA

Cultural sites

- Australian Convict Sites
- Budj Bin Cultural Landscape
- Royal Exhibition Building and Carlton Gardens, Melbourne
- Sydney Opera House

Natural sites

- The Wet Tropics of north Queensland, an area of virgin rainforest.
- Heard and McDonald Islands in the Southern Ocean.
- The Great Barrier Reef off the Queensland coast.
- Fraser Island – the world's largest sand island – also off the coast of Queensland.
- The Gondwana Rainforests (formerly the Central Eastern Rainforest Reserves) in Queensland.
- The Blue Mountains in New South Wales, much of which is true wilderness despite its proximity to Sydney.
- Lord Howe Island, situated 700 kilometres north-east of Sydney in the Tasman Sea, is a semi-tropical paradise for nature lovers.
- Shark Bay in Western Australia, noted for its marine life.
- The Riversleigh and Naracoorte fossil mammal sites, situated in Queensland and South Australia respectively.
- Macquarie Island, situated in the Southern Ocean, where the Earth's mantle is exposed.
- Ningaloo Coast in Western Australia, noted for its reef and biodiversity.
- Purnululu National Park in Western Australia is noted for its unique landforms.

Mixed sites (cultural and natural)

- Kakadu National Park in Northern Territory, an area of tropical wetland and savanna.
- Tasmanian wilderness, much of which is almost impenetrable temperate rainforest.
- Uluru-Tjuta National Park (Ayers Rock) in Northern Territory.
- Willandra Lakes in New South Wales, actually dry clay pans that hold evidence of aboriginal cultures.

Source: https://whc.unesco.org/en/states/parties/au

These landscapes provide great opportunities for tourism. Tourists can go 'bushwalking', prospect for gold or gemstones, go on whale or dolphin-watching trips, take part in four-wheel-drive vehicle safaris that allow visits to remoter areas away from the all-weather roads, or try adventure sports such as abseiling and white-water rafting. The Australians are leaders in minimising the environmental impact of these recreational activities, and there are a number of state and federal ecotourism strategies and awards for sustainable tourism practices.

The size of Australia and its geographical location in the Southern Hemisphere means that it experiences a wide range of climatic conditions without the prolonged winter cold typical of northern lands. Most of Australia, with the exception of Tasmania, lies within tropical or sub-tropical latitudes. The desert interior has a more extreme climate; in July and August pleasantly warm days are followed by nights with temperatures dropping below 0°C. The northernmost region of Australia around Darwin experiences a tropical monsoon type of climate with a rainy season known as 'the wet' between December and May, accompanied by high temperatures and humidity. The great majority of Australians live in the southeastern part of the country and enjoy a warm, temperate climate, which, in general, is ideal for outdoor recreation. Even so, summer temperatures often exceed 35°C due to winds from the desert interior. Australia is highly exposed to climate change, and this means that the risk of bushfires is increasing, threatening coastal communities and towns across the country. The impact on tourism is as yet unknown. Snowfall is rare, except in Tasmania and the southern sections of the Great Dividing Range, and even here, it cannot always be guaranteed to provide good skiing conditions during the Southern Hemisphere winter, which lasts from June to September. Perhaps the best climate is around Perth in Western Australia, where summers are dry but not excessively warm due to a constant sea breeze.

Cultural features

The population of Australia is almost 26 million, of which only 3 per cent are Aborigines. The boomerang-shaped coastal belt extending from Brisbane to Adelaide, while only accounting for 5 per cent of the area of the country, contains 80 per cent of its inhabitants. Until the 1980s, most Australians were the descendants of British and Irish settlers. Still, the population composition has changed with the influx of immigrants from southern and eastern Europe in the latter half of the twentieth century and, more recently, from Asian countries. In contrast to its outdoor image, the nation is highly urbanised, with almost a third of the population living in Sydney and Melbourne. The urban character of Australia's population has an important influence on the patterns of tourism which have developed. A developed and diversified economy means that Australians enjoy a high standard of living. Car ownership, for example, approaches North American levels, and the effects are seen in suburban sprawl around the major cities. Participation in outdoor activities is high by European standards. The most popular participant sports are tennis, swimming, sailing, and surfing. Sports facilities are excellent, boosted by the Sydney Olympics in 2000 and the Commonwealth Games in 2018, and spectator sports include football, cricket, and horseracing – epitomised by the Melbourne Cup. Gambling is also popular, with casinos and clubs producing considerable revenue and attracting foreign visitors, particularly from Asia.

CASE STUDY 22.1
THE ABORIGINAL HERITAGE: A NEGLECTED RESOURCE?

Only recently have white Australians recognised that the history of their country did not begin with Captain Cook, and the arrival of the First Fleet at Port Jackson in 1788. Aboriginal tribes had been living there for many thousands of years. The archaeological evidence suggests that their occupation even pre-dates the arrival of the Cro Magnon people in Europe during the last Ice Age. As hunter-gatherers they successfully adapted to a range of challenging environments, including tropical northern Queensland, the arid 'red centre' of Australia, and the dank rainforests of Tasmania. However, their long isolation from other cultures ensured that their level of technological development remained in the Stone Age, to be dismissed as primitive by the European settlers. The petroglyphs or rock art of the native Australians is not only comparable to the cave paintings of Ice Age Europe, but is a tradition preserved and added to by many generations until recent times. These paintings provide an invaluable record of how the Aborigines observed the natural world, including animals that have long been extinct. There are an estimated 100,000 rock shelters containing aboriginal art, although a systematic inventory has yet to be made. Some of the most significant of these sites are in the Arnhem Land region of Northern Territory and the Pilbarra region of Western Australia. Unlike European cave paintings, most sites are exposed to erosion, to which must be added damage through vandalism, urban development and mining activity. Many aboriginal communities have also lost their connection with this aspect of their heritage as a result of the demoralising impact of contact with Europeans.

Nevertheless, aboriginal arts and crafts are now increasingly appreciated as part of the Australian heritage, and a number of communities are participating in tourism in the following ways:

- As guides and trackers on eco-tours.
- By selling artwork based on traditional themes directly to tourists or through art dealers.
- By hosting cultural tours, which may include traditional dances. or
- By owning and operating heritage sites or tourism ventures.

The Jawyn people, who live around the Nimuluk Gorge, 300 kilometres south of Darwin, are one example of an aboriginal group that has directly benefited from tourism. In 1989 they won a land claim under the Aboriginal Land Rights Act, but instead of excluding outsiders, the community association embarked on a tourism project. The land was leased back to the Northern Territory government as a national park jointly managed by the community association and the territory's Parks and Wildlife Service. The project includes an interpretation programme, flight-seeing tours and private boat tours of the Nimuluk Gorge. An eco-lodge using natural materials and aboriginal artwork in its design aims to attract up-market tourists from Europe. The Nimuluk National Park is visited by around 270,000 people each year, most of whom stay in self-catering accommodation. The profits from the venture are primarily used to support training and employment in tourism for the young people of the Jawin community. The Nimuluk National Park is generally regarded as a model for cooperation between aboriginal peoples and governments throughout Australia.

Demand for tourism

Domestic tourism

Each year Australians take, on average, at least two pleasure trips involving a stay away from home, and travel has become an important element of discretionary spending, increasing travel propensities. The domestic market is significant simply because of the wide range of experiences on offer in the continent, and it is the mainstay of the tourism economy. Although only a small proportion of trips cross state boundaries, partly because of the distances involved, domestic travel has increased in the early years of this century as international travel has been depressed by world events. The deregulation of domestic airlines in the early 1990s led to lowering airfares and boosting the domestic industry. The majority of holidays are taken in December and January, mainly to the beach resorts between Sydney and north Queensland. During the winter months there is a smaller but much more concentrated migration to the semi-tropical beaches of Queensland, and large numbers also head for the ski slopes of the Australian Alps, while others seek the unspoiled desert scenery around Alice Springs.

Outbound tourism

Australia is the largest generator of international tourism in the Southern Hemisphere, with 11.6 million trips taken in 2019. Despite their distance from other destinations, Australians feel a strong need to explore other parts of the world. The majority of Australian tourists who travel abroad are residents of the two most prosperous states, New South Wales and Victoria, which between them contain over half the population. Despite the high costs involved, large numbers of Australians visit Europe on holidays extending over a few weeks, during which several countries may be visited. They include a high proportion of young people combining a European tour with work experience, some travelling overland from Singapore via India and the Middle East. Other popular destinations are the United States, including Hawaii, New Zealand and the Pacific islands such as Fiji, Vanuatu and New Caledonia. A glance at the world map will show that Australia is, in fact, much closer to Southeast Asia than it is to Europe or North America, with Indonesia being less than 1000 kilometres from Darwin. This accounts for the popularity of the beach resorts of Bali, Thailand and Malaysia.

Inbound tourism

- Only a small percentage of foreign visitors to Australia come on inclusive tours, and VFR tourism is decreasing in importance from Britain and Ireland as holiday tourism becomes more important. The main inbound markets for Australia are New Zealand, North America, the United Kingdom and Asia – particularly Japan. In the early years of the twenty-first century the Japanese and North American markets were affected by 9/11 and also by the collapse of Ansett, Australia's second airline, but they have largely recovered. The Japanese are predominantly in the younger age groups and are mainly attracted to the resorts of the Queensland coast. The Americans, on the other hand, are generally older with a high propensity to travel; they feel an affinity with the pioneering spirit of Australia and are most likely to take a touring holiday. A growing number of tourists come from China, Singapore, Hong Kong, and other Asian countries, and many of these are in the student category. Such has been the turnaround in the demand for tourism that Australia now runs a surplus on its travel account, and tropical destinations such as Cairns and the Whitsunday Islands are taking market share from places such as Fiji. However, Australia's strict lockdown policies in response to COVID-19 meant that demand for tourism was devastated in 2021 and 2022.

The supply side of tourism

The tourism industry in Australia caters in the main for the significant domestic demand, and until the 1980s, little attention was paid to the needs of foreign visitors. Choice was limited and service standards were indifferent, partly because of the egalitarian attitudes prevalent in the country. Change has come about mainly as a result of the influx of large numbers of immigrants from southern Europe and Asia. These 'New Australians' have expanded the range of entertainments and restaurants on offer in their adopted cities and greatly improved standards in Australia's hotels, of which there are over 6,000 in total.

Transport

The great majority of foreign visitors to Australia arrive in the international airports serving Sydney and Melbourne and relatively few travel beyond New South Wales or Victoria to take advantage of lower domestic fares. This is despite attempts to spread arrivals to other gateways such as Cairns – where Qantas' budget holiday airline Jetstar is based (www.jetstar.com). Deregulation of the domestic airlines in 1991 attracted new airlines to Australia, but none succeeded until the arrival of Virgin Blue (now Virgin Australia Airlines) (www.virginaustralia.com) and Jetstar in 2001. In that year, more services were developed, and air fares fell – such that by 2022 passenger numbers had reached 54 million. Airports across Australia are also being privatised and upgraded. In contrast, surface transport in such a vast, sparsely populated country can be problematic; for example, travel across the continent from Perth to Sydney (3,300 kilometres) involves a two-hour time change and a journey by train or bus lasting three days. Despite its length (almost 41,000 kilometres), the Australian rail system is not a viable alternative to flying as the network is incomplete and interrupted by changes in gauge at state boundaries. An exception is the *Indian Pacific Express* which allows direct travel from Sydney to Perth. Dedicated rail services for tourism are also being developed, including the *Great South Pacific Express* between Sydney and Cairns and *The Ghan* between Adelaide and Darwin.

Organisation

Each state has a tourism marketing agency, and most also have a government tourism department. At the federal level, tourism began to be taken seriously in the early 1990s with several strategy initiatives and the appointment of a tourism minister to the cabinet. The federal Department of Foreign Affairs and Trade co-ordinates policy and action plans, while Tourism Australia (www.tourismaustralia.com) is responsible for tourism marketing internationally and is funded by the federal government with contributions from the tourism industry. Australia's long-term national visitor economy strategy THRIVE 2030 was launched in March 2022 to help the visitor economy rebuild and return to long-term sustainable growth.

Despite a very well organised tourism sector at both state and federal levels, apart from some significant destinations – Sydney, Melbourne and the Gold Coast – the tourism organisation is weak at the local level.

Tourism resources

New South Wales

Australia's most populous state accounts for half of all trips by international visitors. Tourism in New South Wales is dominated by its capital, Sydney. The city has developed around one of the world's finest harbours, and the beaches of the Pacific are within easy reach by hydrofoil or ferry. Sydney's attractions include:

- The famous suspension bridge across the harbour, which visitors can now ascend.
- Harbour-side attractions such as the Sydney Opera House (www.sydneyoperahouse. com), the ferry terminal at Circular Quay, shopping, restaurants and hotels on the

waterfront and revitalised areas such as 'The Rocks', with art galleries and specialist shopping.

- Darling Harbour has been revitalised with Sealife Sydney Aquarium (www.syd-neyaquarium.com.au), the Maritime and Powerhouse Museums, and an IMAX Cinema.
- Around the harbour are heritage sites and buildings such as Fort Dennison and Man-ley's Quarantine Station, where emigrants first landed, now converted into a hotel (www.qstation.com.au).
- The city has many cultural attractions such as the Art Gallery of New South Wales (www.artgallery.nsw.gov.au) and a range of museums.
- Districts such as Paddington and Kings Cross with their distinctive lifestyles.

The best known of Sydney's beaches is Bondi, with superb surfing conditions. Still, since the strong tidal surges can be dangerous, many families prefer the more sheltered beaches of Port Jackson or the small seaside resort of Manly with its Oceanworld attraction. Sydney's hosting of the 2000 Olympics gave tourism a significant boost and involved building 14 new hotels, improving the transport infrastructure and providing new sports facilities.
Recreational areas within easy reach of the city include:

- The Snowy Mountains with ski resorts such as Thredbo and Perisher.
- The gorges of the Hawkesbury River.
- The Hunter Valley vineyards.
- The Blue Mountains, a scenic area of hard limestone features such as the Jenolan Caves, forested ridges, deep valleys and waterfalls. Cable cars and a funicular railway provide access from the resort of Katoomba to a variety of viewpoints.

From Sydney a scenic coastal route passes north through resorts such as Coffs Harbour, Port Stephens, Port Macquarie, Byron Bay (a famous surfing beach) and the rainforest in the Dorrigo National Park.

Queensland

This largely tropical state is predominantly a destination for beach tourism, accounting for a quarter of overnight stays by foreign visitors. The area 50 kilometres south of Brisbane, known as the **Gold Coast**, is one of the most popular holiday regions for Australians but also caters for international visitors, particularly the Japanese. The coast is a highly developed strip of resorts, 70 kilometres in length, with Surfer's Paradise at its heart. Much of the development is badly planned and commercialised with many high-rise hotels, and parts of the area need revitalisation. The Gold Coast is the setting for both sporting events and a number of major theme parks reminiscent of Florida, namely:

- Seaworld (https://seaworld.com.au)
- Warner Brothers Movie World (https://movieworld.com.au)
- Paradise Country (https://paradisecountry.com.au)

- Wet'n Wild waterpark (https://wetnwild.com.au)
- Dreamworld (https://www.dreamworld.com.au), a Disney-type park.

Lamington National Park in the hinterland of the Gold Coast is well known for its birdlife.

Brisbane, the state capital, received a boost to tourism in 1988 by hosting the Expo, and the site has been redeveloped as the Southbank Parklands - a cultural and park area on the south bank of the Brisbane River. The city has a spectacular setting on the river where *CityCat* catamarans ferry visitors and commuters, offering various cultural venues, museums, and galleries. The city is set to host the Olympic Games in 2032.

Near the coast of Brisbane is Fraser Island, the world's largest barrier island composed of sand deposits. Other offshore islands are recreational areas for Queenslanders and good locations for dolphin and whale watching. To the north of Brisbane, the **Sunshine Coast** has excellent beaches stretching from Caloundra to Rainbow Beach and a theme park – Aussie World (https://aussieworld.com.au). One resort, Noosa Heads, has specialised in fine dining. In the hinterland are the Noosa and Cooloola national parks.

CASE STUDY 22.2
THE GREAT BARRIER REEF

One of Australia's unique tourist attractions, visited by over 24 million people annually, the Great Barrier Reef begins 350 kilometres north of Brisbane and extends north-wards for 2,000 kilometres to Cape York. It consists of about 2000 individual reefs, which provide a habitat for 350 species of hard corals, 1,500 fish species, and 240 bird species. It is designated as a marine park and is managed by the Great Barrier Reef Marine Park Authority (GBRMPA) (www.gbrmpa.gov.au) which shares responsibility with the state government of Queensland. The reef provides opportunities for scuba diving that are unequalled elsewhere, but there are fears that global warming and the 'crown of thorns' starfish are damaging the coral. Between the reef and the coast lies an enormous sheltered lagoon dotted with hundreds of islands. Some of these have been developed as exclusive holiday resorts with marinas, golf courses, and other sports facilities, while others cater more for campers. Examples include:

- Hamilton Island in the Whitsunday group has its own jetport with flights from Brisbane.
- Green Island specialises in eco-friendly tourism.
- Great Keppel Island is for young travellers.
- Bedarra specialises in honeymooners.

Pollution and over-fishing are problems on the more popular islands with consequent danger to the reef ecosystem; some areas have been designated as nature reserves to remedy this. The ports of the Queensland coast, notably Cairns, Townsville and

Port Douglas is the starting point of excursions to the reef and offshore islands by boat and helicopter.

Discussion point

Discuss the effectiveness of the various measures to protect the Great Barrier Reef, including zoning, the issue of permits, and management plans to control fishing and pollution, cope with the tourist influx, avoid conflicts between a diverse range of recreational activities, and not least, educate the public on conservation and sustainability issues.

In northern Queensland, Cairns is now an important international gateway, particularly for Asian visitors, and is a booming resort city offering a range of hotels and a casino. Inland sugar plantations, the rainforests of the Daintree National Park and the Atherton Tablelands provide the main interest away from the coastal resorts. The Kurunda Skyrail (www.skyrail.com.au) provides a 7.5-kilometre ride over the rainforest canopy, with the Tjapukai Aboriginal Cultural Park at its foot (www.tjapukai.com.au). From Cairns northwards to Cape York lie the excellent and largely deserted white beaches of the Marlin Coast; however, transport can be problematic in much of northern Queensland during the cyclone season, due to widespread flooding.

Victoria

Victoria experiences more variable weather conditions than other states of mainland Australia, with rural tourism playing a more important role. Melbourne rivals Sydney as the country's commercial capital but with a more conservative, less flamboyant lifestyle. The city has a wide range of retailing, restaurants, cultural and sporting attractions and is almost as cosmopolitan as Sydney, with large Italian and Greek communities. The capital of Victoria offers major sporting venues such as the Melbourne Cricket Ground (MCG) (https://www.mcg.org.au) and Albert Park, where the Australian Formula One Grand Prix is held; however, it is the Melbourne Cup – not only a sporting event but a fashion show – that attracts the most interest. The city has its beach resort at St Kilda and is conveniently placed for touring the vineyards of the Yarra River. Other tourist resources accessible from Melbourne include:

- The Victorian Alps, a popular region for hiking, skiing (in resorts such as Mount Buller) and white-water rafting.
- The Great Ocean Road drive along the picturesque Victoria coast with rock features such as the *Twelve Apostles*.
- Phillip Island with its burrowing penguins.
- The Gippsland Lake District.
- Reminders of Victoria's nineteenth-century mining heritage with 'living museums' at Ballarat (www.sovereignhill.com.au) and Bendigo re-creating the 1850s Gold Rush, and Beechworth, which is associated with Ned Kelly, Australia's most famous outlaw.
- Old-style steamboat trips on the Murray River, an important commercial waterway before the coming of the railways.

Australian Capital Territory

Canberra is the capital of Australia and is spaciously planned in a beautiful lakeland setting near the Snowy Mountains. It is a relatively small city and cannot compare in vitality to Sydney or Melbourne, but boasts major cultural attractions, including the National Gallery (https://nga.gov.au) and Museum (www.nma.gov.au), as well as national institutions such as the Australian Institute of Sport and Parliament House (www.aph.gov.au).

Tasmania

The small island state of Tasmania is separated from the mainland by the Bass Strait and accounts for only 3.5 per cent of overnight stays by foreign visitors in Australia. It can be reached by ferry or fast catamaran from Melbourne or by air to Launceston or Hobart. With its mild oceanic climate and perpetually green countryside, Tasmania contrasts with the rest of Australia and has flora and fauna – such as the Tasmanian Devil. The small resorts along the north coast (such as Stanley) are not unlike those of England's West Country and are particularly attractive for senior citizens escaping the summer heat and more hurried lifestyle on the mainland. Inland there is mountain and lake scenery in the Cradle Mountain - Lake St Clair National Park and the Cataract Gorge, a spectacular ravine popular for adventure sports. Ben Lomond is an important ski resort, with a season lasting from July to late September. The island's southwest receives the heaviest rainfall in Australia and is covered by barely explored rainforest. Once used for transporting minerals, the Tasmanian West Coast Wilderness Railway has been restored as a 30-kilometre journey through virgin wilderness (https://www.wcwr.com.au). The island has a range of heritage attractions such as the Port Arthur historic site, a reminder of Australia's most notorious penal settlement (https://portarthur.org.au).

Western Australia

The largest and most thinly populated of the states, Western Australia suffers as a destination due to its great distance from the more popular tourist regions of the east coast. As a result, it accounts for only 11 per cent of trips by foreign visitors. It is nevertheless developing markets based on ecotourism, adventure tourism and its mining heritage. Perth is a green, spacious city close to good surfing beaches (such as Scarborough and Margaret River) fronting the Indian Ocean. At the same time, Fremantle gained wide publicity by hosting the America's Cup yacht race and now has a maritime museum. The city has a variety of attractions including the Perth Mint (www.perthmint.com), Perth Cultural Centre (www.mra.wa.gov.au), and gemstone shopping in the suburbs. Perth is also a good base for exploring the Outback, including:

- The Punululu/Bungle Bungle National Park with its multi-coloured rock formations.
- The even more remote Kimberley region, over 2,000 kilometres north of Perth, a wilderness of sandstone gorges, transformed during the rainy season into a riot of

vegetation and cascading waterfalls. The El Questro wilderness park provides a variety of accommodations for tourists.
• Kalgoorlie and Coolgardie with their gold mining heritage.

Attractions along the coast include:

• Shark Bay which is renowned for its marine wildlife, including the dolphins of Monkey Mia that interact freely with visitors, but this situation could change if tourist numbers become excessive.
• Exmouth on the **Coral Coast** is the base for exploring the Ningaloo Reef.
• Broome, famous for its former pearl diving industry, and now an up-market beach resort.

South Australia

South Australia's attractions are less well known than those of NSW, Queensland or Victoria. Consequently, the state receives less spending from international tourists in the holiday and business categories. Over 75 per cent of the population live in and around the capital, Adelaide, which is promoted as the 'Festival City' with a range of event attractions. Adelaide is close to the coastal resort of Glenelg and the vineyards of the Clare and Barossa Valleys. Elsewhere in the state, attractions are dispersed, including the Eyre Peninsula, offering the rich marine resources of the Southern Ocean and the scenic Flinders Ranges. To the south, Kangaroo Island can be reached by ferry services and is noted for its coastal scenery and remarkable variety of wildlife. These resources are protected by a comprehensive plan for sustainable tourism, including the Flinders Chase National Park, tragically ravaged by bushfires in the summer of 2019–2020. The north of the state is desert country. Here, Lake Eyre, on the rare occasions it partially fills with water, is the main feature of interest. The opal mining town of Coober Pedy is located deep in the interior, where visitors can stay in the Desert Cave Hotel, built underground like most dwellings in this community to avoid the extreme summer heat (www.desertcave.com.au).

Northern Territory

The Stuart Highway links Australia's southern city of Adelaide with the northern city of Darwin. The only city of any size in the 'Top End', Darwin itself has a limited range of attractions but is used as a base for exploring the region's tourism resources. These include Australia's tropical northlands with game-rich grasslands and reserves on which the Australian aborigines continue their traditional lifestyle. In the Tiwi Islands, visitors can interact with the aborigines. A number of areas significant for tourism are accessible from Darwin:

• The Kakadu National Park is probably the most popular attraction in this region. It was the setting for the movie *Crocodile Dundee*, and is rich in the wildlife of tropical wetlands.

- Litchfield National Park is closer to Darwin, famous for wildlife, aborigine rock art and the Gagudju Crocodile Hotel – so-called because of its design.
- Arnhem Land is a large unspoiled wetland area under aborigine management, where a permit system strictly controls visitor numbers.

Further south lies the 'red heart' of Australia, an area of spinifex desert, salt lakes, and strange rock formations such as the Olgas (known as Kata Tjuta in the local aboriginal language) and the more famous Uluru, better known as Ayers Rock. The only town in the region, Alice Springs, offers a range of attractions such as:

- The Telegraph Station, a reminder of the city's pioneering role in communications (https://alicespringstelegraphstation.com.au).
- The Alice Springs Cultural Precinct showcasing the history of central Australia.
- The School of the Air Outback Radio Service.
- The base of the Flying Doctor Service.

CASE STUDY 22.3
ULURU: AN AUSTRALIAN NATIONAL ICON

Alice Springs owes its importance as a tourist centre more to its function as the gateway to the Uluru National Park and its prime attraction – the Rock, despite an intervening distance of 300 kilometres. The Rock has achieved internal recognition as an icon of Australia, due to its unique character as the world's largest monolith – it measures nine kilometres in circumference and 300 metres in height – and how the rock changes colour at sunrise and sunset. The Rock became much more accessible with the opening of an airport and purpose-built resort at Yulara in the 1980s. This provides a range of accommodation from budget camping to the five-star Ayers Rock Resort Hotel (www.ayersrockresort.com.au). Guided tours of the Rock and the surrounding area interpret aborigine culture and legends of the *Dreamtime*, and visitors can sample *bush tucker* – the natural foods of the outback. Nevertheless, the ever-growing number of visitors raises a number of issues regarding the future of tourism in the area, namely:

- **Sustainability** Burgeoning demand may exhaust groundwater supplies, already under pressure from the cattle industry. Although the Yulara resort is built to an aesthetically high standard, it is challenging to justify air conditioning and swimming pools as being compatible with ecotourism.
- **The potential for conflict between tourists and the host community** Uluru is a sacred site for the aboriginal people who were granted land rights to the area in 1984. For most tourists, it is a photo-opportunity and an objective to be climbed for some. Many Aborigines regard this as an act of desecration, and in 2019, the trail along the ridge to the summit was closed for good. Some non-indigenous Australians argue that Uluru, as a World Heritage Site and national park, should be free for everyone to enjoy.

New Zealand (Aotearoa)

Although New Zealand shares cultural similarities with Australia, including a love of sport and outdoor life and a certain informality of outlook, it is different in many other respects in terms of its physical geography and culture.

The setting for tourism

The Tasman Sea separates New Zealand from Australia, which is 1,900 kilometres wide and often stormy. New Zealand is scenically very different from its big neighbour, boasting volcanoes, glaciers and fjords among its natural attractions – the backdrop for filming the *Lord of the Rings* trilogy. The native flora and fauna are quite unlike that of Australia. Much of this, including the unique flightless birds, was threatened with extinction as a result of the introduction of new species by Europeans in the process of clearing 'the bush' for farmland. New Zealand was among the first countries to establish national parks on the American model to conserve what remained of the natural heritage. There is a widespread interest in environmental issues, exemplified by the opposition to the French nuclear testing in the Tuamotu Islands. New Zealand has also actively protected its extensive coastline and offshore waters with a system of marine reserves.

Physical features

Most of New Zealand is hilly or mountainous; the country's greatest tourist asset is the beauty and variety of its scenery. The two large islands that comprise New Zealand's bulk offer quite different environments. Much of the North Island consists of a volcanic plateau, while the South Island is dominated by a range of high fold mountains, the Southern Alps, which contain glaciers, snowfields, and a rugged, profoundly indented fjord coastline.

The climate of New Zealand favours the more active types of outdoor recreation, with its equable temperatures and pollution-free atmosphere. Although the islands enjoy more sunshine than the British Isles, sunshine is not guaranteed, and the range of latitude occupied by the islands means that while Auckland has a sub-tropical climate, at Invercargill and Stewart Island 1,600 kilometres further south the temperatures more closely resemble those experienced in the western islands of Scotland. This puts domestic tourism at a disadvantage compared to foreign destinations such as Australia's Gold Coast, Bali, and the islands of the Pacific. The mountains in the North and South Islands are high enough to receive heavy snowfalls, with the skiing season lasting from July through October.

Cultural features

New Zealand's cultural heritage includes an export-oriented pastoral economy and a nineteenth-century gold rush in Westland and Otago reminiscent of the Australian experience. However, New Zealand was colonised by the British from the outset with free settlers, in contrast to the convict origins of Australia's first British and Irish colonists. The indigenous Maori people had a highly developed, if warlike, culture derived from their homeland in Polynesia. They now account for some 17 per cent of the population and their cultural heritage, expressed in crafts and dances, forms an important ingredient in New Zealand's tourist appeal. The Maori have become more fully integrated into the mainstream national culture than the native peoples of Australia. However, unemployment and other social problems in Maori communities are higher than the national average.

Tourism demand

Domestic and outbound tourism

Three-quarters of New Zealand's population live in North Island, and of these, 40 per cent are concentrated in the country's largest city, Auckland. The standard of living is high, with motor vehicle ownership approaching Australian levels. The economy is still dependent on the export of primary products such as meat and wool, but the service sector, including tourism, is becoming increasingly important. Nevertheless, despite the distances that must be covered and the high cost of airfares, New Zealanders have a high propensity to travel abroad and have the same preferences regarding destinations as Australians. About half of all overseas visits are to Australia, with the encouragement of cheap airfares.

A much greater number of New Zealanders take annual summer holidays in their own country, mainly during the six weeks from mid-December to the end of January. Since this coincides with the peak period of arrival for foreign visitors, there is considerable pressure on hotel rooms in most resort areas. Motels are the accommodation most favoured by domestic holidaymakers, although caravanning, camping and youth hostelling are also popular. Many families also own or share a second home, a holiday cottage known as a 'bach' or 'crib', at the coast. In the past, most of these were basic, albeit brightly painted, corrugated iron structures. Still, thousands of 'designer' beaches have increased, and 'bach-hopping' using the Internet has become popular.

Inbound tourism

Tourism is a significant foreign exchange earner; international visitor arrivals in 2019 approached 4 million, compared to only 100,000 in 1970. This growth has been achieved despite the remoteness of this small island nation from the world's major trade routes and centres of population. Geographical isolation made it easier to enforce strict quarantine regulations during the COVID-19 pandemic, but this devastated the tourism sector, such that arrivals fell by over 90 per cent by 2021. Australia provides around 40 per cent of incoming tourists, followed by the United States and Canada, where many visitors are interested in hunting and fishing holidays. East Asian countries like China, Japan and South Korea are significant source markets. The Japanese are interested in New Zealand as a destination for skiing holidays, when the Northern Hemisphere season and other outdoor activities have ended. The UK market has stayed fairly constant at between 5 and

10 per cent of arrivals since the 1950s. But its composition has changed, with fewer British visitors falling into the VFR category, and an increasing number opting to purchase tailor-made holidays rather than inclusive tours. The choice of New Zealand as the host nation for the 2011 Rugby World Cup underlined the country's appeal to sport-lovers.

The supply side of tourism

Transport

The great majority of visitors to New Zealand arrive at the international airports serving Auckland (the busiest), Wellington and Christchurch. The mountainous topography has encouraged the widespread use of domestic air services connecting the main cities and the resort areas. Specially equipped light aircraft bring the Southern Alps within easy reach of tourists, while hiking trails and scenic mountain highways are used by the more adventurous. Rail transport is much less significant, except on a few scenic routes. A network of bus services provides access to most parts of the country, while the Wellington-Picton ferry service across Cook Strait is a vital link between the North and South Islands.

Auckland and Wellington are important gateways to the South Pacific region and major business travel centres.

Accommodation

Most tourism enterprises in New Zealand are small enterprises catering mainly for domestic demand. However, foreign visitors are often attracted to remote and sparsely populated rural areas, where it has been uneconomic for the private sector to develop resort facilities of international standard. The government previously intervened by financing the Tourist Hotel Corporation to operate quality hotels in scenic locations. Since the 1980s, international hotel chains have developed large hotels in the main resorts, catering mainly for the inclusive tour market, while luxurious lodges cater for the top end of the independent traveller market. Farm stays are also available throughout New Zealand, providing welcome income to the agricultural sector without government subsidies.

Organisation

The New Zealand government was one of the first to recognise the importance of tourism, setting up an official tourist organisation as far back as 1901. The Ministry of Business, Innovation and Enterprise (MBIE) is responsible for tourism. Tourism New Zealand (TNZ) is a public body which markets the country internationally. It has successfully promoted and developed the country's resources, and clever use of the islands as the setting for the *Lord of the Rings* films. Tourism New Zealand works closely with the private sector to attract the more adventurous type of tourist interested in scenery, meeting people and outdoor life. Marketing is focussed on 'the 100% Pure New Zealand' brand. New Zealand can offer the unique resource of uncrowded countryside, with only 5 million occupying an area comparable to the British Isles. Regional Tourist Organisations (RTOs) are essential, taking on a leadership role in development and marketing through destination management plans.

Tourism resources

New Zealand has an extensive resource base for sightseeing, ecotourism and adventure tourism, which includes some unusual, if not risky, pastimes such as jet-boating, para-penting, zorbing and bungee jumping, as well as sea kayaking and white-water rafting. Beach tourism, catering mainly for domestic demand, is well developed on the east coast of North Island, with resorts such as Hastings and Napier, and surfing is a popular activity. Auckland, Rotorua, and Wellington are the major tourist centres in **North Island**, catering for the bulk of the international demand.

- **Auckland**, sited between two fine harbours, is known as 'The City of Sails' and attracted the world's attention in the summer of 1999/2000 when it was the venue for the Americas Cup yacht race. New Zealand's largest city has a population of over 1.5 million, including many Polynesian immigrants from the islands of the South Pacific. Auckland is the centre for touring the sub-tropical north of the country with its kauri forests, surfing beaches and opportunities for game-fishing.
- **Rotorua** is situated in the volcanic plateau in the centre of North Island, which contains some of the world's most unusual scenery, including the Pohutu geyser, and Mount Tongariro – which is still active. Rotorua became a resort in the late nineteenth century when bathing in the hot springs was fashionable. It is also the centre of traditional Maori culture as interpreted by tourists. Although tourism employs Maori entertainers and craftsmen, most business enterprises are owned by *pakehas* (white New Zealanders), resulting in fewer economic benefits to local communities.
- **Wellington**, the capital of New Zealand, has a harbour setting reminiscent of San Francisco and a range of cultural attractions. The city is convenient for visiting the vineyards of the Marlborough Sounds area of South Island, New Plymouth with its rugby football museum, and the beaches of Hawkes Bay, where Napier is noted for its Art Deco architecture – the legacy of reconstruction following the 1931 earthquake. Egmont National Park surrounding volcanic Mount Taranaki (regarded as a sacred mountain by the Maori) is also within easy reach of Wellington.
 South Island was the setting for much of the filming of *Lord of the Rings*. The Mount Cook National Park boasts New Zealand's highest mountain and the Tasman Glacier, one of the largest in the Southern Hemisphere outside Antarctica. In the Westland National Park, glaciers flow almost to the sea amid dense evergreen forests. Ecotourists are particularly attracted to Fiordland, a barely explored wilderness of New Zealand's largest national park. One of its most spectacular features is Milford Sound, which can be reached by boat or overland on a popular hiking trail. Another vital centre for ecotourism is Kaikoura, a Maori community not far from Christchurch, which has become world famous for whale watching. In contrast to Rotorua, tourism enterprises are operated by local people, who claim exclusive use of marine resources in a bid to discourage competition by white New Zealanders. Other essential tourist centres include:
- **Christchurch** is the international gateway to the South Island and a garden city with a reputation as the most English city in New Zealand. It is now attempting to

Photo 22.1
Lyttleton Harbour, the port for Christchurch, New Zealand
Source: ©istockphoto.com/Daniel Thomson

diversify this image by promoting the scenic attractions and ski resorts of the Southern Alps, which are within easy reach. The city's Canterbury Museum (https://www.canterburymuseum.com) focusses on Antarctica, a reminder that Christchurch has been the point of departure for many expeditions to the 'white continent' (Photo 22.1). In 2010 and 2011, the city suffered a devastating earthquake which severely affected its tourism sector and infrastructure.

• **Queenstown** on Lake Wakatipu has two tourist seasons, as a ski resort in winter, and as a centre for mountain climbing, hiking, and a whole range of activity holidays in summer, including 'extreme sports' for adrenalin addicts. Queenstown also has a vibrant entertainment scene, attracting young people from all over New Zealand.

Chatham Islands

New Zealand includes a number of outlying islands. Of these, only the Chatham Islands, 800 kilometres east of Christchurch, are inhabited. As we mentioned in Chapter 5, they are located near the International Date Line with their own time zone, so its people claim to be 'the first to see the sunrise'. This remote community with its wildlife and indigenous Moriori heritage has been put on the tourist map thanks to the regional airline Air Chathams.

The Pacific Islands

The 'South Sea Islands' image of blue lagoons, palm-fringed coral beaches, lush scenery and hospitable islanders has a powerful appeal to would-be escapists from the industrialised societies of the West. So far, the great distances separating the Pacific islands from the tourist-generating countries have prevented the development of mass tourism, based on sun, sand, and sea, so collectively they only account for 0.15 per cent of world arrivals. The exceptions are Hawaii and, to a lesser extent, Fiji. There is little demand for domestic or outbound tourism, and most of the arrivals at airports in many islands are returning emigrants visiting their families.

Most Pacific islands have a tropical humid climate, characterised by abundant rainfall and intense solar radiation, with air and sea temperatures averaging well above 20°C throughout the year. Sea breezes mitigate the heat and humidity, especially in Polynesia, but tropical storms are frequent during the rainy season and can cause widespread damage. The larger islands are generally of volcanic origin, mountainous, and covered with luxuriant vegetation, with fringing coral reefs along the coast. The smaller islands are primarily coral atolls, low-lying and consisting of little more than a narrow strip of sand, almost enclosing what may be an extensive lagoon.

Inter-island distances are great compared to the Caribbean, making it difficult to visit more than a few countries in one itinerary. At the same time, the lack of inter-line agreements between the various national airlines adds to the cost of travel. In the past, shipping services connected the islands, but these have long been in decline. However, most governments in the region recognise that, given their limited financial resources, some degree of international cooperation is necessary. The Tourism Council of the South Pacific (SPTO) was established in 1983 and is vital in promoting most regional countries. (https://southpacificislands.travel). Investment for the development of facilities has to come mainly from external sources of capital, not only in the West but also increasingly in Asian countries such as Japan and South Korea. Hotel accommodation is generally of a high standard, designed in sympathy with the environment and local building traditions. The main problems are a lack of infrastructure, deplorable roads, and an insufficiently skilled local workforce.

Tourism and other aspects of Western consumer society have been a mixed blessing to the Pacific islands. Most islanders have lost their skills for self-sufficiency in agriculture and fishing and have come to rely heavily on imported foods, with a negative effect on dietary standards. The native culture had been under severe pressure for two centuries from Western missionaries, traders, and administrators imposing their own value systems. Governments in the region see tourism as almost their only chance of raising living standards and reducing the islands' dependence on world markets for their exports of copra and other products. Tourism has helped revive the islanders' folklore and provide new markets for their traditional handicrafts. However, much of the tourist spending fails to benefit the local economy as it does not stay on the islands. Most of the hotels are owned by foreign companies, and considerable imports of food and drink must be made to meet tourist requirements. Unless tourism development is carefully planned about carrying capacity, further damage is likely to be inflicted on the traditional culture of the islands and the fragile marine environment that is their primary resource. The latter is already under threat from the effects of climate change, with higher sea temperatures resulting in a massive die-off of corals throughout large areas of the Pacific. At the same time, low-lying atolls are exposed to rising sea levels and more frequent storm surges.

As with the Caribbean, it is a mistake to stereotype the Pacific islands as offering similar tourism products. We need to distinguish three culturally distinct regions, namely:

- **Micronesia** in the western Pacific, lying to the east of the Philippines.
- **Melanesia**, with its darker-skinned peoples, in the south-west Pacific.
- **Polynesia**, roughly forming a triangle drawn between Hawaii, Fiji, and Easter Island, covering a vast expanse in the centre of the Pacific Ocean.

Micronesia

The thousands of small islands that make up Micronesia total less than 3,000 square kilometres in area scattered over 8 million square kilometres of ocean. Except for the Marianas, which are volcanic and mountainous, most of the islands are coral atolls, with Kiribati claiming the world's largest atoll – Christmas Island. Following Japan's defeat in the Second World War, most of the region, except for the former British colonies of Kiribati and Tuvalu, was administered by the United States, until the islands gained independence in the early 1990s as four separate republics, namely:

- The Northern Marianas, including Saipan
- Palau
- The Federal Republic of Micronesia (formerly the Caroline Islands)
- The Marshall Islands, including Majuro

Micronesia's main tourism resources are the beaches and lagoons, which are ideal for sailing and diving. Palau boasts some of the world's best dive sites, including the Truk Lagoon, a major naval battle scene in the Second World War. The wrecks of numerous Japanese ships and aircraft have been transmuted with time into colourful artificial reefs.

Guam is the most developed tourism destination in Micronesia. It was acquired by the United States from Spain in 1898, continues to be administered as a US territory and, offering more attractions and facilities than the other islands, receives many tourists. Some of the other islands have important American military bases, and US aid is crucial in developing infrastructure projects such as airports and harbours. As a result, tourism has grown rapidly, although, as yet, it has made little impact on the more remote islands. The United States, Japan and South Korea provide the majority of tourists to Micronesia, some of whom are the families of ex-servicemen revisiting the battlefields of the Second World War.

Melanesia

Melanesia mainly consists of fairly large, mountainous and densely forested islands. Commercial logging has become a major earner of foreign exchange. Still, the rapid depletion of the forest cover could have a severe effect on the islands' wildlife, water supplies and offshore coral reefs. Melanesia includes the following destinations:

- **Papua-New Guinea** is the second largest country in Australasia, boasting its highest mountains, its largest area of rainforest and a great variety of wildlife, including the bird of paradise. In addition to the eastern half of New Guinea, it includes a number of other islands, notably New Britain, where Rabaul is a tourist centre of some significance. Until the 1930s thousands of native communities in the interior highlands were completely isolated from contact with the outside world. Pidgin-English, as elsewhere in the western Pacific, became the means of communication in a country where there are no less than 800 different tribal languages. With surface transport poor or non-existent, domestic air services play an essential role, and most tribes, especially those in the central highlands, have moved from the Stone Age to the Jet Age within a generation. There are few tourist facilities, but a number of tour circuits have been established based in the capital, Port Moresby, where the Kokoda Trail evokes memories of the Second World War and at Mount Hagen in the central highlands. The majority of foreign visitors to Papua-New Guinea and Melanesia generally come from Australia and New Zealand.

     The **Solomon Islands** to the east of New Guinea form part of the 'Pacific Ring of Fire'. Tourism is a fledgling industry, with only 30,000 arrivals in 2019, mainly visiting Guadalcanal and the capital Honiara. This is due to infrastructural problems, namely an inadequate road network, limited air connections and substandard inter-island ferry services. Nevertheless, the islands have considerable potential for diving, surfing and ecotourism.
- **Vanuatu** comprises the volcanic islands known before independence as the New Hebrides when they were ruled jointly by Britain and France. This unique arrangement did little to encourage the country's development, although the legacy of bilingualism has probably been an advantage for tourism. Vanuatu also earns considerable revenue from its status as a tax haven and flag of convenience. Tourist facilities have developed based on water sports and 'safaris' to native villages. Pentecost Island is celebrated for the ritual in which young tribesmen leap from towers with a jungle vine securing their ankles. It may be that bungee jumping, developed as a commercial activity in New Zealand, originated in Vanuatu.
- **New Caledonia** offers more sophisticated facilities and an attractive coastline, protected by an extensive barrier reef which is a World Heritage Site. The capital of this French overseas territory, Nouméa, has been styled with some exaggeration as 'the Paris of the Pacific', but there is unrest among the indigenous Kanaka community seeking greater autonomy from France. Nevertheless, New Caledonia attracts substantial numbers of tourists from Australia and Japan.

Polynesia

Polynesia arguably contains the most attractive islands of the Pacific, offering a climate in which malaria and other tropical diseases are largely absent, lush scenery, and a culture in which music, dance and seafaring play major roles. The various island groups are separated by vast expanses of ocean, but the Maohi (Polynesians) developed the double-hulled outrigger canoe and the navigation skills to make long voyages.

Tourism has developed most on those islands as staging points on the trans-Pacific air and shipping routes. This is particularly true of Hawaii and Fiji and, to a lesser extent, Tahiti and Samoa. At the other extreme, the most remote islands – such as Pitcairn (of *Mutiny on the Bounty* fame) lack airports and are served by very infrequent shipping services. Cruise ships call at an increasing number of Pacific islands, but this can be a mixed blessing. As in the Caribbean, the economic benefits of cruising compared to long-stay hotel tourism have been questioned, while the arrival of a thousand Western visitors at a time can cause considerable disruption to a small, unsophisticated island community.

Since their 'discovery' by European explorers such as Cook and Bougainville in the eighteenth century the islands of the South Pacific have captured the Western imagination. This is particularly true of Tahiti and the other islands that make up French Polynesia.

CASE STUDY 22.4
TAHITI: PARADISE LOST?

Five separate archipelagos spread out over 4 million square kilometres of ocean are usually promoted as 'Tahiti and her islands', after the largest and best known of these islands. This contains the capital, Papeete, and neighbouring Mooréa, most tourist accommodation. In contrast, the outlying Marquesas and Austral Islands are much less developed. French Polynesia received a degree of autonomy in 1977 and has its airline – Air Tahiti Nui – linking Papeete to Los Angeles, Tokyo, Honolulu, and Auckland (https://www.airtahitinui.com).

Tahiti's romantic image owes much to French writers and artists such as Pierre Loti and Gauguin. This was amplified by Hollywood in the twentieth century with 'South Pacific', based on a novel by Michener, and the various movie versions of 'Mutiny on the Bounty'. European sailors enjoyed the hospitality of the seemingly free-spirited islanders and readily adopted the Tahitian custom of tattooing. Despite the impression of carefree sensuality and simplicity, Tahitian society was hierarchical and governed by strict rules that gave the word 'taboo' to the English language. Human sacrifice was also occasionally practised at the outdoor temples known as *maraes*, the remains of which can still be seen, half overgrown by tropical vegetation.

Contact with Western civilisation had a devastating impact. The population was decimated by imported diseases, while European missionaries, supported by Tahiti's rulers, all but destroyed the traditional culture. However, in 1881, France annexed the islands, and the influence of Protestant missionaries has since been less evident than elsewhere in the South Pacific, with Bastille Day being used as a pretext for celebration. Since the 1950s there has been a solid movement to re-invent the traditional dances, which the missionaries had suppressed as immodest and immoral. These are showcased in the annual festival known as *heiva* which involves the whole population of French Polynesia, and which also features outrigger canoe races along with other traditional sports (www.heiva.org). Tahitians now take pride in their cultural heritage, and largely due to tourism, the weaving of *pareos* (sarongs) and other handicrafts has been encouraged.

Next to subsidies from the French government, tourism is the main pillar of the economy. Promotion is the responsibility of Tahiti Tourisme, which focusses on the islands' natural beauty. Forested mountain peaks, waterfalls and sheltered lagoons make up a landscape that provides a lush backdrop to the seemingly idyllic lifestyle of the islanders. Much of the tourist accommodation is in the form of *fare*, Polynesian-style bungalows built on stilts over the waters of a lagoon. Although the beach and water sports are the main attractions, golf, health and wellness tourism, and mountain trekking are also encouraged. Given the romantic image of islands such as Bora Bora, it is not surprising that weddings and honeymoons are the largest segment of the tourism market. The United States contributes a third of tourist arrivals, overtaking France, where most overnight stays are in the VFR category. Demand from other European countries is affected by the strength of the Pacific franc (CPF) which is pegged to the euro. In contrast, Japan, Australia, and New Zealand are much more significant as tourist markets.

Nevertheless, the average number of tourist arrivals is little more than 200,000 annually, with few repeat visitors. This is partly due to high aviation costs and a shortage of trained personnel. Although French Polynesia is an expensive destination, few hotels are profitable due to high labour costs. Tahiti should be agriculturally self-sufficient, but 85 per cent of foodstuffs are imported, along with other supplies for the hotel sector. Much of Papeete is marred by pollution and ramshackle development. This is a destination that has probably been 'over-hyped', where reality often fails to measure up to the image of a 'tropical paradise' populated by alluring *vahines*.

Fiji

As an ex-British colony, where rugby and cricket are the national sports, Fiji has a different appeal. The country consists of two large volcanic islands – Viti Levu and Vanua Levu – which contain most of the population and hundreds of small coral islands. As a nation, Fiji faces the problem of reconciling the aspirations of two distinct ethnic groups – the native Fijians and the descendants of Hindu immigrants from India, brought in under British rule to work the sugar plantations, who now dominate the commercial sector of the economy. Although ethnic tensions have contributed to civil unrest, resulting in temporary downturns in tourist arrivals, multi-culturalism is also one of Fiji's assets as a destination.

Viti Levu contains the capital, Suva – which is a major port of call for cruise ships and the hub for domestic air services to outlying islands. Nadi is one of the most important airports in the South Pacific, with the national airline Fiji Airways (www.fijiairways.com) providing direct flights to Los Angeles, Tokyo, and a number of cities in Australia and New Zealand. Tourism development is well established along the drier west coast of Viti Levu and the 'Coral Coast' to the south, which offers fine beaches and water sports facilities. Australians and New Zealanders have for long been the most important tourist markets, but visitors from the United States, Japan, Britain, and other EU countries are now growing in number. Many tourists, especially honeymooners, are seeking out the outlying islands, such as Wakaya, which offer tranquillity. Resort hotels vary from the luxurious, with spa and golf facilities, to those with impeccable 'green' credentials. All boast beaches of fine white sand and unpolluted seas offering ideal conditions for diving. Fiji also offers a number of cultural attractions, which include fire-walking and traditional war dances, but these tend to be of secondary importance compared to the beaches and duty-free shopping.

Samoa

The islands of **Samoa** are divided between the United States and an ex-British colony, now independent. American Samoa centres on the important harbour of Pago-Pago. Western Samoa offers a more traditional lifestyle, where much of the tourist accommodation is in the form of beach *fales* with an open verandah and thatched roof, operated by local families and located in village communities. Most tourist attractions, including waterfalls and the former home of the great writer Robert Louis Stevenson, are located on the island of Upolu.

Tonga

Tonga is unique as the only South Pacific country that has never been colonised by Europeans and has retained among other traditions a native monarchy which exercises considerable authority. Most visitors arrive by cruise ship at Nuku'alofa, but since the airport's expansion in the early 1990s, the number of long-stay tourists has been steadily increasing. Tonga provides opportunities for surfing and other water sports, and a mix of accommodation that includes resort villages and guest houses.

The Cook Islands and Niue

While these islands are self-governing, New Zealand is responsible for their defence and external affairs. The Cook Islands have encouraged tourism to the extent that it now dominates the economy and the native culture, particularly on the main island – Rarotonga – which is often visited by cruise ships. On the other hand, Niue is much less visited and has retained its traditions without the commercialisation that characterises Tahiti and other islands.

Summary

- Australasia is located mainly in the Southern Hemisphere, consisting of Australia, New Zealand and many relatively small islands separated by wide expanses of ocean.
- The development of air transport is now overcoming the friction of distance from the rest of the world, but the distance from the major tourist-generating countries of the Northern Hemisphere has prevented the region from becoming a major holiday destination.
- Australia and New Zealand belong to the affluent West, while most Pacific islands have more in common with the Third World developing countries.
- The tourism industries of Australia and New Zealand have primarily developed to satisfy demand from their own populations, and incoming tourism is not nearly as significant or as vital to the economy as it is to the smaller, poorer islands of the Pacific.
- Australasia is primarily a destination area for those travelling for recreational rather than cultural reasons, although ecotourism is of growing importance in most of these countries.
- The climates of Australasia are generally favourable for tourism, and there is less population pressure on available resources than is the case elsewhere. Environments such as the Australian outback, the Great Barrier Reef, the Southern Alps of New Zealand, and the atolls of the South Pacific, offer a range of opportunities for adventure holidays.
- Another factor favouring tourism development is the political stability prevailing in most of the region, creating good conditions for investment.

Assignments

1. Compare a specific area of the Australian outback with the Fiordland National Park in New Zealand as a destination for adventure tourism and ecotourism. You should consider factors such as accessibility, climate, the physical resources for different types of activity, and the available support facilities.
2. Compare the role of indigenous communities in tourism development in Australia, New Zealand, and French Polynesia. To what extent have they benefited from tourism?
3. The Sydney Opera House and Ayers Rock are widely recognised 'tourist icons' for Australia. Identify features that could similarly be used to promote the following destinations, giving reasons for your choice of icon:

    - French Polynesia
    - Fiji
    - Papua-New Guinea

4.   Explain why zoning and visitor management are necessary to protect vulnerable tourism resources, giving examples from Australia, New Zealand and the smaller oceanic islands.

Further reading

Organization for Economic Co-operation and Development (annual) *Tourism Policy and International Tourism in OECD Member Countries*, OECD, Paris

Turton, S. (2023) *Surviving the Climate Crisis: Australian Perspectives and Solutions*, CRC Press, Abingdon

https://www.unwto.org/tourism-data/unwto-tourism-dashboard

The Americas

23 The tourism geography of North America

Learning objectives

After reading this chapter, you should be able to:

- Describe the major physical regions of North America and understand their importance for tourism.
- Appreciate the scale and character of domestic tourism, especially in the United States.
- Understand the transport system in the United States and the impact on tourism.

DOI: 10.4324/9781003406853-29

- Describe the demand for tourism in the United States and Canada and the economic importance of the industry for both countries.
- Demonstrate knowledge of the tourist regions, resorts, business centres, and tourist attractions of North America.

Introduction

Although the UN World Tourism Organisation treats the Americas – North and South – as one region, the two continents need to be investigated separately in view of their extent and the striking differences between North and South America, particularly in terms of ecology and culture. In our definition, North America excludes Mexico, which we treat as part of Central America in Chapter 25, but includes Hawaii, which is one of the constituent states of the United States.

Both the United States and Canada boast a wealth of natural resources in a vast physical setting. Although the contribution of the native peoples is increasingly recognised, both countries are predominantly 'nations of immigrants' who have blended to produce a distinctly North American culture. The English language is dominant, despite being challenged by Spanish in Florida and the southwestern United States and French in parts of Canada, notably Québec. Both countries have developed democratic federal structures of government and legal systems largely inherited from Britain. They are informal and competitive in their outlook and share similar attitudes to business enterprise and the individual's freedom. This has favoured an innovative approach to leisure activities and tourism, especially in visitor management, marketing, and merchandising.

In 2021, North America received more than 13 per cent of the world's international tourist arrivals and accounted for one-third of the world's hotel capacity. From a visitor's point of view, the continent's size is important – extending over eight time zones and including most of the world's climates – but equally important is the rich variety of landforms and ecosystems. The western part of North America is dominated by high mountain chains, including the spectacular scenery of the Rockies and the Sierra Nevada. Near the eastern seaboard rise the forested Appalachians, much lower in altitude than the Rockies. Between these two mountain systems lie vast interior plains, drained by great rivers such as the Mississippi and its tributaries in the south, and by the St Lawrence, Athabasca, and Mackenzie in the north.

The climate of North America is largely determined by relief and tends to be more extreme than similar latitudes in Western Europe, with warmer summers and colder winters. In winter, Arctic winds penetrate far to the south, occasionally bringing freezing temperatures to the Gulf Coast and northern Florida. Yet in summer, most of the continent is open to tropical airstreams originating in the Gulf of Mexico, so that humidity tends to be high in the eastern half of the United States. Along the western seaboard, high mountain ranges intercept moisture-bearing winds from the Pacific Ocean, bringing heavy rainfall to coastal areas, which also experience much milder temperatures than the interior and eastern seaboard. Most of the western United States, however, has a dry climate due to its situation in the 'rain shadow' of the mountain barriers. The most important climatic divide is between the *Frostbelt*, consisting of Canada and the northern states of the United States, and the *Sunbelt* stretching from California to the Carolinas. This has far-reaching social and economic implications in that industry and population as well as tourism increasingly gravitates from the northern states, with their declining industries and cold winters, to more attractive environments in the south and west.

Compared to the rest of the world, North Americans have been profligate in their use of natural resources, favoured by relatively low energy costs. This has not encouraged sustainable forms of development, as shown by the dominance of the automobile and the prevalence of urban sprawl. Nevertheless, the United States and Canada are very much involved with issues of environmental protection. Despite the fact that the great majority of the population lives in cities, the unsettled wilderness is very much part of the national heritage in both countries, and determined efforts have been made to save areas of unique scenery from development. The United States was the first country in the world to designate a system of national parks, starting with Yellowstone in 1872 (https://www.nps.gov/yell); Banff (https://www.pc.gc.ca.pn-np/ab/banff) in the Canadian Rockies followed in 1885. Such areas are owned and managed by the federal government with the objectives of conservation and providing access to outdoor recreation. Most of the services required by tourists are, however operated by the private sector on a concession basis. The national parks are widely regarded as a major North American contribution to world tourism and a role model for good practice in both landscape and wildlife conservation and interpretation. However, national parks tend to be resource-oriented, and they are mostly located in areas distant from the major centres of the population. Closer to urban areas, this has led to the development of recreation areas that are more user-orientated, providing a range of facilities, such as the state parks in the United States and some of the provincial parks in Canada.

North America also offers a host of man-made attractions celebrating its achievements in science, technology and the arts. Canada and the United States are 'young nations' compared to those of Europe, while their cities are undergoing a continual process of renewal and reinvention so that historical buildings are few. Those who have survived tend to be associated with celebrities or important events in the process of nation-building. They have been carefully restored, or in some cases reconstructed, as heritage attractions, with costumed guides and craft workers interpreting the lifestyle of the past – Colonial Williamsburg (https://www.colonialwilliamsburg.com) in Virginia is an outstanding example. This, like many others, operates as a non-profit-making trust. Theme parks, on the other hand, along with a great number of smaller visitor attractions, are part of the much larger private sector of the tourism industry.

Big cities play a major role in the cultural life of the United States and Canada, with significant museums, theatres, and art galleries. There are 35 such 'metropolitan areas' with populations exceeding 1 million in the United States and another three in Canada. As population centres, they generate most of the demand for holiday travel, and as commercial centres, they attract a considerable amount of business travel. The *convention* (conference) industry plays an important role, with city governments competing to increase market share with ever-more impressive facilities. Sports events are of major significance, although soccer has only a limited following in the United States and Canada, compared to the huge interest in the Super Bowl (https://www.nfl.com/superbowl) and the World Series (http://eorldseries.com), not to mention basketball and ice hockey. The United States is the world's largest sports market and boasts many of the world's largest sporting venues.

However, from the viewpoint of European tourists, relatively few North American cities are attractive in themselves, and the street layout places obstacles to the free movement of pedestrians, as distinct from vehicles. In the United States 'the flight to the suburbs' by the middle class has left areas of dereliction and deprivation around the downtown area. The pattern of high-rise central business districts, commercial strip development along 'the highways, and low-density suburbs is repeated throughout the continent. A number of cities have attempted to regenerate their run-down inner city areas, with projects aimed at attracting leisure shoppers and tourists. Many visitors from Europe and Asia find the out-of-town shopping malls more appealing, although they are no longer as unique to North America as they were in the 1980s.

The United States

The period since 1918 has been called the 'American Century', during which the United States has consistently been one of the world's leading generators in international tourism, especially long-haul travel. With a wealth of natural resources and technical know-how, the United States boasts the world's largest economy, and since the collapse of the Soviet Union, it has become the only superpower. Although there is a tendency towards cultural homogeneity, regional differences persist. Each of the 50 constituent states is self-governing to a large extent, and Americans retain a strong attachment to their home state. US territory also extends beyond the North American continent to the islands of the Caribbean – specifically Puerto Rico and the US Virgin Islands – (see Chapter 24) and to the Pacific – Guam and American Samoa (which we described in Chapter 22).

The United States is also one of the world's leading destinations, with tourism accounting for 2.9 per cent of the gross domestic product, and employing 3.8 million people. In contrast to some other sectors of the economy, the tourism industry is made up largely of small and medium-sized enterprises, and these have contributed substantially to the high rate of economic growth and job creation that the country enjoys. In contrast to the United Kingdom, the industry is not dominated by large tour operators and has developed regionally over time, to serve a particular emigrant group such as Irish-Americans, for example.

The demand for tourism

Domestic tourism

The United States can offer an unrivalled range of natural attractions and opportunities for outdoor recreation, so it is not surprising that domestic tourism is many times larger than outbound tourism. Also, in the event of a recession, Americans are much more likely to forego a holiday trip than is the case in Europe. Some 30 per cent of American households do not take a holiday away from home, a 'staycation' in the true sense.

An important constraint on the demand for tourism is the limited leisure time available to most Americans of working age. The United States is an affluent but 'leisure poor' society compared to most European countries, and predictions made in the 1970s of a 'leisure boom' have not materialised. Since that decade productivity has trebled but the amount of leisure time has been reduced substantially over the same period, despite the introduction of flexible working hours. Thanks to 'downsizing' and the resulting job in-security Americans are working harder than before. For example:

- The average working week in the United States is over 40 hours, compared to 36 hours in the United Kingdom;
- Workers in the United States, on average, have 18 days of paid annual leave (includ-ing public holidays) compared to 37 days for workers in France;
- In the United States, the amount of leave is negotiated between the individual and his/her employer and is usually tied to the length of service with a particular com-pany. Moreover, the corporate culture at the workplace tends to discourage employ-ees from taking two weeks off at a time;
- Almost two-thirds of American workers take substantially less than their full leave entitlement.

This means that holidays for middle-income families tend increasingly to be in the form of short weekend breaks rather than long summer vacations. There continues to be a peak in demand for domestic holidays in July and August so beaches are generally deserted before Memorial Day in late May and after Labor Day in early September. Thanksgiving in late November is the time when family reunions, often necessitating long journeys by car or by air, are almost obligatory.

Outbound tourism

Almost half of the trips are to overseas destinations, and by 2019, it was estimated that around 37 per cent of Americans owned passports (compared to 80 per cent in the United Kingdom). National tourism organisations in Europe and elsewhere know that the US market is lucra-tive but volatile, notoriously sensitive to any hint of unrest in a particular region. Moreover, retired people generate a higher proportion of the demand for foreign travel than in Europe.

Foreign travel by Americans has grown steadily since the 1990s, despite a downturn in the aftermath of 9/11, to reach 93 million trips in 2019. Nevertheless, over half of all outbound tourism is to Canada and Mexico. Much of this is business travel, stimulated by the success of the North American Free Trade Agreement (NAFTA) to which the three countries belong. Trips to Canada tend to be short-stay and undertaken mainly by car, whereas visits to Mexico tend to be of longer duration and involve air travel to the des-tination. The major overseas destinations for American tourists are the United Kingdom, Italy, and Japan. The Caribbean attracts a large number of leisure tourists, including a major share of the growing cruise market.

Inbound tourism

Inbound tourism continued to grow steadily over the last two decades of the twentieth century, exceeding 50 million arrivals a year by 2000 but then falling back to 41 million as a result of 9/11. Tourism has since made a healthy recovery, to 79 million arrivals in 2019, half of whom came from overseas.

Canadians make up almost one-third of tourist arrivals, and many more day visitors. Mexico generates around a quarter of arrivals, but this tends to be a low-spend market, with a high volume of trips in the VFR category due to the close family ties with Mexican-Americans. Important overseas markets are Japan, South Korea, Brazil, and China. Among European countries, the United Kingdom is by far the most important generator of demand, followed by Germany, France, and Italy. The most popular destinations for foreign tourists are New York, California, and Florida, which account for almost 75 per cent of arrivals.

The supply side of tourism

The resource base for tourism

In the public sector, a number of organisations are involved with the supply of recreational resources at the federal level of government. These include:

- The National Park Service (NPS), the Fish & Wildlife Service, and the Bureau of Land Management, which come under the jurisdiction of the Department of the Interior.
- The Forest Service, which is part of the Department of Agriculture.

The NPS is responsible for a range of protected areas, variously designated as National Parks, National Recreation Areas, National Seashores, and National Monuments (which are usually specific sites rather than large areas). Most of the national parks are located in the western states and can be visited in practice only by private transport, making them inaccessible to the inner city populations of the north-east. Nevertheless, the number of visitors to the national parks trebled between 1960 and 1994, and is now over 31 million trips annually. This has caused the following problems:

- Popular attractions and campgrounds in the most visited parks regularly reach their capacity at peak holiday times.
- Traffic on access routes and roads within the parks has also risen considerably.
- Footpath erosion is severe in the most visited areas, while vegetation and wildlife have been disturbed by trail bikes, hiking off the designated trails and careless behaviour by campers.

Measures to curb car use in a few of the most popular parks, namely Yosemite, the Grand Canyon, and Zion, have met with some success, but the size and physical configuration of most national parks makes it difficult to implement 'park and ride' schemes and circular bus tours. Underfunding of the national park system is a matter of concern, given the mandate of the NPS that it should both promote outdoor recreation and protect nature.

The Forest Service is responsible for the National Forest system, where the emphasis is on multiple-use management, including grazing, watershed control and wildlife conservation as well as forestry and recreation. Some 17 per cent of National Forest land is classified as *wilderness areas* under a 1964 Act of Congress prohibiting road building and other development for the benefit of backpackers and canoeists seeking unspoiled nature and physical challenge.

The coastline of the United States provides a more accessible and popular resource, particularly the beaches of Southern California, the Gulf of Mexico, and the Eastern Seaboard from Cape Cod to Florida. Nevertheless, extensive residential development and a lack of public pathways can make access to many beaches problematic. Off the Atlantic coast is the world's longest series of *barrier islands*, acting as natural sand breakwaters that form parallel to a low-lying coastal plain. Miami Beach and Atlantic City are the best-known examples of resort development on such offshore islands. Unfortunately, these resources are threatened by massive population growth in coastal communities, over-development, pollution from effluents, rising sea levels, not to mention the occasional hurricane sweeping up from the Caribbean. Many coastal communities have built sea walls as protection from destructive waves, but these merely accelerate erosion elsewhere. Others, like Miami Beach, have called upon the US Army Corps of Engineers to carry out beach re-nourishment using sand dredged from other locations. However, the best long-term solution is for the state governments to introduce land use management regulations in the coastal zone.

CASE STUDY 23.1
THE RESPONSE OF THE NATIONAL PARK SERVICE TO CLIMATE CHANGE

American visitors to the national parks expect to see a landscape that has remained essentially unchanged over time. The NPS was created by Congress in 1916 with the mandate of leaving the landscape and wildlife in the parks 'unimpaired for the enjoyment of future generations'. This was interpreted by park managers as the preservation of natural attractions, along with the plants and animals that existed at the time Europeans first appeared on the scene. This ignored the impact of pre-Columbian Native Americans on ecosystems through, for example, their widespread use of fire.

From the 1980s onwards, scientists came to accept that environmental changes were taking place and that rather than resisting change, park managers might need to adapt. However, the notion of climate change due to human agency was regarded as controversial, with political implications that might affect federal funding.

National parks in various parts of the United States face the following challenges that can be attributed to climate change:

- Along the Atlantic coast the intensification of storm surges and the general rise in sea levels is causing widespread erosion and flooding. This is most evident in the barrier islands such as Assateague Island and Cape Hatteras, which are designated as National Seashores. In the past NPS managers resisted change, for example, by relocating a lighthouse on Cape Hatteras almost a kilometre inland. Lack of funds makes repeated restoration of other structures, bridges and car parks increasingly impractical, and alternatives have to be improvised.

- The vulnerability of the Florida Everglades to ecological changes as freshwater in these wetlands becomes increasingly brackish.
- The acidification of the ocean along the Pacific coast, affecting marine ecosystems.
- The retreat of the glaciers in the Rocky Mountains and the migration of wildlife to higher altitudes, which is most evident in the Glacier National Park.
- The vulnerability of protected species in California to prolonged periods of drought and the increased incidence of wildfires. This includes the sequoias of the Sierra Nevada and the Joshua trees of the desert.

The role of national park managers is increasingly to 'manage for continuous environmental change' rather than rigorously following the principles of conservation.

Theme parks and similar visitor attractions now account for over 375 million visitors annually and provide half a million jobs. Although its antecedents can be found in the amusement parks, seaside piers, and fairgrounds of nineteenth-century Europe, the theme park is an American invention and has reached its fullest expression in the United States. Old-style amusement parks such as New York's Coney Island found it challenging to compete with other forms of entertainment and are mainly places for young people to meet, rather than being regarded as suitable destinations for family outings. Theme parks fulfil this function and differ from old-style amusement parks in the following ways:

- Development is planned around a single theme, with the rides, shows, shopping and catering facilities promoted as a co-ordinated set of attractions.
- Location is all-important – they are market-oriented attractions. Theme parks are built between major cities and near motorway interchanges so that as large a population as possible lives within a 160-kilometre radius.
- There is an all-inclusive admission charge.
- Theme parks are imaginatively landscaped. Millions of dollars are spent on maintenance, upgrading facilities, and on new rides and shows using the latest technology.
- Theme parks are staffed by young people who are well-motivated and trained to provide a high standard of service.

Theme parks require massive capital investment and are therefore owned by large corporations with interests in television, the film industry, or – in the case of Busch Gardens, Florida – a major brewing company. The Disney theme parks are world-class destinations in their own right, and Walt Disney must certainly be regarded as one of the greatest innovators in leisure and tourism. In 1955, he opened his first theme park – Disneyland – at Anaheim, near Los Angeles, on a 60-hectare site developed around five themed areas. Disneyland's success encouraged a sprawl of development in its vicinity. To avoid repetition, the second theme park – Walt Disney World (WDW), was constructed on 1,000 hectares of swampland in central Florida, over which Disney had complete planning control. It is a self-contained destination with its own transport system, hotels, and facilities for various outdoor activities. Disney theme parks aim to insulate the visitor from the world of reality by means of:

- The Disney corporate ethos; staff are known as 'cast members'.
- The concepts of 'imagineering' and 'animatronics', using cutting edge of technology.
- A sophisticated infrastructure, concealed from the visitor and the use of non-polluting transport modes within the park.

The Disney theme parks provide a clean, safe, and wholesome environment for families, but some would argue that the experience is too sanitised and that too much control is exercised over visitors and staff.

In contrast to the large theme parks such as Six Flags and Disneyland, there are a vast number of small-town attractions, each striving to boost the local economy. Some showcase aspects of the American heritage, notably achievements in sport, industry, and entertainment, while others attempt to replicate the cultures of Europe and Asia in the New World. Many of these attractions lack authenticity or an appropriate setting. A number of communities have also re-invented themselves to attract heritage tourism. These include the 'Danish village' of Solvang (https://www.solvangusa.com) in California, Nauvoo (https://beautifulnauvoo.com/) in Illinois with its Mormon associations, and the Alpine theme town of Helen (https://www.helenga.org/) in Georgia. By the 1960s, this former gold mining and lumber town in the Appalachians was in poor shape economically, but thanks to the local business initiative, the buildings were remodelled and painted in Bavarian style, while event attractions such as 'Octoberfest' were introduced. As a result, Helen is now the most popular destination in Georgia after Atlanta and Savannah.

Transport

Transport in the United States is highly developed, as you might expect from a nation constantly on the move. The following characteristics are worth emphasising:

- The private car is the dominant transport mode for all types of journeys.
- Domestic air services are widely used.
- Public transport, except in some major cities, is poorly developed.

The United States has the highest car ownership in the world, with the number of motor vehicles in some states exceeding the resident population. Well over 80 per cent of holiday trips are taken by car. Although the internal combustion engine was not an American invention, the world's first car show was held in New York in 1900, and it was largely due to Henry Ford that ownership of an automobile was brought within reach of people on modest incomes. As a result, by 1930, there were 23 million cars registered in the United States, whereas in Europe, similar levels were not reached until the late 1950s. Demand from vehicle manufacturers and motorists led to much-needed road improvements, such as the legendary Route 66 from Chicago to Los Angeles. Scenic routes or *parkways*, such as the Skyline Drive in the Blue Ridge Mountains of Virginia, were designed in the 1930s to encourage sightseeing by car. From the late 1950s onwards, some of the older highways – including Route 66 – were superseded by the Interstate Highway system, financed largely by the federal government. This provided a nationwide motorway network – 78,000 kilometres in length – linking most of the major cities and resulted in a threefold increase in the number of kilometres travelled by car between 1950 and 1980. Motoring in the United States is subject to fewer inconveniences than elsewhere, and fuel costs are relatively low. However, the American love affair with the car has had an adverse environmental impact, including:

- Pollution – despite strict regulations on motor vehicle emissions. These measures have been rendered less effective by the growth in four-wheel drive sports utility vehicles (SUVs) since the 1990s.
- Visual blight – with large areas given over to parking lots.
- Urban sprawl – which in turn necessitates ever-lengthening journeys to work, shopping, and recreational facilities.

Since the early 1990s, even cities as wedded to cars as Los Angeles and Miami have realised that road building alone cannot solve traffic congestion, and they have invested heavily in rapid transit schemes.

Air transport accounts for some 8 per cent of domestic holiday trips, and most medium-sized towns in the United States have an airport within easy reach by car. Some 30 airports now serve as international gateways. Airfares are relatively cheap, largely due to competition between the airlines. After 1978, when the civil aviation industry was deregulated, routes were organised on a 'hub and spoke' system, with a few major airports handling the bulk of the traffic. As a result of deregulation, many small airlines came into service, but some old-established carriers failed to adjust to the new conditions. The largest casualty was undoubtedly Pan-Am, which had largely pioneered intercontinental air services before the Second World War. The airlines that have clearly emerged as front-runners include United (https://www.united.com), American (https://www.aa.com), and Delta (https://www.delta.com), while Denver, Chicago, Atlanta, and Dallas have developed as major hubs. A large number of regional carriers, often code-sharing with one of the major airlines, provide feeder services.

The Federal Aviation Administration (FAA) (https://www.faa.gov/), the agency responsible for the safety of air travel, came under scrutiny as a result of 9/11. A new agency, the Transport Security Administration (TSA) (https://www.tsa.gov/), now oversees airport security. Stricter controls are problematic given the vast scale of air travel in the United States. For example, on a typical day, there are 45,000 flights in US air space. There are also some 8,000 small airports and airfields that are used by charter airlines catering mainly for business executives.

Public transport by road and rail compares unfavourably with the situation in most other developed countries. The major bus company – Greyhound (https://www.greyhound.com/) – does provide an extensive network of intercity services, as well as inclusive tours and bargain fares for foreign tourists. Nevertheless, coach travel (in its British rather than American meaning) accounts for less than 3 per cent of the domestic market and is widely regarded as downmarket. The train provides a more stylish alternative. To a large extent, the railroad 'made America', but in the 1950s, passenger services declined due to competition from airlines and the private car. They might have disappeared altogether from the long-distance routes had not the federal government intervened in 1970 with the introduction of Amtrak (https://www.amtrak.com/), a semi-public corporation that operates passenger trains over the network of a dozen private railroad companies. Amtrak has upgraded rolling stock, in some cases introducing double-decker 'superliners' for scenic viewing. Historic routes have been revived, such as the 'Empire Builder', which takes 46 hours to cover the 3,500 kilometres from Chicago to Seattle. The introduction of high-speed trains is inhibited by the cost of upgrading track, some of which dates from the nineteenth century; also much of the network is single-track, with precedence given to freight trains. Amtrak has achieved the most success in the densely populated 'north-east corridor' linking Washington with Boston via Baltimore, Philadelphia, and New York City. This is by far the most important route, accounting for 50 per cent of Amtrak's revenue, and where *Acela Express* trains compete effectively with the airlines for the lucrative business market. Elsewhere in the United States, train services, where they exist, tend to be infrequent. This situation may change as Americans feel the impact of higher fuel costs, and become more aware of the safety and environmental issues posed by growing congestion on the highways, at airport terminals, and in the airways. For this reason, plans for a second high-speed corridor in California, linking San Diego with San Francisco, are under consideration. Congress has been reluctant to further subsidise Amtrak's investment programme, as politicians are inclined to take the short-term view of reducing public spending.

Accommodation

Americans have long demanded high standards of convenience in their accommodation, resulting in the concept of the hotel in holiday destinations as a 'resort', a self-contained leisure complex. Across North America, the supply of accommodation is closely linked to patterns of transport. In the largest cities, hotels are most numerous in the *downtown* areas or CBDs. Elsewhere, the distribution tends to be peripheral, with hotels clustering around an airport or located in the commercial strip developments fanning out along the main highways, alongside restaurants and other businesses. The first motels developed in the 1930s as family enterprises offering fairly basic accommodation. From the 1950s, following the example of the *Holiday Inns* chain (https://www.ihg.com/holidayinn/), the trend was to go more up-market with facilities such as swimming pools and towards standardisation of the product in terms of service and décor. Hotels themselves have become increasingly innovative, with such features as the atrium lobby pioneered by Regency Hyatt and the concept of theming, which is best seen in Las Vegas, to appeal to niche markets. Bed and breakfast in private homes is a growing sector, although it has a more up-market image than its British counterpart, particularly in New England, where much of the accommodation is in restored colonial buildings. Apartments in condominiums, campsites, and trailer parks for recreational vehicles are a major part of the accommodation sector.

Organisation

The promotion and development of tourism have generally been weak at the national level of government. This is primarily due to two factors:

- The belief in free enterprise with the minimum of government interference; and
- The division of responsibilities between the federal government in Washington and the state governments.

It was not until 1981 that the United States Travel and Tourism Administration (USTTA) was set up to co-ordinate federal government policies regarding tourism and to promote the country more effectively abroad. The demise of the USTTA meant that the United States entered the new millennium without an overall tourism strategy or tourist information service for the whole country. Following 9/11, the federal government reappraised the role of tourism. The National Travel and Tourism Office (NTTO) within the International Trade Administration of the US Department of Commerce is now in charge of tourism in the United States. It co-ordinates tourism statistics, and 'Brand USA' promotes inbound travel.

On the other hand, the states have some kind of official tourism organisation. For the most part, these are concerned with marketing, and few have policies on sustainable tourism development. At the local level, most cities and some counties have a convention and visitors bureau, although these vary considerably in their effectiveness. This situation has led a number of state governments to combine their resources to promote a particular region on the international stage.

The regional distribution of tourism resources

The North-East

The Northeastern states constitute the most densely populated and one of the most visited parts of the country, including the four major gateway cities of Boston, New York, Philadelphia, and Washington. The urbanised belt – 'Megalopolis' – extending from Boston to Washington contains well over 50 million inhabitants and has excellent transport facilities in the form of road, rail, and shuttle air services. In contrast, there are large areas of forested wilderness in the mountains of the northern Appalachians.

New England is probably the most interesting region in the United States from a historical standpoint. In the seventeenth century, it was occupied by English settlers who were Puritans seeking freedom to practice their religious beliefs. What came to be known as the 'Yankee' traits of hard work, thrift, and ingenuity, and the American belief in their country's 'exceptionalism', was forged in the struggle to wrest a livelihood from a harsh environment of cold winters and infertile soils. This explains the importance of the region's history of fishing, whaling, overseas trade, and manufacturing industry. New England played a crucial role in the struggle for independence from British rule in the 1770s, notably the 'Boston Tea Party' and the battle of Lexington. The region has a strong cultural tradition, as shown by the international reputation of its universities – particularly Yale, Harvard, and the Massachusetts Institute of Technology – and has produced many famous writers. Since the mid-nineteenth century, New England has become a multicultural society due to further immigration, particularly from Ireland and Italy.

The rural interior is noted for its forested mountains and picturesque villages of clapboard houses grouped around a wooden church; two of the most visited examples are Sturbridge and Pittsfield in western Massachusetts. Many of the farms have long been abandoned and are now used as weekend or summer retreats by city dwellers. In the fall (autumn), the brilliant foliage displays attract crowds of weekend visitors, particularly to the state of Vermont. During the snowy winters, skiing is a major activity, particularly at Bretton Woods and Mount Washington Valley in New Hampshire and Stowe in Vermont.

The coast is equally appealing. In the state of Maine, it is rugged, deeply indented, and backed by a sparsely populated hinterland of rivers and forests; sailing, fishing, and canoeing are popular activities. Further south, there are many fine beaches and a number of historic seaports. Tourists are particularly attracted to the following areas:

- The Cape Cod peninsula, with its extensive sand dunes. Summer resorts such as Hyannisport cater for wealthy second-home owners, while ferries connect to the islands of Nantucket and Martha's Vineyard. At Plymouth, there is a 'living museum' (https://www.plimoth.org) commemorating the original settlement of the Pilgrim Fathers in 1620.
- Newport, Rhode Island, was once the exclusive summer resort for America's millionaires. It is now a major yachting centre and a popular venue for music festivals.
- Salem is mainly visited because of its association with the witch trials of 1692, an example of Puritan intolerance.
- New Bedford and Mystic are historic seaports associated with the nineteenth-century whaling industry.
- Boston is a major North American city that has retained its compact character and mellow brick buildings, although these are often overshadowed by examples of modern architecture such as the Government Center. The 'Freedom Trail' commemorates Boston's role in the American struggle for independence.

The **Middle Atlantic Region** is less easily defined. Even in colonial times, it was settled by immigrants from a variety of origins, including English Quakers, Irish Catholics, Dutch, Germans, and Scandinavians. The mountainous interior, which forms part of the Appalachians, the beach resorts of Long Island, New Jersey, and the Delmarva Peninsula (Delaware, Maryland, and Virginia east of Chesapeake Bay) are mainly visited by domestic tourists. The attractions of most interest to foreign tourists are to be found in the big cities, for example:

- **New York** owes a great deal to its historic role as the major port of entry to the United States, with the advantages of a deepwater harbour and access via the Hudson River to the interior of North America. Until the 1960s, the Statue of Liberty was, for most immigrants and visitors, their first sight of the New World. It is the largest city in North America, with almost 24 million people living in the metropolitan area. The

terrorist attacks of 9/11 on the World Trade Center further highlighted its importance as one of the world's top ten destinations. Tourism is of major importance to
the city's economy, supporting around 375,000 jobs, almost 10 per cent of the total
employment. Although it is not an administrative capital, New York is the nation's
primary city in almost every other respect. It is, for example, the USA's leading financial centre and conference venue and also a major centre for fashion and the
arts. New York City boasts world-class cultural attractions such as the Metropolitan
Opera House (https://www.metopera.org/) and Carnegie Hall (https://www.carnegie-
hall.org/), while the Madison Square Garden and Flushing Meadows (https://www.
nycgovparks.org/parks/flushing-meadows-corona-park/) are among the country's top
sports venues. New York has an international role as the seat of the United Nations
Assembly, but transactions on Wall Street have an even greater impact on the global
economy.

- **Philadelphia**, the fourth largest city in the United States, is regarded as the birthplace
  of the nation, witnessing the Declaration of Independence (1776) and the ratification
  of the US Constitution (1788). Independence Hall, The Liberty Bell and Congress Hall
  are examples of this heritage. It is a major sports venue and cultural centre, while
  Penn's Landing is a maritime heritage attraction.

- **Washington**, DC, has a unique appeal as the capital of the United States. It was
  planned as such at the beginning of the nineteenth century, with wide avenues lined
  with Neo-classical buildings, attractive parks, and a skyline protected by a limit on
  the height of buildings. The most important feature is the Mall, extending from the
  Lincoln Memorial to the Capitol, housing the American Congress; grouped nearby
  are other important public buildings such as the White House (https://www.nps.gov/
  wtho/index.htm), the Smithsonian museums (https://www.si.edu/), and the National
  Gallery of Art (https://www.nga.gov/). The federal government and various international agencies, such as the World Bank (https://www.worldbank.org/), generate a considerable volume of business travel. The capital is served by three international airports
  – Reagan National (https://www.flyreagan.com/), Dulles International (https://www.
  flydulles.com), and Washington-Baltimore (https://www.bwiairport.com/).

The Northern Appalachians constitute the rural hinterland of the cities of the Eastern
Seaboard. They are made up of forested mountain ridges, narrow river valleys, and rolling
hill country. In parts of West Virginia and Pennsylvania, the landscape has been blighted
by coal mining and heavy industry, leaving behind polluted rivers. However, there are
widespread opportunities for field sports, white-water rafting (mainly in West Virginia),
and skiing during the winter months.

- 'Upstate' New York boasts a variety of scenic attractions, providing a contrast to the
  bustle of New York City. These include the Finger Lakes and the Adirondack Mountains, which contain extensive wilderness areas, as well as Lake Placid, the venue for
  the 1980 Winter Olympics. The Catskills have long been popular as a resort area for
  New Yorkers. The Hudson Valley, with its vineyards, historic mansions, and wooded

scenery, has been called 'the Rhineland of North America'. Two tourist centres in New York State deserve special mention – Cooperstown, 'the home of baseball' – and Rochester, where George Eastman made photography accessible to a mass market. The state's most famous attraction – although half of it lies in Canada – is Niagara Falls (https://niagarafallsusa.com/). Since the nineteenth century, a variety of facilities has been provided for viewing the spectacle, but some of the development, particularly on the American side, is excessively commercialised and inappropriate for the setting.

- Pennsylvania offers the Pocono and Allegheny Mountains, the Civil War battlefield of Gettysburg (https://www.nps.gov/gett), and Lancaster County, famous for its Amish communities of German origin who have rejected technological progress. The Amish have accepted tourism on their own terms, but it nevertheless poses a threat to their traditional way of life.

The coastal resorts. These include the Hamptons on Long Island, Atlantic City, and Cape May in New Jersey, and Ocean City in Maryland. Although some resorts aimed for exclusivity, Atlantic City, in particular, was the creation of the railroad and developed to meet the needs of the growing numbers of industrial workers, the main focus being the elevated *boardwalk* (promenade) along the beach. In the 1920s, the resort achieved fame for its event attractions, such as the Miss America beauty pageant. After the Second World War, fashions changed as alternative destinations such as Florida became more accessible, and Atlantic City entered a long period of stagnation. The resort's fortunes revived in the late 1970s following the decision of the state government to legalise gambling. For a time, its casinos attracted more visitors than those of Las Vegas, although their length of stay tended to be much shorter. Since the 1990s, Americans have been able to gamble in many places outside Nevada and Atlantic City, as well as online. Unlike Las Vegas, Atlantic City has failed to diversify and upgrade its attractions and now faces the decline stage of the tourist area life cycle.

The South

The South is the most distinctive region of the United States, although its boundaries are difficult to define. Many regard the Ohio River and the Mason-Dixon Line separating Virginia from Pennsylvania as the northern limit. We can regard the South as having these features:

- A climate characterised by long sultry summers, short, mild winters, and abundant rainfall.
- The importance given by Southerners to the American Civil War (1861–1865), in which the Confederacy, made up of 11 slave-holding states, was defeated in its attempts to secede from the United States.
- The presence of a large Black minority, who for a century after the Civil War continued to suffer from many forms of discrimination.

- A lifestyle that is more traditional, family-orientated, and religion-based than other regions of the United States. The strength of fundamentalist Christianity explains the use of the term 'Bible Belt' for much of the region.
- An economy where areas of dynamic growth and prosperity – the so-called 'New South' – contrast with pockets of rural poverty.

The heritage of the period before the Civil War, often highly romanticised, is an important part of the South's appeal to tourists. This has tended to focus on the plantation houses of the former slave owners, although the cabins of the former slaves have, in some cases, been renovated to give a more inclusive narrative. Of wider significance is the contribution the region has made to literature and popular music, including jazz, country and western, rhythm and blues, and gospel. The South is also well endowed with recreational resources, which include:

- Large areas of forest, particularly in the Southern Appalachians.
- The wetlands of the coastal plains, such as the Okefenokee Swamp in southern Georgia and the *bayous* of the Mississippi delta, provide a unique refuge for wildlife.
- A number of large man-made lakes provide facilities for water sports. These are a legacy of the hydroelectric power projects of the Tennessee Valley Authority (TVA). This was a federal government agency set up to boost the region's economy as part of President Franklin D. Roosevelt's New Deal in the 1930s.
- The abundance of golf courses, particularly in the hilly, well-wooded Piedmont zone between the Appalachians and the coastal plains. Pinehurst in North Carolina and Augusta in Georgia are the most popular golfing resorts.
- The barrier islands of the Atlantic and Gulf coasts provide many fine beaches. Some have been developed as resorts – Hilton Head Island is one example - while others, such as Cape Hatteras and Cumberland Island, are preserved from development by federal and state governments.

We can divide the South for tourism purposes into a number of sub-regions, starting with Virginia.

Virginia was the first English colony in the New World. It played a major role in the struggle for independence – George Washington and Jefferson were both Virginians. During the American Civil War, Richmond, less than 200 kilometres from Washington, DC, was the capital of the Confederacy. Not surprisingly, heritage attractions play an important role. They include:

- George Washington's home at Mount Vernon (https://www.mountvernon.org/).
- The Civil War battlefield site at Fredericksburg (https://www.nps.gov/frsp/).
- 'The Historic Triangle', consisting of Jamestown – the site of the first English settlement; Yorktown; and Williamsburg, the capital of Virginia in colonial times. Of these, Williamsburg is the most popular, and it has become a role model for similar attractions in other countries due to its meticulous attention to detail.

- The western part of the state includes the scenic Blue Ridge Mountains and the Shenandoah Valley National Park. All these attractions are within easy reach of Washington.

The South-east consists of Georgia and the Carolinas, states which have shown remarkable economic growth since the 1950s.

- Atlanta is the main conference venue of the southeast with its modern hotels and excellent communications. As a major hub, its airport has overtaken Chicago regarding domestic traffic. It is growing in importance as an international gateway – one of the main reasons it was chosen as the venue for the 1996 Olympics. As a major centre for finance and broadcasting, Atlanta is a symbol of the 'New South'. The city also has important associations with Martin Luther King and the Civil Rights movement of the 1960s. Other attractions include 'Underground Atlanta' (https://undergroundatl.com/) – a project to revive the decaying inner city; the 'World of Coca Cola' museum (https://www.worldofcoca-cola.com/) celebrating the city's best-known product; and Stone Mountain (https://www.stonemountainpark.com/) – reputedly the world's largest granite monolith.
- The seaports of Savannah and Charleston have based their tourism industries on the heritage of the Old South. Charleston attracts a large number of foreign as well as domestic tourists to its well-preserved *'ante-bellum'* (pre-Civil War) mansions, with garden tours being especially popular. Strict zoning regulations ensure that the tourist facilities are kept separate from the historic district of Old Charleston.

The Southern Appalachians, a series of forest-covered ranges separated by deep valleys, rise to the north of Georgia and the west of North Carolina, accounting for most of Tennessee and Kentucky see photo 23.1. In the more remote mountain valleys, the persistence of craft industries is a legacy of the old pioneering days. Gatlinburg and Cherokee, on the fringes of the much-visited Smoky Mountains National Park, are examples of rural communities exploiting this heritage. To the west of the mountains lie the fertile Nashville Basin and the 'Bluegrass Country' of Kentucky – an area noted for its bourbon distilleries and equestrian sports. Kentucky also boasts the world's most extensive cave system in the Mammoth Cave National Park. In Tennessee, Nashville and Memphis rank among the most important tourist centres in the South:

- Nashville is widely regarded as the 'capital' of the country and Western music industry. This is showcased in the Grand Old Opry Auditorium (https://www.opry.com/) and a number of theme parks in the area, but many find that the clubs and bars in 'Music Row' provide a more authentic experience.
- Memphis is particularly rich in musical traditions, focussing on the historic district of Beale Street, known as the 'birthplace of the blues'. However, the most popular attraction is undoubtedly Graceland (https://www.graceland.com/), visited by Elvis Presley fans from all over the world.
- Louisville has opened the 101 Afro-American Museum.
- At Pigeon Forge, Tennessee, the 'Skyfly Soar America' is a new ride experience simulating a flight over the United States.

Photo 23.1
A view from the Appalachian Trail
Source: ©istockphoto.com/Richard Mirro

The Deep South usually refers to the states of Alabama, Mississippi, and Louisiana, where Southern traditions are strongest. Tourism is of particular importance to Louisiana, where the economy is dependent upon oil prices. This state is renowned for the spicy cuisine associated with its Creole and Cajun communities and the cultural heritage of French and Spanish rule.

- New Orleans is a major port on the Mississippi River, and prior to the Hurricane *Katrina* disaster in 2005, it ranked among the five most popular cities visited by foreign tourists and Americans. Much of the city lies below river level and is protected by high artificial banks or *levees*. Tourists are mainly attracted to the historic core of the city, known as the Vieux Carré or the French Quarter, focussed on Bourbon Street and St Louis Cathedral (https://www.stloiiscathedral.org/). New Orleans has a long-established reputation for entertainment and gambling, but its tourism industry is firmly based on conventions and sporting events. The city's fame as the birthplace of jazz appeals to many tourists, and the annual Mardi Gras carnival (https://www.mardigrasnworleans.com/) is one of the USA's most popular event attractions. The Mississippi's historical role as a major transport artery is recalled in the sternwheeler steamboats that are now used for short river cruises.
- Other tourist centres include Lafayette for visiting 'Cajun country', Natchez, famed for its pre-Civil War plantation houses, and the beach resorts of Gulfport and Biloxi,

severely damaged by the *Katrina* disaster. In 2010, the BP oil spill in the Gulf of Mexico had a severe impact on the shrimp fishing industry and marine wildlife generally.

The **Ozarks** in Arkansas and southern Missouri are similar in many respects to the Appalachians. Tourism centres on the spa resort of Hot Springs and the small town of Branson, which boasts no less than 40 theatres featuring big-name performers in the music industry. This success is difficult to explain in resource terms, but it is clearly demand-led, with most of the 7 million annual visitors arriving from other parts of the South and the Mid-West.

Florida

Although the northern part of the state – particularly the 'Panhandle' west of Tallahassee is typically 'Southern', most of Florida is quite different from the rest of the South in the following ways:

* Its tourism industry is on a larger scale, with a constant flow of visitors all year round.
* Retired people from the northern states make up a high percentage of its population.
* The influx of Cuban immigrants to southern Florida since 1960 has made Miami a largely Spanish-speaking city and effectively the financial centre of Latin America.

Florida is among the world's leading holiday destinations, with an annual income from tourism exceeding Spain's receipts from its foreign visitors. Orlando alone receives over 75 million visitors a year as the world's 'theme park capital'. At the beginning of the twentieth century, Florida was largely wilderness, one of the least developed and most sparsely populated regions of the United States. Tourism was to change all that, along with the development of large-scale agriculture and the aerospace industry after the Second World War. The population grew from 2.7 million in 1950 to almost 22 million in 2021. This growth has put enormous pressure on the water resources and fragile ecosystems of the Florida Peninsula, which is low-lying and of limestone formation.

   The great majority of Florida's visitors are Americans, mainly from the states east of the Mississippi, and Canadians. Overseas tourists come mainly from Latin American countries and Western Europe, where the United Kingdom is the leading market for air-inclusive holidays. Florida's success can be attributed to its subtropical climate, a coastline of white sandy beaches, and, not least, to a major investment by the private sector in sports facilities, theme parks, and other man-made attractions. Florida is readily accessible, with domestic air services to all parts of the United States and three international airports – Miami, Orlando, and Tampa. The main east coast highway (US 1) brings the Atlantic coast resorts within the reach of the family motorists living in the cities of the Eastern Seaboard.

   Florida originated as a winter destination for wealthy Americans in the 1890s, with the opening of hotels in the old Spanish town of St Augustine. By the 1920s, with the extension of the railroad, Palm Beach (catering exclusively for the wealthy) and Miami Beach (for those a little less affluent) had been established on barrier islands off the Atlantic coast. Since the 1950s, with the vast improvement in road and air transport, Florida has broadened its appeal to become a summer destination within reach of the majority of Americans. However, the southern third of the state has retained its image as a winter haven for Northerners and Canadians, and this is reflected in lower hotel prices during the summer months. Large numbers of foreign visitors have invested in holiday and retirement homes.

The city of Miami (as distinct from Miami Beach) is primarily a business centre with a population of over 3 million. Miami Airport (https://www.miamiairport.com/) is the major gateway to the Caribbean islands and the countries of Central and South America, while the port of Miami is the base for most Caribbean cruises.

In the southeast of Florida, a string of resorts have developed, including:

- Fort Lauderdale, known as the 'Venice of Florida', with its extensive marina facilities. During 'spring break' the resort has long hosted an influx of fun-seeking college students, but fashions change and this market is now more widely dispersed.
- Miami Beach, with its concentration of high-rise accommodation, suffered from a period of stagnation in the 1960s and 1970s with an ageing clientele and falling property values. It has since restored its Art Deco hotels, reclaimed its beachfront and re-invented its image as a centre of fashion.
- The Florida Keys – a chain of coral islands to the south of Miami – provide ideal opportunities for scuba diving. Key West, with its Hemingway associations, is the most developed tourist centre.

The development of tourism on such a large scale has created problems. Many hotels and condominiums have been built so close to the sea that the beaches have been badly eroded, while a great deal of the best recreational land has been bought up as sites for private homes. The demand for water by large-scale agriculture and the residents of Greater Miami has endangered the unique wetland ecosystem of the Everglades.

The south-west of Florida along the Gulf Coast is much less developed, with the exception of the Tampa Bay area. The most important resorts are St Petersburg – one of America's largest retirement centres, Sarasota, and Clearwater, each catering for different markets. Further south, Naples and Fort Myers provide less expensive self-catering accommodation.

The beaches of the northern Gulf Coast cater for summer visitors from Alabama and Georgia rather than foreign tourists, with Panama City Beach being the clear favourite. Another important recreational resource in this part of Florida is the hundreds of crystal-clear freshwater springs underlying the surface. Some of these have been developed as secondary attractions, a notable example being Weeki Wachee Springs (https://weekiwachee.com/) with its 'mermaid show'.

Central Florida is the fastest-growing tourism area, thanks largely to the success of Disneyworld since its opening in 1971. In 2019, the most popular part of this theme park complex – the Magic Kingdom – received almost 21 million visitors, falling to 12.7 million in 2021 due to the COVID-19 pandemic. The success of Disneyworld has encouraged other leisure projects. The main impact has been on Orlando – a medium-sized town noted only for its citrus industry before 1971 but now an international gateway. The other major attraction in Central Florida is the NASA space research centre at Cape Canaveral (https://www.kennedyspacecenter.com).

The Mid-West

In marked contrast to Florida, this region, with its cold winters and hot humid summers is a tourist-generating area and a zone of passage rather than a destination. Lying to the west of the Appalachians and south of the Great Lakes, the Mid-West is one of the world's most productive agricultural areas. From the air, the landscape from Iowa to Ohio appears like a huge chessboard, with fields, roads, and settlements laid out on a regular grid pattern. Further north in Wisconsin, Minnesota, and Michigan, the scenery is much more diverse with innumerable lakes and landforms resulting from past glaciation and giant forest areas. The Great Lakes themselves are a major attraction; there are fine beaches along the southern shores of Lakes Michigan and Huron, while Lake Superior, the largest and deepest, has a shoreline of spectacular cliffs. Nevertheless, the lakes, which contain 20 per cent of the world's freshwater, have been damaged by pollution, and this is being addressed by a water quality agreement between the US and Canadian governments. The state of Michigan has a well-established tourism industry based on its lake and forest resources. The resorts cater mainly for the demand from the region's cities, including Lake Geneva, 30 kilometres from Chicago and Kensington, which serves Detroit. In winter large areas of northern Minnesota and northern Wisconsin are set aside for snowmobile trails, while Upper Michigan provides facilities for skiing.

Some of the cities of the Mid-West are important cultural as well as business centres:

- Detroit in the 1950s was the world's leading city for motor vehicle manufacturing, but it suffered severely from the recession in the 1980s and 'white flight' to the suburbs. This city is now a byword for urban decline, with large areas of dereliction and a population that has halved since its boom years. At nearby Dearborn, Henry Ford revolutionised transport and tourism with the Model T and later founded Greenfield Village (https://www.thehenryford.org/) as an open-air museum of small-town America prior to the advent of the automobile.
- Cleveland offers the Rock n' Roll Hall of Fame (https://rockhall.com/), mainly because this industrial city provides some of the largest audiences for this type of music, an example of an attraction based on demand.
- Chicago can claim to be the transportation centre of the United States and is its second largest city. O'Hare Airport (https://flychicago.com/ohare/) is one of the world's busiest. The city is a major rail terminal, and despite its distance from the sea, it is also a port - thanks to the St Lawrence Seaway. Chicago is renowned for its architectural achievements, particularly those associated with Frank Lloyd Wright and Mies Van de Rohe. Its many cultural attractions include the Museum of Science and Industry (https://msichicago.org/) and the Art Institute (https://www.artic.edu/). As a commercial centre it has excellent facilities for conventions and trade fairs. The city is also a major sports venue and its recreational facilities include 24 kilometres of public

beaches, yacht marinas, and parks along the shores of Lake Michigan. The popular perception of Chicago, however, owes more to its reputation for gangsterism in the Prohibition era of the 1920s and early 1930s, an image that the city has tended to downplay although it appeals to many visitors.

- Indianapolis boasts the Motor Speedway stadium (https://www.indianapolismotor-speedway.com/), where the world's oldest and largest motor racing event takes place.
- Dayton, Ohio is famous in aviation history as the hometown of the Wright brothers.
- St Louis historically played a major role in the nation's westward expansion, which is commemorated by the iconic Gateway Arch monument (https://www.gatewayarch.com/). The city is a major centre for music and the performing arts.

The West

The West is defined by American geographers as the part of the United States lying beyond the 100th meridian, where the climate becomes too dry in most years to support arable farming, and ranching is more significant. Most of this vast region is sparsely populated and its appeal for tourism is based on the 'great outdoors', and the heritage of the frontier. This has been evoked in countless 'western' movies, which have also made the extraordinary landscapes of the region familiar to millions. The West also contains the great majority of the Indian reservations – tribal lands set aside by treaty with the federal government – where the Native American way of life continues to flourish. Amerindian handicrafts are much in demand, and Amerindian traditions have influenced white Americans to seek alternative, more holistic lifestyles. Tourist accommodation is available on some reservations, while a few Amerindian nations have taken advantage of their special status in relation to federal and state law to open gambling casinos. On the other hand, tourism may prove to be a threat as well as an opportunity to communities already under pressure, with levels of unemployment and alcohol abuse well above the national average.

Tourism ranks as the most important employer in four western states – Colorado, Nevada, New Mexico and Wyoming – and is second in five others. Because of its extent, we need to divide the West into a number of sub-regions as follows:

1. The **High Plains** stretching from Oklahoma to North Dakota. This was the setting of the 'dustbowl' of the 1930s and is often afflicted by extreme weather events such as tornadoes. It is for the most part relatively featureless. One major exception is the granite Black Hills of South Dakota that rise abruptly from the surrounding prairies. The famous sculptures of Mount Rushmore are located in this area, along with the Crazy Horse Memorial (https://crazyhorsemonument.org/) commemorating the Native American resistance led by the Sioux chief of that name. Another tourist attraction is the former mining town of Deadwood (https://www.deadwood.com/) – notorious in 'Wild West' mythology. Further south in Nebraska, the Scotts Bluff National Monument was one of the landmarks on the trail of the covered wagons that carried great numbers of pioneers westward during the nineteenth century.

2. The **Rocky Mountains** form a barrier 2,000 kilometres in length, 500 kilometres wide, and reach a height of 4,000 metres. They are a series of ranges separated by a number of enclosed basins. Winters provide dry 'powder' snow for skiing in the mountains of Idaho – where Sun Valley was developed in the 1930s – and in Colorado, where Aspen, Vail, and other resorts became established in the 1950s. These are easily reached from the gateway city of Denver. Aspen, in particular has a fashionable reputation and hosts an all-year programme of cultural events. Wyoming boasts two world-class national parks – the Tetons with their glaciated landscapes, and the better-known Yellowstone, which contains many remarkable geothermal features. A touring circuit 237 kilometres in length provides access to the popular sites – Yellowstone Falls, Mammoth Hot Springs, and Old Faithful – the most famous of the 200 or so geysers. These parks also provide a refuge for wildlife, notably bears, buffalo, antelope, elk, and beaver. The National Parks Service has aroused controversy by introducing wolves to Yellowstone and using controlled forest fires to create a more balanced ecosystem. Further to the north, Montana is less visited. It contains a number of old mining towns, forests and ranchlands, and the lake and mountain scenery of the Glacier National Park.

3. **The Southwest** is distinguished by its cultural heritage as well as its climates and scenery. The whole of this region, along with Texas and California was once part of the Spanish Empire and later Mexico, before its acquisition by the United States in 1848. Most of the Southwest is a desert 'basin and range' country with a sparse cover of sagebrush and mesquite vegetation or high plateaus dissected by deep gorges or canyons. The tourist appeal of the region is based on these features:

- The warm, dry, sunny climate has long attracted winter visitors and a growing number of retired people to cities such as Phoenix and Tucson. Health and wellness tourism is particularly important in Arizona with its many spa facilities.
- The facilities for water-based recreation, unusual in a desert region, in Lakes Powell, Mead, and Havasu. These lakes were created by the damming of the Colorado River in the 1930s for power generation and irrigation projects.
- *Dude ranches* provide tourists with accommodation, riding expeditions, and the opportunity to sample the cowboy lifestyle. Many communities also hold rodeos, where professionals display the horsemanship and other traditional skills associated with cattle ranching.
- A wealth of scenic attractions, including the Grand Canyon, Monument Valley – a much-photographed group of *mesas* (flat-topped landforms formed by erosion) and the lesser-known Bryce and Zion Canyons in Utah.
- The Native American heritage. Archaeological excavations at Canyon de Chelly and the Mesa Verde National Park provide evidence of an advanced Amerindian culture centuries before the arrival of the Spanish missionaries and colonisers. The contrasts between the Hopi and Navajo in Arizona

illustrate the diversity of Native American culture today. The Navajo's lifestyle is semi-nomadic, based on stock-raising, and their reservation occupies an area the size of Belgium. The Hopi and the Zuni in New Mexico, live in *pueblos*, permanent farming communities where religious ceremonial continues to play an essential role. To respect these traditions, tourism needs to be carefully managed.

• The heritage of the 'Wild West'. In the late nineteenth century, the region's rich mineral resources supported thriving mining communities, which have now become 'ghost towns'. Some of these have been restored, notably Tombstone in Arizona, scene of the shoot-out at the OK Corral.

CASE STUDY 23.2
THE GRAND CANYON

Over millions of years, the Colorado River has carved its way through many layers of sedimentary rocks to create one of the world's most spectacular features – the Grand Canyon (see photo 23.2). It is almost 2000 metres deep, 300 kilometres long and on average 25 kilometres wide, and is distinguished from the surrounding plateaus by the colour of its redwall limestone cliffs. The North Rim of the canyon at an altitude of 2700 metres has a climate not unlike that of Scandinavia, with forests of pine, spruce, and aspen covering this part of the Colorado Plateau. In contrast, the canyon floor is characterised by extreme summer heat and an annual rainfall of fewer than 20 centimetres, which can support only sparse desert scrub.

Although the Canyon had been 'discovered' by the Spanish over three centuries earlier, it was not systematically explored until 1869. Recognition of its unique character led to its designation as a National Monument by President Theodore Roosevelt in 1902, followed by national park status in 1919. In the meantime the Topeka & Santa Fe Railroad had made the area more accessible, opening a spur line from Flagstaff to the South Rim of the canyon, where several resort hotels were built for wealthy tourists. The 1950s saw a massive increase in the number of tourists arriving by car, which resulted in the closure of the Grand Canyon Railway in 1968. It has since been revived, this time as a tourist attraction in its own right.

The vast majority of the Canyon's 6 million annual visitors are based in Las Vegas and Phoenix and spend only a few hours at vantage points on the South Rim. Flightseeing tours give some idea of the immensity of the Canyon, but for a true appreciation, it needs to be explored on foot or by mule, camping overnight. Another alternative is to follow the example of the explorer John Wesley Powell by participating in one of the white-water rafting expeditions on the River Colorado that are organised by specialist tour operators.

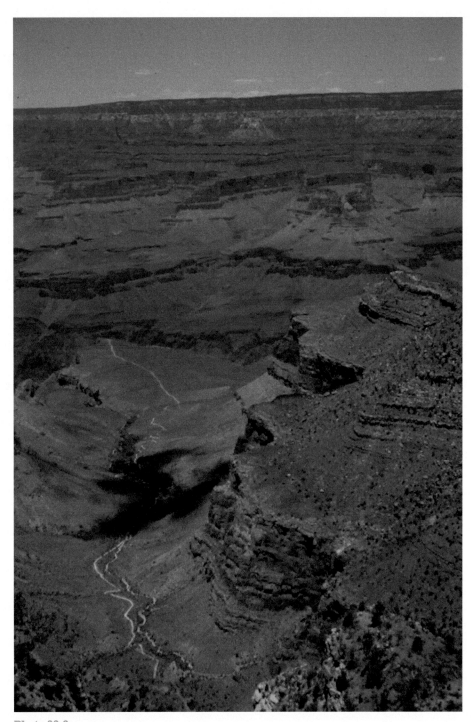

Photo 23.2
Grand Canyon

Source: Brian Boniface

Substantial areas of the Grand Canyon lie outside the boundaries of the National Park and belong to Indian reservations. As full owners of the land, these Native American tribes are not subject to the same regulations as the NPS as regards 'flightseeing' tours and the operation of boats and rafts on the Colorado River. For this reason, the Haalapai were able to go ahead with the 'Skywalk' project that allows sightseers an uninterrupted view of the canyon floor 1,200 metres below. The Haalapai see this as an economic opportunity for their isolated community, but the skywalk has been strongly criticised, not only by conservationists but also by other Native American groups.

Discussion point

Should access to the Grand Canyon be 'available to all', rather than restricted in practice to the energetic (and affluent) minority of tourists? What activities and facilities, in your view, are appropriate for such a unique location?

Tourism in **Nevada** is a special case, thanks to this state's liberal attitudes to marriage and divorce and above all to gambling, which elsewhere in the United States was illegal for most of the twentieth century. The sex industry also flourishes, legally in most of the state, where it is tightly regulated, and illegally in Las Vegas; as a result, most of the proceeds go to organised crime rather than generating revenue for the city government. However, the legalisation of prostitution is opposed by religious groups and the convention industry, which accounts for a quarter of the city's income.

Despite its desert location, Las Vegas has developed rapidly since the 1940s, sustained by power generated from the Hoover Dam on the Colorado River. Its airport – McCarran International – is linked to all major cities in the United States and a growing number of foreign countries. It is now a city with almost 3 million inhabitants in the Greater Valley Area, and one of the world's top tourist destinations, attracting around 42 million visitors a year, almost half of whom are foreign tourists. It offers over 150,000 hotel rooms, almost twice the capacity of New York City. Activity is centred on the Strip, a 6-kilometre-long boulevard flanked by casinos and large hotels. The enormous revenues from the casinos have made Las Vegas the 'world's entertainment capital', offering 'the total leisure experience'. In response to the competition from other gambling centres, the city has invested on a major scale in theme parks, shopping malls, and museums while also going up-market with luxury hotels and golf courses.

Arguably, Las Vegas represents the tourism of the future, in which themed attractions provide a simulated, risk-free substitute for an authentic destination or an imagined past. The first themed hotel was Caesar's Palace (https://www.caesars.com/) in the 1960s, based on Ancient Rome (as interpreted by Hollywood). Since then, advances in technology have made it possible to replicate a volcanic eruption (The Mirage) (https://mirage.mgmresorts.com); Arthurian legend (Excalibur) (https://excalibur.mgmresorts.com); and a foreign destination (such as Venice).

Two other tourist centres in the Southwest deserve specific mention, both very different in character from Las Vegas:

- Santa Fe is the historic capital of New Mexico, with a well-preserved Spanish-Amerindian heritage of adobe buildings and traditional handicrafts. Large numbers of artists have been attracted to the city and nearby Native American communities such as Taos.
- Salt Lake City is both a business and religious centre, where the Church of Latter Day Saints (Mormon Church) plays a dominant role. As a consequence, in most of Utah alcohol is prohibited. Visitors are attracted to the Mormon Tabernacle (https://www.templesquare.com/explore/tabernacle/) and the Family History Library (https://templesquare.com/explore/family-history-library/), which contains the world's largest collection of genealogical records. The Wasatch Mountains provide first-class ski facilities, largely explaining why Salt Lake City was chosen as the venue for the 2002 Winter Olympics. The Great Salt Lake has been used for attempts on the world land speed record.

Texas

For historical reasons, the 'Lone Star State' is as much part of the South as the West, while its closeness to Mexico is reflected in its food, architecture, and music. Texas has a booming economy that has generated a considerable volume of business travel to its major cities. Dallas is a major financial and distribution centre, while the neighbouring city of Fort Worth takes pride in its cattle industry heritage. Houston is noted for its oil and aerospace industries, where the major attractions are the Space Center (https://spacecenter.org/) the Astrodome – the world's largest covered sports facility – and the Astroworld theme park. The fine beaches of the Gulf Coast are within easy reach, notably those of Galveston and Padre Island. Other tourist centres include Austin, the state capital with an important music-recording industry, and San Antonio which celebrates its 'Latin' traditions. This city's best-known tourist attraction is the Alamo (https://www.thealamo.org), the old Spanish mission that played a major role in the Texan struggle for independence from Mexico and is presented as a site of 'Anglo' rather than Latino heritage. The Paseo del Rio (Riverwalk) (https://thesanantonioriverwalk.com/) is a fine example of a major event attraction – the 1968 Hemisfair Spanish American Exposition – providing the impetus for inner city regeneration.

California and the Far West

The West Coast, particularly California, is much more populated, cosmopolitan and dynamic in its outlook than the interior. It faces the other countries of the Pacific Rim and is at the cutting edge of new technology – 'Silicon Valley' around San Jose and the Boeing plant outside Seattle are just two examples. Since 1849, when gold was discovered near Sacramento, Americans have regarded California as the land of opportunity. It has long been the wealthiest state, with a population that is extraordinarily mobile even by American standards. The 'Golden State' is renowned for its warm, sunny climate and the remarkable variety of its scenery. This includes lush farmlands, forests of giant redwood and sequoia, strange volcanic landforms, and the high peaks of the Sierra Nevada – contrasting dramatically with Death Valley, one of the lowest, driest, and hottest locations on Earth. All these, and a wealth of man-made attractions, explain why California is the primary holiday destination for Americans and one of the most popular states for foreign tourists. However, tourism is less important to the Californian economy than the engineering industries and agriculture, unlike the situation in Florida, where tourism is the primary source of income.

There are important differences in climate between the Pacific coast, which is cooled by the California Current, and the Central Valley east of the Coast Ranges where summer temperatures frequently exceed 40oC. Northern California also has a generally cooler and wetter climate than the south, where conditions are ideal for outdoor recreation. Nevertheless, California has its share of environmental problems. These include:

- The earthquakes associated with the San Andreas Fault and other lines of weakness in the Earth's crust. These destroyed San Francisco in 1906 and threatened Los Angeles in 1998.
- The devastating fires that occur in summer in the dry *chaparral* scrub, and the equally destructive floods and landslides affecting slopes cleared for development.
- The severe air pollution in Los Angeles which occupies a valley hemmed in by mountains.
- The water demands that may not be sustainable in the long term.

Tourism in California is mainly concentrated in the following areas:

- **Los Angeles**. 'LA' is not so much a city as a sprawling conurbation covering an area of 2,000 square kilometres and consisting of no less than 82 separate local authorities and many ethnic communities. It is held together by the most extensive freeway network in the United States, and the automobile is the only practical way of visiting the dispersed attractions. Los Angeles has grown to prominence on the basis successively of the citrus industry, oil, motion pictures, aerospace, and music recording. The city's tourism industry was given a major boost by the 1984 Olympic Games. With the San Bernardino Mountains and the Mojave Desert at its backdoor, and with an extensive shoreline along the Pacific, Los Angeles offers a wide range of recreational opportunities. The beach resorts of Santa Monica and Venice Beach have been trend-setters in leisure fashions, epitomising the Californian obsession with youth and physical fitness. Southern California can claim to be the birthplace of the American theme park, the best known being Disneyland, but in this respect, it now suffers in comparison with Florida. The glamorous image of Hollywood is a major draw for visitors, and some of the film studios have been transformed into tourist attractions. Even the desert interior has been affected by tourism by its closeness to Los Angeles, and in some areas trail bikes and 'dune buggies' have had a severe environmental impact. Within easy reach of Los Angeles are:
  - Palm Springs, an 'oasis' of golf courses amid the Mojave Desert.

- Santa Barbara, which deserves special mention out of the many beach resorts of Southern California for its attractive Spanish-style architecture. The city originated, like so many others in California, as a Spanish mission. However, its buildings are not relics from colonial times but the result of a deliberate planning initiative following an earthquake in 1925.
- The resort island of Santa Catalina offers a tranquil semi-natural environment where the automobile is restricted, with golf carts providing personal mobility (see Photo 23.3).
- **San Francisco**. The 'City on the Bay' is very different from Los Angeles. It is relatively compact, with a good public transport system, and is widely regarded as the most scenic and 'European' of all North American cities. San Francisco has also acquired a reputation for tolerance of lifestyles that do not conform to the mainstream culture; it played a prominent role in the 'hippy' movement of the 1960s, centred on the district of Haight-Ashbury, and it has attracted a large gay community. The city developed after the 1849 Gold Rush as a major seaport on one of the world's finest natural harbours. Much of the waterfront is now devoted to tourism, restaurants, and entertainment, notably at Fisherman's Wharf. Other major attractions include the largest Chinese community in North America, the famous 'cable cars' (actually nineteenth-century trams), a flourishing theatre and arts scene, and the Golden Gate Bridge (https://www.goldengate.org) spanning the entrance to the harbour. The cold

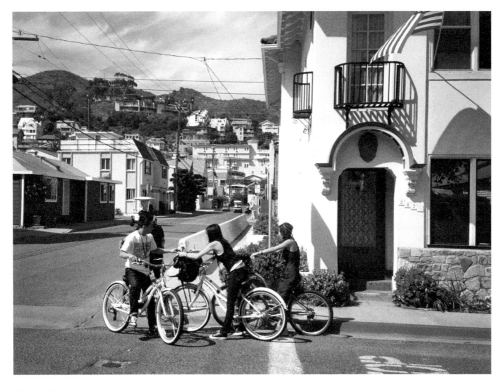

Photo 23.3
Catalina Island

current offshore deterred would-be escapers from the former prison on Alcatraz Island (https://www.nps.gov/alca/), and results in San Francisco having the lowest summer temperatures of any major city in the United States, often accompanied by coastal fog.

Within easy reach of San Francisco are:

- The exclusive beach resorts of Carmel and Monterey.
- The wine-producing area of the Napa Valley, including the spa town of Calistoga.
- The ski resorts around Lake Tahoe and the Sierra Nevada mountains.
- The Yosemite National Park with its spectacular waterfalls and sheer granite cliffs. Yosemite Valley is crammed to capacity on summer weekends.
- The redwood forests to the north of San Francisco, reached by a scenic coastal highway.
- **San Diego** is the third gateway city to California, lying close to the Mexican border. The city is primarily a naval port, but visitors are attracted by the ideal climate and the excellent beaches such as those of La Jolla, with facilities for sailing and sport fishing.

The North-West

The other states of the Far West – Oregon and Washington – have been less affected by tourism. The environmentally-conscious state government of Oregon has severely limited development along its coastline. The unspoiled national scenery provides the main appeal for tourists. Outstanding attractions include:

- Crater Lake, a perfect example of a volcanic caldera.
- The Olympic National Park, an area of heavy rainfall that supports dense temperate rain forests.
- The Mount Rainier National Park, which boasts large numbers of glaciers, lakes, and waterfalls. This forms part of the Cascades Range, which includes a number of active volcanoes such as Mount St Helens.

Portland and Seattle are the gateway cities to the North-west. Seattle has the advantage of an attractive coastal setting. One of its main landmarks is the Space Needle (https://www.spaceneedle.com/), erected for the 1962 World Fair. Seattle is also the main gateway to Alaska for visitors by sea.

Alaska

As much of Alaska lies within the Arctic Circle, it is climatically distinct from the rest of the United States. It is isolated from the 'lower 48' states by some of Canada's most difficult mountain terrain. Only the narrow Bering Strait – ice covered in winter – separates it from Siberia on the other side of the International Date Line. In fact, Alaska was purchased from the Tsar of Russia in 1867, and the Orthodox cathedral in Sitka is one of a number of sites that evoke the Russian heritage. To most Americans, Alaska is the 'last frontier' – a wilderness image that has persisted since the 1898 Gold Rush. The gruelling Iditarod dog sled rally from Anchorage to Nome is an annual reminder of those pioneering days. Nowadays air transport is crucial to this sparsely settled state, and Alaska's main external links are also by air. Its major city, Anchorage, lies on the trans-polar route from Europe to Japan. However, there are alternative ways of reaching Alaska, namely:

*   The Alcan Highway, over 2,000 kilometres in length, was constructed during the Second World War from Edmonton to Fairbanks, and remains the only practical overland route from Canada.
*   The Alaska Marine Highway System operates ferry services linking Prince Rupert in British Columbia to the coastal communities of southern Alaska, including Juneau, the state capital, which is not accessible by road or rail.

In most of Alaska, the climate is a major constraint on tourism development. The southeast of Alaska has the greatest tourism potential, offering spectacular fjords, rugged mountain scenery, and some of the largest glaciers in the Northern Hemisphere. The climate here is relatively mild but excessively rainy. A sheltered coastal waterway – the Inside Passage - provides a route for summer cruises operating out of Long Beach, San Francisco, and Seattle. However, the rapid expansion of cruise tourism, now over 1 million passenger arrivals a year, has brought problems to the small coastal communities in the form of overcrowding, intrusive sightseeing by visitors and marine pollution – a sensitive issue since the 1989 *Exxon Valdez* oil spill disaster. Ports that respond by levying higher passenger taxes risk alienating the powerful cruise operators based in Miami.

Elsewhere in Alaska ecotourism and adventure tourism are growing in popularity, bringing some economic benefit to the native Amerindian, Aleut, and Inupiat (Eskimo) communities. On the other hand, the growing energy crisis has led to renewed demands to exploit wilderness areas for their mineral resources. One high-profile example is the Arctic National Wildlife Refuge, a tundra wilderness that is under threat from proposals to expand the oil industry already well established at Prudhoe Bay. These are supported by the Inupiat but not by the neighbouring Amerindian community, whose traditional way of life is based on the caribou. With less than a million people inhabiting an area the size of Western Europe, the majority of Alaskans are not opposed to development, and some resent what they see as interference by environmentalists from the 'lower 48'.

The Denali National Park – boasting Mount McKinley, North America's highest summit – is already experiencing visitor pressure despite its rigorous sub-arctic climate and lack of tourist facilities. Denali can be accessed by road and rail from Anchorage, whereas other natural attractions, such as the volcanic landscapes of Katmai National Park, are even more remote and, as a result, much less visited.

Hawaii

The location of the Hawaiian Islands in the mid-Pacific, 4,000 kilometres southwest of California, sets them apart from the rest of the United States as a destination. Hawaii received 10 million visitors in 2019, two-thirds of whom are Americans from the mainland.

The Japanese market is much smaller in volume but highly significant regarding visitor spend. Hawaii has become one of the world's best-known holiday destinations based on the climate, superb volcanic scenery and surfing beaches of the islands, and their Polynesian heritage, romanticised by the Hollywood film industry. These resources have become accessible to the North American mass market through cheap domestic airfares and competitive tour pricing.

Oahu is the most visited of the islands, and most tourism development has been concentrated there. It contains 75 per cent of the population, the naval base of Pearl Harbor (https://pearlharborhistoricsites.org/), and the state capital, Honolulu, which is the gateway to the islands. It is also a major city that has become increasingly important as a business centre for trade between North America and the East Asia-Pacific region. The 'North Shore' (the northwest coast of Oahu) offers some of the best conditions for surfing, a sport invented by the native Hawaiians.

CASE STUDY 23.3
WAIKIKI: PLAYGROUND OF EAST AND WEST

The lighting of tiki torches at sunset, Hawaiian dance performances, the *wahine* carrying her surfboard to the beach, and the streets thronged day and night with people of all ages and ethnic origins – these features give Waikiki an ambiance that is different from any other American resort.

Waikiki is the recreational business district (RBD) of Honolulu, located a few kilometres to the east of downtown. This compact and densely built-up area, consisting mainly of high-rise hotels, is marked off from the sprawl that characterises most of the city, by the Ala Wai Canal and yacht harbour to the north and west. To the east is the green expanse of Kapolani Park and the cliffs of Diamond Head, an extinct volcanic crater, which forms an impressive backdrop to the world-famous beach.

Waikiki provides a range of accommodation for the 80,000–90,000 visitors who arrive each week. The most expensive hotels occupy prime sites near the beachfront, while lower-value properties, including time-share apartments, are located further back, between the commercial artery of Kuhio Avenue and the Ala Wai Canal. Two of the flagship hotels – the elegant Moana Surfrider (https://marriotthawaii.co/hotels/moana-surfrider-a-westin-resort-spa/) with its carriage entrance (1901) and the art deco Royal Hawaiian (1927) – were built long before the age of mass tourism and still retain something of their former exclusivity. Their individuality in design and décor contrasts with the standardised 'leisure factories' developed since the 1950s.

The beach itself is not particularly wide and is slowly eroding. In the central section, public access to the foreshore is restricted to narrow passageways between the hotels and areas of beach have been roped off for the private use of their clients. The eastern shore towards Diamond Head has been designated a marine conservation area.

Although the restaurants and entertainment cater mainly for the middle-income North American family market, Waikiki is also a Japanese resort. It particularly attracts groups of young people who during their brief stay can experiment with a more re-laxed 'Western' lifestyle than is available back in Japan. Users of the trolley (tram) service to the Ala Moana shopping centre (https://www.alamoanacenter.com/) and downtown Honolulu are predominantly middle-aged Japanese tourists. Many busi-nesses are Japanese-owned, while many more, such as the indoor shooting ranges, are geared to the Japanese market. One emporium selling duty-free merchandise has signs and literature exclusively in the Japanese alphabet. Some of Waikiki's hotels are popular wedding locations for Japanese couples, who insist on a formal Western-style ceremony.

Tourists looking for authentic Hawaiian arts and crafts in Waikiki, however, will probably be disappointed. The numerous ABC convenience stores supply an almost identical range of leisurewear and souvenirs, as with the International Marketplace, where the stalls display an array of kitsch merchandise, much of it imported from Taiwan.

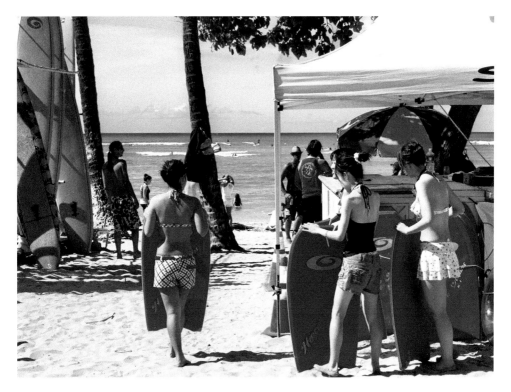

Photo 23.4
Boogie board hire at Waikiki, a favourite destination for young Japanese tourists.
Source: Brian Boniface

Since the 1960s, the state government, increasingly concerned about the undesirable impacts of mass tourism on Oahu, has encouraged quality development projects on the other major islands. Maui contains the Haleakala National Park with its impressive volcanic scenery and the former whaling port of Lahaina. Kauai is particularly renowned for its lush landscapes, exemplified by the Fern Grotto at Wailua, the Waimea Canyon, and the beaches at Hanalei, (the location for 'Bali Hai' in the film *South Pacific*). The 'Big Island' of Hawaii (from which the state takes its name) offers great climatic and scenic variety, due to the effect of the high volcanic peaks of Mauna Loa and Mauna Kea on the prevailing trade winds. Hilo, on the windward side of the island, receives heavy rainfall, whereas Kona on the West Coast is much drier. Frequent volcanic eruptions have created a lunar landscape of craters and lava caves in the southeastern part of the island, in contrast to the rainforests, coffee plantations, and cattle ranches elsewhere. The reality of this volcanic landscape was felt in 2018 and 2021 when Kilauea erupted, causing significant disruption to tourism and the closure of the Hawaii Volcanos National Park. Molokai and Lanai are islands as yet little influenced by tourism, and sparsely populated Niihau has rejected it altogether. The remote and uninhabited north-western islands (including Midway of Second World War fame) have been designated a National Monument – in effect, the world's largest marine reserve – after the US government was alerted to the environmental disaster unfolding in the North Pacific.

Canada

Canada is second only to the Russian Federation in area and is larger than the United States, but has only a tenth of its population (38 million compared to almost 332 million). Climatic factors, such as the chilling effect of Hudson Bay and the Labrador Current, largely explain why the great majority of Canadians occupy a narrow belt of territory lying within 200 kilometres of the US border. Tourism is also unevenly distributed, with most foreign visitors shunning the prairies of central Canada and concentrating their attention on Vancouver and the Rockies in the west, and Toronto or Montréal in the southeast. In economic and cultural terms Canada tends to be overshadowed by its powerful neighbour, and this together with a more northerly location, has resulted in an image problem.

About 80 per cent of this vast country is classified as wilderness, mainly boreal forest and tundra, while Canada boasts some of the world's largest lakes and 15 per cent of its freshwater resources. Not surprisingly, the promotional literature highlights the unspoiled scenery and the great outdoors, but since most Canadians are city dwellers, the campaigns also emphasise the sophistication of Canada's cities, contrasting the traditional appeal of Québec with the contemporary attractions of Montréal. Canada's separate identity is demonstrated by its political institutions, strict gun control laws, and a number of heritage attractions commemorating French and British rule, including resistance to US expansion in the War of 1812. Even so, Canada's quest for national unity is made problematic by the existence of two official languages, representing two different cultural traditions.

Domestic and international tourism account for 2 per cent of Canada's gross domestic product and around 10 per cent of employment. The tourism sector is almost entirely made up of small and medium-sized enterprises. As early as 1929 tourism was a major earner of foreign exchange, and in 1934, the Canadian Travel Bureau was established under the Department of Commerce to carry out promotion abroad.

The demand for tourism

Domestic tourism

As in the United States, domestic tourism is far larger in volume and expenditure than inbound or outbound tourism. Canadians make well over 300 million domestic trips annually, but most are within their home province. British Columbia and Prince Edward Island are the destinations most favoured by Canadian holidaymakers.

Outbound tourism

The Canadian winter partly explains why Canadians have a high propensity to travel outside their own country, with around one-third of the population taking a trip abroad any year. This, combined with a high travel frequency, results in a massive deficit in Canada's international tourism account. The American border states of New York, Vermont, Michigan, and Washington are the most visited destinations. Florida is also popular with Canadians, particularly in winter, with many retired people spending several months there or in Hawaii. This exodus of 'snowbirds' may well increase with the general ageing of the population, while the open skies agreement between the US and Canadian governments will favour greater use of the airlines rather than travel by private car. Other destinations include Mexico, the Caribbean islands, Europe, and East Asia. Most of the expenditure on foreign travel, especially to Europe, is generated by the more prosperous and urbanised provinces, such as Ontario, British Columbia, and Manitoba.

Inbound tourism

In 2019, the majority (70 per cent) of Canada's 22 million foreign tourist arrivals came from the United States, and less than 10 per cent originated in European countries. Americans also account for the large volume of excursionists whose numbers fluctuate according to differences in prices on either side of the border and the strength of the two currencies. This does leave Canadian tourism vulnerable to a downturn in the US economy. The great majority of American tourists arrive by car, return frequently, and are attracted mainly by the recreational facilities of the Canadian countryside. Canada's cities are also perceived to be safe compared to those of the United States, the language and culture are familiar, and crossing the world's longest undefended border is an easy matter for Americans. Overseas visitors tend to spend much more per head than Americans, the leading markets being the United Kingdom, France, Germany, Japan, and increasingly China. Most overseas visitors arrive by air in Toronto or Montréal, and almost half of these stay primarily with friends and relatives. Canada's tourism was severely impacted by the COVID-19 pandemic, with international tourist arrivals falling to 3.1 million in 2021.

The supply side of tourism

The resource base

Canada does not have such a wide range of resources for recreation as the United States, while theme parks and similar demand-based visitor attractions are less prominent. Foreign tourists are attracted to the country's mountains, lakes, and forests rather than its extensive coastline. Most of the national parks are situated in the more scenic western part of Canada. The Canadian Pacific Railway (CPR) was largely instrumental in their creation, specifically as a tourist attraction. The national parks, together with a large number of National Historic Sites (NHS), are administered by a federal agency – Parks Canada (https://www.pc.gc.ca). In Canada's national parks, the emphasis is on conservation rather than outdoor recreation, and, due in part to the shorter season, visitor impacts are less than in the parks of the United States. Each of the provinces and territories has an agency responsible for the conservation of natural resources, with a remit for recreation and tourism. The provincial parks are widely distributed, and while some provide a variety of recreational facilities, others are less developed than the national parks.

The severity and length of winter – most of southern Canada is snow-covered for three months of the year – is seen as a challenge, rather than a constraint on tourism development. Canadians invented the snowshoe and snowmobile, and regard winter as a time for participation in a wide range of recreation activities. Snowmobile trails thread the countryside, and many ski resorts have developed to meet domestic demand within reach of all the major cities. Snowfall is heavier in southern Québec than in the Prairies, with lower temperatures. Some resorts in the Laurentian Mountains of Québec and the Canadian Rockies attract a growing international market. Canadian cities are well equipped to deal with winter; in some, underground shopping centres provide full protection from the weather.

Summers, at least in southern and western Canada, are warm enough for a wide range of outdoor activities, including beach tourism and water sports. Transport and equipment for fishing and hunting trips is provided by specialist *outfitters* in even the most remote areas of Canada. Boating and canoeing are especially popular in the many lakes and rivers of the Canadian Shield – the vast expanse of forest lying to the north of the Great Lakes and the St Lawrence River. Canada's waterways played a crucial role in the early development of the country. Unlike the French *voyageurs* and the Hudson Bay Company fur traders, today's canoeists have the advantage of lightweight equipment. The old canoe trails form the basis for a system of 'heritage rivers'. This is a good example of cooperation between the public and private sectors in resource management; stakeholders include the federal government, provincial or territorial governments, the local communities – especially those of the 'First Nations' or native Amerindians, and tour operators. The activities of the users – anglers, campers, and ecotourists as well as canoeists – are carefully monitored to avoid environmental damage. The new Trans-Canada Trail, 13,000 kilometres long, exemplifies the nation's commitment to 'green' tourism.

Transport

In most of Canada, winter poses problems for vehicles and road maintenance. As in the United States, the railways played a major role in opening up the western part of the country to settlement, and the scenic mountain areas to tourism. After the 1950s, they faced severe competition from domestic air services. In 1972, the passenger services of the CPR and the state-owned Canadian National Railways (CNR) were combined under the banner of VIA Rail (https://www.viarail.ca), an independent Crown corporation that is subsidised by the federal government. By the late 1980s, scheduled train services had been drastically reduced on most routes with the exception of the Toronto-Montréal corridor. VIA Rail still provides a trans-continental service, but at a frequency of only three trains a week in either direction, while sightseeing tours by train are available in the Rocky Mountains in the summer months. The great majority of domestic trips are now undertaken by private car. Most major cities, from Vancouver to Halifax, are linked by the world's longest national road – the Trans-Canada Highway. Domestic air travel is dominated by Air Canada, which ranks as one of the world's leading airlines. There are a number of regional carriers and air charter companies serving the vast areas that are virtually inaccessible by surface transport.

Accommodation

At the end of the nineteenth century, the CPR was responsible for developing luxury hotels across the country, including the impressive Chateau Frontenac overlooking St Lawrence in Québec and at scenic locations in the Rocky Mountains, such as Banff and Lake Louise. Canada offers a wide range of accommodation, including the popular holiday homes known as 'cabins' or 'cottages'. In remote areas, fly-in camps and eco-lodges serve adventure-seekers.

Organisation

Since the late 1960s, the federal government in Ottawa has become directly involved in tourism. It is in charge of policy through the office of the Minister of Tourism and the Associate Minister of Finance (supported by the Department of Innovation, Science and Economic Development). Marketing is carried out by the Canadian Tourism Commission (CTC), created in 1995 as a partnership between the federal government and the domestic travel industry and now branded as 'Destination Canada'. The governments of the ten provinces and the three territories are also involved in product development and overseas promotion, with all levels of government in Canada having tourism responsibilities.

The regional distribution of tourism resources

Ontario

Ontario accounts for over half of Canada's industrial production, and has a number of cities, apart from Toronto and Ottawa, that rank as major business centres. It is the most visited province, containing Canada's largest English-speaking city, is easily reached by road from New York in the south and Michigan to the west and has a third of Canada's hotel capacity. Many holiday homes are located in the Muskoka Lakes area north of Toronto. Most of the population of Ontario is concentrated in the fertile peninsula lying between three of the Great Lakes – Huron, Erie, and Ontario. Relatively few live in the

Canadian Shield to the north of Lake Superior – a vast area of granite outcrops separated by lakes and *muskeg* (swamps) and covered with forests of spruce and fir.

- Toronto is Canada's most cosmopolitan city, with a vibrant nightlife and cultural scene – a far cry from its staid reputation in the 1950s, when it was known as 'Toronto the Good'. Attractions include Ontario Place – a major waterfront recreation area; the CN Tower (https://www.cntower.ca/); the Ontario Science Centre (https://ontariosci-encecentre.ca/) – one of the first interactive museums; and the Hockey Hall of Fame (https://www.hhof.com/), celebrating Canada's national sport.
- Ottawa as the federal capital attracts sightseers to its impressive Gothic-style Parliament Buildings, the National Gallery of Canada (https://www.gallery.ca/), and other important museums.
- The Niagara area includes not only the famous waterfalls but also the resort of Niagara-on-the-Lake, famous for its theatre festival and a popular wine route.
- Stratford is famed throughout North America as a theatrical centre.
- Kingston is important for its historical associations and as a base for visiting the scenic Thousand Islands.
- Georgian Bay and the Algonquin Provincial Park offer large areas of unspoiled lake and forest scenery on the southern edge of the Canadian Shield.

Québec

Québec Province is culturally distinct from the rest of Canada, an 'island' of French speakers in an English-speaking continent. Until the 1960s, it was predominantly rural and traditional in outlook, but since that time there has been rapid economic growth, based largely on the province's huge resources of hydroelectric power. The great majority of the population live in a relatively narrow strip bordering the St Lawrence River. The influence of Catholicism remains strong, as shown by the popularity of pilgrimages to the shrine of St Anne de Beaupré (https://sanctuairesainteanne.org/).

- Montréal is Canada's largest city and the world's second largest French-speaking metropolis, with restaurants and *boîtes de chanson* (nightclubs) to match those of Paris. It vies with Toronto as the gateway to Canada, with Montreal-Trudeau International Airport – and is a port on the St Lawrence Seaway linking the Atlantic to the Great Lakes. This has made Montréal a major financial centre. The 1967 World Exposition and the 1976 Olympic Games did much to improve the city's transport and recreation facilities, including a new entertainment amphitheatre. Other facilities include Le Souterrain (https://montrealundergroundcity.com/) – an underground shopping area served by an efficient metro system centred on Place Ville-Marie. The city also hosts the annual Canadian Formula One Grand Prix.
- Québec City is less cosmopolitan than Montréal, and its historic core has preserved the ambiance of eighteenth-century France. Most of the tourist attractions are in the fortified Upper Town. Québec is also famous throughout Canada for the ice sculptures and exuberance of its Winter Carnival (https://carnaval.qc.ca) and as the home of the famous circus troupe known as Cirque du Soleil (https://www.cirquedusoleil.com).

- Downstream from Québec City are two scenic areas – the fjord-like Saguenay River – increasingly popular for whale-watching – and the picturesque Gaspé Peninsula with its fishing villages.
- Ski resorts in Québec Province include Mont-Tremblant in the Laurentian Mountains and Mount Orford in the Notre Dame Range.

The Atlantic provinces

The provinces along the Atlantic seaboard of Canada are relatively poor, due to the decline of traditional industries such as fishing. International tourism is handicapped by the region's peripheral location and an indifferent climate.

Newfoundland, consisting of the island of that name and the coastal areas of Labrador, typifies these conditions. The climate is influenced by the cold Labrador Current, and for this reason, the Atlantic coast is called the 'Iceberg Alley'. This results in the late arrival of spring, frequent fog, and a short, cool summer. Scores of small fishing villages cling to the rocky coastline, where ecotourism in the form of bird-watching and whale-watching may provide an alternative livelihood. St John's has an interesting heritage, while the interior offers opportunities for hiking and adventure tourism.

Newfoundland is the nearest part of North America to Europe, and this was significant in the early days of trans-Atlantic communications; in the pre-jet era, Gander Airport (http://www.ganderairport.com) was an important staging point, and as 9/11 showed, it continues to play an important role as a diversionary airport. Coastal shipping services are a lifeline for many isolated communities, and Labrador's rugged 'Ghost Coast' is featured on summer cruises.

Prince Edward Island, the smallest of the three Maritime Provinces, enjoys a warmer climate and a flourishing tourism industry, although this caters mainly for the domestic market. The island's resources include fine sandy beaches, attractive countryside, golf courses, and its literary associations – the town of Cavendish is the setting for *Anne of Green Gables*, which makes it popular with Japanese tourists among others. The island is now linked to the mainland by the Confederation Bridge.

Nova Scotia offers a variety of coastal scenery and an interesting French and Scottish cultural heritage. Tourism is based on many touring routes such as Evangeline Trail, but some communities might benefit from a greater influx of long-stay visitors. The capital, Halifax, is a major seaport with a marine heritage that includes its association with the *Titanic*. Louisbourg on Cape Breton Island is a former French fortress that has been restored as a 'living history' attraction.

New Brunswick is less orientated towards the sea, although the Bay of Fundy is famous for its tides, and there are beach resorts such as Shediac Bay. The extensive forests and rivers of the interior attract hunters, anglers, and canoeists. The main tourist centres are Fredericton, which has an impressive art gallery, St John and Moncton.

The Prairie provinces

The heartland of Canada consists of two provinces – Manitoba and Saskatchewan – that are mainly known for their vast wheat-growing prairies. Winters are comparable with those of Siberia, but Lake Winnipeg is a major focus for water sports during the short, hot summers. Further north the prairies give way to forests, where fly-in camps and lodges provide accommodation for anglers. Although the scenery may be low-key, the region is culturally diverse, with large communities of Ukrainians, Germans and Icelanders that have retained the traditions of their homelands. Winnipeg is the main business and cultural centre of the region, followed by Regina, home of that world-famous national institution, the Royal Canadian Mounted Police.

CASE STUDY 23.4
ECOTOURISM NEAR HUDSON BAY

The isolated community of Churchill in northern Manitoba (it can only be reached by air, or slow train from Winnipeg) is an example of how ecotourism can revive a local economy. A former Hudson Bay Company fur trading post, it is now visited by tourists in summer for whale-watching, and in October to view polar bears from the safety of 'tundra buggies' – four-wheel-drive all-terrain vehicles. Churchill is well suited for ecotourism as the meeting point of three ecosystems – the boreal forest to the south, the tundra to the northwest, and the frigid waters of Hudson Bay. (This may explain why Churchill, which is on the same latitude as Inverness in Scotland, experiences a rigorous sub-arctic climate.) The town is situated on the migration route for polar bears making their way on and off the sea ice of Hudson Bay to hunt and is one of the few places where a community co-exists with these formidable predators. Accommodation is provided in eco-lodges and the Churchill Northern Studies Centre, a research facility for studying the wildlife of the area.

Polar bear watching is an integral part of Churchill's economy, but there is evidence that this resource may be at risk from climate change. However, although the ice-free season in western Hudson Bay has lengthened in recent decades, some experts claim this has not had a major impact on polar bear numbers.

The West

The provinces of Alberta and British Columbia offer some of the most spectacular scenery and wildlife to be found in North America. The Rocky Mountains contain no less than seven of Canada's national parks. Most of the tourism development is on the Alberta side, and includes the following attractions:

* Banff National Park is the most popular area, attracting 4 million visitors annually, mainly in July and August. It contains two world-famous resorts – Banff and Lake Louise. Banff was initially developed as a spa by the CPR based on its hot springs and attracted a wealthy international clientele in the early twentieth century. With the development of skiing after the Second World War, it became an all-year resort, with a winter sports season lasting from November to May. It is now a major urban centre with attractions, restaurants, golf courses, and other facilities that may seem

inappropriate to the setting and the national park ethos. Banff also offers major cultural events, such as art and film festivals.

- Jasper National Park lies close to the Yellowhead Pass, the route across the Rockies followed by the CNR. Major attractions include the Columbia Icefield and Maligne Lake, both superb examples of glacial scenery. Outside the park boundaries, heli-skiing and heli-hiking allow access to the most remote mountain areas.
- Calgary is the gateway to the Canadian Rockies. It is also the centre for the ranching industry of southwestern Alberta, hence the significance of the 'Stampede' (https://www.calgarystampede.com/) – a world-famous event attraction celebrating the cowboy lifestyle. The winter climate of this area is often affected by warm, dry *chinook* winds – similar to the *föhn* of the Alps – that can raise temperatures by as much as 25°C. This would be disastrous for the ski resort operations were it not for the availability of computerised snow-making systems covering most of the pistes. Waterton Lakes near Calgary was the venue for the 1988 Winter Olympics.
- Edmonton has long been regarded as the gateway to the Canadian North. Its modern prosperity is largely based on the oil industry, and the city boasts the largest shopping mall in North America – Edmonton West – offering a range of themed attractions.
- The arid landscapes of the Alberta Badlands are unlike any other part of Canada. They are noted for their dinosaur fossil beds and the landforms resulting from wind erosion known as *hoodoos*.

The coastal region of British Columbia offers many attractions, including:

- A climate characterised by the mildest winters of Canada – with temperatures 20°C higher than in Labrador at the same latitude – and in the south, warm summers with abundant sunshine.
- A spectacular coastline backed by mountains, deeply indented with fjords, and with many offshore islands.
- Diverse ecosystems, including the rainforests of Vancouver Island, and rivers teeming with salmon. An extensive area including Haida Gwaii (formerly the Queen Charlotte Islands) has been designated as Canada's largest marine reserve.
- The Native American heritage. The abundance of natural resources allowed the Haida and other coastal tribes to develop a sophisticated culture. This was severely disrupted by contact with Europeans, but the totem pole survives as the best-known example of traditional skills and beliefs.

The main tourist centres are Vancouver and Victoria:

- Vancouver is Canada's third largest city, with a large Chinese community, and serves as a major gateway to the East Asia-Pacific Region. This makes the city particularly appealing to visitors from Japan, Hong Kong, and other Asian countries. The superb natural setting means sailing, golf, and skiing can be enjoyed on the same day.
- Victoria, on Vancouver Island, is a major holiday resort and retirement area with a strong English ambiance that makes it appealing to American tourists from the West Coast.

The interior of British Columbia comprises high mountain ranges, broad plateaus, and deep, canyon-like valleys. The climate is much drier than the coast, with cold winters but very warm summers. This is particularly true of the sheltered Okanagan Valley, where sailing and water skiing are popular at the lake resorts of Penticton and Kelowna. On the Fraser River visitors can experience white-water rafting or pan for gold near former mining towns. Excellent winter sports facilities are available in the Selkirk Mountains at Kimberley, and at Kamloops, the heart of British Columbia's cattle-ranching country.

Discussion point
Much of British Columbia is impossible to reach except by air transport. These mountain and forest areas are nevertheless sought-after destinations for hikers, skiers and nature lovers. Proponents of heli-hiking and heli-skiing downplay the environmental impact of helicopters and claim that with improved technology they are now much safer than in the past. Road building, they argue, would produce much more pollution, while hiking to the destination would be a feat of endurance given the trackless terrain. Anyway, such hikers would produce waste, light fires and scare wildlife.
    Discuss the pros and cons of heli-touring, heli-hiking, and heli-skiing in remote areas of North America.

The North

Most Canadians perceive James Bay, Nunavik (the predominantly Inuit northern part of Québec Province), and Labrador as part of the North, but despite having a sub-arctic climate, these locations are on the same latitude as Britain. The Canadian North is generally defined as comprising the territories of Yukon, Northwest Territories (NWT), and Nunavut which lie north of 60° latitude. Here, tourism development is constrained by the high costs of transport and construction.

- **The Yukon Territory** is more accessible than other parts of the Canadian North, and although winters are just as severe, summers are much warmer than in Nunavut to the east. The Yukon's tourism industry is mainly based on the heritage of the 1898 Gold Rush, Canada's equivalent of the 'Wild West' – at Dawson City and Whitehorse. The Kluane National Park provides limited facilities for adventure tourism.
- **The NWT** have substantial indigenous communities, belonging to the Dene Indian and Inuit cultures. Although there is road access to Yellowknife and to Inuvik on the Mackenzie delta, most of the NWT can only be reached by air, while in winter ice roads on the frozen waterways serve some communities. The problems caused by even a limited amount of tourism are becoming evident in the region's main natural attraction – the Nahanni National Park Reserve. This World Heritage Site includes the spectacular Virginia Falls and an extensive karst limestone system – unusual in such high latitudes. Although this remote area is only accessible by air, it is already experiencing severe impacts, resulting from the growth of white-water rafting on the South Nahanni River.

- **Nunavut** covers most of the Canadian Arctic and was created by the federal government in 1999 specifically for the Inuit people. Visits to the region are part of the growing ecotourism movement, and this is a sector in which Inuit guides and outfitters, with their intimate knowledge of the country, are playing an important role in sustaining both their economy and culture. Nunavut's rigorous climate, the vast distances between the few settlements, and the forbidding terrain hinder tourism development and discourage independent travel. The resource base includes:
- The spectacular glaciated mountain and fiord scenery of Baffin Island, culminating in the Auyuittuq National Park.
- The pristine lakes and rivers of the Barren Grounds, the tundra plains extending from Hudson Bay north-westwards to the Arctic Ocean.
- The marine wildlife of Hudson Bay and Lancaster Sound.
- Inuit handicrafts based on their hunting traditions.

CASE STUDY 23.5
THE NORTHWEST PASSAGE

The impact of climate change on the Arctic regions has revived interest in the centuries-old quest for a commercial shipping route linking the Atlantic and Pacific oceans. As explorers such as Franklin and McClure found to their cost, navigation was not feasible, due to year-round sea ice blocking the maze of channels between the islands of Canada's Arctic archipelago.

Now accessible to large ships due to climate change, the Passage would greatly reduce transport costs by sea between Europe and East Asia. It is also attracting attention from cruise operators as one of the 'last frontiers' of tourism. There is a demand, particularly in the United States, for

- The opportunity of seeing Arctic wildlife in a natural habitat under threat from 'global warming'.
- Retracing the route of past explorers in a cruise ship equipped for luxury travel, with the voyage taking two weeks to a month (whereas it took Amundsen three years to complete the Passage in 1903–1906).

The use of the Northwest Passage for luxury cruise ships is problematic, given the unpredictability of ice and weather conditions, and the fact that supply and rescue facilities in Arctic Canada are few and far between. It also raises a number of environmental and social issues, namely:

- Pollution. The environmental impact of cruise liners is considerable, with air pollution caused by emissions of fuel with a high sulphur content. The average cruise ship with 3,000 passengers and crew produces 21,000 gallons of sewage a day, plus a much larger volume of 'grey water' from sinks, showers and baths. The

Canadian Arctic is one of the world's most pristine environments, with ecosystems that are highly vulnerable to air and marine pollution. The cruise industry itself is also contributing to climate change.

- Impact on local communities. The Inuit villages on the cruise route have only a few hundred inhabitants and lack infrastructure. The government of Nunavut, along with other organisations, calls for controls, claiming that these small communities cannot manage the influx of tourists.

Greenland (Kalaallit Nunaat)

As described in Chapter 4, a permanent ice cap thousands of metres thick covers 84 per cent of Greenland, acting as a laboratory for climate change. Inuit mainly live in scattered communities along the western and southeastern coasts (www.visitgreenland.com). To the north and east, a barrier of pack ice prevents circumnavigation of the world's largest island. A self-governing Danish territory and a member of the Nordic Council, Greenland has nevertheless shunned incorporation in the European Union. Greenland's economy remains highly dependent on Denmark, and it is more accessible by air services from Copenhagen or Reykjavik than Canada. Most visitors arrive via the airport at Kangerlussuaq (formerly Sondre Stromfjord), but this may change with the expansion of the airport serving Nuuk, Greenland's capital. The exploitation of rare minerals, now accessible due to climate change, may encourage Greenlanders to seek greater autonomy and closer links with their Inuit neighbours in Nunavut.

Greenland's main tourism resource is its fjord and mountain scenery, culminating in Disko Bay, where glaciers reach the sea to spawn a myriad of icebergs (the ice here is claimed to be the world's purest). Narsarsuaq in the extreme south is the main focus for activities such as hiking and mountain climbing, while dog-sledding is offered by Inuit communities on the southeast coast. Prospects for tourism development are limited by the high costs of accommodation and transport. Even in summer, the coastal ferries and the system of air services (mainly using helicopters) are likely to be disrupted by a sudden deterioration in weather conditions, including fog and strong winds.

St-Pierre and Miquelon

This French overseas territory consists of two small rocky islands off the south coast of Newfoundland. Not just the language but many aspects of everyday life are French, so the islands have curiosity appeal, attracting Canadians on shopping trips. With only 6,000 inhabitants, a climate characterised by frequent fog, and few resources, the islands' tourism capacity is limited. The territory relies on Metropolitan France for economic support and a direct air service between St- Pierre and Paris was inaugurated in 2018.

Plans to attract more visitors to the islands have included French language schools for American students, but St-Pierre would have to compete against destinations that are more accessible, which offer a more agreeable climate and a greater range of activities. The islands' maritime heritage and history of smuggling during the era of Prohibition in the United States are themes that would interest niche markets.

Summary

- North America is a vast continent of scenic and climatic contrasts.
- With the exception of northern Canada and Greenland, it is highly developed economically.
- Urban landscapes, lifestyles, transport systems, and tourist facilities are broadly similar throughout both the United States and Canada, and there is considerable travel between the two countries.
- The main problem for the overseas visitor is the great distances involved, which has been largely overcome by excellent highways and an extensive network of air services, with rail transport now playing only a minor role.
- Tourist facilities have been developed mainly to serve the enormous domestic market, and it is only recently that federal, state, and provincial governments have become directly involved in encouraging inbound tourism.
- North Americans spend heavily on travel abroad, resulting in Canada continuing to have a large deficit in its international tourism account.
- Overseas visitors to the United States and Canada are attracted to the cities for cultural and business reasons, and there is a large VFR market. Florida on the other hand is regarded mainly as a beach and theme park destination.
- Both the United States and Canada have realised the importance of conservation and their state-controlled national parks and forest reserves are probably the world's finest.
- The native peoples of North America, marginalised in the past, are now taking a more active share in tourism development.
- The private sector of tourism is very much larger than the state sector and is responsible for all profit-making enterprises; sports facilities and theme parks are particularly important.

Review questions

1. A group of students is planning a tour of the United States. They are particularly interested in places associated with the nation's musical heritage. Suggest a suitable itinerary for the tour, including Route 66, giving brief descriptions of the places to be visited.
2. Describe how the dominance of the private car has influenced the pattern of domestic tourism and the landscapes and townscapes of North America.
3. Justify the statement that the United States is a 'land for all seasons', catering for many types of outdoor recreation and tourism.
4. Compare and contrast Las Vegas and Disneyworld, Florida as tourist destinations.

5.   Discuss the achievements of the conservation movement in the United States and Canada, and identify the ways in which natural resources are being put at risk by climate change and developmental pressures.

Further reading

Ioannides, D. and Timothy, D. (2010) *Tourism in the USA: A Spatial and Social Synthesis*, Routledge, New York

Organization for Economic Co-operation and Development (annual) *Tourism Policy and International Tourism in OECD Member Countries*, OECD, Paris

https://www.unwto.org/tourism-data/unwto-tourism-dashboard

The tourism geography of the Caribbean Islands

Learning objectives

After reading this chapter, you should be able to:

- Describe the major physical features and climate of the region and understand their importance for tourism.
- Appreciate the significance of tourism to the economies of the Caribbean islands.
- Outline the development of tourism in the Caribbean and be aware of the impact of cruising and all-inclusive resorts.

DOI: 10.4324/9781003406853-30

- Appreciate the diversity of resources and tourism development across the region.
- Appreciate the importance of the North American market in the demand for tourism across the region.

Introduction

The islands of the Caribbean are often considered to be part of Latin America, but in fact, this is strictly true only of Cuba (https://www.cubatravel.cu/en), the Dominican Republic (https://www.godominicanrepublic.com/) and Puerto Rico (https://www.discoverpuertorico.com/), which are Spanish-speaking, along with most of the countries on the mainland of South and Central America. Although Columbus 'discovered' and named most of the other islands and claimed them for Spain, these were later colonised by the British, the Dutch, and the French. The colonists imported slaves from Africa to provide labour, and their descendants contributed a major ingredient to the cultural makeup of the Caribbean. The cultural heritage reflects the colonial past; most of the region is at least nominally Roman Catholic in religion, but some of the Commonwealth Caribbean islands are strongly Protestant with traditional views on moral behaviour.

Physical features

The islands of the Caribbean form a chain, extending for some 4,000 kilometres from Florida to the northern coast of South America. The Caribbean Sea is almost enclosed and has been called, with some justification, 'the American Mediterranean'. However, it is warmer and less polluted than its Old World counterpart, with a greener coastline and finer beaches.

The islands are generally healthier than most tropical destinations, although this is due to medical advances since the nineteenth century rather than any climatic advantage. The northeast trade winds do moderate the relatively high temperatures and humidity, bringing heavy rainfall to the windward coasts; this means that locations on the sheltered side of a mountainous island and low-lying islands generally have a much drier climate, as evidenced by cacti and other drought-resistant vegetation. The best time for visiting the Caribbean is from December through April when the weather is pleasantly warm, sunny, and relatively dry. This has long been the high season for winter sun-seekers, arriving mainly from North America. Summer temperatures are appreciably higher, and there is a greater probability of rain. Hotel prices are generally lower in summer, attracting a younger, less affluent type of holidaymaker, including many from Europe. The Caribbean is no longer primarily a winter destination, as over 60 per cent of its visitors now arrive during the summer months. From July to November there is the risk of hurricanes occurring in some parts of the region, and these tropical storms can cause immense damage to the tourism infrastructure of the islands and the Caribbean coast of Central America, as evidenced in the 2019 season.

While climatic conditions are fairly uniform throughout the region, there are considerable differences between the landscapes of the various islands. There are also great disparities in size – from tiny Saba (https://www.sabatourism.com/), with just under 2,000 inhabitants, to Cuba which is comparable in area and population to a medium-sized European country. The Greater Antilles – Cuba, Hispaniola, Puerto Rico, and Jamaica – could be described as 'continents in miniature'. The smaller islands or Lesser Antilles tend to fall into two categories:

- The 'low islands' of limestone formation. These are scenically less interesting but boast fine beaches of white coral sand.
- The 'high islands' of volcanic origin in the eastern Caribbean. These are mountainous and often densely forested, with fewer beaches and a wetter climate, while rugged terrain makes road building and airport expansion difficult. There have been few volcanic eruptions in recent centuries – Mont Pelée in Martinique (1902) and Montserrat (1995–97) are notable exceptions – but there are significant geothermal resources in most of these islands.

Cultural features

The islands are a mosaic of different races, languages, and religions, with a cultural heritage resulting from successive phases of European colonisation, namely:

- **The age of discovery**: The arrival of the Spanish under Columbus had a fatal impact on the native Amerindians, particularly the Taíno of the Greater Antilles. They have left few physical traces of their culture, but the words barbecue, canoe, hammock, iguana, cassava, tobacco, and hurricane are derived from the Taíno language. The Caribs of the eastern Caribbean put up a longer resistance, and a small community still survives in Dominica.
- **The age of piracy**: The buccaneers of the seventeenth century used the smaller islands abandoned by the Spanish as bases for their expeditions, which were directed mainly against the Spanish treasure fleets from Mexico and South America.
- **The plantation era**: The plantation economy developed in the eighteenth century when sugar was a valuable commodity, and the islands a prize to be acquired by Britain, France, Holland, Denmark (St Thomas, St John, and St Croix – now the US Virgin Islands), and Sweden (St Barts – now French). As we saw in Chapter 19, the transatlantic slave trade provided the workforce for the plantations. The legacy of the plantation is still evident in the attitude of many Afro-Caribbeans towards tourism.
- In the course of the nineteenth century, slavery was abolished, and large numbers of indentured workers were brought in from China and the Indian subcontinent to fill the gap in the labour market.

685

Development of tourism in the Caribbean

English is the most widely spoken language in the Caribbean, and this, together with proximity to the United States has been a factor encouraging tourism development. The region is however highly fragmented politically. The islands collectively known as the West Indies or the Commonwealth Caribbean, retain cultural ties with Britain but comprise no less than ten independent nations and five British colonies. Nevertheless, there is an increasing awareness of the advantages of cooperation in the fields of tourism planning and promotion. Most remaining islands retain close links with France, the Netherlands, and the United States. Cuba, the Dominican Republic, and Puerto Rico have strong cultural ties with Spain and the other Spanish-speaking countries of Latin America. There has been some progress toward economic integration through CARICOM (The Caribbean Community) (https://caricom.org/). At the same time, the Caribbean Tourism Organization (CTO) (https://www.onecaribbean.org/) carries out joint promotion with member countries in Europe and North America. The COVID-19 pandemic was particularly challenging for the Caribbean islands with their small populations and limited resources. Governments responded effectively by closing borders, while regional organisations such as CARICOM and the Organisation of Eastern Caribbean States (OECS) worked together to manage and contain the pandemic.

Most Caribbean islands are over-populated in relation to their limited resources for economic development. Tourism is encouraged by most governments in the region who perceive that beaches, sunshine, and scenery are more marketable assets than sugar or bananas. Since 1997, agriculture has become even less profitable, as the islands are no longer guaranteed a market for their produce in the European Union, thanks to the ruling of the World Trade Organisation. Tourism has the advantage of creating jobs in a region where unemployment is high, where emigration to Europe and the United States is no longer an option, and where manufacturing industry is generally not viable. Tourism is now the major earner of foreign exchange, the fastest-growing sector of the economy, contributing as much as 25 per cent of the GDP and accounting for over a third of the workforce in many of the islands. According to the CTO the region as a whole received around 32.0 million international tourist arrivals in 2019, representing a 2.2 per cent share of the world total.

Since 1985, the Caribbean's hotel capacity has grown rapidly to exceed 150,000 rooms. However, the region is highly dependent on the North American market, which supplies over half of all stayover visitors and over 90 per cent of cruise passengers, and is vulnerable to the effects of recession in the United States. Most national currencies are tied to the US dollar, and resort accommodation is designed and priced to meet North American expectations. Foreign tour operators also tend to regard the islands as offering an interchangeable holiday product, disregarding the considerable cultural differences that exist within the Caribbean and national aspirations. Domestic tourism is less significant due to the small size of most countries in the region, but there is a substantial volume of inter-island tourism.

The dependence on international tourism does mean that the islands are highly vulnerable to negative publicity on crime. Much of this is linked to drug running since the Caribbean Sea lies between some of the world's major suppliers and the world's largest market for narcotics. The many harbours and airfields are challenging to patrol effectively, with under-resourced police forces helping the US Coast Guard to intercept the traffickers. This is another area where greater cooperation between island governments would be advantageous.

An island's success as a tourist destination depends to a large extent on its accessibility to air and shipping services. Inter-island ferry services tend to be less reliable than air transport, making 'island hopping' problematic. There are many small regional airlines in the Caribbean, but only a few international airports with the capacity to handle a large volume of long-haul traffic. Barbados (https://www.visitbarbados.org/), for example, acts as a regional hub, providing services to the less developed islands such as St. Vincent and Dominica. The vital air links to North America and Europe are dominated by airlines based outside the Caribbean. However, Caribbean Airlines, based in Trinidad and Jamaica (https://www.caribbean-airlines.com), is gaining a larger market share. Tourism within the region is hindered by insufficient air services, and the Caribbean has been criticised by IATA as being a very expensive place for airlines to do business, due to airport taxes and high fuel charges. This places the Caribbean at a disadvantage in competing with other long-haul destinations for the European market.

Tourism in the Caribbean has had negative as well as positive impacts on host communities. This is particularly true of two holiday types which have been encouraged by most governments as a means of maximising income from visitors, namely cruising and all-inclusive.

Cruising

The Caribbean has maintained its position as the world's most popular cruise destination due mainly to competitive pricing by the shipping lines, aimed particularly at middle-income groups in the United States. Although Canada and the United Kingdom are important markets, they each account for less than 10 per cent of cruise tourists in the Caribbean, and the great majority are Americans. Cruising has shown a faster growth rate than stayover tourism, from less than a million passengers in the early 1980s to around 11 million in 2021, while the ships boast a far higher occupancy rate than most resort hotels. In winter the Caribbean has unrivalled natural advantages, but in summer, it faces strong competition from other destinations, leading some cruise lines to re-position their vessels in Alaskan or Mediterranean waters. Both the number of ships and their overall size are increasing, with the largest accommodating more than 7,000 passengers and over 2,000 crew. Size is an advantage for cruise operators regarding yield, while stricter environmental and safety regulations also discourage the use of smaller, older vessels. Although providing terminal facilities is costly for island governments, an equivalent number of staying tourists would require a much greater investment in hotel building. Nevertheless, the economic benefits of attracting the multi-billion dollar cruise market have been disputed, and there are also negative environmental and cultural impacts (Pattullo, 2005). We can summarise the objections to cruising as follows:

- Cruise lines offer unfair competition to Caribbean hoteliers, as they pay little in the way of taxes to island governments.

- Cruise lines provide few employment and business opportunities to island communities. They source most of their food requirements from outside the Caribbean, claiming that local farmers cannot provide supplies to the quantity or quality required.
- Cruising is high volume but low-spend tourism, with cruise passengers accounting for only 8 per cent of the annual visitor spend in the Caribbean. With increasingly sophisticated on-board facilities for shopping, leisure, and gambling, there is less incentive for passengers to spend in the ports of call. Duty-free goods – most of which have to be imported – account for half the spend ashore, which puts the smaller, less developed islands at a disadvantage.
- The sheer volume of passengers is difficult for some communities to handle, given the limited number of taxis and buses available.
- Cruising is 'convenience travel'. In contrast to the Mediterranean and other cruise destinations, the Caribbean attracts 'sun and fun' holidaymakers rather than those interested in sightseeing, while the ship is often promoted as the primary attraction. With just a few hours ashore, passengers receive only a stereotyped impression of the Caribbean, and the commercialisation of the ports of call can be demeaning to both the visitors and the host community.
- Cruise ships generate an enormous amount of waste, and island governments are ill-equipped to carry out clean-up operations on the scale required.

All-inclusive resorts

Although Club Méditerranée (https://www.clubmed.co.uk/) pioneered the all-inclusive principle in their villages in the French islands of Martinique and Guadeloupe, the idea did not spread to the rest of the Caribbean until the late 1980s, following the example of the Sandals group (https://www.sandals.co.uk/) in Jamaica. All-inclusive have the following advantages:

- For tourists, they offer value-for-money holidays, as there is no need to budget for 'extras' such as drinks and the use of sports facilities.
- For tour operators they boost profits by stimulating sales.
- For the hotelier they improve occupancy rates, allowing more staff to be employed year-round.

On the other hand, all-inclusive has been accused of widening social divisions between the tourists, who see little needs have to venture beyond the security of their hotels, and the host community. Also, most are owned by multinationals, which reduces their benefits to the local economy.

Leakages of the earnings from tourism to import goods, which the foreign tourist demands are a feature of most destinations, but they are problematic in islands lacking a diversified economy. Some forms of tourism allow more visitor spending to be retained locally by encouraging *linkages* with suppliers in the islands. They include:

- **Yachting** Whereas only a small number of harbours in the Caribbean can accommodate 100,000-tonne cruise ships, yachtsmen from Europe and North America have an almost unlimited choice of natural anchorages. Purpose-built marinas are available on many islands, providing facilities for both bareboat charter and crewed vessels. Nautical tourists are predominantly from the upper-income groups, but tend to be more informal in their dealings with local people than their counterparts in the luxury resort hotels, and are likely to buy supplies from local farmers and businesses.
- **Diving** Some of the world's finest coral reefs fringe the Caribbean islands. The invention of the self-contained underwater breathing apparatus (scuba) in the 1950s revolutionised diving and opened up a new frontier for tourism. With more than 5 million practitioners in the United States alone, scuba diving is one of the world's fastest-growing sports, and divers are among those campaigning against the depletion of the reef ecosystem by over-fishing and marine pollution. A number of resorts provide facilities for divers, but the best sites tend to be in areas that can only be accessed by *live-aboards*, boats specially designed and chartered for diving expeditions.
- **Ecotourism** Columbus was the first European visitor to describe the Caribbean islands, with their profusion of plant and bird life, as a 'paradise on earth'. Although the original forest cover has long since disappeared on most low islands, the Greater Antilles and the volcanic Windward Islands retain much to attract nature lovers.
- **Cultural and heritage tourism** Most Caribbean islands can offer an interesting colonial heritage and a vibrant contemporary culture, expressed particularly in music and dance (most 'Latin' rhythms are in fact Caribbean in origin) and to a lesser extent in the visual arts. The colourful Carnivals staged by many islanders, and other event attractions such as *Reggae Sunsplash* in Jamaica, *Junkanoo* in the Bahamas (https://www.bahamas.com/junkanoo), *Cropover* in Barbados (https://www.visitbarbados.org/crop-over-festival), and *'Pirates Week'* in the Cayman Islands (https://www.piratesweekfestival.com/) – are showcases of national identity, allowing tourists to interact with the host community. We will now look at some of the islands in more detail, starting with the English-speaking countries of the Commonwealth Caribbean.

The Bahamas

Of the 700 islands that make up the Bahamas, only 30 are inhabited. Poor soils and a lack of surface water mean that only 5 per cent of the land is suitable for agriculture, forcing the islanders to find alternative sources of income. The vulnerability to hurricanes was also evident with the devastation in the 2019 season. Nassau became fashionable as a winter destination for wealthy Americans in the late nineteenth century, but it was not until the 1960s, in the aftermath of the Cuban Revolution, that mass tourism developed. Proximity to Miami has ensured that the Bahamas are the most popular ports of call for cruise ships, including a number of private islands, where passengers are free of the unwelcome attentions of the beach vendors and hustlers prevalent in many Caribbean resorts. Most of the hotels and other facilities are concentrated on two islands:

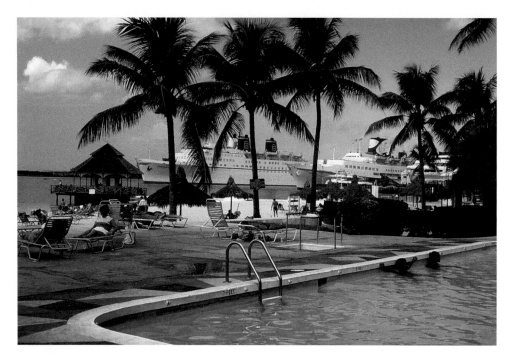

Photo 24.1
Nassau

Source: Brian Boniface

- New Providence contains the capital, Nassau, and the resort areas of Paradise Island (https://www.nassauparadiseisland.com/) – which boasts casinos and the Atlantis hotel and leisure complex (https://www.atlantisbahamas.com/) among its attractions – and Cable Beach, lined with expensive hotels.
- Grand Bahama (http://grandbahamavacations.com/) offers two purpose-built resorts – Freeport and Lucaya, based on golf, duty-free shopping and gambling.

In contrast, the 'Family' or 'Out Islands' are less developed, but provide for a range of outdoor activities and low-impact ecotourism. Abaco (https://abacobeachresort.com/) has a long-established boat-building industry and is a yachting centre; Eleuthera and Bimini are noted for game fishing, while the exceptionally clear waters around Andros are ideal for scuba diving.

Discussion point

It is proposed to develop one of the Out Islands, which contains large areas of mangrove swamp, as a luxury resort with a marina and golf course. Most of the labour for the hotels will be imported from other Caribbean islands and South America. The project is opposed by most local people and pressure groups such as Tourism Concern (https://www.tourismconcern.org.uk/). Present arguments for supporting the project as well as opposing it.

The Turks and Caicos Islands

These islands to the south of the Bahamas are flat and relatively arid, but upmarket tourism has developed on Providenciales (https://www.visittci.com/providenciales), which offers fine beaches and world-class diving and is easily accessible with frequent air services from the United States.

Bermuda

We feel justified in including Bermuda as part of the Caribbean in view of the cultural and physical similarities. Nevertheless, you should be aware that this British overseas territory is situated in the North Atlantic, well outside the tropics, and is closer to North Carolina than to the Bahamas. A group of interlinked coral islands, Bermuda offers world-class beaches of pink sand, facilities for sailing and diving, as well as golf, cycling and riding among its attractions. Bermuda was originally developed as a winter resort for wealthy Americans from New York and Boston, but since beach tourism became fashionable, visitors prefer the summer months, and seasonality is a problem. The islands have retained their exclusive appeal, primarily by careful resource management, given that the total land area is only 50 square kilometres. For example:

- Hotel capacity is limited to 10,000 bed spaces, although accommodation disrupter Airbnb now accounts for 10 per cent of overnight stays.
- The number of cruise arrivals is restricted, to protect the hotel sector from competition and the shopping and port facilities of Hamilton from congestion. Nevertheless, cruises accounted for two-thirds of visitor arrivals in 2019.
- The environment is safeguarded by a ban on car rentals (other than electric cars) and roadside advertising.

To reduce its dependence on beach tourism, the Bermuda Tourism Authority is promoting the island's naval heritage, yachting facilities, and music festival scene.

Jamaica

Jamaica (https://www.visitjamaica.com/) is located in the centre of the Caribbean and is the largest of the English-speaking islands, with a more diversified economy and a higher international profile than most countries in the region. Elite tourism was well-established before the Second World War, with writers such as Ian Fleming taking up residence near Port Antonio. However, large-scale development did not take place until the 1960s. Jamaica's image has since been damaged by internal political strife and drug-related crime. The government countered the effect of negative publicity with infrastructural improvements, event attractions, and currency devaluation to attract foreign visitors. Domestic tourism has also been encouraged, with residents being offered reduced hotel rates, while companies received tax credits if they gave their employees incentives to holiday in Jamaica. This has helped to change local attitudes of negativity towards tourism. In 2019, Jamaica received 2.7 million stayover visitors, of whom 83.5 per cent were from North America and 8.5 per cent from the United Kingdom. The government responded to the COVID-19 crisis with a tourism recovery plan emphasising sustainability. The island has been able to develop new markets in Eastern Europe and Latin America by forging alliances with airlines such as Copa.

Outside Kingston, which is a major business centre for the Caribbean but which has a reputation not conducive to leisure tourism, most of the hotel development is concentrated along the north coast, at Montego Bay (https://montego-bay-jamaica.com/), Ocho Rios – a major port of call for cruise ships – and Negril (https://negril.com/). Here, the fine beaches are backed by forest-covered mountains, the best-known attractions being Dunns River Falls (https://www.dunnsriverfalls.net/) near Ocho Rios, and rafting on the Rio Grande near Port Antonio. Jamaica can offer excellent sports facilities, particularly at Negril which was developed in the 1970s to cater for the younger, more active type of holidaymaker. Much of the accommodation is all-inclusive, but most of these are Jamaican-owned. Market segmentation is evident, with different hotels catering for young singles seeking a hedonistic lifestyle, couples, and families with young children. Jamaica can also offer the following alternatives to beach tourism:

- Ecotourism in the Blue Mountains and the karst limestone Cockpit Country based on small resorts such as Discovery Bay and Mandeville.
- The colonial heritage, including the great houses built by wealthy plantation owners, the historic town of Falmouth, the old pirate stronghold of Port Royal in Kingston harbour and the Seville Heritage Park.
- Contemporary West Indian culture, particularly the musical legacy of Bob Marley.

The Cayman Islands

These small islands lying to the west of Jamaica are the best known of a number of Caribbean territories that provide offshore financial services to the international business community. Grand Cayman (https://www.visitcaymanislands.com) is a developed upmarket holiday destination, while the islands offer world-class diving, including the 'drop-off' known as Bloody Bay Wall off Little Cayman.

The Leeward Islands and the Windward Islands

The islands of the eastern Caribbean fall into two major groups:

- The Leeward Islands, clustering around Antigua (https://visitantiguabarbuda.com/).
- The Windward Islands to the south, forming a chain from Dominica (https://discoverdominica.com) to Grenada (https://www.grenadagrenadines.com/).

The two groups share a common currency – the East Caribbean dollar – and belong to the Organisation of Eastern Caribbean States (OECS) (https://www.oecs.org).

Antigua is the most developed of the Leewards, in contrast to its dependent island, Barbuda. It has an international airport handling direct flights from London and North America and a network of regional services. Most of the island is low-lying and suffers from chronic water shortages, and has few natural attractions other than a coastline indented with coves and harbours, and boasting many fine beaches. Tourism dominates the economy of this small island nation and, with tourist arrivals greatly outnumbering the resident population, has been a mixed blessing. For example:

*   Most jobs in tourism are low status, with managerial posts usually filled by expatriates. Antiguans have been criticised for their attitude to service work.
*   Antiguan popular culture has been stereotyped to meet tourist expectations.
*   The island's ecosystems have been damaged by beachfront development.

Antigua offers a major heritage attraction in English Harbour (http://nationalparksantigua.com/marina/), an attractive yachting centre where Nelson's Dockyard is a reminder of the island's former importance to Britain's Royal Navy.

The other Leeward Islands can offer a greater variety of scenery than Antigua and have not embraced mass tourism to the same extent, retaining a mix of small hotels, inns, and guest houses. **Anguilla** (https://visitanguilla.com/), with its pink and white sand beaches, and **Nevis** (https://www.nevisisland.com/) are small-scale upmarket destinations reflecting a more traditional Caribbean lifestyle. Tourism on **Montserrat** (http://www.visitmontserrat.com/) was curtailed after a series of volcanic eruptions in 1995 destroyed the capital, Plymouth, and made two-thirds of the island an exclusion zone. **St Kitts** (https://www.stkittstourism.kn/) in its Frigate Bay development has sought the middle-income market, particularly from Canada, and the island is a venue for a number of cultural events such as music festivals.

St Lucia (https://www.stlucia.org) is the most developed of the Windward Islands, and for many visitors, it represents the ideal holiday destination. Fine beaches of coral sand, as at Marigot Bay, contrast with the mountainous interior. The twin peaks of volcanic origin known as the Pitons must rank among the most spectacular attractions of the Caribbean and provide St Lucia with a unique selling point (USP) that few other islands can offer. However, the international airport is inconveniently located at the southern tip of the island, a fair distance from the capital, Castries. Tourism developed rapidly during the 1990s, and most resort hotels are now all-inclusive.

Ecotourism and adventure tourism have been promoted by the governments of Dominica, St Vincent, and Grenada based on similar resources. **Grenada**, known as the 'Spice Island of the Caribbean', does have the attraction of white sand beaches, coral reefs, and the fine harbour of St Georges, which is a major yachting centre. For **St Vincent** (https://www.discoversvg.com/), cruise excursionists are almost as important to the economy as stayover tourists, while the chain of small coral islands known as the Grenadines offer a number of small resorts catering for divers and yachtsmen, and hideaways for the rich and famous.

CASE STUDY 24.1
ECOTOURISM IN DOMINICA, 'NATURE ISLAND
OF THE CARIBBEAN'

Dominica was a latecomer to tourism, with its lack of white sand beaches, rugged terrain, rainy climate, and relative inaccessibility. This small island nation has set out to attract nature-loving tourists to its mountainous interior, which offers pristine rainforest, waterfalls, sulphur springs, and a 'boiling lake' of volcanic origin. There are two marine reserves and two national parks that attract hikers, nature lovers, and bird watchers. Accommodation is in small hotels and guest houses that are locally owned and managed, with strong linkages to the island's farms and craft industries. Dominica was the first country in the world to be officially benchmarked by Green Globe 21 (https://greenglobe.com/) as an ecotourism destination. However, tourism growth since the 1990s – including a tenfold increase in cruise passenger arrivals in Roseau, the capital – has put the more accessible sites such as Trafalgar Falls under severe pressure. Some would argue that cruise tourism on this scale is incompatible with ecotourism and that Dominica's unique appeal as the 'nature island of the Caribbean' is at risk. The island could also do more to reduce its dependence on imported fuels by using more renewable energy sources – at present the island's water resources supply half its electricity demand. Since the destructive hurricanes of 2017, Dominica has a new 'Sustainable and Resilient Energy Plan' (S-REP), hoping to become the 'world's first "hurricane-proof" country' and climate-resilient nation.

Barbados

Barbados is the easternmost of the Caribbean islands, with a long-established tourism industry. In 2019, Barbados received almost 1 million arrivals, and this is one of the few destinations in the region where British visitors outnumber those of North American origin. The legacy of four over three centuries of uninterrupted British rule is evident. The appeal of Barbados lies in its cultivated countryside – 'the garden of the West Indies', and the superb beaches. The importance of sports tourism to the country is evident, with Barbados hosting the World Golf Championships (https://www.worldgolfchampionships.com/) in 2006 and the ICC Cricket World Cup (https://www.cricketworldcup.com/) in 2007. As a consequence, the government's 'Legacy Barbados' policy aimed to make the island 'the number one place to live, work, play and invest', by changing from an import to an export economy, developing new markets, and improving the quality of life of the community.

Most of the resort development is on the west coast near the capital, Bridgetown, where land prices are among the highest in the world, fuelled by the influx of 'new money'. The rugged east coast, exposed to the Atlantic surf, is protected from development. Tourism has to compete with other land uses on this small densely populated island. To meet the challenge, the government has an effective coastal zone management plan to prevent beach erosion and is reducing the country's dependence on fossil fuels by encouraging solar energy use, with the aim of being 100 per cent dependent on renewable energy by 2030. The tourist authorities have tried to maintain the exclusive appeal of Barbados while at the same time encouraging middle-income holidaymakers on air-inclusive charters. The COVID-19 crisis impelled the Barbados Tourism Product Authority to find ways of competing with other destinations, such as encouraging culinary tourism.

Trinidad and Tobago

The large island of Trinidad (https://www.gotrinidadandtobago.com/) lies outside the hurricane belt close to the mainland of South America. It has a fairly developed economy based on petroleum and a vibrant culture in which Asian as well as African and European influences are evident. The capital, Port of Spain (http://cityofportofspain.gov.tt/) is an important regional gateway and business centre, with good conference facilities. The collapse of oil prices in the 1990s induced the government to place more emphasis on tourism. Trinidad is famed for its steel bands, calypso singers, and limbo dancers, and its Carnival (http://www.ncctt.org) must rank as one of the most spectacular event attractions in the Caribbean. The island also boasts a geological curiosity – Pitch Lake – and the Caroni Swamp with its wildlife resources (https://caronibirdsanctuary.com/). The much smaller island of Tobago offers a more relaxed lifestyle than Trinidad and an environment better suited to beach tourism and water sports.

The proximity of Trinidad to Venezuela has placed the island at the forefront of a major refugee crisis in recent years.

The Virgin Islands

This cluster of islands is divided between Britain and the United States. **The US Virgin Islands** (https://www.visitusvi.com/) have the advantage of free access to sources of investment in the United States and, in the case of St Thomas, frequent air and shipping services from the US mainland. The port of Charlotte Amalie is thronged with American cruise passengers seeking duty-free shopping bargains. St John's marine resources have been given National Park status (https://www.nps.gov/viis/index.htm). **The British Virgin Islands** (BVI) (https://www.bvitourism.com/) are much less developed in terms of hotel capacity and although Tortola and Virgin Gorda are on the cruise circuit they receive far fewer visitors than St Thomas. The sheltered waters between the islands provide an ideal environment for flotilla sailing.

The French Antilles

The former French colonies of Martinique (http://tourisme-centre-fr/en/) and Guadeloupe (http://www.visitguadeloupe.co.uk/) have opted for closer association with

France, as overseas *départements*, instead of independence. This has advantages in guaranteeing a higher standard of living than their Commonwealth Caribbean neighbours and frequent flights to and from Paris. The influence of French culture is apparent in the cuisine and architecture, and the islands cater mainly for French holidaymakers. Of the two main islands, **Martinique** is scenically the most attractive, with its volcanic peaks and lush vegetation, and Fort de France is one of the most sophisticated cities in the Caribbean. **Guadeloupe** is less popular as a destination, despite the fine beaches along its eastern coast, and is the setting for a popular television detective series. The outlying island of St Barts (St Barthelémy) (https://www.st-barths.com/en) has become a 'jet-set' resort.

The Dutch Caribbean

Six Caribbean islands were former Dutch colonies known as the Netherlands Antilles. In 2010, Curaçao (https://www.curacao.com/en/) and St Maarten (http://www.visit-stmaarten.com/) became independent states, following the example of Aruba (https://www.visitaruba.com/), leaving Saba, St Eustatius (https://www.statia-tourism.com), and Bonaire (https://www.tourismbonaire.com/) under Dutch administration.

- Saba, St Eustatius and St Maarten are situated among the Leeward Islands. Of these St Maarten (St Martin) is by far the most developed, and it is a major port of call for cruise ships. Part of the appeal lies in the fact that this small island is divided between the Netherlands and France, so that the visitor has the choice of shopping in either Philipsburg or Marigot (on the French side).
- The southern group, known as the 'ABC Islands' (Aruba, Bonaire, and Curaçao), lie outside the hurricane belt, close to the South American mainland and the oilfields of Lake Maracaibo in Venezuela – hence the oil refineries on Curaçao and Aruba. The inhabitants speak a language – Papamiento – which is a mixture of Dutch and Spanish. The main attraction to tourists lies in the excellent beaches, facilities for water sports and duty-free shopping, rather than the relatively arid landscapes. Aruba has set out to attract the mass market in the United States with casinos and non-stop entertainment, whereas Bonaire is much less developed, being mainly known for windsurfing and world-class diving. Curaçao has more diversity although it attracts far fewer visitors than Aruba. Its capital, Willemstad is a vibrant cosmopolitan seaport, with a townscape of picturesque canals and Dutch-style buildings, very different from the pastiche development that characterises most Caribbean resorts. Curaçao appeals to visitors from Europe and South America as well as the United States.

The Dominican Republic and Puerto Rico – along with Cuba – share a heritage from the time of the Spanish Empire in the Americas. During the twentieth century, they followed very different political paths, which has affected the type of tourism that has developed.

Puerto Rico

Puerto Rico is associated with the United States as a self-governing commonwealth. With the advantage of ready access to markets and sources of finance in the United States, a large manufacturing and service sector has developed on an island that, prior to 1950, was one of the poorest in the Caribbean. The capital, San Juan (https://sanjuanpurtorico.com) is a major business centre and one of the main gateways to the Caribbean. With a number of beaches within easy reach, it is also an important holiday destination with hotel accommodations geared to a clientele that is 80 per cent North American. Another major source of visitors is the large number of Puerto Ricans resident on the US mainland, but these usually fall into the VFR category. Puerto Rico's major attractions include:

- Old San Juan, the fortified colonial city, showcasing the Spanish heritage.
- El Yunque National Park (https://www.fs.usda.gov/elyunque/), an area of rainforest in the eastern highlands.
- Cultural events such as the Pablo Casals music festival.

Many Puerto Ricans now view their Amerindian heritage as part of their national identity, as shown through re-enactments of Taíno dances and the revival of indigenous crafts.

The large island of **Hispaniola** is divided on cultural and political lines between the Spanish-speaking Dominican Republic and French Creole-speaking Haïti (https://visithaiti.com/), where African influences are predominant. Between 1980 and 1995, the fledgling tourism industries of the two countries took a very different course; the Dominican Republic experienced a phenomenal rate of tourism growth, to become the most popular holiday destination in the Caribbean, while arrivals in Haïti declined considerably during the same period.

The Dominican Republic

The Dominican Republic has been much more successful than Haïti in attracting foreign investment and has become the most popular destination in the Caribbean. In 2019, it received 7.5 million stayover visitors, while tourism accounts for around 8 per cent of GDP. Americans account for over a third of visitors, including many seeking medical and dental treatment. The Dominican Republic's success has been achieved through effective promotion by the Ministry of Tourism, which has tourist offices in North America, Europe, and the EAP region, and the forging of strategic alliances with a number of major airlines. The country has eight international airports, of which Punta Cana is the busiest, and there are five ports of call for cruise ships. Development is mainly in tourist enclaves on the 'Amber Coast' in the north and southeast, with all-inclusive dominating the accommodation sector. More recently, Airbnb has made significant inroads, attracting part of the European low-cost holiday market. The infrastructure for tourism is generally adequate, including a good highway network.

Tourism resources

The Dominican Republic's resource base includes 1600 kilometres of coastline fringed by many resorts offering a wide variety of water sports. There has been considerable investment in golf course development, particularly around Punta Cana and La Romana. (Golf participants have a spending power four times that of the average tourist.) Yet the Dominican Republic is more than just a 'sun, sand and sport' destination, offering sensuous *merengue* rhythms, rum, and cigars, and like Cuba, it has a strong cultural heritage. The capital, Santo Domingo, was the springboard for the Spanish conquest of the Americas, boasting the first cathedral in the New World. The former residence of Diego Colón, the son of Columbus and 'governor of the Indies', is one of the number of early sixteenth-century buildings. This heritage was given further emphasis in 1992, with the inauguration of the controversial Faro á Colón (Columbus Lighthouse) commemorating the great explorer's achievement.

The interior offers scope for adventure tourism with a diverse landscape that includes Pico Duarte, the highest mountain in the Caribbean region, rainforest, and desert. Much of this is protected in a number of national parks, where conservation is integrated with forestry and hydroelectric power generation.

Haïti

Haïti occupies the western third of Hispaniola and ranks among the poorest countries in the Western Hemisphere. Yet Haïti was the first country in the region to achieve independence from colonial rule, as a result of a slave revolt against the French. France subsequently demanded reparations to compensate the former plantation owners, and Haïti has struggled for many decades to repay the debt. It has also suffered more than other Caribbean destinations from misgovernment, political instability, and negative publicity – including an AIDS scare in the early 1980s, that had a severe impact on its tourism industry. Prospects for recovery were not improved by a major earthquake in 2010 that devastated the capital, Port-au-Prince. Haitian emigrants provide much of the labour for tourism developments in the English-speaking Caribbean, leading to social problems, as in the Turks and Caicos Islands. Population pressures have resulted in ecological disaster, and only 1 per cent of the original forest cover now remains.

Haïti's major cultural resource is the skill displayed in the locally-made paintings and handicrafts, in contrast to the imported souvenirs available elsewhere in the Caribbean. The rituals of voodoo – an alternative African religion – attract the more intrepid type of tourist. Most of the limited hotel capacity is located in Port-au-Prince and Cap Haïtien in the north. The latter is visited for the remarkable citadel of Laferrière built by Henri Cristophe, one of the leaders in the war of independence against the French. Cruise ships on the eastern Caribbean circuit tend to use the private island of Labadee, with its fine beaches, in preference to calling at Port-au-Prince or Cap Haïtien – yet another example of 'enclave tourism'. Cross-border traffic with the Dominican Republic mainly involves Haitians on temporary work contracts.

Cuba

Cuba, which has the only centrally-planned economy in the Western Hemisphere, is a unique destination. Separated from the United States by only the 150-kilometre-wide Florida Strait, this large island is far more than a beach destination and can appeal to a wider range of markets than most Caribbean countries. It has a vibrant Spanish and African cultural heritage, and Cuban dance rhythms – notably rumba and salsa – have done much to promote the country's image in Europe. More than six decades of trade sanctions imposed by the US government has resulted in a '1950s time-warp' with *clasicos* – American cars of that era – still in use as taxis on the streets of Havana. Cuba has nevertheless achieved a high reputation for health care, attracting visitors from a wide range of countries seeking medical treatment.

The demand for tourism

Tourism has gone through the following phases, in response to political changes:

- **'Elite tourism'** From 1902 until 1959, Cuba's economy was controlled by US interests. Tourism was concentrated, as it is today, in Havana and the beach resort of Varadero, which largely developed in the 1920s with American investment. Havana was renowned for its uninhibited nightlife and casinos, catering for a wealthy and predominantly American clientele. In the 1950s, Cuba was the leading destination of the Caribbean.
- **'Socialist tourism'** Fidel Castro's revolution in 1959 was followed by an exodus of middle-class Cubans to the United States. Subsequently, Cuba lost 80 per cent of its international tourist market as a result of the trade and travel embargo imposed by the US government. Castro turned to the USSR for economic aid, and tourism subsequently followed a similar pattern to the countries of Eastern Europe, with the state ownership of hotels, an emphasis on social tourism for the domestic market, and cultural exchanges with other members of the Soviet bloc. Visitors from Western countries were largely restricted to group tours, organised by specialist tour operators who were broadly in sympathy with the regime and its achievements in education and health care.
- **Incipient mass tourism** During the 1980s, the government modified its attitude to international tourism while remaining firmly in control. Joint ventures between Cubanacán (https://www.cubanacan.cu/en), the state-owned tour operator and foreign companies, such as the Spanish Meliá group (https://www.melia.com/en) were encouraged, with the aim of expanding and modernising the hotel sector. Cuba became popular as a low-cost winter sun destination for Canadians. With the collapse of the Soviet Union, Cuba was deprived of cheap oil imports and a guaranteed market for its sugar, so that tourism was increasingly seen as a lifeline for the economy. Cuba was now offered as a package holiday destination by the leading tour operators of Western Europe, and the US dollar, later replaced by the convertible peso (CUC), became the only acceptable currency for most transactions involving tourists. Small business enterprises were allowed limited participation in the tourism sector, such as the *paladares* (restaurants in private homes).

There is an apparent contradiction between the government's socialist principles and its support for a free market that benefits tourists, not the Cuban people. Western-style tourism has created divisions in Cuban society between those with access to hard currency – in effect those in direct contact with tourists – and the 95 per cent of the population who are paid entirely in almost worthless Cuban pesos. Sex tourism, which was rife in pre-1959 Havana and prohibited after the Revolution, is now evident in places frequented by foreign tourists. In 2008, some of the restrictions preventing domestic tourists from staying in hotels used by foreign visitors were relaxed, but Cubans wishing to travel abroad continued to face many obstacles.

The restoration of diplomatic relations between the US and Cuban governments in 2015 and the subsequent relaxation of travel restrictions, resulted in cruise ships being allowed to dock in the port of Havana for the first time since 1959, followed by an influx of almost half a million American visitors in 2017. With a new administration in Washington, some of the restrictions on trade and travel were re-imposed, including a ban on cruise visits in 2019. The eventual lifting of the US embargo is expected to bring about economic and social change and will have an impact on the type of tourism on offer. Some question whether Cuba will be able to preserve its unique appeal to foreign visitors in the process, as the long-suppressed demand from ordinary Cubans for the consumer lifestyle becomes an effective demand. The future of tourism in Cuba depends on improved relations with the United States and a peaceful transition to a more liberal regime, in which the Cuban exile community in Miami is bound to play an important role.

Tourist arrivals grew from 30,000 in the late 1970s to 4.3 million in 2019. In response to the COVID-19 pandemic, Cuba closed its borders until its own vaccination programme was effective. In 2022, arrivals were down to 1.6 million arrivals, in contrast to the post-COVID recovery in tourism evident elsewhere in the Caribbean.

In 2021, Russia was Cuba's main source of tourists followed by Canada and the Cuban diaspora, mainly resident in the United States. Europe accounts for over 20 per cent of arrivals, including Spain, Germany, Italy, and the United Kingdom. In Latin America, Argentina and Mexico lead the field. Foreign visitors are mainly concentrated in tourist enclaves such as Varadero – located on a sand spit with restricted access and which has its own international airport (http://www.varadero-airport.com/) – and Cayo Largo, a beach resort that has been developed on a small offshore island. Tourism receipts now exceed those from sugar exports, but the net gain to the economy is much less due to the need to import materials that Cuban industry and agriculture cannot provide, and the repatriation of profits by foreign investors. Tourism developers also have to cope with a deteriorating infrastructure – including frequent power cuts, shortages of food supplies, poor roads, and inadequate public transport. On the other hand, Cuba has one of the best-educated workforces in Latin America.

Tourism resources

Cuba's resource base includes extensive sandy beaches, coral islands for scuba diving, well-preserved ecosystems, and picturesque mountain scenery. The best-known scenic area is the Sierra Maestra in the south-east of the island. The Viñales region, closer to Havana, also offers attractive landscapes characterised by karst features known as *mogotes*, and, as the main tobacco-growing area, supplies Cuba's most famous export. Heritage attractions include the colonial cities of Trinidad and Santiago de Cuba. The latter is almost 1,000 kilometres from Havana and is best reached by air rather than the unreliable rail service.

Havana can offer ballet, art galleries, and other cultural attractions comparable with those of Europe, and is arguably the most sophisticated city in the Caribbean region. One of Havana's biggest attractions is the Tropicana floorshow (https://www.cabaret-tropicana.com/en/), a reminder of pre-Revolution Cuba that has been revived for tourists.

CASE STUDY 24.2
TOURISM AND CULTURAL HERITAGE IN OLD HAVANA

In the eighteenth century, Havana became the wealthiest city in the Spanish empire, thanks to its exports of sugar and tobacco, and the plantation owners had the means to build magnificent townhouses, as well as endowing convents, churches, theatres, and universities. However, in the course of the twentieth century, the capital expanded to the west to accommodate its growing population, while the historic core of Old Havana declined due to lack of investment.

When the historic core of Havana was declared a World Heritage Site in 1982 most of its buildings were run down and occupied by impoverished families, while the Plaza Vieja, the market square of the colonial city was derelict. Once-elegant mansions, with their airy balconies, wide vestibules, and interior patios showed the effect of decades of neglect, with peeling plasterwork and crumbling facades. With part-funding from UNESCO, a team of architects and planners has embarked on a systematic programme of restoration and reconstruction, using old plans, paintings, and photographs to ensure that the end result is an authentic version of nineteenth-century Havana. Since the old city covers an area of 5 square kilometres and has about 100,000 residents this is a major undertaking.

In 1992, the Cuban government set up a state agency, Habaguanex to provide the goods and services for tourists that were largely lacking in the old city. The income from tourism was intended to finance the restoration work, but it soon became expedient to allocate some of the proceeds to improve housing and infrastructure for the local community. Even so, some allege there is insufficient 'grassroots' consultation, while many of those displaced by the renovation schemes have been relocated far from Havana to housing estates that lack adequate services (Hoffman, 2016).

Old Havana is no museum piece but a place full of vibrant activity. Former mansions have been converted to a variety of uses, such as art galleries, dance academies, gymnasiums, craft shops, bars, and restaurants. El Floridita, the bar frequented in the 1950s by Ernest Hemingway and famous in the history of cocktails, has become a popular tourist attraction. Tourism has brought new opportunities to local artists and craftsmen, who display their wares in the cathedral square. Tourism may also have trivialised Cuban culture, with the controversial revolutionary Che Guevara appearing as a tourist icon on a wide range of souvenirs.

Summary

- The Caribbean is well endowed with tourism resources, making the region one of the world's most important destinations.
- On many islands tourism has replaced agriculture as the main source of income.
- The English language is widespread throughout the islands, so there are few language barriers to English-speaking tourists.
- The islands cater mainly for beach tourism and recreation rather than cultural tourism.
- The United States dominates the market, particularly for winter sun tourism and cruising.
- An island's success as a destination depends largely on its accessibility to air and shipping services.
- On many of the smaller islands, tourists and cruise passengers outnumber the local population, and this has significant environmental and social consequences.

Review questions

1. Explain why the Caribbean has become the world's premier cruise destination.
2. Compare and contrast Cuba and the Dominican Republic as holiday destinations.
3. Apart from beach tourism, what other tourism products can the smaller Caribbean islands offer, and what are their prospects for success?
4. Explain why leakages significantly reduce the economic benefit of tourism to the islands. Suggest solutions to the problem, such as developing linkages between tourism and other sectors of the economy.

References

Hoffman, L. (2016) In Havana, tourism development before the US Tsunami *Metropolitics* 22 (3) 1–6

Pattullo, P. (2005) *Last Resorts: The Cost of Tourism in the Caribbean* 2nd edition, New York University Press, New York

The tourism geography of Central and South America

Learning objectives

After reading this chapter, you should be able to:

- Describe the major physical features and climates of the region and understand their importance for tourism.

- Appreciate the cultural heritage of Mexico, Central America, and the South American countries, and their appeal to tourists.

- Assess the potential of South American countries as long-haul destinations.

- Understand the patterns of inbound and outbound tourist demand in the region.

DOI: 10.4324/9781003406853-31

- Recognise the importance of adequate infrastructure and political stability in encouraging tourist development.
- Demonstrate knowledge of the tourist regions, resorts, business centres, and tourist attractions of the region.

The countries south of the US border share many social and economic features, and while Mexico is part of North America in its physical geography, culturally, it has more in common with its neighbours in Central America. Mainland Latin America contains 16 Spanish-speaking countries and Portuguese-speaking Brazil. Belize in Central America and the Guianas in South America were colonised later by the British, the Dutch, and the French, and are culturally similar to the Caribbean islands. Most of the countries in the region have Amerindian communities practising a traditional, rural way of life, while the majority of the population are *mestizos* of mixed European and Amerindian origin. As in the Caribbean islands, the Spanish and Portuguese colonists imported slaves from West Africa to provide labour, and their descendants contribute a major ingredient to the cultural mix, particularly in Brazil. The total population of Latin America is about 650 million and includes two of the world's mega-cities with over 20 million inhabitants – São Paulo and Mexico City. Most of the region is Roman Catholic in religion, so that religious festivals and pilgrimages to shrines such as Guadalupe (Mexico), Esquipulas (Central America), and Luján (Argentina) play an important role in the culture. However, evangelical movements are challenging the dominance of the Church in parts of Latin America. In many countries, the indigenous peoples are increasingly finding a voice in determining their destiny, including the management of tourism in their communities.

Most Latin American countries are at the emerging market stage of economic development. During the 1990s, governments throughout the region adopted free-market and privatisation policies in place of the protectionism of earlier decades to stimulate economic growth and reduce dependence on the export of minerals or cash crops. With the new millennium, most of Latin America experienced an economic malaise more severe in its impact than the Asian currency crisis of 1997/1998. Some blame this on globalisation, but much can be attributed to excessive borrowing by the public sector. Governments have been forced to adopt austerity measures and divert a high proportion of their resources to repay huge debts to foreign creditors. Since 2005, a number of countries in the region, particularly Brazil, have achieved substantial economic growth, but social inequalities remain evident, with around one-quarter of the population living below the poverty line. There are usually great disparities in wealth between the major cities, resembling those of Europe or North America, and the more remote rural areas where pre-industrial lifestyles persist. Rural poverty, in turn, has led to a massive exodus to the cities, where most migrants live in crime-ridden shanty towns on the periphery, deprived of basic services.

In 2019 the region accounted for just over 3 per cent of the world's total of international tourist arrivals. Latin America includes some major destinations, while in a few countries, tourism is in its infancy. However, we can make the following generalisations about tourism in the region:

- The wealthier socio-economic groups often prefer to travel abroad, particularly to the United States, rather than take holidays in their own countries.
- Visitors from other countries in the region, usually short stay, make up the bulk of arrivals.
- The United States provides the majority of tourists from outside the region to Mexico and Central America, but some South American countries attract a large proportion of their tourists from Europe.
- Tourism is much less significant as a source of foreign exchange in South America than it is to the Caribbean islands.
- The region's airlines have long struggled to compete with US carriers, which account for two-thirds of the Latin American market. Unlike their North American competitors, they can count on little support from their governments, who, with few exceptions, see aviation as a cash cow, imposing taxes on airlines and their passengers. Countries in Latin America benefit from a multilateral open skies agreement, although fares are high compared to equivalent distances in Europe, yet average incomes are much lower. Nevertheless, IATA predicts that Mexico and South America will experience a doubling in passenger numbers by 2040. Some airports have already reached saturation, among them Mexico City and Bogotá, where plans for expansion are being given priority.

There is a great variety of tourism resources in a region that includes some of the world's highest mountains and is greater in latitudinal extent than either North America or Africa, with climates ranging from the equatorial to the sub-Antarctic. Products include beach tourism, adventure travel, and ecotourism in the mountains and forests of the interior, and cultural tourism in the Andes of South America and the 'Maya Route' of Central America.

Mexico

The heartland of Mexico (https://www.visitmexico.com/en/) is a high plateau – the Meseta Central – separated by the mountain barriers of the Sierra Madre from the tropical coastlands to the east and west. To the north are semi-desert landscapes similar to those of the southwestern United States, whereas central and southern Mexico, along with the countries of Central America, forms part of the much more diverse region known to anthropologists as Mesoamerica.

Mexico is the second-largest economy in Latin America and, with a population approaching 130 million, is the world's most populous Spanish-speaking country, boasting important publishing and film-producing industries. Unlike most countries in the region, it has experienced political stability since the 1920s, after one of the few Latin American revolutions that resulted in lasting social and economic change. The Revolutionary Party (PRI) had a near monopoly of political power in all 31 states of the federal republic until the Presidential elections in 2000 when the more conservative Nationalist party (PAN) won control. In 2018, a left-wing coalition of three parties gained power. The nationalist and socialist aspirations of the Mexican Revolution remain largely unfulfilled, in part due to Mexico's situation in the economic shadow of the United States. Moreover, Mexico's impressive economic development scarcely keeps pace with rapid population growth, and there are regional disparities in wealth distribution. This has caused a massive flow of emigration – much of it illegal – to the United States, where the economic opportunities are so much greater. Mexico's membership of NAFTA has opened up the economy to foreign investment and stimulated business travel to and from the United States and Canada.

Mexico's appeal to North Americans is partly based on its beaches and sunny winter climate, but the cultural contrasts which the country offers to the United States are equally important. Although the majority of Mexicans are *mestizos* (of mixed Spanish and Amerindian origins), the Amerindian heritage, as expressed in the distinctive cuisine, folklore, and handicrafts, is regarded as central to the national identity. There is a contradiction here, as the majority of present-day Amerindians are socially and geographically marginalised in the poorer southern states. The most significant features of this rich cultural heritage are:

- The pre-Columbian heritage represented by the impressive remains of advanced Amerindian civilisations that flourished in Mexico before the Spanish conquest. The best known of these are the step pyramids of Teotihuacán and Tula in central Mexico, and the cities of the Mayas in Yucatán and Chiapas in the south. These form part of the Ruta Maya tourist circuit, which also takes in neighbouring Belize, Honduras, and Guatemala.
- The legacy of the Spanish colonial period, particularly the numerous Baroque churches and picturesque towns such as Quéretaro, Morelia, San Miguel Allende (https://visitsanmiguel.com/) and Guanajuato in central Mexico, is associated with the Mexican struggle for independence and has been meticulously preserved. Most of the colonial *haciendas* (country estates), on the other hand, were destroyed during the Mexican Revolution (1910–1920). Other legacies of Spanish rule, such as bullfighting and the fiestas of the Catholic Church, continue to flourish in the popular culture. Although many Catholic countries observe the 'Day of the Dead' (November 2), in Mexico it is celebrated with particular fervour, incorporating pre-Hispanic traditions.
- The artistic legacy of the Mexican Revolution is expressed by painters such as Frida Kahlo (now a feminist icon), Diego Rivera, and many others, who are noted for their murals decorating public buildings that celebrate Mexican folk traditions and the pre-conquest civilisations.

Tourism demand

Domestic and outbound tourism

While traditional Mexico embodies the tourist image, modern Mexico – particularly the wealthier northern states – has adopted many aspects of the lifestyle of the United States. A substantial middle class generates a considerable demand for domestic tourism and international travel, despite several economic crises that have led to the devaluation of the peso against foreign currencies. Many Mexicans, particularly in the rural areas, do not have sufficient disposable income to take holiday trips.

Inbound tourism

Mexico is one of the world's leading travel destinations, attracting over 45 million foreign tourist arrivals in 2019, plus another 52 million day visitors. Tourism supports around 2 million jobs, contributes 8 per cent of GDP, and is second only to petroleum exports and remittances from Mexicans working abroad as a source of foreign exchange. However, the tourism industry is highly dependent on the US and Canadian markets, leaving it vulnerable to 'shocks' to tourism demand.

The supply side of tourism

Transport

As in most Latin American countries, domestic air services and long-distance bus travel are more important than rail transport. Approximately 50 per cent of foreign tourists arrive in Mexico by air. The major cities are linked by modern highways to the United States, but east-west communications are less adequate.

Organisation

In an attempt to improve the economic situation, the federal government has given tourism a prominent role in national planning since the 1950s. Foreign developers are encouraged to participate in large hotel projects that will stimulate job creation, especially in the less developed regions. There is a strong Ministry of Tourism (SECTUR) (https://www.gob.mx/sectur/) responsible for policy-making. The federal government has also taken a direct role in tourism development through the FONATUR funding agency (http://www.fonatur.mw/en), responsible for several comprehensively planned resorts such as Ixtapa on the Pacific coast and Cancún. There is an Interministerial Tourism Commission, while the National Tourism Conference co-ordinates planning at the three levels of government – federal, states, and local authorities.

Nevertheless, tourism development faces a number of problems. Water supplies and sanitation are defective in many rural areas, falling far short of those considered acceptable in the United States. Drug-related organised crime has spread in recent years from its focus in Sinaloa to Monterey, Mexico's second city, and the towns on the US border, particularly Ciudad Juárez. Many see this as a major threat to the country's stability and well-being.

Tourism resources

Mexico can offer a great variety of colourful traditions showcased by the Ballet Folklórico (https://www.balletfolkloricodemexico.com.mx/) in the capital, as well as contrasting landscapes. We can divide the country into the following regions:

The north and west

The northern part of Mexico is basin and range country with large areas of desert, similar to those across the US border in Arizona. The Barranca del Cobre (Copper Canyon) is the best-known natural attraction, accessed by the spectacular Chihuahua-Pacific railway. Visitors to Tijuana and other border towns tend to be cost-conscious, and numbers vary according to the strength of the dollar against the peso. Also, liberal attitudes towards gambling and sex tourism are less important motivators for young Americans now that such attractions are widely available nearer home, and drug-related violence has deterred visitors in recent years. Monterrey is the major city of northern Mexico, with an important manufacturing base, rivalling the capital as a business centre.

The **peninsula of 'Baja'** (Lower California) in the northwest is separated from the rest of Mexico by the Gulf of California, also known in the travel industry as the Sea of Cortéz. The peninsula is largely desert, but temperatures along the Pacific coast are moderated by the cold California Current. The beaches and game-fishing attract large numbers of Americans, thanks to an excellent highway running the length of the peninsula from the border town of Tijuana. Ensenada and La Paz have become major tourist centres and cruise ports, while the federal government has developed purpose-built resorts at Loreto and Los Cabos (https://visitloscabos.travel/).

The **'Mexican Riviera'** further south has a tropical climate with a long dry season corresponding to winter in the United States. This stretch of the Pacific coast has become popular with North Americans as a winter sun destination and retirement area. Acapulco is the most important centre, with good air and road communications to Mexico City. The historic seaport is now overshadowed by a vast agglomeration of hotels and condominiums surrounding the famous bay. Other resorts have developed from fishing ports, such as Puerto Vallarta (https://visitpuertovallarta.com/) and Mazatlán (https://gomazatlan.com/).

The Gulf coast of Mexico, with its more humid climate, is less popular as a holiday area but offers the historic port of Veracruz among its many cultural attractions.

Central Mexico

The area richest in cultural attractions is the southern part of the Meseta Central, which is dominated by volcanoes such as Popocatepetl. These attractions include the archaeological sites and colonial cities mentioned earlier, as well as many others such as Puebla, noted for fine ceramics, and Taxco, which grew rich from its silver mining industry. All of these are easily reached from the capital.

- Mexico City (http://www.mexicocity.gob.mx/), situated at an altitude of 2700 metres, is the world's fastest-growing metropolis; however, this growth has been accompanied by severe air pollution, depletion of water supplies, and acute traffic congestion. While few traces remain of the Aztec city of Tenochtitlán, destroyed by Cortéz, the central square or Zocalo, adjoined by the cathedral and Presidential Palace, occupies the site of its most important temples. The capital's attractions include:

    - The National Museum of Anthropology (https://www.mna.inah.gob.mx/), celebrating the achievements of the Aztecs and other Amerindian civilisations.
    - The Basilica of Guadalupe (https://virgendeguadalupe.org.mx/), has particular resonance for Mexicans and is among the world's most visited Marian shrines. The Virgin of Guadalupe is regarded as the Patroness of the Americas.

- The floating gardens of Xochimilco, popular for Sunday excursions. This is all that remains of the lake that once surrounded the former Aztec city, but the attraction is increasingly threatened by a lowering of the water table.
- The Casa Azul in Coyoacán, the former home of Frida Kahlo, which is now a museum showcasing her life and work.

Southern Mexico and Yucatán

Southern Mexico, particularly the states of Chiapas and Oaxaca, is also noted for its Amerindian heritage. Along with the Yucatán Peninsula, this region forms part of the area covered by the *Mundo Maya* (World of the Maya) tourism development plan (http://mundomaya.travel/), which also encompasses four Central American countries – Belize, El Salvador, Guatemala, and Honduras. This is an example of regional co-operation between governments, tour operators, and the local communities, with the aim of achieving sustainable development. Plans are well advanced for a Meso-American 'ecological corridor' to provide more adequate protection for the rich biodiversity of southern Mexico and Central America.

Tourism is mainly focussed on the fine beaches of the Yucatán Peninsula facing the Caribbean. The interior of Yucatán is a low limestone plateau dotted with *cenotes* (sinkholes) that have yielded much archaeological evidence of the ancient Maya civilisation. The region was isolated from the rest of Mexico until the 1970s, when the federal government improved the infrastructure and developed facilities, notably at Cancún. This part of Mexico can be included in the western Caribbean cruise circuit and also has the advantage of greater proximity by air to Miami and the cities of the eastern United States. Cancún is a good example of both mass tourism and 'enclave tourism', a self-contained 'mega-resort' where holidaymakers and conference delegates have little contact with the indigenous Maya population. South of Cancún, development is taking place along the so-called Mayan Riviera, but on a smaller scale and with more respect for traditional values. The hinterland, with its impressive Mayan sites of Uxmal and Chichen Itza, is of more interest for cultural tourists.

Central America

Central America is a mountainous neck of land linking the continents of North and South America. The region is prone to natural disasters such as earthquakes, volcanic eruptions, and hurricanes, and also has a reputation for political instability. It consists of three main physical divisions:

- The coastal lowlands along the Caribbean, often densely forested and sparsely inhabited by Afro-Caribbean and Amerindian communities, many of which are English-speaking.
- The central volcanic highlands, which contain the majority of the population and much of the cultural heritage.
- The Pacific coast, which has better beaches and a drier climate than the Caribbean lowlands.

Central America consists of six Spanish-speaking republics and English-speaking Belize, which is culturally and economically part of the Commonwealth Caribbean. The majority of tourists – other than those from neighbouring countries – come from the United States. Most of these use air transport, especially from Miami, rather than the Pan-American highway system. Much of the region – notably Guatemala, El Salvador, and Nicaragua – has only recently recovered from a long period of violent political strife. This, together with a continuing problem posed by criminal gangs in Honduras and El Salvador, has held back the development of tourism. During the 1990s, Central America experienced a higher growth rate in tourist arrivals than either the Caribbean or South America, but from a very low base. Costa Rica and Belize have concentrated on the development of ecotourism while in Guatemala, cultural tourism is dominant. However, other countries in the region have been arguably less successful in defining their tourism product. In most of these countries, the capital city is a major destination for business travel rather than leisure tourists.

While Central America attracted 11.1 million visitors in 2019, only a small percentage came from Europe. Co-operative marketing by the seven national governments is expected to increase demand from Europe and Asia, particularly China, which is already a major investor in the region. The main obstacle is the lack of direct flights to Europe and Asia, and the obstacles to intra-regional travel. This is being addressed with the growth of low-cost carriers, while Copa (https:/www.copair.com/en), the national airline of Panama, is one of the success stories of Latin America.

Guatemala

Guatemala (https://visitguatemala.com) has a legacy of ethnic division between the Ladinos (Spanish-speakers), who are the dominant group, and the Amerindian majority speaking Mayan languages, who still live in traditional communities where the value systems are quite different. Guatemala has great scenic and cultural diversity for such a small country, and this is its strength as a tourist destination, attracting 1.8 million arrivals in 2018. Its tourism resources include:

- The colonial heritage. This is based mainly on Antigua, the former capital, which has become an important centre for Spanish-language tuition.
- Traditional Amerindian culture. Each Mayan community has its own distinctive costume, making their markets exceptionally colourful, with the best-known example being that of Chichicastenango in the northern highlands. Here, ancient Mayan beliefs coexist with the Catholicism introduced by the Spanish.
- The volcanic mountain scenery around Lake Atitlán and the Cuchumatanes range.
- The Tikal National Park (http://www.tikalnationalpark.org/) in the Petén rainforest, protecting one of the most important Maya sites in Central America. This city, with its stepped pyramid-temples and ceremonial plazas, was abandoned to the jungle centuries before the Spanish conquest, and was only rediscovered in the nineteenth century.

Belize

Belize (https://www.travelbelize.org/) can also claim large tracts of pristine forest, important Mayan sites, and the world's second-largest barrier reef. The policy of the government is to encourage 'community-based ecotourism' but also to use it as a means of earning foreign exchange to finance economic development. In other words, Belize is an excellent example of how a country can use the notion of sustainability to promote the development of new types of tourism (Mowforth and Munt, 2008). Much of the tourism industry is owned by expatriates, mostly US citizens, and although some reefs have been designated as marine reserves, others are likely to develop as exclusive resorts.

El Salvador

This small country (https://elsalvador.travel/) is the most densely populated in Latin America and one of the most developed. Salvadoreans are renowned for their business enterprise, and El Salvador has been at the forefront of attempts at regional economic co-operation. While little of the original forest cover remains, the landscape of coffee plantations in a setting of volcanic mountains is attractive and is now promoted as a tourist route – La Ruta de las Flores. The Pacific coast offers world-class surfing. El Salvador's spas and beach resorts cater mainly for the domestic market and the large number of Salvadorean emigrants living in the United States.

Honduras

Honduras (https://www.honduras.travel) is better known for the banana plantations around San Pedro Sula than for tourism. The interior is rugged mountain country, making air transport almost essential. The country is one of the poorest in Latin America and its plans for economic development were dealt a heavy blow by Hurricane 'Mitch' in 1998. Nevertheless, there were almost 0.9 million tourist arrivals in 2019. Honduras has significant wildlife resources, while Comayagua, the former capital, offers heritage attractions. The Bay Islands in the Caribbean Sea, particularly Roatan, have good diving facilities. Copán (https://whc.unesco.org/en/list/129/) is one of the most important Maya sites in Central America.

Nicaragua

The international spotlight fell on Nicaragua (https://www.visitnicaragua.us/) in the 1980s when the United States sought to bring down the left-wing Sandinista regime through economic sanctions and support for the 'Contra' rebels. The present government has given generous tax breaks to foreign investors, and the country is becoming a retirement haven for US citizens, following the examples of Costa Rica and Honduras. Nicaragua received around 1.5 million tourist arrivals in 2019, with attractions that include:

- The spectacular scenery of Lake Nicaragua, studded with volcanic islands.
- The cities of Granada and León with their fine colonial heritage.

There is some small-scale development of beach tourism along the Pacific coast, catering mainly for middle-class visitors from other parts of Central America.

Costa Rica

Costa Rica (https://www.visitcostarica.com/en) has a well-developed infrastructure and accommodation sector, and unlike other countries in the region, has a long-established reputation for democracy and political stability. Tourism accounts for 4.8 per cent of GDP.

The demand for tourism

Domestic and outbound tourism

A large middle class generates a demand for tourism, mainly to neighbouring countries and the United States.

Inbound tourism

Costa Rica boasts an ecotourism industry with a worldwide reputation, and the capital, San José, also attracts visitors from the United States on account of the low-cost medical services that are on offer. Beach tourism, dolphin watching, surfing and diving are important. In 2019 Costa Rica received 3.1 million tourist arrivals, of which 40 per cent came from the United States and 16 per cent from Europe, mainly Germany, France, and Spain.

Organisation

The Costa Rica Tourism Institute (ICT) is a public agency responsible for tourism policy, reporting to the Ministry of Tourism.

CASE STUDY 25.1
COSTA RICA AS A MODEL FOR SUSTAINABLE DEVELOPMENT

This small, mountainous country is exceptionally rich in biodiversity. For example, there are no fewer than 1,300 kinds of orchids, not to mention a great variety of birds, reptiles, amphibians, and butterflies. This is due to the country's location at the meeting-point of the ecosystems of North America and South America, its altitudinal range, and a coastline fronting two oceans. Since the 1960s, the government has designated national parks and reserves to include a range of ecosystems and a number of volcanoes such as Irazú. Many rural communities now see ecotourism as a viable alternative to cattle farming, mining, and commercial logging. As a result, the damage to wildlife habitats that occurred between 1950 and 1987, during which Costa Rica lost 25 per cent of its forest cover, has been stemmed to a large extent.

In addition to its natural resource base, Costa Rica has the following advantages for ecotourism:

- Most hotels are small, with less than 20 rooms, locally owned, and serve as examples of good practice in resource conservation.
- The Institute of Tourism (ICT) (https://www.ict.go.cr/en/) encourages sustainable development by a voluntary programme of certification for all types of tourism enterprises (https://www.turismo-sostenible.co.cr/).
- There is a strong environmental lobby supporting the government's conservation policies.
- Costa Rica has technical and financial support from the IMF and the US government for its conservation programmes.

Moreover, Costa Rica is at the forefront of countries aiming to be carbon-neutral in the near future.

With improved road access from San José and the port of Puntarenas, which receives a growing number of cruise passengers, some of the most popular national parks now receive a thousand visitors a day during the high season. There is a real danger that environmental capacities will be exceeded, resulting in disturbance to wildlife. With this rate of growth, the drive for profit in the short term may lead to a relaxation of conservation rules by national park staff. Other concerns include the following:

- The development of golf courses and a large resort complex in the Nicoya Peninsula has been criticised by environmentalists as being incompatible with Costa Rica's image as a destination for ecotourism. These projects are driven by the government's need for a higher-yield type of tourism to service the country's large foreign debt.
- Although 25 per cent of the country is designated for protection, most of the land remains in private ownership so that enforcement of conservation measures can be problematic.
- The certification scheme has been criticised as 'greenwashing', where, for example, a large hotel can be awarded the same environmental rating as a small jungle lodge by complying with waste management and recycling targets (Dasenbrock: 2002).
- The growth of adventure tourism, which includes activities such as bungee-jumping, mountain bike riding, and canyoning, as well as kayaking, white-water rafting, and horse riding. Although most of these activities take place outside national park boundaries, some eco-tour operators view adventure tourism as a threat to their business. Zip-wires enable tourists to cross fast-flowing rivers but cause disturbance to wildlife, while developments such as a 'nature theme park' including an 'Indian village' are not really compatible with a nature-based tourism claiming it

has 'no artificial ingredients'. On the other hand, some tour companies combine adventure with nature study and work closely with local communities. It is claimed that if the young people of the community are involved in these activities, they will be more inclined to conserve the natural environment for future generations.

Panama

Panama (https://www.visitpanama.com/) received 1.8 million tourist arrivals in 2018. The country owes much of its importance as a tourist destination to the famous Canal (https://www.pancanal.com/eng/), which passed from United States to Panamanian control at the end of 1999, along with the surrounding territory known as the Canal Zone. Some 40 to 50 ships pass through the Canal each day. The locks at Gatún, where the Canal crosses the Continental Divide, must count as one of the world's major feats of engineering. The city of Panama, with its mixture of high-rise modern buildings and Asian bazaars, is a major centre of international commerce, encouraged by the country's liberal banking laws and use of the dollar as the national currency. The Biomuseo celebrates Panama's biodiversity. The free port of Colón, at the western (Caribbean) end of the Canal, is another important trading centre. However, Panama has yet to realise its full potential as 'the crossroads of the Americas', due to the jungles of Darien only 200 kilometres to the east. These pose a formidable barrier – the notorious 'Darien Gap' – to the completion of the Pan-American highway system, and any projected route must respect the land claims of the local Amerindian tribes.

Panama's holiday attractions mainly lie in the offshore islands. Of these, the Pearl Islands (https://pearl-islands.com/) have received the most attention from tour operators. The most important of these – Contadora – is a luxury resort and conference venue. The San Blas Islands (https://sanblas-islands.com/) are noted for game-fishing, but here the local Kuna tribe have kept development at arms length – tourism has to be on their terms.

It is likely that the former Canal Zone will be developed to yield maximum revenue, with marinas, hotels, and timeshare apartments. In the past, the Canal itself was too restricted for the largest cruise ships, and so a third set of locks to accommodate cruise ships was completed in 2016 – but this development could have an adverse environmental impact, affecting water supplies to the city of Panama. In contrast, ecotourism is being encouraged in other parts of the country, along with projects to restore the old Spanish seaport of Portobelo – a reminder that the isthmus was an important transit corridor for trade centuries before the opening of the Canal.

South America

South America receives around 2.6 per cent of the world's international tourist arrivals. The high cost of air fares and the lack of charter flights partly explains why this continent remains a destination for the wealthy or adventurous traveller. There is also a shortage of suitable hotels for the inclusive tour market. Long-term planning and investment in the tourism industry have been discouraged by political instability and inflation.

Climatic conditions, dense vegetation, and rugged terrain have been great obstacles to road and railway construction in many areas. In the west, the Andes – the world's longest mountain range, and second only to the Himalayas in altitude – pose a formidable barrier. Most of South America lies within the tropics, and the continent includes the world's largest rainforest in the Amazon Basin. Water transport is still widely used wherever there are navigable rivers – such as the Amazon and the Paraná – but shipping services are usually slow and uncomfortable. Transport infrastructure is gradually improving with the expansion of the Pan-American highway network and the development of internal air services. Rail systems in South America tend to be rudimentary, but some of the world's most spectacular lines are to be found in the Andes, and these have become tourist attractions in their own right.

A number of countries in South America are undergoing rapid industrialisation, resulting in an increase in business travel from Europe and the United States. As for the holiday market, national tourist offices in South American countries are generally underfunded, so overseas promotion has been left to the national airlines or to specialist tour operators in the tourist-generating countries. Closer international co-operation, as among the Andean Community (http://www.comunidadandina.org/) countries and those belonging to MERCOSUR (The Common Market of the South) (https://www.mercosur.int/en), should facilitate travel within the region and bring about more effective tourism promotion.

Brazil

Brazil (https://www.visitbrasil.com/) occupies almost half of South America and is a leading member of MERCOSUR. Unlike most Latin American countries, Brazil has a well-defined image, based on its beaches, the Rio de Janeiro carnival (https://www.rio-carnival. net/EN/), and the Amazon rainforest. The country is comparable in size to the United States – spanning three time zones – and is the world's sixth most populous country, with over 200 million inhabitants, mainly concentrated along the Atlantic seaboard. Brazilians are essentially the result of a fusion of three cultures – Portuguese, African, and Amerindian. Since the nineteenth century, the country has also attracted many millions of immigrants from all over the world, including Germany, Italy, and Japan, but it has arguably been more successful than the United States in blending different races and cultures.

Brazil's market potential for tourism is closely linked to the development of the economy, now the largest in Latin America, which has grown rapidly since 2001. Brazil is now one of the five leading 'emerging market' economies, but it remains to be seen whether the 'boom and bust' cycle, so evident in the past, has been resolved. Most of the country's industrial wealth is concentrated in the Rio de Janeiro – São Paulo – Belo Horizonte triangle, while other regions, notably the North-east, remain poor and underdeveloped.

Demand for tourism

Domestic and outbound tourism

The growth in the economy has swelled the ranks of the Brazilian middle class, who now have discretionary income for both domestic and international tourism. Under the country's labour laws, employees are guaranteed a 44-hour week and an annual paid holiday of 30 days, but many are excluded from becoming tourists by low incomes, especially in the rural areas. However, recreational facilities are provided by the state governments in city areas, while the beaches are freely available to rich and poor alike. Domestic tourists tend to use small hotels and campgrounds or stay with friends and relatives. As a result of competition between the airlines, the number of domestic trips doubled between 2005 and 2013, reaching almost 90 million. Although Brazilians are beginning to travel widely in their own country, they tend to be far more interested in beach holidays than in trips to the Amazon, as the beach and the cult of the 'body beautiful' occupies a central place in the nation's hedonistic lifestyle. Television through the popular *tele-novelas* (soap operas) plays an important role in opening up new coastal areas for the domestic market.

Outbound travel has also shown rapid growth, to approach 10.8 million trips in 2019. For many Brazilians, it is their first experience of travelling abroad, so group tours are preferred to independent travel, and with the advantage of a strong currency, spending levels, particularly on shopping, tend to be high. While the United States remains the most popular destination, more Brazilians than before are travelling to European countries, particularly Portugal and Spain, taking advantage of the competitive fares offered by Emirates and LATAM (https://www.latam.com/), South America's leading airline. As the result of expenditure on foreign travel, Brazil has a substantial deficit on its tourism account.

Inbound tourism

Brazil received 6.4 million tourist arrivals in 2019, and tourism ranks fifth in the country's foreign exchange earnings. Most tourists come from neighbouring countries, particularly Argentina, but the United States is an important market. The FIFA World Cup exceeded expectations, with a million extra arrivals in 2014 for this event, from a wide range of countries. There is a strong business travel sector, and São Paulo and Rio de Janeiro are among the world's leading cities for international conferences. The demand for holiday travel tends to be seasonal, with the greatest tourist activity taking place during the months of Carnival, which is also the hottest and most humid time of the year in most of Brazil. Nature, ecotourism, and adventure are the motivators for 20 per cent of foreign tourists.

The supply side of tourism

Transport

To reduce dependence on imported petroleum, Brazil pioneered the use of biofuels, with most motor vehicles using ethanol derived from sugarcane produced in the state of São Paulo. The recent discovery of vast offshore oil reserves near Rio de Janeiro has helped the country to aim for self-sufficiency in energy, while Petrobras, the state-owned petroleum corporation, has invested in environmental projects.

The vast size of Brazil poses a major problem for overland transport, especially during the rainy season from December to May. The Amazon and its tributaries provide 20,000 kilometres of navigable waterways, but these are far from the major populated areas, and port facilities are inadequate. The national transport strategy is to construct a number of major highways through the rainforest to improve access to the Amazon and eventually link up with the road system of neighbouring countries. However, the road network has not opened up the interior for development to the extent the government envisaged; rather, it has facilitated rural out-migration and contributed to the decline of Brazil's antiquated railway system. On the other hand, Brazil's internal air network is well-developed, with nine international airports and hundreds of airfields allowing access to even the most remote areas. Facing a financial crisis, the national airline VARIG was acquired by the low-cost carrier GOL (https://www.voegol.com.br/en) in 2007, and its competitor LATAM now provides a greater choice of domestic and international services. There is a frequent shuttle service between São Paulo and Rio de Janeiro for business travellers.

Organisation

Tourism development since the 1960s has been the responsibility of Embratur (http://www.embratur.gov.br), a federal government agency, but until 2003, Brazil did not have a Ministry of Tourism with dedicated funding. Previously, the sector had been the remit of the Ministry of Sport and before that, to the Ministry of Foreign Trade. The federal government now recognises the central importance of tourism to the economy with more effective marketing, national tourism plans, investment in training to improve professionalism, and expanding the infrastructure. There has also been considerable investment by state governments and the private sector in hotels, theme parks, and other attractions. The government invested heavily in facilities for the FIFA World Cup in 2014, sparking widespread protests in this 'football-mad' nation at the exorbitant expense, and resulting in a legacy of underused stadiums that are costly to maintain.

Tourism resources

Brazil offers a wide diversity of landscapes, ranging from *caatinga* - thorny scrubland in the northeast, tropical savanna – *campo cerrado* – occupying the Planalto or central plateau, and the large areas of rainforest for which the country is best known. Much of this natural resource is protected in a large number of national parks managed by the Chico Mendes Institute for Biodiversity Conservation (ICMBio). However, problems of accessibility and lack of facilities mean that most parks are underused.

Brazil has five tourism regions, each offering a different appeal:

* **Amazonia** (http://www.visitamazonia.org/en) forms the major part of the world's greatest river basin, covering 5 million square kilometres and containing 20 per cent of the planet's freshwater resources. The region's rainforests hold a fascination for foreign visitors as an ecological resource threatened with destruction. This is a good example of a change in perception, exemplified by the film *The Emerald Forest*, contrasting with the earlier view of the Amazon as a 'green hell' vividly described by

Colonel Fawcett and other explorers. In Brazil itself, there is a growing environmental movement, following the Rio Summit in 1992, to prevent further exploitation of the region for large-scale cattle ranching, mining, dam construction, and road-building, but this faces opposition from powerful vested interests. Most tourists to Amazonia arrive by air at Manaus or Belém. Both cities have fine buildings dating from the rubber boom of the 1890s, particularly Manaus with its magnificent opera house. After a long period of decline, this city has been revitalised with its development as a free port. Santarem, at the confluence of the Amazon and the Tapajoz, is another important tourist centre. Ecotourists seeking a closer encounter with the rainforest are accommodated in a number of lodges, some of which are built in the tree canopy, while others use 'floatels' moored at the river bank. Sustainable tourism is aimed for in the following ways:

- By restricting lodge capacity to a small number of guests.
- By keeping facilities simple, using solar power and local food supplies wherever possible, and dispensing with air-conditioning.
- By maintaining remoteness, with the journey from, say, Manaus being undertaken by boat and canoe rather than by air.
- Visits to Amerindian villages are controlled by FUNAI (http://www.funai.gov.br/), the Indian Protection Agency. Tourists are taken to visit local families, but no family is visited regularly, so minimising impact.
- As a result of these policies the natural resources are protected, and the quality of the experience for the visitor is also maintained.
- The rivers of Amazonia are a resource for sport fishing, which is also managed sustainably. Americans account for 95 per cent of foreign tourists in this market. (According to the US Fish and Wildlife Service, there are 37 million sport fishing participants in the United States).

- **The North-east** consists of a fertile coastal belt and the semi-arid scrublands in the interior known as the *sertão* or backlands, an area prone to devastating droughts and often described as the 'Triangle of Thirst'. This is a poverty-stricken region that has traditionally exported millions of rural migrants to the cities of southern Brazil. The coast is very popular with Brazilians, as it offers many fine beaches. Former fishing villages are 'discovered' and then cease to be fashionable in the never-ending quest for the 'perfect beach'. The coast is the subject of a tourism development programme, resulting from an agreement between the state governments of the region and the Inter-American Development Bank (IDB) (https://www.iadb.org/en). International hotel groups have moved in, particularly along the 'Golden Coast' south of Recife, creating tourist enclaves. In contrast accommodation is in short supply and often substandard in the sertão, which has an important place in Brazilian folklore as former bandit country. The major tourist centres of the North-east include:

  - Salvador de Bahia, one of the major cultural centres of Brazil, famed for its attractive colonial architecture, and as the birthplace of the samba, hosting a carnival that rivals the more famous one in Rio de Janeiro.
  - Fortaleza, noted for its fine beaches.
  - Recife the international gateway to the region, known as the 'Venice of Brazil' on account of its many waterways.

- The remote island of Fernando do Noronha, located in the Atlantic Ocean 400 kilometres from Recife, has become a fashionable destination, with world-class resources for surfing and diving. Designation as a national park means that the number of visitors is strictly limited, with each visitor paying an entrance fee, and the island remains difficult and expensive to reach.

- **The Centre-West** is Brazil's underdeveloped heartland, although it received a major boost in the 1960s with the establishment of Brasilia as the new federal capital. Most of the region consists of savanna grassland, with extensive wetlands near the Paraguayan border. This area, known as the Pantanal, is rich in wildlife that had previously co-existed with cattle ranching. This unique environment is now under threat from the activities of poachers and loggers, the expansion of agriculture, and projects to improve navigation on the Rivers Paraná and Paraguay that interrupt the annual flood cycle. The government-sponsored National Environment Agency has designated a number of natural reserves in the region, but these are relatively small and underfunded. In contrast, Brasilia is noted for its freeways and the visionary architecture of Oscar Niemeyer, epitomised by the Palace of Congress and the National Museum of the Republic. Although the capital is attractively landscaped, it lacks the vibrancy of other cities, particularly at night, as most workers have to live in dispersed suburbs.

- **The South** is the only region of Brazil to experience a temperate climate, with occasional frosts during the winter months. It is home to many migrants from Europe, including a large German-speaking community. Florianopolis is a popular beach resort for domestic tourists and well-off Paraguayan visitors, while Curitiba is one of the most progressive cities in the Americas. The major attraction for foreign tourists is Iguaçú Falls (www.iguacubrasil.com) on the border with Argentina. This is actually a series of cataracts three times larger in volume than Niagara. Walkways have been built in the Garganta de Diablo gorge at the edge of the biggest waterfall. The resort of Foz de Iguaçú has good communications by air and is a major conference venue.

- **The South-east** receives the most foreign tourists, largely because it contains Rio de Janeiro. This is one of the world's great tourist cities, for the following reasons:

  - Approximately 80 kilometres of fine sandy beaches, the best known being Copacabana and the more fashionable Ipanema. These are ideal for people-watching (but not for bathing due to the heavy Atlantic surf).
  - The uninhibited dance rhythms and extravagant costume parades of the Rio Carnival, which is a showcase for Brazilian creativity. There is the official Carnival, a sponsored event held in the Sambadrome, in which only the members of the top 'samba schools' participate, and then there are the popular street parties and parades which last for five days. Carnival attracts 5 million visitors, of whom 10 per cent are foreign tourists.
  - The spectacular beauty of Rio's setting, on one of the world's finest harbours, backed by the granite peaks of Sugarloaf and Corcovado (https://www.bondinho.com.br/), which is crowned by the iconic statue of Christ the Redeemer.

To complement these resources, the city has a well-developed transportion infrastructure, including two major airports and world-class hotels concentrated in the Copacabana area.

Photo 25.1

Rio de Janeiro receives the majority of Brazil's foreign tourists

Source: ©istockphoto.com/Luoman

CASE STUDY 25.2
TOURISM AND POVERTY ALLEVIATION
IN RIO'S FAVELAS

Mudslides, resulting from exceptionally heavy rains in May 2010, led to hundreds of deaths in the *favelas*, the shanty towns that sprawl down the hillsides and overlook the wealthiest neighbourhoods of the city. While their inhabitants may enjoy some of the best views, they are deprived of basic sanitation and other services. About 20 per cent of Rio's population resides in these slums. In response to the disaster, the government initiated a programme to relocate the slum-dwellers. However, many residents suspect that this was a pretext to clear prime sites for redevelopment in preparation for the World Cup and the Olympic Games.

Contrary to popular belief, the vast majority of favela-dwellers are not criminals but work in low-paid jobs in the city, mainly in the informal sector of the economy. Roçinha, the largest of the favelas with an area of 144 hectares and a population estimated at 150,000, supports many small businesses, cybercafes, bars, and even a local TV station, all established through local initiative. The city authorities are unable to control tax evasion, the establishment of businesses without legal permit, and the illegal tapping of electricity from the municipal grid. A semblance of order and so-cial aid for those in need is provided by well-organised gangs involved in the illegal drugs trade. So far, tourism has done little to benefit the people of the favelas, but Roçinha has been the subject of a private initiative to train local guides to show tourist groups the hidden face of Rio and help regenerate the area.

This policy is now being adopted by the city authorities, but only in those favelas that have been 'pacified' by removing them from gang control. It became imperative to reduce the high levels of street crime for which Rio is notorious and provide a se-cure environment for foreign tourists arriving for the FIFA World Cup. A special police force, the UPP, has been deployed for this purpose, using less draconian methods than in the past. This policy has had some success, even in Cidade de Deus, a favela made internationally famous through the movie *City of God*. However, some critics allege that the problem of criminal gangs is simply transfered from the south and west of the city, the areas most visited by tourists, to favelas on the outskirts.

The coastline between Rio and Santos, set against the lush mountain scenery of the Serra do Mar, has been designated for major tourism development. A number of beach re-sorts, are increasingly popular with foreign visitors, such as Buzios, Angra dos Reis, and Sepetiba. However, development poses a threat to the Atlantic rainforests, already under severe pressure. The interior of this part of Brazil also has much to attract the cultural tourist, including the picturesque colonial towns of Mariana and Ouro Preto (https://ouropreto.org.br/), which prospered from the silver and diamond mining boom of the eighteenth century. Business travellers gravitate toward the big modern cities of Belo Horizonte and São Paulo.

- São Paulo diversified from coffee production to become one of the world's great man-ufacturing and financial centres during the twentieth century. Until recently, the city was primarily a business destination, and leisure tourism held little significance. Brazil's largest city now vigorously promotes its sporting, cultural, and entertainment attractions, making it the country's leading destination, although only 15 per cent of its visitors are international tourists. The city exemplifies the contrasts that exist in Brazil between private wealth and social deprivation; it boasts South America's highest car and helicopter ownership, along with major pollution and water supply problems. On the other hand, the state of São Paulo has pioneered an outstanding example of social tourism for low-income families.

Northern South America

We could include the northern countries of South America as part of the Caribbean re-gion; in fact, Venezuela and Suriname belong to the CTO, while Guyana and Suriname are members of Caricom. Colombia and Venezuela share an extensive coastline on the

Caribbean, and the cities of Cartagena and La Guaira (serving Caracas) feature prominently on some cruise itineraries. Guyana, Suriname, and French Guiana have cultural similarities with the West Indies and maintain close links with Britain, the Netherlands, and France respectively. Moreover, the music of the tropical coastlands of Colombia, Venezuela, and the Guianas is African rather than Amerindian in origin.

Colombia

The political and economic situation in Colombia has improved considerably in recent years with the end of the long-running conflict between the government and the FARC guerrilla movement, which had affected large areas of the country. Another, more romantic image is provided in the novels of García Márquez, epitomised by Mompox on the River Magdalena. Nowadays, it is a picturesque backwater, but in colonial times, the town was a major commercial centre. Colombia has made significant progress in industrial development and is also the world's chief exporter of coffee and emeralds.

The demand for tourism

Domestic and outbound tourism

Rising incomes and competition between low-cost carriers, such as Viva Air (https://www.vivaair.com/co/en), have made holiday travel more affordable for Colombians, resulting in approximately 4.5 million foreign trips in 2019. The primary destinations include the United States, followed by Mexico, Spain, Panama, and Ecuador.

Inbound tourism

Colombia received 4.5 million tourist arrivals in 2019, and tourism is a major source of employment. Most visitors arrive overland from Ecuador and Venezuela, attracted by shopping bargains. Promotion is mainly aimed at the US market, although growing numbers of tourists are coming from Germany and France.

The supply side of tourism

Transport

The national airline, Avianca (https://www.avianca.com/uk/en/), was among the first to pioneer domestic air services in the Western Hemisphere; this was largely in response to the difficult topography. Colombia is compartmentalised by the Andes, which here form a triple chain of mountains, acting as a formidable barrier to east-west communication. Not surprisingly, small regional airlines, often employing robust aircraft that can use short runways, are the lifeline for many communities. As elsewhere in South America, long-distance bus services play a much more important role than the limited rail network.

Accommodation

Most of the international hotel chains have invested in Colombia, particularly in the major cities. In addition, the former Corporación Nacional de Turismo (CNT) developed a network of *paradors* (luxury hotels) along the main tourist routes.

Organisation

Tourism policy is based on the National Development Plan, which changes every four years. The Ministry of Commerce, Industry, and Tourism (MINCIT) has overall responsibility for the sector. At the national level, MINCIT works with three main agencies:

*   FONTUR (The National Tourism Fund).
*   ProColombia is the agency charged with international promotion and attracting foreign investment.
*   Colombia Productiva assists the private sector in providing a quality service.

At the regional level, each of the 32 departments has responsibility for tourism development.

Tourism resources

Although Colombia has an extensive share of the Amazon rainforest and a long Pacific coastline, factors such as climate, accessibility, and security determine that the most popular tourist area is the Caribbean coast. Here, tropical beaches are backed by the snow-capped mountains of the Sierra Nevada. The beach resort of Santa Marta and the historic seaport of Cartagena de Indias (https://www.cartagenadeindias.travel/), the key fortress of the 'Spanish Main' in colonial times, offer vibrant *cumbia* rhythms and beauty pageants among their attractions. The outlying islands of San Andrés (https://sanandres-colombia.com/) and Providencia in the Caribbean Sea attract domestic tourists with duty-free shopping.

Medellín is the second-largest city of Colombia and a major cultural centre. A high-capacity cableway links the city centre with the hillside communities. The department of Antioquia is one of the most progressive regions of the country, with a long-established social tourism programme providing recreation facilities and accommodation to low-income workers and their families. Cali is primarily a business destination but also offers salsa-based entertainment. For foreign visitors, the main tourist attractions are smaller cities such as Popayán, located in beautiful mountain valleys that still retain much of their Spanish colonial heritage. Bogotá is noted for its Gold Museum, a collection of artefacts from the pre-conquest Amerindian civilisations, while San Agustin (https://whc.unesco.org/en/list/744/) is one of the largest archaeological sites in the Americas.

Venezuela

As a major petroleum producer, Venezuela enjoyed the highest per capita income of any Latin American country before the fall in oil prices in the early 1990s. Middle-class Venezuelans travelled abroad in large numbers, particularly to Miami. Governments since 1999 have been committed to social change under the so-called Bolivarian Revolution, which takes its inspiration from Simón Bolívar, who liberated Venezuela and five other South American countries from Spanish rule in the early nineteenth century. The regime has failed to diversify the economy, which remains overwhelmingly dependent on oil exports. Consequently, Venezuela has suffered for many years from soaring inflation, a shrinking GDP, a shortage of everyday commodities, and a surge in crime, making Caracas and the states bordering Colombia the most violent areas in South America. The government has devalued the currency and imposed strict exchange controls, but this has led to a parallel economy based on an unofficial exchange rate. The outcome is widespread civil unrest and a massive flow of refugees to neighbouring countries, and many governments, including the United States, advise against travel to Venezuela.

The demand for tourism

The economic crisis has prompted the government to show a greater interest in promoting inbound tourism. Nevertheless, Venezuela has the reputation of being an expensive destination and receives fewer than half a million tourist arrivals anually. The loss of the American market has only been partially offset by visitors from Russia and some European countries. About half of the visitors are on business trips, and many are VFR tourists, a result of substantial immigration in the last century from Spain and Italy.

The supply side of tourism

Venezuela's shortcomings as a destination include an outdated infrastructure, insufficient co-ordination between the public and private sectors in tourism development, and, at the government level, the lack of a clear strategy for tourism.

The private car is the dominant mode for domestic tourists, thanks to cheap gasoline. Domestic air fares are high, restricting tourism despite the large number of airports throughout the country. Hotel capacity is mainly concentrated in the capital and the beach resorts of the Caribbean coast. Timeshare apartments are an important part of the accommodation sector, particularly for domestic tourists.

Tourism resources

Venezuela offers exceptional scenic variety, much of which is protected by the National Institute for Parks. Caracas is one of South America's largest cities and a major gateway to the continent. It is primarily a business destination, and most of the colonial heritage was swept away in the 1960s to be replaced by *superbloques* (neighbourhoods consisting of high-rise apartments) and modern highways. One important exception is the birthplace of Simón Bolívar (https://casa-natal-del-libertador.webnode.com.ve/). Most of Venezuela's attractions lie beyond the capital and include:

- The beach resorts of the Caribbean coast. The most important of these are Puerto La Cruz on the mainland and Porlamar on the island of Margarita, which comprises most of the state of Nueva Esparta. The climate here is dry and sunny throughout the year.

- The coral reefs of Los Roques attract divers.
- A section of the Andes, including the colonial city of Mérida.
- The vast grasslands known as the Llanos, and the Guiana Highlands south of the River Orinoco, offer many possibilities for ecotourism. Fly-in camps in this remote, sparsely populated region provide a base for exploring the strange landscapes of the *tepuys* – sheer-sided, flat-topped mountains that inspired Conan Doyle's *Lost World* – and viewing the world's highest waterfall – Angel Falls. The Orinoco is navigable for shipping as far inland as Ciudad Bolívar, while the delta is famous for its biodiversity. However, compared to similar waterways in other parts of the world, the river is greatly under-utilised for transport and tourism.

The Guianas

The Guianas are isolated from the rest of South America, and in Guyana, Suriname, and French Guiana, tourism is in its infancy, so that these countries receive fewer than 0.5 million visitors a year. Throughout the region, there is a contrast between the low-lying coast, with its plantation economy, and the forested interior, where Amerindian tribes maintain their traditional way of life. As in the Caribbean islands, the plantation economy was based on slavery, and after abolition, it relied on indentured labour from India and other Asian countries. The majority of the population live on the coast and are mainly of African or Asian origin. The coast lacks the beaches and coral reefs that make other tropical destinations appealing. Instead, the main resource is biodiversity, and poor infrastructure means that ecotourism is often the only viable form of tourism. A coastal highway linking the three countries was only completed in 1998, while the rivers and internal air services provide the only access to the interior.

- **Guyana** (https://guyanatourism.com) boasts some of South America's finest rivers and one of its highest waterfalls – Kaieteur – yet it remains barely exploited as a tourist attraction. The few hotels are primarily located in Georgetown, additional accommodation provided by forest lodges elsewhere. The Guyana Tourism Authority's Vision 2025 aims to protect the natural and cultural heritage, offer authentic experiences, and maximise the benefit to local communities. The Rupununi savanna region (http://www.visitrupunini.com/) in the south-west of the country is a good example of sustainable development, integrating ecotourism and forest management while involving local Amerindian communities.
- **Suriname** (https://www.surinametourism.sr/) has strong cultural and business ties with the Netherlands, and the capital, Paramaribo is one of the most cosmopolitan cities in South America, blending African and Indonesian cultures. The Suriname Hospitality and Tourism Association (SMATA) focusses its promotion campaigns on selected markets in co-operation with the Department of Trade, Industry, and Tourism. Ecotourism is centred on the Big Pan nature reserve and several lodges in the

interior, where tourists can also interact with communities of Maroons, the descendants of fugitive slaves who have evolved their own unique culture.

- **French Guiana** benefits from direct flights between Paris and the capital, Cayenne, due to its status as an overseas *département* of France, while Kourou serves as the base for the European Space Agency's 'Ariane' programme. Although ecotourism is being promoted, the country is better known as a 'dark tourism' destination due to its former role as a penal colony. St Laurent du Maroni in the interior served as the processing centre for incoming convicts, and the infamous Devil's Island, where 'Papillon' was imprisoned, is now on the tourism circuit.

The Andean republics

Peru, Ecuador, and Bolivia share a similar physical environment dominated by the Andes and a cultural heritage in which Amerindian influence is more prominent than elsewhere in South America. The region consists of three major physical divisions:

- The Pacific coastal lowlands of Ecuador and Peru, where there is some development of beach tourism.
- The High Andes, actually two mountain chains separated by a series of intermontane basins and high plateaux. Here, cultural tourism and, more recently, adventure tourism are important.
- The forested lowlands to the east of the Andes, forming part of the vast Amazon Basin, where ecotourism is being developed.

The majority of the attractions are found in the Andes, where there is a great variety of climates and landscapes due to differences in altitude. The arrangement of zones is similar to that of Mexico and Central America, but there are also extensive areas above 4,000 metres altitude, known as *puna*, where the climate is bleak and dry, or as *páramo*, where it is cold and damp year-round. Although *soroche* (mountain sickness) is a distinct possibility due to the altitude, climbers from all over the world are attracted to the challenge of peaks such as Chimborazo, Huascarán (https://whc.unesco.org/en/list/333/), and Illimani, while the spectacular scenery attracts growing numbers of trekkers from Europe and North America. There is also much to interest the cultural tourist. Intricate cultivation terraces on steep mountainsides, and the remains of temples and fortresses bear witness to the achievements of the Incas who ruled this part of South America prior to the Spanish conquest. The Amerindian influence is also evident in the artistic heritage of the colonial period in cities such as Quito (https://quitotravel.ec/en/), Cuzco, and Sucre, as well as in the folklore and plaintive music of the Andes.

Due to the difficult terrain, road transport in the Andean republics is inadequate. However, air travel within the region has been facilitated since the early 1990s under the terms of the Andean Community. Accommodation varies widely in quality, standards of service, and cost. There is a large informal sector of hostels, often with very basic facilities, that caters for the backpacker market.

Peru

Peru (https://www.peru.travel/en) is the largest of the Andean republics with a population of around 30 million. For centuries, Peru has been mainly renowned for its mineral
wealth, and gold is the reason the country boasts the world's highest permanent settlement, La Rinconada, at an altitude of 5000 metres (over 16,000 feet). Lacking basic
services and grossly polluted, this is few people's idea of a tourist destination. In contrast,
the Inca ruins at Machu Picchu are among South America's most iconic images and have
put Peru firmly on the tourist map. Tourism accounts for 3.9 per cent of GDP and directly
provides 4 per cent of employment. The COVID-19 pandemic had a devastating impact,
particularly on the informal sector of tourism and Andean rural communities. With no
markets for their handicrafts, many had to return to subsistence farming for a livelihood.

The demand for tourism

Domestic and outbound tourism
A growing middle class generates a substantial demand for tourism, amounting to over 40
million domestic trips a year. The Pacific coast is the most popular destination, especially
during the Christmas and New Year holidays. Peruvians also travel abroad, mainly to
Chile but also to the United States and Spain.

Inbound tourism
Peru received 4.4 million tourist arrivals in 2019. Tourists from Western Europe and the
United States each account for about a quarter of all arrivals. Peru appeals both to the luxury tour market, which has proved resilient to the effects of recession, and to the young
traveller on a budget who sees the country as an adventure destination.

The supply side of tourism

Transport
The government's open skies policy has attracted foreign airlines, including European
carriers. The rail system – primarily developed for conveying minerals from the Andes
to coastal ports – is being revitalised for tourism. It includes the highest narrow-gauge
railway in the world (from Callao to Huancayo – reaching 4,800 metres) and the 'Inca
Rail' from Cuzco to Machu Picchu, Peru's best-known attraction. However, most domestic
travel is by road or by air.

Organisation
The Ministry of Foreign Trade and Tourism (MINCETUR) has overall responsibility for
tourism policy, while tourism promotion abroad is carried out by PROMPERU (https://
www.promperu.gob.pe/), with private sector backing. The Ministry also oversees COPE-
SCO, which is concerned with restoring historic sites. The National Council for Handicraft

Development recognises the importance of this sector for tourism, particularly in rural communities. In a country that is more than twice the size of France, regional governments play an important role in tourism development.

Tourism resources

Most of the tourist attractions in Peru are located in the Andes, although Lima is the usual starting point for cultural tours. Cuzco is said to be the oldest continuously inhabited city in the Americas, where Spanish buildings have been erected on Inca foundations. Cuzco and the 'sacred valley' of the Urubamba provide the best examples of the heritage of this advanced Amerindian civilisation. These include:

* The Inca fortresses of Sacsahuamán and Ollantaytambo, built of intricate masonry without the use of mortar or iron tools.
* The 'lost city' of **Machu Picchu** (https://whc.unesco.org/en/list/274/), abandoned for centuries in the forest and rediscovered by an American archaeologist in 1911. By 2020, the site attracted around 1 million visitors a year, with a few arriving by helicopter, and the majority making the journey by rail and road along the Urubamba Valley. Approximately 20 per cent of visitors followed the classic 'Inca Trail' – actually one of three trekking routes, originally used by Amerindian couriers and llama pack trains. This popularity has had a negative impact in the form of widespread erosion, discarded toilet paper, and other refuse, as well as damage from illegal campfires. In 2001, the authorities closed the trail to all but authorised trekking companies employing local guides and porters and imposed an upper limit of 500 trekkers a day.

Discussion point
Some argue that the ban on independent hikers, most of whom are environmentally aware, is indiscriminate. Another controversy concerns the transport of tourists from the hotels in Aguas Calientes, the railhead, and service centre for Machu Picchu, to the actual site. This involves replacing the diesel minibuses that are currently used by an aerial cableway, but this project has aroused a storm of opposition and is currently in abeyance. An alternative proposal is to develop another Inca site in a remote location 70 kilometres away, with an aerial cableway providing access. This would take the pressure off Machu Picchu. In class, debate these issues, considering visitor safety, the economic advantages of improved access, and the impact on the environment.

Alternative attractions to Cuzco and Machu Picchu include:

* The attractive city of Arequipa (https://www.arequipa.com/) with its colonial architecture and the nearby Colca Canyon.
* The Callejón de Huaylas in the north of the country with its spectacular mountain scenery.

- Lake Titicaca, shared with Bolivia – at almost 4,000 metres (12,500 feet) altitude, this is the world's highest navigable body of water.

The Peruvian coast is mainly desert, although temperatures are moderated by the cold Humboldt Current, and fogs known as *garua* are a feature of the climate of Lima. Periodically, the Humboldt Current is displaced by a warm current flowing from the Equator; because this occurs around Christmas, the phenomenon is known as El Niño (the Christ Child in Spanish). El Niño episodes bring abundant rainfall and dramatic changes to the arid coastal region, including:

- Destruction of marine life; with warmer sea temperatures, fish stocks decline, and this has can have a disastrous impact on the important fishing industries of Peru and Ecuador.
- Impacts on the distribution and diversity of the wildlife resources of the Galápagos Islands.
- Disruption by mudslides and flooding to coastal communities and infrastructure.

An El Niño event is sometimes followed by its female counterpart – La Niña – a period of exceptionally cool sea surface temperatures, which has a reverse effect. El Niño is related to a wider climatic phenomenon in the Southern Hemisphere known to meteorologists as the Southern Oscillation (ENSO). This is responsible for extreme weather events in many parts of the world, such as droughts in Australia, and there are concerns that El Niño episodes will become more severe with 'global warming'.

The beaches of Peru's coastal region now feature on the international surfing circuit. The coastal desert has yielded many relics of ancient Amerindian civilisations long predating the Incas, including the mysterious Nazca Lines and the Moche culture, celebrated for its pottery and advanced irrigation systems. This heritage is increasingly at risk from treasure seekers and the illicit trade in pre-Columbian artefacts.

Lima, with a population approaching 10 million, is one of the largest cities in the Americas, including the *barriadas* (squatter settlements) named more euphemistically, *pueblos jovenes*, housing thousands of rural immigrants. In contrast, the historic centre has many cultural attractions as a reminder of its role as the power base for Spanish rule in South America. These include the Palacio de Torre Tagle, which is an outstanding example of colonial architecture.

Peru also includes a large part of the Amazon Basin. Iquitos is the main tourist centre although it is yet inaccessible by road, and during the rubber boom around 1900, this was an important centre of commerce, despite being 3,700 kilometres from the Atlantic Ocean.

Ecuador

Ecuador has many natural advantages as a tourist destination, containing a range of attractions within a relatively compact area. To an extent, Ecuador is South America in miniature, characterised by a high rate of population growth and a high rate of urbanisation – both Quito and Guayaquil have grown tenfold since 1957.

The demand for tourism

Domestic and outbound tourism

Domestic tourists visit spas such as Baños in the Andes noted for its thermal springs or the beach resorts of the Pacific coast, particularly Atacames and Suá near Esmeraldas, while Salinas and Playas are within easy reach of Guayaquil.

Inbound tourism

Tourism is an important earner of foreign exchange for Ecuador, and accounts for 5 per cent of GDP. Tourist arrivals reached 2.1 million in 2019, but many of these are low-spending backpackers. The United States accounts for a quarter of arrivals, followed by Colombia, Peru, and Chile. Ecotourism is the largest growth market. Adventure tourism is also important, and the up-market holiday options available include stayovers on colonial-style *haciendas* in the Andean region of Ecuador.

The supply side of tourism

Transport

The airports of Quito and Guayaquil are linked to a number of major cities in North and South America. Internal transport is facilitated by domestic air services or by road. One of South America's most spectacular railways, linking Quito to Guayaquil, has been revived as a heritage tourist route using authentic steam locomotives and traditional rolling stock. The Tren Crucero or 'Cruise Train' has been promoted successfully in the United States and Britain with the growing interest in 'slow travel', and as such, it provides a market for the indigenous communities along its route.

Organisation

The aim of the Ministry of Tourism is to improve the profile of Ecuador by attracting more 'high-value' visitors.

Resources

Ecuador has few rivals for biodiversity. This is particularly true on the western flanks of the Andes, where constant humidity supports a narrow zone of 'cloud forest' at altitudes between 900 and 2,500 metres. This resource is under threat from illegal logging and mining, but the government has designated a system of national parks and nature reserves, which provide a measure of protection for 17 per cent of the country. The effectiveness of conservation is held back by underfunding and the lack of trained guides. The Cotopaxi National Park, centred on South America's most famous volcano, is under pressure from tourism development.

We can divide Ecuador into four contrasting regions:

- The Sierra or Andean region
- The coastal lowlands
- Ecuador's section of the Amazon Basin, known as the Oriente
- The Galápagos Islands (https://whc.unesco.org/en/list/1/), situated in the Pacific Ocean, about 1,000 kilometres west of Guayaquil. Nevertheless, they are the best-known part of Ecuador due to wildlife programmes in the media and generate much of the country's revenue from tourism (see the case study).

Within the Sierra are the series of intermontane valleys known as the 'Avenue of the Volcanoes'. An attractive countryside, framed by mountains and eucalyptus trees, along with picturesque markets selling a variety of handicrafts, explains the Sierra's appeal. The cities have a rich cultural heritage, especially the following which are both World Heritage Sites:

- Quito, known as 'the city of eternal spring' is celebrated for the number of Baroque churches and convents in its historic centre. Located nearby is the much-visited Mitad del Mundo (Middle of the World) attraction, which commemorates the French scientist La Condamine's determination of the Equator (and the origins of the metric system of measurement). The capital's reputation as a tourist centre is suffering from runaway growth, air pollution, and the consequences of the economic crisis that has afflicted Ecuador since the early 1990s.
- Cuenca (https://whc.unesco.org/en/list/863/), Ecuador's third-largest city, has similar cultural attractions but fewer social and environmental problems.

The coastal lowlands offer a very different environment to the Sierra, with a plantation economy geared to export markets. The toquilla fibre produced here is used to manufacture Panama hats. The seaport of Guayaquil is Ecuador's main business centre.

The Oriente is an area of rainforest that was undeveloped prior to the discovery of oil in the 1950s. Adventure tourism, including canoeing on the River Napo, is organised by tour operators based in Quito, who also promote the region for ecotourism. However, much of this so-called ecotourism is merely another form of exploitation that fails to benefit the local Amerindians. The exceptions are the Cuyabeno Reserve and Yasuni National Park, which are partly under the control of indigenous tribal communities. Here, tourist groups are limited in numbers, and sustainable forms of transport and accommodation are used. Nevertheless, the region's ecosystems continue to be under threat from oil spillages and its indigenous people from diseases against which they have little resistance.

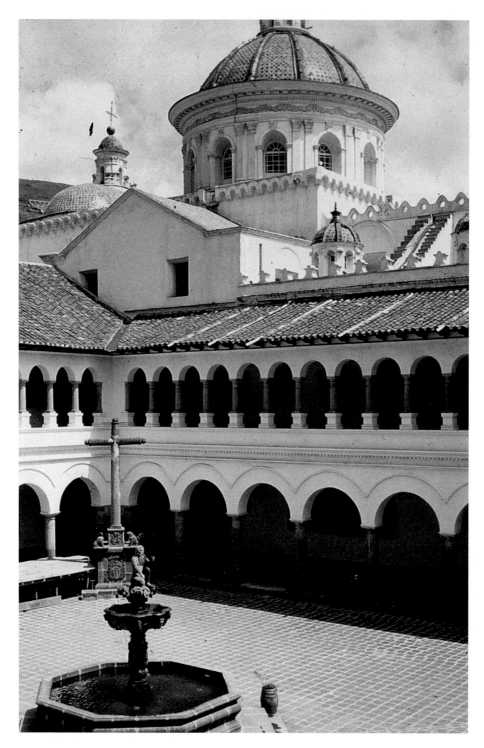

Photo 25.2
La Merced Convent, Quito

Source: Brian Boniface

The Galápagos are a group of 19 volcanic islands. The vegetation is far from exuberant, but the unique wildlife is a world-class attraction for ecotourists, and in 1959, 97 per cent of the land area was designated as a national park. The Galápagos have also been given international recognition as a World Heritage Site and Biosphere Reserve. The animals have no fear of human beings, as there are no natural predators. Although the islands are situated on the Equator, penguins and sea lions flourish alongside tropical species, due to the cold ocean currents offshore. The best-known animals are the giant tortoises and marine iguanas, with 14 distinct species on the different islands. This provided the inspiration for Darwin's theory of evolution by natural selection, and the value of the islands as a 'living laboratory' has long been recognised.

Ecotourists arrive at the Galápagos on domestic flights from Guayaquil or Quito and are then transfered to a live-aboard boat for a cruise lasting several days, visiting several islands. The number of vessels is controlled by a permit system to reduce the risk of contamination. Visitor impacts on the wildlife are minimal, due to the controls imposed by the Galápagos National Park Service (GNPS). These include:

- Fixed itineraries, with a naturalist-guide accompanying groups of visitors on the trail.
- A limitation on the number of visitor sites.
- A limitation on the number of visitors at any particular site.
- Visitors are prohibited from approaching wildlife too closely.
- Visitors are prohibited from taking 'souvenirs' such as shells or coral.

Furthermore, the GNPS can close sites or change itineraries in response to growing pressures. A visitor's initial impression of the islands before making a 'wet' or 'dry' landing by *panga* (an inflatable motorised dinghy) is of a pristine environment 'on the first morning of Creation'.

Although visitor management has been successful at site level, there is an absence of a long-term strategy for the growth of tourism in the region of Galápagos as a whole. The number of visitors has increased from less than 60,000 in 1997 to over 270,000 in 2022. Of these, 46 per cent were foreign tourists (who pay the full $100 US National Park entrance fee), and 54 per cent were Ecuadorians from the mainland, who may be not as environmentally aware. The growth of tourism has been fuelled by low-cost air travel and the opening of a second airport on the islands. The resident population of the islands increased from less than 2,000 in 1959 to over 33,000 in 2020. This has been largely due to immigrants from the mainland, many of whom are not registered, seeking economic opportunities. This, in turn, has increased the islands' dependence on food imports and the consequent risk of introducing invasive species of plants and animals, which may soon outnumber those native to the islands.

Photo 25.3
On the trail in Galapagos

Moreover, the number of tourists staying in hotels or low-budget accommodation has now surpassed those who are sea-based. Many of these visitors are attracted by opportunities for adventure tourism and sport fishing rather than nature-based tourism. If these trends continue, the Galápagos will no longer be truly unique, as similar attractions can be found elsewhere.

Although it would be desirable to limit hotel capacity and restrict further immigration from the mainland, the goal of sustainable tourism will probably not be achieved unless the local community are involved.

Bolivia

Until recently, Bolivia was a byword for political instability, where the Amerindian majority were marginalised and without a voice in the government of the country. In the new millennium, under a government committed to social change, Bolivians now take pride in their Inca heritage, traditional festivals such as the Oruro carnival, and the wearing of traditional costumes are encouraged, and new public buildings incorporate Amerindian motifs in their design. The Ministry of Cultures, Decolonisation and Depatriarchalisation underlines this radical ethos and is responsible for tourism policy.

Tourism in Bolivia is handicapped by the country's land-locked situation, inadequate communications, and a poorly developed accommodation sector. Nevertheless, it appeals to adventure-seekers and received over a million tourist arrivals in 2019. The country has as great a variety of landscapes as any in South America, including vast salt lakes in the south-west, which are being exploited for their mineral resources such as lithium, lush subtropical valleys on the northern flanks of the Andes, and tropical rainforests, swamps, and savannas in the eastern part of the country. Here, Santa Cruz has a booming economy, based on the region's oil and natural gas resources. Although a number of national parks, such as Madidi, and trekking routes – notably the Che Guevara Trail – have been designated, the number of tourists is small compared to those using the Inca Trail to Machu Picchu.

The Altiplano, at an average altitude of 4,000 metres, is Bolivia's heartland, a bleak plateau characterised by intense sunshine during the day and sub-zero temperatures for much of the year at night. The majority of the population are Amerindians, speaking the Quechua and Aymara languages rather than Spanish. Attractions include:

- The mysterious ruins of Tiahuanaco near Lake Titicaca are a reminder of a pre-Columbian civilisation that flourished here many centuries before the Incas.
- The Baroque architecture of the city of Potosi. This was made possible by the silver mines of the mountain known as the Cerro Rico overlooking the city, and the back-breaking labour of untold millions of Amerindians.
- Bolivia boasts the world's highest capital and international airport, La Paz (http://www.sabsa.aero/), which is now linked to the even higher city of El Alto by one of the world's longest, and most heavily used aerial cableways (http://www.miteleferico.bo/).
- The vast salt flats of Salar de Uyuni.

Temperate South America

Argentina, Chile, Uruguay, and Paraguay are in the part of South America lying outside the tropics. Due to its triangular shape, with the Patagonia peninsula tapering towards Antarctica, this region is known as the 'Cono Sur' (Southern Cone) by Spaniards and Latin Americans. Distance from the main generating countries in both Europe and North America has been a major disadvantage for the development of international tourism. Nevertheless, with the exception of Paraguay, these countries share a relatively high level of economic development and educational attainment. Since the nineteenth century, they have attracted large numbers of immigrants from Europe – particularly Italy and Germany – as well as Spain, and this has strongly influenced the culture, while the Amerindian heritage is less evident than elsewhere in Latin America. Tourism industries are well established, and there is a substantial middle class providing a large domestic market.

Paraguay

Paraguay (https://visitparaguay.travel/) is an enigma; one of the poorest, least developed and least publicised countries in the Western Hemisphere. Despite having a central location in South America, it is somewhat isolated, with few border crossings. The Rivers Paraná and Paraguay are fine waterways but are under-utilised. In consequence, Paraguay does not rank high as a destination, with little more than a million tourist arrivals a year. The National Secretariat of Tourism (SENATUR) aims to address this situation.

West of the River Paraguay lies the Gran Chaco, an expanse of scrubland characterised by drought, extreme summer heat, and occasional winter cold associated with the *Pampero* winds from the south. A few Mennonite settlements of German origin have achieved success in taming this wilderness, but most remain isolated from the outside world. Not surprisingly, the great majority of the population live in the eastern part of the country. Here, the scenery is also much more luxuriant, and attractions such as Lake Ypicaraí are popular with domestic and foreign tourists. An important part of Paraguay's appeal lies in the music and handicrafts of the Guaraní people. This is a legacy of the Jesuit missions that flourished here until 1767 when they were suppressed by the colonial authorities, a tragedy recounted in the movie *The Mission*. Paraguay's membership of MERCOSUR provides access to funding from the wealthier South American countries for much-needed infrastructural improvements. At present, there are few hotels outside the capital Asunción and the border town of Ciudad del Este, which has developed largely due to the Itaipú Dam project, and which offers shopping bargains to Argentinian and Brazilian visitors.

Uruguay

Uruguay's (https://turismo.gub.uy) position as a small country between two big neighbours – Argentina and Brazil – and its reputation for political stability, explains why the capital, Montevideo, has become an important venue for international conferences.

The demand for tourism

Domestic and outbound tourism

There is a strong domestic demand for tourism, particularly from Montevideo, which contains over a third of the country's population. In 2019, there were 2.1 million outbound departures, mainly to Argentina and Brazil. Travel further afield is constrained by Uruguay's relatively poor connectivity by air to other parts of the world.

Inbound tourism

Uruguay is a major destination for leisure tourists, attracting around 3 million arrivals in 2019. Two-thirds of these come from Argentina, followed by Brazil. This dependence on two markets is a problem, along with seasonality and a geographical concentration of tourism in Montevideo and the south-east coastal resorts.

The supply side of tourism

Transport

In such a relatively small compact country, transport is not a major problem and Uruguay has a good network of inter-city bus services.

Organisation

There is a Ministry of Tourism responsible for promotion, emphasising Uruguay's natural attractions and culture.

Tourism resources

The scenery is relatively low-key, and Uruguay's main tourist asset is 500 kilometres of fine beaches, many of which offer opportunities for surfing. Punta del Este is one of South America's most important holiday destinations, attracting the 'jet set' (mainly wealthy Brazilians and Argentinians) to its casinos, luxury hotels, boutiques, and sports facilities in the short summer season between December and February. A number of satellite communities supply the labour force for this exclusive resort, where access is determined by price. Other resorts along the Atlantic coast cater for large numbers of middle-class domestic tourists and Argentinians from Buenos Aires on the other side of the Rio de la Plata.

Uruguay is best known internationally for sport – it was the first country to host the FIFA World Cup (in 1930), commemorated by the Centenario Stadium in Montevideo. It shares much of the cultural heritage of Argentina, including gauchos and tango rhythms. The estancias or country estates in the interior are developing rural tourism in response to the fall in beef and wool prices on the world market. The abundant geothermal resources near Salto and Paysandú have been utilised for spa tourism. The following tourist centres merit special attention:

- The historic town of Colonia del Sacramento, which preserves the heritage of Portuguese and Spanish colonial rule.
- The town of Fray Bentos on the River Uruguay supplied meat products to a Europe devastated by the Second World War, when feeding the population was a more urgent need than foreign holidays. With growing prosperity in Europe, the decline in demand led to the closure of the factory, which is now a World Heritage Site and an unusual tourist attraction.

Argentina

Traditionally, Argentina (https://www.argentina.travel/) has looked towards Europe rather than the rest of South America for trade and cultural inspiration. The financial crisis of 2001 devastated the economy and dealt a severe blow to the country's self-image. Yet the world's largest Spanish-speaking country has vast natural resources, including cheap energy supplies and the fertile farmlands of the Pampas. These resources made Argentina one of the world's richest countries in the early part of the twentieth century, when Buenos Aires (https://turismo.buenosaires.gob.ar/en) was known as the 'Paris of South America'. However, much of this wealth was expended due to the social and economic projects of the Perón regime, and the decades of political strife that followed. One of the country's main problems is outdated infrastructure – most of the road and railway systems were built in the early twentieth century. Another issue is the imbalance between Buenos Aires – which has a disproportionate share of the wealth and population – and the provinces, which are deprived of political and financial influence despite a federal system of government.

The demand for tourism

Domestic and outbound tourism

Until the 1980s, incoming tourism was of little importance to the country's economy and better-off Argentinians spent much more on travel abroad – particularly to neighbouring Chile, Uruguay, and Brazil. Domestic tourism in Argentina is much larger in volume than either outbound or outbound tourism. With the revival of the economy in recent years, Argentinians are making over 12 million foreign trips a year, resulting in a substantial deficit on the country's travel account. Europe accounts for 20 per cent of outbound tourism, where close ethnic and cultural ties with Spain and Italy make these countries favourite destinations for Argentinians. To encourage domestic tourism and divert Argentinians away from the beaches of Brazil, Chile, and Uruguay, the federal government increased the number of public holidays from 11 to 19, benefitting the popular resort of Mar del Plata.

Inbound tourism

Argentina received 7.4 million tourist arrivals in 2019, mainly from Brazil, Uruguay, and Chile. Tourism is a now an important earner of foreign exchange and employs over 10 per cent of the workforce.

The supply side of tourism

Transport

Aerolineas Argentinas is one of the largest airlines in South America with its hub in Buenos Aires, while Flybondi is a low-cost carrier serving mainly domestic destinations. The Argentinian rail network in the early part of the twentieth century was one of the largest in the world. It now carries only a small volume of passenger traffic compared to road or rail transport.

Accommodation

Over half a million bed spaces are available in hotels, mainly concentrated in Buenos Aires and the second city of Argentina – Córdoba. There is a tendency for new projects to be located in outlying regions such as the Andes.

Organisation

The National Institute for Tourism Promotion (INPROTUR) has positioned Buenos Aires both as a destination in its own right and as the gateway to the rest of Argentina. There are also a number of regional tourist organisations responsible to the Ministry of Tourism.

Tourism resources

Argentina can offer the tourist a great variety of scenery, much of which is protected in a large number of national parks. In recent years, there has been a growing movement among conservationists towards re-wilding the landscape by introducing species such as the puma that had been decimated by the activities of ranchers. In Patagonia, former cattle and sheep ranches have become nature reserves, while the Iberá wetlands in the north-east provide a refuge for animals that have become extinct elsewhere. However, the introduction of beaver from North America has brought devastation to the forests of Tierra del Fuego, which are slow-growing due to the rigorous sub-Antarctic climate.

The **Pampas** are the heartland of Argentina, but these featureless grasslands are of little interest to foreign visitors, except as the setting for the gaucho (cattleman), who plays an important role in national folklore. Some of the *estancias* provide visitors with accommodation, an *asado* (barbecue), as well as displays of horsemanship and other traditional skills. In contrast, Buenos Aires is a cosmopolitan city displaying architectural styles from France, Italy, Spain, and Britain. Attractions include:

- The waterfront district known as La Boca, which is claimed to be the birthplace of the tango, Argentina's best-known contribution to the world of music and dance.
- The Teatro de Colón (https://teatrocolon.org.ar/en) rivals Milan's La Scala as one of the world's great opera houses.
- La Recoleta Cemetery is the resting place of Eva Perón, an outstanding feminist icon and social reformer in a continent noted for social inequality and *machista* attitudes.
- The beaches of Mar del Plata (http://www.turismomardelplata.gov.ar/), within easy reach of the capital, offer relief from the humid summers.

Most of Argentina's attractions are located in outlying regions of this vast country:

- The **north-east** offers Argentina's share of Iguazú Falls (https://iguazuargentina.com/en) and former Jesuit missions that are now World Heritage Sites (https://whc.unesco.org/en/list/275).
- The **north-west** is characterised by landscapes similar to those of neighbouring Bolivia. In the cities of Salta (http://www.turismosalta.gov.ar) and Jujuy (http://www.turismo.gov.ar/), the colonial heritage of Spain is much more evident than in Buenos Aires.
- The **Cuyo** region in the west includes spectacular mountain and desert landscapes, the vineyards around Mendoza, and the important ski resort of Las Leñas (https://www.laslenas.com/en/) in the foothills of the Andes. Here, the mountains form a formidable barrier between Argentina and Chile. The only major route linking the two countries is over the Uspallata Pass, with its famous statue of 'Christ of the Andes'.

Nevertheless, cross-border traffic forms a large percentage of the tourist arrivals in both countries.

- The **Argentine Lake District** includes the important resort of San Carlos de Bariloche (https://www.barilocheturismo.gob.ar/en) on Lake Nahuel Huapi, which is both a summer and winter destination for domestic tourists.
- **Patagonia** is the vast, sparsely settled expanse south of the Rio Negro. It lies in the rain shadow of the Southern Andes and as a result, is mostly a windswept semi-desert. Nevertheless, ecotourism and adventure tourism are significant, based on the marine wildlife resources of the Valdés Peninsula and the mountain, lake, and glacier scenery of Los Glaciares National Park. The heritage of the Welsh settlers in the Chubut Valley and the foothills of the Andes attracts growing numbers of domestic as well as foreign tourists, an example of tourism acting as a force for the revival of a language.
- The island of **Tierra del Fuego** is divided between Argentina and Chile. Ushuaia situated on Beagle Channel is Argentina's gateway to Antarctica but is also a tourist destination in its own right.

Chile

Chile is a narrow expanse of territory, situated between the world's largest ocean and the Andes, further isolated by the world's driest desert – the Atacama – to the north. As part of the 'Pacific Ring of Fire', the country is prone to devastating earthquakes. The latitudinal extent of the country, over 4000 kilometres from Arica to Cape Horn, results in striking contrasts in climate from tropical desert to the sub-Antarctic. Most of the population is concentrated in the central region which enjoys a Mediterranean climate.

The demand for tourism

Domestic and outbound tourism

Chile is one of the most successful economies in Latin America and is a leading member of the Pacific Alliance trade bloc. A substantial middle class generates a significant demand for tourism, encouraged by competitive air fares, to a wide range of destinations, including the United States. Domestic tourism is promoted by the government's 'Chile es tuyo' (Chile is yours) campaign (https://www.chileestuyo.cl/). This has stimulated Chileans to experience, many perhaps for the first time, the variety of landscapes their country can offer.

Inbound tourism

Tourism is a major growth sector of the economy, accounting for 3.3 per cent of GDP.

Chile received 5.4 million international tourist arrivals in 2019. The majority of these come from Argentina and Peru, but the United States is an important market, accounting for 4 per cent of arrivals.

The supply side of tourism

Transport

Air transport is a major part of the tourism infrastructure, overcoming the friction of distance in reaching this destination, which is geographically remote from the world's major tourist-generating countries. Coastal shipping services link Puerto Montt to Punta Arenas, providing a lifeline to communities in southern Chile. There is a good highway network serving most of the country, while in the south, the gravel-surfaced Carretera Austral plays an important role, extending the frontier of settlement in Chilean Patagonia. Travellers wishing to venture further south find the route overland blocked by the largest glaciers in the Southern Hemisphere outside Antarctica.

Organisation

The Ministry of Economy, Development and Tourism has the overall responsibility for tourism. The National Tourism Service, SERNATUR (https://www.sernatur.cl/), is responsible for promoting Chile as a destination. It has offices in each region working with the Chilean Economic Development Agency to improve tourism infrastructure. The post-COVID recovery plan includes a number of priority areas:

* Rural and indigenous tourism.
* Wine and gastronomy.
* Cultural and heritage tourism.
* Adventure tourism, working closely with the National Forest Corporation (CONAF), which administers Chile's national park system.

Tourism resources

Each region of Chile has different attractions to offer:

* **Northern Chile** is for the most part desert, much of it situated at high altitudes. The region was the setting for an important mining industry for nitrates and copper in the early part of the twentieth century, which brought prosperity to cities such as Antofagasta. Many former mining communities have since become 'ghost towns' amid a landscape of salt lakes and sand dunes. The Lauca National Park (https://www.conaf.cl/parques/parquenacional-lauca/) includes volcanoes and caldera lakes among its natural attractions and provides opportunities for ecotourism. Temperatures on the coast are greatly modified by the cold Humboldt Current, and there has been some development of beach tourism around ports such as Iquique, catering for domestic demand.
* **Central Chile** can be compared to California, with a fertile central valley lying between the Pacific coastal ranges and higher mountains to the east. Here, Santiago is one of the major gateways to South America. The ski resorts of Portillo (https://www.skiportillo.com/en/en) and Los Nevados (https://vallenevado.com/en/) are within easy reach, and these attract skiers from the United States during the Northern Hemisphere summer. The vineyards of the Maipó Valley provide Chile's best-known

export. The Pacific coast offers fine beaches, although heavy surf and strong currents discourage bathing. Viña del Mar (http://www.visitevinadelmar.cl/) is Chile's major beach resort and is also an important cultural centre. Valparaíso (http://www.vlpo.cl/) has a similar setting to that of San Francisco, but its prosperity declined with the opening of the Panama Canal, and the port needs urban regeneration.

- The **Lakes Region** around Temuco has a cooler, wetter climate that supports extensive forests of Araucaria pine. It boasts some of the world's most spectacular lake and mountain scenery, culminating in the active volcano of Osorno. The region is also the homeland of a substantial Amerindian minority – the Mapuche – that has been in dispute with the government over land rights since the return of democracy to Chile in the 1990s.

- **Southern Chile:** In contrast to the rest of the region, the island of Chiloé was settled early in the colonial period, and due to its former isolation, the fishing communities here are distinctive in their timber architecture and cultural traditions. Further south is one of South America's most challenging environments, a wilderness of fjords, glaciers, forests of evergreen beech, while the islands on the western fringes are exposed to the full force of the 'Roaring Forties' and 'Furious Fifties'. When Charles Darwin visited in the *Beagle*, he noted that the islands extending south of Tierra del Fuego to Cape Horn were inhabited by an indigenous people who had seemingly adapted to the cold, damp climate without clothing or basic shelter. Between these rain-swept islands and the mainland is an intricate network of relatively sheltered channels that nowadays provide a route for summer cruises.

  To the east, the Southern Andes are dissected by a number of valleys that have a much drier climate. Development in this part of Patagonia followed a similar path to that of Argentina, namely the removal of the indigenous population and the fencing off of large areas as sheep farms. The Aisén region contains a number of national parks and wildlife reserves, but conservation efforts are threatened by commercial logging and mining. Nevertheless, despite the rigorous climate, southern Chile offers considerable scope for adventure tourism. This is particularly true of the Torres del Paine National Park, which contains some of the most spectacular peaks in the Andes. Despite its remoteness, this attracts around 250,000 visitors a year, putting considerable pressure on the limited infrastructure.

Tourism has led to the revival of Punta Arenas, once a major port on a world shipping route through the Strait of Magellan, which became obsolescent with the opening of the Panama Canal. Although strong winds rather than warm sunshine characterise the weather here, the UV Index is frequently high, due to the depletion of the ozone layer over Antarctica. Puerto Williams claims to be the world's southernmost town and is a base for some cruises to Antarctica.

The island territories of Chile

Chile owns a number of islands in the Pacific Ocean, including the Juan Fernández archipelago almost 700 kilometres west of Valparaíso, and the much more distant Easter Island.

The main island of **Juan Fernández** is promoted as 'Robinson Crusoe Island' based on associations with the castaway Alexander Selkirk, the historical inspiration for Defoe's Robinson Crusoe. Uninhabited at the time of its discovery by Europeans, the archipelago has been designated a national park and World Biosphere Reserve, due to the unique character of the plants and bird life. With a population of less than a thousand, the infrastructure for tourism is limited.

Easter Island (Isla de Pascua in Spanish and Rapa Nui in the Polynesian language) (https://whc.unesco.org/en/list/715/) is the most enigmatic of all Pacific destinations. Since 1969, scheduled air services by LATAM have crossed the 3500 kilometres of ocean separating this remote island from mainland Chile and provide a link to Tahiti, which lies an equivalent distance to the west. Although there are world-class opportunities for surfing and scuba diving, tourists are attracted by the *moai*, mysterious stone statues serving as mute reminders of a vanished civilisation. Some experts theorise that these monuments were erected centuries ago as a form of competition between rival clans, and in so doing the inhabitants of Rapa Nui exploited the natural resources to the point of ecological collapse. The island was once covered with palm forest but is now treeless and windswept.

The future of Easter Island is tied to the growth of international tourism. In 1990, this small island received 6000 visitors; but with the extension of the airport to accommodate the largest jets (carried out by the US military), arrivals had increased to 45,000 in 2007. By 2020, the number of flights had increased to three per day, and the number of arrivals had more than doubled. Tourism has brought economic benefits but not without social tensions between the native Polynesians and the growing number of immigrants from mainland Chile. Without effective visitor management, historic sites are under threat, notably the Orongo crater associated with the 'Birdman' cult.

Discussion point

Small, formerly isolated islands are especially vulnerable to introduced species of plants and animals that wreak havoc with their ecosystems. Here, tourism is both part of the problem and also part of a solution. In class, debate this statement with reference to Cocos Island (https://isladelcoco.go.cr/) (which belongs to Costa Rica), the Juan Fernández Islands, Easter Island, and the Galápagos, explaining the differences between these four destinations and the approach to conservation by the authorities concerned.

The Falkland Islands

The Falklands (https://www.falklandislands.com/) are a group of islands in the South Atlantic some 500 kilometres east of Patagonia. Since 1833, they have been a British overseas territory, but Argentina has a long-standing claim to the islands it calls 'Las Malvinas', along with South Georgia and the South Sandwich Islands. In scenery, climate, and the lifestyle of its people, the Falklands more closely resemble the Scottish Hebrides than mainland South America. The penguins and sea mammals are representative of the sub-Antarctic zone, and this resource is marketed by the Falkland Islands Tourist Board as an international wildlife destination. The opening in 1985 of a modern airport near Stanley made the islands more accessible from Britain, but most tourists arrive via Santiago. In 2019, the Falkland Islands received 6,950 tourist arrivals, plus over 70,000 day visitors from cruise ships and expedition vessels. The Falklands and South Georgia are included in the itineraries of many cruises to the Antarctic, which we cover in Chapter 26.

Summary

- The countries of the Western Hemisphere south of the US border form a cultural entity where, for historical reasons, the Iberian culture and languages are dominant.
- The United States dominates the market for tourism to Mexico and Central America, but tourists from Western Europe are of growing importance to most South American countries.
- Beach tourism is of major importance in Brazil and Mexico, but elsewhere cultural tourism, based on traditional lifestyles and heritage sites is of more significance.
- Ecotourism is growing in importance, particularly in the more remote areas of Central and South America, but it has often failed to benefit indigenous communities.
- 'Soft' and 'hard' adventure tourisms are other growth markets, mainly in South America, based on spectacular scenery and vast areas of wilderness.
- Business tourism is also likely to increase in those countries which are undergoing rapid economic development, such as Brazil.
- Political instability, inadequate infrastructure, and ineffective marketing have held back tourism in most of the region.
- Although incomes are generally low throughout Latin America, domestic tourism is significant, and there is a considerable demand for outbound tourism to Europe and the United States from a growing middle class.

Review questions

1. Identify the opportunities for ecotourism in Central America and South America, and explain why these natural resources may be at risk.
2. Describe the pre-Columbian Amerindian cultures of Central and South America, and explain the importance of this heritage to certain countries for domestic and international tourism.
3. Analyse the strengths and weaknesses of Brazil as a destination for business and leisure tourism.
4. Investigate the role of sport and water-based recreation in attracting tourists to Central and South America.

References

Dasenbrock, J. (2002) The pros and cons of ecotourism in Costa Rica, *Trade Environment Database Case Studies* 648, 1–12

Mowforth, M. and Munt, I. (2008) *Tourism and Sustainability*, 2nd edition, Routledge, Abingdon

Organization for Economic Co-operation and Development (annual) *Tourism Policy and International Tourism in OECD Member Countries*, OECD, Paris

https://www.unwto.org/tourism-data/unwto-tourism-dashboard

26 The tourism geography of Antarctica

Learning objectives

After reading this chapter, you should be able to:

- Understand that ecotourism may be the only type of tourist activity compatible with the polar environment.

- Recognise that there are significant differences between Antarctica and other wilderness areas visited by ecotourists.

- Understand that the great majority of tourists arrive on cruise ships and spend only a short time ashore.

DOI: 10.4324/9781003406853-32

- Be aware that the greatest challenge is from the growth of adventure tourism and the resulting demand for tourist facilities in Antarctica.
- Understand the special political status of Antarctica and how this could be threatened by external pressures.

Introduction

Aside from space, Antarctica is probably the most hostile environment known to humankind. Indeed, for most of the twentieth century, the extreme climate and the remote location of Antarctica posed a major constraint on any type of human activity, let alone tourism. The bases dotted around the continent that provide accommodation for scientists and support workers are, in effect, life support systems, for which everything needed for survival has to be brought in from outside.

As shown in Figure 26.1, the 'white continent' is not the elongated strip at 'the bottom of the world' on Mercator maps, rather it is a vast expanse, roughly circular in shape, centred on the South Pole. There are only two seasons (the austral summer, cold but light, and winter, very cold and dark) and without any time zones. Representing the major part of the Earth's cryosphere, Antarctica contains around 70 per cent of the world's fresh water, frozen in the form of glaciers, ice shelves, and ice sheets. Antarctica is, by far, the world's largest wilderness but differs from other destinations for sightseers, nature lovers, and adventure-seekers in not having any indigenous communities to be affected by tourism. Thanks to ecotourism, Antarctica is no longer perceived as the 'white hell' of the early explorers. In the 1970s, this was tourism's last frontier; now there are guidebooks dedicated to the Antarctic, feature films such as *March of the Penguins* have sparked popular interest, and the number of tourists arriving during the austral summer months, from November through March, exceeds the resident population at the bases (Antarctica is off-limits for tourists from April through October). Nature-loving tourists are attracted by the unique wildlife, the awe-inspiring glacial scenery, and the heritage of polar exploration, associated with such figures as Amundsen, Byrd, Mawson, Ross, Scott, and Shackleton.

Although they feature in Antarctic cruise itineraries and guidebooks, it is crucial to initially distinguish the **Sub-antarctic islands of the Southern Ocean**, which are situated in middle latitudes, from the continent of Antarctica. The Southern Ocean is the realm of the albatross, containing only a few small, uninhabited islands, which are exposed to the 'Roaring Forties' and the 'Furious Fifties'. These islands lie close to the Antarctic Convergence, where the cold surface water spreading outwards from the frozen continent meets warmer water from the north. The climate is characterised by poor weather and overcast skies year-round, but the temperatures are mild compared to Antarctica. The islands' marine resources were exploited in the nineteenth century by whalers, sealers, shipwreck survivors, and even would-be colonisers, who introduced alien species that devastated the native plants and birds. Unlike Antarctica, these islands are under the sovereignty of a specific country. As mentioned in Chapter 22, volcanic Heard Island and Macquarie are Australian World Heritage Sites. The Auckland and Campbell Islands

Figure 26.1
Antarctica

belong to New Zealand, while Marion Island is South African territory. Some of these islands feature on cruise itineraries to Antarctica, but shore visits are restricted to protect the remaining wildlife. The Antarctic and Southern Ocean Coalition (ASOC) is a group of NGOs concerned with protecting the marine environment and monitoring the impact of climate change.

South Georgia is a British overseas territory administered by the government of the Falkland Islands. It is mountainous and has many glaciers, but the millions of seals and penguins crowding the beaches are the main reason it attracts tourists on Antarctic cruises, as well as the island's associations with Shackleton. In the early part of the twentieth century, this was the hub of a major whaling industry. The volcanic South Sandwich Islands are much less inviting, as they are ice-capped, fogbound, and almost inaccessible.

The mysterious island of **Kerguelen**, which is part of the French Southern and Antarctic Territories (TAAF), is one of the world's most remote locations. It is rarely visited by cruise ships, although a supply ship services the French research base four times a year from Réunion, more than 3,000 kilometres to the north.

Over 99 per cent of the continent of Antarctica's 14 million square kilometres of land surface (larger than Australia or Europe) is permanently covered by ice. This immense ice sheet is bisected by the Transantarctic Mountains, one of the world's longest mountain ranges. The coast is fringed by ice shelves formed where glaciers flow into the ocean and coalesce to form vast floating platforms of ice, which spawn huge tabular icebergs. Because of its high altitude, the interior of Antarctica is extremely cold and very dry (so that dehydration is a serious problem), while much of the coast is swept by pitiless winds. Nevertheless, the Antarctic atmosphere is remarkably clear, while the ultraviolet (UV) index in summer is often high. The few ice-free areas can only support fragile mosses and lichens. However, due to the low temperatures and lack of vegetation, Antarctica is free of the insect pests that can make life irksome in other parts of the world.

As a destination, Antarctica differs from the Arctic in the following ways:

- It is much less accessible. Antarctica is separated from the nearest populated lands in the Southern Hemisphere by vast expanses of stormy ocean and is moreover, encircled by a barrier of pack ice for most of the year. It is, therefore, unlikely that Antarctica was visited by man at any time before its recorded discovery by American, British, and Russian explorers in the early nineteenth century. Permanent scientific bases have only been established since the 1940s. No international air routes cross the southern polar regions. Travel from the major tourist-generating countries is expensive and time-consuming, involving up to two days of air travel, plus a sea voyage lasting from two to ten days from the nearest ports in South America, South Africa, Australia, and New Zealand.

- The Antarctic south of latitude 60 degrees is politically 'no-man's land'. Under the terms of the 1959 Antarctic Treaty, the territorial claims made by seven of the signatory governments, namely Argentina, Australia (Australian Antarctic Territory), Britain (British Antarctic Territory), Chile, France (Adèlie Land-TAAF), New Zealand (Ross Dependency), and Norway (Queen Maud Land), are in abeyance. Under the Antarctic Treaty System (ATS), Antarctica is a 'global commons', serving as a vast laboratory for international co-operation in scientific research, currently involving 29 different countries, which have established permanent bases.

- Discoveries in astronomy, meteorology, seismology, and other disciplines made in Antarctica 'have dramatically changed the way we see our world' (Walker, 2012, xiv). For example, deep ice cores extracted from the East Antarctica ice sheet have provided a record of changes in 'greenhouse gas' emissions over many millennia. The hole in the ozone layer was identified at Halley, a British Antarctic Survey base in the 1980s, and it is in Antarctica that global pollution trends are monitored. Under the 1991 Madrid Protocol on Environmental Protection, conservation is given priority, and there is a moratorium on mineral exploitation.

- While the adjoining seas teem with marine life, the interior of Antarctica is virtually sterile, in contrast to the Arctic tundra. The coast provides a summer habitat for penguins, which are more adept at home in the sea than on dry land. The largest of these – the iconic Emperor penguin – is the only species of bird to over-winter in Antarctica.

Antarctica comprises three distinct regions:

- West Antarctica between the Ross and Weddell Seas
- The Antarctic Peninsula and the South Shetland Islands
- East Antarctica

Although West Antarctica includes the highest part of the continent – the Vinson Massif, most of the region under the ice sheet lies below sea level, making it potentially vulnerable to the impact of climate change; here the Thwaites Glacier has become the focus of scientific attention. This region is the most remote part of the continent, as it is difficult to access by air or by sea.

A rise in temperatures over the last century is already evident in the **Antarctic Peninsula.** This is the most accessible part of the continent, separated by the stormy waters of the Drake Passage from South America. The Peninsula, along with the South Sandwich Islands and South Orkney Islands, is held by geologists to be a southern continuation of the Andes, so it is not surprising that Britain's claims to the region's offshore mineral resources have been strongly contested by Argentina and Chile. The Peninsula's coastline is deeply indented, with tidewater glaciers and many offshore islands. The west coast of the Peninsula and the South Shetland Islands to the north is the most visited part of Antarctica, since it is has a milder climate, although summer temperatures struggle to reach 6°C (43°F). It is relatively close to the ports of Punta Arenas and Ushuaia, and cruise itineraries can include the Falklands, South Georgia, and the fjords of southern Chile.

The interior of **East Antarctica** is a high plateau covered by an ice sheet 2,300 metres thick. The rugged peaks of Queen Maud Land rise above the ice sheet, while sub-glacial lakes lie buried deep below its surface. Investigation of the largest of these – Lake Vostok – poses a dilemma for scientists because of the risk of contamination to an unknown ecosystem that has been isolated for many millions of years. There is less evidence of climate change in East Antarctica, with the possible exception of the moss beds near the Australian (AAT) base of Casey.

The demand for tourism

Antarctica, unlike other parts of the world, has no permanent inhabitants to generate a demand for domestic or outbound tourism. The scientists and support personnel live and work at the bases for periods varying from a few months to a maximum of two to three consecutive years, after which they return to their countries of origin. Compared to the 1980s, the bases are no longer a male preserve. However, only Chile and Argentina have made provision for staff to live with their families at two of their bases, allegedly with a view to future colonisation. The number of summer residents in Antarctica can be around 4,000, whereas in winter, it is just over a thousand. The US base of McMurdo is by far the largest, offering some of the facilities of a small town and occasionally hosting VIPs, artists, writers, and musicians who are invited by the US National Science Foundation (NSF).

Under the terms of the Antarctic Treaty, tourists require authorisation from the governments of their home countries to visit Antarctica.

Tourism to Antarctica began in the 1920s with mail ships based in the Falkland Islands, carrying a few paying passengers to the whaling stations in the South Shetland and South Orkney Islands. In the late 1950s, the first charter flights took place from Chile and New Zealand. In 1966, Lars Lindblad organised the first expedition cruise, appealing to tourists who prefer informative lectures given by professionals to shipboard entertainment (https://world.expeditions.com/). However, it was not until an Antarctic Treaty conference in 1977 that tourism received official attention. In 1991, the International Association of Antarctica Tour Operators (IAATO) was founded, and this organisation has a co-ordinating role with the objective of promoting 'safe and environmentally responsible travel' (https://www.iaato.org.). As a result of competition between tour operators, technological advances, and the growing demand for ecotourism and adventure tourism, the number of arrivals grew from less than a thousand a year in the 1980s to 48,000 in the 2007–2008 summer cruising season. As a result of the 2008 world financial crisis and a ruling by the International Maritime Organisation (IMO) banning the use of heavy fuel oil, arrivals fell to around 37,000 in the 2012–2013 season. However, by the 2019–2020 season, tourist numbers had increased to more than 74,000, two-thirds of whom made shore landings (IAATO, 2019). Many visitors do not actually set foot in Antarctica, being content to view the coast from the deck of a cruise liner or from the air on a flight-seeing tour based in Australia or Chile. In contrast, a number of cruises offer a closer experience of the white continent through activities such as sea kayaking and camping. Less than 1 per cent of visitors participate in expeditions and adventure tourism, organised by a few specialist tour operators to the interior of Antarctica, but demand for this is expected to grow.

Although tourists to Antarctica come from many countries, the United States is the biggest generator of demand, accounting for a third of all arrivals. Europe accounts for another third, with Germany and Britain in the lead. In the Southern Hemisphere, only Australia and New Zealand are considered important markets.

Tourists are predominantly from the older age groups and are motivated to undertake the long air and sea journey by an interest in nature. Travel usually involves a long-haul flight to Santiago or Buenos Aires, followed by a flight to Punta Arenas or Ushuaia. For some, this is the trip of a lifetime, whereas others see it as a prestige opportunity to add a seventh continent to an already extensive world travel portfolio. Aware of the threat of global warming, many visit Antarctica as the 'last chance' to see a pristine wilderness before it changes irrevocably. Ironically, the carbon footprint of these tourists is itself a contributory factor to climate change. A typical cruise generates significantly higher amounts of CO_2 emissions per passenger than the average international trip, apart from the carbon footprint of the outward and return flights from the tourists' home countries.

The future expansion of tourism is likely to include source markets in Asia, as countries such as China, India, Japan, and South Korea already play an important role in scientific research in Antarctica. Japan was one of the original 12 signatories of the Antarctic Treaty, whereas China became a signatory in 1983 and established its first base – Cheng Chang (Great Wall) – in the South Shetland Islands. China now spends more on its research programme than any other country, constructing a fifth base in the Ross Sea region before an Environmental Impact Statement was completed, as required by the ATS. China has overtaken Japan as a source market, and the numbers of visitors increased from little more than a thousand in the 2010–2011 season to almost 8,000 in 2019–2020, reflecting the growth of a middle class that can afford the expense of travel to Antarctica. Three Chinese tour operators are registered as IAATO members, but none are licensed as yet by the Chinese government (Cheung et al., 2019). Chinese tourists differ from Western visitors in their cultural background, being motivated by curiosity or status-seeking, rather than an interest in a wilderness experience per se, and find it more difficult to adhere to strict IAATO guidelines.

The COVID-19 pandemic, particularly its impact on South Africa, highlighted the vulnerability of Antarctica to external pressures and put tourism on hold. The Council of Managers of National Antarctic Programs (COMNAP) co-ordinated a major reduction in personnel at the bases to ensure a strict quarantine and testing regime. This inevitably had an adverse impact on research into climate change and other scientific programmes. Tourism has shown a full recovery in the 2022–2023 season, surpassing 100,000 arrivals.

The supply-side of tourism

Transport

Five cities in the Southern Hemisphere serve as gateways to Antarctica from a logistical viewpoint, each transporting people and supplies to the research stations directly to the south:

- Ushuaia, only 1,000 kilometres from the Antarctic Peninsula, is the most popular departure point for tourist expeditions by sea.
- Punta Arenas is the hub for over 20 national Antarctic programmes carried out by the large number of scientific research stations located on the South Shetland Islands and the Antarctic Peninsula. Rothera, the main British Antarctic Survey (BAS) base, is also accessed from the Falklands.
- Cape Town lies at a much greater distance from Antarctica, but nevertheless is more convenient than Argentina or Chile as a transit point for scientists on the national programmes of South Africa, Scandinavia, Russia, India, and Japan. Cape Town is linked by long-range aircraft to Troll airfield in East Antarctica, which is operated by the Norwegian Polar Institute. Troll provides feeder services to a number of bases in Queen Maud Land, a project involving 11 countries, which is a good example of international co-operation.
- Christchurch is the key gateway to Antarctica, as it is linked by long-range aircraft to New Zealand's Scott Base and McMurdo, which serves as the logistics centre for the US National Science Foundation (NSF) programme.
- Hobart is the headquarters of the Australian Antarctic Division (AAD), with world-class research and educational institutions.

Overland travel in Antarctica is problematic due to the extreme conditions and the risk posed by crevasses in the ice. Almost all transport is by short take-off and landing (STOL) aircraft, usually equipped with skis. Aviation in Antarctica is difficult, as there is often little visual difference between ice, sea, sky, and mountain. Some airfields have 'blue ice' runways in the few locations where glacial ice is exposed. A marked trail (the South Pole Operations Traverse) used by specialised tractor convoys connects McMurdo to the Amundsen-Scott base operated by the NSF at the South Pole, providing an alternative to air transport to bring in vital supplies and reduce fuel costs.

We can distinguish between the following types of tourism, based on transport arrangements:

- Land-based, with air support
- Over-flights
- Sea-based, where the ship provides the accommodation and all other facilities. Visits from expedition vessels carrying less than 500 passengers account for the great majority of tourist arrivals in Antarctica. Cruise ships carrying more than 500 passengers are not allowed to make landings.

Land-based tourism: Compared to the Arctic regions of North America, there is a lack of infrastructure for commercial aircraft. Although the bases and their associated field camps are served by a network of airfields, fuel depots, supply ships, and specialised vehicles, this is very costly to maintain. Most governments are, therefore, reluctant to support tourism ventures because of the health and safety issues involved, and the possible disruption to scientific programmes. While some Chilean and Russian bases have provided tourist accommodation in the past, the ATS has so far resisted demands for permanent facilities. A tour operator based in Punta Arenas flies wealthy clients and expeditioners to a tented camp at Union Glacier in the Ellsworth Range, where activities include mountain climbing, ski touring, and flights to the South Pole. In response to growing demand, some experts predict that tourists will stay in prefabricated mobile 'pods' which can be set up in the most remote locations with minimal impact on the environment (a tour operator based in Cape Town already flies clients to an ice-free 'oasis' in Queen Maud Land using this type of accommodation). Such 'glamping' (luxury camping) is a far cry from the basic tents used by the Amundsen and Scott expeditions.

Over-flights: In the 1970s, over-flying Antarctica was popular in New Zealand, until an Air New Zealand Boeing 747 crashed on Mount Erebus, killing all 257 on board. In 1994, a Melbourne-based company resumed flight-seeing tours from Australian cities, and by 2001, over 10,000 passengers had viewed the spectacular icefalls and glaciers of the Transantarctic Mountains from the air.

Sea-based tourism: This includes a few expeditions by private yacht, but cruising is far more significant, with most of the ships carrying between 40 and 150 passengers. Ushuaia is the starting point for most cruises, followed by Punta Arenas, Puerto Williams, and Puerto Madryn. As an alternative, tourists can avoid the notorious Drake Passage south of Cape Horn by taking a two-hour flight from Punta Arenas to Chile's Teniente Marsh airport (TNM) in the South Shetlands where they begin their cruise.

Organisation

Antarctica is in effect ruled by a committee made up of those nations that are signatories to the Antarctic Treaty. The Secretariat of the Antarctic Treaty, based in Buenos Aires, is the closest thing to a government, overseeing 54 member states. The Antarctic Treaty Consultative Meeting (ATCM) is a conference of 'interested parties' held every year in a different host city, and it includes IAATO representing the travel industry. Any new binding agreement on the lines of the Madrid Protocol must be based on consensus. This has worked fairly well in the past, but according to some, the ATS is too unwieldy and insufficiently proactive to face the major challenges posed by the growth of commercial fishing in the Southern Ocean and the boom in adventure tourism. The number of member states with voting rights has grown from 13 in 1980 to 30 in 2019, while the number of research stations now exceeds 75. The regulation of tourism is left to IAATO and is based on voluntary agreements, so much depends on common sense and goodwill. IAATO's membership consists of over 100 tour operators and associated companies, based in 16 countries. To meet the growth in demand, some 20 new expedition vessels were under construction in 2018, adding to the 33 already registered with IAATO. Private yachts and private expeditions flying direct to Antarctica sometimes flout the rules, which are difficult to enforce.

Tourism resources

Conservation of the natural environment of Antarctica is the main priority of the Madrid Protocol, which specifies that an Environmental Impact Assessment is carried out every time a new activity is proposed. The Committee for Environmental Protection (CEP) makes provision for Antarctic specially protected areas (ASPAs) and specially managed areas (ASMAs), which are deemed to have environmental, scientific, aesthetic, or historic value. ATS member states are required to develop a management plan regulating human activities in detail in these areas or prohibiting access altogether. Visitor guidelines are available for the most frequently visited sites.

Although over 200 landing sites are available, 90 per cent are in the Antarctic Peninsula region, and only a small number of these are regularly visited as they offer the most spectacular scenery and variety of wildlife. The most popular sites are located in the South Shetlands and on the west coast of the Antarctic Peninsula, where Marguerite Bay south of the Antarctic Circle is the limit for expedition vessels. Such is the growth in tourism in recent years, slots for popular landing sites have to be booked months in advance. Inflatable zodiac landing craft carry groups of tourists ashore, accompanied by a naturalist-guide to visit penguin rookeries. Here, it is worth noting that Adélie penguins, which are adapted to sea ice, are declining in numbers and have been replaced in some locations by gentoo penguins, which prefer open water. A selection of sites would include:

- Deception Island in the South Shetlands, a volcanic caldera with a geothermal spring.
- Paradise Harbour for whale-watching.
- Cuverville Island.
- Port Lockroy – a former British Antarctic Survey base, which is now a heritage attraction visited by over a hundred ships each season.
- Lemaire Channel, one of the most photogenic locations.

- Some research stations, where tourists are usually welcome, providing a break in routine for scientists and support workers, and (in the case of the bases run by less wealthy countries) some much-needed revenue.
- Brown Bluff, a feature of volcanic origin at the entrance to the Weddell Sea.
- Detaille Island, an abandoned research station.

There is also a human face to Antarctica, with heritage sites testifying to the fortitude of the scientists from many nations in the quest for knowledge. The legacy of two centuries of exploration is commemorated in around 85 historical sites and monuments that have been proposed by member countries and which are protected under the ATS. These include relics of the heroic age of exploration in the early part of the twentieth century, those relating to the sealers and whalers who first exploited the marine resources of Antarctica in the nineteenth century, and in more recent times, memorials to those scientists and support workers who have lost their lives in this unforgiving environment. The remains of explorers' huts and former research bases, in varying states of preservation, are important tourist attractions.

The story begins with the recorded discovery of the northernmost part of Antarctica in 1819, an event shrouded in mystery, controversy, and tragedy. The British navigators Smith and Bransfield are generally held to be the discoverers. However, the anchor stock of a Spanish warship, the *San Telmo,* found by Smith on Livingston Island, part of the South Shetland archipelago, provided mute evidence that they were not the first. The *San Telmo* was the 74-gun flagship of a naval expedition that had left Cadiz in May 1819 with the aim of suppressing the independence movement in Peru. In attempting to round Cape Horn, the ship's rudder and rigging were damaged, and at the mercy of winds and currents, she was driven far to the south. She was last seen on September 2, 1819, at latitude 62° south and longitude 70° west. There is evidence that some of the 644 soldiers, sailors, and marines aboard later made landfall in Antarctica. The castaways, unlike today's tourists, were unprepared for Antarctic conditions and faced the grim problem of survival on an uncharted island, for the most part covered in glaciers. It is interesting to compare their predicament with the situation confronting Shackleton a century later, following the wreck of his ship, *Endurance,* and the prospect of an open boat voyage across the Southern Ocean to seek help. In 2019, the Spanish representative at the ATCM held in Prague proposed that the site of the *San Telmo* wreck, which, unlike *Endurance* has not been identified, should be designated for protection to forestall private diving expeditions.

Ironically, the South Shetland Islands were very soon to yield a rich harvest for British and American seal hunters suppling the demand for furs and oil in the markets of New England, London, and Canton, China. A decade of slaughter in the 1820s without any concern for sustainability resulted in the near-extinction of the islands' fur seals and elephant seals. Today, the wildlife has recovered, while the relics of the sealing and whaling eras are visited as part of the Antarctic heritage.

A much smaller number of cruises, using ice-breaker ships and departing from Fremantle and Hobart in Australia, and Christchurch and Bluff in New Zealand, undertake the long voyage to the **Ross Sea**, which is geographically much closer to the South

Pole than the Antarctic Peninsula. The cruising season is shorter, lasting from late December to late February. Tourists can view colonies of Emperor penguins and other attractions such as:

- Cape Evans – with its relics of Shackleton, and Scott's ill-fated expedition to the South Pole.
- New Zealand's Scott Base.
- The Mount Erebus volcano.
- The cliffs marking the edge of the immense Ross Ice Shelf, called 'The Barrier' by its discoverer James Ross, as it prevented further southward exploration in his ships *Erebus* and *Terror*.

The ice-free 'Dry Valleys' – said to be the nearest thing on Earth to the landscape of Mars – can be reached by on-board helicopters.

CASE STUDY 26.1
THE DAVIS AERODROME PROJECT

Australia lays claim to the largest sector of Antarctica (almost 6 million square kilometres), and with three permanent bases on the coast – Davis, Mawson, and Casey – takes its responsibilities for conservation and scientific research very seriously. There is also the possibility that base personnel may have to be evacuated for urgent medical reasons, necessitating a fast and reliable link to Hobart, 5,400 kilometres away. Since 2004, the Australian Antarctic Division has depended on Wilkins airfield, which is about 70 kilometres from Casey but at a much greater distance from Davis (1,400 kilometres) or Mawson (over 2,000 kilometres). This is a 'blue ice' runway, which is operational for inter-continental flights only for a short period during the austral summer.

To improve access and boost scientific programmes, in 2018, the Australian government proposed an airfield with the first paved runway in Antarctica, 2.7 kilometres in length. (By way of comparison, McMurdo is served by runways built on sea ice which have to be constantly cleared of snow.) The site chosen was in the Vestfold Hills, an ice-free area close to the Davis base where the local meteorological conditions were favourable. An Environmental Impact Statement was submitted as required by the Madrid Protocol, which met with little opposition from other ATS member countries. Nevertheless, in 2021, the Australian government cancelled the project, citing environmental concerns. Some allege that the financial cost played a part in the decision.

The fact that such an infrastructural project is feasible could encourage China to expand its programme from its bases deep in the interior of East Antarctica. Although tourism was not envisaged as part of the project, long-range aircraft such as the Airbus A340 will inevitably provide an alternative to the ageing ice-breaker fleet for tour operators.

The impacts of tourism

Tourism in Antarctica is an outstanding example of co-operation between the various stakeholders, which include:

1. The commercial sector, represented by the IAATO.
2. The governments that are signatories to the Antarctic Treaty and the Madrid Protocol on Environmental Protection.
3. The tourists themselves.

    Cruise operators to Antarctica generally subscribe to strict codes of conduct laid down by IAATO. Passengers, during their two-hour ashore, are kept under constant surveillance, for their own safety, and to prevent pollution, disturbance to wild-life, and contamination by non-indigenous pathogens. (It is for the last reason that dogs, widely used in earlier polar expeditions, are banned by the Madrid Protocol.) Conservation measures include:

-   The separation of poultry products from other food waste, to prevent the spread of avian flu to penguins.
-   The shipping out of waste of any kind.
-   Tourists are prohibited from approaching wildlife too closely.
-   The prohibition on taking 'souvenirs' other than photographs or videos.
-   The disinfection of tourist's boots between shore trips.
-   A guide to passenger ratio of 1:20.

Despite the vast extent of Antarctica, tourists following established routes are concentrated in a relatively few sites during the short summer season between November and March, and the time interval between visits by different groups to a site is often only a few hours. A number of sites are approaching their psychological carrying capacity – 10,000 visitors a season – at which point the nature-loving tourist feels that his/her experience is being diminished by the presence of others (Lamers et al., 2011). There has been serious trail erosion at some sites, such as Hannah Point on Livingston Island. Many believe tourism has an adverse effect on the breeding patterns of seals and penguins, but others argue that the presence of human visitors protects young birds from predators. Emissions from the outboard motors of the zodiacs pollute the water, while not all cruise ships dispose of waste in accordance with environmental guidelines, and there is always the risk of a major oil spill. The sinking of the *MS Explorer* – the veteran of many Antarctic cruises – in November 2007, was a wake-up call for cruise operators to use ice-strengthened ships and led to demands that the International Maritime Organisation (IMO) should impose stricter controls on Antarctic cruise tourism. Nevertheless, land-based tourism represents a much greater threat to the environment, if we consider the impact already made by the permanent scientific research stations. Tourism accounts for less than 1 per cent of all person-days logged in Antarctica compared to more than 99 per cent for personnel at the research stations, who arguably do much more damage. Ironically, it was the negative publicity generated by returning cruise passengers about the garbage at one American base that forced the authorities to clean up their act. Tourism also funds conservation programmes; most cruise operators connect passengers with a range of citizen science projects, such as participating in surveys.

It is not just the growth in the numbers of tourists that threatens the environment but the changing nature of the demand. The typical Antarctic cruise passenger is predominantly from the older age groups and is content with a passive role as an eco-tourist, seeing Antarctica from a distance and responding positively to the restrictions imposed by tour operators. They are also good ambassadors for Antarctica; without publicity in the media, it would be difficult to gain popular support for the idea that the 'white continent' should remain purely a preserve for scientific research. The future is likely to witness a growth in adventure tourism, attracting younger visitors who may show less concern for the environment and their own safety. The range of activities on offer is increasing, showcasing new technology and 'pushing boundaries'. With no one country able to enforce planning controls, this could lead inexorably to a demand for more ground facilities, as in other destinations. This could lead, for example, to a ban on activities such as jet skiing and heli-skiing.

A future energy crisis could pose an even greater problem, as it would set off a 'free for all' among competing nations for mineral rights in Antarctica, effectively putting an end to the ATS, as the Madrid Protocol is due for renewal in 2048.

Summary

- Antarctica can support only a limited range of tourist activities, and even these can have a negative impact on wildlife.
- Tourism is highly concentrated in a very small part of Antarctica, so visitor sites are under pressure.
- There is an increasing diversity of tourism activities.
- The infrastructure and facilities for tourism in Antarctica are extremely limited, and any expansion of tourism would contravene the Antarctic Treaty that protects its unique environment.
- The environmental guidelines for tourists depend on the willingness of stakeholders to comply, as no one country can enforce rules or effectively monitor tourist activity.

Discussion points

1. Many scientists believe that tourists have no reason to be in Antarctica, while those in the travel industry maintain that is the right of humankind to see and experience the world's wild places. In class, debate these opposing viewpoints, bearing in mind that the average tourist trip to Antarctica emits approximately 5.44 tonnes of CO_2 per passenger. Role-play the various stakeholders involved in Antarctic conservation and tourism.

2. The melting of the ice shelves of the Antarctic Peninsula is often described by the media as evidence of global warming and an imminent world-wide rise in sea level.

By using data from the British Antarctic Survey and other scientific organisations, assess the evidence for climate change in Antarctica and the effect on plant growth and animal behaviour.

3. Discuss the extent to which the professionalism of the naturalist-guides contributes to the success of the Antarctic cruise experience.

References and further reading

Aston, F. (2013) *Alone in Antarctica*, Summersdale, Chichester

ATCM42 (2019) Proposals for inclusion of the San Telmo Wreck in the Antarctic Treaty List of historic sites and monuments, Secretariat of the Antarctic Treaty, Buenos Aires

Bastmeijer, C.J. (2003) Tourism in Antarctica: Increasing diversity and the legal requirements for authorization, *New Zealand Journal of Environmental Law* 5 (7), 85–118

Bauer, T. (2002) Antarctic tourism: Where are the limits? *Tourism 2002*, Tourism Society, 18–20

Cheung, W. et al. (2019) The growth of Chinese tourism to Antarctica: A profile of their connectedness to nature, motivations and perceptions, *The Polar Journal*, 9 (1) 197–213

Davis, P.B. (1998) Beyond headlines: A model for Antarctic tourism, *Annals of Tourism Research* 23 (3), 546–553

Dove, J. (1997) Antarctica: tourism's last frontier, *Geography Review* (March), 14–18

Fretwell, P. (2020) *Antarctic Atlas*, Penguin Books, London

Hall, C.M. and Johnston, M. (1995) *Polar Tourism*, Wiley, Chichester

Lamers, M., et al. (2011) Last chance tourism in Antarctica – Cruising for change, pp. 23–40, in Lamelin, H., Dawson, J., Stewart, E. (eds.) *Last-Chance Tourism: Adapting Tourism Opportunities in a Changing World*, Routledge, London

Sánchez, R. (2007) *Antártida: Introducción a un continente remoto*, Albatros, Buenos Aires

Thomas, T. (1994) Ecotourism in Antarctica: The role of the naturalist-guide in promoting places of natural interest, *Journal of Sustainable Tourism* 2 (4), 204–209

Walker, G. (2012) *Antarctica: An Intimate Portrait of the World's Most Mysterious Continent*, Bloomsbury, London

Web sites

www.quarkexpeditions.com

https://www.coolantarctica.com

International Association of Antarctica Tour Operators: https://www.iaato.org

Tourism futures

After reading this chapter, you should be able to:

- Appreciate the need for a disciplined approach to predicting the future of tourism.
- Understand the geographical impact of crises and shocks on the tourism system.
- Appreciate the role of technology in shaping the future geography of travel and tourism.
- Understand the changing behaviour of tourists.
- Recognise the importance of the environmental movement in tourism.
- Understand the changing nature of tourism destinations.
- Recognise the trend towards the globalisation of the tourism sector.

DOI: 10.4324/9781003406853-33

Introduction

The twenty first century has witnessed severe shocks to the tourism system – 9/11, terrorist bombings in holiday resorts and cities, disrupting events such as the Boston Marathon, clear evidence of climate change, a number of natural disasters such as earthquakes, tsunamis, and hurricanes, and revolutions against long-established regimes in North Africa and the Middle East, the COVID-19 pandemic and the Ukraine war. These 'wild card' events emphasise the fact that we cannot manage tourism if we do not understand how it reacts to change. Making predictions is fraught with problems, especially with a sector as fickle as tourism; but if we are to successfully manage tourism in the future, that is what we must do. This means identifying the drivers of future trends, recognising that while some forces of change, such as demographics and technology, are already clearly evident, others have yet to emerge. We therefore set out to identify the key trends and issues that will reshape the geography of travel and tourism through the twenty-first century under the following headings:

- Changing markets
- Changing destinations
- Developments in transport and the tourism sector
- Globalisation and the new world order

Common to each of these themes are other agents of change, such as technology, the search for sustainability in tourism allied to responses to climate change, and changes in consumer behaviour. These trends are interlinked and are combining to accelerate the pace of change. For example, tourists are increasingly knowledgeable and sophisticated and can now be catered for by a tourism sector that is firmly embracing marketing and research strategies, facilitated by technological developments such as the Internet and mobile commerce - where the mobile phone becomes the medium for guiding, visitor information, and increasingly to seek out products and book them. At the same time, the sector is becoming truly global as larger organisations operate across different cultures and time zones. In combination with continued shifts in the world economic and political situation, these trends will influence tourism flows as new generators and new destinations emerge. Underlying all of these trends are two imperatives. Firstly, the pressure for sustainable development and solutions to climate change will ensure that destinations are better planned and managed, and will show more concern for their environment and host community than did their earlier counterparts, while tourists contemplate about the impact of their activities (see Fennell and Cooper, 2020). This is supported by annual UN meetings on climate change and the UNWTO's global code of tourism ethics. Secondly, since 9/11, the tourism sector has recognised the imperative to develop crisis management response strategies covering all sectors of the tourism industry to anticipate future 'shocks' to the system and ensure that tourism can recover from any future crises.

   One of our consistent themes in this book is that we can only understand tourism if we recognise the inter-relationships between the various elements in the system. This is equally true in attempting to understand the future. Here, the concept of 'product markets' is helpful; these recognise the relationship between the changing demands of tourists and the need to develop tourism products to meet their needs. For example, we know that the 'new tourist' demands low-impact tourism, active involvement, and environmentally and socially acceptable tourism – hence the development of eco-tourism products and companies specialising in carbon off-setting. At the same time, there is a trend towards greater market segmentation and the development of a vast range of personalised products to meet specialised demands.

Markets

Patterns of demand

Undoubtedly, since the 1950s, a wave of leisure and travel has broken across the globe pushing the frontier of tourism further outward as more and more people have enjoyed access to both domestic and international travel. This trend continued as the global economy expanded but was severely checked by COVID-19. Along with the pandemic and the economic impact of the war in Ukraine, forecasters also suggest that both demand and supply side constraints may slow the growth of tourism:

- On the demand side, some countries are reaching ceilings in airport capacity and available leisure time that will constrain further growth. The UNWTO study on leisure time, for example, has shown that leisure is under threat from the pressures of changing work practices, technology, and competition.
- On the supply side, the threat of terrorism, political instability, ethnic strife, further health risks, climate change, and capacity ceilings in transport infrastructure may also discourage tourism growth in some areas.

There is no doubt that the distribution of tourism by the year 2030 and beyond will therefore be different from that of the first 15 years of this century. The countries of the East Asia and Pacific (EAP) region are emerging as important generators of tourism and as major tourist destinations. China and India, in particular, will become major generators of both domestic and outbound tourism, changing the nature of travel across the globe. The EAP region will rival Europe and North America in its significance for tourism. To some extent, the success of the EAP region is at the expense of Europe's traditional dominance. Europe's share of international tourism will continue to erode as more long-haul destinations grow in popularity. The principal long-term factors affecting demand for tourism are demographic changes, the amount of leisure and holiday time available, consumer preferences, and the economic performance of the main generating countries. In the short term, as well as the sectors recovering from the pandemic and ongoing war in Ukraine, other factors such as relative prices and exchange rates affecting the cost of travel and effective marketing and promotion will also be important. Although forecasters say that long-haul travel will continue to increase, short-haul travel – especially to neighbouring countries – will still account for a very high proportion of international trips; furthermore, there is evidence that responses to climate change are slowing the growth of long-haul flights. Business tourism will remain as an important segment of the market but developments in communications, such as video-conferencing and videophones, may reduce the need. Indeed, with face-to-face meetings impossible, the pandemic has left a legacy of meetings held on social media platforms such as Zoom and Microsoft Teams.

Changing market demands

While there is no doubt that social and economic trends will encourage the growth of tourism, the nature of the market will change, with consequent implications for the type of development at the destination. The tourists of tomorrow will be more discerning, seeking to 'co-create' a quality experience, conscious of the continuing risks from COVID-19, and, in the developed world, increasingly drawn from an older age group. They may subscribe to the principles of sustainable development, but they also know their rights and, as an empowered group, will complain and seek compensation if their travel experience is disappointing. Demographic changes can be forecast to an extent – we know, for example, that as the baby boom generation ages, there will be a large 'grey tourism' market. It is also difficult to track the influence of changing values among the travelling public. For example, motivations for travel are moving away from passive sunlust towards active participation and curiosity about other cultures. As everyday life and work becomes safer, more predictable, and less physically demanding, there will be a greater demand, at least in the youth market, for extreme sports, 'hard adventure', and other high-risk activities. More leisure should be available through flexible working practices, sabbaticals, study leave, and early retirement. On the other hand, if the United States is any guide, the corporate workplace could become the chief provider of recreation opportunities for many employees, thus blurring the boundaries between work and leisure. Lifestyle changes, such as the growing numbers of 'singletons' (young single person households), and 'downshifting', where an individual changes from a highly paid, high pressure job to one with less income but more free time- will have an impact on the demand for tourism. Travel will also be tailor-made to suit other groups in society, such as single parents. Intensive marketing research on consumer preferences, allied to technology, will increasingly allow more sophisticated market segmentation of tourists, so that product development can be engineered to deliver quality experiences. Use of the Internet allows modularisation of the elements of travel packages so that consumers can co-create and customise their own holidays by trading directly with suppliers – an innovation with significant implications for the way travel has traditionally been distributed. As a consequence, travel intermediaries are re-inventing their role in the tourism system in order to survive. In essence, tourism is becoming less passive and less dominated by the mass market, and more geared to active involvement, individual preferences, and direct purchase of tailor-made products.

Destinations

In tandem with market changes is the realisation by tourism developers that destinations are unique, special, and fragile places that have to be carefully managed if they are to retain their appeal. The United Nations Environment Program (UNEP, 2002) has identified three environmental concerns for the future:

1. Climate change
2. Depletion of natural resources (energy, water, and land use)
3. Loss of biodiversity

Of these, climate change has become a key concern for destinations. The scientific evidence is compelling, but tourism is also a climate-sensitive sector. Climate determines tourism seasons, determines destination choice, and impacts upon tourism product development. The other concerns raised by UNEP will also impact on the future of tourism (see Day and Chin, 2018). Water will become a precious asset in some regions of the world; indeed estimates suggest that by 2025 1.8 billion people will live in areas of absolute water shortage (see Gössling et al., 2015). Tourism is a significant consumer of energy. In the future, this will have to be carefully managed, as the years of 'peak oil' approach when the maximum amount of petroleum is being extracted. There is now a growing dialogue supporting the transition to a low-carbon economy. This will depend upon the development of renewable energy technologies for tourism operations and 'fossil fuel free', efficient, and smart transport systems (Becken, 2015). Biodiversity too is being impacted upon by development in many regions of the world and by climate change. For destinations that depend upon natural resources as a major part of their attraction, this remains a serious issue for tourism.

As a result, the destination of the future will use sustainability and product differentiation – based on a unique selling proposition (USP) – to remain competitive. Attitudes on the part of both consumers and suppliers are changing as the result of pressure from the environmentalist movement, media exposure of bad practices, and a more mature tourism industry. In particular, we are only just beginning to understand how destinations can adapt to climate change. Sustainability has gained prominence through high-profile conferences, initiatives from representative bodies for the industry such as the World Travel and Tourism Council (WTTC), and by tour operators themselves. In particular, the realisation of the negative impacts of tourism upon host environments, societies, and developing economies has prompted the search for alternative forms of tourism – such as eco-tourism – and a critical attitude towards mass tourism (although we must recognise that mass tourism will remain a very substantial part of the market, and indeed is becoming more enlightened). Sustainable tourism ensures that the tourism sector is sympathetic to host environments and societies. An increasing number of public agencies are drawing up guidelines for the reduction of tourism impacts, and there is no doubt that the consumer of the future will avoid destinations that are not 'environmentally sound'. Increasingly, this will include concerns for basic infrastructure, for example potable water and electricity supply, as well as indicators such as biodiversity and changes in land use. Interestingly, some enlightened destinations are discouraging certain types of undesirable tourists, such as stag and hen parties (Amsterdam is an example here). In essence, we are seeing a move towards the responsible development and consumption of tourism through:

*   Greater local control of tourism development, as recommended by the Agenda 21 initiatives of the Rio+20 Earth Summit in 2012.

765

- Translation of the *principles* of sustainability into *practice* through codes of conduct, accreditation schemes, eco-labelling, best practice guidelines, and industry self-regulation.
- Initiation of 'climate action plans' for destinations following the 'Glasgow Declaration Climate Action in Tourism' as the COP 26 in Glasgow (UNEP, 2021).
- Pro-active adoption of professional approaches to the integrated management of visitors, traffic, and resources at tourist destinations, instead of reacting to problems as they arise.
- Use of marketing and information management to influence the behaviour of visitors at destinations.
- Initiatives such as the UNWTO's drive to use tourism as an agent of poverty alleviation, and its global code of tourism ethics.
- Efforts by destinations to respond to climate change by diversifying their products (from *beach* to *beach plus* for example).
- An enhanced awareness of the impacts of tourism on the part of both the sector and tourists themselves.

Discussion point: destination response to climate change

As the evidence for climate change grows, many destinations are considering how to respond. Traditional beach destinations are adding other products such as theme parks, and winter sports resorts are developing summer products to compensate for poor snow cover and a shortened season. When examining a destination of your choice, how might it be affected by climate change, and how should it respond?

It is perhaps inevitable that these ideas will find more fertile ground in the developed world than in most developing countries, where the short-term imperatives of obtaining foreign exchange and job creation will still dominate and may eclipse the longer-term objectives of sustainable development. Destinations are responding to these demands in a variety of ways:

- Resource-based destinations, i.e., those based on elements of the natural or cultural heritage, are adopting sophisticated planning, management, and interpretive techniques to provide both a welcome and a rewarding experience for the tourist, while at the same time ensuring protection of the resource itself. It is felt that once tourists understand why a destination is significant they will want to protect it. Protection here may be not only in terms of changed behaviour but also through *enhancive sustainability* initiatives where the visitor 'leaves the destination in a better condition than before'. These initiatives include:

  1. 'Visitor payback' where visitors become financial supporters of a site.
  2. Voluntary 'eco-taxes' to protect and repair tourist destinations suffering environmental and social damage.

3. New products publicised as 'working holidays', voluntourism to aid poor communities, and 'volunteer tourism' to 'clean up' degraded destinations.

- Good planning and management of the destination lie at the heart of providing the tourism consumer of the future with a high-quality experience. To achieve this, it may be that tourists of the future will have to accept increasingly restricted viewing times at popular sites, comply with destination 'codes of conduct', be content with replicas of the real thing (as at the caves of Altamira and Lascaux), or even a 'virtual' substitute in cyberspace using computer technology such as Oculus Rift.
- As resource-based destinations come under increased pressure, we are seeing a greater emphasis on purpose-built, demand-led attractions that merge tourism and entertainment. The trend to more frequent trips taken closer to home will demand 'synthetic' attractions such as artificial ski slopes and those which combine leisure, entertainment, retailing, accommodation, and quality catering in a single setting. The emergence of totally enclosed and controlled tourist environments such as theme parks, mega-cruise ships, and vacation islands will be promoted as a 'market-oriented' alternative to the real, and increasingly fragile, 'resource-based', non-reproducible attractions of natural, historic, or cultural destinations. Such artificial settings have many advantages and can provide the safe and secure environment sought by most tourists – already destinations such as Dubai and Las Vegas are bringing these trends to life.

In the future, destinations will be affected by climate change, with rising sea levels creating problems for coastal resorts, the erosion of the ozone layer modifying the traditional beach holiday to 'beach plus' tourism, and the generally more volatile weather conditions worldwide affecting the profitability of the sector. There is also a real threat that climate change will destroy some tourism icons, such as Australia's Great Barrier Reef and the Alpine glaciers. However, a more insidious threat could be posed by the growth of tourism itself. In the 1950s, the polar regions and the Himalayas were the ultimate frontier for tourism; nowadays, they are exposed to the assault of thousands of adventure-seeking tourists, and climbers have to 'book' Everest several years in advance. Having visited most of the world's wild places and cultural sites, the well-heeled tourist is seeking new horizons and challenges. The frontiers of tourism will, therefore, expand ever-outwards, with new destinations being created under the oceans and in space. In fact, we know less about the ocean depths than we do about the surface of the Moon or Mars, and this knowledge is vital if we are to combat marine pollution, particularly the scourge of plastic, which poses a threat to the entire planet. The development of submersibles capable of withstanding the immense pressures would enable tourists to view the *Titanic* wreck site and the strange life-forms of the ocean floor. On the continental shelves, projects for undersea hotels are already underway as with the Poseidon resort in Fiji. Yet, it is space that is much more likely to appeal to the imagination of future tourists.

Discussion point: new realities: travel in cyberspace as an alternative to real travel?
Virtual reality (VR) sparks controversy between futurists: some argue that it will never replace the real experience of travel, while others foresee the home becoming the centre for all leisure activities – a total immersive cave or experience chamber – with VR software available for tourism destinations as 'tasters', the ultimate replacement for the travel brochure or DVD. In some respects, this is the perfect form of tourism – the destination receives a royalty for the software but receives none of the negative impacts of tourists actually on-site. The *cybernaut* would have the advantage over a real tourist in being able to view a historic building, for example, Spain's Alhambra, in its entirety, without the intrusive presence each day of this attraction's 9,000 visitors. He/she can also receive the sensory experience of a destination, for example, the sounds, humidity, and aromas of the rainforest, without irksome transport and border delays, or the risk of crime and disease. In the future, VR technology will ensure that the experience is neurologically indistinguishable from the real; and this technology is advancing today, with headsets such as that developed by Oculus Rift being bought by Facebook in recognition of its potential.

Discuss whether virtual journeys represent tourism in the true sense, or are better used as a 'taster' to try out new destinations.

CASE STUDY 27.1
OUR FUTURE LIES IN SPACE?

Despite the fact that space is cold, dark, and deadly, it is set to become the destination of the future. Indeed, simulated space travel experiences and tours of space research centres are already popular (see Spector and Higham, 2019). Although NASA first landed astronauts on the Moon in 1969, space tourism – as distinct from space travel for scientific or military reasons – did not become a reality until 2001, when an American millionaire became the first space tourist, visiting the International Space Station as a paying passenger on a Russian space mission. Space tourism has been defined as the 'taking of short pleasure trips in low earth orbit by members of the public' (Collins and Ashford, 1998). Until recently, tourism in near space was prohibitively expensive because of the high cost of launches. This situation is set to change as a result of international competition between three rival companies, namely 'Space Adventures' (https://spaceadventures.com), 'Virgin Galactic' (https://www.virgingalactic.com/), and SpaceX (https://www.spacex.com/) to produce a re-usable space vehicle. Of course, passenger safety will be a real issue for space tourism and despite the Virgin Galactic crash in 2014, space-planes would pose a much lower risk than the existing space shuttles that use ballistic missile technology (see Ashford, 2003). Health risks are perhaps less significant, although the susceptibility to nausea in space is an issue. The condition of weightlessness, due to zero gravity in space, offers recreational opportunities as well as challenges to would-be tourists. Long-term health issues such as a loss in bone density, as well as exposure to cosmic and solar radiation, are unlikely to affect tourists – as distinct from astronauts or crew members – on a sub-orbital flight lasting only a few hours. Still, those staying at a 'space hotel' would need to have adequate protection. Inter-planetary voyages in outer space are some decades in the future, awaiting new technology or the application of cryonics that will overcome the tyranny of time and distance.

Website

http://www.spacetourismsociety.org

Developments in transport

We have already touched on some of the future developments in transport (see Figure 5.1). These are notoriously difficult to predict, and forecasts made in the 1950s have proved to be wide of the mark half a century later. Technology and changing business practices will have a major impact on transport systems. Development of the rechargeable lithium-ion battery and the hydrogen fuelcell have been hailed as the answer to our energy problems. Battery technology is advancing quickly, with talk of battery-powered aircraft, while the hydrogen fuel cell is more problematic because the production of hydrogen results in as much pollution as the burning of fossil fuels. However, by mid-century batteries, hydrogen, and new types of biofuels should replace petroleum and kerosene as the main source of motive power, with zero emissions of pollutants.

In civil aviation, long-haul airline operations will be characterised by the use of a new generation of aircraft with a capacity for as many as 700 passengers. The application of space technology will enable these aircraft to achieve hypersonic speeds and a much greater range so that the flying time between London and Tokyo could be reduced to two and a half hours, without stops for re-fuelling. Nevertheless, speed is not the only consideration, and many long-haul travellers may opt for the greater comfort provided by improved aircraft configurations, so that the journey itself becomes a pleasurable experience rather than a cramped ordeal. For short-haul operations, the use of VTOL (vertical take-off and landing aircraft) would provide more flexibility. The trend towards deregulation will continue across the world. In the United States and Europe, deregulation has led to domination of the market by a few major airlines and the forging of strategic alliances, a trend which is emerging in other sectors of the tourism industry. In such an environment, competitive advantage will not come from government protection. On regional and short-haul flights, 'budget' airlines already dominate, competing from a different business model based on Internet reservations, ticketless travel procedures, and 'no frills' service. The major airlines will concentrate on hub-and-spoke operations. Airlines based at a 'hub' airport in a prime geographical location will co-ordinate their schedules, enabling travellers to make onward connections between flights on routes radiating from the central hub. This gives the hub airline a strong competitive edge and leads to a system of 'fortress hubs', keeping out newcomers. However, this could result in some communities having less choice in their travel arrangements than was the case hitherto.

Although VTOL aircraft and new versions of seaplanes could eventually take some of the pressure, airports will need to be built on a major scale to cope with the anticipated growth in air traffic; this will be greatest in the East Asia-Pacific region. Local communities and environmentalists from different countries will launch co-ordinated protest campaigns through the Internet, but these may largely be ineffective. However, governments, particularly in the West, will increasingly be faced with the dilemma of balancing the benefits of economic growth against the environmental damage, and climate change has already become the new watchword for protestors. Government policies favouring airport expansion can be criticised for the following reasons:

- The predicted growth rate for air traffic is based on the rapid increase since the 1970s. However, the demand for air travel will slow down as the market matures and environmental factors dominate.
- The growth in demand for cheap air travel cannot be sustained indefinitely, as the true cost in environmental terms is not borne by the airline or the passenger.

In surface transport, the desire for personal mobility will have to be reconciled with the need for an efficient form of mass transit, one that truly responds to public demand. In parts of the world, particularly in developing countries and economies such as India and China, car ownership continues to grow as suppressed demand becomes effective demand as a result of economic growth and democratic structures of government that allow freedom of choice. We can expect developments in automotive technology to make driving safer and more environmentally acceptable, including networked driverless cars, intelligent satellite navigation systems, and the penetration of the market by electric vehicles (see Cohen and Hopkins, 2019). We can be sure that the car of the future will be quite different from the vehicle that has evolved with the internal combustion engine in the twentieth century. However, until the infrastructure is in place, cars powered by hydrogen or electricity have been slow to capture the market. Highway networks will continue to develop around the world and the capacity of busy routes could be greatly increased with the use of computer-controlled guideways; this will make motoring safer but at the cost of the driver's independence.

As the century unfolds, it is likely that car use will decline for inter-city travel and for trips within large cities for the following reasons:

1. Within the world's major cities, rapid transit systems will reduce car use, as is now occurring in some Asian countries.
2. The development of high-speed inter-city rail links could result in the train being preferred over the car or air transport for journeys of less than 500 kilometres, due to the following:
    (a) Congestion on the roads and airways.
    (b) The train is perceived as a 'greener' form of travel.
    (c) A range of new rail-based leisure and business tourism products will be developed.
    (d) 'Green' taxes will penalise car users.

(e) The application of innovative technology, such as magnetic levitation or repulsion in which the train 'flies' above a track at speeds of up to 500 kilometres/hour. This will transform the image of rail travel and bring it firmly into the twenty-first century.

On the world's oceans, high-speed vessels and passenger-carrying submarines will be developed. Mega-cruise ships carrying over 5,000 passengers will cater for the mass market, possibly with 'satellite' vessels for diving and shore excursions. A variety of much smaller ships would provide nature-based cruises to island destinations such as the Galápagos, linking up with local hotels on a 'cruise and stay' programme.

The tourism sector

As the tourism market matures, the sector is striving for acceptability not only in terms of (i) environmental practices such as auditing and total quality management, but also (ii) sustainable behaviour, including moving to a low-carbon future and embracing business ethics and social responsibility as short-term, profit-driven operations become less acceptable. There will be an increasing consideration for all stakeholders involved in the business, including the well-being of the destination and its residents. For example, it makes increasing commercial sense for tour operators to invest in destinations and their facilities, while leading companies such as Accor and Tui have integrated sustainability in their business models.

In response to these trends, the tourism sector is rapidly becoming more professional and embracing developments in technology. According to the UNWTO, technology will penetrate all aspects of life, determining and facilitating tourism futures. The most successful technology will be invisible to the user, and where it does interface with the user, the experience will be organic and seamless. The fusion of information and communication technologies (ICTs) allows tourism enterprises to become more efficient and competitive, not simply by lowering costs and facilitating market access, but also by allowing them to network and integrate with other enterprises – and their consumers. Indeed, everything and everyone will be connected in the future. ICTs and Big Data will increasingly allow customisation of products and real-time access to demand, allowing flexible pricing and segmentation down to the individual consumer. Innovations such as facial recognition technology, allied to Big Data, will allow each and every individual visit to an event, museum, or theme park to be personally curated. In the market, we are also seeing the growth of online tourism communities; here, the evolution of the Internet is transforming the way that business is done. The fusion of Internet technologies with social activities such as blogging facilitates the use of websites rich in content and enables networked online tourism communities. User-generated content (such as TripAdvisor) will displace more traditional ways of seeking information about destinations. Effectively, technology has increased the connections between the actors in the tourism system. Finally, with the fourth industrial revolution, or Industry 4.0, breaking like a wave over the tourism sector, we have to consider the impact of the development of artificial intelligence (AI) and robotics. There is now a convergence of robotics, artificial intelligence, and automation technologies (RAIA) driving the future of tourism employment and the way the sector will be managed in the future. The use of robots in the hospitality industry is already evident in the cities of Japan, and the trend is spreading to other destinations where suitable labour is in short supply.

Globalisation and the new world order

The tourism sector does not operate in a vacuum and is affected by political trends – the election of a climate change sceptic as the President of the United States, for example, had implications for how research on climate change was funded. Globalisation is the trend for markets and production to become inter-dependent worldwide, regardless of government policies in any particular country. Globalisation can be defined as 'the interaction, and sometimes integration of industries, peoples, governments, and economies through international arrangements, trade, travel, information technology' (Timothy, 2018, 570).

Smeral (1998) has identified the key drivers of globalisation in tourism as:

*   The adoption of free trade agreements, removing barriers to international transactions.
*   Digital and communications technology encouraging networked 'e-business'.
*   Worldwide-acting suppliers utilising CRS and global distribution systems (GDS); examples here include the major airlines, hotel chains, and tour operators, as well as their strategic alliance partners in the supply chain.
*   Decreasing costs of international travel allowing access to most markets in the world.
*   Increasing levels of income in the generating countries, allied to the 'new tourist' who is experienced and discerning.
*   The emergence of 'new' destinations, fuelling the demand for more international travel.

The consequences of globalisation for the tourism sector include:

*   Standard procedures and quality control (as in the accommodation sector); there are concerns that this could result in a worldwide homogenisation of tourism products.
*   Increased competition.
*   Head office decisions on marketing and technology in the larger companies.
*   Forging of strategic alliances (as in the airlines sector).
*   Adoption of global brands (such as American Express, Sheraton, and Disney).
*   Changing management approaches.
*   Adoption of new ways of doing business, such as the approaches used by budget airlines.
*   Adoption of global distribution systems and yield management.
*   More challenging trading conditions for small- and medium-sized tourism enterprises (SMTEs).

> **Discussion point: global, local or 'glocal' tourism?**
>
> There is a danger that globalisation creates uniform landscapes, cultures, and brands of tourism; for example, Hilton, Coca Cola, Starbucks, Avis rental cars, and carriers such as British Airways can become ubiquitous with the spread of tourism around the world. But is this a good thing? While the global brands and companies certainly provide quality assurance and service, they may erode the special 'sense of place' and cultural identity of a destination. And this is the challenge: how can we deliver a quality-assured, top-class tourism experience to international standards at the local level? Here, we encounter the hybrid word 'glocal', combining global standards of expertise with the best in local products and skills. How might this be achieved at the destination of your choice?

On this latter point, there is scope in tourism for both the large organisation and the small independent operator supplying niche markets to co-exist (see Dwyer, 2014). However, the medium-sized enterprises have neither the power of the large firms, nor the opportunities to specialise and will therefore struggle to survive in a globalising sector. In fact, the competitive dominance of larger corporations in tourism will continue through their strict quality control and global branding, which is designed to reduce the perceived risk of a tourism purchase. This has implications for tourism destinations that may become increasingly dependent upon decisions made by such corporations. Nonetheless, we must never lose sight of the fact that tourism will continue to be delivered at a destination by local employees, within the context of a local culture.

The futures of tourism cannot be divorced from political events and trends. Initiatives at different geographical scales are changing the world order, and these will impact upon tourism. At the national level, a major shift has been the way that the role of government in tourism has changed since both 9/11 and the COVID-19 pandemic. These events displaced the view that tourism was a private sector activity. Following both 9/11 and COVID-19, governments recognised the potentially devastating impact on the whole tourism and transport sectors as well as whole destinations. In response, governments provided assistance to businesses and employees through state funding and rescue packages, as well as the co-ordination and promotion of tourism at ministerial level.

At the international level, tourism in the future will be facilitated by the free trade agreements under the umbrella of the General Agreement on Trade in Services (GATS) signed in 1994. GATS is based on the principle that free market forces are the best means of providing consumers with the best products at the best prices. The role of GATS is controversial, since:

- On the one hand, supporters of GATS point to the elimination of barriers to tourism growth, removing restrictions on hiring staff from other countries, establishment of management operations, and franchises in other countries, easier transfers of currency, and other payments.
- On the other hand, opponents of GATS maintain that freedom for companies to operate where they wish, to hire non-local staff, and to franchise their products flies in the face of the development of sustainable tourism, as there will be few controls on the activities of companies in the tourism sector.

There are two opposing trends to the world order implied by GATS:

- First, the formation of a number of trading blocs across the globe as country group-ings come together in economic alliances is evident. Notable here are the North American Free Trade Agreement (NAFTA), the creation of the European Union under the 1992 initiative, the Association of South East Asian Nations (ASEAN), and MER-COSUR covering most of South America.
- Second, regional and national politics are also at variance with the spirit of GATS. The rise of regionalism (for example, in Scotland or Catalunya), 'city states', and a search for cultural identity – particularly amongst ethnic minorities – has led to conflict in some parts of the world (as in the republics of the former Yugoslavia and Ukraine), but elsewhere the trend is less sinister. In the midst of this contradiction, 'city states' are emerging as major tourist destinations, whether it be as cultural centres, or sim-ply competing with others to stage mega-events such as the Olympic Games or the soccer World Cup. Brexit – the UK's vote to leave the European Union – is an extreme example of this trend towards national and regional power in the face of trade blocs.

As the millennium unfolds, the new world order and the global tourism industry will continue to be threatened by terrorism. This, along with natural disasters, epidemics, and inter-communal violence, will particularly affect developing countries who can ill-afford the loss of foreign exchange. It is likely that tourists themselves will be a primary target for terrorists rather than being incidental victims. The effect of 9/11 and subsequent disasters has been to tighten security and immigration procedures, and for crisis and risk manage-ment plans to be developed for many destinations and the tourism sector generally. Crisis and risk management recognises that we must be prepared for man-made and natural disasters and lays down a response pattern to such events. The most significant risks are determined, and strategies implemented to deal with them. Although international organ-isations will be important, the onus will be on individuals, private businesses, and govern-ments to be vigilant concerning future crises, but not to the extent of being risk-averse. For tourism, the dilemma is that absolute security achieved by 'lockdown' is not possible: the destination/attraction has to be welcoming while remaining vigilant (see Beirman, 2015).

Trends towards a new tourism?

A number of commentators have attempted to synthesise the trends identified earlier. Poon suggests that the future will see a flexible, segmented, customised, and diagonally integrated tourism sector rather than the mass market, rigid, standardised, and packaged tourism of the 1970s (see Figure 27.1). Poon (1989, 92) identifies the key trends leading to this new tourism as follows:

- The diffusion of a system of new information technologies in the tourism industry
- Deregulation of the airline industry and financial services
- The negative impact of mass tourism on host countries
- The movement away from sunlust to sun-plus tourism

- Environmental pressures
- Technology
- Competition
- Changing consumer tastes

Figure 27.1
International tourism in metamorphosis

Source: Poon (1989)

There is no doubt that the maturing and changing tourist market will have major implications for the geography of travel and tourism. This will manifest itself in changing patterns of tourism around the world as new destinations emerge and older ones decline, while conflict reduces some localities to no-go areas for tourism. Climate change too is beginning to influence global tourism patterns. The nature of the impact at the destination will increasingly depend on the type of tourism, and those charged with planning for the industry will respond more positively to the needs and desires of visitors. Above all, the challenge for this century, taking climate change into account, will be the balancing of the environmental and social impacts of tourism against its perceived economic gains. It is here that geography as a discipline will continue to play a valuable role in providing us with:

1. A holistic approach to tourism.
2. The specialised knowledge needed to plan and manage low-impact tourism.

As a postscript to this trend to a new tourism, optimistic commentators hoped that as tourism emerged into a post-COVID world, the sector would see sense and move towards a low-carbon, sustainable, and smaller scale operation. Depressingly, within two years of the world opening up from the pandemic, we are almost back to pre-COVID levels of travel, with the consequent and all too familiar impacts on the environment and society.

Summary

- The future geography of travel and tourism will be influenced by a number of inter-related trends. These can be summarised as the changing tourism market place, new trends at the destination, the changing world situation, and the effects of globalisation on the tourism sector.
- In line with these forces for change are other influences such as technology, consumer behaviour, crisis management, and the rise of environmental awareness, particularly climate change.
- Technology is forcing the pace of change in the transport sector, mobile commerce, and the Internet. This is linked to changing consumer behaviour, particularly in the ageing markets of the developed world. Here, knowledgeable, discerning tourists are seeking independent travel and active involvement.
- Destinations will respond through positive planning, showing more concern for the environment and host community, and by providing a quality experience.
- Finally, the world is changing, and tourism will be affected by the developing economies of the East Asia-Pacific region, the rising number of signatories to GATS, and the expansion of the tourism frontier into space.
- There is no doubt that the skills of geographers and their understanding of these global issues will be a valuable contribution to the 'knowledge-based' management of the tourism sector in the twenty-first century.

Assignment: 'Leisure landscapes of tomorrow'

Put forward your own ideas (not those derived from the writers of science fiction) on the 'ideal resort community' that will meet the environmental and social requirements of the mid-twenty-first century. This should include considerations of transport infrastructure, public utilities and waste disposal, the form of accommodation, and the types of recreation, shopping, and entertainment on offer. Your planning brief should take account of the needs of individuals and special interest groups as well as the demands of society as a whole.

References

Ashford, D. (2003) *Spaceflight Revolution*, Imperial College Press, London

Becken, S. (2015) *Tourism and Oil*, Channel View, Clevedon

Beirman, D. (2015) Tourism crisis and safety management, pp. 154–170 in Cooper, C., Volo, S., Gartner, W.C. and Scott, N. (eds) *The Sage Handbook of Tourism Management*: *Applications of Theories and Concepts to Tourism*, Sage, London

Cohen, S. and Hopkins, D. (2019) Autonomous vehicles and the future of urban tourism, *Annals of Tourism Research* 74, 33–42

Collins, P. and Ashford, D. (1998) Space tourism, *Ada Astronautica* 17 (4), 421–431

Day, J. and Chin, N. (2018) Tourism, energy, oil and water, pp. 466–481, in Cooper, C. et al. (eds) *The Sage Handbook of Tourism Management: Theories, Concepts and Disciplinary Approaches to Tourism*, Sage, London

Dwyer, L. (2014) Transnational corporations and the globalisation of tourism, pp. 197–209, in Lew, A.L., Hall, C.M. and Williams, A.M. (eds) *The Wiley Blackwell Companion to Tourism*, Wiley, Chichester

Fennell, D.A and Cooper, C. (2020) *Sustainable Tourism: Principles, Contexts and Practices*, Channel View, Bristol

Gössling, S., Hall, C. M., & Scott, D. (2015). *Tourism and Water* (Vol. 2). Channel View Publications, Bristol

Poon, A, (1989) Competitive strategies for a 'New Tourism', pp. 91–102 in Cooper, C. (ed.), *Progress in Tourism, Recreation and Hospitality Management*, Belhaven, London

Smeral, E. (1998) The impact of globalization on small to medium sized enterprises, *Tourism Management* 19 (4), 371–380

Spector, S. and Higham, J. (2019) Space tourism in the anthropocene, *Annals of Tourism Research* 79, doi.org/10.1016/j.annals.2019.102772

Timothy, D. (2018) Globalisation, supranationalism and tourism, pp. 569–581 in Cooper, C. et al. (eds) *The Sage Handbook of Tourism Management: Theories, Concepts and Disciplinary Approaches to Tourism*, Sage, London

UNEP (2002) *Global Environment Outlook 3 – Past, Present and Future Perspectives*, United Nations Environment Program, New York

UNEP (2021) *Glasgow Declaration Climate Action in Tourism. Recommended Actions, Examples by Pathway*, UNEP, Nairobi

III Useful sources

Sources to support work on worldwide destinations

This section is designed to support your reading of this book. While we have provided a set of relevant sources in this section, there is also a range of other material that you will find useful including trade publications (*Travel Trade Gazette* for example). We have not included these for two reasons: first, there will be different trade journals and newspapers available to you depending upon which part of the world you live in, and second, in our view, the material tends to date rapidly. We have also decided not to provide a list of academic tourism journals, simply because their number is constantly expanding and we are seeing a rise of open-access and online journals.

Of course, the World Wide Web is now a major source of information about tourism and destinations. Remember though that the Web is disorganised and lacks any form of information quality control. Nonetheless, the official tourism sites in particular provide instant access to countries, cities and resorts. Other sites are now available that provide destination accounts, reviews, photographs and statistics. However, we would not recommend that you use only Internet sources, but use the Web to *supplement* print sources and keep up to date. You will also find that there are now collections of tourism cases published, many of which are destination based. These include for example CABI's collection of 'Tourism Cases' focused on tourism development (https://www.cabidigitallibrary.org/journal/tcs), and the excellent range of cases and teaching resources developed by the 'building excellence in sustainable tourism education network' (BESTEN) (https://www.besteducationnetwork.org/). This list of sources is organised to cover the following types of reference material:

1. General texts on tourism and the geography of travel and tourism;
2. Reports, dictionaries, yearbooks, handbooks and encyclopaedias; and
3. Statistical sources.

Books on tourism and the geography of travel and tourism

Agarwal, S. and Shaw, G. (2007) *Managing Coastal Tourism Resorts*, Channel View, Bristol

Airey, D. and Chong, K. (2011) *Tourism in China: Policy and Development Since 1949*, Routledge, London

Almuhrji, H., Alriyami, H. and Scott, N. (eds.) (2017) *Tourism in the Arab World. An Industry Perspective*, Channel View, Bristol

Andrews, H. (2011) *The British on Holiday: Charter Tourism, Identity and Consumption*, Channel View, Bristol

Andrews, H. (2020) *Tourism and Brexit, Travel, Borders and Identity,* Channel View, Bristol

Aramberri, J. and Butler, R. (2004) *Tourism Development*, Channel View, Bristol

Ashford, D. (2003) *Spaceflight Revolution*, Imperial College Press, London

Ashworth, G.J. and Tunbridge, J.E. (1990) *The Tourist-Historic City*, Belhaven, London

Ateljevic, I., Pritchard, A. and Nigel, M. (2007) *The Critical Turn in Tourism Studies*, Elsevier, Oxford

Backer, E. and Lane, B. (2015) *VFR Travel Research*, Channel View, Bristol

Baggio, R. and Baggio, J. (2020) *Modeling and Simulation for Tourism and Hospitality. An Introduction*, Channel View, Bristol

Ball, S., Horner, S. and Nield, K. (2007) *Contemporary Hospitality and Tourism Management Issues in China and India*, Elsevier, Oxford

Becken, S. (2015) *Tourism and Oil. Preparing for the Challenge*, Channel View, Bristol

Becken, S. and Hay, J. (2007) *Tourism and Climate Change*, Channel View, Bristol

Berger, A.A. (2010) *Tourism in Japan*, Channel View, Bristol

Bhandari, K. (2014) *Tourism and National Identity*, Channel View, Bristol

Bierman, D. (2003) *Restoring Destinations in Crisis*, Allen and Unwin, London

Borsay, P. and Walton, J.K. (eds.) (2011) *Resorts and Ports: European Seaside Towns since 1700*, Channel View, Bristol

Buckley, R. (2008) *Environmental Impacts of Ecotourism*, CABI, Wallingford

Buhalis, D. and Costa, C. (2006) *Tourism Management Dynamics: Trends, Management and Tools*, Elsevier, Oxford

Buhalis, D. and Darcy, S. (2010) *Accessible Tourism: Concepts and Issues*, Channel View, Bristol

Buhalis, D., Taheri, B. and Rahmi, R. (2022) *Smart Cities and Tourism: Co-creating Experiences, Challenges and Opportunities*, Goodfellow, Oxford

Burns, P.M. and Novelli, M. (2007) *Tourism and Politics*, Elsevier, Oxford

Buswell, R.J. (2011) *Mallorca and Tourism: History, Economy and Environment*, Channel View, Bristol

Butler, R.W. (2006) *The Tourism Area Life Cycle Volumes, 1 and 2*, Channel View, Bristol

Cetron, M.J., DeMicco, F.J. and Davies, O. (2010) *Hospitality 2015 the Future of Hospitality and Travel*, American Hotel & Lodging Educational Institute, Orlando

Church, A. and Coles, T. (2006) *Tourism, Power and Space*, Routledge, London

Conlin, M.V. and Baum, T. (1995) *Island Tourism*, Wiley, Chichester

Connell, J. (2010) *Medical Tourism*, CABI, Wallingford

Cooper, C. (2011) *Essentials of Tourism*, Pearson, Harlow

Cooper, C. and Hall, C.M. (2012) *Contemporary Tourism*, Goodfellow, Oxford

Costa, C., Panyik, E. and Buhalis, D. (2013) *Trends in European Tourism Planning and Organisation*, Channel View, Bristol

Crotts, J.C. and Van Raaij, W.F. (1993) *Economic Psychology of Travel and Tourism*, Haworth Press, New York

Daher, R. (2006) *Tourism in the Middle East*, Channel View, Bristol

Davidson, A. (1994) *Business Travel*, Addison, Wesley and Longman, Harlow

Daye, M., Chambers, D. and Roberts, S. (2008) *New Perspectives in Caribbean Tourism*, Routledge, London

De Kadt, E. (1979) *Tourism: Passport to Development*, Oxford University Press, Oxford

Decrop, A. (2006) *Vacation Decision Making*, CABI, Wallingford

Dixit, S.K. (ed.) (2021) *Tourism in Asian Cities*, Routledge, London

Doganis, R. (2006) *The Airline Business*, Routledge, London

Dowling, R. (2006) *Cruise Ship Tourism*, CABI, Wallingford

Drakakis-Smith, G. and Lockhart, D. (1997) *Island Tourism: Trends and Prospects*, Pinter, London

Dredge, D. (2006) *Tourism Planning and Policy*, Wiley, Chichester

Dumazedier, J. (1967) *Towards a Society of Leisure*, Free Press, New York

Duval, D. (2007) *Tourism and Transport. Modes, Networks and Flows*, Channel View, Bristol

Dwyer, L., Edwards, D., Mistilis, N., Scott, N., Cooper, C. and Roman, C. (2007) *Trends Underpinning Tourism to 2020: An Analysis of Key Drivers for Change*, STCRC, Brisbane

Dwyer, L., Forsyth, P. and Dwyer, W. (2020) *Tourism Economics and Policy*, Channel View, Bristol

Erfurt-Cooper, P. and Cooper, M. (2009) *Health and Wellness Tourism*, Channel View, Bristol

Faulks, R.W. (1990) *The Principles of Transport*, 4th edition. McGraw Hill, New York

Fayos Sola, E. and Cooper, C. (eds.) (2019) *The Future of Tourism. Innovation and Sustainability*, Springer, Cham

Fennell, D. (2006) *North America*, Channel View, Bristol

Fennell, D. and Cooper, C. (2020) *Sustainable Tourism: Principles, Contexts and Practices*, Channel View, Bristol

Fennell, D.A. (2008) *Ecotourism*, Routledge, London

Frechtling, D. (2001) *Forecasting Tourism Demand*, Elsevier Butterworth-Heinemann, Oxford

Frost, W. and Hall, C.M. (2008) *Tourism and National Parks: International Perspectives on Development, Histories and Change*, Routledge, London

Fyall, A. and Garrod, B. (2004) *Tourism Marketing*, Channel View, Bristol

Goeldner, C.R. and Ritchie, J.R.B. (2011) *Tourism: Principles, Practices, Philosophies*, Wiley, Chichester

Gössling, S. and Hall, C.M. (2006) *Tourism and Global Environmental Change*, Routledge, London

Gössling, S., Hall, C.M. and Scott, D. (2015) *Tourism and Water*, Channel View, Bristol

Graham, A. (2009) *Managing Airports*, Elsevier Butterworth Heinemann, Oxford

Gray, H.P. (1971) *International Travel-International Trade*, Heath Lexington Books, Lexington

Gross, S. and Klemmer, L (2014) *Introduction to Tourism Transport*, CABI, Wallingford

Guichard-Anguis, S. and Moon, O. (2008) *Japanese Tourism and Travel Culture*, Routledge, London

Gunn, C.A. (1997) *Vacationscape: Designing Tourist Regions*, Van Nostrand Reinhold, Hawthorne

Gunn, C.A. and Var, T. (2002) *Tourism Planning*, Routledge, London

Hall, C.M. (1994) *Tourism and Politics*, Wiley, Chichester

Hall, C.M. (2007) *Tourism Planning: Policies, Processes and Relationships*, Pearson, Harlow

Hall, C.M. and Higham, J. (2005) *Tourism, Recreation and Climate Change*, Channel View, Bristol

Hall, C.M. and Jenkins, J.M. (1994) *Tourism and Public Policy*, Routledge, London

Hall, C.M. and Lew, A. (2009) *Understanding and Managing Tourism Impacts: An Integrated Approach*, Routledge, London

Hall, C.M., Müller, D.K. and Saarinen, J.J. (2009) *Nordic Tourism: Issues and Cases*, Channel View, Bristol

Hall, C.M. and Page, S. (2002) *The Geography of Tourism and Recreation*, Routledge, London

Hall, C.M. and Williams, A. (2008) *Tourism and Innovation*, Routledge, London

Hall, D. (2020) *Tourism and Brexit*, Channel View, Bristol

Hall, D., Smith, M. and Marcisweska, B. (2006) *Tourism in the New Europe*, CABI, Chichester

Hanley, K. and Walton, J.K. (2010) *Constructing Cultural Tourism: John Ruskin and the Tourist Gaze*, Channel View, Bristol

Hannam, K. and Knox, D. (2010) *Understanding Tourism: A Critical Introduction*, Sage, London

Hara, T. (2008) *Quantitative Tourism Industry Analysis*, Elsevier, Oxford

Harrison, D. (2002) *Tourism in the Less Developed World*, CABI, Wallingford

Hayllar, B., Griffin, T. and Edwards, D. (2008) *City Spaces - Tourist Places*, Elsevier, Oxford

Heeley, J. (2011) *Inside City Tourism: A European Perspective*, Channel View, Bristol

Henderson, J.C. (2007) *Tourism Crises*, Elsevier, Oxford

Hill, M. (2004) *Coasts and Coastal Management*, Hodder Murray, London

Hinch, T. and Higham, J. (2011) *Sport Tourism Development*, Channel View, Bristol

Holden, A. (2008) *Environment and Tourism*, Routledge, London

Holloway, C. and Humphreys, C. (eds.) (2012) *The Business of Tourism*, Pearson, Harlow

Horner, S. and Swarbrooke, J. (2003) *International Cases in Tourism Management*, Elsevier Butterworth-Heinemann, Oxford

Hottola, P. (2009) *Tourism Strategies and Local Responses in Southern Africa*, CABI, Wallingford

Hsu, H.C. (2008) *Tourism Marketing*, Wiley, Chichester

Huang, S. and Chen, G. (2015) *Tourism Research in China*, Channel View, Bristol

Hudman, L.E. (1980) *Tourism: A Shrinking World*, Wiley, Chichester

Hudman, L.E. and Jackson, R.H. (1999) *The Geography of Travel and Tourism*, Delmar, New York

Inskeep, E. (1991) *Tourism Planning: An Integrated Planning and Development Approach*, Van Nostrand Reinhold, Hawthorne

Ioannides, D. and Debbage, K.G. (1998) *The Economic Geography of the Tourist Industry*, Routledge, London

Ioannides, D. and Timothy, D. (2009) *Tourism in the USA: A Spatial and Social Synthesis*, Routledge, London

Jeffries, D. (2001) *Governments and Tourism*, Elsevier Butterworth-Heinemann, Oxford

Jennings, G. (2001) *Tourism Research*, Wiley, Chichester

Kelly, J.R. (1990) *Leisure*, Prentice Hall, Harlow

Kolb, B. (2006) *Tourism Marketing for Cities and Towns*, Elsevier, Oxford

Kotler, S., Makens, J., Bowen, D. and Baloglu, S. (2020) *Marketing for Hospitality and Tourism*, 8th edition. Prentice Hall, Harlow

Kozak, M. and Andreu, L. (2006) *Progress in Tourism Marketing*, Elsevier, Oxford

Krippendorf, J. (1987) *The Holidaymakers. Understanding the Impact of Leisure and Travel*, Butterworth Heinemann, Oxford.

Lansing, J.B. and Blood, D.M. (1960) *The Changing Travel Market*, Institute for Social Research, Michigan

Laws, E., Prideaux, B. and Chon, K. (2006) *Crisis Management in Tourism*, CABI, Wallingford

Leiper, N. (1990) *The Tourism System*, Massey University Press, Massey

Lenček, L. and Bosker, G. (1999) *The Beach: The history of Paradise on Earth*, Pimlico Press, London

Lennon, J. and Foley, M. (2002) *Dark Tourism*, Continuum, London

Lennon, J.J. (2003) *Tourism Statistics*, Allen and Unwin, London

Leslie, D. (2008) *Tourism Enterprises and Sustainable Development: International Perspectives on Responses to the Sustainability Agenda*, Routledge, London

Li, Y. (20923) *The Rise of Tourism in China: Social and Cultural Change*, Channel View, Bristol

Liburd, J. and Edwards, D. (2010) *Understanding the Sustainable Development of Tourism*, Goodfellow, Oxford

Maitland, R. and Newman, P. (2008) *World Tourism Cities: Developing Tourism Off the Beaten Track*, Routledge, London

Mason, P. (2008) *Tourism Impacts, Planning and Management*, Elsevier, Oxford

McCabe, S. (2007) *Marketing Communications in Tourism and Hospitality*, Elsevier, Oxford

McCabe, S., Minnaert, L. and Diekmann, A. (2011) *Social Tourism in Europe: Theory and Practice*, Channel View, Bristol

Mercer, D. (1980) *In Pursuit of Leisure*, Sorret, Publishing Melbourne

Middleton, V.T.C. and Hawkins, R. (1998) *Sustainable Tourism: A Marketing Perspective*, Elsevier Butterworth-Heinemann, Oxford

Middleton, V.T.C. and Lickorish, L.J. (2007) *British Tourism*, Elsevier, Oxford

Mill, R.C. and Morrison, A. (1992) *The Tourism System: An Introductory Text*, Prentice Hall, Harlow

Miller, G. and Twinning Ward, L. (2005) *Monitoring for a Sustainable Tourism Transition. The Challenge of Developing and Using Indicators*, CABI, Wallingford

Morgan, M., Lugosi, P. and Brent Ritchie, J.R. (2010) *The Tourism and Leisure Experience: Consumer and Managerial Perspectives*, Channel View, Bristol

Morpeth, N.D. (2007) *Religious Tourism and Pilgrimage Management an International Perspective*, CABI, Wallingford

Morrison, A. (2023) *Marketing and Managing Tourism Destinations*, Routledge, London

Morrison, A. (2023) *Marketing and Managing Tourism Destinations*, Routledge, London

Mowforth, M., Charlton, C. and Munt, I. (2007) *Tourism and Responsibility*, Routledge, London

Mowforth, M. and Munt, I. (2008) *Tourism and Sustainability*, Routledge, London

Muller, D.K. and Jannson, B. (2006) *Tourism in Peripheries*, CABI, Wallingford

Muller, D.K and Saarinen, J. (2008) *Nordic Tourism*, Channel View, Bristol

Murphy, P.E. (1991) *Tourism: A Community Approach*, Methuen, London

Murphy, P.E. and Murphy, A. (2004) *Strategic Management for Tourism Communities Bridging the Gaps*, Channel View, Bristol

Newsome, D., Moore, S.A. and Dowling, R.K. (2013) *Natural Area Tourism Ecology Impacts and Management*, Channel View, Bristol.

Niewiadomski, P. (2023) *Tourism in Post-Communist States Central and Eastern Europe*, Routledge, London

Nordin, S. (2005**)** *Tourism of Tomorrow – Travel Trends and Forces of Change*, European Tourism Research Institute, Stockholm

Orams, M. (1999) *Marine Tourism*, Routledge, London

Page, S. (2008) *Tourism Management: Managing for Change*, Elsevier Butterworth-Heinemann, Oxford

Page, S. (2009) *Transport and Tourism: Global Perspectives*, 3rd Edition. Pearson, Harlow

Page, S. (2011) *Tourism Management*, 4th edition. Routledge, London

Page, S.J. and Connell, J. (2014) *Tourism: A Modern Synthesis*, Cengage Learning, New York

Pattullo, P. (2007) *Last Resorts: The Cost of Tourism in the Caribbean*, 2nd edition. New York University Press, New York

Pearce, D. (1989) *Tourist Development*, Longman, Harlow

Pearce, D. (1992) *Tourist Organizations*, Longman, Harlow

Pearce, D. (1995) *Tourism Today: A Geographical Analysis*, Longman, Harlow

Pearce, D. and Butler, R. (1995) *Change in Tourism: People, Places, Processes*, Routledge, London

Pearce, D.G. and Butler, R.W. (2001) *Contemporary Issues in Tourism Development*, Routledge, London

Pearce, P.L. (2011) *Tourist Behaviour and the Contemporary World*, Channel View, Bristol

Peisley, T. (2006) *The Future of Cruising*, Pearson, Harlow

Poon, A. (1993) *Tourism, Technology and Competitive Strategies*, CABI, Wallingford

Poon, A. (2018) *Overcoming Overtourism*, LEVE-Global, Trinidad and Tobago

Prideaux, B., Timothy, D. and Chon, K. (2007) *Cultural and Heritage Tourism in Asia and the Pacific*, Routledge, London

Rathee, R. and Rajain, P (2022) *Destination Marketing Creating Memorable Tourism Experiences*, Routledge, London

Reisinger, Y. and Dimanche, F. (2008) *International Tourism*, Elsevier, Oxford

Ritchie, B.W. (2009) *Crisis and Disaster Management for Tourism*, Channel View, Bristol

Ritchie, J.R.B. and Crouch, G.I. (2003) *The Competitive Destination*, CABI, Wallingford

Ron, A. and Timothy, D. (2019) *Contemporary Christian Travel*, Channel View Publications, Bristol.

Ross, G.F. (1996) *The Psychology of Tourism*, Hospitality Press, New York

Ryan, C. (2002) *The Tourist Experience*, Continuum, London

Ryan, C. (2003) *Recreational Tourism*, Channel View, Bristol

Ryan, C. (2007) *Battlefield Tourism*, Elsevier, Oxford

Ryan, C. and Huang, S. (2013) *Tourism in China*, Channel View, Bristol

Ryan, C. and Huimin, G. (2008) *Tourism in China: Destination, Cultures and Communities*, Routledge, London

Saarinen, J., Becker, F.O., Haretsebe, M. and Wilson, D. (2009) *Sustainable Tourism in South Africa*, Channel View, Bristol

Scott, N., Baggio, R. and Cooper, C. (2008) *Network Analysis and Tourism*, Channel View, Bristol

Shackley, M. (2001) *Managing Sacred Sites*, Thomson, London

Sharpley, R. and Kato, K. (2021) *Tourism Development in Japan Themes, Issues and Challenges*, Routledge, London

Sharpley, R. and Stone, P. (2009) *The Darker Side of Travel: The Theory and Practice of Dark Tourism*, Channel View, Bristol

Sharpley, R. and Telfer, D. (2015) *Tourism and Development*, Channel View, Bristol

Shaw, G. and Williams, A. (1994) *Critical Issues in Tourism*, Blackwell, Oxford

Sinclair, T. and Stabler, M. (1991) *The Tourism Industry: An International Analysis*, CABI, Wallingford

Sinclair, T., Stabler, M. and Papatheodorou, A. (2009) *The Economics of Tourism*, Routledge, London

Smith, M. (2003) *Issues in Cultural Tourism Studies*, Routledge, London

Smith, M., MacLeod, N. and Hart Robertson, M. (2010) *Key Concepts in Tourist Studies*, Sage, London

Smith, M. and Robinson, M. (2006) *Tourism in a Changing World*, Channel View, Bristol

Smith, S.L.J. (1996) *Tourism Analysis: A Handbook*, Addison Wesley Longman, Harlow

Smith, V. and Brent, M. (2003) *Hosts and Guests Revisited*, Cognizant, New York

Smith, V.L. (1989) *Hosts and Guests*, University of Pennsylvania Press, Philadelphia

Smith, V.L. and Eadington, W.R. (1995) *Tourism Alternatives: Potential Problems in the Development of Tourism*, University of Pennsylvania Press, Philadelphia

Snyder, J. and Stonehouse, B. (2007) *Prospects for Polar Tourism*, CABI, Wallingford

Stonehouse, B. and Snyder, J. (2010) *Polar Tourism*, Channel View, Bristol

Stronza, A. (2008) *Ecotourism and Conservation in the Americas*, CABI, Wallingford

Su, X. and Teo, P. (2008) *The Politics of Heritage Tourism in China: A View from Lijiang*, Routledge, London

Su, J. (2023) *Intangible Cultural Heritage and Tourism in China*, Channel View, Bristol

Swarbrooke, J. (2001) *The Development and Management of Visitor Attractions*, 2nd edition. Elsevier Butterworth-Heinemann, Oxford

Swarbrooke, J. and Horner, S. (2007) *Consumer Behaviour in Tourism*, Elsevier, Oxford

Telfer, D.J. and Sharpley, R. (2007) *Tourism and Development in the Developing World*, Routledge, London

Terrell, S. (2004) *The Geography of Sport and Leisure*, Hodder & Stoughton, London

Theobald, W.F. (1994) *Global Tourism: The Next Decade*, Butterworth-Heinemann, Oxford

Thomas, R. and Augustyn, M. (2007) *Tourism in New Europe*, Elsevier, Oxford

Timothy, D.J. (2011) *Cultural Heritage and Tourism: An Introduction*, Channel View, Bristol

Timothy, D.J. (2023) *Cultural Heritage and Tourism in Africa*, Routledge, London

Timothy, D.J. and Boyd, S.W. (2003) *Heritage Tourism*, Prentice Hall, Harlow

Timothy, D.J. and Boyd, S.W. (2015) *Tourism and Trails*, Channel View, Bristol

Timothy, D.J. and Nyaupane, G. (2008) *Cultural Heritage and Tourism in the Developing World*, Routledge, London

Towner, J. (1994) *An Historical Geography of Recreation and Tourism*, Belhaven, London

Travis, A. (2015) *Planning for Tourism, Leisure and Sustainability. International Case Studies*, CABI, Wallingford

Tribe, J. (2011) *The Economics of Recreation, Leisure and Tourism*, 4th edition. Routledge, London

Tribe, J. and Airey, D. (2007) *Developments in Tourism Research*, Elsevier, Oxford

Turner, L. and Ash, J. (1975) *The Golden Hordes: International Tourism and the Pleasure Periphery*, Constable, London

UNWTO (2001a) *Tourism in the Least Developed Countries*, UNWTO, Madrid

UNWTO (2001b) *The Tourism Satellite Account as an Ongoing Process: Past, Present and Future Developments*, UNWTO, Madrid

UNWTO (2002a) *Tourism and Poverty Alleviation*, UNWTO, Madrid

UNWTO (2002b) *Enhancing the Economic Benefits of Tourism through Poverty Alleviation*, UNWTO, Madrid

UNWTO (2002c) *Sport and Tourism*, UNWTO, Madrid

UNWTO (2003a) *Worldwide Cruise-ship Activity*, UNWTO, Madrid

UNWTO (2003b) *Global Code of Ethics for Tourism*, WTO, Madrid

UNWTO (2005a) *Tourism's Potential as a Sustainable Development Strategy*, UNWTO, Madrid

UNWTO (2005b) *City Tourism and Culture*, UNWTO, Madrid

UNWTO (2005c) *Making Tourism More Sustainable. A Guide for Policy Makers*, UNWTO, Madrid

UNWTO (2007) *A Practical Guide to Destination Management*, UNWTO, Madrid

UNWTO (2007) *Policies, Strategies and Tools for the Sustainable Development of Tourism*, UNWTO, Madrid

UNWTO (2008) *Climate Change and Tourism. Responding to Global Challenges*, UNWTO, Madrid

UNWTO (2009) *From Davos to Copenhagen and Beyond. Advancing Tourism's Response to Climate Change*, UNWTO, Madrid

UNWTO (2011a) *Communicating Heritage: A Handbook for the Tourism Sector*, UNWTO, Madrid

UNWTO (2011b) *Manual on Tourism and Poverty Alleviation – Practical Steps for Destinations*, UNWTO, Madrid

UNWTO (2011c) *Tourism towards 2030 – Global Overview*, UNWTO, Madrid

UNWTO (2023) *Climate Action in the Tourism Sector – An Overview of Methodologies and Tools to Measure Greenhouse Gas Emissions*, UNWTO, Madrid

Urry, J. (2000) *Sociology Beyond Societies. Mobilities for the Twenty-First Century*, Routledge, London

Urry, J. and Larsen, J. (2011) *The Tourist Gaze*, Sage, London

Van Egmond, T. (2007) *Understanding Western Tourists in Developing Countries*, CABI, Wallingford

Veal, A.J. (2011) *Research Methods for Leisure and Tourism*, Pearson, London

Vickers, A. (2012) *Bali: A Paradise Created*, 2nd edition. Tuttle, North Clarendon

Vikneswaran, N. Amran, H. and Ghazali, M. (2020) *Responsible Rural Tourism in Asia*, Channel View, Bristol

Vogel, M., Papathanassis, A. and Wolber, B. (2011) *Business and Management of Ocean Cruises*, CABI, Wallingford

Wall, G. and Mathieson, A. (2006) *Tourism: Change, Impacts and Opportunities*, Pearson, Harlow

Weaver, D. (2008) *Ecotourism*, Wiley, Chichester

Weed, M. (2007) *Olympic Tourism*, Elsevier, Oxford

Whitford, M., Ruhanen, L., and Carr, A. (eds.) (2017) *Indigenous Tourism: Cases from Australia and New Zealand*, Goodfellow, Oxford

Wilks, J., Pendergast, D. and Leggat, P. (2006) *Tourism in Turbulent Times*, Elsevier, Oxford

Williams, S. (2004) *Tourism, Critical Concepts in the Social Sciences*, Routledge, London

Williams, S. (2009) *Tourism Geography*, Routledge, London

Winter, T., Teo, P. and Chang, T.C. (eds.) (2008) *Asia on Tour: Exploring the Rise of Asian Tourism*, Routledge, London

Woodside, A. and Martin, D. (2008) *Tourism Management: Analysis, Behaviour and Strategy*, CABI, Wallingford

Yeoman, I. (2008) *Tomorrow's Tourist*, Butterworth Elsevier Heinemann, Oxford

Yeoman, I. (2012) 2050 *Tomorrow's Tourism*, Channel View, Bristol

Reports, dictionaries, yearbooks, handbooks and encyclopedias

There are a number of useful sources to be found in consultant's reports (including those online such as www.euromonitor.com), tourism dictionaries, yearbooks and encyclopaedias. In the past decade publishers have also capitalised on synthesising tourism, knowledge into handbooks. Some of the key sources include:

Baggio, R. and Klobas, J. (2011) *Quantitative Methods in Tourism: A Handbook*, Channel View, Bristol

Ballantyne, R. (2013) *International Handbook on Ecotourism*, Edward Elgar, Cheltenham

Beaver, A. (2002) *A Dictionary of Travel and Tourism Terminology*, Oxford University Press, Oxford

Cater, C.I. and Garrod, B. (2015) *Encyclopedia of Sustainable Tourism*, CABI, Wallingford

Cooper, C. (2013) *Contemporary Tourism Reviews*, Goodfellow, Oxford

Cooper, C. and Hall, C.M. (2005) *Oceania. A Tourism Handbook*, Channel View, Bristol

Cooper, C. and Lockwood, A. (1989) *Progress in Tourism, Recreation and Hospitality Management*. Vols 1–6. Belhaven and Wiley, Chichester

Cooper, C., Volo, S., Gartner, W.C. and Scott, N. et al. (eds.) (2018a) *The Sage Handbook of Tourism Management: Theories, Concepts and Disciplinary Approaches to Tourism*, Sage, London

Cooper, C., Volo, S., Gartner, W.C. and Scott, N. et al. (eds.) (2018b) *The Sage Handbook of Tourism Management: Applications of Theories and Concepts to Tourism*, Sage, London

Dwyer, L. and Forsyth, P. (2008) *International Handbook on the Economics of Tourism*, Edward Elgar, Cheltenham

Economic Intelligence Unit Publications. EIU, London

Euromonitor Publications, London

Europa Publications (annual) *The Europa World Yearbook*, Europa Publications, Brussels

Gursoy, D. and Nunkoo, R (2019) *The Routledge Handbook of Tourism Impacts Theoretical and Applied Perspectives*, Routledge, London

Huang, S and Ganghua, C. (2020) *Handbook on Tourism and China*, Elgar, London

Jafari, J. (2001) *The Encyclopedia of Tourism*, Routledge, London.

Jones, I. and Mason, P. (2008) *Routledge Dictionary of Leisure and Tourism*, Routledge, London

Hall, C.M., Gossling, S. and Scott, D. (2015) *The Routledge Handbook of Tourism and Sustainability*, Routledge, London

Holden, A. and Fennell, D. (2012) *The Routledge Handbook of Tourism and the Environment*, Routledge, London

Khan, M., Olsen, M. and Var, T. (1993) *Encyclopedia of Hospitality and Tourism*, Van Nostrand Reinhold, New York

Lew, A.L., Hall, C.M. and Williams, A.M. (2014) *The Wiley Blackwell Companion to Tourism*, Wiley, Chichester

Luck, M. (2008) *The Encyclopedia of Tourism and Recreation in Marine Environments*, CABI, Wallingford

Medlik, S. (2002) *Dictionary of Transport, Travel and Hospitality*, Butterworth-Heinemann, Oxford

Page, S. and Connell, J. (2014) *The Routledge Handbook of Events*, Routledge, London

Paxton, J. (annual) *The Statesman's Yearbook*, Macmillan, New York

Ritchie, J.R.B. and Goeldner, C.R. (1994) *Travel, Tourism and Hospitality Research: A Handbook for Managers and Researchers*, Wiley, Chichester

Ritchie, J.R.B. and Hawkins, D. (1991–1993) *World Travel and Tourism Review*. Vols 1–3. CABI, Wallingford

Seaton, A., Wood, R., Dieke, P. and Jenkins, C. (1994) *Tourism: The State of the Art: The Strathclyde Symposium*, Wiley, Chichester

Smith, M. (2012) *The Routledge Handbook of Cultural Tourism*, Routledge, London

Stephenson, M. (ed.) (2023) *Routledge Handbook on Tourism and Small Island States in the Pacific*, Routledge, London

Stone, R., Hartmann, P., Seaton, A., Sharpley, R. and White, L. (eds.) (2018) *The Palgrave Handbook of Dark Tourism Studies*, Palgrave, London

Weaver, D. (2001) *The Encyclopaedia of Ecotourism*, CABI, Wallingford

Wilson, J. (2012) *The Routledge Handbook of Tourism Geographies*, Routledge, London

Witt, S.F. and Mountinho, L. (1995) *Tourism Marketing and Management Handbook*, Student edition. Prentice Hall, Harlow

World Tourism Organisation (2001) *Thesaurus on Tourism and Leisure Activities*, UNWTO, Madrid

World Travel and Tourism Council Special Country Reports, WTTC, London

Xie, P.F. (2023) *Handbook on Tourism Planning*, Elgar, London

Useful statistical sources

This section is designed to support your reading of this book by guiding you through the minefield that is tourism statistics. There is still only a limited range of sources that draw together *reliable* tourism statistics and trends.

At the global the scale we find the reports from the UNWTO (https://www.unwto.org/statistics) and the OECD (https://www.oecd.org/cfe/tourism/tourism-statistics.htm) are the most reliable. You will also find that the WTTC has a range of statistics, particularly for the economic impact and value of tourism but these are drawn from their own calculations and should be treated with care (see https://www.wttc.org/economic-impact/country-analysis/data-gateway/). Nonetheless, the UNWTO's increasingly user-friendly reports are well worth consulting for both global and regional trends – but beware the distinctions between travellers, tourists and day visitors in the tables. The UNWTO also has a very useful searchable statistics web site - https://www.unwto.org/tourism-data/unwto-tourism-dashboard.

There are a number of sources at the regional level:

- Eurostat provide a good statistical service (https://ec.europa.eu/eurostat/statisticsexplained/index.php/Tourism_statistics).
- The Pacific Asia Travel Association has a comprehensive set of statistics and forecasts.
- The Association for Southeast Asian Nations (ASEAN) also has a web-based tourism statistics service (https://data.aseanstats.org/dashboard/tourism) for its ten members.

- The Caribbean Tourism Organization has a statistics portal which is free to researchers and students (https://www.onecaribbean.org/statistics/).

At country level, governments collect and submit their tourism statistics to the UNWTO and to the OECD (where they are members) so there is no need to go the individual country sources unless you are seeking more detail.

The key print sources are:

Organization for Economic Co-operation and Development (annual) *Tourism Policy and International Tourism in OECD Member Countries*, OECD, Paris

Pacific Asia Travel Association (PATA) (annual) *Annual Statistical Monitor*, PATA, Bangkok

Pacific Asia Travel Association (PATA) (quarterly) *Quarterly Tourism Monitor*, PATA, Bangkok

Pacific Asia Travel Association (PATA) (2019) *Asia Pacific Visitor Forecasts 2020–2024*, PATA, Bangkok

Pacific Asia Travel Association (PATA) (2019) *Asia Pacific Destination Forecasts 2019–2023*, PATA, Bangkok

United Nations World Tourism Organisation (annual) *Compendium of Tourism Statistics*, UNWTO, Madrid

United Nations World Tourism Organisation (annual) *Tourism Highlights*, UNWTO, Madrid

United Nations World Tourism Organisation (annual) *Yearbook of Tourism Statistics*, UNWTO, Madrid

United Nations World Tourism Organisation (monthly) *World Tourism Barometer*, UNWTO, Madrid

United Nations World Tourism Organisation (1994) *Recommendations on Tourism Statistics*, UNWTO, Madrid

United Nations World Tourism Organisation (1999) *Observations of International Tourism Volume 1*, UNWTO, Madrid

United Nations World Tourism Organisation (1999) *Observations of International Tourism Volume II*, UNWTO, Madrid

United Nations World Tourism Organisation (2010) *Tourism Satellite Account Data around the World: Worldwide Summary*, UNWTO, Madrid

United Nations World Tourism Organisation (2011) *Tourism towards 2030 – Global Overview*, UNWTO, Madrid

United Nations World Tourism Organisation (2019) *UNWTO Tourism Definitions*, UNWTO, Madrid. https://www.unwto.org/tourism-data/unwto-tourism-dashboard

World Travel and Tourism Council (annual) *Travel and Tourism. Economic Impact (Year) World*, WTTC, London

Selective Place Names Index

NOTE: Page numbers in *italics* refer to illustrations.

Subject Index

NOTE: Page numbers in *italics* refer to illustrations.

Transantarctic Mountains
750
transit routes 9
transport 102, 574;
costs and pricing
104–107; elements of
transport 102–104;
future developments
in transport 769–771;
integration 107;
transport modes 107;
transport networks
109–110; transport
routes 109; *see also* air
transport, road and rail
transport, water-borne
transport; supply *for
specific countries*
travel experience phases
19–20
travellers/tourists,
classifications 7
travel motivators 35
travel propensity and
travel frequency 25–27
trekking 485, 552–553
trends towards a new
tourism 774–776

tropics, the (tropical
climates) 73–75, 85–86,
87

undersea tourism 767
UN Universal Declaration
of Human Rights 24
UNWTO *see* World
Tourism Organization
urban tourism 15
UV Index 80, 742

vertical take-off and
landing (VTOL) aircraft
116, 267
VFR tourism 17
virtual reality 768
visitor payback 766
voluntourism 767

wanderlust 35
water-borne transport
121–126; inland
waterways 126; long-
haul/line shipping
routes 109, 123–124;
short sea routes 124;
vessels 121–123

wildfires 89, 620,
664
wind-chill factor 82
wine tourism 296
winter sports tourism *see*
skiing
World Biosphere Reserve
519
World Health Organisation
38, 51
World Heritage Sites 55,
610–611, 731, 733, 748
World Tourism
Organization (UNWTO)
14, 24, 39
World Travel and Tourism
Council (WTTC) 14

yachting 59, 126, 289, 307,
327, 345, 358, 402–403,
625, 689, 691, 693, 695,
755
Yamassoukro Decision 491
youth hostel movement
265

Zeppelin airship 267
zoning 297–298

Printed in the United States
by Baker & Taylor Publisher Services